THE ANCHOR BIBLE REFERENCE LIBRARY

THE BIRTH
OF THE MESSIAH

A COMMENTARY
ON THE INFANCY NARRATIVES
IN THE GOSPELS OF
MATTHEW AND LUKE

BY

Raymond E. Brown, S.S.

NEW UPDATED EDITION

ABRL

Doubleday

NEW YORK   LONDON   TORONTO   SYDNEY   AUCKLAND

THE ANCHOR BIBLE REFERENCE LIBRARY
PUBLISHED BY DOUBLEDAY
a division of Random House, Inc.
1540 Broadway, New York, New York 10036

THE ANCHOR BIBLE REFERENCE LIBRARY, DOUBLEDAY, and the portrayal
of an anchor with the letters ABRL are trademarks of Doubleday,
a division of Random House, Inc.

First Anchor Bible Reference Library edition published October 1993
by special arrangement with Doubleday, a division of Random House, Inc.

The Library of Congress has cataloged
The Anchor Bible Reference Library hardcover edition as follows:
Brown, Raymond Edward.
The birth of the Messiah : a commentary on the infancy narratives
in Matthew and Luke: new updated edition / by Raymond E. Brown.—
1st Anchor Bible reference library.
p.   cm.—(Anchor Bible reference library)
Includes bibliographical references and indexes.
1. Bible. N.T. Matthew I–II—Criticism, interpretation, etc.
2. Bible. N.T. Luke I–II—Criticism, interpretation, etc.
3. Jesus Christ—Nativity.   I. Title.   II. Series.
BS2575.2.B76   1993
226.2′06—dc20   93-11256
CIP

Nihil Obstat
Myles M. Bourke, S.T.D., S.S.L.
Censor deputatus
Imprimatur
✝ Patrick J. Sheridan, D.D.
Vicar General, Archdiocese of New York
June 22, 1993
The *nihil obstat* and *imprimatur* are official declarations that a book or pamphlet
is free of doctrinal or moral error. No implication is contained therein that
those who have granted the *nihil obstat* and *imprimatur* agree with the contents,
opinions, or statements expressed.

ISBN 0-385-49447-5

5   7   9   10   8   6   4

THE BIRTH OF THE MESSIAH

THE ANCHOR BIBLE REFERENCE LIBRARY is designed to be a third major component of the Anchor Bible group, which includes the Anchor Bible commentaries on the books of the Old Testament, the New Testament, and the Apocrypha and the Anchor Bible Dictionary. While the Anchor Bible commentaries and the Anchor Bible Dictionary are structurally defined by their subject matter, the Anchor Bible Reference Library serves as a supplement on the cutting edge of the most recent scholarship. The series is open-ended; its scope and reach are nothing less than the biblical world in its totality, and its methods and techniques the most up-to-date available or devisable. Separate volumes will deal with one or more of the following topics relating to the Bible: anthropology, archaeology, ecology, economy, geography, history, languages and literatures, philosophy, religion(s), theology.

As with the Anchor Bible commentaries and the Anchor Bible Dictionary, the philosophy underlying the Anchor Bible Reference Library finds expression in the following: the approach is scholarly, the perspective is balanced and fair-minded, the methods are scientific, and the goal is to inform and enlighten. Contributors are chosen on the basis of their scholarly skills and achievements, and they come from a variety of religious backgrounds and communities. The books in the Anchor Bible Reference Library are intended for the broadest possible readership, ranging from world-class scholars, whose qualifications match those of the authors, to general readers, who may not have special training or skill in studying the Bible but are as enthusiastic as any dedicated professional in expanding their knowledge of the Bible and its world.

David Noel Freedman
GENERAL EDITOR

To the
Theological Faculties of the
Universities and Colleges
who have nominated me
for Honorary Doctorates in
Divinity, Theology, and Letters
in the years 1972 through 1992
as a most inadequate expression
of my deep gratitude

FOREWORD
(ORIGINAL EDITION)

In some ways the narratives of Jesus' birth and infancy are the last frontiers to be crossed in the relentless advance of the scientific (critical) approach to the Gospels. For more conservative Christians this frontier may be completely without demarcation, since there are still many who do not recognize that the infancy material has an origin and a historical quality quite different from that of the rest of the Gospels. For such Bible readers the coming of the magi and the appearance of angels to the shepherds have exactly the same historical value as the stories of Jesus' ministry. Yet the stories of the ministry depend, in part at least, on traditions that have come down from the disciples of Jesus who accompanied him during that ministry, while we have no reliable information about the source of the infancy material. This does not mean that the infancy narratives have no historical value, but it does mean that one cannot make assumptions about their historicity on the basis of their presence in the Gospels.

For many less conservative Christians the frontier demarcating the infancy narratives as a separate evangelical province is all too clear. They know that this territory has been "scouted" in the past, but in their judgment it is not worth permanent settlement. For them the popular character of these narratives with exotic magi, a birth star, angelic messengers, etc., means that we have here legends unworthy to be a vehicle of the pure Gospel message. In their opinion this folklore devoid of real theology is fit only for romantics or the naive. As a result the infancy narratives are often overlooked or treated cursorily in seminary courses, even though those ordained to parish ministry will have to face them every Christmas. Books of NT introduction generally give them short shrift, disproportionate to their role in Christian theology, art, and poetic imagination. This disproportion does no justice to the fact that people who know little of Jesus, beyond his death on the cross and his resurrection, are often acquainted with the Christmas story, which accordingly offers a channel through which the Gospel can be made intelligible to them. Perhaps the most visible sign of neglect is the absence, in all the languages of biblical scholarship, of a major modern commentary which treats the two infancy narratives together.

It was from a felt need, then, that this commentary was undertaken. Faithful to the insights of historical criticism, I shall not avoid historical problems. But I am primarily interested in the role these infancy narratives had in the early Christian understanding of Jesus. By treating the two infancy narratives within the same volume, I hope to point out their common tendencies and emphases. By giving them separate treatments (the volume is divided into Book One and Book Two), I hope to show how each fits into the theology of its respective Gospel, and thus offer some reasons for differences between the infancy narratives. It is the central contention of this volume that the infancy narratives are worthy vehicles of the Gospel message; indeed, each is the essential Gospel story in miniature. The appreciation for them among ordinary Christians may in part reflect sentimentality, as well as the fact that they are stories well told. But on a much deeper level it reflects a true instinct recognizing in the infancy narrative the essence of the Good News, namely, that God has made Himself present to us in the life of His Messiah who walked on this earth, so truly present that the birth of the Messiah was the birth of God's Son. I maintain that genuine biblical criticism, for all the historical problems that it raises, sets this claim in clear perspective.

The commentary is meant to be both scholarly and intelligible—the reader may judge my success—and to reach a variety of audiences: fellow scholars, students of theology and of the Bible, and interested Christians. The way in which I have structured it reflects this anticipated variety. The biblical narrative has been divided into sections reflecting units in the evangelists' structures. Each section begins with a translation of the Scripture. That is followed by detailed NOTES which proceed verse by verse. It is here that I have included the technical information needed by those more professionally interested in exegesis: textual questions, problems of translation, disputed interpretations, historical background. Neither exegesis nor biblical theology should be without a detailed factual basis, and I hope that there will be things in the NOTES which will interest all. Nevertheless, it is in the COMMENT, which follows the NOTES and can be read without them, that I discuss the basic meaning of the biblical scene: how it is organized, how it fits into the evangelist's theology and message, and how he may have drawn upon pre-Gospel material or OT background in constructing it. (Such reconstruction of the pre-Gospel history involves considerable theorizing; and I have generally treated it last in each section so that it will be clear that my interpretation of the meaning of the scene in the Gospel does not depend for its validity on accepting a disputable reconstruction.) In order to keep the COMMENT readable, pertinent information of a more scientific or technical nature is given in footnotes. There are ample bibliographies, both general and sectional, to encourage further reading. I hope that my personal insights have value, but it is also my goal to have summarized for the reader a broad range of scholarship. I shall be flattered if this commentary has covered previous work with enough thoroughness and fairness that it can provide a convenient basis for subsequent reflection and a text presupposed in continuing study.

I have taught a course on the infancy narratives a number of times both in Rome and New York, and I am grateful to my students for deepening my understanding through their questions and observations. Mary Callaway and Richard Sturm checked the bibliographies for accuracy. Professor John Kselman of St. Mary's Seminary, Baltimore, has helped me significantly as he read through the whole volume in typescript; there will be fewer mistakes because of his observant eye. Peerless, devoted copy editing by Robert Hewetson and the friendly help of a host of friends at Doubleday, including Judith Dollenmayer, John Delaney, John Miles, and Robert Heller, have bettered the book and eased the burden.

I acknowledge my scholarly debt to many writers both Jewish and Christian. In particular, as the reader will see, the infancy narratives have been an area in which Roman Catholic writers have shown considerable interest because of their devotion to Mary; and from such detailed research this commentary has profited. However, historical criticism of the New Testament is relatively new on the Catholic scene, and many of those studies were written at a time or with a mentality that I shall have to reject as uncritical. As a Roman Catholic myself, I share their faith and their devotion; but it is my firm contention that one should not attempt to read later Marian sensibilities and issues back into the New Testament. (I do not mean that there is no need to relate the NT to later theology, but one must respect historical development.) I see no reason why a Catholic's understanding of what Matthew and Luke meant in their infancy narratives should be different from a Protestant's.

In closing, I realize that many ordinary readers will find the critical approach in this volume quite different from what they learned about the infancy narratives in their early religious education. It is my hope that, once they have adjusted to the different approach, they will recognize that I have in fact preserved much of what they cherished in their memories of the newborn Messiah.

Advent 1976
Union Theological Seminary, N.Y.C.

FOREWORD TO THE NEW UPDATED EDITION

It is more than fifteen years since I wrote the above Foreword to *The Birth of the Messiah*. I was very encouraged by the reception given that work, especially on the part of those who wrote or told me that it made the Gospel infancy narratives truly meaningful. In the scholarly world the book seems to have catalyzed new attention to the infancy narratives, liberating them from comparative neglect, so that the literature on the subject in the years following 1976 was extraordinarily abundant— nearly five hundred books and articles that are known to me! In the 1986 *Catholic Biblical Quarterly* I attempted a brief summary; but when Doubleday offered me the opportunity for a new updated edition, I realized that something like that would be totally inadequate. In the updating I have attempted to read thoroughly and reflect on this flourishing new literature. Some of it was very enlightening and gave me ideas that I could accept enthusiastically. In particular, contributions from narrative and literary criticism seemed to add new depth. With other contributions I wanted to enter into debate and argue out merits. Yet even then I often saw ways in which I could clarify my ideas and organize them better. Still other contributions I am convinced are wrong, but I needed space to explain why.

To make available the contributions of the last fifteen years and to organize what I learned from them, the best idea seemed to be a Supplement that could be added to *The Birth of the Messiah*, leaving intact the original work, which has proved enduringly helpful and popular. When I began, I never dreamed that the Supplement would run more than a quarter of the size of the original work, increasing the total size of the book from just under six hundred pages to over seven hundred and fifty. Indeed, the Supplement is almost a small book in itself! As I explain on the first page of the Supplement, I have constructed it in such a way that it is very easy to use in coordination with the original work.

I thank the publishers and editors at Doubleday for their generosity in allowing me to do this and for their efficiency (almost taken for granted now, after twenty-five years of working together on books). John Kselman (now professor at Weston School of Theology in Cambridge, MA), who was of so much help in reading and correcting

typescript for the original edition, has continued that service for this
updated edition. Friends at universities and seminaries throughout the
country have helped by photocopying articles; and, in particular, Dr.
Cecil White, librarian at St. Patrick's Seminary, Menlo Park, CA, has
rendered yeoman service in tracking down fiendishly hard-to-get items
in the Bibliography of the Supplement. I write with the hope that this
major updating will serve into the next millennium.

Feast of the Presentation of Jesus in the Temple
February 2, 1993

CONTENTS

INTRODUCTION

BOOK ONE: THE MATTHEAN INFANCY NARRATIVE

BOOK TWO: THE LUCAN INFANCY NARRATIVE

APPENDIXES

SUPPLEMENT (1993)

INDEXES

List of Illustrative Tables in the Volume:

ABBREVIATIONS

AB	The Anchor Bible
ABJ	R. E. Brown, *The Gospel According to John* (AB 29, 29A; Garden City, N.Y.: Doubleday, 1966, 1970)
AER	*American Ecclesiastical Review*
AJT	*American Journal of Theology*
Ant.	The *Antiquities* of Flavius Josephus
AP	R. H. Charles, ed., *Apocrypha and Pseudepigrapha of the Old Testament* (2 vols.; Oxford: Clarendon, 1913)
ASNU	Acta Seminarii Neotestamentici Uppsaliensis
ATD	Das Alte Testament Deutsch
ATR	*Anglican Theological Review*
A.U.C.	*anno urbis conditae* or *ab urbe condita* (in the year specified from the founding of Rome)
BAA	M. Black, *An Aramaic Approach to the Gospel and Acts* (2nd ed.; Oxford: Clarendon, 1954)
BAG	W. Bauer, W. F. Arndt, and F. W. Gingrich, *Greek-English Lexicon of the New Testament and Other Early Christian Literature* (Cambridge University, 1957)
BBM	R. E. Brown, *The Birth of the Messiah* (Garden City, N.Y.: Doubleday, 1977)
BC	F. J. Foakes Jackson and K. Lake, *The Beginnings of Christianity* (5 vols.; London: Macmillan, 1920–33)
BDF	F. Blass, A. Debrunner, and R. W. Funk, *A Greek Grammar of the New Testament* (University of Chicago, 1961)
BDM	R. E. Brown, *The Death of the Messiah* (2 vols.; New York: Doubleday, 1994)
BET	Beiträge zur Evangelischen Theologie
BETL	Bibliotheca Ephemeridum Theologicarum Lovaniensium
BibKir	*Bibel und Kirche*
BibLeb	*Bibel und Leben*
BibOr	*Bibbia e Oriente*
BibSac	*Bibliotheca Sacra*
BibTrans	*The Bible Translator*
BJRL	*Bulletin of the John Rylands Library of the University of Manchester*
BNTC	Black's New Testament Commentaries
BR	*Bible Review*
BS	Biblische Studien
BTB	*Biblical Theology Bulletin*
BVC	*Bible et Vie Chrétienne*
BWANT	Beiträge zur Wissenchaft vom Alten und Neuen Testament
BZ	*Biblische Zeitschrift*
BZNW	Beihefte zur ZNW
CBNTS	Coniectanea Biblica: New Testament Series
CBQ	*Catholic Biblical Quarterly*
CD	Cairo (Genizah text of the) Damascus (Document)
CJ	*Cahiers de Joséphologie*

CJT — *Canadian Journal of Theology*
CKC — *Chronos, Kairos, Christos*, eds. J. Vardaman and E. M. Yamauchi (J. Finegan Festschrift; Winona Lake, IN: Eisenbrauns, 1989)
CNT — Commentaire du Nouveau Testament
CQR — *Church Quarterly Review*
CSEL — Corpus Scriptorum Ecclesiasticorum Latinorum
DAICC — W. D. Davies and D. C. Allison, ICC commentary on Matt. See Supplement Bibliography.
DBSup — *Dictionnaire de la Bible, Supplément*
EA — *Erbe und Auftrage*
EB — *Estudios Bíblicos*
EE — *Estudios Eclesiásticos*
EKKNT — *Evangelisch-Katholischer Kommentar zum Neuen Testament*
EphMar — *Ephemerides Mariologicae*
ETL — *Ephemerides Theologicae Lovanienses*
ETR — *Études Théologiques et Religieuses*
EV — *Esprit et Vie*
EvQ — *Evangelical Quarterly*
ExpTim — *Expository Times*
ExTh — P. Benoit, *Exégèse et Théologie* (4 vols.; Paris: Cerf, 1961–82)
FGN — *The Four Gospels 1992*, eds. F. Van Segbroeck *et al.* (F. Neirynck Festschrift; BETL 100; 3 vols.; Leuven Univ., 1992)
FRLANT — Forschungen zur Religion und Literatur des Alten und Neuen Testaments
GCS — *Die Griechischen Christlichen Schriftsteller* (Berlin)
GL — *Geist und Leben*
GP2 — *Gospel Perspectives 2*, eds. R. T. France and D. Wenhem (Sheffield: JSOT, 1981).
HJ — *Hibbert Journal*
HKNT — Handkommentar zum Neuen Testament
HNT — Handbuch zum Neuen Testament
HPG — C. Kopp, *The Holy Places of the Gospels* (New York: Herder and Herder, 1963)
HPR — *Homiletic and Pastoral Review*
HTKNT — Herders Theologischer Kommentar zum Neuen Testament
IBS — *Irish Biblical Studies*
ICC — International Critical Commentary
IEJ — *Israel Exploration Journal*
IER — *Irish Ecclesiastical Record*
ILS — H. Dessau, *Inscriptiones Latinae Selectae* (3 vols.; Berlin: Weidmann, 1892–1914)
ITQ — *Irish Theological Quarterly*
ITS — *Indian Theological Studies*
JAAR — *Journal of the American Academy of Religion*
JBap — John the Baptist
JBC — *The Jerome Biblical Commentary*, eds. R. E. Brown *et al.* (Englewood Cliffs, N.J.: Prentice-Hall, 1968). See NJBC
JBL — *Journal of Biblical Literature*
JBR — *Journal of Bible and Religion*
JETS — *Journal of the Evangelical Theological Society*
JJS — *Journal of Jewish Studies*
JQR — *Jewish Quarterly Review*

JR	*Journal of Religion*
JSNT	*Journal for the Study of the New Testament*
JSNTSup	Journal for the Study of the New Testament—Supplement Series
JSOTSup	Journal for the Study of the Old Testament—Supplement Series
JSS	*Journal of Semitic Studies*
JTS	*Journal of Theological Studies*
KJ	The *King James* or *Authorized Version* of the Bible
KMRL	*Kecharitōmenē: Mélanges René Laurentin*, eds. C. Augrain and T. A. Koehler (Paris: Desclée, 1990)
LD	Lectio Divina
LTK	*Lexikon für Theologie und Kirche*
LXX	Septuagint Greek Translation of the OT
MGNTG	J. H. Moulton, *Grammar of New Testament Greek* (4 vols.; Edinburgh: Clark, 1908–76)
MIE	S. Muñoz Iglesias, *Los Evangelios de la Infancia.* See Supplement Bibliography
MK	H. A. W. Meyer, Kritisch-exegetischer Kommentar über das Neue Testament
MNT	*Mary in the New Testament*, eds. R. E. Brown *et al.* (Philadelphia: Fortress; New York: Paulist, 1978)
MS	*Marian Studies*
MT	Mas(s)oretic Text of the OT or standard Hebrew Bible
MTC	B. M. Metzger, *A Textual Commentary on the Greek New Testament* (New York: United Bible Societies, 1971)
NAB	*New American Bible*
NJBC	*The New Jerome Biblical Commentary*, eds. R. E. Brown *et al.* (Englewood Cliffs, N.J.: Prentice-Hall, 1990)
NovTest	*Novum Testamentum*
NovTestS	Novum Testamentum Supplements
NRT	*Nouvelle Revue Théologique*
NS	new series
NT	The New Testament
NTA	*New Testament Abstracts*
NTApoc	E. Hennecke and W. Schneemelcher, *New Testament Apocrypha* (2 vols.; Philadelphia: Westminster, 1963–65)
NTD	Das Neue Testament Deutsch
NTR	*New Theology Review*
NTS	*New Testament Studies*
NTSMS	New Testament Studies Monograph Series
OL	The Old Latin Version of the Bible
OS	The Old Syriac Version of the Bible
OS^{cur}	The Curetonian tradition of the OS
OS^{sin}	The Sinaitic tradition of the OS
OT	The Old Testament
PG	J. Migne, Patrologia Graeca–Latina
PL	J. Migne, Patrologia Latina
PS	*Parola e Spirito*, ed. C. C. Marcheselli (Onore de S. Cipriani; 2 vols.; Brescia: Paideia, 1982)
QJRAS	*Quarterly Journal of the Royal Astronomical Society*
RB	*Revue Biblique*
RBR	*Ricerche Bibliche e Religiose*
RechScRel	*Recherches de Science Religieuse*

RevExp	*Review and Expositor*
RHE	*Revue d'Histoire Ecclésiastique*
RHPR	*Revue d'Histoire et de Philosophie Religieuses*
RivBib	*Rivista Biblica*
RSPT	*Revue des Sciences Philosophiques·et Théologiques*
RSV	*Revised Standard Version* of the Bible
RTP	*Revue de Théologie et de Philosophie*
SBFLA	*Studii Biblici Franciscani Liber Annuus*
SBLMS	Society of Biblical Literature Monograph Series
SBLSP	Society of Biblical Literature Seminar Papers
SBS	Stuttgarter Bibelstudien
SBT	Studies in Biblical Theology
SBU	Symbolae Biblicae Upsalienses
SC	Sources Chrétiennes
ScEccl	*Sciences Ecclésiastiques*
SeB	*Sémiotique et Bible*
SJT	*Scottish Journal of Theology*
SLJT	*Saint Luke's Journal of Theology*
StANT	Studien zum Alten und Neuen Testament
St-B	H. Strack and P. Billerbeck, *Kommentar zum Neuen Testament aus Talmud und Midrasch* (6 vols.; Munich: Beck, 1926–61)
StEv	Studia Evangelica
TalBab	The Babylonian Talmud
TalJer	The Jerusalem Talmud
TBT	*The Bible Today*
TD	*Theology Digest*
TDNT	G. Kittel and G. Friedrich, *Theological Dictionary of the New Testament* (10 vols.; Grand Rapids: Eerdmans, 1964–76; German original 1928–73)
THKNT	Theologischer Handkommentar zum Neuen Testament
TKP	*Zur Theologie der Kindheitsgeschichten; der heutige Stand der Exegese*, ed. R. Pesch (Munich: Schnell & Steiner, 1981)
TPQ	*Theologish-Praktische Quartalschrift*
TQ	*Theologische Quartalschrift*
TS	*Theological Studies*
TU	Texte und Untersuchungen
TZ	*Theologische Zeitschrift*
v.c.	virginal conception (an abbreviation used only in APPENDIX IV of the Supplement)
VCBRJ	R. E. Brown, *The Virginal Conception and Bodily Resurrection of Jesus* (New York: Paulist, 1973)
VetTest	*Vetus Testamentum*
VetTestS	Vetus Testamentum Supplements
VF	*Virgo fidelis*, eds. F. Bergamelli and M. Cimosa (D. Bertetto Festschrift; Rome: Centro Liturgico Vincenziano, 1988)
VK	*Vivarium*, eds. E. Dassmann and K. Thraede (T. Klauser Festschrift; Münster: Aschendorff, 1984)
ZBG	M. Zerwick, *Biblical Greek* (Rome: Pontifical Biblical Institute, 1963)
ZDMG	*Zeitschrift der Deutschen Morgenländischen Gesellschaft*
ZDPV	*Zeitschrift des Deutschen Palästina-Vereins*
ZNW	*Zeitschrift für die Neutestamentliche Wissenschaft*

ZTK   *Zeitschrift für Theologie und Kirche*

Standard abbreviations are used for the biblical books and for the Dead Sea
Scrolls (for the latter see NJBC, article 67, ##82–95). An asterisk after a
biblical version indicates the original hand of the copyist of the ms., as distinct
from later correctors.

There are seventeen sections in this book (see Contents); cross-references are
to sections (indicated by the § sign) and their subdivisions. The system of
bibliographical references is explained at the beginning of the Bibliography
for § 1.

INTRODUCTION

SCHOLARSHIP AND THE
INFANCY NARRATIVES (§ 1)

Two of the four Gospels, Matthew and Luke, begin with a story of Jesus' conception, birth, and childhood. Although coincidentally each consists of two chapters, the Lucan narrative is more than twice the length of the Matthean. The term "infancy narrative" is customary in English[1] and will be used, even though inaccurate and inadequate. Actually, only Matt 2 and Luke 2:1–40 describe Jesus' *infancy*, while the first chapter in each Gospel describes the period before Jesus' birth, and Luke 2:41–52 portrays Jesus at the age of twelve. As for *narrative*, one may well wonder whether the term is applicable to a series of short scenes with accompanying Scripture citations, such as we find in Matt 2:13–23.

Although they constitute a total of four out of eighty-nine Gospel chapters, the infancy narratives have an importance far greater than their length. They have offered abundant material for reflection both to Christian and non-Christian, to saint and skeptic. For orthodox Christians they have helped to shape the central doctrine of Jesus God and man. On the one hand they leave no doubt that Jesus was the Son of God from the moment of his conception; on the other hand the portrayal of physical birth (plus the Lucan reference to the manger) has underlined the true humanity of Jesus' origins. As a provocative Gospel subject for artists, storytellers, and poets, only the passion has rivaled the infancy narratives. Nevertheless, these narratives have also been a prime target for rationalistic scoffing. The frequent angelic appearances, the virginal conception, a marvelous star guiding magi from the East, a child prodigiously endowed with wisdom—to many these are patently legendary themes. In part, such a judgment reflects a general incredulity about the supernatural and the miraculous, an incredulity that is often just as unscientific as the credulity it

---

[1] The term "Prologue" also appears, but certainly the introductory chapters of Matthew and Luke are more closely integrated into their respective Gospels than is the Johannine hymn we call the Prologue (John 1:1–18). "Infancy narrative" renders the usual German designation *Kindheitsgeschichte*; but occasionally *Vorgeschichte*, "pre-history," is used, on the analogy of the first chapters of Genesis. French commentators tend to speak of "infancy gospels," a terminology which reflects the purpose of the evangelists. Since the two infancy narratives are so different, it may be asked whether the same designation is applicable to both.

replaced; but in part it reflects the observations of critical scholarship[2] on historical problems in the infancy narratives.

It is appropriate, then, to begin this commentary with a simplified analysis of the development of a scholarly understanding of the infancy narratives. To an extent, such an analysis reflects the past history of scholarship. Yet it also describes a growth that each person who reflects seriously on the problems will have to experience for himself or herself. This is an area where it is difficult to avoid reliving personally the history of thought. We may distinguish three stages in a deepening scholarly penetration of the infancy narratives: (A) The perception that the infancy narratives differ significantly from the main body of Gospel material; (B) The problem of historicity becomes more acute through the perception of the degree to which the two canonical infancy narratives differ from one another; (C) The historicity problem is somewhat relativized by the perception that the infancy narratives are primarily vehicles of the evangelist's theology and christology.

A. *The Infancy Narratives and the Rest of the Gospels*

Both in the lateness of their incorporation into the written Gospels and in their very origins the infancy narratives are unusual. To see this we must trace, first, the process of Gospel formation, and, then, the development of christology.

1. The Formation of the Gospels

Paradoxically, one may speak of the Gospels as developing backwards. The oldest Christian preaching about Jesus concerned his death and resurrection, as may be seen in the formulas of Acts 2:23,32; 3:14–15; 4:10; 10:39–40; and I Cor 15:3–4. Not only did these events constitute the clearest instance of God's salvific action in Jesus, but also it was through them that the disciples came to a more adequate understanding of who Jesus really was. The preaching was eventually shaped into an account of the passion which constituted the oldest consecutive narrative about Jesus.

Christian preachers also turned their attention to the deeds and words that came down to them from the traditions of Jesus' ministry. These were

2 By "critical scholarship" I mean a study of the Bible which employs scientific historical and literary methods. Such biblical criticism implies the recognition that, as a set of written documents, the Bible is open to the same methods of study as any other collection of literature. To many scholars who maintain a religious faith, such a recognition does not detract from the belief that the Bible is the word of God. Nor does it necessarily deny the inspiration of the Bible, unless inspiration is equated with divine dictation and seen as the basis of a simple theory of inerrancy in all matters.

particularly useful as further teaching[8] for those who had come to faith through the proclamation of the death and resurrection (see I Cor 7:10). Collections of sayings, parables, and miracles grew; and the evangelists drew upon these in composing accounts of the ministry of Jesus. The ministry narratives, however, were much less a consecutive unity than the passion narrative. Since no one of the four evangelists was himself an eyewitness of the ministry of Jesus, the arrangement of ministry material in the Gospels was logical rather than chronological.[4] Our written Gospels emerged from the prefixing of the ministry material to the passion accounts. The oldest example, the Gospel of Mark,[5] starts with the encounter of Jesus and JBap at the Jordan as "the beginning of the Gospel of Jesus Christ" (1:1), and it terminates with the angelic proclamation of the resurrection at the empty tomb (16:1–8).[6] Mark tells the reader nothing about Jesus' birth or youth, not even the name of his father (Joseph). An outline similar to Mark's may be detected in the sermon in Acts 10:37–41 —no mention of the birth, but a sequence beginning with the baptism and ending with the resurrection. This sermon is Luke's distillation from the Gospel account. We find the same pattern in the Fourth Gospel which (after an introductory hymn, the Prologue[7]) begins the story line with JBap's testimony about Jesus and ends with the appearances of the risen Jesus. John too tells the reader nothing about Jesus' birth, not even the name of his mother (Mary).

In such a process of Gospel formation, selection and emphasis were dictated by the fact that a message of salvation was being preached and taught. Biographical interest was not primary, for only a very unusual biography would begin with the subject's death and report little or nothing about his birth and parentage. This understanding of the Gospels obviates a problem that puzzled those ages when the Gospels were thought to be

---

8 Not only *kerygma* (proclamation) but also *didachē* (teaching) was a major factor in Gospel formation; see D. M. Stanley, CBQ 17 (1955), 336–48. It is noteworthy that the first written Gospel, Mark, contains a smaller body of *didachē* than do Matthew and Luke, and that is why in the past the Church has favored these later Gospels over Mark in its own teaching. Other factors in Gospel formation included apologetics, reflections on the OT, the usages of Christian cult and liturgy, etc.

4 It is interesting that the Roman Catholic Pontifical Biblical Commission, which at the beginning of this century insisted that Matthew and John were substantially eyewitness Gospels, now states: "The evangelists relate the words and deeds of the Lord in a different order, and express his sayings not literally but differently, while preserving (their) sense." See JBC, article 72, ##6,28,35.

5 The majority scholarly opinion is that Mark was written in the late 60s; Matthew and Luke in the 80s; and John in the 90s—approximations allowing a five-to-ten-year margin of error. The Roman Catholic Church was one of the last major Christian bodies to regard the date and authorship of biblical books as a doctrinal issue, but see below, § 2, footnote 2.

6 Mark 16:9–20 was a later addendum to the original Gospel.

7 The Johannine Prologue was often seen as giving the heavenly origin of Jesus, while Matthew and Luke gave the earthly origin, especially in their genealogies. Thus, Matt 1:1–17 was counterposed to John 1:1–18.

lives of Christ,[8] namely, the absence of infancy narratives in Mark and John. Sometimes these Gospels were deemed to be later compositions because of that absence;[9] but it is the other way around: the earlier one goes, the less emphasis one finds on the birth and family of Jesus. There is no reference at all to the birth in the sermons of Acts, and only one specific reference to it in the main Pauline letters.[10] In the early Christian preaching the birth of Jesus had not yet been seen in the same salvific light as the death and resurrection.

This brings us to a double question: Why were infancy narratives composed and why were they finally brought into the Gospel outline in the instance of Matthew and of Luke? First, the reasons for composition. *Curiosity* certainly played a role in both the canonical and apocryphal infancy stories.[11] Christians wanted to know more about their master: his family, his ancestors, his birthplace. And, on the implicit principle that the child is the father of the man, the marvelous aspects of Jesus' public life were read back into his origins. *Apologetics* may explain certain aspects of the infancy stories. Some would see an apologetic against non-Christian followers of JBap in the Lucan stories of JBap's birth,[12] e.g., in order to protect the superiority of Jesus, Luke describes JBap as acknowledging Jesus even before birth (1:41,44). Others would see an anti-Docetist aspect in the emphasis on the birth of Jesus.[13] More plausible is the suggestion that the story of Jesus' birth in Bethlehem was intended as a response to a Judaism skeptical about a Messiah who came from Galilee (John 7:41–42,52). If Judaism was already beginning to charge that Jesus was illegitimate (Appendix V), the virginal conception offered an explanation

---

[8] The oldest understanding of the Gospels was not so simplistically historical. In the early second century Papias wrote in reference to Mark: "When Mark became Peter's interpreter, he wrote down accurately, though by no means in order, as much as he remembered of the words and deeds of the Lord; for he had neither heard the Lord nor been in his company, but subsequently joined Peter, as I said. Now Peter did not intend to give a complete exposition of the Lord's ministry but delivered his instructions to meet the needs of the moment. It follows, then, that Mark was guilty of no blunder if he wrote, simply to the best of his recollections, an incomplete account" (Eusebius *Eccl. Hist.* III xxxix 15). Papias may have simplified Mark's relationship to Peter, but he makes clear that the Gospel is not a chronological or verbatim history.

[9] Clement of Alexandria (Eusebius *Eccl. Hist.* VI xiv 5) thought that the two Gospels with genealogies were written before the two Gospels without them. The thesis that Mark was an abridgment of Matthew and Luke, which omitted areas in which they did not agree, was used to explain the lack of an infancy narrative in Mark.

[10] Gal 4:4–5; see Appendix IV A.

[11] The apocryphal gospels most important for our purposes in this book are the *Protevangelium of James* (ca. A.D. 150) and the *Infancy Gospel of Thomas* (late second century). See the collection in Hennecke, NTApoc, I, 363–417.

[12] This proposal is related to the thesis that Luke drew upon a collection of JBap stories and modified them. I do not accept this thesis (below § 10D), and I find no anti-JBap apologetics in the Lucan infancy narrative.

[13] In later Christianity the creedal slogans "Born of the Virgin Mary" and "Suffered under Pontius Pilate" were employed to refute the Docetist claim that Jesus was not really human; they proved that he was born and died like other human beings (Appendix IV, footnote 3). But I fail to detect anti-Docetist apologetics in the infancy narratives.

that allowed for an irregularity in the birth, but at the same time, defended the purity of the mother and the sanctity of the child. Partly apologetic and partly *theological* factors may have been involved in the development of a pre-Matthean story that drew a parallel between Joseph the legal father of Jesus and Joseph the patriarch who dreamed dreams and went to Egypt (see Table VII). This same story had Jesus delivered from the hands of a wicked king who slaughtered male children—a deliverance no less dramatic than that of Moses from the hands of a wicked Pharaoh who slaughtered male infants. Such OT parallels and reminiscences would have served well in a counterapologetic against Jewish positions; they would have served even more fruitfully in developing a Christian understanding that Jesus the Messiah relived the history of his own people. Thus, many factors, some no longer to be detected with certitude, went into the development of infancy stories—besides the most obvious possible factor: a Christian memory of events that happened.

This leads us to the second part of our question: Why were certain infancy stories (whether pre-Gospel in origin or composed by the evangelists themselves) finally incorporated into the written Gospels of Matthew and Luke? If Mark could write a Gospel and be satisfied to have the heavenly voice at the baptism make the first declaration of Jesus' identity, why did Matthew and Luke feel impelled to preface the baptism with two chapters of infancy narrative? This addition to the Gospel is best explained in the light of the development of christology. Matthew and Luke saw christological implications in stories that were in circulation about Jesus' birth; or, at least, they saw the possibility of weaving such stories into a narrative of their own composition which could be made the vehicle of the message that Jesus was the Son of God acting for the salvation of mankind. When the infancy narratives conveyed that message, it became quite appropriate to prefix them to the main body of Gospel material about Jesus, which had the same message.

2. The Development of Christology

Several times throughout the commentary I shall have occasion to refer to and reflect upon the development of early christology, but it may be useful to the reader if I sketch it briefly here as part of the introduction to the infancy narratives. In a pre-Gospel period, as attested by Paul and the sermons in Acts, the *resurrection* was the chief moment associated with the divine proclamation of the identity of Jesus.[14] When God raised Jesus

---

14 At an earlier stage in Christian thought, the second coming (parousia) may have been the christological moment—when Jesus would return in glory, then God would fully reveal him as Messiah, Lord, and Son of Man. This outlook would have required very little change in standard Jewish expectations about the coming of the Messiah, except that Christians would have worked out a thesis of two comings, with the second constituting the moment of final victory, of the subjugation of God's enemies, and of universal peace and abundance.

from the dead and/or elevated Jesus to His right hand, God made or proclaimed him Lord, Messiah, and Son of God. Note the following texts:

■"This Jesus God raised up. . . . God has made him both Lord and Messiah, this Jesus whom you crucified" (Acts 2:32,36).

■"God exalted him at His right hand as Leader and Savior" (Acts 5:31).

■"What God promised to the fathers, He has fulfilled for us their children by raising Jesus, as it is written in Ps 2: 'You are my son; today I have begotten you'" (Acts 13:32–33).

■"Born of the seed of David according to the flesh; designated Son of God in power according to the Holy Spirit [Spirit of Holiness] as of resurrection from the dead" (Rom 1:3–4).

■"[Jesus] became obedient unto death, even death on the cross. Therefore God has highly exalted him and bestowed on him the name [i.e., 'Lord'] which is above every name" (Philip 2:8–9).

As can be seen from some of these texts, the resurrection was originally contrasted with a ministry of lowliness, so that through the resurrection Jesus became greater than he had been in the ministry.[15] (This is what scholars mean by a "two-step" christology.) This view can be easily understood in light of the fact that through the resurrection his first disciples learned what they had not known clearly before. But such a view became inadequate as Christians reflected further upon the mystery of Jesus' identity; and by the time the Gospels were written (beginning in the 60s), a more developed view was dominant whereby Jesus was seen already to have been the Messiah and Son of God during his ministry, so that the resurrection simply revealed more publicly what was there all the time. Mark tells *the reader* that already at the *baptism* Jesus was the Son of God (1:11).[16] Yet the disciples never recognized Jesus' glorious identity during his lifetime; and Jesus never openly reveals it to his disciples, presumably because (in Mark's judgment) they would not have been able to comprehend such a revelation. We detect this lack of comprehension in the transfiguration scene: when Jesus takes select disciples aside and unveils his majesty, and when God's voice declares that Jesus is His Son, they are afraid and do not understand (Mark 9:2–8). In Mark's Gospel, only after

---

15 I speak of the original import of the texts; I do not mean that they continue to have that connotation in Acts. Luke/Acts has diverse statements about the "christological moment"; some of them associate it with the resurrection, some with the baptism, and some with the virginal conception. Presumably, in his own mind Luke had harmonized these "moments," even as did later theology, e.g., the secret of Jesus' identity was revealed to Mary at the conception and revealed more widely at the baptism and the resurrection. He has woven into a sequence a movement from conception to baptism to resurrection (and to second coming)—a movement which, in terms of Christian growth of perception, went in the other direction.

16 On the one hand, it is simplistic to think that a divine voice spoke audibly at the baptism and was heard by those who stood around—no human being in Mark seems to be aware of what was revealed. On the other hand, it is just as simplistic to think that this was the moment when Jesus found out who he was. The evangelists are interested only in telling the reader who Jesus is, not in analyzing Jesus' growth in self-understanding.

the death of Jesus is the mystery finally unraveled by a human witness: "Truly this was God's Son" (Mark 15:39). Thus Mark has partially preserved the older understanding. He insists that Jesus was already Son of God and Messiah during his lifetime, but this was not publicly known; and so it becomes understandable why Christians might speak of his becoming Messiah and Son of God through the death and resurrection.

In the later Gospels the synthesis that Mark fashioned breaks down in two ways. First, the mystery of Jesus' identity begins to become apparent to his disciples already during his lifetime. In Matthew there are confessions of Jesus as God's Son where Mark has none (cf. Matt 14:33 with Mark 6:51–52; and Matt 16:16 with Mark 8:29). In the Fourth Gospel Jesus speaks openly as a pre-existent divine figure (John 8:58, 10:30; 14:9; 17:5). Second, the question of Jesus' identity is pressed back beyond the baptism in different ways. The Johannine Prologue presses it back to pre-existence before creation, while Matthew and Luke press it back to Jesus' *conception*.[17] The same combined ideas that early Christian preaching had once applied to the resurrection (i.e., a divine proclamation, the begetting of God's Son, the agency of the Holy Spirit), and which Mark had applied to the baptism, are now applied to the conception of Jesus in the words of an angel's message to Joseph and to Mary (respectively, in Matthew and in Luke). And once the conception of Jesus has become the christological moment, the revelation of who Jesus is begins to be proclaimed to an audience who come and worship (the magi, the shepherds), while others react with hostility (Herod in Matthew; those who contradict the sign in Luke 2:34). And thus the infancy stories have become truly an infancy gospel.

The addition of these stories to the Gospel proper is thus intelligible as part of a christological process—a process which explains well why they appear in the later Gospels rather than in Mark. (John took another christological route, namely through pre-existence.) Once they were attached, however, they did begin to give a biographical cast to Matthew's and Luke's account.[18] These Gospels now began with a conception and birth, continued through a public life, and ended with a death and resurrection. On first reading, such a biography makes perfect sense, but upon reflection many features are puzzling. If Herod and all Jerusalem knew of the birth of the Messiah in Bethlehem (Matt 2:3), and indeed Herod

17 In the commentary I shall stress that Matthew and Luke show no knowledge of preexistence; seemingly for them the conception was the becoming (begetting) of God's Son. The harmonization whereby John's pre-existent Word takes on flesh in the womb of the Virgin Mary (spoken of by Matthew and Luke) is attested only in the post-NT period; see § 5, footnote 27.

18 The correct insistence that the Gospels did not have biography as their original focus has led to a neglect of this fact. For a modern attempt to reintroduce the biographical into Gospel discussion without becoming simplistic, see G. N. Stanton, *Jesus of Nazareth in New Testament Preaching* (NTSMS 27; Cambridge University, 1975).

slaughtered the children of a whole town in the course of looking for Jesus (2:16), why is it that later in the ministry no one seems to know of Jesus' marvelous origins (13:54–55), and Herod's son recalls nothing about him (14:1–2)? If it was made clear through an angelic message to the parents of Jesus who Jesus was (the Davidic Messiah, the Son of God), why is it so difficult for his disciples to discover this later on, even though Mary was alive at the time of the ministry? Indeed, why does Mary herself seem to be an outsider to the family of true disciples (Matt 12:46–50)?[19] If JBap was a relative of Jesus who recognized him even before his birth (Luke 1:41,44), why does JBap give no indication during the ministry of a previous knowledge of Jesus and indeed seem to be puzzled by him (7:19)? Ingenious harmonizing has been invoked to solve such conflicts, e.g., JBap really did know about Jesus but was sending his disciples so that they could discover for themselves; or it was modesty that prevented Mary from telling the disciples that her son was the Son of God. But such ingenuity may be dispensed with when the backwards process of Gospel formation and christological development is understood. The stories of the ministry were shaped in Christian tradition without a knowledge of the infancy material; and the evangelists never really smoothed out all the narrative rough spots left by the joining of two bodies of once-independent material, even though in their own minds they presumably would have reconciled the different theologies therein contained (footnote 15 above).

B. *The Infancy Narratives as History*

What has been said about the difference of the infancy narratives from the rest of the Gospel material has implications for historicity which must now be pursued.

1. The Problem of Corroborating Witnesses

The main body of Gospel material has a claim to be anchored in the reminiscences of those who accompanied Jesus from shortly after his baptism until his death (see Acts 1:22) and to whom he appeared after his resurrection (Acts 10:41; I Cor 15:3). If the readers of the Gospel ask how do they know that Jesus was baptized, or that he preached in Galilee, or that there was a supper on the night before he died, or that there was a death, burial, and resurrection, one can reply (as did Paul who also was

---

19 In Mark 3:31–35 this scene (which is even harsher since it follows 3:21 where Jesus' "own" think he is frenzied) offers little difficulty, for Mark communicates no awareness of an infancy story or of a virginal conception (Appendix IV A). If Matthew did not see the difficulty, apparently Luke did; for Luke 8:19–21 is a drastic modification so that the mother of Jesus becomes part of the family of disciples (see § 11D).

not present at many of these events) that there was a tradition passed on about such things (I Cor 11:23; 15:3). But how do we know what happened at Jesus' birth? Certainly none of the apostolic preachers of the Jerusalem community who accompanied Jesus during his ministry and whose tradition is at the basis of the Gospel stories of the ministry (from the baptism to the resurrection) was present at the birth. (This difference is reflected in the situation discussed above wherein the birth of Jesus is not the subject of early apostolic preaching.) Indeed, the body of the Gospel shows that the people among whom Jesus had been reared knew nothing about an extraordinary infancy (Matt 13:53–58; Luke 4:31–32, 36–37). A common *guess* has been that the tradition about Jesus' infancy came from Joseph or Mary. Yet Joseph never appears during the ministry of Jesus and seems almost certainly to have been dead by that time,[20] so that it is really pure speculation to posit him as a source. Mary does not seem to have been close to the disciples of Jesus during the ministry (Mark 3:31–35; Matt 12:46–50; John 2:4), although there is NT evidence that she was part of the post-resurrectional community (Acts 1:14). While there is no *a priori* impossibility that she was the source of the material in the Lucan infancy narrative which describes experiences for which she would be the most plausible witness, there is an *a priori* unlikelihood that she was the source for the material in the Matthean infancy narrative which centers upon Joseph and in which she figures only on a secondary level. In the second century, James the "brother of the Lord" who lived into the 60s, was thought to be a plausible source for information about Jesus' infancy, but the resultant *Protevangelium of James* is highly legendary, makes elementary mistakes about Temple procedure, and is more obviously folkloric than the canonical infancy narratives.[21] All of this means that, in fact, we have no real knowledge that any or all of the infancy material came from a tradition for which there was a corroborating witness.

2. The Problem of Conflicting Details

If all the facts discussed thus far have raised doubts about the historicity of the infancy narratives,[22] how are these doubts to be resolved? The the-

[20] The failure to mention him in Mark 6:3, where the list of Jesus' family at Nazareth is being invoked, would otherwise be inexplicable. On the question of family reminiscences, see also footnote 25.

[21] The relative sobriety of the canonical infancy narratives when compared to the non-canonical ones has been used as an argument for their historicity. But is this a difference of kind (history vs. fiction) or a difference of degree? One might argue that both canonical and non-canonical narratives result from the attempts of Christian imagination to fill in the Messiah's origins, and that in the case of the apocryphal narratives the imagination had a freer and further exercise.

[22] Protestant biblical scholarship recognized these difficulties and began to wrestle with them seriously already at the end of the last century. The confrontation was postponed in

sis of inspiration may not be invoked to guarantee historicity, for a divinely inspired story is not necessarily history. Any intelligent attempt to combine an acceptance of inspiration with an acceptance of biblical criticism must lead to the recognition that there are in the Bible fiction, parable, and folklore, as well as history. Nor will it do to argue that the infancy narratives must be historical or else they would not have been joined to the main body of Gospel material which had its basis in history. That argument wrongly supposes that history or biography was the dominant optic of the evangelist, and also that the evangelist could tell whether the stories he included had a historical origin. We must rather face a gamut of possibilities. Although both treat the same period of Jesus' life, the respective approaches of the two infancy narratives may be different: both may be historical; one may be historical and the other much freer; or both may represent non-historical dramatizations.

In order to decide among these varied possibilities, let us make a detailed comparison of the two narratives to see whether they confirm or contradict each other. Since it is generally agreed among scholars that Matthew and Luke wrote independently of each other, without knowing the other's work, agreement between the two infancy narratives would suggest the existence of a common infancy tradition earlier than either evangelist's work—a tradition that would have a claim to greater antiquity and thus weigh on the plus side of the historical scale. The following eleven points are shared by the two infancy narratives:

a) The parents to be are Mary and Joseph who are legally engaged or married, but have not yet come to live together or have sexual relations (Matt 1:18; Luke 1:27,34).
b) Joseph is of Davidic descent (Matt 1:16,20; Luke 1:27,32; 2:4).
c) There is an angelic announcement of the forthcoming birth of the child (Matt 1:20–23; Luke 1:30–35).
d) The conception of the child by Mary is not through intercourse with her husband (Matt 1:20,23,25; Luke 1:34).[23]
e) The conception is through the Holy Spirit (Matt 1:18,20; Luke 1:35).
f) There is a directive from the angel that the child is to be named Jesus (Matt 1:21; Luke 1:31).
g) An angel states that Jesus is to be Savior (Matt 1:21; Luke 2:11).

Roman Catholicism because the anti-Modernist decrees of the Pontifical Biblical Commission in the period 1905–1915 blocked the development of biblical criticism until the pontificate of Pope Pius XII. When critical scholarship was finally encouraged, the delicate question of the historicity of the infancy narratives became the subject of debate immediately before Vatican II. It was because of his cavalier rejection of the infancy narratives that Jean Steinmann's *La Vie de Jésus* (1959) received the dubious distinction of being the last book to be placed on the Roman Catholic *Index of Forbidden Books*.

23 Some scholars have questioned whether Luke intended to portray a virginal conception (see below § 11, B1).

h) The birth of the child takes place after the parents have come to live together (Matt 1:24–25; Luke 2:5–6).

i) The birth takes place at Bethlehem (Matt 2:1; Luke 2:4–6).

j) The birth is chronologically related to the reign (days) of Herod the Great (Matt 2:1; Luke 1:5).

k) The child is reared at Nazareth (Matt 2:23; Luke 2:39).

As we evaluate these common points, it is striking that all but the last are found in one section of the Matthean narrative (1:18 – 2:1), and the last is something that could have been known by both evangelists from the public ministry. Moreover, even in the restricted section of Matthew where the parallels occur, there is often a significant difference from Luke, e.g., in (c) the angel speaks to Joseph in Matthew, while he speaks to Mary in Luke.

The rest of the Matthean infancy narrative is quite different from Luke's infancy narrative. The genealogy in Matt 1:1–17 is very unlike the genealogy that Luke has placed outside the infancy story (3:23–38). The whole of Matt 2:2–22 has no parallel in Luke, just as most of Luke 1 (outside 1:26–35) and most of Luke 2 have no parallel in Matthew. The Lucan account alone depicts the following: the story of Elizabeth, Zechariah, and the birth of JBap; the census which brings Joseph to Bethlehem; the acclamation of Jesus by the shepherds; the presentation of Jesus in the Temple as the parents return to Nazareth; and the loss and finding of Jesus in the Temple at the age of twelve. Matthew concentrates on a different series of happenings of which Luke makes no mention: the star, the magi, Herod's plot against Jesus, the massacre of the children at Bethlehem, and the flight into Egypt.

Commentators of times past have harmonized these different details into a consecutive narrative,[24] so that the ordinary Christian is often not even aware of a difficulty when Lucan shepherds and Matthean magi fraternize in the Christmas crib scene. But if originally there was one narrative, how did it ever become fragmented into the two different accounts we have now? As I hinted above, the suggestion that Matthew is giving Joseph's remembrance of the events, while Luke is giving Mary's, is just a pious deduction from the fact that Joseph dominates Matthew's account, and Mary dominates Luke's. In point of fact, how could Joseph ever have told the story in Matthew and not have reported the annunciation to Mary? And how could Mary have been responsible for the story in Luke and never have mentioned the coming of the magi and the flight into Egypt?[25]

---

24 See the attempt by Machen, *Virgin Birth*, 191ff. The normal harmonized sequence is Luke 1; Matt 1; Luke 2:1–38; an unmentioned return to Bethlehem; Matt 2.

25 At most, only one of the narratives can stem from family reminiscences, with the tacit assumption that most of the other is not historical. Moderately critical scholars who recognize this have generally opted for the Lucan account as the more likely family tradition. The research done in this commentary points to the implausibility of this thesis.

This leads us to the observation that the two narratives are not only different—they are contrary to each other in a number of details. According to Luke 1:26 and 2:39 Mary lives in Nazareth, and so the census of Augustus is invoked to explain how the child was born in Bethlehem, away from home. In Matthew there is no hint of a *coming* to Bethlehem, for Joseph and Mary are in a house at Bethlehem where seemingly Jesus was born (2:11). The only journey that Matthew has to explain is why the family went to Nazareth when they came from Egypt instead of returning to their native Bethlehem (2:22–23). A second difficulty is that Luke tells us that the family returned peaceably to Nazareth after the birth at Bethlehem (2:22,39); this is irreconcilable with Matthew's implication (2:16) that the child was almost two years old when the family fled from Bethlehem to Egypt and even older when the family came back from Egypt and moved to Nazareth. Of the options mentioned before we made the detailed comparison of the two narratives, one must be ruled out, i.e., that both accounts are completely historical.

Indeed, close analysis of the infancy narratives makes it unlikely that either account is completely historical. Matthew's account contains a number of extraordinary or miraculous public events that, were they factual, should have left some traces in Jewish records or elsewhere in the NT (the king and all Jerusalem upset over the birth of the Messiah in Bethlehem; a star which moved from Jerusalem south to Bethlehem and came to rest over a house; the massacre of all the male children in Bethlehem). Luke's reference to a general census of the Empire under Augustus which affected Palestine before the death of Herod the Great is almost certainly wrong (Appendix VII), as is his understanding of the Jewish customs of the presentation of the child and the purification of the mother in 2:22–24. Some of these events, which are quite implausible as history, have now been understood as rewritings of OT scenes or themes. For instance, Matthew's story of the magi who saw the star of the Davidic Messiah at its rising is an echo of the OT story of Balaam, a type of magus from the East, who saw the star rise out of Jacob (§ 6, C2). The story of Herod seeking the life of the infant Jesus and massacring the male children at Bethlehem is a reapplication of the OT story of the wicked Pharaoh who sought the life of the infant Moses and slaughtered the male children of the Israelites, even as the story of Joseph, the father of Jesus, who dreams dreams and goes to Egypt is a reapplication of the story of the patriarch Joseph who does the same thing (§ 4, B2). Luke's description of Zechariah and Elizabeth, the parents of JBap, is taken, at times almost verbatim, from the OT description of Abraham and Sarah.

It was at this point in the history of the investigation of the infancy narratives that the term "midrash" began appearing in the discussions. The

term came from the ancient Jewish interpretations of the OT which
popularized and expanded the biblical accounts (Appendix VIII). While
this term has helped to focus attention on the importance of OT motifs in
the infancy narratives, ultimately it does not do justice to them. The purpose of midrash was to make the OT account intelligible, and that is not
the purpose of the infancy narratives. They were written to make Jesus'
origins intelligible against the background of the fulfillment of OT expectations. The style of the use of the OT is very different in the two infancy
narratives (and so the same term derived from a method of interpreting
Scripture can scarcely be used to describe both); but the common instinct
to draw so heavily upon the Scriptures suggests that for each evangelist the
infancy narrative was to supply a transition from the OT to the Gospel—
the christological preaching of the Church presented in the imagery of Israel.

C. *The Infancy Narratives as Vehicles of the Evangelist's Theology*

With the remarks at the end of the last paragraph we have moved into the
present stage of scholarly research on the infancy narratives: the quest for
the evangelist's intent. If I spend only a few paragraphs developing this
quest here in the introduction, it is because that is the task of the whole
commentary.

Previous investigation with all its "hard-nosed" probing of historicity
was necessary, even if it discovered that the probabilities were more often
against historicity than for it.[26] Necessary too was the quest for sources,
even if it has led only to possibilities, and so was the quest for literary
genre (the midrash discussion), even if attempts at classification have not
been totally successful. Much of permanent value was discovered in all
those quests, and it will be digested and preserved in the pages that follow.
Nevertheless, the end result from some aspects of this past research has
been almost an embarrassment about the value of the infancy narratives
for educated Christians, as I pointed out in the Foreword.

Now biblical scholarship seems to be moving into a more fruitful stage
of research as it seeks to recover the value of the infancy stories as theology. In the last twenty years in general Gospel research, attention has
shifted away from the pre-Gospel history of narratives and sayings about

26 As I shall point out in Appendixes II, III, and IV, I think an intelligent case can be
made for the historicity of some of the details in the infancy narratives that have a close
relationship to Christian doctrine. I speak here of the historicity of the overall narratives.

Jesus to the role of those narratives and sayings in the finished Gospels.[27] What message is the evangelist trying to convey to the Church through them? This shift of focus can be dangerous if it leads to a neglect of questions of source, historicity, and literary genre; but it is healthy in its reaffirmation that the primary task of exegesis is to make sense of the existing text.

That the infancy narratives do make sense as part of their respective Gospels will be the *leitmotif* of this commentary. Whether or not the infancy narratives were historical, whether or not they were based on eyewitness testimony, whether or not they had a pre-Gospel existence, Matthew and Luke thought they were appropriate introductions to the career and significance of Jesus. To give them less value than other parts of the Gospels is to misread the mind of the evangelists for whom the infancy narratives were fitting vehicles of a message they wanted to convey. Indeed, from this point of view the infancy narratives are not an embarrassment but a masterpiece. Perhaps precisely because the material had been less fixed in the course of apostolic preaching, the evangelists exercised greater freedom of composition in the infancy narratives. One is hard pressed to find elsewhere in the Gospels theology so succinctly and imaginatively presented. It is my sincere hope that in this commentary I can effectively share with the reader my own discovery that the first two chapters of Matthew and Luke are just as profoundly Christian and as dramatically persuasive as the last two chapters, the story of the passion and resurrection.

---

[27] I refer to the development of *Redaktionsgeschichte,* but I am not overly content with some of the aspects of *redaktionsgeschichtlich* research. In this commentary I think of the evangelists as truly creative authors and not mere redactors. Moreover, I hope to avoid the abuse of having to find in every detail of the evangelist's work an example of his master plan. While the infancy narratives do fit into the respective evangelist's plan, there remain inconsistencies stemming from the different origin of the material contained therein.

GENERAL BIBLIOGRAPHY FOR THE
TWO INFANCY NARRATIVES

(The bibliographies of this book will contain works directly pertinent to the infancy narratives. If works on other topics are cited, the complete information about the work will be given at the place and moment of citation. There will be three types of bibliographies, proceeding from the general to the more specific, matching the focus of the works listed. The bibliography here is the most general, containing works that treat the two infancy narratives together or indiscriminately. For works that treat only the Matthean or only the Lucan infancy narrative, see the bibliographies at the end of §§ 2 and 9, respectively. Lastly, works treating a specific topic, passage, or verse within one of the infancy narratives will be listed in the bibliography at the end of the appropriate section.

Citations to works listed in one of the bibliographies will be given in a shortened form consisting of: the author's last name, one or two significant words, usually from the beginning of the title, and the page numbers (without the abbreviation "pp."). Thus, Strecker, *Weg*, 17. The complete bibliographical information pertinent to a work so cited may be easily found by consulting the Bibliographical Index at the end of the book. All abbreviations used in the bibliographies may be found in the list of Abbreviations on pp. 19–22 above.)

Bishop, E. F. F., "Bethlehem and the Nativity: Some Travesties of Christmas," ATR 46 (1964), 401–13.

Bornhäuser, K., *Die Geburts- und Kindheitsgeschichte Jesu* (Beiträge zur Förderung christlicher Theologie, 2nd series, 23; Gütersloh: Bertelsmann, 1930).

Box, G. H., "The Gospel Narratives of the Nativity and the Alleged Influence of Heathen Ideas," ZNW 6 (1905), 80–101.

Briggs, C. A., "The Gospel of the Infancy," *New Light on the Life of Jesus* (New York: Scribner's, 1904), 159–66.

Bultmann, R., *History of the Synoptic Tradition* (New York: Harper, 1963), esp. 291–301.

Cabaniss, A., "Christmas Echoes at Paschaltide," NTS 9 (1962–63), 67–69.

Daniélou, J., *The Infancy Narratives* (New York: Herder & Herder, 1968).

Delorme, J., "À propos des Evangiles de l'Enfance," *Ami du Clergé* 71 (1961), 760–64.

Derrett, J. D. M., "Further Light on the Narratives of the Nativity," NovTest 17 (1975), 81–108.

de Solages, B., "Réflexions sur les Evangiles de l'Enfance," *Bulletin de Littéra- ture Ecclésiastique* 72 (1971), 39–42.

Dibelius, M., *From Tradition to Gospel* (New York: Scribner's, 1935; orig. 1919), esp. 123–31.

Edersheim, A., *The Life and Times of Jesus the Messiah* (8th ed., 2 vols.; New York: Longmans, Green, 1897).

Erdmann, G., *Die Vorgeschichten des Lukas- und Matthäus-Evangeliums und Vergils vierte Ekloge* (FRLANT 47: Göttingen: Vandenhoeck, 1932).

Goodman, F. W., "Sources of the First Two Chapters in Matthew and Luke," CQR 162 (1961), 136–43.

Graef, Hilda, *Mary: A History of Doctrine and Devotion* (2 vols.; London: Sheed & Ward, 1963), esp. I, 1–31.

Kattenbusch, F., "Die Geburtsgeschichte Jesu als Haggada der Urchristolo- gie," *Theologische Studien und Kritiken* 102 (1930), 454–74.

Klostermann, E., and H. Gressmann, *Die Synoptiker Evangelien* (HNT; Tübingen: Mohr, 1919), esp. 151–67, 361–410.

Knox, W. L., *The Sources of the Synoptic Gospels* (2 vols.; Cambridge Univer- sity, 1957), esp. II, 39–44, 121–28.

Laurentin, R., "Bulletin sur la Vierge Marie," RSPT 54 (1970), 269–317; 56 (1972), 433–91. A survey of infancy narrative literature.

Leaney, R., "The Birth Narratives in St Luke and St Matthew," NTS 8 (1961–62), 158–66.

McHugh, J., *The Mother of Jesus in the New Testament* (Garden City, N.Y.: Doubleday, 1975).

Mann, C. S., "The Historicity of the Birth Narratives," in *Historicity and Chronology in the New Testament* (Theological Collection 6; London: SPCK, 1965), 46–58.

Minear, P. S., "The Interpreter and the Birth Narratives," SBU 13 (1950), 1–22.

Nellessen, E., "Zu den Kindheitsgeschichten bei Matthäus und Lukas," *Trier Theologische Zeitschrift* 78 (1969), 305–9. A survey of German literature.

Ortensio da Spinetoli, *Introduzione ai Vangeli dell'Infanzia* (Brescia: Paideia, 1966). Good bibliography.

Räisänen, H., *Die Mutter Jesu im Neuen Testament* (Annales Academiae Scientiarum Fennicae, Series B, 158; Helsinki: Suomalainen Tiedeaka- temia, 1969), esp. 52–137.

Riedl, J., *Die Vorgeschichte Jesu. Die Heilsbotschaft von Mt 1–2 und Lk 1–2* (Biblisches Forum 3; Stuttgart: Katholisches Bibelwerk, 1968).

Schelkle, K. H., "Die Kindheitsgeschichte Jesu," *Wort und Schrift* (Düssel- dorf: Patmos, 1966), 59–75.

Schmidt, K. L., *Der Rahmen der Geschichte Jesu* (Berlin: Trowitzsch, 1919), esp. 309–16.

Schubert, K., *Jesus im Lichte der Religionsgeschichte des Judentums* (Vienna: Herold, 1973), esp. 11–40.

Schürer, E., *A History of the Jewish People in the Time of Jesus Christ* (5 vols.; Edinburgh: Clark, 1885–90).

Stauffer, E., *Jesus and His Story* (London: SCM, 1960), esp. 22–43.

Streeter, B. H., *The Four Gospels* (rev. ed.; London: Macmillan, 1930), esp. 266–68.

Thomas, J., *Our Records of the Nativity and Modern Historical Research* (London: Sonnenschein, 1900).

Thompson, P. J., "The Infancy Gospels of St. Matthew and St. Luke Compared," StEv, I (TU 73; Berlin: Akademie, 1959), 217–22.

Vögtle, A., *Das Evangelium und die Evangelien* (Düsseldorf: Patmos, 1971), 43–102.

Völter, D., *Die evangelischen Erzählungen von der Geburt und Kindheit Jesu kritisch untersucht* (Strasbourg: Heitz, 1911).

Winandy, J., *Autour de la Naissance de Jésus* (Lire la Bible, 26; Paris: Cerf, 1970).

BOOK ONE

THE MATTHEAN INFANCY NARRATIVE

(Matt 1–2)

I. GENERAL OBSERVATIONS ON THE MATTHEAN GOSPEL AND INFANCY NARRATIVE (§ 2)

We shall begin with Matthew's infancy narrative which is shorter and more easily manageable than Luke's. Before reading this commentary, the reader is urged to go through Matt 1–2 carefully, noting what is in Matthew and expunging from mind details about Jesus' birth known from the Lucan infancy narrative. Methodologically, it is imperative to ask oneself: What would I learn about Jesus' birth if I possessed only Matthew's Gospel.

A. *The Matthean Gospel*

Most scholars today maintain that the Gospel was written in Syria by an unknown Greek-speaking Jewish Christian, living in the 80s in a mixed community with converts of both Jewish and Gentile descent. This is the theory presupposed in my discussion of the Matthean infancy narrative. (I hope that discussion will have its own merit, but I do not wish to detract from its utility by adopting a distinctly minority approach to the Gospel.) A standard NT introduction[1] will give detailed supporting arguments for this position, and in footnotes I shall alert the reader where there is serious dissent from it. I wish to explain here only the elementary reasoning behind it, so that the reader may appreciate the Christian community situation seen in and through the infancy narrative.

There would be nearly unanimous agreement in scientific circles today that the evangelist is unknown, although we continue the custom of referring to him as "Matthew." His dependence upon Mark (and upon Q, a body of Jesus' sayings in Greek, known also to Luke) indicates that he was not an eyewitness of the ministry of Jesus;[2] for presumably an eyewit-

---

[1] For example, W. G. Kümmel, *Introduction to the New Testament* (rev. ed.; Nashville: Abingdon, 1975).

[2] Roman Catholics were among the last to give up defending officially the view that the Gospel was written by Matthew, one of the Twelve—a change illustrated in 1955 when the secretary of the Roman Pontifical Biblical Commission gave Catholics "full liberty" in reference to earlier Biblical Commission decrees, including one which stipulated that Greek

ness with his own memories would not draw so totally upon "secondhand" collections. The fact that he improves upon Marcan Greek and that no major portion of his work shows signs of being a direct translation from Semitic suggests that we should think of the evangelist as a Greek-speaking Christian. Yet, at least in some of his formula citations of Scripture (Table V below), the evangelist seems to have a control of Hebrew; and so many scholars add the detail that he was a Greek-speaking *Jewish* Christian.[3] His respect for the details of the Law (5:17–18) and for the authority of scribes and Pharisees (23:2), combined with a fierce hostility toward scribes and Pharisees who oppose Jesus (23:13,15,23,25,27,29), would be explicable if he was a scribe of the Pharisee party who had come to believe in Jesus. Indeed, the praise of the scribe "who has been trained for the kingdom of heaven," which comes at the end of Jesus' sermon in parables (13:52), may be autobiographical.

The relationship to Mark (written *ca.* A.D. 70?), as well as the polemics with the Synagogue reflected in Matthew, make a date in the 80s plausible.[4] After the failure of the Jewish revolt against the Romans in the 60s and the destruction of the Temple in 70, the pluralism of Judaism rapidly diminished, as the Pharisees attained exclusive domination. Around the year 85, the twelfth of the *Eighteen Benedictions* (*Shemoneh Esreh:* one of the principal prayers in synagogues) was reformulated so as to include a curse on *minîm* or heretics, including, or even primarily, Jews who believed in Jesus as the Messiah.[5] This traumatic expulsion (which in many ways cut the umbilical cord that had joined the Church, or at least the Jewish-Christian churches, to Judaism) increased the bitterness of Christians toward the Pharisees who opposed Jesus.[6] This appears in the apologetic overtones of the christology of the infancy narrative with its stress on Jesus' genealogy as the son of David, and its contention that he

---

Matthew was identical in substance with a Gospel written by the apostle in Aramaic or Hebrew. (See JBC, article 72, ##25,28.) A group of Protestant scholars (mostly American, e.g., W. R. Farmer) who have argued that Matthew was *not* dependent on Mark do not interpret Matthean priority to mean that the evangelist was an eyewitness. Whether or not Papias of Hierapolis was factual when he reported that Matthew collected the sayings of the Lord in the Hebrew language (Eusebius *Eccl. Hist.* III xxxix 16), no such collection was preserved for us; and there is no way of knowing whether canonical Matthew drew even indirectly (through translation) on such a collection.

[3] There are exceptions on both points. J. Jeremias, ZNW 50 (1959), 270–74, argues that the evangelist's mother tongue was Aramaic and his prayer tongue was Hebrew. That the evangelist was not a Jew is argued by Strecker, *Weg,* 34. See also P. Nepper-Christensen, *Das Matthäusevangelium—ein juden-christliches Evangelium?* (Aarhus University, 1958); and K. W. Clark, JBL 66 (1947), 165–72.

[4] Matthew is thought to have written before the time (*ca.* 110) of Ignatius of Antioch who knew Matthean tradition.

[5] Davies, *Setting,* 275ff.; J. L. Martyn, *History and Theology in the Fourth Gospel* (New York: Harper & Row, 1968), 31ff. The Fourth Gospel was written after this action (John 9:22); it is more difficult to be certain about Matthew.

[6] R. Hummel, *Die Auseinandersetzung zwischen Kirche und Judentum im Matthäus-evangelium* (BET 33; 2nd ed.; Munich: Kaiser, 1966). He and others suggest that Matthew was engaged in another polemic as well: against Gentile Christians who were antinomians or depreciated the Law.

was born in Bethlehem. Indeed, as we shall see in § 4, A1, there is probably a hint of polemic in the way the evangelist cites Scripture.

But apologetics does not dominate the Matthean Gospel; it is primarily
an instruction and exhortation to a Christian community consisting of both
Jews and Gentiles, enlightening and confirming them in their faith.[7]
Matthew stresses that Jesus directed a ministry only to Israel (10:5–6;
15:24); yet the risen Christ sent forth his followers to make disciples of
the Gentiles (28:18).[8] This is more than a remembrance of what had happened about the year 30; it is an analysis of the way evangelization had
proceeded since then. A Christian community, at first Jewish, had seen an
increasing number of Gentiles come to believe; and with the rejection of
Christians by the Synagogue, it now seemed as if the kingdom were being
taken away and given to a "nation" that would bear fruit (21:43). In this
situation of a mixed community[9] with dominance now shifting over to the
Gentile side, Matthew is concerned to show that Jesus has always had
meaning for both Jew and Gentile. (And nowhere does he do this more
consistently than in the infancy narrative.) Such a reconstruction of
Matthew's situation has led scholars to localize the author and his community in Syria,[10] as a place near Palestine where there would be many
Greek-speaking Jews as well as Gentiles, where there would be a strong
presence of the Synagogue, and where one could plausibly encounter a
converted scribe who wrote Greek and knew Hebrew. Other factors con-
tributing to a localization in Syria are the importance of Peter in this
Gospel (he is placed at Antioch in Syria in Gal 2:11), some close similarities between Matthew and the *Didache* (thought to have been composed
in Syria), and a knowledge of Matthean tradition by Ignatius of Antioch.

A final introductory detail is that the evangelist shows himself to be systematic and a good organizer, collecting into topical and thematic units
material that was once scattered. His intent was to instruct his community
about the kingdom of heaven, and his sense of organization made this
Gospel the best adapted of the four to serve as a catechetical text. In detecting organization some scholars have found in chs. 3–25 five "books,"
each ending with a refrain in which it is stated that Jesus had finished his

---

[7] Even the apologetics may have been catechetical in intent: not primarily intended to
convert or change hostile Pharisee authorities, but to give confirming, defensive arguments
to Jewish Christians who had been bombarded by Jewish arguments against Jesus.

[8] See J. P. Meier, CBQ 37 (1975), 204–7; D. R. A. Hare and D. J. Harrington, *ibid.*,
359–69; J. P. Meier, CBQ 39 (1977), 94–102.

[9] Jewish and Gentile elements in the Matthean community are recognized widely by
scholars; but some, e.g., Trilling and Strecker, do not think of them as stemming from the
same period of time. They attribute the strongest Jewish interests in Matthew to an early
stage of Gospel transmission and community life, and the Gentile interests to a later stage
(which was the time of the evangelist).

[10] Antioch is frequently suggested; but B. W. Bacon has argued strongly for eastern Syria,
a thesis that would explain why the first to accept Jesus (the magi) are described as coming
from the East. Goulder, *Midrash*, 12ff., argues strongly for Matthew as a small-town or provincial scribe in this area.

sayings (7:28; 11:1; 13:53; 19:1; 26:1). These five books have been seen
to constitute a Christian Pentateuch based on a typology between Christ and
Moses. In particular, the Sermon on the Mount and the Beatitudes have
been compared with the scene of Moses on Sinai and the Ten Commandments. There are real difficulties about this theory,[11] even though it may
contain elements of truth. It is important background for the thesis to
be mentioned below that the Matthean infancy narrative deliberately
patterns the birth of Jesus on the birth of Moses, and that there are five
episodes in the infancy narrative centered around the five fulfillment
citations.

B. *The Matthean Infancy Narrative*

Two main problems concern us here: the external relation of Matt 1–2 to
the rest of the Gospel, and the internal organization or structure of Matt
1–2.

1. The Relation of Chs. 1–2 to the Rest of the Gospel

We saw in § 1 that the birth stories had an origin and transmission
different from that of the stories of Jesus' ministry, death, and resurrection. Yet it is the same evangelist who put these two bodies of material
together.[12] How did he effect this union? The more obvious supposition is
that from the start he had the infancy material in mind, so that he began
writing at 1:1 and continued right into the account of the ministry. However, since we are following the majority hypothesis that Matthew drew
upon Mark's Gospel, which began with the baptism and the ministry, it is
not inconceivable that Matthew at first planned a Gospel with the same
general outline as Mark, and only as an afterthought prefixed the infancy
narrative. Let us evaluate these two proposals.

Certainly the infancy narrative is no alien intrusion in the Matthean
Gospel, for many of the same thought patterns are shared by the infancy
narrative and the Gospel proper.[13] For instance, the Matthean hallmark of
explicit citations of Scripture, introduced by a formula stressing fulfillment,
runs through both bodies of material (Table V). But when we go beyond
the general similarity of style and thought, we run into difficulty. The Gos-

---

11 The great proponent of this theory was Bacon who, in his *Studies*, traced it back in
Christian tradition to the very origins of exegesis. It is seriously criticized by Davies, *Setting*,
and Kingsbury, *Matthew*.

12 The general similarity in style between the Matthean infancy narrative and the rest of
the Gospel precludes the possibility that the first two chapters are the work of another
hand.

13 See Racette, "L'Evangile," 77–78, for a list of common themes; but he adds that the
evangelist seems to work with more personal freedom of composition in the infancy narrative than in the rest of the Gospel.

pel proper never refers back to the special information supplied by the infancy narrative, e.g., to a birth at Bethlehem, to a major stir caused by that birth when the magi came to Jerusalem, or even to the virginal conception.[14] No one in the ministry appears to have profited from the christological insights revealed during Jesus' conception and infancy. If the first two chapters had been lost and the Matthean Gospel came down to us beginning with 3:1,[15] no one would have ever suspected the existence of the missing chapters. The title in 1:1, "The Birth Record of Jesus Christ," if it refers just to chs. 1–2, might conceivably be the title of a separate and independent work.

However, in my judgment these difficulties reflect more on the unique *origins* of the infancy materials rather than on the process of Matthean composition; and there are other factors that relate chs. 1–2 very closely to what follows and point toward unified composition. Indeed, there has been a serious attempt to identify 4:17, rather than 3:1, as the opening of a new section in Matthew's Gospel plan, so that the opening section would run from 1:1 through 4:16.[16] The geographic motif in ch. 2 that runs from Bethlehem (2:1) to Nazareth (2:23) would then continue from Nazareth to Capernaum in 4:13; and Capernaum would be the center of the ministry proper which opens in 4:17 with the words: "From that time on Jesus began to preach." The pattern of frequent formula citations (five in chs. 1–2) would be continued with two more in 3:3 and 4:14–16.[17] A christology of Jesus as "son of David, son of Abraham" in chs. 1–2 (see 1:1) would be continued in 3:1 – 4:16 with a christology of him as "Son of God" (3:17).[18] Some would argue that the title in 1:1 should be translated: "The Book of the Origin of Jesus Christ," and that it covers all the preliminaries up to 4:16. (This is quite dubious; the noun *genesis* clearly means "birth" in 1:18, and should be translated as "birth" rather than "origin" in 1:1). Finally, if one of the primary analogies for chs. 1–2 is the legend that grew up around Moses' birth (§ 4, B2 below), then the

14 One would have expected some of this information to appear in Matt 13:53–58 where those in Nazareth who know Jesus and his family betray no understanding of his greatness. Matthew 13:55 refers to Jesus as "the son of the carpenter." In a small northern town would they not have inquired about the strangers who came from Bethlehem in the South? If it was known that their son was born there, would it not have been the talk of Nazareth that he had escaped the terrible massacre?

15 The introductory words of that verse, "In those days," might serve as the opening of a book. The phrase appears in the opening of the *Gospel of the Ebionites* (Epiphanius *Adv. Haer.* XXX xiii 6): "Now it happened in those days when Herod was king of Judah [with Caiaphas as high priest], that John came baptizing" (a combination of Matt 3:1 and Luke 3:1–2). It is not a reference to the days of the infancy narrative or of Jesus' childhood (which occurred many years before), but is an eschatological expression indicating the time chosen by God (Jer 33:15; Joel 4:1 [RSV 3:1]).

16 Krentz, "Extent"; Kingsbury, *Matthew*, 1–37.

17 The four citations in ch. 2 mention place names, as do those in 3:3 ("the desert") and 4:15 ("Galilee of the Gentiles"). If the seven citations are taken as a sequence, the first and last are from Isaiah.

18 Or one could find the "son of David" motif in chs. 1–2 (1:20; 2:6), the "son of Abraham" motif in 3:8–9, and the "Son of God" motif in 3:17.

history of Moses as a young man (Exod 2:11ff.), preceding his great mission, may be a parallel to Matt 3:1 – 4:16.

I find the evidence for the unity of Matt 1:1 – 4:16 interesting but not compelling. The very arguments advanced for it, however, have enough value to tip the scales decisively in favor of the thesis that Matthew composed the infancy narrative as an integral part of his Gospel plan. The Matthean infancy narrative was not an afterthought.

2. The Internal Organization of Chs. 1–2

The outline or structure that one detects in chs. 1–2 reflects a decision about the main emphases in the narrative and about whether the evangelist was joining material from different sources (oral or written). To facilitate that decision let me list the facts which must be dealt with.

a) The genealogy in 1:1–17 has its own unity and organization, based on patterns of fourteen generations. This genealogy is set off as a unit by an inclusion[19] between the introduction in vs. 1 and the conclusion in vs. 17. Both these verses relate Jesus to David and Abraham.[20]

b) The unity of the genealogy is not absolute, for it is connected to the account of Jesus' conception which follows in 1:18–25. The genealogy is introduced in vs. 1 with a reference to the *genesis* of Jesus Christ, and vs. 18 continues that motif: "Now, as for [Jesus] Christ, his *genesis* ('birth') took place in this way." The section in 18–25 explains the "How" of Jesus' Davidic descent which is at the core of the genealogy, and clarifies the peculiar wording with which the genealogy describes Jesus' parentage in vs. 16: "Jacob was the father of Joseph, the husband of Mary; of her was born Jesus, called the Christ."[21]

c) While the section in 1:18–25 is closely related to the genealogy which precedes it, that section is also related by stylistic patterns to what follows in ch. 2. There runs through 1:18 – 2:23 a pattern of five explicit citations of OT prophecy, introduced by a formula stressing that these prophecies are fulfilled in the events pertinent to Jesus (see Table V below). There is also a pattern of three dream appearances by an angel of the Lord who gives Joseph a command that he carries out to the letter (see Table VI).

d) Despite this continuity of pattern, there are reasons for a separation between chs. 1 and 2. The first verse of ch. 2 has the air of beginning a new story,[22] and there is nothing in that story which presupposes information from ch. 1. And so, one might agree with the ancient scholar who divided

---

19 Inclusion is a stylistic technique for marking off or·"packaging" a unit: a detail mentioned at the beginning of a section is alluded to or repeated at the end.

20 This is clear in the Greek: vs. 1 speaks of the *genesis* of Jesus Christ, son of David, son of Abraham, while 17 speaks of the *geneai* ("generations") from Abraham to David to the Christ.

21 The wording is peculiar because the pattern in the genealogy would have led one to expect: "Jacob was the father of Joseph; Joseph was the father of Jesus by Mary."

22 Strecker, *Weg*, 52–53, argues that there was a pre-Matthean unity of material in chs. 1–2, but Matthew added 1:18 and 2:1a, breaking up the existing sequence. I reject this

the Bible into chapters and settle on two parallel units (chs. 1 and 2), each terminating on the note of what the child was called, namely, "Jesus" (1:25) and "Nazorean" (2:23).

e) If one does consider ch. 2 to be a unit, two distinct strands of narrative seem to be woven together imperfectly within its verses. In one strand (vss. 1–2,9–11) the magi are illumined by a star as to the birth of Jesus, a star which leads them to Bethlehem and the house. In the other strand (vs. 3–8) they are advised to go to Bethlehem by Herod who inquires about the child. The implication of hostility in this second strand is developed in 13–23, and, as we shall see, really constitutes a story in itself.

f) A geographical motif runs through ch. 2, so that birth in *Bethlehem,* flight to *Egypt,* and journey back to *Nazareth* constitute a divinely guided itinerary. A grammatical pattern of "Now, when [or after] . . . , behold"[23] marks the opening of the subsections dealing with the three geographical locations (2:1; 2:13; 2:19), and each location becomes the subject of a Scripture citation.[24]

No one outline of Matt 1–2 can do justice to all these facts, and the two most popular outlines have favored some of the facts, with the resultant neglect of others. The first outline we shall discuss detects an introduction and five scenes built around the five formula citations of Scripture.[25]

Introduction:	1:1–17		The genealogy
Scene One:	1:18–25	(Isa 7:14)	First dream of Joseph
Scene Two:	2:1–12	(Micah 5:1)[26]	Herod, magi, Bethlehem
Scene Three:	2:13–15	(Hosea 11:1)	Second dream of Joseph
Scene Four:	2:16–18	(Jer 31:15)	Herod, children, Bethlehem
Scene Five:	2:19–23	(Isa 4:3?)	Third dream of Joseph

This outline takes into account points (a), (c), and (e) above, but does little justice to (b), (d), and (f). Although some find a fivefold division in

---

theory, for I hope to show that it is Matthew who unified pre-Matthean elements; but it does illustrate the abruptness of 2:1.

23 This pattern of a genitive absolute with a postpositive *de,* followed by *idou,* is also found in 1:20 (see Table VI) where there is no geographical reference. On the other hand, the grammatical patterns in 1:20; 2:13; and 2:19 are set in the context of an angelic dream appearance, and that is not true in 2:1.

24 The pattern, however, is not perfectly clear. Besides the difficulties mentioned in the preceding footnote, we should note that still another formula citation of Scripture appears in 2:18 with a geographical location (Ramah) that does not fit into an itinerary for Jesus going from Bethlehem through Egypt to Nazareth.

25 Galbiati, "L'adorazione," supports the fivefold division by pointing out that it is not dependent solely on five formula citations, for he finds the pattern of a secondary allusion to the OT in each section. In Scene One, "He will save his people from their sins" (21) echoes the Samson story in Judg 13:3–5; in Scene Two the coming of the magi and the list of their gifts echo the visit of the Queen of Sheba to Solomon in I Kgs 10:1–13; in Scenes Three and Four Herod's actions echo the Pharaoh's killing of the newborn in Exod 1:22; and in Scene Five the command in 2:20 echoes the Moses story in Exod 4:19–20. However, while these echoes of the OT give clues as to the background and origin of Matthew's narrative, they are scarcely systematic enough to constitute proof for a fivefold division.

26 To be exact, no complete formula of fulfillment introduces this compound citation of Micah 5:1 and II Sam 5:2, even though it is identified as a prophecy (see § 6, B1, below).

the body of the Gospel, as we saw above, it is questionable whether formula citations should constitute a basis for divisions in the infancy narrative, since in the body of the Gospel they are scattered and do not seem to serve as indicators of a division.[27] What they indicate are areas of theological significance which might otherwise be overlooked. Consequently, an outline which features them has the advantage of highlighting the theological character of the events narrated—events that Matthew has chosen because they are related to the expectations of Israel, and because they fulfill prophecy, as he understands it.

A second and even more popular outline[28] supposes that the division of the infancy narrative into two chapters has preserved the evangelist's intention. Sometimes this division is made fourfold through subdivision,[29] thus:

ch. 1: 1:1–17:   Genealogy
          1:18–25:   The conception of Jesus
ch. 2: 2:1–12:   The coming of the magi to Bethlehem
          2:13–23:   Flight of the family to Egypt and return to Nazareth

In a brilliant article entitled *"Quis et Unde?"* Stendahl has concisely picked out a theological motif for each chapter. The first chapter would answer the question "Who?" (*Quis*): Jesus is "son of David, son of Abraham" (1:1) and Savior of his people (1:21)—a chapter of names. The second chapter would answer the question "Whence?" (*Unde*)—a chapter centered around locales (Bethlehem, Egypt, Ramah) offering a geographical/theological itinerary. This outline does justice to points (b), (d), and (f) above, but less justice to points (a), (c), and (e).

There is both plausibility and difficulty, then, in each of the outlines. In part, as we shall see, this situation reflects the history of the composition of Matthew's infancy narrative. In my judgment, Matthew has incorporated into the final narrative several different kinds of raw materials: lists of names of patriarchs and kings, and a messianic family tree; an annunciation of the Messiah's birth patterned on OT annunciations of birth; a birth story involving Joseph and the child Jesus, patterned on the patriarch Joseph and the legends surrounding the birth of Moses; a magi-and-star story patterned on the magus Balaam who came from the East and saw the Davidic star that would rise from Jacob; and finally some carefully chosen citations of Scripture. (Each of these will be discussed in the commentary.) Some of this raw material had its own outline and organization (e.g., a sequence of angelic dream appearances in the birth story patterned

----

27 Yet see § 4, footnote 5.

28 A basic division into two parts is supported by Bonnard, Bultmann, Léon-Dufour, Milton, Rasco, and Stendahl, among others.

29 Racette, "L'Evangile," 79, finds a further pattern of three in each of the four subdivisions, e.g., three sections in the genealogy, three scenes in 2:13–23. It is difficult to find three scenes in 2:1–12, however, and virtually impossible to find three in 1:18–25. If one breaks down ch. 2 beyond the two subdivisions, one can find five scenes, as I shall illustrate in § 6, A1, below.

on the patriarch Joseph and Moses); and the pre-Matthean outline has not
been completely covered over in the final product. Thus some of the patterns that we have detected in points (a) through (f) above are really pre-
Matthean patterns that have not been erased.

In another way, the difficulty of detecting an outline stems from the in-
terlocking character of Matthean thoughts. Stendahl's analysis of the
themes (which I shall expand below) is true if one underlines the fact that
the geographical names in ch. 2 continue the motif of the "Who" in ch. 1:
Jesus is born at Bethlehem because he is the son of David; he goes to
"Galilee of the Gentiles" (4:15) because he is son of Abraham by whom
"all the nations of the earth shall bless themselves" (Gen 22:18). Moreover, because of the virginal conception through the Holy Spirit (1:18–
25), Jesus has been revealed as the Son of God; and ch. 2 recounts the
proclamation of that through the star and the Scriptures, as well as the
twofold reaction of belief/homage (magi who are Gentiles) and of rejec-
tion/persecution (Herod, "all the chief priests and scribes of the people,"
"all Jerusalem"). No single outline can do justice to such intertwined motifs.

Nevertheless, an expansion of Stendahl's formula[30] offers a basic approach—not simply *Quis et Unde* but *Quis et Quomodo, Ubi et Unde*
(Who, How, Where, Whence):

  1:1–17: The *Quis* (Who) of Jesus' identity as son of David, son of
  Abraham, as illustrated through his ancestors—a double motif
  catalyzed by the mixed character of the Matthean community, Jew
  and Gentile. Women from the OT are mentioned to prepare for the
  way in which the Spirit will work through Mary: "of her was begotten Jesus, called the Christ."

  1:18–25: The *Quomodo* (How) of Jesus' identity: he is son of David
  not through physical begetting, but through an acceptance by the
  Davidid Joseph of a child conceived through the Holy Spirit. This
  conception further clarifies the *Quis* of Jesus' identity: he is the Son
  of God, Emmanuel.

  2:1–12: The *Ubi* (Where) of Jesus' birth, at Bethlehem, underlines
  his identity as son of David. The paradox that Gentiles (the magi)
  react to this birth by belief and homage begins to explain how Jesus
  is to function as son of Abraham.[81]

[30] I owe the idea of doubling Stendahl's formula to A. Paul, *L'Evangile*, 96; for I have
put into Latin *with adaptation* his suggestion that Stendahl's *"Qui et d'Où"* needs a *Comment* and a *Quand*. For my difficulties with the way Paul himself develops the outline, see
§ 6, C2.

[81] P. J. Thompson, "Infancy," 219, finds the son of David theme in the persecution of
Jesus by a king (=Saul's persecution of David) and Jesus' finding protection in a foreign
land (=David's flight to Philistia). He finds the son of Abraham motif also in Jesus' flight
to Egypt, because Abraham found shelter in Egypt but Isaac did not remain there (Gen
26:2). The connections are ingenious, but we have not the slightest evidence that Matthew
intended them.

2:13–23: The *Unde* (Whence) of Jesus' destiny is set in motion by the hostile reaction of Herod and the Jewish authorities.[32] Jesus providentially relives the experiences both of Moses in Egypt and of Israel in the Exodus. He is led away from Bethlehem, the city of the King of the Jews, to Galilee of the Gentiles; and his taking up residence at Nazareth supplies the final touch to his identity and destiny, for it is as Jesus the Nazorean that he will begin his ministry (4:13).

In the commentary that follows I shall seek to uncover the wealth of thought simply hinted at in this brief outline.

[32] See NOTE on "those who were seeking the child's life" in 2:20.

BIBLIOGRAPHY FOR THE MATTHEAN INFANCY NARRATIVE

(This Bibliography contains works pertinent to *the whole* of Matt 1–2; see also the material pertinent to Matthew in the General Bibliography in § 1.)

Allen, W. C., *A Critical and Exegetical Commentary on the Gospel according to S. Matthew* (ICC; New York: Scribner's, 1907), esp. 1–22.

Bacon, B. W., *Studies in Matthew* (New York: Holt, 1930), esp. 145–64.

Bonnard, P., *L'Evangile selon saint Matthieu* (CNT; 2nd ed.; Neuchâtel: Delachaux, 1970; orig. 1963), esp. 13–30.

Bornkamm, G., with G. Barth and H. H. Held, *Tradition and Interpretation in Matthew* (Philadelphia: Westminster, 1963).

Cavalletti, S., "I sogni di San Giuseppe," BibOr 2 (1960), 149–51.

Cave, C. H., "St. Matthew's Infancy Narrative," NTS 9 (1962–63), 382–90.

Crossan, D. M., "Structure & Theology of Mt. 1.18 – 2.23," *Cahiers de Joséphologie* 16 (1968), 119–35.

Danieli, G., "Traditiones evangelii infantiae secundum Matthaeum earum origo," *Verbum Domini* 45 (1967), 337–41.

———— "Storicità di Matteo I–II: Stato presente della discussione," *Cahiers de Joséphologie* 19 (1971), 53–61.

Davies, W. D., *The Setting of the Sermon on the Mount* (Cambridge University, 1964).

Davis, C. T., "Tradition and Redaction in Matthew 1:18 – 2:23," JBL 90 (1971), 404–21.

Didier, M., ed., *L'Evangile selon Matthieu: Rédaction et Théologie* (BETL 29; Gembloux: Duculot, 1972).

Filson, F. V., *A Commentary on the Gospel according to St. Matthew* (BNTC; London: Black, 1960), esp. 51–62.

Goulder, M. D., *Midrash and Lection in Matthew* (London: SPCK, 1974), esp. 228–42.

Green, F. W., *The Gospel according to Saint Matthew* (Oxford: Clarendon, 1936), esp. 101–14.

Grundmann, W., *Das Evangelium nach Matthäus* (HKNT; Berlin: Evangelische Verlag, 1968), esp. 59–89.

Hartman, L., "Scriptural Exegesis in the Gospel of St. Matthew and the Problem of Communication," in Didier, *L'Evangile,* 131–52.

Kilpatrick, G. D., *The Origins of the Gospel according to St. Matthew* (Oxford: Clarendon, 1946), esp. 51–58.

Kingsbury, J. D., *Matthew: Structure, Christology, Kingdom* (Philadelphia: Fortress, 1975).

Knoch, O., "Die Botschaft des Matthäusevangeliums über Empfängnis und Geburt Jesu vor dem Hintergrund des Christusverkündigung des Neuen Testaments," in *Zum Thema Jungfrauengeburt* (Stuttgart: Katholisches Bibelwerk, 1970), 37–59.

Krämer, M., "Die Menschwerdung Jesu Christi nach Matthäus (Mt 1)," *Biblica* 45 (1964), 1–50.

Krentz, E., "The Extent of Matthew's Prologue," JBL 83 (1964), 409–14.

Lohmeyer, E., and W. Schmauch, *Das Evangelium des Matthäus* (MK; 2nd ed.; Göttingen: Vandenhoeck, 1958), esp. 1–33.

McCasland, S. V., "Matthew Twists the Scripture," JBL 80 (1961), 143–48.

Milton, Helen, "The Structure of the Prologue to St. Matthew's Gospel," JBL 81 (1962), 175–81.

Muñoz Iglesias, S., "El género literario del Evangelio de la Infancia en San Mateo," EB 17 (1958), 243–73.

Ortensio da Spinetoli, *Matteo* (2nd ed.; Assisi: Cittadella, 1973), 23–61.

Paul, A., *L'Evangile de l'Enfance selon saint Matthieu* (Lire la Bible 17; Paris: Cerf, 1968).

Peretto, E., *Ricerche su Mt. 1–2* (Rome: Marianum, 1970).

Pesch, R., "Eine alttestamentliche Ausführungsformel in Matthäus-Evangelium," BZ 10 (1966), 220–45; 11 (1967), 79–95.

Plummer, A., *An Exegetical Commentary on the Gospel of Matthew* (London: Clarke, 1915), esp. 1–20.

Ponthot, J., "L'Evangile de l'enfance selon S. Matthieu. Perspectives doctrinales de Mt 1–2," *Revue Diocesaine de Tournai* 19 (1964), 615–37.

Racette, J., "L'Evangile de l'enfance selon saint Matthieu," ScEccl 9 (1957), 77–82.

Rasco, E., *Synopticorum Quaestiones Exegeticae* (Rome: Gregorian, 1965–66), 1–106.

———— "Matthew I–II: Structure, Meaning, Reality," StEv IV (TU 102; Berlin: Akademie, 1968), 214–30.

Sabourin, L., *Il Vangelo di Matteo* (Marino: Fede ed Arte, 1975), I, esp. 183–254.

Schlatter, A., *Der Evangelist Matthäus* (6th ed.; Stuttgart: Calwer, 1963; orig. 1929), esp. 1–50.

Schniewind, J., *Das Evangelium nach Matthäus* (NTD, 5th ed.; Göttingen: Vandenhoeck, 1950), esp. 9–20.

Schweizer, E., *The Good News according to Matthew* (Atlanta: Knox, 1975), esp. 31–45.

Smith, B. T. D., *The Gospel according to S. Matthew* (Cambridge University, 1927), esp. 75–81.

Stendahl, K., "Matthew," in *Peake's Commentary on the Bible* (London: Nelson, 1962), esp. ※※674a–675g.

———— *"Quis et Unde?* An Analysis of Mt 1–2," in *Judentum, Urchristentum, Kirche,* ed. W. Eltester (Festschrift J. Jeremias; BZNW 26; Berlin: Töpelmann, 1964), 94–105.

Stramare, T., "I sogni di S. Giuseppe," *Cahiers de Joséphologie* 19 (1971), 104–22.

Strecker, G., *Der Weg der Gerechtigkeit* (FRLANT 82; 2nd ed.; Göttingen: Vandenhoeck, 1966).

Tatum, W. B., "The Matthean Infancy Stories. Their Form, Structure and Relation to the Theology of the First Evangelist" (Duke University, unpublished doctoral dissertation, 1966).

Trilling, W., *Das wahre Israel* (StANT 10; 3rd ed.; Munich: Kösel, 1964).

Vögtle, A., *Messias und Gottessohn. Herkunft und Sinn der matthäischen Geburts- und Kindheitsgechichte* (Düsseldorf: Patmos, 1971).

———— "Die matthäische Kindheitsgeschichte," in Didier, *L'Evangile,* 153–83.

II. THE GENEALOGY OF JESUS (§ 3)

Translation of Matt 1:1–17

1 [1] The birth record of Jesus Christ, son of David, son of Abraham:
[2] Abraham was the father of Isaac;
Isaac was the father of Jacob;
Jacob was the father of Judah and his brothers;
[3] Judah was the father of Perez and Zerah by *Tamar;**
Perez was the father of Hezron;
Hezron was the father of Aram;
[4] Aram was the father of Amminadab;
Amminadab was the father of Nahshon;
Nahshon was the father of Salmon;
[5] Salmon was the father of Boaz by *Rahab;*
Boaz was the father of Obed by *Ruth;*
Obed was the father of Jesse;
[6] Jesse was the father of David the king.

David was the father of Solomon by *Uriah's wife;*
[7] Solomon was the father of Rehoboam;
Rehoboam was the father of Abijah;
Abijah was the father of Asaph;
[8] Asaph was the father of Jehoshaphat;
Jehoshaphat was the father of Joram;
Joram was the father of Uzziah;
[9] Uzziah was the father of Jotham;
Jotham was the father of Ahaz;
Ahaz was the father of Hezekiah;
[10] Hezekiah was the father of Manasseh;

---

* To facilitate reader recognition I have italicized the five women mentioned in the list, for they will be the subject of special discussion.

Manasseh was the father of Amos;

Amos was the father of Josiah;

[11] Josiah was the father of Jechoniah and his brothers
at the time of the Babylonian Exile.

[12] After the Babylonian Exile,

Jechoniah was the father of Shealtiel;

Shealtiel was the father of Zerubbabel;

[13] Zerubbabel was the father of Abiud;

Abiud was the father of Eliakim;

Eliakim was the father of Azor;

[14] Azor was the father of Zadok;

Zadok was the father of Achim;

Achim was the father of Eliud;

[15] Eliud was the father of Eleazar;

Eleazar was the father of Matthan;

Matthan was the father of Jacob;

[16] Jacob was the father of Joseph, the husband of *Mary;*
of her was begotten Jesus, called the Christ.

[17] Thus the total generations from Abraham to David were fourteen generations; and from David to the Babylonian Exile fourteen more generations; and finally from the Babylonian Exile to the Christ fourteen more generations.

NOTES

1:1. *birth record.* Literally "book of the genesis." A more precise translation of the Greek word *genesis* here might be "genealogical"; but the same word means "birth" in 1:18, and to translate it differently in the two instances would be to destroy the relationship Matthew intended between 1:1–17 and 18–25. *Genesis* gives us the leitmotif of the passage: the related verbal form *egennēsen* (from *gennan,* "to beget, be the father of") is used throughout the list, and the noun *genea,* "generation," appears in the summary statement at the end (1:17).

The translation "book" is favored over "record" by those who think that 1:1 is a title for the first two chapters or even for the whole Gospel. However, *biblos geneseōs* is generally thought to reflect Hebrew *sēper tôlᵉdôt* (or *toledoth*, "generations"), a title which Gen 5:1 gives to a genealogical record. Others would relate *biblos geneseōs* to the rabbinic formula *sēper yûḥăsîn* ("book of family [genealogical] records"). Whichever background one posits, it is unlikely that Matthew means his title to cover more than the genealogy (1:2–17), with 1:18–25 included if that section is looked on as explaining 1:16. The very reuse of *genesis* in 1:18 shows that Matthew is thinking here of the birth of Jesus. To stretch the term to cover the whole Gospel, which then has to be understood as "the book of the origins of Jesus Christ," is fanciful.

of Jesus. Another form of the theory just rejected is to understand "Jesus" as a subjective genitive: "the book of the genesis (new creation) brought about by Jesus." (A similar problem occurs in translating the genitive "Jesus Christ" in the title in Mark 1:1.) Again I would judge this fanciful since there immediately follows a genealogy of which Jesus is the object, not the subject. See the discussion in Davies, *Setting*, 70.

Christ. In the infancy narrative Matthew uses *Christos* five times, but it is not feasible to keep the same translation in all instances. In 2:4, preceded by a definite article, it has its most original meaning as a translation of Aramaic *mᵉšîḥă'*, "the Messiah" or "the anointed one," i.e., the anointed king of the House of David. That could also be the meaning in 1:16 ("Jesus, called the *Christos*") and in 1:17 ("from the Babylonian Exile to the *Christos*"). Yet those verses are meant to refer back to the present verse where "Christ" must be the translation, since what was originally a title has become so appropriated to Jesus that it has become part of his name. "Jesus the Messiah" became "Jesus the Christ" which, in turn, became "Jesus Christ." Only here (1:1) and in 1:18 (see NOTE there) does the name "Jesus Christ" appear in Matthew's Gospel.

son of David, son of Abraham. It has been argued that since "son of David" comes before "son of Abraham," Matthew is placing more emphasis on Jesus' Davidic origins. However, the arrangement is logical: the fact that Abraham's name comes last in the title enables that title to lead into the first line of the genealogical record which will begin with Abraham. David is the middle item in the sequence both in 1:1 (Jesus Christ/David/Abraham) and in 1:17 (Abraham/David/the Christ)—an inclusion. It may well be that Matthew is more interested in Jesus' Davidic descent than in his Abrahamic descent, but one cannot conclude that from the order in 1:1.

2. *was the father of. Egennēsen* is literally "begot." The formula "A begot B; B begot C" is a standard one in OT genealogies; see especially Ruth 4:18–22 and I Chr 2:10–15, the OT genealogies which are closest to the pre-Davidic section of Matthew's record. In the post-Davidic genealogy of I Chr 3:10ff., however, another formula is employed: "The sons (i.e., descendants) of Solomon: Rehoboam, his son Abijah, his son Asa. . . ." Matthew maintains the "A begot B" throughout.

3. *Perez was the father of Hezron.* While there are OT stories about the first four names in Matthew's record (Abraham, Isaac, Jacob, Judah), there is no real narrative about the names he gives between Judah and Boaz. The OT authority for these names are genealogical lists such as found in Ruth 4:18–22 and I Chr 2:5ff.

Aram. In the names in this record I have normally not transcribed Matthew's Greek forms literally but have accepted the standard OT forms of the names. Here, however, I preserve Matthew's variant form of "Ram," the name given to the son of Hezron in the MT of Ruth 4:19 and I Chr 2:9. The LXX of Ruth has "Arran," while the LXX of I Chr has *two* sons of Hezron "Ram" and "Aram," but it is Aram who begets Amminadab (2:10). While there is a possibility that the LXX was translating a Hebrew text other than the one we know in the MT and that this divergent Hebrew text was used by Matthew, we shall see other reasons for suspecting that Matthew's record had immediate Greek rather than Hebrew ancestry.

Aram's father, Hezron, is connected in the OT (Gen 46:12) with the period of Joseph and the going down to Egypt; Aram's son Amminadab is connected (Num 1:7) with Moses and the desert wanderings after the Exodus. Thus Matthew allots one name, Aram (never mentioned in the Pentateuch), and only two generations to a period which traditionally (and perhaps factually) lasted some 400 years (Gen 15:13; Exod 12:40). Probably the genealogical heritage on which Matthew is drawing has been influenced by a different biblical tradition about the length of the period in Egypt, e.g., Gen 15:16: "And they shall come back here in the fourth generation."

4. *Amminadab was the father of Nahshon.* Numbers (2:3; 7:12) speaks of Nahshon as a leader of the tribe of Judah during the desert wandering and describes how he offered sacrifice at the Tabernacle. Exodus 6:23 tells us that his sister Elisheba, or Elizabeth (Amminadab's daughter), married Aaron the levitical high priest. In both Matthew and Luke we shall find an interesting mixture of Judah and Levi in Jesus' putative ancestry.

5. *Salmon was the father of Boaz by Rahab.* Although Salmon (or Salma) is named as the father of Boaz in the genealogies of Ruth 4:21 and I Chr 2:11, his name occurs nowhere in the biblical narrative. The statement that Boaz was the child of Rahab (*Rachab* in Matthew's orthography) has no other biblical support and is curious since the famous Rahab (LXX orthography *Raab*) lived at the time of the conquest, nearly two centuries before Boaz' time. Despite the difference of spelling, it is virtually certain that Matthew means the Rahab of the conquest. In rabbinic tradition she married Joshua.

7. *Asaph.* This is the best attested reading. Later copyists observed that Matthew's record had confused the psalmist Asaph (title of Pss 50, 73-83; I Chr 16:5-37; II Chr 29:30) with King Asa of Judah (I Kgs 15:9); and so they changed the text to Asa, a reading common in the Byzantine Greek tradition and in the Latin and Syriac versions. See NOTE on Amos in vs. 10.

8. *Joram was the father of Uzziah.* This notice embodies the first omission in the Matthean list of the Davidic kings. Three kings, three generations, and some sixty years separated Kings Joram and Uzziah. A complete list would have the sequence Joram, Ahaziah, Jehoash, Amaziah, and Uzziah (see Table III). This omission will be discussed in the COMMENT. At times we know of both birth and regnal names for the kings of Judah; in this instance Azariah was the king's birth name and Uzziah was his regnal name.

10. *Amos.* This is the same type of problem as with Asaph/Asa in vs. 7.

Later copyists observed that Matthew's record had confused the prophet Amos with King Amon of Judah (II Kgs 21:19); and so they changed the text to Amon. Some commentators would attribute the historically correct readings "Asa" and "Amon" to Matthew and blame copyists for the confused "Asaph" and "Amos." The desire to spare Matthew an error may stem from a theory of inerrancy or from an overestimation of Matthew's knowledge of the Scripture (Bornhäuser, *Kindheitsgeschichte*, 12). In 27:9 Matthew attributes to Jeremiah a citation that comes from Zechariah; and in 23:35 Matthew confuses the prophet Zechariah, the son of Berechiah, with another Zechariah who was killed in the Temple three centuries earlier (II Chr 24:20–22). Other commentators admit that it was Matthew who wrote "Asaph" and "Amos" but contend that he did so deliberately, to bring wisdom and prophetic strains into Jesus' ancestry. That suggestion is highly imaginative for a list of Davidic kings.

11. *Josiah was the father of Jechoniah and his brothers.* In this instance Matthew prefers the birth name Jechoniah to the regnal name Jehoiachin, the opposite of his choice in regard to Azariah/Uzziah in vs. 8. This notice contains the second omission in the Matthean list of the Davidic kings. Historically Josiah was the *grandfather* of Jechoniah who, as far as we know, had only one brother. The listing would be correct if Matthew read: "Josiah was the father of *Jehoiakim* and his brothers at the time of the Babylonian Exile"; for Jehoiakim, Josiah's son, had two brothers (Jehoahaz II and Zedekiah; see Table III) who were also kings. Indeed, Zedekiah's kingship was precisely "at the time of the Babylonian Exile," for he was reigning when the second deportation to Babylon began in 587 B.C. Thus it appears that Matthew has confused Jechoniah (Jehoiachin) the grandson of Josiah with Jehoiakim the son of Josiah and thus has omitted a generation. This omission will be discussed in the COMMENT.

12. *Shealtiel was the father of Zerubbabel.* That Zerubbabel was the son of Shealtiel, the first son of King Jechoniah, is affirmed by Ezra 3:2,8; 5:2; Neh 12:1; Hag 1:1,12,14; 2:2,23; and by the LXX of I Chr 3:19. However, the MT of I Chr 3:19 makes Zerubbabel the son of Pediah, who was the brother of Shealtiel and the third son of King Jechoniah. Zerubbabel, who was active in 520–515 B.C. in the rebuilding of the Temple after the Babylonian Exile, seems to have been appointed *peḥah* or governor in Judah by the Persian king. He became the focus of messianic, Davidic expectations in the immediate post-exilic period, whence his appearance in both the Lucan and Matthean lists of Jesus' ancestors. He is the last figure in Matthew's record about whom we have any OT information.

13. *Zerubbabel was the father of Abiud.* The latter does not appear among the list of Zerubbabel's eight children in I Chr 3:19–20.

16. *Jacob was the father of Joseph, the husband of Mary; of her was begotten Jesus, called the Christ.* One can translate the last phrase as "called the Messiah," but Matthew probably means to refer back to "Jesus Christ" in 1:1 (see NOTE). As for "was begotten," the Greek form *egennēthē* (*gennan*) is ambiguous when used of a pregnant woman, for it can mean "was begotten" or "was born," two successive stages in the generative process. In 1:20 the related form

to gennēthen refers to the child begotten in Mary's womb, whereas *tou gennēthentos* in 2:1 refers to the child that has already been born. Since in the rest of the genealogy *gennan* means "beget" (A begot [was the father of] B), the meaning "was begotten" seems better here, with the proviso that such a translation does not mean that the child was naturally begotten by Joseph. If Matthew meant that (and 1:18–25 is clear proof that he did not), why would he have departed from the usual formula which would have affirmed it clearly: "By her Joseph was the father of Jesus, called the Christ." The very shift of pattern implies that Matthew did not want to say that Joseph was the biological father of Jesus.

a) The reading I have accepted I shall designate as (a). It makes room for the virginal conception of Jesus as Matthew will describe it in 1:18–25 and is supported by the best Greek textual witnesses, including Codices Vaticanus and Sinaiticus. However, there are two other readings with minor textual support which I shall discuss at length below as (b) and (c). These would attract little attention if scholars had not seen in them a hint, direct or indirect, of a natural conception of Jesus with Joseph as the biological father. The reader should keep separate the two questions: First, is there any real likelihood that either of these variants is to be preferred as the original reading in the genealogy as Matthew gave it to us, or even in a pre-Matthean genealogy (if there was one)? Second, whether or not there is such a likelihood, does the variant imply that Joseph was the biological father of Jesus? An affirmative answer to the latter would have its importance, even in face of a negative answer to the former; for if the variant is attributed to a later copyist, that copyist would have intended to deny the virginal conception.

b) There is minor Greek (Codex Koridethi and the Ferrar family of mss.) and some ancient versional (Old Latin) support for a reading which (with insignificant variations) can be translated thus:

> Jacob was the father of Joseph, to whom the betrothed
> virgin Mary bore [gave birth to] Jesus, called the Christ.

To be noted is that Joseph is not called the husband of Mary and she is specifically designated a virgin. These details, plus the fact that this reading also breaks the formula-pattern of the genealogy (which should have produced: "Joseph was the father of Jesus"), means that it gives even less support than reading (a) to Joseph's biological fatherhood. The possible origins of this reading will be discussed below.

c) A reading with even less textual support may be translated thus:

> Jacob was the father of Joseph; and *Joseph,* to whom
> the virgin Mary was betrothed, *was the father of Jesus,*
> called the Christ.

Although, like reading (b), this reading avoids calling Joseph the husband of Mary and specifically designates her a virgin, it is the only one of the three readings to preserve in part the formula-pattern of the genealogy (italicized). The only clear support for the reading is the Old Syriac (Sinaiticus) version. B. Metzger, "On the Citation" and "The Text," has shown how dubious is the other support frequently cited for it. For instance, there is a Palestinian church lectionary with the reading: "Joseph, the husband of Mary, *him* from whom was born Jesus"; but this is seemingly a scribal blunder for "her from whom" (see Burkitt, *Evangelion*, II, 264). The following is found in the fifth-century *Dialogue of Timothy and Aquila:* "There is a genealogy . . . in Matthew, and it reads in this manner: Jacob was the father of Joseph, the husband of Mary; of her was born Jesus, called the Christ. *And so Joseph was the father of Jesus, called the Christ*." This seems in its last line, which I have italicized, to echo the Sinaitic Syriac reading (c). But the whole passage is part of a dialogue between a Christian and a Jew; and the italicized words, which are part of the Jew's remarks, may well constitute the conclusion he has drawn, rather than a continued and tautological quotation from the genealogy. The two other times that the *Dialogue* quotes Matt 1:16 support the (a) reading not the (c) reading.

How can we explain the origins of the three different readings? One way is to suppose a simple original reading (no longer extant) in the style of the rest of the genealogy: "Jacob was the father of Joseph; and Joseph was the father of Jesus." The three extant readings, (a), (b), and (c), would then stem from scribal attempts to modify the impact of the genealogical statement which seemed to deny the virginal conception. Yet, can we really believe that Matthew wrote that Joseph begot Jesus when he also wrote 1:18–25 which disproves this? If Matthew wrote "Joseph was the father of Jesus," he would have had to understand this in a non-biological way. Nor does it prove satisfactory to argue that "Joseph was the father of Jesus" was the reading of the pre-Matthean genealogy, preserved only in (c); and that (a) and (b) reflect a change wrought by Matthew in the standard genealogical formula in order to bring it into line with a virginal conception. In that case one would have to claim either that the Sinaitic Syriac translator knew the pre-Matthean formula (highly implausible) or that he made a shrewd guess and undid Matthew's correction.

A far more satisfactory approach is to regard one of the extant readings as original and the other two as copyists' "clarifications." It has sometimes been argued that (c) was the original Matthean reading, that it meant that Joseph was the biological father of Jesus, and that scandalized copyists changed it to readings (b) or (a). No part of this argument is very convincing. If reading (c) meant to make Joseph the biological father of Jesus, why did it not simply say: "Joseph was the father of Jesus by Mary," the formula employed in the genealogy when women are mentioned? Rather it stresses that Mary is a virgin and does not call Joseph her husband. And if the composer of reading (a) was correcting reading (c) in order to protect the virginal conception, why did he suppress these features that would have aided his cause? (It gets needlessly complicated if the supporter of the originality of [c] argues that it is not preserved in its pristine form and that "virgin" is a later insertion. The very mention of Mary, even without the designation "virgin," indicates that Matthew posits some special role for her involving irregularity in the marital union, as we shall see in the COMMENT discussing the presence of the women in the genealogy.)

A far simpler solution is to suppose that the best attested reading (a) was original and that (b) and (c) are stages of copyists' corrections of (a). Why might a copyist feel uneasy about (a) when that reading allows for the virginal conception? He might have been bothered by the designation of Joseph as "the husband of Mary," an indelicacy in the light of the growing Christian tradition of Mary's perpetual virginity, i.e., her continued virginity after the birth of Jesus, which was a topic of major theological discussion from the second to the fourth centuries. The substitution of a neutral clause "to whom was betrothed (the virgin) Mary," which is attested in readings (b) and (c), would have been an attempt to avoid the indelicacy. But that substitution would have produced a grammatical difficulty about the antecedent of the "begetting" clause; notice the awkwardness of reading (b). The grammatical difficulty may have led the translator of the Sinaitic Syriac to modify further by producing reading (c) which, while preserving the virginity of Mary, employs the standard genealogical formula "Joseph was the father of Jesus." As I have mentioned in ABJ, II, 821, the Sinaitic Syriac translator was a free spirit who did not hesitate to make major "improvements" in the textual tradition that came to him. A Semite, he could have understood "Joseph was the father of Jesus" not in a biological way that would contradict Matthew's emphasis in 1:18–25 but in terms of legal paternity (i.e., the view that a man's acceptance of a child as his son is what makes him a father—see the discussion of levirate marriage in Appendix I).

COMMENT*

To the modern reader there are few things in the Bible less meaningful than the frequent lists of descendants or ancestors. Those who read the Bible from cover to cover tend to develop an elastic conscience when they come to the first nine chapters of I Chronicles. Geneaologies often become the butt of risqué humor, as in the mockery from "Finian's Rainbow": once Adam and Eve ate from the apple tree, "they began the begat." Even in scholarly circles genealogical research fell on hard times, once Wellhausen showed that the name-lists of the Pentateuch generally belonged to its latest stratum and were worthless as sources for early Israelite history. But now, with the resurgence of interest in biblical factors other than the historical, new life has come back into the study of biblical genealogies.[1] Re-

---

* I stated in the Foreword that it was my goal that the COMMENT on each Gospel scene be intelligible to the general reader. Perhaps, then, I should warn such a reader that this section on the genealogy of Jesus is intrinsically more difficult than any other COMMENT in the book.

[1] An important factor has been the 1966 publication of the genealogy of the Hammurapi Dynasty by J. J. Finkelstein and the evaluation of it by A. Malamat. The impact of this research is conveniently summarized by R. R. Wilson, "OT Genealogies," 171–78. The "new" genealogical research involves a careful comparison between modern oral genealogies and ancient Semitic written genealogies, a distinction between genealogies that existed independently and genealogies that took shape as part of an attached narrative, and a diagnosis of the differences between a linear genealogy (direct paternal descent) and a segmented

cent major works by M. D. Johnson (*Purpose*) and R. R. Wilson ("Genealogy") show that renewed investigations into OT genealogies have implications for the birth records of Jesus as well. Perhaps the most important single factor is the recognition that genealogies serve different purposes[2] and that an individual can be accorded two or more different genealogies according to the purpose for which they were drawn up. Only rather rarely and to a limited depth do ancient Semitic genealogies afford us a list of strictly biological ancestry—a factor that does not necessarily make them inaccurate since the intention of those who preserved them was not strictly biological. Too often the genealogies of Jesus have been read with the same expectations with which one reads the list of grandparents and great-grandparents constituting the frontispiece of the family Bible.

Let me illustrate how biblical genealogies serve different functions.[3] The very interest in ancestry reflects Israel's tribal origins where one's provable identity as a member of the tribe is a passport to survival: the tribe cares for its members.[4] Besides establishing identity, biblical genealogies are sometimes used to undergird status, especially for the offices of king and priest where lineage is important (see Ezra 2:62–63; Neh 7:64–65). The closest parallels to Matthew's genealogy of Jesus, the anointed king (Messiah), are found in the genealogies of the Pentateuch and those of the Chronicler—in short, in genealogies where the primary concern is to structure history into epochs and to authenticate a line of (cultic) office holders. Another aspect of genealogies may be related to the biblical concept of collective personality: if something of the ancestor is thought to reappear in the descendant, then one's genealogy may reflect on one's character, personality, or traits. Related to this is the tendency to narrate stories about famous ancestors or descendants within the framework of a genealogy, so that history becomes an expansion of a genealogy (see Gen 10).[5]

genealogy (lateral branches). Wilson's working definition is that a genealogy is a written or oral expression of one's descent from an ancestor or ancestors by enumeration of intermediate persons. It may appear in the format of either a narrative or a list.

[2] Wilson, "OT Genealogies," 180–81, classifies the social areas of life served by oral genealogies as domestic (to show family, economic, or geographical relationship), political-jural (to support a line of hereditary office holders), and religious (to support a cultic office).

[3] Johnson, *Purpose*, represents a major attempt to analyze these functions; a convenient summary and critique is supplied by Wilson, "OT Genealogies," 172–73.

[4] It should be added that in a society where a person receives only one name, it is necessary to mention a father or grandfather to distinguish between homonyms. In Palestine, Jesus could be distinguished from his homonyms by being designated as Jesus *of Nazareth*. In Nazareth he could be distinguished from other residents named Jesus by being designated as Jesus (son) of Joseph.

[5] The practice continues into modern times; for the history of the Ta'amireh Bedouin (finders of the Dead Sea Scrolls) has been committed to writing from tribal legends in terms of a genealogical tree (going back as far as ten generations), with interruptions to develop narratives about individuals. See B. Couroyer, RB 58 (1951), 75–91. However, Wilson, "Genealogy," stresses that genealogies are not normally *created* to link such narratives; rather existing genealogies are adapted.

Granted this background, it would really be surprising if the NT did not give us a genealogy of Jesus as part of its attempt to explain his significance. (In a sister religion, Islam, there are comparable attempts to trace the ancestors of Mohammed as far back as twenty-two to thirty generations; indeed, to Adam, even as Luke traces Jesus back through Adam to God.[6]) Later on we shall discuss in detail the differences between the two NT genealogies, a set of differences for which we have no adequate OT analogy. But we do have biblical precedent for the different localization of the two genealogies. In Matthew the genealogy opens the story of Jesus, a localization resembling the sequence in Gen 5–9 where a genealogy prefaces the story of Noah. Similarly the genealogy of Gen 11:10–32 prefaces the story of Abraham (chs. 12ff.). In Luke the genealogy (3:23–38) is given after Jesus' baptism and just before he takes up the ministry of proclaiming the kingdom, a localization resembling that of the genealogy of the tribes and of Moses in Exod 6:14–25 which is given after the call of Moses and just before he begins his mission of leading the tribes out of Egypt.

A. *Matthew's Purpose in the Genealogy*

For the moment let us confine our attention to Matthew's genealogy, and let us use the background gained from a study of OT genealogies in order to interpret it.

1. General Observations

Matthew begins his work with a title (1:1): "The birth record [*biblos geneseōs*—see NOTE] of Jesus Christ, son of David, son of Abraham." We are immediately reminded of similar titles or formulas found in Gen 2:4a; 5:1; and 6:9.[7] The closest of these in wording to Matt 1:1 is that of Gen 5:1: "The record of the genesis [*biblos geneseōs;* Hebrew *sēper tôlᵉdôt*]

---

[6] According to Wilson, "OT Genealogies," 179, *oral* genealogies are strictly limited in depth (i.e., in the number of generations recorded). A linear genealogy (see footnote 1) may reach a depth of nineteen generations, while a segmented genealogy rarely stretches beyond ten to fourteen. Greater depth is achieved through attachment to a written genealogy —an observation worth remembering when studying how Matthew's third section in the genealogy (containing nine names of persons without biblical attestation) is related to the second section (the known kings of the Davidic dynasty in the history of Judah). From Wilson's study, it seems that the longest genealogies are those designed to root a person in an office or power.

[7] It is not impossible that Matthew's use of *genesis* in the title may mean to evoke the first book of the Greek Bible, which contains the best parallels to his title. The word *genesis* occurs some ten times in that book; and perhaps already by the first century A.D. "Genesis" was the formal title of the book in Greek-speaking Jewish communities. (In Hebrew the book was known as "In the beginning," and John 1:1 plays on the Hebrew title.)

of Adam," a formula that, as we saw, introduces the Noah story[8] even as Matthew's formula introduces the Jesus story. But there is a major difference. The genealogy in Gen 5 leads from Adam to Noah, for the genealogy of Adam is a genealogy of his descendants, while the genealogy of Jesus is a genealogy of his ancestors. In Christian salvific history there can be no genealogy of Jesus' descendants because history has reached its goal in Jesus.

Besides entitling the record of begettings that follows (1:2–17), Matt 1:1 with its emphasis on "Jesus *Christ*" and on "son of David" and "son of Abraham" calls the reader's attention to the basic themes of the infancy narrative. The name "Jesus Christ" (see NOTE) binds the title "Messiah" indivisibly to Jesus and serves as a good preparation for a genealogy and a narrative both of which will stress that Jesus is the fulfillment of Jewish messianic hopes.[9] The sonship of David will be the special theme of Matthew's first chapter; for not only is the Davidic theme lucidly clear in the genealogy,[10] but it reappears in the angelic revelation to Joseph who is addressed as "son of David" (1:20). It is imperative in Matthew's mind that Joseph, a Davidid, accepts Jesus as his son. The theme of the "son of Abraham" is more subtle. As we have seen, Matthew is very concerned with justifying the coming of large numbers of Gentiles into Christianity. In 8:11, in commenting on the faith of the Roman centurion, Matthew will record Jesus' saying: "Many will come from east and west and sit at table with Abraham, Isaac, and Jacob in the kingdom of heaven." In 3:9,

---

8 Within the story of Noah, the title in Gen 6:9, "These are the generations of Noah," comes after Noah has been introduced and leads into the story of the flood. There is a question about the role of the title in Gen 2:4a: "These are the generations of the heaven and the earth" (LXX: "This is the record of the genesis [*biblos geneseōs*] of heaven and earth"). Modern interpreters attach it to what precedes (Gen 1:1–2:3), i.e., as a summary of the first or priestly-document creation story, with the *generations* of the heavens and the earth being related to the numerical pattern of the seven days. But the LXX editors (and perhaps Jewish opinion in Matthew's time) seem to have regarded 2:4a as an introduction to what follows, namely, the second or Yahwist (J) creation story.

9 The history of Messianism is complex. In pre-exilic Israelite history when there was an anointed king of the House of David (and thus a messiah) reigning in Jerusalem, hopes for deliverance from enemies or catastrophe were attached to that monarch. If he was bad, these hopes were attached to his successor, as we see eloquently in Isa 7 where the prophet despairs of King Ahaz and attaches his hopes to the royal child who will soon be born (King Hezekiah?). However, when the Babylonian Exile of 587–539 B.C. brought an end to the reigning Davidic monarchy, and when in the early post-exilic period the dreams centered around Zerubbabel and the Davidic descendancy came to nought, the expectations surrounding the anointed kings of the House of David shifted to an anointed king of the indefinite future. And thus hope was born in *the* Messiah, the supreme anointed one who would deliver Israel. This hope is given voice in the first century B.C. in the *Psalms of Solomon* 17:23(21): "O Lord, raise up for them their king, the son of David, at that time in which you, O God, see that he may reign over Israel your servant."

10 Perhaps even to the point where the fourteen pattern into which it is organized (1:17) may reflect the numerical value of David's name—see footnote 38 below. The title "son of David" does not occur in the OT; but its appearance in the *Psalms of Solomon* (previous footnote) supports the evidence of Mark 10:47 that it was a title equivalent to "Messiah" in the first century A.D. (E. Lohse, TDNT, VIII, 481). It is the most frequently used messianic designation in the Talmud and many of the Midrashim. See Appendix II.

when the Pharisees and Sadducees are presumed to claim, "We have Abraham as our father," Jesus warns them that God is able to raise up new children to Abraham. Thus, for Matthew the designation of Jesus as "son of Abraham" may indicate that he is the seed of Abraham by whom "all the nations of the earth shall bless themselves."[11] This will be fulfilled in the second chapter of the infancy narrative when the magi (who are clearly meant to be Gentiles) come to pay homage to the King of the Jews.

The special relation of Jesus to David and Abraham is a pre-Matthean insight, for it is attested in the Pauline letters of the 50s (Rom 1:3; Gal 3:16).[12] But Matthew has woven both themes into the genealogy and respectively into 1:18–25 (son of David) and 2:1–12 (children of Abraham) to appeal to the mixed constituency of his community of Jewish and Gentile Christians. From the first words of the Gospel both segments of the community are in sight: Jesus is heir to the promises made to David and kept alive in Judaism; he is also heir to the wider promise of blessings to the Gentiles made through Abraham. In Matthew's view the two ancestors (David and Abraham) and their ultimate offspring (Jesus) are evidence of God's planning. Thus, the genealogy is not a record of man's biological productivity but a demonstration of God's providence. Although the standard formula "A was the father of [begot] B" (see NOTE on vs. 2) seems to emphasize man's role,[13] in the biblical mentality a "begetting" does not involve only the passing of physical life from parent to child. In the process of begetting, which fulfills God's command to increase and multiply and have dominion over the earth (Gen 1:28), there is transmitted the likeness to God given to Adam (i.e., to humans, male and female) in Gen 1:27. A genealogy, then, reflects the working out of God's plan of creation in a history of salvation.

Matthew expresses awe at this providential plan in 1:17 where he explains that the genealogy of the Messiah can be divided into three sections of fourteen generations each and that each section matches nicely a major

11 The theme of universal blessing through Abraham's seed is frequent in Genesis (some nineteen times), but we may consider Gen 22:18 a model passage. The import of the Hebrew is that in Abraham's seed all the peoples of the earth will bless themselves or invoke blessings on another (i.e., wish to be blessed as Abraham was). However, the Christian understanding exemplified in Acts 3:25 and Gal 3:8,16 follows the LXX reading: "In your seed shall all the nations of the earth be blessed."

12 Indeed, the special combination of David and Abraham probably occurred in pre-Christian Judaism. Johnson, *Purpose*, 149–51, refers to rabbinic genealogies that make David and Abraham pivotal points. S. Cavalletti, *Studi e Materiali di Storia e Religione* 35 (1964), 251–65, points to the tendency in post-biblical Judaism to make Abraham a messianic figure to whom Ps 110 could be applied—a king who recapitulates the history of his people.

13 Some individual births in the genealogy were possible only through divine assistance (e.g., Isaac's birth from the sterile Sarah); and, as we shall see, the presence of women in the list stresses the role of providence. The emphasis on man's role, especially on the male's role, is much less than the formula would indicate.

portion of salvation history. In the first or pre-monarchical section from
Abraham to David, we are shown how the divine selective process pro-
duced the Davidic line. Jesus is Abraham's son not through the older Ish-
mael but through Isaac (Gen 16–17); Jesus is Isaac's son not through the
firstborn Esau but through Jacob (Gen 27). Among the twelve sons of
Jacob, it is from Judah, the fourth son, that Jesus is descended, for to
Judah was promised the eternal scepter (Gen 49:10). Yet the brothers of
Judah are not forgotten by Matthew, since Jesus is related to the whole of
Israel (the twelve tribes)[14] and will call to himself twelve disciples to symbolize that (Matt 10:1; 19:28). Within the tribe of Judah it is to the
House of David that the scepter is entrusted, and so the first section of
Jesus' ancestors comes to a triumphant close with "David the king," who
by the grace of God supplanted Saul. In the second section of the
genealogy Matthew lists the kings of the Davidic line who reigned in
Jerusalem. This monarchical section concludes with Jechoniah who, despite the Babylonian Exile, begot an heir and thus enabled the Davidic line
to survive.[15] The last section of fourteen generations connects the end of
the monarchy with the appearance of the final anointed king, the Messiah
(Christ) Jesus. The Fourth Gospel uses its "genesis" Prologue ("In the
beginning") to speak of the incarnation of God's timeless Word; Matthew
uses his introductory book of genesis (*biblos geneseōs,* "birth record") to
stress Jesus' insertion into a history and a people.

2. How Matthew Composed the Genealogy

Anticipating what I hope to show from the evidence discussed in subsequent pages, I think it may be helpful at the beginning of the treatment of
the birth record itself (1:2–16) *to summarize Matthew's process in
composing that record.* Naturally, this involves a choice among various
hypotheses that have been advanced. The first question affecting composition is whether the evangelist constructed the genealogy himself or copied
it from a predecessor. The answer to this question is intimately related to
whether Matthew discovered the 3×14 structure mentioned in vs. 17 or
created it by deliberate omissions. I am inclined to a nuanced response,
namely, that Matthew drew upon two genealogical lists[16] already in ex-

---

14 Bornhäuser, *Kindheitsgeschichte,* 10, reports a dispute in Jesus' time as to whether the
ten tribes of the Northern Kingdom would have a place in the age-to-come. In light of that,
the inclusion of the twelve tribes of the sons of Israel in Rev 7:4–8 is significant.

15 I Chronicles 3:17 simply mentions his fatherhood of Shealtiel, but there were rabbinic
legends about the marvel of his begetting a son while in prison (see Davis, "Fulfillment,"
530).

16 Although I speak of two lists (one for the pre-monarchical period, the other for the
monarchical), it is possible that the joining of them was pre-Matthean. The sign of the joining is the title in 1:1: "son of David, son of Abraham"; but the title could represent
Matthew's analysis of an already joined list. (I find quite implausible the suggestion that the

istence in Greek—lists which, in turn, were partially dependent on genealogies to be found in the LXX. One of these lists covered the pre-monarchical period and was similar to those found in Ruth 4:18–22 and I Chr 2:5ff. Matthew made some changes in it, especially by adding the names of women who, despite the irregularity of their history or marital situation, were employed by God to accomplish His plan and to preserve the messianic line. Matthew noted that in this list, which covered the period from Abraham to David inclusive, there were fourteen names and thus implicitly fourteen generations. The other list, which covered the monarchical and early post-monarchical period was a popular genealogy of the Royal House of David, containing the names of the kings who ruled in Judah and some generations of the descendants of Zerubbabel, i.e., the post-exilic Davidic scions. The monarchical section of this list was dependent on OT information, but its circulation in a popular rather than archival context is suggested by its errors and omissions, probably stemming from confusing similarities in the Greek forms of the royal names.

Matthew noticed that in the (accidentally abbreviated) monarchical section there were again fourteen generations. Moreover, in the post-exilic section which listed putative descendants of Zerubbabel, a pattern of fourteen names emerged again if one added Joseph and Jesus. Giving rein to a predilection for numerical patterns,[17] Matthew thought that he had discovered the key to God's plan of salvation, a 3×14 pattern. In this hypothesis, then, the numerical pattern would stem partly from coincidences in the genealogies that Matthew knew and partly from Matthew's own additions (Joseph and Jesus) and his insight into how to divide the genealogy. As concerns Jesus, I doubt both that Matthew found an existing genealogy of Jesus or that he created one *in toto*. He added Joseph and Jesus[18] to existing genealogies, including a popular genealogy of the Davidic Messiah, which he adapted and combined. The end product (1:1–17), then, is very much a Matthean product in all its important theological and structural emphases.[19]

---

pre-Matthean list was entitled "Jesus Christ, son of Abraham," and that Matthew added "son of David." What would have been the purpose of a genealogy whose exclusive purpose was to show that Jesus was descended from Abraham? All Jews were thought to be Abraham's descendants.) P. Parker, EA 48 (1972), 467–69, thought that the Qumran fragment 7Q5 might represent a piece of genealogy that could serve as a prototype for Matthew's genealogy; but the latest photos published by P. Benoit, RB 79 (1972), 321–24, make Parker's identification of the piece impossible. It was this same fragment that was earlier (erroneously) identified as a fragment of Mark.

17 See Allen, *Matthew*, 6; Johnson, *Purpose*, 211–14.

18 He may also have added Matthan, Jesus' great-grandfather (compare Matthat in Luke's list), but that would imply that he had knowledge of Jesus' family beyond what came to him in the tradition from the public ministry. See footnote 55 below.

19 The amount of adaptation allows me to agree with Johnson, *Purpose*, 214–28, that linguistically and theologically the genealogy is in harmony with the Gospel proper. Vögtle, *Messias*, 164, points out that this is certainly the dominant view in modern scholarship.

3. Why the Women?

In addition to Mary, the mother of Jesus, Matthew includes four women in his genealogy: Tamar, Rahab, Ruth, and (Bathsheba) the wife of Uriah, women whose names I have italicized in the translation to make clear that they need special consideration. True, it may be a slight exaggeration to treat separately the problem presented by the presence of these women. One could argue that it is necessary to give equal attention to every instance where Matthew has departed from the stereotyped formula "A was the father of B."[20] But it is reasonably clear that the Matthean variations in reference to males ("Judah *and his brothers*"; "Perez *and Zerah*"; "Jechoniah *and his brothers*") are his way of calling attention to the selectivity practiced by God and thus of the work of divine providence in the ancestral list of the Messiah. It needs to be seen if the four OT women play the same role and to ask how they are related to Mary. Their presence in a genealogy is unusual according to biblical patterns.[21] It is a fact that Tamar is mentioned in I Chr 2:4, a genealogical list to which Matthew is at least indirectly indebted; but while that might have served as a catalyst, it can scarcely explain Matthew's choice of the other three OT women. What did the four women have in common that prompted Matthew's choice? There have been three main explanations.

The *first proposal*, already espoused by Jerome (*In Matt.* 9; PL 26:22), is that the four OT women were regarded as sinners;[22] and their inclusion foreshadowed for Matthew's readers the role of Jesus as the Savior of sinful men. Some would even see in Matthew's usage a cryptic apologetic against the Jewish claim that Mary was an adulteress who conceived Jesus as the fruit of a sinful relationship—Matthew would be rebutting this by pointing to irregularities on the part of women in the acknowledged

20 Davis, "Fulfillment," 523, thinks he can find five critical points where the rhythmic formula of the genealogy is broken, e.g., a point centered around Judah ("Jacob was the father of Judah *and his brothers; Judah* was the Father of Perez *and Zerah by Tamar*"), and a point centered around Boaz ("Salmon was the father of Boaz *by Rahab; Boaz* was the father of Obed *by Ruth*"). He sees the five points as moments of "five major threats to the fulfillment of the promise" and as particularly related to the creation motif. While these are all instances of God's overcoming human obstacles, Matthew's treatment of them is not so systematic as Davis would make it.
21 David's wives are named in the list in I Chr 3:1–10, including Bathsheba; but there is no evidence that this led Matthew to mention "Uriah's wife." In the OT Rahab is never connected with the Davidic line, and so the Scriptures are not Matthew's direct source for including the four OT women in the genealogy.
22 Stauffer, "Jeschu," 123–25, supports this thesis and calls attention to the (late) *Midrash Rabbah* VIII 1 on Ruth. David is portrayed as protesting the charge that his descent is tainted because of Ruth the Moabitess, and he countercharges that the tribe of Judah as a whole is descended from Tamar whose union with Judah was reprehensible. For an opposed view and a thorough refutation of this "sinner" hypothesis see Spitta, "Die Frauen."

genealogy of the Messiah.[23] In weighing this understanding of the women, we should note, however, that the Bible does not make all these OT women sinners. It is not clear, for instance, that Ruth sinned with Boaz.[24] Moreover, while in the OT the other women were guilty of unchastity in varying degrees (Tamar was a seductress and pretended prostitute; Rahab was a prostitute; Uriah's wife was an adulteress), in the Jewish piety of Jesus' time these women came off quite well. Tamar[25] was esteemed as a saintly Jewish proselyte (a "convert" Canaanite); for by her initiative she had perpetuated the family line of Judah's son who was her deceased husband. She is said to have done this because she had faith in the messianic promise concerning Judah's lineage, and she wanted to share in its blessing. Rahab, also classified as a proselyte, was looked on as heroine for having helped in Israel's victory at Jericho; and in early Christian writing she was hailed as a model of faith (Hebr 11:31; *I Clement* 12:1). Even Bathsheba's adultery was not always condemned in rabbinic literature because she ultimately gave birth to Solomon.[26] Thus, there is little likelihood that Matthew's readers would have understood the women as sinners.

The *second proposal,* one made popular by Luther, has more to recommend it, namely, that the women were regarded as foreigners and were included by Matthew to show that Jesus, the Jewish Messiah, was related by ancestry to the Gentiles.[27] According to the Bible, Rahab and (probably) Tamar were Canaanites,[28] while Ruth was a Moabite. Bathsheba is not identified in the OT as a foreigner; but it is as the wife of Uriah (*the Hittite*) that Matthew identifies her, and indeed this peculiar designation constitutes the strongest argument for the proposal that the four women were to be thought of as foreigners in the genealogy of the Messiah. But there are two objections against this proposal or, at least, against

---

23 The logic of this rebuttal is not entirely convincing. If Mary had committed adultery, the presence of other sinful women in the Messiah's ancestry would not really absolve her or make Jesus' origins more acceptable.

24 Some have thought that seduction and fornication are described euphemistically in Ruth 3:6–9,14; but certainly that is not the overall impression of the book. Or perhaps Ruth came under the general Israelite contempt for the Moabites who had their origins in incest (Gen 19:30–37) and whose offspring were impure to the tenth generation (Deut 23:3).

25 Bloch, "Juda," comments on the high respect enjoyed by Tamar in post-biblical Judaism; indeed, her basic righteousness was already recognized in Gen 38:26. For the other women, see Paul, *L'Evangile*, 31–35; also Johnson, *Purpose*, 159–75.

26 St-B, I, 28. The evidence for the praise of Bathsheba, however, is not impressive; and therefore Johnson, *Purpose*, 176–78, argues that there is no uniform Jewish attitude of praise for the four OT women mentioned by Matthew. He thinks that these women are mentioned because they all figured in intra-Jewish polemic against the Pharisees' expectation of the Messiah. These women constituted a blot on the purity of the Davidic Messiah and may have been cited by those who preferred a priestly Messiah of pure lineage.

27 This thesis has been strongly defended by Stegemann, "Uria," who points to its possibilities for diagnosing the theology of the evangelist.

28 The pre-Christian *Book of Jubilees* (41:1) calls Tamar an Aramean.

it as the *sole* explanation of the presence of the women. First, one would think that the four OT women constitute some preparation for the role of Mary, and yet Mary was not a foreigner.[29] Moreover, it is not clear that the Jews of the first century would have regarded the women as foreigners despite the OT evidence. In the post-biblical Jewish literature Rahab and Tamar were not presented as Gentiles but as proselytes or converts to Judaism.[30] Now, if Matthew introduced them into the genealogy to appeal to the Gentile Christian segment of his community and to show these Gentiles that their presence was foreshadowed in the messianic genealogy, how would the Gentiles understand the proselyte status of the women? The Gentile Christians had *not* become Jewish proselytes in order to accept Jesus. Or is one to maintain that in a community that had consisted predominantly of Jewish Christians, the Gentile Christians were looked on as proselytes not to Judaism but to Jewish Christianity?

The *third proposal,* which has considerable following today, finds two common elements in the four OT women, elements that they share with Mary: (a) there is something extraordinary or irregular in their union with their partners—a union which, though it may have been scandalous to outsiders, continued the blessed lineage of the Messiah; (b) the women showed initiative or played an important role in God's plan and so came to be considered the instrument of God's providence or of His Holy Spirit. Tamar took the initiative in bringing about her somewhat scandalous union with Judah. We know nothing from the OT of Rahab's union with Salmon, but it had to be somewhat irregular since she had been a prostitute; and it was her initiative that made it possible for Israel to come into the Promised Land. The union of the Moabite Ruth with Boaz had a certain irregularity if not scandal (footnote 24) and was brought about by Ruth's initiative; without that initiative the Davidic line might not have come into being. Uriah's wife (Bathsheba) had an adulterous union with David; yet it was through her intervention that Solomon, their son, succeeded David. In post-biblical Jewish piety these extraordinary unions and initiatives were seen as the work of the Holy Spirit.[31] These women were held up as examples of how God uses the unexpected to triumph over human obsta-

---

[29] The implausible thesis that Mary was a Gentile has been proposed; see R. Seeberg, "Die Herkunft der Mutter Jesu," *Theologische Festschrift für G. N. Bonwetsch* (Leipzig: Deichert, 1918), 13–24. For obvious reasons it had a certain following in the Third Reich.

[30] See Paul, *L'Evangile,* 32–33; St-B, I, 22.

[31] Bloch, "Juda," 386–87, has collected many texts from targumim and midrashim (i.e., Aramaic translations of OT books and rabbinic commentaries on them) to show that Tamar was a holy vessel of God's providence. (The texts that relate the "Holy Spirit" to Tamar, however, are mostly from medieval works, like the *Midrash Ha-Gadol.*) The late *Midrash Rabbah* II 1 on Ruth 1:1 tells us: "The Holy Spirit rested on Rahab before the Israelites arrived in the Promised Land."

cles and intervenes on behalf of His planned Messiah.[32] It is the combination of the scandalous or irregular union and of divine intervention through the woman that explains best Matthew's choice in the genealogy. There was divine intervention in several other births he lists (e.g., in overcoming the sterility of Sarah, Rebekah, and Rachel), but Matthew does not mention the women involved because there was nothing scandalous about their union. The latter element is important because Matthew has chosen women who foreshadow the role of Mary, the wife of Joseph. In the eyes of men her pregnancy was a scandal since she had not lived with her husband (1:18); yet the child was actually begotten through God's Holy Spirit, so that God had intervened to bring to fulfillment the messianic heritage. And this intervention through a woman was even more dramatic than the OT instances; there God had overcome the moral or biological irregularity of the human parents, while here He overcomes the total absence of the father's begetting.

The third proposal, then, seems to fit most smoothly into Matthew's overall view in the infancy narrative. But we should not rule out a subordinate motif stemming from the second proposal. It was to Matthew's interest that the four OT women were also Gentiles or associated with Gentiles (Uriah's wife).[33] This did not foreshadow the role of Mary, but it did foreshadow the role of the Messiah who was to bring Gentiles into God's plan of salvation—people who, though not Jews, were like Jesus in their descent from Abraham. These suggestions about how the presence of the women in the genealogy can be related to Matthew's theology and purpose imply that the inclusion of the women belongs to the stage of Matthew's editing or writing rather than to a pre-Matthean level.

4. Fourteen—the Magic Number

The Matthean genealogy is "artificial" rather than strictly "historical" in its structure, although neither term is really precise if we consider that the primary purpose of a biblical genealogy is rarely involved with purely biological descent. What I mean by "artificial" is that even God did not arrange things so nicely that exactly fourteen biological generations separated such crucial moments in salvation history as the call of Abraham, the accession of David, the Babylonian Exile, and the coming of the Messiah. The spans of time covered by the three sections of the genealogy are too great to have contained only fourteen generations each, since some 750 years separated Abraham from David, some 400 years separated David

---

[32] This motif is also found in some of the references to males in Matthew's genealogy where the "A was the father of B" pattern is broken. Matt 1:3 mentions "Perez *and Zerah*" because it was by divine intervention that Perez replaced Zerah (Gen 38:27–30).

[33] But I remind the reader of the problem (not insuperable) of the proselyte status accorded to these women in Judaism, as discussed under the second proposal.

from the Babylonian Exile, and some 600 years separated the Babylonian Exile from Jesus' birth.[84]

A glance at Tables III and IV will show that for the monarchical and post-monarchical periods Luke allows many more generations than does Matthew; and an examination of the OT evidence shows that Matthew omits names in the pre-monarchical and monarchical periods (NOTES on vss. 3,5,8,11).[85] Such omissions in a genealogy are a problem to the Western mind with its quest for biological accuracy and completeness, but are well attested in both ancient and modern tribal genealogies.[86]

In light of these facts, how do we interpret Matthew's insistence (1:17) on the 3×14 pattern? It seems to indicate that the evangelist was not aware of the omissions in his list, or at least that he did not make such omissions himself. It would be strange for him deliberately to have omitted generations in order to create the pattern and then to have called the reader's attention to it as something marvelous and (implicitly) providential. What suggested the number fourteen? We know of no special symbolism attached to this number in terms of its being twice seven, the perfect number. True, some have calculated that Matthew's 3×14 is equal to 6×7, so that six periods of seven generations preceded Jesus and he opens the seventh or final period, a division of time attested in the *Book of Enoch,* as we shall see. But if that were Matthew's idea, one would have expected him to speak of 6×7 rather than 3×14. (A genealogy built on sevens is a perfect possibility, as we shall see in Luke.) Moreover, there is no explicit emphasis in the Matthean infancy narrative on Jesus' closing one period and opening another.

Could Matthew have discovered the pattern of fourteens in whole or in part in the material that came to him? This is not implausible as regards

---

[84] The calculations are based on dating Abraham *ca.* 1750 B.C., the accession of David *ca.* 1000, the beginning of the Babylonian Exile at 597–587, and the birth of Jesus at *ca.* 5 B.C. Generations average out about twenty-five to thirty years (see footnote 78 below), so that fourteen generations would cover little more than 350 years. We have accurate knowledge about only the middle section of Matthew's genealogy: in fact, there were eighteen generations of kings of Judah in the 400 years that separated David from the Babylonian Exile. (See Table III.)

[85] Artificial sub-patterns within the overall patterns of 14s may be present. Although Matthew has shortened impossibly the number of generations in Egypt (NOTE on vs. 3), his list has five names (Judah to Amminadab) to cover the period in Egypt, and five names (Nahshon to Jesse) to cover the period of the settlement in Canaan before the Davidic monarchy.

[86] Wilson, *Genealogy,* stresses that these omissions occur for various reasons and that they are not usually found at the beginning of the list (founders are important) or at the end of the list (which involves living memory), but in the middle of the list—just as in Matthew. As for OT genealogies, the author of I Chr 6:18–28 (=RSV 6:33–43) could scarcely have missed the fact that for the same time span (between Levi and David) he allotted to Heman twenty-one ancestors and to Asaph, Heman's relative, fourteen ancestors. The list in Ezra 7:1–5 stretching from Seriah to Aaron is five names shorter than the similar list in I Chr 5:29–40 (=RSV 6:3–14), namely, the five names between Azariah and Meraioth. As for Matthew's formula "A was the father of [begot] B," there is a corrective rabbinic principle: "Grandchildren are counted as children" (TalBab, *Kiddushin* 4a).

TABLE I: THE GENEALOGY OF JESUS ACCORDING TO LUKE 3:23–38

Now, as Jesus began his ministry, he was about thirty years of age,

POST-MONARCHICAL

1. the supposed son of Joseph
2. the son of Eli (Heli)
3.   "   "   "   Matthat*
4.   "   "   "   Levi*
5.   "   "   "   Melchi
6.   "   "   "   Jannai
7.   "   "   "   Joseph

8.   "   "   "   Mattathias*
9.   "   "   "   Amos*
10.   "   "   "   Nahum
11.   "   "   "   Hesli
12.   "   "   "   Naggai
13.   "   "   "   Maath*
14.   "   "   "   Mattathias

15.   "   "   "   Semein
16.   "   "   "   Josech
17.   "   "   "   Joda
18.   "   "   "   Joanan
19.   "   "   "   Rhesa
20.   "   "   "   Zerubbabel
21.   "   "   "   Shealtiel

MONARCHICAL

22.   "   "   "   Neri
23.   "   "   "   Melchi
24.   "   "   "   Addi
25.   "   "   "   Cosam
26.   "   "   "   Elmadam (Elmodam)
27.   "   "   "   Er
28.   "   "   "   Jesus (Joshua)

29.   "   "   "   Eliezer
30.   "   "   "   Jorim
31.   "   "   "   Maththat* (Matthat)
32.   "   "   "   Levi*
33.   "   "   "   Simeon
34.   "   "   "   Judah
35.   "   "   "   Joseph

36.   "   "   "   Jonam
37.   "   "   "   Eliakim
38.   "   "   "   Melea*
39.   "   "   "   Menna*
40.   "   "   "   Mattatha(n)
41.   "   "   "   Nathan
42.   "   "   "   David

PRE-MONARCHICAL

43. the son of Jesse
44.   "   "   "   Obed
45.   "   "   "   Boaz
46.   "   "   "   Sala (Salmon)
47.   "   "   "   Nahshon
48.   "   "   "   Amminadab* (Amminadam)
49.   "   "   "   Admin*
50.   "   "   "   Arni*
51.   "   "   "   Hezron
52.   "   "   "   Perez
53.   "   "   "   Judah
54.   "   "   "   Jacob
55.   "   "   "   Isaac
56.   "   "   "   Abraham

PRE-ABRAHAMIC

57.   "   "   "   Terah
58.   "   "   "   Nahor
59.   "   "   "   Serug
60.   "   "   "   Reu
61.   "   "   "   Peleg
62.   "   "   "   Eber
63.   "   "   "   Shelah

64.   "   "   "   Cainan
65.   "   "   "   Arphaxad
66.   "   "   "   Shem
67.   "   "   "   Noah
68.   "   "   "   Lamech
69.   "   "   "   Methuselah
70.   "   "   "   Enoch

71.   "   "   "   Jared
72.   "   "   "   Mahalaleel
73.   "   "   "   Cainan
74.   "   "   "   Enos
75.   "   "   "   Seth
76.   "   "   "   Adam
77.   "   "   "   God

* A name missing in some manuscripts, versions, or citations of Luke.

TABLE II: THE PRE-MONARCHICAL PERIOD IN THE GENEALOGIES

Matthew's Fourteen Generations from Abraham to David	The Lists in I Chr 1:28,34; 2:1-15 and Ruth 4:18-22	The List in Luke 3:31-34
Abraham was the father of Isaac [1]	Abraham; Isaac	56. Abraham
		55. Isaac
Isaac " father " Jacob [2]	Israel	54. Jacob
Jacob " father " Judah [3]	Judah	53. Judah
Judah " father " Perez and Zerah [4]	Perez	52. Perez
Perez " father " Hezron [5]	Hezron	51. Hezron
Hezron " father " Aram [6]	Ram (Aram, Arran in LXX)	50. Arni*
		49. Admin*
Aram " father " Amminadab [7]	Amminadab	48. Amminadab* (Amminadam)
Amminadab " father " Nahshon [8]	Nahshon	47. Nahshon
Nahshon " father " Salmon [9]	Salma (Salmon in LXX)	46. Sala (Salmon)
Salmon " father " Boaz [10]	Boaz	45. Boaz
Boaz " father " Obed [11]	Obed	44. Obed
Obed " father " Jesse [12]	Jesse	43. Jesse
Jesse " father " David the king [13]	David	42. David

* A name missing in some manuscripts, versions, or citations of Luke.

TABLE III: THE MONARCHICAL PERIOD IN THE GENEALOGIES

Matthew's Fourteen Generations from David to the Babylonian Exile	A List of the Kings of Judah† from Information in I-II Kgs	The List in Luke 3:27-31
		(42. David)
		41. Nathan
		40. Mattatha(n)
		39. Menna*
		38. Melea*
		37. Eliakim
		36. Jonam
		35. Joseph
		34. Judah
		33. Simeon
1. David was the father of Solomon	Solomon (961–922 B.C.)	32. Levi*
2. Solomon " father " Rehoboam	Rehoboam (922–915)	31. Maththat*
3. Rehoboam " father " Abijah	Abijah or Abijam (915–913)	30. Jorim
4. Abijah " father " Asaph	Asa (913–873)	29. Eliezer
5. Asaph " father " Jehoshaphat	Jehoshaphat (873–849)	28. Jesus (Joshua)
6. Jehoshaphat father " Joram	Jehoram or Joram (849–842)	27. Er
	Ahaziah (842)	26. Elmadam (Elmodam)
	Queen Athaliah (842–837)	25. Cosam
	Jehoash or Joash (837–800)	24. Addi
	Amaziah (800–783)	23. Melchi
7. Joram " father " Uzziah	Uzziah or Azariah (783–742)	22. Neri
8. Uzziah " father " Jotham	Jotham (742–735)	
9. Jotham " father " Ahaz	Ahaz or Jehoahaz I (735–715)	
10. Ahaz " father " Hezekiah	Hezekiah (715–687)	
11. Hezekiah " father " Manasseh	Manasseh (687–642)	
12. Manasseh " father " Amos	Amon (642–640)	
13. Amos " father " Josiah	Josiah (640–609)	
14. Josiah " father " Jechoniah and his brothers	Jehoahaz II or Shallum (609) / Jehoiakim or Eliakim (609–598) / Jehoiachin or Jechoniah (597)	Zedekiah or Mattaniah (597–587)

* A name missing in some manuscripts, versions, or citations of Luke.

† In instances of alternative forms of the kings' names which involve a regnal and a birth name, the regnal name appears first and the birth name is italicized.

TABLE IV: THE POST-MONARCHICAL PERIOD IN THE GENEALOGIES

Matthew's Fourteen Generations from the Babylonian Exile to the Messiah	Post-Monarchical Davidids† (1 Chr 3:19-24)	The List in Luke 3:23-27
Jechoniah was the ¹father of Shealtiel	Shenazzar or Sheshbazzar‡ (595)	(22. Neri)
Shealtiel " " ²father " Zerubbabel	Zerubbabel (570)	21. Shealtiel
		20. Zerubbabel
Zerubbabel " " ³father " Abiud	Hananiah (545)	19. Rhesa
Abiud " " ⁴father " Eliakim	Shecaniah (520)	18. Joanan
		17. Joda
		16. Josech
		15. Semein
Eliakim " " ⁵father " Azor	Hattush (495)	14. Mattathias
Azor " " ⁶father " Zadok	Elioenai (470)	13. Maath*
		12. Naggai
Zadok " " ⁷father " Achim	Anani (445)	11. Hesli
		10. Nahum
Achim " " ⁸father " Eliud		9. Amos*
Eliud " " ⁹father " Eleazar		8. Mattathias*
		7. Joseph
Eleazar " " ¹⁰father " Matthan		6. Jannai
		5. Melchi
Matthan " " ¹¹father " Jacob		4. Levi*
		3. Matthat*
Jacob " " ¹²father " Joseph, the husband of Mary		2. Eli (Heli)
of her ¹³was born Jesus, called the Christ		1. Joseph of whom Jesus was the supposed son

* A name missing in some manuscripts, versions, or citations of Luke.
† The approximate birth dates are those assigned by F. M. Cross, JBL 94 (1974), 17.
‡ This son of Jechoniah, whose Babylonian name was Sin-ab-uṣur, was uncle of Zerubbabel.

the first section of names, since with effort one can find in the lists of I Chr 1–2 exactly fourteen names from Abraham to David inclusive.[87] As for the second section of the names, Matthew may have had available a monarchical list containing accidental omissions (to be discussed below) and he may have noticed that if one broke the continuity of the list at the Babylonian Exile and counted several of the last kings as one ("Jechoniah and his brothers"), the result was fourteen generations. A catalyst to such Matthean calculation may have come from gematria, since in the ancient Hebrew orthography the numerical value of David's name was fourteen.[38] The fact that such gematria would fit with Matthew's purpose in the genealogy to show that Jesus was "son of David" constitutes another argument for attributing the whole structure of the genealogy to Matthew. Accordingly, I would presume that it was Matthew himself who carried the fourteen pattern into the post-monarchical section by adding the names of Joseph and Jesus to a traditional genealogy of Davidids who traced their descent from Zerubbabel.

Through combining sources and working with imagination, Matthew, then, would have "discovered" a 3×14 pattern in God's messianic plan. This numerical pattern in the genealogy of Jesus Christ would be an instance of the same outlook expressed in the five quotations of Scripture scattered in the succeeding scenes of the infancy narrative. Four of those quotations are introduced by a formula indicating that the scene in Jesus' infancy took place *in order to fulfill the Scriptures*. God planned from the beginning and with precision the Messiah's origins.

The idea that the list of ancestral names of a famous man, beginning with Abraham, could be divided sequentially into equal numerical parts would not have been foreign to the Jewish mind.[39] The list of priestly

87 But note fourteen *names*, not fourteen generations, even as Matthew has fourteen names in his first section despite his reckoning of fourteen generations in 1:17. The sons of Abraham are listed in I Chr 1:28, those of Isaac in 1:34, of Israel (Jacob) in 2:1, of Judah in 2:3, of Perez in 2:5, and of Hezron in 2:9. Then in 2:10–12 there are eight consecutive names from Ram to Jesse (connected by the same "was the father of" formula that Matthew uses), and David is named as Jesse's seventh son in 2:15. The fact that this enumeration is scarcely obvious in I Chronicles has been a factor in the judgment that Matthew is no more than *indirectly* dependent on I Chronicles or on Ruth 4:18–22 (ten names from Perez to David). See also footnote 21 above.

38 The most common MT orthography of the name is *dwd* (=14), not *dwyd* (=24). But from the Qumran evidence it is clear that the *plene* writing (*dwyd*) would have been more common in Jesus' time (F. M. Cross, "The Contribution of the Qumran Discoveries to the Study of the Biblical Text," IEJ 16 [1966], 89–90). But the numerical value of the older orthography may have become a tradition. As early as the fifth century B.C. and the composition of the Book of Proverbs, the accepted value of David's name seems to have been fourteen (P. W. Skehan, CBQ 29 [1967], 179, #6). In my hypothesis the evangelist is imposing this Hebrew gematria on a list of *Greek* names and so is not necessarily drawing it from the contemporary Hebrew spelling of one of those names. (That such a linguistic mixture is possible can be seen from Rev 13:18 where an author writing in Greek draws symbolism from the numerical value of Nero Caesar's *Hebrew* name.)

39 Kaplan, "Generation," makes the interesting suggestion that the pattern of *fourteen* for generations reflects the division of a lunar month of twenty-eight days (fourteen waxing, fourteen waning). Abraham would have begun the fourteen waxing generations with David as the full moon; then there would be fourteen waning generations to the eclipse of the

names from Aaron to the Exile in I Chr 5:27–41 (=RSV 6:1–15) is
divided into equal parts by a time indicator attached to the name of
Azariah "who served as a priest in the Temple which Solomon built in
Jerusalem" (5:36=RSV 6:10). In later Judaism *Midrash Rabbah* XV 26
on Exod 12:2 divides the period from Abraham to Solomon into fifteen
generations (listing the same male names as does Matthew) and the period from Solomon to Zedekiah into 15 generations (more historically correct than Matthew). Numerical patterns are also familiar in reference to
the coming of the messianic era. According to Jer 25:11–12 the Babylonian servitude would last seventy years; but by the second century B.C. as
witnessed by Dan 9:24–27, this number had been expanded to seventy
weeks of years (490) in order to describe the period from the beginning
of the Babylonian Exile to the coming of God's kingdom.[40] In *Enoch*
93:1–10 and 91:12–17 world history is divided into ten weeks of years,
the first three of which are pre-Israelite, so that from Jacob (Israel) to the
end there are seven weeks of years. *Pirke Aboth* 5:2–3, a work of early
post-biblical Judaism, counts ten generations from Adam to Noah, and
then ten more from Noah to Abraham. In *II Baruch* 53–74 world history
from Adam to the Messiah is divided into twelve periods with the messianic period as the last.[41] If these enumerations are more often begun
with Adam (in this connection note that Luke takes Jesus' ancestry back
through Adam to God), there is also evidence for starting with Abraham.
In *IV Ezra* 6:7–8 we are told that the era of Abraham, Isaac, and Jacob
marked the dividing of times, i.e., the end of the first age and the beginning of the age to come. To be sure, none of these enumerations is so deliberate as Matthew's but they share with Matthew an eschatological outlook, so that the coming of the Messiah marks the end of God's carefully
delineated plan.[42]

5. Could Matthew Count?

Although Matthew (1:17) insists on the presence of a 3×14 pattern of
generations in the genealogy of Jesus, when one actually counts the generations in the three sections of the list, it seems as if Matthew's arithmetic
leaves something to be desired.[43] In the *first section,* from Abraham to

---

Babylonian Exile, followed by fourteen more waxing generations to the Messiah as the full
moon again. Moreton, "Genealogy," calls attention to the fact that 3×14 yields 42, and
that in Rev 13:5 a period of forty-two months is allotted to evil before God's final intervention.

40 It has been pointed out that if the generations are counted at thirty-five years each,
then Matthew's fourteen generations from the Babylonian Exile to Jesus would yield 490
years. See St-B, IV, 996–1011.

41 There may be a pattern of fourteen links in the Pharisees' computation of tradition
from Moses to Shammai/Hillel (Johnson, *Purpose,* 202–7).

42 Johnson, *Purpose,* 219–23, compares Matthew's genealogy and his Gospel on this subject.

43 F. V. Filson, "Broken Patterns in the Gospel of Matthew," JBL 75 (1956), 227–31,
shows that, while some numerical patterns are worked out in Matthew, others are not.

David, there are fourteen names but only thirteen generations or begettings (see Table II). Of course, Abraham, whose name is listed first, had
to be begotten; and so Matthew may intend the unmentioned generation of
Abraham to be counted as the fourteenth generation. Only in the *second
section,* from David to the Babylonian Exile, are there fourteen gener-
tions explicitly listed (but at the price of omitting four historical generations and six kings who actually ruled—see Table III). In the *third section,* from the Babylonian Exile to Jesus, there are again only thirteen
generations; and this time apparently one cannot solve it by appealing to
the unmentioned generation of the first person named (Jechoniah) because his generation was the last of the second section!

Let us probe more closely by considering the omissions in Matthew's
second section, omissions not known to us in any OT list of kings. (For
instance, I Chr 3:10–14 has sixteen names inclusive from Solomon to
Josiah, compared to Matthew's thirteen.) In the NOTE on vs. 8, we have
seen that between Kings Joram and Uzziah ("Joram was the father of Uzziah") Matthew skipped some sixty years and the three generations of
Kings Ahaziah, Jehoash, and Amaziah. It has been suggested that these
three kings were omitted from the ancestral list of the Messiah because
they were wicked[44] (but even more wicked was Manasseh who was included in the list), or because they were assassinated (but so was Amon
who is included). A further refinement of this theory is that the three
omitted kings were regarded as accursed.[45] A more plausible explanation
is that the omission was accidental caused by the similarity between the
Greek forms of the names of Uzziah (Azariah) and Ahaziah, so that
"Joram was the father of Uzziah" is a mistake for "Joram was the father
of Ahaziah."[46] Certainly there are other instances of confusion in the
monarchical list, e.g., Asaph for King Asa, and Amos for King Amon
(NOTES on 7 and 10). If there is truth in the theory expounded above that
Matthew found the basis for his pattern of fourteen in genealogical lists
that served as his sources, then the lists were already in Greek and already
contained errors.[47]

---

[44] For the implication that great sinners were not included in genealogies, see the rabbinic
argument reported by Bornhäuser, *Kindheitsgeschichte,* 18–19, that Phinehas, son of Eli,
was not a sinner (despite I Sam 2:12,22) because his name is included in a genealogy in I
Sam 14:3. See also Mal 2:12.

[45] A curse on the House of Ahab, king of Israel, levied in I Kgs 21:21, may have been
brought over to the royal house in Judah through Ahab's daughter Athaliah, wife of King
Joram. According to biblical rules this curse would have affected Joram's offspring even to
the third and fourth generation (Exod 20:5), thus his son Ahaziah, his grandson Jehoash,
and his great-grandson Amaziah—the three kings omitted in the Matthean list. See also the
curses on these kings in II Chr 22:7; 24:22; and 25:16.

[46] There are at least two ways the mistake may have occurred. The copyist's eye may
have slipped down a royal list from *Ochozias* (Greek for Ahaziah) to *Ozias* (Greek for
Uzziah). Another way of explaining the confusion stems from the fact that Codex
Vaticanus of the LXX uses *Ozeias* rather than *Ochozias* as the Greek form of Ahaziah.
The possibility of confusing *Ozeias* (Ahaziah) and *Ozias* (Uzziah) would be great.

[47] See Johnson, *Purpose,* 186. While, as we have seen, a logical explanation can be offered
for the "errors," we must remember the caution of Wilson, "Genealogy," that omissions are

In the NOTE on vs. 11, I have called attention to the second omission in the monarchical section of Matthew's list, namely, that instead of saying "Josiah was the father of *Jechoniah* and his brothers," Matthew would have been true to history if he said, "Josiah was the father of Jehoiakim and his brothers [King Jehoahaz II and Zedekiah]); Jehoiakim was the father of *Jechoniah*." Once again we may be dealing with an omission caused by confusion between similar names, viz., the name of Jehoiakim, the son of Josiah, and that of Jehoiachin (Jechoniah), the grandson of Josiah. The fact that both Jehoiakim and Jehoiachin had a brother named Zedekiah (the former's brother was King Zedekiah; the latter's brother never ruled) already caused confusion in antiquity as we see in II Chr 36:10 which incorrectly identifies King Zedekiah as Jehoiachin's brother. The confusion between Jehoiakim and Jehoiachin (Jechoniah) may have been facilitated by Greek orthography since occasionally the LXX uses the same spelling (*Iōakim*) for both names.[48]

This explanation may also help us with another difficulty about Matthew's arithmetic. In the third section of the genealogy, from the Babylonian Exile to Jesus, there are only thirteen generations. There have been many proposals for finding a fourteenth generation, some highly ingenious. For instance, it has been argued that, while Jesus is the thirteenth generation, the Messiah is the fourteenth generation; for Jesus became the Messiah only after the resurrection which was a new birth! Yet this is certainly not Matthew's understanding, since he writes the infancy narrative to show that Jesus was the Messiah from conception; and in the Gospel proper Jesus is acknowledged as the Messiah during the ministry (Matt 16:16). Another proposal brings Mary into the fourteenth generation since she, not Joseph, is the natural parent of Jesus. But that still leaves only thirteen generations, since one can scarcely count his not being begotten by Joseph as the thirteenth and his being born of Mary as the fourteenth. A more plausible explanation traces the difficulty to the *beginning* of the third section. If the last listing in the second section should have read "Jehoiakim and his brothers," then there would have to be another listing for the begetting of Jechoniah: "Jehoiakim was the father of Jechoniah." Could Matthew have recognized that a generation was omitted and counted this implicit generation by mentioning Jechoniah at the beginning of his third section, even as he counted the implicit generation of Abraham at the beginning of his first section?[49] With ingenuity,

---

frequent particularly in the middle section of contemporary tribal genealogies for reasons that do not seem logical to the Western scientific mind and that the designation "error" may be gratuitous here.

48 See the LXX of II Kgs 23:36 and 24:8; also the uses of *Iōakim* as an orthography for Jehoiachin in II Kgs 25:27; Jer 52:31; and Ezek 1:2. Of course, such confusion was more likely when the king's regnal name (Jehoiachin) was involved rather than his birth name (Jechoniah, rendered in Greek as *Iechonias*). Since Matthew employs the latter, the confusion is most likely pre-Matthean, existing in the list Matthew drew upon.

49 Many have argued that if Matthew knew there was a confusion at the end of the second section of the genealogy, he would have corrected it. That is not so certain. First,

then, one can salvage Matthew's reputation as a mathematician. But from the viewpoint of a modern reader, he certainly could have been of more assistance in clarifying the 3×14 pattern of generations that he claims for the genealogy of the Messiah.

B. *Matthew's Genealogy Compared to Luke's*

Already, in the course of studying Matthew, we have come upon points that invited a comparison with the genealogy that Luke gives of Jesus, the Son of God (3:23–38). The time has come for a systematic comparison of the two genealogies, at least as regards their significant differences. By way of background the reader should first consult Table I which enumerates the names in Luke's list and divides them into four time periods (three of which correspond to Matthew's sections).[50] Then the reader should turn to Tables I, III, and IV to survey the differences between Matthew and Luke. The following are general observations:

■*Overall:* Matthew's list descends from Abraham to Jesus and uses the formula: "A was the father of B; B was the father of C" (NOTE on vs. 2), while Luke's list ascends from Jesus through Adam to God and uses the formula: "A, (son) of B, (son) of C."[51] Since Luke includes a pre-patriarchal (pre-Abrahamic) period, his list is much longer than Matthew's—some seventy-seven names compared to Matthew's forty-one. Even in the three periods in which the two genealogies overlap (between Abraham and Jesus), Luke's is longer—some fifty-six names compared to Matthew's forty-one.

■*The pre-monarchical period* covering some 750 years between Abraham

---

Matthew may have regarded the genealogical list that he was using as sacred. Second, in order to correct it he would have had to bring fifteen generations into the second section. He could not solve this by inserting the missing generative notice ("Jehoiakim was the father of Jechoniah") as the first of third section rather than as the fifteenth of the second section, for the third section is dated "After the Babylonian Exile," and the begetting of Jechoniah took place before the Babylonian Exile. See the exhaustive discussion of this and other hypotheses in Vögtle, "Josias."

50 The reader should also note the context of the genealogy in Luke. Jesus had just been baptized, and a heavenly voice has proclaimed him as "My beloved Son" (3:22). Thus Luke's tracing Jesus' sonship back to God is quite intelligible. The opening line which leads into Luke's genealogy ("Now, as Jesus began his ministry, he was about thirty years of age") is phrased in awkward Greek. The first words could be translated: "Now, as this Jesus," i.e., the Jesus referred to by the heavenly voice. The participle *archomenos*, translated "as he began his ministry," is literally "as he began." Its abruptness has caused some to prefer *erchomenos*, "as he came (from being baptized)." The initial filiation, "being the son (as it was supposed) of Joseph," may contain an older formula ("being the son of Joseph") which Luke has modified in harmony with his presentation of the virginal conception (1:26–38).

51 As pointed out in the NOTE on vs. 2, Matthew's formula has exact parallels in the OT. Parallels to Luke's ascending pattern and formula are harder to find. The levitical genealogies of Heman and Asaph in I Chr 6:18–28 (=RSV 6:33–43) are a close parallel, except that in the LXX those genealogies have the word "son" (*huios*), whereas Luke implies it. MGNTG, I, 236, ref. to p. 84, cites an inscriptional genealogy in Palmyrene-Aramaic and Greek that matches the Lucan formula.

and David (Table II): This is the only area in which the two genealogies have any extended agreement, the one significant difference occurring in the names between Hezron and Amminadab. In that slot Matthew has Aram, while Luke has Arni and Admin.[52]

■*The monarchical period* covering some 400 years from David to the Babylonian Exile (Table III): Here the two lists are totally different, agreeing only on David. Luke has twenty-one names, compared with Matthew's fifteen; and of the twenty-one only David and Nathan have attestation in the OT history of the monarchy.[53]

■*The post-monarchical period* covering some 575 years from the beginning of the Babylonian Exile to the birth of Jesus (Table IV): The Matthean list with thirteen names and the Lucan list with twenty-two agree only in the first two (Shealtiel[54] and Zerubbabel) and in the last two (Joseph and Jesus).[55] And these four names are the only ones in either list for which we have any biblical information. The other persons are completely unknown from the OT and from the intertestamental literature.

In face of these enormous differences it may be well to repeat the admonition offered by R. R. Wilson ("OT Genealogies," 182). It is possible to have conflicting genealogies of the same person if those genealogies have different functions. Only one or neither of them may be historical in terms of traceable biological lineage, but both of them may be accurate in terms of the function they serve, e.g., Matthew's intention to show that Jesus is the Davidic Messiah, and Luke's intention to show that Jesus is the Son of God. Nevertheless, modern readers cannot help wondering about the biological lineage of Jesus, and so let us begin by discussing how the two genealogies differ regarding Jesus' immediate ancestry, a problem that will enable us to become more precise about the origins of Matthew's genealogy.

52 While Matthew's (A)ram is attested in the genealogies of Ruth and I Chr 2, there is no biblical support for Arni and Admin. The scribes who copied Luke's Gospel had difficulty identifying them as we can see from the ms. variants. Admin has been judged a corruption of Amminadab, so that Luke would have given us the same man twice, under two different names. Similarly Arni has been judged a corruption of (A)ram. Neither solution is very persuasive.

53 As for Luke's choice of a messianic line through Nathan (II Sam 5:14) rather than through Solomon, this may reflect a popular Jewish uneasiness about the taint attached to Solomon's scandalous life. See Johnson, *Purpose*, 135–36.

54 Matthew and Luke attribute different parentage to Shealtiel. Matthew's attribution (son of King Jechoniah) has biblical support (I Chr 3:17); for Luke he is the son of Neri of whom the OT tells us nothing. Jeremias, *Jerusalem*, 296[91], thinks that Luke may be right in making Zerubbabel the descendant of a non-reigning Davidic branch. The post-exilic concentration on Zerubbabel as the "white hope" of the Davidic line would favor creating for him a direct royal lineage if he did not already have one, e.g., by making King Jechoniah his grandfather. (There is confusion in the OT itself about Zerubbabel's lineage; see NOTE on vs. 12.) But that observation does nothing to confirm Luke's statement that he was the grandson of Neri.

55 A fifth agreement has been proposed through the identification of Matthan, whom Matthew lists as Joseph's grandfather, with the Matthat whom Luke lists as Joseph's grandfather. Yet the intervening generation (Joseph's father) is different in the two lists.

1. Who Was Jesus' Grandfather?

This question, which may seem naively curious, is raised by the blatant disagreement between Matt 1:16, which identifies Joseph's father as Jacob, and Luke 3:23, which identifies that gentleman as Eli. A discussion of this disagreement leads us into an evaluation of the third section of Matthew's genealogy (from the Babylonian Exile to Jesus) and indeed into an analysis of how Matthew gave final form to his genealogy. While his first and second sections are made up of names known to us from the OT, we are faced with unknowns in the nine names of the third section between Zerubbabel and Joseph (Table IV). There are three major explanations of how Matthew got these names: (a) he invented them; (b) he copied them from a list which traced the post-exilic royal lineage of the House of David; (c) he copied them from Joseph's family records.

a) *Invention by Matthew.* This suggestion has had less acceptance than the others because Matthew showed no tendency to invent ancestors in the earlier two sections of the genealogy. There Matthew depended on sources, differing slightly from the OT genealogies known to us; and one might suspect that he did the same thing in the third section. Moreover, the marvel implicit in recognizing the pattern of 3×14 seems strange (at least in our eyes) if Matthew simply invented the last grouping. And if the genealogy was to have any probative value in dealing with the Jews, sheer invention would be risky.

The only real argument for invention is the claim that genealogical records of individuals were rare in Jesus' time. However, J. Jeremias (*Jerusalem*, 275–97) argues that both for public and private individuals genealogical traditions were kept alive among the Jews and that some of these traditions had historical value. For instance, when Israel returned from the Babylonian Exile, genealogical records were an absolute necessity to establish rights and privileges. That is why the Chronicler, who reflects the post-exilic mentality, opens his book with a series of genealogies (chronicles). Ezra 9:1 – 10:44 stresses that at this period families of pure lineage kept themselves separated from families that had intermarried with Gentiles. Our most frequent later references to the lineage of individuals pertain to the members of the tribe of Levi[56] and of the tribe of Judah,[57] especially of the House of David.

---

[56] There is considerable evidence that written genealogical records of the priestly families were kept in Jerusalem; see Johnson, *Purpose*, 96–101. Josephus (*Life* 1;≹≹1–6), who was of priestly descent, names ancestors six generations back and over a span of almost 200 years. He claims his pedigree can be found in the public registers.

[57] The most frequent claims to belonging to a tribe other than Levi or Judah are to Benjamin (Judah's reluctant ally in the Southern Kingdom; see I Kgs 12:21); and it is interesting that Paul professes to be a Benjaminite (Rom 11:1; Philip 3:5).

b) *Copying from a Davidic List*. This brings us to the second suggestion whereby Matthew used an existing Davidic genealogy. We may distinguish two different types of supporting evidence, the first pertaining to individuals who claim to be of Davidic descent, the second pertaining to the survival of a post-exilic royal lineage. As for individual Davidids, the great Rabbi Hillel is said to have been of Davidic descent on the maternal side; and well into the first Christian millennium, the exilarch or head of the Jewish community in Babylon claimed Davidic descent. Eusebius (*Eccl. Hist.* III xii, xix–xx, xxxii 3–4) mentions persecution of Jews of Davidic descent under the Roman Emperors Vespasian (A.D. 79), Domitian (96), and Trajan (120). It is difficult to evaluate the historicity of these scattered claims to Davidic ancestry,[58] but their very existence increases the possibility that a list supporting Davidic descent (historical or fictional) may have been available to Matthew.

As we move to the second type of evidence pertaining to the Davidic royal family,[59] we find that scholars like E. Sellin and J. Jeremias have argued that the House of David remained the foremost lay family in post-exilic Judaism, at least until Maccabean times (*ca.* 150 B.C.). Since there was discussion about the Davidic ancestry of the Messiah among Jews in Jesus' time, there may well have been attempts to trace genealogically the royal (and messianic) line within the House of David. But were there *official* lists of the post-exilic royal family in existence in the first century A.D.? The possibility that there were is raised by the information (stemming from Julius Africanus[60]) that Herod the Great burned the archives of Jewish families (including those descended from Ruth, and thus Davidic), so that he would not be embarrassed by references to his own base origins. Presumably he would have been most interested in genealogies that could challenge his position as king; presumably, too, he would not have been successful in destroying all the lists, so that some birth records of the Davidic royal family could have survived. The OT itself gives us a list of five descendants of Zerubbabel,[61] the last well-known scion of

---

[58] Liver, "Problem," argues that there are no reliable extra-biblical genealogies; he dismisses Hillel's Davidic claim (*Midrash Rabbah* XCVIII 8 on Gen 49:10). For Liver, the talmudic genealogies of the Babylonian exarchs are a jumble based on I Chronicles. Jeremias, *Jerusalem*, is less negative, but on pp. 285–90 he discusses falsified genealogies. Johnson, *Purpose*, 108–15, treats the role of popular and imaginative midrash in forming genealogies.

[59] We are naturally pushed in that direction since Matthew has attached his post-exilic names to a list of the kings of Judah—unlike Luke who gives Jesus only one ancestor who reigned as king, David.

[60] Cited by Eusebius *Eccl. Hist.* I vii 13. Josephus, *Contra Apion* I 7;⍭31, speaks of archives of genealogies. One may compare Jeremias, *Jerusalem*, 281–82, and Johnson, *Purpose*, 102–8. Johnson is more skeptical of the existence of written genealogical records for laymen, as distinct from valid oral memories of ancestors going back as far as ten generations.

[61] The names Hananiah, Shecaniah, Hattush, Elioenai, and Anani are found in I Chr 3:19–24, and there is comparative evidence for dating Anani to *ca.* 445–405. See J. M. Myers, *I Chronicles* (AB 12; Garden City, N.Y.: Doubleday, 1965), 21; and F. M. Cross, "A Reconstruction of the Judean Restoration," JBL 94 (1975), 4–18.

David, a list that would reach to *ca.* 400 B.C.; but it is debatable how such a list would have been continued and preserved with any completeness through the period from 400 to 200 from which virtually no other memories have survived in Judaism.

Matthew's list of names for the post-exilic period is too short to cover the span of time, and neither his names nor those of Luke's longer list coincide with the descendants of Zerubbabel listed in the OT (Table IV), even though both Matthew and Luke trace the lineal descent of Jesus from Zerubbabel. And so, even if there were official genealogies of the royal House of David in the post-exilic period, there is nothing to support the thesis that Matthew drew upon one.[62] It is far more plausible to assume that, at most, he may echo a popular genealogy of the royal lineage that circulated in Greek-speaking Jewish circles as part of their speculations about the coming of the Messiah. (I say "Greek-speaking" since the confusions in the second section of Matthew's genealogy and the "Aram" of the first section are best explained on the basis of a Greek tradition of the names.) Such a popular tradition would have been subject to changes, losses, inaccuracies, and vagaries of the imagination.[63]

If Matthew drew upon this hypothetical popular list of royal Davidic descendants, he must have added to it at least the two names that now come last in the genealogy, the names of Joseph and Jesus known to him from the tradition of the public ministry. (Anticipating the study in Appendix II, I contend that the tradition that Jesus was a Davidid is independent of and older than the attempts of Matthew and Luke to find a Davidic genealogy for him.) In point of fact, if Joseph and Jesus were Davidids, they must have belonged to a lateral branch of the family rather than to the direct royal lineage. There is not the slightest indication in the accounts of the ministry of Jesus that his family was of ancestral nobility or royalty. If Jesus were a dauphin, there would have been none of the wonderment about his pretensions. He appears in the Gospels as a man of unimpressive background from an unimportant village.

c) *Copying from Joseph's family records.* Before we can accept as least objectionable the theory that Matthew added the names of Joseph and Jesus to a popular list of the royal descendants, we must discuss the third possibility, namely, that Matthew gives us Joseph's real family tree. This

---

62 It is surprising to find the priestly name of Zadok in Matthew's list (1:14) of Jesus' post-exilic ancestry. Does the list echo that stage of Jewish history when the high priests of the line of Zadok replaced the Davidic princes as the effective rulers? See a critical discussion of Zech 6:11 where in the standard Hebrew Bible the recipient of the royal coronation has been changed from Zerubbabel, a Davidid, to Joshua the high priest.

63 Johnson, *Purpose*, 179–80, points out that Matthew's post-exilic names from Abiud to Matthan do not occur in the *Corpus Papyrorum Judaicarum* and so are scarcely attested in the last centuries B.C. They may be adaptations of names from the pre-exilic period found scattered in the Greek Bible, especially in I Chronicles.

brings us face to face with the problem that Luke's list of Jesus' post-exilic ancestors is very different from the list given in Matthew,[64] with the possible exception of Joseph's grandfather who is Matthan in Matthew and Matthat in Luke. There have been many attempts to solve this problem. The most simple and best-known is the attempt to treat them both as family records, with Matthew giving us Joseph's record, and Luke giving us Mary's.[65] What influences this suggestion is the centrality of Joseph in Matthew's infancy narrative, as compared with the spotlighting of Mary in Luke's. Even at first glance, however, this solution cannot be taken seriously: a genealogy traced through the mother is not normal in Judaism,[66] and Luke makes it clear that he is tracing Jesus' descent *through Joseph*. Moreover, Luke's genealogy traces Davidic descent and, despite later Christian speculation, we really do not know that Mary was a Davidid.[67] The tradition that she was a Davidid may have been fostered in Gentile Christian circles where the force of Jesus' legal descent from David through Joseph would not have been appreciated, and so it would have been felt necessary to make Jesus a blood descendant of David through Mary.

Another proposed solution to the differences between the two lists of post-exilic ancestors is in terms of a levirate marriage (Deut 25:5–10)—the custom, when a husband has died childless, of having his next of kin marry the widow in order to beget children to continue the de-

[64] Origen, *Against Celsus* II 32, reports that the discrepancies between the genealogies were already a problem among Christians in his time. In the same century (third) Porphyry used the divergencies as an argument against Christianity. In the OT period, less dominated by formal logic, the presence of variant genealogies seemingly caused no problem, e.g., I Chr 2:19–20 gives Bezalel the builder of the Tabernacle, more ancestors than does Exod 31:2.

[65] This thesis is presented in the writings of Annius of Viterbo (*ca.* 1500). It is expounded in detail in Vogt, *Stammbaum*, and Heer, *Stammbäume*. A converse situation with Matthew giving Mary's ancestors (and Luke giving Joseph's) has minor support—perhaps Tertullian, *De carne Christi* xx–xxii. A modern variant is supplied by Blair, "Matthew," who thinks that the Joseph in Matthew's genealogy was the father (not the husband) of Mary, that Joseph's begetting Mary is the missing and fourteenth generation in Matthew's third section, and that thus Matthew gives us a genealogy of Mary. Seethaler, "Eine kleine," accepts the rather desperate hypothesis that Matthew and Luke give us the genealogies of two different Josephs.

[66] TalBab, *Baba Bathra*, 109b, gives the principle: "The family of the father is regarded as the proper family, but the family of the mother is not regarded as proper family." Nolle, "Old Testament," 40–42, argues against this by pointing to Num 26:33 which gives the names of the daughters of Zelophehad, and to I Chr 2:16–17 which mentions David's two sisters and their children. However, these would offer no real parallel to a long list of Mary's ancestors. The Numbers passage, for instance, is deliberately inserted to prepare for Num 27:1–11 where there is a legal discussion about the rights of these daughters as heiresses. The particular twist in Nolle's thesis is that Joseph, son of Jacob (Matthew's genealogy), married Mary the heiress daughter of Eli (see Luke's genealogy), so that Joseph became Eli's heir as well, incorporated into Eli's family tree—the type of case envisaged in the legal discussion in Numbers. Related to this is the thesis supported by B. Weiss, requiring an extraordinary translation of Luke 3:23: "Jesus . . . being the son (as it was supposed) of Joseph, [but really the grand]son of Eli," the latter being the father of Mary. See the refutation in Johnson, *Purpose*, 143–44.

[67] This question will be discussed in reference to Luke 1:27, see NOTE there.

ceased husband's lineage. According to this theory both evangelists give us family records of Joseph, but one traces the ancestors through Joseph's natural father, and the other through Joseph's legal, deceased father. We shall discuss the intricacies of this thesis in Appendix I, noting here only that the difficulties it faces are formidable.

In light of these difficulties, most scholars today have rejected the explanation that both the Matthean and Lucan genealogies are family lists. A possible solution, corresponding to what we have already seen, would be that Matthew's genealogy represents a popular tradition about the royal Davidic lineage (to which the names of Joseph and Jesus have been joined), while Luke's genealogy may be the family list of Joseph's ancestors. To test the Lucan side of that theory we need now to look at the Lucan genealogy in more detail, even though by its localization in ch. 3 it lies outside the direct scope of a commentary dedicated to the infancy narratives. By way of preparing the reader, let me report here that the Lucan genealogy is no less theological in purpose than Matthew's and no freer of historical difficulties.

2. The Family Tree of the Son of God

At the very beginning of this section when we were comparing the two genealogies, I summarized the main differences, section by section. Many of the Lucan peculiarities may be traced to the author's theological intent. If his is the only genealogy in the Bible to trace a man's origins to God, that is because his genealogy comes after the baptism where a voice from heaven proclaimed Jesus as God's Son.[68] If Luke traces Jesus to Adam, that may reflect the fact that his is a Gospel written for the Gentiles of the Pauline churches. In a mixed community, Matthew could appeal to Gentile Christian interest by tracing Jesus to Abraham, whom Jews called "our father," but in whom all the nations of the earth were to be blessed (footnote 11 above). But since the Pauline preaching not only related Jesus to Abraham (Gal 3:16) but drew a parallel between Jesus and Adam (Rom

[68] There are Greek and Roman attempts to establish the divinity of a ruler by tracing his pedigree to a god, but there are too many Jewish elements in the Lucan genealogy to doubt its Jewish provenance. It is not clear how Luke understood Jesus as "the son of Adam, the son of God." Later Christian orthodoxy understood Jesus to have pre-existed as God's Son in a non-corporeal manner from all eternity, but that view is closer to John's theology than to any explicit Lucan thought. A complicating factor in our diagnosis of the theology of the Lucan genealogy is the possibility that it may have been part of the Gospel plan from the beginning, whereas the Lucan infancy narrative may have been prefixed after the body of the Gospel was written. (See § 9, B1 below.) The placing of the genealogy after the baptism may reflect a stage in Gospel christology (shared by Mark) wherein the baptism was the moment of the principal revelation of Jesus as the Messiah and Son of God. As explained in § 1, A2, the infancy narrative may reflect a later stage of christology wherein the conception of Jesus has become the moment of this revelation. (For an adaptation of the Lucan genealogy to the Lucan infancy narrative, see footnote 50 above). The theme of Jesus as God's Son appears in the Lucan infancy narrative in 1:35 and 2:49.

5:12–21; I Cor 15:22,45), Luke may have felt impelled to include both
figures in the genealogy.[69] The mention of Adam ("Man") as well as God
emphasizes the paradox that Jesus had human and divine origins, and that
the human origins are those shared by all who walk the face of the earth,
Gentile and Jew.[70] Also the reference to Jesus as "the son of Adam" immediately precedes the scene in Luke 4:1–13 where Jesus is tempted by
Satan, an echo of Adam's struggle with Satan in Eden.[71]

Although Luke does not specify that his genealogy follows a system of
numerical organization, many have detected a pattern of 11×7.[72] There
are many features in the genealogy that support the thesis of a pattern of
7s: e.g., there are seven patriarchs from Adam to Enoch, and then seventy
names between Enoch and Jesus, perhaps reflecting the tradition (see
Enoch 10:12) that there would be seventy generations from the sin of the
angels until the judgment. Again, Luke has twenty-one (3×7) names in
the post-exilic period, as Matthew has fourteen (Table IV). This is also
true of the monarchical period (Table III), while in the pre-monarchical
period Abraham is fourteen (2×7) names before David (Table II), and
God is twenty-one (3×7) names before Abraham. Thus, the total Lucan
list has a pattern from Joseph to God of 21+21+14+21 (Table I).
The fact that David (※42) and Abraham (※56) appear as a multiple
of seven may also be important.[73]

However, there are also problems about detecting a pattern of 7s. Those
who count seventy-seven names in all are not in agreement as to whether
Jesus himself should be counted as ※1, with God omitted from the calculation at the end (so Heer, *Stammbäume*); or, as I have done, Joseph
should be counted as ※1, and God counted as ※77 (perfection?). Indeed, it might be more honest to count both Jesus and God and to admit a
pattern of seventy-eight names. Moreover, the count of seventy-seven is
uncertain on purely textual grounds; for there are many manuscript variants, and the number of names in different textual witnesses runs the
gamut from seventy-seven to sixty-three.[74] The most that can be said is

---

69 At the beginning of Book Two (§ 9) I shall discuss Luke's Gospel and the community
to which it was directed. The thesis that Luke wrote to a community in the Pauline tradition
does not necessarily imply that the evangelist was a companion of Paul.

70 There may be another, indirect reference to the Gentiles in the fact that the number of
Jesus' ancestors in the Lucan list is close to the number of the nations of the world
(seventy-two) descended from Noah in Gen. 10. See footnote 74 below.

71 J. Jeremias, TDNT, I, 141ff.

72 Such a pattern began to be detected already in the fourth century by Augustine and by
the Cappadocian Church Fathers. Some have proposed as a parallel for the Lucan
genealogy a division of world history into twelve parts (*II Baruch* 53–74; *IV Ezra* 14:11).
There would be the eleven divisions of seven names each (seventy-seven) from God to
Joseph, and Jesus would begin the twelfth.

73 One can point also to Enoch (※70) and God (※77). Bruns, "Matthew's Genealogy,"
982, finds a significant name and turning point at the end of almost every seven, e.g., Joseph
(※7), Shealtiel (※21), Jesus (※28), Joseph (※35). This requires considerable imagination.

74 A list of the varying enumerations in the different textual witnesses is given by Heer,
Stammbäume, 3; they include seventy-six names in Vaticanus, seventy-five in the Sinaitic

that there are patterns of 7s in parts of the Lucan genealogy and that they may be connected with the view of a predetermined world history coming to an end—a view that may have been inherent in a pre-Lucan form of the genealogy.

The very presence of these numerical patterns calls into question the likelihood that Luke's genealogy is any more historical (in a biological sense) than Matthew's. As we press that question our chief concern must be the section of the Lucan record from David to Jesus. In the monarchical period from David to Neri, who was the father of Shealtiel (Table III), Luke may be less pretentious than Matthew in tracing Jesus' lineage through Nathan rather than through the ruling kings descended from Solomon, but that does not necessarily mean that he is more historical.[75] Some of the names that he assigns to this pre-exilic period (Levi, Simeon, Joseph, Judah) seem to be anachronisms, for the custom of naming children after the patriarchs did not develop until after the Exile.[76] Indeed, another sequence of names, Jesus, Eliezer, Jorim, Maththat, and Levi (※※28–32 in Table I) is very close to a sequence of names at the beginning of the list: Jesus, Joseph, Eli, Matthat, and Levi (※※1–4); so that one begins to wonder if the names of the monarchical period have not in part been supplied from names of the post-monarchical (post-exilic) period.[77] This wonderment is increased when we notice that the name Joseph appears three times in the list (※※1,7,35), while six men have the very similar names of Matthat, Mattathias, Maath, Maththat, and Mattatha(n) (※※3,8,13,14,31,40)—a name associated with the Maccabean or Hasmonean family of the House of Levi in the second century B.C. (I Macc 2:1), rather than with the House of David, especially as we know it in the monarchical period.

In the post-monarchical period (Table IV) Luke has a more plausible

---

Syriac, and seventy-four in Alexandrinus. Heer himself opts for seventy-two as the original number. Since Luke does not spell out a numerical pattern as Matthew did, his long list was more open to omissions; and the fact that almost half the Lucan names are not attested in the OT led to textual corruptions.

[75] See footnote 53 above. That there was a subdivision of the Davidic line claiming descent from Nathan is attested by Zech 12:12–13, which compares the division between the House of David and the House of Nathan to the division between the House of Levi and the Shimeites (a levitical subdivision). I prefer this explanation to the thesis that Luke has confused Nathan, David's son, with Nathan, David's prophet, and that his preference for descent through Nathan over descent through Solomon was dictated by his strong interest in Jesus as a prophetic figure. (See Johnson, *Purpose*, 240–52; and Abel, "Genealogies.")

[76] Jeremias, *Jerusalem*, 296. The fact that Luke gives to one ancestor of Jesus the name Jesus (※28) has raised the possibility that other ancestors have been given the names of Jesus' brothers (James, Joseph, Simon, and Judah, according to Matt 13:55), especially in the combination Simeon, Judah, and Joseph (※※33,34,35). This is dubious, however, since, although Luke knows of the brothers of Jesus (8:19–21; Acts 1:14), he never gives them names.

[77] G. Kuhn, "Geschlechtsregister," 208–9, works out an elaborate thesis whereby the Lucan list from Jesus to Mattathias (※※1–14) is a duplicate of the list from Jesus to Mattatha(n) in ※※28–40.

number of generations (twenty-two from Shealtiel to Jesus) than does Matthew (thirteen),[78] but again that is no historical guarantee. The whole Lucan picture from David to Jesus is complicated by the fact that, having avoided the direct royal line throughout the monarchy by tracing the genealogy through Nathan rather than through Solomon, Luke rejoins the royal line after fall of the monarchy by listing Shealtiel and Zerubbabel (※※21,20), who appear also in Matthew's list.[79] Some have been impressed that, despite all biblical evidence (footnote 54), Luke makes Shealtiel the son of the otherwise unknown Neri rather than of the last king Jechoniah; but his motivation may have been theological, namely, to avoid having in Jesus' ancestry a figure whom Jeremiah cursed thus: "Write this man down as childless . . . for none of his offspring shall succeed in sitting on the throne of David and ruling again in Judah" (Jer 22:30). In the list from Zerubbabel to Jesus there are signs of confusion. Besides the duplicate sequences of names and the occurrence of levitical names mentioned in the preceding paragraph, there is a curiosity such as Rhesa (※19). Is this a personal name, or is it a misunderstanding of the Greek transcription of Aramaic *rēšā'*, "prince"? If the latter, then as Jeremias (*Jerusalem*, 296) points out, the pre-Lucan reading may have been *"Prince* Joanan, the son of Zerubbabel,"* a reading that raises the possibility of identification with the Hananiah whom I Chr 3:19 designates as a son of Zerubbabel.

In summary, then, the Lucan list, while in some ways more plausible than Matthew's list, scarcely constitutes an exact record of Jesus' biological ancestry. One can always speculate that the last few generations of immediate ancestors might be correct, but the same speculation is possible for Matthew's list—with no chance of proving either and with little in the rest of the list to warrant much confidence in such speculation. What one may say with surety of Luke's list is that, in part, it is artificially arranged in numerical patterns of seven and that it contains enough inaccuracies and confusions to suggest a popular provenance (rather than an archival provenance) among Greek-speaking Jews.[80] Luke adopted this list and

[78] Almost exactly 600 years separated the birth of Shealtiel from the birth of Jesus; Matthew's numbers would lead to about forty-six years per generation, while Luke's numbers would lead to about twenty-seven years. Jeremias, *Jerusalem*, 294, points out that Josephus' list of post-exilic high priests yields an average generation of about twenty-seven years, a calculation that should be lessened to about twenty-five years by F. M. Cross' observation that Josephus has omitted several names (*art. cit.* in footnote 61).

[79] I find no plausibility in the suggestion that the Shealtiel and Zerubbabel of Luke's list are not the same men mentioned by Matthew; in the two lists the men appear together about halfway between David and Jesus.

[80] Some of the possible confusions, e.g., regarding Rhesa, can be more easily explained in a list of Greek names. Moreover, the name of Cainan (※64), which appears in the Lucan list between Shelah and Arphaxad, is not found in I Chr 1:24 (a section of a list often assumed to be Luke's source) but in the LXX (not the MT) of Gen 10:24; 11:12–13. True, it appears in *Jubilees* 8:1–4, but dependence of the genealogy upon the LXX is more likely than dependence on *Jubilees*.

adapted it for theological purposes by placing it between the baptism of Jesus and his temptations.

This means that, while the two NT genealogies tell us how to evaluate Jesus, they tell us nothing certain about his grandparents or his great-grandparents. The message about Jesus, son of Joseph, is not that factually he is also (grand)son of either Jacob (Matthew) or of Eli (Luke) but that theologically he is "son of David, son of Abraham" (Matthew), and "Son of God" (Luke).

SECTIONAL BIBLIOGRAPHY (§ 3)
(MATT 1:1–17)

Abel, E. L., "The Genealogies of Jesus *Ho Christos*," NTS 20 (1973–74), 203–10.

Blair, H. A., "Matthew 1,16 and the Matthean Genealogy," StEv II (TU 87; Berlin: Akademie, 1964), 149–54.

Bloch, Renée, " 'Juda engendra Pharès et Zara, de Thamar' (*Matt* 1,3)," in *Mélanges bibliques rédigés en l'honneur de André Robert* (Paris: Bloud & Gay, 1957), 381–89.

Braude, W. G., "A Rabbinic Guide to the Gospels," *Scripture* 19 (1967), 33–45, esp. 40–45.

Bruns, J. E., "Matthew's Genealogy of Jesus," *The Bible Today* 1 (Dec. 1964), 980–85.

Burkitt, F. C., *Evangelion Da-Mepharreshe* II (Cambridge University, 1904), 262–66 on Matt 1:16.

Davis, C. T., "The Fulfillment of Creation. A Study of Matthew's Genealogy," JAAR 41 (1973), 520–35.

Heer, J. M., *Die Stammbäume Jesu nach Matthäus und Lukas* (BS 15[1–2]; Freiburg: Herder, 1910).

Hood, R. T., "The Genealogies of Jesus," in *Early Christian Origins* (Studies in Honor of H. R. Willoughby; Chicago: Quadrangle, 1961), 1–15.

Jeremias, J., *Jerusalem in the Time of Jesus* (Philadelphia: Fortress, 1969), 275–97.

Johnson, M. D., *The Purpose of the Biblical Genealogies with Special Reference to the Setting of the Genealogies of Jesus* (NTSMS 8; Cambridge University, 1969).

Kaplan, C., "The Generation Schemes in Matthew I:1–17, Luke III:24ff.," BibSac 87 (1930), 465–71.

Kuhn, G., "Die Geschlechtsregister Jesu bei Lukas und Matthäus, nach ihrer Herkunft untersucht," ZNW 22 (1923), 206–28.

Lambertz, M., "Die Toledoth in Mt 1,1–17 und Lc 3,23bff.," in *Festschrift Franz Dornseiff*, ed. H. Kusch (Leipzig: VEB Bibliographisches Institut, 1953), 201–25.

Léon-Dufour, X., "Livre de la genèse de Jésus-Christ," *Etudes d'Evangile* (Paris: Seuil, 1965), 47–63.

Leuba, J.-L., "Note exégétique sur Matthieu 1,1a," RHPR 22 (1942), 56–61.

Liver, J., "The Problem of the Genealogy of the Davidic Family after the Biblical Period," *Tarbiz* (1957), 229–54. In Hebrew; see NTA 2 (1957–58), ※20.

Metzger, B. M., "On the Citation of Variant Readings of Matt 1:16," JBL 77 (1958), 361–63.

——— "The Text of Matthew 1.16," in *Studies in New Testament and Early Christian Literature: Essays in Honor of Allen P. Wikgren,* ed. D. E. Aune (Leiden: Brill, 1972), 16–24.

Moreton, M. J., "The Genealogy of Jesus," StEv, II (TU 87; Berlin: Akademie, 1964), 219–24.

Nineham, D. E., "The Genealogy in St. Matthew's Gospel and Its Significance for the Study of the Gospel," DJRL 58 (1975–76), 421–44.

Nolle, L., "Old Testament Laws of Inheritance and St. Luke's Genealogy of Christ," *Scripture* 2 (1947), 38–42.

Pascual Calvo, E., "La genealogía de Jesús según San Mateo," EB 23 (1964), 109–49.

Ramlot, L., "Les généalogies bibliques, un genre oriental," BVC 60 (1964), 53–70.

Seethaler, Paula, "Eine kleine Bemerkung zu den Stammbäumen Jesu nach Matthäus und Lukas," BZ 16 (1972), 256–57.

Spitta, F., "Die Frauen in der Genealogie des Matthäus," *Zeitschrift für Wissenschaftliche Theologie* 54 (1912), 1–8.

Stegemann, H., " 'Die des Uria': Zur Bedeutung der Frauennamen in der Genealogie von Matthäus, 1,1–17," in *Tradition und Glaube* (Festgabe K. G. Kuhn; Göttingen: Vandenhoeck, 1972), 246–76.

Vögtle, A., "Die Genealogie Mt 1,2–16 und die matthäische Kindheitsgeschichte," BZ 8 (1964), 45–58, 239–62; 9 (1965), 32–49. Reprinted in his *Das Evangelium und die Evangelien* (Düsseldorf: Patmos, 1971), 57–102.

——— " 'Josias zeugte den Jechonias und seine Brüder' (Mt 1,11)," in *Lex tua Veritas* (Festschrift H. Junker; Trier: Paulinus, 1961), 307–13.

Vogt, P., *Der Stammbaum bei den heiligen Evangelisten Matthäus* (BS 13³; Freiburg: Herder, 1907).

Waetjen, H. C., "The Genealogy as the Key to the Gospel according to Matthew," JBL 95 (1976), 205–30.

Wilson, R. R., "Genealogy and History in the Old Testament" (Yale University Dissertation, 1972; Ann Arbor: University Microfilms).

——— "The Old Testament Genealogies in Recent Research," JBL 94 (1975), 168–89.

III. THE COMPOSITION OF THE
BASIC MATTHEAN NARRATIVE (§ 4)
(1:18–2:23)

We were able to discuss the genealogy as a unit; for despite the fact that it is clearly related to what follows (especially to 1:18–25), Matthew marks off its inner unity by pointing out the pattern of fourteens. We now turn to the narrative unit, the story of Jesus' conception, birth, and infancy, which runs from 1:18 to 2:23. In § 2, B2, I pointed out the difficulties in determining an outline that does justice to the different factors within this narrative. Two structures proposed by scholars were discussed, each with its supporting arguments; and the suggestion was made that the key to why two different structures have plausibility may lie in the recognition of a pre-Matthean composition underlying the present Matthean narrative. It is now time to test that suggestion by studying the compositional history of 1:18 – 2:23. The most prominent visual feature in this narrative is the presence of four or five explicit citations of Scripture introduced by a fulfillment formula. So prominent are these that they constitute the backbone of one of the structures discussed in § 2. (See p. 51 for an arrangement of the narrative into five scenes, each containing a citation.) A study of the technique of formula citations throughout Matthew's Gospel will enable us to determine whether their presence in the infancy narrative should be attributed to the evangelist himself, rather than to a pre-Matthean stage. After this first step, a study of the relation of the citations to their immediate context may tell us whether the rest of the narrative had the same origin as the citations. Thus, the citations can become the key to the composition of 1:18 – 2:23.

A. *Matthew's Formula Citations of Scripture*

In 1:22–23 Matthew cites the OT directly; and he introduces this citation with the words: "All this took place to fulfill what the Lord had spoken by the prophet who said." This is the first instance in the Gospel of formula citations or fulfillment citations,[1] i.e., citations of the Scriptures (usually of

1 The German term *Reflexionszitate*, which appears as early as the 1889 edition of H. J. Holtzmann's commentary on the Synoptics, emphasizes that the citations have been added

the prophets) introduced by a *formula* which indicates that the NT event took place in order to *fulfill* the OT passage which is being cited. In Matthew there are some ten to fourteen of these, eight of them citations of Isaiah. A glance at Table V shows that, when this phenomenon is made the subject of a comparison between Matthew and the other Synoptic Gospels, formula citations are almost a Matthean peculiarity.[2] That Jesus is to be related to the Scriptures is a commonplace in early Christianity, but Matthew has uniquely standardized the fulfillment of the prophetic word. In finding this fulfillment, Matthew makes no attempt to interpret what we might consider the full or contextual meaning of the OT text that he cites; rather he concentrates on features of the text wherein there is a resemblance to Jesus or the NT event. His method of quoting the prophet directly rather than weaving an allusion into the wording of the Matthean narrative is an indication of a Christian effort to supply the story of Jesus with OT background and support. Let us discuss the purpose of such citations, their relation to the story they illustrate, and their source.

1. Purpose of the Citations

Scholars have interpreted Matthew's "in order to fulfill" as a pointer toward an apologetic motif in the citations. Taken from the prophets sacred to the Jews, were the citations perhaps meant to prove to the Synagogue that God had foretold the career of Jesus?[3] Yet, if the primary purpose of the formula citations was to mount an apologetic against the Synagogue, one would have expected more of these citations in reference to the passion and crucifixion of Jesus, the "stumbling-block to the Jews."[4] A more

---

to the common Gospel material as a personal *reflection*. The more recent term *Erfüllungszitate*, "fulfillment citations," employed by W. Rothfuchs, is descriptive rather than analytical.

[2] The only uncontested formula citation in the other Synoptics is Luke 22:37, which speaks of accomplishment rather than fulfillment. John, with nine fulfillment formulas, can be compared to Matthew in frequency; but Matthew's usage is more standardized than John's. Five times John refers in a vague manner to a fulfillment of "the Scripture," and only once to a fulfillment of "the prophet" (12:38, citing Isa 53:1). In fact, in two instances (John 18:9,32) the fulfillment citation refers to previous words of Jesus rather than to the OT. When John's citations are from the OT, they are not always easily identifiable, e.g., John 15:25, which speaks of fulfilling the Law, draws not on the Law but on Pss 35:19 and 69:5(4); John 19:36 cites one or all of the following: Exod 12:10 (LXX Vaticanus); 12:46; Num 9:12; Ps 34:21(20). For further discussion, see E. D. Freed, *Old Testament Quotations in the Gospel of John* (NovTestS 6; Leiden: Brill, 1965); and J. O'Rourke, "John's Fulfillment Texts," ScEccl 19 (1967), 433–43.

[3] See Lindars, *Apologetic*. Moule, "Fulfilment-Words," distinguishes three sets of possible correlatives in the idea of fulfillment: prediction/verification, beginning/completion, and covenant obligation/consummation. On pp. 297–98, he indicates that most of the Matthean formula citations belong to the first set of correlatives, for they show the truthfulness of God in carrying through His predetermined plan. Matthew's usage, however, has an element of the second and third correlatives as well.

[4] I Cor 1:23. In Table V only the last two Matthean citations are from the passion narrative, and one of them is dubiously classified as a formula citation. The many references to the OT in the passion narrative are by way of allusion woven into the story, rather than by direct citation.

TABLE V: FORMULA OR FULFILLMENT CITATIONS
IN THE SYNOPTIC GOSPELS

Matt 1:22–23 citing Isa 7:14.
       *2:5b–6 citing Micah 5:1 and II Sam 5:2.ᵃ
        2:15b citing Hosea 11:1.
        2:17–18 citing Jer 31:15 (LXX Vaticanus 38:15).
        2:23b citing perhaps Isa 4:3 and Judg 16:17.
       *3:3 citing Isa 40:3.ᵇ
        4:14–16 citing Isa 8:23 – 9:1 (=RSV 9:1–2).
        8:17 citing Isa 53:4.
        12:17–21 citing Isa 42:1–4.
       *13:14–15 citing Isa 6:9–10.ᶜ
        13:35 citing Ps 78(77):2, even though the formula speaks of "the prophet [Isaiah]."
        21:4–5 citing Isa 62:11 and Zech 9:9.
       *26:56—a formula (cf. Mark 14:49) without any citation.
        27:9–10 citing Zech 11:12–13, perhaps combined with echoes of Jeremiah (32:6–15;
        18:2–3) to whom the formula attributes the citation.

Mark*15:28 citing Isa 53:12.ᵈ
        It is dubious that we should list Mark 1:2–3 (=Matt 3:3) or Mark 14:49 (partially
        parallel to Matt 26:56) as formula citations.

Luke*18:31—a formula without any citation.ᵉ
        22:37 citing Isa 53:12.ᵉ
       *24:44—a formula without any citation.ᶠ
        It is dubious that we should list Luke 3:4–6 (=Matt 3:3) or the general references
        to fulfillment in 4:21 and 21:22.

* Imperfections in the formula create uncertainty as to whether this passage should be classified as
  a formula citation.
a. This citation is not a comment of the evangelist but appears as part of the words of Herod's
   advisors. The unusual introduction does not specifically mention fulfillment ("for thus it is written
   by the prophet").
b. A brief formula, for which there is a parallel in the other Gospels (Mark 1:2–3; Luke 3:4–6),
   does not specifically mention fulfillment (". . . spoken of by the prophet Isaiah when he said").
c. There is no explicit expression of purpose in the formula ("With them indeed is fulfilled the
   prophecy of Isaiah which says"). The text, cited from the LXX, appears also in John 12:40 (not
   from the LXX).
d. This is a textually dubious verse, omitted by Nestle and Aland. It may be borrowed from Luke
   22:37, although it employs *pleroun* ("to fulfill"—influence of Matthew on a scribe?) rather than
   the Lucan *telein* ("to accomplish").
e. Luke speaks of accomplishing (*telein*) rather than of fulfilling (*pleroun*).
f. A general statement: "Everything about me in the law of Moses, the prophets, and the psalms
   must be fulfilled."

plausible explanation is that the formula citations had a didactic purpose, informing the Christian readers and giving support to their faith. Some of the citations are attached to the minutiae of Jesus' career, as if to emphasize that the whole of Jesus' life, down to the least detail, lay within God's foreordained plan.

The uneven frequency of the formula citations is noteworthy. Five out of fourteen (or four out of ten, depending on the count) are found in the infancy narrative, which constitutes two chapters out of the Gospel's twenty-eight.[5] This concentration of formula citations may mean that the evangelist regarded the infancy as a section of Jesus' life still relatively unexplored in reference to the OT. In this it might be contrasted to the passion which had been studied against an OT backdrop from the beginning of Christian preaching. The readers of the passion story would not have been in such need of Matthew's *nota bene* technique of formula citations.

Thus, it seems likely that in his usage of formula citations Matthew is continuing the invocation of Scripture begun in early Christian preaching, but is doing so at a time when the preaching has become less missionary and more didactic, since the preachers are often now addressing settled Christian communities.[6] Even in this situation, however, there were Christians of Jewish descent in Matthew's community who may have found such citations useful when they were called on to defend their adherence to Jesus in the course of discussions with their Jewish neighbors who remained in the Synagogue. But primarily the scriptural insights were directed to believers.

2. Relation of the Citations to Their Context

If the presence of the formula citations is generally attributed to the evangelist, it becomes crucial to determine how they are related to the narrative they illustrate. (To discuss all the Matthean citations in detail would lead us too far afield; and so let us concentrate on the citations in the infancy narrative, using the citations in the rest of the Gospel only as a guide.) In this matter there have been two general lines of scholarly opinion, namely, that the citations gave rise to the infancy narrative, or that they are appended to a narrative that already existed. With the many variant forms of the first thesis, that the citations gave rise to the narrative, may be associated the names of Kilpatrick, Soltau, and Vaganay. To illustrate the variants, it could be proposed that the evangelist really created the narrative by reflecting imaginatively on the citations; or, more subtly, one might suggest that the citations were the focal points for gathering very fragmented early traditions into a consecutive story. In either case, the narrative becomes almost entirely Matthean in origin. With the many variant forms of the second thesis, that the citations were added to an earlier narrative, may be associated the names of Bultmann, Dibelius, Hirsch, and Strecker. To illustrate the variants, it could be proposed that a virtually complete pre-Matthean narrative existed as a written document,

---

[5] Van Segbroeck, "Les citations," calls attention to the concentration of five formula citations in chs. 4–13, but it is difficult to see a significance in this.

[6] Thus Gärtner, "Habakkuk," and Rothfuchs, *Erfüllungszitate.* This thesis does not necessarily exclude Kilpatrick's contention that liturgy influenced the selection of citations, for preaching to the community sometimes took place in the context of eucharistic celebrations (Acts 20:7–12).

so that all that Matthew did by way of editing was to add the citations. Or one might speak of substantially formed pre-Matthean stories and traditions woven by Matthew himself into a consecutive story with the citations appended as a final touch. Let us begin by trying to determine which is the more plausible of the two general theses, and later we can study the variations of that thesis in light of the evidence.

Several factors favor the thesis that in chs. 1–2 Matthew added the citations to an already existing narrative. *First,* in a section like 2:13–23 it is extremely difficult to imagine how the narrative could ever have been made up by reflection on the three formula citations contained therein, since the citations deal with aspects that are only minor in the story line. The same may be said of the citation of Micah 5:1(2) in Matt 2:5b–6. Reflection on that citation might have caused a Christian to compose a story locating Jesus' birth at Bethlehem, but it could scarcely have led him to the narrative about the magi. Reflection on the LXX of Isa 7:14 (cited in Matt 1:22–23) might have caused a Christian to compose a story about Jesus' mother being a virgin, but it could scarcely have led him to compose a narrative wherein Joseph was the main figure.

Second, four of the five formula citations in the infancy narrative have a definite air of being appended. The reader should make the experiment of reading the stories in 1:18–25 and 2:13–23 omitting four of the formula citations (1:22–23; 2:15b; 2:17–18; 2:23b). The story line not only makes perfect sense without them but even flows more smoothly. The only citation that is woven into the plot is the one that is dubiously a formula citation (2:5b–6). This observation weakens even the more subtle form of the thesis that Matthew composed his narrative on the basis of the citations, for they are too tangentially related to the plot to have served as a nucleus in gathering fragmented traditions into a consecutive story.

Third, we have other instances of Matthew's appending formula citations to stories that already came to him. For instance, Mark 1:14 and Luke 4:14 agree that after his baptism Jesus went to Galilee, but only Matt 4:12–16 comments on this with a formula citation from Isa 8:23 – 9:1 (=RSV 9:1–2) which speaks of the land of Zebulun and Naphtali, toward the sea, Galilee of the Gentiles. Matthew prepared for the introduction of the citation by reporting not only that Jesus went to Galilee, but also that he went to Capernaum by the sea in the territory of Zebulun and Naphtali. The citation could not have caused Matthew to create the story of Jesus' going to Galilee—he had that in Mark—but it did cause him to color and adapt the Marcan narrative, so that the correspondence to the prophecy might be more obvious.[7] We have a good anal-

---

[7] Similarly the formula citation of Zech 11:12–13, introduced by Matt 27:9–10 in reference to Judas' violent death, did not cause the evangelist to invent the story that money received by Judas was used to buy the Field of Blood—that basic story is attested inde-

ogy then for arguing that the same process occurred in the infancy narratives where we do not have a control coming from comparative Synoptic material.[8]

3. Origin of the Formula Citations

If we judge as more probable the thesis that Matthew added formula citations to a pre-existing narrative or body of infancy traditions (a narrative and traditions that we have yet to discuss), we must still ask the question of how Matthew obtained or arrived at the particular citations he introduced. Were they the product of his own reflection and study, or were they already known in the Christian tradition?[9] Some have even proposed that Matthew drew upon a collection of texts developed in early Christian preaching.[10] Three avenues of argumentation have been followed by scholars in their attempts to answer this question. The first concerns the possibility of a broader use of the citations; the second concerns the wording of the citation in relation to the Hebrew and Greek OT; the third concerns the relation of the citation to Matthean theology.

a) *The possibility of a broader use of the citations.* There are instances where the study of the common Synoptic tradition suggests a pre-Matthean use of a prophecy, so that Matthew has simply made earlier Christian usage more explicit. For instance, Mark 4:12 describes the reaction to Jesus' parables in the language of Isa 6:9–10, but Matt 13:14–15 introduces the explicit citation of the Isaian passage to accompany the description that came from Mark. Among the Synoptic Gospels, only Matt 21:4–5 supplies a formula citation from Zech 9:9 in the description of Jesus' entry into Jerusalem; yet the same scriptural association is made in John 12:15–16. In other instances, then, where we have no comparative control, we may suspect that, at least sometimes, Matthew is bearing testi-

---

pendently by Acts 1:18–19. But the Zechariah passage did influence the Matthean narrative in the mention of the thirty pieces of silver (Matt 27:3 and 26:15, contrasted with Mark 14:11).

8 We have a partial control in relation to the formula citation: "He will be called a Nazorean" (Matt 2:23). That citation did not cause Matthew to invent the information that Jesus' family dwelt "in a city called Nazareth." Such geographical information was part of the common Gospel tradition.

9 Such tradition may have been written (Bacon, Lohmeyer, Strecker) or oral. See also footnote 6 above.

10 The existence of an early collection of scriptural "testimonies" was posited by J. Rendel Harris (*ca.* 1915) who thought that debate with the Jewish authorities may have caused Christian preachers to develop an arsenal of texts. (*Testimonia* did exist in later times, e.g., in the works of Cyprian, Tertullian, and Gregory of Nyssa.) After a period of popularity, Harris' theory fell into disfavor until the discovery of a form of testimony literature among the Dead Sea Scrolls. But the frequency of this literature at Qumran is not clear. For instance, J. Allegro's detection of testimonies in *4Q Florilegium* and *4Q Testimonia* is probably wrong. See JBC, article 68, ##79–80.

mony to passages well known to Christians. The only way this insight can be applied to the formula citations used in the infancy narrative, a narrative that is peculiar to Matthew, is to ask whether conceivably the citations could have been useful to Christians independently of their present context. But, in fact, one would be hard put to think of a general or a different usage that Christians might have made of Hosea 11:1, "Out of Egypt have I called my son" (Matt 2:15b), or of Jer 31:15, "A voice was heard in Ramah, weeping and loud mourning, Rachel crying for her children" (Matt 2:17–18).[11] A complicated composite reference to Micah and II Samuel (Matt 2:5b–6) is more easily attributed to the evangelist than to a hypothetical pre-Matthean collection of OT passages. Thus, while it is difficult from this avenue of argumentation to give an absolute answer to the problem of whether Matthew borrowed the formula citations in the infancy narrative from a wider Christian usage, there is little conceivable wider usage of most of the infancy narrative citations.[12]

b) *The wording of the citation in relation to the Hebrew and Greek OT.* Many have found a more fruitful approach in a detailed study of the wording of the Matthean citations. For instance, Stendahl, *School,* maintains that when the common Synoptic tradition uses Scripture, *exclusive of the formula citations,* the usage conforms to the LXX wording. Matthew, following Mark, attests this LXX usage; yet in his formula citations the wording often does not correspond to the LXX but is closer to the Hebrew text or to other known variants of an OT passage. This leads Stendahl to maintain that formula citations are original with Matthew and are the product of a school of writers who studied the OT carefully,[13] finding among various texts and versions a wording that would best enable the passage to be related to a NT event.

Recently, however, Stendahl's approach and analysis have been challenged by Gundry[14] who maintains that only when Matthew is copying ci-

---

11 Lindars, *Apologetic,* 17–24, 216, has contested the force of this argument. A citation may have been used in an earlier stage of Christian apologetics to make a point totally different from that now made by Matthew. Yet one needs considerable imagination to create other-than-Matthean applications for all five formula citations in the infancy narrative.

12 In § 5, B3, I shall discuss the possibility of a wider use of Isa 7:14 (LXX).

13 While such research was carried on in the later rabbinical schools, a closer analogy in time and style would be the scriptural studies of the Qumran community; for among the Dead Sea Scrolls are *pesharim* (plural of *pesher*) or commentaries on OT books, applying their words to the situation of the Qumran sect. However, there is a significant difference between Matthew's technique of telling a story about Jesus and accompanying it with OT citations which find fulfillment therein, and the *pesher* technique of Qumran where the method is a line by line analysis of the OT. See Davies, *Setting,* 208–9, in critique of Stendahl; also Gärtner, "Habakkuk." It is worth noting that the almost stereotyped formula that Matthew uses to introduce his fulfillment citations has no real parallel at Qumran (Fitzmyer, "Use," 303), nor in the Mishnah (Metzger, "Formulas," 307).

14 Gundry, *Use,* 172–74, offers a "targumic" explanation for the Matthean citation of Scripture. (The targums were translations, often remarkably free and interpretative, of the Hebrew Scriptures into Aramaic.) He maintains that there were various forms of the He-

tations found at least implicitly in Mark is there a very close adherence to the LXX wording (an adherence that is therefore Marcan, not Matthean). In non-Marcan usage of Scripture, whether formula citations or not, Matthew is freer with regard to the LXX wording.[15] Thus, the contention that in formula citations alone a Matthean school gives us the benefits of their research is weakened, for eclecticism in wording is found in Scripture passages that Matthew shares with pre-Matthean (but non-Marcan) tradition. Even if one does not fully agree with Gundry, it is a fact that Stendahl's suggestion of a school has not won the field and, indeed, has been modified by Stendahl himself.[16]

Stendahl's great contribution (and in this he has been followed) was to remind us that there were available in the first century a multiplicity of textual traditions of Scripture—not just a standardized Hebrew (MT) and Greek (LXX) tradition, but variant Hebrew wordings, Aramaic targums, and a number of Greek translations, including some that conformed more closely to the MT than does the LXX. When we add to these the possibility of a free rendering by the evangelist himself, the avenue of deciding what citation is Matthean and what is pre-Matthean on the basis of wording becomes uncertain.[17] If one maintains that sometimes Matthew introduces as a formula citation a passage that was already known in Christian usage, one would expect that he would reproduce the familiar wording, a wording that may or may not reflect the LXX, depending on when and where the citation entered into circulation. On the other hand, when Matthew himself was the first to see the possibilities of an OT fulfillment, he would presumably choose or even adapt a wording that would best fit his purposes.

c) *The relation of the citation to Matthean theology.* The implicit argumentation is that, if the point made by a formula citation fits closely Matthew's overall theological interests, this favors the thesis that Matthew

---

brew text in circulation (a fact that can be verified from Qumran), and that Christian preachers orally and freely translated the Hebrew text of their choice into Aramaic and Greek as part of their mission to their fellow Jews. Sometimes these translations were original; sometimes they reflect in whole or in part existing Aramaic and Greek translations. The Matthean evangelist served as his own targumist or translator. See also Rothfuchs, *Erfüllungszitate,* 105–7.

15 Gundry makes part of his case depend on allusions to Scripture as distinct from direct citations. But when an allusion differs from the LXX wording, can we be sure that behind it there is a variant textual tradition of the OT, or is it simply an inexact recollection?

16 The original Stendahl position has not been accepted by the works of McConnell, Rothfuchs, and Van Segbroeck (besides Gundry). For Stendahl's later reflections, see the Preface to the second edition of *School.*

17 I speak here about the citation itself, not about the formula that introduces the citation. Strecker, *Weg,* 50, points out that the almost stereotyped introductory formula is composed of words characteristic of Matthew's Gospel. (For a discussion of minor differences in the formulas, see Pesch, "Gottessohn," 397–400.) Thus, there is little doubt that, no matter where the citation came from, the introductory formula was composed by the evangelist.

himself found the citation he has used, while if the point made does not fit
Matthean theology particularly well, this favors the thesis that Matthew is
using citations already in Christian usage. G. Strecker, *Weg,* contends that
the citations illustrate details of the career of Jesus but are of very secondary importance for the theology of the Gospel. The books of McConnell
and Rothfuchs, written almost as a dialogue with Strecker, have exactly the
opposite contention. The citations are seen as closely related to Matthew's
thought and so are looked on as the work of the evangelist himself. It is
difficult to be certain, for often a scholar diagnoses the theological point of
the citation precisely against the background of what are recognized as
Matthean interests; and so in judging conformity to Matthean theology,
there is danger of circular reasoning. As we shall see, the formula citations
in the infancy narrative can be interpreted to relate Jesus to the main
themes in Israelite history: the Davidic Messiah, the Exodus, the Babylonian Exile, etc. While that makes the overall thought of the infancy narrative fit in with the Gospel, can we be sure that Matthew saw in the citations what we see in them?

All that we can come to is a convergence of probabilities giving us the
following results.[18] It is Matthew himself who added the formula citations
to the Gospel tradition. In many instances, he was the one who first recognized the applicability of a particular text to a particular incident in Jesus'
career. In such cases he seems to have chosen the OT text tradition that
best illustrated this applicability or even to have made his own translation
into Greek to heighten the applicability. In fewer instances, the applicability of a text was detected in a pre-Matthean stage of tradition, and
Matthew was satisfied to reproduce the citation as it was already known.
For Matthew, these citations did more than highlight incidental agreements between the OT and Jesus. He introduced them because they fit his
general theology of the oneness of God's plan (a oneness already
implicitly recognized by the appeal to the OT in early Christian preaching)
and, especially, because they served some of his own particular theological
and pastoral interests in dealing with a mixed Christian community of
Jews and Gentiles.

B. *The Detection of Pre-Matthean Material*

An application of these probabilities to the infancy narrative leads to the
judgment that the four or five formula citations therein, whether or not

18 See Van Segbroeck, "Les citations," 129–30. They will be defended in detail in my
commentary.

previously used by Christians, owe their presence in the birth stories to Matthew's own hand. We must now study more carefully the implications of that judgment for the pre-Matthean history of the infancy narrative. We can exclude from the start the thesis that there was a completely formed and preserved non-Matthean narrative to which Matthew's sole contribution was the formula citations. There is too much that is Matthean in 1:18 – 2:23, even when the formula citations are left aside. For instance, there is a relatively high percentage of Matthean vocabulary in this narrative.[19] Some of the narrative is so phrased as to continue the emphasis of the genealogy, which in its present form, as we saw, is a Matthean construction.[20] Indeed, the narrative has a pattern of five alternating episodes which is attested elsewhere in Matthew.[21] Therefore, while Matthew may have added the citations to a narrative in which they originally had no part, he must have also had a considerable role in fashioning the narrative into its present form.

1. The Method Employed in the Detection

Scholars have used three basic guides in determining what is Matthean and what is pre-Matthean. No one of them is foolproof; but when taken together, they put the detection on a reasonable basis. The *first* guide is the amount of Matthean vocabulary, style, and organizational pattern in verses or sections of the infancy narrative. (The criterion for "Matthean" is derived from comparing Matthew with Mark and Luke in the main body of the Gospel.) If a passage in the infancy narrative is almost purely Matthean in vocabulary and style, it is more likely that Matthew has com-

---

19 Pesch, "Ausführungsformel," 81–88, and Nellessen, *Kind*, 50–56, discuss the Matthean features in 1:18–25 and 2:1–23, respectively. Of some ninety-five words or phrases that can be considered characteristic of Matthew (see R. Morgenthaler, *Statistik des neutestamentlichen Wortschatzes* [Zurich: Gotthelf, 1958]), about twenty-five can be found in the infancy narrative. However, one should be cautious about such statistics; some of these words occur in the introductory formulas for the citations, and so tell us little about the narrative. Lohmeyer, *Matthäus*, 9, comments that the language of 1:18 – 2:23 is rather uniform, sometimes with parallels elsewhere in Matthew, sometimes not. Knox, *Sources*, II, 125, claims "that Matthew is not responsible for more than his normal amount of editorial revision in the infancy narrative"—normalcy being judged by Matthew's revision of Mark in the main Gospel narrative.
20 For instance, 1:18 echoes 1:1 (birth of Jesus Christ) and 1:16.
21 The alternating episodes involving Joseph and Herod in 1:18 – 2:23 may be compared with the five alternating episodes at the end of the Gospel (27:57 – 28:20) involving the body of Jesus and the guards set to watch the tomb. (See J. C. Fenton, "Inclusio and Chiasmus in Matthew," StEv, I [TU 73; Berlin: Akademie, 1959], 174–79.)

Joseph	(1:18–25)	Jesus	(27:57–61)
Herod	(2:1–12)	Guards	(27:62–66)
Joseph	(2:13–15)	Jesus	(28:1–10)
Herod	(2:16–18)	Guards	(28:11–15)
Joseph	(2:19–23)	Jesus	(28:16–20)

posed the passage himself. If Matthean peculiarities are mixed with neutral or non-Matthean features, the possibility increases that Matthew has edited a pre-Matthean tradition or narrative. The *second* guide is the presence of internal tensions or conflicts (aporias) within a passage, indicating that two bodies of material may have been joined. At times, this guide can be combined with the first guide, so that in the case of conflicting material, one section may be seen to be more Matthean than the other. The *third* guide is the presence of parallels to other material. In § 1, B2 above, I listed eleven points that the Matthean and Lucan infancy narrative have in common, eight of them found in Matt 1:18–25. Some of them are strong indicators of pre-Matthean material or traditions upon which both Matthew and Luke drew. Also we shall see that some of the story lines in the Matthean infancy narrative have close parallels in the OT and in Jewish legend, and these parallels may offer a guide to what is likely to have been in a pre-Matthean narrative, especially when they agree with results gained through the first and second guides offered above.

Let me illustrate the way these three guides have been employed in the study of a short section of the infancy narrative, 2:19–23.[22] Verse 23b is a formula citation, having the quality of an appendix to the story of Joseph's leaving Egypt. But how much of vss. 19–23a is Matthean and how much is pre-Matthean? If we apply the second guide mentioned above, there is an internal tension. There are two different geographical thrusts in the passage, namely, that Joseph should take child and the mother "to the land of Israel" and that he should go "to the district of Galilee," with Nazareth as a specification of the latter. Each geographical goal is the product of a divine command in a dream. If this story were a unity, why would there be two different dreams? Why did not the angel tell Joseph in the first dream to "go to the land of Galilee"?

Yet, we must be aware that what seems illogical to the modern reader may not have seemed illogical to the ancient writer. The questions we have raised are not probative in themselves without an appeal to the first guide, namely, the presence of Matthean style. The "district of Galilee, city called Nazareth" direction is harmonious with Matthew's formula citation; the land of Israel direction is not related to the formula citation. Thus, the strong possibility begins to emerge that onto a tradition about Joseph being sent from Egypt to Israel, Matthew has tacked a specification about Galilee and Nazareth to prepare for the formula citation. This possibility is virtually confirmed when we compare the Galilee-Nazareth verses

---

[22] An invaluable help here is Davis, "Tradition," 406–9. Careful attention to methodology is apparent also in the treatments of Vögtle and Nellessen. The fact that the results and reconstructions differ in minor points is a caution about the limits of our methods.

(2:22–23) to 4:12–16, a passage written in Matthean style, as we can determine from a comparison with Mark 1:14 and Luke 4:14:

2:22–23	4:12–16
But when he heard that Archelaus was king over Judea . . .	But when he heard that John had been arrested . . .
he went off to the district of Galilee. There he went to dwell in a city called Nazareth	he went off to Galilee. There, leaving Nazareth, he went to dwell in Capernaum
so that what was spoken by the the prophets might be fulfilled [formula citation].	in order that what was spoken by Isaiah the prophet might be fulfilled [formula citation].

The pattern, the grammar, and the vocabulary of the two passages are clearly the same, and since the second is Matthean, so is the first. By contrast, we may infer that Matthew is not the creator of 2:19–21, "the land of Israel" section,[23] which stands in tension with the Galilee-Nazareth geographical direction.

This emerging conclusion is reinforced when we bring into play the third guiding principle, namely, parallels. Matthew did not invent the idea that Jesus grew up in Nazareth; that is a commonplace of the Gospel tradition. Having an infancy narrative that is set in Bethlehem, Matthew is forced to explain how the family got to Nazareth. Luke is faced with the same problem;[24] but the very different Lucan account of how the family went to Nazareth (2:39) suggests that there was no common pre-Gospel story explaining the geographical move. Rather each evangelist has chosen his own way of working a move from Bethlehem to Nazareth into the infancy narrative.

Parallels are also informative about the origin of 2:19–21 and the return from Egypt. The setting ("when Herod died") and the divine directive to Joseph in Egypt ("take the child and his mother and go back to the land of Israel, for those who were seeking the child's life are dead") are literally evocative of the divine directive to Moses in Midian when the hostile Pharaoh had died: "Go to Egypt, for all those who were seeking your life are dead" (Exod 4:19). A quasi-quotation from the early chapters of Exodus, which deal with the infancy and youth of Moses, is important; for, as we shall see, a basic narrative interwoven into Matt 1:18 – 2:23 draws parallels between the infancy of Jesus and the infancy of

---

[23] There are some Matthean features in 2:19–21 as well (see footnote 30 below), but not so many. Thus, while we may posit a pre-Matthean origin of the material in these verses, Matthew has certainly edited it.

[24] Luke's problem is less acute, for he portrays Joseph and Mary as residents of Nazareth who have gone only temporarily to Bethlehem for the census. But Matthew implicitly portrays them as having their home in Bethlehem (2:11), and so must account for a change of domicile after the Egyptian interlude.

TABLE VI: THE PATTERN OF ANGELIC DREAM APPEARANCES
(comparing three Matthean scenes: [A] 1:20–21, 24–25; [B] 2:13–15a; [C] 2:19–21)

An introductory resumptive clause[a] connecting the appearance with what precedes:
A) 1:20   As he was considering this, behold . . .
B) 2:13   When they had gone away, behold . . .
C) 2:19   When Herod died, behold . . .

1) An angel of the Lord *appeared*[b] to Joseph in a dream (1:20; 2:13; 2:19).

2) The angel gave a *command*, saying[c]:
A) 1:20   Joseph, son of David, do not be afraid to take Mary your wife into
               your home . . .
   1:21   She will give birth to a son; and you will call his name Jesus . . .
B) 2:13   Get up; take the child and his mother and escape to Egypt. Stay there
               until I tell you . . .
C) 2:20   Get up; take the child and his mother and go back to the land of
               Israel . . .

3) The angel offered a *reason*[d] for the command:
A) 1:20   for the child begotten in her is through the Holy Spirit.
   1:21   for he will save his people from their sins.
B) 2:13   for Herod is going to search for the child to destroy him.
C) 2:20   for those who were seeking the child's life are dead.

4) Joseph got up[e] and *fulfilled* the command:
A) 1:24–25   So Joseph got up from sleep and did as the angel of the Lord had com-
               manded him. He took his wife home, but he had no sexual relations
               with her before she gave birth to a son. And he called his name Jesus.
B) 2:14–15a   So Joseph got up, took the child and his mother by night, and went
               away to Egypt, where he stayed until the death of Herod.
C) 2:21   So Joseph got up, took the child and his mother, and went back to
               the land of Israel.

a. Consisting of a genitive absolute with a postpositive *de*, and followed by *idou*.
b. Aorist tense in 1:20; historical present in 2:13 and 2:19. The latter is not a usual tense for
   Matthew.
c. Consistently the participle *legōn*.
d. Consistently a postpositive *gar* introduces the reason.
e. Consistently *egertheis* with a postpositive *de*. The verb "took" is consistently *paralambanein*.

Moses. Beyond the OT parallel to Matt 2:19–21, the structural parallels to
other sections within the Matthean infancy narrative itself are most important. The structure in 2:19–21 involves the appearance of an angel of the
Lord in a dream, his command to Joseph, a reason offered for the command, and the carrying out of the command by Joseph. This is a stereotyped pattern found also in 1:20,21,24,25 and in 2:13–15a (see Table
VI). If 2:19–21 is pre-Matthean, so probably are these two passages which
constitute the skeleton of the material resembling the infancy of Moses.
Thus, the probabilities converge to suggest a pre-Matthean narrative patterned on the infancy of Moses and built around angelic dream appearances to Joseph.

TABLE VII: A RECONSTRUCTION OF THE MAIN
PRE-MATTHEAN NARRATIVE

A) Now, when Mary had been betrothed to Joseph, behold an angel of the Lord appeared to him in a dream, saying, "Take Mary your wife into your home, for she will give birth to a son who will save his people from their sins." So Joseph got up from sleep and took his wife home, and she gave birth to a son.

Now Jesus was born in the days of Herod the king. When Herod the king heard this [in a dream], he was startled, and so was all Jerusalem with him. Assembling all the chief priests and scribes of the people, he inquired of them where the Messiah was to be born. "In Bethlehem of Judea," they told him. Then he sent (secretly) to Bethlehem with the instruction: "Go and search diligently for the child."

B) Now, when [Herod had done this], behold an angel of the Lord appeared to Joseph in a dream, saying, "Get up; take the child and his mother and escape to Egypt. Stay there until I tell you, for Herod is going to search for the child to destroy him." So Joseph got up, took the child and his mother by night, and went away to Egypt, where he stayed until the death of Herod.

Then Herod [when the search for the child was unsuccessful] fell into a furious rage. He sent into Bethlehem and the regions all around it and massacred all the boys of two years of age and under [according to the time he had ascertained from the dream].

C) Now, when Herod died, behold an angel of the Lord appeared in a dream to Joseph in Egypt, saying, "Get up; take the child and his mother and go back to the land of Israel, for those who were seeking the child's life are dead." So Joseph got up, took the child and his mother, and went back to the land of Israel. . . .

---

2. Summary of the Results

I have now illustrated the methodology used by scholars in detecting pre-Matthean material in 1:18 – 2:23. This study of one passage (2:19–23) needs to be complemented by studies of other passages, a study to be done in this book as we move consecutively through the Matthean scenes. However, for the reader it is important from the start to understand the logic of the procedure and to be assured that the results reflect something more than guesswork. It may also be useful to summarize in advance the total picture of the pre-Matthean material that emerges from this process of methodical detection. I do not pretend that all scholars, working with the same tools, will agree with my results, although every factor that I have isolated will be recognized by them in their own way.[25] May I emphasize that what follows is only a *summary* so that the

---

[25] Besides the studies mentioned in footnote 22, see Bultmann, *History*, 291–94; Pesch, "Ausführungsformel," 79–91; Lohmeyer, *Matthäus*, 12; Schmidt, *Rahmen*, 309–10; Knox, *Sources*, II, 121–28; Soares Prabhu, *Formula*, 294–300.

reader will know beforehand the direction in which the discussion in subsequent chapters is going.

a) *The Pre-Matthean Material.* We may distinguish several bodies of infancy narrative material that predated Matthew's present narrative. It is convenient to discuss this material under two headings: first, the main pre-Matthean narrative, which is the most substantial; second, a grouping of other, more episodic narratives. Treating these narratives separately is for the sake of clarity; it does not prejudice the possibility that they may have already been joined in the pre-Matthean stage.[26]

THE MAIN PRE-MATTHEAN NARRATIVE. Scholars[27] have drawn attention to the very stylized pattern of angelic dream appearances to Joseph found in three places in the Matthean infancy narrative: (A) 1:20–21, 24–25; (B) 2:13–15a; (C) 2:19–21. A schematic analysis of the pattern is presented in Table VI. On the facing page, in Table VII, is a reconstructed pre-Matthean narrative built around these dream appearances. The reader should be alerted about several points in studying the two Tables. While, as we have seen, there is good evidence that the substance of the angelic dream appearance in 2:19–21 is pre-Matthean,[28] it is chiefly by analogy that scholars have judged that all three angelic dream appearances are pre-Matthean. One could dispute this and argue, for instance, that while the angelic dream appearances in ch. 2 (thus B and C) are pre-Matthean, Matthew himself took over the pattern and constructed on his own the angelic dream appearance in ch. 1 (A), which has peculiar features.[29] I myself will argue that the substance of 1:20–21,24–25 belongs

---

[26] "Pre-Matthean" need mean no more than predating Matthew's present narrative. I know of no way of deciding whether there were two stages of Matthean composition in the infancy narrative, e.g., the composition of a basic narrative by Matthew, and then his later glossing of it by the addition of the formula citations. Nevertheless, the general supposition is that "pre-Matthean" antedates the evangelist's work.

[27] In particular, Knox, *Sources,* II, 122. For other ways of schematizing the pattern, see Paul, *L'Evangile,* 143–47; and Malina, "Matthew," 291. The latter finds a chiastic pattern by bringing into consideration the additional dreams of 2:12 and 2:22–23a. These dreams, however, which do not involve an angel, differ in format from the three angel dream appearances of Table VI. They are probably secondary Matthean additions to the basic narrative.

[28] The "angel of the Lord" and the dream are two different vehicles of revelation in the OT. B. T. D. Smith, *Gospel,* 77, argues that it was Matthew who caused the duplication by introducing the dreams into the infancy narrative where originally only the angel of the Lord was involved. He points to 27:19, a Matthean scene that involves the dream of Pilate's wife. However, the pre-Matthean narrative is closely patterned on the model of Joseph the patriarch in Egypt, and Joseph was the dreamer of dreams (Gen 37, esp. 37:19). If it seems likely that dreams belonged to the pre-Matthean narrative, Matthew has used his own phrase (*kat' onar;* see NOTE on 1:20) to describe the dream.

[29] Vögtle, *Messias,* 85: "The evangelist has in a certain sense enlarged the pre-Matthean infancy narrative basic to ch. 2 by adding to it ch. 1, a demonstrative piece essentially composed by him, showing that the prehistory which began with Abraham leads to the birth of Jesus, the promised Messiah, who is son of David, son of Abraham, and the Son of God." Yet Vögtle believes that there was pre-Matthean theological material behind ch. 1, the adaptation of which was encouraged by the presence of similar elements in the pre-Matthean story behind ch. 2.

to the main pre-Matthean narrative, and that the peculiar features result from the addition of a secondary episode. But no certainty can be claimed.

Another caution concerns a distinction between pre-Matthean content and pre-Matthean wording. The narrative given in Table VII is often in clearly Matthean wording,[30] *Any pre-Matthean material has been edited so thoroughly that often we cannot get behind the Matthean wording,* a fact that is evidenced by the disagreements among the scholars who have attempted to so do (footnote 25). *The most that I claim is that the reconstruction shows partially and approximately the content of the narrative that Matthew drew upon.* The joining of the pre-Matthean narrative with other pre-Matthean material to be mentioned below makes exact reconstruction impossible.

A final caution concerns the relation of the dream appearances to the rest of the basic narrative. These appearances (Table VI) were only the framework or skeleton of the narrative; they tell us that Joseph was commanded by an angel in a dream to take Mary his wife to his home, to escape with her and the child into Egypt, and to return to the land of Israel. Obviously, in Matthew's infancy narrative as it now stands there is much more narrative material concerning Mary's pregnancy, the messianic child, the coming of the magi, and Herod's attempt against the life of the child. It is very difficult to decide which of that material came from the same source or tradition as the angelic dream appearances. My decisions on this score depend heavily on the second and third guidelines mentioned above in the discussion of methodology, namely, the presence of internal tensions as a sign that two bodies of material have been joined, and the guide supplied by parallels in Jewish traditions.[31]

Let us now turn to the Jewish traditions that serve as a background and a parallel for the reconstructed pre-Matthean narrative, so that the reader may see how these traditions flesh out the skeleton supplied by the pattern of the three angelic dream appearances. That Jesus was "son of Joseph" was part of the common Gospel tradition. If little were known of this Joseph (and, in fact, he never appears in the stories of the ministry), a characterization may well have been supplied by the famous patriarch

[30] This is true also of the pattern in Table VI. The introductory resumptive clause in the genitive absolute, followed by *idou* (a feature found also in 2:1), occurs eleven times in Matthew, as compared to once in Luke.

[31] As an anticipated instance of my application of these guides, I omitted the magi material from the basic narrative because of internal tensions visible in 2:1–3,9, where the star and the Scriptures constitute competing divine indicators of where Jesus might be found and where implausibly the king cannot find Jesus although the magi have led the way. On the other hand, I included Herod's massacre of the young boys in Bethlehem on the basis of parallelism to the Pharaoh's killing of the Hebrew male children. The reconstruction of Davis, "Tradition," omits the massacre of the children and includes the magi. In judging our two reconstructions, the reader should keep in mind that I plan to mention other pre-Matthean material (which will include the magi story); but I differ from Davis in my estimation of whether all the pre-Matthean material originally belonged together.

Joseph of the Book of Genesis.[32] Two very memorable items in the saga of
Joseph the patriarch were his ability to interpret dreams (Gen 37:19: a
"man of dreams" or "specialist in dreams")[33] and his going down to Egypt
where he was involved with the Pharaoh. These are the same two items
that characterize the Joseph of Matthew's infancy saga. Joseph consistently
receives revelation in dreams and he goes down to Egypt, the only man
in the NT to do so. And the NT Joseph is involved with a king (wicked)
even as the OT Joseph was involved with the Pharaoh.

One may object that the Pharaoh whom the patriarch Joseph served was
a benevolent figure. Yet there was another Pharaoh who was not benevolent, the Pharaoh "who knew not Joseph" (Exod 1:8), who killed the
male infants of the Israelites, with only Moses escaping, and who later
sought to kill Moses, so that Moses could not return from exile until this
Pharaoh was dead (Exod 4:19). The NT king who seeks to kill the infant
Jesus takes on the physiognomy of the second Pharaoh; and the basic
story line is established on the parallel between OT Joseph/wicked
Pharaoh/infant Moses and NT Joseph/wicked King Herod/infant Jesus.
The OT tells us nothing of the history of the Hebrews in Egypt between
the descent into Egypt associated with Joseph and the Exodus under Moses.
The NT abbreviates even further, for the one king deals with both Joseph
the father who went to Egypt and the infant Jesus who will come back
from Egypt to the land of Israel. (We remember that Matthew's genealogy
allots only one name, Aram, to the Egyptian period; NOTE on 1:3.) If the
parallelism between the two Josephs depends on the similarity of name
and is made possible by the lack of historical knowledge about the career
of the NT Joseph, the parallelism between Jesus and Moses is deeply
rooted in early Christian thought[34] and is particularly prominent in Matthew's picture of Jesus' ministry, as we saw in § 2. Matthew's appreciation
of this parallelism explains why he has chosen an infancy narrative which
fills out the parallelism more perfectly. Just as there is an infancy narrative
of Moses in the Book of Exodus showing God's hand in his career even

---

[32] The fact that Joseph (one of the twelve sons of Jacob/Israel) was betrayed by his brothers created a parallelism with Jesus who was betrayed by Judas (=Judah), one of the
Twelve. Another common feature was the forgiveness manifested by both. Thus, the patriarch
Joseph was part of the Christian picture of salvation history (Acts 7:9ff.) before his mirror-
image appearance in the Matthean infancy narrative.

[33] The Hebrew expression *ba'al haḥalōmôt* is more dramatic than the usual English translation "dreamer." Besides the association of dreams with Joseph, divine messages are given
in Genesis in dreams to Abimelech (20:3), to Laban (31:24), and especially to Jacob/
Israel (46:2–4): "God spoke to Israel in a dream of the night saying, 'Jacob, Jacob . . .
do not be afraid to go down to Egypt." Although the main OT inspiration for the pre-
Matthean infancy narrative comes from the Joseph and Moses stories in Egypt, there are
also plausible echoes of the Abraham and Jacob/Israel patriarchal cycles. See Appendix VI.

[34] Among the items illustrative of this parallelism are the association of Jesus with Moses
(and Elijah) in the Transfiguration accounts, Jesus' death at Passover time and as the
paschal lamb, the covenant theme in the eucharist, the Prophet-like-Moses motif (Acts
3:22–23; 7:37; and the Johannine references to "the Prophet"), and the comparision between Moses and Jesus in Hebr 3:2ff.

before he began his ministry of redeeming Israel from Egypt and of mediating a covenant between God and His people, so Matthew has given us an infancy narrative of Jesus before he begins his ministry of redemption and of the new covenant.[85]

It is important that we review what was said about the pre-ministry career of Moses in Jewish tradition both biblical and non-biblical. *First, the biblical account.* According to Exodus, the Pharaoh, alarmed at a population explosion among the Hebrews who had multiplied despite poverty and forced labor, ordered the Hebrew midwives and ultimately the Egyptians themselves to kill the male children born to the Hebrews. When Moses was born, he was spared this fate because his mother floated him in a basket on the Nile, where the Pharaoh's daughter found and saved him. Brought up at the Egyptian court, Moses killed an Egyptian who had been inflicting brutality upon a Hebrew. This enraged the Pharaoh, and so Moses had to flee for his life to the land of Midian. From the biblical account the following points of resemblance to Matthew may be listed:[86]

■Matt 2:13–14   Herod was going to search for the child to destroy him, so Joseph took the child and his mother and went away.

Exod 2:15   The Pharaoh sought to do away with Moses, so Moses went away.[87]

■Matt 2:16   Herod sent to Bethlehem and massacred all the boys of two years of age and under.

Exod 1:22   The Pharaoh commanded that every male born to the Hebrews be cast into the Nile.

■Matt 2:19   Herod died.

Exod 2:23   The king of Egypt died.

■Matt 2:19–20   The angel of the Lord said to Joseph in Egypt: ". . . go back to the land of Israel, for those who were seeking the child's life are dead."[38]

Exod 4:19   The Lord said to Moses in Midian: ". . . return to Egypt, for all those who were seeking your life are dead."

■Matt 2:21   Joseph took the child and his mother and went back to the land of Israel.

Exod 4:20   Moses took along his wife and his children and returned to Egypt.

---

85 Although chapter divisions are a later precision, it is noteworthy that there are two chapters of "early Moses" material in Exodus before Moses is solemnly called by the voice of God in the burning bush episode of ch. 3, just as there are two chapters of "early Jesus" material in Matthew before Jesus is solemnly designated by the voice of God in the baptism episode of ch. 3.

86 See Strecker, *Weg,* 515.

87 The verb "went away" (*anachorein*) is the same in Matthew and the LXX of Exodus; the verb "do away with" (*anairein*) used in the LXX of Exod 2:15 appears in Matt 2:16 where Herod *massacres* the boys.

88 The puzzling plural verb in Matthew (when only Herod has died) may be a direct quotation from the LXX of Exod 4:19; but it has the effect of joining the chief priests and scribes of Matt 2:4 with Herod in seeking the life of Jesus.

Second, the non-biblical tradition. This list of parallels is greatly enlarged when we turn to the Jewish midrashic tradition about the infancy of Moses (see Appendix VIII).[89] Our sources for this tradition date from the first century A.D. to the medieval period; they include targums or Aramaic translations of Exodus (which were at times quite free in adding details not found in the Hebrew), and midrashim or homiletic expositions of Exodus, and some lives of Moses. It is difficult in sifting these works to determine how much of the material is ancient and might have been known to the Jews of the period when Matthew's infancy narrative was taking shape. Fortunately, the *Life of Moses* by Philo and the account of Moses' birth in Josephus' *Antiquities* (II ix; ※ ※ 205–37)[40] offer indisputable examples of midrashic tradition circulating in the first Christian century. The following details, taken mostly from Josephus, heighten the already-noted biblical parallels between the infancies of Moses and Jesus:

▪The Pharaoh was no longer seeking simply to control the Hebrew population but had been marvelously forewarned of the birth of a Hebrew who would constitute a threat to the Egyptian kingdom. This brings the story closer to that of Herod who is seeking the life of the newborn King of the Jews.

▪According to Josephus, this forewarning came from one of Pharaoh's "sacred scribes."[41] In the pre-Matthean story Herod finds out from the chief priests and the scribes where the Messiah (or promised King of the Jews) was to be born.

▪According to other and later stories, the Pharaoh got his forewarning of the birth of the Hebrew deliverer from a dream[42] that had to be interpreted by his magicians (magi) or specialists in the occult. It is the *possibility* that this tradition was already known in NT times that caused me to insert in brackets in Table VII the suggestion that in the pre-Matthean story Herod heard of the birth of Jesus the Messiah in a dream. The absence of this dream in the final Matthean account is explicable on the

---

[89] In post-exilic Judaism (after 500 B.C.) there was an exaltation of the Mosaic Law as the center of religious life and, correlatively, a popular interest in the origins of Moses who gave Israel this celestial teaching. Obbink, "Legends," 252, points out that many features in the burgeoning Moses legends appear also in the stories surrounding the origins of other religious leaders. See also Erdmann, *Vorgeschichten*, 58–59.

[40] Strecker, *Weg* 51–55, agrees with Erdmann and others that the story in Matt 2 reflects specifically the form of the Moses legend found in Josephus. A wider (and later) midrashic tradition about Moses is appealed to by Bloch, "La naissance"; Muñoz Iglesias, "Los Evangelios"; and Perrot, "Les récits."

[41] *Ant.* II ix 2; ※205 uses the word *hierogrammateis*. The components of this appear in Matthew's chief priests (*archiereis*) and scribes (*grammateis*).

[42] A dream motif is widespread and may be original in the Moses legend. The dream is attributed to Pharaoh in the Jerusalem Targum and in the *Chronicle of Moses;* the latter and Pseudo-Philo also have a dream attributed to Miriam, Moses' sister; and, as we shall see, Josephus attributes a dream to Amram, Moses' father. Obviously this motif helps to explain the ease with which the pre-Matthean story has brought together Joseph the dreamer and the infancy of Moses.

grounds that a once independent magi-and-star story has been introduced, displacing the dream as the source of the wicked king's information. If there were magi in the Moses legend in the first century, we can
see why the pre-Matthean narrative of Jesus' infancy, which was based on
the Moses legend, would have easily attracted to itself this other birth
story involving the magi and the star.[43]

▪The Pharaoh was alarmed at hearing of the coming birth of the Hebrew
deliverer; indeed the thought of that birth filled the Egyptians with dread
(Josephus *Ant.* II ix 2,3; ※ ※206,215). Similarly when Herod heard of
the birth of Jesus the Messiah, "he was startled, and so was all Jerusalem
with him."

▪The Pharaoh's plan to assure the death of the promised child by execut-
ing all the male Hebrew children was frustrated because God appeared in
a dream to Amram (Moses' father), a Hebrew whose wife was already
pregnant, and told him not to despair of the future. His child about to be
born would escape those who were watching to destroy him and would
"deliver the Hebrew race from their bondage in Egypt" (*Ant.* II ix
3; ※ ※212,215–16). The parallels with the situation of Joseph, Jesus' father, are obvious. Like Moses, Jesus "will save his people from their sins"
(Matt 1:21).[44]

Indeed, the parallels between the Moses legend and the pre-Matthean
Jesus infancy narrative may have been more obvious than we can now
perceive. In the reconstruction in Table VII, I have followed the story line
in the sequence of Matt 1:8 – 2:23, even though, as we saw in footnote 21,
that sequence with its alternating pattern reflects Matthew's sense of organization. Perhaps one should be more adventurous in the reconstruction
and propose an older, pre-Matthean sequence in which the warning to
Herod (in a dream) about the forthcoming birth of the Messiah in Bethlehem *preceded* the angel's dream appearance to Joseph telling him of the
future of the child. In the Josephus form of the Moses legend the sacred

---

43 While some forms of the Moses legend have magi-magicians interpret the Pharaoh's
dream, other forms have magi-astrologers advise the Pharaoh about the birth of a Hebrew
deliverer (TalBab, *Sanhedrin*, 101a; *Midrash Rabbah* I 18 on Exod 1:22). There is a later
Moses legend (Bloch, "La naissance," 115–16) wherein at the birth of Moses a great light
like that of *a star* or of the sun and moon fills the house. Yet, I stress that, while the magi-
and-star story known to Matthew may have been attracted to the Moses legend by such features, its origin was independent of the Moses legend. The Matthean magi are favorable
to the child and opposed to the wicked king; the magi in the Moses legend abet the
Pharaoh and his murderous scheme.
44 This statement in the pre-Matthean narrative about the future of Jesus is an implicit interpretation of his name. Yet I suspect that the angelic directive to name the child Jesus
(Matt 1:21) does not belong to the Joseph-and-the-wicked-king narrative but to an annunciation of birth that will be discussed under other pre-Matthean episodes. In the early forms
of the Moses legend, his name is not prescribed before his birth. This feature does appear in
Pirke Rabbi Eleazar 32 (see Muñoz Iglesias, "El género," 257). In TalBab, *Sotah*, 12b, the
Pharaoh's magi are said to have foreseen the birth of "the savior of Israel," a phrasing
remarkably close to Matthew's description of Jesus.

scribes warn the Pharaoh about the forthcoming birth of the Hebrew deliverer before God tells Amram in a dream about the future of the child Moses. Before that dream there had been a hesitancy on Amram's part about his pregnant wife, since he saw no purpose in having a child that would be exterminated.[45] A change of sequence in the pre-Matthean story might enable us to explain along similar lines Joseph's hesitancy about taking Mary his wife into his home. In such a hypothesis Matthew would have changed the order of the story because there had been introduced into it the theme of the virginal conception. To explain such a suggestion let us now turn to other pre-Matthean material that was ultimately combined with the main pre-Matthean narrative of Table VII.

OTHER PRE-MATTHEAN EPISODES. Seemingly already before Matthew's editing, the main narrative of angelic dream appearances to Joseph and his struggle with the wicked king had attracted to itself other episodes in the infancy of Jesus. The word "episode" is chosen precisely because we can reconstruct only short vignettes. I shall leave full reconstructions until the respective sections of the commentary (pp. 154, 192 below) and only list the episodes now:

▪An annunciation of birth narrative. This was added to the angelic dream appearance now preserved in 1:18–25. If my readers will study the pattern in Table VI, they will note that in items 2 and 3 Scene A differs from Scenes B and C, in that Scene A has two angelic commands and two reasons. The duplication results from the combination of two different literary forms, the angelic dream appearance and the angelic annunciation of birth. The latter as an independent literary form is well attested in the OT (see Table VIII in § 5C) with stereotyped features like the naming of the visionary ("Joseph, son of David"), the injunction not to fear ("Do not be afraid"), the message that the pregnant woman will give birth ("She will give birth to a son"), and the name by which the child is to be called ("You will call his name Jesus"). That one may postulate for Jesus a separate annunciation of birth narrative with just these features is

---

[45] In later forms of the Jewish legend, Amram had actually repudiated his wife Jochebed; yet, at the insistence of his daughter Miriam, he took Jochebed as wife once more in order to beget Moses. This leads us to the tradition of an angelic appearance to Miriam (see footnote 42). In the first-century A.D. work, the *Biblical Antiquities* of Pseudo-Philo (ix 10), the Spirit of God came over Miriam, and a man (angel) in linen garments appeared to her in a dream. She was told to inform her parents that through the child to be born to them God would save His people. Since Miriam is the Hebrew form of Mary's name, alongside the tradition of an angelic appearance to the father of the savior (which has echoes in Matthew), there was the tradition of an angelic appearance to a woman named Mary (which has echoes in Luke). Le Déaut, "Miryam," points out that in the early Targum Neofiti on Exod 1:15, Miryam of the tribe of Levi was considered to have received the crown of royalty, for she was to be the ancestor of David. Luke's Mary, who is betrothed to Joseph of the House of David (1:27) has a relative, Elizabeth, who is of the House of Levi, descended from Aaron (1:5,36).

confirmed by Luke's story of an angelic annunciation to Mary in 1:26–38 ("Mary, do not be afraid . . . you will give birth to a son and you will call his name Jesus"). Seemingly it was this annunciation of birth narrative and not the angelic dream narrative that contained the theme of the conception of the child through a Holy Spirit, for that is common to both the Lucan (1:35) and Matthean (1:20) annunciations.

■A narrative of magi from the East who saw the star of the King of the Jews at its rising and were led by it to Bethlehem. While this narrative reflects the general belief that the birth of great men was augured by astronomical phenomena, its immediate inspiration came from the story of Balaam in Num 22–24, a man with magical powers who came from the East and predicted that a star would rise from Jacob.[46] Since in Jewish tradition this star was interpreted as a reference to the royal House of David, the narrative of the magi involved a public heavenly proclamation of the birth of the Messiah. It is notable that functionally the pre-Matthean story of the appearance of a star to the magi after Jesus' birth is matched by the Lucan story of the appearance of angels to the shepherds. The joining of the magi-and-star story with the Joseph-and-Herod narrative required minor adjustments in the A and B scenes of the latter (Table VII). The magi now become the ones who inform Herod of the birth of the child, and he sends them to Bethlehem to search for the child. Clauses pertaining to the magi in 2:13 ("when they had gone away") and 2:16 ("when he saw how he had been deceived by the magi") have replaced the clauses of the original Joseph-and-Herod narrative, leaving us with no more than a guess about the original.

We have now surveyed all the major pre-Matthean elements that went into the infancy narrative. It is more than likely that several or even all of these elements were already combined when the story came to Matthew, or, at least, before Matthew's final editing (see footnote 26).

b) *The Matthean Editing.* The word "editing" is used in a neutral sense here; it does *not* mean that Matthew simply put the final touches on a completed body of material. Matthew rearranged that material, retold it in his own language (see footnote 19), and fitted it carefully into his own theological vision. But here I wish to list only some specific Matthean contributions that were clearly distinct from the pre-Matthean material.

---

[46] In footnote 43 I pointed out that the possible presence of magi in the Moses legend may explain why a magi-and-star story was easily attracted to the basic pre-Matthean narrative of Joseph and Herod. In later forms of the Moses legend (TalBab, *Sotah*, 11a; *Midrash Rabbah* I 9 on Exod 1:9) Balaam appears as a counselor of the Pharaoh; and elsewhere Jannes and Jambres (see II Tim 3:8), the Pharaoh's chief magi, are identified as Balaam's sons (*Sepher ha-Yashar*). One wonders if this association of Balaam with the Pharaoh's court springs from the mention in Balaam's oracle of God bringing Israel out of Egypt (Num 24:8).

▪The addition of five formula citations which gave new highlighting and emphasis in the story. The virginal conception was clearly implied in the begetting through a Holy Spirit motif which was part of the pre-Matthean annunciation of birth material, but Matthew added the citation of Isa 7:14 to show that the continuation of the Davidic line by virginal conception had long been an aspect of the divine plan revealed through the prophets. This citation underlines the themes of the "Who" (*Quis*) and the "How" (*Quomodo*) that dominate the two sections of ch. 1, respectively, the genealogy and the annunciation (see the outline on p. 53 above). The pre-Matthean narrative of Joseph and Herod already had the motif of birth of the Messiah at Bethlehem, but Matthew's addition of Micah 5:1(2) supplied the scriptural basis for that localization and underlined the theme of "Where" (*Ubi*) which dominates the first half of ch. 2. The fact that the Micah passage is combined with II Sam 5:2 ("who will shepherd my people Israel") sets the tone for Matthew's understanding of the way in which the newborn ruler will exercise his rule (see Matt 20:25–28). The addition of Hosea 11:1, "Out of Egypt have I called my son," by calling attention to the Exodus of Israel, helped to underline the analogy between Moses and Jesus that was crucial in the pre-Matthean story. Further attention to the parallelism between the history of Jesus and the history of Israel was called by the addition of Jer 31:15, with Rachel in Ramah crying over the exile of her children, the Northern Tribes. Finally, the addition of "He will be called a Nazorean" showed that paradoxically Jesus fulfilled two Jewish expectations: the Messiah would be born in Bethlehem and yet he would be a Nazorean, which Matthew interprets to mean "from Nazareth." After the mention of Bethlehem in the Micah citation, the place names in the three subsequent citations (Egypt, Ramah, Nazareth) constitute a theological geography evocative of three important stages in salvation history: the Exodus in Egypt; the Exile; and the ministry of Jesus. From the "Where" (*Ubi*) of Jesus' birth, they turn the reader's attention to the "Whence" (*Unde*) of his destiny.

▪Some changes in the context were required by the additions of the five formula citations. For instance, to preserve the motif that a virgin would give birth to a son (Isa 7:14), Matthew added the assurance that Joseph did not have sexual relations with Mary before she gave birth to Jesus (1:25). And to make it possible to include the Nazareth citation, Matthew supplied a plausible reason for the family's move from Bethlehem (2:22–23a).

▪The joining of the narrative to a genealogy that Matthew himself had put into final shape also required editorial touches. For instance, Matthew fashioned an introduction (1:18) that gave a smooth sequence: the narrative that would follow would tell the story of the birth of Jesus Christ whose birth record was given in 1:1–17 and would explain the peculiar way in which his name had been introduced into that record in 1:16, where noticeably it was *not* said, as would have been expected, that Joseph begot (was the father of) Jesus. It should be added here that the joining of the genealogy to 1:18–25, the presence therein of two pre-Matthean episodes (angelic dream appearance; annunciation of birth), and the incorporation of a fulfillment citation makes 1:18–25 the most complicated section in the whole infancy narrative—the one with the heaviest Matthean rewriting and the one whose prehistory is the most difficult to determine.

These editorial additions to a rewritten earlier narrative have left some slight inconsistencies of logic and style which are very useful to us in detecting the material that came to Matthew. But such inconsistencies do not detract in any real way from the success of the end product—a powerful story of the confrontation between God's will and man's machinations in the birth of Jesus, a story that grips the imagination and remains in the memory. No matter what the prehistory of his material, Matthew has made the narrative an effective vehicle of *his* theology and message. If this section (§ 4) has been devoted to detecting the elements that have gone into Matthew's narrative, it was because I felt that, having an overview of the history of composition, the reader would move more smoothly through the commentary. In no sense are the reconstructed pre-Matthean elements with all their uncertainties comparable in importance to the final Matthean narrative, the only compositional stage for which we have surety. (It may be noted, however, that many of the OT motifs we have discussed, e.g., Joseph, Moses, Balaam, are essential aspects of the final narrative, independently of the value of the reconstruction.) As we begin the commentary on the narrative, I wish it to be clear that this will not be a commentary on a reconstruction but a commentary on what Matthew has given us. The evangelist's intent will have first place, and the prehistory of his material will be discussed to the extent that it may enlighten that intent.

SECTIONAL BIBLIOGRAPHY (§4)

A. MATTHEW'S FORMULA CITATIONS OF SCRIPTURE

Fitzmyer, J. A., "The Use of Explicit Old Testament Quotations in Qumran Literature and in the New Testament," NTS 7 (1960–61), 297–333.

Gärtner, B., "The Habakkuk Commentary (DSH) and the Gospel of Matthew," *Studia Theologica* 8 (1954), 1–24.

Gundry, R. H., *The Use of the Old Testament in St. Matthew's Gospel* (NovTestS 18; Leiden: Brill, 1967), esp. 89–104.

Kilpatrick, G. D., *Origins,* esp. 52–57, 93–95.

Knox, W. L., *Sources,* II, 121–32.

Lindars, B., *New Testament Apologetic* (London: SCM, 1961), esp. 189–221.

McConnell, R. S., *Law and Prophecy in Matthew's Gospel. The Authority and Use of the Old Testament in the Gospel of Matthew* (Theologische Dissertationen 2; Basel University, 1969).

Metzger, B. M., "The Formulas Introducing Quotations of Scripture in the New Testament and the Mishnah," JBL 70 (1951), 297–307.

Moule, C. F. D., "Fulfilment-Words in the New Testament: Use and Abuse," NTS 14 (1967–68), 293–320.

Pesch, R., "Der Gottessohn im matthäischen Evangelienprolog (Mt 1–2). Beobachtungen zu den Zitationsformeln der Reflexionzitate," *Biblica* 48 (1967), 395–420.

Rothfuchs, W., *Die Erfüllungszitate des Matthäus-Evangeliums* (BWANT 88; Stuttgart: Kohlhammer, 1969).

Soares Prabhu, G. M., *The Formula Quotations in the Infancy Narrative of Matthew* (Analecta Biblica 63; Rome: Pontifical Biblical Institute, 1976).

Stendahl, K., *The School of St. Matthew* (Philadelphia: Fortress, 2nd ed. 1968; orig. 1954).

Strecker, G., *Weg,* esp. 49–63.

Van Segbroeck, F., "Les citations d'accomplissement dans l'Evangile selon Saint Matthieu d'après trois ouvrages récents," in M. Didier, *L'Evangile,* 107–30. (Analysis of Gundry, McConnell, Rothfuchs.)

B. Background for Matthew's Narrative in Jewish Midrashic Traditions

Bloch, Renée, "La naissance de Moïse dans la tradition aggadique," in *Moïse, l'Homme de l'Alliance* (Paris: Desclée, 1955), 102–18.

Bourke, M., "The Literary Genus of Matthew 1–2," CBQ 22 (1960), 160–75.

Daube, D., *The New Testament and Rabbinic Judaism* (London: Athlone, 1956), 189–92.

Galbiati, E., "Genere letterario e storia in Matteo 1–2," BibOr 15 (1973), 3–16.

Ginzberg, L., *The Legends of the Jews* (7 vols.; Philadelphia: Jewish Publication Society, 1909–38).

Le Déaut, R., "Miryam, soeur de Moïse, et Marie, mère du Messie," *Biblica* 45 (1964), 198–219.

Muñoz Iglesias, S., "Los Evangelios de la Infancia y las infancias de los héroes," EB 16 (1957), 5–36.

———— "Midráš y Evangelios de la Infancia," EE 47 (1972), 331–59.

Neff, R. W., "The Birth and Election of Isaac in the Priestly Tradition," *Biblical Research* 15 (1970), 5–18.

———— "The Annunciation in the Birth Narrative of Ishmael," *Biblical Research* 17 (1972), 51–60.

Obbink, H. W., "On the Legends of Moses in the Haggadah," in *Studia Biblica et Semitica T. C. Vriezen Dedicata*, ed. W. C. van Unnik and A. S. van der Woude (Wageningen: Veenman, 1966), 252–64.

Perrot, C., "Les récits d'enfance dans la Haggada antérieure au IIᵉ siècle de notre ère," RechScRel 55 (1967), 481–518.

Tuñi, J. O., "La tipologia Israel-Jesús en Mt 1–2," EE 47 (1972), 361–76.

Winter, P., "Jewish Folklore in the Matthean Birth Story," HJ 53 (1954–55), 34–42.

IV. THE CONCEPTION OF JESUS (§ 5)

Translation of Matt 1:18-25

1 [18] Now, as for [Jesus] Christ, his birth took place in this way. His mother Mary had been betrothed to Joseph; but before they began to live together, it was found that she was with child—through the Holy Spirit. [19] Her husband Joseph was an upright man, but unwilling to expose her to public disgrace; and so he resolved to divorce her quietly.

[20] Now, as he was considering this, behold, an angel of the Lord appeared to him in a dream, saying, "Joseph, son of David, do not be afraid to take Mary your wife into your home, for the child begotten in her is through the Holy Spirit. [21] She will give birth to a son; and you will call his name Jesus, for he will save his people from their sins."

[22] All this took place to fulfill what the Lord had spoken by the prophet who said,

> [23] "Behold, the virgin will be with child
> and will give birth to a son,
> and they will call his name Emmanuel
> [which means 'God with us']."

[24] So Joseph got up from sleep and did as the angel of the Lord had commanded him. He took his wife home, [25] but he had no sexual relations with her before she gave birth to a son. And he called his name Jesus.

NOTES

1:18. *Now, as for [Jesus] Christ.* The overwhelming majority of textual witnesses read *Tou de Iēsou Christou;* and this reading fits well with the thesis that the opening of the narrative is related to the last line of the genealogy, namely, "Joseph, the husband of Mary; of her was begotten *Jesus,* called the *Christ"* (1:16). The word order also indicates a reference to someone already mentioned. Nevertheless, the presence of "Jesus" is suspect for several reasons: (a) the name is omitted in a minor Greek ms., in Irenaeus, and in some Latin and Syriac evidence; (b) the position of "Jesus" varies in the witnesses that have it—often the sign of a scribal addition; (c) while one could explain its omission on the grounds of a scribal assimilation to 1:17 (which has simply "the Christ"), it is easier to explain its presence as a scribal addition in imitation of 1:16; (d) there is no other uncontested instance in the NT of an article preceding the compound *Iēsous Christos,* a difficulty that disappears if *Iēsous* is not original.

birth. The same word, *genesis,* as in 1:1, another tie in with the genealogy. A respectable number of less important textual witnesses read *gennēsis,* which also means "birth" but does not have the same wide range as *genesis* ("birth, creation, genealogy"; see NOTE on 1:1). Davies, *Setting,* 69, wonders if *gennēsis* was not original, with *genesis* being introduced as a scribal assimilation to 1:1. It seems more likely that *gennēsis,* which became the common word in patristic literature for the Nativity, was introduced by scribes to replace the less familiar *genesis* (Metzger, MTC, 8).

betrothed. Both Luke (1:27; 2:5) and Matthew use the middle or passive of the verb *mnēsteuein,* "to be betrothed, engaged," to describe the relationship between Joseph and Mary; they avoid the more usual verbs for marrying, *gamein* and *gamizein,* as well as the related noun *gamos,* "wedding, marriage." It may have been as difficult for them in Greek as it is for us in English to find the exact word to cover the appropriate stage in the Jewish matrimonial procedure. This procedure, which is implicit in some biblical passages, is spelled out in the later rabbinic documents. (See Jeremias, *Jerusalem,* 365–68; St-B, I, 45–47; II, 393.) It consisted of two steps: a formal exchange of consent before witnesses (Mal 2:14) and the subsequent taking of the bride to the groom's family home (Matt 25:1–13). While the term marriage is sometimes used to designate the second step, in terms of legal implications it would be more properly applied to the first step. The consent (*'ērûsîn,* "betrothal"), usually entered into when the girl was between twelve and thirteen years old, would constitute a legally ratified marriage in our terms, since it gave the young man rights over the girl. She was henceforth his wife (notice the term *gynē,* "wife," in Matt 1:20,24), and any infringement on his marital rights could be punished as adultery. Yet the wife continued to live at her own family home, usually for about a year. Then took place the formal transferral (*nîsû'în*) or taking of the bride to the husband's family home where he assumed her support. According to later Jewish commentary (Mishnah *Kethuboth* 1:5; TalBab *Kethuboth* 9b, 12a), *in parts of Judea* it was not unusual for the husband to be alone with his wife on at least one occasion in the interval between exchange of consent and the move to the home (and so interim marital relations were not absolutely condemned). But *in Galilee* no such leniency was tolerated and the wife had to be taken to her husband's home as a virgin. It is clear, explicitly in Matthew and implicitly in Luke (since Mary is betrothed but still a virgin) that Joseph and Mary are in the stage of matrimonial procedure between the two steps. But it is risky to apply the difference between Judean and Galilean sensibilities to them. First, many think that the difference arose because of the danger that occupying Roman troops might rape or seduce a betrothed virgin; and so the difference may well stem from a post-A.D. 70 period. Second, for Matthew (unlike Luke) Mary and Joseph live in Bethlehem of Judea and have their home there (2:11); and so, if the Judean/Galilean marriage customs were already different, Mary and Joseph would more likely have come under the less stringent Judean practice. Yet the tone of scandal implicit in the Matthean narrative would better fit the Galilean practice.

before they began to live together. That is, before the second step in the matrimonial practice described above. There is a wide range of meaning in *synerchesthai:* common habitation, sexual relations, and the constitution of a family. Lohmeyer, *Matthäus,* 13[1], cautions that sexual relations are not necessarily implied by this verb; but certainly that it is a very common meaning (Josephus *Ant.* VII viii 1;⚒168; ix 5;⚒⚒213–14; Philo *De virtutibus* xxii ⚒⚒111–12).

it was found that she was. Literally "she was found to be." This need not have the sense of a secret discovered by a busybody. A weakened sense in which "found to be" simply means "was" is to some extent present in English as well as Greek: "He found himself in the country."

with child. Literally "having in the womb"; no Greek substantive for "child" appears either here or in 1:20.

through the Holy Spirit. I have separated this expression by a dash in order visually to mark it off as an explanation that Matthew offers to the reader. The fact that the child was conceived through the Holy Spirit is not part of the narrative flow here; rather that news comes to the dramatis personae from an angel's revelation in vs. 22. But Matthew wants the reader to know more than do the characters in the story, so that the reader will not entertain for a moment the suspicion that grows in Joseph's mind. Literally, the expression is genitive and has no definite article: "of a Holy Spirit." However, when one has supplied the word "child" (previous NOTE), the reading "child of the Holy Spirit" gives the false impression that Matthew has said that the Holy Spirit is the father of the child. There is never a suggestion in Matthew or in Luke that the Holy Spirit is the male element in a union with Mary, supplying the husband's role in begetting. Not only is the Holy Spirit not male (feminine in Hebrew; neuter in Greek), but also the manner of begetting is implicitly creative rather than sexual. The lack of the definite article (also missing in the parallel description of pregnancy in Luke 1:35) tempts one to speak of "a holy spirit," but that is probably too indefinite to do justice to Matthew's theology. In the COMMENT (C2) I shall contend that the relationship of the Holy Spirit to Jesus' divine sonship was articulated first in reference to the resurrection (Rom 1:4) and then in relation to the ministry beginning with the baptism (Matt 3:16–17). Thus, an articulation of this relationship in reference to Jesus' conception came after considerable Christian reflection upon the Spirit of God. If most commentators try to catch this by supplying the definite article before "Holy Spirit," this should not lead the Christian reader to assume that either Matthew or Luke has developed a theology of the Spirit as a person, much less the Third Person of the Trinity. Perhaps the broader category of divine agent best covers the evaluation of the Spirit throughout most of NT Christian thought (with the Johannine Paraclete passages moving toward personality). Behind such a conception would be the images of the spirit as the God-given life breath (Ps 104:30; Matt 27:50), as the force by which God moved the prophets to speak (Matt 22:43), and as the animating principle of Jesus' ministry which descended upon him at the baptism (Matt 3:16) and was communicated by him to his followers after the resurrection (John 20:22; Acts 1:8). As for capitalization I follow recent Bible custom, without implying that a passage conveys either personality or a Trinitarian concept of divinity. Early English Protestant Bibles capitalized neither "holy" nor "spirit"; the Rheims Catholic edition capitalized both; the Authorized (King James) Version capitalized only "Spirit" until the eighteenth century.

19. *Her husband.* Joseph was so designated in 1:16; but variants there (calling Mary Joseph's betrothed) reflected the sensitivities of later scribes that such a designation might compromise Mary's virginity. For Matthew, of course, since Joseph and Mary have taken the first step in the matrimonial procedure by exchanging consent (betrothal), they are truly "husband" and "wife" (1:20,24). It is interesting that Luke uses neither term for Joseph and Mary (cf. 1:34), remaining content with "betrothed."

an upright man. Four OT women were mentioned by Matthew in the genealogy as preparation for Mary's role as the instrument of the Holy Spirit in the begetting of the Messiah. But in two of those instances the man involved was not upright, Judah and David. (In fact, in Gen 38:26 Judah says, "Tamar is more upright than I.") But both of Jesus' parents are models of virtue. Although *dikaios,* "upright, just," is a favorite Matthean word (nineteen times, compared to twice in Mark), I do not agree with Davis, "Tradition," 413, who would classify this description as Matthean rather than pre-Matthean. The most likely meaning of "upright" here, namely, observant of the Law, is not the usual meaning of *dikaios* for Matthew, and theme of the uprightness of parents as observers of the Law appears in the Lucan infancy narrative (1:6). Thus, Joseph's uprightness may well have been a feature of the pre-Matthean annunciation of birth narrative. Above, I spoke of the "most likely" meaning of "upright," precisely because there has been considerable scholarly dispute about the way in which Joseph's decision to divorce Mary quietly stems from or is related to his being "an upright man." Was his uprightness or justice exemplified in his not wishing to expose Mary to public disgrace or was the latter a touch of mercy that modified his justice? There are three current explanations of Joseph's justice, the first two of which understand the opening clauses of vs. 19 in this way: "an upright man *and therefore* unwilling to expose her publicly," while the third would read: "an upright man *but* unwilling to expose her publicly." Let me discuss each of the three explanations, for they reflect a considerable body of scholarly literature:

a) *Kindness or mercy* was the key factor in Joseph's uprightness or justice, a theory defended by Pesch, "Ausführungsformel," 91, and by Spicq, "Joseph," 206–9. The latter invokes Clement of Alexandria as an early proponent. Adherents of this theory differ among themselves on whether Joseph judged that Mary had committed adultery, or refrained from passing judgment; but they agree that he showed himself upright (merciful) in his unwillingness to enforce the law against adultery rigorously and in his desire to get Mary off as easily as possible. Such an understanding of uprightness is foreshadowed in Ps 112:4 which joins justice (RSV: righteousness) to graciousness and mercy. In Ps 37:21 we are told, "The upright man is kindly"; and Wisdom 12:19 declares, "Those who are upright must be kind." In Philo's portrayal, an upright man emerges as equitable, moderate, and clement—in short, a gentleman. (Spicq, "Joseph," 209–13—one of Philo's examples of an upright man is Noah; see footnote 20 below.) However, in reading such passages, one is not certain that justice or uprightness is presented as *consisting* in mercy, as distinct from being tempered by mercy. If being upright is being merciful, why is Joseph told in vs. 20: "Do not be afraid to take Mary your wife into your home"? The angelic message implies that Joseph had a scruple against the completion of the matrimonial process, a scruple that should logically be related to his being an upright man.

b) *Respect or awe* for God's plan of salvation was the key factor in Joseph's uprightness or justice, a theory defended by Schlatter, *Matthäus*, 13; Krämer, "Menschwerdung," 26–33; and in greatest detail by Léon-Dufour, "L'annonce." This interpretation requires the omission of the dash in 1:18. "It was found that she was with child through the Holy Spirit" means that Joseph knew that Mary's pregnancy was the result of a divine intervention—a position held in antiquity by Eusebius, Ephraem, and Theophylact. In typical Jewish awe or fear at the presence of God, Joseph drew back: he could not take as spouse the woman whom God had chosen as His sacred vessel. (This is sometimes designated as the "fear" hypothesis, in distinction from the "suspicion" hypothesis in which Joseph suspects that Mary has been unfaithful—a hypothesis operative in explanations [a] and [c].) The angelic message "Do not be afraid to take Mary your wife into your home" was intended to assure Joseph that God's plan included the final step in the matrimonial process, so that Joseph might give his name and Davidic heritage to the child. While attractive, this explanation faces serious difficulties. It is true that *dikaios* can mean pious or saintly, so that the interpretation of uprightness as religious awe is possible. But how would Joseph have known that Mary's pregnancy was the result of divine intervention? If we are to imagine that he had received a previous revelation to that effect, would that revelation not have included the instruction to complete the matrimonial process by taking Mary to his home? The suggestion that it was Mary who told

Joseph about the divine origins of her pregnancy is questionable inasmuch as it presupposes something like the Lucan annunciation to Mary, a scene of which Matthew betrays no knowledge. Even more questionable is the romantic suggestion that Joseph guessed that the child had been divinely conceived on the basis of his character estimation of Mary who, he was sure, could not have sinned.

As I have stated in the NOTE on "through the Holy Spirit" in 18, that information is meant for the reader and tells us nothing about the knowledge of the dramatis personae. It is fairly obvious that Joseph *learns* from the angel the divine origin of the child in Mary's womb. Moreover, even if one were willing to grant the improbability that Joseph already knew this, how would his decision to divorce Mary out of a motive of religious awe have protected Mary? He could scarcely have hoped that the people who heard of the pregnancy followed by a divorce would jump to the conclusion that the child had been begotten through the creative action of the Holy Spirit. He would, in fact, be manifesting his uprightness at the expense of Mary's reputation.

c) *Obedience to the Law* was the key factor in Joseph's uprightness or justice, a theory that seems to have been common in antiquity (Justin, Ambrose, Augustine, and Chrysostom) and which is defended in recent literature by Hill, "Note," and Descamps, *Les Justes*, 34–37. This is certainly the sense of "upright" in the Lucan infancy narrative (1:6) when that term is applied to Zechariah and Elizabeth who were "blamelessly observing all the commandments and ordinances of the Lord." This understanding of the uprightness of Joseph is attested in the second-century *Protevangelium of James* 14:1: "If I hide her sin, I am fighting the Law of the Lord." The particular law that would have concerned Joseph was Deut 22:20–21, which deals with the case of a young woman who is brought to her husband's home and found not to be a virgin. Deuteronomy required the stoning of the adulteress; but in a less severe legal system the command to "purge the evil from the midst of you" could have been met by divorcing her. In this interpretation, while Joseph's sense of obedience to the Law forced him in conscience to divorce Mary, his unwillingness to expose her to public disgrace led him to proceed without accusation of serious crime (see NOTE on "quietly" below). He was upright *but* also merciful. This theory demands no special understanding on Joseph's part about the origins of Mary's pregnancy: he assumes that she has been unfaithful. It also makes perfect sense of the angel's instructing Joseph not to be afraid to take Mary his wife into his home—the Law was not being broken because Mary was not an adulteress; she had conceived through the agency of the Holy Spirit with her virginity intact. Léon-Dufour, "L'annonce," 70, objects that this theory makes Joseph a formalist who keeps the letter of the Law but tries to avoid its harsh effects; but in the eyes of others that might illustrate an intelligent combination of principle and compassion.

Of the three explanations, I would judge that only the third is convincing. I deem it no accident that the first and second are popular among Roman Catholic scholars, for those explanations are more adaptable than the third to later pious sensitivities about Jesus' parents. Many today might be offended by the thought that Joseph could regard Mary as an adulteress; but among first-century Christians of Jewish origin this would in no way detract from his upright character illustrated in his willingness to obey the Law against his own inclinations. I doubt the plausibility of a compromise solution, namely, that in the pre-Matthean stage uprightness meant obedience to the law concerning an adulteress, but that Matthew, by adding "through the Holy Spirit" in 1:18, has shifted over the meaning to reverence or awe (the second explanation). Even the Matthean stage is perfectly consonant with the third explanation.

but unwilling. The "but" translation of *kai* is consonant with the third explanation of Joseph's uprightness. "Unwilling" is a negated participle, "not willing," an expression not characteristically Matthean (BDF 101, p. 52 on *thelein*).

to expose her to public disgrace. Sometimes translated as "to put to shame, make an example of," *deigmatizein* has the connotation of public display and was used, even in secular Greek, in reference to convicted adulteresses. It should be translated more strongly than does Krämer, "Menschwerdung," 32 ("to give her secret away") or Germano, "Nova" ("to investigate her [involvement in the divine mystery]").

to divorce her. Some scholars, particularly those sensitive to later piety, have tried to avoid the idea that Joseph would have divorced Mary. One suggestion for what was involved is a "separation of bed and board," even though there had as yet been no union of bed and board, and we have little evidence for such "separations" in the Judaism of Jesus' time. Another dubious solution is that Joseph was going to abandon or leave Mary rather than divorce her, and thus make himself appear as the guilty party (Suhl, "Davidssohn," 64–67). Both of these theories run against the fact that elsewhere in Matthew (5:31–32; 19:3,7–9), the verb used here, *apolyein*, means "to divorce." Interestingly, an Aramaic act of marriage repudiation, dating from A.D. 111 and involving a certain Joseph and Mary, has been found among the Dead Sea Scrolls (Mur 19 ar).

quietly. It is not clear what this means or how Joseph hoped to accomplish it. According to the practice known from later rabbinic writings, a totally secret divorce was not possible, since the writ of repudiation had to be delivered before two witnesses (St-B, I, 304–5). Nor could Joseph have kept Mary's shame hidden indefinitely; for, no matter what reason he alleged in the divorce proceedings, Mary's pregnancy would eventually have become a matter of public knowledge, and her neighbors would have concluded that her adultery was the real reason for the divorce. Probably, all that Matthew means is that in the divorce Joseph was not going to accuse Mary publicly of adultery and thus not going to subject her to trial. (If Num 5:11–31 was still effective in NT times, a trial by ordeal was the procedure when there were no witnesses to the adultery.) To avoid the accusation of adultery, Joseph could have offered less serious grounds, as acknowledged by the Pharisees of the school of Hillel. (Jewish debates between the followers of Hillel and Shammai about the grounds for divorce are in the background of the question raised in Matt 19:3.) Thus, "to divorce quietly" may mean to divorce leniently.

20. *Now, as he was considering this, behold.* This stereotyped pattern of a

genitive absolute, with a postpositive *de*, continued by the demonstrative particle *idou*, is found also in 2:1,13,19 (see Table VI). Elsewhere the basic pattern occurs some seven times in Matthew. Here the verb is aorist, an unusual tense for expressing continued action. Some have proposed to understand the aorist as ingressive (BDF 331): "as he began to consider this" or "as he had made up his mind to do this." This verb *enthymesthai* is found in the NT only here and in Matt 9:4.

an angel of the Lord. This figure will reappear in 2:13,19. Most often the OT "angel of the Lord" is not a personal, spiritual being intermediate between God and man, but is simply a way of describing God's visible presence among men. For the interchangeability of the angel and God, compare Gen 16:7 and 13; Gen 22:11 and 14; Exod 3:2 and 4; Judg 6:12 and 14; Hosea 12:5(4); Isa 63:9. Only in post-exilic Jewish thought was wide acceptance given to angels as intermediate beings with their own personalities and names. See NOTE on Luke 1:11. Outside of the infancy narrative "an angel of the Lord" appears only at the empty tomb (28:2)—a datum in harmony with my contention in §1, A2, that the infancy narrative is the vehicle of post-resurrectional christology.

in a dream. The expression *kat' onar* occurs five times in the infancy narrative, namely, in the three angelic dream appearances (here; 2:13,19) and in the two supplementary divine communications (2:12,22). The only other occurrence in the Bible is Matt 27:19. In the LXX the words used for the dream revelations to the patriarchs (footnote 33, § 4) include *enypnion, hypnos* ("sleep"), and *horama nyktos* ("vision of the night"); but Josephus, *Ant.* II v 1;⊁63, uses *onar* for a dream interpreted by the patriarch Joseph. It is noteworthy that Matthew's dreams are not like the apocalyptic dreams in Daniel, puzzles that need an interpreter; nor do the dreams themselves carry the revelation. In three of the passages they are simply a context for the angel of the Lord who conveys the message. See Acts 16:9; 18:9; and 27:23–24 for appearances in a dream, a vision, and at night—of a man, of the Lord, and of an angel of the Lord, respectively.

Joseph, son of David. Compare Luke 1:27: "a man of the House of David whose name was Joseph."

do not be afraid. The aorist *mē phobēthēs* (compare the present tense *mē phobou* in Luke 1:30) may have the sense of "do not hold back out of fear" (BDF 336[8]).

to take Mary your wife into your home. Literally, "to take [*paralambanein*] Mary your wife"; similarly in 1:24: "he took Mary his wife." Some would understand *paralambanein* to mean "take as" and would translate "to take Mary as your wife." But in the Jewish understanding of the matrimonial procedure (NOTE on "betrothed" in 1:18), Mary was already Joseph's wife, though they had not yet come together to share bed and board. The Syriac translator (OS[cur]), since he has "Mary your betrothed," not "Mary your wife," clearly understood *paralambanein* to mean "take home." A related sense of *paralambanein* as "take along, take with" appears in 2:14,21. Chrysostom attempted to interpret Matt 1:20 as "to *retain* Mary *as* your wife," an interpretation used by others to support the thesis that Mary was already at Joseph's home. This is most unlikely; see J. Delorme, *Ami du Clergé* 66 (1956), 774.

for. This *gar*, followed by a *de* at the beginning of vs. 21, is translated in a non-causal way by Léon-Dufour ("L'annonce," 73–74), as part of his argument for the "fear hypothesis" in relation to *dikaios* in vs. 19 (see explanation [b] in the NOTE there on "upright"). Since Léon-Dufour thinks that Joseph already knew the divine origins of the child, he cannot have Joseph learn that from the angel. He translates: "Do not be afraid to take Mary your wife into your home; true [*gar*], the child begotten in her is through the Holy Spirit, but [*de*] she will give birth to a son and you will call his name Jesus." He points to the meaning of *gar . . . de* (*gar . . . plēn*) in Matt 18:7; 22:14; 24:5–6. However, the "but" clause remains awkward in Léon-Dufour's translation; and his interpretation of *gar* would better fit a *men gar . . . de* construction (Pelletier, "L'annonce"). The other two instances of *gar* in the Matthean angelic dream pattern (Table VI) in 2:13,20 have Joseph being told something that he does not already know. By analogy, the translation "for" is more plausible here than the translation "true." Krämer, "Menschwerdung," 26, speculates that in a supposed Aramaic original there would have been no such connective; but there is no real evidence that the pre-Matthean narrative existed in Aramaic.

the child begotten. Literally "what was begotten"; see NOTE on "with child" in 1:18. *Gennēthen*, "begotten," is related to *genesis* of 1:1,18, and more closely to *egennēsan* ("begot, was the father of") used regularly in the genealogy. It is closest to the *egennēthē* ("was begotten, born") in 1:16.

is through the Holy Spirit. See the NOTE on this phrase in 1:18. The problems that occur there occur here also and are complicated by the fact that "Holy" and "Spirit" are separated by the verb "to be"; literally "is of a Spirit which is Holy."

21. *She will give birth to a son.* The *texetai de huion* may be compared to the *kai texei huion* ("and you will give birth to a son") of Luke 1:31. The Old Syriac versions of Matthew add "for you"; and Bultmann, *History*, 292, regards this reading as plausibly more original and indicative of the lack of a theme of virginal conception in the pre-Matthean narrative. Yet this reading is intimately associated with the reading of the Old Syriac Sinaiticus in 1:16: "*Joseph*, to whom the virgin Mary was betrothed, *was the father of Jesus*, called the Christ." As I pointed out in the NOTE there, the reading is not original but a scribal "improvement," to which OS[sin] is particularly susceptible. Since the virginity of Mary was safeguarded for the Syriac translators of vs. 21 by the context, they did not hesitate to stress Joseph's legal paternity. The "for you" addition brings the Matthean statement closer to OT usage, e.g., Gen 17:19, "Behold, Sarah your wife will give birth to a son for you."

you will call his name Jesus. The awkward expression "to *call* someone's *name* X" is a Semitism for "to call someone X" (Matt 2:23; Luke 1:59) or "to name someone X" (BDF 157[2]). The expression reappears in 1:23,25 and Luke 1:13,31. In Matthew Joseph is to name the child, whereas in Luke 1:31 Mary is told to name the child (cf. Luke 1:62). In patriarchal times either father (Gen 4:26; 5:3) or mother (Gen 4:25) could name the child.

for he will save. The "for" indicates that "he will save" is an etymological interpretation of the name given the child. *Iēsous* is a Hellenized rendering of the Hebrew *Yēšûa'*, often shortened to *Yēšû'* (BDF 53²ᵇ). This Hebrew name is already a shortened form of *Yᵉhôšûa'* or Joshua, the name borne by Moses' successor. The original meaning of *Yᵉhôšûa'* was "Yahweh helps," from the root *šw'*, "to help" (M. Noth, *Die israelitischen Personennamen* [BWANT, 3rd series, 10; Stuttgart: Kohlhammer, 1928], 107). However, a popular etymology connected the name and its shortened form with the root *yš'*, "to save," and the noun *yᵉšû'â*, "salvation." It is this popular etymology that is reflected in Matthew's interpretation of "Jesus" as "God saves"; see also Acts 4:12. The argument that this etymology indicates a Semitic origin for the Matthean or pre-Matthean narrative is false. Undoubtedly the etymology of the savior's name could have been taught to Greek-speaking Christians as well. Certainly, Greek-speaking Jews knew the Hebrew etymology of Joshua's name; for in Alexandria Philo explains: "Jesus [Joshua] is interpreted salvation of the Lord, a name for the best possible state" (*De mutatione nominum* xli;121, on Num 13:16). In vs. 23 Matthew will interpret a Hebrew name, Emmanuel, of which Greek-speaking Christians would not be likely to know the meaning.

his people. Israel, for Matthew, included both Jews and Gentiles. It is more difficult to interpret the reference to "His people" in Luke 1:77a in connection with JBap; there it might refer only to Jews.

22. *took place.* I have interpreted this perfect tense as an instance of the perfect used for the aorist. But there may be a cumulative sense of accomplishment: "had come about" (see BDF 343⁸).

to fulfill. For the stereotyped fulfillment formula in Matthew, see Table V.

what the Lord had spoken. Matthew's formula citations involve a fulfillment of the *words* of Scripture, not simply of a plan or intention of God. Ten of the formula citations (Table V) refer to fulfilling the prophet's word, and twice there is a reference to what is written by the prophet.

by the prophet. Codex Bezae and the OL and OS add "Isaiah," a scribal clarification, but in imitation of good Matthean style since in six of the Matthean formula citations, Isaiah is mentioned by name.

23. *they will call.* As we shall see in the COMMENT, the LXX of Isa 7:14 reads: "you [sing.] will call"; and this reading appears in Codex Bezae of Matthew (and in Luke 1:31). There is also very slight textual evidence for "she will call," a reading that may represent a harmonization with the MT.

24. *So Joseph got up from sleep.* All three angelic dream appearances (Table VI) begin the description of Joseph's response with: "So Joseph got up" (2:14,21); but only the first adds "from sleep."

and did as the angel of the Lord had commanded him. This is also a specification found only in the first angelic dream appearance. Like the patriarchs, Joseph shows himself obedient to God's command. Motté, "Mann," tries to connect this obedience to Joseph's being an "upright man" (*dikaios*) in 1:18. The righteousness (*dikaiosynē*) of Abraham was in one way or another associated with his obedience to God's commands (Rom 4:2; Gal 3:6; James 2:21). But Matthew mentions Joseph as *dikaios* not in relation to a personal divine command but in reference to Mary's divorce and the general law concerning adultery.

He took his wife home. For *paralambanein,* see NOTE on "to take Mary your wife into your home" in vs. 20.

25. *he had no sexual relations with her before.* Literally, "he did not know her until." The OL and OS omit this. Burkitt, *Evangelion,* 261, suggests that the clause may have been added by a scribe in order to support the idea of the virginal conception. More likely it was omitted by scribes who saw in it an obstacle to the thesis of Mary's continued virginity after Jesus' birth. (The Diatessaron reads: "he lived with her purely until.") This leads us to the problem of the implications of 1:25 for the perpetual virginity of Mary which has become a divisive issue among Christians. Leaving aside post-Reformation quarrels, we must seek to reconstruct Matthew's intention, first from the immediate context and then from the whole Gospel. How does "not know her until" fit into the immediate context? In English when something is negated *until* a particular time, occurrence after that time is usually assumed. However, in discussing the Greek *heōs hou* after a negative ("not . . . until, not . . . before"; BAG, 335, 1b, alpha), K. Beyer, *Semitische Syntax im Neuen Testament* (Göttingen: Vandenhoeck, 1962), I, 132[1], points out that in Greek and Semitic such a negation often has no implication at all about what happened after the limit of the "until" was reached. (Since there is no real proof of an Aramaic original behind Matthew's account, there is no sense to prolonged discussion of the thesis of Krämer, "Menschwerdung," 37–40, that *heōs hou* is a mistranslation of *'ad dī:* "Although he had not known her, still she bore a son." See the refutation by Vögtle, "Mt 1,25," 34–36.) The immediate context favors a lack of future implication here, for Matthew is concerned only with stressing Mary's virginity before the child's birth, so that the Isaian prophecy will be fulfilled: it is as a virgin that Mary will give birth to her son. As for the marital situation after the birth of the child, in itself this verse gives us no information whatsoever. In my judgment the question of Mary's remaining a virgin for the rest of her life belongs to post-biblical theology, and Matt 1:25 relates to that issue only when it is joined to two other passages in the Gospel (12:46–50; 13:55–56) where Mary is mentioned alongside the brothers (and sisters) of Jesus. In antiquity there were debates whether these were stepbrothers of Jesus (sons of Joseph by a previous marriage—*Protevangelium of James;* Epiphanius), or cousins (sons either of Joseph's brother or of Mary's sister—Jerome), or blood brothers (children of Joseph and Mary—Helvidius). Besides the question of fact, one has to ask whether Matthew was in a position to know the facts. Did he think that the brothers were children of Mary born after Jesus; and if so, was this simply an assumption on his part?

she gave birth to a son. Later Greek mss. add "her firstborn," a scribal borrowing from Luke 2:7. The OS[sin] adds "for him"; see the NOTE on "She will give birth to a son" in vs. 21.

he called. The Greek *ekalesen* does not specify whether the subject is "he" or "she." The OS[sin] took the subject as masculine; the OS[cur] took it as feminine. It is almost certainly masculine in light of vs. 21 where Joseph is told to name the child and in light of Matthew's thought that by accepting the child as his own Joseph gives Jesus a Davidic genealogy.

COMMENT

We shall begin the treatment of 1:18–25 with a discussion of the two themes that constitute Matthew's main message: who Jesus is and how this identity has been effected. Then we shall turn to the formula citation that Matthew has included in the scene to see how this reinforces the main themes of his message. Last of all, we shall analyze the pre-Matthean elements of the scene and Matthew's utilization of them in the service of his message.

A. *Matthew's Message: the Who and the How— a Christological Revelation*

This scene begins the actual narrative in Matthew's infancy account and thus to some extent points ahead. The angelic dream visions that commence here will be continued in ch. 2. Yet, to an equal extent 1:18–25 continues the theme of the genealogy. Even grammatically the opening vs. 18 (see NOTE), "Now, as for [Jesus] Christ, his birth took place in this way," refers back to the first verse of the genealogy, "The *birth* record of *Jesus Christ*" (1:1) and to the unexpected last verse, "Joseph, the husband of Mary; of her was begotten Jesus, called the Christ"—unexpected because it did not read "Joseph begot [or was the father of] Jesus, called the Christ." Matthew is now going to explain to us the reason for this departure from the usual formula of the genealogy. It is this pointing backwards that has caused Stendahl to classify 1:18–25 as "the enlarged footnote to the crucial point in the genealogy."[1] However, I do not think that such a classification does sufficient justice to the progression of thought involved in the scene. It is now time to justify my contention in § 2, B2, that the theme of ch. 1 goes beyond the *Quis* (Who) of the genealogy. The scene in 1:18–25 goes onto a deeper *Quis*—not merely the son of David, but the Son of God—and to the *Quomodo* (How) of both identities.

1. The *Quis*: Who Jesus Is

The genealogy has told the reader that Jesus is "son of David" and "son of Abraham." Matthew leaves the "son of Abraham" motif and its Gentile

---

1 Stendahl, "Quis," 102.

connections until the story of the magi in ch. 2, and concentrates first on Jesus as son of David. In so doing, he moves to a motif of divine sonship. To understand this some general background is needed.

Matthew shows a particular interest in the title "son of David" for Jesus. John never uses it, and Mark and Luke use it only four times;[2] but Matthew uses it a total of ten times.[3] In fact it is not uncommon to find the affirmation that for Matthew "son of David" is the most important title applied to the Jesus of the ministry,[4] with such titles as "Lord" or "Son of Man" kept principally for the exalted or risen Jesus. This claim is somewhat exaggerated. It is true that Matthew confines "son of David" to the earthly career of Jesus, a sign that the title does not capture the mystery revealed through the resurrection—the mystery of a Jesus to whom all power in heaven and earth has been given (Matt 28:18). Yet, "son of David" is not even a title that captures the mystery of the earthly Jesus. It is chiefly given to him by outsiders when they come to recognize him as the Messiah because of the miraculous healings he has performed, but it is never used by Jesus himself or by his close disciples and thus it never signifies an intimate penetration of Jesus' identity. In passages like 22:41–46 (see Appendix II), the Matthean Jesus, while not denying Davidic sonship, points to an exalted status for the Messiah, a status that cannot be explained by mere descent from David, since the Messiah has a lordship even over David. Thus, "son of David" is a correct but inadequate title for the Jesus of the Matthean ministry. A comparison of Matt 22:41–46 and 16:16–17 shows that the adequate answer to the question, "What do you think of the Messiah—whose son is he?", is not "son of David" but "Son of God."[5]

In § 1, A2, I discussed in general the "backwards development" of NT christology whereby the evaluation of Jesus that came to Christian consciousness after the resurrection was gradually read back and allowed to interpret the Jesus of the ministry.[6] But let me concentrate here on that backwards development in relation to divine sonship. Association of the title "Son of God" with the risen Jesus was part of early Christian creedal affirmation; see the contrast between "son of David" and "son of God" in

2 In two passages: two times in Mark 10:47–48=Luke 18:38–39; and two times in Mark 12:35–37=Luke 20:41–44. The respective Matthean parallels are 20:30–31; 22:41–45.

3 Besides the four times mentioned in the previous note, which are taken over from Mark, there are 1:1 and five additional passages in the ministry: 9:27; 12:23; 15:22; 21:9,15. See Kingsbury, *Matthew*, 99–103; Gibbs, "Purpose"; Suhl, "Davidssohn." Also the bibliography of Appendix II.

4 See Bornkamm, *Tradition*, 32–33; Strecker, *Weg*, 118–20, corrected by Kingsbury, "Title."

5 For a discussion of the title "Son of God" in Matthew, see Pesch, "Gottessohn"; Kingsbury, *Matthew*, 40–83.

6 Perhaps it is worth reaffirming here that orthodox Christians need have no conflict with such a thesis of a growing retrospective evaluation of Jesus, provided it is understood that the evaluation involves an appreciation of a reality that was already there—Jesus was who he was during his lifetime, even if it took his followers centuries to develop a partially adequate theological vocabulary in which to articulate his greatness.

Rom 1:3–4. By the time the Gospels were written (the last one-third of the first century), it was well established that Jesus was Son of God not only after the resurrection but already during his ministry. Mark 1:11 has a heavenly voice declare Jesus' divine sonship at the time of his baptism. But in Mark that declaration provides information for the *reader* of the Gospel; it does not inform Jesus' disciples since they never recognize Jesus as God's Son during his lifetime.[7] The first believing confession of divine sonship comes after Jesus dies.[8] Matthew differs sharply from Mark on this point; for in several scenes that he shares with Mark, Matthew introduces confessions by the disciples that Jesus is the Son of God. Compare Mark 6:51–52 with Matt 14:32–33; and Mark 8:29 with Matt 16:16. The latter scene is particularly important, for it illustrates the adequacy of confessing Jesus as Son of God. Jesus blesses Peter for that confession and declares that it is not a human insight but a revelation from "my Father in heaven" (Matt 16:17).

This same relationship between "son of David" (true but inadequate) and "Son of God" (revealed as adequate) which exists in the Matthean account of the ministry is found in the infancy narrative. Jesus is truly "son of David" as the genealogy shows, a sonship the "how" of which 1:18–25 will spell out. The genealogy, however, being basically an OT witness, cannot do more than establish the divinely intended Davidic character of the Messiah. The fact that Jesus is "God with us" comes not from the genealogy but from a divine revelation through "an angel of the Lord" (see NOTE). Originally in Christian thought, it was God's raising Jesus from the dead that brought the designation of Jesus as God's Son (Rom 1:4: He was "designated Son of God in power through a Spirit of Holiness as of resurrection from the dead"). Then it was God's voice at the baptism and the concomitant descent of the Holy Spirit (Matt 3:16–17). Here it is God appearing in His customary guise as "an angel of the Lord" to tell Joseph of the action of the Holy Spirit. It is noteworthy how consistent the christological language has remained in this development, a language involving divine revelation, and the designation of Jesus as related to God, and the action of the Holy Spirit. Joseph can acknowledge Jesus by naming him, and that makes him "son of David"; the Holy Spirit has to act and God has to designate Jesus through revelation to make him "Son of God."[9]

---

[7] Jesus is confessed as Son of God by demons in Mark 3:11 and 5:7 because, though evil, they have a "supernatural" insight into realities.

[8] The centurion's confession at the end of the Gospel in 15:39 ("Truly this man was the Son of God!") may be contrasted to the deepest but quite inadequate disciple's confession halfway through the Gospel: Peter's confession "You are the Messiah" in 8:29.

[9] It is true that the title "Son of God" does not appear in 1:18–25; yet the theme of divine sonship is present there because "begotten . . . through the Holy Spirit" is offered as a counterexplanation to human parentage in 1:20. The fact that Isa 7:14 gives Jesus the revealed name Emmanuel, "God with us," may have constrained Matthew from giving Jesus

In the formula of Rom 1:3–4 the two titles "son of David" and "Son of God" are contrasted (yet see footnote 46, § 11); for Matthew, however, while one is more adequate than the other, the two are harmonious and interrelated. This is again understandable if we know the history of the terms, for divine sonship made its appearance in Israelite thought in relation to Davidic royal descent.[10] The constitution justifying the claims of the House of David was the promise of God by the mouth of Nathan the prophet: God would raise up a son after David and establish the throne of his kingdom forever; God would be a father to this king and the king would be God's son (II Sam 7:8–17).[11] Sonship here is in an adopted sense: the coronation of the king would make him God's representative before the people. If we may judge from Ps 2:7, at the moment of coronation a prophetic oracle explained to the people what God in heaven was saying of the king: "You are my son; today I have begotten you."

In early Christian preaching, the resurrection was looked on as the moment of the enthronement of Jesus: the moment when he was placed at God's right hand and made Lord and Messiah (Acts 2:32–36).[12] The very language of sitting at God's right hand (see also Matt 26:64) echoes the Davidic coronation psalm (110:1) where the prophetic oracle reports how God installs the king: "The Lord [God] said to my lord [the king], 'Sit at my right hand' " (see Matt 22:44).[13] This type of coronation psalm reference is applied verbatim to the resurrection of Jesus in Acts 13:32–33: "What God promised to the fathers, He has fulfilled for us their children by raising Jesus—as it is written in Ps 2: 'You are my Son; today I have begotten you.' " (See the use of the same citation in Hebr

another revealed title in this first scene. He holds off the specific designation of Jesus as God's Son until 2:15, where the revelation is attributed directly to "the Lord" rather than to an angel of the Lord. I shall explain in §§ 6 and 7 that the hostility of Herod, the chief priests, and the scribes against Jesus and the attempt on his life is Matthew's foreshadowing of the passion and death, while God's sparing Jesus by taking him to Egypt and bringing him back again is a foreshadowing of the resurrection. It may be significant that the title of the divine Son appears first in the Lord's dictum "Out of Egypt have I called my Son"; this may be a reminiscence of the post-resurrectional origins of that title.

10 The OT designation "son (sons, children) of God" had a wide range, describing angels (Job 1:6; Ps 29:1), the people of Israel collectively (Exod 4:22; Deut 14:1; Hosea 11:1), and the upright or pious (Sirach 4:10; Wisdom 2:18). But in terms of describing an individual in a precise role, the designation of the king as the divine son is the most prominent. This idea may have had pagan origins.

11 Precisely in light of the previous footnote, it is sometimes objected that while God calls the king His son (see also Ps 89:27–28[RSV 26–27]), the king never bears the title "son of God." I do not see this as a particularly significant observation, and it may now no longer be accurate. In the Dead Sea Scrolls (4QpsDan Aª or 4Q243) an enthroned king is called "the son of God" and "son of the Most High." J. A. Fitzmyer, NTS 20 (1973–74), 393, suggests that the reference is to a Jewish king.

12 I am not suggesting that in Acts Luke gives us an exact record of early Christian sermons delivered by Peter and Paul. Yet the christology of the sermons is more primitive than Luke's own christology and may echo or imitate early Christian kerygma. See S. Smalley, "The Christology of Acts," ExpTim 73 (1961–62), 358ff.

13 For the use of Ps 110 in reference to Jesus, see the literature cited in Appendix II, esp. Hay, *Glory*.

1:3–5.) When the christological declaration of divine sonship was moved
to the beginning of the ministry and to the baptism, the coronation language
was also moved. The voice from heaven that speaks over Jesus at the baptism, saying "You are my beloved Son" (Mark 1:11), combines the "You
are my son" of Ps 2:7 with the beloved servant motif of Isa 42:1. In the
Western tradition of Luke 3:22 the reference to Ps 2 is made more explicit
since the voice goes on to say, "Today I have begotten you." Now, the
begetting of Jesus as God's Son was clearly figurative[14] when it was attached to the resurrection or the baptism. (There may have been a
symbolic connection between coming forth from the tomb or from the
water and coming forth from the womb. That the death and resurrection
of Jesus was a type of messianic birth is implied in John 16:20–23 and
Rev 12:5. And NT thought frequently associates baptism with participation in the death and resurrection of the Lord and with coming forth as
reborn or as a "new man.") But when the complex of Davidic messiahship
and divine sonship is moved back to the conception of Jesus, the imagery
of begetting is now in a context where it is capable of a more realistic
sense. Yet, neither in Matthew or Luke does the divine begetting of Jesus
become a sexual begetting. The Holy Spirit (see NOTE on vs. 18) is the
agency of God's creative power, not a male partner in a marriage between
a deity and a woman (*hieros gamos*).

When Matthew tells us that Jesus, who through Joseph's acknowledgment is the descendant of the royal Davidic line, has been begotten in
the womb of a virgin through God's Holy Spirit, he sees a very tight connection between Davidic and divine sonship. For Matthew it is a most literal fulfillment of the promise of God to David through Nathan: "I shall
raise up *your son* after you. . . . I shall be his father, and he will be *my
son.*" As we shall see, the formula citation of Isa 7:14, dealing both with
the House of David and with God's presence among his people, reinforces
the connection. Before Jesus has ever raised the problem, Matthew in the
infancy narrative has told the reader that, although the messianic king is
David's son, David can call him "Lord" (Matt 22:41–46).

Before we leave the discussion of the "Who'" element in 1:18–25, we
should notice that besides the designations "son of David" and "Emmanuel," there is an identity involved in the name "Jesus" itself, a name
which Matthew carefully interprets for us (1:21). While the covenant
with David was important in OT history, it was only a modification of the

---

14 The Dead Sea Scrolls have shown us that the figurative use of the divine begetting of
the Messiah may have been fairly wide in Judaism and have certainly disproved the contention of those who maintained that it was necessarily borrowed by Christians from pagan
sources or that is was known only in Greek-speaking Judaism. In the context of a banquet,
presumably an eschatological banquet (and therefore, a context where "begetting" is clearly
figurative), we have a provision for the possibility that God may *beget* the Messiah (1QSa
2:11).

great covenant with Israel ratified through Moses. We saw in § 4B that the story underlying Matt 1:18 – 2:33 is the story of Moses in Egypt; and so it is not surprising that Moses motifs, so important on the pre-Matthean level, surface here. The role that Jesus will have ("he will save his people from their sins") is parallel to the role that Moses would have, for according to Josephus God told Moses' father in a dream that the child would "deliver the Hebrew race from their bondage in Egypt."[15] Yet, while Moses did deliver God's people from Egypt, it was not he but Joshua who led the people into the promised land. Jesus, whose name is a form of Joshua (see NOTE on vs. 21), is like Moses in being spared as an infant from the murderous plans of a wicked king; but in his lifetime his accomplishments will match those of Joshua as well. The fact that he is given this name before birth underlines the motif of divine preparation that has dominated the genealogy.[16]

2. The Quomodo or the "How" of Jesus' Identity

The section in 1:18–25 not only tells us that Jesus is son of David and "God with us," but also tells us how that came about. The "How" of Davidic sonship is through the agency of Joseph. We have seen that Matthew uses the title "son of David" for Jesus more frequently than do the other NT authors; but Matt 1:20, "Joseph, son of David," is the only instance in the NT of the title being applied to someone other than Jesus. Having drawn attention to Joseph as the source of Jesus' Davidic descent, Matthew takes pains to stress that this descent was not communicated through normal sexual relations between husband and wife. He is so careful on this point that he violates the normal pattern of angelic revelation whereby the reader should learn of God's action through the words addressed to the visionary. Although Joseph learns from the angel that the child is through the agency of the Holy Spirit, Matthew refuses to allow the reader to misunderstand Mary's situation the way Joseph does in 1:19. Rather he tells the reader ahead of time in 1:18 that Mary's pregnancy is through the Holy Spirit. If Matthew rules out any human sexual agent in the begetting of the child, he goes further by denying sexual relations between Mary and Joseph after the child has been conceived (1:25). Davidic descendancy is to be transferred not through natural paternity but through legal paternity.

For Matthew this is emphatically *God's will,* since the two steps in the legal paternity are dictated by the angel and carried out by Joseph exactly

15 *Ant.* II ix 3;⁂216. See § 4, footnote 44.
16 Plummer, *Luke,* 13, cites rabbinic tradition (unidentified) that the names of six were given before birth: Isaac, Ishmael, Moses, King Solomon, King Josiah, and the Messiah. Four of the six appear in the Matthean genealogy.

"as the angel of the Lord had commanded him" (1:24).[17] The first step is: "Do not be afraid to take Mary your wife into your home." By doing this rather than divorcing Mary as he had proposed (1:19), Joseph assumes public responsibility for the mother and the child who is to be born. The second and more important step is: "You will call his name Jesus." By naming the child, Joseph acknowledges him as his own. The Jewish position on this is lucidly clear and is dictated by the fact that sometimes it is difficult to determine who begot a child biologically. Since normally a man will not acknowledge and support a child unless it is his own, the law prefers to base paternity on the man's acknowledgment. The Mishna *Baba Bathra* 8:6 states the principle: "If a man says, 'This is my son,' he is to be believed." Joseph, by exercising the father's right to name the child (cf. Luke 1:60–63), acknowledges Jesus and thus becomes the legal father of the child.[18]

Legal paternity is not an easy concept for the non-Semite. The whole idea of levirate marriage (Appendix I) strikes us as odd because offspring are attributed to the dead father, not to the biological father. In NOTES on 1:16,20,25 I have reported that the Syriac Sinaiticus (OS[sin]) translation does not hesitate to say that Joseph begot Jesus, and that Mary gave birth to a son *to Joseph*. Modern commentators have often jumped to the conclusion that such a translation was denying the virginal conception, even though OS[sin] firmly describes Mary as a virgin. The seeming contradiction disappears if we realize that the OS[sin] translator (presumably a Semite translating into a Semitic language) did not deny the virginal conception but accepted legal paternity as real paternity. Another example of the failure to appreciate the reality of legal paternity is the contention that basically the genealogy and 1:18–25 are contradictory and of separate origin, on the grounds that if someone traced a genealogy through Joseph, he must have believed Joseph to be the biological father. Stendahl may not do sufficient justice to 1:18–25 by speaking of it as a footnote to the crucial point in the genealogy, but his instinct for joining the two parts of ch. 1 is much to be preferred to any theory of contradiction between them.[19]

17 If one studies the pattern of the angelic dream appearances in Table VI, such a specification is not found in reporting Joseph's actions after the second and third angelic visitations. Thus, its inclusion here by Matthew is quite deliberate and is reminiscent of his style in 21:4–6 where, after a formula citation (comparable to 1:22–23), we are told, "The disciples went and did as Jesus had commanded them." The pattern for such a clause is found also in the OT, e.g., "They went and did as the Lord had commanded them" (LXX Job 42:9; see also Exod 1:17; Num 20:27). Davis, "Tradition," 421, therefore, treats it as pre-Matthean in 1:24; I would regard it as Matthean imitation of OT style.

18 Legal father is a better designation than foster father or adoptive father. Joseph does not adopt someone else's son as his own; he acknowledges his wife's child as his legitimate son, using the same formula by which other Jewish fathers acknowledged their legitimate children.

19 A milder form of the contradiction theory is the paradoxical relationship that Helen Milton, "Structure," would find between the two parts. Jesus' origins are supernatural according to 1:18–25; yet he is no phantom, as some Gnostic thought would contend, since

The two parts of Matt 1 (the genealogy of Jesus introduced by the rubric *biblos geneseōs* in 1:1, and the narrative about Jesus introduced in 1:18 by the rubric "Now, as for [Jesus] Christ, his birth [*genesis*] took place *in this way*") fit together just as smoothly as do the genealogy from Adam to Noah in Gen 5:1–32 (introduced by the rubric *biblos geneseōs* in 5:1) and the narrative about Noah (introduced in 6:9 by the rubric "Now, *these* are the generations [*genesis*] of Noah").[20] Indeed, Matthew's two ways of telling us about the *genesis* of Jesus, by a numerically structured genealogy followed by a narrative, may be compared to the two genesis or origin accounts in Gen 1:1ff. and Gen 2:4ff., the first being the numerical pattern of the creation of six days, the second being the narrative account.[21]

With much less detail Matthew narrates the "How" of Jesus' other identity as "God with us" or Son of God. This sonship is through the Holy Spirit. Under the "Who" of divine sonship I have already discussed the way in which the divine declaration of Jesus' identity, the agency of the Holy Spirit, and begetting are interlocked in christological thought about the resurrection, about the baptism, and finally about the conception. While Matthew reflects this tradition of interlocked ideas in his angelic declaration about the child "begotten . . . through the Holy Spirit," he is much less specific about the "How" of the Holy Spirit's action than is Luke 1:35, where, as we shall see in Book Two, the echoes of early Christian kerygmatic formulas are stronger.[22]

The fact that Matthew can speak of Jesus as "begotten" (passive of *gennan*) in 1:16,20,[23] suggests that for him the conception through the agency of the Holy Spirit is the *becoming* of God's Son. In tracing the "backwards" application of christological language (see the texts in § 1, A2), one observes that, besides "beget," the verbs "make" (Acts 2:36), "elevate" (5:31), "designate" (Rom 1:4), and "give [a name] to" (Philip

the genealogy in 1:1–17 shows that he has human ancestors. However, there is little evidence of an anti-Gnostic motif in Matthew.

20 The similarity to Matthew is heightened if we note that the next clause in Gen 6:9 states "Noah was an upright man" (*anthrōpos dikaios*) just as the next verse in Matthew states "Joseph was an upright man" (*anēr dikaios*).

21 While I believe that Matthew understands the action of the Holy Spirit in the begetting of Jesus as a creative rather than a sexual action, I hesitate to use the analogy between Matt 1 and Gen 1–2 to argue that Matthew is thinking of the Spirit of God that moved over the waters in Gen 1:2. (See Davies, *Setting*, 70–72.) The reference to the Holy Spirit came to Matthew (indirectly) from early christology, and we do not have enough evidence to know what, if any, specific OT background it may have evoked.

22 Yet, while Luke stresses the supernatural element in the "How" more eloquently than Matthew does, neither author has the kind of biological interest in the virginal conception that marks subsequent discussions. In my judgment, both Matthew and Luke think that Jesus was conceived without human father, but are more interested in theological import than in historicity. Accordingly, the broader questions of historicity raised in later theology will be reserved till Appendix IV.

23 The present passive of *gennan* appears in reference to Jesus in Luke 1:35 but seemingly with the connotation of birth: "The child to be born" (see NOTE there).

2:9) are used to describe the way in which the christological titles came to
Jesus from God after the resurrection (or exaltation). This vocabulary, at
least sometimes, reflects a stage of thought wherein Jesus *became* God's
Son (or Messiah or Lord) only at the resurrection—a thought pattern
corrected by the movement of the christological moment to the baptism.
Yet, even after this correction, the divine baptismal declaration of Jesus as
Son without any prehistory (as in Mark 1:11), left open the possibility of
understanding the baptism as an adoption,[24] so that Jesus would not have
been God's Son before the baptism. This impression has been corrected by
the further movement of the christological moment to conception, as
witnessed in Matthew's and Luke's infancy narratives. However, there was
another direction in the backwards movement of the christological moment in early Christian thought, a movement toward pre-existence, exemplified best in the hymns of the NT (Philip 2:6; Col 1:15; John
1:1).[25] Conception christology and pre-existence christology were two
different answers to adoptionism. In the former, God's creative action in
the conception of Jesus (attested negatively by the absence of human
fatherhood) begets Jesus as God's Son. Clearly here divine sonship is not
adoptive sonship, but there is no suggestion of an incarnation whereby a
figure who was previously with God takes on flesh. Incarnational thought
is indicative of pre-existence christology ("emptied himself taking on the
form of a servant"; "the Word became flesh"); and works reflecting that
christology show no awareness of or interest in the manner of Jesus' conception. For pre-existence christology the conception of Jesus is the beginning of an earthly career, but not the begetting of God's Son. It is no accident that John never speaks of the "begetting" of Jesus,[26] for Jesus simply
is ("I AM"). I stress this difference between conception christology and
pre-existence christology, because Christian theology soon harmonized the
two ideas, so that the pre-existent Word of God was described as taking
flesh (John) in the womb of the virgin Mary (Matthew and Luke).[27] The
virginal conception was no longer seen as the begetting of God's Son but

24 I do not think that Mark intended an adoptionist christology, but the ambiguous description of the baptism was the mainstay of adoptionism in early Christianity.

25 See also John 17:5. These texts may represent different forms of pre-existence
christology, e.g., pre-existence after creation as an Adam-like figure in the image of God, or
pre-existence as the firstborn of all creation, or pre-existence before creation. Some scholars
do not think that Philip 2:6 refers to pre-existence.

26 The only indisputable instance of *gennan* used of Jesus is John 18:37, where it has the
sense of being "born," as the parallelism with "I have come into the world" shows. The singular reading "he who was begotten" in 1:13 (rather than "those who were begotten") is
not attested in any Greek ms., and it is uncertain that *ho gennētheis* in I John 5:18 refers
to Jesus (see footnote 10, Appendix IV). That the Johannine *monogenēs* does not mean
"only begotten," see Brown, ABJ, 13.

27 This thought process is probably already at work at the beginning of the second century in Ignatius of Antioch (Hoben, *Virgin Birth*, 20–21). It is clear in Aristides *Apology* xv
1; Justin *Apology* I xxi and xxxiii; and Melito of Sardis *Discourse on Faith* 4 (*Corpus
Apologetarum* 9:420).

as the incarnation of God's Son, and that became orthodox Christian doctrine (Appendix IV).

If in both Matthew and Luke the Holy Spirit is the main agent in the begetting of God's Son, it is also in relation to this sonship that Mary plays her role—a minor role in the Matthean infancy narrative, a major role in the Lucan. We saw that the two steps in the "How" of Davidic sonship were actions of Joseph explicitly commanded by the angel (Matt 1:20-21: "Do not be afraid to take Mary your wife into your home . . . you will call his name Jesus"). The same angelic command spells out Mary's role in the "How" of divine sonship: "She will give birth to a son"; "the child begotten in her . . . through the Holy Spirit." But Matthew's narrative offers no more detail than that. The fact that Mary is a virgin is mentioned specifically only in the formula citation (to be discussed below) —a notable difference from Luke's insistence on Mary's virginal state (1:27 [two times]; 1:34). Matthew does not stress the virginal conception as a miracle but as the fulfillment of God's plan made known in prophecy. Beyond that, Matthew sees it simply as the other side of the coin of the "How" of Davidic sonship, i.e., a sonship not through sexual relations with Joseph, but through acknowledgment by Joseph. On the whole, then, the two parents have a harmonious role in making Jesus who he is. Although they do not join physically in the begetting, Joseph is the one through whom Jesus is begotten as son of David, and Mary is the one through whom he is begotten as Son of God. Matthew has made the theme of a divinely arranged conception support, rather than destroy, the concept of human genealogical descent.

While Matthew's discussion of this double "How" is primarily theological, we cannot overlook the possibility of an apologetic motif in his presentation. In Appendix V we shall see the history of the Jewish charge that Jesus was illegitimate. *If* that charge were already in circulation when Matthew was writing, his narrative could be read as an effective response to it, even as the peculiarly Matthean narrative of the guard at the tomb (27:62-66; 28:11-15) constituted an effective response to the Jewish charge that Jesus' disciples had stolen his body from the tomb. (For a structural resemblance between the two narratives, see footnote 21 in § 4.) If the marital situation between Joseph and Mary were not a fact and could have been created according to the dictates of Christian imagination, it is difficult to see why a situation less open to scandal was not contrived.[28] For instance, instead of picturing Mary as already pregnant, the

---

[28] It is true that in Hellenistic literature favorable to heroes or immortals, sometimes a superficially scandalous birth situation is part of the legend. In Plutarch's *Romulus,* the mother is a vestal virgin who is discovered to be with child, and she would have been punished had not the king's daughter mediated for her. In the biography of Alexander the Great by Pseudo-Callisthenes, his mother becomes pregnant while his father Philip is away from home. (The reader finds out that in both cases it is by intervention of the gods.) How-

narrator could have imagined her as betrothed to Joseph but without child. Then he could have had the angel of the Lord appear and begin his message with "Joseph, son of David, hasten to take Mary your wife into your home." Everything else in 1:20–25 could follow, and there would be no hint of scandal. (Basically, the setting in Luke is exactly like the one I have just presented, with the exception that the angel appears to Mary.) However, as Matthew's account now stands, it means that Jesus will necessarily be born early after the parents come to live together—too early to escape notice and gossip. But suppose that the marriage situation and the pregnancy as described were historical facts rather than the product of imagination, then we can understand why a charge of illegitimacy arose among Jesus' opponents, a charge that may be foreshadowed in 1:18–19. In responding to this charge, Matthew would not have been free to change the fact that Jesus was born noticeably early. But he could brand the Jewish interpretation of that fact as calumny and offer a (or the) Christian explanation of it.[29] His naming the four OT women in the genealogy would have been part of the same apologetic. There was something extraordinary or irregular in the unions of those women with their partners (see § 3, A3). Yet they played an important role in God's plan and were instruments of His providence (or of the Holy Spirit). If to outsiders their lives seemed scandalous (as in the case of Tamar), it was through them that the blessed lineage of the Messiah was continued. The same is true of Mary, Matthew would be arguing; but instead of continuing the line of the Messiah, her pregnancy had brought it to fulfillment.

B. *The Formula Citation of Isaiah 7:14*

Thus far I have interpreted Matthew's message in 1:18–25 without major reference to the clearest guide he has given us, namely, the indicator that "the birth of [Jesus] Christ . . . took place in this way" (1:18) "to fulfill what the Lord had spoken by the prophet" (1:22). It is now time to study how well the prophetic guidance corresponds to my deduction from the context, namely, that Matthew is concerned with the Who and the

---

ever, I am not sure that such parallels remove the element of scandal in Matthew's account. Matthew's world view and that of his opponents is not one in which deities have sexual relations with men or women and beget children. He is in confrontation with Pharisees and in his account of the ministry he is most careful not to give them anything they can use against Jesus (e.g., his omitting the spittle miracle narrated in Mark 8:22–26). If the situation described in Matthew is not a factual one but is the product of Christian romantic imagination, one must deem it a great religious blunder; for it gave rise to the charge of illegitimacy against Jesus that was the mainstay of anti-Christian polemic for many centuries.

29 In the second century we find the explanation circulating among Jewish Christians (whom eventually Gentile Christians regarded as heretical) that Jesus was the natural son of Joseph.

How of Jesus' identity as an instruction to his Christian community of Jews and Gentiles, and possibly as a refutation of the calumny circulating among their adversaries.[80] In order to do that well, I shall have to ask the reader to work through with me the details of Matthew's handling of Isa 7:14, his first formula citation (see § 4A).

1. The Placing of the Citation

Occurring where it does, the citation in 1:22–23 is intrusive in the flow of the narrative. In my translation I have set it off as a paragraph to show that 24–25 is the real continuation of the angelic appearance in 20–21 and that 22–23 is obviously an insertion—a characteristic of formula citations in the infancy narrative as we have seen. Yet, why does Matthew insert this citation so awkwardly in the middle of the narrative?[81] Why does he not follow the procedure that he will establish in 2:15,17–18,23 of inserting his formula citations at the end of episodes? In other words, why does he not place the formula citation after 1:24–25 when Joseph has fulfilled the angel's command and Mary has given birth to the promised son? The most plausible explanation is that Matthew wanted the episode to end with the words with which it now ends: "He [Joseph] called his name Jesus." This would be in harmony with the emphasis that we have diagnosed on the "Who" and the "How" of Davidic sonship. If the formula citation had been placed at the end, the Davidic emphasis would have been obscured; for the climactic line would have been: "They will call his name Emmanuel [which means 'God with us']." While Matthew is interested in the divine element in the identity of Jesus, as indicated in the interpretation "God with us" which he supplies, he is not interested in Emmanuel precisely as a name. It reappears neither in the infancy narrative nor in the rest of the Gospel.[82]

In any case, the arrangement that results from the insertion of Isa 7:14 into the middle of the scene is peculiarly Matthean. The same pattern is

---

[80] In discussing Matthew's message, I have stressed as his main goal didactic explanation for a believing community, with apologetic refutation as possibly a secondary motif. Davies, *Setting*, 66–67, argues that the infancy narrative is not primarily didactic but kerygmatic—a kerygma, however, not directed to the world but to the Church to whom it expounds the mystery of the Lord through his birth. I would agree with Davies' analysis of the audience and the goal, but I hesitate to call the method kerygmatic. The systematic inclusion of formula citations and the numbered genealogy are not indicative of a proclamation to arouse belief (which is what I understand by kerygma) but more the mark of a teaching technique designed to offer background for those who already believe.

[81] The position is so strange that, since the time of Irenaeus, commentators (including Zahn and B. Weiss) have suggested that we are to look on the formula citation as the words of the angel! Nowhere in the Bible does an angel cite Scripture in this fashion.

[82] The inclusion between 1:23 and the end of the Gospel in 28:20 is not based precisely on Emmanuel but on Matthew's interpretation of the name as "God with us"—"*I am with you* all days till the end of the world."

found in 21:1–7, where we can see Matthew's editorial hand by comparison with Mark 11:1–7.[33] The pattern may be schematized thus:

Setting of the scene:	1:18–19	21:1
Command:	1:20–21	21:2–3
Formula citation:	1:22–23	21:4–5
Execution of the command:	1:24–25	21:6–7

Within this pattern the closest parallels are the style of the insertion of the formula citation, and the statement about doing what had been commanded (see footnote 17 above).

2. Isaiah 7:14 in the Hebrew and Greek Bibles

The text of Matthew's citation of Isa 7:14 may be compared to the text of the prophet in the MT and the translation in the LXX, thus:

Matt: "Behold the virgin [*parthenos*] will be with child [*en gastri hexei*]
and will give birth to a son,
and they will call his name Emmanuel."

LXX: "Behold the virgin [*parthenos*] will conceive [*en gastri lēpsetai*][34]
and will give birth to a son,
and you [sing.] will call his name Emmanuel."

MT: "Behold the young girl ['*almâ*] is (will be) with child
and will give birth to a son,[35]
and she will call his name Emmanuel."

The variation between "young girl" (MT) and "virgin" (LXX, Matt) has given rise to some of the most famous debates in the history of exegesis, ranging from debates between Jews and Christians as early as Justin's *Dialogue with Trypho* in the mid-second century,[36] to debates provoked by

33 See Pesch, "Ausführungsformel."

34 Codices Alexandrinus and Sinaiticus of the LXX read *hexei* (literally, "*have* in the womb") rather than *lēpsetai* (literally, "*receive* in the womb"). This reading presumably represents a Christian scribe's adaptation of the Isaian LXX text to Matthew's wording of it. However, J. Zeigler, the distinguished LXX specialist, has accepted *hexei* as the correct reading in the Göttingen edition of the LXX.

35 Although I have offered the same translation "give birth" in the MT and the Greek, there is no mention of the womb in the Hebrew as there is in the Greek (see preceding NOTE). We are dealing with the idioms of two different languages for saying the same thing, and so the difference is not significant.

36 In *Dialogue* lxvii 1, Trypho the Jew tells Justin: "The passage is not, 'Behold the *virgin* will conceive and will give birth to a son,' but, 'Behold the *young girl* will conceive and will give birth to a son.'"

ultraconservative readers of the RSV translation in 1952.[37] In part these debates reflect different understandings of the nature of prophecy. Before the advent of the modern critical method it was generally accepted by religious Jews and Christians that the Hebrew prophets foresaw the distant future. In particular, Christians thought that the prophets had foreseen the life and circumstances of Jesus the Messiah. A prime example of this was Isa 7:14 where the reading "virgin" seemed to imply that, 700 years before Jesus, the prophet had predicted a virginal conception, something unparalleled in history that would have had to involve foreknowledge of Jesus' conception.[38] The OT prophecy and the NT event gave each other support. The NT fulfillment verified the conception of prophecy as prediction and proved that God had planned the whole history of salvation; the OT prophecy helped to establish the facticity of the NT event. The reaction to the RSV showed that, for many, to deny that Isaiah was thinking of a virginal conception was to deny that the virginal conception of Jesus took place.

However, this conception of prophecy as prediction of the distant future has disappeared from most serious scholarship today, and it is widely recognized that the NT "fulfillment" of the OT involved much that the OT writers did not foresee at all.[39] The OT prophets were primarily concerned with addressing God's challenge to their own times. If they spoke about the future, it was in broad terms of what would happen if the challenge was accepted or rejected. While they sometimes preached a "messianic" deliverance (i.e., deliverance through one *anointed* as God's representative, thus a reigning king or even a priest), there is no evidence that they foresaw with precision even a single detail in the life of Jesus of Nazareth.[40] If one accepts this approach, the following remarks about the MT and LXX form of Isa 7:14 are appropriate.

[37] The RSV was burned by fundamentalists in some parts of the United States because it used "young woman" rather than "virgin" in Isa 7:14–a sign to the book burners that the translators were denying the virginal conception of Jesus! The reading "virgin" was imposed by a decision of the American bishops on the reluctant Catholic translators of the NAB.

[38] Justin, *Dialogue* lxvi 3, states: "Now it is plain that in the race of Abraham according to the flesh, no one has ever been born from a virgin, nor has been said to be so born, save this our Christ."

[39] For the notion of fulfillment see footnote 3, § 4. One must not assume that the modern analysis, although it may be factually correct, was the view shared by Jesus or his contemporaries. The Qumran sectarians, who were responsible for the Dead Sea Scrolls and whose community existed from *ca.* 140 B.C. to A.D. 70, thought that the ancient prophets, like Habakkuk, had foretold the existence of the Qumran group and written about its history and destiny line by line. The Pharisees and their successors, the rabbis, thought that, since every important event was intended by God, it must be found in the Scriptures. Thus, Matthew's insistence on fulfillment in Jesus is typical in its presupposition of prophetic foresight.

[40] Those who accept a theory of inspiration wherein a distinction is made between the divine author and the human author, sometimes posit a "fuller sense" of Scripture, i.e., a predictive sense of the *words* of the prophets (NOTE on vs. 22), not clearly known by them but intended by God. See JBC, article 71, ##32ff., esp. 56–70.

The Hebrew form of Isa 7:14. The interpretation of this passage by modern scholars may be summarized under these points:

▪It was to the wicked King Ahaz (ca. 735–715 B.C.) that Isaiah spoke the oracle involved in 7:14. It was intended as a sign to this disbelieving monarch during the Syro-Ephraimite war of 734[41] and must refer to something that took place during that year or shortly thereafter.

▪The child to be born was not *the* Messiah, for messianism had not yet developed to the point of expecting a single future king (footnote 9, § 3).[42] Scholars are not agreed on the identity of the child, but *at most* it may refer to the birth of a Davidic prince who would deliver Judah from its enemies. An ancient Jewish interpretation, known to Justin (*Dialogue* lxvii 1) identified the child as Hezekiah, Ahaz' son and successor, one of the few truly religious monarchs of the House of David.

▪The word *'almâ,* used to describe *the woman,* normally describes a young girl who has reached the age of puberty and is thus marriageable. It puts no stress on her virginity, although *de facto,* in the light of Israelite ethical and social standards, most girls covered by the range of this term would be virgins.[43]

▪The presence of the definite article, "the young girl," makes it likely that

41 The Aramean King Rezin of Damascus (Syria) and King Pekah of Israel (Ephraim: the Northern Kingdom) were organizing a revolt against Assyria, the "superpower." When King Ahaz of Judah refused to join the revolt, they turned on him, surrounded Jerusalem, and plotted to put a vassal on the throne of Judah. To save himself, Ahaz planned to appeal for aid to King Tiglath-Pileser of Assyria; but Isaiah opposed this, knowing that, while the Assyrians would destroy Judah's enemies, they would also reduce Judah to vassalage. Isaiah urged Ahaz to have faith in Yahweh's power to deliver Jerusalem and Judah, and he offered the king a sign from Yahweh. When the king refused, Isaiah angrily proclaimed that a sign would still be given to him—the sign of Isa 7:14. The name given to the child to be born, "Emmanuel," would incline us to think that the sign involved something beneficial for Judah, but the context in Isa 7:15ff. seems to predict disaster after the birth of the child. A supposition of editing and re-editing of his chapter of Isaiah is required in order to make sense of the whole picture.

42 When expectations of *the* Messiah did develop and many OT passages were reinterpreted as references to him, Isa 7:14 was *not* applied messianically in Jewish usage. A list of 456 such "messianic passages" is given in Edersheim, *Life,* II, 710–41; and Isa 7:14 is not among them. Knowing this, Justin, already in the second century, was accusing (correctly or incorrectly) Jewish scholars of tampering with OT evidence pertinent to the Messiah (*Dialogue* lxxi–lxxiii).

43 See Bratcher, "Study," for an accurate summary of the immense literature on this question. *'Almâ* is used only nine times in the Hebrew OT, and two passages demonstrate how poorly it would underline virginity: in Cant 6:8 it refers to women of the king's harem, and in Prov 30:19 an *'almâ* is the object of a young man's sexual attention. We have no clear instance in the OT of *'almâ* being applied to a woman already married, so that Martin Luther could still win the bet of 100 florins he was willing to make on that point. However, there is a Ugaritic text (*Keret* 128, II, 21–22) that puts the cognate word *ǧlmt* in poetic parallelism (and thus rough equivalence) with *'att,* "wife." The closeness of the two languages raises the possibility that in Hebrew as well, a young wife might be called an *'almâ.* Although it does not have the clinical precision of *virgo intacta,* the Hebrew word *betûlâ* is the normal word for "virgin." It appears some fifty times in the OT and seemingly never for a woman who is not literally a virgin (Ezek 23:1–8 and Joel 1:8 are debatable). The reference to a *betûlâ* giving birth in the "Hymn to Nikkal" (Ugaritic text 77, line 5) is now generally discounted as an incorrect reading, although line 7 still has the interesting *hl ǧlmt tld bn* ("Behold, the *'almâ* will give birth to a son").

Isaiah was referring to someone definite whose identity was known to him and to King Ahaz, perhaps someone whom the king had recently married and brought into the harem. The proposal that the '*almâ* was Isaiah's own wife, "the prophetess" mentioned in 8:3, is most unlikely; for the fact that she had already borne Isaiah a son old enough to walk with him (7:3) makes such a designation for her implausible.

■From the Hebrew participial construction it is not possible to know whether Isaiah meant that the '*almâ* was already pregnant or would become pregnant.[44] The birth, however, was almost certainly future; yet even in that judgment we are hampered by the temporal vagueness of the Hebrew conjugations.

In summary, the MT of Isa 7:14 does not refer to a virginal conception in the distant future. The sign offered by the prophet was the imminent birth of a child, probably Davidic, but naturally conceived, who would illustrate God's providential care for his people. The child would help to preserve the House of David and would thus signify that God was still "with us."

The Greek form of Isa 7:14. In Alexandria, some time in the last centuries before Jesus' birth, the LXX translator rendered '*almâ* by *parthenos*, a Greek word more regularly used to translate *bᵉtûlâ* (see footnote 43) and which normally means "virgin."[45] The normal rendering of '*almâ* would be *neanis*, "young woman";[46] and it is quite understandable that the post-LXX translations of the Hebrew Bible into Greek (Aquila, Symmachus, Theodotion), which are consistently closer to the MT, employed *neanis* in Isa 7:14. When the Jewish opponent of Justin tried to tell him that the Christians were misunderstanding Isa 7:14, he insisted that *neanis* and not *parthenos* was the correct rendering.[47] Granted this, surely the choice of *parthenos* by the LXX translator represented a deliberate preference for understanding the young woman of Isa 7:14 as a virgin.[48] But that should not lead us to jump to the conclusion that he was speaking of

[44] If we compare two OT scenes where this grammatical construction is used in a birth announcement to women, in Gen 16:11 the woman (Hagar) is already pregnant, while in Judg 13:3,5,7 the woman (mother of Samson) becomes pregnant afterwards.

[45] No more than *bᵉtûlâ* is *parthenos* so clinically exact that it necessarily means *virgo intacta*. The Liddell and Scott Greek Lexicon gives several instances of the secular use of *parthenos* for women who were not virgins. But the word seems to have become more specialized in later Greek (Bratcher, "Study," 112), and most of the sixty-five LXX usages are clear references to virgins.

[46] For example, Exod 2:8; Ps 68:26 (RSV 25); Prov 30:19; Cant 1:3; 6:8.

[47] *Dialogue* xliii 8, lxvii 1, lxxi 3, lxxxiv 3. However, the Jewish opponent never denies Justin's explicit claim that *parthenos* is the LXX reading; and so it can scarcely be claimed that the presence of *parthenos* in the LXX manuscripts (which were copied by Christians) is an interpolation from Matt 1:23.

[48] It is true that in one other instance, Gen 24:43, the LXX renders '*almâ* by *parthenos*, but that is not a good parallel for explaining the choice in Isa 7:14. The translator in Gen 24 is simply being consistent and using the word he had been using throughout for Rebekah; see *parthenos* in 24:14,16.

a virginal conception of the Messiah.[49] While, as we saw, the Hebrew is vague about whether the conception had already taken place or would take place in the future, the Greek is not vague and the conception is definitely future. Therefore, all that the LXX translator may have meant by "the virgin will conceive" is that a woman who is *now* a virgin will (by natural means, once she is united to her husband) conceive the child Emmanuel. He may have felt that the "sign" offered by Isaiah required more than that someone who was already pregnant would bear a child and that it would be more manifestly reflective of divine providence if a well-known woman who was still a virgin would become pregnant as Isaiah had prophesied. And so the LXX language makes it clear that the providential child to be born would be a firstborn.

For both the MT and the LXX, then, the sign offered by Isaiah was not centered on the manner in which the child would be conceived, but in the providential timing whereby a child who would be a sign of God's presence with His people was to be born precisely when that people's fortunes had reached their nadir. Neither the Hebrew nor the Greek of Isa 7:14 referred to the type of virginal conception of which Matthew writes, and his Christian use of the passage has added a great deal to the literal meaning. If my remarks have pointed toward a rejection of a naive or fundamentalist use of OT prophecy, they also constitute a rejection of an overly simple liberal explanation of how the idea of the virginal conception of Jesus arose. It has been suggested that reflection on Isa 7:14 and on its prediction that a virgin would give birth gave rise to Christian belief in the virginal conception of Jesus. I am maintaining that there was nothing in the Jewish understanding of Isa 7:14 that would give rise to such a belief nor, *a fortiori*, to the idea of a begetting through the creative activity of the Holy Spirit, an idea found explicitly in both Matthew and Luke but not in Isa 7:14. At most, reflection on Isa 7:14 colored the expression of an already existing Christian belief in the virginal conception of Jesus.[50]

3. The Matthean Use of Isaiah 7:14

If the Isaian prophecy did not give rise either to the idea of the virginal conception or to Matthew's narrative, nevertheless, its use by Matthew in that narrative is remarkably felicitous. Matthew saw in it scriptural support for both the Davidic and the divine aspects of the Who and the How of Jesus' identity. The Isaian verse immediately preceding (7:13) has

---

49 There is no evidence that the presence of *parthenos* in the LXX gave rise in Alexandrian Jewry to an expectation of the virginal conception of the Messiah. Despite claims to the contrary, Alexandrian paganism had no myths of virginal conceptions by the mothers of the Pharaohs—only myths of male gods *using their divine seed* to beget royal children of women. See Appendix IV, B1.

50 As we shall see, it is not clear to what extent, if at all, Isa 7:14 entered into Luke's description of the virginal conception.

Isaiah introduce his prophetic sign by addressing the king as "House of David." Matthew has been trying to explain that Jesus is truly of the House of David, a Davidic descent that is not at all negated by the fact that Joseph begot him legally rather than naturally. And here he has a text addressed to the House of David which speaks of a virgin being with child and giving birth to a son.[51] Not only through the women mentioned in the genealogy, but also through this virgin foretold in His word spoken by the prophet, God had prepared for the birth of Jesus the Messiah "in this way" (Matt 1:18). But Matthew has also been trying to explain that "this way," which involves the creative action of the Holy Spirit rather than the sexual action of a man, means that Jesus is God's Son as well as David's. And *mirabile dictu,* the same text that foretold to the House of David the unique manner in which the messianic child would be conceived also foretold that the child would be Emmanuel, "which means, 'God with us.' "[52] The same Lord who had laid out the genealogical record of the Messiah with meticulous mathematics (1:17) had planned the Who and the How of the genesis of the Messiah down to the last detail. And if there were those in Matthew's ken who were calumniating that genesis as illegitimacy, let them know that they were blaspheming against what the Lord Himself had spoken.[53]

Having seen that the citation of Isa 7:14 fits Matthew's theological (and perhaps apologetic) message, let us now turn to the details of his handling the text. (The reader is reminded of the general discussion of Matthew's originality in relation to formula citations in § 4, A3.) In three details he departs from the LXX form of Isa 7:14 as seen on p. 145 above: (1) the use of *hexei* rather than *lēpsetai;* (2) the third person plural "they will call," rather than "you [sing.] will call"; (3) the supplied interpretation of Emmanuel as "God with us." One by one we shall seek the explanation of these features.

---

[51] Lindars, *Apologetic,* 215, makes the interesting suggestion that Isa 7:14 was first used by Christians in its Hebrew form to support the Davidic origins of Jesus, and only later in its Greek form to support the virginal conception of Jesus.

[52] Just as one should not confuse the conception christology found in Matthew's and Luke's infancy narratives with the pre-existence christology of John's Prologue, as if one could speak of an incarnation in Matthew and Luke, so also one should not read "God with us" in a Nicaean sense, as if it were identifying Jesus as God. For Matthew Jesus is the expression of God's presence with His people, and to him God has given all power in heaven and on earth (28:18). Matthew's Gospel is not one of the NT works that begins to call Jesus "God"; and, of course, no NT work achieves the clarity of the Council of Nicaea in calling him "true God of true God." See R. E. Brown, "Does the New Testament Call Jesus God?" in *Jesus God and Man* (New York: Macmillan, 1967).

[53] These statements may seem odd to the reader after I have shown that, according to a critical analysis of prophecy, Isa 7:14 was not referring to Jesus or to the Messiah or to the virginal conception. But see footnotes 39 and 40 above. Matthew interpreted Scripture according to the religious presuppositions of his time, and it would be a naïve modern scholar who would deny that Matthew may have reached a truth unobtainable by critical analysis of the literal sense of Isa 7:14.

First, the use of hexei *rather than* lēpsetai. If *lēpsetai* is the original reading of the LXX (footnote 34), the simplest (but not a demonstrable) explanation of the Matthean reading is that he was using a variant Greek translation only partly similar to the LXX.[54] If the clause in Matt 1:18, "it was found that she was with child," belonged to one of the pre-Matthean strata (see § 4, B2), the appearance of *en gastri hexousa* there may have prompted him to adapt Isa 7:14 to agree. (Many, however, think that the adaptation was in the other direction, namely, that, finding *en gastri hexei* in Isa 7:14, Matthew wrote the clause in 1:18 to prepare for it.) My own suggestion is that the Matthean narrative, involving an annunciation of birth by the angel of the Lord, is highly evocative of the birth stories of the Patriarchs and the Judges, and that *en gastri echein* is a standard LXX idiom for pregnancy in those narratives (Gen 16:11; 17:17; Judg 13:3,7). Matthew wrote 1:18 in that idiom[55] and adapted the Isaian passage to match it.

Second, the use of "they will call" rather than "you will call." In this instance there is a greater possibility that Matthew used a Greek translation that varied from the LXX, for the LXX is a mistranslation. The MT has the consonants *qr't* which would normally represent a second person singular form of the verb "to call," whence the LXX reading "you will call." However, most scholars agree that here the Hebrew preserves an old third person feminine form: "she will call." Another possibility is that Matthew has corrected the LXX in light of the Hebrew, but not the Hebrew found in the MT. Another Hebrew reading appears in one of the Dead Sea Scrolls of Isaiah (1QIsa), namely, *qr'*, which may be translated "his name will be called"—a translation equivalent to Matthew's "they will call."[56] Perhaps the most commonly accepted explanation is that Matthew deliberately changed the LXX reading to suit his own narrative.[57] In that narrative the angel has already told Joseph, "You will call his name Jesus," and so it would be awkward to have the prophecy read, "You [Joseph] will

54 That there were two Greek forms of Isa 7:14 in Christian circulation is possible (see Lindars, *Apologetic*, 214).

55 As we shall see below, I do not rule out the possibility that the pre-Matthean stratum had a reference to Mary's pregnancy; but precisely because I think that Matthew rewrote the pre-Matthean material in his own way, arguments drawn from the hypothetical Greek phrasing of the pre-Matthean stratum are precarious. The expression *en gastri echein* occurs again in Matt 24:19 but can scarcely be considered peculiarly Matthean Greek (see also I Thes 5:3; Rev 12:2).

56 Germano, "Privilegium," 153–55, discusses vocalizations and translations of the Hebrew. See A. Baumstark, ZDMG 89 (1935), 116, for the possibility that Matthew drew upon an Aramaic targum rather than a Hebrew text, but also the critical reaction to this theory in Stendahl, *School*, 983.

57 This explanation may be combined with the previous explanations by the proposal that Matthew deliberately sought out a reading different from that of the LXX in order to suit his own narrative.

call his name Emmanuel." By changing the prophecy to "they will call," Matthew has shifted the action away from Joseph's naming of the child to a larger audience's appreciation of the meaning of the child. What larger audience is meant by the "they"? Presumably the "they" refers to the "people" of vs. 21: "You will call his name Jesus, for he will save his people from their sins."[58] If "his people" includes the Gentiles (see NOTE), then their recognition of Jesus as Emmanuel or God's presence with them would be an aspect of Jesus' being "son of Abraham" (1:1). Herein would be fulfilled the prophecy that in Abraham's seed all the nations of the earth would be blessed (footnote 11, § 3).

Third, the supplied interpretation of Emmanuel. Strecker has argued for a pre-Matthean Christian employment of Isa 7:14 on the basis of the ending of the citation in Matthew: "Emmanuel [which means (*methermēneuomenon*) 'God with us']." He points out that this interpretation of the name Emmanuel is quite different stylistically[59] from the interpretation of the name Jesus in 1:21: "You will call his name Jesus, for he will save his people from their sins"; and so he argues that the interpretation of Emmanuel is pre-Matthean. (I would argue exactly to the contrary: the meaning of the name Jesus was a commonplace among Christians, and so Matthew did not have to spell out "Jesus which means. . . ." But "Emmanuel" would not be generally known, especially to Gentile Christians; and the meaning would have to be given formally.) Strecker argues that Matthew himself would not have bothered to interpret the name Emmanuel, because that interpretation focuses attention on the very thing that Matthew would have liked to avoid, namely, the embarrassing fact that the name given to the child in the Isaian prophecy was not the name given to the child born of Mary. However, if we wish to be precise, while Matthew shows no interest in Emmanuel as a real name for the child, he has a definite interest in the significance of that name. I would maintain that he draws the interpretation of the name from Isa 8:10, a passage

---

[58] It has been argued that this verse echoes Ps 130:8: "He [Yahweh] will redeem Israel from all its iniquities"—an implicit citation that would attribute to Jesus the task of Yahweh and thus supply a reason for seeing in him and his activity God's presence among His people (Emmanuel). Stendahl, "Quis," 102[59], denies the allusion to the psalm; but Gundry, *Use*, 127, thinks that Matthew made a free translation of it (e.g., by substituting "save" for "redeem" because he was explaining the name Jesus which he took to be derived from the verb "to save"—see NOTE on 21). We know that this psalm was in Christian usage in the first century for it is cited in Titus 2:14, in a form closer to the LXX. Kilpatrick, *Origins*, 93, makes the suggestion that the introductory fulfillment formula of 1:22 originally referred to 1:21b and to the implicit citation of the psalm, and that its reference was changed when the Isaian passage was introduced in 1:23. In my opinion the "citation" of Ps 130:8 is too allusive to have constituted a formula citation. Matthew's "he will save his people from their sins" probably echoes a mélange of passages of which Ps 130 would be only one, e.g., "He will begin to save Israel" in Judg 13:5, the angelic announcement pertaining to the forthcoming birth of Samson (so F. Danker); and/or "Save your people" in Ps 28:9 (so Lindars, *Apologetic*, 2142).

[59] The verb *methermēneusthai* occurs nowhere else in Matthew but occurs three times in Mark and twice in John.

that follows immediately upon the second mention of Emmanuel in 8:8: "Speak a word [you peoples] but it will not stand; for *God is with us.*"[60] Matthew is interested in this interpretation because, as I have mentioned above, it helps to support Jesus' divine sonship,[61] alongside his Davidic sonship. Moreover, it enables him to set up an inclusion[62] between the first words spoken about Jesus at the beginning of the Gospel and his own last words at the end of the Gospel: "Behold, *I am with you* all days till the end of the world" (28:20—notice that the angel of the Lord from ch. 1 reappears at the tomb of Jesus in 28:2). Indeed, the inclusion reflects Matthew's understanding that in the coming of Jesus the Messiah, the presence of God has made itself felt in an *eschatological* way. Even if the intervention of God through the Holy Spirit had been required many times in the long genealogical record of the Messiah, His intervention through the Spirit in the conception and birth of Jesus is not just one more in a series. Jesus is the final and once-for-all manifestation of God's presence with us, which is so much the work of the Spirit that for the first time in the genealogical record of the Messiah no human begetter can be listed.

In my judgment, then, Matthew has not only inserted the formula citation of Isa 7:14 but has adapted that citation to its context and to his purpose. But was he the first or only NT Christian to see the applicability of the Isaian passage, or was he utilizing a passage already well known in Christian reflection on the OT? To a large extent the answer to this depends on one's analysis of Luke 1:26–38. Luke never cites Isa 7:14, but is his double reference to Mary as a *parthenos* in 1:27 an echo of Isaiah? And in the angel Gabriel's words to Mary, "Behold you will conceive in your womb and will give birth to a son, and you will call his name Jesus," is the Lucan *syllēmpsēi [syllambanein] en gastri* an echo of Isaiah's *en gastri lē[m]psetai [lambanein]*? Is Luke's description of Joseph as a man "of the House of David" an echo of the address in Isa 7:13 "O House of David"? Scholars have taken a stance on both sides of this question;[63] but the language of birth annunciations, ranging from the accounts in Genesis and Judges through Isaiah to Luke, is so stereotyped that judgments about implicit citations of one passage (Isa 7:14) are very precarious.

60 Matthew uses the same inverted order of the Greek words ("with us God") found in Isa 8:10.

61 Indeed, the interpretation of Emmanuel may be part of Matthew's apologetic motif. Lindars, *Apologetic*, 214, thinks Matthew may be answering a Jewish objection that Isa 7:14 was not applicable to Jesus precisely because he was not named Emmanuel. Matthew responds by showing that the interpretation of the name Emmanuel is applicable to him.

62 For inclusion, see § 2, footnote 19. Its most frequent modern appearance probably would be in the sermon where it is good style to come back at the end to the citation with which one began.

63 Neirynck, *Noël*, 30, contends that there is no real evidence that Luke's scene reflects Isa 7:14, while Schürmann, *Lukasevangelium*, I, 58ff., is insistent on the influence of the Isaian passage. Vögtle, "Offene," 46, comments on how difficult it is to decide.

C. *Matthew's Use of Pre-Matthean Material*

We have analyzed Matthew's message in 1:18–25, a message of a Davidic and a divine Who and How in Jesus' identity, and we have seen how Matthew used the formula citation of Isa 7:14 both to illustrate and to support his message. It is now appropriate to discuss the raw material that Matthew used in the composition of his scene and to see how he bent that to his purpose. In Table VII in § 4, B2, I reconstructed what I called the main pre-Matthean narrative underlying the whole of 1:18 – 2:23 and based on a pattern of angelic dream appearances. I explained there that this main narrative drew upon the motifs of the patriarch Joseph, the "man of dreams" who went to Egypt, and of the birth of Moses, who escaped the wicked Pharaoh's attempt to kill him and who came back from Egypt. Let me isolate here the part of that reconstructed pre-Matthean narrative that is pertinent to 1:18–25:[64]

> Now when Mary had been betrothed to Joseph, behold an angel of the Lord appeared to him in a dream, saying, "Take Mary your wife into your home, for she will give birth to a son who will save his people from their sins." So Joseph got up from sleep and took his wife home, and she gave birth to a son.

The reconstruction hews very close to the pattern of introduction, appearance, command, reason, and fulfillment that occurs in all three angelic dream appearances, as can be seen from Table VI.[65] However, this reconstruction is obviously shorter than what is now found in Matt 1:20–21,24–25—the core of the angelic appearance to Joseph, without the inserted formula citation:

> Now, as he was considering this, behold, an angel of the Lord appeared to him in a dream, saying, *"Joseph, son of David, do not be afraid to* take Mary your wife into your home, *for the child begotten in her is through the Holy Spirit. She will give birth to a son; and you will call his name Jesus, for* he will save his people from their sins.

---

[64] May I ask the reader to recall the several cautions that accompanied my reconstruction in § 4. While we may attain to pre-Matthean content, we are able to reconstruct the content only in highly Matthean wording. Also what we reconstruct may represent only the skeleton of a more complex narrative. I have also allowed that the main pre-Matthean narrative may have already been joined to other pre-Matthean material before it came to be worked upon by the evangelist.

[65] In the other scenes in ch. 2, where my reconstruction goes considerably beyond the basic angelic dream pattern, I shall have to offer detailed reasons for the additional material that I have included.

So Joseph got up from sleep and did as the angel of the Lord had commanded him. He took his wife home, but he had no sexual relations with her before she gave birth to a son. And he called his name Jesus.

Now, as we have seen, some of this additional material is clearly the product of Matthean editing, as the evangelist made the narrative fit his theological purpose. For instance, the point that Joseph "did as the angel of the Lord had commanded him" is a Matthean touch encountered elsewhere (footnotes 17, 33), and points up the extent to which the divine plan specified a legal Davidic paternity through Joseph's accepting and naming the child. The point that Joseph "had no sexual relations with her before she gave birth to a son" was meant by Matthew to protect the virginity of the mother as predicted by Isaiah, as well as to protect Jesus' divine sonship.[66]

But not so easily explicable as Matthean editing is the material I have italicized. This material, which is not found in my reconstruction of the main pre-Matthean narrative, gives important information about the conception and birth of the child: Joseph is identified as a son of David; Mary is already pregnant; this pregnancy is through the Holy Spirit and not by sexual relations with another man; and the child is named before birth.[67] Where did Matthew get this information? In § 4, B2, I spoke of pre-Matthean material other than that recounted in the main narrative of angelic dream appearances, and I called specific attention to an annunciation of birth narrative. It is now time to ask whether the additional information in Matt 1:20–21,24–25 comes from such a pre-Matthean annunciation.

1. The Annunciation of Birth

As I pointed out in the brief previous reference to this literary form, our attention is called to its existence in Matthew by the fact that the angelic dream appearance to Joseph in 1:20–21,24–25 (which we may call Scene A) differs in a notable way from the angelic dream appearances to Joseph in 2:13–15a (Scene B) and 2:19–21 (Scene C). The three scenes are compared in Table VI, and Scene A alone has two angelic commands and two reasons offered for those commands. In addition there is a difference of context, for although the angelic dream appearance initiates Scenes B and C,[68] in Scene A it is prefaced by two verses of introduction

---

66 See footnote 69 below for an instance of Matthean editing in 1:18–19.

67 In footnote 44, § 4, I explained that this last feature was probably not a part of the main pre-Matthean narrative based on the birth of Moses.

68 That is why I have made the angelic dream appearance initiate my reconstruction of Scene A in the main pre-Matthean narrative.

TABLE VIII: BIBLICAL ANNUNCIATIONS OF BIRTH

The Five Steps:

1. The *appearance* of an angel of the Lord (or appearance of the Lord)
2. *Fear* or prostration of the visionary confronted by this supernatural presence
3. The divine *message*:
   a. The visionary is addressed by name
   b. A qualifying phrase describing the visionary
   c. The visionary is urged not to be afraid
   d. A woman is with child or is about to be with child
   e. She will give birth to the (male) child
   f. The name by which the child is to be called
   g. An etymology interpreting the name
   h. The future accomplishments of the child
4. An *objection* by the visionary as to how this can be or a request for a sign
5. The *giving of a sign* to reassure the visionary

Biblical references for the five steps:

	Ishmael	Isaac	Samson	John Baptist	Jesus	Jesus
1.	Gen 16:7	Gen 17:1; 18:1	Judg 13:3	Luke 1:11	Luke 1:26	Matt 1:20
2.	16:13	17:3; 18:2	13:22	1:12	1:29	
3a.	16:8	(17:15)		1:13	1:30	1:20
3b.	16:8	(17:15)			1:28	1:20
3c.			(13:23)	1:13	1:30	1:20
3d.	16:11		13:3		1:31	(1:20)
3e.	16:11	17:19; 18:10	13:4	1:13	1:31	1:21
3f.	16:11	17:19		1:13	1:31	1:21
3g.	16:11	17:17; 18:13–15	13:5	1:15–17	1:32,33,35	1:21
3h.	16:12	17:16,19			1:31	1:21
4.		17:17; 18:12	13:8,17	1:18	1:34	
5.		(17:20–21)	13:9,18–21	1:20	1:36–37	

Parentheses are used to indicate verses where the substance of the step is present but in an unusual form.

(1:18b–19).[69] I am suggesting that at least a partial reason for these peculiarities in Scene A is the presence, intermingled with an angelic dream appearance, of an angelic annunciation of birth.

In the adjacent Table VIII I present the five steps typical of the rather stereotyped biblical annunciations of birth,[70] with references that enable the reader to compare the Matthean annunciation with the OT annunciations of Ishmael, Isaac, and Samson, and those of JBap and Jesus in Luke. Matthew does not meet the standard five-step pattern nearly so well as does Luke, whose annunciations are nearly perfect examples of the genre. The absence of steps 2, 4, and 5 in Matthew is easily explained by the fact that the annunciation has been fitted into the dominant angelic dream pattern and suffered dislocations accordingly. Scenes B and C in the angelic dream appearances (Table VI) had no pattern of fear on Joseph's part or a questioning of the angel; and there was no reason why such features should have been introduced into Scene A since they were not essential to the story line. It is in step 3, the message, that Matthew comes very close to the annunciation pattern, and by so doing breaks the angelic dream pattern found in Scenes B and C. Let me compare the messages of some of the other birth annunciations with that of Matthew (continuing the device of using italics to indicate the words that I have not considered to be part of the main pre-Matthean narrative, based on the angelic dream appearances—words that I would attribute to the once-separate angelic annunciation of birth):

> Gen 16:8,11: "Hagar, maid of Sarah, . . . you are with child and will give birth to a son; and you will call his name Ishmael [i.e., God hears], for the Lord has been attentive to your humiliation."

> Gen 17:19 (to Abraham): "Sarah, your wife, will give birth to a son for you; and you will call his name Isaac [i.e., he laughs—see 17:17 and 18:13–15 where Abraham and Sarah laugh]."

> Luke 1:13 (to Zechariah): "Zechariah, do not be afraid, . . . your wife Elizabeth will bear you a son, and you will call his name John."

---

69 I have already pointed out that 1:18a ("Now, as for [Jesus] Christ, his birth took place in this way") is Matthew's editorial work, effecting a transition from the genealogy to the narrative.

70 Léon-Dufour, "L'annonce," 77, rightly points out that similar steps appear in divine commissions to heroes—commissions that are going to change their lives and thus, in a sense, give them a new birth:

Step	1.	Moses in	Exod	3:2;	Gideon	in	Judg	6:12
Step	2.	"	" "	3:6;	"	"	"	6:22
Step	3a.	"	" "	3:4;				
Step	3b.				"	"	"	6:12
Step	3c.				"	"	"	6:33
Step	3h.	"	" "	3:10;	"	"	"	6:14,16
Step	4.	"	" "	3:11;	"	"	"	6:15,17
Step	5.	"	" "	3:12;	"	"	"	6:19–22

Luke 1:28,30–31: "Hail, O favored one . . . do not be afraid, Mary, . . . you will conceive in your womb and will give birth to a son; and you will call his name Jesus."

Matt 1:20–21 (to Joseph): *"Joseph, son of David, do not be afraid to* take Mary your wife into your home, *for the child begotten in her is through the Holy Spirit.* She will give birth to a son *and you will call his name Jesus, for* he will save his people from their sins."

It is quite clear that the italicized Matthean material matches very closely the standard annunciation message. So does some non-italicized material like "she will give birth to a son" and "he will save his people from their sins"; but that is because in those clauses there coincided the two literary forms in the pre-Matthean stratum, the angelic dream pattern and the angelic annunciation of birth. In other words, those are clauses that had a function (and sometimes a different one) in both patterns. For instance, in the angelic dream pattern, "for he will save his people from their sins" serves as the standard *reason* offered by the angel for his command (Table VI), while in the annunciation pattern it is the etymology of the name Jesus.[71]

Thus, I would explain Matthew's "Joseph, son of David, do not be afraid" as the standard 3a–c of the annunciation pattern,[72] and Matthew's "The child begotten in her. . . . She will give birth to a son; and you will call his name Jesus, for he will save his people from their sins" as the standard 3d–g of the annunciation pattern. The same features, 3a–f, without the formal etymology,[73] appear in the Lucan annunciation to Mary. Matthew's "Joseph, son of David, do not be afraid" is matched by Luke's "O favored one . . . do not be afraid, Mary." And Matthew's "The child begotten in her. . . . She will give birth to a son; and you will call his name Jesus" is matched by Luke's "You will conceive in your womb and

[71] Of course, I am not suggesting that this was mere coincidence. The angelic dream narrative has formulated the reason out of the implicit etymology of the name Jesus, which probably was well known to Christians (see NOTE on vs. 21). Although I am separating the two literary forms to help the clarity of our study, their content overlaps; and reflection on Jesus was not neatly compartmentalized.

[72] Burger, *Jesus*, 103–4, argues that the "son of David" designation of Joseph is an editorial addition by Matthew in order to promote his explanation of Jesus' Davidic descent. I doubt this on two scores. First, the qualifying phrase describing the visionary is a standard feature (3b) of the annunciation pattern, and normally that qualification has something to do with the story. Gideon is called "mighty man of valor" in Judg 6:12 (see footnote 70) precisely because he will employ that valor, along with God's help, in smiting the Midianites. Mary is called "favored one" in Luke 1:28 because the conception of Jesus will be a sign that she has "found favor with God" (1:30). Second, the Davidic motif is found also in the Lucan annunciation of Jesus' birth: Joseph is "a man of the House of David" in 1:27 and the Lord God will give Jesus "the throne of his father David" in 1:32.

[73] Perhaps the etymology appears after Jesus' birth in the angelic annunciation to the shepherds: "To you this day there is born in the city of David a *Savior* who is Messiah and Lord" (Luke 2:11).

will give birth to a son; and you will call his name Jesus." The two major points of variance between Matthew and Luke are perfectly tolerable within the range of variants allowed by OT examples of the annunciation of birth narratives. Matthew has the annunciation addressed to the man, and the wife is already pregnant; Luke has the annunciation addressed to the woman, and she will become pregnant. In the annunciations of the births of Ishmael and Isaac given above, in one case (Ishmael) the annunciation is to the woman who is already pregnant, while in the other case (Isaac) it is to the man whose wife will become pregnant.[74]

The resemblance between the Matthean and Lucan messages is strengthened when we look at similarities that spill over into the context. Joseph, who is addressed as "son of David," in the Matthean message, is called "a man of the House of David" in the Lucan introduction to the annunciation (1:27). The salvation theme that appears in the Matthean message appears in the Lucan annunciation after the birth of Jesus.[75] The description of Joseph as "upright" in the Matthean introduction to the annunciation matches the description of Zechariah and Elizabeth as "upright" in the Lucan introduction to the annunciation of JBap's birth. Since it is almost unanimously agreed by scholars that the Matthean and Lucan infancy narratives are independent of each other (see § 1, B2), and since so many similarities can scarcely have arisen by accident, we are led to the probability of a basic pre-Gospel annunciation tradition that each evangelist used in his own way. And since both annunciation messages mention David (Matt 1:20; Luke 1:32), this pre-Gospel tradition presumably concerned the birth of Jesus as the Davidic Messiah.[76]

---

74 The problem of present versus future pregnancy is inherited from the ambiguity of the Hebrew participial construction used to describe the pregnancy (footnote 44 above). That the Matthean annunciation is directed to Joseph, rather than to Mary, is dictated by the fact that it has been joined to the main narrative of angelic dream appearance to Joseph. That the Lucan annunciation is to Mary was influenced in part by Luke's deliberate imitation of the Genesis stories of the births of Abraham's sons, Isaac and Ishmael. (As we shall see in § 10A, Luke modeled Zechariah and Elizabeth after Abraham and Sarah.) The annunciations of the births of those two sons were given to a man (Abraham) and a woman (Hagar) respectively. Luke has the annunciation of JBap's birth given to a man; the Genesis analogy would suggest that the annunciation of Jesus' birth be given to a woman. See also footnote 45, § 4.

75 See footnote 73 above. The theme of salvation also appears in the Lucan insertion into the Benedictus, "But you, child, will . . . grant to His people knowledge of salvation in the forgiveness of their sins" (1:76–77), a wording close to Matthew's: "He will save his people from their sins." In Book Two of this commentary I shall seek to show that Luke wrote some of his description of the infancy of JBap in imitation of material that came to him about Jesus.

76 The reference to salvation discussed in the previous footnote fits well into the Davidic motif, even as it does into the Moses motif (footnote 44, § 4), whence my tendency to regard "he will save his people from their sins" as having a place in both the angelic dream appearance and in the annunciation (in the latter alone, however, as an etymology of "Jesus"). In the first-century B.C. work, the *Psalms of Solomon* (17:23–28 or 21–26), "the son of David" who is to be raised up is expected to thrust out sinners from the inheritance of Israel in order to gather a holy people—in short, to save his people from their sins.

2. Begotten of a Virgin through the Holy Spirit

Our discussion of the similarities between Matthew and Luke, which has led us to posit a pre-Gospel annunciation tradition drawn on by both evangelists, has now reached the point where we can no longer ignore those startling similarities that have no forerunner in an OT annunciation of birth. Matthew and Luke agree that the annunciation came after the "betrothal" of Mary and Joseph (NOTE on vs. 18) but before Mary had come to live at Joseph's house,[77] so that Mary was a virgin at the time of the annunciation (Matt 1:23; Luke 1:27). In both Matthew and Luke the angelic message states that Mary will give birth to a son through the action of the Holy Spirit (Matt 1:20–21; Luke 1:35). Let us begin our consideration of these two points, begotten of a virgin, begotten through the Holy Spirit, with the latter.

At the beginning of this section, when treating Matthew's message, I discussed the background of the concept of begetting through the Holy Spirit. The phrase echoes the language of early Christian preaching about Jesus as the Son of God. In its earlier usage the begetting of God's Son was associated with the resurrection (Acts 13:33) and with the baptism (Matt 3:17; Western text of Luke 3:22). In a later stage, but still one that would antedate both Matthew and Luke, it obviously had been associated with the conception of Jesus. That such an association would find articulation in an annunciation tradition of the birth of the Davidic Messiah is not surprising. An angelic annunciation of birth was the usual biblical format for dealing with questions of the begetting of salvific figures, and the notion of God's Son had been consistently set alongside the notion of David's son in early preaching. At first, the comparison of the two designations, Son of God and son of David, involved a sharp contrast. Two distinct phases were spoken of in Rom 1:3–4: "Born of the seed of David according to the flesh; designated Son of God in power according to the Holy Spirit [Spirit of Holiness] as of resurrection from [of] the dead." The discussion about whose son the Messiah was (Mark 12:35–37 and par.) contrasted his being the son of David with his exalted status in being called Lord (Appendix II). Yet significantly, even in such contrasts, it was never denied that Jesus was son of David. By the time that the concept of the begetting of God's Son had begun to be applied to Jesus' conception,

---

[77] Luke 1:27 speaks of Mary as "betrothed," using the same verb that Matthew uses in 1:18. The fact that Mary has not yet had sexual relations with her betrothed (Luke 1:34) implies that she has not yet been taken to her husband's house. Three months later, after the visitation to Elizabeth, Mary is pictured as returning to *her* home (1:56). If Luke is being exact (and if he knew of Palestinian customs), this would suggest that Mary's pregnancy was far advanced by the time she came to live with Joseph and thus to travel with him (2:4–5).

the relationship between Davidic sonship and divine sonship had become complementary. The Davidic psalm, "You are my son; today I have begotten you" (2:7) was not now being applied to a symbolic begetting (e.g., the resurrection) which had to be contrasted with the more humble natural begetting; it was being applied to the real begetting of Jesus, so that Jesus was both David's son and God's Son from the moment of conception. And if the Holy Spirit had been consistently associated with divine sonship in Christian preaching, a mention of the role of the Spirit of God was not at all out of place in the coronation (begetting) of a Davidic king and hence of the Messiah.[78] Isaiah had prophesied to the House of David the coming birth of a wonderful child who would be the sign of God's continued presence (7:13–14). That child was to be given governance and to sit upon the throne of David, and to be called, "Wonderful Counselor, Mighty God, Everlasting Father, Prince of Peace" (Isa 9:6–7). And upon this new branch or shoot that would spring from the Davidic line of Jesse would come the Spirit of the Lord (11:1–2).

There is no real difficulty then in explaining how a christological statement about the begetting of God's Son and the accompanying role of the Holy Spirit became attached to the conception of Jesus in the literary framework of annunciation of the Messiah's birth. But why was the action of the Holy Spirit related to a begetting of the Messiah *on the part of a virgin?* If the action of God through the Holy Spirit was involved in the conception, the narrative pattern would require the overcoming of some human obstacle to demonstrate this. But the OT examples on which the Christian storytellers drew would suggest the obstacle of sterility or barrenness on the mother's part. There was nothing in the OT (including the Hebrew and the Greek of Isa 7:14) that would have suggested the obstacle of a virgin who was not to have marital relations with her husband. In Appendix IV I shall explain the various theories that have been proposed to account for this unusual concept of a virginal conception. Here I would stress only that it was not the creation of either Matthew or Luke, but seems to have come to them both from a pre-Gospel tradition. It is true that Matthew alone brings up the question of scandal caused by the virginal conception, since it involved Mary's being pregnant before she went to live with Joseph. Yet as I mentioned in A2 above, even this scandal is not easily classified as the evangelist's dramatic creation (footnote 28). What Matthew did (with possible apologetic aim) was to bring into open discussion the problem raised by a pre-Gospel narrative of the annunciation of the Davidic Messiah's birth from a virgin through the creative power of the Holy Spirit.

---

[78] For both evangelists, the birth of Jesus constituted his coronation as the Davidic king. Matthew 2:2 has the magi speak of "the newborn King of the Jews"; Luke 1:32 has the angel promise that to the son whom Mary will bear "the Lord God will give . . . the throne of his father David."

3. Summary

I trust that the reader can now see the various pre-Matthean elements that I am positing and the way in which I think they coalesced. First, I posit a kerygmatic proclamation of Jesus as God's Son begotten through the Holy Spirit—a christological affirmation that only after considerable Christian reflection was applied to the conception of Jesus in the womb. Second, I posit a tradition of an angelic annunciation of the birth of the Davidic Messiah, an annunciation fashioned in popular circles on the pattern of OT annunciations of birth. At least by the time that the annunciation tradition (which may have various forms) came into the immediate pre-Matthean and pre-Lucan background, the christological formulation of the begetting of God's Son through the Holy Spirit had been incorporated into the message section of the annunciation,[79] a union catalyzed by the fact that (adoptive) divine sonship had long been associated with Davidic expectations and by the further fact that "Son of God" and "son of David" were set side by side (in contrast) in Christian preaching. The marital situation that constituted the setting of this annunciation tradition (with its christological message) was one in which Mary and Joseph were betrothed, but Mary was still a virgin.[80]

This pre-Gospel annunciation pattern developed in each evangelist's tradition in a different way.[81] As part of an elaborate parallelism between the infant JBap and the infant Jesus, Luke rewrote it and used it to fashion a companion annunciation of the birth of JBap. Since he directed the JBap annunciation to Zechariah, he directed the Jesus annunciation to Mary (footnote 74). Matthew (or his tradition) combined the pre-Gospel angelic annunciation of the birth of the Davidic Messiah (with its christological message of begetting through the Holy Spirit) with a popular narrative in which a story of Joseph and the infant Jesus had been modeled upon the adventures of the patriarch Joseph and the infant Moses, a narrative structured on a series of angelic dream appearances. The first of the angelic dream appearances, which had a relatively simple message, was enlarged through the inclusion of the message from the annunciation of birth narrative, giving us substantially the story which now appears in Matthean language in 1:18b–21,24–25.

---

79 I see no way of knowing whether this annunciation ever existed in a form in which the Messiah was begotten without mention of the Holy Spirit. Thus, in distinguishing between the first and second elements, I am not necessarily positing separate existence but separate origins.

80 The historicity of this marital situation will be discussed in Appendix IV.

81 I am being deliberately vague in referring to the evangelist's "tradition." The Matthean annunciation of Jesus' birth has come down to us in Matthean style; the Lucan annunciation, in Lucan style; and so each evangelist has rewritten whatever tradition came to him. It is impossible to distinguish *with precision* how much development had already taken place in the respective traditions before the rewriting.

This combined story (and its sequence in ch. 2) fitted perfectly into Matthew's overall purpose. The strains of Davidic and divine sonship that had emerged he used to gloss a genealogy, the numerical pattern of which he had half discovered and half worked out. This genealogy traced Jesus from Abraham through David to Joseph, but Matthew concluded it in such a way that Jesus could be seen to be descended from David without it being said that he was begotten by Joseph. How that was so, the annunciation narrative explained. As for the patriarch Joseph and infant Moses motifs (which will grow stronger in ch. 2), these enabled Matthew to connect Jesus, Son of God, son of Abraham, and son of David, with one great episode in Israelite history to which the genealogy had failed to call attention, namely, the Egyptian bondage and the Exodus. It was perfectly fitting that the child named after Joshua who was to save his people from their sins should echo in his origins the historic deliverance of Israel from Egypt.

SECTIONAL BIBLIOGRAPHY (§ 5)
(MATT 1:18–25)

A. EXEGESIS OF THE PERICOPE

Descamps, A., *Les Justes et la Justice dans les évangiles et le christianisme primitif hormis la doctrine proprement paulinienne* (Dissertationes Theologicae Lovanienses, Series II, 43; Gembloux: Duculot, 1950), 34–37 on Matt 1:19.

Germano, J. M., "Nova et vetera in pericopam de sancto Joseph (Mt 1,18–25)," *Verbum Domini* 46 (1968), 351–60.

———— "Privilegium nominis messianici a S. Joseph imponendi (Is 7,14; Mt 1,21.23.25)," *Verbum Domini* 47 (1969), 151–62.

———— " 'Et non cognoscebat . . .' Inquisitio super sensu spirituali seu mystico Mt 1,25," *Marianum* 35 (1973), 184–240.

Graystone, J. M., "Matthieu 1:18–25. Essai d'interprétation," RTP 23 (1973), 221–32.

Hill, D., "A Note on Matthew i. 19," ExpTim 76 (1964–65), 133–34.

Léon-Dufour, X., "L'annonce à Joseph," in *Etudes d'Evangile* (Paris: Seuil, 1965), 65–81. From two previous articles: "L'annonce à Joseph," in *Mélanges bibliques rédigés en l'honneur de André Robert* (Paris: Bloud & Gay, 1957), 39–97; and "Le juste Joseph," NRT 81 (1959), 225–31.

Motté, Magda, " 'Mann des Glaubens': Die Gestalt Josephs nach dem Neuen Testament," BibLeb 11 (1970), 176–89.

Pelletier, A., "L'annonce à Joseph," RechScRel 54 (1966), 67–68.

Pesch, R., "Ausführungsformel," esp. 79–91.

Spicq, C., " 'Joseph, son mari, étant juste . . .' (Mt., I, 19)," RB 71 (1964), 206–14.

Stramare, T., "Giuseppe, 'Uomo Giusto,' in Mt. 1,18–25," *Rivista Biblica* 21 (1973), 287–300.

Trilling, W., "Jesus, der Messias und Davidssohn (Mt 1,18–25)," in *Christus-verkündingung in den Synoptischen Evangelien* (Munich: Kösel, 1969), 13–39.

Vögtle, A., "Mt 1,25 und die Virginitas B. M. Virginis post partum," TQ 147 (1967), 28–39.

B. Information on Isaiah 7:14

(I shall make no attempt at a complete bibliography, which would necessarily include the numerous commentaries on Isaiah. I list only a few works helpful as background for Matthew's use of the text.)

Bratcher, R. G., "A Study of Isaiah 7:14," BibTrans 9 (1958), 97–126.

del Olmo Lete, G., "La profecía del Emmanuel (Is. 7,10–17): Estado actual de la interpretación," EphMar 22 (1972), 357–85.

Kilian R., *Die Verheissung Immanuels Jes 7,14* (SBS 35: Stuttgart: Katholisches Bibelwerk, 1968).

McNamara, M., "The Emmanuel Prophecy and Its Context—III," *Scripture* 15 (1963), 80–88.

C. Special Details

Formula (Fulfillment) Citation: see Bibliography for § 4.
Davidic Descent: see Bibliography for Appendix II.
Virginal Conception: see Bibliography for Appendix IV.

V. THE MAGI COME TO PAY HOMAGE
TO THE KING OF THE JEWS (§ 6)

Translation of Matt 2:1–12

2 ¹ Now, after the birth of Jesus in Bethlehem of Judea in the days of Herod the king, behold, magi from the East came to Jerusalem ² asking, "Where is the newborn King of the Jews? For we have seen his star at its rising and have come to pay him homage." ³ When King Herod heard this, he was startled, and so was all Jerusalem with him. ⁴ Assembling all the chief priests and scribes of the people, he inquired of them where the Messiah was to be born. ⁵ "In Bethlehem of Judea," they told him; "for thus it is written by the prophet:

⁶ 'And you, O Bethlehem (in the) land of Judah,
   are by no means least among the rulers of Judah;
   for from you will come forth a ruler
   who will shepherd my people Israel.' "

⁷ Then Herod summoned the magi secretly and ascertained from them the exact time when the star had appeared. ⁸ And he sent them off to Bethlehem with the instruction: "Go, search diligently for the child. As soon as you find him, bring me word that I too may come and pay him homage." ⁹ Obeying the king, they set out; and behold, the star which they had seen at its rising went before them until it came to rest over the place where the child was. ¹⁰ When they saw the star, they were greatly overjoyed. ¹¹ And entering the house, they saw the child with Mary his mother; and they bowed down and paid him homage. Then they opened their treasure-boxes and brought out gifts for him: gold, frankincense, and myrrh. ¹² But, since they had been warned in a dream not to return to Herod, they went away to their own country by another route.

NOTES

2:1. *Now, after the birth of Jesus . . . behold.* The construction of a genitive absolute with a postpositive *de* ("Now"), followed by *idou* ("behold"), is used by Matthew to mark developments in the narrative (1:20; 2:13,19). See Table VI.

Bethlehem. Five miles south of Jerusalem, this was the ancestral town of David where he was anointed by the prophet Samuel as king over God's people (I Sam 16:1–13; 17:12,15; 20:6,28). Matthew does not tell us precisely where in Bethlehem Jesus was born, but vs. 11 suggests that the birthplace was the house where Mary (and Joseph) lived. The Lucan version (2:7; see NOTE), wherein Mary and Joseph were visitors to Bethlehem without a place to stay and the child was placed in a manger, led to the subsequent Christian tradition that Jesus was born in a cave. The basilica at Bethlehem built by Constantine (A.D. 325) and rebuilt by Justinian (*ca.* 550) stands over a series of caves.

of Judea. In the OT (Judg 17:7,9; 19:1,2; Ruth 1:1,2; I Sam 17:12) there is a tendency to specify "Bethlehem of Judah," probably to distinguish it from the Bethlehem in the territory of Zebulun (Josh 19:15). If the latter is to be identified with the modern Beit Lahm, seven miles NW of Nazareth, a similar desire to prevent confusion may have governed Matthew's use of "of Judea" (see also Luke 2:4). However, most scholars have detected a more theological intent, e.g., to prepare for the citation in vs. 6 ("Bethlehem [in the] land of Judah") or to underline that Jesus is descended from Judah, as indicated in the genealogy (1:2,3). Yet, one must then explain why Matthew uses "Judea" (*Ioudaia*) instead of "Judah" (*Ioudas*)—cf. "Judah" in Hebr 7:14; Rev 5:5. Probably the key is found in 2:2 where the magi seek the "King of the Jews" (*Ioudaiōn*). By using a related word, Matthew shows that the King of the Jews was born in a town in Jewish territory (Judea).

in the days of. This is a frequent OT chronological expression; the absence of the article before "days" leads Klostermann, *Synoptiker*, 161, to suggest a Semitism.

Herod the king. Luke 1:5 sets the annunciation of JBap's birth "in the days of Herod, king of Judea"; see NOTE there. In *Ant.* XVII vi 4; ⚹167 and ix 3; ⚹213, Josephus fixes the death of Herod the Great shortly after an eclipse of the moon and before a Passover. In 750 A.U.C. (4 B.C.) there was an eclipse on the night of March 12/13th, one month before Passover. While other possibilities are 5 B.C. and 1 B.C., the best evidence favors March/April 4 B.C. as the time of Herod's death. See the attempt of W. E. Filmer, JTS 17 (1966), 283–98, to establish the case for 1 B.C., and the convincing refutation by T. D. Barnes, JTS 19 (1968), 204–8. A birth of Jesus dated two years (Matt 2:16) before the death of Herod in 4 B.C. would be consonant with the information in Luke 3:23 that Jesus was "about thirty years of age" in the fifteenth year of the reign of Tiberius Caesar (Luke 3:1), a year reckoned at October A.D. 27 to October A.D. 28, following the Syrian calendar, with antedating. For a full discussion of Jesus' age, see G. Ogg, NTS 5 (1958–59), 291–98. The anomaly that Jesus was born "before Christ" results from an ancient mistake in calculating the year of his birth. In 533 Dionysius Exiguus (Denis the Short) proposed to reckon years no longer from the foundation of Rome (A.U.C.) but from the birth of the Lord; he chose 754 A.U.C. as A.D. 1, a date too late since Herod died in 750.

   magi. What does Matthew mean by *magoi?* Long before, Herodotus (*Histories* I) had intrigued his Greek readers with a description of a priestly caste of magi among the sixth-century Medes, a caste that had special power to interpret dreams. The magi survived both the transfer of power from the Medes to the Persians (*ca.* 550 B.C.) and the emerging religious dominance of Zoroastrianism, so that by Herodotus' time (*ca.* 450) the magi were Zoroastrian priests. In the subsequent centuries there was a diversification in the functions of magi as the title was loosely applied to men adept in various forms of secret lore and magic. In the Greek form of the Book of Daniel (second century B.C.) the author can describe *magoi* as flourishing in every corner of the Babylonian kingdom of Nebuchadnezzar. Along with the enchanters and astronomers, they were thought to have the power of interpreting dreams and visionary messages (Dan 1:20; 2:2; 4:4; 5:7). A contemporary of Jesus, Philo of Alexandria (*De legibus specialibus* III 18;※※100–1) knows both of scientific magi and of magi who are charlatans and magicians. In his account of the early first century A.D., Tacitus (*Annals* II 27–33) mentions as absurdities popular in Rome predictions by astrologers, rites practiced by magicians, and the reading of dreams. Suetonius (*Tiberius* 36)tells us how that emperor banished all astrologers *ca.* A.D. 19. In Acts 8:9–24 Luke tells the story of Simon, a magus in Samaria in the 30s who amazed everyone with his magical powers; later, Acts 13:6–11 tells of Elymas or Bar-Jesus, a Jewish magus and false prophet on the island of Cyprus. A contemporary of Luke, Josephus (*Ant.* XX vii 2;※142) writes of Atomos, a Cypriot magus who functioned at Caesarea Maritima in Palestine in the 50s. Thus, the term "magi" refers to those engaged in occult arts and covers a wide range of astronomers, fortune tellers, priestly augurers, and magicians of varying plausibility (Delling, *"Magos,"* 356–57).

   Matthew's description of the magi as interpreting the rise of a star tips the scales in favor of his considering them to be astrologers. Is Matthew carrying on an implicit apologetic against false magi and particularly against astrology? This is the view of Mann, "Epiphany," 496, who draws upon Clarke, *Divine Humanity,* 41–51, pointing out that *magos* is always pejorative elsewhere in the NT and that a Christian is commanded in *Didache,* ii 2, not to act the part of a *magos.* Mann sees the Matthean magi as Babylonian Jews who dabbled in black magic and star worship but are now giving up the tools of their trade in homage to Jesus. He points to the Greek magical papyri for the use of incense and myrrh as accompaniments of incantation. Davies, *Setting,* 79, thinks that, just as the sorcerers of Egypt were vanquished by Moses, so the power of the astrologers was broken at the advent of Christ. He sees the homage of the magi in vs. 11 as their being "led to kneel at the feet of the greater Moses." These are variations of an ancient theory; for *ca.* 110 Ignatius, *Ephesians* xix 3, argued that by means of the star which manifested Jesus to the world "all magic [*mageia*] was dissolved." Justin, *Dialogue* lxxviii 9, followed by Augustine, thought of the magi as formerly having been loaded down with sin, but now being turned from superstition to the adoration of the true God. My own opinion is that such references reflect a Christian use of Matthew in an apologetic against magic rather than a true exegesis of Matthew. There is not the slightest hint of conversion or of false practice in Matthew's description of the magi; they are wholly admirable. They represent the best of pagan lore and religious perceptivity which has come to seek Jesus through revelation in nature. In Philo's *Vita Moysis* (I L; ※※276–77), the pagan magus Balaam receives from the God of Israel an authentic prophetic spirit; so too the Matthean magi receive a further revelation from the Jewish Scriptures.

from the East. The phrase *apo anatolōn* occurs in the Balaam story (LXX of Num 23:7) which, as we shall see in the commentary, is part of the background of Matthew's magi story; and so it may be a borrowing which designates no precise locality. (It gave Matthew's story a touch of the exotic, and fitted in well with contemporary visits to Palestine and Rome made by Oriental potentates—see NOTE on "homage" in vs. 2.) Nevertheless, interpreters have drawn on Matthew's use of the term *magoi*, on his reference to the rising of the star, and on his description of the gifts for indications as to what section of "the East" may have been meant. I shall match these three indications to three frequently proposed localizations, moving from the farthest East toward Palestine.

a) **Parthia or Persia**—a localization favored by the history of the term *magoi*, originally associated with the Medes and the Persians. For about five hundred years between 250 B.C. and A.D. 225 the Arsacid dynasty established itself as heirs to the Persian Empire. In early Christian art the NT magi were depicted in Persian or Parthian dress, i.e., in belted tunics with full sleeves, in trousers, and wearing Phrygian caps (Marsh-Edwards, "Magi," 3). This depiction led to a famous incident in the history of the basilica at Bethlehem built by Constantine and rebuilt by Justinian. In 614 the armies of Chosroes of the Sassanid dynasty of Persian kings swept over Palestine, wreaking havoc and setting churches to the torch. They spared the Bethlehem church, however, because of a mosaic picturing the magi as Persians—they recognized their countrymen. (This was reported in a letter of 836, associated with the Synod of Jerusalem.) A further argument for Persian localization is provided by the Zoroastrian background of the magi proposed by the Church Fathers beginning with Clement of Alexandria (*Stromata* I 15). Indeed, there was a patristic belief that Zoroaster was a prophet who had predicted the coming of the Messiah. Clement, *Stromata* VI 5, quotes Paul the Apostle to the effect that in the *Oracles of Hystapes* (a first-century B.C. or A.D. mixture of Persian apocalyptic and Jewish lore) there is a clear reference to the Son of God and his coming. The later *Arabic Gospel of the Infancy*, 7:1, reports that "some magi came to Jerusalem according to the prediction of Zoroaster." Messina, "Una profezia," analyzes the development of this legend in Christian circles which ultimately identified Zoroaster and Balaam. He sees the possible origins of the whole idea in the doctrine of the Avesta concerning the expectation of the Saušyant, a son to be born after Zoroaster's death. (The seed of Zoroaster was preserved in a lake; and when a preordained virgin would bathe there, she would be impregnated by it.) This salvific figure was to raise the dead and crush the forces of evil. However, there is no evidence that Christians in Matthew's time knew of this expectation. A minor variant of the Parthian/Persian hypothesis is the theory that the magi came from Commagene on the border area NE of Syria, standing on the fringes of the Roman Empire facing the Parthian domains. This area was close to eastern Syria where, according to scholars like Bacon (*Studies,* 23), Matthew's Gospel was written; and a great Christian center arose at Edessa, some 50 miles SE of the Commagene border. There was much Persian influence on Commagene, and astrology flourished there. Burrows, *Oracles,* 99, points out that Nemrud Dagh, a famous site in Commagene, has yielded a horoscope of the Roman client king Antiochus I (69–31 B.C.), and so we have evidence that the astral lore of the region was applied to royal births. He thinks this significant background for Matthew's reference to a star whose rising announces the birth of the King of the Jews.

b) **Babylon**—the localization most favored by the astrological implications of the rising of the star. The Babylonians or Chaldeans had developed a great interest in astronomy and astrology. Moreover, after the Babylonian Exile in the sixth century, a large colony of Jews had remained on, so that Babylonian astrologers could have learned something of Jewish messianic expectations and might have associated a particular star with the King of the Jews. As we saw in the preceding NOTE, *magoi* occur most frequently in the OT in Daniel's description of the Babylonian court.

c) **Arabia or the Syrian desert**—a localization favored by the gifts that the Matthean magi bring. Gold and frankincense are gifts that Isa 60:6 and Ps 72:15 associate with the desert camel trains coming from Midian (NW Arabia) and from Sheba (the kingdom of the Sabeans in SW Arabia). In the OT the "people of the East" or Qedemites are most often desert Arabs. That there might be magi or wise men among them would not be surprising, for they had a reputation for wisdom (I Kgs 5:10 [RSV 4:30]; Prov 30:1; 31:1 [Massa is an Arabian kingdom]). Astrology was not unknown to the Arabs, and four of the Arabian tribes took their names from stars (Bishop, "Some Reflections," 38). Moreover, Arabia had Jewish contacts. Commercial relations between Israel and South Arabia went back to Solomon's time; in the Yemen an Arab king, Dhu Nowās, embraced Judaism; and there were Jewish colonies around Medina. While the thesis that the magi came from Persia became the dominant view among the Church Fathers, the thesis that they came from Arabia is the earliest attested view. About A.D. 160 Justin, *Dialogue* lxxviii 1, wrote: "Magi from Arabia came to him [Herod]." Some fifty years later Tertullian, *Adversus Marcion* iii 13, working by deduction from the gifts, linked the magi with Damascus and Arabia. And independently of the magi question, as early as A.D. 96, Clement of Rome, *I Corinthians* 25:1–2, associated frankincense and myrrh with "the East, i.e., the districts near Arabia." A special variant of the Arabian theory is proposed by Bultmann, *History,* 292: "Indeed, it is not impossible that the story of the Adoration of the Magi had its origin in the Arabian cult of

Dusares, which had its shrines in Petra and Hebron, and perhaps also in Bethlehem. The feast of the birth of the God from his virgin mother was celebrated (on December 25th?) with the presentation of gifts such as money, ointments and incense." Bultmann has had little following in this thesis; for Matthew's story of the magi is not closely attached to the theme of the virginal conception, and the association of the magi theme to December 25th came much later than Matthew's time.

came to Jerusalem. Here and in vs. 3 there appears the Hellenized form *Hierosolyma,* as in nine other instances in the body of the Gospel. Only in Matt 23:27 does the more Semitic form *Hierousalēm* occur (BDF 56⁴).

2. *the newborn King of the Jews.* The order of the Greek is article, participle, noun (an order that appears also at the end of vs. 7)—this is unusual, for in Matthean style the attributive participle with its article normally follows the noun. Consequently, some translate appositively: "he who has been born, namely, the King of the Jews." The title "King of the Jews" may have had a nationalistic overtone of political independence: it seems to have been used first by the Hasmonean priest-kings (Josephus *Ant.* XIV iii 1;※36, mentions its use by Alexander Jannaeus). Since Herod the Great was known by this title (*Ant.* XVI x 2;※311), the suggestion that a new King of the Jews had been born was a challenge to him.

his star. Matthew's age would not have found bizarre the claim that a star rose to herald the birth of the King of the Jews and subsequently guided magiastrologers in their quest to find him. Virgil (*Aeneid* II 694) reports that a star guided Aeneas to the place where Rome should be founded. Josephus (*War* VI v 3;※289) speaks of a star that stood over Jerusalem and of a comet that continued for a year at the time of the fall of the city. He says (v 4;※※310, 312): "God has a care for men and *by all kinds of premonitory signs* shows His people the way of salvation," and relates this to the Jewish belief that "someone from their country would become ruler of the world" (see also Tacitus *Histories* V 13). It is true that Pliny (*Natural History* II vi 28) combats the popular opinion that each person has a star which begins to give light when he is born and fades out when he dies; yet the thesis that at least the births and deaths of great men were marked by heavenly signs was widely accepted. Cicero (*De divinatione* I xxiii 47) reports that on the night that the great temple of Diana at Ephesus burned, when the light began to dawn, the magi who were wise and learned among the Persians clamored that this presaged the birth of one who would be a great peril for Asia, one who turned out to be Alexander of Macedon. Suetonius (*Augustus* 94) records a tradition stemming from Julius Marathus that a public portent alerted the Roman people some months before the birth of Augustus that Nature was making ready to provide them with a king, and this so frightened the Senate that it issued a decree forbidding the rearing of any male child for a year. The births of Mithradates and of Alexander Severus were among the many births thought to have been accompanied by the appearance of a new star in the heavens. Suetonius (*Nero* 36) tells us how alarmed that emperor was when a comet appeared several nights in succession, for a comet was popularly supposed to herald the death of a person of great importance. Superstitiously prudent, Nero fulfilled the portent by having some of the notables of his realm put to death.

Thus, not only the appearance of a star heralding the birth of the Messiah, but also Herod's attempt on the life of the child would have been motifs familiar to the times. Now we must investigate whether, in fact, there was an astronomical phenomenon at the time of the birth of Jesus that, in the light of such beliefs, might have been interpreted as the "star" indicating the birth of the Messiah. (This question is meaningful even if one doubts the historicity of the story of the magi, for subsequent Christian believers in retrospect may have *fastened on a remembered phenomenon as a sign of Jesus' birth*.) Since the time of Johannes Kepler in the seventeenth century there have been careful astronomical studies of peculiar celestial phenomena in the decade before Jesus' birth, namely 14–4 B.C. (The brochure of the Adler Planetarium in Chicago, "The Star of Bethlehem," gives a very readable discussion of the astronomy involved.) Three candidates have been proposed, with the third as the most important.

a) **A supernova or "new star."** This was Kepler's own suggestion and corresponds literally to Matthew's description of a star. A nova or supernova involves a faint or very distant star in which an explosion takes place so that for a few weeks or months it gives out a great deal of light, sometimes to the point of being visible even in the daytime. A supernova can be brighter even than the moon, since the star involved may be a hundred million times more luminous than our sun. About a dozen novae are discovered each year, but the ones visible to the naked eye are much rarer. There is no record of a nova or supernova just before Jesus' birthdate; for surely the statement of Ignatius (*Ephesians* xix 2) is poetic rather than scientific: "A star shone in heaven beyond all the stars; its light was beyond description, and its newness caused astonishment; all the other stars, with the sun and the moon, gathered in chorus around the star, but it far exceeded them all in its light." Thus, the theory of a "new star" is purely a guess.

b) **A comet.** This phenomenon has caught human imagination throughout all recorded history. Comets move in regular but elliptical paths around the sun. In the distant part of their orbit they cannot be seen from earth; but when they come close to the sun and to the earth, they can be striking, especially if they develop a luminous tail of gasses and dust. Remarkably bright comets appear only a few times each century; and, in particular, the history of the comet now named after E. Halley (d. 1742) has fascinated astronomers from early days. Recorded appearances of this comet, which occur every seventy-seven years, date back to 240 B.C. in Europe, China, and Japan. By astronomical calculations we know that Halley's comet made its appearance in 741–742 A.U.C. or 12–11 B.C. In our own times it was last visible in 1911; and Père Lagrange, the famous Dominican biblical scholar who was living in Jerusalem at the time, saw it come from the East, fade while it was overhead, and then "reappear" several days later as it set in the West. Burrows, *Oracles,* 100, says that when it appeared before Jesus' birth (dated by Chinese records to 26 August, 12 B.C.), it would have been in the zodiacal region of Gemini with its head toward Leo.

This raises the possibility of a zodiacal interpretation of the astronomical phenomenon (e.g., Leo might have been associated with the lion of Judah). Zodiacal interest can be traced as far back as the second millennium B.C. and the classical zodiac became current in the early first millennium B.C. Burrows shows the possibility of zodiacal influence on the wording of the oracles of Jacob and Balaam. While we have ample proof of interest in the zodiac in post-Christian Judaism, we do not have exact details about such an interest in Jesus' time—a lacuna that may be filled when the astrological texts of Qumran are published. Besides this uncertainty, the comet interpretation of Matthew's "star" faces several difficulties. First, a comet is not a star. Yet, already by the third century Origen (*Against Celsus* I 58) had concluded that the star of the magi was not an ordinary fixed star, "but is to be classified with the comets which occasionally occur, or meteors, or bearded or jar-shaped stars, or any other such name by which the Greeks like to describe the different forms." Thus, a popular understanding of a comet as a bearded star may solve this difficulty. Second, and more seriously, a comet was usually thought to herald a catastrophe, so that it would be unusual to interpret its appearance as heralding the birth of a salvific figure. Third, the date of 12 B.C. would be very long before the date of 6 B.C. usually assigned for Jesus' birth. However, this argument loses its force if one is arguing, not that Matthew's account is historical, but that it has reinterpreted by association with Jesus an astral phenomenon which occurred in the general time period of his birth. It is possible that the appearance of Halley's comet in 12 B.C. and the coming of foreign ambassadors two years later to hail King Herod on the occasion of the completion of Caesarea Maritima have been combined in Matthew's story of the star and the magi from the East.

c) **A planetary conjunction.** Jupiter and Saturn are the slowest of the visible planets in their orbit around the sun: for Jupiter there is an orbit every twelve years; for Saturn, every thirty years. In the course of these orbits the two planets pass each other every twenty years; and in so passing, even though they may be considerably north or south of each other, they are said to be in conjunction. A much rarer occurrence is when a third planet, Mars, passes during or shortly after the conjunction of Jupiter and Saturn, so that the three planets are close together. Kepler saw this occur in October 1604. He calculated that it happens every 805 years and that it had happened in 7–6 B.C. Mention seems to have been made of this phenomenon in cuneiform texts (see Schaumberger, "Textus," 446–47—two works indicate close attention to planetary movements in Jesus' time: the "Berlin Table," copied on Egyptian papyrus and covering from 17 B.C. to A.D. 10; and the "Star Almanac" of Sippar, written in cuneiform on a clay tablet and prognosticating planetary movements from 7 B.C. [Stauffer, *Jesus*, 36–37]). From calculations we know that the three high points of the conjunction of Jupiter and Saturn were in May/June, September/October, and December of 7 B.C.—a rare triple conjunction (Holzmeister, "La stella," 12–15)—and that Mars passed early the next year. This "great conjunction" of Jupiter and Saturn took place in the zodiacal constellation of Pisces. I have pointed out in the previous paragraph that we are uncertain of the style of zodiacal calculations among Jews in Jesus' time; but

Pisces is a constellation sometimes associated with the last days and with the Hebrews, while Jupiter (an object of particular interest among Parthian astrologers) was associated with the world ruler and Saturn was identified as the star of the Amorites of the Syria-Palestine region. The claim has been made that this conjunction might lead Parthian astrologers to predict that there would appear in Palestine among the Hebrews a world ruler of the last days. (Rosenberg, "Star," 108–9, points to the connection of Jupiter and Saturn with justice, a messianic notion in Jer 23:5–6; 33:15–16.) But all of this is very speculative; for we really have no contemporary evidence justifying the reference to such a conjunction of planets as a "star" or attaching a particular astrological effect to it, even if there is later Jewish support for that.

At the risk of a digression, let me mention this later Jewish support for the messianic interpretation of the conjunction of Jupiter and Saturn in the constellation of Pisces. Abraham Bar Hiyya (*ca.* A.D. 1100) thought that the phenomenon occurred every 2,859 years (actually it occurs every 257 years), and that the last conjunction was in 1395 B.C., heralding the promulgation of the Torah through Moses. He expected that the Messiah would appear before the next conjunction which was to occur in A.D. 1464. This next conjunction occurred during the lifetime of Isaac Abravanel (1437–1508) who was deeply interested in the coming of the Messiah. Working with Bar Hiyya's calculations, Abravanel estimated that the Exodus took place eighty-three years after the conjunction of 1395 B.C. and that, correspondingly, the Messiah would come within an eighty-three-year period after the conjunction of A.D. 1464—to be precise, in the year 1503. (See J. Sarachek, *The Doctrine of the Messiah in Medieval Judaism* [2nd ed.; New York: Hermon, 1968], 326; A. H. Silver, *A History of Messianic Speculation in Israel* [Boston: Beacon, 1959], 124–25.) It is interesting that Abravanel did not know that the phenomenon to which he gave such attention had occurred just before Jesus' birth.

at its rising. The OS^sin reads "from the East" as in vs. 1. The former expression was *apo anatolōn;* the expression here is *en tē anatolē,* and so it is not surprising that some translators have rendered it "in the East." (The related verb *anatellein* means "to rise," and the East is the place of the sun's rising.) However, prepositions governing points of the compass usually do not take the article (BDF 253⁵). There may be a play on the rising of the star and the birth of the king, since an underlying Aramaic term *mwld* can refer to the birth both of a star and of a person. (This brings us into the discussion of a Qumran document about "The Elect of God" that is disputedly messianic and disputedly astrological—see J. A. Fitzmyer, CBQ 27 [1965], 367–68, 370.) The principle of astrology is to establish a horoscope based on the sign of the zodiac that is rising in the eastern horizon when a person is born. In reference to the discussion in the previous note about astronomical phenomena occurring near the time of Jesus' birth, the appearance of a supernova or of a comet might be called a "rising"; but the term could only with difficulty be applied to the almost contemporary heliacal or elliptic ascent of two planets. (See Boll, "Stern," on astronomical vocabulary.) It is interesting that the noun *anatolē* occurs also in the Lucan infancy narrative (1:78—see NOTE on "rising light") where once again it is difficult to translate.

and have come. If we abandon the translation "in the East" for *en tē anatolē,* there is no indication that the magi followed the star to Jerusalem. Rather, having seen the rise of the star which they associate with the King of the Jews, they have come to the capital city of the Jews for more information. Only in vss. 9 is it clear that the star served as a guide—from Jerusalem to Bethlehem.

pay him homage. The verb *proskynein* occurs three times in this section (here; vss. 8,11), and ten times in the rest of Matthew. Often involving an act of prostration (vs. 11), it describes homage offered to a person of dignity (Philo *De Josepho* xxviii ✸164) or of authority (Josephus *Ant.* II ii 2;✸11), as well as adoration or worship paid to a deity. H. Greeven, *"Proskyneō, proskynētēs,"* TDNT, VI, 763–64, points out that the general usage of this term in the NT is centered on divinity and maintains, "The proskynesis of the wise men . . . is truly offered to the Ruler of the world." However, the association of the action with the title "King of the Jews" in vs. 2 directs the reader's thought to homage paid to royalty rather than to worship of divinity. Of course, the distinction may be tenuous, for the reader knows that this child has been conceived through God's Holy Spirit and is God's Son (2:15).

The picture of magi coming from the East to pay homage to a king and bring him royal gifts (vs. 11) would not have struck Matthew's readers as naively romantic. When King Herod completed the building of Caesarea Maritima in 10–9 B.C., envoys from many nations came to Palestine with gifts (Josephus *Ant.* XVI v 1;✸✸136–41). In A.D. 44 Queen Helen of Adiabene, a kingdom that paid tribute to the Parthians, converted to Judaism and came to Jerusalem with bounteous gifts for those affected by the famine which was devastating the land. In A.D. 66 there took place an event that captured the imagination of Rome (Dio Cassius *Roman History* lxiii 1–7; Suetonius *Nero* 13). Tiridates, king of Armenia (a kingdom that was neighbor to Commagene—see NOTE on "from the East" in vs. 1), came to Italy with the sons of three neighboring Parthian rulers in his entourage. Their journey from the East (the Euphrates) was like a triumphal procession. The entire city of Rome was decorated with lights and garlands, and the rooftops filled with onlookers, as Tiridates came forward and *paid homage* to Nero. Tiridates identified himself as a descendant of Arsaces, founder of the Parthian Empire, and said, "I have come to you, my god, to pay homage, as I do to Mithras." After Nero had confirmed him as king of Armenia, "the king did not return by the route he had followed in coming," but sailed back a different way. It is significant that Pliny (*Natural History* XXX vi 16–17) refers to Tiridates and his companions as magi.

3. *he was startled.* The verb *tarassein* occurs one other time in Matthew (14:26), after the epiphany of Jesus walking on the sea, on which occasion the disciples confess Jesus as "God's Son" (14:33).

all Jerusalem with him. Josephus (*Ant.* II ix 2–3;✸✸206,215) describes the terror of both the king (the Pharaoh) and the Egyptians at the news that a child (Moses) was going to be born to the Israelites, a child who would threaten the king's sovereignty.

4. *Assembling.* The verb *synagein* is frequent in Matthew's passion narrative (absent in Mark's; once in Luke's) to describe the assembling of Jesus' enemies against him, especially the chief priests, the scribes, and the elders (26:3,57;

27:17,27,62). It also appears in Ps 2:2 where the rulers assemble against the anointed king (the messiah).

all the chief priests and scribes. The Sanhedrin consisted of the priests, the scribes, and the elders; and so we may be meant to think of a session of that body. The reference to "all" broadens the responsibility, a tendency seen in the references to "the whole Sanhedrin" in the passion narrative (Matt 26:59; Mark 15:1). The reference in the plural to "chief priests" need not mean that Matthew erroneously thought there was more than one high priest at a time (cf. 26:3), for the plural is an accepted idiom found in Josephus and the Mishnah. Under the rubric of "chief priests" were included the incumbent high priest, deposed but still living high priests, and members of the privileged families from which the high priests were chosen. See Schürer, *History*, II, I, 203–6.

of the people. In 27:1 we hear of "all the chief priests and elders of the people." The shift from "elders" to "scribes" as the companions to the priests may be explained by Matthew's dependence here on a pre-Matthean narrative based on the birth of Moses, wherein "priestly scribes" advised the Pharaoh. See footnote 41 in § 4. The reference to the people may be another way of broadening the responsibility (cf. 27:25). It also raises the possibility that Matthew no longer considers himself part of that people. In any case, there is an implicit contrast between these religious authorities "of the people" and Jesus, "a ruler who will shepherd my people Israel" (2:6).

of them. The phrase is omitted in Codex Bezae.

the Messiah. The magi asked for "the King of the Jews"; Herod speaks of "the Messiah." For the same interchangeability, see Matt 26:63 where in the Sanhedrin the chief priest asks about Jesus as "the Messiah" and 27:37 where Jesus is crucified by the Romans as "the King of the Jews."

5. *the prophet.* The citation is compound, from Micah 5:1 (RSV 5:2) and II Sam 5:2. As in 1:22, some manuscripts betray scribal attempts to supply the name of the prophet, e.g., Micah or even Isaiah.

6. *(in the) land of Judah.* The Greek is awkward, as if "land of Judah" were in apposition to "Bethlehem." Codex Bezae and the OL have substituted an easier reading: "Bethlehem of the land of Judea," in imitation of "Bethlehem of Judea" in 2:1.

7. *Then. Tote* (here, 16, and 17) is Matthew's favorite connective, contrasted with the typical Marcan use of *kai.*

ascertained . . . the exact. This translates the verb *akriboun,* a technical term used in astronomical observations. Matthew is preparing for the order by Herod in 2:16 to massacre all the boys "of two years of age and under."

the star had appeared. Boll, "Stern," points out that the verb *phainesthai* applied to the star here covers the same event as "we have seen his star at its rising" in vs. 2. It refers to the time when the star came up over the horizon, the year, the month, and the day.

8. *the child.* Beginning here, Matthew will use *paidion* nine times to refer to Jesus, while using *pais* and *teknon* for the massacred children of Bethlehem and of Rachel (2:16,18). Luke uses *paidion* three times for Jesus (2:17,27,40), but also *pais* (2:43), *teknon* (2:48), and *brephos* (2:12,16).

bring me word. The verb, meaning "to report, announce," does not make clear whether the magi are to send word or to bring it themselves. The latter is implied by 2:12.

9. *Obeying.* Literally, "Having listened to."

at its rising. See NOTE on vs. 2.

the place where. The Greek has simply a relative pronoun; only in vs. 11 is a house mentioned. While the motif of a star leading people to a destination is known in antiquity (NOTE on "his star" in vs. 2), the precision of leading them to a house is unusual.

10. *were greatly overjoyed.* Literally, "rejoiced exceedingly with great joy." There is a certain intensity in having a cognate accusative ("rejoiced with joy"); it is heightened by the modifying adjective ("great joy"; BDF 153[1]); and here it is further heightened by the adverb "exceedingly."

11. *house.* Presumably this was the house which served as the home of Joseph and Mary who were inhabitants of Bethlehem. The view is quite different from that of Luke 2:1–7. There have been many attempts, often quite forced, to harmonize the information. An ingenious explanation has been offered by Bartina, "Casa": here *oikia* does not mean "house" but the "village" of Bethlehem. He argues that in Matt 10:12–14 a related word *oikia* is interchangeable with *kōmē*, "village," and that in Micah 5:1 (LXX) Bethlehem is described as an *oikos* ("village"?) of Ephrathah. The latter argument has little force: Matthew can scarcely have had the LXX usage in Micah in mind since he quotes the Micah passage without using the LXX expression.

treasure-boxes. In this instance, *thēsauros* is probably not the accumulated treasure itself (as in Matt 6:21) but the coffer that held it. The *Protevangelium of James*, 21:3, speaks of their knapsack (*pēra*, a noun also used for a shepherd's bag); and Epiphanius thought that this was the correct reading for Matthew. However, the second-century *Protevangelium* here, as elsewhere, probably represents a combination of Matthean and Lucan traditions (e.g., the star brings the magi *to the cave*), and the idea of a sack may echo the Lucan theme of shepherds.

gold. It has been suggested that in some instances (especially those dealing with Sheba in Arabia) where the Bible seems to speak of gold, the translation is an error. The Hebrew word for gold is *zāhāb*, reflecting a proto-Semitic root *dhb*, "gold." However, South Arabic has a word from the root *dhb* referring to an aromatic substance. Therefore, there may have been a word *dahab* (Hebrew *zāhāb*) referring both to gold and to a type of incense. In most Semitic languages the more common usage as "gold" would have eventually drowned out the usage as "incense." Ryckmans, "De l'or," suggests that in Isa 60:6 ("The young camels from Midian and Ephah, all those from Sheba will come; they will bring *gold* and frankincense") Hebrew *zāhāb* may refer to incense rather than to gold, since it is yoked to frankincense. Obviously, by the time Matthew wrote, the meaning "gold" was accepted.

12. *warned in a dream.* The *Protevangelium of James*, 21:4, specifies that the warning came from an angel; but that information has been deduced from the other angel/dream scenes in the Matthean infancy narrative (1:20; 2:13,

19). The failure to mention an angel here and in 2:22 is a reason for suggesting that the pertinent material was not part of the pre-Matthean narrative of angelic dream appearances. The verb *chrēmatizein* is not unusual for divine revelations and admonitions.

COMMENT

There is a smoother narrative flow in ch. 2 than was possible in ch. 1 in which genealogy and narrative had to be combined; for that reason ch. 2 is more easily seen as a unit. Nevertheless, a division within this chapter is quite plausible, as can be seen from the fact that 2:1–12 is centered on Bethlehem with the magi foiling Herod, while 2:12–23 moves the action from Bethlehem through Egypt to Nazareth with Joseph foiling Herod. Consequently, although below I shall make some general remarks about Matthean thought in the whole of ch. 2, the detailed exegesis of the chapter will be divided into two sections.

A. Matthew's Message: the Where and the Whence— Reactions to a Christological Revelation

It is noteworthy that in both the Matthean and Lucan infancy narratives, the description of the birth of Jesus and its aftermath (the second chapter in each) constitutes almost a separate narrative in independence of what has gone before.[1] In both, one could read the second chapter and understand it perfectly without knowing or even suspecting the material in the first chapter.[2] Again in both, the first mention of Bethlehem does not occur until the second chapter, a chapter that ends with a subsequent move of the parents and the child to Nazareth.[3] As for Matthew, I shall eventually seek to explain some of this independence in terms of new pre-Matthean

[1] In Luke this is more obvious since ch. 2 has a self-sufficient introduction. In Matthew the beginning of the chapter is too brief and would have to be expanded were that chapter to mark the beginning of the Gospel.

[2] The virginal conception, for instance, is not mentioned or even clearly presupposed either in Luke 2 or in Matt 2. See footnote 32 below.

[3] Once again, in Luke this is more understandable since Mary and Joseph live in Nazareth and are brought to Bethlehem only by the census. The contention of Machen, *Virgin Birth*, 175, that Bethlehem is not mentioned in ch. 1 of Matthew because the events narrated there did not take place in Bethlehem, is dubious harmonization with Luke. Matthew gives the strong impression that Mary and Joseph lived in Bethlehem (NOTES on "house" in 2:11 and on "to return there" in 2:22).

material in ch. 2 (especially in 2:1–12) that had a different origin from the pre-Matthean material in the narrative of angelic dream appearances, the beginning of which we saw in ch. 1.[4] But first I am concerned to show that in the overall Matthean conception of the infancy narrative, ch. 2 is the logical sequel to the revelation of the Who and the How of Jesus' identity that was the message of ch. 1 (pp. 53–54 above). Let us first consider the plan of ch. 2 and then discuss how that plan is related to Matthew's message.

1. The Place of 2:1–12 in the Plan of Chapter Two

This chapter consists of two acts that spell out Matthew's theological conception of the narrative. The first act (vss. 1–12) is dominated by the magi from the East and their positive response to the revelation of the birth of the King of the Jews. The evil Herod lurks in the background with his coterie of chief priests and scribes; but his malevolent plan does not come to light until the second act (vss. 13–23), when the magi are off the scene. There we see that his reaction to the birth of the King of the Jews is to seek to kill the child, an attempt that is foiled by God's guidance of Joseph through an angel. Interwoven with the respective good and evil reactions to Jesus in the two acts is a geographical concentration. The chapter opens in Bethlehem and closes in Nazareth, major sites in Jesus' life. The first act moves toward Bethlehem and reaches a culmination there; the second act moves away from Bethlehem to the extent that Joseph (and Jesus) cannot return there. Also interwoven, and related to the geographical concentration, is a theme of the fulfillment of Scripture. We may schematize all of this in the following plan wherein the two acts are divided into five scenes:[5]

Act I (2:1–12): The magi from the East, representing the Gentiles, receive God's revelation about the birth of the Messiah through a proclamation in nature, a star. They come to Jerusalem and are further enlightened about the place of the Messiah's birth through the Jewish Scriptures. They go to Bethlehem to pay him homage with gifts, and then return another way.

Scene 1 (2:1–6): The magi come from the East to Jerusalem and are directed to Bethlehem. Concluded by a formula citation from Micah 5:1 and II Sam 5:2 mentioning Bethlehem.

---

[4] The pattern of 1:20 (Table VI) is continued in 2:13 and 2:19, but is not found in 2:1–12. See NOTE on "warned in a dream" in 2:12.

[5] A pattern of five divisions is perceptively suggested by Hengel and Merkel, "Magier," 141–42, but their treating these five as if they were of equal status does not do justice to the themes that unite Scenes 1 and 2 into Act I, and Scenes 3–5 into Act II.

> Scene 2 (2:7–12): The magi go to Bethlehem where they pay homage to the king and offer him gifts. There is an implicit citation of Ps 72:10–11 and Isa 60:6 concerning foreigners bringing gifts of gold and frankincense in homage to the king, God's royal son (Ps 72:1).

Act II (2:13–23): Despite a knowledge of the Scriptures in which he has been instructed by Jewish officialdom, Herod seeks to kill the newborn king. But through God's planning the Messiah is taken away to Egypt and brought back alive (to Nazareth).

> Scene 3 (2:13–15): The flight of Joseph with the child and his mother to Egypt. Concluded by a formula citation of Hosea 11:1 mentioning Egypt.
>
> Scene 4 (2:16–18): The massacre of the children at Bethlehem by order of the wicked Herod. Concluded by a formula citation of Jer 31:15 mentioning Ramah (thought to be near Bethlehem).
>
> Scene 5 (2:19–23): The return of Joseph with the child and his mother, not to Bethlehem of Judea, but to Nazareth of Galilee. Concluded by a formula citation (of Isa 4:3 and Judg 16:17?) mentioning derivation from Nazareth.

2. The Relation of the Plan to Matthew's Message

Stendahl has analyzed the motif of ch. 2 in terms of the question *Unde* ("Whence?"), corresponding to the question *Quis* ("Who?") which he detected as the theme of ch. 1. We saw that the theme of ch. 1 was more complicated since it contained a revelation not only about the *Who* (*Quis*) of Jesus' identity (namely, the messianic son of David, and "God with us" or Son of God), but also about the *How* (*Quomodo*)[6] of this identity (namely, Emmanuel by being begotten of Mary through the Holy Spirit; son of David by being named and accepted by Joseph, a son of David). Similarly here the situation is more complicated than Stendahl's formula indicates. The "Whence" motif appears in Act II with the geographical move from Bethlehem through Egypt and back to Nazareth of Galilee. The motif of Act I, however, is better described as *Ubi* ("Where?"), since that act focuses attention on Bethlehem as the Davidic city, the birthplace of Israel's ruler.

The double motif of *Ubi et Unde* has some of the same apologetic goal that the double motif of *Quis et Quomodo* had in ch. 1. Matthew's presentation of Jesus as son of David and Emmanuel was in part inspired by controversy with Jews who did not believe in Jesus—Jews who denied his

6 See footnote 30 in § 2.

divine origin because they knew of his humble human family, and indeed may have questioned even the family origin by a charge of illegitimacy. The geographical theme of ch. 2 seems to have been aimed at the very same group. His opponents mocked the fact that Jesus was from Nazareth in Galilee, an obscure locale that lent little support to either Davidic or divine origin. Our best evidence for Jewish polemic on this score comes from the Fourth Gospel which in dealing with the Synagogue is not too far in stance from Matthew (footnote 5, § 2). In John 1:45–46, when Jesus of Nazareth is hailed as the one described in the Mosaic Law and the prophets, Nathanael retorts, "Can any good come from Nazareth?" In 7:52, the Pharisees[7] challenge Jesus' supporters: "Look it up [in Scripture], and you will not find the Prophet arising in Galilee." And in 7:41–42 the objection to Jesus as the Messiah is quite specific: "Surely the Messiah isn't to come from Galilee? Doesn't Scripture say that the Messiah, being of David's family, is to come from Bethlehem, the village where David lived?" Matthew's story in ch. 2 answers these Jewish objections in a double way, by the *Ubi* and the *Unde*. The "Where" motif of Act I (2:1–12) shows that Jesus did meet the strictest Jewish expectations about the Messiah: as a true son of David, he was born in Bethlehem, the ancestral Davidic home.[8] The "Whence" motif of Act II (2:13–23) shows that it was no historical accident that Jesus came from Nazareth and was known as a Nazorean. The same God who had spoken through the prophet to predict that the ruler would come forth from Bethlehem also spoke through the prophets of a Nazorean. Far from detracting from Jesus' claims, the designation of him as a Nazorean underlined his status as the messianic *nēṣer* or "branch" and the *nāzîr* or "holy one" of God. (See NOTE on "Nazorean" in 2:23.)

Within this double-pronged answer to his opponents' objections about Bethlehem and Nazareth (which supplies the opening and closing geographical motifs of the chapter), Matthew is able to squeeze in an added apologetic use of geography. In moving Jesus from Bethlehem to Nazareth, he has him go to Egypt and return; and he has the massacre of the children at Bethlehem commented upon in the words that Jeremiah used to describe the exiled northern tribes. Thus, in a certain sense, the Matthean Jesus relives the Exodus and the Exile and fulfills the history of Israel.

Nevertheless, Matthew's apologetic motif is secondary: his first goal is not to refute the opponents of Jesus, but to explain the Christian mystery

---

[7] They would constitute the sole effective Jewish party in last third of the century when Matthew and John were writing.

[8] That Jesus' opponents could have been totally ignorant of this constitutes a difficulty, but not so great a difficulty as the fact that few of his followers seem to have known of it. There are only two clear references in the NT to Jesus' birth at Bethlehem, namely, Matt 2 and Luke 2. For a discussion of the historical problems, see Appendix III.

to a believing community of Jews and Gentiles. In the genealogy of ch. 1, especially in the mention of the "son of Abraham" alongside the "son of David" and in his inclusion of the foreign women, we saw Matthew hinting that Jesus was destined for Gentiles as well as Jews—a hint that reflected the mixed nature of the Matthean community (§ 2). However, in what followed in ch. 1, Matthew concentrated on Jesus as the son of David; and so it is fitting that now in 2:1–12 he turns his attention to the ramifications of Jesus as son of Abraham. He does this by showing that the first to pay homage to the newborn King of the Jews were Gentiles from the East.[9] In these magi Matthew sees an anticipation of Jesus' promise: "Many will come from East and West and sit at table with Abraham, Isaac, and Jacob in the kingdom of heaven" (8:11).

To understand the appropriateness of a reference to Gentiles here, let us recall what has been said previously (§ 1, A2; § 5A) about the christology of the conception of Jesus. I pointed out that the christological moment (i.e., the moment of the revelation of who Jesus is—the Messiah— the Son of God in power through the Holy Spirit), which was once attached to the resurrection and then to baptism, has in the infancy narratives been moved to the conception: it is the virginal conception that serves now as the begetting of God's Son. Historically, when the christological moment was attached to the resurrection, those who saw the risen Jesus went forth proclaiming who he was: Jesus is Lord, Jesus is Son of God. That post-resurrectional proclamation produced a twofold reaction: some believed it and paid homage[10] to the exalted king (first Jews, then Gentiles); others rejected both the message and the preachers. In short, the christological revelation was followed by proclamation and by the twofold reaction of acceptance/homage and rejection/persecution. When the evangelists looked back into the ministry of Jesus with the insight they had gained after the resurrection, they saw that the baptism which began the ministry was already a christological moment revealing to those who had the eyes and ears of faith that Jesus was God's Son endowed with the Spirit during the ministry. They also saw the same sequence of proclamation and the twofold reaction of acceptance and rejection. As soon as Jesus was baptized, he went forth proclaiming the good news (Matt 4:23). On the one hand, some accepted him as having the power of God and paid him homage as "God's Son" (14:33). On the other, the Pharisees rejected him; and "all the chief priests and elders of the people" (27:1) delivered him to the Roman ruler to be put to death. If the sequence of christological

9 There is no reasonable doubt that Matthew presents the magi as Gentiles. We can see this from the history of the term, from its use in Daniel, from the fact that they do not know the Scriptures, and from the implication that the "King of the Jews" is for them the king of another people. See the NOTE on "magi" in vs. 2.

10 In Philip 2:10 we have a description of the homage in terms of the bending of every knee, and so it is not surprising to find the magi bowing down to pay homage in Matt 2:11.

revelation, proclamation, and twofold reaction was verified in relation to the resurrection and the baptism, it is not surprising that it holds true in the infancy narrative as well. Chapter 1 told us of a christological revelation by an angel of the Lord in reference to the conception of Jesus; ch. 2 is the story of the proclamation of good news and the twofold reaction it received.

In shaping his story of that sequence, Matthew is affected by developments that had taken place in the Christian mission in the last third of the first century and by the history of his own community. Although the proclamation had been first made to the Jews who had the Scriptures to proclaim to them who Jesus was, the major part of the Jewish people had rejected Jesus as the Messiah, so that in Matthew's time the Pharisee authorities in the Synagogue were hostile to the claims made for Jesus, even as the chief priests and elders had been hostile during Jesus' lifetime. The Christian preachers had been delivered up to sanhedrins, flogged in synagogues, and dragged before kings for bearing testimony to Jesus (Matt 10:17–18) Meanwhile, Gentiles were flocking into the Christian communities, so that the apostolate had become one of going and making disciples of the Gentiles (28:19). As we saw in § 2A, in Matthew's own community the Gentiles had increased to the point that Matt 21:42–43 could interpret the parable of the vineyard to mean that the kingdom of God was being taken away from those who read the Scriptures and being given to a nation that would bear fruit. It is this particular twofold reaction to the Christian proclamation that Matthew anticipates in ch. 2.

The proclamation of Jesus as the Messiah is given to magi from the East, the wise and learned among the Gentiles.[11] Precisely since they are Gentiles, they receive their proclamation through created nature (see Rom 1:19–20; 2:14–15); but, like Balaam of old[12] who also came from the East and was endowed with special insight, they recognize the salvific import of the Davidic star. Although they hasten to Jerusalem to pay homage, the full revelation of the Messiah cannot be gleaned from nature: it is a secret found in the Scriptures, the special revelation that God has given to the Jews alone. And so the magi must learn from the Jewish Scriptures God's plan of salvation before they can find the Messiah and pay him homage. Therein lies a paradox: Jews who have the Scriptures and can plainly see what the prophets have said are not willing to worship the newborn king. In the twofold reaction to this combined proclamation by the

---

11 In the NOTE on "magi" in vs. 2 I reject the thesis that Matthew thinks of them as false astrologers. Luke 2 also hints at the impact of the birth of the Messiah on the Gentiles, but does so in reference to Rome and the West, personified in the might of the Caesars (2:1), while Matthew speaks of the East. This geographical difference probably reflects the respective sites of the Lucan and Matthean communities.

12 Below, in part C of this section, I shall comment on both the Balaam background and the impact of contemporary astrological beliefs on Matthew's story.

star and the Scriptures, the wise men of the Gentiles accept and pay homage; but the ruler of Jerusalem and all the chief priests and scribes of the people do not believe. Rather, they conspire against the King of the Jews and seek to put him to death.[13]

I have said that in this portrayal Matthew is echoing the history of his own times, with the conversion of the Gentiles and persecutions before synagogues and sanhedrins and kings.[14] But he is also thinking of the passion of Jesus. At Jesus' trial and crucifixion, the secular ruler in Jerusalem and "all the chief priests and the elders of the people" (27:1) were arraigned against Jesus. Modeled on them are the characters in ch. 2: the king in Jerusalem and "all the chief priests and scribes of the people." In the passion (27:25) "all the people" accepted the responsibility for Jesus' blood; in 2:4 "all Jerusalem" joins the authorities startled by the birth of the Messiah.[15] (There is a motif of judgment in their being startled: the same verb and form [*etarachthē*] appears in Dan 5:9 where the king is startled along with his advisors when his magi have failed to read the handwriting on the wall, a handwritten message telling him that his kingdom will be taken from him.) And the same title is in question: "The King of the Jews" was the charge placed over Jesus' head as he hung on the cross (27:37); and the only other place outside the passion that designation is applied to Jesus is here—a title given him by the magi but rejected by Herod and implicitly by those who advise him. In the crucifixion Jesus dies but is brought back to life through the resurrection; in the infancy narrative Jesus is taken away to another land and returns. In each instance God has confounded the kings and rulers who assembled against Him and His Messiah (Ps 2:2, which uses *synagein* as does Matt 2:4).

Thus understood, ch. 2 is the necessary completion of ch. 1 in the sequence of revelation, proclamation, and twofold reaction, a sequence that gives to the infancy narrative its status as a gospel in miniature. The gospel is the good news, but that gospel must have a passion and rejection, as well as success.

13 Although Herod alone commands the massacre at Bethlehem, he has sought his information about the place where the Messiah might be from "all the chief priests and scribes of the people" (2:4); and the plural reference in vs. 20 ("those who were seeking the child's life") places guilt on those others as well. The reaction of the Jewish authorities after reading the Scriptures reminds us again of a charge that the Fourth Gospel levels against "the Jews" who sought to kill Jesus: "You search the Scriptures . . . they also testify on my behalf. Yet you are not willing to come to me to have life" (5:39–40).

14 In light of Matthew's use of this terminology in 10:17–18, the language of 2:4 (see NOTES) is significant in the use of *synagein* (a verb related to "synagogue") and the hint of a session of the Sanhedrin called by the king.

15 I repeat the cautions I gave in ABJ, I, 368; II, 792, 802, 895, namely, that such attributions of guilt, while somewhat intelligible in the heat of a polemic between the Synagogue and the Church in the late first century, are not religious attitudes to be promoted. The imperfect, alas, mars even great religious insights. Repeated through the centuries, they have fostered a hatred against the Jews that has made a mockery of the Gospel.

B. *Matthew's Use of Scripture in the Service of His Message*

As we shall see in C below, there are themes from Scripture (e.g., the Balaam story) essentially interwoven in the very origins of the magi story in 2:1–12. But first, attention must be paid to the Scripture that surfaces in the final Matthean level of composition, either by formula or by implicit citation.

1. The Formula Citation of Micah 5:1 and II Sam 5:2 in Scene 1

We have seen that the coming of Gentiles from the East begins to illustrate the theme that Jesus is the son of Abraham by whom "all the nations of the earth will bless themselves" (Gen 22:18). In 1:1 the "son of Abraham" theme stands alongside the "son of David" theme, and so it is not surprising that Matthew continues the son of David motif in 2:1–12 by a formula citation joining two passages, namely, Micah 5:1 (RSV 5:2) and II Sam 5:2. The first of these states that from Bethlehem will come one who is to be a ruler in Israel. It is a very appropriate passage for the context in which Matthew has placed it, for the next line in Micah uses birth terminology: "until the time when she who is in travail has given birth." Since Bethlehem was David's place of origin, Micah was speaking of a Davidic king. The Davidic implication is made explicit by the addition of II Sam 5:2 ("You will shepherd my people Israel"); for that line was spoken to David when, as King of Judah, he was being asked by the tribes of Israel to extend his sovereignty over them as well. This shepherd motif of the II Samuel passage[16] protects against an interpretation of Micah that would support an absolute ruler and offer backing for a tyrant like Herod.[17]

The combined citation does not reflect exactly either the standard Hebrew (MT) or the standard Greek text (LXX) of the OT passages:

Matt: "And you, O Bethlehem (in the) land of Judah,
         are by no means least among the rulers [*hēgemōn*] of Judah;
         for from you will come forth a ruler [*hēgoumenos*]
         who will shepherd my people Israel."

16 The addition of a line pertinent to a shepherd may have been suggested by the context in Micah, for in Micah 5:3 (RSV 5:4) there is a reference to shepherding (feeding) the flock.

17 For Matthew's ideal of the humble king, see 21:5. The "son of David" in Matthew is a healer (9:27; 15:22; 20:31–32).

LXX: "And you, O Bethlehem, house of Ephrathah,
    are too small to be among the thousands [*chilias*] of Judah;
    from you there will come forth for me a leader [*archōn*] of
    Israel."
  "You will shepherd my people Israel."

MT: "And you, O Bethlehem Ephrathah,
    small to be among the clans [literally, "thousands"] of Judah;
    from you there will come forth for me one who is to be a ruler
    in Israel."
  "You will shepherd my people Israel."

We notice the following differences in Matthew's version:

■*Line 1:* All reference to Ephrathah[18] is absent. In its place the "land of Judah" appears as a modifier of Bethlehem. Some see this as Matthew's attempt to make the citation match the mention of Judea in 2:1,5a, although the majority of scholars think the influence was in the opposite direction and that the context was worded to match the citation. (Neither explanation is very plausible; see NOTE on "of Judea" in vs. 1.) Matthew's purpose is probably theological: "Ephrathah" would add little meaning, but "Judah" reminds the reader of the Messiah's descent from Judah (1:1,2).[19]

■*Line 2:* Matthew categorically denies the insignificance of Bethlehem as it is stated in both the LXX and the MT; for the greatness of Bethlehem hinted at in the earlier renditions of Micah[20] had been realized through Jesus' birth there. If this seems to be a deliberate Christian change of the text rather than a variant reading,[21] the second Matthean difference in line 2 can plausibly be explained as a variant reading—an interpretation of the Hebrew consonants *'lpy* as *'allupē*,[22] "rulers, head of clans," instead of *'alpē*, "clans, thousands."

18 The clan of Ephrath or Ephrathah, an ally of Caleb (I Chr 2:19,24,50), was installed in the region of Bethlehem (I Sam 17:12; Ruth 1:2); and their name passed to the city (Gen 35:19; 48:7; Ruth 4:11). See Burrows, *Oracles*, 51–60, for an elaborate theory about the history of the Ephrathite city of Shiloh. The original text of Micah 5:1 probably read "And you, O Beth-Ephrathah"; and a scribe, in an attempt to clarify this ancient designation, changed it to "Bethlehem Ephrathah."

19 A remembrance that Ephrathah stood in apposition to Bethlehem may explain the appositional reading "land of Judah" rather than simply "of Judah."

20 Although both the MT and the LXX state the insignificance of Bethlehem, this insignificance enhances the greatness to be, as described in the lines that follow. Matthew anticipates this greatness by affirming it already in line 2. Gundry, *Use*, 91⁵, thinks that the Matthean interpretation is insinuated in the targum of Micah.

21 Lohmeyer, *Matthäus*, 23, and Allen, *Commentary*, 13, argue for a variant reading, namely, that Matthew's rendition reflects not the *lhywt* (*lihyôt*, "to be") of the MT but *l'hyyt* (*l'* being the Hebrew negative *lō'*—thus, "you are not"). For the original meaning of *lhywt*, see J. A. Fitzmyer, CBQ 18 (1956), 10–13.

22 In three passages in the LXX *hēgemōn* (the word Matthew uses) renders the Hebrew *'allûp*. Lindars, *Apologetic*, 193², sees the possible influence of Ps 68:28(27) on Matthew's

▪*Line 3:* Matthew's shorter version drops the mention of Israel, for he will mention it in an appended fourth line from II Sam 5:2. The omission of "for me" may be also part of the general shortening of the line, although the originality of the phrase in the MT has been questioned.[23] The use of *hēgoumenos* was dictated by a desire to match the *hēgemōn* of line 2.
▪*Line 4* (II Sam 5:2): Here Matthew has made only a slight grammatical change necessitated by the joining of the two passages.

An evaluation of these differences suggests a scholarly care applied to OT texts. While the citation of II Sam 5:2 is in almost verbatim agreement with the standard Hebrew and Greek texts, the citation of Micah differs in many important details. Of the twenty-two words in the LXX form of Micah, only eight are found in the Greek of Matthew's citation. One may theorize that the text of Micah 5:1 came to Matthew in a form already fixed by Christian usage[24]—a form different from the standard versions we know—and that Matthew added a line from II Sam 5:2 in a Greek form identical with the standard versions. Matthew himself would have us believe that Micah 5:1 was accepted by Jews as referring to the birthplace of the Messiah, a thesis partially supported by John 7:41–42 which quotes people in Jerusalem: "Doesn't Scripture say that the Messiah, being of David's family, is to come from Bethlehem?" A Jewish polemic based on this text would lead Christians to develop a counterpolemic, interpreting it.[25]

A doubt has been expressed as to whether Matt 2:5b–6 is truly to be classified as a formula or fulfillment citation, since it lacks the usual formula: "(All) this was to fulfill what the Lord had spoken by the prophet." Moreover, the citation is not presented as the evangelist's comment but is part of the direct speech of the chief priests and scribes. However, the latter point explains the former: since the priests and scribes are speaking, they could scarcely have been quoted using the fulfillment formula. In this instance, Matthew has chosen to make the citation part of the direct speech of his opponents to show their obduracy. Even though they can read the Scriptures correctly, they do not choose to believe. That 2:5b–6 is truly a Matthean addition is suggested by the fact that, like the other formula citations in the infancy narrative, it could be omitted and no one

---

choice of words: "There is Benjamin, the youngest, in the lead; the princes of Judah and their rulers [*hēgemōn*]."

[23] According to Fitzmyer (footnote 21 above), the "for me" is a misunderstanding of a more ancient construction.

[24] If the text was already fixed, one can explain more easily the lack of conformity between Matthew's own "Bethlehem of Judea" in 2:1,5a and the pre-Matthean reading in the citation: "Bethlehem (in the) land of Judah." It is more difficult to attribute both forms to Matthew. Strecker, *Weg*, 57, argues that the form in the citation is not Matthean style.

[25] See also § 14, C1 below, on the possible role of Micah 4–5 in the background of Luke 2:8.

would notice its absence. Moreover, like the other three formula citations in Matt 2, it mentions a geographical place name.

2. The Implicit Citation of Isa 60:6 and Ps 72:10–11 in Scene 2

If Matthew has added a formula citation to the first scene of 2:1–12, seemingly he has added an implicit citation to the second scene. Under C below we shall discuss the Balaam narrative in Numbers which forms the background of the magi story. While, like the magi, Balaam acknowledges the greatness of the Israelite ruler who is symbolized by the rising star, there is nothing in the Balaam narrative about the offering of gifts. But the mention of the rising star in the Balaam narrative (Num 24:17) may have suggested to Matthew another OT passage that speaks of a rising light. Isaiah 60:1 is a passage addressed to Zion or Jerusalem as it awaits for its deliverer (see 59:20): "Be enlightened, O Jerusalem, for your *light* has come; and the glory of the Lord has *risen* upon you." A few verses later we hear: "The wealth . . . of nations will come to you . . . all those from Sheba will come bringing gold and frankincense, and proclaiming the salvation of the Lord" (60:5–6 LXX). If, as we shall see, the outlines of the magi were copied from Balaam, a seer from the East who saw the Davidic star rise, those outlines have been filled in from the Isaian description of the representatives of the nations who bring gold and frankincense to Jerusalem because the light and glory of the Lord has risen upon her. The Isaian citation helps to underline the Gentile character of the magi. In Matthew the place of the presentation of the gifts has shifted from Jerusalem to Bethlehem, but that shift is seen in Luke's use of Scripture in the infancy narrative as well (§ 14, C1) and is part of the newness of fulfillment. Added coloring probably came from a second passage that mentions Sheba and gifts *and homage*—the full combination echoed in Matt 2:11. This passage is Ps 72:10–11:[26] "May the kings of Sheba and Saba bring gifts; may all kings pay him homage." Later Christian reflection on the magi detected Matthew's use of the psalm, for the magi were quickly transformed into kings (see D below).

If one evaluates the two sets of Scripture citations that Matthew has used here, they catch very nicely what he has told us of Jesus in 1:1. The formula citation of Micah 5:1 and II Sam 5:2 in Scene 1 emphasizes his Davidic character and the fact that he is a King who will rule over Israel. The implicit citation of Isa 60:6 and Ps 72:10–11 in Scene 2 emphasizes

---

26 Gundry, *Use*, 129–30, treats Matt 2:11 as an allusive citation of the LXX of Ps 72:10–11 and Isa 60:6, since almost all its vocabulary (not necessarily in the same grammatical forms) is attested in those two OT passages. Non-canonical passages where Gentiles bring gifts to Jerusalem and Israel's God included *Enoch* 53:1; *Psalms of Solomon* 17:32–33.

his role as son of Abraham in whom all the nations of the earth are blessed, for at his birth are fulfilled the expectations that people, nay kings, from Sheba and Saba would bring gifts and pay the King homage. The star that rose in the East is the star of the King of the Jews, but this King rules over the nations as well.

C. *The Pre-Matthean Background of the Magi Story*

The two main lines in popular and scholarly thought about the magi story are that it is history or that it is the product of reflection on OT themes. First, then, let us turn to some questions of history and the related issue of verisimilitude. After that, we can turn to the main candidate in the proposals for OT background, namely, the Balaam narrative.

1. History and Verisimilitude

The simplest explanation of the pre-Matthean background of the magi story is that it is factual history passed down from the time of Jesus' birth in family circles. As I have explained in § 1, I refuse to dismiss such an explanation simply on the grounds that the events described are supernatural; for a presupposition that miracles are impossible is unscientific. Nevertheless, even without such a prejudice, those who wish to maintain the historicity of the Matthean magi story are faced with nigh insuperable obstacles.

a) *Intrinsic unlikelihoods.* A star that rose in the East, appeared over Jerusalem, turned south to Bethlehem, and then came to rest over a house would have constituted a celestial phenomenon unparalleled in astronomical history; yet it received no notice in the records of the times.[27] The narrative of how Herod assembled the priests and scribes for consultation betrays no awareness of the bitter opposition that existed between Herod and the priests, nor of the fact that the Sanhedrin was not at his beck and call. In vs. 4 the birthplace of the Messiah seems to be abstruse knowledge known only to theological specialists, while in John 7:42 the crowd speaks as if everyone knows that the Messiah is to be born in Bethlehem. The suspicious Herod makes no attempt to follow the magi in their five-mile journey from Jerusalem to Bethlehem. One can imagine the impression that exotic magi from the East with royal gifts would make in a small vil-

---

[27] Skepticism on this point has a venerable history. Chrysostom, *Homilies on Matthew* VI 2 (PG 57:64), pointed out that Matthew's account cannot fit any natural phenomenon. It really does not solve the problem of historicity to argue that the star was a purely internal vision seen by the magi alone—that is not what the narrative describes.

lage; yet when they go away, Herod's intelligence system cannot discover which child they visited. His slaughter of all the male children beneath the age of two is not mentioned in Josephus' detailed account of the horrors of Herod's reign.

b) *Irreconcilability with Luke.* Although Luke 2 also has Jesus born at Bethlehem, there is no mention of an intervention by Herod, of the coming of the magi, of a massacre, or of a flight to Egypt. Even the most determined harmonizer should be foiled by the impossibility of reconciling a journey of the family from Bethlehem to Egypt with Luke's account of their taking the child to Jerusalem when he was forty days old and their going on from Jerusalem to Nazareth where they stayed.

c) *Conflict with the accounts of the ministry.* The statement that all Jerusalem was startled over the birth of the King of the Jews and that there was widespread awareness of the King's birth at Bethlehem (Herod, chief priests, scribes, and, to their regret, the people of Bethlehem) conflicts with the Gospel accounts of the public ministry where the people in Nazareth do not know this and are amazed that Jesus has special pretensions (Mark 6:1-6 and par.) and where people in Jerusalem do not know that Jesus was born at Bethlehem (John 7:40-42). According to the Synoptic Gospels (Mark 6:14-16 and par.), Herod Antipas, the son of Herod the Great, despite the measures his father is supposed to have taken against Jesus, is perplexed by Jesus and seems to have no previous knowledge of him. A possible explanation may be found for one or the other of these difficulties,[28] but the overall thrust is clearly against historicity.

But, one may argue, there are also plausibilities in the Matthean narrative. There was an expectation that a ruler of the world would come from Judea.[29] There were remarkable astronomical phenomena in the period around the birth of Jesus. There was a general interest in astrology and in the relation of celestial events to human destiny. Magi were famous among both Jews and Gentiles as having special powers, good and bad. There were instances in the first century of potentates from the East bringing regal gifts to Jerusalem and Rome. I have called attention to these facts in the respective NOTES on "magi," "from the East," "his star," and "pay

[28] Richards, "Three Kings," exemplifies an intelligent attempt in this direction. Even though I think that the weight of the evidence casts very serious doubt on the overall historicity of the Matthean account of the magi, it is impossible to be certain about individual details. Therefore, sweeping statements (e.g., "There were no magi!") are quite unprovable.

[29] Josephus (*War* VI v 4; #312) reports this expectation and applies it to Vespasian, and it is repeated with that application by Tacitus, *Histories* V 13, and Suetonius, *Vespasian* 4. Obviously it served the political purposes of the Flavian emperors; but that very propaganda value makes it dubious how widespread among Gentiles the expectation was, independently of the political use. Nevertheless, Virgil's Fourth Eclogue (Appendix IX) bears witness to wide expectation of a world ruler who would bring peace.

him homage"; and I would presume that the readers of Matthew were aware of many aspects of this background. But this constitutes evidence of verisimilitude, not of history. Inclusion of these details would make Matthew's story intelligible and would be a natural way of expression. Christians who believed that Jesus was the Messiah might well explain him to Gentiles as the fulfillment of the expectation of a world ruler from Judea. If in the East, where there was contact with large Jewish colonies, some Gentiles were familiar with Jewish messianic expectation, this could easily have been dramatized by Christians as a readiness to accept the birth of Jesus.[30] Christians, sharing the general belief that celestial phenomena marked the birth of great men, may have reflected on astronomical peculiarities at the time of Jesus' birth, e.g., a supernova, or Halley's comet, or a conjunction of Jupiter, Saturn, and Mars, and, in retrospect, may have fastened on one or the other as a sign from God that His Son was going to be born. Yet, these contacts of the Matthean story with culture of its time do little to establish that the story is factual or to account for what originally inspired it. The original inspiration, in the judgment of many scholars, is to be sought in popular reflection on the OT.

2. The Balaam Narrative

In Table VII I gave a reconstruction of the main pre-Matthean narrative, structured around a pattern of angelic dream appearances and deriving its content from OT and Jewish stories about the patriarch Joseph, the interpreter of dreams who went to Egypt, and about the birth of Moses, the infant who was delivered from the murderous plans of the Egyptian king in order to become the savior of his people and lead them back from Egypt. While this narrative gives us the substance of almost the whole story in Act II of chapter 2 (13–23), it offers little background for most of Act I (1–12). The only details in Act I that have parallels in the angelic dream appearance narrative are Herod's being informed (in a dream?) that the messianic child had been born, and his inquiry from the priests and the scribes as to the exact locale, with the concomitant disturbance of all Jerusalem. There is nothing in the narrative (or in the stories about Moses[31] from which it was derived) to account for magi coming from the East or for the rising of a star to herald the birth of the child. And so already in § 4, B2, I suggested that we have intermingled in 2:1–12 another pre-Matthean narrative.

---

[30] In the NOTE on "from the East" I pointed out how second-century Christians converted Zoroastrian predictions of a savior into prophecies of the birth of Christ. Similarly Virgil's Fourth Eclogue was converted into a prophecy by Christian interpreters.

[31] At least in the stories about Moses which we can date to the first century A.D. (e.g., in Philo, Pseudo-Philo, and Josephus). I cautioned in § 4, B2, about the indiscriminate use of later targums and midrashim to reconstruct what a first-century Jew would have thought of Moses.

A general objection to this hypothesis is offered by scholars who have argued for the indissoluble unity of the composition in 2:1–12, as witnessed in the carefulness of its arrangement. For instance, Lohmeyer (*Matthäus*, 19) sees a parallel arrangement of six short episodes, with episode 1 matching episode 4, etc.:

1	Magi come to Jerusalem led by star (vss. 1–2)	4	Magi go to Bethlehem led by star (9–10)
2	Herod asks scribes where the Messiah is to be born (3–6)	5	Magi find the child and offer royal gifts (11)
3	Herod instructs magi to find the child and return (7–8)	6	Magi warned not to return to Herod (12)

André Paul (*L'Evangile*, 97–98) has built upon Lohmeyer's suggestion by detecting a Jerusalem setting and a question by Herod in each episode on the left side of the schema, and a Bethlehem setting and a response in each episode on the right side. However, some of this parallelism is clearly the evangelist's work, e.g., the citations of Scripture (formula and implicit) in 5b–6 and 11. Moreover, part of the parallelism is more in the exegete's eye than in the text. In episode 1 the magi are *not* led by a star to Jerusalem, and there is no question by Herod (who does not figure at all, except as a chronological setting). The first three episodes concern Jerusalem and the last three concern Bethlehem simply because in the story the magi come to Jerusalem before they go to Bethlehem. The apparent "unity" of 2:1–12 may easily be explained as the result of intelligent editing and does nothing to disprove the inclusion of once independent material.

The features noted above as *not* stemming from the main pre-Matthean narrative (Table VII), namely, the coming of the magi from the East after the rising of the star, create certain conflicts or tensions within 2:1–12 which support the thesis of the joining of independent narratives. Why does the star, which eventually leads the magi to the house where Jesus is, not lead them directly to Bethlehem from the East, so that a stop at Jerusalem would not be necessary? We seem to have two different stories pointing to Bethlehem, one through investigation of the Scriptures, the other through the star. Herod's failure to find the child at Bethlehem would be perfectly intelligible in a story in which there were no magi who came from the East and where he had only general scriptural knowledge about Bethlehem to guide him. It becomes ludicrous when the way to the house has been pointed out by a star which came to rest over it, and when the path to the door of the house in a small village has been blazed by exotic foreigners. The total absence of Joseph in 2:1–12 is inexplicable if that story came from the main pre-Matthean narrative which is centered around Joseph (notice how prominent Joseph is in 2:13–23); it is quite intelligible if the substance of 2:1–12 came from another story in which Joseph had no major part.[32] Thus, according to the criteria proposed in § 4, B1, there is justification for isolating the following reconstructed pre-Matthean narrative about magi from the East:[33]

> Now, after the birth of Jesus in Bethlehem of Judea,[34] behold, magi from the East came to Judea[35] saying, "Where is the newborn King of the Jews? For we have seen his star at its rising and have come to pay him homage." And behold, the star which they had seen at its rising went before them until it came to rest over the place where the child was. (When they saw the star they were greatly overjoyed.)[36] And entering the house, they saw the child with Mary his mother; and they bowed down and paid him homage.[37] Then[38] they went away to their own country.[39]

[32] The clause "They saw the child with Mary his mother" has been brought forward, erroneously in my opinion, as the (only) indication in ch. 2 supporting the theme of a virginal conception. The failure to mention Joseph has been seen as a hint that Jesus had no human father. On the level of Matthean composition, this is a strange argument, for Joseph is the central figure in the annunciation of the virginal conception in ch. 1. Moreover, the phrase "the child and his mother" occurs four times in the second part of ch. 2 (13,14,20,21) precisely in terms of their being with Joseph, so that the ordinary reader would scarcely see a hint of the absence of a human father in the reference to "the child with Mary his mother" in vs. 11. On the pre-Matthean level, to those familiar with the OT the occurrence of this phrase in the magi story would scarcely suggest a virginal conception, an idea totally unattested in the OT. Rather, since the magi story puts so much emphasis on homage paid to a Davidic king in Bethlehem of Judah, "the child with his mother" might evoke the peculiar importance given to the queen mother (*gebîrāh*, "the Great Lady") of a newborn or newly installed king in the Davidic dynasty. (On this point, see R. de Vaux, *Ancient Israel* [New York: McGraw-Hill, 1961], 117–19.) The honor paid to the king and his mother is attested in I Kgs 2:19 and Jer 13:18. The queen mother had an official position in the Davidic monarchy in Judah (but not in the Northern Kingdom), and her name is always mentioned in the introduction to each reign in the Book of Kings.

[33] As in my previous attempts to reconstruct pre-Matthean material, I warn the reader that there is no way to divorce this material from Matthean wording, since it has been thoroughly rewritten. What can be reconstructed here is of necessity much more fragmentary and incomplete than the reconstructed narrative of Table VII.

[34] Matthew 2:1, "Now, after the birth of Jesus in Bethlehem of Judea in the days of Herod the king," has elements of the two pre-Matthean narratives, both of which had the motif of birth in Bethlehem.

[35] Matthew 2:1 has them come to Jerusalem, but this specification was probably dictated by the combination with the other pre-Matthean narrative wherein Herod was at Jerusalem.

[36] The language of this verse is almost entirely Matthean, but there may have been a theme of exuberant joy in the pre-Matthean narrative. See in Luke 2:10 the "great joy" of the shepherds.

[37] I have omitted "they opened their treasure-boxes and brought out gifts for him: gold, frankincense, and myrrh" because this theme is not found in the Balaam story. We saw above that it may constitute an implicit Matthean citation of Ps 72:10–11 and Isa 60:6, catalyzed by the themes of rising light and paying homage.

[38] The "since they had been warned in a dream" of 2:12 stems from the joining with the Herod story and is in the same language as 2:22, which we saw in § 4, B1, to be a Matthean creation.

[39] "By another route" in Matt 2:12 was necessitated by the joining of the magi story to the Herod story. The stratagem may have been suggested by I Kgs 13:10; see also Tiridates in the NOTE on "pay him homage" (vs. 2).

If the background of the main pre-Matthean narrative (Table VII) was the combined story of Joseph in Egypt and Moses, what is the background of this narrative? Many suggestions have been made (Appendix VI), including the stories of the birth of Abraham, the visit of the Queen of Sheba to Solomon, and the struggle between Laban and Jacob. Nevertheless, the most likely background is offered by the episode centered on Balaam in Num 22–24.[40] The setting is the plot of Balak, the Transjordanian king of Moab; he feared the Israelites who were being led by Moses out of Egypt and sought to destroy them. Since I maintain that this pre-Matthean narrative based on Balak and Balaam was joined to a pre-Matthean narrative based on the birth of Moses, it is significant that both stories involve the attempt of wicked kings to destroy Moses. The Matthean Herod resembles both the Pharaoh and Balak.[41]

To accomplish his purpose, King Balak summoned a famous seer named Balaam to put a curse upon Israel. He was a curious figure: obviously a non-Israelite, an occult visionary, and a practitioner of enchantment (see Num 23:23). Small wonder that Philo, *Vita Moysis* I L;⨳276, calls him a *magos*. And as is true of magi in general (see NOTE) he is thought of as both evil and good. After Balaam came to Moab, Israelite men were seduced into idolatry by Moabite women (Num 25); and so a biblical tradition blamed Balaam for this stratagem and listed him as slain by the Israelites along with the kings of Midian (Num 31:8). This hostile view of Balaam is known in the NT (Rev 2:14; see also Jude 11; II Peter 2:15–16).[42] But in Num 22–24 itself Balaam is looked on in a positive way, for he prophesied good for Israel. The Philo passage that calls him a magus goes on to say that he was filled with an authentic prophetic spirit (⨳277), and in this view he would be very close to Matthew's magi. Like them, and indeed in the same phraseology, he comes "from the East" (LXX Num 23:7),[43] accompanied by two servants (22:22)—thus a party of three, even as Christian tradition came to settle on three magi (see D below). And when he came, he foiled the hostile plans of King Balak by

---

40 Paul *L'Evangile*, 101–3, gives a detailed list of parallels, some of which I have omitted as too tenuous.

41 Balak was from the Transjordan; Herod was an Idumaean, descended from the Transjordanian Edomites.

42 It is this pejorative view of Balaam that facilitated the identification of Laban and Balaam. See Appendix VI.

43 Where is this "East" in the Balaam story and does it help us to identify what Matthew meant by "the East" (see NOTE for various candidates)? On the one hand, Balaam is said to be from Pethor near the Euphrates river (Num 22:5; Deut 23:5[4]). This is the Pitru known to us from Accadian sources as being NE of Syria in the region of the Upper Euphrates and the Balikh—a localization that would favor the candidacy of Commagene as the home of Matthew's magi. However, another tradition in Num 31:8 and Josh 13:21–22 associates Balaam with the Midianites, a connection that would favor the candidacy of Arabia as the home of the Matthean magi.

delivering oracles that foretold the future greatness of Israel and the rise of its royal ruler. In other words, the wicked king sought to use the foreign magus to destroy his enemy, but the magus actually honored his enemy. Obviously this is very close to the story of Herod and the magi.

Our hypothesis of the joining of two pre-Matthean stories becomes very plausible at this point. In the story of the birth of Moses (which underlies the main pre-Matthean narrative of Table VII), as Josephus tells it, "sacred scribes" advised the wicked Pharaoh both of the birth of the Hebrew deliverer and how to destroy this child. The adapted latter function is reserved in Matthew's account for "all the chief priests and the scribes," a terminology that echoes the language of Josephus (footnote 41, § 4). But the former function is shifted over to the magi who, like Balaam, receive a revelation that will frustrate the king. The joining and realignment would be easily intelligible if, in Jesus' time, the sacred scribes in the birth of Moses' story were thought to be magi, even as Philo calls Balaam a magus. (In later Jewish tradition they were indeed thought to be magi and Balaam was named among them,[44] but it is not wise to use this later tradition as specific background for the NT.) Such an identification is suggested when we remember that the popular, midrashic first-century Jewish picture of the Pharaoh and his advisors conspiring against Moses even before his birth is certainly a reflection of the biblical picture of the Pharaoh and his advisors opposing Moses later in life. The LXX of Exod 7:11 speaks of the later advisors as "learned men, sorcerers, and charmers"; but Philo, *Vita Moysis* I xvi;⋇92, speaks of them as "magi" and "learned men."[45] Thus, we know of a contemporary picture wherein the Pharaoh was advised against Moses by magi possessing occult knowledge. Matthew's Herod is also advised by magi; but the Matthean magi have the added coloring of the magus Balaam who comes to the king from the East only to frustrate his designs.

Let us now turn to the oracles and visions of Balaam. The MT of Num 24:15–16 relates Balaam's vision to ecstasy,[46] but according to the LXX of 24:4,16 the vision of Balaam is the vision of one who sees God in his sleep. (A dream motif would constitute another similarity to the Joseph-Moses story.) The contents of the vision about the future leader begin to become explicit in 24:7 (LXX): "There will come a man out of his [Israel's] seed, and he will rule many nations . . . and his kingdom will be

---

44 Ginzberg, *Legends*, II, 254ff.

45 Josephus, *Ant.* II xiii 3;⋇285, calls them "priests," so that first-century Jews thought of scribes, priests, and magi advising the wicked Pharaoh.

46 Balaam's oracle is "the oracle of the man *whose eye is opened,* the oracle of him who hears the word of God, and knows what the Most High knows, and sees what the Almighty sees, *falling down but having his eyes uncovered.*" The word translated "opened" is of uncertain meaning, and some think it should be translated "shut."

increased." The most famous description, however, is that of Num 24:17 which differs notably in the MT and the LXX:

> "I see him, though not now;
> I behold him, though he is not near;
> a star will come forth from Jacob,
> and a scepter will rise from Israel" (MT).

> "I will point to him, though not now;
> I bless him, though he has not drawn near;
> a star will rise from Jacob,
> and a man will stand forth from Israel" (LXX).

Modern critics often suggest that the historical background for this oracle was the emergence of the Davidic monarchy, over two centuries after Moses' time: David was the star and the scepter ruling over the united kingdom of Judah and Israel. In any case, in the Judaism before Jesus' time, this passage had already been applied to the Messiah, the anointed king.[47] In several targums or Aramaic translations of Numbers, the fact that the star is a reference to a king is made specific.[48] And in the second century A.D. Rabbi Aqiba hailed as the Messiah the revolutionary Simon ben Kosibah, who was popularly known as Bar Cochba, i.e., *bar Kôkᵉbâ,* "son of the star."

Thus, beside similarities between the magus Balaam and the Matthean magi in title, origin, and role, we have the similarity whereby Balaam foretold that a star symbolizing the Messiah[49] would rise (LXX) and Matthew's magi saw the star symbolizing the Messiah (2:4) at its rising.

---

[47] We see this in the messianic interpretation of the passage by the Qumran community. The references to it in *4QTestimonia* (which is *not* a list of messianic prophecies—see JBC, article 68, #79) and 1QM xi 6 are not particularly helpful. But in CD vii 18–20, written at a stage when the Qumran community looked for the coming of two Messiahs, the star and scepter of Num 24:17 are seen as referring to two different figures. The *star* from Jacob is "the Interpreter of the Law," while the *scepter* from Israel is "the Prince of the whole congregation," respectively then, the levitical High Priest of the end times and the Davidic Messiah. (See R. E. Brown, CBQ 28 [1966], 55–56.) A similar exegesis is found in the *Testaments of the Twelve Patriarchs.* When *Levi* 18:3 speaks of the new priest whom the Lord will raise up in the last times, it says: "His *star* will rise in heaven, as if he were king." But it is to Judah that the *scepter* is applied (*Judah* 24:5). However, *Judah* 24:1 seemingly applies both star and scepter (="a man"—cf. LXX) to the (Davidic) Messiah from Judah, an interpretation that may reflect a later editing of the *Testaments.*

[48] Our copies of the targums date from the Christian era. Targum Neofiti I and the Fragmentary Targum (Jerusalem II) have: "A king will arise from the house of Jacob, and a savior and sovereign from the house of Israel." Targum Pseudo-Jonathan (Jerusalem I) has: "When the powerful king of the house of Jacob will reign, and when the Messiah, the powerful scepter of Israel, will be anointed." Targum Onkelos has: "A king will arise from Jacob, and the Messiah will be anointed from Israel."

[49] I refer to the interpretation of the Balaam oracle current in the first century, not to its original meaning. Matthew uses *astēr* for "star," while the LXX of Num 24:17 uses *astron* —scarcely a significant difference.

Some have objected that in the Balaam oracle the star is the king, while for the magi the star was the sign of the king;[50] but such a shift of imagery is quite intelligible once the king has been born. Another objection is that the Matthean star leads the magi (2:9), a feature not found in the Balaam story. However, we may have here another motif from Israel's wandering in the desert toward the Promised Land (the context of the Balaam story), namely, that of a light which brightened the night and went before Israel, leading it.[51] For Matthew, this privileged light has now been accorded to the Gentiles.

After the acknowledgment of the king in both the Balaam and the magi stories, there is a departure of the main characters: "Balaam went off to his home" (Num 24:25), and the magi "went away to their own country" (Matt 2:12). This ending was useful when the pre-Matthean magi story was joined to the pre-Matthean story based on the Joseph-Moses legends, for it explained why Herod could not interrogate the magi. And it remained useful on the Matthean theological level. We saw in A above that the magi are believers who have reacted in faith to the christological proclamation centered on the conception and birth of Jesus. Now, historically, there were no such believers present when Jesus' ministry opened with the baptism; and so it was imperative that the magi be made to depart from the scene immediately. Luke (2:20) shows exactly the same sensibility in having the shepherds return to their fields after glorifying God in Bethlehem.

This reference to Matthew's theological concerns reminds us how well the Balaam background fits in with the Gospel's ultimate use of the combined pre-Matthean stories.[52] The main pre-Matthean narrative (Table VII) placed around Herod only characters hostile to Jesus (chief priests and scribes); but the introduction of the magi/Balaam narrative brought positive characters on the scene. Thus the *twofold* reaction to revelation and proclamation was exemplified. The echoes of the Balaam story would remind the reader familiar with the Bible and Jewish midrashic tradition that already in the OT God had revealed His salvific intent to Gentiles. The presence of Gentile worshipers in Matthew's community was not the result of a failure in God's plan for Israel; it was the continuity and fulfillment of a plan of salvation for those from afar to be accomplished through the Messiah and Israel.

[50] An instance in the NT where the star is Jesus is found in Rev 22:16: "I Jesus . . . am the root and offspring of David, the bright morning star."

[51] This pointed out by Hengel and Merkel, "Magier," 153. See Exod 13:21; 40:38; Neh 9:19; Ps 78:14; 105:39.

[52] I have several times suggested that these stories were probably already combined on a pre-Matthean level. However, Matthew's reworking of the material makes judgment difficult (see footnote 38 above, and footnote 45 in § 7).

D. *The Magi in Subsequent Christian Piety*

The mysterious "wise men" from the East caught popular Christian fancy earlier and more often[53] than did Luke's rather pedestrian shepherd-visitors to Bethlehem. In the *Protevangelium of James* (second century) only magi come to pay homage at the Bethlehem *cave*—an interesting mixture of Matthew and Luke. In the Roman catacombs the magi made their pictorial debut a good two centuries before the shepherds, who belatedly appear in the fourth century in Sts. Peter and Marcellinus as subsidiary to the magi. If interest in relics is taken as a gauge, there is simply no contest between the magi and the shepherds. Indeed, the corporeal relics of the magi traveled on a grander scale than their original owners, to the point that in the twentieth century the relics were still traveling and even going back to their earlier home "by another route." We are told that the relics of the magi were brought from Persia to Constantinople in 490 by the Emperor Zeno. Relics (the same or others) appeared much later in Milan, and from there they went to Cologne in 1162 as part of the booty dispersed by the Emperor Frederick Barbarossa who had ravaged Italy. The magi's remains were none the worse for travel, apparently, for the report speaks of still incorrupt bodies. Today these relics remain in Cologne in a magnificently enameled shrine, although in 1903 the cardinal of Cologne sent some of the relics back to Milan as a gift to the cardinal of that city.

It is only in comparatively recent times that the magi encountered opposition and competition. According to Marsh-Edwards ("Magi," 1), under the influence of anti-symbolic feelings aroused by the Protestant Reform, the shepherds began to take the place of the magi, particularly as the mainstay of Christmas carols: "Being free from all taint of the 'Popish superstition' of relic adoration, they could be safely lauded." The battle over the magi was to come later in Catholicism. On the American Catholic scene in the early 1960s, when the effects of biblical criticism were beginning to be felt on a practical level, disbelief in the magi was used by reactionaries as a barometer to test just "how far out" an exegete was. And it must be admitted, with a mixture of sadness and amusement, that some of those who circulated the "good news" of biblical reform seem to have had

---

[53] Our information here is drawn from the works of Kehrer, Leclercq, Marsh-Edwards, and Metzger in the accompanying bibliography. The last mentioned ("Names," 79–80²) gives a short scientific bibliography, and Leclercq provides reproductions of ancient illustrations.

as their chief kerygmatic proclamation: "There were no magi!"[54] It is told that one such magi-debunker received a hand-painted Christmas card depicting three very angry Orientals in royal garb, accompanied by camels, knocking at the door of his study, demanding by name to see him.

The enrichment that imagination and devotion have brought to the Matthean story of the magi is a remarkable example of Christian midrash. In Appendix VIII I shall discuss the problematic use of the term "midrash" to explain the literary form of the Matthean and/or Lucan infancy narrative and the relation of that narrative to the OT. But if midrash is understood as the popular and imaginative exposition of the Scriptures for faith and piety, then the term may quite appropriately be applied to the way the infancy narratives were interpreted and enlivened in subsequent Christianity. As applied to the magi, the first step in the midrashic process seems to have been that of elevating them to royalty, a step encouraged by Matthew's implicit citation of Ps 72:10–11: "May the kings of Sheba and Saba bring gifts; may all kings *pay him homage*" (see B2 above).[55] By the end of the second century Tertullian reports, "The East considers magi almost as kings" (*Adversus Marcion* iii 13). In the West, by the time of Caesar of Arles (*ca.* 500), it was taken for granted that the magi were kings. Another step in the midrashic process was the specification of the number of magi-kings. In light of the mention of three gifts (2:11), most often (and now exclusively) the number has been set at three. Yet other numbers appear: two in the above-mentioned catacomb art of Sts. Peter and Marcellinus; four in the third-century catacomb fresco at St. Domitilla; and twelve (with names!) in some medieval Eastern lists.[56]

In the East the earliest known attempt to give the magi names identifies them as: Hormizdah, king of Persia; Yazdegerd, king of Saba; and Perozadh, king of Sheba.[57] In a Christian work preserved in Ethiopic, the *Book of Adam and Eve* (iv 15), the magi are Hor, king of the Persians; Basanater, king of Saba; and Karsudan, king of the East. Better known to most Christians is the Western tradition whereby the names of the magi are Balthasar, Melchior, and Gaspar. The first (and somewhat corrupt) literary reference to this tradition is in the *Excerpta Latina Barbari,* a Latin translation of a sixth-century Greek chronicle. Three magi appear clearly in the famous sixth-century mosaic of the church of St. Apollinaris (Nuovo) at Ravenna, but the legend over their heads supporting the

---

[54] See footnote 28 above.

[55] Also Isa 49:7: "Kings will see and arise; princes will pay homage"; Ps 68:30(29): "Because of Your Temple in Jerusalem, kings bring gifts to You."

[56] Leclercq, "Mages," col. 1066; Metzger, "Names," 83.

[57] Marsh-Edwards, "Magi," 6, attributes these names to the fourth-century Syrian writer Ephraem, but gives no reference. Metzger, "Names," 82, attributes these names to the sixth-century Syriac work *Cave of Treasures* and gives the reference. Unless otherwise noted, the information about names is taken from Metzger.

Western tradition of their names is of uncertain date.[58] These names and
the hint that the magi represent different races appear in a classical description of them:[59]

> The magi were the ones who gave gifts to the Lord. The first is said to
> have been Melchior, an old man with white hair and a long beard
> . . . who offered gold to the Lord as to a king. The second, Gaspar
> by name, young and beardless and ruddy complexioned . . . honored
> him as God by his gift of incense, an oblation worthy of divinity. The
> third, black-skinned and heavily bearded, named Balthasar . . . by
> his gift of myrrh testified to the Son of Man who was to die.

It would be considerably later, however, before a black king made his appearance in art. The symbolism of the gifts in this quotation goes back to
the second century, for it is found in Irenaeus (*Against the Heretics* III ix
2) and in a fourth-century hymn of Prudentius on the Epiphany (PL
59:904–5). Eventually, alongside this symbolism which related the gifts to
different aspects of Jesus (king, God, suffering redeemer), there developed
a symbolism relating them to different aspects of Christian response: gold
symbolizing virtue, incense symbolizing prayer, and myrrh, suffering.

Further information is supplied with charming naivete by the obituary
notice in the calendar of saints at Cologne,[60] where the magi finally came
to rest:

> Having undergone many trials and fatigues for the Gospel, the three
> wise men met at Sewa (Sebaste in Armenia) in A.D. 54 to celebrate
> the feast of Christmas. Thereupon, after the celebration of Mass, they
> died: St. Melchior on January 1st, aged 116; St. Balthasar on Janu-
> ary 6th, aged 112; and St. Gaspar on January 11th, aged 109.

We may smile at the anachronisms in such descriptions, but this imaginative reflection on the magi is not too far from Matthew's own intent. In
the persons of the magi Matthew was anticipating the Gentile Christians of
his own community. Although these had as their birthright only the revelation of God in nature, they had been attracted to Jesus; and when instructed in the Scriptures of the Jews, they had come to believe in and pay
homage to the Messiah. Subsequent Christian midrash continued this
process of coloring-in the outline of the magi with hues familiar from the

---

[58] See the photo in the *New Catholic Encyclopedia* (New York: McGraw-Hill, 1967), IX,
62.

[59] This appears in the treatise *Excerpta et Collectanea* (PL 94:541CD) associated, probably incorrectly, with the saintly Anglo-Saxon historian, "the Venerable Bede," of Jarrow
(*ca.* 700).

[60] Marsh-Edwards, "Magi," 9.

lives of Christians of later centuries. The king was now described in the incarnational terminology derived from the creeds—the magi honored him as God and man. The gifts were related to the spirituality of ordinary Christian lives, filled with good deeds, prayer, and sacrifice. And the homage paid to Jesus was reinterpreted in terms of the main Christian act of homage, the Eucharist (Mass). Naive? Yes, but a valid hermeneutic instinct nevertheless.

SECTIONAL BIBLIOGRAPHY (§ 6)
(MATT 2:1–12)

Adler Planetarium and Astronomical Museum, "The Star of Bethlehem" (Chicago, 1961).

Bartina, S., "Casa o caserío? Los magos en Belén (Mt 2:11; 10:12–14)," EB 25 (1966), 355–57.

Bishop, E. F. F., "Some Reflections on Justin Martyr and the Nativity Narratives," *Evangelical Quarterly* 39 (1967), 30–39.

Boll, F., "Der Stern des Weisen," ZNW 18 (1917–18), 40–48.

Bruns, J. E., "The Magi Episode in Matthew 2," CBQ 23 (1961), 51–54.

Burrows, E., *The Oracles of Jacob and Balaam* (Bellarmine Series, III; London: Burns Oates, 1938), 97–100, on the magi.

Clarke, W. K. L., *Divine Humanity* (London: SPCK, 1936), 41–51, on the magi.

Daniélou, J., *The Theology of Jewish Christianity* (Chicago: Regnery, 1964), esp. 214–24, on Balaam's star.

Davies, W. D., *Setting*, 72–82, on the magi.

Delling, G., *"Magos,"* TDNT, IV, 356–59.

Denis, A. M., "L'adoration des mages vue par S. Matthieu," NRT 82 (1960), 32–39.

Dieterich, A., "Die Weisen aus dem Morgenlande," ZNW 3 (1902), 1–14.

Filas, F. L., "The Star of the Magi," IER 85 (1956), 432–33.

Galbiati, E., "L'adorazione dei Magi," BibOr 4 (1962), 20–29.

Hengel, M., and H. Merkel, "Die Magier aus dem Osten und die Flucht nach Ägypten (Mt 2) im Rahmen der antiken Religionsgeschichte und der Theologie des Matthäus," in *Orientierung an Jesus*, ed. P. Hoffmann (Festschrift Josef Schmid; Freiburg: Herder, 1973), 139–69, with detailed bibliography.

Holzmeister, U., "La stella dei Magi," *La Civiltà Cattolica* 93 (1942), 1–22.

Kehrer, H., *Die heiligen drei Könige in Literatur und Kunst* (2 vols.; Leipzig: Seemann, 1908–9).

Leclercq, H., "Mages," *Dictionnaire d'archéologie chrétienne* (Paris: Letouzey, 1931), X[1], cols. 979–1067.

McNamara, M., "Were the Magi Essenes?" IER 110 (1968), 305–28.

Mann, C. S., "Epiphany—Wise Men or Charlatans?" *Theology* 61 (1958), 495–500.

Marsh-Edwards, J. C., "The Magi in Tradition and Art," IER 85 (1956), 1–19.

Messina, G., "Una presunta profezia di Zoroastro sulla venuta del Messia," *Biblica* 14 (1933), 170–98.

—————— "Ecce Magi ab Oriente venerunt (Mt. 2,2)," *Verbum Domini* 14 (1934), 7–19.

Metzger, B. M., "Names for the Nameless in the New Testament," in *KYRIAKON*, eds. P. Granfield and J. A. Jungmann (Festschrift Johannes Quasten; Münster: Aschendorff, 1970), 79–99.

Montefiore, H. W., "Josephus and the New Testament," NovTest 4 (1960), 139–60, esp. 140–48 on the star.

Muñoz Iglesias, S., "Les mages et l'étoile," in *Assemblées du Seigneur* 12 (2nd series, 1969), 19–31.

Nellessen, E., *Das Kind und seine Mutter: Struktur und Verkündigung des 2. Kapitels im Matthäusevangelium* (SBS 39; Stuttgart: Katholisches Bibelwerk, 1969).

Richards, H. J., "The Three Kings (Mt. ii. 1–12)," *Scripture* 8 (1956), 23–38.

Rosenberg, R. A., "The 'Star of the Messiah' Reconsidered," *Biblica* 53 (1972), 105–9.

Ryckmans, G., "De l'or (?), de l'encens et de la myrrhe," RB 58 (1951), 372–76.

Schaumberger, P. I., "Textus cuneiformis de stella Magorum?" *Biblica* 6 (1925), 444–49.

Turner, N., "The New-Born King (Matthew ii. 2)," ExpTim 68 (1956–57), 122.

Vitti, A., "Apocryphorum de Magis enarrationes," *Verbum Domini* 7 (1927), 3–13.

Vögtle, A., "Das Schicksal des Messiaskindes. Zur Auslegung und Theologie von Mt 2," BibLeb 6 (1965), 246–79.

Zani, L., *"Abbiamo visto la sua stella": Studio su Mt 2,1–12* (Padova, 1973: excerpt from a doctoral dissertation at the Gregorian University).

VI. HEROD UNSUCCESSFULLY SEEKS TO DESTROY THE KING OF THE JEWS (§7)

Translation of Matt 2:13–23

2 [13] Now, when the magi had gone away, behold, an angel of the Lord appeared to Joseph in a dream, saying, "Get up; take the child and his mother and escape to Egypt. Stay there until I tell you, for Herod is going to search for the child to destroy him." [14] So Joseph got up, took the child and his mother by night, and went away to Egypt, [15] where he stayed until the death of Herod. This was to fulfill what the Lord had spoken by the prophet who said,

"Out of Egypt have I called my Son."

[16] Then, when Herod saw how he had been deceived by the magi, he fell into a furious rage. He sent into Bethlehem and the regions all around it and massacred all the boys of two years of age and under, according to the exact time he had ascertained from the magi. [17] Thus was fulfilled what was spoken by the prophet Jeremiah who said,

[18] "A voice was heard in Ramah,
weeping and loud mourning,
Rachel crying for her children;
and she would not be consoled,
because they are no more."

[19] Now, when Herod died, behold, an angel of the Lord appeared in a dream to Joseph in Egypt, [20] saying, "Get up; take the child and his mother and go back to the land of Israel, for those who were seeking the child's life are dead." [21] So Joseph got up, took the child and his mother, and went back to Israel.

[22] But when he heard that Archelaus was king over Judea in place of his father Herod, Joseph was afraid to return there. And being warned in a dream, he went off to the district of Galilee. [23] There he went to dwell in a city called Nazareth, so that what was spoken by the prophets might be fulfilled:

"He will be called a Nazorean."

NOTES

2:13. *Now.* . . . Much of the vocabulary and grammar of this sentence reflects the stereotyped pattern found in the angelic dream appearances (Table VI). NOTES discussing these points are found in connection with 1:20.

the magi. The Greek has simply "they."

appeared. Although the verb in 1:20 is in the aorist tense, a historical present is employed here and in 2:19. Codex Vaticanus "improves" by using the aorist.

child. Paidion; see NOTE on 2:8.

for. The *gar* clause offering a reason for the command (Table VI).

is going to search. The idea is one of imminence (BDF 356): he has made up his mind to search.

to destroy him. The same verb (*apollynai*) appears in the passion narrative in Matt 27:20: "The chief priests and the elders had persuaded the crowds to ask for the release of Barabbas and *to destroy Jesus.*"

14. *So.* . . . Consistently in this pattern (Table VI), Joseph's action follows to the letter the angel's command.

went away to Egypt. Herod's power would not reach to Egypt which had been under Roman control since 30 B.C. It was a classic land of refuge for those fleeing from tyranny in Palestine. When King Solomon sought to put him to death, Jeroboam "arose and fled to Egypt" (I Kgs 11:40, a passage with close verbal similarity to Matt 2:14). When King Jehoiakim sought to kill him, the prophet Uriah, son of Shemaiah, fled and escaped to Egypt (Jer 26:21 [LXX 33:21]). About 172 B.C. the high priest Onias IV fled to Egypt to escape from King Antiochus Epiphanes, who had killed Onias' uncle (Josephus, *Ant.* XII ix 7;≯387). The likelihood that this refuge-in-Egypt tradition has influenced Matthew's story renders irrelevant the insistence of conservative scholars (anxious to protect historicity) that the family did no more than cross the border and went no farther than Gaza which was in the confines of Roman Egypt. Such a minimalist surmise is no more scientific and no more likely than the imaginative Coptic legends which have the family sailing several hundred miles down the Nile.

As a continuation of Christian midrash on the infancy narratives (§ 6D), a few of the charming Christian tales from Egypt are worth mentioning (see Meinardus, *Steps*). It is told that the journey of the family to Egypt was made easier by many miracles worked in their favor: they were protected from dragons, reverenced by lions and leopards who wagged their tails in homage, marvelously fed by palm trees that bent down before them (*Gospel of Pseudo-Matthew* 18–20; fourth to eighth century). As for their destination, one very popular tradition (*Arabic Infancy Gospel* 24; translated from a Syriac original of the fifth century or earlier) brings the family to Matariyah, just NE of Cairo, near ancient On (Heliopolis) and near the Jewish center at Leontopolis. Here Jesus was responsible for the growth of balsam trees or palm trees, a tradition that made its way with alterations into the Muslim Koran; for the balm from the balsam trees of Matariyah was used by both Christians and Muslims of the Middle Ages as a cure-all, healing anything from snake bite to running nose. Another tradition associates the holy family with Babylon, the Roman garrison post or colony over which Cairo was built. Accordingly, the church of Abu Serghis (Sargah), near the ancient Qaraite Jewish synagogue of Cairo, contends today to be the site of the home of the holy family in Egypt. There are also traditions associating the holy family with Middle Egypt. Hermopolis Magna (El Ashmûnein), some 175 miles south on the Nile from Cairo, was an important tax collecting center, and we are told that the pagan idols of the city temple fell to the ground as the holy family passed through (*Gospel of Pseudo-Matthew* 22–24). A famous site of pilgrimage, about 50 miles farther south, is the monastery Deir el-Muharraq, near El Qûsîya (Cusae or Kuskam), where the family lived for six months. Here is localized the story of the *Arabic Infancy Gospel* (23) wherein they were set upon by two robbers who attempted to plunder them, but one repented when he saw Mary's tears—these were the same two robbers who were to be crucified with Jesus on Calvary, and the one who repented was the Good Thief. It was also here, according to legend, that the report reached the family of what Herod had done in Bethlehem.

15. *the death of Herod.* For the dating of this to March/April 4 B.C., see NOTE on "Herod the king" in 2:1.

This was to fulfill. For fulfillment citations see Table V.

the prophet. Hosea (11:1) is meant. OS^sin wrongly identifies the prophet as Isaiah, probably an incorrect scribal inference from Matthew's general preference for Isaiah in fulfillment citations. Klostermann, *Synoptiker,* 165, thinks that the Syriac reading may be original and that the dropping of the name "Isaiah" may be an improvement by scribes who were embarrassed that Matthew made a wrong attribution. This is unlikely although there are instances of wrong scriptural attributions by Matthew (13:35; 27:9).

16. *Then, when Herod.* The same *tote* construction introducing Herod's action was seen in 2:7, also following a formula citation and marking a shift of scenes within the Act.

deceived. The verb *empaizein* has a tone of mockery or ridicule. The chief other use of it in Matthew (27:29,31,41) is for the mockery of Jesus as king during the passion narrative—another point of contact between that narrative and the infancy narrative.

He sent into Bethlehem . . . and massacred. Literally, "And having sent, he massacred in Bethlehem. . . ."

all the boys. The plural of *pais,* as contrasted with the plural of *teknon* ("children") in the citation from Jeremiah which Matt 2:17–18 applies to this event. The double use of "all" ("regions all around it") in this verse gives the impression of large numbers. Despite the obvious storytelling atmosphere, those interested in establishing the historicity of the event have calculated how many children there would have been in a village like Bethlehem and its surroundings. Because of the high infant mortality rate, we are told that if the total population was one thousand, with an annual birthrate of thirty, the male children under two years of age would scarcely have numbered more than twenty. In this thought pattern the lowness of the number is judged to increase the likeli-hood, as opposed to the tendency in later writing to exaggerate the number. Justin, *Dialogue* lxxviii 7, has Herod ordering the slaughter of all the boys with-out mention of an age limit. The Byzantine liturgy sets the number of "Holy Children" (or "Holy Innocents" in Western hagiography) at 14,000; Syrian menologies or calendars of saints set it at 64,000; and by accommodation with Rev 14:1–5 the number has reached even 144,000 (equaling the number of "those who have not defiled themselves with women"—a safely attributed vir-tue at the age of two). The speculation about numbers is another instance of Christian midrash.

of two years of age and under. This notice, fixing the age limit according to the rising of the birth star of the King of the Jews (2:1–2,7), has led scholars to date Jesus' birth *ca.* 6 B.C., two years before Herod's death (NOTE on "Herod the king" in 2:1). Matthew's opinion on this interval (and probably that of his source) is not to be easily discounted since Luke dates JBap's con-ception (some fifteen months before the birth of Jesus) "in the days of Herod the king."

17. *Thus was fulfilled.* Literally, "Then"—an awkward second *tote*, following the *tote* that introduced vs. 16. This fulfillment formula relative to Jer 31:15 differs from those in 1:22; 2:15b; and 2:23b (see Table V) in that it does not explicitly mention the notion of purpose; there is no "[in order] to fulfill," with the conjunction *hina* or *hopōs*. Probably this reflects Matthew's reluctance to attribute to God an evil purpose: that He would have brought about the death of the children in order to fulfill a prophecy. See in 27:9 the same handling of the fulfillment formula pertinent to Judas and the thirty pieces of silver.

18. *Ramah.* Why is Rachel's voice associated with Ramah? We are told in Gen 35:19 and 48:7 that Rachel died and was buried "on the way to Ephrath-[ah]." Since the veneration of Rachel's burial place would have been likely among a tribe that claimed descent from Rachel, I Sam 10:2 is plausible in lo-calizing Rachel's tomb "in the territory of Benjamin at Zelzah," i.e., near Bethel, about eleven miles N of Jerusalem. The same localization is implicit in the Ramah reference of Jeremiah: Rachel's voice could be heard in Ramah, about five miles from Bethel and halfway between Bethel and Jerusalem. How-ever, as we saw in footnote 18 in § 6, some of the clan of Ephrath(ah) eventu-ally settled in the region of Bethlehem and the name of (Beth-)Ephrathah was associated with Bethlehem (Micah 5:1). The tradition that Rachel died and was buried "on the way to Ephrath[ah]" was then also associated with Bethlehem, as indicated by the parenthetical gloss that has become part of the text in Gen 35:19 and 48:7: "Ephrath (that is, Bethlehem)." It is this late (and mistaken) form of the tradition that Matthew has drawn upon in associat-ing Rachel's mourning with a happening at Bethlehem, S of Jerusalem, even though the Jeremiah text he cites more correctly associates it with Ramah and the region N of Jerusalem. The transplanted tradition has endured, for to this day Muslims venerate the tomb of Rachel at a site just outside of Bethlehem.

loud mourning. Literally, "much mourning."

Rachel crying. For Jeremiah the figurative allusion to Rachel crying for her children is probably a reference to the captivity and deportation of the tribes of the Northern Kingdom by the Assyrians in 722–721 B.C., since some of the principal northern tribes (Manasseh and Ephraim) were reckoned as her descendants, along with Benjamin. Yet there is a possibility that Jeremiah is referring just to the Benjaminites whose fate was entwined with the Southern Kingdom of Judah, overrun by the Babylonians in 597 and 587. After the fall in 587, Jer 40:1 tells us that the captives from Judah and Jerusalem were taken to *Ramah*. In addition to the problem as to which captivity was in Jeremiah's mind, we have the problem of how Matthew understood Jeremiah. The fact that Matthew has previously cited Micah 5:1 (RSV 5:2) is ambivalent, for Micah 4:10 mentions captivity in Babylon, while Micah 5:4–5 (RSV 5:5–6) mentions the Assyrian invasion. In any case, Matthew changes the force of the Jeremiah text. Although Jeremiah describes Rachel as crying for her children, God's message to her is to stop weeping and crying, since the children are going to come back from the land of the enemy (31:16–17). In other words this is a message of joy and hope, none of which appears in Matthew. Later rabbinic writings attributed to Rachel a successful intercessory role on behalf of her children (St-B, I, 99), but there is no evidence that Matthew has speculated on the future fate of these massacred children. In piety the "Holy Innocents" became Christian martyrs and saints.

children. See NOTE on "all the boys" in vs. 16.

19. *Now. . . .* Much of the vocabulary and grammar of this sentence and of the next reflect the stereotyped pattern found in the angelic dream appearances (Table VI). NOTES discussing these points are found in connection with 1:20.

appeared. See NOTE on 2:13.

20. *the land of Israel.* This expression occurs only here in the NT. A possible background for Matthew's use of it is supplied by Ezek 20:36–38: "As I entered into judgment with your fathers in the desert of the land of Egypt, so I shall enter into judgment with you. . . . They will not enter into *the land of Israel*" (Paul, *L'Evangile*, 162).

for those who were seeking the child's life are dead. While it is true that Matthew is citing almost verbatim the LXX of the Lord's words to Moses in Exod 4:19 ("for all those who were seeking your life are dead"), Matthew's use of the plural remains a bit strange, since he has mentioned only the death of Herod. The plural is an allusive plural (BDF 141): others joined Herod in hostility to Jesus (2:3–4: "all Jerusalem"; "all the chief priests and scribes of the people"); but with Herod's death, the plot against Jesus' life has failed.

21. *So. . . .* Consistently in the angelic dream pattern (Table VI), Joseph's action follows to the letter the angel's command.

22. *when he heard.* Seemingly the information about Archelaus is described as coming to Joseph from a source other than revelation. This is awkward since the information that comes before and after it (the message that Herod has died and they are to go back to Israel; the warning not to go to Judea) does come from revelation. The awkwardness reflects Matthew's addition of 22–23 to a basically pre-Matthean story that ended in 21.

Archelaus was king over Judea. Literally a present tense, as if in direct discourse (BDF 324). At Herod's death in 4 B.C., his kingdom was split into three parts which were accorded to his sons. The full brothers *Archelaus* and

Herod Antipas (sons of the Samaritan Malthace) got Judea-Samaria-Idumea and Galilee-Perea respectively; their half-brother *Philip* (son of Cleopatra of Jerusalem) got the regions E and N of the Lake of Galilee. Technically an ethnarch in Judea, not a king, Archelaus was the least liked of the three because of his dictatorial ways. The Jewish deputies who went to Rome to protest against his becoming ruler stated that he had ushered in his reign with a massacre of three thousand people (Josephus *War* II vi 2;⚹89). He persisted till his brutality became intolerable; and at the request of his subjects he was deposed by Rome in A.D. 6, thus enjoying the shortest reign of the three heirs (Josephus *Ant.* XVII xiii 2;⚹⚹342–44). By having Joseph avoid a Judea ruled by Archelaus and go to a Galilee ruled by Herod Antipas, Matthew is reflecting correctly the situation of greater political tranquillity in Galilee.

to return there. Joseph's first thought was to return to Judea, i.e., to "Bethlehem of Judea" (2:1), because he and Mary lived in a house there (2.11). Since Joseph and Mary were citizens of Bethlehem, Matthew takes pains to explain why they went to Nazareth. In Luke's account, where they are citizens of Nazareth, the painstaking explanation is centered on why they went to Bethlehem (2:1–5).

to the district of Galilee. In 20,22,23 there are three neatly balanced geographic phrases governed by *eis* ("into, to") with ever narrowing coverage: "the land of Israel"; "the district of Galilee"; "a city called Nazareth." Herod Antipas, the Herod of the stories of the ministry of Jesus, ruled in Galilee from 4 B.C. to A.D. 39, until finally, like his brother, he was deposed by Rome.

23. *Nazareth.* Although shown by archaeological investigations to have been occupied continuously since the seventh century B.C., Nazareth is never mentioned in any pre-Christian Jewish writing, a lacuna that is unfortunate since there is a problem in the NT about the form of the name. Of twelve NT occurrences the name appears ten times as *Nazareth* or *Nazaret* (most frequent), and two times as *Nazara* (Matt 4:13; Luke 4:16). If the latter instances reflect the Q source common to the two Gospels, then the one reference to the town in Q would have been in the form *Nazara*—a neuter plural form, but understood as a feminine singular in Matt 4:13. (See the same confusion about *Hierosolyma*, "Jerusalem," which is neuter plural in Matt 4:25, but a feminine sing. in 2:3.) The *Nazara* form appears also in the first non-biblical Greek reference to the town by Julius Africanus, a native of Palestine, writing *ca.* 221 (Eusebius *Eccl. Hist.* I vii 14). These facts have led some scholars to suggest that *Nazara* is the older form of the name; but Albright, "Names," 398, has argued that the form *Nazaret(h)* gives evidence of the retention of the feminine "t" ending, common in Galilean place names. When the name finally appears in post-Christian Hebrew writings (eighth century), it appears as *Naṣrat(h)*. If there was a ṣade (ṣ) in the Hebrew/Aramaic form of the town's name, it is curious that this should appear in the Greek form of the name as a zeta (z); for the normal transcription should yeild a sigma (s—*Nasareth*). Yet there are exceptions, e.g., the land called *'ûṣ* in the Hebrew of Job 1:1 appears in some LXX mss. as *ōz;* and the *Ṣō'ar* of Gen 13:10 appears as Zogora in Greek copies of Jer 48:34 (LXX 31:34). Moreover, we may be dealing with a peculiarity of the Palestinian Aramaic dialect wherein a ṣade (ṣ) between two voiced (sonant) conso-

nants tended to be partially assimilated by taking on a zayin (z) sound. In the Jerusalem church lectionary, reflecting Christian Palestinian Aramaic pronunciation, the name of the town appears as *Nāzōrăt(h)*. This form cannot be dismissed as a retroversion from Greek, for the names in this version of the Scripture usually have a correct Aramaic form (Albright, "Names," 400). I have given so much attention to the form of the name because of the problem of deriving "Nazorean" from it, to be discussed below.

what was spoken by the prophets. The citation given by Matthew is not a verbatim form or even a clear adaptation of any known OT passage, and there have been at least four directions in the attempts of scholars to explain what Matthew meant. (a) Matthew was quoting from known prophetic passages but combining them very freely. In the commentary we shall explore the possibility that he meant Isa 4:3 and Judg 16:17. (b) Matthew was citing a sacred book or books that later Judaism and Christianity did not accept as canonical and did not preserve for us, a suggestion already made by John Chrysostom. It is quite clear now that the canon of the Jewish Scriptures had not been completely fixed in NT times (JBC, article 67, ※※31–39); yet the ambiguity about books was chiefly in relation to *the Writings*, the third section of the Jewish Scriptures, coming after *the Law* and *the Prophets*. Matthew refers to "the prophets," a relatively fixed part of the canon. However, the reference may be a broad one—in 13:35 "the prophet" is used as a designation for the psalmist, and the Psalms belong among the Writings. A NT parallel for citing a (section of a) lost non-canonical book may be found in the presumed citation from the *Assumption of Moses* in Jude 9. The main objection to this explanation is that all the other times Matthew mentions a prophet in his fulfillment formulas, he is citing *known* OT books. (c) Matthew was citing a text whose OT source he did not know, and that is why he spoke so vaguely of "the prophets." This is proposed by Lindars, *Apologetic,* 196, who thinks that Matthew derived the citation from the storehouse of early Christian usage of Jewish writings. (d) Matthew did not intend to cite a specific text here. This general explanation has many different forms. Some have interpreted "the prophets" as a generic plural referring to the overall message of the OT concerning Jesus as a Nazorean. Others have noted that the expression "who said" does not appear after "the prophets"—contrast its presence in 1:22; 2:15b; 2:17b; and, indeed, in all the non-asterisked Matthean formula citations in Table V. On that basis they have interpreted vs. 23 thus: "so that what was spoken by the prophets might be fulfilled *by the fact of* his being called a Nazorean." Or as Holzmeister, "Quoniam," 25, phrases it: "so that what was spoken by the prophets might be fulfilled, namely, that he is called a 'Nazorean.'" The grammar behind this proposal is that the *hoti* which introduces the seeming citation is not a *hoti recitativum* (the equivalent of our quotation marks) but a brachyology for *touto hoti* ("by the fact that") and that the future tense of the verb is an equivalent for the present. Such grammatical suppositions are weak, e.g., the *hoti recitativum* is more normal and is attested, though not frequent, in Matthew (at least thirteen times; BDF 470[1])—there are two instances where a *hoti recitativum* introduces a citation of Scripture (4:6; 21:16). And it is against the general pattern of the fulfillment formula not to have it introduce a direct citation

(Rembry, "Quoniam," 48–57). In fact, the expression that appears here, "What was spoken" (*to rēthen*), occurs thirteen times in Matthew, and only once does it not refer to a Scripture citation.

He will be called. The "he" is Jesus, even though the "he" at the beginning of this verse is Joseph. This is another instance of awkwardness arising from Matthean editing: if 22–23 constitute a Matthean addition to a pre-Matthean narrative, the citation is, in a sense, an addition to the addition.

a Nazorean. The problem discussed above about whether and what Matthew is citing in this seeming citation depends in part for its solution on the meaning and derivation of *Nazōraios*, a subject of much scholarly discussion. This discussion is complicated by some dubious presuppositions. *First*, much of it centers on derivations possible according to strict phonological rules; but biblical derivations and etymologies are rarely accurate by scientific criteria. They are often the product of analogy rather than of phonology. *Second*, some of the theories are proposed with exclusivity: one derivation is brilliantly defended, but with the contention or implication that other derivations are wrong. However, the biblical attitude is often a "both . . . and," rather than an "either . . . or," and we should recognize that Christians may have been attracted by the wealth of possible allusions in a term applied to Jesus. With these cautions in mind, let us examine three theories for the meaning and/or derivation of "Nazorean."

a) **Derived from Nazareth.** Philologists have questioned the correctness and even the possibility of such a derivation, but it is certainly one that Matthew accepted. No contrary interpretation of 2:23 is possible. In discussing the point, we should distinguish two gentilic adjectives applied to Jesus in the NT: *Nazarēnos*, "Nazarene," which occurs four times in Mark, twice in Luke, but never in John or Matthew; and *Nazōraios*, "Nazorean," which occurs eight times in Luke/Acts, three times in John, and twice in Matthew. (The same variance occurs in the Greek adjectives for Essene: *Essēnos* is more frequent in Josephus, and *Essaios* in Philo.) There is a certain equivalence in the usage of the two adjectives, e.g., in the story of Peter's denial, where Mark 14:67 has *Nazarēnos*, Matt 26:71 has *Nazōraios*. Some scholars, like Kenard, argue that neither adjectival form should come from *Nazaret(h)*; he would expect *Nazarethēnos* or *Nazarethaios* ("Capernaum," 131). But a larger group of scholars recognize that *Nazarēnos*, at least, is derivable from the place name, especially if it had the form *Nazara* discussed above. (Parallels are offered by *Magdalēnos* and *Gadarēnos*, derived from Magdala and Gadara.)

And so most of the questioning has centered on the form *Nazōraios*, which has its clearest analogy in adjectives referring to sects or parties, e.g., *Saddoukaios* and *Pharisaios*, "Sadducee, Pharisee"; and indeed in Acts 24:5 Christians are called "the sect of the *Nazōraioi*." This fact has led to the suggestion that Jesus was called a Nazorean, not because he came from Nazareth, but because he belonged to a pre-Christian sect of that name. Disputable evidence is found in later Mandaean writings for a group related to JBap's movement calling themselves *nāṣōrayyā*, "Observants," and in later Church Fathers for a pre-Christian group called *Nasaraioi*. However, all of this is very speculative and perhaps unnecessary. Such highly competent Semitists and exegetes as Albright, Moore, and Schaeder, in their articles cited in the bibliography, argue on purely philological grounds that the form *Nazōraios* is quite defensible as a derivation from Nazareth, if one takes into account dialectal phonology in Galilean Aramaic. Nevertheless, if one accepts as correct Matthew's contention that Jesus was called a Nazorean because he came from Nazareth, Sanders, "*Nazōraios*," is correct in insisting that this does not exclude a secondary messianic association of the term and that it was remembered precisely in the form *Nazōraios* (not *Nazarēnos*) because of that secondary association. Thus, the following theories, though often presented as alternatives to the Nazareth theory, need not be so.

b) **Derived from Nāzîr.** This is a theory defended, with different nuances, by Bonnard, Rembry, Sanders, and Schweizer. *Nāzîr* means one consecrated or made holy to God by a vow. It has been suggested that originally the Nazirite was one who received a charismatic call and that only secondarily was a vow introduced into the concept; but the relation of the word to the Semitic root *nḏr* (Hebrew *ndr*), "to vow," implies that the idea of being vowed to divine service may be primary. The classic description of the Hebrew Nazirite appears in Num 6:1–21: he was to separate himself from other men by not drinking wine or strong drink, by not cutting his hair, and by having no contact with the dead. In practice, however, our knowledge of the Nazirite comes from the birth stories of Samson and Samuel. (The latter is never called a *Nāzîr* in the MT; but one of the old, fragmentary Hebrew mss. of I Sam 1:22, found in Cave IV at Qumran, says of him: "He will be a *Nāzîr* forever.") In Judg 13:2–7 we are told that an angel of the Lord told the wife of Manoah that she would conceive and give birth to a son (Samson), and that no razor should touch his head, for he would be a Nazirite to God from birth and would begin to deliver Israel from the power of the Philistines. During her pregnancy the mother was forbidden to touch wine or strong drink. In I Sam 1:11 we hear the barren Hannah pleading with God for a son (Samuel), promising that she would give him to the Lord all the days of his life and that no razor would touch his head. The ideal of the Nazirite carried over into Jewish Christian memory. For instance, the asceticism of JBap, known to Luke from a saying in the ministry of Jesus (7:33), is translated into the JBap infancy narrative by describing him as a Nazirite: "And he will drink no wine or strong drink. And he will be filled with the Holy Spirit even from his mother's womb." James, the brother of the Lord and the head of the Jerusalem church, is also considered a Nazirite from birth in the account of Hegesippus (*ca.* A.D. 180), preserved in Eusebius *Eccl. Hist.* II xxiii 4–5): "He was holy [*hagios*—one of the Greek translations of *Nāzîr*] from the womb of his mother; he drank no wine or strong drink and ate no animal food; no razor touched his head." A more temporary Nazirite vow seems to be envisaged in Acts 21:23–26.

Granted this background, have we any way of deciding whether Matthew had the Nazirite model in mind when he cited the prophets, speaking of Jesus as a Nazorean? That the citation is made in an infancy narrative is helpful since most of our knowledge of Nazirites has a birth setting. And from many indications in the Lucan birth story, we know that a parallel was drawn between the infancy of Jesus and the infancy of Samuel the Nazirite, e.g., Mary's canticle in Luke 1:46–55 and Hannah's canticle in I Sam 2:1–10; the description of Jesus in Luke 2:52 and the description of Samuel in I Sam 2:26; etc. One may well object that Jesus demonstrated none of the asceticism that made it appropriate to think of JBap as a Nazirite (Matt 11:18–19); however, perhaps he was considered a Nazirite in the sense that he was consecrated to God's service from the womb (cf. Judg 13:3b,5b and Matt 1:21).

Further evidence that Jesus was thought of as a Nazirite comes from a knowledge of the Greek rendition of *Nāzîr*. In the LXX the word was either virtually transliterated as *Naziraios*, "Nazirite," or translated as *hagios*, "holy, holy one." For instance, while the Codex Alexandrinus renders the *Nāzîr* of Judg 13:5,7 and 16:17 by *Naziraios*, in those passages Codex Vaticanus has respectively *Nazir, hagios, hagios*. A curiosity is Lam 4:7 where the Hebrew *nāzîr* means "prince," not "Nazirite", but the LXX has *Naziraios* (an interpretation of the verse known to Tertullian, *Adversus Marcion* iv 8, who renders it, "Her Nazirites were whiter than snow," and sees it as a foreshadowing of the Christians being called Nazarenes). There is an obvious similarity between the one Greek rendering of *Nāzîr* as *Naziraios* (with LXX ms. variants of *Nazaraios, Nazēraios,* and even *Nazōraios*) and the designation of Jesus as *Nazōraios* because he came from Nazareth, and so Matthew may have delighted in the irony that the title that Jesus received from his unlikely home town gave him a similarity to heroes like Samson and Samuel. (Schweizer, "Nazoräer," 93, sees the development in the opposite direction: primarily *Nazōraios* means that Jesus was a Nazirite, and only secondarily was the term associated with Nazareth.) And the other Greek rendering of *Nāzîr* as *hagios* may show up in the tradition that Jesus was known as "the Holy One of God" —a title that occurs in Mark 1:24; Luke 4:34; and John 6:69; and for which we may have the Matthean equivalent in the title Nazorean. This point will be considered in more detail in the commentary as we seek for the prophetic texts from which Matthew may have culled "He will be called a Nazorean."

c) **Derived from Nēṣer.** Scholars such as M. Black, Médebielle, and Stendahl have related Nazorean to the messianic *nēṣer*, "branch." The key OT passage is Isa 11:1: "There will come forth a shoot from the root [Greek *riza*] of Jesse [David's father], and from his roots a branch [Hebrew *nēṣer*; Greek *anthos*] will blossom." In Isaiah the passage refers to the appearance of a king of the House of David in succession the reigning monarch, and in Judaism it was eventually applied to the Messiah, as we see in the Aramaic targums and in the rabbinic literature (Edersheim, *Life*, II, 723–24). In Christian circles the passage was the subject of christological reflections. The theme of the *riza* is the focus of Jesus' words in Rev 22:16: "I am the *root* and the offspring of David." Justin, *Dialogue* cxxvi 1, fastens on the theme of the *anthos*, "Blossom" in application to Jesus. That in the Post-NT period *nēṣer* was applied to Jesus is attested in the writing of Jerome to Pammachius *ca.* 395 (Letter 57; PL 52:574) who cites the second line of the Isaian verse thus: ". . . and from his root will grow (the) Nazorean." In Jewish tradition (TalBab *Sanhedrin* 43a) the authorities challenge a disciple of Jesus named *Nēṣer* in reference to

Isa 11:1; they argue, rather, that it is Isa 14:19 that this Christian name recalls: "You are cast out, away from your tomb, like a loathed branch [nēṣer]." A remembrance of the nēṣer may also be reflected in the common Hebrew designation of Jesus as the Nôṣrî and of Christians as Nôṣᵉrîm.

Granted such general evidence, what is the likelihood that Matthew had the nēṣer of Isa 11:1 in mind as background for the designation of Jesus as "a Nazorean"? The strongest positive indication lies in the fact that the branch which will blossom from the root of Jesse (Isa 11:1) is the child Emmanuel whose forthcoming birth had been announced in Isa 7:14. Since Matthew applied the latter passage to Jesus in 1:22–23, it is not unlikely that he was still thinking in terms of the Isaian description of the Davidic royal child. Médebielle, "Quoniam," 323, makes the interesting point that between Isa 7:14 and 11:1 there is much reference to devastation and injustice, even as between Matt 1:23 and 2:23 there is the description of Herod's persecution of Jesus.

But objections have also been raised. First, there is the phonological problem of positing an unusual representation of the ṣade (ṣ) in nēṣer by the Greek zeta (z) in Nazōraios. However, even on purely philological grounds we saw that this was not an insuperable difficulty when we discussed the relationship of Semitic Naṣrat(h) and Greek Nazaret(h)/Nazara (NOTE on Nazareth in vs. 23). And a purely philological objection is less serious if we treat a relation to nēṣer as a secondary connotation of Nazorean, with the primary derivation of the term from Nazareth. The second objection is that nēṣer, meaning "branch," occurs only four times in the Hebrew Bible, and that in the other three passages it is not messianic (Isa 14:19; 60:21; Dan 11:7). However, we must ask which of these meanings of "branch" had the most influence among the Jews of NT times. In the Dead Sea Scrolls (1QH vi 15, vii 19, vii 6,8,10) nēṣer is used in reference to the chosen community of Qumran, so that the word had an eschatological significance in God's plan of salvation. Indeed, the fact that a community could see itself as a nēṣer (also Isa 60:21) is interesting in light of the subsequent designations of Christians as Nazoreans, the same term that Matthew applies to Jesus.

In considering the messianic impact of nēṣer, we must reflect on the import of a group of words with the same idea. For instance, the ṣemaḥ, "branch," shoot," is to appear on the day of the Lord (Isa 4:2); and Jer 23:5 has the Lord say: "I shall raise up a righteous shoot for David; as king he will reign and govern wisely" (also Jer 33:15; Zech 3:8; 6:12). The Suffering Servant Song of Isa 53:2 compares the servant to a yônēq, "sapling," and a šōreš, "root" (one of the terms for Jesse's root in Isa 11:1). The Qumran community (1QH vi 15, viii5) uses maṭṭa'at to describe itself as "an everlasting planting" or "a planting for Your glory," probably an echo of Isa 60:21, "a branch of His planting" (neṣer maṭṭa'aw, usually corrected to "My planting"). Thus, a secondary connection of Nazorean and nēṣer may have involved the application to Jesus of a number of passages involving Davidic or messianic "plant" words. (And some have used this to explain the plural in Matthew's "what was spoken by the prophets.") Zolli and Gärtner have argued that a connection with nēṣer would also bring into the picture other meanings of the root nṣr, particularly the verb nāṣar in the sense "to watch, observe, keep." Zolli,

"Nazarenus," calls attention to Jer 31:6–7: "For there will be a day when watchmen [nōṣᵉrîm] will call out in the hill country of Ephraim . . . 'The Lord has saved His people, the remnant of Israel.'" If the first part of that passage is related to the mention of Nazorean in Matt 2:23, the last part of it resembles what is said of Jesus in 1:21: "He will save his people from their sins." Gärtner, "Die rätselhaften," calls attention to the use of *nāṣar* in two of the Suffering Servant Songs. In Isa 42:6 the Lord says: "I have called you . . . I have *kept* you; I have given you as a covenant to the people, a light to the nations." And in Isa 49:6: "It is not enough for you to be [called (LXX)] my servant to raise up the tribes of Jacob and to restore the *'preserved'* [nᵉṣîrê, to be corrected to nᵉṣûrê] of Israel; I shall give you as a light to the nations so that my salvation will reach the end of the earth." In the first passage it is the servant who is the object of *nāṣar* and there is a reference to being "called," even as Jesus is "called a Nazorean" in Matt 2:23. In the second passage the Israelites are the object of *nāṣar*, "the preserved of Israel," and the idea of being "called" appears in the LXX. As we have seen before, the term *Nazōraios* can similarly be applied both to Jesus and to the Christians. (On p. 15, Gärtner would use the form *nāṣûr*, which appears in the second passage, to explain the *ō* vowel in *Nazōraios,* since a change from *û* to *ō* is phonologically well attested.) As support for his appeal to these Isaian passages, both of which mention "a light to the nations," Gärtner points to the occurrence of that phrase in Simeon's canticle in Luke 2:32, where Jesus is "a light to be a revelation to the Gentiles." We shall see, when treating Luke 2, that certain underlying OT passages have been interpreted in different ways in the second chapters of the two infancy narratives.

COMMENT

The Matthean Plan for ch. 2 was outlined and discussed in § 6A. I shall not repeat what was said there but simply bring some of the salient points to bear on the second Act (2:13–23) which is under discussion here.

A. *Matthew's Message as Enhanced by His Use of Scripture*

In § 6A we saw that the two Acts of the chapter portray a *twofold reaction* to the christological revelation involved in the virginal conception of Jesus, now proclaimed through the birth star and the Scriptures. Act I (2:1–12) described the acceptance of that revelation by the Gentiles as the magi came to pay homage. Act II will now describe the rejection of that revelation by the Jewish authorities and their persecution of Jesus.

Lest Matthew's description of this twofold reaction seem simplistic, let me insist that the rejection and persecution of Jesus is not by "the Jews" (as in John's Gospel) but by the secular ruler, the high priests, the scribes of the people, and Jerusalem.[1] Matthew knows well that many Jews did accept Jesus, for they are part of his own community; and so he patterns the opponents of the child Jesus on the opponents of Jesus in the passion narrative (and to some extent on the Jewish authorities in the synagogues who continue to oppose believers in Jesus). And since Matthew must remain true to the historical course of events in the passion and resurrection of Jesus, he does not allow the hostile Jewish authorities in the infancy narrative to destroy Jesus, any more than they were able to destroy him by the crucifixion. God delivers His Son by having him taken away and brought back again.[2] The human instrument in this deliverance is Joseph, through his absolute obedience to the divine commands—a Joseph who has already been described as "an upright man" (1:19), i.e., a Jew totally faithful to the Law. In Matthew's mind, Jews who are true to the Law and the Prophets stand alongside the Gentile magi in accepting Jesus, while the authorities reject him.

The main motif of a twofold reaction to the christological revelation and proclamation is enhanced in Act II by related themes worked into the three scenes (2:13-15,16-18,19-23), scenes that we shall now consider one by one. Each scene terminates in a formula citation (Table V), and I shall discuss the theological import of that citation in explaining the scene. We can leave to section B below the more detailed discussion of the relation of the citations to the MT and the LXX.

Chapter Two, Scene 3 (vss. 13-15)

The basic story line concerns the rescue of the child savior from the machinations of the wicked king by flight to Egypt. This echoes in part the rescue of the infant Moses from the machinations of the wicked Pharaoh in Egypt and comes from the main pre-Matthean narrative (Table VII), as does the format of the angelic dream appearance in which it is cast (Table VI). We shall discuss the pre-Matthean level of this story in section C below; but here, on the Matthean level, it is important to note that Matthew's formula citation of Hosea 11:1 ("Out of Egypt have I called my Son") is not foreign to the historical setting of the basic story to which

---

[1] For Matthew's intent to involve more than Herod in the plot against Jesus, see the NOTE on "those who were seeking the child's life" in vs. 20. For cautions on the attribution of guilt, see § 6, footnote 15.

[2] I see a parallel between burial in the tomb and a reappearance of the risen Jesus after three days in the one instance, and flight to Egypt and return to the land of Israel in the other. The child who returns from Egypt is Emmanuel, "God with us" (1:23); the Jesus who returns from the tomb says: "I am with you always" (28:20).

it has been appended. Originally the Hosea passage referred to the Exodus of *Israel* from Egypt, but Matthew sees that the filial relationship of God's people is now summed up in Jesus who relives in his own life the history of that people. If the whole people was God's "son," how much the more is that title applicable to him who "will save His people from their sins" (Matt 1:21). In 1:1 Matthew himself designated Jesus as "son of David, son of Abraham," titles that he expounded in 1:18–25 and 2:1–12 respectively. But the designation of Jesus as God's "Son" is left to God speaking through the prophet;[3] for divine sonship is a matter revealed by the Father in heaven and does not come from a human source (16:16–17).

The combination of divine sonship and the Exodus found here is also found in the story of the baptism.[4] There, after God has said of Jesus, "This is my beloved Son" (3:17), Jesus is led into the desert for forty days and forty nights before he returns to take up his ministry—a symbolic re-enactment of Israel's forty years in the desert before entering the Promised Land.[5] In both instances we are dealing with a basic Christian intuition that the preparation for the ministry of Jesus was the history of Israel, and so Jesus' (largely unknown) career before he began his ministry is filled in with descriptions redolent of the history of Israel. Not only was the story of Israel in Egypt and of the Exodus one of the most important events in that history; but also, involving as it did the giving of the covenant, it was the ideal model on which to pattern the opening of the story of the new (i.e., renewed) covenant.

I have said that the story line in 2:13–15 echoes *in part* the story of Moses in Egypt and the Exodus.[6] (The echo is so brief that clearly Matthew had no primary interest in storytelling as such[7]—indeed, he may

---

[3] Vögtle, *Messias*, 18, stresses the sequence: son of David, son of Abraham, Son of God; but I am hesitant to judge that the *main* point in 2:15 is the proclamation of divine sonship. There is a more solemn and direct proclamation of the Son of God at the baptism in 3:17, so that the sequence is worked out perfectly for those scholars who consider 1:1 – 4:16 a unit. I suggest that Matthew keeps the reference to divine sonship in 2:15 indirect (through the prophet) and "low-key" because of his remembrance that only with the ministry of Jesus did that revelation become public and direct.

[4] As we have seen, the baptism and the conception are major moments in the "backwards" development of christology, and the theological descriptions of these two moments inevitably involve many of the same features (§ 1, A2; § 5, A1).

[5] The Exodus-and-Desert-Wandering background of Jesus' temptations in the desert is highlighted by his citation of three passages from Deuteronomy, the book that has its setting in those Wanderings (Deut 8:3; 6:16; 6:13 in Matt 4:4,7,10 respectively).

[6] The Exodus motif in the *story line* is by association: the child Moses whose life is sought will lead the Hebrews out of Egypt, and the kind of persecution suffered by Moses and the other children will make the Exodus necessary. I am more dubious about a direct reference to the Exodus in the fact that the flight is "by night" (Matt 2:14), a detail that some have seen as evocative of the night setting of the Exodus (Exod 12:29).

[7] Bultmann, *History*, 244–45, gives "legend" as the classification for the Matthean infancy narrative, i.e., a story, religious and edifying in character, sometimes told for biographical purposes. But, as we see in Act II, this is a story stripped to bare bone, in which (as in 2:16–18) the appended Scripture citation may be as long as the narrative. See also footnote 17, § 16.

well have cut out details from the pre-Matthean narrative. What would have happened were he interested in legend is seen in the folkloric accounts of the journey to Egypt in Christian midrash; see NOTE on "went away to Egypt" in 2:14.) But there is one important part of the Matthean story that must have another explanation, namely, that the child is saved by flight *to Egypt*. Jesus relives not only the Exodus of Israel from Egypt but also (and first) the departure of Israel from Canaan into Egypt. This detail is to some extent explained by the fact that the main figure in the flight to Egypt is Jesus' legal father Joseph, who plays the role of Joseph the patriarch bringing Jacob/Israel down to Egypt. Yet it was not persecution that caused Jacob/Israel to go to Egypt under Joseph's guidance. Consequently, some scholars have turned for background to an earlier incident in the career of Jacob/Israel when he fled persecution by Laban (Gen 31). This is an important suggestion, but I shall leave it to Appendix VI where we can see the Jacob-Laban story as a whole.

Chapter Two, Scene 4 (vss. 16–18)

The story line here, involving the massacre of the male children in Bethlehem and the surrounding regions, echoes faithfully Pharaoh's slaughter of the male infants of the Hebrews. But Matthew works to connect this event in Egypt with another major tragedy in Israelite history, the Exile of the tribes to Assyria and Babylon.[8] In the theology of Israel the persecution in Egypt and the Exile were the two greatest trials to which God's people had been subjected; and the Exodus and the return from Exile were the two greatest manifestations of Yahweh's protective power. This parallelism is prominent in Deutero-Isaiah who described the return as a second Exodus through the desert (40:3; 52:3–6). If Matthew is interested in the Exodus motif because of his dependence on a pre-Matthean narrative which imitated the story of Moses, he is no less interested in the Exile, which is an event demarcating a major division in the genealogy of Jesus (1:11–12).[9] His ingenuity lies not so much in connecting the two events, as in relating them to what happened at Bethlehem. The massacre of male children was a clear reminder of the persecution in Egypt; Bethlehem, where this happened, was also the place on the way to which Rachel was buried; Jeremiah (31:15) referred to the Exile in terms of Rachel weeping over her children; and now her voice is heard from the tomb again, nay heard as far as Ramah, as the children of Israel suffer

---

[8] In the NOTE on "Rachel crying" in vs. 18, I pointed out how difficult it is to decide which Exile is meant, and Matthew may have intended a conglomerate picture.

[9] The other event demarcating a division is the kingship of David (1:6,17), and Matthew has used a previous formula citation (2:5–6) to refer to Bethlehem, the city where David was born and anointed king.

persecution once more. But, just as God ultimately broke the power of tyrants who persecuted Israel in Egypt and in the Exile, so will He frustrate the power of this tyrant.[10] Thus Jesus, who is to save God's people (1:21), relives both great past moments of divine salvation. A modern interpreter may regard Matthew's exegesis of Jeremiah as fanciful (and, in fact, incorrect as regards the burial place of Rachel—NOTE on "Ramah" in vs. 18); but it is an exegesis that detects a divine master plan of salvation. The three formula citations thus far discussed in ch. 2, by mentioning *Bethlehem,* the city of David, *Egypt,* the land of the Exodus, and *Ramah,* the mourning-place of the Exile, offer a theological history of Israel in geographical miniature. Just as Jesus sums up the history of the people named in his genealogy, so his early career sums up the history of these prophetically significant places.

Chapter Two, Scene 5 (vss. 19–23)

In § 4, B1, these verses were carefully analyzed as a parade example of Matthean composition: we saw that while 19–21 are drawn from the main pre-Matthean narrative (rewritten by Matthew), vss. 22–23 represent his own appended composition. It is this history of composition that explains the awkwardness of the several revelations involved in the return from Egypt. Here, however, we are interested in the final narrative (composite though it may be) as reflective of Matthean thought. The story line, which thus far has echoed primarily the infancy of Moses, now shifts to echo his career as an adult. The angel's explanation to Joseph in 2:20 that "those who were seeking the child's life are dead" is almost a verbatim repetition of the Greek form of the Lord's words to Moses in Exod 4:19, pertaining to the Pharaoh's death. And just as that death freed Moses to begin his mission of return to the Promised Land, so the death of Herod enables a return from Egypt that will lead Jesus to the starting place of his mission.

Three geographical indications, each a phrase governed by *eis* (2:20,22,23) and each more specific, form the backbone of this scene, guiding the Exodus and the return of Joseph with the child. First, the angel tells Joseph to go *to the land of Israel,* and he does. Second, and more specifically,[11] Joseph is warned in a dream to go *to the district of Galilee.* Third, and still more specifically, he goes to dwell *in a city called Nazareth,*

---

10 The promise of victory, so far as Matthew's account is concerned, lies in the subsequent narrative where Herod dies and Jesus returns safely. In the citation of Jeremiah, Matthew gives no hint of the consolation or victory for the children envisaged by Jeremiah; see NOTE on "Rachel crying" in vs. 18.

11 Granted the editorial history of this scene wherein the mention of Galilee in 22–23 was joined to the mention of Israel in 19–21, "the land of Israel" was certainly meant to include the whole of Palestine (and therefore, both Judea and Galilee). That is why Matthew must explain why Galilee, and not the more likely Judea where they had a house, was the choice. See NOTE on "to return there" in vs. 22.

so that the words spoken by the prophets might be fulfilled. The direction to all three places is divinely given,[12] and so we must ask how Matthew understood God's plan working out in each of the three geographical directions. The purpose of the directive to go "to the land of Israel"[13] is easily detected: Jesus, reliving Israel's experience under Moses after the escape from the Pharaoh, is to go the Promised Land of God's people. The divine purpose that Matthew finds in the second specification, "to the district of Galilee," is probably to be related to the motif explicated in 4:14–16: Galilee is the land of the Gentiles, and Jesus goes there in order that the people who sit in darkness and death may see the light.[14] This reference to Galilee comes in vs. 22, which is Matthew's own composition. Thus, by combining the reference to Israel in the pre-Matthean narrative with the Galilee of the Gentiles of his own theology,[15] Matthew has Jesus divinely directed to the two groups that make up the Matthean community: Jew and Gentile.

The divine purpose in relation to the third geographical direction, "in a city called Nazareth," needs no angelic vision or dream to be articulated; long before had the prophets spoken: "He will be called a Nazorean." The birth of the Messiah at Bethlehem was predicted by the prophet, as we learned at the beginning of ch. 2; and so was the fact that Nazareth, not Bethlehem, should serve as his home. (In § 6, A2, I suggested that both these points were made, in part, to answer Jewish polemics against Jesus, to the effect that the Messiah was not to come from Galilee or, *a fortiori*, from Nazareth.) Thus, if the formula citations in 2:1–18 gave us three names, Bethlehem, Egypt, and Ramah, evocative of great moments of OT history, 2:19–23 gives us three names, Israel, Galilee, and Nazareth, anticipatory of the career of Jesus and the membership of his church. The infancy narrative ends in the place from which Jesus will go forth to begin his mission (Matt 3:13; Mark 1:9).

But "Nazorean" evokes more than the name of a place. In a long NOTE I have discussed the various scholarly derivations of *Nazōraios*, pointing out that they are not mutually exclusive but reflect the allusive wealth of

---

[12] On a practical level, the decision not to go to Judea is determined by the political circumstance that the tyrannical Archelaus is king there, but the direction to Galilee must be related to the divinely given dream in vs. 22. In fact, of course, Matthew had no choice in describing where Joseph was to go, since Matthew knew the incontrovertible tradition that Jesus was a Galilean. But for Matthew there are no historical accidents in relation to Jesus: the God who planned the genealogy of Jesus so carefully could scarcely have left his homeland to chance.

[13] See the NOTE on vs. 20 for Ezekiel's use of this phrase in relation to the Exodus.

[14] In 4:14–16 Matthew is citing Isa 9:1–2, one of the Isaian Emmanuel passages. Matthew has already cited Isa 7:14, and we shall see the possibility that "Nazorean" in Matt 2:23 reflects the *nēṣer*, "branch," used to describe Emmanuel in Isa 11:1. Thus, we are really dealing with a chain of Emmanuel passages.

[15] Notice that Matthew does not wish to expand the message of the pre-Matthean dream in 2:19–20 by having the angel direct Joseph "to the land of Israel, to the district of Galilee"—that would violate the analogy with the Moses story. And so in 2:22 Matthew introduces a second, warning dream (even as he introduced a warning dream in 2:12).

the term. Nazareth is providentially the home of the child Jesus because it gives him a gentilic designation "Nazorean" that reminds us that he is a Nazirite (*Nāzîr*)—a select holy one set aside to God's service from his mother's womb, like Samson and Samuel. In this motif Matthew may be reflecting an earlier infancy tradition, for we shall see that the Samson/ Samuel pattern greatly influenced the Lucan infancy narrative.[16] The gentilic designation "Nazorean" also reminds us that Jesus is the messianic "branch" (*nēṣer*)—the blossom from the Davidic root predicted in Isa 11:1, as part of Isaiah's continued description of Emmanuel. Thus, with ingenious symmetry Matthew brings together Isaian themes in his first and last formula citations in the infancy narrative: "They will call his name Emmanuel" (Isa 7:14), and "He will be called a Nazorean" (the *nēṣer* of Isa 11:1). The first citation concerned the conception, birth, and identity of the prophesied child; the last citation concerns his mission and destiny. The annunciation of the birth of the child (Matt 1:18–25) closed with Joseph calling the child *Jesus*; the aftermath of the birth of the child (2:1–23) closes with Joseph bringing the child to Nazareth so that all may call him a *Nazorean*. We now have the full identity of the son of David, the son of Abraham, the Son of God, as he will be known for all time: JESUS THE NAZOREAN.[17]

B. *The Three Formula Citations*

Nowhere in the Gospel do formula citations come in such proximate abundance as in 2:13–23 (see Table V), where they constitute about one-third of the content. Although we have already discussed some of the theological usage to which Matthew puts them, we have now the opportunity of testing theories about the origin of the formula citations (§ 4, A3), both as regards the kind of biblical text cited and possible previous Christian use.

1. The Citation of Hosea 11:1 in Matt 2:15b

Commentators have been struck by the peculiar localization of this citation. Although it deals with the Exodus or coming "out of Egypt," Matthew inserts it as a comment on Joseph's taking the child and his mother *to* Egypt. One suggestion as to why Matthew did not wait until after 2:21 to insert this citation is that he wanted to give a different geo-

---

16 The Nazirite image in Jesus' infancy story (which inevitably evokes Samson and Samuel) is probably the retrojection into his origins of the tradition that he was the "Holy One" (*Hagios*, an alternative rendering of *Nāzîr*) during his lifetime. See NOTE on "Nazorean" in vs. 23.

17 Almost by way of inclusion (§ 2, footnote 19), Matthew will join the components "Jesus" and "the Nazorean" at the end of the ministry in the scene of Peter's denial (26:71).

graphical thrust to the return journey—not so much a journey from Egypt, but a journey to Nazareth. Consequently, one may theorize, Matthew chose to bring out the Egypt/Exodus motif at the first mention of Egypt in his story, namely, in 2:13–14.[18] He may also have wanted the reference to the Exodus to precede the reference to the Exile in 2:17–18.

The citation of Hosea 11:1 is so short that it gives little scope for a detailed comparison of Matthew's text with the standard Hebrew and Greek forms of the passage:

Matt: "Out of Egypt have I called [*kalein*] my Son [*huios*]."
LXX: "Out of Egypt have I summoned [*metakalein*] his children [*tekna*]."[19]
MT: "From [or out of] Egypt have I called my son."

It is quite clear that Matthew has not taken his citation from the LXX but prefers a Greek rendition that is literally faithful to the Hebrew.[20] This is a simpler and better explanation than the theory that Matthew used the LXX but changed "his children" to "my Son" as part of his theological emphasis on Jesus as the Son of God.[21] Are we to think that Matthew was the first to apply this Hosea passage to Jesus or was it already in the Christian arsenal? *A priori* the latter suggestion is not impossible; for the passage deals with the Exodus, and Exodus motifs were popular among Christians. But this is a reference to an Exodus *from Egypt,* and it is difficult to imagine how such a reference could be applied to the career of Jesus, other than in the circumstances that Matthew envisages.[22] And those Christians who used the LXX would certainly have seen no reference to Jesus in "Out of Egypt have I summoned his children." Indeed, the context of the Hosea passage in either Hebrew or Greek would do nothing to favor an application to Jesus, for the prophet speaks of the chastisement of the child(ren) whom God has called out of Egypt.[23] Probabilities, then,

---

18 Thus Stendahl, "Quis," 97.

19 While the Hebrew speaks of "son" for Israel as a collective, the LXX uses the plural "children," since in subsequent verses Hosea will deal with the Israelites as a plurality ("they, them").

20 It is noteworthy how close Matthew comes to the Greek translation of Aquila which is generally more faithful to the MT: "From [*apo* instead of Matthew's *ex*] Egypt have I called [*kalein*] my son [*huios*]."

21 Of course, in choosing to stay close to the Hebrew which spoke of "son," Matthew was favoring his own theology: he speaks of Jesus absolutely as "the Son" three times and as "the Son of God" twelve times.

22 I find a bit fanciful the suggestion of Lindars, *Apologetic,* 217, that the Hosea text may have been in pre-Matthean usage in reference to the resurrection of Jesus, in light of Rev 11:8 which mentions "the great city which is spiritually called Sodom and *Egypt* where their Lord was crucified."

23 If we consider the context, only the first line of Hosea 11:1 would be easily applicable to Jesus: "When Israel was a child, I loved him." Matthew may have interpreted this to mean that God showed His love for Jesus as a child by helping him to escape Herod's plot. But granted the general inapplicability of the Hosean context to Jesus, what drew Matthew's attention to Hosea 11:1? Lindars, *Apologetic,* 217, makes an interesting suggestion. Presumably Matthew recognized the connection between the story of the magi and the biblical account of Balaam which we saw in § 6, C2. The phrase "out of Egypt" occurs twice in

favor Matthean originality in the application of Hosea 11:1 to Jesus. It is noteworthy that of the four passages used in formula citations thus far, the two that may have been already used by other Christians (Isa 7:14; Micah 5:1) are cited in a form noticeably divergent from the MT, while the two that are seemingly Matthean discoveries (II Sam 5:2; Hosea 11:1) are cited in a form very close to the MT. Yet the latter consist of one line apiece, so that the basis for comparison is inadequate. And as for the former, even if they were used by other Christians, we have no way of knowing that they were used in exactly the textual form in which they appear in Matthew.

2. The Citation of Jer 31:15 (LXX 38:15) in Matt 2:18

This is the longest single passage cited by Matthew in the infancy narrative. As we compare his version of Jeremiah with the standard Hebrew and Greek, we face the particular difficulty of two divergent LXX traditions represented by Codices Alexandrinus (A) and Vaticanus (B) respectively, with A closer to the Hebrew.

Matt: "A voice was heard in Ramah,
        weeping and loud mourning,
        Rachel crying for her children [*tekna*];
        and she would not be consoled,
        because they are no more."

LXX B: "A voice was heard in Ramah
        of lamentation and weeping and mourning;
        Rachel, who was crying,
        would not cease on behalf of her sons [*huioi*],
        because they are no more."

LXX A: "A voice was heard on high
        of lamentation and weeping and mourning,
        of Rachel's crying over her sons [*huioi*];
        and she would not be consoled,
        because they are no more."

MT: "A voice is [or was] heard in Ramah,
        lamentation and bitter weeping,
        Rachel weeping over her sons [*bānîm*],
        refusing to be consoled over her sons,
        because he is no more."

---

the oracles of Balaam (Num 23:22; 24:8), and that phrase may have reminded Matthew of Hosea 11:1. The LXX of Num 24:7–8 is particularly interesting in this regard: "There will come a man out of his [Israel's] seed, and he will rule over many nations. . . . God led him out of Egypt."

We notice the following details in Matthew's version:

▪*Line 1:* Matthew joins the MT and LXX B in considering Ramah a proper name and not attempting to translate it, as did LXX A (and Codex Sinaiticus*, the Aquila translation, and Targumic tradition).

▪*Line 2:* Matthew agrees with the MT in understanding the grammatical relationship of the nouns involved. In Hebrew there are three nouns; but the second and third are bound together in a construct formation, so that one of them is best rendered as an adjective; the LXX has missed this nuance.[24] Matthew also agrees with the MT in seeing the nouns as nominative appositives to the "voice" of the first line, whereas the LXX has shifted them into a genitive construction. To an extent, but this is harder to judge, Mathew's "weeping . . . mourning" has reversed the order of the Hebrew nouns "lamentation . . . weeping," an order preserved in the first two nouns of the LXX.

▪*Line 3:* In some ways the *huioi* of the LXX is closer to MT *bānîm* than is Matthew's *tekna;* yet *teknon,* "child," is used elsewhere in the Gospels to render Hebrew *bēn,* "son" (Matt 22:24 and Mark 12:19 rendering the "not having a son" of Deut 25:5, where the LXX uses *sperma,* "seed"). If Matthew himself were responsible for the Greek of his Jeremiah citation, it is odd that he chose the plural of *teknon* rather than the plural of *pais,* "boy," the word he used in speaking of Herod's massacre in 2:16. If it is objected that this would be too narrow a rendition of Jeremiah's *bānîm* which was meant to include both male and female, the plural *paides* covers both sexes. The only solution seems to be that sometimes Matthew adapts the citation to his context, while other times he retains a standard Greek way of rendering Hebrew,[25] even if this leaves a slight difference from his context.

▪*Line 4:* Matthew's "she would not be consoled" is identical with LXX A, and both are close to the MT's "refusing to be consoled," whereas LXX B diverges noticeably with its "would not cease." Yet, in another detail, namely, a repetitive mention of "sons," the LXX B agrees with MT, while both Matthew and LXX A omit. However, this may not be a true divergence between Matthew and the Hebrew, since many scholars think that the MT is corrupt here and the original Hebrew of Jeremiah lacked this second reference to "sons."

---

[24] Since the two LXX codices, A and B, give exactly the same second line in the Jeremiah passage, they are not totally independent of each other. This raises the likelihood of A being a partial revision of the LXX tradition in favor of the Hebrew; see Gundry, *Use,* 97.

[25] The thesis that Matthew favors the word *teknon* is dubious. It appears most often in passages where Matthew draws upon Mark (two passages that have no Synoptic parallel are 21:28 and 27:25).

•*Line 5:* None of the Greek renditions follows the awkward reading of the MT. Once again the MT may represent a corruption of a more original Hebrew Jeremiah.[26]

To sum up the above observations, it is clear that Matthew's version of the Jeremiah citation is closer to the MT than to LXX B; and its similarities to LXX A are explicable precisely because LXX A itself resembles the MT (probably through a deliberate process of being made to conform more closely to the Hebrew). The few differences between Matthew and MT are easily explained if Matthew's Greek rendered a better Hebrew text of Jeremiah than that preserved in the MT.

We saw at the end of the previous discussion (of the Hosea passage) that the two short formula citations where Matthew is close to the Hebrew are also the citations less likely to have had extra Matthean Christian usage. That holds true here as well; for, of all the formula citations in the infancy narrative, this is the most difficult to imagine being applied to Jesus in circumstances other than those described by Matthew.[27]

3. The Citation of Isa 4:3 and Judg 16:17 in Matt 2:23?

"He will be called a Nazorean" is the most difficult formula citation in the Gospel since it is not indisputably related to an identifiable OT text. In the NOTES I have surveyed four diverse ways of solving this difficulty and explained at length three different proposed derivations of "Nazorean." I trust that I shall not be deemed arbitrary if here I state my own view without repeated cautions about all the other interpretations previously discussed. "Nazorean" is primarily applicable to Jesus because he has dwelt at Nazareth; and therefore the formula citation contains a place name, as do all the other formula citations in this chapter. "Nazorean" is secondarily applicable to Jesus because he is the messianic *Branch* of the House of David (the *nēṣer*) and because he is a Nazirite (*Nāzîr*), the Holy One, dedicated to God's service from birth. It is this last derivation that Matthew has in mind when he says "that what was spoken by the prophets might be fulfilled, 'He will be called a Nazorean.' " He is citing known Scripture and has two definite prophetic passages in mind. The passages are Isa 4:3 ("*He* who is left in Zion and remains in Jerusalem *will be called*

---

26 It has been suggested that the Hebrew originally had "her son" (singular) in line 3, so that "he is no more" would have been in numerical agreement with that.

27 In discussing Luke 2:8–20 (§ 14, C1), I shall point out the background influence of Gen 35:21 which has a reference to Migdal Eder, "the Tower of the Flock," as if it were in the vicinity of Ephrath-Bethlehem where Rachel was buried (35:19). The Genesis reference to Bethlehem (a mistaken reference, as we have seen) and the Micah reference to Bethlehem underlie both Matthew and Luke. But Matthew alone seems to have made the connection between the Genesis passage with its mention of Rachel and the Jeremiah passage which also mentions Rachel.

holy")[28] and Judg 16:17 ("I have been a Nazirite of God from my mother's womb"). The relationship between Matthew's citation and these texts has been complicated by the way Matthew dealt with the Hebrew.[29]

Matt:	"He will be called a Nazorean [*Nazōraios klēthēsetai*]"
LXX (Isa 4:3):	"They will be called holy [*hagioi klēthēsontai*]."
MT (Isa 4:3):	"He will be called holy [*qādôš*]."
LXX B (Judg 16:17):	"I am a holy one [*hagios*] of God."
LXX A (Judg 16:17):	"I am a Nazirite [*Naziraios*] of God."
MT (Judg 16:17):	"I have been a Nazirite [*Nāzîr*] of God."

Two facts are necessary to understand Matthew's association and rendition of these texts: first, that Hebrew *Nāzîr* is rendered in Greek both by *hagios* ("holy") and *Naziraios;* second, that Jesus was known in the ministry as "the Holy One of God" (*Hagios Theou*).[30] The latter title was unusual, having been employed for an individual only once in the whole Greek Bible, namely, of Samson in Judg 16:17 (Vaticanus). Knowledge of this would tell Matthew that a special title of Jesus appeared in one of the prophetic books.[31] However, the Hebrew of this unique passage called Samson a Nazirite, so that a more literal Greek rendition (like Alexandrinus) would reproduce the title as *Naziraios*. We would thus have an association of the *Hagios Theou* title of Jesus with *Naziraios,* which, in turn, is a close echo of *Nazōraios,* the designation borne by Jesus because of his home town Nazareth. The *Hagios/Naziraios* interchangeability presumably reminded Matthew of another prophetic passage where it was actually promised "He will be called (a) *Hagios*" (Isa 4:3).[32] Knowing the equivalence, Matthew was perfectly free to read it: "He will be called a *Naziraios.*" He thus had a citation with the place name Nazareth and a prophecy that Jesus would be a Holy One of God set aside like Samson from his mother's womb. The memory of Samson the Nazirite could not have been divorced from the words spoken by the angel of the Lord to his mother: "The boy will be a Nazirite [LXX B: *Naziraios*] of God from

28 The LXX of Isa 4:3 reads: "And it will be that the remnant in Zion and the remnant in Jerusalem . . . they will be called holy." Although, as we shall see, Matthew's primary interest is in the interchangeability of the designation "Holy (One)" with "Nazirite," the fact that the passage refers to the remnant of God's people is an added value, since Matthew has already worked with the theme of Jesus' reliving the history of Israel.

29 I am indebted here to Rembry, "Quoniam," for his study of Isa 4:3 and to Schweizer, "Nazoräer," for his study of Judg 16:17.

30 Both of these points are explained in detail in section (b) of the NOTE on "Nazorean."

31 In the Hebrew arrangement of the biblical books, Judges was listed as one of the Former Prophets.

32 I have accepted the thesis that "Nazorean" is related secondarily not only to *Nāzîr* but also to *nēṣer,* the messianic branch of the House of David (Isa 11:1); and in the NOTE on "Nazorean" I pointed out that this involved a connection with other "plant" words, such as *ṣemaḥ,* "branch, shoot." It is scarcely accidental that the verse which precedes Isa 4:3 reads: "In that day will the shoot [*ṣemaḥ*] of the Lord be beautiful and glorious."

birth, and he will begin to save [LXX A] Israel from the hand of the Philistines" (Judg 13:5). Had not the angel of the Lord said a very similiar thing of Jesus the *Nazōraios:* "He will save his people from their sins" (Matt 1:21)?

This style of exegesis is complicated, but no more complicated than Matthew's connection of Jer 31:15 to the massacre at Bethlehem by a chain of ideas stretching from Rachel in the Jeremiah passage through the reference to Rachel's burial place on the way to Ephrath-Bethlehem in Gen 35:19, and the reference to Bethlehem as the birthplace of the Messiah in Micah 5:1. It is an exegesis that finds its justification in the view that, though the prophetic voices have a different timbre, it is the one God who has spoken through them—a God who planned for the birth and career of His Son in intricate detail. If "Matthew" could recognize this intricate plan, it was because he was a scribe well versed in the Law and the Prophets and the subtleties of translating them[33]—a "scribe trained for the kingdom of heaven . . . who brings out of his treasure what is new and what is old" (Matt 13:52).

C. *The Pre-Matthean Background of the Herod Story*

We must ask the same question of this story that we asked in relation to the magi. Is the narrative of the flight to Egypt and the massacre at Bethlehem history or is it the product of speculation on OT and Jewish themes? Let us consider these alternatives in order.

1. History and Verisimilitude

Once more, the simplest explanation is that the events of this story are factual history. Yet, for *the flight to Egypt,* some of the same objections to historicity mentioned in § 6, C1, obtain here. There is no remembrance in the accounts of the ministry of Jesus of such an extraordinary event in his background, and a journey to Egypt is quite irreconcilable with Luke's account of an orderly and uneventful return from Bethlehem to Nazareth shortly after the birth of the child. An attempt has been made to detect independent support for an Egyptian sojourn in the Jewish stories of the sec-

---

[33] It remains unclear to me whether Matthew made his own translations from the Hebrew or had available to him various Greek translations closer to the Hebrew than was the LXX. We know of attempts by Jewish scholars about this period to make available Greek translations literally faithful to the Hebrew (JBC, article 69, ##60ff.). Zuckschwerdt, "*Nazōraios*," thinks that Matthew worked directly from the Hebrew, and that by a *Kethib-Qere* pattern he read *qādôš*, "holy," for *Nāzîr* in Judg 13:5,7; 16:17. (The *Kethib-Qere* pattern means that while one word is written, another word is read.) Indeed, Zuckschwerdt makes the ingenious suggestion that it was the combination of the written consonants for *Nāzîr* (Nzr) read with vowels of *qādôš* (āô) which explains the vocalization of *Nazōraios*.

ond century which have Jesus going to Egypt (Appendix V). However, these stories introduce Egypt as a place where Jesus or his mother sought refuge because of the scandalous (adulterous) character of his birth and as a place where he became adept in black magic which he then used to deceive people. Most likely this is Jewish polemic against the Gospel picture of Jesus (including the Matthean infancy narrative) and can scarcely be invoked as independent support for the historicity of that picture.

As for *the massacre at Bethlehem,* Josephus, the Jewish historian, documents thoroughly the final years of the reign of Herod the Great, concentrating on his brutal deeds; yet he never mentions a massacre of children at Bethlehem.[84] Independent support for this tragedy has been sought in the story that Macrobius reports in his *Saturnalia,* II iv 11, written *ca.* A.D. 400: "When it was heard that, as part of the slaughter of boys up to two years old, Herod, king of the Jews, had ordered his own son to be killed, he [the Emperor Augustus] remarked, 'It is better to be Herod's pig [*hys*] than his son [*huios*].'" The relation of the story to Augustus has been thought to guarantee its antiquity. However, a closer observation shows that what is directly related to Augustus is a pun on Herod's brutality in killing his son while, according to Jewish practice, he would not deal thus with a pig. Now, it is well attested that Herod was given to fits of ungovernable rage and had three of his own children put to death; and so the Augustus pun may be historical. But that pun has nothing to do with a massacre of children at Bethlehem. The reference to "the slaughter of boys up to two years old" is part of the setting supplied by Macrobius writing three centuries after the Christian Gospel had been proclaimed. The likelihood is that the setting in Macrobius has been influenced by the story in Matthew.

The passage in Rev 12:1–5 has been advanced as another support for the Matthean narrative of Herod's attempt against Jesus. There a dragon stands before the woman who brings forth the messianic child in order to devour and thus destroy the child. Even were we sure that the author of Revelation was referring to the physical birth of Jesus, it would be hazardous to identify the dragon as a symbol for Herod. In fact, however, a good case can be made for the thesis that Rev 12:1–5 does not refer to Jesus' physical birth but to his death and resurrection, the climactic event which

---

84 S. Perowne, *The Life and Times of Herod the Great* (Nashville: Abingdon, 1956), 152: "However we look at them, Herod's last years were tragic; but Josephus has made them seem more repulsive than they were." Perowne points out that, since Josephus was writing for the Emperor Titus whose Jewish mistress, Berenice, was descended from the Hasmoneans, Herod's priestly enemies, it was to Josephus' interest to blacken Herod. This interest would overshadow the fact that Josephus got some of his information from Nicolas of Damascus, Herod's friend. One can always argue that Nicolas omitted mention of the massacre at Bethlehem because it was too unfavorable to Herod, and so Josephus did not know of it. But if it acquired any widespread notoriety, Josephus should have heard of it; and if he knew of it, he would have mentioned it, as suiting his purposes.

constituted his birth as the Messiah.[85] In this interpretation there is no possible reference to Herod. Still one more passage has been brought forward, namely, the *Assumption of Moses* 6:2–6:[86] "An insolent king will succeed them [the Hasmonean priests]. . . . He will slay the old and the young [*juvenes*], and he will not spare. And he will execute judgments on them, just as the Egyptians did." The general statement, "He will slay the old and the young," is not precise enough to be a certain reference to the Bethlehem massacre.[87] But if the comparison of the foreigner King Herod, an Idumaean, to the Pharaoh was widespread, we may have the key to why a story with its roots in the Pharaoh's attempt to kill Moses might eventually be attached to Herod.

And so once more we are led to verisimilitude. There are serious reasons for thinking that the flight to Egypt and the massacre at Bethlehem may not be historical. Yet, at the same time, if one can trace the basic story to another origin, there are good clues to why it has been cast in its present form. A story of a massacre, based on the Pharaoh's massacre of the male children in Egypt, could plausibly be attributed to Herod, especially amid the horrors of the last years of his life. To ensure mourning at his funeral, Herod wanted his soldiers instructed to kill notable political prisoners upon the news of his death. His goal was expressed thus:[88] "So shall all Judea and every household weep for me, whether they wish it or not"—we are not far from Matthew's scriptural comment upon the Bethlehem scene in terms of Rachel mourning for her children. Plausible too is the Matthean story's insistence that the massacre at Bethlehem came out of Herod's fear of the birth of a rival king.[89] Josephus (*Ant.* XVII ii 4; ✕43) tells us that the Pharisees had predicted that Herod's throne would be taken from him and his descendants, and that power would go to Pheroras (his brother) and his wife and any children to be born to them;

[85] See A. Feuillet, "The Messiah and His Mother according to Apocalypse XII," *Johannine Studies* (Staten Island: Alba, 1964), 257–92. For the analogy of birth applied to Jesus' departure in death and subsequent return, see John 16:21–22; for the analogy of begetting applied to the resurrection, see Acts 13:32–33.

[86] Charles, AP, II, 411, dates this book to A.D. 7–30; others (G. Hölscher, S. Zeitlin) have opted for a later (second-century) date. Recently there has been an attempt to associate its thought and milieu with that of the Dead Sea Scrolls and the Essenes, an association that would favor Charles' dating and an origin in Palestine. (See M. Delcor, RB 62 [1955], 60–66; and D. H. Wallace, TZ 11 [1955], 321–28.) The *Assumption* has been preserved for us in a sixth-century Latin ms. (probably translated from Greek, which was translated from Hebrew).

[87] Here I disagree with Stauffer, *Jesus*, 39, who states: "Therefore the paragraph about the murder of 'the young' can only be pointing to a massacre of children *en masse*, in the Pharaonic manner."

[88] Josephus *War* I xxxiii 6; ✕660; *Ant.* XVII vi 5; ✕✕174–78.

[89] There are many ancient literary accounts of attempts by a wicked ruler to kill the hero whose birth had been foretold. They appear in India, Persia, Mesopotamia, Greece, and Rome, and involve such notables as Gilgamesh, Sargon, Cyrus, Perseus, and Romulus and Remus. See P. Saintyves, "Le massacre des Innocents ou la persécution de l'Enfant predestiné," in *Congrès d'histoire du Christianisme*, ed. P.-L. Couchoud (Jubilé A. Loisy; Paris: Rieder, 1928), I, 229–72.

and King Herod put those Pharisees to death and all who agreed with
them. Even the setting of the tragedy at Bethlehem is plausible; for Herod
was buried in the Herodium a few miles from there, easily visible; and so
the contrast between the city where David was anointed and the tomb of
the wicked king was easily made. As for the flight to Egypt, as I have mentioned in the NOTE on vs. 14, Egypt was the standard place of refuge for
those fleeing the tyranny of kings in Palestine. As with the story of the
magi, such plausible details tell us nothing about historicity but tell us a
great deal about intelligibility. Matthew's story would not be fantastic to
the reader who knew the history of Herodian times.

2. The Joseph/Moses Narrative

Once again I suggest that Matthew did not draw upon an account of his-
torical events but rewrote a pre-Matthean narrative associating the birth of
Jesus, son of Joseph, with the patriarch Joseph and the birth of Moses.
From the reconstruction of the whole pre-Matthean narrative (Table
VII), let me reproduce here the section pertinent to Matt 2:13–23:[40]

> Now, when Herod had done this [i.e., sent to Bethlehem to search for
> the newborn Messiah],[41] behold, an angel of the Lord appeared to
> Joseph in a dream, saying, "Get up; take the child and his mother and
> escape to Egypt. Stay there until I tell you, for Herod is going to
> search for the child to destroy him." So Joseph got up, took the child
> and his mother by night, and went away to Egypt, where he stayed
> until the death of Herod.
> Then Herod [when the search for the child was unsuccessful] fell
> into a furious rage. He sent into Bethlehem and the regions all around
> it and massacred all the boys of two years of age and under [accord-
> ing to the time he had ascertained from the dream].[42]

[40] I repeat the usual caution that the reconstruction does not pretend to be in pre-Matthean language, for Matthew has so rewritten the narrative that recovery of the original
phrasing is guesswork. It is noteworthy that this section of the narrative remains closer
to the biblical account of the Pharaoh and Moses without major recourse to the non-biblical
tradition discussed in § 4, B2. I have already called attention to the virtual citation of Exod
4:19 in Matt 2:20, and Exod 2:15 is echoed in Matt 2:13–14.

[41] I have supplied a vague introduction in place of Matthew's "Now, when they [the
magi] had gone away." Knox, *Sources*, II, 122, suggests that the original opening of this
section was what now appears in 2:1: "Now, after the birth of Jesus in Bethlehem (of
Judea) in the days of Herod the king."

[42] The chronological reference to the two years belonged to this narrative rather than to
the story of the magi. In Matt 2:7 Herod is supposed to have ascertained from the magi the
exact time that the star appeared, but why then did the massacre have to cover such a wide
range as "two years old and under"? If in the original pre-Matthean narrative Herod found
out *through a dream* that the Messiah had been born and through the chief priest and the
scribes that the birthplace was at Bethlehem, he may not have known the exact date of the
birth, whence the wide range in the command for the massacre. In my opinion, the
specification "two years" is a Christian recollection that Jesus was born several years before
Herod's death (see NOTE).

> Now, when Herod died, behold an angel of the Lord appeared in a dream to Joseph in Egypt, saying, "Get up; take the child and his mother and go back to the land of Israel, for those who were seeking the child's life are dead." So Joseph got up, took the child and his mother, and went back to the land of Israel.

I have reconstructed this narrative according to the order of events now found in Matthew. It remains possible that for his own purpose Matthew has reordered[43] the material taken from the pre-Matthean narrative. For instance, the paragraph concerning Herod's sending to Bethlehem to massacre the children may originally have preceded the dream warning to Joseph in the first paragraph.[44]

If one removes the formula citations from Matt 2:13–23, one sees that the evangelist has added very little to the pre-Matthean narrative. I pointed out in § 6, C2, that the magi story came from a different pre-Matthean narrative, echoing the story of Balaam. The fusion of that with the Joseph/Moses narrative has left seams in only three places:

2:13a: "when they [the magi] had gone away"

2:16a: "when he [Herod] saw that he had been deceived by the magi"[45]

2:16d: "according to the exact time he had ascertained from the magi."

The fact that the two pre-Matthean narratives are so easily separable is the strongest argument for their original independence of each other. If I am right in my reconstruction of the narrative in Table VII patterned on Joseph and Moses, it already contained the motif of a hostile reaction in Israel to the revelation of the Messiah's birth, and the motif of God's deliverance of Jesus. The former of these themes appears in Luke 2:34–35 in the aftermath of the birth of the Messiah—a good confirmation that we are dealing with an infancy narrative motif that predates either evangelist. It was Matthew who integrated his source into a true Gospel message (§ 6, A2), but the source was not just interesting folklore; it already had a salvific message that Matthew could develop harmoniously.

---

[43] In footnote 21, § 4, I pointed out that the present order with its alternating episodes is quite Matthean.

[44] In the non-biblical developments of the Moses story, God appeared in a dream to Amram (Moses' father) to tell him that the child about to be born would escape those who were watching to destroy him. Obviously that is a pattern for the angelic dream appearance to Joseph in Matt 1:18–25. If it is also a pattern for the angelic dream appearance to Joseph in 2:13 (and therefore an exception to the general *biblical* antecedents for this section, as noted in footnote 40 above), it is noteworthy that in Josephus (*Ant.* II ix 2–3;⧽⧽205–216) the Pharaoh's order to kill the children precedes the dream of Amram.

[45] These two "when" clauses are genitive absolutes in typical Matthean style, especially the "when he saw" pattern (Matt 27:3,24). While I have suggested that the joining of the two pre-Matthean narratives may have antedated the evangelist, the presence of Matthean style in the seams is another reason to be cautious (see footnotes 38 and 52 in § 6).

SECTIONAL BIBLIOGRAPHY (§ 7)
(MATT 2:13–23)

(Some of the articles in the preceding sectional Bibliography cover the whole of ch. 2.)

Albright, W. F., "The Names 'Nazareth' and 'Nazorean,'" JBL 65 (1946), 397–401.

Black, M., BAA, 143–46, on *Nazōraios*.

Blinzler, J., "Die Heimat," on Nazareth.

Conti, M., "Nuove scoperte a Nazaret," BibOr 4 (1962), 17–19.

Gärtner, B., *Die rätselhaften Termini Nazoräer und Iskariot* (Horae Soederblomianae, 4; Uppsala: Gleerup, 1957), esp. 5–36.

Holzmeister, U., "Quot pueros urbis Bethlehem Herodes rex occiderit?" *Verbum Domini* 15 (1935), 373–79.

——— "'Quoniam Nazaraeus vocabitur' (Mt. 2,23)," *Verbum Domini* 17 (1937), 21–26.

Lyonnet, S., "'Quoniam Nazaraeus vocabitur' (Mt. 2,23)," *Biblica* 25 (1944), 196–206.

Médebielle, A., "'Quoniam Nazaraeus vocabitur' (Mt. 2,23)," in *Miscellanea Biblica et Orientalia A. Miller Oblata,* ed. A. Metzinger (*Studia Anselmiana,* 27–28; Rome: Herder, 1951), 301–26.

Meinardus, O. F. A., *In the Steps of the Holy Family from Bethlehem to Upper Egypt* (Cairo: Dar Al-Maaref, 1965).

Moore, G. F., "Nazarene and Nazareth," in *The Beginnings of Christianity,* ed. F. J. Foakes Jackson and K. Lake (London: Macmillan, 1920–33), I, 426–32.

Rembry, J., "'Quoniam Nazaraeus vocabitur' (Mt 2. 23)," SBFLA 12 (1961–62), 46–65.

Sanders, J. A., "*Nazōraios* in Matt. 2:23," JBL 84 (1965), 169–72.

Schaeder, H. H., "*Nazarēnos, Nazōraios,*" TDNT, IV, 874–79.

Schweizer, E., "'Er wird Nazoräer heissen' (zu Mc 1,24; Mt 2,23)," in *Judentum, Urchristentum, Kirche,* ed. W. Eltester (Festschrift J. Jeremias; BZNW 26; Berlin: Töpelmann, 1960), 90–93.

Zolli, E., "Nazarenus vocabitur," ZNW 49 (1958), 135–36.

Zuckschwerdt, E., "*Nazōraios* in Matth. 2,23," TZ 31 (1975), 65–77.

VII. EPILOGUE (§ 8)

As we look back briefly on Matthew's infancy narrative, the skill of the evangelist is admirable. He has woven disparate pre-Matthean material into a remarkable preface to his Gospel. The Jesus of Nazareth who after his baptism began to preach the kingdom of heaven (4:17) did not come without preparation. The immediate preparation within the context of the ministry was JBap who preached the kingdom of heaven before him (3:2). The remote preparation was the whole of God's activity in Israel as told in the Law and the prophets. In the two chapters with which he prefaces the ministry Matthew shows how this was so—by a genealogy ranging over the whole of Israel's history from father Abraham to Jesus, by a narrative based on some of the main events in the Law,[1] and by explicit citations of the prophets. Of course, Matthew could have written an impersonal summary of Israel's history; but he chose to make the preparation more intimate by having Jesus relive that history. This infancy story then becomes as integral for Jesus' ministry as the infancy and youth of Moses (and the genealogy) in Exod 1–6 were for Moses' ministry.

As Matthew narrates the infancy narrative, it is the place where the OT and the Gospel meet. If he brought forward some themes from the OT with which to clothe the infant Jesus, he also brought back from the Gospel some evaluations of Jesus by the Christian community: son of David, son of Abraham, and messianic Son of God. He attaches the basic Gospel revelation, "You are the Christ, the Son of the living God" (16:16), to the conception of Jesus. He has this revelation proclaimed to Gentiles and Jews, to be received by the former and rejected by the authorities among the latter. But he does not lose the continuity with Israel, for the figure of Joseph holds the narrative together. He is a Jew who is "upright" (1:19), i.e., scrupulously faithful to the Law; and he protects Jesus from the hos-

---

[1] I use "the Law" here as Matthew uses it when he designates a part of Scripture, namely, the *Torah* or Pentateuch. In particular, the Matthean infancy narrative echoes Genesis and Exodus. We shall see that the Lucan infancy narrative also echoes Genesis, for Zechariah and Elizabeth are modeled upon Abraham and Sarah. The Johannine Prologue takes as its first words the opening of the Book of Genesis: "In the beginning"—the words that supplied the name of the book in the Hebrew Bible. The tendency to resort to Genesis to explain Jesus' origins reflects the Christian concept of a new creation or a new beginning. The tendency to resort to Exodus and the Moses story reflects the Christian concept of a new (or renewed) covenant. For an interesting analysis of common theological tendencies in the prologues to the Gospels (with the infancy narratives understood as prologues), see O. J. Seitz, JBL 83 (1964), 262–68.

tile authorities of his own people and brings him safely to Galilee of the Gentiles. And so we have the Gospel and its destiny in miniature. If the Gentiles are becoming the dominant factor in the Church as Matthew knows it, and if the Jewish authorities have rejected Jesus as the Christ, faithful Jews did heed God's message about Jesus and have defied the Jewish authorities to bring Christ to the Gentiles. In so doing, they were being faithful to the Law and the prophets (5:17–18).

The effectiveness of Matthew's dramatization of these conceptions is attested by the fact that his infancy story is known by many who know little else of the Gospel. The subject of countless plays, poems, hymns, and pictures, the Matthean magi and star have come from the East into places where the cross cannot be publicly displayed. There are preachers who are uneasy about the popularity of this story, feeling that it serves as a palliative for true Gospel. But this is to neglect the fact that the infancy narrative contains both the cross and the God-given triumph. Herod stalks the trail of the magi, a menacing reminder that, while the star of the newborn King has shone forth in purity and simplicity, there are those who will seek to blot out that light. If the infancy story is an attractive drama that catches the imagination, it also is a substantial proclamation of the coming of the kingdom and its possible rejection. The dramatis personae may be exotically costumed as Eastern potentates and as a Jewish king and priests, and for that reason they are not easily forgotten. But beneath the robes one can recognize the believers of Matthew's time and their opponents. And, indeed, a perceptive reader may even recognize some of the drama of the Christian proclamation and its fate in all times.

BOOK TWO

THE LUCAN INFANCY NARRATIVE

(Luke 1–2)

I. GENERAL OBSERVATIONS ON THE LUCAN GOSPEL AND INFANCY NARRATIVE (§ 9)

In discussing Luke we have an advantage that we did not have with Matthew, namely, that the Gospel is part of a larger work which terminates in the Book of Acts, a book that aids in diagnosing the interest, style, and techniques of the evangelist.

A. *The Lucan Gospel*

Most scholars today would maintain that Luke's Gospel was written in a church of the Gentile mission in the 70s or 80s. As with my general statements about Matthew's Gospel, I recommend to the reader a standard introduction for detailed arguments (footnote 1, § 2) and explain here only the elementary reasoning behind this position, so that the reader may appreciate the Lucan community situation as it affects the infancy narrative.

The Greek of Luke is the best of the four Gospels, and it is likely that Greek was the evangelist's native tongue. Indeed, he is so at home in it that he seems able to adapt his style to different circumstances and sources.[1] The Gospel is noticeably lacking in Hebrew words, local Palestinian color, and direct OT citations. In this it is in marked contrast to Matthew; and so many scholars judge Luke's audience to be predominantly Gentile Christian, roughly contemporary with but quite different in membership from Matthew's mixed community of Jewish and Gentile Christians. The emphasis placed on Paul in the second half of Acts would be explicable if Luke was writing for a Gentile church that was an outgrowth of the Pauline missionary effort.[2]

By the end of the second century a tradition is recorded (Muratorian Canon, Irenaeus) identifying the evangelist, who never identifies himself,

---

[1] For instance, the Greek of the Prologue (1:1–4) is imitation classical; the Greek of the infancy narrative is Semitized; the Greek of the sermons in Acts is sometimes affected by the circumstances of the speaker. Many have detected a strong influence of the LXX upon Luke. See footnote 14, § 15, for the suggestion that Luke was a Gentile convert to Judaism.

[2] I would be no more specific than that. Antioch is reported by Eusebius to have been Luke's place of origin, and some would localize the composition of the Gospel there. But Syria begins to become a bit crowded as the conjectured place of NT authorship: Matthew and John are often localized there, and occasionally so is Mark.

as Luke, a companion of Paul. This tradition probably stems from an early analysis of the "We Sections" of Acts (16:10–17; 20:5–21:18; 27:1–28:16): Paul and the author were thought to constitute the "we," and the evidence was studied to see which of the Pauline companions might have feasibly been with Paul in the places covered by the "We Sections." This identification is now widely questioned because of the author's inaccuracies about Paul's career (Gal 1:16–17 versus Acts 9:19–29) and differences from Paul's thought as we know it from the Pauline Epistles. In fact, the author's identity is not so crucial for a discussion of the infancy narrative as it would be for a discussion of Acts. We shall continue to speak of the evangelist as "Luke" without prejudice to the question of whether or not he really was Luke. More important for our discussion is the clear recognition since antiquity that the evangelist was not an eyewitness of the ministry of Jesus, a fact that can be deduced from his own statement (1:2). The features separating "Luke" from Paul would be more easily explained if the writing of Luke/Acts came at least a generation after Paul's literary activity in the 50s,[8] when it was no longer possible to seek from Paul himself the details of his life, and when the changing Christian scene had modified Pauline thought even in those churches evangelized by him. A date in the 80s, give or take ten years, would also fit well the ecclesiology of Acts.[4]

Jervell and others have argued for an admixture of Judaism in the ambiance of Luke's community, either in terms of many Jewish Christian members or of active Jewish adversaries. I find no real plausibility in such a thesis. Luke's interest in Judaism reflects an attempt at self-understanding on the part of a Gentile Christian community. For Luke, the mission to the Gentiles was no aberration nor a desperate alternative for the mission to Israel. Rather it had been God's plan from the beginning that Jesus should be both a revelation to the Gentiles and the glory of the people of Israel (2:32). In the opening chapters of the Gospel and of Acts Luke portrays many Jews as seeing this and accepting Jesus; but there were also

---

[8] A date after 70 would be indicated by Luke's dependence upon Mark (and Q). The tradition of Luke's living in Greece in the 80s is our oldest tradition. A later tradition of the composition of Luke/Acts in Rome in the 60s stems from a false analysis of the purpose of Acts as a biography. It is defended by the argument that, if Luke wrote after Paul's death, he would not have ended the story with Paul as a captive in Rome. But Luke is not interested biographically in either Peter or Paul, the two main figures of Acts. He thinks of them as instruments in the plan of God whereby witness to Jesus should be borne "in Jerusalem, in all Judea and Samaria, and to the ends of the earth" (1:8). Peter dominates the first half of Acts because he was a major apostolic figure in the mission to Jerusalem, Judea, and Samaria. However, once Peter is instrumental in approving Paul's mission to the Gentiles (Acts 15), Luke betrays no more interest in Peter. The focus in the second half of Acts shifts to Paul who is brought to Rome, the capital of the Empire, and thus symbolically fulfills the promise of witness "to the ends of the earth." The ending of the story at Rome tells us about the purpose of Acts, not about the date of its composition.

[4] For instance, the simplified identification of "apostles" with the Twelve has become dominant; and there is a structure of presbyters in the churches (Acts 14:23; 20:17).

Jews who blinded themselves to the clear line of salvation history which, for Luke, connected Jesus to the history of Israel. Their blindness did not cause the mission to the Gentiles—that came under the guidance of the Holy Spirit—but it offered an explanation as to why the mission to Israel was now no longer a major issue in the churches Luke knew. On the part of Christians in Jerusalem there was "one mind" on the harmony between the mission to Israel and the mission to the Gentiles (Acts 15:25); but as the mission to the Gentiles reached to the ends of the earth (symbolized by Rome), the hardness of the hearts of "the Jews" meant almost exclusive attention to the Gentiles (Acts 28:25–28). If Paul is pictured as an observant Jew (Acts 21:26—a picture that may well be historical), it is not because Luke is appealing to Jewish Christians but because he wants to assure the Gentile children of Paul's mission that they were not fathered by a renegade but by one who was totally faithful to the witness of the Law and the prophets (28:23).[5] The active apologetic tone so visible in Matthew is greatly subdued in Luke's Gospel (and infancy narrative) since missionary confrontation with the Jews is a more distant issue geographically and temporally. Unlike the Paul of Rom 11, the Lucan Paul of Acts 28:25–28 seems to be resigned to a Gentile Church. Since that Paul reflects Luke's mind, we can understand a Lucan view of the Jewish Temple and its ritual more in terms of nostalgia for things past, rather than of hostility for an active and seductive enemy.

The geographic interest visible in Acts should be kept in mind while reading the Gospel and the infancy narrative. The writer who composed Acts to show how both geographically and theologically the focus of Christianity passed from Jerusalem of the Jews to Rome of the Gentiles is quite deliberate in framing the Gospel of Jesus in scenes involving the Jerusalem Temple (1:8 and 24:53),[6] with a miniature framework of Temple scenes for the infancy narrative (1:8 and 2:41). The worldwide interest of Acts will bring mention of Roman emperors in both the infancy narrative and the Gospel proper (Augustus and Tiberius; 2:1 and 3:1). Harmonious with the relative lack of apologetics is the gentleness of many Lucan scenes, especially those dealing with women[7]—some of them the

---

5 Luke's stress that Christianity was not just a sect of the Jews but the true Way of worshiping the God of the patriarchs (Acts 24:14) may be further explicable as an attempt to identify the Christians in the Roman world, e.g., they were not one of those Jewish sects who had caused the recent revolt in Palestine, but rather a peaceful religious group with ancient roots.

6 The context for almost half the ministry is the journey of Jesus toward Jerusalem (beginning in 9:51), a journey with a theological goal since "no prophet should perish anywhere away from Jerusalem" (13:33). It is consonant with Luke's interests that he mentions no Galilean appearances of the risen Jesus but has the whole post-resurrectional scenario take place in the Jerusalem area.

7 For example, the healing of the son of the widow of Nain, the penitent woman at Jesus' feet, the weeping women on the way to the cross. Luke alone gives us the parables of the Good Samaritan and the Prodigal Son.

most poignant in Christian memory. It is no accident, then, that Mary, the humble handmaid of the Lord, dominates the Lucan infancy narrative in a way clearly different from the Matthean insistence on Joseph.

But before we pass on to discuss the infancy narrative itself, I wish to mention two deductions from the Gospel at large that have been used to support the historicity of the infancy narrative. The first involves the interrelationships of the Third and Fourth Gospels. In ABJ, I, XLVI–XLVII, I pointed out that most of the unquestionable parallels between Luke and John are best explained on the pre-Gospel level of contact, e.g., a source, oral or written, behind John was known to the Lucan tradition, or vice versa. The main features shared by the two Gospels appear so differently that it is difficult to posit much direct copying of one evangelist by the other. Consequently, attempts to appeal to Lucan-Johannine parallelism as support for the infancy narrative are very dubious. For instance, it is true that JBap is mentioned both in John's Prologue (1:6–8,15) and in Luke 1; but the presence of these references (which have no real similarity to each other) can be explained by the common Christian memory that JBap preceded Jesus and, therefore, JBap should be mentioned before the narrated opening of Jesus' career. In particular, there is little merit in the thesis that links together Luke and John by a number of unsubstantiated guesses in order to explain the origins of the infancy narrative: the Beloved Disciple was John son of Zebedee (dubious); the highly symbolic scene in John 19:27 was historical and Mary lived at John's home for a number of years[8] (very dubious); Mary told John of the events surrounding the birth of Jesus (pure guess); and Luke got that information from his contacts with the Johannine tradition, contacts justified by the parallels just mentioned. This theory[9] makes the tradition behind the Fourth Gospel responsible for the material in Luke 1–2, even though John shows no awareness of the birth story[10] and in 1:31 seemingly contradicts the relationship between JBap and Jesus postulated by Luke 1:36!

The second deduction regarding the infancy narrative is drawn from the Lucan Preface (1:1–4) which is interpreted to mean that Luke used historical sources with extreme care and that therefore the infancy narrative is historical, based on reliable sources. However, that most perceptive commentator H. J. Cadbury[11] has quite correctly warned us against in-

---

8 Either in Jerusalem or at Ephesus (according to unreliable legends about John's subsequent history). Luke, as part of the "we" in Acts is thought to have had contact with John and/or Mary at one or other of those places (Acts 20:17; 21:15).

9 It is found in works that present themselves as modern biblical treatments, e.g., McHugh, *Mother*, 8–10, 147–49.

10 A possible exception is John's knowledge that Jesus was born at Bethlehem *if* John 7:41–42 is interpreted ironically. See footnote 6, Appendix III.

11 *Making*, 345–47, also an appendix in BC, II, 489–510. I am presuming that the outlook of the Preface to the Gospel is applicable to Acts as well.

terpreting the Preface to mean that Luke conducted research in the modern sense. If Luke mentions traditions from "those who were from the beginning eyewitnesses and ministers of the word" (1:2), primarily he means the companions of Jesus' ministry and the apostolic preachers, as indicated in Acts 1:21–22. It is unjustified to claim that this statement would substantiate his dependence upon family eyewitness tradition about Jesus' birth. Luke's intention "to write an orderly account" (1:3) does not imply that he gives us exact history or chronology. A study of Luke/Acts shows that Luke had shortcomings as a historian, e.g., in Acts 5:36 he has Gamaliel in the mid-30s refer in the past to a revolt by Theudas which did not occur till the 40s—and then Luke compounds the confusion by having Gamaliel refer to the revolt led by Judas the Galilean (A.D. 6) as if it came after the revolt of Theudas! There is every reason to believe that Luke himself composed many or all the speeches he has placed on the lips of Peter and Paul in Acts. To be sure he may be reusing older material in these speeches, but Luke weaves it together in a dramatic setting. And Luke's sense of "order" is often logical rather than chronological. For instance, in 4:31 – 5:11 he reverses the order he found in Mark 1:16–31: the Marcan Jesus called four disciples and then healed Peter's mother-in-law; but Luke seems to have thought it more logical to have the miracle precede the call, so that the disciples would have a reason to follow Jesus. Thus, if one wishes to use the statements in the Lucan Prologue to make prejudgments about the amount of historical precision one can expect in the infancy narrative, one must first interpret the Prologue in the light of Luke's procedure in the body of Luke/Acts—a procedure that gives evidence of considerable freedom of composition, occasional historical inexactitudes, and a primary interest in the logical rather than the chronological.

B. *The Lucan Infancy Narrative*

Two main problems concern us here: the relation of Luke 1–2 to the rest of Luke/Acts (under which heading I shall treat questions of sources and languages), and the internal organization or structure of Luke 1–2.

1. The Relation of Chs. 1–2 to the Rest of Luke/Acts

Here we must ask the same question that we asked in reference to Matthew's infancy narrative. Granted that the birth material had an origin and transmission different from the stories of Jesus' ministry, how did the evangelist proceed in joining birth material to the story of the ministry? Did he begin writing with the birth stories, or did he begin with the account of the ministry and, as an afterthought, prefix the birth stories?[12] In the case of Matthew the evidence clearly favored the thesis that the evangelist began with 1:1 and composed the Gospel in the order in which it has come to us. In the case of Luke the evidence points in the opposite direction. Although there have been occasional attempts to join the infancy story to the next two chapters, so that a continuous narrative-unit of the Gospel would extend from 1:5 to 4:15,[13] the solemn beginning of the ministry in 3:1-2 has proved an almost insurmountable obstacle to such a joining. Indeed, historiographical parallels in other Greek writing suggest that Luke 3:1-2 could well have served as the original opening of the Lucan Gospel.[14] Support for this is found not only in the fact that Mark and John open the Gospel story with the events surrounding the baptism of Jesus, but also in the reference to this baptism by JBap as a *beginning* in Acts 1:22. (The latter passage suggests that the infancy narrative may have been prefixed to the Gospel after the Book of Acts was completed.) The placing of the genealogy in the third chapter of Luke makes more sense if that had been done before an infancy narrative had been prefixed.[15] As was true also with Matthew's Gospel, none of the Lucan infancy narrative has had major influence on the body of the Gospel,[16] so that, if the first two chapters had been lost, we could never have suspected their existence. Since Luke was somewhat affected by the procedure of the classical historians, it is noteworthy that there is precedent for composing an infancy or early-youth narrative as part of the biography of a man whose public career was well known.[17]

[12] A third possibility worthy of serious consideration is that, while Luke began with the account of the ministry and later prefixed the birth stories, they were no afterthought—he had in mind from the beginning the whole scope of the work, even if he composed last a section that he placed at the beginning.

[13] See Schürmann, *Lukasevangelium*, I, 19, for these attempts. We remember that a similar (and more plausible) proposal was made to see Matt 1:1–4:16 as a continuous narrative-unit (§ 2, B1).

[14] Cadbury, *Making*, 204–9, offers parallels to Luke 3:1-2 from various ancient authors, including Josephus, *War* II xiv 4;#284, and Thucydides, *History* II ii 1. These are not the physical beginnings of the respective books; and so Cadbury comments: "The completest parallels to Luke [3:1-2] occur, however, in special passages in other historians where they are marking like the evangelist the real starting-point of their narrative." Streeter, *Four Gospels*, 209, considers 3:1-2 to have been the beginning of "Proto-Luke," to which Luke prefixed chs. 1-2. For the beginning of the *Gospel of the Ebionites*, which echoes Luke 3:1-2, see footnote 15, § 2.

[15] However, as I pointed out at the beginning of § 3, there is a precedent in the biblical account of the career of Moses for localizing a genealogy just before the hero of the story begins his ministry, rather than before he is born.

[16] There are occasional touches which bring ministry material into harmony with the infancy narrative. Luke 3:2 identifies JBap as the "son of Zechariah," the only reference in the Gospel proper to his parentage. (It is curious that Luke never takes up again the family relationship between Jesus and JBap that he has established in 1:36.) Because he has mentioned the virginal conception, Luke qualifies the description of Jesus as the "son of Joseph" (3:23) with the parenthetical clause "as was supposed." In 4:13 Luke speaks of Nazareth as the place where Jesus was "brought up," presumably because of the information in ch. 2 that he was not born there.

[17] Erdmann, *Vorgeschichten*, 8, insists that this practice was not unusual in Greek writing, e.g., Plutarch's treatment of Coriolanus, Fabius Maximus, etc.

Even if the infancy narrative was prefixed after the Gospel and Book of Acts had been completed, this reverse order of composition raises no doubt that it was Luke himself who prefixed it.[18] But it does add to the problem of Luke's technique in the composition of the infancy narrative. Were these two chapters composed entirely by Luke himself, so that they correspond closely to his thought? Or was Luke dependent here upon pre-Lucan sources[19] whose thought, even when modified, is not really consonant with Lucan theology? If there were sources, were they early Jewish Christian and originally composed in either Hebrew or Aramaic? And was there perhaps even a non-Christian source pertaining to JBap? Scholars have raised these questions, and the answers to them have serious implications both for the history and the theology of the Lucan infancy narrative. Here let me simply survey the various opinions of scholars, indicating briefly the type of solution I favor, but leaving detailed proof till the commentary. In line with the questions I have asked, I shall treat three areas: first, the relation of the theology of the infancy narrative to the theology of the Gospel proper; second, the nature and extent of the possible sources; third, the language of the sources.

THEOLOGICAL RELATIONSHIP OF LUKE 1–2 TO LUKE/ACTS. If there is a close theological relationship, Luke may still have used sources but the material taken from the sources would have been brought into real harmony with Luke's own views. If there is no close theological relationship, the theory of pre-Lucan sources becomes the most plausible explanation for such a divergent infancy narrative. The most famous modern analyst of Lucan theology, H. Conzelmann (*Theology*) virtually ignores the infancy narrative, for he has found it different from and even contrary to the main thought of Luke/Acts. Conzelmann maintains that Luke divided his account of salvation history into three periods: the period of Israel (3:1–4:13); the Satan-free period of Jesus (4:13–22:3); the period of the Church and of the Spirit (22:3 through Acts). According to Conzelmann, the Lucan JBap was not a precursor of Jesus and did not proclaim the kingdom of God or know anything about it; he was the last of the

---

[18] Marcion seemingly omitted the infancy material from his form of the Gospel of Luke, but that was probably because of the OT atmosphere which he would find objectionable. F. C. Conybeare (ZNW 3 [1902], 192–97) pointed to a note in a medieval Armenian copy of Ephraem's *Commentary on the Diatessaron* which seemed to speak of Luke as beginning with the baptism of John, as contrasted with another Gospel (Matthew?) which began with Abraham. Although the note was garbled, Conybeare thought that Ephraem might have had access to an old ms. in which the infancy narrative was omitted from Luke. Subsequent studies (D. Völter, ZNW 10 [1909], 177–80; F. Herklotz, BZ 8 [1910], 387–88) have offered completely different understandings of the note.

[19] In the discussion that follows I am using the term "source" in a technical way: an oral or written consecutive narrative or collection of material. As I shall make clear, even where I doubt the existence of a source, I admit that Luke picked up items of information or tradition, historical and non-historical, from which he shaped the narrative. But the question of a "source" asks whether someone shaped such a narrative before Luke.

prophets and belonged to the period of Israel (Luke 16:16). One can understand how poorly the infancy narrative fits into this schema, for there JBap is clearly part of the good news of salvation fulfilling the prophets (1:19,70,76).

Some scholars, like Oliver, Tatum, and Voss, while accepting Conzelmann's general analysis of Lucan theology, have sought to work the infancy narrative into that analysis. Oliver,[20] for instance, has argued that even in the infancy narrative JBap belongs to the period of Israel, for his parents are described as a Jewish priest and a daughter of Aaron, "observing all the commands and ordinances of the Lord" (1:5–6). Still others, like Audet, Minear, and Songer, have used the infancy narrative to challenge the validity of the Conzelmann analysis. Since personally I think the Conzelmann analysis is wrong, let me expand on this last approach.

The infancy narrative can be seen as a true introduction to some of the main themes of the Gospel proper,[21] and no analysis of Lucan theology should neglect it. In many ways, one may compare the relation of Luke 1–2 to the rest of the Gospel and the relation of Acts 1–2 to the rest of Acts. The first two chapters of Acts supply a transition from the story of Jesus to the story of the Church. The apostles are the principal connecting element, for they were with Jesus in his ministry and they will be the chief human agents in the early days of the Church. The risen Jesus appears to them and instructs them,[22] so that the continuity with what has preceded will be clear; the Holy Spirit comes upon them after Jesus departs, so that the continuity with what follows will be clear. Similarly in the first two chapters of the Gospel there is a transition from the story of Israel to the story of Jesus. There appear, almost from the pages of the OT, characters like Zechariah and Elizabeth, Simeon and Anna, who are the final representatives of the piety of Israel, while Mary recites a hymn that vocalizes the aspirations of the remnant (the "poor ones" who constitute God's servant Israel—1:54). The voices of these figures form a chorus to hail the new era marked by the advent of JBap and of Jesus. Thus, one may wish to keep Conzelmann's analysis of three periods (Israel, Jesus, Church), but see the scriptural representatives of the three periods as: (1) the Law and the prophets, i.e., much of what we call the OT; (2) the Gospel ac-

---

[20] "Lucan Birth," 217–19. He agrees with Conzelmann that in the Lucan account of the ministry JBap is not a precursor of Jesus, but he thinks that is because JBap already played that function in the infancy narrative. I shall contend that the picture of JBap in Luke is reasonably consistent throughout.

[21] Audet, "Autour," 412–13, says that chs. 1–2 were conceived by Luke in the manner of the classical and Hellenistic *prooimia* ("prefaces"), the functions of which were described in Aristotle's *Rhetoric* iii 14. These prefaces prepared the reader to understand the body of the work, since otherwise there was a danger of misunderstanding the author's purpose.

[22] It is Jesus who gives the outline of the Book of Acts in 1:8. Luke might have done this himself in the Prologue to Acts; but by having Jesus do it, Luke shows the continuity between the Church and Jesus.

count of the ministry, beginning with JBap;[23] (3) the account of the post-pentecostal period in the Book of Acts. Between (1) and (2) there is a transitional narrative, the infancy story of Luke 1–2; between (2) and (3) there is a transitional narrative, the story of the ascension of Jesus and the coming of the Holy Spirit at Pentecost in Acts 1–2.[24]

This analysis of Lucan theology helps to explain something that is a real puzzle for Conzelmann's analysis, namely, the atmosphere of the period of the Church in the infancy narrative.[25] If Luke composed the infancy narrative last of all (and thus after Acts) and if he intended a certain parallelism between the two transitional sections (Luke 1–2, Acts 1–2), it is not surprising that in many ways the infancy narrative is closer in spirit to the stories in Acts than to the Gospel material which Luke took from Mark and Q. The outpouring of the prophetic spirit which moves people to act and speak (Luke 1:15,41,67,80; 2:25–27) is not well attested in the ministry[26] but resembles very closely the pentecostal and post-pentecostal outpouring of the prophetic spirit in Acts 2:17: "I shall pour out my Spirit upon all flesh, and your sons and daughters will prophesy." The speeches of Acts and the hymns of the infancy narrative are both compositions reflecting older material, but compositions which convey to the reader the tonality of the character to whom they are attributed and which comment upon the significance of the context in which they are uttered. The angelic appearances which are frequent in the infancy narrative (1:11,26; 2:9) have little parallel in the ministry of Jesus, but close parallels in Acts (5:19; 8:26; 10:3; 12:7; 27:23). The title "Messiah Lord" (*Christos Kyrios*) given by the angels to the infant Jesus in 2:11 echoes the christology of the post-resurrectional speeches in Acts, e.g., "God has made him both Lord [*Kyrios*] and Messiah [*Christos*], this Jesus whom you crucified" (2:36). The artistry that Luke manifests in the parallelism that he establishes between JBap and Jesus in the infancy narrative[27] is also at work in the parallelism in Acts between the careers of Peter and Paul.[28] All of this shows that the infancy narrative is much more Lucan in thought and pattern than Conzelmann allows.

[23] Although Conzelmann understands Luke 16:16 ("The Law and the prophets were until John; since then the good news of the kingdom of God is preached") to exclude JBap from the period of Jesus, that verse can be understood to confirm the first two divisions I propose.

[24] Admittedly I am speaking with a certain vagueness when I refer to Acts 1–2, for I do not mean that precisely with Acts 3:1 the story of the Church begins. It begins in ch. 2; and there is no such clear line of demarcation in Acts between the transitional material and the narrative proper, such as we find in Luke 3:1–2.

[25] See Minear, "Luke's Use," 116. Minear's article is a thorough and persuasive challenge to the Conzelmann hypothesis.

[26] In the ministry the Spirit is related to Jesus himself who is a prophet, but there is no outpouring of the Spirit on others.

[27] In a saying of the Q tradition (Matt 11:16–19; Luke 7:31–35) JBap and Jesus are set side by side, but Luke has developed this into a major parallelism.

[28] Like Peter, Paul preaches kerygmatic sermons and performs the same type of miracles. It is interesting how Luke handles the interplay of two characters when he intends to pursue

NATURE AND EXTENT OF POSSIBLE SOURCES. While we are not compelled, then, by differences in theology to posit a pre-Lucan source for the infancy narrative, similarities in theology do not resolve that question. It is more correctly a question of a *plurality* of sources, and one may posit sources for a part of the infancy narrative and reject them for another part. There are three frequently proposed types of sources: (*1*) *A special source for the canticles* or hymns, i.e., for the Magnificat (1:46–55), the Benedictus (1:67–79), the Gloria in Excelsis (2:13–14) and the Nunc Dimittis (2:29–32).[29] The style of these canticles is more poetic and Semitized than the style of their context; indeed, the Magnificat and Benedictus have only minor touches that make them Christian. They seem to be appendages and can be easily excised so that the reader would never miss them.[30] It has been suggested that these were originally Jewish hymns (even Maccabean war songs!) or Jewish Christian hymns (of the Jerusalem community which is so prominent in Acts 2–6). (*2*) *Sources for one or more units in ch. 2*, e.g., for 2:1–20; 2:22–39; or 2:41–51. Chapter 2 is completely separable from ch. 1: it has its own introduction, and presupposes nothing from ch. 1, neither the virginal conception nor the identity of the parents.[31] Although prominent in ch. 1, JBap has completely disappeared from the scene. Within ch. 2 itself, the story in 2:41–51 is quite separable from the rest. Not only does it deal with a different phase of Jesus' life, but in its emphasis on the parents' lack of understanding (2:48–50) it seems to clash with the revelations given to them in what has gone before. One could argue that 2:40 was the original conclusion and that a story of different provenance was added, requiring a second and duplicate conclusion in 2:52. (*3*) *Sources for the JBap and Jesus stories of ch. 1*. Since these stories contain intimate detail about the conception of each child, those who regard them as historical often tend to trace them

---

the career of only one of them: JBap and Jesus both appear in Luke 1, but only Jesus appears in Luke 2; JBap and Jesus both appear in Luke 3, but JBap is removed from the scene in 3:20 so that Jesus has the field to himself; Peter and Paul both appear in Acts 15, but Peter is not mentioned afterwards and Paul has the field to himself. George, "Le parallèle," 156–58, points to a somewhat similar parallelism in Greco-Roman literature (*synkrisis*: Homer/Hesiod; Aeschylus/Euripides) but often by way of contrasting the two figures. Could Luke by his parallelism be reacting to early rival groups who tended to set up an opposition between JBap and Jesus, between Peter and Paul?

29 Since the Gloria and the Nunc Dimittis are so short, most of the judgments about the canticles are made on the basis of the Magnificat and the Benedictus. One could posit a source for those two canticles, and attribute the Gloria or the Nunc Dimittis to Lucan imitation.

30 Luke 1:45 can be connected directly to 1:56; 1:66 to 1:80; and 2:28 to 2:34b. If we accept the reading "angel" (singular), 2:15 can be joined to 2:12.

31 In 2:4 it is repeated that Joseph is of the house of David, although the reader was told that in 1:27. There is nothing in ch. 2 that is based on Jesus having been virginally conceived. The angelic annunciation to the shepherds in 2:8–12 has been thought to duplicate the angelic annunciation to Mary in 1:26–38 as a means of revealing that the child is the Messiah.

back to family traditions.[82] The thesis of a Marian source has its advocates today largely in Roman Catholic circles, and usually supposes an oral communication of Mary's experiences, upon which Luke has drawn directly or indirectly.[83] Many critical scholars posit a Baptist source, sometimes thought to have had Christian origins, but more often thought to have been composed by followers of JBap.[84] Indeed, it is posited that the Baptist source once contained not only the material in Luke 1 that now refers to JBap but other material which has been reapplied to Jesus, e.g., the Magnificat (originally spoken by Elizabeth), the annunciation in 1:26–38 (originally addressed to Elizabeth, as a parallel to the annunciation to Zechariah), and even the presentation in the Temple in 2:22–39 (a continuation of the Samuel motif evident in the picture of JBap as a Nazirite).[85]

Various aspects of these suggestions will have to be discussed in detail in the commentary. Inevitably, the source proposals have been combined in complicated theories. C. A. Briggs[86] thought he could detect a pattern of seven poems, reflected not only in the obvious poetry of the canticles, but also in the prose account. K. L. Schmidt[87] has found seven separate traditions or narratives cemented together by Lucan additions. Most recently, H. Schürmann[88] has found five separate tales about Jesus, in addition to a JBap narrative, and at least three different hymns.

THE LANGUAGE OF THE PUTATIVE SOURCES. Although content has been a guide in the detection of sources, linguistic analysis has often been pro-

---

[82] Either to two family traditions, or to Mary alone as knowing the story of both births through the visitation.

[83] The classic argument is that, since Mary is pictured alone on the occasion of the annunciation, only she could be the source of the dialogue found therein. This argument has lost much of its force since it is now clear in Roman Catholic thought that inspiration of the Scriptures does not guarantee historicity. There is no reason now why a Roman Catholic could not judge the scene to be the product of Luke's creative imagination, so long as he or she did not deny the theological truths contained therein. See footnotes 28 and 29 in Appendix IV.

[84] Either by followers who were anti-Christian (maintaining that JBap, not Jesus, was the Messiah) or by followers who did not become Christian. The suggestion that the JBap source was composed by followers who became Christians leads us into the thesis of the origin of the source in early Jewish Christianity. Among those who posit a Baptist source in one form or another can be listed Bultmann, Dibelius, Gunkel, Leaney, Vielhauer, and Völter. For an example of the theory in practice, see Wilkinson, *Johannine Document*.

[85] Geyser, "Youth," proposes that there was a lost sequel which once came after 1:80 and described JBap's youth, how he was raised in the desert and became subject to Essenes as to adoptive parents. The theory approaches fantasy.

[86] "Gospel," 162–63. He finds a pattern for these poems in the *Psalms of Solomon*. For an even more complicated arrangement, see Thompson, "Infancy," 220.

[87] *Rahmen*, 309–14. The seven are: (a) 1:8–25,57–66, a narrative about JBap; (b) 1:26–38, a narrative where Mary lives in Nazareth; (c) 1:39–45; 2:21–40, a narrative where Mary lives in Jerusalem; (d) 2:6–20, a shepherd folk story; (e) 2:41–49, a narrative where Jesus' family lives in Nazareth; (f) and (g) 1:46–55 and 67–79, two separate canticles.

[88] "Aufbau," 110–11. The five Jesus tales are: (a) 2:6, enlarged into 2:1–7; (b) 2:22–39—these two tales arose in early Palestinian Jewish Christian circles; (c) 2:8–20, a later composition but still Palestinian; (d) 1:26–38, a Gentile Christian development around a Jewish Christian kernel in vss. 30–33; (2) 2:41–51, a Gentile Christian story.

posed as the ultimate control. The Greek of the infancy narrative is more Semitized than the Greek of most of the Gospel, and so it has been argued that we have here translation from oral or written sources in Aramaic (Dibelius, Michaelis, Plummer, Spitta, B. Weiss), or in Hebrew (Box, Dalman, De Lagarde, Gunkel, Laurentin, Streeter, Torrey), or in both languages (Winter).[39] A counterargument is that there is highly Semitized Greek in Acts as well, and that its presence does not seem to be traceable to any uniform source. If the proponents of a Semitic source single out phrases which, they claim, must be translation Greek, Minear[40] can supply lists showing that fifty-five significant words or phrases which appear in the infancy narrative are found more often in Luke/Acts than in the rest of the NT. A frequent explanation for the presence of both Lucan and Semitic features is the proposal that Luke himself made the translation, although others (e.g., Schelkle) argue for a pre-Lucan translation of the sources.

Firmly opposed to the thesis of extended Semitic sources for the infancy narrative (with the occasional exception of allowing a source for the canticles) is an equally impressive number of scholars: Benoit, Cadbury, Goulder and Sanderson, Harnack, Turner, and Wellhausen, to name a few. They speak of Luke's deliberate use of Semitized Septuagintal style when he was composing a narrative imitative of the OT. They do not necessarily deny that Luke had items of information (footnote 19 above), but they think that it was Luke who first gave form to the narrative we now know, a narrative that never existed other than in Lucan Greek.

The reason for such a serious division among scholars is well phrased by Cadbury (*Making,* 67): "The Third Evangelist's personal style is never so totally wanting as to prove alien origins for a passage, and is never so persuasive as to exclude the possibility that a written source existed, although the source be no longer capable of detection by any residual difference of style." Following that caution, although in the NOTES I shall point out both Semitisms and "Lucanisms," I abandon in this commentary the thesis that by style and language one can decide the question of sources. The linguistic opponents have fought one another to a draw at the present moment of our scientific research, and so I shall appeal more to arguments of content and thought pattern.

For the reader's guidance let me summarize here my own position. I see no need of positing either a JBap source or a Marian source for ch. 1. For that chapter Luke had some items that came to him from tradition, e.g.,

---

[39] Machen, *Virgin Birth,* 104, traces the scholarly debate about the Lucan and putative non-Lucan character of the language in the infancy narrative back to Gersdorf in 1816. See the bibliography carefully analyzed by McHugh, *Mother,* 435–37.

[40] "Luke's Use," 113–15. He builds upon Morgenthaler and points out that, of sixty-two favorite Lucan words, forty-six appear in the infancy narrative. He discusses stylistic and thought patterns as well.

the names of JBap's parents. Also pre-Lucan was a tendency to compare the conception of Jesus to the conception of OT salvific figures by the use of an annunciation pattern, and the idea of a virginal conception which took place while Mary was contracted to Joseph as a bride but had not yet come to live with him.[41] But it was Luke himself who combined and fleshed out these traditions, incorporating a Christian creedal formula about Jesus as son of David and Son of God, and portraits of JBap and Mary gleaned from the Gospel account of the public ministry. With a sense of parallelism, he constructed an annunciation of JBap's conception to match the annunciation of Jesus' conception, exhibiting theological care to keep JBap on a lower level. The characters of JBap's parents he constructed on the pattern of Abraham and Sarah from the OT, as part of his plan to make the infancy narrative a bridge between Israel and Jesus. After the main lines of his composition in ch. 1 were clear, Luke added (with adaptation) two canticles, the Magnificat and the Benedictus, which may have come to him from a Jewish Christian community. These canticles would have been the longest "prefabricated" elements Luke used in ch. 1.

For explaining the composition of ch. 2 a source theory has greater possibility. The story in 2:41–51 seems to have been appended late in the process of composing the infancy narrative. Plausibly it stemmed from a popular tradition of pre-ministry marvels, seemingly attested in John 2:1–11 and clearly attested in the apocryphal gospels. The story or stories in 2:6–20 and 2:25–38 are more difficult to analyze. Luke fashioned the setting in 2:1–5 and 2:40, as well as the connective material in 2:21–24; but the core of the Lucan post-birth narrative has some deep (not surface) resemblances to the post-birth narrative in Matt 2. It is not only a question of a similar story line and theology, but also of a common underlying association of the Bethlehem and Migdal Eder motifs in Micah 4–5 and Gen 35:19–20. I hesitate to posit a source in the sense of footnote 19 above, but Luke has built upon and dramatized earlier reflections (and added the Gloria and the Nunc Dimittis).

All these judgments will be further explained in the commentary, with a rationale supplied. If I have resorted to qualifying adverbs like "plausibly" and "seemingly," it is because of the skillful character of Lucan redaction —more thorough and more subtle than the Matthean redacting of pre-Matthean material. Frequently, it is not possible for us to have surety about the nature of the pre-Lucan material underlying the infancy narra-

---

41 My judgment on what was pre-Lucan, even as my judgment on what was pre-Matthean, is heavily influenced by what Matthew and Luke have in common. One may hypothesize that independently Matthew and Luke hit upon the pattern of an annunciation, the idea of a virginal conception, etc.; but it is more plausible that these are earlier ideas that each has taken over and developed in his own way. I find totally implausible that they would independently chance upon the same peculiar marital situation as a setting for the annunciation.

TABLE IX: ANALYSES OF THE STRUCTURE OF LUKE 1–2

(A) ANALYSES INTO THREE DIVISIONS

(Galbiati)

I	II	III
A ANNUNCIATION before birth To Zechariah (1:8–25) *Notice* of Birth (1:57–58) *Scene* of Circumcision and Naming (1:59–66) B PROPHETIC REVELATION By Zechariah (1:67–79) (Benedictus) *Refrain* about growth; JBap stayed in desert (1:80)	ANNUNCIATION before birth To Mary (1:26–38) PROPHETIC REVELATION By Elizabeth and Mary (1:39–55) (Magnificat) Mary remained three months; then returned home (1:56)	*Scene* of Birth (2:1–7) ANNUNCIATION after birth To the Shepherds (2:8–20) *Notice* of Circumcision and Naming (2:21) PROPHETIC REVELATION By Simeon and Anna (2:22–38) (Nunc Dimittis) The family returned to Galilee (2:39) *Refrain* about growth (2:40) *Scene* of Jesus in the Temple (2:41–50) Jesus went back to Nazareth (2:51) *Refrain* about progress (2:52)

(Burrows)

A	B
I ANNUNCIATION to Zechariah (1:5–23) plus two intermediary verses (1:24–25) II BIRTH of JBap (1:57–79) plus an intermediary verse (1:80) III TEMPLE MYSTERY: Presentation of Jesus (2:22–39) plus an intermediary verse (2:40)	Scene 1. ANNUNCIATION to Mary (1:26–38) Scene 2. Visitation of Mary to Elizabeth (1:39–56) BIRTH of Jesus (2:1–21) Scene 1. Annunciation to Shepherds (2:1–15) Scene 2. Visitation of Shepherds to Bethlehem (2:15–20) plus an intermediary verse (2:21) TEMPLE MYSTERY: Finding of Jesus (2:41–51) plus a concluding verse (2:52)

(Dibelius)

	A	B
I	ANNUNCIATION of Birth of JBap by angel Gabriel (1:5–25)	ANNUNCIATION of Birth of Jesus by angel Gabriel (1:26–38)
	Parallel Greetings of Two Mothers ([Magnificat] 1:39–56)	
II	BIRTH, CIRCUMCISION, NAMING of JBap with accompanying wonders (1:57–66)	BIRTH, CIRCUMCISION, NAMING of Jesus with accompanying wonders (2:1–21)
III	GREETING of JBap by inspired Zechariah (Benedictus); growth of child (1:67–80)	GREETING of Jesus by inspired Simeon and Anna (Nunc Dimittis); growth of child (2:22–40)
		Surpassing behavior of Jesus in the Temple (2:41–52)

(B) ANALYSES INTO TWO DIVISIONS

(Gaechter)

I THE TWO ANNUNCIATIONS:
1. Annunciation of JBap's birth (1:5–25)
2. Annunciation of Jesus' birth (1:26–38)
3. Visitation of Mary to Elizabeth (1:39–56)

II THE TWO BIRTHS AND MANIFESTATIONS:
4. Birth and Manifestation of JBap (1:57–80)
5. Birth and Manifestation of Jesus (2:1–21)
6. Presentation of Jesus in Temple (2:22–40)
CONCLUSION:
7. Finding Jesus in Temple (2:41–52)

(Lyonnet)

I THE TWO ANNUNCIATIONS:
    Annunciation to Zechariah
    Annunciation to Mary
        First Supplement: Visitation
II THE TWO BIRTHS:
    Birth of JBap
    Birth of Jesus (2:1–20)
        First Supplement: Circumcision, Presentation (2:21–40)
        Second Supplement: Jesus amidst Teachers

(Laurentin)

I THE TWO ANNUNCIATIONS:
1. Annunciation of JBap's birth
2. Annunciation of Jesus' birth
3. Complement: Visitation
Conclusion: 1:56

II THE TWO BIRTHS:
4. Birth of JBap
    His Circumcision and Manifestation
5. Birth of Jesus
6. His Circumcision and Manifestation
7. Complement: Finding Jesus in Temple
Conclusion: 2:52

tive. If for the ministry account the Gospel of Mark had not survived, but one knew that Luke had used an earlier Gospel, it would be enormously difficult, working from Luke, to reconstruct the Marcan material. Reconstruction in the infancy narrative offers a similar, and probably greater, difficulty.

2. The Internal Organization of Chs. 1–2

There is common agreement today that Luke arranged these chapters with careful artistry, even though scholars do not agree in their analyses of that arrangement.[42] In part, I suspect, the disagreement stems from not recognizing that there were two stages of Lucan composition, namely, a basic narrative constructed by Luke, and later additions by Luke. However, before I develop that suggestion, let me present in simplified form in Table IX some structural analyses of the Lucan infancy narrative, so that the reader may study the points on which there are agreements and disagreements.[43] The following factors must come into play in analysis of Lucan structure:

▪There are basically seven episodes: (1) Annunciation about JBap; (2) Annunciation about Jesus; (3) Visitation; (4) Birth/Circumcision/Naming of JBap; (5) Birth/Circumcision/Naming of Jesus; (6) Presentation in Temple; (7) Finding in Temple.

▪All the analyses agree that Luke intended to show parallels between JBap and Jesus.[44] When that parallelism is found in adjacent episodes, the term diptych is often used. The closest parallelism is between episodes 1 and 2—the two annunciations. There is also parallelism between episodes 4 and 5; but it is less close.[45] These four episodes, arranged in diptych fashion, are the backbone of the analyses into two divisions.

[42] For longer discussions of these analyses, see Laurentin, *Structure*, 23–33; and George, "Le parallèle."

[43] For the analyses into three divisions, see Galbiati, "La circoncisione," 38–40; Burrows, *Gospel*, 5–6; and Dibelius, *Überlieferung*, 67—the last is presented in English with adaptation by Wink, *John*, 59. Galbiati gives only the raw material for the diagram that I have constructed. For the analyses into two divisions, see Gaechter, *Maria*, 11–12; Laurentin, *Structure*, 32–33, Lyonnet, "Le récit," 6—the last is presented in English in Lyonnet, "St. Luke's," 148–49.

[44] This parallelism is a Lucan feature found in the Gospel proper:
   JBap and Jesus both in the desert (3:2; 4:1);
   JBap and Jesus both written of by Isaiah (3:4–6; 4:17–19);
   JBap and Jesus both issued warnings drawn from OT (3:7–9; 4:24–27);
   JBap and Jesus both questioned about identity (3:15; 4:34);
   JBap and Jesus both preached the good news (3:18; 4:43).
The last point challenges the Conzelmann analysis of Luke's attitude toward JBap.

[45] As Galbiati's analysis underlines, there is just a *notice* of the birth of JBap (1:57–58) but a *scene* built around his circumcision and naming (1:59–66). The situation of Jesus is just the opposite: a *scene* of birth (2:1–20) and a *notice* of circumcision and naming (2:21).

■Episode 3, which brings the mothers of JBap and Jesus together, does not fit either side of a diptych arrangement. However, since it exalts Jesus, there is a tendency to put it on Jesus' side of the diptych pattern (Burrows, Laurentin). Dibelius' schema is the clearest visually in treating this episode of the visitation as a connective.

■There are no narrative parallels in the JBap story for episodes 6 and 7, and so these episodes cause difficulty for those who analyze into two divisions. Laurentin tries to join 6 with 5 as an unbalanced parallel to 4.[46] Most analyses treat 7 as an unbalanced factor; but Burrows (and Lyonnet to some extent) sets up a parallelism between 6 and 7, even though both deal with Jesus. Dibelius sees a certain likeness between 3 and 7, since both are outside the structure of parallels between JBap and Jesus.

■There are statements concerning the growth or progress of the child at the ends of 4, 6, and 7, the first statement referring to JBap, and the second and third to Jesus.[47]

■The canticles fit only awkwardly into the various analyses: (a) The second canticle or Benedictus refers to JBap, while the first and fourth, the Magnificat and Nunc Dimittis, refer to Jesus. (b) In terms of parallelism, the Magnificat and Benedictus are close to each other in length, tone, and speakers (respective parents); yet the episodes in which they are placed (3 and 4) are not parallel. (c) In terms of episodes, the Benedictus and Nunc Dimittis are close to each other: each is a prophetic canticle uttered after the birth/naming/circumcision of the child, and each refers to the child's destiny, especially in relation to Israel. (d) The shortest canticle, the Gloria, is more general than the others.

I cannot pretend to propose an analysis that will do justice to all these confusing factors, for some of them are inherent in the fact that Luke worked into his infancy narrative material of different provenance. Nevertheless, as a step toward dealing with many of the factors, let me suggest that Luke composed his narrative in two stages. The *first stage* was based on establishing a parallelism between JBap and Jesus. It resulted in the following arrangement of two diptychs:

I. Two Annunciations of Conception:
    1. Annunciation about JBap (1:5–23);
       plus Elizabeth's pregnancy and praise of God (1:24–25).
    2. Annunciation about Jesus (1:26–38);
       plus Elizabeth's praise of Mary's pregnancy (1:39–45,56).

---

[46] There is a statement about the growth of the child at both the end of 4 (1:80) and the end of 5–6 (2:40). There is a canticle about the future greatness of the child and his relation to God's people at both the end of 4 (Benedictus) and the end of 5–6 (Nunc Dimittis).

[47] Some would compare these statements to the summaries in Acts (major summaries in 2:42–47; 4:32–35; 5:11–16; minor summaries in 1:14; 6:7; 9:31, etc.), which can be interpreted, at times, to mark divisions in the action.

II. Two Narratives of Birth/Circumcision/Naming and Future Greatness:
  1. Narrative about JBap (1:57–66);
     plus a growth statement transitional to his ministry (1:80).
  2. Narrative about Jesus (2:1–27,34–39);
     plus a growth statement transitional to his ministry (2:40).

The first diptych, based on annunciations (see Table XI), consists of sections of equal length, i.e., twenty-one verses each. The visitation (with the Magnificat omitted) does not constitute a separate episode; rather, as an epilogue, it is the fulfillment of the annunciation to Mary and the verification of the sign given to her, even as 1:24–25 is the fulfillment of the annunciation to Zechariah, and 1:22 is a verification of the sign given to him. The fact that the first diptych culminates with the mother of JBap praising Mary as the mother of Jesus already hints at Luke's attitude: although they are parallel, Jesus is superior to JBap. The second diptych, based on birth narratives (see Table XIV), makes this superiority explicit by giving much more attention to the future greatness of Jesus than to the future greatness of JBap. The wonders surrounding the birth, circumcision, and naming of JBap cause all who hear of him to ask, "What then is this child going to be?" The birth of Jesus is heralded by an angel who identifies the child as Messiah and Lord. And after Jesus is circumcised, he is brought to the Temple so that Simeon, filled with the Holy Spirit, can predict his future (2:34–35).[48]

The *second stage* of Lucan composition added valuable material, but at the same time unbalanced the neat pattern of diptychs. The canticles are beautiful but structurally awkward (see footnote 30 above). The presence of the Magnificat, for instance, makes a separate episode of the visitation, which is now too long to serve as a balance for 1:24–25 in the first diptych. It was in this second stage that Luke also added the episode of finding the child Jesus in the Temple[49]—an episode of another origin and subject matter that cannot be fitted into a diptych structure. Its addition after the original concluding growth statement of 2:40 required the appending of a second growth statement transitional to Jesus' ministry (2:52).

---

[48] The first Lucan stage of composition was marked off by a perfect inclusion: it began with Zechariah who had come into the Temple to burn incense, but was struck mute and was unable to bless the people; it ended with Simeon who was led into the Temple by the Spirit and enabled to bless the parents and the child. In each case the principal male figure is associated with a woman (Elizabeth and Anna) whose age, tribal derivation, and piety are mentioned.

[49] When I discussed the possibility of pre-Lucan sources above, I suggested that two areas in which such a theory had the most probability were the canticles and this episode in 2:41–51. Therefore, it seems likely that in this second stage of composition Luke was making his additions from sources that had come to his attention—sources that had no previous connection to infancy tradition.

With these brief suggestions as an overall guide to Luke's procedure, let me now turn to a detailed study of each Lucan episode. The reader will discover that rarely has theology been dramatized with more artistry and delicacy.

BIBLIOGRAPHY FOR THE LUCAN INFANCY NARRATIVE

(This Bibliography contains works pertinent to *the whole* of Luke 1–2; see also the material pertinent to Luke in the General Bibliography.)

Audet, J.-P., "Autour de la théologie de Luc I-II," ScEccl 11 (1959), 409–18.

Burrows, E., *The Gospel of the Infancy and Other Biblical Essays* (London: Burns Oates, 1940), esp. 1–58.

Cadbury, H. J., *The Making of Luke-Acts* (rev. ed.; London: SPCK, 1958; orig. 1927).

Conzelmann, H., *The Theology of St. Luke* (New York: Harper, 1960).

Creed, J. M., *The Gospel according to St. Luke* (London: Macmillan, 1957), esp. 6–46.

Danker, F. W., *Jesus and the New Age according to St. Luke* (St. Louis: Clayton, 1972), esp. 6–41.

Dibelius, M., "Jungfrauensohn und Krippenkind. Untersuchungen zur Geburtsgeschichte Jesu im Lukas-Evangelium," in *Botschaft und Geschichte: Gesammelte Aufsätze von Martin Dibelius* (Tübingen: Mohr, 1953; orig. 1932), I, 1–78.

Ellis, E. E., *The Gospel of Luke* (rev. ed.; London: Oliphants, 1974), esp. 68–86.

Flender, H., *St. Luke: Theologian of Redemptive History* (Philadelphia: Fortress, 1967).

Gaechter, P., *Maria im Erdenleben* (Innsbruck: Tyrolia, 1953).

George, A., "Le parallèle entre Jean-Baptiste et Jésus en Luc 1–2," in *Mélanges Béda Rigaux*, eds. A. Descamps and A. de Halleux (Gembloux: Duculot, 1970), 147–71.

Goulder, M. D., and M. L. Sanderson, "St. Luke's Genesis," JTS 8 (1957), 12–30.

Grundmann, W., *Das Evangelium nach Lukas* (THKNT; 4th ed.; Berlin: Evangelische Verlag, 1966), esp. 46–98.

Harnack, A. von, *Luke the Physician* (London: Williams and Norgate, 1907), esp. 96–105, 199–218.

Jervell, J., *Luke and the People of God* (Minneapolis: Augsburg, 1972).

Keck, L. E., and J. L. Martyn, *Studies in Luke-Acts* (P. Schubert Festschrift; Nashville: Abingdon, 1966).

Lagrange, M.-J., *Evangile selon Saint Luc* (7th ed.; Paris: Gabalda, 1948; orig. 1921), esp. 7–98.

Laurentin, R., *Structure et Théologie de Luc I–II* (Paris: Gabalda, 1957).

——— "Traces d'allusions étymologiques en Lc 1–2 (I,II)," *Biblica* 37 (1956), 435–56; 38 (1957), 1–23.

Leaney, A. R. C., *The Gospel according to St. Luke* (BNTC; New York: Harper, 1958), esp. 20–27, 78–103.

Lyonnet, S., "St. Luke's Infancy Narrative," in *Work and Mystery*, ed. L. J. O'Donovan (New York: Newman, 1968), 143–54. Translation of part of Lyonnet, "Le récit."

MacNeill, H. L., "The *Sitz im Leben* of Luke 1:5 – 2:20," JBL 65 (1946), 123–30.

Marshall, I. H., *Luke: Historian and Theologian* (Exeter: Paternoster, 1970), esp. 96–105.

Minear, P. S., "Luke's Use of the Birth Stories," in Keck, *Studies*, 111–30.

Morgenthaler, R., *Die lukanische Geschichtschreibung als Zeugnis* (2 vols.; Zurich: Zwingli, 1949).

Neirynck, F., *L'Evangile de Noël selon S. Luc* (Paris: Pensée Catholique, 1960).

——— ed., *L'Evangile de Luc: Problèmes littéraires et théologiques* (BETL 32; Gembloux: Duculot, 1973).

Oliver, H. H., "The Lucan Birth Stories and the Purpose of Luke-Acts," NTS 10 (1963–64), 202–26.

Plummer, A., *A Critical and Exegetical Commentary on the Gospel according to S. Luke* (ICC, 4th ed.; Edinburgh: Clark, 1901), esp. 6–80.

Ruddick, C. T., Jr., "Birth Narratives in Genesis and Luke," NovTest 12 (1970), 343–48.

Sahlin, H., *Der Messias und das Gottesvolk. Studien zur protolukanischen Theologie* (ASNU 12; Uppsala: Almqvist, 1945).

Schlatter, A., *Das Evangelium des Lukas* (2nd ed.; Stuttgart: Calwer, 1960; orig. 1931), esp. 152–207.

Schürmann, H., "Aufbau, Eigenart und Geschichtswert der Vorgeschichte von Lukas 1–2," BibKir 21 (1966), 106–11.

——— "Der 'Bericht von Anfang,'" StEv, II (TU 87; Berlin: Akademie, 1964), 242–58.

——— *Das Lukasevangelium*, I (HTKNT 3; Freiburg: Herder, 1969), esp. 18–145.

Songer, H. S., "Luke's Portrayal of the Origins of Jesus," RevExp 64 (1967), 453–63.

Talbert, C. H., *Literary Patterns, Theological Themes and the Genre of Luke-Acts* (SBLMS 20; Missoula: Scholars Press, 1974).

Tatum, W. B., "The Epoch of Israel: Luke I–II and the Theological Plan of Luke-Acts," NTS 13 (1966–67), 184–95.

Tsuchiya, H., "The History and the Fiction in the Birth Stories of Jesus—An Observation on the Thought of Luke the Evangelist," *Annual of the Japanese Biblical Institute* 1 (1975), 73–90.

Turner, N., "The Relation of Luke I and II to Hebraic Sources and to the Rest of Luke-Acts," NTS 2 (1955–56), 100–9.

Vögtle, A., "Offene Fragen zur Lukanischen Geburts- und Kindheitsgeschichte," BibLeb 11 (1970), 51–67. Reprinted in Vögtle, *Das Evangelium,* 43–56.

Voss, G., "Die Christusverkündigung der Kindheitsgeschichte im Rahmen des Lukasevangeliums," BibKir 21 (1966), 112–15.

Weiss, B., *Die Quellen des Lukasevangeliums* (Stuttgart: Cotta, 1907), esp. 195–200.

Wilson, R. M., "Some Recent Studies in the Lucan Infancy Narrative," StEv, I (TU 73; Berlin: Akademie, 1959), 235–53.

Winter, P., "The Cultural Background for the Narrative in Luke I and II," JQR 45 (1954), 159–67, 230–42, 287.

———— "Some Observations on the Language in the Birth and Infancy Stories of the Third Gospel," NTS 1 (1954 55), 111 21.

———— "The Proto-Source of Luke I," NovTest 1 (1956), 184–99.

———— "On Luke and Lucan Sources," ZNW 47 (1956), 217–42. Response to Turner, "Relation."

———— " 'Nazareth' and 'Jerusalem' in Luke chs. I and II," NTS 3 (1956–57), 136–42.

———— "On the Margin of Luke I, II," *Studia Theologica* 12 (1958), 103–7.

———— "Lukanische Miszellen," ZNW 49 (1958), 65–77. Treats 1:17,48–52, 68,72,73; 2:11,38.

———— "The Main Literary Problem of the Lucan Infancy Story," ATR 40 (1958), 257–64.

Zedda, S., "Un aspetto della cristologia di Luca: il titolo *Kyrios* in *Lc* 1–2 e nel resto del III Vangelo," *Rassegna di Teologia* 13 (1972), 305–15.

Zimmermann, H., "Evangelium des Lukas, Kap. 1 und 2," *Theologische Studien und Kritiken* 76 (1903), 247–90.

II. THE ANNUNCIATION OF THE BIRTH OF JOHN THE BAPTIST (§ 10)

Translation of Luke 1:5–25

1 ⁵In the days of Herod, king of Judea, there was a certain priest named Zechariah who belonged to the division of Abijah. He had a wife descended from Aaron, and her name was Elizabeth. ⁶In God's sight they were both upright, blamelessly observing all the commandments and ordinances of the Lord. ⁷Yet they had no children, inasmuch as Elizabeth was barren, and both were on in years.

⁸Now, while Zechariah was serving as priest, during the time that his division was on Temple duty in God's presence, ⁹there were lots cast according to the custom of the priesthood; and he won the privilege of entering the sanctuary of the Lord to burn the incense. ¹⁰At this hour of incense the whole multitude of the people was there, praying outside. ¹¹There appeared to Zechariah an angel of the Lord, standing at the right side of the altar of incense. ¹²On seeing him, Zechariah was startled, and fear fell upon him. ¹³However, the angel said to him: "Do not be afraid, Zechariah, for your prayer is heard.

¹³ᵈ And your wife Elizabeth will bear you a son,
¹³ᵉ and you will call his name John.
¹⁴ᵃ And you will have joy and gladness,
¹⁴ᵇ and many will rejoice at his birth.

¹⁵ᵃ For he will be great before the Lord,
¹⁵ᵇ and he will drink no wine or strong drink.
¹⁵ᶜ And he will be filled with the Holy Spirit even from his mother's womb,
¹⁶ and he will turn many of the sons of Israel to the Lord their God.

¹⁷ᵃ And he will go before Him
¹⁷ᵇ in the spirit and power of Elijah
¹⁷ᶜ to turn the hearts of the fathers to the children
¹⁷ᵈ and the disobedient unto the wisdom of the just,
¹⁷ᵉ to make ready for the Lord a prepared people."

¹⁸ But Zechariah said to the angel, "How am I to know this? I am an old man, and my wife is on in years." ¹⁹ The angel responded, "I am Gabriel; I stand in the presence of God. I have been sent to speak to you and announce to you this good news. ²⁰ And behold, you will be reduced to silence and unable to speak until the day that these things will happen, because you did not believe my words which, nevertheless, will be fulfilled in due time."

²¹ Meanwhile, the people were waiting for Zechariah, astonished at his delay in the Temple sanctuary. ²² And when he did come out, he was not able to speak to them; so they realized that he had seen a vision in the Temple sanctuary. For his part, Zechariah communicated with them by signs, remaining mute. ²³ When his time of priestly service was completed, he went back to his home.

²⁴ Afterwards Elizabeth his wife conceived, and for five months she kept herself in seclusion. ²⁵ "The Lord has dealt with me in this way," she reflected, "in the days when He looked to take away my disgrace among men."

NOTES

1:5. *In the days of Herod, king of Judea.* In general, this is a semitized Greek expression, similar to Matt 2:1, "In the days of Herod the king," except that Luke uses the article after "king" and before "Judea"—a rather classical touch. Most scholars assume that Luke means Herod the Great (but see Appendix VII, footnote 2). For the dates of Herod's reign and the implications for Jesus' age see the NOTE on Matt 2:1. Technically, Herod was king over all Palestine, not only over Judea, a smaller area eventually placed under the rule of his son Archelaus (Matt 2:22). The use of "Judea," then may be anachronistic, or perhaps simply the use of the part for the whole, as in Luke 7:17 and Acts 10:37, where "Judea" must include Galilee. (A modern equivalent would be the tendency to use "Holland," a province, as a name for the Netherlands.) The usage is explicable here since the action to follow takes place in Judea.

a certain priest. The indefinite Greek expression (good LXX style) eliminates the possibility that Luke thought of him as the high priest, despite the *Protevangelium of James* (see NOTE below).

named Zechariah. Literally, "by name" (*onomati,* used over twenty-five times in Luke/Acts). "Zechariah" appears as a priestly or Levite name some seven times in I–II Chronicles. The most famous "Zechariah," the son of Berechiah, was a sixth-century prophet whose name identified the next-to-the-last book in the collection of Minor Prophets. Since Matt 23:35 confuses him with Zechariah (the son of Jehoiada the priest) who was stoned to death in the Temple court at the end of the ninth century (II Chr 24:20–21), some have thought that the Lucan "a certain priest named Zechariah" is an imaginative creation based on such a confusion (see COMMENT). However, the parallel passage in Luke 11:51 avoids Matthew's confusion between the prophet and the priest. That this confusion ultimately did enter the picture we see in the *Protevangelium of James* (23–24) where Herod murders the *high priest* Zechariah at the altar for refusing to disclose JBap's hiding place. Origen compounds the confusion with his report that when, after giving birth to Jesus, Mary came to worship in the Temple, Zechariah the priest defended her for daring to stand with the virgins, as a result of which defense he was killed between the Temple and the altar (*Commentatorium Series* 25, *In Matt.* 23:35; GCS 38:43, lines 5ff.). This story played an important part in patristic tradition about the continued status of Mary as a virgin.

who belonged to the division. The noun *ephēmeria* can refer to the term of priestly service (Neh 13:30), or, as here, to the course or division of priests who were on duty (I Chr 23:6). According to I Chr 24:1–19 there were twenty-four divisions of priests; however, since only four of the original twenty-four returned from the Babylonian Exile (Ezra 2:36–39; 10:18–22), it is inferred that the four were redivided into twenty-four divisions and given the old names (cf. Neh 12:1–7). Nevertheless, Josephus (*Contra Apion* II 8; ※108) speaks for four families of priests, each containing over 5,000 men. Jeremias, *Jerusalem,* 198–206, estimates that there were some 18,000 priests and Levites in Palestine in Jesus' time.

a wife descended from Aaron. Literally, "of the daughters of Aaron." A priest did not have to marry a woman of a priestly (Levitical, Aaronic) family; but rabbinic sources reproached women descended from a priestly family who did not marry a priest (St-B, II, 68–70).

and her name was Elizabeth. This construction (found in the LXX of Gen 17:5,15) is unusual for Luke, being found only in the parallel annunciation of Jesus' birth (1:27: "and the virgin's name was Mary"). The only Elizabeth mentioned in the OT was Elisheba, the wife of the high priest Aaron (Exod 6:23); see NOTE on Matt 1:4.

6. *In God's sight.* Luke indicates that, while their lack of a child might be deemed by many a sign of sin or guilt (1:25: "my disgrace among men"), such was not the judgment of God.

upright, blamelessly observing all the commandments and ordinances. Literally, "righteous, walking in all . . ." These are Semitized Greek expressions, echoing the LXX (I Kgs 8:61). Matthew (1:19) describes Joseph, the legal father of Jesus, as "upright," because he feels obliged to obey the Law.

of the Lord. In the Gospel proper Luke uses "Lord" both for God (the Father) and for Jesus; but in the OT atmosphere of the infancy narrative, of twenty-six instances only two refer to Jesus (1:43; 2:11).

7. *Yet.* An adversative "and"; despite their piety, God had not blessed them with children.

inasmuch as. Kathoti is exclusively a Lucan word in the NT, meaning "because" and "according as."

both were on in years. Literally, "advanced in days," a Hebrew expression. Technically, this clause does not explain why "they had no children," but why they were not likely to have children. Luke is simply stressing the human impossibility.

8. *while Zechariah was serving as priest.* Literally, "in his priesting"; the same type of grammatical construction is found in 3:21.

the time that his division was on Temple duty. Each of the twenty-four divisions served one week every half-year.

9. *there were lots cast . . . and he won.* Literally, "it happened he won by lots." In the infancy narrative there occurs with frequency a Lucan pattern of an initial *egeneto* ("it happened") followed by a finite verb (twenty-two times in the Gospel) or by *kai* ("and") plus a verb (twelve times). E. Schweizer, "Eine hebraisierende Sonderquelle des Lukas," TZ 6 (1950), 163, supplies these statistics and uses the presence of this feature in certain sections of the Lucan writings as an indication of a semitized source (see also BDF 472[3]). The same verb means "to cast lots" and "to win by lot," and I have woven both meanings into my translation. During the division's term of office, lots decided who did the various tasks. There were four lots in the morning, the third of which determined who offered incense. (The others were for the burnt animal offering, the meal offering, and the maintenance of the candlestick in the Holy Place.) The only afternoon lot was for incense. Thus was fulfilled the command of Exod 30:7–8 that fragrant incense be burned "by Aaron" morning and evening.

the privilege . . . to burn the incense. To facilitate reading, I have supplied "the privilege." Offering incense was a high privilege that generally came only once in a lifetime, since the priest who won it was ineligible in future selections until all the other priests of his division had had it. See A. Edersheim, *The Temple, Its Ministry and Services as They Were at the Time of Jesus Christ* (London: Clarke, 1959 reprint; orig. 1908), 157–73; also Schürer, *History,* II, 1, 275, 292–99.

entering the sanctuary of the Lord. Here and in 1:21–22 Luke uses *naos,* the term for the Temple sanctuary, as distinct from *hieron,* the Temple in general or the Temple courts (2:27,37,46). The priest would enter the Holy Place, not the inner Holy of Holies (entered only by the high priest on the Day of Atonement, as described in Hebr 9:1–7). He would take the incense from a bowl, put it on the burning coals, and scatter it. The ceremony is described in Mishnah *Tamid* 3:6,9; 6:3.

10. *the whole multitude of the people was there.* "Multitude" is so stereotyped a Lucan expression (twenty-five times) that one may wonder whether it constitutes any estimate of number. Nevertheless, from the large number of people it has been argued that we are dealing with the evening incense offering, *ca.* 3 P.M. That hour (the ninth hour) is called by Acts 3:1 the "hour of prayer." The second OT appearance of Gabriel (Dan 9:21) takes place at the time of the evening sacrifice.

praying outside. Presumably the smoke of the incense was the signal for prayer. Except for the offering of the first fruits (Deut 26:13–15), the prayer of the people is not mentioned in the OT in the context of the times of sacrifice; yet prayers were certainly offered (I Kgs 8:33–49; II Chr 6:12ff.; Ps 141:2). The people would have been in the courts of the men and the women, separated from the Temple sanctuary by the court of the priests. Of course, we cannot be sure that Luke knew the exact geography of the Temple. "Outside" is omitted by the OS^sin, perhaps because the scribe recognized that it was unnecessary—the people could not have been inside.

11. *There appeared.* Literally, "was seen"; in terms of comparative Synoptic usage, *ōphthē* is Lucan. It is used for the appearance of the "tongues as of fire" (Acts 2:3), the appearance of God to Abraham (7:2), of Jesus to Paul (9:17), and for other Pauline visions (16:9); and so one can draw from it nothing specific about the manner or reality of the appearance. The related noun *optasia,* "vision," occurs in vs. 22. In an earlier period of Hebrew thought angels did not need to "appear" in the Temple, since cherubim and flying seraphim accompanied God's presence in the Holy of Holies.

an angel of the Lord. This figure is quite common in annunciation narratives (Table VIII); and as I pointed out in the NOTE on Matt 1:20, it is not usually a personal, spiritual being intermediate between God and man, but a way of describing God's visible presence among men. However, Luke 1:19 will identify the angel of the Lord as Gabriel; and so Luke is writing in the context of post-exilic angelology with the concept of personal, intermediate beings. This new concept in Judaism had been accepted by the Pharisees but rejected by the Sadducees.

the right side of the altar of incense. This altar is described in Exod 30:1–10; 37:25–29. The Temple faced east; and the right side, the place of honor, was toward the south, between the altar itself and the golden candlesticks.

12. *startled, and fear fell upon him.* Throughout the Bible this is the standard reaction in the presence of the divine, whether encountered directly, or through an angel, or through some exercise of extraordinary power (Exod 15:16; Judith 15:2; Matt 28:4; Luke 2:9; Acts 19:17).

13. *Do not be afraid.* Since the fear of the visionary is one of the five standard steps in the biblical annunciation of birth (Table VIII), the revealer must urge the visionary not to be afraid (Matt 1:20; Luke 1:30; 2:10).

your prayer is heard. Not directly the general prayer for Israel offered by the priest during the incense ceremony, but the unspoken prayer for a child implied in vss. 6–7. Indirectly, the prayer for Israel is also heard, since the child "will turn many of the sons of Israel to the Lord their God" (vs. 16).

And your wife Elizabeth. The oracular message is delivered in a semipoetic style, but it is extremely difficult to reach surety in detecting lines and strophes. Grundmann, for instance, finds here seven bicola; Sahlin finds two strophes of four cola each. In my division into three strophes, the first strophe of four lines deals with the participation and reaction of others, while the second strophe tells us what the child will do. As I shall mention in the COMMENT, the third strophe consisting of vs. 17 repeats some of the themes in the second strophe.

you will call his name John. For this Semitism, which appears in the parallel annunciation in 1:31, see the NOTE on Matt 1:21. The name Yehoḥanan or Yoḥanan ("Yahweh has given grace," associated with the root *ḥnn*) was not uncommon at this period; it occurs in the Maccabean priestly family (for the grandfather of Judas Maccabeus in I Macc 2:2; and for John Hyrcanus).

15. *before the Lord.* The idea is borrowed from Mal 3:1, "I send my messenger to prepare the way *before me*" (LXX: "before my face"), even though Luke uses a different preposition (*enōpion*) from the *pro* of the LXX. Luke uses *pro* in 7:27 when he cites Malachi directly in relation to JBap, but here in free composition he resorts to his own style. *Enōpion* occurs thirty-seven times in Luke/Acts, once in John, and never in Matthew or Mark. See also footnote 36 below.

wine or strong drink. A set OT expression (Lev 10:9; Judg 13:4; Prov 20:1; Micah 2:11). The "strong drink" covers intoxicants not made from grapes, e.g., cider, beer.

filled with the Holy Spirit. The expression "filled with" occurs some twenty-two times in Luke/Acts, as contrasted with once each in Mark and Matthew. Here the Greek for "Holy Spirit" is anarthrous. (The same usage was found in Matt 1:18; see NOTE there for why it should not be rendered as "a holy spirit," as if there had been no peculiarly Christian reflection on the Holy Spirit by the time Matthew and Luke were written, and yet why we cannot simply assume a Trinitarian concept.) In the infancy narrative Luke prefers the anarthrous form five times (1:15,35,41,67; 2:25) to one (2:26); in Acts the usage is very mixed: eighteen times *pneuma hagion*, sixteen times *to pneuma to hagion;* and seven times *to hagion pneuma*. No theological difference can be deduced from this variety, as a comparison of Luke 2:25 and 2:26 shows.

even from his mother's womb. This Semitism can refer to the time when the child is still in the womb (Judg 13:3–5) or to the time of emergence from the womb ("from birth"—see the parallelism in Ps 22:11[10]). From 1:41 we know that the former is meant here.

17. *go before Him in the spirit and power of Elijah.* Elijah was known for his power of miracles and his gift of the prophetic spirit, both of which were passed onto Elisha (see II Kgs 9:15). Just as "before the Lord" in Luke 1:15 (see NOTE) echoes Mal 3:1, so this phrase which is a specification of 1:15 echoes the specification of Mal 3:1 found in Mal 3:23 (RSV 4:5): "I send you Elijah the prophet before [*pro*] the great and terrible day of the Lord." The parallelism with 1:15 makes it clear that the "Him" is the Lord God, not Jesus. Some have used this as an argument for the thesis that Luke was quoting from

a non-Christian JBap source which preserved the original theology of JBap himself wherein his task was to precede the Lord God—a view of his role contrary to Christian theology which would have JBap precede Jesus. (See footnote 42 below.) However, even though Luke thought that JBap preceded "the Lord" in the sense that he preceded Jesus who was the Lord's instrument and presence, he could scarcely have had Gabriel announce to Zechariah that JBap would precede Jesus, since he had not yet informed the reader of the Messiah's coming birth. He was content to use vague OT language from Malachi (who mentions "the Lord" in both 3:1 and 3:23) which he could interpret later when it is revealed that Jesus is "Lord" (Luke 1:43; 2:11). See NOTE on vs. 6 above.

to turn the hearts of the fathers to the children. As we shall see, Luke borrows this phrase from Mal 3:24 (RSV 4:6) and Sirach 48:10 which describe Elijah as one who will "turn the heart of the fathers toward the children." The Hebrew of these two passages has a singular noun for "heart" and a plural noun for "children"; the LXX has two singular nouns, "heart" and "son"; and Luke has two plural nouns. Moreover, he uses a different preposition of direction, *epi,* "to, upon," rather than the LXX *pros,* "toward." (See the *enōpion/pro* problem in the NOTE on 1:15, "before the Lord.")

the disobedient unto the wisdom of the just. The preposition *en* normally means "in." However, parallelism with *epi* in the preceding line suggests that here *en* has the sense of *eis,* "into" (BDF 206) and justifies the translation "unto." Note that the disobedient are turned "unto wisdom." One would expect a change from disobedience to lawful behavior; but a change from disobedience to wisdom may reflect the atmosphere of the post-exilic sapiential literature where wisdom is identified with the Law (Baruch 4:1).

to make ready . . . a prepared people. Grammatically, it is probable that "to make ready" in 17e is to be read in parallelism with "to turn" in 17c, and both verbs continue the "he will go before Him" of 17a. While "to make ready a people" is LXX style (II Sam 7:24; Sir 49:12), the joining of "make ready" and "a *prepared* people" is odd. The latter reflects Mal 3:1 ("to prepare the way before me") as applied to JBap in Luke 7:27—the only other passage in Luke/Acts in which the verb *kataskeuazein,* "prepare," occurs.

19. *Gabriel.* For the departure from the "angel of the Lord" concept, see NOTE above on 1:11. The name, a typical formation in the angelic onomasticon (similar to "Michael, Raphael, Phanuel"), means "Man of God" or "God has shown Himself strong"; and in his only previous biblical appearances (Dan 8:15–16; 9:21) he is described as a man. *Enoch* 40:2 describes him as one of the four presences who look down from heaven (9:1), a holy angel (20:7), set over all powers (40:9). He is the angel set over Paradise, over the serpent and the cherubim (20:7), with the power to destroy the wicked (9:9–10; 54:6).

I stand in the presence of God. Besides the just-mentioned thesis of four angels in the divine presence, there was also a thesis of seven such angels (*Enoch* 20; *Testament of Levi* 8; Ezek 9:2; Tobit 12:15; Rev 8:2,6). For the idea of angels "standing" before God, see Job 1:6; Dan 7:16.

I have been sent. The word for "angel" in Hebrew (*mal'āk*) has the sense of messenger.

to announce to you this good news. Euangelisthai, a verb related to *euangelion,* "gospel." The birth of JBap is part of the Gospel.

20. *And behold. Idou,* "behold," occurs ten times in the Lucan infancy narrative, even as it occurred six times in the shorter Matthean infancy narrative, where it featured in the pattern of angelic dream appearances (Table VI). Of the ten Lucan occurrences, four of them are in the formula *kai idou* (here; 1:31,36; 2:25), a formula that occurs twenty-seven times in Luke and only nine times in Acts. As with the *egeneto* pattern (first NOTE on vs. 9 above), E. Schweizer would use these statistics as an indication of a semitized source. Of the six *idou* occurrences in the Matthean infancy narrative, *kai idou* appears in 2:9.

you will be reduced to silence. Seemingly he became deaf as well as mute, for the people have to communicate with him in signs in 1:62.

my words which. Luke uses the relative *hostis* (which often denotes a characteristic quality) as if it were a simple relative (BDF 293[8]).

fulfilled. The same verb that Matthew uses for his fulfillment formulas (Table V) in relation to OT prophecies.

in due time. Kairos, a divinely appointed time.

21. *astonished at his delay.* This may be simply a touch of pathos to lend interest to the narrative. Nevertheless, some would find here the echo of a Jewish legend: an old man appeared and went into the Temple with Simon the Just each year in association with the offering on the Day of Atonement; and one year, when the man did not come out, Simon knew he was about to die. Simon the Just was high priest about 300 B.C., but the legend of the old man (an angelic appearance?) is attested only long after NT times (TalBab *Yoma* 39b). The idea that the priest should not tarry in the sanctuary is found in Mishnah *Yoma* 5:1.

in the Temple sanctuary. See NOTE on 1:9 above.

22. *he was not able to speak to them.* Zechariah and the assisting priest should have pronounced the Aaronic blessing (Num 6:24–26) from the steps of the sanctuary building, as described in Mishnah *Tamid* 7:2. Luke seems to think that Zechariah was alone in the sanctuary, unless the isolation of Zechariah is part of his storytelling technique.

they realized that he had seen a vision in the Temple sanctuary. The seeming illogic in this guess may be solved if there was a tradition of appearances in the sanctuary. Josephus, *Ant.* XIII x 3;⋇⋇282–83, tells us of a divine revelation that came to the high priest John Hyrcanus while offering incense in the Temple sanctuary (also TalJer *Yoma* 5:42c).

23. *his time of priestly service.* The period of Temple duty mentioned in vs. 8. The conclusion of the annunciation scene resumes motifs introduced in the setting (vss. 8–10).

he went back. Literally, "it happened he went back," an *egeneto* construction as in vs. 9. A theme of departure terminates six of the seven Lucan infancy narrative scenes: *aperchesthai* here and in the parallel annunciation (1:38); *hypostrephein,* "return," in 1:56; 2:20,39; *erchesthai,* "go," in 2:51.

to his home. A city of Judea in the hill country (1:39).

24. *Afterwards.* Literally, "After these days."

for five months she kept herself in seclusion. That is, for the first half of her pregnancy. Although there are passages in biblical literature. (II Macc 7:27; *II Esdras [IV Ezra]* 4:40) which refer to a nine months pregnancy, a more common reckoning seems to have been one of ten (lunar) months (Wis 7:2–3), i.e., forty weeks, 280 days. Apparently Luke follows the latter, since Elizabeth is in her sixth month at the time of the annunciation to Mary (1:36), and then Mary stays with her three months (1:56) and can still leave before the baby is born. As for the seclusion, in the *Protevangelium of James* 12:3, during the three months that Mary visits Elizabeth, it is Mary who hides herself from the children of Israel. They know her as a dedicated virgin, and yet she is pregnant.

25. *The Lord.* This verse is introduced by *hoti* which most interpret as a *hoti recitativum*, introducing a direct quotation. P. Winter, ZNW 46 (1955), 261–63, argues for a causal tone in the *hoti*, "since," pointing to the Vulgate *quia*.

He looked to take away my distress. Some translations supply an object for "looked," e.g., "on me," or else anticipate the object of the second verb: "He looked on my disgrace to take it away." Still other translations modify the meaning of the verb, e.g., "He condescended to take away."

COMMENT

Luke begins his infancy narrative with a self-contained story of a divinely prepared conception of JBap. It lends itself to a division into three parts:

> 1:5–7:   *Introduction* of the dramatis personae.
> 1:8–23: *Annunciation* of the conception, delivered by an angel of the Lord (Gabriel) to Zechariah in the Temple sanctuary:
>   8–10: Setting;
>   11–20: Core;
>   21–23: Conclusion.
> 1:24–25: *Epilogue* concerning Elizabeth's pregnancy and her praise of God.

Both in structure and in features of style there are remarkable similarities between this scene and the scene that follows, i.e., the story of the divinely prepared conception of the birth of Jesus, with an annunciation by Gabriel to Mary. The similarities are so close (Table X) that they cannot be accidental. A parallel between the two stories has been deliberately established. Relatively few scholars have proposed that the annunciation of the birth of Jesus was original, and that on the basis of it Luke created the story of an annunciation of the birth of JBap.[1] More have proposed that the story of the annunciation of JBap's birth was original, and that on the basis of it Luke created the story of an annunciation of Jesus' birth.[2] Finally, some have proposed a simultaneous creation of both narratives, either in a pre-Lucan stage or by Luke. The first proposal, since it involves the originality of the annunciation to Mary, may be left for discussion until our treatment of the next section (§ 11). Here, as we move systematically through 1:5–25, we may test the last two proposals. Did Luke invent all the information about JBap; or did he receive it, in whole or in part, from tradition? If the latter, was the tradition a complete JBap source[3] or only items of information? If the latter, what was Luke's theological motif in developing the narrative of 1:5–25 from such items of information?

A. *The Introduction (1:5–7)*

Here we are given four items of information: the time setting for the infancy story was the reign of Herod the Great; the names of JBap's parents were Zechariah and Elizabeth; they and he were of priestly descent; they were aged and Elizabeth was barren. Is this information invented by Luke, or did he receive at least some of it from tradition (historical or non-historical)? In answering this question, I shall take the first three items together and only later turn to the fourth.

The fact that, independently of Luke, Matthew relates the birth of Jesus to the last days of Herod the Great makes it quite plausible that Luke did not invent the first item.[4] The second and third items are more difficult since there is no other indication in the NT of JBap's priestly stock or of the names of his parents.[5] Inevitably, ingenious theories have been proposed as to how Luke might have invented such information.[6] Since Mal 3:1 is a text frequently associated with JBap (Luke 7:27), and since Malachi addressed much of his prophetic message to priests (1:6; 2:1), it has been proposed that a chain of association led to the creation of a priestly descent for JBap. In the OT Zechariah is the name of the pro-

[1] Thus, Benoit, "L'enfance," 191–94. As the reader will see, I agree with Benoit as to the priority of an annunciation of Jesus' birth; but I disagree with his thesis that a high amount of family tradition has gone into the Lucan story of that annunciation.
[2] This theory is held by most of the scholars who posit Lucan dependence upon a JBap source (footnote 34, § 9).
[3] A variation upon this thesis is the suggestion that vss. 8–23 came from the JBap source, and that, using that material, Luke himself composed the introduction in vss. 5–7. (See Schmidt, *Rahmen*, 310.) One must then posit that earlier (unpreserved) material in the source introduced Zechariah and Elizabeth.
[4] See the NOTE on "two years of age" in Matt 2:16; also Appendix VII.
[5] The designation of JBap as "the son of Zechariah" in Luke 3:2 is a harmonization with the infancy narrative and scarcely an independent tradition.
[6] See Goulder and Sanderson, "Genesis," 15–16.

phetic book that immediately preceded Malachi, and so that name is thought to have been seized upon for JBap's priest father.[7] The mother of JBap, who is the wife of the priest Zechariah, is thought to have been given the name Elizabeth because it was the name of the wife of Aaron, even as Mary, the mother of Jesus, bore the name of Miriam, the sister of Aaron. One can never disprove such a theory, but it demands remarkable ingenuity and fails to explain many factors. The Malachi text is applied to JBap in Matthew and Mark, as well as in Luke; yet the other two evangelists never derive from it a hint of JBap's priestly lineage. The proposed derivation of the name Zechariah from the order of the books in the prophetic canon does not explain such a recherché detail as Zechariah's belonging "to the division of Abijah." One has to account for the accurate knowledge shown in 1:8–10 about priestly terms of service, the incense offering, and the cult.[8] Even the detail that Zechariah did not live in Jerusalem (1:23), but in the hill country of Judea, betrays a knowledge of the priesthood in the first century (NOTE on 1:39).

In my opinion, then, the names of the parents and the priestly lineage are better explained, along with the Herodian dating, as items of tradition (historical or non-historical) that came to Luke, rather than as the product of Lucan invention. In dealing with the annunciation itself we shall have to ask what kind of tradition: a full-scale JBap source narrating his origins, or stray items about JBap known in Christian circles? Luke mentions a group of JBap disciples in Acts 19:1–7. He also shows a knowledge of the Jerusalem Christian community which frequented the Temple (Acts 2:46; 3:1; 5:21,42; 21:23–26) and to which there were converted a "great many of the priests" (6:7). Traditions about JBap's priestly lineage and details about the cult might have been known in such circles.

This may be the appropriate place to discuss a theory proposed by Wink, building upon Laurentin. He denies the existence of a full-scale pre-Lucan JBap narrative and posits only JBap tradition, probably brought over to the church by former followers. "Or, to state it perhaps more accurately, the church possessed these traditions from the very beginning by virtue of the fact that it was itself an outgrowth of the Baptist movement." On a pre-Lucan level these traditions and the traditions of Jesus' birth were worked into an artful symmetry, treating *JBap and Jesus as the two Messiahs, one from Aaron and one from David.*[9] It is the latter point

---

[7] This identification would have been helped by the confusion between Zechariah the prophet and Zechariah the priest (NOTE on 1:5).

[8] Some of Luke's information would seem to go beyond a deduction from the OT. Moreover, one must realize that Luke's knowledge of Jewish cultic practice is not always accurate, e.g., his confused picture of presentation and purification in 2:22–24.

[9] Wink, *John,* 72–79. Wink and Laurentin (*Structure,* 110–16) recognize that Luke himself did not share the view that JBap was the Messiah from Aaron; but Laurentin suggests that Luke mentions Mary's relationship to Elizabeth (1:36) to insinuate that Jesus himself fills the role of the priestly Messiah.

that must be examined. In the post-exilic period with the absence of a monarchy, the ceremony of anointing was shifted over to the high priest who thus became a messiah, an anointed one, and who *de facto* was the political leader in Judah. Just as before the Exile Isaiah had yearned for an ideal king, so now the pious yearned for an ideal high priest, as we see in the panegyric of Simon, son of Onias, "the pride of his people," in Sirach 50. Among the "pious ones" (presumably Essenes) who broke away from the Maccabean revolt and founded the Qumran settlement (*ca.* 150 B.C.) the idealization of the high priest descended from Zadok was heightened and "eschatologized," so that an ideal high priest of the last times was expected.[10] He would exist alongside the Davidic Messiah, so that the full Qumran expectation involved "the coming of a prophet and the Messiahs of Aaron and Israel."[11] In arguing that the pre-Lucan tradition described JBap as the Messiah of Aaron, Wink points out that JBap resembles Elijah, "the great prophet priest of old." I question this hypothesis on almost every point. It is true that in the infancy narrative JBap is likened to Elijah (1:17), but we have no datable evidence that *in this period* Elijah was already thought of as a priest.[12] It is very dubious that Qumran would ever have identified him as the eschatological Messiah of Aaron, since there is no evidence of his having had a Zadokite lineage and that was a *sine qua non* at Qumran for legitimate high priesthood. Rather, the Qumran Essenes probably colored Elijah with some of the features of the prophet-like-Moses of Deut 18:18 and fitted him into their future expectations as the "prophet" who was to come before the two Messiahs. And it is precisely as a prophet who is to come before the one Messiah (Jesus) that JBap is presented in the Lucan infancy narrative.

Rejection of a priestly Messiah role for JBap (even on a putative pre-Lucan level) highlights an important point in interpreting 1:5–25. Although Luke gives JBap levitical parents, Luke makes nothing whatsoever of JBap himself as a priest. Thus his interest in the priesthood is on the level of *preparation* for JBap and ultimately for Jesus. This is part of his theology that the institutions of Judaism, when they were "observing all the commandments and ordinances of the Lord" (1:6), were receptive to Jesus and not opposed to him. Luke underlines the same motif when he has Mary and Joseph bring Jesus to the Temple to fulfill the rituals of purification and presentation (2:22–40).[13] By the time that Luke/Acts

---

[10] For a brief history of Qumran community origins as a protest against the Maccabean (non-Zadokite) usurpation of the high priesthood, see JBC, article 68, ##84–87.

[11] For a discussion (and bibliography) of the idea of the two Messiahs and the texts that support it in the Dead Sea Scrolls, see R. E. Brown, CBQ 19 (1957), 54–66; 28 (1966), 51–57.

[12] The evidence that Wink cites on p. 74 is talmudic. The idea that Elijah was a priest was in vogue by the 2nd cent. A.D. Earlier, *Biblical Antiquities* 48:2 is uncertain.

[13] The Lucan infancy narrative (and Acts) has a context of "Temple piety," a quasi-technical term used to describe devout observance of the Law, coming to the Temple "to see the

was written, the Temple had been destroyed and the priesthood had lost much of its *raison d'être;* and Christians were beginning to look on this development as God's punishing judgment. But Luke wants to make it clear that if opposition arose between the Temple/priesthood and the following of Jesus, it was not because there was an inherent contradiction between Christianity and the cult of Israel. Rather there was continuity, as illustrated both in Jesus' origins and in the origins of the Church.[14] That continuity was broken because of hostility on the part of the high priests (Acts 4:1–3; 5:17; 23:2). Combining priestly origins and blameless observance of the Law, Zechariah and Elizabeth were for Luke the representatives of the best in the religion of Israel;[15] and as a remnant which received the "good news" (1:19), they personified the continuity in salvation history.

The fourth item of information in the introduction, namely that Zechariah and Elizabeth had no hope of children (1:7), also reflects a Lucan theological utilization of the parents of JBap (about whom he may have known little more than their names and priestly descent). Of course, historically the parents could have been aged—a suggestion that they died when JBap was young may lie behind 1:80. But the motif of barrenness is so common in OT annunciations of birth that I suspect Luke is establishing a connection with the OT rather than writing intimate family history. In particular, he has Zechariah and Elizabeth figuratively relive the careers of two OT sets of parents. The message in the annunciation (1:15) describes JBap as a Nazirite, drinking no wine or strong drink.[16] One of the most famous Nazirites of the OT was Samuel, and Luke draws a parallel between the parents of Samuel and the parents of JBap. The opening of the Samuel story is found in I Sam 1:1: "There was a certain man . . . whose name was Elkanah . . . and he had two wives; the name of one was Hannah." This is quite close to the Lucan opening in 1:5: "There was a certain priest named Zechariah . . . he had a wife . . . and

---

face of God," offering of gifts, taking part in the cult, and the recitation of the psalms. See R. Schnackenburg, "Tempelfrömmigkeit," LTK (2nd ed.), IX, cols. 1358–59.

14 Above I pointed out the many references in Acts to a Jerusalem (Hebrew) Christian community which frequented the Temple. Luke also knows of a Hellenist Christian community at Jerusalem. (I interpret "Hellenist" as a designation for Jews who spoke only Greek and were theologically opposed to the centralization of cult in Jerusalem.) Their spokesman Stephen was hostile to the Temple (Acts 7:48–51). Luke preserves a remembrance of the Hellenists because their views ultimately won out in Christianity, after the death of James the brother of the Lord in the 60s and the expulsion of the Hebrew Christian community from Jerusalem in the revolt against Rome.

15 Schürmann, *Lukasevangelium,* I, 21, is correct when he insists that, even if Luke is drawing upon items of tradition in his characterization of Zechariah and Elizabeth, his primary interest is not biographical. Schürmann speaks of his giving an air of plausibility and trustworthiness to the narrative; I would not neglect that but would insist on the theological utility of the information he transmits.

16 For information on the Nazirite, see part (b) of the NOTE on "Nazorean" in Matt 2:23. As I point out there, Samuel is called a Nazirite in an old Cave IV Qumran Hebrew ms. of I Sam 1:22.

her name was Elizabeth." The revelation to Hannah that her petition for a child would be heard comes through the priest Eli during the annual journey to the sanctuary at Shiloh to offer sacrifice (I Sam 1:3,17), even as it is revealed to the priest Zechariah in the sanctuary of the Jerusalem Temple that his prayer is heard (1:13). The motifs of the Samuel story will continue throughout Luke 1–2, as we shall see.

The other pair of OT parents whom Luke has in mind, and even more clearly, are Abraham and Sarah. While there are several examples of barren women who are made capable of childbearing through divine intervention,[17] in only one other instance in the Bible are both parents incapacitated by age as well: "Abraham and Sarah were old, on in years; Sarah had ceased to have her periods" (Gen 18:11). The parallel to Luke 1:7 is obvious: "Elizabeth was barren, and both were on in years."[18] Another parallel is that in the Abraham/Sarah story the annunciation of birth is made to the father rather than to the mother. More parallels will be cited below in discussing the conclusion of the annunciation and the epilogue.

This parallelism with two sets of OT parents, Elkanah/Hannah and Abraham/Sarah, places the annunciation of JBap's birth in continuity with the births of famous figures in the salvific history of Israel. I contend that JBap himself belongs to the period of Jesus in Luke's divisions of salvific history (§ 9, B1, above); that is why this birth is accompanied with the messianic joy that surrounds the coming of Jesus. But his parents and the circumstances of his origins belong to the period of Israel. In particular, the strong Abraham/Sarah motif connects the infancy narrative with the patriarchal narratives of Israel's beginnings in the Book of Genesis. In footnote 1, § 8, at the close of my discussion of Matthew, I pointed out that it was a common trait for Matthew, Luke, and John to turn to Genesis in their efforts to push back their understanding of Jesus beyond the beginnings of the ministry (the baptism) to his origins. It is their way of teaching us that his origins were in Israel and that his coming involves a new creation or a renewal of the covenant made with the patriarchs.[19]

Thus, the few items of tradition in the introduction (1:5–7) have been dramatized and woven skillfully into theology. That the theology is truly Lucan will be the burden of our discussion as we turn to the annunciation itself.

---

[17] Rebekah in Gen 25:21; Rachel in 29:31; the mother of Samson in Judg 13:2; Hannah in I Sam 1:2.

[18] It is interesting to note how Luke reuses the two details of barrenness and age. In the objection that Zechariah poses to the angel (1:18), only age is mentioned, while Gabriel speaks to Mary of both Elizabeth's old age and barrenness (1:36).

[19] Other examples of this tendency would be the Lucan genealogy tracing Jesus back through Adam to God; the Matthean genealogy tracing Jesus back to Abraham; the Jesus/Adam parallelism in Rom 5; and the references to Abraham in Gal 3.

B. *The Annunciation (1:8–23)*

This part of the scene is divisible into three subsections: the setting (8–10), the core (11–20), and the conclusion (21–23). I shall not spend time on the setting since the cultic details it relates (with remarkable accuracy) have been explained in the NOTES. This setting reveals to the reader why Luke mentioned in vs. 5 that Zechariah was a priest of the division of Abijah: the annunciation to Zechariah was going to come during the incense offering, at the time when the division of Abijah was on duty in the sanctuary. The "good news" of the inauguration of God's definitive plan of salvation was to be heralded first in the Holy Place associated with His presence in Israel.

1. Echoes of Daniel in the Appearance of Gabriel

We have seen that Zechariah and Elizabeth recall the figures of Abraham and Sarah from Genesis, the book which stands at the beginning of the sacred writings of Israel. The angel Gabriel who appears to Zechariah at the hour of incense had his only previous biblical activity in Dan 8:16ff. and 9:21ff., and Daniel belongs to the last books of Israel's collection.[20] If Luke was conscious of this, he may have intended the characters involved in the annunciation, Zechariah and Gabriel, to span the sacred history of Israel from beginning to end, from the *Law* to the *Writings*.[21] In any case, there can be no doubt that in his description of Gabriel's appearance Luke intends to evoke the atmosphere of Daniel. We may note the following points shared by Luke 1:8–23 and by Daniel:[22]

▪In 1:22 the appearance is called a vision; *optasia* is found six times in the Theodotion of Dan 9–10.[23]

---

[20] In the period when Luke was writing there was no official canon of sacred writings, although his contemporaries mention twenty-four books (*II Esdras* or *IV Ezra* 14:45) or twenty-two books (Josephus *Contra Apion* I 8; ##39–41). Daniel was listed among the *Writings*, the last section of the Hebrew canon to be shaped, after the *Law* and the *Prophets*.

[21] However, Luke 24:44 speaks of "the Law of Moses, the Prophets, and the Psalms," so we have no way of knowing where Luke would place Daniel.

[22] Neirynck, *Noël*, gives much attention to the Danielic background of the Lucan infancy narrative. The points cited in my text come from Daniel's description of Gabriel; but we may add Dan 7:16 where Daniel approaches "one of those who stood there," i.e., in God's presence—a passage not unlike Luke 1:19 where Gabriel can say: "I stand in the presence of God."

[23] The Greek text of Daniel has come down to us in two forms, the LXX and a version commonly attributed to Theodotion. The latter is closer to the Hebrew and Aramaic of Daniel.

■In 1:10–11, as in Dan 9:20–21, Gabriel appears at the time of liturgical prayer.

■In 1:13 we find that Zechariah had uttered a personal prayer of distress (see Note), even as Daniel had been praying in distress (9:20).

■In 1:12, as in Dan 8:17 and 10:7, fear greets Gabriel's appearance.

■In 1:19 Gabriel says, "I have been sent to speak to you"; in Dan 10:11 the angel[24] refers to "the words which I am speaking to you."

■In 1:13, as in Dan 10:12, Gabriel tells the visionary not to fear.

■In 1:20,22, as in Dan 10:15, the visionary is struck mute.

By these echoes Luke is giving a new application to a common Christian reflection in which such Gospel motifs as the Son of Man and the Kingdom of God were related to Dan 7:13–14.[25] In particular, the famous Danielic vision of the seventy weeks of years had figured in the Gospel reference to the "abominating desolation" in the Temple, seemingly interpreted as the Roman action against Jerusalem (Dan 9:27; Mark 13:14; Matt 24:15; Luke 21:20).[26]

The theme of the seventy weeks of years, as interpreted by Gabriel in Dan 9:24–27, serves Luke as the background for the annunciation by Gabriel to Zechariah. In 9:21 we are told that Gabriel appeared to Daniel when he was occupied in prayer at the time of the evening sacrifice; this helps to explain the temporal setting of Luke's account at the "hour of incense," when "the multitude of the people was there, praying outside," especially if Luke means the evening incense offering (see Note). For Daniel (9:24) the end of the seventy weeks of years is the time when "everlasting justice will be introduced, vision and prophecy will be ratified, and a Holy of Holies will be anointed."[27] Luke thinks that these last times have come (see Acts 2:16–17); and so he may have thought it appropriate, since Zechariah was a priest, to have the inaugural annunciation of this take place in the sanctuary (the Holy Place), adjacent to the Holy of Holies which was to be anointed.[28] The eschatological atmosphere evoked from Daniel is echoed in the tone of the message that follows.

24 The angel (called "a man") in 10:5, while not identified, is probably the Gabriel of 9:21 (called "a man" in 8:15–16).

25 See Mark 13:26 (Luke 21:27) and Mark 14:62 (Luke 22:69.)

26 For the thesis that much of the apocalyptic discourse in Mark 13 (with parallels in Luke 21) is an interpretation of Daniel, see L. Hartman, *Prophecy Interpreted* (CBNTS 1; Lund: Gleerup, 1966).

27 It is difficult to know what Daniel means by "a Holy of Holies," for it could describe a thing, a place, or a person. The whole context of Daniel, which rails against the profanation of the Temple, and the immediate context with its mention of the sanctuary, sacrifices, and offerings (9:26–27), would favor the thesis that primarily Daniel is thinking in terms of the Temple.

28 It should be added to the preceding footnote that the context also mentions an anointed prince, a messiah, or in the Greek of Theodotion, a *christos*. Could Luke be playing on both motifs: although the annunciation pertaining to JBap takes place in the Temple, the real Holy of Holies is Jesus, the one who "will be called holy" (Luke 1:35)?

2. The Message (13–17)

In Table VIII I listed five steps in the typical biblical annunciation of birth, and I showed that all five are found in Luke 1:11–20, which constitutes the core of the annunciation scene. Having seen the coloring that comes to Luke's model annunciation pattern from the portrayal of the dramatis personae along OT lines (of Abraham in Genesis and of Gabriel in Daniel), let us now concentrate on the origins of the material that Luke fits into the pattern, especially into the message of vss. 13–17.

THE FIRST STROPHE (*vss. 13–14*). The first four lines of the message delivered by Gabriel concern participation in and reaction to the birth of JBap, primarily on the part of Elizabeth and Zechariah, but then also on the part of "many." The format in vs. 13 in almost totally that of the standard annunciation pattern (3a,c,e,f in Table VIII). Specifically, we may compare the words to Abraham in Gen 17:19, "Sarah your wife will give birth to a son for you," and the words to Zechariah in Luke 1:13, "Your wife Elizabeth will bear you a son." The name "John" is given before birth to signify that God has a special role for this child,[29] but there is no explicit etymology. Some have found an implicit etymology in the joy and gladness mentioned in vs. 14, seen as a response to a name which means "Yahweh has given grace" (see NOTE); but I doubt that Luke's Greek readers would have understood such a subtle play on a Semitic name.[30] More simply, "joy and gladness" are sparked by the divine announcement of the birth of a child who is to have a role in salvation history, and they form a response quite intelligible in the eschatological atmosphere evoked by the presence of Gabriel. If there is anything implicit in vss. 13–14, rather than a play on the name "John," it is the end of the seventy weeks of years signaled by the reappearance of the angel who announced that time span. In § 1, A2, I have insisted that the key to understanding the infancy narratives is the realization that the christology once attached to the resurrection (and later to the ministry) has been moved back to the conception and birth of Jesus. "Joy" greets the risen Jesus in Luke 24:41; and the Psalm passage, "My heart was happy; my tongue was

---

[29] See footnote 16, § 5. The biblical pre-natal namings are retrospective interpretations: the career and accomplishments which are already known are used to interpret the subject's name. This is a symbolic way of telling the reader that God foresaw and ordained the role the subject was to play.

[30] Gentile converts might have been taught the Hebrew meaning of Jesus' name, not necessarily that of John's name. Of course, those who posit a Semitic pre-Lucan source think that the original audience for that source would have understood the play on the name. However, even on the putative Semitic level the connection between "Yahweh has given grace" and "joy and gladness" is a guess.

glad," is cited in Acts 2:26 as a response to the last days ushered in by the resurrection. It is no surprise then to find the same terms appearing in the infancy narrative in order to tell the reader that the power of God which was visible in the resurrection is at work here.[81]

THE SECOND STROPHE (*vss. 15–16*). The second four lines of the message concern the future career of the child and what he will do. Those who argue for a JBap source find here an exuberant language that betrays the beliefs of a sect which has made a Messiah[32] or even more[33] out of JBap, perhaps by way of opposition to Jesus. But I detect nothing that goes beyond common Christian belief in JBap as attested in the accounts of Jesus' ministry. For instance, in 15a it is promised that JBap "will be great"; this is an echo of Luke 7:28 where Jesus says, "Among those born of women, none is greater than John." That JBap will be great "before the Lord" seems to echo the Malachi prophecy (3:1) applied to JBap in Luke 7:27, "Behold, I send my messenger before your face who will prepare your way ahead of you."[34] The statement in 15b that JBap "will drink no wine or strong drink" is an echo of Luke 7:33: "JBap has come eating no bread and drinking no wine." Of course, this ascetical motif from the ministry account has now been translated into terms that are appropriate for an annunciation of birth. Two of the most famous OT birth annunciations concerned the Nazirites Samson and Samuel.[35] To the mother of Samson it was said by the angel, "Beware, and drink no wine or strong drink . . . for you will conceive and bear a son . . . the boy will be a Nazirite to God from birth" (Judg 13:4–5). When the mother of Samuel prayed "before the Lord,"[36] she promised that, if God would give her a son, she would give him to the Lord all the days of his life; and she stressed that she had drunk neither wine nor strong drink (I Sam 1:9–15). Using this stereo-

[81] I shall maintain that what is said about JBap in the annunciation message is little more than a digest of the general knowledge about JBap gleaned from the ministry tradition in the Gospels. John is a Gospel with interesting parallels to Luke; and in John 3:29 JBap greets Jesus with "joy" and in 5:35 people are "glad" to bask for a while in the light cast by JBap.

[32] For the question of whether JBap was the Messiah, see Luke 3:15 and John 1:20. In the Latin of the Pseudo-Clementine *Recognitions* (I 54 and 60; PG 1:1238,1240) we find JBap sectarians stressing that their master, not Jesus, was the Messiah.

[33] The designation "great" for JBap has suggested to some the pretensions of Simon Magus, "the Power of God which is called Great" (Acts 8:10). The connection is far-fetched since "great" could be used without pretensions of a figure in salvation history, e.g., of Isaiah in Sirach 48:22. Thus, correctly Wink, *John*, 69.

[34] The word for "before" (*enōpion*) in Luke 1:15 is different from the words for "before" and "ahead of" in 7:27 (*pro, emprosthen*); see NOTE on 1:15.

[35] I have already called attention to the parallels between the birth annunciations of Samuel and of JBap, especially in their cultic setting. It is worth noting that there is also a cultic setting of a cereal offering in the angelic appearance associated with Samson's birth (Judg 13:19–20).

[36] The phrase *enōpion Kyriou* in the LXX of I Sam 1:9,15 may help to explain Luke's preference for *enōpion Kyriou* in 1:15a; see footnote 34 above.

typed language, Luke is portraying JBap, traditionally an ascetic, as a Nazirite from his infancy, even as Matthew portrayed Jesus as a Nazirite from his infancy (§ 7, B3 above).

The statement in 1:15c, "He will be filled with the Holy Spirit even from his mother's womb," is a key passage for those who argue for a JBap source or a non-Christian origin of this material. The contention is that in the Gospel proper the Holy Spirit is associated with Jesus, not with JBap; and attention is called to Luke 3:16 where JBap says, "I baptize you with water; but he who is mightier than I is coming . . . he will baptize you with the Holy Spirit and with fire." In Acts 19:2-3 those who have been baptized with the baptism of JBap have not even heard that there is a Holy Spirit. But is the association of the Holy Spirit with JBap in the infancy narrative really irreconcilable with this picture? A distinction must be made in thinking of the Spirit. It is the Spirit of Jesus that is associated with Christian baptism—a Spirit of life and power that was his during his lifetime and which he has transmitted to his followers after the resurrection. Obviously Christians would not associate this baptismal Spirit with JBap. But there is also the Holy Spirit of God associated with the prophets.[87] This is the Spirit that came upon Saul and turned him into a prophet (I Sam 10:10), the Spirit that spoke through David (II Sam 23:2), and above all the Spirit that filled the prophets Elijah and Elisha (II Kgs 2:9-16). In the Gospel account of the ministry, JBap is presented as a prophet, indeed greater than any other prophet (Luke 7:28; 20:6);[88] and so it would follow logically that JBap was filled with the prophetic Holy Spirit.[89] If one compares the OT passages where the *Spirit* of the Lord is said to come upon a prophet to enable him to speak God's message (Isa 61:1; Ezek 11:5; Joel 3:1 [RSV 2:28]) with the passages where the *word* of God is said to come to a prophet for the same purpose (Isa 2:1; Jer 1:2; Joel 1:1), it becomes clear that when Luke 1:15c says that JBap "will be filled with the Holy *Spirit* even from his mother's womb," he is saying exactly the same thing as he says in 3:1-2: "In the fifteenth year of the reign of Tiberius Caesar . . . the *word* of God came

[87] This distinction is well made by Tatum, "Epoch," 189-92.

[88] Luke 16:16 reports the "Q" saying, "The Law and the prophets were until John" (see Matt 11:13). I have already mentioned Conzelmann's attempt to use this verse to separate JBap from the period of Jesus (§ 9, B1), but for Luke Jesus is a prophet too (4:24; 7:16; 13:33; 24:19).

[89] It may be accidental that Luke states this explicitly only in the infancy narrative and not in the Gospel proper. Or perhaps there was less danger in the infancy context of confusing the prophetic Holy Spirit given to JBap and the Holy Spirit given to the followers of Jesus in baptism. Readers familiar with later theology may be asking whether this distinction implies that there are two Holy Spirits. No. But to the idea of the Spirit of God taken over from Judaism, Christianity made its distinctive contribution. The Spirit poured out at Pentecost after the resurrection is described as having both aspects, prophetic and baptismal (Acts 2:17,38).

to John, the son of Zechariah, in the desert." These are simply alternate ways of describing the beginning of the career of a prophet. In the former Lucan statement, when the career is traced to infancy, the dominating model is that of a prophet like Samson ("a Nazirite to God from my mother's womb," Judg 16:17; 13:7)[40] or Jeremiah ("Before I formed you in the womb, I knew you . . . I appointed you a prophet to the nations," Jer 1:14). In the latter Lucan statement, when the career is traced to the beginning of a preaching ministry, the dominating model is the standard opening of several prophetic books, e.g., "In the second year of Darius, the word of the Lord came to Zechariah, the son of Berechiah" (Zech 1:1).[41]

In vs. 16 Luke begins to specify the role that this forthcoming prophet will have: "He will turn many of the sons of Israel to the Lord their God." The idea of "turning" or "returning" to the Lord God is standard OT language for the repentance of a people (Deut 30:2; Hosea 3:5; 7:10); and sometimes such a "turning" is proclaimed by a prophet upon whom the Spirit of God has come (II Chr 15:1,4). The idea that JBap's prophetic task is to affect Israel (see also 1:68,80) appears in the words attributed to him during the ministry in John 1:31: "I came baptizing with water that he might be revealed to Israel." In summary, the second strophe (vss. 15–16) transposes to the conception and phrases poetically the ministry portrayal of JBap as an ascetic prophet calling upon Israel to repent, an image found in Luke 3:1–3 and 7:24–35.

THE THIRD STROPHE (*vs. 17*). More specifically, the final strophe of the angelic oracle proclaims that JBap will carry out his prophetic mission of repentance and reconciliation "in the spirit and power of Elijah." Again we seem to have an anticipation of a theme that is common in the Synoptic accounts of the ministry. For instance, in the Gospel of Mark (9:13), Jesus says, "I tell you that Elijah has come, and they did to him whatever they pleased, as it is written of him." Whatever this vague statement may have meant on Jesus' own lips,[42] it is probable that Mark interpreted it as a reference to JBap, since he has described JBap as wearing Elijah-like

---

40 While Samson is a Judge, the Book of Judges was ranked by the Jews among the "Former Prophets," even as Jeremiah was ranked among the "Latter Prophets."

41 I have chosen the example of the opening of Zechariah, precisely because JBap's father bore the name of that prophet (see NOTE on 1:5, and footnote 7 above).

42 Some would maintain that Jesus originally identified himself (rather than JBap) as the Elijah-prophet of the last times, or that the earliest stage of Christian thought so identified him. For complications involved in this thesis, see R. E. Brown, "Jesus and Elisha," *Perspective* 12 (1971), 85–104. What is reasonably certain is that Christians clarified the once obscure relations between JBap and Jesus, not by rejecting JBap from salvation history, but by attributing to him the subordinate role of Elijah, who was thus conceived as going before the Messiah rather than going before God.

clothing,[48] and he has dramatized the violent death of JBap (6:14–29), a death suffered precisely because, like Elijah, JBap dared to challenge kings (Herod and Herodias resemble Ahab and Jezebel). Matthew removes all doubt by offering an interpretation (17:13) of the saying of Jesus: "Then the disciples understood that he was speaking to them of JBap" (see also Matt 11:13–14).

But if, by attributing to JBap the role of Elijah,[44] Luke is voicing a Synoptic theme in his infancy narrative, this very identification raises another question about the harmony between the infancy narrative and the Gospel proper. In his account of the ministry does Luke give JBap an Elijah-like role; or does he hold a position similar to that of John 1:21 where JBap denies that he is Elijah?[45] Wink asserts, "Luke has retained nothing of JBap's role as Elijah."[46] The fact that Luke gives no parallel to Mark 9:9–13, where Jesus says that Elijah has already come, has been looked upon as a deliberate omission directed against the thesis of JBap equaling Elijah. And Luke 4:25–26 and 9:54 have been invoked as proof that for Luke it was Jesus, not JBap, who had the Elijah role.[47] Yet in 7:27 Luke follows "Q" in applying to JBap Mal 3:1, a passage associated with Elijah (see Mal 3:23 below). Perhaps one may speak of traces in Luke of two different Christian views of the Elijah role (see footnote 42). An earlier stage, dominant in Luke's account of the ministry, would have identified Jesus as the Elijah-like eschatological prophet of the last times (7:16). A later stage, dominant in the Lucan infancy narrative (perhaps composed after the Gospel and Acts), would have stressed Jesus as God's Son. Such a shift would have freed the Elijah role for JBap, an association only hinted at in the Lucan account of the ministry but made specific in the infancy narrative.

If 1:17b gives us this specific association of JBap and Elijah, that asso-

---

[48] In II Kgs 1:8 Elijah is said to have worn "a garment of haircloth, with a leather girdle about his waist"; in Mark 1:6 we hear that JBap "was clothed with camel's hair and had a leather girdle around his waist." (Yet, according to Zech 13:4 "a hairy mantle" was the ordinary prophetic dress.) Mark 1:2 introduces JBap by citing Mal 3:1, a passage associated with Elijah in Jewish exegesis (Mal 3:23 [RSV 4:5]).

[44] Some would make a sharp distinction between JBap "in the spirit and power of Elijah" (Luke 1:17) and JBap identified as Elijah (Matt 11:14; 17:13). I do not think that the Matthean passages can be interpreted so literally—the Transfiguration scene wherein Elijah and Moses are heavenly figures (Matt 17:3) precludes a literal identification of JBap with Elijah. I doubt that Matthew means any more than that the precursor role given to Elijah in Jewish expectations has been played by JBap.

[45] The negative attitude of the Fourth Gospel on this question has been influenced by increasing hostility between JBap sectarians and Christians (see ABJ, I, LXVII–LXX). A possible exception occurs in John 5:35 which compares JBap to a burning lamp, perhaps echoing the description of Elijah in Sirach 48:1: "Then the prophet Elijah arose like a fire, and his word burned like a torch."

[46] Wink, *John*, 42; yet he makes this statement in the light of a distinction I rejected in footnote 44. He contends that Luke has no Elijah typology but does have an Elijah midrash. He says that for Luke neither JBap nor Jesus fulfill anything as "new Elijahs," but Luke does use Elijah as a basis for comparison. This overstresses a difference in tone.

[47] See the list of passages cited by Wink, *John*, 44.

ciation is echoed in the other lines of 17. To see this, let us recall a series of OT texts:

Mal 3:1:   "I send my messenger to prepare the way before me,[48]
                    and the Lord whom you seek will suddenly come to
                    His Temple."

Mal 3:23–24:
(RSV 4:5–6)   "I send you Elijah the prophet
                    before the great and terrible day of the Lord comes.
                    He will turn the heart of the fathers toward the
                       children,
                    and the heart of the children toward the fathers,
                    lest I come and smite the land with a curse."

Sirach 48:10:   "[Elijah], it is written, you are destined in time
                    to put an end to wrath before [. . .]
                    to turn the heart of the fathers toward the children
                    and to restore the tribes of Jacob."

Luke 1:17a: "And he will go before Him
       17b: in the spirit and power of Elijah
       17c: to turn the hearts of the fathers to the children
       17d: and the disobedient unto the wisdom of the just,
       17e: to make ready for the Lord a prepared people."

In studying these texts, we see that, while the "messenger" in Mal 3:1 was not identified (and was perhaps an angel), by the time that Mal 3:23 had been appended, the messenger had been identified as Elijah. Also the coming of the Lord had been interpreted as the coming of "the great and terrible day of the Lord." Both Mal 3:24 and Sirach 48:10 gave Elijah a task of reconciliation before that terrible day. Thus Luke 1:17a,b is simply following an established exegesis in introducing the Elijah motif as part of the association between Mal 3:1 and JBap. And Luke 17e is also an example of established exegesis when it associates Mal 3:1 and Isa 40:3. The first time that JBap is introduced in Mark (1:2–4), the OT text that is applied to him is Mal 3:1 combined with Isa 40:3 ("The voice of one crying in the desert: 'Make ready the way of the Lord.' "). The parallel Lucan scene (3:4) has only the Isaiah text, and some have attributed the omission of the Malachi text to Luke's refusal to give JBap an Elijah-like role (despite the citation of the Malachi text in 7:27!). But there is a simpler explanation. Luke agrees with Mark that the combined Malachi/

48 The LXX of Mal 3:1 reads: "I send forth my messenger, and he will survey the way before my face." Luke 7:27 cites Mal 3:1 (combined with Isa 40:3) thus: "I send my messenger before your face who will prepare your way ahead of you."

Isaiah text should be applied to JBap when he is first introduced, to serve as a leitmotif. However, Luke introduces JBap not at the baptism but in the annunciation; and so 17e both continues the Malachi motif ("prepared") and begins an Isaiah motif ("make ready for the Lord"). It is this combination that explains the awkwardness of this line mentioned in the NOTE.

The most difficult lines in this third strophe are 1:17c,d. To understand them we must recall that the third strophe (vs. 17) is a specification of the second strophe (vss. 15–16).[49] If vs. 15a stated that JBap would be great before the Lord, 17a,b specifies that JBap will "go before Him in the spirit and power of Elijah." If 16 promised that JBap would "turn many of the sons of Israel to the Lord their God," 17c,d specify how that turning will take place in order to make ready a prepared people. The wording of vs. 16 echoed the last line of Sirach 48:10 ("to restore the tribes of Jacob"), while 17c,d has a phrasing close to the penultimate line of the Sirach passage ("to turn the heart of the fathers toward the children"), which in turn recalls Mal 3:24. That leads us to compare the peculiar phrasing of Luke in the light of Malachi:

Mal 3:24:   "He will turn the heart of the fathers toward the children,
                   and the heart of the children toward the fathers"[50]
Luke 1:17c: "to turn the hearts of the fathers to the children
       17d: and the disobedient unto the wisdom of the just"

The Lucan parallelism is difficult; for, while the two lines in Malachi clearly involve a reciprocal turning, that is not clear in Luke. To achieve a reciprocal turning one must read the Lucan lines chiastically, with the last mentioned group in the second line ("just") corresponding to the first mentioned group in the first line ("fathers"), so that the disobedient children are turned unto the wisdom of the just fathers. It would be more normal, however, to read the Lucan lines in synonymous parallelism whereby the "disobedient" are the fathers, and the "just" are the children.[51]

While this second interpretation may seem strange, one may find some interesting support for it in Lucan theology. In Luke's view of salvation history, most of the Jews rejected Jesus, while large numbers of Gentiles accepted him (Acts 28:25–28). Thus, while the "fathers" were disobe-

49 Schürmann, *Lukasevangelium*, I, 36, raises the possibility that 17 is a secondary reinterpretion of 15–16. This theory might imply that 15–16 came from a source, and 17 from Luke's hand. That is possible but not necessary.

50 The LXX of these lines is somewhat different: "He will return the heart of the father to the son, and the heart of a person toward his neighbor." The next verse in Malachi reads: "Remember the Law of Moses my servant as I entrusted it to him on Horeb, commands and regulations for all Israel." Is this line in Luke's mind in 1:17d?—in the NOTE I pointed out that the peculiar idea of moving from disobedience to wisdom implied that wisdom was equivalent to law.

51 In Malachi and in the chiastic interpretation of Luke 1:17c,d there is guilt on both sides, whence the reciprocal turning. In this second, synonymous interpretation of Luke 1:17c,d there is only one turning and one guilt or disobedience, i.e., that of the fathers.

dient, the unexpected "children" of Abraham, the Gentiles, were justified and found the wisdom of God (11:49) in Jesus. Is it accidental that most of the vocabulary of Luke 1:17c,d occurs in Gospel passages involving JBap and castigating the lack of acceptance on the part of the Jewish crowds? In a "Q" saying which Matt 3:7 has addressed to the Pharisees and Sadducees but which Luke 3:8 addresses to the crowds, JBap warns, "Do not begin to say to yourselves, 'We have Abraham as our *father*,' for I tell you God is able from these stones to raise up *children* to Abraham."[52] In Luke 7:31–35 Jesus says by way of rebuke: "To what then shall I compare the people of this generation? . . . For JBap has come eating no bread and drinking no wine; and you say, 'He has a demon.' . . . Yet *wisdom is justified by all her children*." One may put these passages together so as to mean that an acceptance of JBap's challenge (which is reinforced by Jesus) produces a new generation of children who possess the wisdom of the just, while those who think of the patriarchs as their fathers are disobedient and not justified in their wisdom. But, whether or not this is the correct interpretation of 17c,d, its language seems to be a borrowing from Malachi and Sirach, reinterpreted with terms that appear in the Lucan ministry accounts of JBap.

In summary, looking back on the angelic message in 1:13–17, I recognize that there is no real way to disprove the theory that Luke drew it in whole or in part from a JBap source. However, I find no convincing reason *by way of content* or *by way of theology*[53] for such a hypothesis, since everything said therein echoes or is consonant with what Luke will say of JBap in 3:1–20 and 7:18–35. The slight differences of tone can be explained by the fact that this material has been fitted into an annunciation of birth pattern and that Jesus has not yet been mentioned.

3. Zechariah's Response (18–20) and the Conclusion (21–23)

The basic pattern of the biblical annunciation of birth is continued in vss. 18–20, i.e., steps 4 and 5 in Table VIII: the objection by the visionary as to how this can be, and the giving of a sign.[54] The coloring of these steps comes from the specific OT antecedents that we have already seen as Lucan background. Thus, the Lucan wording of Zechariah's objection, "How am I to know this?", is a verbatim quotation from Abraham's reaction to divine revelation in Gen 15:8. And so that the reader will not miss

---

52 See O. Seitz, JBL 79 (1960), 247–54, for the suggestion that this passage may echo the story in Joshua of the replacement of the disobedient generation of Israel in the wilderness by a new generation as they entered the Promised Land.

53 In discussing language in § 9, B1, and the problem of a Greek that is more semitized than usual, I declared that I abandon the thesis that by style and language one can decide the question of Lucan sources. Therefore, the failure of difference in content and difference in theology to establish a convincing case for a source is of major importance.

54 See also § 5, footnote 70.

this allusion, Luke has Zechariah continue in vss. 18 with a reminder of his own and his wife's age—the feature in which Zechariah and Elizabeth most resemble Abraham and Sarah (Gen 17:17). In giving the sign the angel explicitly recalls the Daniel background of the annunciation by identifying himself as Gabriel (Dan 8:16; 9:21) who stands in the presence of God (Dan 7:16); and, as mentioned above, the sign of being struck mute echoes Dan 10:15. The recognition of the extent to which Luke is following a stereotyped pattern and an OT background makes otiose the question of whether Zechariah's punishment was just. Many of the Church Fathers wrote severely about the stubborn disbelief implied in Zechariah's question (vs. 18); and yet it is not noticeably different from the objection that Mary will pose in 1:34, and she is not punished. The literary pattern virtually required a sign, and the parallel with Daniel[55] suggested the sign of being struck mute.

The conclusion (vss. 21–23) forcefully brings us back to the atmosphere of the Temple that was so dominant in the setting of the annunciation in vss. 8–10. Gabriel has promised Zechariah something positive, that his wife Elizabeth will bear him a son, and something negative, that he will be struck mute. The fulfillment of the positive promise requires a lapse of time; but Luke uses the people's expectation of a blessing and the inability of Zechariah to respond (NOTE on vs. 22) to demonstrate the immediate fulfillment of the negative promise. If Luke's Gentile readers can be presumed to have known that the phrase "he was unable to speak to them" meant that Zechariah was unable to bless them, we have here a remarkable instance of Luke's love of symmetry. The priestly blessing that could not be given at the beginning of the Gospel by Zechariah will be given at the end of the Gospel by Jesus. In 24:50–52 we are told that Jesus led his disciples out to Bethany, lifted his hands over them, and blessed them; then they worshiped him, and returning to Jerusalem with great joy, they were continually in the Temple praising God. It has been recognized that this ending of Luke is remarkably like the ending of the praise of the ideal high priest, Simon son of Onias, in Sirach 50:19–23.[56] There we are told that the high priest, when he completed his service of offering sacrifice, would come down (the Temple steps) and lift his hands over the congregation of Israel, and bless them; meanwhile the people would be prostrate in worship and would be urged to praise the God of all who would grant them joy of heart. It is not farfetched to think that Luke has attached to the risen Jesus the fulfillment or replacement of the Tem-

---

[55] Even though Gabriel appears in both Lucan annunciations (to Zechariah and to Mary), it is the annunciation to Zechariah (a man) that is the most closely conformed to Gabriel's appearances to Daniel.

[56] See P. A. Van Stempvoort, NTS 5 (1958–59), 30–42. We saw that in his description of JBap in 1:17 Luke seems to have Sirach 48:10 in mind, and so it is not unlikely that in describing Jesus Luke would turn to Sirach 50.

ple ritual. That theme is explicit in Hebrews and is hinted at in the Gospel accounts of the death of Jesus (e.g., Mark 15:38).

The final detail in the annunciation scene, the notice that Zechariah "went back to his home" (vs. 23), supplies a connection to the epilogue where Luke will tell us how the positive side of Gabriel's promise worked out and Elizabeth conceived a child. As I pointed out in the NOTE, the theme of departure is Luke's way of marking the termination of scenes in the infancy narrative.

C. *The Epilogue (1:24–25)*

These brief verses have been the subject of considerable discussion. Among those who argue for a JBap source, some contend that vss. 24–25 may once have been followed by what is now in vs. 57 ("Now the time came for Elizabeth to give birth"), so that Luke has broken the original sequence of the source to insert the annunciation of Jesus' birth and the visitation. Other proponents of the source theory suggest that the abruptness and obscurity of the epilogue results from the omission or loss of pre-Lucan JBap material, e.g., of an annunciation to Elizabeth which would have come after vs. 23 (and which Luke may have converted into an annunciation to Mary).[57] Such theories are just as difficult to disprove as to prove.

But several facts are worth noting. That Elizabeth conceives without receiving an annunciation corresponding to the annunciation to her husband is not strange; the same is true in the Abraham/Sarah story of the birth of Isaac. Also the sequence from vs. 23 to vs. 24 is plausible and shows no sign of omission. In fact Luke's statements, "He went back to his home. Afterwards Elizabeth his wife conceived," seem to echo once again the theme of the parents of Samuel: "Then he went to his home at Ramah . . . and in due time (his wife) Hannah conceived" (I Sam 1:19–20).[58] Among the words I omitted from this Samuel citation are "The Lord remembered her," which are quite close to Elizabeth's first words in Luke 1:25: "The Lord has dealt with me in this way," even as the rest of her words ("He looked to take away my disgrace among men") echoes Rachel's reaction to conception in Gen 30:23: "God has taken away my disgrace."[59]

Much of the theorizing that something has been omitted before or after

---

[57] See Dibelius, "Jungfrauensohn," 6–7.

[58] The LXX has "he went"; the MT has "they went."

[59] Sarah's reaction to conception and birth in Gen 21:6 was: "God has given me cause to laugh [a play on the name Isaac, 'he laughs'], and all who hear of it will rejoice together with me." Luke takes up this reaction (which followed the birth of Isaac) after the birth of JBap: "When Elizabeth's neighbors and relatives heard that the Lord had shown His great mercy to her, they rejoiced together with her" (1:58).

the epilogue depends on the supposed obscurity of the detail that for five months Elizabeth kept herself in seclusion. Commentators have seen here various theological motifs, e.g., a response of awe and silence before the workings of the divine, corresponding to her husband's fear (1:12) and inability to speak (1:22). The mention of the "five months," combined with references to "the sixth month" (1:26), "three months" (1:56), and "eight days" (2:21), has induced the more imaginative to read into Luke a calculation that would total out 490 days, corresponding to the Danielic seventy weeks of years.[60] Personally I see no need to posit any mystique or obscure purpose in the Lucan mention of the five months of seclusion: it is a literary device to prepare for the sign to be revealed to Mary in 1:36: "And behold, your relative Elizabeth, despite her old age, has also conceived a son; indeed this is the sixth month for a woman who was deemed barren." Since Elizabeth had been in seclusion for five months, no one could have known of her pregnancy;[61] and therefore the angel's knowledge of the otherwise unknown increases the sign value of the annunciation to Mary and helps to show that the conception of JBap really was the work of God. This close connection between 1:24 and 1:36 shows that the epilogue is totally a Lucan composition.

Indeed, in the theory of composition proposed on pp. 251–52 above, I suggested that, rather than being an awkward addendum, the epilogue was part of Luke's original plan. The annunciations of the births of JBap and of Jesus (Table XI) were each followed by an epilogue in which the work of God in the respective conception could be praised (1:24–25; 1:39–45). The "Afterwards" (literally, "After these days") introducing the first epilogue is matched by the "At this time" (literally, "In these days") introducing the second epilogue. And each epilogue is dated by a time reference to Elizabeth's pregnancy (five months in 1:24; three months in 1:56).

D. *The Relationship between John the Baptist and Jesus*

If Luke was drawing upon a JBap source which contained an annunciation of birth, there is little reason to ask why 1:5–25 appears in the Gospel in

---

[60] I would see this interpretation reaching the point of eisegesis when commentators begin to supply numbers that Luke does not mention. For example, Burrows, *Gospel*, 41–42, followed by Laurentin, *Structure*, 49, calculates the 490 from "In the sixth month" of 1:26 (read arbitrarily as six months or 180 days), from the nine months of Mary's pregnancy (not mentioned by Luke, but calculated at 270 days), and from the forty days before the presentation of 2:22 (also not mentioned by Luke). This thesis has the added difficulty of calculating pregnancy as nine months, instead of ten lunar months which seems to be the calculation in Luke's sequence (see NOTE on 1:24).

[61] I speak of a literary device because the whole purpose of the seclusion is in relation to the annunciation to Mary. There would be no purpose for a seclusion during the *first* five months of pregnancy (the less visible period) if the prime concern was the reaction of the neighbors. The dating of the seclusion is to make certain that Mary is the first to know (by divine revelation)—after that there is no need for seclusion.

its present place and form. But if Luke was composing the infancy narrative freely on the basis of a few items of information (see A above), then one must ask why he composed an annunciation of JBap's birth and inserted it at the beginning of his narrative. In the next section (§ 11), drawing upon points of similarity between Matthew and Luke, I shall suggest that there was a pre-Gospel tradition of an angelic annunciation of the birth of Jesus as the Davidic Messiah; and I think that Luke used the annunciation of Jesus' birth as a pattern in composing the annunciation of JBap's birth (Table XI). However, what theological insight would have led him to do this? Why did Luke not begin, as Matthew did, with the annunciation of Jesus' birth?

To answer this, let me attempt a brief critical reconstruction of the historical relationship between the careers of JBap and Jesus, probing beneath the later rethinking of that relationship in the Gospels.[62] Historically, Jesus was baptized by JBap and may have gone so far in identifying himself with JBap's movement as to have become temporarily a disciple of JBap or, at least, to have imitated his baptizing ministry (John 3:22,26).[63] But after JBap's arrest, Jesus went his own way with a ministry of preaching and healing. And so in Palestine in the late 20s there were two salvific figures, each proclaiming the imminence of God's eschatological action[64] and each dying a martyr's death, after having had contact with each other during their ministries and having shared a certain harmony of thought. The last observation is justified not only by Jesus' having accepted baptism from JBap, but also by an acceptance of Jesus on the part of some of the followers of JBap.[65] Because of this harmony we find no tendency in the Christian records to excise the memory of JBap.

However, there was a tendency among Christians to reinterpret these almost parallel careers by subordinating JBap to Jesus, so that he was seen as a forerunner of Jesus or one who prepared the way for Jesus. While one can find some historical basis for this view in the fact that JBap began preaching first and died first, the idea that he was preparing the way for the Messiah whom he identified as Jesus (John 3:28, most explicitly) is a Christian adaptation of JBap's own thought that he was preparing the way for God. As part of this Christian reinterpretation, JBap was attributed the role of Elijah through an exegesis of Mal 3:1,23, combined with Isa

---

[62] The brevity of my sketch conceals much scholarly dispute. Two attempts in English to reconstruct the history of JBap are: C. H. Kraeling, *John the Baptist* (New York: Scribner's, 1951) and C. H. H. Scobie, *John the Baptist* (Philadelphia: Fortress, 1964).

[63] In ABJ, I, 165, I argue that John 4:2 is a redactor's attempt to offset the clear indication of 3:22 that Jesus baptized. There is no way to prove the historicity of the latter, but I find it more easily explicable as early tradition than as Christian theological creation, granted the tendency to make Jesus superior to JBap.

[64] From the words attributed to them, there is a greater sense of realization in Jesus' proclamation. For JBap the intervention of God would come frighteningly soon; for Jesus it was already making itself felt in his own words and actions.

[65] Passages like Acts 1:21–22 and John 1:35–43 suggest that members of the Twelve had been disciples of JBap, including Peter, Andrew, and Philip.

40:3,[66] with Jesus seen as the Lord whose coming was thus heralded. The "Q" passage in Matt 11:2ff. and Luke 7:18ff. is a good example of the Christian attempt to work out the relationship between JBap and Jesus in a way that does justice to JBap's having had a preparatory role without understanding it.

If the struggle to fit JBap into a schema of salvation history was a necessary step in the process of Christian self-understanding, the results may also have been meant to persuade unconverted disciples of JBap. Yet, as time went on and some of those unconverted disciples seemingly turned hostile to the Christian movement, the motif of subordinating JBap became stronger in Christian writing, so as not to offer ammunition to possible rivals. This is particularly apparent in the Fourth Gospel where it is underlined that JBap was not the light (1:8), not the Messiah nor Elijah (1:20–21), and was to decrease while Jesus increased (3:30). Indeed, he becomes an incipient Christian, for the whole purpose of his ministry was to testify to Jesus (1:7,30–31). Such apologetics does not cause JBap to be mentioned less. Rather, the historical fact that JBap preceded Jesus is freely admitted and indeed insisted upon, so long as the proper subordination is recognized. This is seen in the Prologue of the Fourth Gospel. The christology that was once associated with the beginning of the ministry of Jesus has here been moved back to the incarnation of the pre-existent Word. However, since JBap had preceded the beginning of Jesus' ministry in order to prepare the way for the divine christological announcement at the baptism, it is seen as logical in the Prologue that JBap should prepare the way for the incarnation (1:6–9,14)—absurd from the viewpoint of chronology but very perceptive from the viewpoint of salvation history!

Such Christian theological developments regarding JBap are reflected in the Lucan infancy narrative in a most graceful way. If the Fourth Gospel has moved the christological moment (i.e., the moment of the revelation of who Jesus is) back to the incarnation of the pre-existent Word (1:14), Luke has moved it back to the virginal conception (1:35). If the Fourth Gospel has JBap prepare the way for the incarnation, Luke has the conception of JBap prepare the way for the conception of Jesus.[67] Subordination is preserved because the miraculous element in Jesus' conception (without a male parent) will be greater than that in JBap's conception (aged, barren parents). When the two pregnant mothers meet, Elizabeth

---

66 I do not wish to exclude the possibility that some of this exegesis began with JBap himself, e.g., the use of Isa 40:3 (as in John 1:23) since that text was also used by the Dead Sea Scroll sectarians as a self-interpretation (1QS viii 13–16).

67 There is no real evidence that Luke knew John's Prologue or that John knew Luke's infancy narrative (or even traditions behind it). Each Gospel is independently preserving the Christian tradition that the good news opened with a preparatory proclamation by JBap. Each Gospel accomplishes this by anticipating JBap material from the ministry account, but the material and the setting are quite different.

will praise Mary as "the mother of my Lord"; and JBap will add his testimony by jumping with gladness in Elizabeth's womb (1:41–45). There is no rivalry between the two figures in salvation history since God sends the same angel Gabriel to announce both conceptions. If in the Fourth Gospel JBap has become an incipient Christian, Luke also brings JBap firmly within the Christian sphere by presenting him as a relative of Jesus on his mother's side (1:36). This latter detail is never suggested anywhere else in the four Gospels, and is very difficult to reconcile with John 1:33 where JBap says that he did not even know Jesus. Indeed, family relationship would make the critical reconstruction given above almost unintelligible, and would make rivalry between the disciples of JBap and disciples of Jesus very hard to understand. But family relationship would be quite intelligible as a symbolic Lucan etiology of the historical relationship between the JBap movement and the Jesus movement, and of the relationship that should exist between the disciples of the two groups.

Thus, without a JBap source, I think it quite possible to attribute to Luke the literary form, the position, the theology, and most of the content of 1:5–25.

Sectional Bibliography (§10)
(Luke 1:5–25)

(Besides referring to the Bibliography for the whole Lucan infancy narrative in § 9, the reader should consult the Bibliography in § 11, since many treat the two annunciations together when studying the annunciation to Mary.)

Benoit, P., "L'enfance de Jean-Baptiste selon Luc I," NTS 3 (1956–57), 169–94. Reprinted in ExTh, III, 165–96.

Dibelius, M., *Die urchristliche Überlieferung von Johannes dem Taufer* (FRLANT 15; Göttingen: Vandenhoeck, 1911).

Wilkinson, J. R., *A Johannine Document in the First Chapters of St. Luke's Gospel* (London: Luzac, 1902).

Wink, W., *John the Baptist in the Gospel Tradition* (NTSMS, 7; Cambridge University, 1968), esp. 58–86.

III. THE ANNUNCIATION OF THE BIRTH OF JESUS (§ 11)

Translation of Luke 1:26–38

1 ²⁶ In the sixth month the angel Gabriel was sent from God to a city of Galilee known as Nazareth, ²⁷ to a virgin betrothed to a man of the House of David whose name was Joseph, and the virgin's name was Mary. ²⁸ He came and addressed her thus: "Hail, O favored one, the Lord is with you." ²⁹ Now she was startled at what he said and wondered what such a greeting might mean. ³⁰ But the angel said to her: "Do not be afraid, Mary, for you have found favor with God.

^{31a} And behold, you will conceive in your womb and give birth to a son,

^{31b} and you will call his name Jesus.

^{32a} He will be great and will be called Son of the Most High.

^{32b} And the Lord God will give him the throne of his father David;

^{33a} and he will be king over the House of Jacob forever,

^{33b} and there will be no end to his kingdom."

³⁴ However, Mary said to the angel, "How can this be, since I have had no relations with a man?" ³⁵ The angel responded,

^{35b} "The Holy Spirit will come upon you,

^{35c} and power from the Most High will overshadow you.

^{35d} Therefore, the child to be born will be called holy—Son of God.

³⁶ And behold, your relative Elizabeth, despite her old age, has also conceived a son; indeed, this is the sixth month for a woman who was deemed barren. ³⁷ Nothing said by God can be impossible." ³⁸ Mary answered, "Behold the handmaid of the Lord. Let it happen to me according to your word." Then the angel went away, leaving her.

NOTES

1:26. *In the sixth month.* That is, of Elizabeth's pregnancy; see NOTE on 1:24. As she had hid herself for the first half of her pregnancy, no outsider could have known that she was pregnant; and it will be revealed to Mary (1:36) before it becomes public.

to a city of Galilee known as Nazareth. In Matthew the annunciation to Joseph apparently takes place in Bethlehem where the child is born (2:1) and where the parents live in a house (2:11). Only after the return from Egypt are we told that Joseph "went off to the district of Galilee . . . to dwell in a city called Nazareth" (2:22–23—for the name and history of the city, see NOTE there). The fact that "known as Nazareth" is omitted from Luke in Codex Bezae and an OL ms. has contributed to the suggestion of Leaney, "Birth Narratives," 161–62, that originally Nazareth was named only in the stories in Luke 2.

27. *to a virgin betrothed to a man . . . whose name was Joseph.* Mary's marital status is described by the same verb (*mnēsteuein*) used in Matt 1:18, "Mary had been betrothed to Joseph," and in Luke 2:5, "Mary, his betrothed, who was pregnant." Although the situation is not spelled out in Luke as it was in Matthew, the fact that Mary is both a virgin and betrothed means that she has exchanged consent with Joseph but not been taken to live with him. For an explanation of this custom, see NOTE on Matt 1:18.

a man of the House of David. In Matthew's annunciation too it was specified that Joseph was a Davidid (1:20). Luke's phrasing is not totally clear; Origen understood "of the House of David" to refer to Mary, and John Chrysostom took it to refer both to Mary and Joseph. Grammatically it stands closer to Joseph; and if Luke meant it to refer to Mary, he would not have needed to reintroduce her as subject in the next clause ("and the virgin's name was Mary"). Elsewhere Luke refers only to Joseph as a Davidid, e.g., in 2:4 he tells us that Joseph went to Bethlehem "because he was of the house and lineage of David," and in 3:23 it is Joseph whose genealogy is traced to David.

If this phrase does not apply to Mary, there is really no other NT evidence that she was a Davidid. The argument that Joseph, a Davidid, would have married within his own tribe and house is offset by the fact that Luke gives to Mary a relative of the House of Levi or Aaron (1:5,36—note also the name "Levi" among the ancestors of Jesus as seen in ⅜⅜4,32 in Table I). The Church writers were divided on this issue. Attributing to Mary a Davidic origin were the *Protevangelium of James*, 10:1; Ignatius *Ephesians*, xviii 2; and Justin *Dialogue* xlv 4; while there are hints of at least partial levitical origins (usually through Mary's father or grandfather) in Hippolytus and Ephraem. The latter position is often involved with identifying the Eli of the Lucan genealogy

(※2 in Table I) as a relative of Mary. Augustine, *Contra Faustum Mani-chaeum* xxxiii 9, takes the trouble to deny that Mary was a priest's daughter. On this question, see Fischer, "Abkunft." Both derivations, Davidic and Levitical, reflect theological conceptions. Gentile writers often did not understand how Jesus could be truly a Davidid through Joseph who did not beget him and so were forced to think of Mary as a Davidid. On the other hand, the designation of Jesus as a priest tended toward the creation of levitic ancestry. We have no idea where the *Protevangelium of James* (1:1; 2:1), which is clearly unhistorical on many points, got the tradition that the names of Mary's parents were Joachim and Anne; but certainly it patterns Anne on her namesake, Hannah the mother of Samuel. For another, unreliable tradition about the names of Mary's forebears, see footnote 7 in Appendix V.

and the virgin's name was Mary. See NOTE on 1:5, "and her name was Elizabeth."

28. *Hail, O favored one.* In the Greek expression *chaire kecharitōmenē,* words of closely related stems are involved. *Chaire* is related to the noun *chara,* "joy." *Kecharitōmenē* is from the verb *charitoun,* a factitive verb, "to make one favored, to give one grace," of the same stem as *charis,* "grace, favor." If one presupposes an underlying knowledge of Hebrew in the account, *kecharitōmenē* virtually translates the name Hannah and may be an echo of motif of the birth of Samuel found in these chapters.

the Lord is with you. The Greek has no verb, and some translators would give it a subjunctive tone ("be with you"). However, W. C. van Unnik has made a minute study of this formula in *New Testament Essays in Memory of T. W. Manson,* ed. A. J. B. Higgins (Manchester University, 1959), 270–305; and he points out (p. 283) that (a) in the instances where a verb is supplied, the note of certainty is stronger than the subjunctive note of wish or possibility; and (b) when a verb is not found (as here), the phrase is practically always a declaration. While the phrase assures Mary of God's support, it does not mean that the Lord Jesus is within Mary's womb. After this phrase the Codices Alexandrinus, Bezae, and many of the versions, including the Latin, add: "Blessed are you among women." This is almost certainly a scribal borrowing from 1:42, but it has influenced the "Ave Maria" prayer.

29. *she was startled.* A stronger variant of the verb which was used in 1:12. Codex Alexandrinus follows it by adding: "when she saw (him)"; but the Vulgate is closer to Luke's meaning when in some mss. it adds: "when she had heard." Many psychological explanations have been advanced for Mary's reaction: a human being's reaction to the presence of an angel; a maiden's reaction to the presence of a man; Mary's modesty. However, disturbance is part of the literary pattern of an angelic annunciation of birth (number 2 in Table VIII); and Mary's wonderment is a reaction to the great grace or favor that the angel has announced. See A. M. Lobina, *Revista Bíblica* (Argentina) 21 (1959), 15–21.

might mean. Literally, "might be"—an optative. BDF 65²: "The optative appears only in the Lucan corpus with any frequency," and only Luke employs the optative in indirect discourse (BDF 386).

30. *you have found favor with God.* The noun is *charis;* see NOTE on "fa-

vored one" in vs. 28. The expression "to find favor" is a Semitism, e.g., "Noah found favor before the Lord God" (LXX of Gen 6:9).

31. *And behold.* See NOTE on this expression (*kai idou*) in 1:20.

you will conceive. As we saw in footnote 44, § 5, the Hebrew participial expression in announcements of birth can be understood as either a present (already pregnant) or a future. Luke's future verb cannot be explained away as a misunderstanding of a putative Semitic original, for the verbs in 1:35 are also future.

you will call his name. A Semitism as in 1:13; see NOTE on Matt 1:21. This is a command and not a simple continuation of prophecy. In Matt 1:21,23 it is Joseph who does the naming; but there are many OT antecedents for the naming of children by divinely favored women, e.g., Hagar (Gen 16:11), Leah (Gen 30:13), the mother of Samson (Judg 13:24), and the mother of Samuel (I Sam 1:20). This naming by Mary constitutes no proof that Luke thinks of Mary as a Davidid. Actually in 2:21 it is not specified who did name the child.

Jesus. For the meaning of this name, see NOTE on "for he will save" in Matt 1:21.

32. *will be called.* In this instance, "calling" brings to expression what one is, so that it means no less than "he will be." Interchangeability of the two phrases is seen by comparing Matt 5:9, "they will be called sons of God," and Luke 6:35, "you will be sons of the Most High."

Most High. In the NT this name for God is encountered most frequently in Luke (1:35,76; 6:35; Acts 7:48; etc.).

34. *How can this be . . . ?* The textual evidence for omitting this question is negligible. See B. Brinkmann, *Biblica* 34 (1953), 327–32, refuting H. Vogels, ZNW 43 (1950–51), 256–60. It is omitted by the OL ms. b, dating from the fourth or fifth century. Perhaps the scribe was embarrassed by the attribution to Mary of seeming disbelief. Or he may have understood the question to mean (as does the curious RSV translation), "How can this be, since I have no husband?", a question that would contradict 1:27 and 2:5 (where this ms. reads "his wife")—Mary has a husband. The eighth-century writer John of Damascus (PG 95:188c) has been cited as evidence for omitting the "since" clause from the question, but his commentary goes on to mention that Mary asked a question about the manner of the conception.

since. The causal conjunction *epei* occurs only here in Luke, and has been used as proof that this verse is non-Lucan. However, it is not a frequent conjunction in the Gospels (Matthew three times, Mark once, John twice), and three times Luke/Acts uses the closely related causal conjunction *epeidē*.

I have had no relations with a man. Literally, "I do not know a man." The verb "to know" is a Semitism for sexual relations; see Matt 1:25: "He did not know her until she brought forth a son." While the tense is present, it describes a state resultant from a past pattern of behavior, as the OL recognized by using a perfect tense (*novi, cognovi*)—see the series of acticles by Quecke. The word for "man" is the specific *anēr*, "male, husband," not the generic *anthrōpos*. Here it should not be translated "husband" since Luke's intent is wider: Mary has not known *any* man and so is a virgin (1:27).

35. *The Holy Spirit.* This expression is anarthrous as it was in the Matthean

annunciation (1:18). See NOTE there justifying the supplying of an article in translation.

will come upon you. Eperchesthai is a Lucan verb, occurring seven times in Luke/Acts, as compared with twice in the rest of the NT. In Acts 1:8 it is used proleptically of the Holy Spirit coming upon the disciples at Pentecost. See also Isa 32:15: "until the Spirit comes upon you [or us] from on high"; and I Sam 16:13: "The Spirit of the Lord came upon David." These parallels make it clear that the sense is not sexual.

power. In this abstract sense *dynamis* occurs some seventeen times in Luke/Acts, as contrasted with twice each in Matthew and Mark. The combination of spirit and power is very Lucan, occurring in Luke 1:17; 4:14; Acts 1:8; 6:5,8; 10:38. Not knowing the rules of parallelism in biblical poetry which make it clear that "power from the Most High" is synonymous with "Holy Spirit," some patristic and medieval theologians thought that the references in 35b,c were respectively to the Third and Second Persons of the Trinity, so that "power" was the Second Person descending to take flesh in Mary's womb. As we shall see, there is no evidence that Luke thought of the incarnation of a Pre-existent.

will overshadow you. In the COMMENT I shall discuss the use of *episkiazein*, "overshadow," in the OT to describe God's presence in the sanctuary, and in the Gospels at the transfiguration—a somewhat literal usage where a cloud of glory overshadows. Two other suggestions have been made, however, which should be discarded. Occasionally, the power overshadowing Mary has been interpreted as a euphemism for a quasi-sexual union, a *hieros gamos.* Strangely enough this appears in one form in the Spanish post-Reformation theologian Cardinal Toletus (1532–96). A modern variation is the thesis of D. Daube, ZNW 48 (1957), 119–20, who sees an allusion to a rabbinic debate over Ruth 3:9 where Ruth presents herself at night to Boaz as his *handmaid* (cf. Luke 1:38) and asks him to *spread* (*periballein*) his mantle *over* her. As I reported in footnote 24, § 3, some saw this as seduction and an invitation to sexual relations. The rabbis denied it by arguing that *ṭallît,* "mantle," had been misread for *ṭallēl,* "overshadow." It is difficult to see how this would affect Luke's meaning; and it is even more difficult to think that Luke was making a subtle allusion to a debate supposing the knowledge of Hebrew or Aramaic, especially since the evidence for the debate is medieval. There is no real evidence for the sexual use of *episkiazein;* and, if anything, the Lucan language of virginal conception is less open to sexual interpretation than Matthew's "begotten . . . through the Holy Spirit" (NOTES on Matt 1:16 and 1:20). Another dubious suggestion was made by H. Leisegang, *Pneuma Hagion* (Leipzig: Hinrichs, 1922), 14–71, esp. 25–33. He sees here a reflection of Hellenistic mystery religions with a spirit-demon overshadowing the mind or spirit of Mary, so that she was possessed by God almost as if she were a mantic or a sibyl. However, there is no other echo of such a pagan context in the scene; and parallelism suggests that overshadowing by the power of the Most High is no more mystical (or sexual) than having the Holy Spirit come upon Mary—a symbolism that, as we saw, is quite biblical. Dibelius, "Jungfrauensohn," 19–22, gives an important refutation of both the sexual and mystical interpretations of *episkia-zein*.

Therefore. Of the nine times *dio kai* occurs in the NT, three are in Luke/Acts. It involves a certain causality; and Lyonnet, "L'Annonciation," 61[6], points out that this has embarrassed many orthodox theologians, since in pre-existence christology a conception by the Holy Spirit in Mary's womb does *not* bring about the existence of God's Son. Luke is seemingly unaware of such a christology; conception is causally related to divine sonship for him.

the child to be born. This translates *to gennōmenon*, a neuter passive partici-ple, present tense, of *gennan*, "to beget (as a father), to bear (as a mother)"; see the NOTES on this verb in Matt 1:16,20 and footnote 23 in § 5. In itself, the translation "the one begotten" is equally possible, and certainly the aorist pas-sive participle has the meaning "begotten" in Matt 1:20. But the situation in Luke is quite different from the situation envisaged by Matthew where Joseph is worried about the paternity of the child. Everything in Luke is from the view-point of the virgin mother, and paternity is not even mentioned. Consequently the verb seems to mean "born" here. In that case the present participle must have future significance (BDF 339[2b]), as recognized by the Vulgate's *quod nascetur*. Why a neuter? This is probably more an instance of the general possibility of using the neuter for persons. BDF 138[1] suggests that we are to understand an implied neuter noun for "child," such as *teknon* (or *paidion*, as in 2:40). A. Fridrichsen, in *Symbolae Osloenses* 6 (1928), 33–36, argues that the participle used by Luke is a recognized idiom for "the child (in the womb)," and that the whole question of "born" or "begotten" can be bypassed. Yet Vicent, "La presunta," insists that the verbal sense is not lost, so that "the child" is not an adequate translation. Greek mss. of minor importance and some versions insert "of you" after *to gennōmenon.* This reading represents the cross influence of Matt 1:20: "the child begotten *in her.*"

will be called holy—Son of God. See NOTE on "will be called" in vs. 32; it is tantamount to saying "he will be." And so I cannot follow those theologians who try to avoid the causal connotation in the "Therefore" which begins this line by arguing that for Luke the conception of the child does not bring the Son of God into being, but only enables us to call him "Son of God" who already was Son of God. The translation of this line is difficult because it is not certain whether the neuter form *hagion*, "holy," modifies the subject ("The holy child to be born will be called Son of God") or is a predicate. If it is a predicate, the translation I have given is more likely than: "The child to be born (will be) holy; he will be called Son of God," since that involves an implicit verb, and an unusual word order for the second clause. The subjectival use of *hagion* is slightly favored by the rhythm of the line and by the fact that it makes "Son of God" the only predicate of "called," thus matching 32a: "will be called Son of the Most High." However, if one examines 32a carefully, a strong argument can be made for the predicate translation I have adopted—in 32a there are two predicates, "great" and "Son of the Most High," even as there are two predi-cates here, "holy" and "Son of God." Moreover, the logic of vs. 35 favors the child being called holy, since the Holy Spirit comes upon Mary. If one looks ahead to 2:23, one finds "holy" as a predicate for the child: "Every male child who opens the womb will be considered consecrated [called holy] to the Lord." Indeed, "to be called holy" is a LXX expression found in Isa 4:3, a passage that, as we saw in § 7, B3, may be the background for Matthew's "He will be called a Nazorean" (2:23). Jesus is called "the Holy One of God" in Mark 1:24; Luke 4:34; and John 6:69; see also Acts 3:14.

36. *And behold*. For the *kai idou* pattern, see NOTE on 1:20, which is exactly parallel to this verse, in terms of giving a sign to Zechariah.

your relative Elizabeth. The degree of family relationship is vague; it was Wycliffe who popularized the idea that "cousin" was meant. For the historical problems raised by Luke's statement, see § 10D.

despite her old age . . . deemed barren. Both these factors were mentioned in 1:7; but only age was mentioned in Zechariah's objection in 1:18.

this is. For the *kai houtos* construction, see Luke 16:1; 20:28.

37. *Nothing said by God can be impossible*. Literally, "Because not impossible will be every word [*rēma*] with God." This OT maxim (cf. Gen 18:14; Job 42:2; Zech 8:6) contains several Semitisms, e.g., the reversed negative pattern of the sentence, and the use of *rēma*, "word," reflecting *dābār*, "word, thing"— I have tried to catch this double meaning with "No*thing said*." See NOTE on "event" in 2:15 for a further play on *rēma/dābār*.

38. *handmaid*. The feminine form of *doulos*, "servant"; see Acts 2:18.

Let it happen to me. Optative; see NOTE on "might mean" in vs. 29. An element of wishing is involved.

according to your word. *Rēma* as in vs. 37.

the angel went away, leaving her. This is an ordinary feature of angelic appearances, since such a heavenly presence has to be temporary (Judg 6:21; Acts 12:10). However, there is a special Lucan pattern whereby departures terminate the scenes of the Lucan infancy narrative; see NOTE on "he went back" in 1:23.

COMMENT

I shall begin with the structure and pattern of this second Lucan annunciation narrative, comparing it to the annunciation of JBap's birth and various OT annunciations. Then I shall concentrate on features that are peculiar to the annunciation of Jesus' birth.

A. *The Structure and the Annunciation Pattern*

The annunciation of the birth of Jesus is parallel in many ways to the annunciation of the birth of JBap. In Table X I have printed side by side the

texts of the two annunciations so that the reader can see the parallels in
the actual Gospel wording. In Table XI I have analyzed the parallels in
terms of diptych which makes the differences apparent as well. The JBap
side of the diptych reminds the reader of the structure of the JBap annunciation scene as spelled out at the beginning of the COMMENT in § 10. The
Jesus side of the diptych shows a somewhat different structure. There is no
full scale introduction corresponding to 1:5–7, for the presentation of the
dramatis personae in 1:27 is very brief and flows right into the narrative
of the angelic appearance.[1] The epilogue of the first stage of Lucan composition (1:39–45,56) was enlarged through the insertion of the Magnificat to form a separate scene, the visitation, which I shall discuss in
the next section (§ 12). And so the real structural parallel is between the
central part of the JBap annunciation (1:8–23) and the whole of the
Jesus annunciation.

The JBap side of the diptych in Table XI shows how I subdivided the
central part of that annunciation into a setting, a core, and a conclusion.
Such a subdivision is not possible for the Jesus annunciation. The appearance of Gabriel to Mary in 1:26–27 mentions only time and place; it is
scarcely equivalent to the detailed setting in the Temple for the appearance of Gabriel to Zechariah in 1:8–10. Nor in the Jesus annunciation is
there a detailed conclusion corresponding to 1:21–23. The fact that the
same angel appears in both annunciations helps Luke to emphasize the
unity of God's salvific plan, but the Danielic atmosphere is absent from the
second annunciation.[2] And so we may narrow further the observation
made above and say that the real structural parallel is between the *core* of
the JBap annunciation (1:11–20) and the whole of the Jesus annunciation (1:26–38). I have led the reader through this close comparison to
make intelligible why I suggested in the previous section (§ 10) that the
core of the JBap scene, i.e., the annunciation itself, might have been composed by Luke on the analogy of the Jesus scene. Comparison in itself
will, of course, not establish the priority of the Jesus scene in the Lucan
process of composition; but it is quite clear that the Jesus scene is the
simpler structure.

[1] This difference between the two annunciations is quite intelligible. Since the parents of
JBap are not mentioned in the Gospel accounts of the ministry, the reader would know
nothing about them and would need more detail. But Mary would have already been known
to Christian readers through the accounts of the ministry, as would also the fact that Jesus
was "son of Joseph," descended from David; and so less detail was needed about the parents of Jesus.

[2] Absent, at least, are the most important motifs I listened in § 10, B1, e.g., appearance at
the time of liturgical prayer when the visionary had been praying in desperation, and the
subsequent effect of the muteness of the visionary. If we could suppose a knowledge of the
extra-canonical imaginings about Gabriel (NOTE on Luke 1:19), the appearance of Gabriel
to Mary might echo his role as the angel set over Paradise (*Enoch* 20:7), who originally
drove Adam and Eve from the garden and who is now undoing the results of that first sin
by proclaiming the birth of the Messiah.

TABLE X: THE TWO LUCAN ANNUNCIATION NARRATIVES

Annunciation of the Birth of John the Baptist
Luke 1:5–23

Annunciation of the Birth of Jesus
Luke 1:26–38

1 ⁵In the days of Herod, king of Judea, there was a certain priest named Zechariah who belonged to the division of Abijah. He had a wife descended from Aaron, and her name was Elizabeth. ⁶In God's sight they were both upright, blamelessly observing all the commandments and ordinances of the Lord. ⁷Yet they had no children, inasmuch as Elizabeth was barren, and both were on in years.

⁸Now, while Zechariah was serving as a priest, during the time that his division was on Temple duty in God's presence, ⁹there were lots cast according to the custom of the priesthood; and he won the privilege of entering the sanctuary of the Lord to burn the incense. ¹⁰At this hour of incense the whole multitude of the people was there, praying outside.

¹¹There appeared to Zechariah an angel of the Lord, standing at the right side of the altar of incense. ¹²On seeing him, Zechariah was startled, and fear fell upon him. ¹³However, the angel said to him: "Do not be afraid, Zechariah, for your prayer is heard.

¹³ᵇAnd your wife Elizabeth will bear you a son,
¹³ᶜand you will call his name John.
¹⁴ᵃAnd you will have joy and gladness,
¹⁴ᵇand many will rejoice at his birth.

1 ²⁶In the sixth month the angel Gabriel was sent from God to a city of Galilee known as Nazareth, ²⁷to a virgin betrothed to a man of the House of David whose name was Joseph, and the virgin's name was Mary.

²⁸He came and addressed her thus: "Hail, O favored one, the Lord is with you." ²⁹Now she was startled at what he said and wondered what such a greeting might mean. ³⁰But the angel said to her: "Do not be afraid, Mary, for you have found favor with God.

³¹ᵃAnd behold, you will conceive in your womb and give birth to a son,
³¹ᵇand you will call his name Jesus.

[32a] He will be great and will be called Son of the Most High.
[32b] And the Lord God will give him the throne of his father David;
[33a] and he will be king over the House of Jacob forever,
[33b] and there will be no end to his kingdom."

[34] However, Mary said to the angel, "How can this be, since I have had no relations with a man?" [35] The angel responded,
[35b] "The Holy Spirit will come upon you,
[35c] and power from the Most High will overshadow you.
[35d] Therefore, the child to be born will be called holy—Son of God.
[36] And behold, your relative Elizabeth, despite her old age, has also conceived a son; indeed, this is the sixth month for a woman who was deemed barren. [37] Nothing said by God can be impossible."

[38] Mary answered, "Behold the handmaid of the Lord. Let it happen to me according to your word." Then the angel went away, leaving her.

[15a] For he will be great before the Lord,
[15b] and he will drink no wine or strong drink.
[15c] And he will be filled with the Holy Spirit even from his mother's womb,
[16] and he will turn many of the sons of Israel to the Lord their God.

[17a] And he will go before Him
[17b] in the spirit and power of Elijah
[17c] to turn the hearts of the fathers to the children
[17d] and the disobedient unto the wisdom of the just,
[17e] to make ready for the Lord a prepared people."

[18] But Zechariah said to the angel, "How am I to know this? I am an old man, and my wife is on in years." [19] The angel responded, "I am Gabriel; I stand in the presence of God. I have been sent to speak to you and announce to you this good news. [20] And behold, you will be reduced to silence and unable to speak until the day that these things will happen, because you did not believe my words which, nevertheless, will be fulfilled in due time."

[21] Meanwhile, the people were waiting for Zechariah, astonished at his delay in the Temple sanctuary. [22] And when he did come out, he was not able to speak to them; so they realized that he had seen a vision in the Temple sanctuary. For his part, Zechariah communicated with them by signs, remaining mute. [23] When his time of priestly service was completed, he went back to his home.

I would now ask the reader to study the Jesus side of the diptych in Table XI against the background of the pattern of angelic annunciations of birth in Table VIII. As indicated by the numbers in the diptych, the five basic steps of the angelic annunciation are all present: (1) the appearance of the angel; (2) fear; (3) the message; (4) the objection; (5) the sign. Within the message seven of the eight usual items are present; the only absent feature is the etymology of the name Jesus ("g" in the enumeration of Table VIII).

From this perfect adherence to literary pattern I would draw two observations. The first is that the stereotyped details in which Luke repeats the pattern need little further commentary. The real concern in this section must be to comment on the material in the Lucan annunciation that is *not* explained by the literary pattern—in other words, the material used by Luke to fill in the pattern. *In particular, this consists of the peculiar manner of the conception (virginal), the description of the future accomplishments of the child (32–33,35), and the portrait of Mary in 34 and 38.* These three items will serve as subject headings in the treatment to follow, in § 11 B, C, and D, respectively.

The second observation is that such a perfect adherence to literary form raises a question about the historicity of the stereotyped features in the Lucan story (as distinct from the filler material mentioned in the preceding paragraph). Of course, one may argue that the annunciation pattern really reflects a reasonable way of procedure. If an angel did appear to Mary, in what other way could Luke (or Mary) have described it? But one may also argue to the opposite effect. If Luke had little more than the idea of a pre-conception proclamation of Jesus' birth, he could fashion a narrative around this idea by incorporating it within the five standard steps of an OT annunciation of birth narrative without any assistance from historical memory. He could read the birth stories of Ishmael, Isaac, Samson, and Samuel and emerge with the story of an appearance of an angel of the Lord[8] to Jesus' mother, fear on her part, an address calling her by name and describing her with a qualifying phrase ("favored one"), a message telling her that she would conceive and bear a son and call his name Jesus, an objection on her part, and a reassuring sign. Luke's tendency to fashion such a story would be even more understandable if in

---

[8] The identification of this angel as Gabriel cannot be explained by the OT annunciation of birth pattern. Luke had a few items of information concerning the priestly origins of JBap (§ 10A). Could this information have given Luke the idea of identifying the angel of the Lord who appeared to Zechariah as Gabriel, a "liturgical angel" who appeared at hours of prayer and sacrifice in the Book of Daniel? (I am supposing that the annunciation of JBap's birth was at least as much a Lucan formation as the annunciation of Jesus' birth.) In that case, by a type of "back formation," Gabriel would have been introduced into the parallel annunciation of Jesus' birth. I say "back formation" because I think Luke first shaped the annunciation of Jesus' birth, and then the annunciation of JBap's birth.

TABLE XI: ANNUNCIATION DIPTYCH
(FIRST STAGE OF LUCAN COMPOSITION)

1:5–25 **Annunciation about JBap**	1:26–45,56 **Annunciation about Jesus**
Introduction of the dramatis personae: Zechariah and Elizabeth, of priestly family, aged, barren (5–7).	The angel Gabriel sent to Mary, a virgin betrothed to Joseph of the House of David (26–38).
Annunciation of the conception of JBap delivered by an angel of the Lord (Gabriel) to Zechariah in the Temple (8–23).	Annunciation of the conception of Jesus delivered by Gabriel to Mary in Nazareth.
Setting (8–10): The priestly customs: Zechariah's turn to offer incense. Core (11–20):*	
1. Angel of the Lord appeared to Zechariah	1. Gabriel came to Mary
2. Zechariah was startled	2. Mary was startled
3. The message: a. Zechariah	3. The message: a. Hail . . . Mary b. Favored one
c. Do not be afraid	c. Do not be afraid d. You will conceive
e. Elizabeth will bear you a son f. You will call his name John	e. and give birth to a son f. You will call his name Jesus
h. He will be great before the Lord, etc. (15–17)	h. He will be great, etc. (32–33)
4. How am I to know this? The angel's response (19)	4. How can this be? The angel's response (35)
5. The sign: Behold you will be reduced to silence.	5. The sign: Behold your relative has conceived.
Conclusion (21–23): Zechariah emerged from the Temple unable to speak. He went back home.	Mary responded with acceptance and the angel went away.
Epilogue: Elizabeth conceived; she reflected in seclusion in praise of the Lord (24–25).	*Epilogue:* Mary went to the house of Zechariah and greeted Elizabeth, who was filled with the Holy Spirit and proclaimed the praise of the mother of the Lord. Mary returned home (39–45,56).

* See Table VIII for the numbered steps in the annunciation.

---

pre-Lucan circles, popular reflection had begun to develop an annunciation tradition about the birth of Jesus.

It is here that we should bring into the discussion the Matthean annunciation narrative which has many of the same stereotyped features, but quite different filler material (except for the virginal conception and Davidic descent). As I argued in § 5, C1, there is reason to posit a pre-Matthean annunciation of birth; and I suggested that this pre-Gospel annunciation tradition upon which both Matthew and Luke drew concerned the birth of Jesus as the Davidic Messiah. Motivated by this tradition,[4] independently each evangelist fashioned a narrative of the annunciation of Jesus' birth which would suit the main lines of the respective infancy narrative. Matthew fashioned the story of an annunciation to Joseph because he was working with an infancy narrative based on the careers of the patriarch Joseph and the baby Moses in Egypt. Luke fashioned the story of an annunciation to Mary in whom he saw symbolic possibilities as a representative of the "poor" remnant of Israel (the *anawim* to be discussed in § 12, C2 below). In footnote 45, § 4, and footnote 74, § 5, we saw OT antecedents for the variation between Joseph and Mary as recipients of the annunciation.

The judgment that the Lucan annunciation pattern may have been borrowed from OT models and that therefore the appearance of an angel to Mary may not be historical tradition should not be equated with a denial of divine revelation pertinent to the birth of Jesus. The discussion of the material that Luke has fitted into the annunciation pattern will begin with the topic of the virginal conception. Precisely since this is a feature that cannot be explained from the OT annunciation pattern, we have to seek other origins for the concept of a virginal conception; and history may enter at this point. If there was a historical factor in the virginal conception (and I show in Appendix IV that this suggestion must be taken seriously), seemingly Mary should have received some divinely given insight. My contention is that, if there was such a revelation, the way in which it could be pictured and described was supplied to Luke by OT birth narratives.[5]

B. *The Virginal Conception (1:34)*

In 1:27 Luke tells us twice that Mary was a virgin at the time of the annunciation. This detail is not something that can be explained from the literary pattern of OT annunciations of birth since none of the classic instances cited in Table VIII concerned a woman who was a virgin. A conception by a virgin who had not known a man (1:34) would be something more startling in the biblical record than the oft-attested conception

---

4 I am deliberately using the vague word "tradition" because I do not want to commit myself to a fixed story that each drew upon. I think rather of a tendency in popular reflection to construct an annunciation of the birth of the Davidic Messiah, perhaps a tendency already at work in Judaism and adapted to Jesus by Christians.

5 The remark of McHugh, *Mother*, 128, is all the more significant because he is conservative: "It is therefore reasonable to begin by asking whether the Annunciation to Mary is not Luke's way of presenting to the reader an account of some more spiritual and wholly interior experience, of which no bystander could have been a witness."

by a set of parents whose barrenness God had overcome. It would be consonant with a theology of a new creation wherein God's Spirit, active in the first creation of life (Gen 1:2), was active again.

However, the existence of the theme of a virginal conception in Luke has been sharply challenged in different ways;[6] and before we can move in the theological direction I have just indicated, we must settle several questions. First, does the present Lucan account truly contain the idea of a virginal conception? Second, if it does, has this idea been secondarily introduced into an account that originally did not contain it? Third, how are we to understand the logic of the question asked by Mary in 1:34?

1. Does the Present Account Contain a Virginal Conception?

While an affirmative answer has usually been assumed, recently J. A. Fitzmyer[7] argued: "When this account is read in and for itself—without the overtones of the Matthean annunciation to Joseph—every detail of it could be understood of a child to be born to Mary in the usual human way. . . ." What has made such an assertion possible is the fact that Luke has no explicit statement that Mary did not have sexual relations with Joseph after the annunciation, a statement comparable to Matt 1:25.[8] Theoretically, if Mary and Joseph had relations and the child was naturally conceived, Luke might still have looked upon the conception as the work of the Holy Spirit, on the grounds that an angel had foretold the conception and that the child was to have a unique role as God's Son.

I would agree with the majority of scholars that Luke *does* intend a virginal conception; but before I present my reasons, I must mention a common argument that in my judgment is not convincing, namely, that the Lucan narrative clearly refers to a virginal conception because it has woven through it an exegesis of Isa 7:14.[9] Two features are often selected as linking Luke 1:26–38 and Isa 7:10–14:[10] (a) In Luke 1:27 Joseph is said to be of "the House of David," and the Isaian sign is addressed to the "House of David" (7:12). (b) In Luke 1:27 Mary is twice called a "virgin," and in 1:31 Mary is told, "You will conceive in your womb and give

6 I am not speaking here of challenges to the historicity of the virginal conception; I shall treat those in Appendix IV. I am speaking of challenges about Luke's intent and/or that of his sources.

7 Fitzmyer, "Virginal Conception," 566–67.

8 We should remember, however, that Matthew asserts this as part of his apologetics against any suggestion of illegitimacy. Luke shows no apologetic tendency here; he does not allow any possibility of scandal to touch Mary, for he introduces her as a virgin. Indeed, Luke omits all mention of when the conception took place or of when Joseph took her to his home.

9 This argument is accepted by such scholars as Vögtle, "Offene," 46; and Schürmann, *Lukasevangelium*, 62–63.

10 There are more points of comparison (see Fitzmyer, "Virginal Conception," 568), but many of them are insignificant, e.g., the common use of "Lord."

birth to a son, and you will call his name. . . ." This is thought to echo Isa 7:14: "Behold, the virgin will conceive and will give birth to a son, and you will call his name. . . ."[11] By way of general comment, let me first note that Matthew added Isa 7:14 to a scene that *already contained* the virginal conception (§ 5, B2), and so we cannot presuppose that only through meditation on that text did Christian writers come to the idea of Mary's virginity. Moreover, the two features that seemingly link Luke and Isaiah are far from convincing. The first feature involving the concept of Davidic descent[12] is shared with Matthew's annunciation scene and may have been part of the pre-Gospel annunciation tradition about the birth of the Messiah, without any necessary reference to Isa 7:14. As for the second feature, much of it is not peculiar to Isa 7:14 but is common to OT annunciations of birth. To Hagar it is said, "Behold, you are with child and will give birth to a son, and you will call his name . . ." (Gen 16:11). And so I would agree with Fitzmyer that there is no way of knowing that Luke was drawing upon Isa 7:14.

However, in disagreement with Fitzmyer,[18] I would use another argument to show that Luke was thinking of a virginal conception. As I indicated in § 10D, while the NT writers admit that JBap preceded Jesus, they make him subordinate to Jesus; and Luke extends this outlook to the infancy narrative by placing an annunciation of JBap's birth before the annunciation of Jesus' birth. Here too JBap comes first, but Jesus is greater. We can see this by comparing the respective descriptions:

- JBap is "great before the Lord" (1:15a), but Jesus is "great" without qualification (1:32a).
- JBap is "filled with the Holy Spirit even from his mother's womb" (1:15c), but the very conception of Jesus involves the Holy Spirit who "comes upon" Jesus' mother (1:35b).
- JBap will "make ready for the Lord a prepared people" (1:17e), but Jesus will actually rule over the house of Jacob/Israel and possess an eternal kingdom (1:33a,b).

Now this build-up of the superiority of Jesus would fail completely if JBap was conceived in an extraordinary manner and Jesus in a natural manner. But it would be continued perfectly if Jesus was virginally conceived, since this would be something completely unattested in previous

---

11 The LXX expression for "conceive" is *en gastri lēpsetai,* or perhaps *en gastri hexei* (footnote 34 in § 5). Luke has *syllēmpsē en gastri.*

12 If it is objected that Luke speaks not only of Davidic descent but more precisely of "the House of David," as does Isaiah, it must be remembered that the theme of the House of David is part of II Sam 7:8ff., the classic passage establishing the Davidic dynasty—a passage associated with the Messiah and definitely in mind in Luke 1:32–33. And so it may have been II Samuel rather than Isaiah which influenced Luke's phrasing. See C1 below.

18 See my answer to Fitzmyer in "Luke's Description."

manifestations of God's power. It is to the virginal conception rather than
to a natural conception that Elizabeth refers when she says of Mary: "Fortunate is she who believed that the Lord's words to her would find
fulfillment" (1:45). No belief would really be required if Mary was to
conceive as any other young girl would conceive.

Moreover, a study of the literary pattern of the two Lucan annunciations points to a virginal conception. In the JBap annunciation, when he
introduces the two parents (1:7), Luke tells us of the human difficulty in
their lives that prevents conception; and it is precisely that difficulty which
is resumed in Zechariah's "How" objection to the angel in 1:18. In the
Jesus annunciation, when he introduces Mary (1:27), Luke mentions
twice that she is a virgin;[14] and it is that factor which is resumed in Mary's
"How" objection to the angel in 1:34: "I have had no relations with a
man." If the age and barrenness of Zechariah and Elizabeth were divinely
overcome in the conception of JBap, the human difficulty of the virginity
of Mary must be overcome by divine power in the conception of Jesus. It
was creatively overcome without loss of virginity through the intervention
of the Holy Spirit, the "power from the Most High" (1:35), with the result that Jesus was only the "supposed son" of Joseph (3:23)—a designation that makes no sense if Jesus was the natural son of Joseph. Indeed, the
totality of the emphasis on Mary in ch. 1 of Luke is curious if Joseph was
equally the parent of Jesus.

2. Did the Original Account Contain a Virginal Conception?

While acknowledging that the present account implies a virginal conception, many scholars have suggested that this concept was added as an afterthought in vss. 34–35 to an account that did not originally contain it.[15]
(Often this theory contains the supposition that without Mary's question
in vs. 34, the conception would be described as natural.[16]) Of this group
relatively few think that the addition was post-Lucan, i.e., by a redactor or
scribe; and in my judgment Taylor has shown conclusively that the lan-

---

14 It is insufficient to claim that the reference to virginity in 1:27 is meant only to underline that Jesus was Mary's firstborn son (2:7,23). In the OT annunciations of birth, there is
never an annunciation to a married virgin; yet all of them are annuciations of the birth of
a mother's firstborn son.

15 Early proponents were H. Usener, *Religionsgeschichtliche Untersuchungen I: Das Weih-
nachsfest* (Bonn: Cohen, 1889), and J. Hillmann, "Die Kindheitsgeschichte Jesu nach Lukas
kritisch untersucht," *Jahrbuch für Protestantische Theologie* 17 (1891), 192–261. It was
made respectable by A. von Harnack, "Zu Lk 1:34–35," ZNW 2 (1901), 53–57. There are
minor variations: Kattenbusch would regard as added just the crucial clause "since I have
had no sexual relations with a man"; on the other hand, Bultmann and Burger would extend
the addition to include 36–37, while Clemen pushes it to 38. Other scholars who hold a
form of this theory are Cheyne, Conybeare, Holtzmann, Loisy, Schmiedel, J. Weiss, and
Zimmermann.

16 I find the virginal conception hinted at in 1:27, 1:45; and 3:23.

guage of 34–35 is Lucan.[17] The real question is whether 34–35 was added by Luke himself to a previous account (Lucan or pre-Lucan) that did not contain those verses.

In proposing his thesis that Luke received the tradition of a virginal conception after he had composed the annunciation narrative and that he intercalated this tradition in 34–35, Taylor has brought forward arguments for an addition; and the following are the most important: (a) 1:30–33 may be smoothly joined to 1:36–37, resulting in a long angelic message similar to that in 1:13–17. However, to argue from the parallelism of the two annunciations backfires in my judgment. The biblical pattern of the annunciation of birth (Table VIII) provides for a "How" question to be posed by the recipient and to be answered by a sign. It is farfetched to posit an earlier annunciation of Jesus' birth which just happened to be missing a regular feature of the annunciation pattern, and that Luke came along with an entirely new theological notion which he was able to fit in by inserting the missing feature. Luke 1:34–35 is perfectly parallel to 1:18–19,[18] and is just as integral to its respective annunciation. (b) The parallelism between 1:34 and 1:18 has been challenged, since Mary's "How" question receives no punishing response, while Zechariah's does, in the form of his being struck mute.[19] This difficulty disappears, however, if one regards both narratives as basically Lucan constructions to fit his theological interests. As I showed in § 10, B1, Luke modeled the Gabriel-Zechariah interchange on the Gabriel-Daniel interchange—Daniel was struck mute, and so was Zechariah. Luke has modeled Mary closely on Hannah, the mother of Samuel, and Mary's Magnificat will echo Hannah's canticle in I Sam 2; and so it does not fit Luke's purpose to have Mary afflicted in any way. (c) It is argued that vs. 35 has a different christology from vss. 32–33. In the earlier passage Jesus is called "Son of the Most High" in a context of Davidic expectations, while in 35 he is called "Son

17 Taylor, *Historical*, 40–87. The only non-Lucan word is *epei*, "since" (see NOTE); and an isolated conjunction amidst thirty-seven words is scarcely probative. The question pattern of 1:34 is Lucan both in wording and narrative style (Gewiess, "Marienfrage," 247–51); the clause "The Holy Spirit will come upon you" resembles the phrasing of Acts 1:8; the combination of spirit and power is Lucan, as is the designation "Most High" (NOTE on vs. 32). The structural resemblance between vss. 34 and 18 must be attributed to the final arranger of the chapter. For a minute analysis of the many Lucan features in 34–35, see Schneider, "Jesu," 109–10.

18 Even to the point that 1:13–17 can be smoothly joined to 1:20 (omitting 1:18–19), just as 1:30–33 can be smoothly joined to 1:36–37 (omitting 1:34–35). It is curious that scholars who have proposed the latter omission have not proposed the former.

19 Scholars concerned to defend the justice of God have tried to detect a subtle difference in the two "How" questions. Zechariah's "How am I to know this?" is said to imply a doubt about God's power, while Mary's "How can this be?" is said to accept God's power and only to wonder about the manner (so Machen). This is pure fancy. It neglects the fact that the answer to Mary assures her of God's power ("Nothing said by God can be impossible"), as well as the more important fact that Zechariah's "How" question is almost verbatim Abraham's "How" question in the LXX of Gen 15:8. Abraham's question is not treated as a doubting question at all; and Abraham is blessed, not afflicted.

of God" in a context of divine begetting. Thus, it is suggested that we have
a Hellenistic addition to a Jewish description of the Messiah. This contention is dubious on every score. An Aramaic fragment from Qumran puts
"son of the Most High" and "son of God" in parallelism,[20] and so the terminology scarcely proves Jewish and Hellenistic differences—a somewhat
dubious distinction in any case at this period of history. Moreover, below
when I discuss the sequence of the Davidic Messiah in vss. 32–33 and the
Son of God in 35, I shall stress that it reproduces a sequence in early
Christian creedal formulae, such as Rom 1:3–4. Thus, the christology in
the Lucan annunciation narrative offers no reason for suspecting a secondary addition.

The lack of persuasiveness in these three arguments leads to the logical
conclusion that the whole annunciation scene was composed by Luke and
that vss. 34–35 were always part of it.[21] However, there remains a fourth
and more difficult argument against integrity, namely, that the peculiar
way in which Mary's "How" question is phrased in 34 makes little sense in
the present context. Let us concentrate on that problem now.

3. The Logic of Mary's Question in 1:34

At the risk of simplifying unduly, I shall divide the scholarly responses
to this problem according to whether the emphasis is placed on the psychological or on the literary.

PSYCHOLOGICAL EXPLANATIONS. In the present sequence Mary is betrothed to Joseph; yet she is a virgin, and this means that she has not yet
been taken to her husband's home where she would have had marital relations with him (NOTE on "betrothed" in Matt 1:18). When she is told by
the angel that she will conceive a child, why does she raise a "How" question, as if there were some difficulty? Why does she not assume that the
conception will occur when she is taken to Joseph's home and has relations with him? If we leave aside the naive suggestion that she did not
know "the facts of life," how can we explain the psychology of her question.

A famous ancient solution is that Mary had already committed herself
to a lifetime of virginity. Her question in 34, which reads literally, "How
can this be, since I do not know a man?", is taken as if the verb were fu-

---

[20] This fragment from Qumran Cave IV (4Q243) is termed pseudo-Danielic; the crucial
line reads: "He will be said to be Son of God, and they will call him Son of the Most
High." See J. A. Fitzmyer, NTS 20 (1973–74), 391–94.
[21] Dibelius, "Jungfrauensohn," 12, makes the general observation that it is bad literary
judgment to excise from a legend the miracle that is at the core of it.

ture: How can this be, since I shall not have sexual relations with a man? Such a theory became popular as part of a belief that Mary remained a virgin all her life, even after the birth of Jesus.[22] It presupposes that her marriage with Joseph was a mutually agreed upon marriage of convenience in which he had agreed to respect her resolve of virginity and to lend her the protection of marriage, lest she be annoyed by more ardent suitors. To support this picture Joseph is portrayed as an elderly widower, in harmony with his statement in the *Protevangelium of James* 9:2: "I already have sons and am old, but she is a girl." This approach flourished at a time when Christian women were entering ascetic or monastic orders to live a celibate life; and so it was even proposed that Mary made a vow of virginity as if she were a nun.[23] The oldest attestation of the vow theory in the East is Gregory of Nyssa in 386 (PG 1140D–1141A), but it spread to the West through Ambrose and Augustine and became the classic interpretation of 1:34. As late as 1975 John McHugh feels compelled to assure his Roman Catholic readers that Mary's vow of virginity need not be considered an infallible teaching of the Church.[24] While such a vow or intention of virginity[25] might make Mary's question in 1:34 intelligible, it is totally implausible in the context supposed by Luke. In our knowledge of Palestinian Judaism, there is nothing that would explain why a twelve-year-old girl would have entered marriage with the intention to preserve virginity and thus not to have children. Luke (1:25,48) uses the words "disgrace" and "low estate" to express what the Jewish mentality toward such childlessness would be. This theory really only makes sense in subsequent Christianity where the virginal conception, plus the virginity of Jesus and Paul, have led to a re-evaluation of celibacy.

Some Roman Catholic scholars have sought to defend the theory of an intention of virginity with more sophisticated arguments. It is claimed, for instance, that the discovery of the Dead Sea Scrolls shows that there was a sect of Jews that placed value on virginity or celibacy. Actually the Scrolls say very little about this question, and our evidence largely comes from

22 The perpetual virginity or *virginitas post partum;* see footnote 2 in Appendix IV.

23 When the Church won acceptance in the Roman Empire with the edict of Milan (A.D. 311), asceticism replaced martyrdom as the chief public expression of sanctity. Mary was held up as a model to Egyptian "nuns" in a Coptic document printed in the proverbs of the Council of Nicaea (325); see the English text in Hilda Graef, *Mary*, I, 50.

24 McHugh, *Mother*, 446. He denies that there was a moral unanimity of the Church Fathers on this as the only interpretation of 1:34. I would be more trenchant and question what value the moral unanimity of the Fathers on such a historical detail might have. Unanimity of the Fathers has value in interpreting God's revelation, but the Fathers of the Church had no more knowledge about Mary's historical intentions than we have and no other way of gaining that knowledge than we have.

25 A recent Catholic writer, Graystone, *Virgin*, has a lengthy defense of Mary's resolve or intention of virginity—a resolve that was not a vow. It is instructive to compare two surveys of Roman Catholic opinions on this verse, Zerwick, "Quoniam," and Gewiess, "Marienfrage," with Zerwick defending the "traditional" view, and Gewiess adopting the position I shall accept.

descriptions of *Essene* celibacy by Josephus, Philo, and Pliny.[26] The most plausible explanation of Essene (Qumran) celibacy is that it was an extension of the abstinence from intercourse demanded of Jewish priests before they offered sacrifice in the Temple; and probably the celibacy was often temporary since the community had to preserve the Zadokite priestly line by having children. Such celibacy practiced in an ascetic, quasi-monastic community withdrawn from the mainstream of Palestinian life throws no light whatsoever on the supposed resolve of virginity made by a young village girl *who had entered matrimony*. Another explanation of Mary's determination to remain a virgin is that she had meditated on Isa 7:14 and had understood that the Messiah was to be born of a virgin.[27] A sophisticated form of this thesis is that the angel's annunciation in vs. 31 reminded her of Isa 7:14, and that her question in 34 is really a question about how the virgin mother of the Messiah was to conceive: "How is this conception to take place, since according to Isa 7:14 I am not to have relations with a man?"[28] This explanation in both its simple and its sophisticated form fails if there is no reference to Isa 7:14 in vs. 31, or if Jews did not understand Isa 7:14 as a reference to the Messiah, or if Isa 7:14 says nothing about a virginal conception—all three conditions are probably true, as we have seen.

A curious variant of the intention-of-virginity theory anticipates the literary explanations to be discussed below. McHugh[29] recognizes that vs. 34 is a Lucan literary device; but he suggests that Luke wrote the words "since I am not to have relations with a man" (note the future) in light of his knowledge that Mary remained a virgin all her life. In other words Mary's words do not reflect a pre-annunciation resolution to remain a virgin, but a resolution that was a response to the annunciation of a virginal conception—a resolution deduced after the fact by Luke. Obviously this theory will have little appeal to Christians who do not accept the lifetime virginity of Mary. But even Christians who do accept it may react negatively to the dubious methodology of assuming without proof Lucan knowledge of Mary's lifetime virginity.[30] There is no indication whatsoever

---

[26] See JBC, article 68, #95; and H. Hübner, "Zölibat in Qumran?" NTS 17 (1970–71), 153–67. The Therapeutae in Egypt had celibate *women* (Philo *De Vita Contemplativa* 68 #155), but we do not know about the Essenes.

[27] Her perception is sometimes traced by Catholics to her immaculate conception, which told her that she was to be the mother of the Messiah. However, an intelligent belief in the immaculate conception does not presuppose any knowledge of it by either Mary or the NT writers. This doctrine is not necessarily based upon intimate information about Mary's origins passed down from the first century; rather, it is based on the insight that the sinlessness of Jesus should have affected his origins, and hence his mother.

[28] Audet, "L'annonce," 365–74.

[29] McHugh, *Mother*, 193–99.

[30] Acceptance of Mary's lifetime virginity does not necessarily posit a knowledge of it by Christians in NT times. If Mary had no further children, that could plausibly have been known and remembered. It is far less plausible, however, to assume that Mary gave a public

that any NT author had an interest in Mary's marital relations after Jesus was born. Such an interest is the hallmark of a later Christianity and cannot plausibly be invoked to interpret a crucial verse in the annunciation scene.

If one abandons the hypothesis of a married girl's resolution or vow of virginity as quite unlikely on the Palestinian scene, other attempts to find psychological plausibility suppose a misunderstanding. One theory is that Mary understood the angel's words in vs. 31 to mean that she was immediately becoming pregnant or was already so—not "you will conceive" but "you are conceiving,"[31] or "you have conceived." Since the child was or is conceived without relations with her husband, Mary is forced to ask the angel, "How can this be, since I have had no relations with a man?"[32] It is true that the Hebrew participial expression in the annunciation of birth narratives can be understood as either a present or a future (footnote 44, § 5), but Luke's Greek is clearly future. Any theory that Luke has mistranslated in vs. 31 is made unlikely by the presence of more future verbs in 35: the conception is yet to happen. And indeed it would violate the genius of the Lucan narrative to have the conception take place before Mary has given her consent in vs. 38.

Another theory posits a misunderstanding introduced by Luke. In a putative original story Mary was an *unmarried* virgin; and so when she was told that she was going to conceive a child, she naturally asked how "since I have no husband" (see NOTE on this translation for vs. 34). However, in the process of incorporating this original story into his infancy narrative, Luke was anxious to connect it to an independent narrative in ch. 2 wherein Mary was Joseph's wife. To make the connection obvious, Luke borrowed from the phraseology of 2:4-5 (Joseph was "of the house and

---

explanation of her subsequent childlessness by telling people that she had no sexual relations with Joseph. The history of the doctrine demands no handed-down family tradition of this type; rather it may have been logically derived from the contention that the "brothers" and "sisters" of Jesus were not truly siblings, when that contention was related to the psychological impact upon Mary of the virginal conception—ideas joined at a time when Christians were putting a priority on freely chosen lifetime virginity (footnote 23 above). For a detailed discussion of ancient Christian theories about the family relationship of the "brothers" of Jesus (Mark 3:31; 6:3; John 2:12; 7:3), see McHugh, *Mother*, 200-54. No NT author directs our attention to such a post-biblical problem.

31 The present translation is not really different from the instant future translation: "you are immediately to conceive." A peculiar variation of this theory was advanced by R. Reitzenstein, *Zwei religionsgeschichtliche Fragen* (Strassburg: Trübner, 1901), 112-31, who drew attention to a poorly preserved fragment from sixth-century Egypt giving the dialogue between the angel and Mary in a form different from that found in Luke and which, Reitzenstein claimed, represented an older story than the Lucan. There is a gap in the manuscript which Reitzenstein interpreted as an omission of "you will conceive in your womb"; and so he argued that in this dialogue Mary thought she was already pregnant; see the refutation by Machen, *Virgin Birth*, 189-90.

32 If one follows the instant future translation (previous footnote), Mary's question may be interpreted somewhat differently, e.g., "How can this be, since I am not supposed to have relations with my betrothed until the (still distant) time when I go to live at his home?" Gaechter, *Maria*, 89-98, proposes such an interpretation, but it makes the understanding of Luke's scene dependent upon information that Luke has not given us.

lineage of David"; Mary was "his betrothed") and introduced a modifying clause into 1:27: "to a virgin *betrothed to a man of the House of David whose name was Joseph.*"[88] This unfortunate addition created a problem for understanding 1:34 which previously made perfect sense. Simple and attractive as this explanation may be, it causes more problems than it resolves. It is always risky methodologically to assume that a writer does not see the contradictions in his own narrative. It is implausible that haphazardly Luke created a situation for Mary exactly like that in Matt 1:18, namely, that she conceived as a virgin betrothed to a Davidid named Joseph. If there was no relationship to Joseph in the original story, how was that story pertinent to the birth of a *Davidic* Messiah?[84] The parallelism that we have seen between the annunciations of JBap and of Jesus favors the originality of the present Lucan form in which both parents and their tribal origin are mentioned in the introduction (compare 1:5 and 1:27).

In the long run, the various attempts to make Mary's reaction in 34 more intelligible by positing a misunderstanding are no more acceptable than the attempts to posit a resolve or vow of virginity.

LITERARY EXPLANATION. This approach contends that 1:34–35 make perfect sense in the context of the annunciation and that these verses were always part of a Lucan scene which would make little christological sense without them. However, it abandons the idea that the scene has a primary concern with Mary's psychology, as if it were meant to explain how she gained a knowledge of the way in which her child was conceived.[85] It is rather meant to tell *the reader* how the child was conceived and hence to explain his identity.

Intrinsic to this explanation is the contention that vss. 34–35 reflect standard features in biblical annunciations of birth. In Table VIII I showed that the fourth step in the annunciation pattern contained an ob-

---

88 The cross-influence is clear; but I join the larger number of scholars who think that it went in the other direction. In order to connect ch. 2 to ch. 1, Luke composed an introduction to ch. 2 that drew upon what he had already written in ch. 1 (see § 14, footnote 7, below).

84 This theory has appealed (with variations) to scholars like Kattenbusch, Sahlin, and Leaney; but the most famous proponent was Dibelius, "Jungfrauensohn," 12, who argued that in the original story Mary was of the House of David. There is no other biblical evidence for such a tradition (see NOTE on 27); and if the genealogy of Luke 3:23ff. has pre-Lucan roots, all the recognizable pre-Lucan or pre-Gospel strata have Joseph as the Davidid.

85 Behind many of the Roman Catholic psychological explanations of 1:34 discussed above, there is the assumption that we are dealing with a conversation that actually took place between Mary and Gabriel. (I have already pointed out in A above that the historicity of 1:26–38 is not the most plausible assumption.) However, even if one recognizes that we are dealing with a narrative constructed by Luke himself, one must still seek to understand the logic of that narrative. I am suggesting that the key to that logic is not a concern with *Mary's* learning about the virginal conception but a concern with the reader's learning about that conception and its christological implications.

jection by the visionary as to how the divinely announced conception could take place (in light of the human obstacles), and that the fifth step involved an angelic reassurance. Such steps enabled the biblical authors to explain to the readers how God's plan was going to work out. Although there was a pre-Gospel tradition of an annunciation of the birth of the Davidic Messiah, it was the (respective) evangelist who shaped that tradition into its present narrative form. And so the phrasing of the "How" question in 34 and the angelic response in 35 is determined by Luke's intention. He wished in these verses to explain the identity of the Davidic Messiah whose birth the angel had proclaimed in 31–33, namely, that he is the Son of God begotten through the creative power of the Holy Spirit. Mary's objection in vs. 34 vocalizes in dialogue what the reader has already learned in narrative in 1:27 (i.e., she is a virgin), even as Zechariah's objection in 1:18 vocalized in dialogue what the reader had learned in narrative in 1:7. The objection in each case calls attention to the human impossibility to be overcome by God. The problem of why Mary would mention her virginity as an obstacle to conception (since she could have had sexual relations with Joseph to beget a child after the annunciation) disappears once we shift away from the psychological quest— Luke phrases Mary's objection the way he does because he has the tradition that the divine plan excluded a human begetting of the child. With male agency excluded by the "since" clause in vs. 34, the "How" part of the objection opens the way for the angel to explain the divine creative begetting in 35. Mary is a spokeswoman for Luke's christological message even as Gabriel is a spokesman; and between them they fill in the picture of the Messiah's conception as God's Son, a conception not through marital intercourse (Mary's contribution) but through the Holy Spirit (Gabriel's contribution).

This interpretation of the logic of 1:34–35 is not purely literary as if Luke could have fitted any content he wished into steps 4 and 5 of the standard pattern. His narrative was determined both by the pre-Gospel tradition of the annunciation of the Davidic Messiah's birth (which dictated the general literary form) and by the pre-Gospel tradition of the christology of divine sonship through begetting by the Holy Spirit—a christology which had been applied to Jesus' birth in terms of a virginal conception.[36] From my analysis of Matthew's narrative of the annunciation to Joseph (§ 5, C2), I concluded that already on a pre-Gospel level these two elements had been joined, and that the popular tradition of the

[36] One must explain why the christology of divine sonship, when it was associated with Jesus' birth, found expression in terms of a virginal conception. In Appendix IV I shall suggest that a historical catalyst was required; and so I do not regard the theologoumenon interpretation of the virginal conception as adequate, as if the concept of divine sonship would have automatically led to the conclusion that Jesus had no human father.

annunciation of the Davidic Messiah's birth had become the vehicle of a christological statement about the begetting of God's Son, which thus became the message (step 3) in the angelic annunciation of Jesus' birth. I think that this literary explanation[87] in which a pre-Gospel tradition plays a role offers a totally satisfactory explanation for Mary's question in 1:34.

C. *The Future Accomplishments of the Child* (*1:32,33,35*)

In A above when I was studying 1:26–38 in the light of the standard annunciation pattern, I pointed out the features in the narrative that are standard to OT annunciations, and I said that our real concern here must be to comment on the material that is *not* totally explained by the annunciation pattern. I mentioned three such items, the first of which (the virginal conception) we have just finished discussing. At the end that discussion led me to mention the content of the angelic message to Mary (step 3 in Table VIII), which constitutes the second of the items to be commented upon. The message consists of vss. 31–33 and 35.[88] Verse 31 needs no comment for it is the standard announcement of pregnancy (step 3, items d,e,f). Verses 32,33,35 constitute item h in step 3 (the future accomplishments of the child), but we must determine whence Luke derived his description of those accomplishments, even as we had to discuss the background of the Lucan description of the future accomplishments of JBap in 1:14–17. In that discussion (§ 10, B2) it seemed that the message about the future of JBap was consonant with and even derived from what Luke knew of JBap in the body of the Gospel describing the ministry of Jesus, i.e., from a Christian picture of JBap which gave him an Elijah-like role as a forerunner of Jesus. Similarly, I shall argue here that Luke composed his description of the future accomplishments of Jesus upon the basis of Christian christological reflection.

We saw that the message of Matthean annunciation to Joseph concerned the Who and the How of Jesus' identity (§ 5A)—he was the *son of David* as the genealogy indicated; yet he was this not through physical conception by the Davidid Joseph but by divine conception through the Holy Spirit, which made him Emmanuel ("God with us") or *God's Son* (Matt 2:15).

---

[87] Since I drew attention above to a number of psychological explanations offered by Roman Catholics, I should note that the literary explanation of the objection in 1:34 is now becoming widely accepted among Catholic scholars in all countries, e.g., Muñoz Iglesias, Ortensio da Spinetoli, Gewiess, and Schürmann. McHugh moves in that direction but then shies away from its full implications (footnote 29 above).

[88] To some extent vs. 35 has a double role: it is part of the annunciation message (step 3) and yet it comes after Mary's objection and is an element in the angelic reassurance (step 5).

Luke's annunciation to Mary has the same two facets of Jesus' identity and the same How. Instead of speaking of Jesus as the "son of David" Luke describes him as the Davidic Messiah in vss. 32–33, but more clearly than Matthew Luke speaks of Jesus as the "Son of God" in 35.

1. The Davidic Messiah (32–33)

Since in my hypothesis there lay behind Luke (and behind Matthew) a pre-Gospel annunciation of the birth of the Davidic Messiah, it is not surprising to find the Davidic theme so strong in the first half of the angelic annunciation of Jesus' future greatness. Indeed, Gabriel's words in 1:32–33 constitute a free interpretation of II Sam 7:8–16, the promise of the prophet Nathan to David which came to serve as the foundation of messianic expectation. We can see this if we set the two passages side by side, italicizing the crucial phrases in II Samuel:

> Luke 1:
> 32a: He will be great and will be called Son of the Most High.
> 32b: And the Lord God will give him the throne of his father David;
> 33a: and he will be king over the House of Jacob forever,
> 33b: and there will be no end to his kingdom.

> II Sam 7:
> 9: I shall make for you a *great* name . . .
> 13: I shall establish *the throne of his kingdom forever*.
> 14: I shall be his father, and he will be *my* son . . .
> 16: And your *house* and your *kingdom* will be made sure *forever*.

The phrases from this promise to David are echoed also in the royal psalms pertinent to the coronation and lineage of the Davidic king, e.g., God calls the king His son in Ps 2:7 (a psalm verse which Luke applies to Jesus in 3:22); and God says in Ps 89:30(29): "I shall establish his lineage forever, and his throne as the days of heaven."[39]

The idea of an annunciation of the birth of the Davidic Messiah, which is pre-Lucan and pre-Matthean, may have already existed in pre-Christian Judaism; and if so, it is not incredible that the message in that Jewish annunciation would have echoed II Sam 7:8–16. We have interesting evidence of the messianic interpretation of it in 4QFlorilegium, a Qumran *pesher* (interpretation) of II Sam 7:10–14, followed by a *pesher* on lines

---

[39] Also in Davidic royalty passages in the prophets, e.g., Isa 9:5–6(6–7): "For to us a child is born; to us a son is given . . . his dominion is vast and peaceful forever, upon the throne of David and over his kingdom . . . from this time forth and forever."

from the psalms.[40] Let us look at a few lines of it, first the text (italicized), then the *pesher* or interpretation:

> *The Lord declares that He will build you a House* (II Sam 7:11). *I shall raise up your lineage after you* (7:12). *I shall establish the throne of his kingdom forever* (7:13). *I shall be his father, and he will be my son* (7:14).
>
> The "he" is the Shoot [*ṣemaḥ*] of David who will arise with the Interpreter of the Law who [will rule] in Zion in the last days. As it is written, "I shall raise up the fallen hut of David" [Amos 9:11]—the "fallen hut of David" is he who shall arise to save Israel.[41]

We note that the Qumran interpretation takes out select lines from II Sam 7, just as Luke apparently did. It has shifted the focus of Nathan's promise from a continual line of kings[42] to a single Davidic king, the messianic "shoot"[43] who will arise in the last days, even as Luke has applied the Samuel passage to Jesus. The "forever" for both Qumran and Luke is, then, not an endless series of reigns by different kings, but an eschatological description. And so there is nothing distinctively Christian in Gabriel's words in vss. 32–33 of Luke, except that the expected Davidic Messiah has been identified with Jesus.

2. The Son of God through the Power of the Holy Spirit (35)

It is in response to Mary's "How" question about the conception of the Messiah (vs. 34) that Luke has Gabriel give us the more important christological aspect of Jesus' identity:

35b: The Holy Spirit will come upon you,
35c: and power from the Most High will overshadow you.
35d: Therefore, the child to be born will be called holy—Son of God.

Of course, even in this christological statement Luke continues to use OT terminology, for all early Christian christology was vocalized in the reinterpreted terms of Jewish expectations. And not surprisingly, the terms which Luke uses in 1:35 have a relation to the description of the Davidic Messiah he has given in 1:32,33. Isaiah 11:1–2 describes a coming of the

---

40 For the nature of this document, correcting J. Allegro's analysis of it as a midrash on the last days, see JBC, article 68, #80. It is noteworthy that the theme of II Sam 7 is carried on by passages from the psalms, including Ps. 2. As I have indicated, Luke may be thinking of II Sam 7 through or along with echoes of it in the psalms.

41 4QFlor or 4Q174, lines 10–13.

42 Notice, nevertheless, that in the lines it quotes from II Sam 7, the "House" of David is mentioned, even as that motif appears in Luke 1:27. See footnote 12 above.

43 For this term, see p. 212 above.

Spirit of the Lord upon the Davidic branch (*nēṣer*). Isaiah 4:2–3 associates being called "holy" with the day of the Davidic "shoot" (*ṣemaḥ*).[44] The term "Son of God" is a parallel to "Son of the Most High" (footnote 20 above), and both echo God's designation of the Davidic ruler as His "son" in II Sam 7:14 and Ps 2:7. But the way these ideas are combined in 1:35 takes us out of the realm of Jewish expectation of the Messiah into the realm of early Christianity. The action of the Holy Spirit and the power of the Most High come not upon the Davidic king but upon his mother. We are not dealing with the adoption of a Davidid by coronation as God's son or representative; we are dealing with the begetting of God's Son in the womb of Mary through God's creative Spirit. If vss. 32–33 could have been part of a purely Jewish narrative announcing the Messiah's birth, as we saw from the Qumran parallel, the same cannot be said of vs. 35, since, as we have seen, there was no Jewish expectation that the Messiah would be God's Son in the sense of having been conceived without a male parent.[45]

The real parallel for the conglomeration of ideas in 1:35 is not an OT passage but the early Christian formulations of christology. I have already discussed these formulations in general (§ 1, A2) and in relation to Matthew's annunciation narrative (§ 5, A1). There I pointed out that the Davidic king language of Ps 2:7 ("You are my son; today I have begotten you") is reinterpreted as applicable to the resurrection in Acts 13:32–33, even as the coronation language of Ps 110:1 ("Sit at my right hand") is made applicable to the resurrection in Acts 2:32–36. A passage that threw light on Matthean thought throws even more light on Lucan phraseology, namely, Rom 1:3–4, which describes God's Son:

3: Born of the seed of David according to the flesh;
4: designated Son of God in power according to the Holy Spirit [Spirit of Holiness] as of resurrection from [of] the dead.[46]

---

[44] For Matthew's application of Isa 4:3 to Jesus, see § 7, B3.

[45] Miguens, *Virgin*, 141–43, is partially right when he claims that the description of Jesus in 1:32,33 does not go beyond the doctrine of the OT; but he is wrong when he goes on to place 1:35 in the same category. He does not distinguish between some of the *terms* in 1:35 (which are echoes of the OT) and the main idea in 1:35.

[46] This text is doubly complicated. First, many think that this formula did not necessarily have the same meaning in the pre-Pauline stage that it has in the Pauline stage. (See H.-W. Bartsch, TZ 23 [1967], 329–39.) By stating that the whole formula applies to God's Son, is Paul correcting the pre-Pauline formula? Is he affirming that in the flesh Jesus was already God's Son and that what the resurrection added or clarified was the element of power? Second, even on the Pauline level the passage is difficult to translate. For Paul's use of *ginesthai* (which I have translated "born") rather than *gennan*, see Appendix IV(A). The verb *orizein* ("designated") can mean "appoint, set up." I have translated the preposition *ek* before "ressurection" with the ambiguous "as of"; it is not clear whether it means "by" or "from the time of." Nor is it clear whether Jesus' resurrection is meant by "resurrection of the deal [plural]." One may debate whether "Spirit of Holiness" (*pneuma hagiōsynēs*) should be capitalized and whether it is exactly the same as "Holy Spirit." Certainly many Christians, accustomed to associate the gift of the Holy Spirit with the resurrection of Jesus, would have interpreted it that way. It is interesting that in referring to the baptism of Jesus,

In the discussion that follows I am not suggesting that Luke drew upon this particular formula.[47] Most scholars agree that it was pre-Pauline, and that Paul used it because it would be familiar to the community in Rome which he himself had not evangelized. If so, it may serve as an example of a widespread christological formulation and thought pattern. The movement in Rom 1:3–4 from Davidic descendant to Son of God is similar to the movement from Davidic Messiah to Son of God that one sees in comparing Luke 1:32,33 and 1:35. The conglomeration of terms that one finds in the second half of the Romans formula (designation as Son of God, power, Holy Spirit) is remarkably like the conglomeration of terms in the second half of the angelic message reported in Luke 1:35 (called Son of God, power, Holy Spirit).

This similarity is not accidental, as may be seen from the "backwards development" of christology which I sketched in § 1, A2. The terms that the Romans formula associates with resurrection appear in the Gospels in the context of the baptism of Jesus. There the Holy Spirit descends upon Jesus as a voice from heaven declares "You are my Son" (Luke 3:22), and then Jesus goes back to Galilee "in the power of the Spirit" (4:14). Luke summarizes the picture in Acts 10:37–38: "After the baptism which John preached, God anointed Jesus of Nazareth with the Holy Spirit and with power." Thus, when the christological moment was moved back from the resurrection to the beginning of the ministry, the christological language of "called Son of God, power, Holy Spirit" was also moved back. And in the Lucan infancy narrative where the christological moment has been moved back still farther to the conception, the christological language has quite consistently been moved back too. That is what I meant when I maintained that the angelic message in 1:35 is simply the Lucan version of an early Christian christological formula. However, whereas the declaration of Jesus as God's Son at the resurrection or enthronement in heaven or at the baptism involved a figurative begetting (see respectively Acts 13:33 and the Western text of Luke 3:22, both of which have God state, "Today I have begotten you"), the association of the christological formula with the conception involves a more literal begetting. The "coming" of the Holy Spirit in 1:35b (which explains why the child is called holy in 1:35d) and the overshadowing by the power of the Most High in

---

Testament of Levi 18:7 says: "A Spirit . . . of sanctification [*hagiasmos*] shall rest upon him in the water."

47 Many authors have drawn attention to the similarities between the formula in Romans and the annunciation message in Luke, e.g., Danell, "St. Paul," 99–100; Orr, *Virgin Birth*, 120–21. Often, however, their conception of the relationship was oversimplified—either that Paul knew Luke's Gospel and was drawing upon it, or that Luke, the companion of Paul, knew Paul's letter to the Romans. (Closely related to this is the thesis that the formula in Romans indicates a Pauline knowledge of the virginal conception; see footnote 6 in Appendix IV.) Much more plausible is the thesis of a common Christian theological statement of divine sonship, formulated and applied differently in Romans and in Luke.

1:35c (which explains why the child is called Son of God in 1:35d) *really* beget the child as God's Son[48]—there is no adoption here.

Yet, as I have emphasized in the NOTES on "come upon" and "overshadow" in 1:35b,c, the begetting is not quasi-sexual as if God takes the place of a male principle in mating with Mary. There is more of a connotation of creativity. Mary is not barren, and in her case the child does not come into existence because God cooperates with the husband's generative action and removes the sterility. Rather, Mary is a virgin who has not known man, and therefore the child is totally God's work—a new creation. If the appearance to Zechariah, a priest, took place in the Jerusalem Temple as a sign of continuity with OT institutions, the coming[49] of Gabriel to Mary takes place in Nazareth, a town to which no OT expectation was attached, as a sign of the total newness of what God is doing.[50] If the prophetic Spirit filled JBap from his mother's womb (1:15,41,44), the Spirit that comes upon Mary is closer to the Spirit of God that hovered over the waters before creation in Gen 1:2.[51] The earth was void and without form when that Spirit appeared; just so Mary's womb was a void[52] until through the Spirit God filled it with a child who was His Son. In the annunciation of the birth of JBap we heard of a yearning and prayer on the part of the parents who very much wanted a child; but since Mary is a virgin who has not yet lived with her husband, there is no yearning for or human expectation of a child—it is the surprise of creation. No longer are we dealing with human request and God's generous fulfillment; this is God's initiative going beyond anything man or woman has dreamed of. If in the message of the JBap annunciation, there was a reminder of evil to be

---

[48] I have stressed in the NOTES on 1:32,35 that being "called" Son of the Most High or Son of God is tantamount here to being God's Son, and that Luke does not think of a preexistent Son of God, as does John. Only in second-century writings do we find the Lucan and Johannine concepts combined into an incarnation of a pre-existent deity (John) in the womb of the virgin Mary (Luke). See Ignatius *Ephesians* vii 2, and *Smyrnaeans* i 1, combined with *Magnesians* viii 2; also Aristides *Apology* xv 1; Justin *Apology* I xxi and xxxiii; Melito *Discourse on Faith* 4 (*Corpus Apologetarum* 9:420). This is treated by Hoben, *Virgin Birth*, 20–21.

[49] I have already noted that Gabriel's annunciation to Mary does not have the Danielic echoes that are so apparent in his annunciation to Zechariah. Similarly we are told in 1:28 that "he came" to Mary, instead of the more apocalyptic "he appeared" (1:11).

[50] Although there are Isaian echoes in the Lucan scene, I see no evidence that "a city of Galilee known as Nazareth" (1:26) is an echo of "Galilee of the Gentiles" from Isa 8:23 (RSV 9:1—cf. Matt 4:15). In Lucan salvation history the passage from Jew to Gentile is dramatized in terms of passage from Jerusalem to Rome rather than in terms of passage from Jerusalem to Galilee.

[51] The author of Genesis may have meant *rûaḥ* (LXX *pneuma*) in the sense of "wind" rather than "spirit"; but certainly later writings understood a reference to God's creative breath or spirit (Ps 33:6; Judith 16:14; *II Baruch* 21:4). The theme is well expressed in Ps 104:30: "When you send forth your Spirit, they are created; and you renew the face of the earth." For references to the creative or life-giving Spirit, see Ezek 37:14; Job 27:3; 33:4; Rom 8:11; John 20:22; and the excellent treatment by Legrand, "Fécondité," 787–88.

[52] In B3 above I pointed out that Luke (1:25,48) uses the words "disgrace" and "low estate" to describe the womb that has not produced the fruit of children. This concept of the womb of Mary as a void that God fills (1:53) is quite the opposite of the vow of virginity theory of later Christian writers. Again see Legrand, "Fécondité."

faced ("the disobedient" in 1:17d), here the message is entirely positive, reflecting the word of the creator God who made everything good.

Perhaps the observant reader has noticed that in tracing 1:35 to early christological formulations reapplied to the conception, while I found background for terms like "Holy Spirit," "power," and "called Son of God," I did not have an example of "overshadow" applied to the resurrection or the baptism. However, this image is applied in a christological setting at the transfiguration. In all three accounts (Luke 9:34 and par.) we are told that a cloud signaling the divine presence *overshadowed* those present, and a voice came from the cloud saying, "This is my [beloved] Son." The parallelism between the baptism and the transfiguration has long been recognized: in one the Holy Spirit descends upon Jesus, while in the other the cloud overshadows;[53] but in both the divine voice speaks the same message from above. The baptism reveals the christological mystery of divine sonship to the reader; the transfiguration reveals it to chosen disciples.[54] From this comparison we may see that descent of the Holy Spirit and overshadowing by the divine presence were alternative ways of expressing how God was active in establishing and confirming that sonship. Thus Luke is perfectly correct in placing the two images in parallelism in 1:35b,c.[55] And this double expression of God's activity makes it clear that when the child is called "holy" and "Son of God," these designations are true to what he is and to his origins.

If I may return to the formulation in Rom 1:3–4, there Davidic descent and designation as Son of God are contrasted. "According to the flesh" and in his lifetime Jesus was recognized as a Davidid; but "according to a Holy Spirit" and as of the resurrection Jesus was designated Son of God. In the Lucan annunciation there is no real contrast between the two parts of Gabriel's message: the Son of the Most High in whom the Davidic royal promise is fulfilled is the child to be called the Son of God, conceived

---

[53] The preference for overshadowing in the transfiguration is to be related to Peter's idea of building *tabernacles* for Jesus, Moses, and Elijah (Luke 9:33 and par.). As we shall see in E below, the OT background of overshadowing is the descent of God's glory upon the Tabernacle or Temple.

[54] Legrand, "L'arrière-plan," 170–83, is excellent on this point. In the transfiguration, he maintains, the apocalyptic coming of the Son of Man with the clouds of heaven (e.g., Mark 14:62, drawing upon Dan 7:13) has been de-apocalypticized for Luke. The cloud of divine presence overshadows one who is already Son of God and Son of Man (Luke 9:44) upon earth.

[55] It is true that the transfiguration has overshadowing with a cloud while Luke 1:35c has overshadowing with power. (The word "power" does not occur in the Lucan transfiguration scene, but see the verse which immediately precedes the transfiguration in Mark 9:1; also II Peter 1:16–17.) Some light is cast on how power might overshadow by the only other use of "overshadow" in the Lucan writings, namely, Acts 5:15–16 wherein Peter's shadow overshadows the sick and they are healed. Peter received the Spirit at Pentecost and this brought divine power: "You will receive power when the Holy Spirit has come upon you" (Acts 1:8); it is by that power that he heals (3:12); and sometimes this life-giving power is brought to bear when his shadow falls upon the sick. The creation of life in the womb of Mary is simply a higher level of the combination of Spirit, divine power, and overshadowing. See P. W. van der Horst, "Peter's Shadow," NTS 23 (1976–7), 204–12.

through the Holy Spirit and power. By moving the christological moment from the resurrection to the conception, Luke tells us that there never was a moment on this earth when Jesus was not the Son of God.[56] Now neither baptism nor resurrection gives a new status in contrast with what went before; these events reveal to a wider audience what was already there.

D. *The Portrait of Mary as Handmaid* (*1:38*)

Mary has two lines of response in the annunciation. We have already seen that the first line, the question-objection of 1:34, represents part of the stereotyped pattern of biblical annunciations of birth (Table VIII). It is Luke's way of calling attention to the virginal conception and offers an entrée into the christological formula of 1:35. If therefore it is likely that this verse does not constitute a historical reminiscence of Mary's reaction to the revelation of the forthcoming conception, some have sought a historical reminiscence in the final response of Mary to the annunciation in 1:38 —*ipsissima verba* expressing her humility as the handmaid of the Lord. This needs comment precisely because the type of response we find in 1:38 is not a step in the stereotyped annunciation pattern. It is lacking even from the JBap annunciation; and it constitutes one of the three items that I have said cannot be explained simply as an expected feature in this literary form.

In treating the previous scene I suggested that Luke drew the portraits of those who are not mentioned in the body of the Gospel (Zechariah and Elizabeth) from OT models (Abraham and Sarah), whereas he drew the portrait of the future JBap from what he knew of the descriptions of JBap in the Gospel story of the ministry. I suggest that he has done the same thing here, and that the portrait of Mary in 1:38 is shaped from Luke's account of her in the ministry.[57]

---

[56] Exactly what Luke means by "Son of God" is not totally clear. I have stressed that pre-existence is not involved (footnote 48 above). I think Lyonnet, "L'Annonciation," 66, is too narrow when he sees only two choices: to take it in a broad sense as equivalent to messianic king or in a proper sense as equivalent to "God." It must be remembered that Luke uses "son of God" for Adam, who had an origin different from other men, because of the direct creative action of God's Spirit (see Luke 3:38). Luke is certainly using "Son of God" in a proper sense in 1:35d, but he is not necessarily saying what Ignatius said twenty or thirty years later: "Our God, Jesus Christ, was conceived of Mary" (*Ephesians* xviii 2; also vii 2).

[57] Filling in a story in this way is a Lucan technique. In the conversation between the risen Jesus and the two disciples on the road to Emmaus, the discussion of the death and resurrection of Jesus in terms of OT fulfillment (Luke 24:19-27) is simply a digest in conversational form of the preaching of the early Church on this problem as Luke presents it in Acts. Luke had no historical tradition of what was said on this occasion; at most he had a tradition of a "private" appearance of the risen Jesus to two disciples, a tradition which he filled in plausibly.

Mary appears in only one scene in the common Synoptic tradition.[58] As it is narrated in Mark 3, it has two parts. First, in 3:20–21 "his own"[59] go out to seize him because the frenzied pace of his ministry is provoking charges of madness. Second, in 3:31–35 his mother and his brothers arrive and stand outside the place where he is, asking for him; but Jesus responds that the listeners seated around him who do the will of God are his mother and brothers. The first part of the Marcan scene reveals the attitude of Jesus' relatives toward him, and it is scarcely one of belief. The second part reveals Jesus' attitude toward family relationship. His true family is established through a relationship to God, not by human origin. (The Johannine parallel is in 2:4 where Jesus resists his mother's interference, seemingly because she has no role in the coming of his "hour.") When the two parts of the Marcan scene are read together, the impact of 3:33–34 is very strong:

> And Jesus replied, "Who are my mother and my brothers?" And looking around on those who sat about him, he said, "Here are my mother and my brothers!"

It is a replacement of his natural family and *might* be read as a rejection of them, especially since Mark 6:4 has Jesus complain that a prophet is without honor among his own relatives and in his own home.

Luke's parallel scene is thoroughly modified.[60] Luke omits the first part of the Marcan scene (Mark 3:20–21) which is so hard on "his own."[61] He also omits the verses just quoted from the second part of the Marcan scene. The total scene in Luke 8:19–21 reads as follows:

> Then his mother and his brothers came to him, but they could not reach him because of the crowd. He was told, "Your mother and your brothers are standing outside, desiring to see you." But he said to

58 Mary is mentioned but does not appear in Mark 6:3 where Jesus returns to Nazareth. There is a parallel in Matt 13:55 and John 6:42, but not in Luke 4:22 which mentions Joseph but not Mary.

59 *Hoi par' autou*, literally "those from him," which theoretically could mean emissaries. But if we consider the sequence in Mark where "they set out to seize him" in 3:21 is followed by "his mother and his brothers came and, standing outside, sent to him" (3:31), it seems likely that Mark understood the *hoi par' autou* to be his mother and his brothers. The absence of an equivalent for Mark 3:21 in Matthew and Luke, plus the fact that the Johannine parallels are widely separated (John 7:4; 2:4), raises the possibility that Mark has joined two once independent traditions. The Johannine parallel confines disbelief to Jesus' brothers; in the NT Mary is never identified as a disbeliever.

60 Matt 12:46–50 follows Mark 3:31–35 closely, so that Luke's differences from the second part of the Marcan scene are probably to be attributed to his editing. The Marcan account itself may be composite, but its prehistory is not of major concern for our purposes here.

61 Matthew also omits it—an indication that both evangelists probably understood it to refer to Mary and found it irreconcilable with the virginal conception. Their reaction to the first part of the Marcan scene constitutes an argument that Mark could write it only because he did not know the tradition of the virginal conception; see Appendix IV.

them, "My mother and my brothers are those who hear the word of God and do it."

This is not to be read as if the hearers of the word of God replace Jesus' mother and his brothers as his real family (so Mark), but as a statement that his mother and his brothers are among his disciples.[62] The physical family of Jesus is truly his family because they hear the word of God. Luke preserves Jesus' insistence that hearing the word of God and doing it is what is constitutive of his family, but Luke thinks that Jesus' mother and brothers meet that criterion. Unlike Mark 6:4, Luke (4:24) does not have Jesus rejected by his relatives. Luke is quite logical, then, in reporting that among the one hundred and twenty "brethren" who constituted the believing community after the resurrection/ascension were "Mary the mother of Jesus and his brothers" (Acts 1:14).[63]

It is this Lucan tradition that already during the ministry of Jesus his mother was one of "those who hear the word [*logos*] of God and do it" which supplied the response placed on Mary's lips at the end of the annunciation scene: "Behold the handmaid of the Lord. Let it happen to me according to your word [*rēma*]" (1:38).[64] Luke needed no special source nor personal reminiscence from Mary for this response; he needed only to make the portrait of Mary in the infancy narrative consistent with what he knew of her from her sole appearance in the common Synoptic tradition of the public ministry. He is voicing a Christian intuition that the virginal conception of Jesus must have constituted for Mary the beginning of her confrontation with the mysterious plan of God embodied in the person of her son.[65] In Jesus' lifetime and after the resurrection, according to Lucan tradition, Mary responded to that confrontation as a true disciple obedient to the word of God; and Luke assures us that her initial confrontation was also that of an ideal disciple.[66] From the first moment that the grace of

---

[62] A few of the Church writers (Tertullian, John Chrysostom) followed Mark in seeing the scene (along with John 2:4) as containing a rebuke to Mary who was not sufficiently obedient to God's word, but the majority followed the more benevolent Lucan form. See Graef, *Mary*, 43, 76.

[63] Other NT works confirm that at least one "brother of the Lord," James, became a prominent believer (Gal 1:19; 2:9; I Cor 15:7). See also Jude 1.

[64] The use of *rēma* rather than *logos* is not a meaningful difference. It was determined by the use of *rēma* in the preceding verse, "Nothing said [*rēma*] by God can be impossible" (1:37), which in turn was determined by Gen 18:14, "Can anything said [*rēma*] by God be impossible?"

[65] It is to this confrontation that Luke refers twice with the formula: "Mary kept with concern all these events [*rēma*], interpreting them in her heart" (2:19,51). Lyonnet, "L'Annonciation," 62–63, maintains that one of the points which Luke wishes to affirm with certainty is that a divine demand was addressed to Mary and that she freely assented to it. I would agree provided it is recognized that this point could have come from Luke's analysis of God's plan known to him from the body of the Gospel and that it does not depend upon Mary's personal recollections.

[66] In a chapter on an ecumenical understanding of Mary in my book *Biblical Reflections on Crises Facing the Church* (New York: Paulist, 1975), 84–108, I have suggested that discipleship is the key to the interpretation of Mary in the NT and, indeed, explains the remarkable plasticity of her image through the ages.

God (the *charis* or "favor" of 1:30) was proclaimed, it began to attract disciples. It is in this sense that Luke has learned from Mary as a "minister of the word" (1:2), the first Christian disciple.

Mary's obedient, and even enthusiastic, acceptance[67] of God's word in 1:38 is highlighted by the context in which Luke has placed it. Verse 36 picks up the theme of the sixth month of Elizabeth's pregnancy—the theme with which Luke introduced the annunciation of Jesus' birth in 1:26. The news of this pregnancy is a sign because it has been hidden from all (1:24). In the annunciation of JBap's birth Luke modeled Zechariah and Elizabeth upon Abraham and Sarah, and so it is not surprising to find the reference to Elizabeth's pregnancy in 1:36 followed by a reintroduction of the Abraham motif. When Sarah heard about the conception of Isaac, she laughed in ridicule, since she knew she was too old to bear a child. God had to challenge her, "Can anything said by God be impossible?" (Gen 18:14). And *Jubilees* 16:12 tells us that it was in the *sixth month* (of the year) that the Lord visited Sarah and made her pregnant according to His word. In the same setting of the sixth month (of Elizabeth's pregnancy) the angel repeats God's challenge, "Nothing said by God can be impossible." Mary's reaction is just the opposite of Sarah's —not a cynical laugh but a total and joyful acceptance. She is closer to Hannah, the mother of Samuel, who reacted to the news that God would grant her petition for a son with the words, "Let your handmaid find favor in your eyes" (I Sam 1:18).[68] Mary, the Lord's handmaid (1:38), has already found favor in His eyes (1:30). Luke's decision to close the scene with an evocation of Hannah is an example of his artistry. The next scene will have Mary recite the Magnificat which is closely parallel to Hannah's canticle in I Sam 2:1–10.

E. *Mary and Old Testament Symbolism?*

In the Lucan infancy narrative the annunciation of Jesus' birth is directed to Mary the mother, rather than to Joseph the legal father. As we have seen, this is a legitimate option within the OT annunciation pattern. However, we may ask whether, having chosen the female figure, Luke intended

---

67 McHugh, *Mother*, 65, criticizes Plummer, *Luke*, 26, for interpreting Mary's response totally in terms of submission, excluding "an expression of joy at the prospect." In an attempt to prove the presence of joy in Mary's response, McHugh may be oversanguine about the extent to which one may depend on the literal meaning of the optative in "let it happen," which he renders as "O may it be so." However, he is certainly right in seeing Mary's response as joyful and enthusiastic. The "word" to which she responds affirmatively is a word of salvation, as she states in her Magnificat: "My spirit has found gladness in God my Savior" (1:47).

68 Note the OT antecedent for the use of *charis* used to describe a divinely guided conception of a son, as in Luke 1:30. "Favor" is also mentioned in the Abraham/Sarah story (Gen 18:3), but with a more general application.

us to recognize OT symbolism that such a female figure might evoke. Many scholars have responded affirmatively to this question, detecting numerous implicit OT echoes in the Lucan portrait of Mary. Yet it is difficult to be certain that Luke intended all these symbolic hints, discovered only with great effort; and so other scholars have classified these efforts as eisegesis.

1. Daughter of Zion in the Old Testament

The most frequent suggestion of OT symbolism attached to Mary in the Lucan account is that of the Daughter of Zion, and as a preliminary step we should review the origins of this phrase in the OT. Zion was the name of the fortified hill of pre-Israelite Jerusalem, so that David's accomplishment was to conquer the "stronghold of Zion" (II Sam 5:6–10), i.e., the southern section of the eastern hill. As the city was enlarged to the north, Mount Zion came to designate the hill on which the Temple stood. Eventually the name was attached to the western hill. For practical purposes, however, Zion in the Bible may be said to serve as a synonym for Jerusalem. With relation to a geographical entity, "daughter" designates a subdivision, e.g., a city, town, or village. Thus, the cities of a country are the "daughters" of that country, so that Ps 97:8 speaks of the "daughters of Judah," with Zion as one of them, and Ezek 16:27 mentions the "daughters of the Philistines." The villages or suburbs of a city are the "daughters" of that city, so that Num 21:25 mentions "Heshbon and its daughters," while Josh 17:11 speaks of "Bethshan and its daughters."

It is in Micah 1:13 (*ca.* 700 B.C.) that we first encounter the phrase "Daughter of Zion"; and Henri Cazelles[69] contends that it referred to a new quarter or suburb of Jerusalem, north of the Temple area (Zion), first inhabited about the time of King Hezekiah by refugees from the Northern Kingdom after the fall of Samaria in 721. Thus it was to a section of Jerusalem filled with poor, displaced people who needed encouragement that Micah addressed his words of hope when he spoke to the "Daughter of Zion" in 4:8,10,13. Eventually, since the part frequently stands for the whole, "Daughter of Zion" would become a personification of Jerusalem (which in turn would become a synonym for all Judah and even Israel);[70] but if Cazelles is right, the connotation of the poor and the dependent may linger in the appellation.

Before we discuss the "Daughter of Zion" symbolism in relation to Mary, we should note a particular aspect of the OT picture, namely, the term "virgin" applied to Zion (or Israel). In 1:27 Luke twice calls Mary a virgin; he is preparing for 1:34 and the virginal conception of Jesus. Is he also evoking the image of the virgin Daughter of Zion or of virgin Israel,

---

[69] "Fille de Sion"; also McHugh, *Mother*, 438–44.
[70] This process would be facilitated by similar biblical personifications: "Daughter of Babylon" (Jer 50:42); "Daughter of Edom" (Lam 4:21).

familiar in the prophets? The ravaging of nations and cities by foreign conquerors is often compared to the rape of a virgin; and so most of the specific OT references to Israel or Zion as a virgin portray her in a state of oppression, and even of waywardness, lusting after foreign lovers and untrue to her God.[71] A partial exception may be Jer 31:3–4: "I have loved you with an enduring love . . . I shall build you again . . . O virgin Israel"; but even there one may find a connotation of Israel's past unfaithfulness. Thus it would seem that the echoes of the "virgin" passages concerning Zion and Israel in the OT are quite inappropriate as background to Luke's description of the virgin Mary. She is to be identified with those of low estate and the poor (the Magnificat); but she is not oppressed or violated, and is totally faithful (1:45) and obedient to God's word (1:38).

2. The Salutation in 1:28

Leaving aside the OT references to virgin Israel, let us discuss the Lucan Mary simply as the "Daughter of Zion," the poor one to whom in the prophets a salvific message of joy and hope is addressed. This is a symbolism that has been accepted by both Roman Catholic (Lyonnet, Laurentin, Benoit) and Protestant scholars (Sahlin, Hebert, Knight, Leaney).[72] A foundation for this symbolism is a particular exegesis of 1:28, wherein three phrases of the angelic salutation are thought to have a deeper connotation than might at first appear. Often the phrases of 1:28 are seen as expanded and interpreted in the second angelic statement of 1:30–31, and so let me set them side by side:

1:28	1:30–31
Chaire ("Hail")="Rejoice"	"Do not be afraid"
kecharitōmenē ("favored one") ="Full of grace"	"You have found favor (*charis*) with God"
"The Lord is with you"	"You will conceive in your womb"

Let us take the three phrases one by one.

CHAIRE AS "REJOICE." While "rejoice" is the literal meaning of the verb *chairein*, the imperative is the normal Greek secular salutation: "Hail, hello, good day, greetings."[78] The Latin translation of Luke's annunciation

---

[71] For oppression, see Amos 5:2 ("Fallen, no more to rise, is virgin Israel, forsaken on her land"); Isa 23:12; 37:22; and Jer 14:17 ("The virgin daughter of my people is smitten with a deep wound"). For waywardness, see Jer 18:13 ("The virgin Israel has done a really horrible thing"); 31:21; 46:11.

[72] It is fascinating to compare two Protestant books on Mary, respectively for and against this symbolism: M. Thurian, *Mary, Mother of All Christians* (New York: Herder & Herder, 1964), 13–65; and S. Benko, *Protestants, Catholics, and Mary* (Valley Forge, Pa.: Judson, 1968), 93–108.

[78] See its use as an ordinary greeting in Matt 27:29; 28:9; II Cor 13:11; James 1:1; II John 10; and in the early Church writers: Ignatius *Ephesians*, initial greeting; *Barnabas* i 1.

reflected in the *Ave Maria* shows that the translators understood the equivalence between *chaire* and the ordinary Latin greeting *ave*. Similarly the Syriac Peshitta rendering as "Peace" shows the equivalence between *chaire* and the ordinary Semitic greeting (Hebrew *shālôm*). However, Lyonnet[74] has made a case for translating it as "Rejoice," so that it evokes highly theological OT passages featuring the Daughter of Zion.

He argues that if Luke wanted the angel to give Mary an ordinary greeting in 1:28, he would have used *eirēnē*, "Peace," reflecting the Hebrew *shālôm*, as he does in 10:5 and 24:36; for that is Luke's custom in scenes set in a Semitic background. If it is objected that Luke uses a form of *chairein* as an ordinary greeting in Acts 15:23 and 23:26, the answer is that there Luke is quoting from letters written in Greek and adapting his style to the Greek context. Before I move onto the theological significance that is drawn from *chaire* taken as "Rejoice" rather than "Hail," I want to point out a weakness in this interpretation of Luke's use of greetings. Luke certainly knows that *eirēnē* translates the ordinary Semitic greeting and that *chaire* is the ordinary Greek greeting. There is good reason to think that when he is freely composing in Greek for his Greek readers, he chooses *chaire* as standard Greek usage. But his choice of *eirēnē* in 10:5 and 24:36 need not mean that he uses a Semitized greeting when the scene has a Semitic background; his usage there is more plausibly explained by the fact that he is following sources that contained a reference to "peace."[75] Accordingly, one may just as well argue that he would have used *eirēnē* as an ordinary greeting in 1:28 only if he was reproducing a source that would have directed him in this way, and that if he was composing freely in Greek (as I think) he would have used *chaire* for the ordinary greeting. The claim that an ordinary greeting would be out of place in a revelation scene does not do justice to the influence of the standard pattern of the annunciation narrative which is so designed as not to alarm the visionary. Laurentin,[76] who opposes the "Hail" meaning of *chaire* as too banal, is forced to admit that the parallel expression in 1:30, "Do not be afraid," is part of the banal and stereotyped language of angelic appearances and has no real psychological import.

But let us move onto the use of *chairein* in the OT: there are some eighty occurrences in the LXX, about one-quarter of which refer to the joy that

[74] He began his reflections with the article *"Chaire"* in 1939 and resumed them with "Le récit" in 1956. In the interim the Daughter of Zion relationship had been developed by Sahlin, *Messias*, 102–4, and popularized in English by Hebert, "Virgin." Lyonnet's translation of *chaire* has been rejected by Strobel, "Gruss," who argues for interpreting it as a secular greeting; and by Räisänen, *Mutter*, 86–92.

[75] Luke 10:5 is from the "Q" source; see the parallel in Matt 10:11–13, and the context in Luke 10:6 which explain why Luke used the greeting "Peace." Luke 24:36 (slightly dubious textually) is parallel to John 20:26, and there is every reason to think that the Lucan and Johannine accounts reflect an earlier form of the narrative.

[76] *Structure*, 66⁴.

greets a divine saving act, announcement, or promise.[77] In Exod 4:31 *chairein* describes the rejoicing over God's having visited His people in their affliction in Egypt; in I Kgs 5:21 it expresses joy that God gave David a son and successor with the wisdom of Solomon; etc. In a particularly relevant scene in Isa 66:7 God promises that He will cause Zion to give birth and bring forth sons, and urges those who love her to *rejoice*—a promise of deliverance from the exilic and immediately post-exilic tragedies. But Lyonnet and Laurentin concentrate on the four instances in which the specific form *chaire* is used in the LXX; or, more exactly they concentrate on three of the four[78] where *chaire* is addressed to the Daughter of Zion (Zech 9:9; Zeph 3:14) or to the land of Israel, the children of Zion (Joel 2:21–23). At least one of the three passages (Zech 9:9: *"Rejoice* greatly, O Daughter of Zion, . . . behold your king is coming to you . . . he is meek and mounted on an ass") was known to early Christians, for it is cited in Matt 21:5 and John 12:14–15—yet it is not cited specifically in Luke, and neither of the authors who cite it quote the *chaire* opening.

It is particularly Zeph 3:14–17 that has been suggested as the Lucan background for 1:28,30. For the sake of comparison, let us juxtapose the two texts, heightening the parallelism by selecting lines from the longer Zephaniah passage:[79]

> *Zeph 3:14–17:*
> Rejoice [*chaire*], O Daughter of Zion, . . .
> The King of Israel, the Lord, is in your midst [*en mesō sou*] . . .
> Take heart, Zion . . .
> The Lord your God is in you [*en soi*];
> the Mighty One will save you.

> *Luke 1:28,30,31:*
> Rejoice [*chaire*], O favored one,
> the Lord is with you [*meta sou*] . . .
> Do not be afraid, Mary,
> for you have found favor with God . . .

[77] There are instances in the LXX where *chairein* serves as the normal Greek greeting (I Macc 10:18,25; 11:30,32; Tobit 7:1; 13:13), but they are dismissed on the grounds that the books which contain them were written originally in Greek (McHugh, *Mother*, 39). That is incorrect: there is very good reason to think that I Maccabees was written originally in Hebrew, and the Qumran discoveries make it virtually certain that Tobit was written in Aramaic.

[78] The fourth passage, "Rejoice [*chaire*] . . . Daughter of Edom . . . you shall become drunk and strip yourself bare" (Lam 4:21) is dismissed by Laurentin (*Structure*, 65[1]) as "very peculiar," since *chaire* seems to be used ironically. In other words, one of the four instances does not fit the theological approach to *chaire* at all! Instead of dismissing it, I would see it as proof that *chaire*, even when understood as "Rejoice," was likely to evoke no specific theological background.

[79] I am following the Greek of Zephaniah. One may highlight the resemblances more by shifting back and forth between the Hebrew and Greek, according to what most resembles

You will conceive in your womb
and give birth to a son.

In part the supposed parallelism is based on relating the phrase "the Lord
is in your midst" to "the Lord is with you," and the phrase "the Lord your
God is in you" to the presence of the child in Mary's womb—points to be
discussed (and challenged) below. If we leave those aside for the moment,
would Luke's readers, because of the use of the word *chaire,* be aware of
the Zephaniah passage (or the other two *chaire* passages) which has nothing to do with childbirth? *Chaire* is not always salvific in the LXX (footnotes 77,78 above), and Luke's readers would hear it used every day of
their lives with the meaning "Hail, hello." If a modern English writer used
"Goodbye" in a farewell without any interpretative comment, would his
readers recognize that he was giving it its ancient religious value as "God
be with you"? If Luke did not want a typical greeting at the beginning of
the annunciation but wanted to evoke messianic joy, why would he not
have used a non-ambiguous verb like *euphranein,* found in Isa 54:1 in the
context of a conception, a verb that Luke uses elsewhere for joy at messianic salvation (15:32; Acts 2:26)? That verb is used in a Daughter of
Zion passage in Zech 2:14–15(10–11), "Rejoice [*euphrainou*][80] O Daughter of Zion, for behold I come and dwell in your midst [*en mesō sou*], says
the Lord."

In short, the *chaire* connection is too fragile to establish either that Luke
had Zeph 3:14–17 in mind or that he was thinking of Mary as the Daughter of Zion. Of course, the typical expectation of divine deliverance
vocalized by Zephaniah, or indeed by Zechariah in the passage just
quoted, played a role in Luke's outlook—but that expectation is a distillation of a whole series of OT passages and not evidence of a particular symbolism. Since Luke's *chaire* leads into the homonym *kecharitōmenē* ("O
favored one") and a reference to God's favor in sending the Messiah who is
His Son, there may well be an element of religious rejoicing in it—but it is
a joy that comes from the context of the annunciation, and not because
chaire should be given an unusual translation which evokes an OT passage.

"THE LORD IS WITH YOU." Part of the case for the resemblance between
Zephaniah and Luke depends on connecting this phrase to Zephaniah's
"The Lord is in your midst." Such a connection is dubious in the extreme.
Zephaniah presumably refers to the presence of the Lord in the Temple or

Luke. For instance, the Hebrew of 3:16 has "Do not be afraid, Zion" instead of "Take
heart, Zion." Laurentin, *Structure,* 68, adds to the parallelism by seeing a connection between "the Mighty one will *save* you" and the meaning of Jesus' name as "God saves"
(NOTE on Matt 1:21)—a dubious connection since Luke draws no attention to this etymology.

80 It is interesting that Justin, *Dialogue* cxv 1, cites this text of Zechariah with *chaire*
rather than the *euphrainou* of the LXX.

to His presence with the forces of His people (Exod 34:9). The Lucan "The Lord is with you" is an ordinary greeting, as exemplified in Ruth 2:4 in the exchange between Boaz and the reapers.[81] In the context of an angelic appearance, the phrase need not be totally banal when addressed to Mary; it reassures her that this divine visitation is benevolent and need not be feared. If Luke is recalling an OT passage, it is not Zephaniah but the scene of the angelic annunciation to Gideon in Judg 6:12. The opening address there, "O mighty man of valor, the Lord is with you," is close in context and wording to Luke's "O favored one, the Lord is with you."

In the attempt to relate Luke to Zephaniah, particularly dubious is Laurentin's shift from the Greek of Zephaniah to the Hebrew in seeking to read *beqirbēk* (the phrase behind "in your midst" and "in you" in 3:15,17) as "in your interior parts" and thus equivalent to Luke's "you will conceive a child *in your womb*." In the many times that the LXX uses the expression "to conceive or have a child in the womb," the noun *qereb* is never in the underlying Hebrew.[82] Such arguments do nothing to strengthen the case based on *chaire*.

KECHARITŌMENĒ AS "FULL OF GRACE." The discussion of this phrase is not directly related to the Daughter of Zion question, but it is illustrative of the tendency to eke every drop of theological and even mariological significance from 1:28. There can be no doubt that *kecharitōmenē*, which I have translated "O favored one," does have theological significance— indeed, more obvious significance than the standard greeting *chaire* and the salutation "The Lord is with you." The use of a qualifying phrase describing the visionary is a standard feature in the biblical annunciation of birth (Step 3b in Table VIII), and the quality that is thus underlined usually has something to do with the message of the annunciation.[83] The difference of rank of the two children Ishmael and Isaac is already hinted at in the different designations of the respective mothers: "Hagar, maid of Sarah" (Gen 16:8), and "Sarah, your wife" (17:15). Joseph is called "son of David" in the Matthean annunciation (1:20) because his role as a Davidid will be to name Jesus and thus give him Davidic descent. Gideon

---

81 Thus McHugh, *Mother*, 48–49, exaggerates when he says that in the OT the formula is never addressed to a person in ordinary circumstances, and that the greeting "The Lord is with you" implies that God has a formidable task in hand for Mary. He is right to point out that many times it serves as an assurance of God's helping presence (Gen 26:24; Exod 3:12; Jer 1:8), although usually not as a greeting but as an affirmative statement that God will be with someone.

82 Laurentin, *Structure*, 68–71, points to this noun in the phrase *beqirbâ* used in Gen 25:22 when the unborn Esau and Jacob are already struggling within Rebekah. Since they are within her womb, he stresses that sense of *qereb*. However, the noun covers various inner organs, including the entrails of animals; and the reference to the womb depends totally upon the context. Translations that say "the children struggled together *within her*" have caught the vagueness of the expression. It is certainly no equivalent for the Lucan *en gastri* (1:31).

83 Audet, "L'annonce," considers these qualifying phrases almost to constitute a new name which fits the addressee for a role in God's plan.

is called a "mighty man of valor" in Judg 6:12 because God will employ his valor to liberate Israel from the Midianites.[84] Thus, Mary's designation in Luke 1:28 as *kecharitōmenē* plausibly has something to do with the annunciation to follow.

How are we to translate this passive participle from the denominative verb *charitoun?* Such a verb has the possibility of reflecting the various ideas contained in the noun *charis,* "grace, favor, charm." Some have chosen the translation "beautiful lady," since a lady who has been "graced" may be considered graceful, beautiful, charming.[85] However, Mary's physical beauty has nothing to do with the scene, and it is more plausible to interpret *kecharitōmenē* to refer to her as one who has been favored or graced by God. It is this interpretation of *kecharitōmenē* that explains why Mary "wondered what such a greeting might mean" (1:29). And Gabriel responded by insisting: "You have found favor [*charis*] with God" (1:30).[86] As the reader will be told, this *charis* which makes her *kecharitōmenē* is the grace of conceiving the Son of the Most High.

Such a theological meaning of *kecharitōmenē* which seems entirely justified by the context is to be kept distinct from another interpretation which has come about by way of the Latin rendering *gratia plena,* "full of grace."[87] It is true that a denominative verb sometimes has the sense of plenitude,[88] and certainly Luke would not be opposed to regarding the grace bestowed upon Mary as a fullness of God's favor. Some modern translations catch this by rendering *kecharitōmenē* as "*highly* favored one." But "full of grace" is too strong. Luke knew that expression since it appears literally in Acts 6:8; yet he chose not to use it here. It is open to the interpretation that Mary already possesses the grace or perfection involved, whereas for Luke Mary's special state is to be constituted by the divine favor involved in the conception of Jesus. Later theology stressed the *fullness* of grace and made it a cardinal principle of mariology, so that Mary was thought to possess every perfection possible for a creature.[89] In-

---

84 An additional example might be that Gabriel addresses Daniel (10:11,19) as "Man greatly beloved," or in the Greek translations as a man to whom (divine) mercy is shown or a man who is the object of (God's) desire.

85 Sirach 18:17 uses *kecharitōmenos* to describe a man who is gracious or charming.

86 The other NT instance of the relatively rare verb *charitoun* is similar in meaning: "The grace [*charis*] with which He has graced us [*charitoun*] in His beloved Son" (Eph 1:6). The verb occurs only about a dozen times in literature between the second century B.C. and the fifth century A.D. (Cambe, "La *Charis,*" 194). It was probably chosen by Luke because of a paronomasia with the preceding *chairein*.

87 The Syriac Peshitta supports this translation. The Old Latin (Codices Palatinus, Monacensis) *gratificata* was more literal but perhaps ambiguous; for the verb *gratificari* may mean "to show oneself gracious," and thus may lose the sense of *gratia* (*charis*) that Luke intended. The translation "full of grace" is not peculiarly Roman Catholic, since it was accepted by Wycliffe, Tyndale, Coverdale, and Cranmer.

88 Yet see MGNTG, II, 393–97: the dominant force of denominative verbs is rather instrumental or factitive. *Charitoun* means to constitute someone in *charis*.

89 The famous medieval *Mariale Super Missus Est,* long thought to be the work of St. Albert the Great, gives almost a classic interpretation of the plenitude of grace: Mary had

deed, it lies at the root of the axiom *numquam satis* (i.e., one cannot claim too much for Mary). No matter what one may think of this theological reasoning (and some within Roman Catholicism today would want to reconsider it), it certainly goes beyond what Luke meant by *kecharitōmenē*.[90] On this point, as on the others, it is wise to be conservative about how much Marian symbolism Luke intended in the relatively stereotyped salutation of 1:28.

3. The Ark of the Covenant in 1:35?

Many of the exegetes (Lyonnet, Sahlin, Hebert, Laurentin) who think that Luke portrayed Mary as the Daughter of Zion also find the symbolism of Mary as the Ark of the Covenant or as the Tabernacle of divine glory. The key to this symbolism is 1:35c: "Power from the Most High will overshadow [*episkiazein*] you." I have shown above (C2) that this clause and its parallel ("The Holy Spirit will come upon you") represent the language of early christology, echoing phrases used in Gospel ministry accounts of the baptism and the transfiguration. Yet the cloud of divine presence that overshadows at the transfiguration is set against the background of Peter's offer to build *tabernacles* for Jesus, Moses, and Elijah (Luke 9:34–35). This reminds us that *episkiazein,* "to overshadow" (along with *skiazein,* "to shadow") was used to describe how the cloud of God's glory cast a shadow upon the Tabernacle in the wilderness (Exod 40:35; Num 9:18,22). Indeed, the verbs for overshadow and shadow described several forms of the divine presence in the OT, e.g., the cloud overshadowing the renewed Mount Zion and its festal assemblies (Isa 4:5); the cloud overshadowing the Israelites when they departed from the desert camp (Num 10:34[36]); God overshadowing His chosen ones (Deut 33:12; Ps 91:4); and the winged cherubim overshadowing the mercy seat or top of the Ark of the Covenant (Exod 25:20; I Chr 28:18).[91]

From this background we may deduce that Luke is thinking of a divine presence overshadowing Mary, a deduction also possible from the parallel line wherein the Holy Spirit comes upon her.[92] The power of that presence creatively brings about the conception of the child, but that is not necessarily the same as Jesus being the embodiment of the divine presence in the womb of Mary.[93] I rejected above the contention that "The Lord is

---

every gift, not only spiritual but secular, even above those given to the angels. See Graef, *Mary,* I, 270–73.

[90] This is admitted by Lyonnet, "L'Annonciation," 68–69, an exegete with a good control of patristic and scholastic interpretations.

[91] This may be related to a bird whose wings overshadow and protect those beneath (Pss 17:8; 57:2[1]).

[92] The parallelism with overshadowing would be heightened if I am right (footnote 51 above) in relating this action of the Holy Spirit to that of the creative Spirit of God which hovered over the face of the waters in Gen 1:2.

[93] It is in *Johannine* theology that the Divine Word "tabernacled" (John 1:14, *skēnoun*) among us, so that Jesus' body becomes the Temple (2:21).

with you" is the same as Zephaniah's "The Lord is in your midst." And it is totally a guess to assume from the verb *episkiazein* that Luke thinks of Mary as the Tabernacle or the Ark of the Covenant overshadowed by or containing the divine presence.[94] To be precise, in the OT the cherubim rather than God are said to overshadow the Ark; moreover, the Ark and Tabernacle are not the only places overshadowed by divine presence.

We have not finished the discussion of Mary as the Ark of the Covenant, for it will reappear in the next scene of the visitation (§ 12B on 1:43), even as will the theme of the Daughter of Zion. If the evidence thus far adduced for either symbolism is not convincing, the proponents argue that the evidence is cumulative. Let me reserve judgment. But in showing myself dubious thus far, I do not wish to convey the impression that in my opinion Luke did not think of Mary against the background of the OT. As I have shown in D above, he draws her dialogue from what he knows of her during the ministry. But her portrayal as a mother conceiving a child is deeply influenced by OT portraits (especially that of Hannah whose very name means "grace, favor"—see NOTE on "favored one" in 1:28), as is the whole annunciation pattern. Moreover, by stressing Mary's acceptance of God's word in 1:38, Luke has begun to associate her with those in Israel who were "poor ones" (*anawim*) in the sense of being totally dependent upon God for support. Luke will develop that theme beautifully in the Magnificat.

[94] Benoit, "L'Annonciation," 207, although not opposed to OT symbolic background for Mary, is uncertain about the applicability of the imagery of the divine presence in the Tabernacle, since the motif of being filled with glory is not present as it is in Exod 40:35. (However, that motif is not in Num 9:18,22.)

SECTIONAL BIBLIOGRAPHY (§ 11)
(LUKE 1:26–38)

(See also the Bibliography for Appendix IV on the virginal conception.)

Audet, J.-P., "L'annonce à Marie," RB 63 (1956), 346–74.

Bauer, J. B., "Philologische Bemerkungen zu Lk 1,34," *Biblica* 45 (1964), 535–40.

Benoit, P., "L'Annonciation," *Assemblées du Seigneur* 6 (1955), 40–57. Cited as reprinted in ExTh, III, 197–215.

Bourassa, B., "*Kecharitōmenē*, Lc 1.28," ScEccl 9 (1957), 313–16.

Brown, R. E., "Luke's Method in the Annunciation Narratives of Chapter One," in *No Famine in the Land*, ed. J. W. Flanagan and Anita W. Robinson (J. L. McKenzie Volume; Missoula: Scholars' Press, 1975), 179–94.

Cambe, M., "La *Charis* chez saint Luc. Remarques sur quelques textes, notamment le *Kecharitōmenē*," RB 70 (1963), 193–207.

Cazelles, H., "Fille de Sion et théologie mariale dans la Bible," *Bulletin de la Société Française d'Etudes Mariales* 21 (1964), 51–71. English summary in McHugh, *Mother,* 438–44.

Cole, E. R., "What Did St. Luke Mean by *Kecharitōmenē?*" AER 139 (1958), 228–39.

Gewiess, J., "Die Marienfrage, Lk 1,34," BZ 5 (1961), 221–54. English summary in TD 11 (1963), 39–42.

Graystone, G., *Virgin of all Virgins: The Interpretation of Luke 1:34* (Rome: Pio X, 1968).

Hebert, A. G., "The Virgin Mary as the Daughter of Zion," *Theology* 53 (1950), 403–10.

Jones, A., "Background of the Annunciation," *Scripture* 11 (1959), 65–81.

Knight, G. A. F., "The Virgin and the Old Testament," *Reformed Theological Review* (Australia) 12 (1953), 1–13.

Legrand, L., "Fécondité virginale selon l'Esprit dans le Nouveau Testament," NRT 84 (1962), 785–805.

——— "L'arrière-plan néo-testamentaire de Lc. I.35," RB 70 (1963), 161–92.

Lyonnet, S., *"Chaire kecharitōmenē,"* *Biblica* 20 (1939), 131–41.

——— "Le récit de l'Annonciation et la Maternité Divine de la Sainte Vierge," *Ami du Clergé* 66 (1956), 33–48. Part of it in English in Lyonnet, "St. Luke's."

——— "L'Annonciation et la mariologie biblique," in *Maria in Sacra Scriptura* (Acta Congressus Mariologici-Mariani in Republica Dominicana anno 1965 Celebrati; Rome: Pontificia Academia Mariana Internationalis, 1967), IV, 59–72.

McHugh, J., *Mother,* 37–72, 173–99.

Muñoz Iglesias, S., "Lucas 1,35b," EB 27 (1968), 275–99.

Prete, B., "Il racconto dell' Annunziazione di Luca 1,26–38," BibOr 15 (1973), 75–88.

Quecke, H., "Lk 1,34 in den alten Übersetzungen und im Protevangelium des Jakobus," *Biblica* 44 (1963), 499–520.

——— "Lk 1,34 im Diatessaron," *Biblica* 45 (1964), 85–88.

———"Lk 1,31 in den alten Übersetzungen," *Biblica* 46 (1965), 333–48.

——— "Zur Auslegungsgeschichte von Lk 1,34," *Biblica* 47 (1966), 113–14.

Schneider, G., "Lk 1,34–35 als redaktionelle Einheit," BZ 15 (1971), 255–59.

——— "Jesu geistgewirkte Empfängnis (Lk 1,34f)," *Theologisch-praktisch Quartalschrift* 119 (1971), 105–16.

Smith, D. M., "Luke 1:26–38," *Interpretation* 29 (1975), 411–17.

Strobel, A., "Der Gruss an Maria (Lc 1,28)," ZNW 53 (1962), 86–110.

Vicent, A., "La presunta sustantivación *to gennōmenon* en Lc 1,35b," EB 33 (1974), 265–73.

Zerwick, M., ". . . Quoniam virum non cognosco. (Conspectus criticus de opinionibus recentioribus)," *Verbum Domini* 37 (1959), 212–24, 276–88.

IV. THE VISITATION OF MARY TO ELIZABETH (§ 12)

Translation of Luke 1:39–56

1 [39] At that time Mary arose and went hastily into the hill country to a Judean city. [40] There she entered the house of Zechariah and greeted Elizabeth. [41] And when Elizabeth heard Mary's greeting, the baby jumped in her womb; and she was filled with the Holy Spirit.

[42] Elizabeth proclaimed with a loud cry:
[42b] "Blessed are you among women,
[42c] and blessed is the fruit of your womb.
[43a] Who am I
[43b] that the mother of my Lord should come to me?
[44a] For behold the moment your greeting sounded in my ears,
[44b] the baby in my womb jumped with gladness.
[45a] Fortunate is she who believed
[45b] that the Lord's words to her would find fulfillment."

[46] And Mary said:*
[46b] "My soul proclaims the greatness of the Lord,
[47] and my spirit has found gladness in God my Savior:

[48a] *Because He has regarded the low estate of His handmaid—*
[48b] *for behold, henceforth all generations will call me fortunate.*
[49a] Because He who is mighty has done great things for me.
[49b] And holy is His name,
[50a] and His mercy is from generation to generation
[50b] on those who fear Him.

---

* Italicization indicates the lines most likely added by Luke to the hypothetical pre-Lucan, Jewish-Christian canticle, in order to fit it into its present context.

51a He has shown His strength with His arm;

51b He has scattered the proud in the imagination of their hearts.

52a He has put down the mighty from their thrones

52b and has exalted those of low degree.

53a He has filled the hungry with good things,

53b and the rich He has sent away empty.

54a He has helped His servant Israel

54b in remembrance of His mercy,

55a as He spoke unto our fathers,

55b to Abraham and his posterity forever."

56 Now Mary remained with Elizabeth about three months and then returned home.

NOTES

1:39. *At that time.* Literally, "In these days." This chronological indication is less definite than the openings of the preceding sections: "In the days of Herod" (1:5); "In the sixth month" (1:26). It is comparable to 2:1 (literally, "In those days") and is a connective in good Lucan style (6:12; Acts 1:15; etc.)

arose and went. The verb "arise" (*anistanai*), which Luke/Acts uses three times more frequently than the rest of the NT taken together, has no precise meaning here, other than to indicate the beginning of an act.

hastily. Why the haste? Psychological reasons have been advanced, e.g., to prevent neighbors at Nazareth from knowing about her pregnancy. B. Hospodar, CBQ 18 (1956), 14–18, protesting that Mary was too thoughtful a person (2:19,51) to act in haste, argues that the phrase means "with serious intent." Philologically that is possible, but it does not fit the logic of the scene. Mary's haste is a reflection of her obedience to the plan revealed to her by the angel, a plan which included the pregnancy of Elizabeth (1:36–37).

into the hill country to a Judean city. Luke has already hinted (1:23) that Zechariah did not live in Jerusalem. It is estimated that only about one-fifth of the priests lived in Jerusalem; many did live in the cities of Judea (Neh 11:3; I Macc 2:1). Some scholars have found Luke's geographical description too telescopic to do justice to a journey of several days from the Galilean hills south across the plain of Esdraelon, through the mountains of Samaria, into the Judean hills. Conzelmann, *Theology,* 69, contends that Luke mistakenly thought that Galilee and Judea were contiguous. Schmidt, *Rahmen,* 311, thinks that in the pre-Lucan form of this tradition Mary lived in Jerusalem rather than in Nazareth. However, Marshall, *Luke,* 71, points out that both Tacitus (*Annals* XII 54) and the NT (Luke 4:44 compared to Mark 1:39) attest to a broad use of "Judea" as a term which includes Galilee, so that the geographical difficulty in Mary's journey need not be exaggerated.

The Lucan phrase is literally "into a city Judah," with no genitive ending on the place name (*eis polin Iouda,* not *eis polin tēs Ioudaias,* as we might have expected from the parallel expression in 1:26, *eis polin tēs Galilaias*). The appearance of the undeclined *Iouda* here (if it is an undeclined form of the name; see BAG, 380) has been interpreted as an indication that we are not encountering Luke's own style. Others have tried to explain it as a translation mistake, e.g., *Iouda* for *Yûṭah,* one of the priestly cities mentioned in Josh 21:16 (cf. 15:55; so B. Weiss); or "city" as a mistranslation of *mᵉdînāh,* which should have been understood as "province" (Torrey)—such explanations generally suppose a pre-Lucan Semitic original. Attention has also been called to Pliny *Natural History* V xv 70, where "Hill Country" is the name of a toparchy of Judea, around Jerusalem. There is no easy solution. I would suggest that Luke had only very general information about the parents of JBap, namely, that they were of priestly stock and that many priests lived in Judea near Jerusalem. To phrase this information, he may have combined a stock biblical phrase (II Sam 2:1: "Shall I go up *into one of the cities of Judah?"—eis mian tōn poleōn Iouda*) with the indication that the parents of Samuel (who were the prototypes for the parents of JBap) lived *in the hill country* (I Sam 1:1). The dependency on OT phrasing would help to explain why Luke speaks of "Judah" rather than of "Judea." (See NOTES on Matt 2:1,6.)

Tradition has not been content that this city of Judah remain anonymous. Since legend erroneously made a high priest of Zechariah (NOTE on 1:5), it is not surprising to find the city identified with Jerusalem where the high priest had his palace. By the sixth century pilgrim tradition was identifying it as Ain Karim, a town five miles W of Jerusalem (HPG, 90–95).

40. *the house of Zechariah.* As a variation in the quest for identification mentioned at the end of the previous NOTE, F. Dattler, *Revista Bíblica* (Argentina) 31 (1969), 202–3, maintains that this is an overly literal translation of the place name Beth-zechariah, mentioned in I Macc 6:32. His argument presupposes a pre-Lucan Semitic original.

41. *the baby jumped in her womb.* This is another *egeneto* construction (NOTE on 1:9): "And it happened when . . . the baby jumped." Grotius and others have raised the possibility that *skirtan* might have been a technical medical term for movement within the womb and thus confirm the theory that Luke the physician (Col 4:14) was the author of the Gospel. But it is a general verb for skipping or leaping, as of sheep in a field, and is applied to a baby already in Gen 25:22. Verse 44 specifies that it was from gladness that the baby moved.

she was filled with the Holy Spirit. In 1:15 the angel promised that JBap would be "filled with the Holy Spirit even from his mother's womb," and his recognition of Jesus shows that this has already happened. The Greek is anarthrous as in 1:15,35. See NOTE on 1:15.

42. *proclaimed with a loud cry.* Luke is almost tautological here to capture the sense of unrestrained joy; and a few scribes tried to "improve" the Greek by substituting "voice" for "cry." The first two lines of Elizabeth's cry are in poetic parallelism; and Plummer, *Luke,* 31, proposes putting all of Elizabeth's words into eight lines of poetry. Certainly the poetry would not be so formal as that of the Magnificat, but still one would be able to speak of two canticles of praise, Elizabeth's uttered in greeting and Mary's uttered in response. The contention that Elizabeth's praise is hymnic is favored by the fact that the verb *anaphōnein,* "proclaim," is consistently used in the LXX for liturgical music (I Chr 15:28; 16:4,5,42).

Blessed are you among women. There are two sets of biblical words (and ideas) involving blessing that should be kept distinct, one set that we may call "participial," and the other "adjectival":

Passive participle: Hebrew *bārûk,* Greek *eulogētos* or *eulogēmenos,*

Latin *benedictus,* English *blessed* (pronounced *blest*);

Adjective: Hebrew *'ašrē,* Greek *makarios,* Latin *beatus,* English *fortunate* or *happy* or *blessed.*

The NT sentences in which the adjectival words are used, e.g., the Beatitudes, are called macarisms (from *makarios*). They do not confer a blessing but recognize an existing state of happiness or blessing; they are an approving proclamation, often signifying that eschatological joy has come. There are macarisms in Luke 1:45,48. But in the present passage Luke employs *eulogēmenos.* In this participial sense "blessed" is properly addressed to God who is to be blessed by human beings. When it is extended to men or women, it invokes on them the blessing of God. Normally such a blessing is a wish: it asks that the one being blessed be granted divine favors; but here the Holy Spirit enables Elizabeth to recognize that the blessing has already been granted by God. Mary is blessed "among women"; this phrase has a comparative (but not an absolutely superlative) value both in Greek (BDF 245[8]) and in Hebrew. It means that Mary has been specially blessed by God, but not necessarily that she is the most blessed woman; for the same thing can be said of other women (Judg 5:24; Judith 13:18).

blessed is the fruit of your womb. Here also the participial form *eulogēmenos* is used. An alternation between *eulogētos* and *eulogēmenos* in parallel lines occurs in Judith 13:18: "Blessed are you . . . among all women on earth, and blessed is the Lord God." The expression "fruit of the womb" is a Hebraism (Gen 30:2; Lam 2:20).

43. *Who am I that.* Literally, "Whence this to me?" The problem of whether we can speak of Elizabeth's words as poetry or not becomes acute here.

the mother of my Lord. Here for the first time *kyrios,* "Lord," refers unmistakably to Jesus. See the opening NOTE on vs. 17.

44. *For behold.* The general Lucan use of *idou,* "behold," was discussed in the NOTE on 1:20. The particular use here is in the expression *idou gar* which appears six times in Luke/Acts and only once in the rest of the NT (II Cor

7:11). Three of the six occurrences are in the infancy narrative (here; 1:48; 2:10).

with gladness. This is not *chara,* "joy" (*chairein* in 1:28) but *agalliasis;* the two are put together in the angelic promise to Zechariah in 1:14: "You will have joy and gladness." See Acts 2:26.

45. *Fortunate.* For the difference between *makarios,* "fortunate," and *eulogēmenos* (or *eulogētos*), "blessed," see the NOTE on vs. 42. Macarisms are particularly frequent in Matthew and Luke.

believed that the Lord's words to her would find fulfillment. Literally, "believed that there would be a completion to the things spoken to her by the Lord." It is equally possible to translate: "believed because there will be a completion," a translation favored by the Vulgate and some of the Reformers. Although the "words" were actually spoken to Mary by an angel of the Lord, Luke can refer to them as spoken by the Lord (see NOTE on Matt 1:20). The word for "fulfillment" here is *teleiōsis,* from *telein,* "to complete"; note that in 1:20, when Zechariah did not believe the words which would be fulfilled, the verb *plēroun* was used. The latter is the more common NT verb for the fulfillment of Scripture, but *telein* and its sister verb *teleioun* are also used (John 19:28).

46. *And Mary said.* This is much less colorful than the introduction to Elizabeth's words in 1:42 or to Zechariah's words in 1:67. The overwhelming textual evidence reads "Mary" in this clause, but there is a variant, "And Elizabeth said." It is found in the following textual witnesses: (a) Three Latin mss. ranging in date from the fourth to the eighth centuries—mss. a,b,1*. (b) One ms. of Irenaeus *Against the Heretics* IV vii 1. The other ms. of that passage has "Mary," as does III x 2. (c) Jerome's Latin translation of Origen, *In Lucam Homiliae* 7 (PL 26:247), in which instance the reference to mss. with "Elizabeth" may have come from Jerome rather than Origen. (d) Nicetas of Remesiana *De psalmodiae bono* (or *De utilitate hymnorum*) ix 11. This bishop lived *ca.* 400 and so may be our earliest witness to the reading. His diocese was in Yugoslavia; thus his evidence joins that of the Latin mss. of Italy and the Balkans.

This textual evidence is so heavily Latin that it would sway few in favor of the "Elizabeth" reading were it not bolstered by a number of other arguments advanced by scholars in the last one hundred years. Benko, "Magnificat," narrates well the interesting development of support for the "Elizabeth" reading. It was defended at the end of the last century by A. Loisy who was still within the Roman Catholic Church and, fearing reprisals, wrote under the pseudonym F. Jacobé. (His fears were not idle, for on June 26, 1912, the Roman Pontifical Biblical Commission issued a decree stating that the Magnificat was to be attributed to Mary, not to Elizabeth. See § 1, footnotes 4,22). In 1900 the great church historian A. von Harnack championed the attribution to Elizabeth, only to be answered ably by F. Spitta and P. Ladeuze who argued for attribution to Mary. Others who have accepted the "Elizabeth" reading include F. C. Burkitt, J. M. Creed, J. G. Davies, B. S. Easton, M. Goguel, J. R. Harris, E. Klostermann, and P. Winter. A neutral explanation is that the original Lucan text read simply "And she said," and that the majority of scribes understood the "she" to be Mary, while a few understood the "she" as Elizabeth. However, that explanation still leaves us with the question of whom Luke meant by "she."

The following factors must be considered: (a) Some lines in the Magnificat fit Elizabeth better than Mary, e.g., the reference to "low estate" in 48a fits barrenness better than virginity and matches Elizabeth's reference to her "disgrace among men" in 25. Similarly, "He who is mighty has done great things for me" in 49a is close to the statement in 58 that "the Lord had shown His great mercy" to Elizabeth. On the other hand, the reference to "His handmaid" in 48a echoes clearly the description of Mary as "the handmaid of the Lord" in 38; and the macarism in 48b matches the macarism applied to Mary in 45a. The argument, then, as to which woman the Magnificat better suits is indecisive and probably invalid, since much of the Magnificat suits neither woman. In the COMMENT I shall contend that the Magnificat was a general hymn applicable to the downtrodden of Israel and that vs. 48 represents Luke's attempt to adapt the hymn to its present context—and 48 matches Mary closer than Elizabeth. (b) It is awkward to have Mary mentioned as the subject in 46 and then to have her name repeated as subject immediately after the Magnificat in 56. The "Now Mary remained with Elizabeth" of 56 would flow more smoothly if 46 read "And Elizabeth said." However, the latter reading would have Elizabeth mentioned as subject twice in a row in 41–42 and 46. Thus, the argument from sequence is also indecisive and once more probably incorrect. In the COMMENT I shall argue that the Magnificat was introduced into the infancy narrative at a second state of Lucan editing and that 45 was originally followed by 56. The awkwardness of having Mary mentioned twice as subject in 46 and 56 results from the intrusive character of 46–55. (c) Why would a canticle of praise spoken by Mary be placed in the midst of the visitation and not after the annunciation of Jesus' birth or after the birth itself? But localization in the visitation is even more awkward if Elizabeth is the speaker, for then we have two exclamations of praise by Elizabeth one after the other. (Scholars who accept the "Elizabeth" reading recognize this, and some propose as a more original setting for the Magnificat a localization after vs. 25 or after 41.) If Mary is the speaker, one can detect a literary design in having Mary's canticle in 46–55 as a response to Elizabeth's "canticle" of praise. (d) The Magnificat is modeled on the canticle of Hannah in I Sam 2; and Elizabeth's situation is closer to that of Hannah than is Mary's—both had been barren. Yet, if Luke thought of Elizabeth as the spokeswoman of the Magnificat, why would he have omitted the passage in I Sam 2:5 where Hannah referred to the barren one bearing children? Moreover, Luke's description of Mary is not without Hannah themes (p. 319 above). (e) The strongest argument for ascription to Elizabeth is that Christian scribes, copying at a later time when Mary was the object of devotion, would scarcely have substituted "Elizabeth" for "Mary" as the speaker, especially in light of the line: "henceforth all generations will call me fortunate" (48b). This argument loses some but not all of its force if "she" was the original reading. (f) The strongest argument for ascription to Mary flows from the contention that, on a second level of editing, Luke inserted the two canticles, the Magnificat and the Benedictus. His intention, then, would be to attribute canticles of praise to the two recipients of the annunciations, Mary and Zechariah. The objection that Mary's canticle should have come after Jesus' birth, just as Zechariah's comes after JBap's birth, has little force; for the birth of Jesus is adequately greeted by an angelic canticle, the Gloria, and by Simeon's canticle, the Nunc Dimittis.

While it is difficult to be certain, in my judgment there are better arguments for the "Mary" ascription than for the "Elizabeth" ascription.

46–47. *My soul . . . and my spirit*. Although in Hebrew and in Greek anthropology *psychē* and *pneuma* are often different human spiritual components, here by way of parallelism they are identical (as also in Job 12:10 and Wisdom 15:11). They mean little more than "I." Compare the parallelism of "my heart" and "my horn" in Hannah's canticle (I Sam 2:1).

46. *proclaims the greatness*. Literally, "makes great, magnifies," as in Ps 69:31(30) and Sirach 43:31(33). I find totally unconvincing the suggestion that the name of the speaker of the Magnificat (Miryam or Mary) is hidden in the Hebrew substratum behind this expression. Laurentin, "Traces, II," would reconstruct the Hebrew consonants *mrymh* or *mrym* (*merîmâ* or *merîm*). However, it is far from certain that the canticle ever existed in Semitic; and if it did, other reconstructions of the Semitic original are just as likely, e.g., *rômēmâ* (Delitzsch), *merabbyâ* (Black).

47. *has found gladness*. The aorist tense of *agallian* (NOTE on "gladness" in vs. 44) contrasts with the present tense in the preceding line. Some would detect the reflection of a Hebrew tense sequence (*waw* consecutive); others speak of an ingressive aorist (BDF 331): "has begun to find."

***God my Savior*.** In the Greek Bible the term *sōtēr* is applied far more often to God (thirty-five times) than to men (five times). For this expression see Ps 24:5 and Isa 12:2.

48. *Because*. Presumably the *hoti* here (or at the beginning of 49) represents the Hebrew *kî* with which the hymns in the psalter frequently begin to list the motives for praising God. See also 68b at the beginning of the Benedictus.

***low estate*.** Other suggested translations of *tapeinōsis* are "humility, humiliation, barrenness, poverty." In the OT it is often descriptive of the persecution or oppression from which God delivers His people, e.g., Deut 26:7; Ps 136:23. In I Sam 1:11 (the Hannah story), which is almost certainly the background for the usage here, *tapeinōsis* translated the Hebrew *'ŏnî*, a word related to the concept of the Anawim (see C2 below). Hannah was one of the "poor ones" because of her barrenness, but *tapeinōsis* can refer to low estate in a much wider sense.

***handmaid*.** The repetition of Mary's self-description in 38.

***for behold*.** See the NOTE on 1:44. A very Lucan expression.

***henceforth*.** The expression *apo tou nyn* occurs six times in Luke/Acts and only once elsewhere in the NT (II Cor 5:16). In most of the Lucan instances there is a reference to the salvific moment (12:52; 22:18; 22:69; Acts 18:6).

***call me fortunate*.** The verb *makarizein*, related to *makarios*; see NOTE on "Blessed" in 42.

49. *He who is mighty*. In the LXX *dynatos* refers more frequently to human

beings, but in Zeph 3:17 the Lord is given this title in the sense of "Mighty Warrior," translating the Hebrew *Gibbôr*.

great things. Megala is a set expression for God's wonderful accomplishments, especially in the Exodus (Deut 10:21; 11:7; Judg 2:7). The poorly attested textual variant here (*megaleia*) may reflect a scribal reminiscence of Acts 2:11: "We hear them telling in our own tongues the mighty acts of God."

holy is His name. While the adjectival sense of *hagios* is indicated, a translation as a title ("the Holy One") is not impossible. The God of Israel is holy (Lev 11:44–45; I Peter 1:16).

50. *His mercy. Eleos* is the normal rendition of the Hebrew *ḥesed,* God's covenant love in choosing Israel (or David) as a covenant partner without merit on the people's part (Exod 34:6; II Sam 7:15).

from generation to generation. Various Greek formulations of this idea occur in the LXX but not this precise wording (*eis geneas kai geneas*) which is found in the *Testament of Levi* 18:8.

those who fear Him. Fear is a basic OT reaction involving recognition of God's sovereignty. See J. DeCantanzero, "Fear, Knowledge, and Love: A Study in Old Testament Piety," CJT 9 (1963), 166–73.

51. *He has shown . . . strength.* Literally, "has made strength"—certainly not a native Greek expression. Some have tried to interpret this verb to govern all that follows, i.e., has shown strength by scattering the proud, by putting down the mighty, etc. However, more likely it is on an equal level with the other verbs and in parallelism with "He has scattered the proud" in 51b. As we shall see in the COMMENT, the recipients of the show of strength are "those who fear Him" in 50b. The strength is manifested in saving the Anawim or poor ones, but it also involves punishing enemies—see Ramaroson, "Structuram," 38–39, for the debate on whether salvation or vindication is intended.

with His arm. Also a Semitism, particularly frequent in reference to God's deeds in delivering Israel from Egypt: "I shall redeem you with an outstretched arm" (Exod 6:6; Deut 4:34).

the proud. A detailed study of the idea behind *hyperēphanos* is presented by P. L. Schoonheim, NovTest 8 (1966), 235–46. The proud look down on others because they do not look up to God, and so in the Bible the proud are constantly presented as God's enemies (Isa 13:11).

in the imagination of their hearts. The reasoning power is localized in the heart (I Chr 29:18), and so it can be the seat of pride: "The pride of your heart has deceived you" (Obadiah 3).

52. *the mighty. Dynastēs* can mean "potentate, prince" (Gen 50:4); and these would be rival to God who is the "only *Dynastēs*" in I Tim 6:15. Luke in vs. 49 has already called God "mighty" (*Dynatos*).

53. *the rich He has sent away empty.* It is a common idea in the Bible that the fortunes of the (wicked) rich will be taken away (Job 15:29; Jer 17:11). However, the imagery of the emptiness of the rich, instead of the impoverishment, is affected by the mention of the hungry being full in the preceding line. Hannah's canticle (I Sam 2:5,7) has a more logical balance in contrasting the hungry and the full, the poor and the rich. In the Gospel parable (Luke

20:10–11) those who seek to collect the rent from the wicked tenants are sent away empty.

54. *He has helped.* The imagery in *antilambanein* is one of taking hold in order to support. The same verb is also used for God's taking Israel His servant from the ends of the earth (Isa 41:8–9).

His servant Israel. This *pais* (not *doulos,* the "handmaid" of 38 and 47) is the term which is found for Jacob or Israel in the Servant Songs of Deutero-Isaiah (41:8; 44:1; 45:4; etc.).

in remembrance of His mercy. Literally an infinitive, "to remember"; yet the connotation is not one of purpose ("in order to remember"). The infinitive is employed, as also in the Benedictus, vs. 72, to supply further definition about the help; it may be a Semitism, reflecting *l^e* plus the infinitive (BDF 391[4]). For "mercy" see the NOTE on vs. 50. The covenant with Abraham is in view here (55).

55. *as He spoke unto our fathers.* Is "unto our fathers" (*pros* with the accusative) in this line in parallelism to "to Abraham" (dative phrase) in the next line? Creed, *Gospel,* 24, and Koontz, "Magnificat," 348, answer affirmatively, placing the two phrases in apposition. Others answer negatively, treating the first line of 55 as parenthetical, so that 55b is the continuation of 54b: "in remembrance of His mercy to Abraham," rather than: "as He spoke unto our fathers, to Abraham." Yet, a parenthetical clause seems out of place in the relatively simple parallelism of the hymn; and a meaningless variation between the dative and a *pros* phrase is not un-Lucan (Tannehill, "Magnificat," 271[19]). Ramaroson, "Structuram," 41–42, argues for the transposition of lines: 54a, 55a,54b,55b.

56. *about three months.* The chronology is in relation to Elizabeth's pregnancy, and this figure is to be added to the sixth month of 1:26,36. The reckoning is presumably of a pregnancy lasting ten lunar months (NOTE on 1:24), so that Mary leaves just before the birth mentioned in 1:57.

returned. Hypostrephein is a Lucan verb, occurring thirty-three times in Luke/Acts as contrasted with four times in the rest of the NT. For the theme of departure serving to terminate scenes in the Lucan infancy narrative, see NOTE on 1:23.

home. At the time of the annunciation Mary had not yet had sexual relations with Joseph, her betrothed, and so had not yet gone to live with him. If the annunciation took place in her own home and after it she went hastily to visit Elizabeth (39), presumably it was to her own home and not to Joseph's that she returned. Luke never specifies when Mary went to live with Joseph, although he has her traveling with him in 2:5. How well did Luke know the Palestinian marriage customs described in the NOTE on "betrothed" in Matt 1:18?

COMMENT

I shall begin with some brief remarks about the structure and composition
of the scene. Then I shall discuss in turn the two main sections of the
scene, the visitation itself (vss. 39–45,56) and the Magnificat (vss.
46–55).

A. *The Structure and Composition of the Scene*

In the general discussion of the organization of chs. 1–2 (§ 9, B2), I
pointed out that the visitation does not fit well into the schema of those
who organize the present Lucan narrative into diptychs centered around
JBap and Jesus (Table IX). The scene is preceded by two annunciations
of conception; it is followed by two stories of birth and circumcision; but it
fits into neither side of these duplicate patterns. This does not mean that
the visitation does not fit smoothly into the overall Lucan story line, for it
serves to bring together the dramatis personae of the two annunciation
narratives and to show the subordinate position of JBap in relation to
Jesus. Yet, while the scene fits Luke's thought, it creates a certain awkwardness in what seems to be a carefully balanced structure.

The difficulty can be alleviated if we posit two stages of Lucan composition. I shall argue below that the Magnificat was added to an already composed Lucan narrative. Without the Magnificat, vss. 39–45,56 cease to be
so clearly an autonomous scene and can be regarded as an epilogue to the
annunciation to Mary. Accordingly, I have proposed the diptych of Table
XI as the earlier Lucan arrangement of the two annunciations. As we shall
see, the information supplied in the first epilogue makes the second epilogue intelligible. In this hypothesis, when Luke decided at a later stage to
add the Magnificat (and the other canticles as well),[1] he sacrificed some of
the perfect balance of his diptych construction in order to strengthen the
theological message of his scene. Obviously, it is the final Lucan scene that
must be the prime object of our study, but I shall contend that the strength
of this analysis is that it helps us to understand better the final scene.

By proposing two stages of Lucan composition, I am implicitly reject-

[1] Since in this hypothesis the canticles are not Lucan compositions, the reason for the
later addition may have been the fact that Luke was not familiar with them when he first
composed the infancy narrative.

ing two other approaches to the scene. *First,* I am rejecting the thesis that a pre-Lucan JBap source, which began in 1:5–25, is being continued here.[2] I have already argued in § 10, B2, that there is no convincing reason either by way of content or by way of theology to posit a JBap source behind the annunciation to Zechariah. Even independently of that, there would be less reason to posit such a source here, since the material in 1:39ff. can scarcely have had much purpose other than to subordinate JBap to Jesus and to prepare for the two birth narratives to follow. With the exception of the Magnificat, the style is clearly Lucan (see NOTES). Against Dibelius[3] who contended that the visitation was a Lucan and not a pre-Lucan composition, Bultmann, Hahn, and others have argued that there is pre-Lucan or non-Lucan material in the scene. I would agree, pointing not only to the Magnificat but also to a geographical detail such as that mentioned in vs. 39. However, the latter represents a small nugget of information about the parents of JBap—the very type of information that we saw in 1:5–7. Here as there I would propose that Luke has woven items of tradition into his own composition, but the dominant story wherein Elizabeth and JBap pay homage to Mary and Jesus is a conception of Lucan theology.

Second, I am rejecting the thesis that there were pre-Lucan *Marian* hymns in the early Church. Virtually no serious scholar would argue today that the Magnificat was composed by Mary. Outside of vs. 48[4] the Magnificat has little direct reference to Mary's situation and is a hymn that describes Israel, specifically the poor and oppressed remnant. Only because Luke thinks of Mary as belonging to this group has the canticle been brought into its present context. But the situation is quite different with the hymn of praise in vss. 42–45 which Elizabeth specifically directs to Mary. J. McHugh has assumed that this hymn is pre-Lucan, and so "there is nothing improbable in the suggestion that early Christians sang hymns of praise in honour of Mary."[5] However, such a suggestion is really quite improbable if one judges the early Christian situation from our earliest writings, the Pauline letters and Mark. Paul never mentions Mary by name and shows no interest in her, and the Marcan scene in which she features is scarcely favorable to her (Appendix IV A). Moreover, vss. 42–45 are replete with Lucanisms, and the main part of Elizabeth's words are an echo of a scene particular to Luke's account of the ministry (11:27–28). In other words, vss. 42–45 may constitute a hymn to Mary, but it was not a pre-Lucan hymn.

[2] Sometimes this thesis includes the assumption that the Magnificat was part of the JBap source and that it was originally spoken by Elizabeth. See the long NOTE on vs. 46.

[3] "Jungfrauensohn," 13–14.

[4] As we shall see below, a plausible case can be made for vs. 48 as a Lucan insertion in the Magnificat and for vss. 76–77 as a Lucan insertion in the Benedictus.

[5] In *Mother* 71–72, McHugh proposes that Luke placed on Elizabeth's lips "a prayer commonly used by Christians of the day to the mother of Jesus."

With these preliminary remarks about composition, let us now consider in detail the two main components of the scene: the visitation and the Magnificat.

B. *The Visitation* (1:39–45,56)

At the end of each annunciation narrative Luke has given us information that was meant to prepare for the visitation. After the annunciation of JBap's birth we were told that, when she had conceived, Elizabeth hid herself for five months, so that her pregnancy was not known to outsiders (1:24–25). The annunciation of Jesus' birth concluded with the angel giving Mary a sign based on Elizabeth's miraculous pregnancy which was then in its sixth month (1:36–37). Having expressed her obedience as the handmaid of the Lord (38), Mary hastens forth to acclaim this marvel of which the angel had spoken. His words, "Nothing said by God can be impossible," were an implicit directive to Mary, with the result that the visitation comes under a divine imperative.

The visitation begins in vs. 40 with Mary's greeting to Elizabeth, a greeting which ends the seclusion that has surrounded Elizabeth's pregnancy (24). Mary could not have known of Elizabeth's status unless God had revealed to her His plan concerning JBap.[6] And Elizabeth is now given in turn a revelation of Mary's status, so that she can return Mary's greeting. This revelation comes to Elizabeth through the action of the child in her womb. In vs. 15 Luke had told us that this child would be filled with the Holy Spirit even from his mother's womb and thus would be a prophet (also vs. 17). Now JBap begins to prophesy in the womb by jumping with gladness (41,44b)—a gladness that hails the advent of the messianic age. Thus, Elizabeth is given to perceive not only that Mary is with child but also that her child is the Messiah. JBap was to be great before the Lord and go before Him (15,17), and his gladness is explicable only if Elizabeth now stands before the mother of the Lord (43b).[7] Each mother has now received a revelation of what God has done for the other, and so Luke gives each a canticle of praise with which to respond to God's mercy, respectively vss. 42–45 and 46–54.[8] And Luke's theological con-

---

[6] Luke's story must be interpreted by the information that he gives us and not by positing any contact between the women other than what is narrated. Luke specifies that it is Mary's greeting that caused the baby to jump in the womb; the greeting itself and not some special message contained in it is the occasion of a revelation to Elizabeth through the action of JBap.

[7] It is this scene, and not merely the supposed family relationship between Elizabeth and Mary (1:36), which offers difficulty in reconciling the Lucan infancy narrative with what we know of JBap and Jesus during the ministry. The critical reconstruction of that relationship given above in § 10D becomes nonsense if JBap and Elizabeth knew from the beginning that Jesus was the Messiah, indeed, the Lord.

[8] In my hypothesis of two stages of Lucan composition, in the first stage, before the Magnificat was added, there was already an interchange between the two women: Mary

cern now becomes apparent, for both canticles praise what God has done for Mary in the conception of the Messiah. From comparing the two annunciations, we were able to deduce the superiority of Jesus over JBap. But now that the dramatis personae from the two sides of the diptych meet each other, that superiority must be made explicit. What God has done for Mary far outshines what God has done for Zechariah and Elizabeth.[9]

Elizabeth's canticle[10] praising Mary (42–45) echoes OT motifs and anticipates motifs that will be found in the Gospel—a combination of elements similar to the portrayal of Mary in the annunciation itself. The initial blessing in vs. 42 illustrates perfectly the double source of Luke's motifs. On the OT side a similar blessing appears in canticles praising women of Israelite history. Just as Elizabeth, filled by the prophetic Holy Spirit, proclaims, "Blessed are you among women," so the prophetess Deborah had proclaimed, "Blessed be Jael among women" (Judg 5:24). And Uzziah, son of Micah, had proclaimed to Judith, "Blessed are you, daughter, . . . among all women on earth" (Judith 13:18).[11] Jael and Judith are blessed because God had used them to slay mighty enemy warriors and deliver Israel—the physically weak used to confound the strong.[12] The blessing of Mary is explained in the next line: "Blessed is the fruit of your womb." (Although the two blessings addressed to Mary are put in parataxis or coordination, reflecting Semitized style, the logic is one of hypotaxis or subordination: Mary is blessed among women in that the fruit of her womb is blessed.[18]) This echoes the blessing promised by Moses to Israel if Israel was obedient to the voice of God (even as Mary obeyed the word of the Lord in 1:38): "Blessed be the fruit [LXX: offspring] of your womb" (Deut 28:1,4). This OT background suggests that Mary's blessing is not a purely personal one. She has a role in God's plan for His people because she has conceived the Messiah who will be the

---

greeted Elizabeth (40) and Elizabeth praised Mary (42–45). The indication that Mary had spoken may have facilitated the later introduction of a canticle which gave her words. Similarly, in the scene after JBap's birth Luke will indicate that Zechariah spoke in praise of God (64), and this may have facilitated the later adding of a canticle which gave him words (67–79).

[9] The complete absence of a mention of Joseph in the visitation scene confirms the fact that Luke really did intend a virginal conception in 1:26–38 (§ 11, B1): there are only three active dramatis personae in the two conceptions, and all three are mentioned in the visitation.

[10] In the initial NOTE I mentioned poetic and vocabulary factors behind the notion that 42–45 constitute a type of canticle. That idea receives support from the fact that the best OT antecedents for vs. 42 are in poetic canticles, as we shall see.

[11] It is not implausible that Luke knew the Book of Judith, which was composed before 100 B.C., probably in Hebrew, and preserved for us in the LXX tradition. See footnote 20, § 10.

[12] Judith, whose name means "Jewess," was not a historical person; her story was modeled on Jael and on God's deliverance of Israel *by the hand* of Moses during the Exodus. See P. Skehan, CBQ 25 (1963), 94–110.

[18] Schnackenburg, "Magnificat," 352. See the last NOTE on vs. 42 for a structural similarity between Judith and Luke in this matter of a double blessing.

glory of Israel (2:32). This salvific role, evocative of Jael and Judith, has been made possible through Mary's obedience.

The latter point is highlighted when we look to the NT background for Elizabeth's blessing. In § 11D I interpreted the portrait of Mary in 1:38 as a Lucan retrojection into the infancy narrative of a picture derived from the one common Synoptic scene wherein Mary appears in the ministry of Jesus. Mary's "Let it happen to me according to your word" was the direct discourse form of Jesus' saying, "My mother and my brothers are those who hear the word of God and do it" (Luke 8:21). But Luke's account of the ministry has a second saying of Jesus pertaining to his mother, a saying for which there is no parallel in the other Gospels. In 11:27–28, to the woman in the crowd who cries aloud the macarism, "Fortunate is the womb that bore you and the breasts you sucked," Jesus responds with a macarism of his own, "Fortunate rather are those who hear the word of God and keep it."[14] It is this scene that provides the background for the beginning and the end of Elizabeth's words to Mary in 1:42,45:

> Blessed are you among women,
> and blessed is the fruit of your womb. . . .
> Fortunate is she who believed
> that the Lord's words to her would find fulfillment.

Like the woman in the crowd, Elizabeth praises Mary's physical motherhood of the Messiah. But such a macarism stemming from Israel's history[15] must be modified in the light of the Gospel. For Luke, Jesus' physical family has to meet the criterion of discipleship which constitutes Jesus' eschatological or real family. Just as in 8:21 the mother was defined in terms of hearing the word of God and doing it, Jesus' response to the woman in the crowd in 11:28 puts the emphasis on hearing the word of God and keeping it. This word of Jesus is a correction of the woman's view; but Elizabeth is the vehicle of the Holy Spirit and so she can supply her own complement to the blessing on physical motherhood. If the opening words proclaimed by Elizabeth with a loud cry are very close to what the woman cried out, her closing macarism is an adaptation of Jesus' macarism in response to the woman. The adaptation consists in joining the hearing and keeping of the word into a picture of believing the word.[16]

14 One may ask whether this peculiarly Lucan scene is a variant of the common Synoptic scene. In each someone says something about Jesus' mother; in each Jesus gives a response which shifts the emphasis from physical maternity to hearing the word (*logos*) and doing or keeping it.

15 The woman's cry is similar in purport to the cry of the disciples as Jesus came toward Jerusalem from the Mount of Olives: "Blessed is the King who comes in the name of the Lord" (19:38): both hail the Messiah.

16 In 1:45 Luke uses for "words" a passive participle of *lalein*, "to speak," rather than the *logos* of 11:28. See also footnote 64, § 11.

The word which Mary accepted in vs. 38 involved a virginal conception, and so it required faith. The conception of the child in her womb which made her blessed among women was entirely through God's creative Spirit, without any physical participation by man; what Mary brought to God's plan of salvation was her faith that the creator God could accomplish this. This faith in the fulfillment of the Lord's words is worthy of a beatitude; for it stands in sharp contrast to the lack of faith upon the part of Elizabeth's husband who did not believe the Lord's words which, nevertheless, would be fulfilled in due time (20).

Having seen that vss. 42 and 45 in Elizabeth's canticle have both OT and NT background, let us turn now to the intermediary verses. The question in vs. 43, "Who am I that the mother of my Lord should come to me?", vocalizes Elizabeth's recognition that Jesus is the Messiah. Both in the Gospel (20:41–44) and in Acts (2:34) Luke uses Ps 110:1, "The Lord said to *my Lord*," to show that Jesus is the Messiah and Son of God; and Elizabeth is recognizing Mary as the mother of "my Lord," i.e., of the Messiah.[17] The implicit citation of a Davidic messianic psalm may have suggested to Luke the reminiscence of a scene in II Sam 6 in which David figured, a scene which, like the visitation, took place in the hill country of Judea near Jerusalem. At David's command the Ark of the Covenant was being brought from the Philistine border country toward Jerusalem, but David hesitated to take it into his city (Jerusalem) because it had caused the death of a man who touched it. He exclaimed, "How can the Ark of the Lord come to me?" (6:9). The resemblance to Elizabeth's question is noteworthy, especially since as the result of David's self-questioning the Ark of the Covenant remained at the house of Obed-edom the Gittite for three months (6:11), even as Mary the mother of the Lord remained with Elizabeth about three months (1:56). This resemblance has been seized upon to defend the (dubious) thesis already mentioned (§ 11, E3) that Luke thinks of Mary as the Ark of the Covenant.[18] However, one should be cautious in drawing an identification from such echoes of an OT scene. It is the Ark's power to kill that causes David to ask his question—a motivation quite different from that of Elizabeth's question. The Ark's eventual journey to Jerusalem after the three-month stay is quite different from Mary's return home.[19] The connecting link in the Lucan reminiscences

---

[17] In the *Ave Maria*, the opening portion, "Hail Mary, full of grace, the Lord is with thee," is taken from 1:28. The next portion, "Blessed art thou among women, and blessed is the fruit of thy womb, Jesus," is taken from 1:42. The salutation in the second part of the prayer, "Holy Mary, Mother of God," echoes the reference to the "mother of my Lord" in 1:43.

[18] This is defended by Laurentin, *Structure*, 79–81, who points to some other resemblances between the two scenes, e.g., the mention of gladness in Luke 1:44 and of rejoicing in II Sam 6:12; the mention of a loud "cry" in Luke 1:42 and II Sam 6:15.

[19] Laurentin calls attention to Mary's going to Jerusalem in ch. 2. Some would press further and speak of Mary's travels in the infancy narrative as a pilgrimage accompanied by hymns!

may be David rather than the Ark. When David goes to Araunah the Jebusite to purchase the threshing floor that will ultimately become the site of the Temple in Jerusalem, Araunah asks, "What is this, that my lord the king has come to his servant?" (II Sam 24:21). This question also resembles Elizabeth's question, and it does not concern the Ark.

In vs. 44 Elizabeth goes on to express in her own words what was already told the reader in the introduction—a Lucan technique that we have seen in the two annunciations (1:7 and 18; 1:27 and 34; see p. 301 above). The repetition is designed to underline that it is through the prophetic action of JBap in Elizabeth's womb that she knows Mary as "the mother of my Lord." The idea that the action of babes within the womb anticipates their future destiny[20] is found in Gen 25:22–23 when Esau and Jacob jump within Rebekah's womb. They are struggling with one another, as they and their descendants will struggle together in life. Luke is doing here exactly what he did in 1:13–17; he is writing the story of the infancy of JBap in light of what he knows from his tradition of the ministry of JBap. That ministry prepared people to recognize "the mightier one who is to come" (3:15–16); it prepared "the way of the Lord" (3:4). That ministry has already begun when JBap causes Elizabeth to recognize the Lord in Mary's womb.[21]

Before going on to Mary's responding canticle, the Magnificat, let us look at the conclusion of the visitation in 1:56. In an earlier stage of Lucan composition vs. 56 probably followed directly after 39–45. The terse statement that Mary remained with Elizabeth about three months and then returned home (to Nazareth) has led to much speculation among those addicted to evaluating the scene as a historical narrative motivated by detectable psychology. Can Luke really have meant that Mary left Elizabeth before the child was born and thus deserted her relative at the time of greatest need? Was Mary's action motivated by the fact that three months had passed in her own pregnancy and that she had to hasten to Galilee to be taken to Joseph's house, lest scandalous rumors start about the origins of her child? Indeed, those who harmonize Matthew and Luke suggest that the scene of the discovery of Mary's pregnancy in Matt 1:18 came about precisely because Mary charitably delayed at Zechariah's home three months to help her relative.

Less imagination and more fidelity to Lucan style suggests that it was Luke's intention to have Mary off the stage before he narrated JBap's birth. The nine months that he has counted off bring the narrative close to

---

20 The same idea is involved in children being named before their conception with a name that is indicative of their future role; see footnote 29, § 10.

21 Luke specifies that JBap leaped "with gladness" (*agalliasis*). Such an emotion is not mentioned in the Synoptic accounts of JBap's ministry; but in John 3:29, JBap says: "The bridegroom's best man, who waits there listening for him, is overjoyed [*chara chairein*] just to hear the bridegroom's voice. That is my joy [*chara*], and it is complete."

the final month of birth in a calculation of ten lunar months of pregnancy, and so the visitation provides a good transition to the birth narratives. But the two birth narratives of JBap and of Jesus have their own balanced scenario. In each the two parents and the newborn child are featured, and it would destroy this careful balance to have Mary the parent of Jesus at the birth of JBap. This literary structure is far more important in the Lucan infancy narrative than the psychology of the characters involved, for we are not dealing with memories from family history but with a carefully planned dramatization of the theology of salvation history. If there is reason to suspect that, as part of an ongoing struggle to bring JBap completely within the framework of Christian theology, Luke made him a relative of Jesus (§ 10D), the visitation scene constitutes a Lucan dramatization of this relationship.

C. *The Lucan Canticles in General*

The Magnificat cannot be discussed in isolation from the other three canticles of the Lucan infancy narrative: the Benedictus (1:67–79), the Gloria in Excelsis (2:13–14), and the Nunc Dimittis (2:28–32). I shall first discuss theories about their composition and then describe the Anawim or "Poor Ones" with whom the canticles have been frequently associated.

1. The Composition of the Canticles

For our present purposes I wish to leave aside the Gloria in Excelsis; not only is it too short to be particularly indicative, but also it constitutes the only instance where the canticle has a speaker who has not hitherto figured in the narrative, i.e., the "multitude of the heavenly host" in 2:13. For the other canticles four different theories have been offered to explain their composition: (a) The canticles were composed by those to whom they are attributed in the narrative, namely, the Magnificat by Mary, the Benedictus by Zechariah, and the Nunc Dimittis by Simeon. This theory dominated in pre-critical times when the infancy narrative was treated as a history stemming from family circles. It is obviously unlikely that such finished poetry could have been composed on the spot by ordinary people,[22] and today there would be no serious scholarly support for such a naive hypothesis. (b) The canticles were composed by Luke at the same

---

[22] This difficulty was overcome by the argument that the Holy Spirit inspired the speakers poetically, not only religiously. Similarities among the canticles could be attributed to the Holy Spirit working in all three speakers and/or to the fact that the speakers shared a common spirituality.

time as he was writing the surrounding narrative. While not naive, this theory also has relatively little following because the canticles fit awkwardly into their present context. If they were omitted, one would never suspect their absence; in fact, the narrative would read more smoothly without them. (c) The canticles were composed by Luke and added subsequently to an already existing (Lucan or pre-Lucan) narrative. (d) The canticles were pre-Lucan or non-Lucan and were added by Luke to an already existing Lucan narrative. Since the canticles stress Israel and David (1:54,69) and speak of "our fathers" (1:55,72), there would be no reason to posit Gentile Christian composition. What has been debated is whether they were composed by Jews or by Jewish Christians and whether they were composed originally in Greek or in Semitic. There is serious scholarly support for theories (c) and (d) and their sub-variations. As I discuss the evidence below, it may assist the reader to know that in my judgment it favors theory (d) and Jewish Christian composition.

In some ways the Lucan canticles resemble the speeches in the Book of Acts:[23] they give voice to general sentiments that are appropriate for the dramatis personae in the setting in which they are placed. It is not a question of a purely fictional creation, for the dramatis personae are remembered or conceived of as representative of a certain type of piety which the canticles vocalize. (In Acts Peter and Paul are remembered as kerygmatic preachers, and therefore the standard Christian kerygma has been woven into speeches attributed to them.) Moreover, the canticles pick up and continue motifs that were already in the infancy narrative pertinent to the three speakers. We are told in 1:40 that Mary greeted Elizabeth, but no words are given; the Magnificat in 1:46–55 supplies Mary with words.[24] We are told in 1:64 that Zechariah began to speak in praise of God, but no words are given; the Benedictus in 1:67–79 supplies Zechariah with words. In 2:34–35 Simeon is said to bless the parents and speak to Mary; the Nunc Dimittis in 2:28–32 supplies Simeon with a companion blessing of God[25]—a blessing which fittingly is put first. Indeed, for the Magnificat there was an added motif on which Luke capitalized in inserting a canticle. In 1:42 Mary received a blessing similar to the blessing received by Judith (13:18). Judith responded to such praise by singing a famous canticle (16:1–17), just as Mary is made to respond with the Magnificat.

---

23 See M. Dibelius, *Studies in the Acts of the Apostles* (London: SCM, 1956; German orig., 1949), 138–85. The resemblance is not perfect, for Luke composed the sermons in Acts while he adapted the canticles. See footnote 70 below.

24 The Magnificat does not concern Elizabeth; but Elizabeth's reaction to Mary's greeting would give one to suppose that the greeting concerned what God had done for Mary.

25 The angel of the Lord announces good news of great joy to the shepherds in 2:10–12; the multitude of the heavenly host with their Gloria in Excelsis supply a companion piece praising God in 2:13–14.

There are both resemblances and differences if we compare the canticles among themselves. By way of resemblances[26] they are all highly evocative of OT and intertestamental passages (Tables XII and XIII), almost to the point that one can speak of them as mosaics pieced together with OT pieces. Yet the poetic patterns vary, with much closer poetic parallelism being found in the Magnificat than in the Benedictus. In a choice between composition by writers of the same circle and composition by the same writer, the resemblances support either theory, while the differences militate against the same author. Nevertheless, Harnack, Goulder and Sanderson, Sparks, and Turner are among those who think that Luke himself may have composed the canticles in the manner of contemporary Jewish psalms by making a mosaic or cento of OT passages, perhaps deliberately imitating the poetic variety of the psalter. In objection to this it has been pointed out that the canticles are considerably more Semitized than the surrounding narrative; but that same phenomenon has been noted in III Maccabees where the prayers have more Hebraisms than the surrounding narrative.[27] The objection becomes more persuasive when it is observed that Lucan stylistic traits are less prominent in the canticles, except for several lines that Luke himself may have added to them to make the canticles fit the context.[28]

The relation between the context and the canticle is really the crucial point here. I have said above that in a general way the canticles vocalize the type of piety that one might expect of the characters to whom they are attributed, but they do not relate to those characters in a specific way. Except for the verses mentioned in footnote 28, the Benedictus does not specifically apply to the situation of Zechariah and JBap, and the Magnificat does not specifically apply to the situation of Mary and Jesus. (The fact that there could be the debate described in the NOTE on vs. 46 as to whether Mary or Elizabeth spoke the Magnificat is eloquent proof of the non-specific character of the canticle.) In fact, there are even lines in the canticles that are awkward when applied to the situation of the speakers. The martial tone in vss. 51 and 52, where the proud have been scattered and the mighty have been put down from their thrones, is scarcely explained by Mary's conception of a child. The birth of JBap scarcely constitutes "salvation from our enemies and from the hand of all those who hate us" (vs. 71). If Luke composed the canticles himself to be spoken by the characters to whom he has attributed them, there should

---

[26] These are stressed by Jones, "Background," 43. For instance, both the Magnificat (1:49) and the Benedictus (1:68) draw upon Ps 111. Also 1:53 and 1:79 draw upon Ps 107.

[27] M. Hadas, *The Third and Fourth Books of Maccabees* (New York: Harper, 1953), 22.

[28] See Machen, *Virgin Birth*, 77–80. In particular, there are many Lucanisms in 1:48 (see NOTES) which is the only verse in the Magnificat which is closely related to the picture of Mary in the context (1:38,45). Also in 1:76–77, the only verses in the Benedictus that pertain specifically to JBap; and in 1:70.

have been much smoother harmony.[29] One cannot avoid this objection by claiming that Luke is adding the canticles he composed himself to a pre-Lucan infancy narrative, e.g., to a JBap source or to a Marian source; for then it becomes unintelligible why there are more Lucan stylistic traits in the narrative than in the canticles.

The most satisfactory solution is that the canticles were composed in a non-Lucan circle and that originally they praised the salvific action of God without any precise reference to the events that Luke was narrating in the infancy narrative. Nevertheless, when Luke considered these canticles,[30] he saw how they might be brought into the infancy narrative with relatively little adaptation (footnote 28). The piety and the concept of salvation found in the canticles corresponded well to the piety and the concept of salvation that one could expect from the main figures of the infancy narrative. (This correspondence is not surprising, granting the fact that the characters of Elizabeth and Zechariah have been sketched according to the models of such OT figures as Sarah and Abraham, and Mary is the forerunner of the Christian disciple.) Accordingly, Luke decided to add the canticles to his infancy narrative. Rather than rewrite the whole narrative to make this addition unnoticeable, Luke was content to leave rough seams. One cannot prove this theory, but it solves more difficulties than any other.

If the canticles came to Luke from a non-Lucan source or circle of writers, what group composed them? They have their closest parallel in the Jewish hymns and psalms attested in the literature from 200 B.C. to A.D. 100, e.g., in I Maccabees, Judith, *II Baruch, IV Ezra,* the Qumran *Hodayoth* (Thanksgiving Psalms), and the Qumran War Scroll. It is not only a parallelism in style (a cento or mosaic of lines taken from earlier poetry) but also in religious outlook (a complete dependence upon God for victory). However, since the comparable Jewish hymns exist both in Hebrew and in Greek (even if the originals were in Hebrew), this parallelism in itself does not tell us whether those who composed the Lucan canticles were Greek-speaking Jews or Hebrew-speaking Jews.[31] At times the Magnificat and the Benedictus seem to depend more closely on the LXX than on the Hebrew Bible (see the asterisked passages in Tables XII and XIII). This may favor their composition among Greek-speaking

---

[29] I am not referring to the lack of smoothness visible in the *joining* of the canticle to the narrative which I mentioned at the beginning of this section in relation to theory (b)—that simply shows that Luke added the canticles after he had composed the narrative. The question here concerns the harmony lacking in the *contents* of the canticle.

[30] See footnote 1 above.

[31] That the Lucan canticles were composed in Hebrew is maintained by Gunkel, D. R. Jones, Laurentin, Torrey, and Winter. An Aramaic original is not often suggested since one would expect canticles to be composed in the sacred cultic language. Machen, *Virgin Birth*, 95–98, proposes Aramaic for the Magnificat since he thinks that it was composed by Mary, a Galilean village girl.

Jews, but others would see it simply as a sign that they were translated from the Hebrew by a writer who knew the LXX.

Scholars like Bornhäuser, Gunkel, Klostermann, Mowinckel, Spitta, and Winter have proposed that the canticles were Jewish (not Christian) compositions taken over and adapted by Luke. Winter, for instance, pointing to the martial references, argues that originally the Benedictus and the Magnificat were Maccabean battle hymns, sung respectively before and after fighting. However, while many of the verses, which echo the OT, would be perfectly at home in Judaism, one would have to find a Jewish situation in the two centuries before Christ which would explain the canticles' tone of salvation *accomplished*. As Winter admits,[32] many of the Jewish hymns cited as parallels in the preceding paragraph reflect the catastrophic conditions of the time of foreign persecution: "One of the rare moments of Jewish thought when despair prevails over hope." For this reason he chose as a setting for the canticles the Maccabean victories, the single bright spot in the whole period. The followers of the Maccabees might well sing of "salvation from our enemies and from the hand of all those who hate us" (Luke 1:71), but would they describe a victory won by their priest leaders of the House of Levi (I Macc 2:1) as God having "raised up for us a horn of salvation in the House of David His servant"?[33] There is really no purely Jewish setting that would explain a tremendous sense of salvation accomplished through the House of David. That theme, plus the fulfillment of the covenant with Abraham (Luke 1:55,73), are very common Christian themes[34] and are better explained if the canticles arose in a Jewish Christian community, a theory defended by such scholars as D. R. Jones, Benoit, Gnilka, and Schürmann.

2. The Canticles and the Jewish Christian Anawim

If the canticles came to Luke from a circle of Jewish Christians, can we identify this group further? An attractive suggestion is that the religious atmosphere of this community was the piety of the Anawim.[35] Although this title meaning the "Poor Ones" may have originally designated the

---

[32] "Magnificat," 330.

[33] The prayer in I Macc 4:30 asks for victory such as was formerly granted to David, but that is not the same as praising a victory accomplished through the House of David.

[34] If one brings the Nunc Dimittis into the discussion, one can scarcely imagine a Maccabean victory being described as "a light to be a revelation to the Gentiles" (Luke 2:32). However, this is the only passage in the canticles that directly concerns the Gentiles, so that conversion of the Gentiles was not a major motif in the Jewish Christian community that composed them. This is another argument against composition by Luke himself.

[35] The word Anawim represents a plural from the Hebrew *'ānāw* which, along with its cognate *'ānî*, is a word for "poor, humble, afflicted." Also of importance is the abstract noun *'ŏnî* "lowliness, poverty." English treatments of the Anawim are found in A. Gelin, *The Poor of Yahweh* (Collegeville, Minn.: Liturgical Press, 1964); L. Sabourin, *The Psalms* (Staten Island, N.Y.: Alba, 1969), I, 98–102; and M. Dibelius, *James* (Hermeneia; Philadelphia: Fortress, 1976; German orig. 1920, 1964), 39–45.

physically poor (and frequently still included them), it came to refer more widely to those who could not trust in their own strength but had to rely in utter confidence upon God: the lowly, the poor, the sick, the downtrodden, the widows and orphans. The opposite of the Anawim were not simply the rich, but the proud and self-sufficient who showed no need of God or His help. There is considerable scholarly debate about the pre-exilic origins of the Anawim, and about the extent to which they constituted a class or community, and not merely an attitude of mind. But a good case can be made for the contention that in post-exilic times the Anawim regarded themselves as the ultimate narrowing down of the remnant of Israel. The concept that God was not going to save His whole people but only a remnant was redefined many times. When the Northern Kingdom (Israel) was destroyed in 722, the Southern Kingdom (Judah) regarded itself as the remnant. When part of the Southern Kingdom was taken into captivity to Babylon (598 and 587), with part of the people left behind in Palestine, both exiles and Palestinians tended to regard themselves as the remnant. Eventually, under the catalyst of defeat and persecution, the remnant was redefined, not in historical or tribal terms, but in terms of piety and way of life.[36] The parallelism in Ps 149:4 equates the people of God with the Anawim: "The Lord takes pleasure in His people; He adorns the Poor Ones with victory" (see also Isa 49:13; 66:2). Very often, woven together with this piety of dependence on God was a "Temple piety" (footnote 13, § 10). The mixture is explained by the fact that the appeal for God's deliverance of His Anawim was made in psalms,[37] and thus in a cultic setting. The "Poor Ones" showed their trust in God by being faithful to the times of prayer and sacrifice.

Of particular interest for our purposes is the possibility of considering the Qumran community as a sectarian group of Anawim. Many scholars think that the origins of the Qumran movement may be found in the Hasidean branch of the Maccabean revolt.[38] In I Macc 2:42 we hear that Mattathias, the father of Judas Maccabeus, was joined by the Hasideans (*Ḥasîdîm* or "pious ones") who were incensed at the religious blasphemies of the Syrian king and his Hellenized Jewish allies. For a while the Hasideans supported the Maccabees; but their interest was primarily religious, while the Maccabees became more and more politically

---

[36] Poverty was the inevitable aftermath of the downfall of the nation. The fact that the rich and the powerful had not been able to prevent that downfall focused the attention of the survivors on God as the only salvation and on poverty as a way of life closer to God than wealth and power. Thus poverty became a religious concept.

[37] There is a considerable literature on the Anawim in the psalms: A. Rahlfs, '*Anî und ʿAnāw in den Psalmen* (Leipzig: Dieterich, 1892; H. Birkeland, '*Anî und ʿAnāw in den Psalmen* (Oslo: Dybwad, 1933); P. Van den Berge, " 'Ani et 'Anaw dans les psaumes," in *Le Psautier* ed. R. De Langhe (Louvain University, 1962), 273–95. God is said to protect, defend, save, and rescue the Anawim, either as individuals or as a group; God does not forget the Anawim but does justice to them. The Anawim both implore God and praise His name.

[38] See JBC, article 68, ##84–87.

oriented, ambitious to establish a dynasty. We read of a split between the two in I Macc 7:9–16, *ca.* 162 B.C.; and we suspect that *ca.* 150, after the Maccabees usurped the high priesthood, a group of the Hasideans followed the Righteous Teacher (of legitimate Zadokite high priestly stock) to the Dead Sea and there became what we know as the Qumran community. These sectarians would have differed from other Jewish Anawim in having their own interpretation of the Law (given by the Teacher), in their withdrawn communitarian existence, in their opposition to the Jerusalem Temple, and in their shifting the messianic hopes over to a Messiah from the House of Aaron (Levi), alongside the Davidic Messiah. But their communal sharing of goods, their intense piety, and their sense of persecution were certainly features common to Anawim thought. The writer of the Qumran *Hodayoth* (Thanksgiving Psalms) frequently designates himself as a "poor one" (1QH v 13–14), a factor of considerable importance if he was, as many think, the founder of the sect. Quite evocative of the Lucan canticles, especially of the Magnificat, is this passage from his writings: "You, O Lord, have assisted the soul of the poor one and the needy against one who is stronger than he. You have redeemed my soul from the hand of the mighty" (1QH ii 34–35). References to the whole Qumran group as Anawim and as the Community of the Poor (*'ebyônîm*) are found in 1QH xviii 14; 1QM xi 9; and 4QpPs 37 (ii 9; iii 10). As already mentioned, the psalms and hymns of Qumran are very close in style to the Lucan canticles.[39]

It is not farfetched then to suggest that Luke got his canticles from a somewhat parallel community of Jewish Anawim who had been converted to Christianity,[40] a group that unlike the sectarians at Qumran would have continued to reverence the Temple and whose messianism was Davidic. Jesus came blessing the poor, the hungry, the downtrodden, and the persecuted (Luke 6:20–22);[41] he himself was persecuted and put to death. Yet Jesus entrusted himself to God's hands (23:46); and God, faithful to His servant Jesus, raised him and exalted him as savior (Acts 5:31)—a savior for Israel coming from David's posterity just as God had promised (Acts 13:23).[42] Jewish Anawim might well have found in him

---

[39] The Therapeutae were an Egyptian group of Jews akin to the Qumran Essenes; and in Philo's *De Vita Contemplativa* x 79–80 there is an important passage describing how the Therapeutae composed hymns.

[40] This thesis is closely associated with Benoit; yet Schnackenburg has also recognized the presence of Anawim mentality in the canticles.

[41] The Beatitudes in their Lucan form stress physical poverty, hunger, and suffering and are sharply opposed to the rich. In their Matthean form the Beatitudes have some interesting resonances at Qumran. The expression "poor in spirit" (Matt 5:3) occurs in 1QM xiv 7. The phrase of Ps 37:11, "The meek will possess the land" (Matt 5:5) is interpreted in 4QpPs 37 (ii 9) as a reference to the Qumran community, the Community of the Poor. It is clear, therefore, that Jesus' sayings could have been interpreted by some Jews against the background of Anawim theology.

[42] I am deliberately showing how much of Luke's own description of Jesus was harmonious with the ideals of the Anawim. If Luke borrowed canticles composed by Jewish Christian Anawim, it was because he felt a kinship to those ideals and to that group.

the fulfillment of their messianic expectations and have used hymns to hail what God had accomplished in Jesus (just as the related Qumran group resorted to hymns to express their thanks to God and to celebrate their anticipated victories in the eschatological war). The Magnificat (without vs. 48) and the Benedictus (without vss. 76–77) would make perfect sense in such a setting. Just as the author of the *Hodayoth* presented himself as a "poor one" and expressed thanks for having been delivered, the Jewish Christian composer of the Magnificat spoke of the mighty things that God had done for him. The collective voice of the Anawim appears later in the Magnificat: "He has exalted those of low degree; He has filled the hungry with good things." Similarly, the Benedictus sings the praise of what God has done for His people "who sat in darkness and in the shadow of death." There is no profound christology in these hymns,[43] only a very Jewish concept of soteriology.[44]

In my hypothesis Luke took these general expressions of the joy manifested by the Jewish Christian Anawim over the salvation accomplished in Jesus and applied them with a specificity that was not in their original purview. By setting them in the context of the infancy narrative, he made them expressions of joy over the conception and birth of Jesus and JBap. This was not a tour de force, for Luke had presented the conception and birth as having salvific significance. Moreover, the characters to whom he attributed the canticles embodied the piety of the Anawim. Mary was the handmaid of the Lord, obedient to His word, believing in the fulfillment of that word which would fill her womb with the presence of the Messiah and make her blessed among women.[45] Zechariah was an upright Temple priest who, along with his wife, blamelessly observed all the commandments and ordinances of the Lord; their disgrace among men consisted in the barrenness of Elizabeth and a childless old age; yet the Lord took away this disgrace and gave them the joy of a son. Simeon was

---

[43] The relative lack of christology in the canticles, when compared with the high christology in the surrounding narrative (e.g., 1:35), is another indication that the narrative and the canticles did not have the same composer. In this feature the Lucan canticles are quite unlike the highly christological canticles in the Pauline letters (Philip 2:6–11; Col 1:15–20).

[44] Were an Orthodox Jew in our times to come to the conclusion that the Messiah had come, I suspect that he could recite the Benedictus (except for vss. 76–77) without any sense of an alien composition. We shall see that the Gloria in Excelsis has been related to Jewish expositions of the trisagion of Isa 6:3. Even the Nunc Dimittis, although it mentions Gentiles (Luke 2:32), may be echoing the idyllic hopes of Isa 2:2–3.

[45] In § 11E we saw that it is far from clear that Luke used Mary as a personification of Israel or the Daughter of Zion. It may be closer to Luke's thought to see Mary as an idealized representative of the Anawim who constituted the remnant of Israel. Schnackenburg, "Magnificat," 354–55, who rejects the former symbolism, is more open to the latter: "Nevertheless, Mary can have a valid role as the deputy of her people who at the same time fulfills its deepest hopes—not in a collective sense, but as an individual who is called to a particular task." I doubted that the *chaire* of Luke 1:28 was meant to evoke the rejoicing of the Daughter of Zion passage in Zeph 3:14. It is easier to relate Mary of the Magnificat to the theme in Zeph 3:12–13: "For I shall leave in the midst of you a people poor ('*ānāw*) and lowly; they shall seek refuge in the name of the Lord, those who are left in Israel."

upright and devout, but aged, waiting for the consolation of Israel; this consolation came to him when he saw the Lord's Messiah brought into the Temple court. Thus the canticles come to us in Luke with a background of two levels of Christian meaning: the original general jubilation of the Christian converts among the remnant of Israel, the "Poor Ones" who recognized that in Jesus God had raised them up and saved them according to His promises; and the particular jubilation of a character in the infancy drama of salvation who is portrayed as a representative of the "Poor Ones."

The existence of these Jewish Christian Anawim is not purely hypothetical. In Acts 2:43–47; 4:32–37 Luke describes with nostalgia (and with some historical simplification[46]) the Jewish Christian community at Jerusalem. These people sold their possessions and gave their wealth for distribution to the needy; thus they certainly qualify to be deemed "Poor Ones." Their poverty was leavened by piety, including "Temple piety," for they devoted themselves to prayer and attendance at the Temple.[47] While Luke does not say specifically that they composed hymns, he does say that they "praised God," which is precisely the leitmotif of the infancy canticles.[48] The legacy of the piety of this Jerusalem group may explain why Luke has all four canticles recited in Judea (the region around Jerusalem and Bethlehem), and the Nunc Dimittis recited in Jerusalem itself. Indeed, there is an unusual concentration upon Jerusalem in the infancy narrative: it begins and ends in that city, and half the action takes place in the Jerusalem Temple.[49] Similarities in language have been pointed out between the canticles and the speeches of the Jerusalem leaders in Acts.[50] Obviously much of this may stem from Lucan editing, but a plausible argument can be constructed for the thesis that Luke got the canticles from the tradition of the Jewish Christian community of Jerusalem.

Would such a suggestion force us to conclude that the canticles were very ancient hymns composed in Semitic, i.e., in the Aramaic or Hebrew

[46] It is not reasonable to consider these Lucan summaries as totally fictional idealization. Luke's description of the structure and ideals of the Jerusalem community comes remarkably close to what we know of Qumran structure and ideals, and so Luke was describing a way of life that was entirely plausible in early first-century Judaism.

[47] As we saw, the Hasidean movement (a branch of which produced the Qumran community) was deeply concerned about purity of cult, Temple, and priesthood. They reflected an early combination of Anawim piety and Temple piety.

[48] The verb that Luke uses in this passage in Acts 2:47 is *ainein*, the same verb he uses in the infancy narrative (2:13,20) for praising God. The noun from that verb, *ainesis*, is a standard translation of *tôdâ*, "praise, thanksgiving," from the same root as *Hodayoth*, the name given to the Qumran psalms of praise and thanksgiving.

[49] I have argued that Luke did not derive ch. 1 from pre-Lucan sources, but that in composing it, he had access to some items of tradition, e.g., about the parentage of JBap. In Acts 6:7 Luke tells us that a great number of Jewish priests were converted to the faith and joined the Jerusalem community. Would it be romantic to suggest that this channel preserved the tradition that JBap had priestly parents and some details of their life and home?

[50] Gryglewicz, "Herkunft," 268, counts eighteen words or terms shared by the Benedictus and the sermon of Peter in Acts 3:12–26.

language spoken by the early Jerusalem community?[51] Not necessarily. In his discussion of the Epistle of James (see footnote 35 above), Dibelius has shown the presence of a dominant Anawim mentality in a strongly Jewish writing composed in Greek quite late in the century.[52] He argues that the traditional attitude of the Poor Ones, seen in Jerusalem Christianity early in the century, continued in the non-Pauline churches of Diaspora Judaism later in the century—churches for which the name of James, the leader of the Jerusalem church, would have had authority. Thus, it is not impossible that, in the last third of the century when he was composing Luke/Acts, Luke came upon these canticles in a Greek-speaking Jewish Christian community in an area influenced by Jerusalem Christianity. The evidence does not permit us to be more definite in resolving the possibilities.

D. *The Magnificat* (1:46–55)

Having treated the Lucan canticles in general, we are now ready to consider in detail the most poetic of the four, the Magnificat. I shall discuss first the structure of the canticle and then its contents.

1. The Structure

In OT research it is customary to classify the psalms into literary types (*Gattungen*). By NT times, as can be seen already in the psalms of Qumran, the classical types had broken down; and we encounter many mixed types.[53] With the caution that we cannot expect a strict adherence to pattern, it is, nevertheless, quite true that the Magnificat resembles in many ways the psalm type known as the hymn of praise.[54] This usually consists of three parts:

   a) An *introduction* praising God.
   b) The *body of the hymn* listing the motives of praise.
      These are often begun by a "because" clause, with the subsequent

---

[51] See footnote 31 above. Gryglewicz, "Herkunft," 272, contending that the canticles stem from liturgical texts originally used by Palestinian Christian communities, thinks that they were first spoken in Aramaic, then written in Hebrew, and finally translated into Greek, only to be stylistically corrected by Luke.

[52] James shares with the canticles a lack of high christology and a lack of major concern with the Gentiles; but one cannot be sure whether silence on these points really indicates the mind of the author or is simply the accidental product of the literary form.

[53] Jones, "Background," 45, insists on this, pointing to H. L. Jansen's study of Jewish psalmody in this period.

[54] In the Psalter the commonly agreed-upon hymns of praise include Pss 8, 19 (combining two hymns), 29, 33, 100, 103, 104, 111, 113, 114, 117, 135, 136, 145, 146, 147, 148, 149, 150.

clauses having different grammatical patterns.[55] The motives for praising God include His deeds for Israel or for the individual, and His attributes (power, wisdom, mercy).

c) The *conclusion*. This is the least defined part, since the conclusion may recapitulate some of the motives, may include a blessing, or make a request.

The Magnificat has an *introduction* (46b–47) which praises God. The *body of the hymn* (48–53) begins with a "because" clause in 48a, or, should that be a Lucan insertion into the original canticle, with a "because" clause in 49a. The motives of praise that are listed involve both God's attributes (mighty, holy, merciful) in 49–50 and His deeds in 51–53. The viewpoint is first that of the speaker ("for me") and then that of the circle of Anawim whom the speaker represents ("those of low degree"; "the hungry"). Thus, the body of the Magnificat can be divided into two stanzas or strophes of equal length.[56] The *conclusion* of the Magnificat (54–55) summarizes what has been said in 49–53, both the deeds of God ("He has helped His servant Israel") and the attributes ("in remembrance of His mercy"). It then puts all this under the rubric of God's fulfillment of His promises to the fathers.[57]

The poetic parallelism of lines is very clear in several parts of the Magnificat, e.g., 46b/47, 51a/51b, 52a/52b, 53a/53b, and perhaps 55a/55b (see NOTE). The real problem is in the first strophe of the body of the hymn, the lines in vss. 48 through 50. Ramaroson thinks that the parallelism there may be improved by regarding 48b as Lucan addition to the original hymn in which the two "because" clauses of 48a and 49a stood in parallelism, each describing what God had done for the speaker. Then he would find a rough parallelism in the two "and" clauses in 49b and 50, each describing an attribute of God.[58] In thus treating 48b as a Lucan insertion, Ramaroson joins the many scholars who have pointed to the several Lucanisms in the line (see NOTES) and the fact that it is related to the Lucan narrative context—Mary was called fortunate in 45a.[59]

---

55 Ramaroson, "Structuram," 30–31, analyzes the grammatical patterns of the motive clauses in Ps 136, and finds the same kind of variety in the Magnificat after vs. 49.

56 Not all would accept this division into 48–50 and 51–53. Vogels, "Magnificat," 280, ignores the OT structural antecedents and joins 46b–47 to 48–49 as one strophe dealing with the first person; the second strophe for him consists of 50–53. However, vs. 50 has a different pattern from the six aorist verbs in 51–53.

57 Others like Gaechter, Gunkel, and Schnackenburg treat the conclusion as a third strophe or a part thereof. Gunkel speaks of the Magnificat as an eschatological hymn ending on the tone of fulfillment of promise. Psalm scholarship is not in agreement on whether eschatological hymns constitute a separate grouping. See Sabourin (footnote 35 above), 146–49.

58 Ramaroson does not divide vs. 50 into two lines, and thus his parallelism between 49b and 50 is between two clauses of very different length. See footnote 67 below.

59 Some, like Mowinckel, also use a metrical argument, i.e., that vs. 48 does not fit the metric pattern of the Magnificat. See also Tannehill, "Magnificat," 270–71. However, Jones, "Background," 21, argues convincingly that metric pattern in this hymn is too uncertain to warrant passing such a judgment.

However, one should probably press further and on the same grounds regard 48a as also a Lucan insertion—Mary was called "the handmaid of the Lord" in 38. Moreover, both 48a and 48b have the same OT matrix, namely, the statements of Leah in Gen 29:32 and 30:13 after the birth of children. If we regard both 48a and 48b as Lucan additions, the original hymn began its list of motives for praising God with the "because" clause in 49a, and the parallelism of clauses is rougher than in Ramaroson's hypothesis.

Of the three canticles attributed to human spokesmen in the Lucan infancy narrative, the Benedictus portrays the reaction of the community of the oppressed but never mentions the speaker in the first person singular; the Nunc Dimittis portrays the reaction of the speaker; and the Magnificat combines both aspects: the reactions of the speaker in the first person singular (introduction; first strophe) and the reactions of the oppressed community (second strophe). Thus, the Magnificat exhibits the features of both the individual hymn of praise and the community hymn of praise.

2. The Contents

I shall presuppose the technical information given in the Notes accompanying the translation. In the accompanying Table XII I have given the background of the Magnificat in terms of the prominent OT and intertestamental passages that may have influenced the author or, at least, reflect the same mentality. This table should illustrate vividly what is meant by the claim that the Magnificat is almost a cento or mosaic. The reader should refer to this table when OT passages are mentioned below.

INTRODUCTION (46b–47). I have proposed that originally the hymn referred to a general salvation in Jesus Christ given by God to Jews who had become Christians. The reference to God as "my Savior," which echoes Habakkuk's hymn, was uttered by a spokesman for such Jewish Christians who believed that Habakkuk's longing for salvation had now seen fulfillment. Luke, who esteems Mary as the first Christian disciple (§ 11D), has placed the hymn on her lips and thus given her the role as spokeswoman of the Anawim. He had an excellent antecedent for this in the OT portrait of Hannah the mother of Samuel, a handmaid of the Lord who sang a hymn of the Anawim (I Sam 1:11; 2:1–10).[60] We shall see that the Mary/Hannah parallelism continues in ch. 2 when Mary brings Jesus to the Temple, even as Hannah brought Samuel to the Tabernacle of Shiloh. Another good antecedent was Judith, "blessed among women," who also sang a song of the oppressed and weak people (Judith 13:18;

---

[60] The literary history of Hannah's hymn is not unlike that of the Magnificat: it is a psalm of a more general nature that has been secondarily inserted into the Hannah story and adapted to her situation.

TABLE XII: THE BACKGROUND OF THE MAGNIFICAT

INTRODUCTORY PRAISE

46b *My soul proclaims the greatness of the Lord,*
47   *and my spirit has found gladness in God my Savior:*
   *Ps 35:9:
   Then my soul will find gladness in the Lord;
   it will take pleasure in His salvation.

   I Sam 2:1–2 (Hannah's hymn):
   My heart is strengthened in the Lord;
   my horn is exalted in my God . . .
   I delight in your salvation.

   *Hab 3:18 (Habakkuk's hymn):
   I shall find gladness in the Lord;
   I shall rejoice in God my Savior.

FIRST STROPHE

48a *Because He has regarded the low estate of His handmaid—*
   I Sam 1:11 (Hannah praying for a child):
   O Lord of Hosts, if you will look on the low estate of your handmaid.

   Gen 29:32 (Leah after a childbirth):
   Because the Lord has regarded my low estate.

   IV Ezra 9:45 (Zion speaking as a barren woman):
   God heard your handmaid and regarded my low estate,
   and considered my distress and gave me a son.

48b *for behold, henceforth all generations will call me fortunate—*
   *Gen 30:13 (Leah after a childbirth):
   Fortunate am I, for all women call me fortunate.

49a *Because He who is mighty has done great things for me.*
   Deut 10:21 (Moses to Israel):
   He is your God who has done great things in you.

   *Zeph 3:17:
   The Lord your God is in you,
   a Mighty One will save you.

49b *And holy is His name,*
   Ps 111:9:
   Holy and awesome is His name.

50a *And His mercy is from generation to generation*
50b *on those who fear Him.*
   Ps 103:17:
   But the mercy of the Lord is from everlasting to everlasting
   upon those who fear Him.

---

* The asterisk denotes passages that are closer to Luke when quoted from the LXX than from the MT.

Psalms of Solomon 13:11:
His mercy upon those who fear Him.

SECOND STROPHE

51a *He has shown His strength with His arm;*
51b *He has scattered the proud in the imagination of their hearts.*
52a *He has put down the mighty from their thrones*
52b *and has exalted those of low degree.*
53a *He has filled the hungry with good things,*
53b *and the rich He has sent away empty.*
I Sam 2:7–8 (Hannah's hymn):
The Lord makes poor and makes rich;
He reduces to lowliness and He lifts up.
He lifts the needy from the earth,
and from the dung heap He raises up the poor
to seat them with the mighty,
making them inherit a throne of glory.

*Ps 89:11(10—a hymn praising God's action for the Davidic king):
You have reduced the proud to lowliness like a wounded thing;
and by your powerful arm you have scattered your enemies.

Sirach 10:14:
He has put down the thrones of princes
and has seated the humble before them.

Job 12:19:
He has overthrown the mighty.

1QM xiv 10–11:
You have raised the fallen by your strength,
and have cut down the high and mighty.

Ezek 21:31(26):
Having reduced the proud to lowliness,
and having exalted the man of low degree.

Ps 107:9:
He has filled the soul of the hungry with good things.

CONCLUSION

54a *He has helped His servant Israel*
54b *in remembrance of His mercy,*
55a *as He spoke unto our fathers,*
55b *to Abraham and his posterity forever.*
Isa 41:8–9:
You, O Israel,
my servant Jacob whom I chose,
seed of Abraham whom I loved,
whom I have helped from the ends of the earth.

*Ps 98:3:
He has remembered His mercy to Jacob
and His goodness to the House of Israel.

Psalms of Solomon 10:4:
And the Lord will remember His servants in mercy.

Micah 7:20:
You will give truth to Jacob and mercy to Israel,
as you have sworn to our fathers from days of old.

II Sam 22:51 (David's hymn at the end of his life):
Showing mercy to His anointed one,
to David and to his posterity forever.

For a comparative table in Greek, see Creed, *Gospel*, 303–4.

16:11).[61] Having the pregnant Mary speak of God as her Savior can make sense because Luke has now associated salvation (once attached to the death and resurrection of Jesus) with the birth of Jesus (1:69; 2:11,30). The Anawim encountered salvation when they proclaimed Jesus as the Messiah, and that truth has already been revealed to Mary. If Luke gives Mary prominence in this hymn by the number of first person pronouns in the initial verses, he never loses the sense that this prominence is totally the gift of God. The opening of the Magnificat is the explication of the *kecharitōmenē* of 1:28; it is a commentary on how Mary has "found favor with God" (1:30) and her resulting eschatological joy.

STROPHE ONE (48–50). As anticipated in a hymn of praise, the body of the hymn commences with the motives for praising God. If I am correct in joining those scholars who regard vs. 48 as a Lucan addition (see above), the motives which begin in 49 were originally more general, as befitting the anonymous spokesman of those who fear God (50b). To speak of the "great things" done by the "Holy" One in His "mercy" was to evoke the language of the Exodus and the Sinai covenant (see NOTES)—a common NT language for communicating the renewal of the covenant in Jesus. The attributes of God that are cited (mighty, holy, merciful) were those most admired by the Anawim who were dependent upon Him.

But Luke has reapplied all these sentiments to Mary, and the focus of her praise is the fulfillment of the Davidic covenant through the conception of the Messiah. As he composed vs. 48, Luke reused vocabulary he had already employed of Mary in 38 ("handmaid") and 45 ("fortunate"), vocabulary that fitted well into the picture of women canticle-singers patterned upon Hannah and Judith, and the picture of patriarchal mothers responding to salivific conceptions (especially, Leah the wife of Jacob/Israel).[62] The stereotyped character of the description of Mary in

[61] Judith, i.e., the "Jewess," is more than a spokeswoman or representative of the Anawim; she is the *personification* of oppressed Judaism. See footnote 12 above.

[62] To be exact, however, the self-description of Mary in the Magnificat goes beyond the self-description of Leah in the LXX of Gen 30:13 ("all women call me fortunate") and

vs. 48 explains the use of "low estate," a term more obviously appropriate to the OT barren woman than to the NT young virgin. But we should not follow the example of scholars who destroy the OT echoes by translating the term as "humility"[63] or of those who use it as the decisive argument for attributing the canticle to Elizabeth rather than to Mary.[64] For Luke, Mary's virginity was like the barrenness of the OT women: both constituted a human impossibility which only the might of God could overcome. In using "low estate" and "handmaid" (i.e., female slave) of Mary, Luke is associating her with all the memories of the Poor Ones evoked by those terms[65]—Poor Ones whom God had helped by His might, whether they were women yearning for children, or Israel reduced by oppression to the status of a "handmaid" (I Macc 2:11) of "low estate" (I Sam 9:16).

In vss. 49–50 too (pre-Lucan components of the hymn), the traditional language of the Anawim takes on a new meaning with Mary as their spokeswoman. For instance, let us consider the designation of God as "He who is mighty" (*ho dynatos*) in 49a. In the OT, as witnessed by Zeph 3:17, God exhibits His might as a warrior in the battle to save Israel. For the Jewish Christian Anawim the salvific might (*dynamis*) of God was made visible in Jesus, "a man attested by mighty works" (Acts 2:22; also 10:38). But Mary had encountered this salvific might long before when "the power [*dynamis*] of the Most High" had overshadowed her in the conception of Jesus (1:35), and she had been assured by the angel, "Nothing said by God can be impossible [*adynatein*]" (1:38). Mary's confession of God in the Magnificat as *ho dynatos* is an anticipation of the Gospel principle: "The things impossible [*adynatos*] for men are possible [*dynatos*] with God" (18:27). Another example of the reinterpretation of language is the Magnificat's confession: "Holy is His name" (49b).[66] This OT insight (Ps 111:9) stems from God's covenant claim

---

even beyond Elizabeth's "Blessed are you among women" (Luke 1:42). Now not only all women but all generations deem Mary fortunate, because her child will bring salvation to all generations.

63 Luke is not referring to Mary's attitude but to her status among men. (As I pointed out in footnote 52, § 11, we are quite far here from the later Christian view where virginity is regarded as a noble status.) Romantic and totally implausible is the suggestion that, having already made a resolve of virginity, Mary had reconciled herself to accept the future abuse of village women who would eventually conclude that she was barren when she had no children.

64 I have shown the weakness of this thesis in the NOTE on vs. 46. Was it this same reasoning by which modern scholars see in "low estate" a reference to Elizabeth that led an ancient Latin scribe to read "Elizabeth" in vs. 46? The thought of Mary being in "low estate" would seem increasingly impossible once the legends of the *Protevangelium of James* were in wide circulation and Mary was pictured as having been raised in the Temple to become the most favored maiden in the country.

65 Tannehill, "Magnificat," 272, is right in insisting that a particular term in the Magnificat must be seen in relation to a whole complexus of terms used in the hymn. Mary is designated as being of low estate to associate her with those of low degree in 52b.

66 The holiness of God's name is related to His might. The "name" of God is the way by which God makes Himself known to human beings. God sanctifies His name by His mighty deeds which cause men to recognize His holiness. In the Lord's Prayer the petition "May your name be sanctified" is parallel to the petition "May your will be brought about."

to be holy (Lev 11:44–45). The Jewish Christian Anawim recognized the crucified and risen Jesus as the embodiment of God's holiness (Acts 3:14; 4:27,30). But again Mary was the first to know that; for, since Jesus had been conceived when God's Holy Spirit came upon her, the child who was to be born would "be called holy" (1:35). And if the Magnificat's reference to the endless mercy of God on those who fear Him (50ab) echoes a commonplace of Israelite thought, Mary coud attest the truth of that verse in a more personal way. She had been told by the angel not to fear (1:30) and that there would be no end to the kingdom over which her child would rule (1:33), so that the new covenant in Jesus is an example of God's mercy (*ḥesed*) from generation to generation.

STROPHE TWO (51–53). The final line in the first strophe of the body of the Magnificat with its reference to "those who fear Him" prepares for a transition to the second strophe where the motives for praising God are less personally those of the spokeswoman and more those of the general group of the Anawim. Of course, there is no reason to think that this shift from the first person to the third reflects separate compositions, for the same phenomenon is found in Hannah's canticle in I Sam 2. It may be the closeness to that canticle (Table XII) which explains the almost classical parallelism in this strophe. (There is even a rhyme established by the last words of the four lines in 52–53: *thronōn* in 52a with *agathōn* in 53a, and *tapeinous* in 52b with *kenous* in 53b—an argument favoring composition in Greek rather than in Semitic.) Yet there is one exception to the parallelism which is indicative of the thought of the hymnologist. In the four lines of 52–53 there are antithetic parallels: the mighty over against those of low degree, the hungry over against the rich.[67] But in 51a there is no group mentioned in antithesis to the proud of 51b. This is probably because the idea of "those who fear Him" is carried over from 50b; they are the Anawim who are the antithesis par excellence of the proud. It is unto them that God "has shown strength with His arm" (51a).[68]

The fact that in this strophe there are six verbs all in the aorist tense has been the center of discussion. Since it takes considerable imagination to think that the embryo in Mary's womb has already put down the mighty from their thrones,[69] it has been suggested that we have here a prophetic

[67] Note the chiastic order in the four terms: mighty, low, hungry, rich (bad, good, good, bad). A lesser chiasmus can be found if we examine the four lines of vss. 49–50; recipient ("for me"), divine attribute ("holy"), divine attribute ("mercy"), recipient ("on those who fear Him"). Thus there is good reason for dividing vs. 50 into two lines, *pace* Tannehill, "Magnificat," 271.

[68] The close connections between the two strophes is further evidence that in those strophes we are not dealing with two originally separate compositions. The theme of God's power is shared by 49a and 51a; the word "mighty" is shared by 49a and 52a; the reference to those of low estate is shared by 48a and 52b.

[69] As mentioned above (see footnote 32), it was the martial atmosphere of these lines that caused Winter to posit that originally the Magnificat was a Maccabean battle hymn sung

aorist: Mary is predicting what will come about through the child to be born. Others have opted for a gnomic aorist (cf. BDF 333) to be translated by a present tense: these lines describe God's normal way of proceeding. However, one wonders then why a present tense was not employed, since Hannah's canticle, which is the model for the Magnificat, used present tenses. The best explanation for the aorists is that the Magnificat is vocalizing literally the sentiments of the Jewish Christian Anawim. The aorists refer to a definite action in the past, namely, the salvation brought about through the death and resurrection of Jesus. That was the supreme manifestation of the strength of God's arm. At that moment He scattered the proud and the mighty, the rulers and the princes who gathered together against His anointed, i.e., the Messiah (Acts 4:24–27); He did this by raising Jesus from death and and *exalting* him at His right hand (Acts 2:33; 5:31).[70] All this praise for what God *had done* could be retroverted and placed on Mary's lips because Luke is interpreting the conception of Jesus in light not only of the post-resurrectional christology of the Church, but also of post-resurrectional soteriology, particularly of the Jewish Christian Anawim of Jerusalem as described in Acts.

The poverty and hunger of the oppressed in the Magnificat are primarily spiritual, but we should not forget the physical realities faced by early Christians. The first followers of Jesus were Galileans; and Galilee, victimized by the absentee ownership of estates (cf. Luke 20:9), was the spawning ground of first-century revolts against a repressive occupation and the taxation it engendered (Acts 5:37; see Appendix VII). There was real poverty among the Jerusalem Christians who became the nucleus of the post-resurrection Church. For this information we are not dependent solely on the voluntary sharing of goods mentioned in Acts 2:44–45; 4:34–35; and 5:1–2, since the need for helping this deprived community was insistently proclaimed by Paul (Gal 2:10; I Cor 16:1–4; Rom 15:25–26). And when the Gospel was proclaimed in the Diaspora among Jews and Gentiles, frequently it attracted the underprivileged social classes. The Epistle of James, with its eloquent denunciations of the rich (5:1–6), may represent Christianity in Diaspora Judaism. There were certainly slaves who were converts in the Pauline communities (I Cor 12:13;

---

after victory. A parallel to their terminology can be found among the words of the Qumran Anawim in the War Scroll (Table XII).

70 The fact that there are similarities of mentality between the Magnificat and the Jerusalem sermons in Acts has already been noted on several occasions (footnotes 23, 42, 50). There are several possible interpretations: (a) both sermons and canticles are total Lucan compositions; (b) neither are Lucan compositions, and they both come from the same community; (c) the sermons are Lucan compositions but incorporating earlier elements, and those elements provide the similarities to the canticles. I think it is the last theory that is probably correct; but I am reluctant to be precise because, if there are reminiscences in Luke/Acts from either the sermons or the hymns of the Jerusalem community, we have them only in edited translation.

Philemon; Eph 6:5).[71] And Luke's peculiar and emphatic castigation of wealth (6:24–26; 12:19–20; 16:25; 21:1–4) points to the existence of many poor in the communities to be served by Luke's Gospel. And so vss. 51–53 of the Magnificat would resonate among such groups;[72] for them the Christian good news meant that the ultimately blessed were not the mighty and the rich who tyrannized them. Reformers of all times have advocated revolutions that would level class distinctions by making the poor sufficiently rich and the powerless sufficiently powerful. But the Magnificat anticipates the Lucan Jesus in preaching that wealth and power are not real values at all since they have no standing in God's sight. This is not an easy message, even for those who profess credence in Jesus. By introducing it as a leitmotiv in the hymns of the infancy narrative, Luke has begun to introduce the offense of the cross into the good news proclaimed by Gabriel. If for Luke Mary is the first Christian disciple, it is fitting that he place on her lips sentiments that Jesus will make the hallmark of the disciple in the main Gospel story (Luke 14:27). It is no accident, then, that some of the offense of the cross rubbed off on Mary. In the early dialogue between Christians and Jews, one of the objections against Christianity is that God would never have had His Messiah come into the world without fitting honor and glory, born of a woman who admitted that she was no more than a handmaid, a female slave.[73]

CONCLUSION (54–55). It now becomes apparent that the Christian Anawim, whose voice has resounded in the body of the hymn, identify themselves as the remnant of Israel—and quite logically so, since Deutero-Isaiah identified Jacob/Israel as a suffering servant.[74] The salvation that has come in Jesus of Nazareth is the definitive act by which God has kept His covenant with Israel, the ultimate manifestation of His mercy (covenant kindness) to His servant people. It is the sense of fulfillment in 54–55 that assures us that the Magnificat is of Christian origin. The statement that God "has helped His servant Israel" is almost an inclusion with the opening line of the hymn: "My spirit has found gladness in God my Savior."[75] Once again the past tense (a bit awkward from the viewpoint

---

[71] It is interesting that when Pliny sought information about Christians (*Epistulae* X 96–97), he sought it from two women slaves, illustrating the status of people associated with Christianity.

[72] This thesis is well expounded by Vogt, "Ecce."

[73] Justin *Dialogue* cxxi 3; Origen *Against Celsus* I 29, 32–33. Vogt, "Ecce," 246–47, points out that Gentiles understood *doulē kyriou* ("handmaid of the Lord") as "slave of her master," an interpretation which may have given rise to the slander that Mary was a concubine. (See Appendix V.)

[74] I have pointed out that the Qumran community had an Anawim mentality; and many scholars think that in the *Hodayoth*, through the first-person-singular voice of the spokesman, the community was identifying itself as the servant of the Lord. See H. Ringgren, *The Faith of Qumran* (Philadelphia: Fortress, 1963), 196–97.

[75] The ideas of God's *salvation* and His *helping* His people (NOTE on 54) are closely joined in Isa 43:3,5 (Ramaroson, "Structuram," 41).

that Jesus has not yet been born) represents the viewpoint of post-resurrectional believers. But since from Luke's theological outlook the "helping" has begun in the conception of the Messiah, Mary can proclaim the fulfillment. If in the original hymn of the Anawim "Abraham and his posterity" (55b) was the same as "Israel" (54a), in Luke's outlook the promise of God to the "fathers" (55a) and His convenant "mercy" (54b) reaches even farther than Israel. Later in the Lucan Gospel, this same JBap, who jumped prophetically in his mother's womb at the first encounter with Jesus, will proclaim a broadening of the concept of the children of Abraham (3:8). The covenant mercy of God in Jesus will reach not only to all generations; it will reach to all peoples.

Mary's canticle (vss. 46–55) in response to Elizabeth's canticle (vss. 42–45) ends the saga of the two annunciations. The dramatis personae of the annunciation scenes have now been brought together. Elizabeth in the shorter canticle has praised Mary the mother, but Mary in the longer canticle has transferred the praise to God who has the principal role in the drama of salvation. The visitation has also confirmed the destinies of the unborn JBap and the unborn Jesus as foretold by the angel. Even before birth JBap has begun to act as a prophet in hailing Jesus as the Messiah. Luke can now move on to tell the stories of the two births.

SECTIONAL BIBLIOGRAPHY (§ 12)
(LUKE 1:39–56)

Aytoun, R. A., "The Ten Lucan Hymns of the Nativity in Their Original Language," JTS 18 (1917), 274–88.

Benko, S., "The Magnificat: A History of the Controversy," JBL 86 (1967), 263–75.

Davies, J. G., "The Ascription of the Magnificat to Mary," JTS 15 (1964), 307–8.

Forestell, J. T., "Old Testament Background of the Magnificat," *Marian Studies* 12 (1961), 205–44.

Galbiati, E., "La visitazione (Luca 1,41–50)," BibOr 4 (1962), 139–44.

Gryglewicz, F., "Die Herkunft der Hymnen des Kindheitsevangeliums des Lucas," NTS 21 (1974–75), 265–73.

Gunkel, H., "Die Lieder in der Kindheitsgeschichte Jesu bei Lukas," in *Festgabe A. von Harnack zum siebzigten Geburtstag dargebracht* (Tübingen: Mohr, 1921), 43–60.

Harnack, A. von, "Das Magnificat der Elisabet (Luk 1,46–55) nebst einigen Bemerkungen zu Luk 1 und 2," *Sitzungsberichte der Kgl. Preussischen*

    Akademie der Wissenschaften zu Berlin 27 (1900), 538–66. Reprinted in *Studien zur Geschichte des Neuen Testaments und der Alten Kirche* (Berlin: De Gruyter, 1931), I, 62–85.

Jones, D. R., "The Background and Character of the Lukan Psalms," JTS 19 (1968), 19–50.

Koontz, J. V. G., "Mary's Magnificat," BibSac 116 (1959), 336–49.

Ladeuze, P., "De l'origine du Magnificat et son attribution dans le troisième Evangile à Marie ou à Elisabeth," RHE 4 (1903), 623–44.

Loisy, A. (writing as F. Jacobé), "L'origine du Magnificat," *Revue d'Histoire et de Littérature Religieuses* 2 (1897), 424–32.

Ramaroson, L., "Ad structuram cantici 'Magnificat,'" *Verbum Domini* 46 (1968), 30–46.

Schnackenburg, R., "Das Magnificat, seine Spiritualität und Theologie," *Geist und Leben* 38 (1965), 342–57.

Spitta, F., "Die chronologischen Notizen und die Hymnen in Lc 1 und 2," ZNW 7 (1906), 281–317.

———— "Das Magnificat, ein Psalm der Maria und nicht der Elisabeth," in *Theologische Abhandlungen: Festgabe zum 17 Mai 1902 für H. J. Holtzmann* (Tübingen: Mohr, 1902), 63–94.

Tannehill, R. C., "The Magnificat as Poem," JBL 93 (1974), 263–75.

Vogels, W., "Le Magnificat, Marie et Israël," *Eglise et Théologie* 6 (1975), 279–96.

Vogt, J., "Ecce ancilla domini: eine Untersuchung zum sozialen Motiv des antiken Marienbildes," *Vigiliae Christianae* 23 (1969), 241–63.

Winter, P., "Magnificat and Benedictus—Maccabean Psalms?" BJRL 37 (1954–55), 328–47.

V. THE BIRTH AND NAMING OF JOHN THE BAPTIST; ZECHARIAH'S PROPHECY (§ 13)

Translation of Luke 1:57–80

1 ⁵⁷Now the time came for Elizabeth to give birth, and she bore a son. ⁵⁸When her neighbors and relatives heard that the Lord had shown His great mercy to her, they rejoiced together with her.

⁵⁹On the eighth day they came to circumcise the child, and they were going to name him Zechariah after his father. ⁶⁰"No, you don't," his mother intervened, "He is to be called John!" ⁶¹But they argued with her, "There is no one in your family with that name." ⁶²So they made signs to the father to find out what he would want the child called. ⁶³He asked for a writing tablet and astonished all by inscribing, "John is to be his name." ⁶⁴With that, Zechariah was able to open his mouth; and with his tongue at last freed, he began to speak in praise of God. ⁶⁵This brought fear upon all their neighbors, and all these events were the talk of the whole hill country of Judea. ⁶⁶All stored up what they heard in their hearts, wondering "What then is this child going to be?" For the hand of the Lord was with him.

⁶⁷But Zechariah his father was filled with the Holy Spirit, so that he uttered this prophecy:*

⁶⁸ᵃ"Blessed be the Lord, the God of Israel:

⁶⁸ᵇ   Because He has visited
⁶⁸ᶜ   and accomplished the redemption of His people,
⁶⁹ᵃ   and has raised up for us a horn of salvation
⁶⁹ᵇ   in the House of David His servant,
⁷⁰   as He spoke by the mouth of His holy prophets from of old:
⁷¹ᵃ   salvation from our enemies
⁷¹ᵇ   and from the hand of all those who hate us,

---

* Italicization indicates the lines most likely added by Luke to the hypothetical pre-Lucan, Jewish-Christian canticle, in order to fit it into its present context.

72a Showing mercy to our fathers
72b and remembering His holy covenant,
73   the oath which He swore to our father Abraham,
     to grant us 74 that, without fear,
     delivered from the hands of our enemies,
     we might serve Him 75 in holiness and justice,
     before Him all the days of our lives.

76a *But you, child, will be called prophet of the Most High;*
76b *for you will go before the Lord to make ready His ways,*
77a *to grant to His people knowledge of salvation*
77b *in the forgiveness of their sins.*

78a Through the heartfelt mercy of our God
78b by which there has visited us a rising light from on high,
79a appearing to those who sat in darkness and the shadow of
79b guiding our feet into the way of peace." | death,

80 And as the child grew up, he became strong in Spirit. He stayed in
the desert until the day of his public appearance to Israel.

Notes

1:57. *the time came for Elizabeth to give birth.* Literally, "for Elizabeth the
time of her bearing was fulfilled." The Semitism, "the *days* of her bearing were
fulfilled," is used in Gen 25:24 to describe Rebekah's delivering Jacob and
Esau, and also in Luke 2:6 for Mary's delivery of Jesus. This statement dates
the birth of JBap in the period after the three months that Mary stayed with
Elizabeth (1:56). For the ten-month pregnancy, see NOTE on 1:24.

bore a son. The same verb, *gennan*, was used in the promise to Zechariah in
1:13.

58. *her neighbors and relatives heard.* They had not known of her pregnancy
because Elizabeth had hid herself (1:24). Mary was the only relative (1:36) to
whom the secret had been revealed.

the Lord had shown His great mercy to her. Literally, "*magnified* His mercy
with her," employing the same verb that we saw in the opening line of the
Magnificat: "proclaims the greatness" (1:46). The theme of mercy occurs in
that canticle as well (1:50). Luke's description may echo Lot's statement in the

LXX of Gen 19:19: "Your servant has found *mercy* before You, and You have *magnified* Your justice which You have done for me." Such an OT pattern explains Luke's phraseology better than the dubious contention that Luke is assuming the reader's knowledge of the meaning of JBap's Hebrew name *Yoḥanan*, "Yahweh has given grace" (NOTE on 1:13).

rejoiced together with her. Both with her and for her. See Gen 21:6.

59. *On the eighth day.* Although originally circumcision may have been performed at the age of puberty, the biblical law specifies the eighth day (Gen 17:12). We find this practice observed both for Isaac (Gen 21:4) and for Paul (Philip 3:5). From what we know of Jewish customs, witnesses (later to be specified as ten) would have been present, and a benediction would have been pronounced.

they came to circumcise. Another *egeneto* construction (NOTE on 1:9): "It happened . . . they came." Circumcision could be performed both by men and by women (see Exod 4:25).

the child. Paidion is used four times in this section (here, 66,76,80). It is used for the newborn in Gen 17:12; 21:8, and also in Matt 2 (NOTE on 2:8) for Jesus—see Luke 2:17,27,40.

to name him . . . after his father. Literally, "call him by the name of his father." This use of the preposition *epi*, "by," with *kaloun*, "to name, call," is found in the LXX of Neh 7:63. Luke uses the dative without a preposition in the similar expression in vs. 61. We are not certain how common it was at this time to have a child named upon the occasion of circumcision, although rabbinic tradition has Moses named on that occasion (*Pirke Rabbi Eleazar* 48 [27c]). In patriarchal times naming often took place at birth (Gen 4:1; 21:3; 25:25–26); but even then the ideas of circumcision and naming were kept proximate (Gen 17:5 and 10; 21:3 and 4). The custom of naming a child after his father is attested in the second-century A.D. Wadi Murabba'at legal documents (Eleazar son of Eleazar, Judah son of Judah). But naming the child after the grandfather (papponymy) seems to have been more common in priestly circles; see JBL 94 (1975), 17, and Josephus *Life* 1.

60. *his mother intervened.* In patriarchal times the child could be named by either father or mother (NOTE on Matt 1:21), but in NT times it is generally thought that naming was the right of the father. Because of the virginal conception, the indication that Mary would name Jesus (1:31) is an understandable exception; yet see 2:21.

"He is to be called John." It would be banal to assume that Zechariah had informed her about the angel's command to name the child John (1:13). Zechariah was mute, and the reader is probably meant to think that Elizabeth's decision was a spontaneous and marvelous confirmation of God's plan.

61. *no one in your family with that name.* Yet "John" is a name known in priestly circles (John grandfather of Judas Maccabeus, John Hyrcanus), and Elizabeth's was a priestly family (1:5).

62. *they made signs.* Some scholars propose a textual emendation so that Zechariah makes the signs because he could not speak. However, Luke thinks of Zechariah as deaf, as well as mute (1:22,64).

63. *astonished.* Precisely since Zechariah was deaf, he had not heard Elizabeth; and so they are surprised when he selects the same name.

inscribing. Literally, "writing, saying"—a Hebraism.

64. *With that.* The word *parachrēma,* "immediately," is typically Lucan (seventeen out of nineteen NT uses).

Zechariah was able to open his mouth; and with his tongue at last freed. Literally, "his mouth was opened and his tongue"—a zeugma, since the verb "open" is not appropriate for a tongue. It is unnecessary to argue for a Hebrew original in which the same verb (niphal of *pātaḥ*) can mean "to open" and "to loose." The poorly attested addition, "and rendered capable of articulate speech," is almost surely a scribal attempt at improvement.

began to speak in praise of God. His first use of speech is appropriate. The OS^sin adds here another expression of marvel by the neighbors.

65. *This brought fear.* Literally, "fear came." Luke likes not only this type of Greek construction but also the theme. With both Zechariah (1:12) and Mary (1:30) there is mention of fear before an awesome divine intervention.

all their neighbors . . . all these events . . . the whole hill country. Bornhäuser, *Kindheitsgeschichte,* 94, is wrong in thinking that Luke's intention is to explain how he found out about JBap's birth, namely, the story was known in the whole hill country. Luke wishes to call attention to the magnitude of the events (the child's unexpected name and the father's regaining speech), as he shows by inserting a canticle of praise. A similar reaction follows the birth of Jesus (2:17–20). For "hill country," see the Note on 1:39.

were the talk of. The verb *dialalein* occurs in the NT only here and in 6:11.

66. *All stored up what they heard in their hearts.* Literally, "All who heard stored them up." This is a Lucan theme (2:19; 3:15; 5:22); with slight prepositional variants it is found in I Sam 21:13(12); Dan (Theodotion) 1:8; Mal 2:2.

"What then is this child going to be?" The use of the neuter "What," rather than "Who," suggests the role of the child is at stake. *Ara,* "then," is frequent in Luke.

the hand of the Lord was with him. An implicit present tense, turning this into direct discourse, is attested in Codex Bezae and some versions (through omission of the copulative). Rather than positing a Hebrew original in which there was no verb, we should probably see the present tense and the direct discourse as a scribal improvement. The "hand of the Lord" is peculiar to Luke in the NT; see particularly Acts 11:21.

67. *But Zechariah his father.* The Greek word order contrasts Zechariah with the "all who heard," the literal subject of the previous verse: they ask what the child will be, but Zechariah knows. The reidentification of Zechariah is consonant with the thesis that Luke added 67–79 in a second stage of editing.

filled with the Holy Spirit. The article is lacking; see the Note on 1:15 for the significance of the anarthrous usage.

68. *Blessed be.* Elizabeth's canticle in 1:42 began with *eulogēmenos;* Zechariah's begins with *eulogētos;* see Note there for the translation. Since this is addressed to God, the blessing is hortatory and "be" is to be preferred to "is."

Because. As in the Magnificat (NOTE on 1:48), the *hoti* clause gives the motive for praise.

visited. The verb *episkeptesthai,* "look over," may have the connotation of inspecting or supervising; but in biblical Greek it also refers to God's gracious visits, helping His people. That usage is frequent in the *Testaments of the Twelve Patriarchs* (*Levi* 4:4; *Judah* 23:5; *Asher* 7:3), a work betraying Jewish-Christian influence, which has vocabulary parallels to the Benedictus.

accomplished the redemption of His people. Literally, "made redemption," a Semitism, although it is not encountered in biblical Greek (the "sent redemption" of Ps 111:9 is close). The redemption is presumably "from our enemies" (71a) or "from the hands of our enemies" (74).

69. *raised up for us a horn of salvation.* An erect horn is an OT metaphor probably coming from the image of an ox or a bull standing alert in its strength, and then transferred to the horns on a victorious warrior's helmet. It fits the Jewish expectation of a triumphant Messiah king from the House of David. In the expression "to raise a horn" the more common verbs in the Greek Old Testament are *hypsoun, epairein,* and *exanatellein,* whereas the verb that is used here, *egeirein,* is more common in the imagery of God's raising up people (judges, priests, and kings). Its usage in a Jewish Christian canticle suggests that the "horn of salvation" has already been personified in Jesus the Savior whom God has *raised up* (Luke 7:16; Acts 4:10,12). Corresponding to this passage in the Benedictus is the reference to "God my Savior" in the Magnificat (1:47). In the Synoptic tradition the various nouns for "savior" and "salvation" (*sōtēr, sōtēria, sōtērion*) are peculiar to Luke and particularly frequent in the infancy narrative.

David His servant. Normally in the Bible, Israel is the *pais,* "servant," of God, as in the Magnificat (1:54). The only other instance in the NT of David being called *pais* is Acts 4:25, but it is well attested in Judaism roughly contemporary with Christianity, especially in prayers (I Macc 4:30; *4 Ezra* [*II Esdras*] 3:23; the Fifteenth Benediction of the *Shemoneh Esreh*). It continues in early Christian liturgical use in *Didache* ix 2.

70. *by the mouth.* The use of this expression to refer to an OT oracle appears in II Chr 36:22, in reference to Jeremiah's words. In the NT it is a Lucan peculiarity and noticeably attested in speeches associated with the early Jerusalem community (Acts 1:16; 3:18,21; 4:25).

holy prophets from of old. The word order distributing the modifiers is good Greek style and resembles that of Acts 3:21. (The Lucanisms in this verse have led some scholars to evaluate it as Lucan addition.) Luke is fond of the adjective "holy"; and this way of expressing "from of old" is found elsewhere in the NT only in Acts (3:21; 15:18; see LXX of Gen 6:4). The expression "holy prophets" occurs only in the later section of the Greek OT (Wisdom 11:1); also *II Baruch* 85:1.

71. *salvation.* See NOTE on this word in vs. 69.

from our enemies. In the psalter this covers either the pagans who are hostile to Israel or the more personal enemies of the psalmist.

72. *Showing . . . remembering.* Literally, "to make mercy . . . to remember." These non-articular infinitives, which define God's help, have a connotation

more of result than of purpose, reflecting a Semitic construction (see NOTE on 1:54, "in remembrance"). The expression "to make mercy with" reflects the Hebrew *'āśâ ḥesed 'im*. It is a reference to God's continuing His covenant kindness (*ḥesed*) which here, as in 1:50, the Greek translates as "mercy."

remembering His holy covenant. Besides the verb "to make," Hebrew uses the verb "to keep" with *ḥesed;* the parallelism of "mercy" and "covenant" catches two facets of the same idea, for it is in the covenant that God's mercy or kindness is expressed. The expression "holy covenant" begins to appear in the Jewish literature of the intertestamental period (I Macc 1:15,63). The parallelism with the next line indicates that the covenant with Abraham and his seed is in mind, but at this period the Mosaic covenant with Israel was thought to be in continuity with the patriarchal covenants.

73. *oath.* As in the Magnificat (NOTE on 1:55), the parallelism of ideas is not always carried over into the grammar: "oath" is in the accusative, while "covenant" in the previous line is in the genitive. Yet there is an apposition (BDF 295); the oath as it is explained in 74–75 constitutes the content (BDF 153²) of the covenant with Abraham (Gen 17:4). God took an oath (Gen 22:16–18), and later words of God hearken back to that oath (Gen 26:3; Deut 7:8). See also the parallelism between "covenant" and "sworn" in reference to David in Ps 89:4(3).

to grant. This articular infinitive does not continue the series of non-articular infinitives of result in 72 (NOTE on "showing"). Rather it is an epexegetical infinitive to express the content of the oath (BDF 400⁸). The same infinitive occurs in exactly the same context in the LXX of Jer 11:5, but there the content of the oath is different (it concerns the gift of the Promised Land).

74. *without fear.* This adverb comes first and may modify both the participle "delivered" and the infinitive construction "we might serve."

delivered. This participle modifies the implied subject ("we") of the infinitive "serve"—a good Greek construction.

enemies. See NOTE on 71.

we might serve. Literally, "to serve." As distinct from the more general *doulein,* this verb *latreuein* in the LXX and NT most often carries a tone of religious or cultic service (Exod 3:12), especially service rendered to the God of the covenant (Deut 11:13).

75. *in holiness and justice.* This pair of nouns occurs in Wisdom 9:3; a similar OT pair of *'emet* and *tāmîm,* sometimes translated as "truth and justice" (Josh 24:14; Judg 9:16,19). These are all covenant virtues.

before Him. The verb "serve" governs both "Him" in 74 and the phrase "before Him" here. The preposition "before" (*enōpion*) is, in Gospel usage, almost exclusively Lucan.

76. *called.* Or "acknowledged as," for the calling brings to expression what the child is (see 1:32,35).

the Most High. See NOTE on 1:32. The expression "prophet of the Most High" is not found in the OT but occurs in *Testament of Levi* 8:15 in reference to a king "who will arise in Judah and establish a new priesthood after the fashion of the Gentiles." Charles, AP, II, 309, takes this as a reference to the

Maccabean priest-kings ruling in Judea; but since the *Testaments* have many
Jewish-Christian features, the passage may refer to Jesus.

go before the Lord. This has been promised of JBap in 1:15,17.

to make ready. An infinitive without an article followed by an infinitive with
an article ("to grant"); see BDF 400⁶. (The same construction occurs in vs.
79: "appearing . . . guiding.") The infinitives are complementary, describing
the same basic action.

77. *knowledge of salvation.* This is not a phrase of the OT whose authors
would think rather of a knowledge of God. "Knowledge" has the sense of experience here; salvation is experienced in the forgiveness of sins.

forgiveness of their sins. Once again this is not an OT phrase, although the
idea of forgiveness occurs there. Clear parallels occur at Qumran; see H.
Ringgren, *The Faith of Qumran* (Philadelphia: Fortress, 1963), 120–25. In
the New Testament the expression is very Lucan (eight out of a total of eleven
occurrences). The amount of Christian theological language in these lines militates against the thesis that this canticle originated among non-Christian disciples of JBap.

78. *heartfelt mercy.* Literally, "the innermost parts of mercy." The *splanchna*
(often rendered as "the *bowels* of mercy") are the upper inner parts of the
body, i.e., the heart, the lungs, and the liver, which were thought to control the
emotions. The idea, then, is of mercy that is genuinely felt in the heart. The expression occurs in *Testament of Zebulun* 7:3; 8:2 (cf. *Naphtali* 4:5); a close
parallel is found in Col 3:12. The exact grammatical antecedent of the phrase
here is difficult to determine; it seems to modify the whole idea of 76–77 rather
than any one clause (and indeed, if 76–77 were added to a pre-Lucan canticle,
originally this phrase may have been related to 75).

by which. Jones, "Background," 38, thinks of a Hebrew original in which this
line was coordinate rather than subordinate: "and there has visited us."

has visited. For the verb, see the NOTE on 68. The manuscript evidence is
divided on whether to read an aorist (many Greek mss. and most of the versions), as I have done, or a future (Vaticanus, Sinaiticus*, OS^sin, Coptic). Some
scholars reject the aorist on the grounds that the scribes have assimilated the
reading to the aorist form of the same verb in 68; but one may just as easily
argue against the future reading as an assimilation to the two future verbs in
the immediate vicinity (vs. 76). The aorist is the more difficult reading (since
in the chronology of the infancy narrative Jesus has not yet "visited us"), and
thus is the tense more likely to have been tampered with in the course of scribal
transmission. Jones, "Background," 38, once more resorts to a Hebrew original
to explain the confusion of tenses (a *waw* consecutive that looks like a future
but should be read as a past); however, the confusion is more likely in transmission, not in translation.

a rising light from on high. The Greek phrase *anatolē ex hypsous* can also
mean "a Messiah from [God] Most High"—presumably "*sent* from the Most
High," unless one wants to read pre-existence into the pre-Lucan hymn (see
Jacoby, "*Anatolē*"). That *anatolē* can be a name for the Messiah we see from
Zech 3:8; 6:12 where the Hebrew makes reference to the Davidic "branch" or
"shoot" (*ṣemaḥ*), and the LXX renders the term by *anatolē* (see p. 212 above;

also the expression "the sprout [*blastos*] of the God Most High" in *Testament of Judah* 24:4). However, the term *anatolē*, literally "rising," besides capturing the burgeoning of a branch, is appropriate to the rising of a heavenly body; see the expression "his star at its rising" in Matt 2:2 and the NOTE there. The qualification "from on high" and the implicit reference to light in the next line (by contrast with darkness) suggests that Luke is thinking primarily of a rising heavenly light; and the analogy from Matthew would suggest a rising star, rather than a rising sun or a dawning day. Of course, Luke thinks of this rising light as the Messiah, and thus catches some of the other meaning of *anatolē*, a combination already found in Num 24:17 (pp. 195–96 above). The Psalms (102:20[19]; 144:7) use the phrase "from on high" to describe the highest heaven from which God extends His help to those on earth.

79. *appearing . . . guiding*. The verb translated "appear" is *epiphainein*, whence "Epiphany." Grammatically, these two verbs are infinitives. The first is inarticular; the second is articular (cf. BDF 400⁶), the same combination we saw in vs. 76, "to make ready . . . to grant." With difficulty one could understand "guiding" ("to guide") to be parallel to "to grant" in 77a, and thus to depend upon "you will go before the Lord" in 76b—a construction that would relegate 78ab and 79a to the status of a parenthesis between the two infinitives (Vielhauer, "Benedictus," 262–63). But this seems a needless complication and would be ruled out if 78–79 were once independent of 76–77, as I shall suggest in the COMMENT. The two infinitives are better seen to express the result of the visitation by the Messiah.

80. *Spirit*. It is difficult to determine whether the Holy Spirit is meant here or not, but the Holy Spirit has been so insistently associated with JBap (1:15,41,67) that a capitalized Spirit seems appropriate.

day of his public appearance. The verb related to *anadeixis* means "to reveal" and "to appoint," so there may be the tone of an appearance to which JBap had been committed by God. The use of "day" for "time" is Hebrew style, as is the use of a genitive for an adjective (BDF 165).

COMMENT

With this scene we come to the second set of diptychs in the Lucan infancy narrative (pp. 251–52 above). Even though the parallelism between the stories of the birth of JBap (1:57–80) and of Jesus (2:1–40) is not so perfect as the parallelism between the stories of the two annunciations (Table XI), the overall pattern is carefully matched. In each there is reference to the birth and the circumcision/naming. In the case of JBap the future greatness of the child is expounded in relation to marvels that surround the circumcision/naming; in the case of Jesus the future greatness of the child is expounded in relation to marvels that surround his birth. In both stories there is a canticle that follows the circumcision/naming: the Benedictus in the case of JBap, and the Nunc Dimittis in the case of Jesus. Here, however, the parallelism becomes more complicated because the Benedictus is closer in length and style to the Magnificat than to the Nunc Dimittis. This irregularity is best explained, as we have seen (§ 12C), from the fact that the canticles have been inserted in a second stage of Lucan composition; this insertion somewhat disrupted the diptych scheme. In this section I shall follow the same procedure as in § 12, namely, to discuss first the surrounding scene, and then the canticle.

A. *The Birth and Naming of John the Baptist (1:57–66,80)*

No more than two verses (57–58) are given by Luke to the birth and the joy that it occasioned. Those verses place us once more in the OT atmosphere of the barren wives of the patriarchs to whom God gives joy through the gift of fertility. As we saw in the annunciation of the forthcoming birth of JBap, the primary patriarchal pattern for Zechariah and Elizabeth is Abraham and Sarah (§ 10A). And so, while the birth description in vs. 57 echoes Rebekah's giving birth to Esau and to Jacob in Gen 25:24 (see NOTE), vs. 58 echoes the aftermath of Sarah's giving birth to Isaac: "God has given me cause to laugh,[1] and all who hear it will rejoice together with me" (Gen 21:6). Mary, the first relative to hear of Elizabeth's fertility, came before the birth to greet her (1:39–40); the other relatives, who have only now discovered it, come after the birth to rejoice with her.

The way they discover that hers is a divinely arranged conception is not through the word of an angel, as in Mary's case, but through the wonders that surround the naming of the child upon the occasion of his circumcision. And it is to these events that Luke devotes the major part of the story (vss. 59–66,80). In the annunciation the angel had predicted that many would rejoice at JBap's birth (1:14b), and that has been fulfilled. Now the other prediction must be fulfilled that the child would be called John (1:13e). The neighbors and relatives do not know of this prediction, but they can sense the stirring of great things in the marvelous agreement between the two parents on the name. The reader sees that, without foreknowledge, Elizabeth has picked the name the angel commanded (NOTE on vs. 60); and the neighbors and relatives see that, without hearing his wife, Zechariah has fixed upon the same unexpected name as she. Zechariah's regaining his power to speak is understandable to the reader because now the things predicted by the angel have happened (1:20: "unable to speak *until the day that these things will happen*"), but that miracle adds all the

---

[1] A play on the name Isaac, "he laughs."

more to the onlookers' astonishment. Well may they wonder, "What then is this child going to be?" In the present sequence of the story, Zechariah answers that question with the Benedictus, a prophecy that repeats Gabriel's promise that JBap will go before the Lord (1:17a). If that canticle was added by Luke in a second stage of composition, the question of the bystanders was originally followed by Luke's assurance to the reader that the hand of the Lord was with JBap (the end of vs. 66), and the information that the child grew up in the desert in preparation for the day when he would be manifested to Israel. The angel had prophesied that the child would be filled with the Holy Spirit from his mother's womb (1:15c), and it is in that Spirit that the child becomes strong (80).

Although the description in 80 fits JBap well, it is actually a stereotyped statement, as we shall see when we discuss the similar affirmation made about Jesus in 2:40 and 52. Thus it is only semibiographical. From the common Synoptic tradition Luke had the information that JBap's career began in the desert; he uses that information in having JBap go off into the desert[2] as part of a technique of ending the scenes of the infancy narrative on a motif of departure (NOTE on "he went back" in 1:23). Luke also had the common tradition that JBap played a quasi-prophetic role in his ministry,[3] and so becoming "strong in Spirit" is a preparation for that.[4] The opening of JBap's ministry in Luke 3:2, "The word of God came to John, the son of Zechariah, in the desert," is an appropriate continuation of 1:80.[5] It is part of Luke's consummate artistry that, in composing such a smooth transition from the infancy narrative of JBap to the ministry of JBap, he has been able at the same time to compose a summary that echoes many of the OT parallels that have run through ch. 1: Isaac, Samson, and Samuel. Of Isaac, the son of Abraham and Sarah, we are told that, after his birth and circumcision, "the child grew up" (Gen 21:8). Of Samson it was said, "The child became mature, and the Lord blessed him;

[2] It is pure fiction to draw upon our knowledge of the priestly Essene community of the Dead Sea Scrolls in order to fashion the theory that JBap was brought to Qumran as the child of a priest and raised there in a desert monastery. It is not impossible that in his adult career in the desert of Judea JBap had some contact with the Qumran group, for there are resemblances between their thought and his. But he is never remembered in the Gospels as a member of a group, and Josephus who knew both of JBap and of the Essenes never connects them. Moreover, the Qumran group was vigorously opposed to worship conducted at the Temple of Jerusalem and to the priesthood that functioned there, so the fact that JBap was the son of a loyal Temple priest would not have been a recommendation for membership.

[3] In Mark 1:6 he is described as wearing the prophetic "hairy mantle"; see footnote 43 in § 10.

[4] As we shall see, this is the feature in the description of the growth of JBap that is missing in the two descriptions of the growth of Jesus. Fridrichsen, *"Sophia,"* points out that, while there are statements in the Greek biographies of great men which mention a growing welfare of body and soul, there is not the precise emphasis on strength, especially strength in Spirit, that we find in Luke.

[5] On p. 275 above I pointed out that the coming of the Spirit of the Lord and the coming of the word of the Lord are alternate ways of describing the beginning of the career of a prophet.

and the Spirit of the Lord began to go with him" (Judg 13:24–25, LXX).
Of Samuel it was written, "And the child waxed mighty before the Lord"
(I Sam 2:21). If JBap's conception and birth echoed the history of these
figures from Israel's past, so also did his growth. Thus, having relived so
much of Israel's history, JBap is made ready for his public appearance to
Israel;[6] and that appearance, which in turn is connected with the appearance of Jesus, will unveil the salvation of Israel (1:77a).

B. *The Benedictus* (*1:67–79*)

As we turn our attention to the hymn of Zechariah, I remind the reader
of the general remarks already made about the Lucan canticles (§ 12C).
There is a wide range of scholarly opinion about the origins of the
Benedictus just as there was about the Magnificat. Distinguished exegetes,
such as Harnack and Erdmann, think of it as a composition by Luke himself, and point to Lucan Greek in the wording of the hymn (see the NOTES
for vocabulary and grammar comparisons). Against this thesis stands the
fact that only a few verses (70,76,77) are heavily Lucan, and these may
be Lucan additions to a pre-Lucan hymn. For the most part the hymn is
less Lucan than the surrounding narrative, and some of the claimed
Lucanisms are really instances of Septuagintal or intertestamental Jewish
Greek style which may have been shared by the composers of the hymn
and by Luke. If we do posit a pre-Lucan hymn, the thesis that it was composed by non-Christian followers of JBap is called into serious doubt by
the reference to a "horn of salvation in the House of David," for JBap was
scarcely a Davidic savior.[7] (Moreover, the language which describes JBap
in 77 is remarkably Christian, as I pointed out in the NOTES; and in the
whole hymn there is not a single reference to baptism, as one would have
expected if it were composed by JBap circles.) This same argumentation
stressing an already accomplished Davidic salvation, with attention to the
aorists in 68–69 and 78, makes it unlikely that the hymn was composed by
Jews who were still awaiting the Messiah.[8]

[6] "Public appearance" is not too strong a term, for in Luke 3:1–2 a solemnity surrounds
the beginning of JBap's ministry: it is dated by the reigns of the Roman emperors, the
Herodian princes, the governor of Judea, and the Israelite high priests.

[7] The thesis of composition by JBap sectarians who gave messianic honor to their master
is supported by scholars like Lambertz and Lohmeyer. The Davidic objection is often
parried by arguing that vs. 69 is a Lucan and Christian addition to the original canticle, but
that argument is highly dubious. The reference to David in 69 fits well with the use of *anatolē* in 78b (see NOTE); also the opening of the canticle is quite amenable to a Davidic reference (see I Kgs 1:48 in Table XIII). A reference to David in the first strophe balances
perfectly a reference to Abraham in the second strophe.

[8] A purely Jewish composition for the greater part of the Benedictus is a thesis supported
by such scholars as Goguel, Gunkel, Klostermann, Spitta, Vielhauer, and Winter. Gunkel
would contend that the Benedictus is an eschatological hymn with prophetic aorists: they
refer to the future with such surety that the future is seen as accomplished. But then one

A hymn composed by Jewish Christians remains the most plausible explanation. Such a group would have shared with their pre-Christian Jewish forebears the martial language of the messianic psalms and even of the Qumran War Scroll (1QM),[9] but that language would now have been cast into a past-accomplished tense rather than a future. More specifically, the group has the Anawim mentality already encountered in the Magnificat. They are hated by enemies (71,74), and they have sat in darkness (79). God's deliverance of them is a sign of His covenant mercy to His people (72–73), for they are the remnant of Israel whose lives enshrine the holiness and justice expected of a covenanted people (75). The description of the deliverance is in Jewish terms which bear no trace of the highly developed christology of the later NT. The agency in the redemption is attributed to God who has raised up the Davidic horn of salvation (68–69) and who visited His people through the *anatolē*, the messianic Branch.[10] If all these indications point to the origins of the Benedictus among early Jewish Christians,[11] especially those of an Anawim mentality, there is a further hint of a connection with Luke's picture of the Jerusalem Christians. Not only are there vocabulary connections with the sermons in Acts (footnote 50, § 12), but also there is the atmosphere of a prophecy uttered by one filled with the Holy Spirit. Obviously that atmosphere is supplied by Luke (67); but at least in Luke's mind, there was a connection with the picture of the Jerusalem community he gives in Acts 2. That was a community filled with the Holy Spirit and speaking prophecy (2:18).[12]

1. The Setting and the Structure

The above remarks constitute a plausible theory about the pre-Lucan history of the canticle, but our main concern is the way in which Luke employs it in the infancy narrative. Even without such a theory, the Benedictus bears the marks of being an addition. If it were omitted, the

---

must ask why certain verses shift to the future tense. An additional argument against this thesis is the hint of Christian phrasing in 69 (see NOTE).

[9] See the parallels in Table XIII. Gnilka, "Hymnus," 225–26, is particularly helpful in stressing the Qumran parallels. It is interesting that the Qumran blessing on the Prince of the Congregation (who is presumably the Davidic Messiah; see JBC, article 68, ≢104) in 1QSb V is cast in the optative future: "May the Lord raise you up. . . . May He make your horns of iron"—a sharp contrast with the Benedictus: "He has raised up for us a horn of salvation."

[10] See the NOTE on "rising light" in 78. It is quite possible that the original hymn meant *anatolē* as "branch" and that Luke reinterpreted it as a rising or dawning light to fit the infancy context better.

[11] Among those who attribute the Benedictus in whole or in large part to such a group are Benoit, Gnilka, Ladeuze, Loisy, Marty, and J. Weiss.

[12] If one objects that the language of the Benedictus about being delivered "from our enemies and from the hands of all those who hate us" (71) is exaggerated and overly stylized as a reference to Jesus' salvific death and resurrection, it is no more so than the language of Acts 2:20 concerning the darkening of the sun and the turning of the moon into blood. In both instances we are encountering Christian exuberance articulated in the language of Israel's expectations.

scene in 1:57–66 would terminate smoothly in 1:80—exactly the same situation we saw with the Magnificat.[13] And the fact that the body of the canticle refers to an already accomplished salvation in Jesus, the Davidic Messiah (not in JBap), is apparent, even if one must interpret this accomplishment as proleptic and read the aorist tenses as a sign of prophetic assurance. Nevertheless, Luke's addition is not maladroit. In the preceding narrative Luke had written that Zechariah, once his tongue was freed, began to speak in praise of God (64).[14] Luke has added the canticle as an expression of that praise: "Blessed be the Lord, the God of Israel" (68a). He thus has brought about an interesting double parallelism. In the preceding scene Elizabeth had uttered a blessing (42); here her husband utters a blessing.[15] The preceding scene moved toward termination with a canticle proclaiming what God had done, a canticle sung by Mary who received the annunciation of Jesus' birth. The present scene moves toward termination with a canticle proclaiming what God has done, a canticle sung by Zechariah who received the annunciation of JBap's birth. Although each canticle primarily concerns salvation already wrought by God in Jesus, Luke has added to each a few lines of future prediction[16] in order to make the canticle appropriate to the new setting wherein it is uttered before the birth of Jesus. And in each instance these added lines concern the figure who has been the subject of the preceding narrative. The Magnificat was preceded by a blessing of Mary, the handmaid of the Lord (1:38,42–45); and so the added lines (vs. 48) refer to the handmaid whom henceforth all generations will call fortunate. The Benedictus has been preceded by a description of the divine wonders surrounding JBap's birth and naming; and so the added lines (vss. 76–77) concern JBap's future role in God's plan of salvation for His people. Since the preceding narrative has the neighbors and relatives ask what the child is going to be, Luke's added lines in the canticle answer that question: he will be the prophet of the Most High going before the Lord to make ready His way.

Those added lines explain why in vs. 67 Luke refers to the canticle as a prophecy uttered by one filled with the Holy Spirit. In the preceding scene it was because Elizabeth was filled with the Holy Spirit (41) that she was able to perceive the true blessedness of Mary; now Zechariah "filled with the Holy Spirit" (67) praises JBap. And both Mary and JBap are praised because they have a preparatory role in the coming of Jesus. Believing the Lord's word about a marvelous conception, Mary came to Elizabeth carry-

[13] If 1:46–55 were omitted, the scene in 1:39–45 would terminate smoothly in 1:56.

[14] The fact that Luke did not put the canticle immediately after vs. 64 is an indication that the canticle belongs to a second stage of composition.

[15] Elizabeth praised the mother of Jesus, but I am not sure that we should press the parallelism to the point of stressing that Zechariah is praising the Father of Jesus. The only hint of that is the reference to "the Most High" in 76a, which may pick up the designation of Jesus as "Son of the Most High" in 1:32a (see 1:35c).

[16] Note that the only indisputable future tenses in both the Magnificat and the Benedictus occur in the verses (48 and 76–77) which for other reasons I regard as Lucan insertions.

ing Jesus in her womb. JBap, who moved Elizabeth to praise Mary on that occasion, has now emerged to begin his career in which he will be the prophet of the Most High going before the Lord to make ready his way. We have seen that in 57–66 Luke was concerned to show that the angelic promises of the annunciation were being fulfilled, e.g., that the barren Elizabeth would bear a son, that his name would be called John, and that many would rejoice at his birth (13–14).[17] In 76–77 another of those promises is seen to be on its way toward realization, the promise that JBap would "go before Him . . . to make ready for the Lord a prepared people" (17ae). Zechariah, who heard that promise, predicts that JBap "will go before the Lord to make ready His ways"; but now that Zechariah knows about Jesus, he knows that making ready the Lord's ways involves making ready for Jesus.[18] As "the prophet of the Most High," JBap is the last of the prophets (Luke 16:16), who at the same time introduces the good news of salvation.

Having discussed the setting, which supplies a key to the way Luke made use of the Benedictus, let us turn to the structure. We saw that, of the various psalm types, the Magnificat most closely resembled a hymn of praise. The same is true of the Benedictus, and I am going to propose that, like the Magnificat, it consists of the three parts usually found in the hymn of praise (§ 12, D1), namely:

     a) An *introduction* praising God, which is found in 68a.

     b) The *body of the hymn* listing the motives of praise, which begins with the "because" clause in 68b. While the original hymn consisted of two carefully balanced strophes (68b–71b; 72a–75), a third strophe has been added in reference to JBap (76a–77b).

     c) The *conclusion* in 78a–79b which recapitulates some of the motives of the hymn.

In proposing this division, I am rejecting several other proposals which should be examined.

---

[17] Another promise of the annunciation was fulfilled at the time of the visitation. The angel said that JBap would be filled with the Holy Spirit even from his mother's womb (15c), and clear signs of that were given by the prophetic movement of the baby in Elizabeth's womb (41,44).

[18] It is difficult to know whether by "the Lord" in 76b Luke means "the God of Israel" or Jesus. We saw the same problem in the phrase "go before Him" in 17, and in the NOTE there I argued that it was the Lord God, not Jesus. I tend to argue the same here, but the case is more complicated. In 1:17 Jesus had not even been mentioned, while 1:76 comes after Zechariah's knowledge of the forthcoming birth of Jesus. However, both texts reflect the ministry tradition which associates Isa 40:3, "make ready the way of the Lord," and Mal 3:1 and 3:23 (RSV 4:5), "before the great and terrible day of the Lord," with JBap. If the Lord is the Lord God, this does not prove that the Benedictus was composed by non-Christians. It simply proves that Luke preserved an older language which reflected JBap's self understanding, even though, as a Christian, Luke has reinterpreted the way in which JBap made ready for the Lord, namely, by making ready for Jesus who was Lord (as Elizabeth already acknowledged in 1:43 by speaking of Mary as "the mother of my Lord").

I have proposed that 76–77 is the Lucan insertion pertinent to JBap,[19] and that 78–79 constitutes the original conclusion of the pre-Lucan canticle. In this proposal I am rejecting the thesis of many scholars[20] who think that the original hymn concluded with vs. 75. Indeed, some speak of two different literary genres: a hymn of praise in 68–75, and a genethliacon or birthday hymn in 76–79 (with the added possibility that JBap sectarians composed the latter). Obviously this thesis would be helped if one reads a future tense rather than aorist for the verb "visit" in 78b (see NOTE), for then 78–79 would have the same overall futurity as 76–77. However, since this is an insoluble textual problem, one must determine the issue on other grounds. Favorable to the thesis of vs. 75 as a conclusion is the fact that expressions of eternity, *similar* to "all the days of our lives," often terminate psalms.[21] However, there are also instances of the same expression that Luke uses occurring in the midst of a psalm, rather than as an ending (Pss 90:14; 128:5). The grammatical argument that there are four infinitives in 76–79 ("to make ready," "to grant," "to appear," "to guide") is not really convincing; for as I have pointed out in the respective NOTES, they are not really coordinate.[22] Favorable to the thesis I have proposed is the fact that the first person plural ("We," "us," "our") which is frequent in 68–75 reappears three times in 78–79, while it is completely absent in 76–77.[23] Moreover, there is in 78–79 neither the distinctive JBap language of 76, nor the Christian phrasing without OT parallel that marks 77. A glance at Table XIII will show that 78–79 has the same kind of background as 68–75. Thus, I think the majority of the evidence favors treating 78–79 as part of the original hymn[24] and as referring to Jesus (a rising light from on high who has visited us[25]) rather than to JBap.

19 Dibelius and Benoit are others who see these verses as the Lucan reference to JBap. With hesitation, Bultmann, *History*, 296, seems to prefer only vs. 76 as "a Christian or a Baptist addition." It is true that the typical JBap language is clear only in 76, but the Christian language of 77 (see NOTES) is unlike the rest of the hymn in having few OT parallels. A totally opposite view is that of Leaney, "Birth Narratives," 161, who would argue on the basis of *Testament of Levi* 8:14–15 that "prophet of the Most High" can refer to a Davidic Messiah and that Luke 1:76 can refer to the same figure as 1:69. However, Luke has clearly indicated that JBap will be the prophet before God (1:17) while Jesus is the *"Son of the most High."* In the NT "going before the Lord to make ready His ways" is a description for JBap, and it is highly dubious that in any stage of the Benedictus it had another reference.

20 For example, Burger, Gnilka, Gunkel, Hahn, Spitta, Winter.

21 Pss 16:11; 18:51(50); 23:6; 28:9; 30:13(12).

22 I have tried to suggest this by translating the third and fourth as participles.

23 The reference to "their sins" in 77b is in noticeable contrast to the sequence which precedes and follows: "our father" (73), "our enemies" (74), "our lives" (75), "our God" (78).

24 As pointed out in the initial NOTE on 78, the grammatical antecedent of 78–79 is not clear; these verses could follow 75 as well as they follow 77. Verses 68–75 constitute one long, rambling sentence, with loosely connected clauses; see footnote 27.

25 Vielhauer, "Benedictus," 40, argues that JBap is the "rising light" (*anatolē*). He proves this from the Fourth Gospel which often directs remarks against the claims of the JBap sectarians: "He was not the light [*phōs*]" (John 1:8). However, a more obvious argument supporting Jesus as the *anatolē* is the clear NT tradition describing Jesus as a light come

The decision about how to treat 76–77 and 78–79 does not solve all the problems of structure, for there are difficulties in the *body of the hymn* (68b–75) as well. Although both the Benedictus and the Magnificat are hymns of praise and have many points in common,[26] the parallelism of lines is much less obvious in the Benedictus. Grammatically, the Benedictus is one long sentence developing the main verbs in 68–69 ("visited . . . accomplished the redemption . . . raised up a horn of salvation").[27] This means that the various attempts to detect strophes or stanzas (and as many as five have been posited) are scarcely on grammatical grounds. On the basis of parallelism of ideas one may detect two strophes of approximately the same length in the original body of the hymn:

First Strophe (68b–71b):
68b Because He has visited
68c and accomplished the redemption of His people,
69a and has raised up for us a horn of salvation
69b in the House of David His servant,
70 as He spoke by the mouth of His holy prophets from of old:
71a salvation from our enemies
71b and from the hand of all those who hate us,

Second Strophe (72a–75):
72a Showing mercy to our fathers
72b and remembering His holy covenant,
73 the oath which he swore to our father Abraham,
to grant us 74 that, without fear,
delivered from the hands of our enemies,
we might serve Him 75 in holiness and justice,
before Him all the days of our lives.

Each begins with what God has done by way of mercy and redemption for His people, our fathers; and then proceeds to how this has been done for

---

into the world or as a light for those who have sat in darkness (Matt 4:16; John 1:9; 3:19; 8:12; 9:4–5; 12:46). And Matt 2:2 uses *anatolē* for the star of Jesus, the newborn King of the Jews.

26 Gryglewicz, "Herkunft," is helpful on the similarities among the four Lucan canticles; he finds fifteen common words shared by the Magnificat and the Benedictus. However, the style of poetry and grammar are different, and the Anawim motif is stronger in the Magnificat. For that reason, although one cannot rule out composition by the same man (there are differences among the Qumran *Hodayoth* which are frequently attributed to one author), it is safer to speak of the canticles coming from a group of writers of the same general theological outlook.

27 The development of those verbs in the succeeding verses is rarely through subordinate clauses (only 70 and 78b). More often it is through coordinate phrases (as in 71, 73, 75, and 78). Most often it is through a bewildering sequence of infinitives. If we count the insert on JBap, there are eight infinitives, which I have translated in various ways (see NOTES): "Showing" in 72a, "remembering" 72b, "to grant" 73, "we might serve" 74, "to make ready" 76b, "to grant" 77a, "appearing" 79a, "guiding" 79b. Since there is only the one set of main verbs at the beginning, insertions do not disrupt the grammar.

us. This salvation is seen, respectively, as fulfillment of promises to David and to Abraham, and it means deliverance from "our enemies."[28]

Verse 70 offers a particular problem in this analysis. It is the only subordinate clause in the two strophes, and its language is much more clearly Lucan than that of the surrounding verses (see NOTES). Perhaps, however, the language may be discounted on the basis that it is most parallel to the material in Acts where Luke describes the Jerusalem Jewish Christian community (which may be the ultimate source of the Lucan canticles). Unlike the Lucan addition in vs. 77, vs. 70 has OT background (Table XIII). Moreover, it is roughly parallel to 73 in the second strophe, and to 55a in the Magnificat. Thus, it seems wiser to treat it as part of the original canticle.

The structure proposed enables us to detect a sequence of thought. The hymn is christological: the main reason for blessing the God of Israel is what He has done for His people in Jesus the Messiah. The two strophes that constitute the body of the hymn stress the fulfillment of the OT expectation: a fulfillment of a promise to David and his House, which was spoken by the prophets, and of an oath to Abraham and his descendants, which was part of the covenant. (It is scarcely accidental that, in expressing the same theme by means of a genealogy, Matt 1:1 mentions David and Abraham in the same order.) After mentioning the OT preparation, Luke mentions JBap who is the bridge between the OT and the Gospel and who terminates the Law and the prophets (16:16). And then the hymn comes to a conclusion with the eulogy of Jesus in 78–79, in whom is realized the theme of God's "visit" which began the first strophe and of God's "mercy" which began the second. This sequence (OT promise/JBap/Jesus) explains why Luke did not tack his addition concerning JBap onto the end of the hymn. Luke wished to preserve the original intent of the canticle which gave priority to the Messiah; and so the canticle must conclude, not with the "prophet of the Most High" who will go before the Lord to make ready His ways, but with the "rising light from on high," who appears to those who have been sitting in darkness. All that Luke added about JBap in 76 he got from the picture of JBap preserved in the accounts of the ministry; and in inserting it into the canticle, Luke remains

---

28 I am consciously rejecting the complicated chiastic structure of the Benedictus proposed by Vanhoye, "Structure." His suggestion is typical of the general theory of chiastic pattern (based largely on selected words) which he and his confrere at Rome, I. de la Potterie, have proposed for several books and sections of the NT. (Elsewhere I have discussed and rejected some of the proposals for the Fourth Gospel.) He finds ten expressions in 68b–72b parallel to ten expressions in 73–79b, and these parallels are arranged in chiastic order. (When a parallel does not fit the chiastic pattern, e.g., "mercy" in 72a and 78a, it is conveniently omitted.) This structure ignores the careful balance that I have pointed out between Strophe One and Strophe Two, the different character of 76–77 (in which 76 has the only clear references to JBap and 77 is singularly lacking in OT echoes), and the fact that 78 (seen as a conclusion) picks up the themes of "visit" and "mercy" which open the two strophes.

faithful to the sequence about JBap supplied by those same accounts: JBap comes before Jesus, and he is the prophet who makes ready for the light.[29]

2. The Contents

Since, like the Magnificat, the Benedictus is a mosaic or cento of OT and intertestamental phrases and ideas, I have given the background of this canticle in the accompanying Table XIII, to which the reader should refer when I discuss OT or other passages in the text below. I shall also presuppose the technical information already given in the NOTES.

INTRODUCTION (68a). While the Benedictus is described as a prophecy (a designation verified in 76–77[30]), it is by literary genre a hymn of praise. Although God has done something new and definitive for His people, the opening line of praise stresses the continuity with what He has done in the past; for it is a well-known refrain from the psalter. Since the Benedictus will celebrate the redemption that God has accomplished through Jesus, the Davidic Messiah, it is not without significance that in I Kgs 1:48 this refrain appears on the lips of David when his son Solomon accedes to the throne, thus guaranteeing the Davidic line of succession. It is noteworthy too that the refrain was used at Qumran to introduce the hymn to be sung after the victory in the war of the last times, a hymn which like the Benedictus speaks of covenant mercy and salvation for a people.

STROPHE ONE (68b–71b). The parallelism with the mentality of the Dead Sea Scrolls continues when we see in CD i 5–12 that the Qumran community spoke of its foundation in terms of God's having *visited* them and having *raised up* the Teacher of Righteousness—the same language used by the Benedictus to describe the renewal of God's people through the raising up of the Davidic Messiah. When we discussed the Magnificat, we found that its OT paradigm was the hymn Hannah sang upon the birth of Samuel. The last verse of that hymn supplies the first known instance of the expression "the horn of His anointed [i.e., Messiah]." Thus, traditional liturgical language is being echoed here.

The reference to the prophets in vs. 70 expresses the early Christian conviction (shared also by Qumran) that God's final action terminates a long line of prophetic preparation. It is vocalized by Peter, speaking for

---

[29] As part of his thesis that 76–79 originated among JBap sectarians and that JBap is the rising light mentioned in 78b (footnote 25 above), Vielhauer says that if the Benedictus was composed by Christians, there would be a clearer subordination of JBap. My analysis of the structure shows a subordination of JBap totally consonant with the general Gospel picture.

[30] In the present setting it is also verified in the fact that, although Jesus has not yet been born, Zechariah already knows of the salvation he has accomplished.

the Jerusalem community in Acts 3:21, when he refers to "the time for establishing all that God spoke by the mouth of His holy prophets from old."[31] The description of God's salvation in terms of deliverance from enemies "who hate us" need not be pressed as if it referred to particular enemies of the Christian community or of Zechariah—the psalter parallels illustrate the stereotyped character of the language (footnote 12 above).

The language of salvation in vs. 71, which terminates the first strophe, may echo the Deutero-Isaian description of the Servant of the Lord who is to serve for "salvation to the ends of the earth." In the conclusion of the canticle (79) we shall hear more Servant language in terms of a light appearing to those who sit in darkness.[32]

STROPHE TWO (72–75). Thus far the redemption and salvation have been described in terms of God's fidelity to His prophets' promises to David. The second strophe shifts the attention from the covenant with David and his descendants to the covenant with Abraham and his seed.[32a] It begins with reference to the primary virtue of God as a covenant partner, i.e., His mercy (*ḥesed*) or covenant kindness in choosing His partner, and continues with an example of His other traditional covenant virtue, i.e., His fidelity (*'emet*) to the covenant, once it has been made.[33] The strophe ends by referring to the virtues of the people as a covenant partner, i.e., the holiness and justice that should mark their lives. The idea that God's fulfillment of the covenant delivers His people so that they may *serve* Him is also found at Qumran (1QH xvii 14), since that group, like the early Christian community, saw in their own history the renewal of God's covenant with Israel.[34] The verb "serve" is often used liturgically (NOTE) and the refrain "all the days of our lives" appears in texts referring to Temple service (Isa 38:2), so that the ideal in the last lines of this strophe would be perfectly appropriate for early Christians in Jerusalem with "Temple piety" (§ 10, footnote 13).

The language of oath, covenant, and covenant virtues, which the Benedictus employs of God's relationship to Abraham and his seed, was

---

31 Above I mentioned the problem of whether 1:70 is a Lucan verse added to the canticle, or whether it was originally a part of the canticle which, along with Acts 3:21, reflects the language used by the Jerusalem Christian community.

32 This is still another argument for the thesis that 78–79 belonged to the original hymn as a conclusion and was not part of the Lucan addition that we find in 76–77.

32a For the close relationship between these two covenants, see R. E. Clements, *Abraham and David* (SBT, 2nd series, 5; London: SCM, 1967), esp. 47–60.

33 God's covenant and oath are the counterparts of His *ḥesed* and *'emet*. For the historical connection in the Abraham story between covenant and oath, and the grammatical connection between these words in the Benedictus, see NOTE on 73.

34 For Qumran, an entrance into the community was an "entrance into the covenant" (1QS i 18,20, etc.). In CD vi 19; xx 12 we hear of the "new covenant" made in the land of Damascus. Both the Qumran group and the Christians took over the expression "new covenant" from Jer 31:31–34 where it also had the sense of renewal, but by the end of the century many Christians had come to understand "new covenant" as a replacement and, indeed, abrogation of the old.

TABLE XIII: THE BACKGROUND OF THE BENEDICTUS

INTRODUCTORY PRAISE

68a *Blessed be the Lord, the God of Israel,*
Pss 41:14(13); 72:18; 106:48 (Ending of three books of the psalter):
Blessed be the Lord, the God of Israel.

I Kgs 1:48 (David, after Solomon's enthronization):
Blessed be the Lord, the God of Israel,
who today has placed one of my offspring upon my throne
and has allowed my eyes to see it.

1QM xiv 4–5 ("Hymn of Return" after victory):
Blessed be the God of Israel,
who keeps mercy toward His covenant
and the appointed times of salvation
with the people He has redeemed.

FIRST STROPHE

68b *Because He has visited*
68c *and accomplished the redemption of His people,*
69a *and has raised up for us a horn of salvation*
69b *in the House of David His servant,*
CD i 5–12:
Three hundred and ninety years after He had given them into the hand of King
Nebuchadnezzar of Babylon, He visited them and caused a root of a plant to spring
from Israel and Aaron to inherit His land . . . He raised up for them a Teacher of
Righteousness to guide them in the way of His heart.

Ps 111:9:
He sent redemption to His people.

Judg 3:9:
And the Lord raised up a savior for Israel.

Ps 132:16–17:
I shall clothe her priests with salvation . . .
I shall make a horn to sprout for David.

Ezek 29:21:
On that day I shall make a horn sprout for all the House of Israel.

I Sam 2:10 (Hannah's hymn):
He will exalt the horn of His anointed [Messiah].

Ps 18:3(2):
My God . . . the horn of my salvation.

Fifteenth Benediction of the *Shemoneh Esreh* (first century A.D.):
Let the shoot of David (Your servant) speedily spring up
and raise his horn in Your Salvation . . .
May you be blessed, O Lord, who lets the horn of salvation flourish.

* The asterisk denotes passages that are closer to Luke when quoted from the LXX than from the MT.

70 *as He spoke by the mouth of His holy prophets from of old:*
II Chr 36:22:
That the word of the Lord through the mouth of Jeremiah might be fulfilled, the Lord
raised up the spirit of Cyrus the Persian king.

Wisdom 11:1:
She made their affairs prosper through the holy prophet.

II Baruch 85:1:
In former times and in generations of old our fathers had helpers, righteous men and
holy prophets.

71a *salvation from our enemies*
71b *and from the hand of all those who hate us,*
*Isa 49:6 (to the Servant of the Lord):
I have placed you as a covenant with the people,
as a light to the nations,
that you should serve for salvation to the ends of the earth.

Psalms of Solomon 10:9:
The salvation of the Lord be upon the House of Israel.

Ps 106:10 (in reference to "our fathers" in Egypt):
He saved them from the hands of those who hated
and redeemed them from the hand of the enemy.

Ps 18:18(17):
He delivered me from my strong enemies
and from those who hate me.

1QM xviii 7–11:
You have kept your covenant with us from of old
and opened the gates of salvation many times.
For the sake of the covenant you have removed our misery . . .
causing the enemy to fall back.

SECOND STROPHE

72a *Showing mercy to our fathers*
72b *and remembering His holy covenant,*
73 *the oath which He swore to our father Abraham,*
to grant us . . .
Micah 7:20:
You will show fidelity to Jacob and mercy to Abraham,
as you have shown to our fathers from days of old.

Exod 2:24 (cf. Lev 26:42):
God has remembered His covenant with Abraham, Isaac, and Jacob.

Ps 106:45:
And for their sake He remembered His covenant
and relented according to the abundance of His mercy.

Gen 26:3 (God to Isaac, giving him Canaan):
I shall stand by my oath which I swore to your father Abraham.

Ps 105:8–9,11:
He is forever mindful of His covenant . . .
the covenant which He made with Abraham
and His oath to Isaac . . .
saying, I shall grant to you the land of Canaan.

Jer 11:5:
That I may stand by the oath which I swore to your fathers
to grant them a land flowing with milk and honey.

Ps 89:4(3):
I have made a covenant with my chosen one;
I have sworn to David my servant.

⁷⁴ . . . *that, without fear,*
delivered from the hands of our enemies,
we might serve Him ⁷⁵ *in holiness and justice*
before Him all the days of our lives.
Ps 18:18(17):
He will deliver me from my mighty enemies.

Josh 24:14:
Fear the Lord and serve Him in truth and justice.

1 QH xvii 13–14:
Those corrected by Your judgments You will deliver
that they may serve You in fidelity,
so that their posterity may be before You all their days.

I Kgs 9:4–5 (God to Solomon):
If you will walk before me as David your father walked, in holiness of heart and uprightness, . . . I shall establish your royal throne over Israel forever.

Isa 38:20:
The Lord is our savior;
we shall sing to stringed instruments
in the house of the Lord
all the days of our lives.

CONCLUSION

⁷⁸ᵃ *Through the heartfelt mercy of our God*
⁷⁸ᵇ *by which there has visited us a rising light from on high.*
Testament of Zebulun 8:2:
Because in the last days God will send his heartfelt compassion on the earth; and where he finds heartfelt mercy, there He will dwell.

Testament of Levi 4:4 (Christian passage):
Until the Lord will visit all the Gentiles in the heartfelt compassion of His Son.

*Isa 60:1:
Be enlightened, O Jerusalem, for your light has come;
and the glory of God has arisen upon you.

Mal 3:20 (RSV 4:2):
For you who fear My name, there will arise
the sun of justice with its healing rays.

*Num 24:17:
A star will arise from Jacob,
and a man will stand forth from Israel.

Testament of Levi 18:3 (Christian passage?):
His star will arise as of a king,
giving light, the light of knowledge.

79a   *appearing to those who sat in darkness and the shadow of death,*
79b   *guiding our feet into the way of peace.*
       Isa 42:6–7 (to the Servant of the Lord):
       A light to the nations
       to open the eyes of the blind,
       to bring out prisoners from confinement
       and from the dungeon, those who sit in darkness.

   *Isa 9:1(2):
       O people walking in darkness, you will see a great light;
       O dwellers in the region and shadow of death, a light will shine upon you.

       Ps 107:9–10:
       He fills the hungry soul with good things,
       those who sit in darkness and the shadow of death.

       Isa 59:8:
       They do not know the way of peace.

       Testament of Judah 24:1:
       Then there will arise for you a star from Jacob in peace,
       and a man from my seed will stand forth,
       as a sun of justice, walking with men in meekness and justice.

---

also employed by Judaism of David and his descendants, as we see in Ps 89:4(3) and I Kgs 9:4–5. Thus the two strophes dealing with David and Abraham are very close to each other in thought and have chosen from the OT the two figures most often mentioned in early Christian preaching as antecedents of Jesus.

STROPHE THREE (76–77). The addition of these verses pertaining to JBap expanded the structure of the hymn with a new strophe. As I explained in discussing the setting of the Benedictus, these are the verses in which we are closest to the narrative context in 59–66 (since, by hypothesis, Luke composed both 59–66 and 76–77); for they answer the question posed in 66: "What then is this child going to be?" I have not included these verses in Table XIII for two reasons: vs. 77 is not composed of OT phrases; and the OT echoes in vs. 76 come by way of other Lucan citations. Verse 76 picks up what was said of JBap in vs. 17; and as we saw (§ 10, B2), vs. 17 was composed from descriptions of JBap in the ministry which combined Isa 40:3 and Mal 3:1,23. Thus, we are hearing in vs. 76 the reverberating echo of Luke 3:4: "The voice of one crying in the desert: 'Make ready the way of the Lord,' "[35] and of 7:27: "Behold I send my messenger before your face who will prepare your way before you." The unique designation of JBap as "prophet of the Most High" in 76 articulates the sentiments of Jesus in 7:26: "A prophet? Yes, and, I tell you, more than a prophet," along with the indication in 16:16 that JBap is the last of the prophets.

85 The desert theme, which is not reproduced in vs. 76, appears in vs. 80.

As for vs. 77, in Luke's account of the ministry it is never said that JBap granted to the Lord's people a "knowledge of salvation in the forgiveness of their sins," although this is Christian and Lucan theological language.[36] But 1:17 has JBap "make ready for the Lord a prepared people"; and 3:6 prophesies that through JBap's preparatory preaching, "all flesh will see God's salvation."[37] Among the evangelists Luke alone (3:10–14) has JBap giving various groups precise instructions about what they must do, thus communicating a type of knowledge of salvation. Finally, 3:3 has JBap come preaching a baptism of repentance "unto the forgiveness of sins." The Lord who made the covenant with Israel (of which we heard in the first two strophes) was a forgiving God (Ps 99:8[7]). It was to be expected that when He would visit His people (vss. 68b and 78b), they would come to know it in the forgiveness of their sins. Thus, by his baptism "unto the forgiveness of sins," JBap gave people an experience or knowledge of God's salvation.

CONCLUSION (78–79). In the hymn of praise the conclusion often recapitulates the motifs of the hymn. The first strophe mentioned God's visitation; the second strophe mentioned God's covenant mercy being shown; the third strophe described JBap as going before the Lord to make ready His ways. The conclusion focuses on "the rising light [*anatolē*] from on high" in whom God has *visited* us[88] and shown His *mercy*, namely, Jesus whom JBap will precede. If one of the key texts behind the description of JBap in 1:76 was Mal 3:1 ("I send my messenger to prepare the way before me, and the Lord whom you seek will suddenly come"), it is noteworthy that a few verses later (3:20[4:2]) Malachi promised that "there will arise the sun of justice with its healing rays."[89] As I have pointed out in the NOTE, *anatolē* was a term used among Greek-speaking Jews to describe the expected king of the House of David. The use of *anatolē* after the birth of Jesus in Matt 2:1 ("his star at its *rising*") may mean that the idea of a rising light had been widely associated with the birth of the Messiah or his coming,[40] perhaps by way of midrashic reflection upon

[36] See NOTES. In particular, notice these passages in Acts: "Let it be *known . . . to all the people of Israel* that . . . there is *salvation* in no one else" (4:10–12); "God raised this *Savior* and Leader to His right hand to give repentance *to Israel and the forgiveness of sins*" (5:31); "To us *the word of this salvation* is sent. . . . To you let it be *known* that through this man *the forgiveness of sins* is being proclaimed to you" (13:26,38). This is part of the evidence for the conclusion that we have a Lucan composition in vs. 77.

[37] Other Gospels apply the quotation from Isaiah (40:3) to JBap, but only Luke extends it to include 40:4–5 and this clause.

[88] In vs. 68 the canticle says that God has visited His people; in 78 the canticle says that it is by the mercy of God that the rising light has visited us. Here Luke moves close to the Emmanuel, "God with us," motif in Matthew's infancy narrative.

[89] Gnilka, "Hymnus," 232, points out that a late second-century fragment of Melito of Sardis on baptism may make the connection between Luke 1:78 and Mal 3:20, for it speaks of "a sun of rising" (*hēlios anatolēs*).

[40] Justin *Dialogue* cxxi 2: "*Anatolē* is his name," and Justin clearly understands *anatolē* as a dawning light.

Num 24:17; Isa 9:2; 42:6–7, etc. In any case, the hymn is internally
consistent in referring twice to God's visitation: in 68–69 in terms of
raising up *a horn of salvation* in the House of David, and in 78 in terms of
a rising light from on high. The Hebrew words underlying these two
symbols had already been joined by Ezek 29:21: "In that day I shall
cause to rise a horn for the House of Israel."

The image of a rising or dawning light leads to the further image of
those sitting in darkness and the shadow of death, awaiting light—an
image particularly dear to the Isaian writers (9:2; 42:6–7). In the preceding paragraph I pointed out how two passages in Mal 3 established a connection between the description of JBap in vs. 76 and the reference to a
rising light in vs. 78. Similarly, we should notice that Isa 40:3 ("Make
ready the way of the Lord") underlies vs. 76, while Isa 42:6–7 underlies
vs. 79. Sequential connections like these may have entered into the logic
and locale of Luke's insertion pertaining to JBap. The language of filling
the hungry and enlightening those who sit in darkness are joined in Ps
107:9–10. The latter occurs in the Benedictus, the former in the
Magnificat (1:53a)—an observation that fortifies our thesis that the two
hymns came from the same ambience of Anawim.

The Benedictus ends (79b) on the theme of the rising light "guiding our
feet into the way of peace." Luke will pick up on that motif in the next
section which describes the birth of Jesus; for he will insert there still another canticle which, despite its brevity, recalls the opening and closing
themes of the Benedictus: praise for God, and peace for those favored by
him (2:14).

We have already studied vs. 80 in the first part of this section, as
belonging to the narrative of the birth and naming. However, as we
prepare to move on to the next section, I would make the brief additional
comment that vs. 80 is a good example of Luke's technique of removing
one person from the scene in order to give the spotlight to another. In ch.
3 Luke describes the whole career of JBap including his imprisonment by
Herod the tetrarch (3:19–20) before he narrates how JBap baptized
Jesus. That may strike some as illogical since obviously the imprisonment
took place *after* the baptism, but it is Luke's way of signaling a shift of attention from JBap to Jesus. Similarly here, Luke describes the growth of
JBap into manhood before he describes the birth of Jesus which took
place only a few months after JBap's birth. Once again Luke is signaling a
shift of attention. Hitherto he has used the diptych pattern to associate
JBap and Jesus in their infancy (even as they were associated in the history of the ministry), but now JBap has served his purpose. He is removed
from the infancy scene by a summary statement and will not be mentioned

at all in ch. 2. Full attention is now to be given to the main protagonist in God's plan of salvation: the *anatolē*.

SECTIONAL BIBLIOGRAPHY (§ 13)
(LUKE 1:57–80)

(The Bibliography of the preceding section covers works on the Lucan canticles in general and combined treatments of the Magnificat and Benedictus.)

Benoit, P., "L'enfance."

Fridrichsen, A., *"Sophia, Hēlikia, Charis* (Luc 1:80; 2:40,52)," *Symbolae Osloenses* 6 (1928), 36–38.

Gertner, M., "Midrashim in the New Testament," JSS 7 (1962), 267–92, esp. 273–82 on the Benedictus.

Geyser, A. S., "The Youth of John the Baptist," NovTest 1 (1956), 70–75.

Gnilka, J., "Der Hymnus des Zacharias," BZ 6 (1962), 215–38.

Jacoby, A., *"Anatolē ex Hypsous* [1:78]," ZNW 20 (1921), 205–14.

Vanhoye, A., "Structure du 'Benedictus,'" NTS 12 (1965–66), 382–89.

Vielhauer, P., "Das Benedictus des Zacharias," ZTK 49 (1952), 255–72. Cited as reprinted in his *Aufsätze zum Neuen Testament* (Theologische Bücherei 31; Munich: Kaiser, 1965), 28–46.

VI. THE BIRTH AND NAMING OF JESUS
(§ 14)

Translation of Luke 2:1–21

2 [1] At that time an edict went out from Caesar Augustus that a census should be taken of the whole world. ([2] This was the first census under Quirinius as governor of Syria.) [3] And so all went to be inscribed in the census, each to his own city. [4] Joseph also went up from Galilee, from the city of Nazareth, into Judea to the city of David which is called Bethlehem, because he was of the house and lineage of David, [5] to have himself inscribed in the census with Mary, his betrothed, who was pregnant.

[6] Now while they were there, the time came for her to give birth; [7] and she gave birth to a son, her firstborn. She wrapped him in strips of cloth and laid him down in a manger, since there was no place for them in the lodgings.

[8] In that same region there were shepherds, pasturing their flock and taking turns watching over it by night. [9] And an angel of the Lord appeared to them, and the glory of the Lord shone around them, so that they were filled with great fear. [10] "Do not be afraid," the angel told them. "For behold, I announce to you good news of a great joy which will be for the whole people: [11] To you this day there is born in the city of David a Savior who is Messiah and Lord. [12] And this will be your sign: you will find a baby wrapped in strips of cloth and lying in a manger!"

[13] Then suddenly there was with the angel a multitude of the heavenly host praising God, saying:

[14a] "Glory in the highest heavens to God,

[14b] and on earth peace to those favored (by Him)."

[15] When the angels had gone from them back into heaven, the shepherds urged one another, "Now let us go over to Bethlehem and see

the event that has taken place, as the Lord has made known to us."
¹⁶ And setting forth with haste, they found Mary and Joseph, with the
baby lying in the manger. ¹⁷ Having seen this, they made known the
event as it was told them concerning this child. ¹⁸ All who heard were
astonished at what the shepherds told them; ¹⁹ but Mary kept with
concern all these events, interpreting them in her heart. ²⁰ And the
shepherds returned, glorifying and praising God for all they had
heard and seen, just as He had told them.

²¹ Now eight days later when the time came to circumcise the child,
he was called Jesus, the name by which the angel called him before
he was conceived in the womb.

Notes

2:1. *At that time.* Literally, "in those days"; compare to "in these days" of
1:39 and "in the days of Herod, king of Judea" of 1:5.

an edict. Luke's use of *dogma*, if it is technical, would imply a formal imperial action taken with the consultation of the Roman Senate, as distinct from
psēphisma, a vote of the assembly of the people. (No such edict is attested in
secular history; see Appendix VII.) Luke uses the expression "edicts of Caesar"
in Acts 17:7.

went out. Literally, "It happened an edict went out"—Semitized Greek, perhaps under the influence of the LXX. For this Lucan *egeneto* construction,
see NOTE on 1:9; also BDF 472⁸.

Caesar Augustus. Octavian, the great-nephew of Julius Caesar, joined with
Mark Anthony after the assassination of Julius in 44 B.C. to punish and defeat
Brutus and Cassius at Philippi in 42. At first a triumvir with Lepidus and Anthony (in a type of troïka), Octavian became the sole ruler after subduing
Lepidus (in 36) and defeating Anthony and Cleopatra at Actium (31). He was
given the title Augustus by the Senate and people in 27. He died in A.D. 14,
having designated Tiberius, a stepson, as his successor; and it was in the
fifteenth year of Tiberius Caesar that Jesus began his ministry (Luke 3:1).

that a census should be taken. Literally, "for the whole world to present itself
for enrollment," if the verb is to be understood as middle rather than passive
(BDF 317). The Greek verb *apographein* and the noun *apographē*, while
having the general sense of enrolling or registering, serve more specifically as
translations of Latin *census* terminology (BDF 5³). Almost certainly Luke
means a census here. (The attempt to see in *apographein* only the initial stage
of a long census process is part of an elaborate effort to protect Lucan accuracy

—since there was, as far as we know, no universal census at the time specified by Luke, it is argued that Luke is referring to the first stage in a census which was actually taken only a dozen years later [see Appendix VII].) The presumed purpose of the census would have been taxation, rather than military service from which the Jews were exempt. Thus, the English translations influenced by Tyndale rendered these Greek words in terms of being valued or taxed.

the whole world. The Greek *oikoumenē* means the *orbis terrarum,* the civilized world of which the Roman Emperor was lord; see the similar Lucan usage in Acts 11:28. Since we know of no single census of the whole Empire under Augustus, some would argue that Luke meant only the provinces. The suggestion of a hypothetical Hebrew original which had "the whole land (of Palestine)" is weak since Luke uses *gē,* not *oikoumenē,* for that expression in 4:25.

2. *This was the first census under.* Greek syntax and textual variants (e.g., with an article) permit other translations: "This first census was under"; or "This census was earlier than the one under" (Lagrange, *Luc,* 67–68); or "This census was before the governorship of" (Higgins, "Sidelights," 200–1). The last two translations, which are further attempts to preserve Lucan accuracy, involve translating *prōtos,* which normally means "first," as equivalent to the comparative *proteros,* "earlier than," or to *proteron* or *prō,* "before." (For objections to this, see Ogg, "Quirinius," 233.) Scholars who maintain the totally unproved hypothesis of several censuses under Quirinius (see Appendix VII) argue that Luke means the first in that series. Rather the census is called "first" because no Roman census had been held in Judea before that of Quirinius in A.D. 6–7 (a census that Luke has wrongly fixed at the time of King Herod through association with 1:5).

Quirinius. Publius Sulpicius Quirinius was made legate of Syria in A.D. 6 and specially charged with restructuring Judea as a Roman province, after the deposing of Archelaus, Herod the Great's son (Matt 2:22), who had ruled from 4 B.C. to A.D. 6. Spellings which end the name in "us" rather than "ius" (Quirinus, Cyrinus) represent a copyist's mistake in the mss.

as governor of Syria. The verb *hēgemoneuein,* like noun *hēgemonos,* was used to translate Latin offices such as *legatus* and *procurator,* with Syria having a *legatus,* and Judea a *prefectus* (or later a *procurator*). Justin, *Apology* I xxxiv, designates Quirinius as a procurator (*epitropos*), probably on the analogy of Pilate. Attempts to render the Lucan verb more generically ("held office," "was in charge of"), although possible as we see from the usage of the noun in reference to Tiberius in 3:1, are part of the unlikely hypothesis that Quirinius had a position in Syria, during the reign of Herod the Great in Palestine, and thus before he became legate there in A.D. 6—another ingenious attempt to save Lucan accuracy (see Appendix VII).

3. *And so.* The sequence is from vs. 1; the intermediary verse is parenthetical.

all. In sequence to "the whole world" of vs. 1, this should mean all the people in the Roman Empire. Our evidence for Augustus' reign, however, points to separate censuses for Roman citizens and non-Roman inhabitants of the provinces, such as Syria. Again to save Lucan accuracy, some have tried to interpret the "all" as those under Quirinius' rule, i.e., the people in Syria; and the *Protevangelium of James*, 17:1, limits the enrollment to the inhabitants of Bethlehem. Historically the census of A.D. 6–7 covered Judeans.

each to his own city. While for Joseph "his own city" means his ancestral city of Bethlehem, Nazareth is designated as "their own city" in 2:39 in the sense of residence. In Roman censuses there is no clear evidence of a practice of going to an *ancestral* city to be enrolled; the oft-cited examples from Egypt are not the same as what Luke describes (NOTE on "of the house and lineage of David" below in vs. 4).

4. *went up*. "To go up" (*anabainein*) is a standard OT expression, carried over to the NT, for ascent to mountainous Judea, especially to Jerusalem (Mark 10:32; John 2:13; Luke 2:42).

from Galilee. Luke seems to assume that the census covered Galilee; but the first Roman census under Quirinius in A.D. 6–7 covered only Judea, where Archelaus had been deposed. (Galilee remained a Roman client kingdom, or more properly a tetrarchy, under Archelaus' brother Herod Antipas, who was the "Herod" of Jesus' ministry.)

from the city of Nazareth. The city where he and Mary lived (2:39), a view that contrasts with the implication in Matt 2:11 that they had their house in Bethlehem.

into Judea . . . Bethlehem. See NOTE on "of Judea" in Matt 2:1.

to the city of David. Normally this is the designation of Jerusalem, as in II Sam 5:7,9—see also the use of "went up" in vs. 4. Bethlehem was the city of David's origin (I Sam 16) to which he returned for family occasions (20:6,28–29).

because he was. The Old Syriac (Sinaiticus) has "because both," implying that Mary was a Davidid; see NOTE on "a man of the House of David" in 1:27.

of the house and lineage of David. Here, as in 1:27, Luke makes reference to Joseph as a Davidid, a lineage affirmed elsewhere in the two genealogies of Jesus and in Matt 1:20. Is there a difference between "house" (*oikos*) and "lineage" (*patria*)? Some have taken *oikos* to mean that Joseph had a home in Bethlehem, or *patria* to mean that he had property there. Still another suggestion is that he was returning to his *home* in Bethlehem ("his own city" of vs. 3) after having gone to Nazareth to claim Mary his bride who lived there. These suggestions run against the reference to Nazareth as "their own city" in 2:39 and against the indication in 2:7 that Joseph had no place to stay in Bethlehem. (Thus we have here no real parallel to the *kata oikian* censuses in Egypt where people were registered in the area where their home [*oikia*] or property was found; Luke refers to a census by ancestry.) It is highly dubious that one can press Davidic lineage to mean direct royal lineage, as Bornhäuser, *Kindheitsgeschichte*, 99, has done when he argues that, while all the Davidids did not have to go to Bethlehem, Joseph did because he was a royal scion. There is nothing in Luke's narrative to suggest that.

5. *with Mary*. Are we to understand that Mary was to be inscribed in the census (this is not an impossibility in Roman practice), or are we to think that she accompanied Joseph so that they would be together when the birth came?

The motive is not clear; but surely we may reject the theory that Joseph brought Mary so that he could still all doubts and clearly acknowledge her child as his own—this thesis is dependent on implicit harmonization with Matthew, for there is no hint of a suspicion of illegitimacy in Luke.

his betrothed. For the previous Lucan use of "betrothed" see 1:27; for the precise marital connotations see the NOTE on Matt 1:18. Some OL and the OS^sin mss. have "his wife" in place of "his betrothed"; some later Greek mss. have a conflated reading: "his betrothed wife." Scholars such as Dibelius, Klostermann, Sahlin, Schmithals, and Taylor, have accepted "wife" as the original reading, sometimes with the suggestion that the story in ch. 2 was once narrated independently of the virginal conception story in 1:26–38, and that in ch. 2 Mary and Joseph were originally ordinary husband and wife, with Jesus as their child. In this hypothesis either Luke or subsequent Christian scribes would have changed "wife" to "betrothed" to harmonize with 1:27. In evaluating this suggestion, I think one should reject the thesis that a pre-Lucan story had "wife" and Luke changed it to "betrothed." In the COMMENT I shall suggest that the substance of 2:1–20 may well have originated independently of the material in ch. 1, but it is likely that the preface in 2:1–5 was composed by Luke himself. Besides, how would the translators of the OL and OS^sin have known the pre-Lucan reading?

It is another question whether Luke himself wrote "wife" and some subsequent copyists changed it to "betrothed," so that OL and OS^sin would be preserving the original Lucan reading. One could argue that in the logic of chs. 1–2 "his wife" would make better sense than "his betrothed," if "wife" means that Mary has now been taken to live at Joseph's home, a situation that was not true in 1:27,34. If Mary were not already living with Joseph, how could she travel with him to Bethlehem? However, this argument presupposes that Luke knew the exact steps in the Jewish matrimonial procedure, a knowledge that is not spelled out here (contrast Matt 1:24–25). A contrary argument would be that Luke, in composing the introduction in 2:1–5, simply reused the term "betrothed" previously employed in 1:27, without any detailed reflection on the steps in the matrimonial procedure. Then, facing the Lucan "betrothed," Semite copyists may have thought that the term "wife" would better indicate that the second step in the marriage procedure had taken place. Or Gentile copyists may have been scandalized at the notion of Joseph traveling with his betrothed, since a Gentile may not have understood that a true marriage was involved in what we have translated as "betrothal." In discussing Matt 1:16 (NOTE there), we saw that copyists had problems about the terminology for the marital relationship between Joseph and Mary, and that they made changes accordingly— and again the OS^sin was involved. In any case, there are good supporting arguments for both readings, "betrothed" and "wife," but I have let the weight of the ms. evidence determine the reading to be preferred. Clearly there is better ms. support for "betrothed."

who was pregnant. Plummer, *Luke,* 53, would translate this in light of Joseph's motivation: "because she was pregnant," Joseph could not leave her behind in Nazareth. However, this is to make the narrative too psychological in its flow. Luke wishes simply to prepare *the reader* for the birth narrative to follow.

6. *while they were there.* Luke places Mary and Joseph at Bethlehem for some time before the child is born. In the *Protevangelium of James* 18:1, the child is born in a cave before they reach Bethlehem.

the time came for her to give birth. Literally, "And it happened, while they were there, that the days of her giving birth were fulfilled." For the Lucan *egeneto* construction, see the NOTE on 1:9. A similar birth description (using the actual word for "time") is found in 1:57, describing Elizabeth's bearing of JBap. Both passages echo Gen 25:24 and Rebekah's delivery of Jacob and Esau.

7. *and she gave birth.* The verb is *tiktein* as in the promise to Mary in 1:31; see the NOTE on 1:57 for the use of *gennan* ("bore") in the instance of Elizabeth.

to a son, her firstborn. Although *prōtotokos*, "firstborn," is sometimes clearly equivalent to *monogenēs*, "only born" (*Psalms of Solomon* 13:8; 18:4; *IV Ezra* 6:58), some would take this to mean "first born among many." And so, since the time of Helvidius (A.D. 380), this verse has played a role in the dispute among Christians as to whether Jesus was Mary's only child (because she remained a virgin), or she had other children, born after Jesus (the brothers and sisters of Jesus, mentioned in Mark 6:3)—see the NOTE on Matt 1:25; and footnote 2 in Appendix IV. In the second century A.D. the Cynic Lucian of Samosata (*Demonax* 29) proposed a dilemma about a philosopher who claimed to be the first and only: "If the first, not the only; if the only, not the first"; and many have seen fit to quote that here. More subtly, Plummer, *Luke,* 53, argues that the evangelist would not have used "firstborn" of Jesus if he knew that Mary had no more children, so that at least in Luke's time there was no well-known tradition that Jesus was an only child. However, the use of *prōtotokos* rather than *monogenēs* proves only that Luke had no interest in presenting Jesus as Mary's only son. Others have seen in "firstborn" an implication of special affection; yet when Luke wants to imply that, as in the case of the widow of Nain, he uses *monogenēs* (7:12; also 8:42; 9:38).

Actually the designation *prōtotokos* tells us only *that there was no child before Jesus,* and that therefore he was to have the privileges and position that Hebrew tradition gives to the firstborn (Exod 13:2; Num 3:12–13; 18:15–16). Luke mentions it here to prepare for the dedication of Jesus as firstborn in 2:22–23. That the designation need not imply the birth of subsequent children is clear from the grave inscription of a Jewish woman named Arsinoe, found near ancient Leontopolis in Egypt and dated to 5 B.C. The Greek text reads: "In the pains of giving birth to a firstborn child, Fate brought me to the end of my life." If she died in giving birth to her firstborn, obviously she had no more children. Thus, despite Lucian's clever dilemma, in that case the child was the "first and only." A full discussion of this Lucan passage is found in Blinzler, *Brüder,* 57–61. See also E. C. Edgar, "More Tomb-Stones from Tell el Yahoudieh," *Annales du Service des Antiquités de l'Egypte* 22 (1922), 7–16; H. Lietzmann, ZNW 22 (1923), 280–86; Frey, "Signification," 385–89; Stoll, "Firstborn," 9.

She wrapped him in strips of cloth. Literally, "She swaddled him." The Greek verb *sparganoun* is derived from the noun *sparganon,* one of the cloths or strips of cloth used to wrap newborn babes. The traditional English rendering, "wrapped him in swaddling clothes," involves both tautology (swaddled in swaddling) and an old spelling of "cloths." To swaddle a baby is a sign of parental care (Wisdom of Solomon 7:4), and the lack of swaddling is seen as neglect in the allegorical description of Jerusalem in Ezek 16:4. From the fact that Mary herself (rather than the father or a midwife) wrapped the child one cannot prove that the birth was miraculous or painless, although the thesis of a miraculous birth soon appeared in Christian tradition, as witnessed in the *Protevangelium of James* 18–19. Goulder and Sanderson have suggested that here Luke wished to foreshadow Jesus' being wrapped in a linen shroud before burial (23:53), but the vocabulary in that passage is entirely different. Just as unlikely is the hypothesis of a play on the Jewish tradition that angels swaddled the first generation of Israel that came forth from Egypt.

and laid him down in a manger. The Greek *phatnē* can mean a "stall" for tying up animals, or a "manger," i.e., a trough for feeding them. (Cadbury, *Making,* 249–50, points out that *phatnē* does not really mean "barn" or "stable.") A stall might be either outdoors or indoors; the latter is implied in Luke 13:15 where a man can set his animals loose from a *phatnē* and lead them out to give them a drink. A manger might be a movable trough placed on the ground, or a cavity in a low rock shelf. Luke does not give us enough context to decide. The fact that the *phatnē* is contrasted with the *katalyma* or "lodgings" may favor the meaning "stall." However, the picture of wrapping the baby and laying him down better suits a cradle-like manger. The Christmas-crib scenes, popularized by Francis of Assisi, have fixed the image of a manger. Oxen and donkeys have been introduced into this nativity scene from a combination of Luke's reference to the *phatnē* (both stall and manger imply animals) with the lament of God in the LXX of Isa 1:3: "The ox knows its owner, and the donkey knows the *phatnē* of its lord [*kyrios* as in Luke 2:11], but Israel has not known me."

since there was no place. The translation "no room" offers the danger of being misunderstood to mean "there was not a room"—that would be too precise. Dibelius, "Jungfrauensohn," 58, thinks that the problem was not of insufficient space but of fitting place. Are we to assume that Mary and Joseph are *in* the lodgings but do not have *place for the baby* (so Miguens, "In una," 194)? Or are they *outside* the lodgings precisely because there was no *place for them* inside. The latter seems more probable, but much depends on precisely what is meant by "lodgings."

in the lodgings. This phrase is omitted by the OS[sin]. The word *katalyma,* which in the LXX represents five different Hebrew terms, is hard to translate here; for again Luke has not given sufficient information. He has told us that the laying of the baby in the *phatnē* was the alternative adopted when the parents did not find room in the *katalyma.* Of itself, this word signifies a place where a traveler lays down (*katalyein*) his baggage in stopping over on a journey. The Vulgate has caught the root meaning when it renders *katalyma* by *diversorium,* i.e., a place for one to turn aside (*divertere*). In the LXX of II

Sam 7:6 *katalyma* describes the dwelling place of the Divine Presence in the desert travels of Israel. More important for the Lucan story, Elkanah and Hannah, the future parents of Samuel, stay in a *katalyma* when visiting the holy place at Shiloh where Hannah's prayers for a child are answered (I Sam 1:18). The Lucan context of a journey to Bethlehem, an ancestral city which is not Joseph's current home, is consonant with the idea of a stop-off place for a traveler. In NT times the religious feeling about hospitality to strangers (characteristic of tribal and nomadic cultures) had declined, so that if the traveler did not have friends or relatives in an area, he had to seek more impersonal shelter. When Luke describes the possibility that crowds of people would unexpectedly have to find overnight lodging in the surrounding villages, he uses *katalyein*, the verb related to *katalyma* (Luke 9:12; also 19:7). Sometimes synagogues provided hospitality in rooms under the main building, while the Romans eventually developed stopping places for merchants (*mutationes* for changing horses; *mansiones* for staying overnight—see John 14:2).

Basically three suggestions have been made for what Luke meant by *katalyma:* (a) A private *home*. For the custom of having travelers stay in a private house, see II Kgs 4:8–10. Yet Luke's use of the definite article seems to preclude his referring to a totally unidentified home. If he meant the home of Joseph's relatives (Benoit, "Non erat," 183–85), more information might have been expected, as well as some explanation for the lack of hospitality to an in-law about to bear a child. Few scholars accept this suggestion. (b) A *room* in an unidentified place (or in the private home of the previous suggestion—Miguens, "In una," 196, suggests a small room in the home of a poor relative). *Katalyma* in Luke 22:11 is used to describe the room where Jesus might eat with his disciples. Sometimes this translation is combined with the suggestion that the *phatnē* was a cradle slung from the ceiling in which Mary placed the baby because there was not enough floor space in the small room (Bornhäuser, *Kindheitsgeschichte*, 102–3). However, the technical Greek name for such a hammock was *aiōra*, not *phatnē*. The definite article before *katalyma* remains an obstacle to translating it "a room." (c) The *inn*, or more specifically, the well-known traveler's inn at or near Bethlehem. The public inns of the time should not be pictured as snug or comfortable according to medieval or modern standards. They were closer to a type of khan or caravansery where large groups of travelers found shelter under one roof; the people slept on cots or on a terrace elevated by a few steps from the floor, with the animals on the floor in the same room. (In this case Luke's contrast between the *katalyma* and the *phatnē* might be a contrast between the place for the people and the place for the animals.) A khan near Bethlehem is designated in Jer 41:17 as the Geruth (lodging place) of Chimham. Unfortunately, the thesis that *katalyma* means "inn" is not helped by Luke 10:34; for there the inn on the road to Jericho where the Samaritan put up the ravaged traveler is called a *pandocheion*, not a *katalyma*. Granting the impossibility of deciding whether Luke meant a home, a room, or the inn, I have employed the translation "lodgings" to preserve the ambiguity of the original. For a full discussion, see Benoit, "Non erat."

Luke excludes the *katalyma* as the place of Jesus' birth, or at least as a place with sufficient space for the baby Jesus to be laid; but Luke does not tell us precisely where Jesus was born. Subsequent piety fixed the site as a cave. That tradition was so well established by the fourth century that the Constantinian basilica marking the site of the nativity was erected in A.D. 325 over a series of caves in Bethlehem; and the greatest biblical scholar of the patristic period, Jerome, spent years in a cave adjacent to the one marked off by tradition as the site of his master's birth. Jerome authenticates the spot by the fact that for 180 years (since A.D. 135, the time of Hadrian and the Second Jewish Revolt) the Romans came there to a grove in honor of Tammuz (Adonis); and "in the cave where the Christ-child once cried, they wept for Venus' lover" (*Epistle 58*, to Paulinus, iii 5; CSEL 54:531–32). In part, the motif of a cave may have come from the mention of a *phatnē*, which is a stall or manger for animals, and from the reference to shepherds for whose animals the cave might have served as a shelter or a feed storeroom. Some scholars have pointed to Isa 33:16 (LXX) as a possible influence: "He will dwell in a high cave of strong rock." However, the frequency of references to a cave already in the mid-second century raises the possibility of an independent (but not necessarily trustworthy) tradition, rather than of a deduction from Luke and the OT. In the *Dialogue* lxxviii 5, Justin reports: "Since Joseph had nowhere to lodge [*katalyein*] in that village, he lodged in a certain cave near the village; and while they were there, Mary brought forth the Messiah and laid him in a manger, where the magi from Arabia came and found him." (Although obviously Justin is to some extent dependent on the canonical Gospels, scholars have suggested his dependence upon another source, e.g., Bishop, "Reflections." Also E. Preuschen, ZNW 3 [1902], 359–60, connects Justin's testimony to the text of Matt 2:9 in the oldest Armenian version where the star comes to rest over a cave.) In the contemporary *Protevangelium of James* 17–18, we read that, as Mary and Joseph came near the third milestone on the journey to Bethlehem, she told him that the child within her was pressing to come forth. Joseph wondered where to take her "to hide her shame," for the place was a desert. "He found a cave and brought her into it." Origen, who frequently resided in Palestine after A.D. 216, wrote: "If anyone wants further proof to convince him that Jesus was born in Bethlehem, . . . he may observe that in agreement with the story in the Gospel about Jesus' birth, the cave at Bethlehem is shown where he was born, and the manger in the cave where he was wrapped in strips of cloth" (*Against Celsus* I 51). This evidence about the localization of the nativity is interesting but, of course, goes beyond Luke's interests.

8. *In that same region.* The Greek *chōra* means "open country." The fields now shown as "Shepherds' Fields" are some two miles from Bethlehem, toward the Dead Sea, below the snow line (see Bishop, "Bethlehem"). Those who regard the Lucan information as historical have tried to date the birth of Jesus between March and November when the shepherds would be out in the fields. Already by the time of Clement of Alexandria (*ca.* 200) there were theories that Jesus was born on May 20 (25 Pachon) or April 20–21 (24–25 Pharmuth), as he mentions in the *Stromata* I 21 (※※145–46). It is most unlikely that any reliable tradition about the exact date of birth would have survived.

taking turns watching over it by night. Literally, "watching the watches of the night"; Luke likes cognate combinations. It is this passage that, for popular piety, has fixed night as the time of Jesus' birth. Midnight was suggested by the application of Wisdom of Solomon 18:14–15 to the birth of Jesus: "When all things were in quiet silence, and *the night in its swift course was half spent,* Your all-powerful word leaped down from heaven's royal throne."

9. *an angel of the Lord.* Luke understands the "angel of the Lord" correctly, for in vs. 15 the angel's message is said to have come from the Lord. See the NOTE on Matt 1:20.

appeared. The verb *ephistanai* (*ephistēmi*) is a Lucan favorite (eighteen out of twenty-one NT usages). See NOTE on 1:11.

filled with great fear. Literally, "feared a great fear," another instance of a cognate combination. Fear is the standard reaction to angelic appearances (1:12–13,29–30).

10. *For behold.* See NOTE on 1:44.

I announce to you good news. Another favorite Lucan verb (ten out of eleven Gospel usages) is *euangelizesthai* (related to *euangelion,* "gospel"), already used of the birth of JBap in 1:19. Conzelmann's thesis that Luke deliberately avoids the noun in the Gospel and thus during the life of Jesus (*Theology,* 221) does not explain its infrequency in Acts. Luke is probably influenced by the LXX which prefers the verb to the noun.

a great joy which. The relative *hostis,* "which," often describes a characteristic quality; thus, "a great joy which has the characteristic of being for the whole people." But Luke uses it almost as if it were a simple relative, as previously noted in treating 1:20.

for the whole people. The dative after the verb "to be" is common in Luke. Codex Bezae reads "also for the whole people." Although some scholars (e.g., Rengstorf, Oliver) have seen a reference to the Gentiles here, arguing that in Acts 15:14; 18:10 the Gentiles are included in the people of God, in the present context the birth of the Davidic Savior is for the (whole) people of Israel (see Luke 3:21; 7:29; 8:47; etc.). This is discussed in S. G. Wilson, *The Gentiles and the Gentile Mission in Luke-Acts* (NTSMS 23; Cambridge University, 1973), 34–35.

11. *To you.* Presumably to the shepherds *and* the people.

this day. A favorite Lucan expression (twenty times), *sēmeron* catches Luke's sense of realized eschatology: the last times are at hand. Winter, "On the Margin," 105, would see a cultic usage (i.e., this day that we are celebrating); and he supposes (without real proof) a shepherd celebration of unknown origin at Bethlehem. Erdmann, *Vorgeschichten,* 18–19, notes that the formula would fit well a feast day of Christ's birth, but such a feast is not attested this early.

the city of David. See NOTE on 2:4.

a Savior. Previously (1:47) Luke has used this term for God, but in 1:69 Jesus was already designated "a horn of salvation." Neither Matthew nor Mark uses *sōtēr* of Jesus; see John 4:42.

Messiah and Lord. The combination *christos kyrios* (literally, "Christ,

Lord") without articles occurs nowhere else in the New Testament; other possible translations are "Christ the Lord" and "the Anointed Lord." The phrase occurs once in the LXX, as a mistranslation in Lam 4:20; it occurs also in *Psalms of Solomon* 17:36. It has been suggested that the Greek is a mistranslation of two Hebrew nouns standing in the construct relationship, which should have been rendered "Anointed or Messiah of the Lord" (*christos kyriou* in 2:26, a more normal Greek expression). Others think that *christos kyriou* was the original reading and that scribes copied it wrongly; for such titles were often abbreviated in Greek mss., leaving open the possibility of confusion (see Winter, "Lukanische Miszellen," 68, 75). Dibelius, "Jungfrauensohn," 62, proposes that Luke added the clause with these titles to a pre-Lucan narrative, creating a certain tension with the other uses of *kyrios* in this section (2:9,15,26) which refer to God; yet see 1:43. Luke is the only Synoptic Gospel to use the title "the Lord" frequently of Jesus (fourteen times, compared to once each in Mark and Matthew).

12. *your sign.* Literally, "a sign to you." This reading is supported by Codex Vaticanus; most other mss., including Codex Bezae, read *"the* sign for you." The definite article appears in OT parallels (Exod 3:12; I Sam 2:34; 14:10; II Kgs 19:29; 20:9; Isa 37:30; 38:7) and is probably borrowed from there.

a baby. The term *brephos* (here and vs. 16) is a newborn child. See the use of *paidion*, "child," in vs. 17.

and lying. This verb is omitted by Codices Sinaiticus* and Bezae.

13. *Then suddenly there was.* Another *egeneto* construction; NOTE on 1:9.

with the angel. The OS^sin reads "with him," and Spitta, "Die chronologischen," 313–15, sees this as an indication that the multitude of angels was with *Jesus* at Bethlehem. This variant and the variant at the beginning of vs. 15 pertinent to the angels point to the awkwardness of 13–14 in the present context. In the COMMENT I suggest that this is another of the four canticles added by Luke in a second stage of editing.

a multitude. The heavenly host is beyond counting; the many who appear here do not exhaust it.

praising. The verb *ainoun* is a Lucan favorite (six or seven times, compared with two non-Lucan usages in the NT). The plural participle modifying a singular noun ("multitude") is a harsh construction (BDF 134^1b), and there may be Semitic influence on the word order (BDF 472^1d).

14. *Glory.* In 2:9 the "glory of the Lord" has a connotation of the visible manifestation of divine majesty; here "glory" is the honor that men and angels pay to God (J. W. Doeve, NTA 7 [1962–63], ✱160).

in the highest heavens. The traditional English rendering, "Glory to God in the highest," is sometimes misunderstood to mean "in the highest degree," which is not at all the force of the Greek.

and on earth peace to those favored (by Him). The way in which the brief angelic hymn is understood depends on the meaning and grammatical force of the last words in the verse: *anthrōpois eudokia(s)*. The oldest and best ms. support is for the genitive *eudokias*, rather than the nominative *eudokia*—a decision on that point will enter into the versification to be discussed below. But, if for the moment we accept a genitive, *anthrōpoi* ("men" in the sense of people) of *eudokia*, what is the precise import of *eudokia* for which dictionaries give a range of meanings: "good will, favor, pleasure, wish, desire"? Is it human or divine? The Syriac Peshitta and Tatian seem to have interpreted the verse as a reference to those who were the object of the "esteem" or "good opinion" of their fellows (See R. Köbert, *Biblica* 42 [1961], 90–1), while the Vulgate and traditional Roman Catholic translation rendered it as "men of good will." Today the tendency among scholars is to evaluate the *eudokia* as divine rather than human, even though one must then supply in translation, as does the Sahidic, an absent reference to God (e.g., "by Him")—a difficulty as Feuillet, "Les hommes," rightly objects. Some would understand this *eudokia* as God's pleasure (Sirach 35:14), thus the RSV: "Among men with whom He is pleased." A parallel expression in the Dead Sea Scrolls (see below and E. Vogt, "Pax") suggests that *eudokia* is God's will or favor in selecting people. Thus, in Luke 10:21 Jesus will praise his Father, the Lord of heaven, for having revealed Himself to some, the little ones, "for such was Your *eudokia*." (The primary object of God's *eudokia* is Jesus himself, as God proclaims at the baptism in Luke 3:22: "You are my beloved Son; with you I am well pleased [*eudokein*].") This meaning of *eudokia* would give the line "and on earth peace to those favored (by him)" the meaning of a peace extended by God to a people He has chosen, as in the *Psalms of Solomon* 8:39: "To us and our children, O Lord our Savior, *hē eudokia* forever; we shall not be moved forever."

Two major versifications have been suggested which I shall translate more literally according to the Greek word order. The lack of a verb suggests a Semitic original or, at least, a Semitic model. Probably there is a jussive force to the construction ("Glory *be* to God") rather than a declarative one ("God is glorified"); see Rom 11:36; Hebr 13:21. But this is not to be understood simply as a wish. What God has done manifests His glory and brings about peace. In "this day" the glory and peace already are, but they need to be proclaimed and acknowledged.

a) a tricolon:

> Glory in the highest to God,
>
> and on earth peace,
> (and) among men divine favor.

In this arrangement there are three elements in the first line, two elements in the second, and two in the third. An element in each line is always a noun in the nominative case, which I have underlined once (respectively, *doxa, eirēnē, eudokia*). The localization phrase (underlined twice) in the first line is matched by a localization phrase in the second line. The directional phrase (underlined thrice) in the first line is matched by a directional phrase in the third line. The versification demands the reading of a nominative *eudokia*, found in the Syriac and Bohairic, and in the majority of later Greek mss., including the Greek tradition known to Luther and to the committee which produced the

Authorized (KJ) *Version*. (For a reconstruction of the putative Hebrew original, see C. C. Torrey, in *Studies in the History of Religions Presented to
C. H. Toy* [New York: Macmillan, 1912], 294.) Most textual critics regard
the nominative as having been introduced by a scribe, since the tendency
of scribes would have been to make *eudokia* match in form the other two
nouns which are nominative. An original genitive *eudokias*, reflecting the
highly Semitic construct arrangement ("men of [God's] favor") may have
struck a polished Greek speaker as a barbarism, whence the tendency to
change. The Syriac has supplied an "and" in the third line without which this
versification is awkward. Flusser, "Sanktus," has argued that the tricolon pattern is really a paraphrase of the threefold "Holy" of Isa 6:3 and is related to
the Jewish Kaddish prayer. It is an interesting thesis; but, as he admits (p. 15),
Luke would then have preserved only in part the original pattern.

b) a bicolon:

> Glory in the highest to God,
>
> and on earth peace among men favored (by Him).

In this arrangement there are three elements in each line: a noun (underlined
once), a localization phrase (underlined twice), and a directional phrase (underlined thrice). The parallelism is imperfect, for the second line is longer. (Because of that many scholars have suggested that the genitive *eudokias* ["of
(His) favor" or "favored (by Him)"] is a later, Lucan addition to an original, perfectly balanced bicolon.) The genitive *eudokias* is supported by the best
Greek mss. and by the Latin and Sahidic. The Dead Sea Scrolls have given us
equivalents both in Hebrew (*beͤnē reͤṣônô*, "children of His good will": 1QH iv
32–33; xi 9) and in Aramaic (*'ĕnôš reͤ'ûtēh*, "a man of His good will": 4Q
'Amram^c 18); see Fitzmyer, "Peace." Indeed, Schwarz, "Lobgesang," who
regards *eudokias* as an addition to the original bicolon, thinks that it was
prompted because the Christian attitude was the same as the Qumran attitude:
God's peace is not for all but only for the chosen community. Yet Luke 2:10
has already indicated that this great joy is "for the whole people," and so in
Lucan thought God's favor is widely directed. A final argument for the bicolon
versification is offered by the parallel in Luke 19:38 which I shall discuss in the
COMMENT (see Spitta, "Die chronologischen," 304–5).

15. *When . . . heaven, the shepherds.* Another Lucan *egeneto* construction;
NOTE on 1:9; literally, "And it happened that when . . . heaven, the shep-
herds." The *hōs temporale* ("when") occurs some fifty-eight times in Luke/
Acts.

the angels had gone. Many of the OL mss. use the singular; see NOTE on
"with the angel" in vs. 13.

urged. Literally, "kept saying."

go over. The verb *dierchesthai* occurs three times more frequently in
Luke/Acts than in the rest of the NT taken together.

see the event. This is a Semitism: the Greek *rēma* means "word"; but here
and in vss. 17,19 it translates the double connotation of the Hebrew *dābār*,
"word, deed." This is a deed that speaks.

the Lord. It was actually an "angel of the Lord" who made the revelation; see NOTES on 2:9 and 1:45.

16. *with haste.* In the NT Luke alone uses *speudein* in a classical intransitive sense whereby it becomes almost an adverb accompanying another verb. Some interpret the haste to imply that the shepherds knew where to go, since the manger served their animals. Rather it implies the ready obedience of the shepherds to the revelation; see NOTE on "hastily" in 1:39.

found. The verb *aneuriskein* is found elsewhere in the NT only in Acts 21:4; a related verb *euriskein* was used for "find" in vs. 12.

Mary and Joseph. The OS^sin reverses the order, and in 2:33 the reading is "the father and the mother." The placing of Mary first may reflect a respect for the mother of the Messiah, as in Matthew's parallel scene with the magi (2:11): "They saw the child with Mary his mother" (see § 6, footnote 32).

17. *seen this.* What they have seen is the baby in the manger, which was the sign given them by the angel (vs. 12) and the event they resolved to go and see (15).

they made known. Seemingly not only to the parents of the child, but also to the audience mentioned for the first time in the next verse.

the event. See NOTE on vs. 15.

this child. The "this" is omitted by Codex Bezae and some of the versions. The designation now shifts from *brephos*, "baby" (vss. 12,16) to *paidion* (here and 2:27,40), the diminutive of *pais*, "boy, servant." (The last term will be used of the twelve-year-old Jesus in 2:43.) *Paidion* is used in a similar scene in Matt 2:11 (see NOTE there).

18. *All who heard.* No mention has hitherto been made of the presence of an audience at the birthplace. The same phrase was used in 1:66 in the aftermath of the circumcision and naming of JBap; but there we were prepared by the information that neighbors and relatives were present and that the news had spread to "the whole hill country of Judea" (1:58,65). The two birth and naming accounts are interdependent.

were astonished. The Greek is typically Lucan, and the same reaction occurs in 1:21,63 and 2:33.

19. *but Mary.* Luke continues the reactions of the cast of characters: the shepherds (17), all who heard (18), and now the mother. In ten other instances in the infancy narrative Mary's name is written in the Hebraized form *Mariam*, but here many mss. have *Maria* (as in 1:41).

kept with concern. Luke uses the verb *synterein* here and *diaterein* in the parallel expression in 2:51. More than simple retention is meant, for *synterein* must be connected with the following verb *symballein:* the difficult events that happened are to be retained in order to be interpreted correctly.

all these events. The plural of *rēma* (NOTE on vs. 15); the position of "all" is emphatic.

interpreting them. The verb *symballein*, often translated "converse with, ponder, meditate upon, compare, meet," is literally "to throw side by side." Rengstorf would understand the verb in this literal sense of Mary's bringing together the individual incidents in order to understand why the shepherds have

come to Bethlehem. However, Van Unnik, "Die rechte," has meticulously examined the usage of this verb in the Hellenistic Greek contemporary with the
New Testament; and he suggests that it means to interpret obscure events, hit-
ting upon the right meaning, often with divine help.

in her heart. Here the phrase modifies *symballein*, "interpreting"; but in the
OT the pattern of *keeping* words in the heart occurs (Gen 37:11), so that the
previous verb in the sentence may also be in mind.

20. *the shepherds returned.* For Luke's use of verbs of departure to end
scenes in the infancy narrative, see NOTE on 1:23.

and praising . . . all. These words are omitted by the OS^sin. The combination
"glorifying and praising" occurs in the LXX of Dan 3:26,55 (in "The Song of
the Three Children"). The combination of praise and glory was already associated with the heavenly host in 2:13–14.

21. *Now . . . when.* The pattern *kai hote* occurs twenty-two times in
Luke/Acts and only three times elsewhere in the New Testament.

eight days later. The circumcision of JBap was dated "on the eighth day"; see
NOTE on 1:59. The same dating is given by Luke 9:28 to the transfiguration
(in preference to the six days of Mark 9:2), but this seems to be coincidental.

when the time came to circumcise the child. Literally, "when the eight days
were fulfilled to circumcise him." The expression "the days were fulfilled" is
also found for Jesus' birth (vs. 6) and the purification (vs. 22), and is Luke's
way of connecting the three events. It is an awkward expression, for it might be
taken to mean that the allotted time for circumcision (or in 22, for purification) *was over.* But in vs. 6 it is clear that the expression means that the allotted time for giving birth *has come,* and that seems to be the meaning here and
in 22 as well. The genitive of the articular infinitive that follows this expression
serves the role of a consecutive clause, describing the event that takes place as
the result of the filled-out period of time (BDF 400²); and it is a construction
that Luke uses relatively often. While the best ms. tradition reads "him," many
scribes were forced, even as I was in my translation, to clarify the sentence by
substituting "the child," i.e., the *paidion* of vs. 17.

he was called Jesus, the name. Literally and tautologically, "his name was
called Jesus," as in 1:34: "You will call his name Jesus"; for this Semitism see
the NOTE on Matt 1:21. The statement about Jesus after his circumcision almost combines the statements made by the two parents of JBap after his circumcision: "He is to be called John" (1:60), and "John is to be his name"
(1:63).

before he was conceived in the womb. Again Luke deliberately evokes the
wording of the angel's message in 1:31: "You will conceive in your womb."

COMMENT

When we discussed the two Lucan annunciation scenes, it was necessary to compare the structure of the Jesus annunciation with the JBap annunciation and to point out the parallelisms. I shall do that here as well, comparing the birth, circumcision, and naming of Jesus to the birth, circumcision, and naming of JBap. After this introductory study of structure, I shall turn to the three basic subdivisions of the scene of Jesus' birth (vss. 1–20), and the concluding notice of his circumcision and naming (21).

A. *The Structure of the Story in 2:1–40*

There is a parallelism between the birth stories of JBap (1:57–80) and of Jesus (2:1–40), even if it is not so perfect as the parallelism between the stories of the two annunciations.[1] In the instance of the annunciations, one could put the scriptural texts side by side to see the similarity (Table X); that would not be too fruitful here, for there are only a few parallels in wording. But once again (see Table XI), one may present the two birth scenes as a diptych (Table XIV), which brings out the general parallels of structure, as well as the differences. The broad sequence of events is clearly the same: a sequence of birth/circumcision/naming which stresses the reactions of the neighbors or hearers; and a terminating refrain about the fact and locale of growth, which serves as a transition to the respective ministries.[2] Yet a close study of the two sides of the diptych shows a different arrangement of the parallel features. Whereas the JBap scene concentrates on the circumcision/naming, with just a notice given to the birth, the opposite is true of the Jesus scene. While the parents appear in relation to the circumcision/naming of JBap, they appear in relation to the birth of Jesus. It is in the setting of an angelic annunciation of Jesus' birth that fear, astonishment, retention in the heart, and praise are mentioned; similar features occur in the JBap story but in a different setting. Moreover, just as in the diptych of the annunciations with regard to the visitation (Table XI), the Jesus side in the birth diptych has a longer aftermath,

---

1 Already at the beginning of the COMMENT on § 13, I pointed out some of the defects in the parallelism.

2 I have constructed Table XIV on the hypothesis that Luke added the canticles (Benedictus, Gloria, Nunc Dimittis) at a second stage of editing. The presence of two canticles on the Jesus side of the diptych, compared to one on the JBap side, creates an unevenness that was not present in the original Lucan scheme.

TABLE XIV: BIRTH DIPTYCH
(FIRST STAGE OF LUCAN COMPOSITION)

1:57–66,80 **Birth/Naming/Greatness of JBap**	2:1–12,15–27,34–40 **Birth/Naming/Greatness of Jesus**
Notice of Birth; rejoicing by neighbors (57–58).	*Scene of Birth* (1–20): Setting (1–7): Census involving the two parents; birth at Bethlehem.

Scene of Circumcision/Naming (59–66): Two parents involved in wonders surrounding the naming, indicating the future greatness of the child.	Annunciation (8–12):*
	1. Angel of the Lord appeared to shepherds nearby
	2. Shepherds filled with fear
	3. The message:
	  c. Do not be afraid; great joy
	  e. This day there is born in the city of David
	  f. A Savior who is Messiah and Lord
	5. The sign: a baby wrapped and lying in a manger
	Reactions (15–20):
	Shepherds went to Bethlehem, saw the sign; made known the event;

All astonished; Zechariah spoke praising God; All the neighbors feared; All who heard stored the events up in their heart.	Hearers astonished; Mary kept these events in her heart; Shepherds returned, glorifying and praising God. *Notice of Circumcision/Naming* (21).
	Scene of Presentation in Temple (22–27,34–38): Setting (22–24): Purification of parents; consecration of firstborn, according to the Law. Greeting by Simeon (25–27,34–35): Moved by the Holy Spirit, Simeon blessed parents, and prophesied the child's future. Greeting by Anna (36–38).
Conclusion (80): Refrain on growth of child. His stay in the desert.	*Conclusion* (39–40): Return to Galilee and Nazareth. Refrain on growth of child.

* See Table VIII for the numbered steps in the annunciation.

---

involving his presentation in the Temple and the greetings by Simeon and Anna. One might be tempted to think that Luke meant this presentation to be totally separate from the birth/circumcision/naming; yet the same type of conclusion that ends the JBap side of the birth/circumcision/naming comes on the Jesus side *after* the presentation. Also, if one considers the second stage of Lucan editing when the canticles were added, Zechariah's canticle predicting the future greatness of JBap was intercalated between the naming and the concluding refrain, even as Simeon's canticle about the future of Jesus was intercalated between the naming and the conclusion.[8] Thus, even though for convenience I shall treat the presentation with the Nunc Dimittis (2:22–40) separately in § 15,[4] there is reason to believe that Luke thought of the whole of 2:1–40 as parallel to 1:57–80.

If Luke has given a whole scene to the birth of Jesus as contrasted to a short notice given to the birth of JBap, that should not disguise the fact that the center of attention for Luke is not Jesus' birth but the angelic annunciation interpreting that birth for the shepherds, and their reaction to the good news. Expanding on the indications in Table XIV, we may trace the flow of action in 2:1–20 thus:

Setting (1–7):
   a) The occasion of the census brings Joseph with Mary to Bethlehem (1–5).
   b) While there, Mary gives birth to Jesus; she swaddles him and lays him in a manger (6–7).
Annunciation (8–14):
   a) Nearby, an angel of the Lord announces to shepherds the birth of the Savior, Messiah, and Lord, giving them the sign of the baby in the manger (8–12).
   b) A multitude of the heavenly host appears and recites the Gloria (13–14).
Reactions (15–20):
   a) The shepherds go to Bethlehem to see the sign; and finding it verified, they make known what was told them (15–17).
   b) The hearers are astonished; Mary keeps these events in her heart; the shepherds return, glorifying and praising God (18–20).

The climax comes in the third part of the scene where the protagonists of the first part (Mary, Joseph, the baby in Bethlehem) are joined by the protagonists of the second part (the shepherds), who praise God for having fulfilled His word to them.[5] Yet it is in the second part that heaven and

---

   [8] Luke underlines the parallelism between the Benedictus and the Nunc Dimittis by having the Holy Spirit move both the elderly spokesmen. In comment on the preceding footnote, one may present the Gloria and the Nunc Dimittis together as a match for the Benedictus, since the Gloria has the same theme as the first part of the Benedictus, i.e., praise for God and peace for his covenanted community on earth.

   [4] Similarly, I treated the visitation with the Magnificat (1:39–56) in § 12, separately from the annunciation. Notice the shift of locale in both the visitation and the presentation.

   [5] I draw here upon the analysis of the scene by Rengstorf, "Weihnachtserzählung," 15; but I disagree with his contention that Mary is the central figure in the scene. Rather, the shepherds are central, even as the magi are central for Matthew. But, as I shall point out in discussing vs. 19, Mary is the only figure kept on stage when the shepherds depart, because she will perdure into the ministry as they will not.

earth touch in and through the angels who interpret the meaning of the birth that has taken place at Bethlehem.[6]

So much do the second and third parts of the Lucan scene dominate over the first (the actual birth) that vss. 6–20 have sometimes been isolated as a pre-Lucan annunciation story for which Luke would have created an introduction in vss. 1–5.[7] In this hypothesis the story began with the merest mention of birth, even as does the story in Matt 2. It has been argued that Luke 2:6–20 is virtually self-contained and presupposes nothing in ch. 1. For instance, vs. 11 proclaims anew that Jesus is the Savior and Messiah as if the reader had not been told this in 1:32–35. The reference to Mary and Joseph in 16 gives no hint of the virginal conception.[8] Indeed, precisely because no virginal conception is involved in 2:6–20, some have thought it was the earliest annunciation narrative.

As will become clear in the discussion of the individual sections, I am dubious of the theory of a pre-Lucan narrative in 2:6–20.[9] True, there is a difference between 1–5 and 6–20; but I think that both are Lucan compositions. The reason for the difference is that they represent narratives developed from two once separate sets of reflections on OT texts. What is pre-Lucan in 6–20 is not a narrative but an interpretative reflection on Gen 35:19–21 and Micah 4–5, which is also found in ch. 2 of Matthew.[10]

The latter observation points to the fact that the real parallel for the annunciation to the shepherds is not the annunciations before Jesus' birth in

[6] Westermann, "Alttestamentliche," 318, argues that 2:1–20 is not primarily the story of a child's birth, but the story of how a divine message preached by angels through a sign became the message of men. This is a moderate corrective of Dibelius, "Tradition," 125, who classifies this as the legend of the heavenly proclamation of the nature and purpose of the newborn child. Yet in "Jungfrauensohn," 53–54, Dibelius makes clear that the angel's message is primary.

[7] Let me survey various theories. Dibelius, "Jungfrauensohn," 59, thinks that there was once another introduction explaining how Mary and Joseph got to the lodgings mentioned in vs. 7, and that Luke replaced it with the census. Schmidt, *Rahmen*, 312, maintains that 2:1–5 is of a literary artistry quite different from 2:6ff., where an older tradition (a folk narrative) begins, and that vss. 1–5 are the work of Luke designed to bring Mary and Joseph to Bethlehem where the birth in the original story was situated. Hahn, *Titles*, 259, thinks that the old beginning was lost but that Luke reworked a census motif which was original. (Of 6–20, Hahn thinks Luke added the last part of 11 and vs. 19.) Burger, *Jesus*, 136, holds that Luke supplied the localization in 1–5 as a contrast to Nazareth, and that it reflects his historical interest as seen in 3:1–2; 13:1; Acts 5:37. Vögtle, "Offene," 54–56, sees only 8–20 as the self-consistent revelatory narrative, with 1–5 as a created introduction, and 6–7 as back-formed from vs. 12.

[8] One could argue that there is even more of a problem about the reintroduction of Joseph and Mary to the reader in 2:4–5, as if this was the first mention of them. But that occurs in verses which are more often attributed to Luke, rather than to a pre-Lucan source. This repetition of material from 1:27 is Luke's way of picking up the sequence from the annunciation after the intervening scenes at the house of Zechariah.

[9] Most of the difficulties mentioned in the preceding paragraph of the text are easily resolved. The annunciation to Mary revealed to her who Jesus was; now the news is given to a wider audience—the same progressive revelation occurs in Matt 1–2. If Mary and Joseph are on a relatively even footing in 2:16 (with Mary mentioned first), Mary alone is singled out in 19, in harmony with ch. 1.

[10] The fact that the same texts appear in Matthew makes me think that the interpretative reflection on them may be pre-Lucan. On the other hand, I suspect that Luke himself may have developed the census motif of vss. 1–5 from reflection on Ps 87:6 (B1 below).

Luke 1:26–38 and Matt 1:18–25, but the magi story in Matt 2:1–12. In both Matthean and Lucan infancy narratives, after a first chapter which informs one parent of the forthcoming birth of Jesus, there is a similar sequence of events early in ch. 2: a brief mention of birth at Bethlehem; the revelation of that birth to a group who were not present (magi, shepherds);[11] the coming of that group to Bethlehem under the guidance of the revelation; their finding of the child with Mary (and Joseph); an acknowledgment on their part of what God has done; and their returning to whence they came. The fact that the group which receives the revelation (magi, shepherds) are the central characters in the respective scenes is explicable once we remember that the conception and birth of Jesus had now become the christological moment. As I indicated in § 6, A2, when the christological moment was the resurrection, the recipients of that revelation became apostles who went forth to proclaim the good news of salvation; and their proclamation of christology was met by the twofold reaction of either acceptance/homage or rejection/persecution. We saw in Matthew's infancy narrative this same sequence of christological revelation, proclamation through a star, and the twofold reaction of acceptance/homage by the magi and rejection/persecution by King Herod, the chief priests and scribes. In Luke's infancy narrative the sequence is also preserved, for the revelatory annunciation in ch. 1 is followed by a proclamation through an angel in ch. 2, with the twofold reaction of acceptance/praise by the shepherds, and of Simeon's warning of rejection/persecution in 2:34–35.[12]

With this general introduction to the structure and theological rationale of the basic Lucan story, let us now turn to the individual components in 2:1–21.

B. *The Setting at Bethlehem (2:1–7)*

There are two parts to the Lucan setting. The first part (vss. 1–5), which describes the census that brought Joseph with Mary to Bethlehem, is paradoxically longer than the second part (6–7) which describes the birth itself. And indeed, in the second part more attention is paid to the placing of the baby in the manger than to the birth.

1. The Census of the Whole World (1–5)

Luke begins his story with a reference to a census of the whole world ordered by Augustus, conducted by Quirinius, and affecting Joseph, a

---

[11] Appropriately revelation by a star for Gentiles and by an angel of the Lord for Jews.
[12] This is another reason for seeing 2:22–40 as forming a unity with 2:1–21.

Galilean inhabitant of Nazareth, so that he had to go to his ancestral city. This supplied the occasion for the birth of Jesus in Bethlehem about the time of the reign of Herod, king of Judea (1:5). As I point out at length in Appendix VII, this information is dubious on almost every score, despite the elaborate attempts by scholars to defend Lucan accuracy. By way of lesser difficulties we have no evidence of one census under Augustus that covered the whole Empire, nor of a census requirement that people be registered in their ancestral cities. While these difficulties can be explained away,[18] we cannot resolve satisfactorily the major objections, namely, the one and only census conducted while Quirinius was legate in Syria affected only Judea, not Galilee, and took place in A.D. 6–7, a good ten years after the death of Herod the Great. Since elsewhere Luke shows himself inaccurate about the dating of events surrounding this census,[14] the evidence favors the theory that the use of the census to explain the presence of Joseph and Mary at Bethlehem is a Lucan device based on a confused memory. Luke may have had a tradition that associated the birth of Jesus with the end of a Herodian reign (a dating confirmed by Matthew) and a time of political trouble. But Luke seems not to have known that, some eighty years before he wrote, there were two such troubled endings of Herodian reigns, namely, the end of the reign of Herod the Great in 4 B.C., when Jews protested against the giving of Judea to Archelaus, and the end of the reign of Archelaus in A.D. 6, when Jews revolted against the census imposed by Quirinius. Consequently he has given a composite scene as a setting for Jesus' birth.[15]

The setting was necessitated in part by Luke's assumption that Joseph and Mary lived in Nazareth before Jesus was born, an assumption challenged by the Matthean picture that they lived in Bethlehem. One may argue which, if either, evangelist was accurate on this point; but the discussions in Appendixes III and VII would suggest that, if one accepts the historicity of both birth at Bethlehem and previous residence at Nazareth, one should find a reason other than the census to reconcile the two facts. Moreover, the probability that the Lucan census picture is not historical raises a serious objection to the theory that Luke's account of the annunciation in 1:26–38 was derived from a family or Marian source (pp.

18 For example, George, "Il vous," 61, suggests that Luke combined into one census censuses that Augustus and his successor conducted over a period of thirty years in various provinces of the Empire. "It is therefore a simplification of history such as one finds in ancient historians who were more interested in literary form than in material details."

14 As pointed out in Appendix VII, in Acts 5:37 Luke mistakenly lists the insurrection of Judas the Galilean (caused by the census of Quirinius in A.D. 6–7) *after* the insurrection of Theudas, which historically occurred in A.D. 44–46. The memory that Judas was from Galilee may have confused Luke as to the territorial extent of the Quirinius census. I doubt that there was a general Lucan confusion about Galilee and Judea (see NOTE on 1:39), since in 3:1 he shows himself capable of distinguishing the political histories of those two areas.

15 This thesis is brilliantly defended by Syme, "Titulus." See the citation related to footnote 22, Appendix VII.

245, 316–19 above and Appendix IV, B2). In themselves the stories in 1:26–38 and 2:1–40 might be independent of each other, but it is difficult to believe that Luke could have had available family reminiscences for the annunciation of Jesus' birth and have had to depend totally upon his own intuitions for the circumstances of the birth itself. There may be historical items within the two narratives,[16] but both involve creative Lucan construction.

Why has Luke given us the elaborate setting in vss. 1–5?[17] I have said that in part it was to move the scene from Nazareth to Bethlehem, but that is not an adequate explanation since Luke could have found a less complicated way to change scene. The census must have suited the Lucan purpose and theological outlook in other ways as well. Several possible motives may be mentioned, and they need not be exclusive of each other.

FIRST, *a solemn beginning.* I have pointed out that at one stage in early Christian thought (a stage associated with the written Gospels) the christological moment was attached to the beginning of Jesus' ministry through his baptism by JBap—that was the moment for God's revelation of who Jesus was. The Gospels tend, each in a different way, to solemnize within history the baptism because of its christological significance. For instance, Mark 1:2 sets the baptism in the context of the fulfillment of the Deutero-Isaian dream of the return of the people from Exile, by echoing Isa 40:3. John 1:19ff. sets JBap's dealings with Jesus in the context of the beginning of the great trial of Jesus of Nazareth which will last throughout the ministry, for JBap is called as the first witness. Luke 3:1–2 depicts the beginning of the ministry as an event of cosmic significance by setting it in the chronological framework of the world and local rulers who will ultimately be affected by it. On the Roman side of the list of rulers, there are Tiberius Caesar, the emperor, and then Pontius Pilate, the local prefect in Judea—Luke and his audience know that the ripples sent forth by the immersion of Jesus in the Jordan will eventually begin to change the course of the Tiber. And so it is not surprising that when Luke moves the christological moment back to the conception and birth of Jesus, he gives the birth too a setting in the chronological framework of world and local

---

[16] For instance, in 2:1–5, birth at the end of the reign of Herod the Great, and perhaps birth at Bethlehem.

[17] See footnote 7 for theories of the composition. I am not convinced by Schmithals, "Weihnachtsgeschichte," who makes a distinction between the composition of vs. 1 and vs. 2, on the grounds that vs. 1 with its mention of Augustus is the typical introduction of a legend (even as was the mention of King Herod in 1:5), while vs. 2 with its mention of Quirinius shows a historicizing tendency. It is true that vs. 2 is parenthetical, and that the dating which it gives produces most of the historical difficulty about the census. Yet there are difficulties about vs. 1 too; and the combination of the emperor Augustus and the governor Quirinius is quite Lucan, as we see from the mention of the emperor Tiberius and the governor Pontius Pilate in 3:1.

rulers, as he mentions Augustus Caesar, the emperor, and then Quirinius, the local legate in Syria.[18] Ironically, the Roman emperor, the mightiest figure in the world, is serving God's plan by issuing an edict for the census of the whole world. He is providing the appropriate setting for the birth of Jesus, the Savior of all those people who are being enrolled.[19]

SECOND, *Augustus, the peaceful savior.* In this solemnizing of the birth of Jesus, Luke may have seen a unique significance in the fact that the birth took place in the reign of Augustus.[20] If Augustus could be pictured by Luke as giving an edict affecting the whole world, it was precisely because he was remembered as the founder of the Empire who had pacified the world. His victories put an end to the internecine wars that had ravaged the Roman realms after the assassination of Julius Caesar, so that in 29 B.C. in the Forum the doors of the shrine of Janus (which stood open in times of war) were at last able to be closed. To the minds of many the promise so mystically described by Virgil in his Fourth Eclogue (Appendix IX) had at last come: a glorious age of pastoral rule over a world made peaceful by virtue. To symbolize this there was erected in 13–9 B.C. the great altar to the peace brought about by Augustus (*Ara Pacis Augustae*), a monument propagandizing Augustan ideals—and incidentally a monument which (rebuilt) still stands to his memory in Rome today. About the same time the Greek cities of Asia Minor (perhaps not far from where Luke was writing) adopted September 23rd, the birthday of Augustus, as the first day of the new year, calling him a "savior"; indeed an inscription at Halicarnassus calls him "savior of the whole world."[21] It can scarcely be accidental that Luke's description of the birth of Jesus presents an implicit challenge to this imperial propaganda, not by denying the imperial ideals, but by claiming that the real peace of the world was brought about by Jesus. The testimony to the *pax Christi* was not a man-made altar such as that erected to the *pax Augusta;* rather there was a

18 Luke 2:1 does not mention the Herodian rulers and the high priests, as does 3:1–2, although Luke 1:5 mentioned "Herod, king of Judea," as part of the setting for the birth of JBap. Interestingly, Matt 2:1,4 mentions Herod the king and the chief priests and scribes as part of the setting for the story of Jesus' birth. Both Luke 2 and Matt 2 show a similar instinct in portraying the birth of Jesus as having an impact on the same types of rulers who will be affected by his death.

19 In § 9, B1, I mentioned resemblances between the Lucan infancy narrative and the first chapters of Acts. In Acts 2:5–11 there is a listing of the peoples of the world, "devout people from every nation under heaven." There, in describing the birth of the Church, Luke is listing the nations by anticipation—eventually they will hear of the mighty works of God. A similar mentality may be at work in the Lucan description of the census.

20 Schmithals, "Weihnachtsgeschichte," is good on this point.

21 Augustus himself refers to the *Ara Pacis* in his famous *Res Gestae* inscription. For the other inscriptions, see *Inscriptions of the British Museum,* #894; and *Inscriptiones Graecae ad Res Romanas Pertinentes,* ed. R. Cagnat (3 vols; Paris: Leroux, 1901–27), III, #719. "Savior" was a frequent title for subsequent emperors; Josephus, *War* III ix 8; #459, tells how the Palestinian city of Tiberias opened its gates to Vespasian and received him as "savior."

heavenly host that proclaimed peace to those favored by God. The birthday worthy of divine honor and marking the true new beginning of time took place not in Rome but in Bethlehem. The claim in the Priene inscription of Augustus, "The birthday of the god has marked the beginning of the good news for the world,"[22] has been reinterpreted by an angel of the Lord with the heraldic cry: "I announce to you good news of a great joy which will be for the whole people: To you this day there is born in the city of David a Savior who is Messiah and Lord" (Luke 2:10–11).[23]

THIRD, *memories evoked by the census.* Luke writes against the background not only of Roman history but also of Jewish history. The former may explain the importance of mentioning Augustus; it is the latter that gives resonance to the theme of a census. There was an infamous census in the OT, and one equally infamous in more recent Jewish memory. Over the objection of his general Joab, King David ordered a census of Israel and Judah (II Sam 24), and for that arrogance incurred the wrath of God in the form of a pestilence.[24] But, in accord with God's ability to bring good out of evil, the place in Jerusalem where the pestilence stopped became the spot for the building of the Temple (II Chr 3:1). If this census may have evoked the memory of the city of David and of the Temple (themes that appear in Luke 2:1–40), the more recent census of Quirinius, which is specifically in Lucan view, had provoked the rebellion of Judas the Galilean,[25] the founder of the Zealot or ultranationalistic movement which culminated a half-century later in the Jewish revolt against Rome. Luke is writing after that Jewish revolt had been suppressed in A.D. 70 (cf. Luke 21:20 and Mark 13:14), at a time when Jewish messianic movements had "bad press" in the Roman Empire. The descriptions of the passion in the Gospels written after 70 are marked by sensitivities about this political situation, for there is a tendency to stress that Jesus was innocent of political ambition and was not a promoter of revolt. In particular Luke (23:4,14,22) has Pilate solemnly affirm three times that Jesus was innocent of the charges against him which involved a refusal to pay Roman taxes (23:2). Has Luke moved this motif back to the birth of Jesus by showing that the Galilean parents of Jesus were obedient to the same

---

22 The Priene inscription is published by W. Dittenberger, *Orientis Graeci Inscriptiones Selectae* (2 vols.; Leipzig: Hirzel, 1903–5), II, #458. See lines 40–42.

23 I shall point out below that Luke derived the titles "Savior, Messiah, Lord" from the early Christian kerygma, as indicated by his use of them in Acts; but here he has recast them into a solemn formula imitative of imperial proclamation. Schmithals, "Weihnachtsgeschichte," 288, wonders if the strange combination *christos kyrios* (NOTE on 2:11) does not come from the combining of a Jewish royal title with an imperial title.

24 There was a constant prophetic fear that the king was intruding on God's sovereignty over His people (I Sam 8).

25 See Acts 5:37 and footnote 14 above; also Josephus *Ant.* XVIII i 1 and 6; ##4–10,23–25.

Roman census (leveled for tax purposes) against which Judas the Galilean and the Zealots rebelled? Is Luke arming his Gentile Christian audience with the knowledge that from birth Jesus was never a party to rebellion against Rome?[26] If so, Luke may also be affirming that, while past censuses brought disaster to Judea (pestilence, rebellion), paradoxically this census brought a peaceful Savior who would be a revelation to the Gentiles and a glory to Israel (2:32).

FOURTH, *the census in Ps 87:6.* If the remarks thus far explain why the worldwide setting and the motifs of Augustus and the census might be very fruitful theologically for Luke, what would have caused him theologically to associate the census with the birth of Jesus? It is possible that he found this association in the Scriptures. Psalm 87 describes with joyous exaggeration how people from various nations come to Jerusalem and gain knowledge of the Lord who Himself registers them as citizens of Zion, so that each finds a spiritual home there. In 87:6 we are told: "The Lord will note in the enrolling of the peoples: 'This person was born there.' "[27] The LXX Greek of that verse reads: "The Lord will recount it in the inscription of the peoples and of the princes who were born in her.' "[28] But in the *Quinta* Greek version,[29] as attested in Eusebius, *Commentary on the Psalms* (PG 23:1052C), the verse reads: "In the *census* of the peoples, this one *will be* born there." Since the LXX speaks of the birth of princes and the Aramaic version of the psalm speaks of the rearing of a king,[30] the *Quinta* version may have been interpreted as a prophecy of the future

---

[26] Braunert, "Provinzialzensus," and Moehring, "Census," affirm this, but I see no way of being certain.

[27] For the Hebrew text of the psalm and some necessary reconstruction (which does not affect our verse), see A. Vaccari, *Biblica* 28 (1947), 394ff.; and P. W. Skehan, AER 124 (1951), 104–5. I am grateful to Msgr. Skehan for very helpful information on this psalm.

[28] The LXX has wrongly read the Hebrew *šārîm*, "singers," from the next verse as *šārîm*, "princes."

[29] At Caesarea in Palestine, before A.D. 245, Origen compiled Hebrew and Greek OT texts and versions into a six-columned work known as the Hexapla Bible (two columns of Hebrew, four of Greek). For the psalms, however, there were extra columns with additional Greek versions. The *Quinta* was the fifth Greek column after the two Hebrew ones (the seventh column in all). Sometime after A.D. 600 the prototype of the Hexapla vanished, so that today we have only fragments of the *Quinta* preserved in ancient writers like Eusebius who had access to the Hexapla. The standard collection is F. Field, *Origenis hexaplorum quae supersunt* (2 vols.; Oxford University, 1875); see JBC, article 69, ##68–71. Nestle, "Schatzung," called attention to the connection between the *Quinta* of Ps 87:6 and Luke 2:1.

[30] The targum on Ps 87:6 reads: "According to the book in which is written the reckoning of all the worlds [or peoples]: 'This king has been brought up there.' " The shift from a birth in Zion to a rearing there probably results from interpreting the "this man and that man" of the preceding verse (5) as a reference to David and Solomon, and the consequent necessity to adapt vs. 6 to King David, who was not born in Zion but did live there. The Midrash on the Psalms, or rabbinic commentary, did interpret part of this psalm as a reference to the Messiah(s). Both the targum and the midrash are quite late and can be used as background for the NT only with extreme caution. Nevertheless, they seem to reflect a direction attested earlier in the LXX.

birth of the messianic king in a census of the peoples. But how ancient is the *Quinta* version and could Luke have known of this reading? Or is the *Quinta* reading (known to us from a fourth-century author) a Christian reinterpretation of the psalm in light of Luke 2? (Eusebius himself drew upon the future tense to claim that a prophecy was involved.) At least one copy of the *Quinta* that Origen used he found *ca.* 212 at Nicopolis near Actium in southern Epirus (Greece),[81] and so the basic version can scarcely be later than the second Christian century. But it is probably older than that, for the textual tradition of the psalms that it represents has close affinities with a revision of the LXX (bringing the Greek closer to the standard Hebrew) which scholars now date to the early first Christian century.[82] And a case can be made from a study of Acts 2:18 that Luke knew the *Quinta* version.[83] If he did and he read in Ps 87:6, "In the census of the peoples, this one will be born there," the reading may have catalyzed his association of the birth of Jesus with the census of Quirinius (which he accidentally associated with the wrong Herodian king). It would further explain why, with a certain exaggeration, he made the census of Quirinius part of a census (of the peoples) of the whole world.

2. The Birth, the Swaddling, and the Manger (6–7)

When Luke shifts from the setting supplied by the imperial census to the actual birth of Jesus, he is very laconic (even as was Matthew) in describing the event: While Mary and Joseph were at Bethlehem, the time came for her to give birth; and she gave birth to a son, her firstborn. (The last mentioned detail is to prepare the way for the story of the presentation of the firstborn in 2:22–40.) Curiously, Luke seems more interested in telling his audience where Mary laid the newborn baby! He is careful to report that Jesus was swaddled and laid in a manger because of the lack of space at the lodgings. The precise picture that he wishes to convey is not clear (see NOTES); but the details about the swaddling and the manger are repeated later (see vss. 12,16) and must be of significance. Most of the popular reflection on vs. 7, however, misses Luke's purpose. Certainly irrelevant are speculations about why there was no room at the lodgings (influx of people for the census; presence of soldiers who took the census

---

81 Eusebius *Eccl. Hist.* VI xvi 2. See P. Kahle, *The Cairo Geniza* (2nd ed.; Oxford: Blackwell, 1959), 242–43.

82 I speak of the *kaige* recension, so-called after its custom of using this Greek expression to render literally the Hebrew particle meaning "and indeed." For a description of that recension and a possible dating to A.D. 30–50, see JBC, article 69, ##57,60,61. H.-J. Venetz, *Die Quinta des Psalteriums* (Hildesheim: Gerstenberg, 1974), 72, argues for the relationship of the *Quinta* to the *kaige*, and (on p. 192) dates the *Quinta* before Aquila, thus before A.D. 130.

83 D. Barthélemy, *Les dévanciers d'Aquila* (VetTestS 10; Leiden: Brill, 1963), 148. Prof. Barthélemy has graciously supplied me with details about the *Quinta* of Ps 87:6.

inscriptions; etc.), especially when these speculations lead to homilies about the supposed heartlessness of the unmentioned innkeeper and the hardship of the situation for the impoverished parents.[84] As the Lucan narrative now stands, the manger does not signify poverty but a peculiarity of location caused by circumstances. The mention of the lodgings is of minor importance; and, if the manger was pre-Lucan in the tradition, the lack of place in the lodgings may have been Luke's vague surmise, in order to explain the use of the manger.

Since the manger appears in all three subdivisions of Luke 2:1-20 (vss. 7,12,16) and Luke himself refers to it as a sign (12),[85] what is its symbolism? Various suggestions have been made. For instance, in a midrashic tradition about the curse on Adam in Gen 3:18, Adam asks, "Shall I be tied to the manger to eat with my donkey?" If this tradition were in Luke's mind,[86] he might be portraying Jesus as a second Adam, fulfilling the situation feared by Adam but turning it to salvific purposes. This is not an impossible suggestion since in his genealogy Luke calls attention to Jesus as "son of Adam" (3:38), but there is no way to prove it. A better suggestion[87] relates the symbolism of the Lucan manger to God's complaint in the LXX of Isa 1:3: "The ox knows its owner; and the donkey knows the manger [*phatnē*] of its lord; but Israel has not known me; my people has not understood me." Luke would be proclaiming that the Isaian dictum is repealed. The shepherds have been sent to the manger to find the Lord who is a source of joy for all the people of Israel; they go and, finding the baby in the manger, begin to praise God. In other words, God's people have begun to know the manger of their Lord. Perhaps the "lodgings" of Luke 2:7 can be brought into this picture through Jer 14:8 addressed to the Lord and Savior of Israel: "Why are you like an alien in the land, like a traveler who stays in *lodgings?*" But now the Lord and Savior of Israel no longer stays in lodgings. The swaddling, far from being a sign of poverty, may be a sign that Israel's Messiah is not an outcast among his people but is properly received and cared for. In Wisdom 7:4-5 Solomon, the wealthiest of Judah's kings, affirms: "I was carefully swaddled and nursed,

---

[84] The popular understanding of Luke 2:1-20 has been shaped, not only by preaching and storytelling, but also by art and especially by the custom of the Christmas crèche or crib scene. This custom was popularized by St. Francis of Assisi, beginning at midnight mass at Greccio in 1223; and the gentle spirit and love of poverty of this saint, called *Il Poverello*, have left their mark on the interpretation of the Lucan birth narrative. For a critique of "crib-scene" hermeneutics of Luke 2:1-20, see Baily, "Crib," 358-66.

[85] This is stressed by Baily, "Shepherds," 1-4. It is not a miraculous sign, any more than is the sign mentioned in I Sam 2:34, but is a constitutive part of the revelation.

[86] Derrett, "Manger," 569-71, cites *Midrash Rabbah* XX 10 on Gen 3:18, and TalBab *Pesachim* 118a; but this is late evidence, not safely used to interpret the NT. Yet Derrett thinks that Luke was aware of the tradition because in Luke 13:15-16 Jesus says, "Does not each of you on the sabbath untie his ox or *his donkey from the manger*," as part of his argument that the woman ought to be loosed from the bonds of Satan on the sabbath.

[87] This is worked out by Giblin, "Reflections," 99-101.

for no king has any other way to begin at birth." Giblin has phrased the total picture well: Jesus is born in the city of David, not in lodgings like an alien, but in a manger where God sustains His people. His swaddling does not belie his royal role.

C. *The Annunciation to the Shepherds (2:8–14)*

Basically there are two subdivisions in this part of the birth scene, centered around the distinct episodes of the annunciation by the angel of the Lord (vss. 8–12) and of the short canticle sung by the heavenly host (13–14). But before treating those subdivisions, let us discuss the symbolism of the shepherds who are the recipients of this double revelation.

1. The Symbolism of the Shepherds (8)

To modern romantics the shepherds described by Luke take on the gentleness of their flocks, and in recent centuries they have triumphed over the magi as a better Christmas symbol for the common man (see § 6D). But such interests are foreign to Luke's purpose. In fact, far from being regarded as either gentle or noble, in Jesus' time shepherds were often considered as dishonest, outside the Law.[88] This has led to the suggestion that for Luke they represented the sinners whom Jesus came to save (see 5:32; 7:34; 15:1; 19:7); yet there is no hint of that in 2:8–20. Let us consider some other suggestions about why Luke has moved the shepherds to front stage in his narrative.

I have pointed out that Luke has placed his narrative against the background of the imperial claims of Augustus. Do the shepherds also have a Hellenistic background? Shepherds appear many times in the legends of Greek religion.[39] In an even wider range of religious backgrounds, attention has been called to the presence of shepherds or domestics in the scene of Mithra's birth and in the infancy story of Osiris,[40] and even to a general

---

[88] TalBab *Sanhedrin* 25b mentions that herdsmen were added by the early rabbis to the list of those ineligible to be judges or witnesses since frequently they grazed their flocks on other people's lands. Thus, they were among the type of dishonest people who were excluded from court. For a general treatment of shepherds, see R. T. A. Murphy, *The Bible Today* 15 (Dec. 1964), 986–91.

[39] See Dibelius, "Jungfrauensohn," 72–73. Swaddling and rearing in a pastoral setting are features in the birth story of Jupiter.

[40] See Creed, *Luke*, 30–31; Dibelius, "Jungfrauensohn," 66–69; and Machen, *Virgin Birth*, 355–58, for a discussion of these ideas. In the representations of Mithra's birth either a man with a staff and animals is standing there, or shepherds are looking on from behind a rock. (The cave motif, which appears at a post-NT period in the story of Jesus' birth [NOTE on "lodgings" in 2:7], is not related to the theme of caves in the Mithra cult, for Mithra was not born in a cave.) The Osiris theory, proposed by H. Gressmann in 1914, is elaborate, for it rewrites the story of Luke 2 in light of the Osiris pattern. In this rewriting Luke 2 was

tendency of pagan deities to show themselves to rustics (Virgil *Eclogues* X 16ff.). Sometimes this search for shepherds in non-Jewish legends is associated with the dubious thesis that the idea of the virginal conception had a similar origin (Appendix IV, B1).

However, if one remembers that the Lucan shepherds are linked very closely with Bethlehem, the city of David the shepherd, it is far more likely that the primary symbolism is to be sought in the Jewish background. In Mishnah *Shekalim* 7:4 we are told that animals found between Jerusalem and Migdal Eder (near Bethlehem) were used for Temple sacrifice, and this tradition has been invoked as support for the idea that the Lucan shepherds in the region near Bethlehem were especially sacred shepherds.[41] I see no hint of that, but the mention of Migdal Eder, "Tower of the Flock," may be the key to a symbolism that attaches the shepherds and their flock to the Bethlehem area. Migdal Eder is mentioned twice in the OT, Gen 35:21 and Micah 4:8, both times in proximity to a mention of Bethlehem (Gen 35:19 and Micah 5:1). I shall suggest that a midrashic reflection associating these texts underlies Luke's narrative in 2:8–20, even as such a reflection entered into the second chapter of Matthew's narrative.

We may begin with Luke's emphasis on the Bethlehem location as an essential part of the "good news of a great joy which will be for the whole people." The angel announces: "To you there is born *in the city of David* a Savior who is Messiah and Lord" (2:10–11). The shepherds respond to this by saying, "Let us go over *to Bethlehem* and see the event that has taken place" (2:15). Now, a scriptural relationship between Bethlehem and the Messiah seems to have been commonplace in first-century Judaism, if we can follow NT indications (Appendix III). In John 7:42 some of the people of Jerusalem say, "Has not the Scripture said that the Messiah is descended from David and comes from Bethlehem, the village where David was?" The "Scripture" referred to was probably Micah 5:1(2), if we may judge from the use of that text as a fulfillment citation in Matt 2:5–6.[42]

Let us consider the overall picture in Micah 4–5. The setting for the prophecy is the humiliation of Jerusalem/Zion by the Babylonian armies, an event which leads the nations to judge that Jerusalem/Zion is finished (4:10–11). But Micah contends that the nations do not know the thoughts of the Lord (4:12). The sufferings of Jerusalem/Zion are not

---

originally the story of a foundling child (royal and divine) in a shepherd's manger; parents were introduced only when the child was identified as Jesus. Such extravagant use of material from comparative religion is less popular today.

41 Plummer, *Luke*, 54. The Mishnah passage must be examined in light of the general prohibition in *Baba Kamma* 7:7 to raise sheep in the land of Israel. Accordingly *Shekalim* may be speaking of strays (perhaps escaped from the Temple pens) rather than of regular flocks.

42 In § 6, B1, we saw that possibly the Christian reflection on Micah 5:1(2) was pre-Matthean.

terminal, but are like those of a woman in labor. When her time to bear
has come, the Lord will rescue her from her enemies (4:10; 5:2[3]).[43]
The final result will be triumph. Jerusalem/Zion is the mountain of the
house of the Lord, and peoples and nations will flow to it (4:1-2). Jerusa-
lem/Zion is Migdal Eder, the Tower of the Flock, to whom the former
kingdom will be restored (4:8). This victory will be achieved by a ruler
from David's place of origin, Bethlehem Ephrathah, among the clans of
Judah (5:1). Thus, in a prophecy concerning the future victory of Jerusa-
lem/Zion through the instrumentality of a ruler from Bethlehem, there is
an identification of Migdal Eder with Jerusalem. It was not inappropriate
for Micah to designate as Tower of the Flock this city of David where a
king descended from a shepherd would rule. Nor was the geography impossible if we may judge from the only other mention of Migdal Eder. In
Gen 35:19 we are told that Rachel died "on the way to Ephrath, i.e.,
Bethlehem" (see NOTE on Matt 2:18), and in 35:21 Jacob/Israel is said to
have "journeyed on and pitched his tent beyond Migdal Eder." The implication is that Migdal Eder was on the road toward Bethlehem, a description that could match Jerusalem, five miles north of Bethlehem.[44]

There are several of these motifs in Micah 4-5 which have parallels in
Luke 2:1-20.[45] Micah's flow of peoples and nations to Jerusalem resembles the movement of the whole world effected by the census of Augustus,
a movement which brought Joseph to the city of David. Micah's twice-
mentioned "woman in birth pangs" resembles the birth motif in Luke.
The "this day" of the birth of Jesus (2:11) is the fulfillment of "the time
when she who is in travail has brought forth" (Micah 5:2[3]). But while
Micah focuses on the triumph of Jerusalem/Zion through the ruler from
Bethlehem, Luke shifts the total attention to Bethlehem.[46] As pointed out
in the NOTES, Luke describes Joseph as *going up* from Galilee to

---

[43] See J. Coppens, "Le cadre littéraire de Michée V:1-5," in *Near Eastern Studies in
Honor of William Foxwell Albright*, ed. H. Goedicke (Baltimore: Johns Hopkins, 1971),
57-62. He argues that the woman in travail who has brought forth (5:2[3]) is the same as
Zion in travail of 4:10, and has nothing to do with the 'almâ of Isa 7:14 nor with the queen
mother (§ 6, footnote 32).

[44] See also *Testament of Reuben* 3:13: "Eder near to Ephrath in Bethlehem." Of course,
the author of Genesis did not think of Jerusalem as Migdal Eder, any more than he thought
of Ephrath as Bethlehem. But the vagueness of his description, plus the later (wrong)
identification of Ephrath as Bethlehem, caused tradition to associate Migdal Eder, a figurative name, with the Jerusalem or the Bethlehem area.

[45] Nestle, "Hirten," argues for the influence of Micah 4 upon Luke; and so does Laurentin, *Structure*, 86-88. In my judgment the latter stretches the parallelism too far. He wishes
to relate the Lucan shepherds to Micah 5:3(4) which mentions a feeding of the flock—a
very different symbolism. And Laurentin seeks to relate "peace on earth" from the canticle
in Luke 2:14 to the mention of future peace in Micah 5:4(5); yet as we shall see, the canticle is probably a later Lucan addition with a very different literary history from that of the
annunciation to the shepherds.

[46] This shift would be further exemplified if the Lucan census reflects the *Quinta* version
of Ps 87:6, a passage which originally referred to a birth in Jerusalem/Zion, reapplied by
Luke to Bethlehem.

Bethlehem, employing the verb that is traditionally used to describe the journey "up" to Jerusalem. In 2:4,11 Luke calls Bethlehem the "city of David," elsewhere a standard designation for Jerusalem. It seems as if, for Luke, Micah's reference to "the mountain of the house of the Lord" has been shifted from Jerusalem/Zion to Bethlehem, since it is there that one must go to see the Lord (2:11–12). Luke's reference to shepherds pasturing their flock in the region of Bethlehem (2:8) may reflect his understanding that Migdal Eder, the Tower of the Flock of Micah 4:8, is in the environs of Bethlehem rather than at Jerusalem.[47] This could have happened if Luke (or a midrashic tradition before him) read in parallelism two verses of Micah:

> "And you, O Migdal Eder,
> hill of the daughter of Zion,
> to you will come back the former dominion,
> the kingdom of the daughter of Jerusalem" (4:8).

> "And you, O Bethlehem Ephrathah,
> small to be among the clans of Judah;
> from you there will come forth for me
> one who is to be a ruler in Israel" (5:1[2]).

In the "Copernican revolution" caused by the birth of Jesus, the city of David and the Tower of the Flock are also the city from which the ruler has come forth, the city to which the kingdom has been restored. Of course, some of this reinterpretation could have begun in Jewish circles with messianic interests. In the Targum Pseudo-Jonathan[48] on Gen 35:21 we read: "The Tower of the Flock, the place from which it will happen that the King Messiah will be revealed at the end of days."

We have already seen that there are functional similarities between Matt 2 and Luke 2. Since Matthew cites Micah 5:1(2) explicitly and Gen 35:19–21 implicitly (NOTE on Matt 2:18), exegesis of these texts may have entered into both these chapters. In the instance of Matt 2, I suggested the existence of a pre-Matthean narrative, with the citations being introduced only at the stage of Matthean composition. The Lucan prehistory is harder to reconstruct since there is no question of citations but only of a reflection upon citations that may have given rise to a motif.

---

47 See Baily, "Shepherds," 6–11. One would still have to ask why Migdal Eder, the Tower of the Flock, is expounded in terms of a story about shepherds instead of a story about a flock of sheep. The fact that David, born in Bethlehem (which Luke calls the city of David), was a shepherd when he was anointed king (I Sam 16) may account for this.

48 This Palestinian Targum to the Pentateuch (also known as Jerusalem I), with its freer translating style, was thought to be later than the literal Babylonian Targum Onkelos. But the free midrashic style has been found in the first-century *Genesis Apocryphon* of Qumran. Still, the absolute date of Targum Pseudo-Jonathan remains uncertain; and J. A. Fitzmyer, CBQ 32 (1970), 525, argues for a date after A.D. 200 for Palestinian targums, even if traditions contained in them may be older.

I speak of a pre-Lucan motif rather than a narrative and suggest that Luke wove this motif into an annunciation narrative which serves to proclaim publicly a revelation already given to Mary in ch. 1.

2. The Annunciation by the Angel of the Lord (9–12)

Having presented the shepherds, the recipients of the annunciation, Luke lets the structure of the subsequent narrative be determined by the standard annunciation pattern (Table VIII). Even though the pattern is not so perfectly preserved as in the annunciations of ch. 1, the main steps are present, as I have numbered them in the diptych of Table XIV. The angel of the Lord, the fear of the shepherds, and the instruction not to be afraid (vss. 9–10) are standard and need no comment.[49] I shall discuss below the christological content of the annunciation message (10–11); but the format of a promised conception has necessarily been changed, since the child is already born. The customary sign is given (12), and the departure of the angel(s) is mentioned in 15. A notable feature of the annunciation pattern is missing, namely, the question asking how this will happen.[50] Perhaps a "how" question simply could not be formulated in the instance of an event that had already taken place. Or else, since the sign offered by the angel was an implicit promise, there may be an implicit "how" in the fact that after the annunciation the shepherds hastened to go and see the event contained in the sign.

The core of the message is the "good news" or gospel proclaimed by the angel of the Lord: "To you this day there is born in the city of David a Savior who is Messiah and Lord" (11). I have pointed out in B1 above that this is cast in the format of an imperial proclamation, as part of Luke's gentle counterpropaganda that Jesus, not Augustus, was the Savior and source of peace whose birthday marked a new beginning of time (i.e., the eschatological "this day"). But that is only a secondary factor in the phrasing of this pronouncement.[51] The primary background seems to be Isa 9:5(6): "To us a child is born; to us a son is given."[52] In the Isaian

---

[49] The message in 2:11 calls Jesus "a Savior." Is this step 3g of Table VIII: the etymology of the child's name "Jesus," given in the previous annunciation to Mary? If so, this would increase the likelihood that Luke himself composed the annunciation to the shepherds.

[50] This is not a required feature (e.g., it is missing from Matt 1:18–25), but it was found in the two previous Lucan birth annunciations (Table XI).

[51] The question as to whether the angelic proclamation in 2:11 is Hellenistic is just as complicated as the question as to whether the sermons of Peter in Acts are Hellenistic. Probably a message shaped by Semitic-speaking Jewish Christians has been increasingly Hellenized, even before Luke passed it on to the Gentile Christians of a Pauline community. In the final product, an angel of the Lord (a purely Semitic figure) speaks with the tone of a Roman imperial herald.

[52] The opening line of this chapter of Isaiah (9:1[2]) was reflected at the end of the Benedictus as part of the description of the *anatolē* or rising light that appears to those who

context this child is the heir to the throne of David, and his royal titles follow: Wonderful Counselor, Divine Hero, Everlasting Father, Prince of Peace. Luke has taken over this Isaian birth announcement of the heir to the throne of David; but for the OT titulary he has substituted three titles taken from the Christian kerygma: Savior, Messiah (Christ), Lord. As we have seen in discussing the content of the previous annunciation messages, these titles were once applied in the descriptions of other christological moments (parousia, resurrection, baptism) and have been reapplied to the conception/birth. Philippians 3:20 applies all three titles to the Jesus of the parousia: "From heaven we await a Savior, the Lord Jesus Christ." In Acts there are combinations of "Lord and Messiah" (2:36) and "Leader and Savior" (5:31) applied to Jesus exalted through the resurrection.[53] The "this day" of Luke 2:11 is the "today" of Ps 2:7 ("You are my son; today I have begotten you"), a verse applied to the resurrection in Acts 13:32, and to the baptism of Jesus in the Western text of Luke 3:22.

If I am correct in seeing Isa 1:3 behind the manger motif which supplies the sign to the shepherds, and Isa 9:5(6) behind the angelic message to the shepherds, the theme of "good news" in Luke 2:10 may echo the "good news" of Isa 52:7. There it is good news of peace and of God's kingship directed to Jerusalem/Zion; and Luke would have once more shifted the message to Bethlehem, the new city of David. Or Luke may be echoing the "good news" of the Lord's anointed (messiah) in 61:1: "The Lord has anointed me to bring good news to the afflicted." Certainly these were passages that Luke knew and had put to service in reference to Jesus.[54]

3. The Canticle of the Heavenly Host (13–14)

We have seen that, introduced by vs. 8, the structure of vss. 9–12 was determined by the angelic annunciation of birth pattern. But suddenly in 13–14 we are no longer in the context of the angel of the Lord (i.e., of the divine messenger who brings God's revelation to this earth), but in the new context of the heavenly host, i.e., of the spirits who dwell in God's

---

sit in darkness. It is possible that Isaiah's "To us a child is born" is related to Micah 5:1(2): "O Bethlehem Ephrathah . . . from you there will come forth for me one who is to be a ruler in Israel." Yet see footnote 43 above.

[53] The fact that already the kerygma associated the three titles that appear in Luke 2:11 makes me skeptical of the thesis that a pre-Lucan form of the pronouncement had "Savior," and that Luke added "Messiah and Lord," or that the pre-Lucan form had "Savior who is Messiah," and that Luke added "Lord." (See NOTE on 2:11). I am even more skeptical of the argument of Burger, *Jesus*, 135–37, that Luke 2:11 must be a Lucan composition since, by applying "Messiah and Lord" to Jesus, it contradicts the usage of the pre-Lucan narrative in which there was no motif of a Davidic Messiah and "Lord" always referred to God. Such contradictory speculations about what was in the pre-Lucan narrative demonstrate how difficult it is to isolate pre-Lucan material from Luke's reworking.

[54] As we shall see Isa 52:10 is part of the background of the Nunc Dimittis (§ 15, C3); and Isa 61:1–2 is cited in Luke 4:18–19.

presence in heaven or in the Temple, singing His praise. Thus, although vs. 15 continues the annunciation pattern of 9–12 by having the angel(s) depart,[55] vss. 13–14 are quite anomalous in an annunciation pattern. These verses contain a brief canticle;[56] and on the analogy of previous canticles we may well suspect the presence of a Lucan addition. But, besides the usual problem of sequence in the case of canticles, we also have here the presence of a different literary genre, namely, a theophany that takes place in the last times.[57] That is why this canticle is attributed to heavenly spokesmen rather than to a character in the narrative. To an extent Luke began to prepare us for this different atmosphere already in vs. 9. When he mentioned the appearance of the angel of the Lord to the shepherds, he added: "The glory of the Lord shone around them." The glory of the Lord is a feature of theophanies, especially those associated with the overshadowing of the Tabernacle and of the Temple (see § 11, E3).[58] Facing the divine presence in the Temple, Isaiah heard the seraphim sing: "Holy, holy, holy is the Lord of Hosts; the whole earth is full of His glory." Certainly, this heavenly canticle served as an antecedent for the canticle that Luke attributed to the heavenly hosts.[59] (It is noteworthy that, although the canticle may have been added at a second stage of Lucan editing, by using a canticle that echoes Isaiah, Luke has been consistent with the previous echoes of Isaiah in the surrounding narrative.) Luke's idea of introducing an angelic hymn in praise of what God had done at Bethlehem corresponds to the idea found in roughly contemporary Jewish literature that, when the angels saw what God had done in creation, they sang a hymn of praise.[60] The "this day" proclaimed by the angel of the Lord in 2:11 has marked an event as worthy of angelic praise as any event that marked the six days of creation.

[55] The only echo of 13–14 in the wording of 15 is the plural "angels," a plural that is not read in some textual witnesses (see NOTE).

[56] The structure of this canticle—two or three lines—is fiercely debated; see NOTE on 2:14.

[57] In identifying literary genre, Westermann, "Alttestamentliche," 323, regards vss. 8–12,15 as an *epiphany* in which God appears to help His people. I prefer to speak of an annunciation of birth; but I agree with Westermann that the divine presence in those verses is not the same as a theophany where God appears in glory. The theophany classification for 13–14 is preferable to the apocalyptic genre invoked by Legrand, "L'évangile," 184; yet see footnote 75 below.

[58] In that previous section the overshadowing of Mary raised the question of whether Luke thought of her as the Tabernacle or the Ark of the Covenant. Here another aspect of the same OT imagery is related to the shepherds. This indicates that Luke is not identifying the characters of his narrative with such symbolism; rather he is associating general pictures and motifs.

[59] Flusser, "Sanktus," 146, sees the trisagion as a direct antecedent for the Lucan canticle, especially if it is structured as a tricolon (NOTE on 2:14). He points out that in the targum there was a tendency to expand the Isaian trisagion by developing each "holy" into a poetic line: "Holy in the highest heavens, the house of His presence; Holy on earth, the work of His might; Holy for endless ages."

[60] *Jubilees* 2:2–3; 11QPsᵃ "Hymn to the Creator"; see P. W. Skehan, CBQ 35 (1975), 343–45.

Once again it seems feasible that this canticle was originally composed by a community of Jewish Christian Anawim. If the Qumran Anawim could compose hymns for the angels to sing, so could a Christian community of similar piety and liturgical interest (§ 12, footnote 47). The Gloria is so brief that one can scarcely compare it to the Magnificat and the Benedictus, although like them it begins on the theme of the praise of God —an occupation of the Jerusalem community described in Acts 2:47. As for the second line of the Gloria, in the NOTE I have pointed out close parallels in the Qumran literature, for both groups of Anawim considered themselves the product of election and divine favor.[61] For the Christians that election and favor centered around the revelation to them that Jesus was the Messiah. In Luke/Acts the closest parallel to the Gloria is the liturgical acclamation at the entry of Jesus into Jerusalem. Only in the Lucan account (19:38) does the multitude of the disciples praise the king who comes in the name of the Lord by shouting aloud:

> "Peace in heaven
> and glory in the highest heavens."

It is a fascinating touch that the multitude of the heavenly host proclaims peace on earth, while a multitude of the earthly disciples proclaims peace in heaven—the passages could constitute antiphonal responses.[62] This parallel hymnic bicolon gives concrete support to my thesis that the canticles of the infancy narrative were once applied to a christological moment later in the career of Jesus. The same kind of poetry used to hail Jesus as the Messiah at the end of his ministry is applicable to the birth of the Messiah. But in the present Gospel sequence, Luke is telling us that the angels of heaven recognized at the beginning of Jesus' life what the disciples came to know only at the end, namely, the presence of the Messiah King who comes in the name of the Lord.

D. *The Reaction as the Shepherds Go to Bethlehem (2:15–20)*

The third scene in 2:1–20 brings together the protagonists from the first and second scenes, as the shepherds come and find Mary and Joseph with the baby (16). In the first scene the reader was told what happened in Bethlehem, viz., that after Jesus was born, Mary wrapped him in strips of cloth and laid him in a manger. In the second scene the shepherds were

---

61 For another contemporary echo of the sentiment of God's selective peace and favor, we may consider *Enoch* 1:8, "He will make peace with his holy ones and will protect the elect."
62 Scholars have argued which of the two Lucan passages (2:14, 19:38) was the more original and the pattern according to which the other was constructed, but it is equally possible that the two are citations from the one, longer pre-Lucan canticle. See Spitta, "Die chronologischen," 305.

told by an angel about this birth in the city of David (11) and were given
as a sign that they would find a baby wrapped in strips of cloth and lying
in a manger (12). And so now they hasten to Bethlehem and find the
baby lying in a manger (16–17). As I pointed out in B2 above, the symbolism, probably borrowed from Isa 1:3, is that of Israel at last coming to
know the manger of its Lord. Luke uses this fulfillment of the angelic sign
and this verification of the angelic joyful good news for the whole people in
order to lead into a dramatic scenario of different reactions by the groups
surrounding the manger (18–20).[63]

After the shepherds tell of the event and the angelic message,[64] the first
reaction is that of "all who heard": they are astonished. This is a clear
parallel with the scene surrounding the circumcision and naming of JBap,
for there also all were astonished (1:63).[65] But whereas all who heard
about JBap (and were astonished) stored up what they heard in their
hearts (1:66), among all those who heard about Jesus and were astonished, only Mary is reported to have kept the events, interpreting them
in her heart (2:19). The contrast between "all who heard" in 18 and
Mary in 19 does not center on the astonishment of the former—Mary is
said to be astonished in 2:33[66]—but on the fact that Mary alone retained
what was heard. For the others the hearing did not lead to further investigation. Perhaps like the audience described in the parable (8:13), "They
hear the word, receive it with joy, but have no root." Whereas Mary is one
of "Those who, hearing the word, hold it fast in an honest and good
heart" (8:15).[67]

Before analyzing in greater depth Mary's reaction in vs. 19, we should
note that it is "sandwiched" between the reactions of all those who heard
with astonishment (18) and of the shepherds who "returned, glorifying
and praising God for all they had heard and seen" (20). Having brought
the angelic good news from the nearby region of the flocks to the site of the
birth, the shepherds are now allowed to depart. These shepherds are

---

[63] Luke's dramatic interests are theological; he does not satisfy a later generation's curiosity about the backdrop of the scene. He does not tell us in what sort of place Jesus was
born (see the end of the last NOTE on 2:7), nor who were the hearers (vs. 18) or where
they came from. He is simply reusing the staging from the JBap scene.

[64] The fact that the shepherds tell the parents what the angel said about the child (vs. 17)
has been used to defend the thesis that this annunciation and the one to Mary in 1:26–38
were once independent narratives. The *origins* of the two stories may well be independent,
but one should not base too much on 2:17. Repetition of message and reiterated astonishment are part of the marvels that surround the birth. Luke is not writing a logical disquisi-
tion but creating an atmosphere.

[65] In the JBap story there was also "fear upon all the neighbors" (1:65). The motif of
fear in the Jesus half of the birth diptych (Table XIV) occurs in the shepherds' reaction to
the angel (2:9).

[66] Astonishment is not necessarily an unworthy or imperceptive reaction, although it can
reflect a failure to understand (9:43–45).

[67] This comparison of the reaction of Mary with the reaction in the parable is probably
deliberate on Luke's part; for the one ministry scene in which Mary appears occurs four
verses later (8:19–21), and there Jesus says, "My mother and my brothers are those who
hear the word of God and do it."

symbolic intermediaries and have no major importance in themselves. It is incorrect to see in them an early apostolic group going forth from Bethlehem to proclaim the Gospel.[68] Rather their comprehension stops at the point where they make the connection between what they have heard and what they have seen (20). They "made known" to those at Bethlehem (17) what the Lord had "made known" to them (15); they return to their flocks, not making it known further, but glorifying and praising God who accomplished such great things. They are the forerunners, not of the apostles, but of future believers who will glorify God for what they have heard and will praise God for what they have seen.[69] There has now begun a praise and glory of God on earth echoing the praise and glory of God by the heavenly host (vs. 20 echoing the language of vss. 13–14).

Luke's instinct to get the shepherds off the scene as soon as they have begun this praise is exactly the same as Matthew's instinct to have the magi depart (2:12) once they have paid Jesus homage.[70] Both evangelists know that when the public ministry of Jesus begins, there is no surrounding chorus of adoring believers, treasuring the memories of the marvels that accompanied his birth at Bethlehem—this memory is completely absent from the records of the ministry. And so the impressed believers of the infancy story are said to have departed; the apostolic task of proclaiming the faith is to begin not now but later.

Only one figure constitutes a bridge from the infancy narrative to the ministry of Jesus, and that is Mary his mother. She is the only adult mentioned in these two chapters who reappears in the body of the Gospel.[71] And so, in vs. 19, by contrast, Luke separates her from the other hearers to report that "she kept with concern all these events, interpreting them in her heart." This verse and its parallel in 2:51 ("His mother kept with concern all these events in her heart")[72] have often been used, particularly by Roman Catholic exegetes, as support for the thesis

68 On this point I agree with Rengstorf, "Weihnachtserzählung," 26, versus Legrand, "L'évangile," 183. There is a proclamation in Luke 2, but it is by the angel of the Lord. The shepherds portray one of the *reactions* to the proclamation: acceptance and homage.

69 It is standard procedure in Luke/Acts for bystanders to glorify and praise God for what they have seen and heard: Luke 7:16; 13:13; 17:15; 18:45; 19:37 (which introduces the hymn parallel to the Gloria); Acts 2:47; 3:8–9; 4:21; 11:18; 21:20.

70 Luke accomplished the departure of the shepherds even more effectively than Matthew accomplished the departure of the magi; for while the magi reappeared in subsequent Christian legends with names and careers (§ 6D above), there was no comparable reappearance of the shepherds.

71 A memory of Joseph's name is preserved in three of the Gospels (not Mark), but Joseph himself never figures during the ministry, presumably because he was dead (Appendix IV A on Mark).

72 One must keep in mind the third parallel, occurring in the aftermath of the naming of JBap: "All who heard stored (them) in their hearts" (a literal translation of 1:66). The statements in 1:66 and 2:19 are part of the diptych pattern and belong to the first level of Lucan composition (Table XIV). But 2:51 was written by Luke in imitation of 2:19 (even as 2:52 was written in imitation of 2:40), as part of a new conclusion of the infancy narrative made necessary by the addition of the story of the boy Jesus in the Temple (§ 16A below).

that the Lucan infancy narrative constitutes eyewitness history, i.e., constitutes the memoirs of all these events that Mary kept in her heart.[73] More subtly, Laurentin thinks that the interpretation by Mary is reflected in the midrashic process whereby OT themes are skillfully interwoven in the description of events.[74] In a certain sense, then, Laurentin puts more emphasis on Mary the theologian than on Mary the composer of memoirs. I think all such suggestions miss the point, since this verse tells us nothing about how the infancy narrative was composed, but only how Mary constituted a bridge between the infancy and the ministry. Precisely because Luke portrays her in the ministry as a believer and a disciple (§§ 11D and 12B above), he must set her on the way to penetrating the deepest meaning of the events that have happened and of the sign that has been given.

The key to the verse lies in her *interpreting* all these *events* or words (NOTE on 2:15) which she has kept with concern in her heart. As Van Unnik has pointed out (NOTE on 2:19), the verb is associated with the divinely given interpretation of obscure events, even as "keep with concern" involves penetrating unclear revelation. Let us look at a few parallels for the Lucan description. In Gen 37:11, after the mysterious dream of Joseph in which a revelation is cloaked in celestial symbols representing the members of his family, we are told, "His father kept with concern this event," obviously puzzling over its meaning. In the LXX of Dan 4:28, after Daniel's interpretation of the obscure dream of the tree, we are told, "Nebuchadnezzar kept with concern these words in his heart" (see also 7:28). In the *Testament of Levi* 6:2, after an angel had opened the gates of heaven and showed Levi the holy temple and the throne of glory of the Most High, and after Levi had been guided to find a mysterious shield, Levi is said to have kept with concern these events in his heart. If these examples indicate the use of the key Lucan verbs in an apocalyptic context, Luke's narrative is not totally devoid of an apocalyptic strain:[75] an angelic messenger has proclaimed "this day" of salvation (11), a sign has been given (12), and the heavenly hosts have appeared (13). These are puzzling events that Mary must keep in her heart. She will interpret them correctly after the ministry when Jesus has been enthroned in heaven. Then, as part of the community that was gathered to receive the gift of

---

[73] Older Protestant critics also accepted Mary as the guarantor of tradition, e.g., B. Meyer, Bornhäuser, and Zahn. But, as Räisänen, *Mutter*, 124, points out, this approach was abandoned in favor of positing a diversity of sources behind the Lucan narrative. I would abandon it further by arguing that the basic narrative or first level was composed by Luke himself, drawing upon items of information and pre-Lucan motifs. Only on the second level of composition, when Luke added the canticles and the story of the boy Jesus in the Temple, would I speak of sources in the proper sense of the word.

[74] Laurentin, *Structure*, 97,100,116–19.

[75] A Roman Catholic, F. Neirynck, *Noël*, 51–57, argues strongly for the apocalyptic background, against any historicizing tendency of Luke 2:19. See also NTA 4 (1960), #669.

Jesus' Spirit at Pentecost (Acts 1:14),[76] she will hear the glorified Jesus proclaimed as "Lord, Messiah, Savior" (Acts 2:36; 5:31) and will come to know fully what the angel meant when he told the shepherds: "To you this day there is born in the city of David a Savior who is Messiah and Lord."

Another background for Luke 2:19 is the biblical wisdom or sapiential tradition.[77] This involves not only interpreting the puzzling words of the past but also observing their message in one's life. The scribe of Sirach 39:1–3 kept with concern the parables, prophecies, and mysterious sayings of the past, reflecting on them in order to understand them and live by them (see also 50:28). In Prov 3:1 the wise man teaches his son and urges him, "Hold in your heart my words." The sage of Ps 119:11 says to God, "I have hidden your sayings in my heart so that I may not sin." If this attitude enters into Mary's quest for the meaning of the events surrounding Jesus' birth, she is once again anticipating the attitude that will be her encomium during the ministry. Placed by Luke in the previous verse among those who hear the events, she is now showing herself (2:20) among those fortunate praised by Jesus "who hear the word of God and keep it" (11:28).

E. *The Circumcision and the Naming (2:21)*

When the shepherds (and presumably the others in the audience) have departed, the circumcision is performed and the child is named. In the JBap story this constitutes the central section of the birth scene, while in the Jesus story it is an attached notice. The parents are prominent in the naming of JBap; they are not even mentioned in the naming of Jesus.[78] The verse describing the circumcision/naming is highly Lucan in construction (see NOTES), and some who posit a complete pre-Lucan narrative behind

---

[76] In Acts 1:12–14, Luke gathers three groups who constitute a bridge between what he has narrated in the Gospel and what he will narrate in Acts: (a) the Twelve, who provide coverage for the general ministry from the baptism to the resurrection, as stressed in Acts 1:22; (b) the women, who provide coverage for the death and the tomb, when the Twelve were absent, as mentioned in Luke 23:49,55; 24:1–2; (c) Mary, who provides coverage for the infancy narrative. She is mentioned with Jesus' "brothers," for it was in their company that she last appeared in the Gospel (8:19–21).

[77] Serra, "Motivi," 249ff., stresses together the sapiential background and the legal background of keeping words in order to understand and observe them. (He cites passages from Deuteronomy, e.g., 4:39–40; 7:17–21; but they are phrased in a Greek vocabulary different from that used in Luke 2:19, and so one would have to suppose a direct influence of the Hebrew.) The two different approaches, the apocalyptic and the sapiential/legal, are less puzzling if we realize that in post-exilic Judaism there was a strong sapiential strain in apocalyptic. See G. von Rad, *Old Testament Theology* (New York: Harper & Row, 1965), II, 306–8.

[78] This is particularly curious since in 1:31 Mary was told to name the child, and we would have expected Luke to tell us that it was she who did the naming.

2:1-20 think of 2:21 as a Lucan addition. However, the threefold use of the expression "the time came" in 2:6 ("for her to give birth"), in 2:21 ("to circumcise the child"), and in 2:22 ("for their purification") indicates a carefully planned schema by the overall author, with the circumcision serving as a chronological intermediary (eighth day) between the birth and the purification/presentation (an unmentioned forty days after birth). Indeed, the circumcision/naming is so intermediary that it can be treated with either the birth scene or with the purification/presentation. My decision to treat it here has been determined by the parallelism with the JBap scene (Table XIV).

In discussing vs. 21, many scholars invoke the general theological import of circumcision and interpret Luke's verse in light of that theology.[79] For instance, since Jesus is the incarnate Son of God, one may be told that his circumcision called attention to his solidarity with the human race, and Rom 8:3 may be cited: "God having sent His own Son in the likeness of sinful flesh." However, there is no evidence that Luke had a theology of incarnation or pre-existence; rather for Luke (1:35) divine sonship seems to have been brought about through the virginal conception. Thus, Luke has no need of the circumcision to establish a pre-existent deity's solidarity with the human race. Jesus was conceived and born, and that is solidarity enough. In addition to the suggestion that circumcision established Jesus' solidarity with the human race, there is the oft-made suggestion that it established his solidarity with Judaism.[80] In support of this Paul is once more cited: "He was born under the Law" (Gal 4:4); or else the passage in Hebr 2:17: "He had to be made like his brethren in every respect." Yet, it is only in relation to the purification/presentation that Luke mentions the Law (2:22-24). He gives no legal context to the circumcision and indeed subordinates it totally to the naming of Jesus. Thus, while the

---

[79] One might have expected commentators to discuss the theology of circumcision earlier, in relation to JBap, where circumcision plays a greater role; but JBap does not lend himself to the same theological reflections as does the incarnate Son of God. In other words, much of the theological reflection on this scene comes from general christology rather than from what Luke actually says. Sometimes the theological reflection draws upon a positive attitude toward circumcision, e.g., as an everlasting covenant in the flesh (Gen 17:13). More often the attitude is negative, in terms of a Christian replacement of circumcision, as in Col 2:11: "In him also you were circumcised and with a circumcision made without hands, by putting off the body of the flesh in the circumcision of Christ."

[80] See J. Jervell, NTA 18 (1973-74), #897. Winter, "Proto-Source," 185, associates the story of the circumcision with James the Just, the "brother" of Jesus, a Christian leader who was traditionally a firm observer of Jewish practices. On the one hand, this association is not provable in terms of positing a historical family tradition behind vs. 21, and Luke would really need no such tradition since it would have been highly unusual if Jesus were not circumcised. On the other hand, we have seen that some of the items about the priesthood of JBap's father and the four canticles may have come to Luke ultimately from the tradition of the Jerusalem community of Jewish-Christian Anawim. James was the first known local leader of that community.

circumcision may lend itself to later theological reflection,[81] we have no evidence that Luke shared these reflections.

Even if one decides to follow Luke's own indication and concentrate on the naming, it is surprising that he does not stop to interpret the name "Jesus," as does Matt 1:21: "You will call his name Jesus, for he will save his people from their sins." There is little doubt that Luke was aware of the popular etymology of "Jesus" as "Yahweh saves"; and some scholars see hints of that either in the scene of the birth (2:11: "To you this day there is born in the city of David *a Savior*") or in the following scene (2:30–31: "For my eyes have seen this *salvation* that you made ready in the sight of all peoples"). These are subtle allusions at most, and certainly not the main Lucan emphasis. What Luke emphasizes is that calling the boy "Jesus" fulfilled the angel's command in 1:31—it was "the name by which the angel called him before he was conceived in the womb." (This is the same emphasis that Luke had [even more dramatically] in the naming of JBap.) When Mary heard that command, enveloped in the heart of an annunciation, she responded, "Let it happen to me according to your word" (1:38). Jesus' parents are obedient to God's word, and the next scene will show that they are also obedient to the Law of the Lord.

---

[81] Still another suggestion is to see the circumcision as an anticipation of the passion, since Jesus sheds his blood for the first time.

SECTIONAL BIBLIOGRAPHY (§ 14)
(LUKE 2:1–21)

(See also the Bibliography for Appendix VII on the Census under Quirinius.)

Baily, M., "The Crib and Exegesis of Luke 2,1–20," IER 100 (1963), 358–76.
——— "The Shepherds and the Sign of a Child in a Manger," ITQ 31 (1964), 1–23.
Benoit, P., " 'Non erat eis locus in diversorio' (Lc 2,7)," in *Mélanges Béda Rigaux*, ed. A. Descamps and A. de Halleux (Gembloux: Duculot, 1970), 173–86.
Derrett, J. D. M., "The Manger: Ritual Law and Soteriology," *Theology* 74 (1971), 566–71.
Feuillet, A., "Les hommes de bonne volonté ou les hommes que Dieu aime. Note sur la traduction de Luc 2,14b," *Bulletin de l'Association Guillaume Budé* 4 (1974), 91–92.
Fitzmyer, J. A., " 'Peace upon Earth among Men of His Good Will' (Lk 2:14)," TS 19 (1958), 225–27. Reprinted in his *Essays on the Semitic Background of the New Testament* (Missoula, Mont.: Scholars' Press, 1974), 101–4.

Flusser, D., "Sanktus und Gloria," in *Abraham unser Vater,* ed. O. Betz *et al.* (Festschrift Otto Michel; Leiden: Brill, 1963), 129–52.

Frey, J.-B., "La signification du terme *prōtotokos* d'après une inscription juive," *Biblica* 11 (1930), 373–90.

Galbiati, E., "La circoncisione di Gesù (Luca 2,21)," BibOr 8 (1966), 37–45.

George, A., " 'Il vous est né aujourd'hui un Sauveur' (Lc 2)," *Assemblées du Seigneur* 10 (2nd series, 1970), 50–67.

Giblin, C. H., "Reflections on the Sign of the Manger," CBQ 29 (1967), 87–101.

Legrand, L., "L'évangile aux bergers. Essai sur le genre littéraire de Luc II,8–20," RB 75 (1968), 161–87.

Meyer, B., " 'But Mary Kept All These Things . . .' (Lk 2,19.51)," CBQ 26 (1964), 31–49.

Miguens, M., " 'In una mangatoia, perchè non c'era posto . . . ,' " BibOr 2 (1960), 193–98.

Nestle, E., "Die Hirten von Bethlehem," ZNW 7 (1906), 257–59.

——— "Die Schatzung in Lukas 2 und Psalm 87(86),6," ZNW 11 (1910), 87.

Pax, E., " 'Denn sie fanden keinen Platz in der Herberge.' Jüdisches und frühchristliches Herbergswesen," BibLeb 6 (1965), 285–98.

Rengstorf, K. H., "Die Weihnachtserzählung des Evangelisten Lukas," in *Stat crux dum volvitur orbis,* ed. G. Hoffmann and K. H. Rengstorf (Festschrift H. Lilje; Berlin: Lutherisches Verlagshaus, 1959), 15–30.

Schmithals, W., "Die Weihnachtsgeschichte Lukas 2,1–20," in *Festschrift für Ernst Fuchs,* ed. G. Ebeling *et al.* (Tübingen: Mohr, 1973), 281–97.

Schwarz, G., "Der Lobgesang der Engel (Lukas 2,14)," BZ 15 (1971), 260–64.

Serra, A., "Motivi sapienziali in Lc 2,19.51," *Marianum* 31 (1969), 248–59.

Stoll, R. F., " 'Her Firstborn Son,' " AER 108 (1943), 1–13.

van Unnik, W. C., "Die rechte Bedeutung des Wortes treffen, Lukas 2,19," in *Verbum—Essays on Some Aspects of the Religious Function of Words,* ed. T. P. van Baaren *et al.* (Festschrift H. W. Obbink; Utrecht: Kemink, 1964), 129–47.

Vogt, E., " 'Pax hominibus bonae voluntatis' (Lc 2,14)," *Biblica* 34 (1953), 427–29. English trans. in *The Scrolls and the New Testament,* ed. K. Stendahl (New York: Harper, 1957), 114–17.

Westermann, C., "Alttestamentliche Elemente in Lukas 2,1–20," in *Tradition und Glaube,* ed. G. Jeremias *et al.* (Festschrift K. G. Kuhn; Göttingen: Vandenhoeck, 1971), 317–27.

VII. THE PRESENTATION; SIMEON AND ANNA PROPHESY ABOUT JESUS (§ 15)

Translation of Luke 2:22–40

2 [22] Now when the time came for their purification according to the Law of Moses, the parents brought Jesus up to Jerusalem to present him to the Lord—[23] as it is written in the Law of the Lord: "Every male child who opens the womb will be considered consecrated to the Lord"—[24] and to offer a sacrifice, according to what is dictated in the Law of the Lord: "A pair of doves or two young pigeons."

[25] And behold, it happened that in Jerusalem there was a man by the name of Simeon who was upright and devout, waiting for the consolation of Israel. The Holy Spirit was upon him; [26] and it had been disclosed to him by this Holy Spirit that he would not see death before he had seen the Lord's Messiah. [27] And so, led by the Spirit, Simeon came into the Temple court. When the parents brought in Jesus to perform for him what was customary according to the Law, [28] Simeon embraced the child in his arms and blessed God, saying:

> [29a] "Mighty Master, now you may let your servant depart
> [29b] in peace, since you have kept your word.
> [30] For my eyes have seen this salvation
> [31] that you made ready in the sight of all the peoples:
> [32a] a light to be a revelation to the Gentiles
> [32b] and to be a glory for your people Israel."

[33] The father and mother were astonished at these things which were said about the child. [34] Simeon blessed them and said to Mary the mother:

> [34c] "Behold, he is set for the fall and rise of many in Israel
> [34d] and for a sign to be contradicted—
> [35a] indeed, a sword will pass through your own soul—
> [35b] so that the inmost thoughts of many may be revealed."

[36] There was also a prophetess, Anna daughter of Phanuel, of the tribe of Asher, who was well on in years; for she had married as a young girl and lived with her husband seven years, [37] and then by herself as a widow for eighty-four years. She never left the Temple courts; day and night she worshiped God, fasting and praying. [38] Now at this very moment she too came on the scene and gave thanks to God; and she spoke about the child to all those waiting for the redemption of Jerusalem.

[39] Then, when they had finished all their duties according to the Law of the Lord, they returned to Galilee and their own city, Nazareth. [40] And the child grew up and became strong, filled with wisdom and favored by God.

Notes

2:22. *when the time came.* Literally, "when the days were fulfilled." Again this expression might be taken to mean that the allotted time for purification *was over;* but the similar pattern in 1:57; 2:6,21 (see Notes there) indicates Luke to mean that the designated time of uncleanness (or interval before purification) was over and that the time *had come* for purification. Birth, not conception, rendered a woman ritually impure; and so a virginal conception did not spare Mary the necessity of being purified.

their purification. This is the best attested reading; and it means the purification of both parents, even though there is no Jewish tradition for the purification of the father. The alternative readings, such as "her purification" or "his [Jesus'] purification," found in the Codex Bezae, Greek cursive ms. 76, OS[sin], and some OL witnesses, represent scribal attempts at improvement. Origen's interpretation that the "their" referred to Mary and Jesus, and the modern suggestion that the "their" is subjective ("their purifying Jesus") are implausible, since the child was to be presented or consecrated to the Lord, but not purified.

the parents . . . Jesus. Luke has simply "they . . . him"; I have anticipated the identification from vs. 27.

brought . . . up. Of the twenty-four times that *anagein/anagesthai* occur in the NT, twenty-one are in Luke/Acts. And so it is questionable whether the current instance is general, or is specific, reflecting the technical OT concept of going *up* to Jerusalem or to the Temple (see Note on 2:4).

Jerusalem. This place name has two orthographies in the NT: *Hierousalēm* which is virtually a transliteration from the Hebrew, and *Hierosolyma* which is a more proper Greek form. The Gospel of Luke shows a marked preference for

Hierousalēm (twenty-six times) over *Hierosolyma* (four times); but in Acts the usage is more evenly distributed (thirty-nine to twenty-five times, respectively). Yet the Lucan pattern is not so clear that the appearance in the Gospel of the rarer *Hierosolyma*, which is the form in this verse, indicates a special source. Dubious is the thesis of J. Kudasiewicz, NTA 19 (1975), ¥120, that Luke uses *Hierosolyma* as a geographical designation, but *Hierousalēm* as an eschatological and ecclesiological term. Luke 13:22 and 19:28 (*Hierosolyma*) are certainly meant to continue 9:51 (*Hierousalēm*), and so the variation of orthography is hardly deliberate.

23. *written . . . "Every.* Literally, "written that 'Every.'" P. Winter raises the possibility that here, as in 1:25 (see NOTE there) and 1:61, the *hoti* is not recitative ("that") but causal ("because").

in the Law of the Lord. Here "law" is anarthrous, while in four other instances (2:22,24,27,39) the article is used. Even though vs. 23 is parenthetical, this is too insignificant a difference to cause us to posit another hand here.

Every male child who opens the womb. The Lucan citation is a mélange of the LXX of Exod 13:2,12,15 and perhaps Num 8:15–16. The phrase means no more than firstborn. Roman Catholic authors have sometimes pointed this out defensively in a desire to show that Luke does not contradict the later tradition and Church doctrine that the birth of Jesus left Mary physically a virgin, with hymen intact and hence without the womb opened (Appendix IV, footnote 2). It is most unlikely, however, that this question ever occurred to Luke; and it is incredible that, if he thought the birth (as distinct from the conception) were virginal in this way, he would have used such an expression (see J. Galot, NRT 82 [1960], 453). Moreover, if the birth were conceived as miraculous, no purification should have been needed.

considered consecrated. Literally, "called holy," the same Greek expression as in 1:35 which Luke intends to echo.

24. *"A pair of doves or two young pigeons."* The phrase is from the LXX of Lev 12:8. These were the only two birds which the Law deemed eligible for sacrifice; and pigeons were sold in the Temple court for that purpose (Mark 11:15; John 2:14). Rock pigeons are a variety found in Palestine throughout the year, as distinct from seasonal species of pigeons. Doves (turtledoves) are a smaller variety of pigeon.

25. *And behold, it happened.* The *kai idou* pattern (NOTE on 1:20) plus the *egeneto* pattern (NOTE on 1:9).

Jerusalem. Here, unlike 22 (see NOTE there), the orthography is *Hierousalēm*.

a man by the name of Simeon. The style of the Greek indicates that an unknown person is being introduced to the reader; and this makes implausible the attempt to identify him as Simeon, the famous son of Hillel and father of Rabban Gamaliel the Elder, *pace* the imaginative attempt to defend that thesis by A. Cutler, JBR 34 (1966), 29–35. The second-century *Protevangelium of James* 24:3–4 turns Simeon into a high priest, the successor of Zechariah, the father of JBap—see NOTE on 1:5 above. (Later, in the *Acts of Pilate* 17:1 it is reported that Jesus raised Simeon's two sons from the dead.) Despite the close relationship that Simeon has to Levi in the patriarchal stories (Gen 29:33–34), there is nothing in Luke's account to favor the idea that Simeon was a levitical priest, although Gentile Christians may have deduced that from his blessing the parents in vs. 34. Luke's description of how Simeon happened to be in Jerusalem and the Temple court contrasts with the description of Zechariah whose priestly duty brought him to the Temple (1:8–9). The reference in the Nunc Dimittis to Simeon's willingness to die has led to the plausible supposition that Luke thinks of him as an old man. The *Gospel of Pseudo-Matthew* 15:2 puts his age at 112; see NOTE on 37 pertaining to Anna's age.

upright. Dikaios is the same adjective used of the parents of JBap in 1:6 and of Joseph in Matt 1:19; it is variously translated as "righteous, pious, holy, saintly." The characters of the infancy narrative who do not otherwise feature in the Gospel story are portrayed as possessing the piety of Israel.

devout. This adjective, *eulabēs,* the NT usage of which is confined to Luke/Acts, denotes a carefulness about religious duties.

waiting for the consolation of Israel. Luke 23:50–51 describes Joseph of Arimathea as "good and upright . . . waiting for the kingdom of God," so that Simeon is his pre-ministry equivalent. Another parallel for this description of Simeon is found in Luke's characterization of the circle to whom Anna proclaimed her message: "All those waiting for the redemption of Jerusalem" (2:38).

The Holy Spirit. No article is used and the adjective is separated from the noun by the verb. We have seen an anarthrous construction before, both in Matt 1:18,20 and in Luke 1:15,35,41,67 (see NOTES); and so I do not agree with Plummer, *Luke,* 66, who translates: "An influence which was holy was upon him." The use with the article in the next verse shows that Luke is thinking of the Holy Spirit, even though we cannot be certain whether Luke thinks of the pre-Christian gift of the Spirit as somewhat different from the post-resurrectional gift.

26. *disclosed.* The verb *chrēmatizein* involves a divine oracle or response, e.g., in Acts 10:22 it is used for the direction of Cornelius by an angel.

by this Holy Spirit. This is the first instance of the use of the definite article in reference to the Holy Spirit in the infancy narrative. See NOTE on 1:15.

not see death before he had seen the Lord's Messiah. Luke's play on the theme of sight prepares for the Nunc Dimittis: "For my eyes have seen this salvation" (2:30). The expression "the Lord's Messiah" appears in *Psalms of Solomon* 18:8, even as the parallel to Luke's "Messiah and Lord" (2:11; see NOTE there) appeared in *PsSol* 17:36.

before. The classical construction of *prin an* with a subjunctive occurs only here in the NT (an optative is employed in Acts 25:16); the normal pattern is accusative and infinitive (BDF 395).

27. *led by the Spirit.* Literally, "in the Spirit"; the article is used. Luke presents the encounter as one prepared for by God. The thesis that Simeon came to the Temple because he had been told about the child by the shepherds of 2:8 (who cared for the Temple sheep) is not only completely fanciful; it misses Luke's intention.

the Temple court. Luke knows the difference between *hieron* (the Temple in

general, or the Temple court), which he uses here, and the *naos* (Temple sanctuary, entered only by priests), which he used in 1:9,21–22. Since Simeon encounters Mary, he is either in the court of the Gentiles or the court of the
women. Later Christians, imagining him to be a priest, often depicted him and
the parents in the Temple sanctuary.

Jesus. Literally, "the child," a designation which I have employed in the next
verse. See NOTE on 2:17.

to perform for him. In Greek "for him" modifies "what was customary according to the Law."

28. *embraced.* Literally, "received" the child into his bent arms (*ankalē*). On
the basis of this verse Simeon became known in Christian hagiography as
Theodochos, the "God-Receiver."

29. *Mighty Master.* The term *despotēs* is not frequently used in the NT for
God, but was employed by the LXX to translate *'ādôn*. Winter, "On the Margin," 106–7, argues that it came to Luke from his Semitic source. The term appears again in Acts 4:24 in the prayer of the Jerusalem Christian community, a
community that may have been the ultimate source of this hymn as well.

you may let. The verb is indicative and declarative; it is not an imperative or
a precative (entreaty), as the traditional English translation "Let" might imply.
BAA, 113–14, suggests an underlying Aramaic participle which perhaps should
have been read as an imperative.

servant. Doulos covers both "slave" and "servant." The use of *despotēs* and
the absoluteness of God's control over death make "slave" appropriate, for the
idea is that of a master setting a slave free to depart (from life). However, the
term "slave" in American English has overtones of the black slavery which was
quite different from slavery in the Greco-Roman world. Since Mary was a *doulē*
in the Magnificat (1:48) and I chose to render that as "handmaid" rather than
"slave," I have preferred "servant" here. Notice the common vocabulary in the
canticles.

depart. Apolyein, "release, deliver," is a euphemism for "die," as in the LXX
of Num 20:29, perhaps in the sense of being delivered from the troubles of life
(Tobit 3:6,13). As part of the theory that the Nunc Dimittis is a hymn of the
pre-Christian Jerusalem liturgy, it has been implausibly suggested that the idea
is "depart from the liturgy." See D. R. Jones, "Background," 40.

30. *my eyes have seen.* This is not to be taken literally as some have done
who maintain that Simeon was blind, even as Zechariah was mute, and that the
healing of each led to the respective canticle.

salvation. Three of the four NT uses are Lucan. In 3:6 and Acts 28:28 the
reference is to "the salvation of God."

31. *made ready.* The verb *hetoimazein* was used of JBap in 1:17,76 (and will
be used in 3:4).

in the sight of all the peoples. In Isa 52:10, which the Lucan canticle draws
upon, the phrase is "all nations," i.e., the Gentiles. Why does the Nunc Dimittis
prefer "peoples"? This plural appears elsewhere in the NT only in Acts
4:25–27 where it refers to (the tribes of) Israel and is contrasted with "nations" (Gentiles). G. D. Kilpatrick, JTS 16 (1965), 127, has argued for the
same meaning here; and he suggests that the next line in the canticle means "a

light for the Gentiles to see," so that the whole canticle refers to Israel. Whatever the term may have meant in the pre-Lucan stage of the canticle's history, it is more plausible that by "peoples" in 31 Luke meant to include the two groups mentioned in the next verse, i.e., the Gentiles (nations) and the people of Israel—two groups that in Luke's view constitute God's people. See COMMENT.

32. *a light to be a revelation.* Literally, "a light unto revelation." The noun "light," which is in apposition to "salvation," is the object of the verb "made ready." It is more difficult to determine the relations of the nouns "light" and "revelation" to the noun "glory" in the next line. "Glory" could stand in apposition to "light" (the terms are in parallelism in Isa 60:1, the type of Isaian passage echoed in the Nunc Dimittis) and thus serve as another object of "made ready." However, it is more likely that "glory" is in apposition to "revelation"; thus, a light both for revelation and for glory. This interpretation supports the position taken in the previous NOTE: revelation for the Gentiles and glory for Israel are two equal aspects of the one salvation and light that God has made ready. Neither is subordinate to the other.

to the Gentiles. The noun "revelation" is followed by a genitive which may be translated "by" (i.e., the Gentiles reveal the light), or "of" (the Gentiles are revealed under the light), or "to, for" (the Gentiles receive revelation from the light). The last seems the most appropriate here, and in the parallel genitive phrase in the next line: "a glory for your people Israel." The lack of articles with these nouns governing genitives is, as BDF 259[3] points out, a mark of the strong Semitic coloring of the Lucan canticles.

33. *The father.* Evidently this designation seemed to subsequent scribes to contradict the virginal conception, whence the substitution "Joseph," especially in the versions.

were astonished. The Greek is typically Lucan, and the same reaction was described in 1:21,63; 2:18. Some have found here an indication that the present story was originally independent of 1:26–38 and 2:1–20 where the parents have already heard of the child's marvelous future (see Creed, *Luke,* 37). But an astonished reaction to divine revelation is too stereotyped to prove anything. Even less likely is the suggestion of Bornhäuser, *Kindheitsgeschichte,* 118, that fear of Herod is involved: the Lucan story should not be interpreted in light of information from Matt 2.

34. *Simeon blessed them.* This action has contributed to the theory that Simeon was a priest (see NOTE on vs. 25).

is set. This verb can mean "to be placed, to lie"; but the imagery is not drawn from the position of the child in the arms of Simeon. It is connected with the imagery of building stones.

rise. Normally *anastasis* means resurrection; here it is more inclusive, being opposed to destruction. The double noun combination, "fall and rise" (like "day and night" and "fasting and praying" in vs. 37), is a Lucan characteristic.

of many in Israel. Jesus will affect the whole nation. As in Mark 14:24, "many" is not by way of exception to "all," but is used to stress the wide-ranging effects (BAG, 694, I 2b).

to be contradicted. A present participle, *antilegomenos,* with a future meaning (BDF 339²ᵇ). Luke has a predilection for compounds with *anti*. See Luke 21:15 which offers a general parallel to Mark 13:11 and Matt 10:19–20 but differs from them in having three *anti* compounds. Six out of ten NT uses of *antilegein* are Lucan.

35. *indeed*. The Greek is *kai sou de*, a construction which Luke uses in 1:76 (the Lucan addition to the Benedictus). I have translated the *sou* as "your own," while the "indeed" renders *kai . . . de*. I interpret this as a specification of the idea in vs. 34: a certain newness is involved, but the thought is progressing in the same direction. Mary too will be affected by the element of contradiction (see Winandy, "La prophétie," 324–25). Other translations of *kai . . . de* are possible, and they would give a different emphasis: "and . . . also," "but . . . also," "and . . . even." The *de* is missing in Vaticanus and is not translated in some of the versions.

a sword. There is some Syriac support for "spear," probably under the influence of John 19:34, since John 19:25–27 was thought of as the fulfillment of this prediction. Although the noun is anarthrous, Winandy, "La prophétie," 326, argues for the possibility of translating with a definite article, which would bind 35a closely to 34d.

pass through. The verb *dierchesthai* is used forty-two times in the NT, about three-quarters of them in Luke/Acts. In the Greek OT it rarely describes the action of a weapon, whence the importance of Ezek 14:17 (see COMMENT).

soul. The *psychē*, the locus of emotions and affections, the heart.

so that. Some give *hopōs an* a consecutive implication ("with the result that"), but it is more normally final ("in order that"). The finality may be to fulfill the Scriptures (see Matt 13:13–15). This subordinate clause is governed by the verb "is set" in 34c. Whether it is also governed by the verb "will pass through" in 35a depends on a decision about the parenthetical nature of 35a. There is a hypothetical element in the *an;* the inmost thoughts will be revealed, but the precise time is not specified.

inmost thoughts. Zahn, Knabenbauer, Lagrange, Plummer, and Creed are among the scholars who take these as both good and bad thoughts; but all thirteen uses of *dialogismos* in the NT are pejorative: bad thoughts, vain thoughts, doubting thoughts. The five other uses in Luke refer to thoughts hostile to Jesus or questioning him. The *dialogismoi* of 35b constitute a continuation of the *semeion antilegomenon*, the "sign to be contradicted," of 34d, for the contradiction is expressed in hostile thoughts.

36. *a prophetess*. Outside of the wicked Jezebel "who calls herself a prophetess" (Rev 2:20), Anna is the only woman in the NT thus entitled, although there are several references to women who prophesied in the Christian community (Acts 2:17; 21:9; I Cor 11:5). In the OT the women called prophetesses included Miriam, Deborah, Huldah, and Isaiah's wife (Exod 15:20; Judg 4:4; II Kgs 22:14; Isa 8:3).

of the tribe of Asher. This genealogical indication is puzzling, for Israelites in Jerusalem were principally of the tribe of Judah ("Jews") or of Benjamin or of Levi; and genealogical memories are normally of those tribes (see § 3, B1 above). As Jeremias, *Jerusalem*, 278, observes, "Naturally there are only very isolated claims to belong to one of the ten or nine-and-a-half 'lost' tribes of Israel." Previous women named Anna in the Bible belonged to those northern tribes: the mother of Samuel was an Ephraimite (I Sam 1:1–2), and the wife of Tobit was of the tribe of Naphtali (Tobit 1:1,9), a Galilean neighbor of Asher, associated with it in Gen 49:20–21 and Deut 33:23–24. The mention by Luke of Anna's lineage has led to the suggestion that she was of a prestigious family, conscious of its ancestors. Yet Asher was not a significant tribe; indeed, it was the last of the sons of Jacob/Israel listed in the blessing of Moses upon the tribes (Deut 33:24). An attempt has been made to explain both Anna's tribe (Asher means "fortunate") and her father (Phanuel means the "face of God") as pure symbolism. It is interesting that Leah's exclamation upon giving birth to Asher, "Fortunate am I, for all women call me fortunate" (Gen 30:13), served as Lucan background in 1:42b,48b.

well on in years. This is a more emphatic form of the expression used to describe Zechariah and Elizabeth in 1:7 (see NOTE there).

she had married as a young girl. Literally, "from her virginity." Presumably she would have been a maiden of about twelve when she married.

37. *and then by herself.* This translation reads the *autē* as an intensive pronoun (*autós*), and not simply meant as a personal pronoun, despite frequent Lucan usage of the latter (ZBG 199).

as a widow for eighty-four years. Literally, "a widow until eighty-four years." The ms. tradition for "about" (*hōs*) instead of "until" (*heōs*) is poor. Are the eighty-four years the length of her widowhood or her total age? If the former, the twelve years (approximate) of her virginity and the seven years of her marriage must be added to give a lifespan of about 103 years. (M. P. John, BibTrans 26 [1975], 247, argues that Luke was precisely trying to call attention to the great length of Anna's widowhood.) The OS[sin] supports an application of the eighty-four years to widowhood, since it allots Anna only seven *days* of marriage; and Judith was a widow who lived to the age of 105 (Judith 16:22–23).

never left the Temple courts. Once again, *hieron* not *naos* (NOTE on vs. 27).

day and night. The idiom is literally "night and day" (also Acts 26:7), but one cannot be certain that it reflects Jewish reckoning whereby the day began at sunset. For the double noun, see NOTE on "rise" in 34.

worshiped. A verb popular in Luke/Acts, *latreuein* may be meant to cover her participation in the hours of sacrifice and in the observance of the weekly fasts.

38. *at this very moment.* Literally, "at the same hour," an expression that occurs nine times in Luke/Acts. BAA, 78–81, regards it as a proof for translation from Aramaic, but MGNTG, IV, 53, disagrees. This verse is marked by typically Lucan vocabulary ("came on the scene," "waiting for").

came on the scene. Of twenty-one NT usages of *ephistanai* (*ephistēmi*), eighteen are Lucan.

spoke. The tense is imperfect: "kept speaking."

waiting for the redemption of Jerusalem. A similar description was used of Simeon in 25: "waiting for the consolation of Israel"; and both refer to messianic deliverance. (Some textual witnesses read "Israel" here in imitation of 25.) Any attempt to interpret the words in purely nationalistic terms, e.g., political freedom of Jerusalem from the Romans, founders on the idealism of the Anawim and on Simeon's prayer for the Gentiles.

39. *they had finished.* The OS^sin specifies the subject as Joseph and Mary, which is almost certainly Luke's intention, even though the next "they" includes the child. The sense of fulfillment in *telein*, "finish," is continued by the use of *pleroun*, "fill, fulfill," in the next verse.

they returned. For Luke's use of verbs of departure to end scenes in the infancy narrative, see NOTE on 1:23.

their own city, Nazareth. Bethlehem was "his own city" for Joseph in 2:3.

40. *the child grew up and became strong.* Verbatim, the same was said of JBap in 1:80.

favored by God. Literally, "the favor of God was upon him."

COMMENT

The general structure of 2:1–40 was discussed in the previous section (§ 14A); and so here, after brief introductory remarks analyzing organization, we shall move directly to a discussion of the four subsections of the pericope.

A. *The Sequence and Internal Structure*

Although the presentation of a male child to the Lord and the purification of the child's mother from giving birth would constitute a normal Jewish sequence to circumcision, there are many reasons for wondering whether Luke has not used this sequence to juxtapose once separate infancy traditions in 2:1–40—separate traditions still discernible in the scenes 2:1–21 and 2:22–40. In discussing the diptych pattern (Table XIV above), we saw that the aftermath of the birth of Jesus differed in many features from the aftermath of the birth of JBap. The salient points of the two structures may be compared thus:

JBap	*Jesus*
Birth	Birth
	Proclamation of Destiny (Angels)
Circumcision and Naming	Circumcision and Naming
Proclamation of Destiny (Zechariah)	Proclamation of Destiny (Simeon)
Conclusion	Conclusion

Why is there a double proclamation of Jesus' greatness and future destiny, one by the angels to the shepherds, the other by Simeon (and Anna)? Why are the parents astonished at Simeon's predictions of the future of the child (2:33) when they have already been apprised of it by the angelic proclamation to the shepherds (2:17–18)?[1] How can Mary be astonished after the revelation given to her in 1:32–35? Why are Joseph and Mary called the parents of Jesus (2:27) and why is Joseph called the father (2:33), if Jesus was virginally conceived?[2] Was the Simeon story shaped in a pre-Lucan context which presupposed neither the annunciation of Gabriel to Mary nor the annunciation of the angel to the shepherds? Were there once three separate and independent narratives: an annunciation to Mary, an angelic pronouncement to shepherds, and Simeon's oracle to the parents—each containing a divine revelation about the identity and future of the child?

Although some of these questions may be easily answered, I have phrased them sharply so that the reader may understand why many scholars maintain that Luke has joined disparate material in ch. 2. But fairness requires that we pay just as much attention to the connected sequence in 2:1–40. I do not mean a connection based simply on the Jewish sequence of birth, circumcision, presentation, and purification; for, as we shall see, these provide no more than a loose frame and are not the substance of the narrative. I mean rather a deep connection in theology and christology. The angelic proclamation to the shepherds which follows the birth of Jesus announces the identity of the child in terms of the expectations of Israel (2:10–11); Simeon's Nunc Dimittis announces the destiny of the child "in sight of all the peoples," including the Gentiles. And so there is no real duplication between the two pronouncements, but rather a development.

We have already seen that the Lucan shepherd story functionally has much the same role as the Matthean magi story (see above, the end of § 14A), since both represent the intuition that the christological event, now centered in the conception and birth of Jesus, should be proclaimed abroad and should be met by belief and adoration. But the Matthean magi story has two elements missing in the Lucan shepherd story: (1) that the belief and adoration would be the response of the Gentiles, and that is precisely the element we find in the second scene of Luke 2 in the Nunc Dimittis; (2) that corresponding to the faith of the Gentiles (magi), there would be a rejection of the newborn king by some of the most potent forces in Israel (Herod, the chief priests, and the scribes of Matt 2:3–4); and once again that element appears in the second scene of Luke 2, for

1 See Note on 2:33.
2 See footnote 25 below.

Simeon's second oracle in 34–35 speaks of the fall of many in Israel and of a sign to be contradicted. Thus, no matter whence Luke drew his material, he has given us in the two scenes of 2:1–40 a narrative of the birth of Jesus and its aftermath that is very close theologically to the narrative of the birth and its aftermath in Matt 2:1–13. The factors that shaped two such very different birth stories and yet resulted in the same theological message[3] may no longer be recoverable with certainty, but we can scarcely think of a haphazard juxtaposition of unrelated material.

Below I shall stress that one of the leitmotifs of 2:22–40 is that both the Law and the prophets are fulfilled in Jesus. Here let me mention some OT passages from Malachi and Daniel that may have contributed to the present Lucan sequence.[4] The story of JBap, which featured prominently in ch. 1, promised that he would go before the Lord in the spirit and power of Elijah (1:17), indeed go before the Lord to prepare his ways (1:76). There is no doubt that such descriptions reflect Mal 3:1: "I send my messenger to prepare the way before me"—a passage that a later addition to Malachi (3:23–24=RSV 4:5–6) interpreted as a reference to Elijah. Now the Mal 3:1–2 passage goes on to promise: "The Lord whom you seek will suddenly come to His Temple. . . . Who can endure the day of His coming?" After the description of JBap in Luke 1, is it accidental that in Luke 2 the child Jesus who has been hailed as Lord (2:11) comes to the Temple to be recognized by Simeon who was "waiting for the consolation of Israel"?[5] And Simeon predicts in 2:34–35 that this coming of the Lord to the Temple is the beginning of his role as a sign of discrimination so that many will fall—or, in the words of Malachi, many will not endure the day of his coming.

Another biblical passage that may have influenced Luke's inclusion of the scene of Jesus at the Temple is Dan 9:21–24, which mentions the angel Gabriel and the seventy weeks of years. Above (§ 10, B1) I pointed out that this passage forms the background of Gabriel's appearance to Zechariah in 1:8–23, an appearance that marks the end of the seventy weeks of years. In Dan 9:24 we are told that when this comes, the Holy of Holies will be anointed. As I pointed out in footnote 27 of § 10, it is difficult to know whether the Holy of Holies or Most Holy means a thing, a place, or a person. Luke may have interpreted it to mean a person. The angel Gabriel told Mary that the miraculously conceived child would "be called holy" (1:35). Now this child is brought to the Temple because he is "considered consecrated [holy] to the Lord" (2:23). Is this the anoint-

---

[3] In § 14, C1, I suggested that one of the factors may have been pre-Lucan reflection on some of the biblical texts that also played a role in the Matthean final narrative.

[4] Helpful here is Galbiati, "La presentazione."

[5] The same sequence of having JBap making straight the way of the Lord and then of having Jesus come to the Temple may be found in John 1–2.

ing of the Most Holy foretold by Daniel for the end of the seventy weeks of years?[6]

Having considered the relationship of 2:22–40 to what precedes in Luke, let us turn now to the inner structure of the scene. It can be subdivided into four parts:

Vss. 22–24:   The setting wherein Joseph and Mary bring the child Jesus to the Temple at Jerusalem.

Vss. 25–35:   The greeting of the child by Simeon and his double oracle about the child's destiny.

Vss. 36–38:   The greeting of the child by the prophetess Anna.

Vss. 39–40:   The conclusion involving a return to Galilee and Nazareth, and a refrain on the child's growth.

But this simple division does not guarantee the internal unity of the parts. The purification and presentation mentioned in the setting play no prominent role in what follows.[7] The two citations in 23 and 24 which refer to the presentation and purification are from the Pentateuch, while the OT background for the Simeon and Anna story is taken from I Sam 1–2 and the figures of Eli and Hannah (Anna), the mother of Samuel. Within the Simeon section of the narrative there are two oracles (29–32 and 34–35), and many scholars have posited that one or the other of these oracles was added to the original story by Luke. Following my thesis of a second stage of Lucan composition in which the canticles were added (§ 9, B2; § 12, C1), I shall propose that the Nunc Dimittis (29–32) was added, and that originally 2:27 was connected directly to 2:34. The greeting by Anna seems to be a duplication of the greeting by Simeon, a fact tacitly recognized by the failure to include any words of Anna. Part of the reason for her presence was probably Luke's desire to have a balance between a man and a woman in the Temple story which began the infancy narrative (Zechariah and Elizabeth in 1:5–25) and a man and woman in the Temple story which closes the infancy narrative.[8] Finally, the conclusion has two unrelated verses, so unrelated that 40 is sometimes connected to 2:41–51 rather than to 2:20–39. As will be seen, I think that there is more Lucan unity than these difficulties seem to indicate, but once more

---

[6] This is as far as I am willing to take Luke's use of Daniel's seventy weeks of years. I find fantastic the attempt to force Luke's chronological indications (and some that he does not give) into a sum of 490 (seventy weeks of seven), thus: six months (Luke 1:26,36) of Elizabeth's pregnancy equals 180; nine months of Mary's pregnancy equals 270; and the forty days of the purification adds a final 40. Luke does not mention the last two numbers, and the pregnancy is probably to be estimated at ten months (NOTE on 1:24).

[7] The purification is completely ignored after vs. 24 and the presentation is mentioned only implicitly in vs. 27.

[8] As I indicated in § 9, B2, I think that on the first level of Lucan composition the infancy narrative ended with 2:40 and that the story of Jesus at age twelve was added only in a later, second stage of composition. The arguments for this thesis will be given in the next section (§ 16).

they may constitute a sign that material of different origins may have been joined.

B. *The Setting Supplied by the Law* (2:22–24)

Two different Israelite customs specified in the Pentateuch serve as background for Luke's scene in the Temple. (Just as the census served as a setting in 2:1–21 by bringing Joseph and Mary from Nazareth to Bethlehem, so the purification and presentation bring Joseph and Mary from Bethlehem to Jerusalem and the Temple.) It is important to see these customs as originally distinct, for Luke seems to have confused them.[9]

First, there was the consecration or presentation of the child to the Lord. Exodus 13:1 and 13:11ff. demand the consecration of all firstborn males to the Lord: "the first to open the womb." This is traditionally related to the Lord's sparing the life of the Israelite firstborn when He slew the firstborn of the Egyptians. The original idea was that the firstborn should then spend his life serving the Lord in a special way; but in fact the tribe of Levi eventually took over the special service of the Lord in cult and thus effectively replaced the firstborn. This change was recognized by the legal provisions in Num 18:15–16 which allowed the firstborn to be bought back from the service of the Lord for five shekels (twenty denarii), while the Levites remained in His service. This sum had to be paid at the sanctuary (the Temple); but there was no obligation (or custom, so far as we know) of bringing the child to the sanctuary for the presentation and redemption.

Second, there was the purification of the mother after the birth of a child. Leviticus 12:1ff. specifies that a woman is to be considered ritually unclean for the seven days before the circumcision of the male child and for the thirty-three days after it,[10] during which time, forty days in all, she could not come to the sanctuary. Then, "when the time comes for her purification" (Lev 12:6), she is to bring to the priest at the door of the sanctuary[11] the offering of a lamb, and a young pigeon or a dove. If she cannot afford a lamb, two young pigeons or doves can be offered.

---

[9] The difficulty caused by the combination of the two customs of presentation and purification in vss. 22–24 has led some scholars to posit a mixed composition. Bultmann, *History,* 299, proposes that 22b–23 pertaining to the presentation are a secondary insertion into 22a, 24 which concerned the purification. Schürmann, *Lukasevangelium,* 122, recognizes that the confusion about the two customs rules out a Palestinian final composition; yet he thinks that there may be a Palestinian source that has been worked over by a Hellenistic Christian writer.

[10] A time period twice as long, totaling eighty days, was specified if the child was female.

[11] In NT times the Nicanor Gate was the customary entrance (St-B, II, 119–20). In the Herodian Temple that gate is generally presumed to have been on the west side of the court of the women, leading into the court of the men (court of Israel); and thus it constituted the farthest point of a woman's entry into the Temple.

In vss. 22–24 Luke is thinking primarily of the second custom. In 21 he has already mentioned the period leading up to the circumcision of the child; and now, following the pattern of Leviticus, he mentions the completion of the period leading up to the purification. His opening words in 22, "when the time came for their purification," is virtually a citation of the law of purification in Lev 12:6; and the offering of the two birds in 24 is a citation from Lev 12:8.[12] Yet he combines all this with a reference to the consecration of the firstborn male to the Lord in 22b–23, and that is the custom alluded to in the narrative that follows (27).[13] The Lucan combination of the two customs has often been thought to reflect popular practice in the Judaism of NT times, i.e., for the sake of convenience, the observance of two different religious duties at the same time. But that explanation does not cover the inaccuracies in the Lucan description of the combined customs. Luke seems to think that both parents needed to be purified, since in 22 (see NOTE) he modifies Lev 12:6 to read "when the time came for *their* purification." He seems to think that the reason for going to the Temple was the consecration or presentation of Jesus (vs. 27), when only the law concerning the purification of the mother mentions the custom of going to the sanctuary. (And it is dubious that a journey to the Temple was still practiced to any great extent in the Judaism of NT times.) He mentions nothing of the price (five shekels) required for redeeming the firstborn child from the service of the Lord; rather he connects with that event the sacrifice of the two doves or pigeons which was really related to the purification of the mother.

If we eschew the elaborate attempts of scholars to save Lucan accuracy on these points (see NOTES), similar to the unsuccessful attempts to save Lucan accuracy on the census, we may conclude either that Luke has misunderstood a tradition which had come down to him or that he has created a setting from an inaccurate reading of OT laws. Several arguments favor the latter: (1) There is little connection between the setting and what follows; (2) We saw a similar creation of a setting in the case of the census, a setting which had the purpose of explaining geographical movement; (3) Luke directly cites the laws involved. In any case, the result is a strange

---

[12] This offering, rather than that of a lamb and a bird, is often adduced as a sign of the poverty of Jesus' parents. However, we are not certain that the alternative offered in Leviticus was still an active custom in Jesus' time. A discussion among several rabbis of a later period (*Midrash Rabbah* XX 7 on Gen 3:16; the rabbis mentioned lived *ca.* A.D. 300) seems to assume that birds would be offered. Quite dubious is the contention of Bishop, "Bethlehem," 408, that the account is probably historical since a purely theological composition would have had a lamb offered. It is John, not Luke, who identifies Jesus as the Lamb of God.

[13] Roman Catholic mariologists have sometimes explained Luke's comparative neglect of the purification on the grounds that Mary did not need such purification (see Burrows, *Gospel,* 20). It is clear from vs. 22 (see NOTE there) that Luke thought she did need purification.

combination of a general knowledge of Judaism with an inaccurate knowledge of details—an indication that the author scarcely grew up in Judaism or in Palestine.[14] The need to explain the customs to the audience supposes that for the most part they also were non-Palestinian Gentiles.

Is there a chance that theological motive rather than ignorance explains some of the inaccuracies? For instance, it has been argued that the reason why Luke does not mention the redemption of the child Jesus through the payment of the five shekels is that he wants the reader to think that Jesus *stayed* in the service of the Lord. Sometimes vss. 22 and 24 have been read together: "The parents brought Jesus up to Jerusalem to present him to the Lord . . . and to offer (him as) a sacrifice," and Mary is thought to have sacrificed her son to God. This can hardly have been Luke's thought. Since he cites Lev 12:6,8, he knew that the sacrifice offered by the parents was the pair of doves or pigeons, and that they offered sacrifice only in the sense that they gave to the priest the animals that he would sacrifice. Other times the explanation has centered not on Jesus as the sacrificial victim but on Jesus as the levitical priest, i.e., that Jesus was not redeemed because he was a Levite left in the service of the Lord. This may be related to the dubious contention that Luke thinks of Mary as a Levite, like her relative Elizabeth (1:5,36).[15] However, since Luke takes pains to stress the Davidic ancestry of Jesus (1:26,32; 2:4; 3:31) and specifically fixes him in the tribe of Judah (3:33), it is hard to believe that he expected his readers to catch such a subtle reference to the non-redemption of Jesus as a Levite—readers to whom he had to explain the basic customs! Still another explanation of the failure to mention a price for Jesus is the contention that he remained in the service of God as His Son (see the use of "my Father" in 2:49). And this may spill over into the thesis that Luke wants us to realize that Jesus was internally dedicated to God's service or consecrated to the Lord,[16] so that the presentation becomes almost the enacting of the sentiment vocalized in Hebr 10:5–7: "Sacrifice and offering you did not desire. . . . Then I said, 'As it is written of me in the book, I have come to do your will, O God.'" Such reflections may be quite appropriate for later Christian theology which bases itself on a total NT picture, but they scarcely constitute an exegesis of Luke's intentions.

14 See § 9A. Much of this could be explained if Luke was a Gentile proselyte to Judaism before he became a Christian: one who had a "book-knowledge" of Judaism through the LXX.

15 See the NOTE on 1:27 for the patristic (mis-)readings of Luke 1:27, applying "House of David" to Mary rather than to Joseph. We simply do not know what Luke thought of Mary's tribal lineage.

16 Burrows, *Gospel*, 45, finds Johannine christology in the Lucan scene, e.g., John 10:36: "The one whom the Father consecrated and sent into the world"; 17:16–17: "As you sent me into the world, so have I sent them into the world. And for their sake I consecrate myself." Burrows fails to recognize that there are no indications of such a pre-existence christology in the Lucan infancy narrative.

If there is any theological explanation for the confusion in vss. 22–24, I think it is of OT derivation. The purification dominates the setting because of the geographical necessity of getting the parents from Bethlehem to Jerusalem. The presentation, however, must be mentioned because it is that custom which leads to the encounter with Simeon and Anna. And although Luke knows something about the custom of presentation as described in the Law, the real model for the presentation motif is the story of Samuel, which, as we have seen, had a strong impact on the narrative in Luke 1. Even though the Law did not require that the child be presented in the Temple, the model of the Samuel story had the child presented in the sanctuary at Shiloh; and it was that model which Luke followed. Even though the Law of presentation had the child redeemed for a price and not left in the Lord's service, Samuel was presented and left at the sanctuary at Shiloh; and so it would not fit Luke's purpose to call attention to the buying back of the child. Thus, the confusion results from a combination of inaccurate knowledge of the exact customs and of the conflict between two motifs.

As a preparation for the narrative to follow, let us explore the Samuel background in more detail. We remember that after the God-given conception and birth of her child, Hannah (or Anna—note the name) brought the child Samuel to the sanctuary at Shiloh and offered him to the service of the Lord (I Sam 1:24–28). There she and her husband encountered the aged priest Eli, even as Mary and Joseph encountered the aged Simeon.[17] We are told that Eli blessed Elkanah and Hannah (I Sam 2:20), even as Simeon blessed Joseph and Mary (Luke 2:34). The Samuel story mentions women who were ministering at the door of the sanctuary (I Sam 2:22), even as Luke describes Anna who "never left the Temple courts; day and night she worshiped God, fasting and praying" (2:37). The conclusion in Luke 2:40, describing how "the child grew up and became strong, filled with wisdom and favored by God," echoes I Sam 2:21,26: "The young child Samuel grew in the presence of the Lord . . . Samuel continued to grow both in stature and in favor with the Lord and with men."

This parallelism between the Samuel story and the account of the presentation of Jesus in the Temple has made scholars wonder whether Jesus was the original subject of the story. Many of the earlier Lucan echoes of the Samuel story pertained to the conception and birth of JBap rather than to the conception and birth of Jesus. I have previously mentioned the theory of a pre-Lucan JBap narrative which was originally longer and contained material that Luke has shifted over to Jesus (p. 245 above); in

---

17 In the NOTE on Simeon in 2:25 mention was made of an early Christian interpretation which turned Simeon into a high priest.

such a theory this would have been a pre-Lucan story of the presentation of JBap in the Temple by Zechariah and Elizabeth. Besides the general objections to a JBap source which I have already discussed, I would contend that the Samuel background is drawn upon by Luke for the whole infancy narrative and not merely for the JBap portion. Thus, the Magnificat of Mary is patterned on the canticle of Hannah.[18] Luke has chosen to continue the infancy story of Jesus rather than the infancy story of JBap; and so, while the conception of JBap was patterned on the conception of Samuel, Luke now shifts the Samuel imagery over to Jesus[19] and patterns Joseph and Mary on Elkanah and Hannah, even as he earlier patterned Zechariah and Elizabeth on the two parents of Samuel. Luke's method is not one of identifying figures in the infancy narrative with OT characters; rather he uses pigments taken from OT narratives to color in the infancy narrative. If there is an echo of the JBap story in Luke 2:22–40, it is not because it originally concerned the presentation of JBap in the Temple. Rather the echo is the result of Lucan artistic inclusion:[20] an infancy narrative that began with an upright and Law-observant man and woman, Zechariah and Elizabeth, the parents of JBap, and a Temple scene ends with an upright and Law-observant man and woman, Simeon and Anna, and a Temple scene—and both the beginning and the ending reflect a Samuel and a Daniel background.

C. *Simeon Greets the Child and Prophesies (2:25–35)*

We shall first discuss the characterization and symbolism of Simeon; then we shall turn our attention to the oracles uttered by him in vss. 29–32 (the Nunc Dimittis) and in 34c–35.

1. The Characterization and Symbolism of Simeon

We have already seen that Luke is not interested in the Jewish customs of purification and presentation for their own value. The custom of purification serves to move the scene to Jerusalem and the Temple. The theme of presentation provides a context for a Samuel-like story involving the parents, the child, and an aged figure at the sanctuary. But it is no ac-

---

18 Unless one adheres to the thesis that the original spokeswoman of the Magnificat was Elizabeth rather than Mary (NOTE on 1:46).

19 We saw a Samuel motif in the Matthean infancy narrative if the Nazorean of Matt 2:23 reflects the theme of the *Nāzîr* (see NOTE there), for Samuel was also a Nazirite from birth. Once again then (§ 14, C1) there may be a connection between the narrative in Luke 2 and the fulfillment citations of Matt 2.

20 For inclusion, see § 2, footnote 19.

cident that Luke mentions the Law three times in vss. 22–24 and continues this theme in vss. 27 and 39. He wishes to underline that this story
which centers on the future greatness of Jesus is made possible through
obedience to the Law of Moses, which is the Law of the Lord.[21] Similarly
it is no accident that the (Holy) Spirit is mentioned three times in vss.
25–27 in reference to Simeon. We saw the prophetic Spirit at work in the
conception stories of Luke 1 (1:15,17,41); and after the circumcision
Zechariah, the father of JBap, uttered the prophecy of the Benedictus
when he was filled with the Holy Spirit (1:67). So now after the circumcision of Jesus, Simeon is led by the Spirit and impelled to utter the Nunc
Dimittis. And in the "one-upmanship" that characterizes the Lucan comparison of JBap and Jesus, whereas one prophet spoke after the circumcision of JBap to predict the future greatness of the child, two prophets,
Simeon and Anna,[22] predict the future greatness of Jesus. Thus, we have
the Law and the prophets, the standard Lucan designation for the heritage
of Israel,[23] coming together to establish a context for the career of Jesus.

We have seen the likelihood that the canticles of the Lucan infancy narrative came out of a circle of Jewish Christian Anawim, the pious ones totally dependent on God who recognized in Jesus the long-awaited
fulfillment of God's promises of help. Simeon and Anna, who have
awaited the consolation of Israel and the redemption of Jerusalem
(2:25,38), are the embodiment of the piety of the Anawim.[24] In § 12, C2,
I pointed out many similarities between the Jewish Christian Anawim and
the Dead Sea Scroll sectarians. Theirs too was a firm expectation of deliverance and of the coming of the Messiah(s). The secrets of the prophets
had been revealed to the Righteous Teacher who was the great hero of the
group, and he saw how those prophecies were being fulfilled in and
through the Qumran community (1QpHab vii 3–5). It is in this sense too
that Simeon is guided by the Spirit of prophecy; for, as we shall see when
we discuss the Nunc Dimittis, he sees how the words of Isaiah are fulfilled
in Jesus and in the community that believes in him. The Qumran Anawim,

---

[21] Bornhäuser, *Kindheitsgeschichte*, 112, has cleverly suggested that the outline of the
Lucan infancy narrative follows Gal 4:4: "When the fullness of time had come, God sent
His Son [=Luke 1:26–38], born of a woman [=Luke 2:1–20], born under the Law
[=Luke 2:21,22–24]."

[22] Anna is specifically called a prophetess in vs. 36, a necessary identification because her
words are not reported. That Simeon is a prophet is evident from the emphasis on the Spirit
that leads him, from his prediction of the future (34c–35), and from the parallelism between the Benedictus (called a prophecy in 1:67) and the Nunc Dimittis. Compare the
prophet Agabus who with the aid of the Holy Spirit can foretell the destiny of Paul in Acts
21:10–11.

[23] Luke 16:16; Acts 13:15; 24:14; 26:22; 28:23.

[24] Although I have proposed that the canticles were added at a second stage of Lucan
composition and that Luke himself did not compose them, I have insisted that they fit the
context into which Luke inserted them, precisely because the characters he describes are the
types of the Anawim who composed them.

even as Simeon and Anna, were upright and devout (Luke 2:25), preparing for the last times by a piety of prayer and fasting (2:37).

Appropriate too for the Anawim motif is the fact that the expectations of Simeon and Anna are fulfilled in the Temple courts. In § 10, footnote 13, and § 12, footnote 47, I pointed out that a spirit of "Temple piety" marks both the Lucan infancy narrative and the theology of the Anawim. Anna who never leaves the Temple courts and who worships God day and night in fasting and prayer is the forerunner of the Jerusalem Christian community which devotes itself to prayer and day by day attends the Temple (Acts 2:42,46), and of its daughter community in Antioch which worships the Lord and fasts and receives the Holy Spirit (13:2). The Lucan infancy narrative opened in a Temple setting with a revelation which came to Zechariah but left him unable to confer the priestly blessing (1:22). Now the light has shone, and the revelation that comes to Simeon in the Temple court enables him to bless the parents of the child (2:34).[25] The Law, the prophetic Spirit, and the Temple cult have all come together to set the scene for the greatness of Jesus. The one who is called "holy" (1:35) has come to the holy place of Israel, and he begins to embody much of what was associated with the Temple. It was predicted that in the last days the Gentiles would come streaming to the mountain of the house of the Lord to be taught His ways (Isa 2:2–3; Micah 4:1). Now in that house Jesus is proclaimed as a salvation made ready in the sight of all the peoples: "A light to be a revelation to the Gentiles" (Luke 2:31–32). It was the proudest boast of the Temple theologians that the glory of God dwelt in the sanctuary (I Kgs 8:10–11; Ezek 44:4); and now as Simeon stands before that sanctuary, he proclaims Jesus to be a glory for God's people Israel.[26]

Before we turn to Simeon's words, let us pay more attention to Luke's description of him as "waiting for the consolation [*paraklēsis*] of Israel."[27]

25 The use of the term "parents" in 2:27 (also 2:41,43) and "father" in 2:33 (also 2:48) has been used as evidence that this scene and the next arose in circles ignorant of the virginal conception. I think that may very well be true of the next scene, but I would not base such a suspicion on the terms "parents" and "father." If Luke, who accepted the virginal conception, found no difficulty in using these terms, how can we be sure what their use by a putative pre-Lucan group would indicate with reference to the virginal conception?

26 It has been suggested that in the Simeon story we have a Hellenistic recognition scene, and parallels have been cited from Greek literature where someone recognizes a marvelous or divine child. It is quite possible that Luke's Gentile readers would interpret the story in such a way; but the origins of Luke's story seem to be totally Jewish. Bultmann, *History*, 299–300, calls attention to a scene in the legend of the Buddha where the aged, ascetic Asita comes to the palace and takes the child in his arms and foretells the great role the child will have, while regretting that he himself will die too soon to see it. However, as Bultmann recognizes, the pattern is too widespread in popular religious literature to detect direct influence upon Luke.

27 The fact that, while waiting for the *paraklēsis* of Israel, Simeon has the Holy Spirit come upon him leads some scholars to see a connection between Luke and John, who designates the Holy Spirit as the Paraclete (*paraklētos*) in 14:26. If one objects that for Luke it

This echoes the language of the second and third parts of the Book of Isaiah, respectively chs. 40–55 and chs. 56–66. Just before the famous passage that the NT associates with JBap (Isa 40:3: "The voice of one crying in the desert: 'Make ready the way of the Lord' "), we hear in the LXX of Isa 40:1: "Console, console [*parakalein*] my people, says your God; speak, priests, to the heart of Jerusalem, for her time of humiliation has been filled out."[28] And in Isa 66:12–13, a LXX passage which speaks of the glory of the Gentiles, we hear: "As one whom a mother consoles [*parakalein*], so also shall I console you; and you will be consoled in Jerusalem." If we look at the companion Lucan phrase in the Anna scene, "waiting for the redemption [*lytrōsis*] of Jerusalem" (2:38), we hear in the MT of Isa 52:9: "The Lord has consoled His people; He has redeemed Jerusalem." We shall see that this same Isaian background dominates the oracles of Simeon in praise of him who is the consolation of Israel and the redemption of Jerusalem.

2. The Problem of the Two Oracles

There are two oracles of Simeon about Jesus, respectively 29–32 and 34c–35. This is not the first instance of doubling in relation to canticles. In 1:42b–45 there was a song of praise by Elizabeth, followed in 1:46–55 by a canticle of Mary, the Magnificat. In 2:10–11 there was an angelic proclamation of Jesus' identity, followed by a canticle of the heavenly host, the Gloria in Excelsis. In the previous instances it seemed best to suppose that the first song or proclamation was part of the original Lucan composition, and that the doubling was caused when Luke added the canticles at a second stage of composition. I think a similar solution is applicable here, with the order reversed, however; for the original oracle seems to be the second.

The awkwardness of the duplication is seen when we compare the two introductions. The Nunc Dimittis (29–32) is introduced in 28: "Simeon embraced the child in his arms and blessed God, saying"; the second oracle (34c–35) is introduced in 34ab: "Simeon blessed them and said to Mary the mother." Verse 33 is a stereotyped reaction to a divine oracle and is supplied as a transition from one to the other. The following reasons suggest that vss. 28–33, containing the Nunc Dimittis, are an addition to an original Lucan account which contained only the oracle in 34–35: (a) There is a smooth transition from 27 to 34: "When the par-

---

is Jesus who is the *paraklēsis*, they point to John 14:16 and I John 2:1 as evidence that in Johannine thought Jesus too is a Paraclete.

28 The fact that in the LXX (not in the MT) the verse pertains to priests may have been another factor in the Christian interpretation of Simeon as a priest (NOTE on vs. 25).

ents brought in Jesus to perform for him what was customary according to the Law . . . Simeon blessed them and said to Mary the mother."[29] However, this argument has limited value, for 34–35 could be just as easily excised as 28–33. (b) The Nunc Dimittis has a clear affinity with the preceding canticles in the infancy narrative, and we have seen the likelihood that they were added at a second stage of Lucan composition. There are vocabulary parallels between the Nunc Dimittis and the Benedictus.[30] All the preceding canticles are introduced by a theme of blessing or praising God (1:46–47; 1:68; 2:13–14), and that is the theme that introduces the Nunc Dimittis. We have seen that there is a generality in the outlook of the preceding canticles. While they praise what God has done in Jesus, they did not originally refer specifically to the conception and birth;[31] and so what they say applies to the whole salvific work and indeed refers to it as something that has already taken place. The same is true of the Nunc Dimittis; it could have been uttered by a pious member of the Anawim just as well after the crucifixion and resurrection as after the birth: "My eyes have seen this salvation that you made ready in the sight of all the peoples." Even the individual reference to "your servant" and to what God has done for the speaker is not unusual in the Qumran hymns which, as we saw, have many parallels to the Lucan canticles of the Anawim; and it is attested in the Magnificat as well: "He who is mighty has done great things for me" (1:49a). (c) On the other hand, the second oracle of Simeon (34c–35) is quite unlike the other Lucan canticles. It is much rougher poetry, and stands in poetic relationship to the Nunc Dimittis the way Elizabeth's oracle (1:42b–45) stands in relationship to the Magnificat.[32] The second oracle is not a general reference to salvation in Jesus and is not phrased in the past tense; it concerns the future of one whose career has not yet begun and is quite appropriate as a prophecy in a birth context. I have proposed that in 1:5 to 2:40 Luke himself composed a basic infancy narrative without using previously composed sources, and then at a second stage of composition he added canticles (and 2:41–52) which were not of his own composition. In the logic of that

[29] If Luke inserted 28–33 into an original narrative in which 27 was followed by 34, the only adjustment he made was to provide an initial *kai,* "and," for vs. 34.

[30] Gryglewicz, "Herkunft," 267ff., detects six. Note the common themes of peace, salvation, people, light, Israel; and some of these would be shared with the other canticles as well. As in the other canticles there are clear Semitisms in the Greek of the Nunc Dimittis (see NOTES) which favor Jewish Christian composition. The theory of pre-Christian Jewish victory hymns would apply to the Nunc Dimittis only with great difficulty.

[31] I have theorized that Luke added 1:48ab to the Magnificat and 1:76–77 to the Benedictus in order make them more specifically applicable to the infancy context.

[32] In the opening of the first NOTE on 1:42, I mentioned the difficulty of determining to what extent Elizabeth's oracle was poetry. It is true that there is at least one similarity of vocabulary between Simeon's second oracle and the previous Lucan canticles, i.e., the *kai sou de* of 2:35 (see NOTE) and the *kai sy de* of the Benedictus. Yet the latter occurs in 1:76, a line which Luke probably added to the original Benedictus.

theory there should be more Lucanisms in the oracle that belonged to the
original stage of composition. Minear has given a list of fifty-five "significant words or phrases which appear both in the birth narratives and in the
rest of Luke-Acts, and which are found more often in these two books
than in the rest of the New Testament." Three of Minear's Lucanisms are
found in Simeon's second oracle;[33] none are found in the Nunc Dimittis.

One may object that, if Luke made an addition of an oracle to his original composition, he should have placed it at the end of the Simeon scene
(as he did in adding the Magnificat and Benedictus to their respective
scenes), rather than in the middle. But here one must recognize that the
order Luke has achieved by inserting the Nunc Dimittis as the first oracle
reflects his schema of salvation history. I have theorized that Luke made
an insertion of vss. 76–77 in the Benedictus. This insertion produced a sequence of a first part which blesses the Lord, the God of Israel (1:68–75),
and a second part where the attention is turned to the destiny of the child
whose birth is being celebrated (1:76–77). The same sequence appears
here: the first oracle of Simeon (the Nunc Dimittis) blesses God, the
Mighty Master, and the second oracle turns to the destiny of the child
whose birth is being celebrated. Another aspect of the Lucan schema of
salvation is that the first oracle of Simeon proclaims that God has given
Jesus as a salvation for all peoples, both the Gentiles and Israel. The second oracle is a specification of that theme, for it points out that all Israel
will not receive him.

With these general remarks in mind, let us now turn to the individual
oracles.

3. Simeon's Nunc Dimittis (29–32)

This has struck many as the loveliest of the Lucan canticles, and its
brevity has made it readily adaptable as a personal prayer of peaceful and
joyful resignation to a call from God which involves separation. D. R.
Jones[34] theorizes that it may early have served as a Christian response at
the death of a believer, when the second coming was still believed to be
imminent. Since the fifth century the canticle has been recited in the night
prayers of the Church, as part of the monastic Office of the Hours.

The brevity of the Nunc Dimittis also obviates the difficulties of structural investigation that we faced in the instances of the Magnificat and the

---

[33] Minear, "Luke's Use," 113; the three are *antilegein, dialogismoi kardiōn,* and
dierchesthai. (Another list of Lucanisms might add *anastasis;* however, it might also include
words found in the Nunc Dimittis, e.g., *sōtēria, despotēs* [for God].) It is noteworthy that
according to Minear's list there are two Lucanisms in 28, *kai autos* and *eulogein ton theon*
—a verse that in my hypothesis Luke wrote as an introduction when he inserted the Nunc
Dimittis.
[34] Jones, "Background," 47.

Benedictus. Basically it consists of three distychs or bicola (29ab, 30–31, 32ab), with the last of the three exemplifying synonymous parallelism.[85]

In the heritage of many peoples there appears the theme of a watchman who expresses his joy upon being released from his duty by the arrival of the one for whom he was watching. For instance, in the *Agamemnon* (1–30) of Aeschylus, the sentinel rejoices at his release from watching for the signal indicating the capture of Troy. But in Simeon's canticle this watchman theme has been combined with that of the last words of the aged or dying. The latter supplies the note of departure in peace, as we see in Gen 15:15 where God promises Abraham, "You will depart to your fathers in peace." The former supplies the note of joy and fulfillment. We see the combination of the two themes, the watchman and the aged, and the two emotions, the joy and the peace, in the statement that the aged Jacob/Israel makes before he dies when, in God's providence, he has found his long lost son Joseph: "Now I am willing to die for I have seen your face" (Gen 46:30).[86]

The messianic context of Simeon's sense of fulfillment is understandable in the Judaism of Jesus' time. In the first-century *Psalms of Solomon* (17:50) we hear: "Blessed are they who will exist in those days to see the good fortune of Israel which God will bring to pass."[87] This same mentality is found in the words of Jesus: "Fortunate are the eyes that see what you see, for I tell you many prophets and kings desired to see what you see and did not see it" (Luke 10:23–24). And Simeon's reference to departure in peace echoes the hopes for peace in the days when God would re-establish the Davidic king. Psalm 72:7 prays: "In his days may uprightness flourish and abundant peace"; Zech 8:12 describes the time of his coming as the "sowing of peace"; and Isa 9:5–6 calls him the "prince of peace." Simeon may depart in peace not because he has finished *his* task but because God has now completed His word. Already the heavenly host has proclaimed, "On earth peace to those favored by Him" (Luke 2:14); and Simeon is one of those so favored.[88]

---

85 It is this parallelism that causes me to reject the division by Plummer (*Luke*, 68) into two tristychs or tricola (29ab–30, 31–32ab).

36 Here, as in the Nunc Dimittis, there is an emphatic "Now," expressing the sense of a felt fulfillment of promise. This parallel with Jacob/Israel has all the more force because of Jewish speculation that, while Jacob saw Joseph, he was still left yearning for God's salvation (Gen 49:18). The targums stress that he was "looking" for the redemption that God would bring to His people; see M. McNamara, *The New Testament and the Palestinian Targum to the Pentateuch* (Analecta Biblica, 27; Rome: Pontifical Biblical Institute, 1966), 243–45.

87 The expression "the Lord's Messiah" of 2:26 is found in *PsSol* 18:8; and a parallel to the end of the Nunc Dimittis is found in *PsSol* 17:34–35: "Nations will come from the ends of the earth to see His glory . . . the glory of the Lord wherewith God has glorified her [Jerusalem]."

38 Originally the early Christian community connected God's giving of peace with the resurrection (Luke 24:36; also John 20:21); but now that the christological moment has been moved back to the conception and birth, the theme of peace appears strongly here.

The vocabulary of the Nunc Dimittis seems to have its primary source in the latter parts of the Book of Isaiah, the influence of which we have already seen on the description of Simeon (and Anna). The following is a list of some of the passages that seem to be echoed in the Lucan canticle:[39]

Isa 52:9–10:
The Lord has comforted His people;
He has redeemed Jerusalem.
The Lord has revealed His holy arm
in the sight of all the Gentiles,
and all the ends of the earth will see
the salvation that comes from our God.

Isa 49:6:
It is insufficient for you to be my servant,
to raise up the tribes of Jacob,
and to recover the diaspora of Israel;
I shall give you as a light to the Gentiles
*that you may bring salvation to the ends of the earth.

Isa 46:13:
I shall put salvation within Zion,
and give to Israel my glory.

Isa 42:6:
I have given you as a covenant to the people,
a light to the Gentiles.

Isa 40:5:
Then the glory of the Lord will be revealed,
*and all flesh will see the salvation of God.

The themes of seeing salvation, the sight of all the peoples, a light to the Gentiles, and glory for Israel, which appear in the Nunc Dimittis, constitute almost a pastiche from the Isaian passages[40]—the same cento technique we have seen in the Magnificat and Benedictus. Of course, they may not have come to the Nunc Dimittis directly from the Book of Isaiah, for they are taken up in other biblical and early Jewish literature. Psalm 98:3 praises God: "He has remembered His kindness and fidelity to the House of Israel; all the ends of the earth have seen the salvation of our God." Baruch 4:24 promises: "The neighbors of Zion . . . will shortly see the

---

39 I am citing these according to the MT, except for the two lines marked with an asterisk where the LXX seems noticeably closer to the thought or wording of the Nunc Dimittis. In Acts 13:47 Luke cites the last lines of Isa 49:6 according to the LXX. Andriessen, "Simeon's Profetie," is helpful with these parallels. See also the end of the NOTE on Matt 2:23.

40 There does not seem to be an exact parallel to the Lucan phrase "salvation that you made ready."

salvation of God come to you with great glory." Among the Dead Sea Scrolls, in 1QM i 5 we are told: "This will be a time of salvation for the people of God" (with "redemption" appearing as a synonym for "salvation" in i 12–see Luke 2:38).[41] And CD xx 20 speaks of "the time when salvation and justice will be revealed to those who fear God," while CD xx 34 continues with a promise: "They will see His salvation."

There is a universalism in the Isaian passages I have quoted, but a subordinated universalism—the light is to come to the Gentiles; but they are to come to Jerusalem, for Israel is God's people. The same may well have been true in the pre-Lucan form of the Nunc Dimittis.[42] But Luke 2:31 has reinterpreted Isa 52:10: the salvation that God has made ready is "in the sight of all the *peoples.*" As the next two lines indicate, the term "peoples" covers the Gentiles and Israel, so that the Gentiles too are God's people. The canticle of Zechariah in 1:68 said that the God of Israel had "visited and accomplished the redemption of His people," but the canticle of Simeon has a wider view of God's redemption. Here in the Second Temple built in obedience to the OT prophet Zechariah, the words of that prophet concerning the Temple and Jerusalem have at last been fulfilled: "Lo, I come and will dwell in the midst of you, says the Lord. And many nations [or Gentiles: *ethnē*] will join themselves to the Lord in that day and will be my people" (Zech 2:10–11).

This opening to the Gentiles in the Nunc Dimittis brings to the Lucan infancy narrative a theme that we saw in Matthew's account of the magi. In their second chapters both evangelists anticipate the future of the Gospel by already bringing into the birth story the theme of Gentiles who are attracted by the light of God's son. Indeed, Luke has Simeon vocalize an understanding that will later be associated with the two great heroes of Acts, Peter and Paul. In Acts 15:14 Simeon Peter (note the spelling of the first name here) relates to the "council" of Jerusalem how God "visited the Gentiles to take out of them a people for His name." The ancient formula describing Israel, "a chosen people out of all the nations [*ethnē*: Deut 14:2; Exod 19:5]," has been reinterpreted—God has chosen for Himself a new people out of the nations (*ethnē*), i.e., a people consisting of Gentiles.[43] This action proclaimed by Peter reaches its conclusion at the end of Acts (28:28) when Paul says, "Let it be known to you that this salvation of God has been sent to the Gentiles." It was then that the vision

---

[41] However, this section of the Qumran War Scroll does not share the universalism of the Nunc Dimittis, for the salvation of the people of God is to be accompanied by a destruction of the Kittim (Romans).

[42] See the theory of Kilpatrick mentioned in the NOTE on "peoples" in vs. 31. Other scholars who favor a Jewish Christian origin for the Nunc Dimittis have tried to interpret away the universalism or at least subordinate it, even on the Lucan level (see Schürmann, *Lukasevangelium*, 126).

[43] See the important article by J. Dupont, "*Laos ex ethnōn* (Acts 15:14)," NTS 3 (1956–57), 47–50.

of Simeon pronounced at the presentation of Jesus in the Temple was verified: "My eyes have seen this salvation . . . a light to be a revelation to the Gentiles."

4. Simeon's Second Oracle (34c–35)

The scene involving Paul at the end of Acts, which I have just mentioned as forming an inclusion with Simeon's Nunc Dimittis, leads us nicely into the second oracle. Paul announced that salvation was sent to the Gentiles because he had just been rejected at Rome by the Jews, and against them he had quoted the words of Isaiah: "You will indeed hear but never understand" (Acts 28:26). So too the second oracle of Simeon concerns the fall of many in Israel and a sign to be contradicted. The dramatic setting of this prophetic woe on Israel (couched in an obscure symbolism worthy of the prophets of the OT) should not be overlooked. The aged Simeon at the end of his life holds in his arms a child that is just beginning his life. Simeon's eyes have peered into the distance and seen the salvation that this child will bring to the Gentiles and Israel alike; but, true prophet, he also sees the rejection and the catastrophe. And his tragic second vision is addressed to the mother of the child,[44] the one to whom the good news about Jesus first came; for as the first to hear the word and accept it, she must encounter in her own soul its challenge and the tragedy of its rejection by many in that Israel whom Jesus was to have helped (1:54a). The opening "Behold" in 2:34c marks the change of tone and thought.[45] The Nunc Dimittis has spoken of messianic peace, but Luke knows what Jesus himself said about peace: "Do you think I have come to bring peace on earth? No, I tell you: rather division; for henceforth in the one house of five they will be divided, three against two and two against three. They will be divided, father against son and son against father, mother against daughter and daughter against mother" (Luke 12:51–53). Simeon's second oracle is the oracle of division.[46]

There are four lines in the oracle, and all have the same theme of a judgment that divides. In the opening line (34c) we are told that Jesus is not simply the occasion of that judgment; rather he is "set" for that purpose, matching the "I have come for division" in the quotation from the

---

[44] The singling out of Mary has nothing to do with the virginal conception in the sense that Luke is trying to tell us that she is the only real parent of Jesus. Luke is simply following the model of Samuel's presentation in the sanctuary by his parents: there Hannah's role dominates over that of Elkanah.

[45] Winandy, "La prophétie," translates it as "Take care."

[46] Since we have seen so many parallels between the story of the presentation of Jesus and that of the presentation of Samuel, it is worth noting that a theme of discrimination and resultant division appears in the Samuel story too. In the canticle of Hannah, Samuel's mother, we hear, "The Lord kills and brings to life; he brings down to Sheol and raises up" (I Sam 2:6).

ministry just given above. The attempts of some commentators to read the fall and rise consecutively (i.e., they shall fall and then rise, as in Micah 7:8) are certainly wrong. Rather there are two groups: those who fall and those who rise. We have here a form of the building-stone image that the NT uses so frequently to explain the mixed fate of the Jews in regard to Christianity. It can be a stone on which people stumble and fall (Isa 8:14),[47] or it can be a cornerstone on which a house is built (Ps 118:22; Isa 28:16); and it is precisely this combination of texts that appears on Jesus' lips in Luke 20:17–18 in a context which concerns the taking of the vineyard from its present tenants and giving of it to others (from Jews to Gentiles). The negative stone text became fixed in the Christian arsenal for explaining why some in Israel rejected Jesus, while the Gentiles were accepting him (Rom 9:30–32; I Peter 2:8). The fact that Luke puts "fall" before "rise" in 34c reflects the history he has recounted in Acts.[48] There were Jews at the beginning who did accept Jesus; but the majority have refused to listen, and the destiny of Christianity is now with the Gentiles.

The pessimistic tone is reinforced by the treatment of Jesus as a sign in 34d. That designation echoes the language of the Davidic oracles of Isaiah. The child that the young woman (LXX: virgin) will conceive and bear and name Emmanuel (Isa 7:14) is *a sign* given by God to the House of David[49]—an Isaian scene that appears in the same context as the stumbling-stone passage (Isa 8:14) we discussed as background for 34c. And if one reads the rest of Isa 7, it becomes clear that the sign has more of a negative than a positive result. So too for Luke the sign of Jesus will be contradicted or spoken against. Thus, in 34d we have moved beyond the discrimination involved in the "fall and rise" of 34c, and only the contradiction is mentioned. The "waters of contradiction" (Num 20:13; Deut 32:51) was the name of the place where Israel spoke against its God, and Simeon is predicting that a rebellious people is about to contradict again. Simeon is anticipating the rejection of Jesus by the Jewish au-

47 This stone text is phrased quite differently in the LXX: "If you trust in Him, He will be a sanctuary for you; and you will not come up against him as against a stumbling stone, nor as against a rock to fall over." Since Luke takes the negative thrust of the MT rather than the positive thrust of the LXX, P. Winter, "Some Observations," 118ff., argues for composition in Semitic. However, we are dealing with a Lucan allusion to Isa 8:14 rather than a quotation; and the allusion has been shaped by general Christian usage (where the negative meaning dominates), so it tells us nothing about the original language of Simeon's second oracle. TalBab *Sanhedrin* 38a applies Isa 8:14 to the Davidic Messiah.

48 Does Luke also think of the fall of Jerusalem, as in 21:24: "They will fall by the edge of the sword and be led captive among all the Gentiles, and Jerusalem be trodded down by the Gentiles"? This oracle is given in the Temple court—a Temple that would be destroyed and every stone of it thrown down (21:5–6).

49 The Hebrew of Isa 7:14 for "sign" is *'ôt*, normally rendered in Greek by *sēmeion*, the word Luke uses. However, Luke could be echoing as well another Hebrew word rendered by *sēmeion* in the LXX, namely, *nēs*, "standard, banner," especially as that appears in Isa 11:10–12: "In that day the root of Jesse . . . will lift up a *sign* to the Gentiles, and will gather up the lost ones of Israel." See Sahlin, *Messiah*, 271.

thorities during his ministry and passion[50] and the rejection of the Christian mission to Israel as described in Acts. (Matthew 2 anticipated the passion in a different way by having aligned against the child Jesus a Jewish king, the chief priests, and the scribes.) A close parallel to Simeon's phrase is the saying of Jesus in Luke 11:29–32 (Matt 12:38–42) that the Son of Man will be *a sign* of judgment given to an evil and unrepentant generation.

Verse 35a with its symbolic reference to a sword that will pass through Mary's soul is obscure, and it has been the subject of extensive patristic and modern mariological reflection. Much of this reflection is poor methodologically, for it seeks to interpret Luke through non-Lucan material—material of which Luke and his community may have been totally ignorant. Let me list some of these interpretations:[51]

▪The most ancient is that of Origen (*Homilies on Luke* 17; PG 13:1845–46) who understands the sword to mean doubt and presumes that Mary was scandalized and doubted during the passion of Jesus. There is little biblical support for the sword as a metaphor for doubt, and no support for the thesis that Mary doubted during the passion. Moreover, Luke has a positive view of Jesus' mother as a disciple (8:21; § 11D above) and shows her as a member of the believing community after the ascension (Acts 1:14).

▪The sword refers possibly to the violent death of the virgin (Epiphanius *Heresies* lxxviii 11; PG 42:716). There is no reliable evidence that Mary died violently.

▪Popular in Marian piety is the interpretation that the sword means suffering (as in Ps 22:21[20]), and that the moment of its passing through Mary's soul was at Calvary when the *mater dolorosa* stood at the foot of the cross and saw her son die, pierced with a lance. However, among the Gospels only John 19:25–27 places Mary at the foot of the cross, and in that highly symbolic scene she is not a *mater dolorosa*. There is no evidence that Luke or his community ever thought that Mary was present at Calvary.[52]

▪A variant of the preceding is the thesis that Mary as the mother of the Messiah underwent the same fate as her son, including rejection and contradiction.[53] Perhaps such a concept may be found in Rev 12:4–6,17 if the woman who bears the Messiah is thought to be Mary, but there is no

---

[50] In Hebr 12:3 the passion of Jesus is described as an *antilogia*, "opprobrium," a noun of the same root as Luke's *antilegein*, "contradict."

[51] Feuillet, "L'épreuve," 248ff., is very helpful here.

[52] That there are similarities between Luke and John does not support the thesis of Lucan knowledge of this Johannine scene which involves the mother of Jesus and the Beloved Disciple. The similarities between the two Gospels break down precisely at the point where the Beloved Disciple is involved, as seen when we compare John 20:2–10 and Luke 24:12.

[53] See Schürmann, *Lukasevangelium*, 129.

evidence of this concept in Luke. Moreover, in NT imagery a sword did not pierce the soul of Jesus—something that would be necessary if Mary's fate in Luke 2:35a is patterned on his. Rather Jesus brought the sword of division (Matt 10:34).

▪An interpretation that the piercing by the sword in 35a is the same as the speaking against the sign in 34d, and that Mary was spoken against because the legitimacy of Jesus' conception was questioned.[54] This is to introduce a motif from Matt 1:18–19 that is totally foreign to Luke's narrative.

▪An interpretation that the piercing by the sword in 35a involves the fall of many in Israel in 34c, and that Mary lived to see the fall of Jerusalem and the rejection of Jesus by his own people.[55]

▪A suggestion made by Ambrose (*In Lucam* II 61; PL 15:1574), and followed by much of Western patristic thought, that the sword represents the word of God. While this symbolism has biblical support, it echoes nothing in Lucan usage. And just when is the moment that the word of God pierces Mary's soul?

▪A reference to the "protevangelium" of Gen 3:15 where there is enmity between the serpent and the woman, between his seed and her seed. This symbolic background catches some of the judgment motif of Luke 3:34c with its "fall and rise"; but it also presupposes a messianic interpretation of Gen 3:15 for which we have no evidence in the pre-Lucan or Lucan tradition. Moreover, it does not do justice to the thrust of 35a where Mary is not a positive figure opposed to the negative, but where the division seems to be brought into her own soul.

Rejecting these interpretations as implausible, let me now turn to interpretations of 35a based on indications from the framework of Lucan thought as attested in Luke/Acts. By way of background it is best to begin with the figure of the *sword passing through*.[56] The closest OT vocabulary parallel is Ezek 14:17 where we are told that by way of judgment the Lord may say, "Let a sword pass through the land so that I may cut off man and beast." Evidently this was a well-remembered oracle; for it is quoted in Greek and adapted in the *Sibylline Oracles,* III 316, to describe

---

54 Burrows, *Gospel,* 43, mentions this with hesitation.

55 Winandy, "La prophétie," 340.

56 It is safer to take as a primary background a text that keeps together the ideas of "sword" *romphaia* and "pass through" *dierchesthai.* Inadequate therefore is the Servant reference in Isa 53:5: "He was wounded [*traumatizein*] because of our sins"; and the "Passion Psalm" 22:17(16): "They have pierced [*orizein*] my hands and my feet," uttered by someone who four verses later pleads "Deliver my soul from the sword." Feuillet, "L'épreuve," 258–61, presses the case for Zech 12:8–14, which he interprets to mean that the representative of the House of David will be pierced through (12:10; see John 19:37: *ekkentein*) and his death will become a source of pardon for the inhabitants of Jerusalem. The Zechariah text is very obscure (the Hebrew has God pierced!), and there is no passing through of a sword, even though a sword is later mentioned (13:7).

the invasion of Egypt by Antiochus Epiphanes (*ca.* 170 B.C.): "For a sword will pass through the midst of you."[57] The image is of a selective sword of judgment, destroying some and sparing others, a sword for discrimination and not merely for punishment (Ezek 5:1–2; 6:8–9; 12:14–16).[58] This is perfectly in harmony with the Lucan thought in 3:34c where the child is set for the fall and rise of many in Israel, and also in harmony with Luke 12:51–53 which I cited above at the beginning of this discussion of Simeon's second oracle: Jesus has come to bring division even among families. It should be remembered that Luke 12:51–53 was probably drawn from the Q source common to Matthew and Luke. The Matthean form of the saying is: "Do not think that I have come to bring peace on earth. I have not come to bring peace *but a sword*" (Matt 10:34–36). Luke's form of the saying omits the reference to the sword, but in 2:35a he refers to the sword of discrimination with the same meaning that it has in Matthew's form of the Q saying.[59]

It is the body of that saying where the sword of discrimination separates even families ("father against son and son against father; mother against daughter and daughter against mother") that may supply the key to how the sword passes through Mary's soul. The one common tradition about Mary in the Synoptic account of the ministry is the scene that distinguishes between Jesus' natural family and the family of disciples created by the proclamation of the kingdom. As we saw in § 11D, in the Marcan form of the scene (3:31–35) Jesus' mother and brothers are replaced by a new family of brother and sister and mother, a family consisting of those who do the will of God. But Luke 8:19–21 modifies this so that the natural mother and brothers passed the test of hearing the will of God and doing it and are thus part of Jesus' true family of disciples. This means that being a natural relative of Jesus or even his own mother does not guarantee that one will stand among those favorably judged in the discrimination that Jesus brings. If his sword of discrimination is to divide families, that is possible even of his own family. In the fall and rise of many in Israel, Mary will stand with the lesser number who rise—she will belong to that handful of one hundred and twenty who emerge from the ministry as a company of believers (Acts 1:12–15)—but only because like the others

[57] The Sibylline form is closer than is Ezekiel to Luke's wording; and so Erdmann, *Vorgeschichten,* 13, suggests that Luke has historicized an oracle of Hellenistic Judaism.

[58] While in Ezek 14:17 the Lord sends the sword of discrimination, in Isa 49:1–2 the Servant of the Lord says, "The Lord called me from the womb; from the body of my mother he named my name; he made my mouth like a sharp sword" (however, the LXX has *machaira* not *romphaia* for "sword"). This would fit Luke's idea that through Jesus a sword of discrimination comes to Israel—presumably through Jesus' mouth (preaching). We have seen the importance of Deutero-Isaiah in this Lucan scene.

[59] The probability is that "sword" (*machaira*) stood in the Q form of the saying and that Luke changed it to "division" for clarity. "Sword" in Luke 2:35a is *romphaia* under the influence of Ezek 14:17.

she has passed the test and recognized the sign. And indeed her special anguish, as the sword of discrimination passes through her soul, will consist in recognizing that the claims of Jesus' heavenly Father outrank any human attachments between him and his mother, a lesson that she will begin to learn already in the next scene (2:48–50).[60]

This interpretation makes Simeon's prophecy of discriminatory judgment for Israel applicable to Mary as an individual Israelite, and more specially applicable to her as a member of Jesus' family. If being an Israelite will not guarantee a share in Jesus' salvation, neither will being a member of his family. It is quite distinct from the thesis that Simeon is speaking to Mary as the personification of Israel who in her own life acts out the history of Israel in face of the Gospel. The latter thesis is associated with the identification of Mary as the Daughter of Zion in previous scenes (§ 11E),[61] an identification that is quite dubious. I think the thesis of personified Israel is quite unsatisfactory here because it fails to do justice to the relationship between 34c and 35a. Mary is not personifying Israel because most of Israel will fall; rather Mary here is part of Israel, to be tested like the rest.

Besides effecting personal discrimination, does the sword that passes through Mary's soul have an effect on others? The answer to that question depends in good part upon whether we think of 35a as parenthetical,[62] or as directly leading into 35b. If the two lines are closely connected, the sword passes through Mary's soul *so that* the inmost thoughts of many may be revealed. However, such an interpretation requires that the last line be taken favorably or at least neutrally, i.e., inmost thoughts accepting Jesus will be revealed, or inmost thoughts both accepting and refusing Jesus will be revealed. (Granting Luke's general respect for Mary, he can scarcely mean that a sword will pass through Mary's soul so that the inmost thoughts rejecting Jesus will be revealed.) Nevertheless, the evidence favors an interpretation of *dialogismoi kardiōn*, "inmost thoughts," entirely as thoughts hostile to Jesus, unbelieving thoughts, doubting thoughts (see NOTE). This makes perfect sense if 35a is taken parenthetically so that 35b continues 34d, giving us this sequence of ideas in the oracle: The

---

60 I think that 2:41–52 was added at the second stage of Lucan composition and thus was not directly in Luke's mind when he wrote this oracle of Simeon (belonging to the first stage of composition). Yet, I maintain that the attitude toward Mary in 2:48–50 is simply an anticipation of Jesus' attitude toward her in the ministry.

61 It is vigorously defended by Benoit, "Et toi-même," an article from which I have drawn liberally in my discussion of OT background.

62 The theory of a parenthesis is said to go back to the early sixteenth century and to Robert Stephanus, the famous Parisian printer and editor of the Greek NT. It is supported by scholars of diverse background, e.g., Creed, Loisy, W. Manson. Another group of scholars think of the line as an addition to a more primitive source (Klostermann, Reuss, J. Weiss), a theory that posits virtually no relationship between the line and its context. I have attempted to show that there is a close relationship between the line and its context, and so I would reject the theory of an addition.

child is set for the fall and rise of many in Israel (34c); but, as the emphasis on "fall" indicates, for the majority he is a sign that will be contradicted (34d) since, as they face him, the hostility of their inmost thoughts toward him will be revealed (35b). As Jesus said about the hostile thoughts of the Pharisees, "Nothing is covered up that will not be revealed; nothing is hidden that will not be made known" (Luke 12:1–2). In this negative sequence, the reference to Mary is parenthetical because Luke knows that, while she cannot be spared the sword of discrimination, she will decide positively.

D. *Anna Greets the Child (2:36–38)*

If this presentation scene once terminated the infancy narrative, Luke is too gentle a theologian to have the story close on such a negative note. Perhaps many in Israel will fall; but Simeon who uttered those words was one who recognized the consolation of Israel (2:25). And he was not the only one, for now Anna comes to "speak about the child to all those waiting for the redemption of Jerusalem." Mary is not the sole parenthetical exception to the contradiction of the sign.

While the joining of the Anna episode to the Simeon scene may seem artificial in the sense that not even a word of hers is recorded,[63] in several ways we have a typical Lucan pattern. She is not so silent as she appears prima facie, for Luke intends that her widowhood devoted to worship, prayer, and fasting should have its own eloquence, vocalizing the ideals of the Anawim. It was this life that opened her to the spirit of prophecy so that she could recognize Jesus and speak about him. On several occasions we have seen a similarity of atmosphere between the infancy narratives and the first chapters of Acts, in part because the Anawim of the infancy narrative are so close to the Jerusalem community of Acts. By placing Anna the prophetess side-by-side with Simeon, Luke is anticipating the atmosphere of Pentecost: "In the last days I shall pour out my Spirit upon all flesh, and your sons and your daughters will prophesy" (Acts 2:17). Moreover, he is duplicating the two waiting figures "on in years" (1:7) with whom he opened the infancy narrative (Zechariah and Elizabeth); for Simeon is ready to die, and Anna is well on in years.[64]

---

63 In one way this is peculiar; for of the four OT women who are called "prophetess" two have canticles associated with them. The canticle of Deborah in Judg 5 is well-known, and a short canticle is attributed to Miriam in Exod 15:21. Miriam was probably the original singer of the canticle that begins in Exod 15:1, although later tradition attributed it to Moses.

64 We have already seen other similarities between Zechariah/Elizabeth and Simeon/Anna: the Samuel motifs that run through both narratives; Zechariah's Benedictus and Simeon's Nunc Dimittis; the secondary dramatic status of Elizabeth and Anna; the pious character of both pairs including the designation "upright" (1:6; 2:25).

To what extent are the details that Luke tells us about Anna symbolic? The Anawim features are hard to evaluate:[65] Luke may be creating a type of Anawim piety, or he may be giving us a woman who was remembered by the Jerusalem Christian Anawim precisely because she was a saintly model of their ideals. The exact details of her age and her genealogy in a minor tribe may be signs of historical memory. Much depends on how literally Luke means the statement: "She never left the Temple courts; day and night she worshiped God." Subsequent Gentile Christian tradition, perhaps influenced by the legend in the *Protevangelium of James* 7–8 that Mary was brought as a child to the altar of the Temple and reared in the Temple confines, read Luke to mean that women lived in the Temple; and that is very dubious.[66] However, Luke may be speaking in hyperbole about faithful visits to the Temple courts, and we should note that in Acts 26:7 the same expression, "to worship day and night," is applied to the Twelve Tribes.

What is of particular interest is the emphasis on Anna's widowhood of eighty-four years. To what extent has this aspect of Anna's portrait been painted in light of an ideal of widowhood that Luke knew in the Pauline churches? Luke mentions widows more than all the other Gospels combined, and there is an awareness of their special place in Christianity in Acts 6:1 and 9:39,41.[67] The most detailed description of Christian widows is in I Tim 5:3–16, many features of which match Luke's description of Anna. To be enrolled the Christian widow must be over sixty years of age (I Tim 5:9), so that clearly she has accepted a life alone and will not remarry (5:5,11,14). The ideal is that she continue "in prayers and supplications day and night" (5:6), even as Anna worshiped God day and night, fasting and praying. It is stressed that the Christian widow should not have been married more than once (5:9), even as Anna had not remarried since the death of the husband of her youth.[68] Yet, while the

[65] In B above we saw that the Samuel story supplied the picture of women who ministered at the door of the sanctuary (I Sam 2:22)—a reference that is missing from the LXX and from one of the Qumran Hebrew mss. of Samuel, but which may still have been known to Luke. The other OT reference to women ministering at the door of the sanctuary is Exod 38:8. The LXX form of that (Exod 38:26) speaks of "the women who fasted" by the doors, an interpretation that might explain why Luke describes Anna as fasting. The Targums Onkelos and Pseudo-Jonathan of Exod 38:8 speak of the pious women who came to pray at the door of the sanctuary, and that tradition might explain why Luke describes her as praying.

[66] Lagrange, *Luc*, 91, speculates that she had a sleeping mat in a corner of the Temple court of the women. Plummer, *Luke*, 72, states that residence within the Temple may have been possible. However, in the passage mentioned in the previous footnote, the Targum Pseudo-Jonathan specifies that the pious women who prayed at the sanctuary went back to their husbands (at night).

[67] The expression "saints and widows" for a Christian group in Acts 9:41 is particularly interesting in light of Luke's juxtaposition of Simeon the "upright and devout" and Anna the widow.

[68] We may speculate whether in Luke's view the celibate status had something to do with the ability to prophesy. The four daughters of Philip who prophesy are unmarried (Acts 21:9).

Christian tradition of widowhood may have influenced Luke's description
of Anna, we should recognize the possibility that such a tradition came
into Christianity precisely from the Jewish Anawim. The Book of Judith is
a product of second-century B.C. piety showing how God delivered His
people through the hands of the weak and lowly rather than through the
strong (Judith 15:5–6). The heroine, who is Judaism personified and thus
called the Jewess (Judith), is a widow of the tribe of Simeon who did not
remarry when her husband died but spent her days observing the Law and
fasting (8:1–8). After she delivered Israel, she gave thanks to God in a
canticle of praise (15:14 – 16:17), even as Anna gave thanks to God before all those waiting for the redemption of Jerusalem.[69] And Judith continued on in her widowhood until she reached the age of 105 (16:23)
which is almost precisely the age Luke seems to attribute to Anna if we
add up his data (see NOTE on 2:36). Thus, there is real verisimilitude in
Luke's portrait of Anna on both the Jewish and the Christian level.

E. *The Conclusion (2:39–40)*

Luke terminates with a twofold conclusion: vs. 39 terminates the immediate scene; vs. 40 terminates the infancy narrative.[70] Both terminations
reflect the Samuel story. It is true that vs. 39a, "when they had finished all
their duties according to the Law of the Lord," is part of the framework of
the presentation scene, related by way of inclusion to 2:22–24. But when
this is woven together with 39b, "they returned to Galilee and their own
city, Nazareth," we have the same combination of motifs as in I Sam 2:20.
There we are told that after Elkanah and Hannah (Anna) came up to the
sanctuary to offer sacrifice and were blessed by the aged Eli for having
dedicated Samuel to the Lord, "they would return to their own home."
This termination is another feature that Luke 2:1–40 shares with Matt
2:1–23. At the end of the Matthean infancy story we hear, "Joseph went
off to the district of Galilee; there he went to dwell in a city called
Nazareth."[71] Both Luke and Matthew had to provide a transition from
the infancy to the ministry which would begin with Jesus as a Galilean from
Nazareth.

[69] In Judith 15:9 Judith is blessed with these words: "You are the exaltation of
Jerusalem; the surpassing joy of Israel; you are the great pride of our race [*genos*]." This
may be compared to "waiting for the consolation of Israel" (Luke 2:25) and "waiting
for the redemption of Jerusalem" (2:38).

[70] Even if one does not accept my thesis that at the first stage of Lucan composition the
infancy narrative ended with 2:40 and that 2:41–52 was added by Luke later, the story of
Jesus *as an infant* still terminates in 2:40. He will be a boy of twelve in the next scene.

[71] For Matthew, unlike Luke, Nazareth is not "their own city," for Joseph and Mary originally dwelt in a house in Bethlehem (Matt 2:11).

The second termination (vs. 40) is part of the diptych pattern comparing the births of JBap and of Jesus (Table XIV) and is parallel to 1:80:[72]

JBap: "And the child grew up and became strong in Spirit."
Jesus: "And the child grew up and became strong, filled with wisdom and favored by God."

When I discussed 1:80 (§ 13A), I listed the OT passages that serve as background for this stereotyped statement. The first part ("the child grew up") is said of Isaac (Gen 21:8); the second part ("the child . . . became strong") resembles what is said of Samson (LXX of Judg 13:24). The relation of the second and third parts in the case of Jesus is like a combination of I Sam 2:21, "And the child waxed mighty before the Lord," and 2:26, "The child advanced and was good in the company of God and men."[73] Thus, the Samuel motif runs through the two verses of the Lucan conclusion.

It is noteworthy that, while Luke says that JBap became strong "in Spirit," he does not use this specification of Jesus. The absence may be accidental, or else Luke may be unwilling to posit a growth in Spirit in one who was conceived of the Holy Spirit (1:35). In any case, in Jewish thought the concept of being filled with wisdom is not so far from that of being strong in the Spirit. For instance, it is said that the Spirit of the Lord, i.e., the spirit of wisdom, will come to rest upon the Davidic king (Isa 11:2).[74] Luke comes closer than does any other Synoptic Gospel to identifying Jesus as the wisdom of God (11:49), a wisdom that can be shared with his followers (21:15). The idea that Jesus was "favored by God" is another bridge connecting the infancy of Jesus with his ministry. At the time of Jesus' conception Mary was told "You have found favor with God" (1:30); here in a context of Jesus' growth we are told that he is favored by God; and in 4:22 at the beginning of Jesus' ministry the people of Nazareth where he grew up will be amazed at "the words of (divine) favor" which come forth from his mouth.

And so the conclusion prepares the reader both geographically and biographically for the appearance of Jesus of Nazareth, coming from Galilee and preaching a message full of wisdom and exemplifying God's gracious favor.

[72] In the stories both of JBap and of Jesus this notice of growth is meant as a transition to the ministry when the respective protagonists will emerge on the scene as grown men.

[73] An even closer parallel to the Samuel pattern is found in the description in Luke 2:52: "And Jesus made progress in wisdom, maturity, and favor before God and men." It is noteworthy that there are two growth formulas for Samuel (I Sam 2:21 and 2:26) and two for Jesus (Luke 2:40 and 2:52).

[74] The notion of the spirit of wisdom appears in Wisdom 1:6; 7:7. In the Judaism of the last centuries B.C. there is a strong emphasis on wisdom as a gift of God (Sirach 1:1; 43:35[33]).

SECTIONAL BIBLIOGRAPHY (§ 15)
(LUKE 2:22–40)

Andriessen, P., "Simeon's Profetie aangaande Maria," *Nederlandse Katholieke Stemmen* 55 (1959), 179–89. See NTA 4 (1959–60), ⅓410.

Benoit, P., " 'Et toi-même, un glaive te transpercera l'âme!' (Luc 2,35)," CBQ 25 (1963), 251–61. Reprinted in ExTh, III, 216–27.

Feuillet, A., "L'épreuve prédite à Marie par le vieillard Siméon (Luc, II 35a)," in *A la Rencontre de Dieu* (Mémorial A. Gelin; Le Puy: Mappus, 1961), 243–63.

Galbiati, E., "La presentazione al Tempio (Luca 2,22–40)," BibOr 6 (1964), 28–37.

Gallus, T., "De sensu verborum Lc. 2,35 eorumque momento mariologico," *Biblica* 29 (1948), 220–39.

Winandy, J., "La prophétie de Syméon (Lc. ii, 34–35)," RB 72 (1965), 321–51.

VIII. THE BOY JESUS IN THE TEMPLE
SPEAKS OF HIS FATHER (§ 16)

Translation of Luke 2:41–52

2 [41] Now every year Jesus' parents used to go to Jerusalem for the feast of Passover. [42] And when he was twelve years old and they had gone up to the feast as usual, [43] and when they had completed the festival days and were returning home, the boy Jesus remained in Jerusalem, unknown to his parents. [44] Thinking he was in the traveling party, they had gone a day's journey before they began to search for him among their relatives and acquaintances. [45] When they did not find him, they returned to Jerusalem to search for him.

[46] Finally, after three days, they found him in the Temple precincts, seated in the midst of the teachers, both listening to them and asking them questions. [47] All who heard him were astounded at his understanding and his answers. [48] When his parents saw Jesus, they were amazed. "Child," his mother said to him, "why have you done this to us? Behold, your father and I have been so worried looking for you." [49] "Why were you looking for me?" he said to them. "Did you not know that I must be in my Father's house?" [50] But they did not understand the event of which Jesus spoke to them.

[51] Then he went back down with them to Nazareth and was obedient to them. His mother kept with concern all these events in her heart. [52] And Jesus made progress in wisdom, maturity, and favor before God and men.

NOTES

2:41. *every year.* This is the only instance in the NT of the expression *kat'etos,* although over half the forty-nine NT usages of *etos,* "year," are in Luke/Acts.

Jesus' parents. Literally, "his parents." Even if this story was once independent (see COMMENT), in its present form it supposes that the reader already knows some details about the child Jesus. Mary and Joseph have been called "parents" in 2:27.

used to go. This is the imperfect of *poreuesthai,* a favorite verb with Luke who uses it more times (49 in the Gospel) than do all the other Gospels together. I do not find persuasive Laurentin's argument (*Jésus,* 98) that, since it appears in theological passages concerning Jesus' destiny, e.g., Luke 22:22, it has a theological symbolism here. Its use is too diversified in Luke to make any judgments.

to Jerusalem for the feast of Passover. Here and in 2:45 the orthography is *Ierousalēm* (NOTE on 2:22). The dative can be just as well translated "at the feast." The expression "the feast of Passover" does not occur in the LXX; *to pascha* (literally, "the Passover"), without the designation "feast," is more usual in the NT. Perhaps the present expression, which is also used in John 13:1, is a clarification for Gentile readers; see also John 6:4: "the Passover, the feast of the Jews." Passover had long been joined to the feast of the Unleavened Bread; thus Luke 22:1 speaks somewhat imprecisely of "the feast of Unleavened Bread, which is called Passover." It was this joining that made Passover one of the three pilgrimage feasts—the other two, besides Unleavened Bread, were Weeks (Pentecost) and Tabernacles—when Jews were to appear "before the Lord" in the Jerusalem Temple to worship (Exod 23:17; 34:23). See John 4:45 for the mention of Galilean Jews going to Jerusalem for Passover. The men were obliged to go and an offering was to be brought (Deut 16:16: "Three times a year all your males will appear before the Lord . . . they will not appear before the Lord empty-handed."). But it is not clear whether women and children were to appear in the Temple with gifts (St-B, II, 142). It is difficult to know how widely the law of the three feasts was observed in Jesus' time: many Jews living outside Palestine may have made the pilgrimage only once in a lifetime, and many Palestinian Jews may have come only once a year.

42. *he was twelve years old.* The verb is *ginesthai* ("become"), but here presumably it is simply equivalent to the verb "to be" (BAG, p. 159; II, 2b). For details on the Jewish customs, see Pax, "Jüdische." The general talmudic principle is that a child reaches manhood at the thirteenth birthday. Yet it was recognized that a child could understand the significance of the commandments and be bound by them before that, e.g., the age of making vows was sometimes set at twelve (TalBab *Nazir* 29b). The age of discrimination was thought to be between twelve and thirteen (TalBab *Kethuboth* 50a). We do not know whether in Jesus' time such later talmudic ideas were already applicable; but *a fortiori* the much later custom of the Bar Mitzvah was not. We do not know whether at age twelve Jesus would have been *obliged* to go to Jerusalem, and nothing in the story indicates that Luke thought of an obligation. It is an example of Jesus' exemplifying "Temple piety."

and they had gone up. For the expression "to go up" (*anabainein*), see NOTE on 2:4. In Greek this is a genitive participial construction (a present participle—awkwardly yoked to the genitive aorist participle "completed" in vs. 43) which is subordinate to the main verb in vs. 43, "remained." Struck by this awkwardness, scribes sometimes changed the participle to an aorist form; and most modern translations have turned the participle into a finite verb. However, in this instance it is important to preserve Luke's sense of subordination. His emphasis is not on the Passover pilgrimage nor on the parents' departure, but on Jesus' action in remaining behind.

to the feast. Literally, "according to the custom of the feast."

as usual. The expression *kata to ethos* is peculiar in the NT to Luke (1:9; 22:39).

43. *completed.* Another genitive participle. For the completion of specified time in 1:23 and 2:6,21,22 ("the time came") Luke used the verb *pimplanai* (*pimplēmi*). Here the verb is *teleioun* which appears in Luke again only in 13:32: "I cast out demons and perform cures today and tomorrow, and on the third day I must *complete* my course." Yet it is probably an exaggeration to see an emphasis on destiny in the current instance, as does Laurentin, *Jésus*, 103. It is similar to 2:39: "when they had finished [*telein*] all their duties."

the festival days. Literally, "the days." Passover was celebrated on the evening concluding the 14th of Nisan, and the seven-day feast of the Unleavened Bread began on the 15th, thus, in sum an eight-day feast (Lev 23:5–6). It was not clearly defined in the Law how long pilgrims had to remain in Jerusalem, other than that they had to stay overnight and were not free to depart before the morning of the second day (St-B, II, 147–48). If Luke knew accurately the duration of the feast, he would seem to be indicating that the parents stayed the whole eight days.

the boy Jesus. Jesus is now a *pais;* previously he was designated by the diminutive form *paidion* (2:17,27,40).

remained. It is useless to speculate whether Jesus' remaining was the result of an accident (they forgot him, or he got lost) or a deliberate act. Nor does Luke mean that, while the parents left early, Jesus remained piously to complete the feast days (*pace* Bornhäuser, *Kindheitsgeschichte,* 127). Romantic is the explanation of J. R. Gray, ExpTim 71 (1959–60), 53, 187, that the parents must have been taking care of their other children, for they could not have forgotten their only child. Verse 49 makes otiose the question of Jesus' motive in remaining behind: his action and that of the parents were for the sake of the story.

44. *Thinking.* Luke favors this verb *nomizein* (nine times in Luke/Acts, compared to six times elsewhere in the NT).

traveling party. This *synodia* consisted of at least relatives and friends from Nazareth. Acts 9:7 uses a verbal form of this word (the only other NT usage) to describe the group with Paul on the road to Damascus.

a day's journey. The same expression (but without Luke's reversed word order) occurs in the LXX of Num 11:31 and I Kgs 19:4. It would cover a distance of about twenty miles, as we know from the range of places listed as a day's journey from Jerusalem in Mishnah *Maaser Sheni* 5:2. (Later Christian legend fixed the end of this day's journey at El Bireh [dubiously biblical Beeroth], ten miles north of Jerusalem.) From the Galilean highlands of Nazareth to Jerusalem was a distance of some eighty miles, and thus a journey of three to four days, even by the direct route through Samaria (Josephus *Life* 52;✗269).

before they began to search. Literally, "and they were searching"; but Luke scarcely means that they spent that first day's journey looking through a long caravan.

relatives and acquaintances. As in 2:34c,37 ("fall and rise," "day and night," "fasting and praying") the pattern of the double expression (*Zweigliedrichkeit*) is a Lucanism; see Morgenthaler, *Die lukanische*, 28.

46. *Finally . . . they found.* Literally, "It happened . . . they found"; another *egeneto* construction as explained in the NOTE on 1:9. It marks the beginning of the main part of the narrative.

after three days. Luke probably means that the finding took place at the end of the third day of their departure from Jerusalem, calculated thus: a day's journey away from Jerusalem; a day's journey back to Jerusalem; a day spent searching. Others have counted the three days from the discovery that the child was missing or even from the return to Jerusalem.

the Temple precincts. Hieron; see NOTE on "Temple court" in 2:27.

seated in the midst of the teachers. Although in the body of the Gospel Jesus is frequently called "teacher" (*didaskalos*), he is not presented as one here. Lagrange, *Luc*, 96, is overly romantic when he imagines the Temple teachers inviting the charming child into their magisterial circle. True, the seated position is often one of a teacher (Matt 23:2; 26:55), and Luke 5:3 describes Jesus thus: "He sat down and taught the people." Yet the seated position also befits a disciple or learner, e.g., Paul is described as having learned at the feet of Gamaliel in Acts 22:3. It is noteworthy that Luke refers to these Jewish leaders as "teachers"; for it is not a term used for them during the public ministry, where they are either "lawyers" (*nomikos*) or "scribes" (*grammateus*). Perhaps by the time that Luke wrote, the Jewish lawyer or scribe was generally thought of as hostile to Jesus (and to Christians), so that in this friendly scene of Jesus' youth Luke preferred a more neutral term. Speculation about whether this was in a school or synagogue in the Temple precincts is unnecessary since Luke is not specific about the context of the teaching. Overall, the scene is not implausible according to Jewish customs where youth learned duties and commandments from the elders; see Pax, "Jüdische," 255.

47. *All who heard.* This includes the teachers but does not emphasize them.

were astounded. This is the first instance of *existanai* (*existēmi*), a verb

Luke/Acts uses eleven times—more than twice the usage of the rest of the NT. Very strong in classical Greek ("out of one's mind"), in the NT it has an attenuated sense of amazement at the miraculous or extraordinary (BAG, 276, 2b). Luke has already recorded astonishment (*thaumazein*) over things said about the child Jesus (2:18,33).

his understanding. The attribute of *synesis* involves perception and intelligence, but not necessarily of a religious nature, e.g., in Acts 13:7 it is used of Sergius Paulus. Its emphasis is on insight rather than on knowledge. Luke sees this *synesis* as an example of the *sophia,* "wisdom," which he stresses in 2:40,52. David prays that the Lord will give Solomon *sophia* and *synesis* in I Chr 22:12, and the spirits of *sophia* and *synesis* constitute a gift for the king in Isa 11:2.

his answers. We were not told in vs. 46 that Jesus was asked *questions.* "Answers" does not necessarily imply that Jesus was teaching the teachers. Like "relatives and acquaintances" in 45, "understanding and answers" may constitute another example of Lucan double expression.

48. *his parents.* Literally, "they"; and grammatically this "they" should refer by proximity to "all who heard him" of vs. 47. However, Luke is simply careless here, for clearly he means to refer to the parents last mentioned in vs. 46. This is one of the factors that have caused some scholars to regard 47 as a late insertion in the development of the narrative.

were amazed. The verb *ekplēssein* occurs in Luke/Acts four times, out of a total of thirteen NT occurrences. It is dubious that it conveys greater intensity than "were astonished" of the preceding verse (Laurentin, *Jésus,* 33–34).

Child. Teknon; see NOTE on "boy" in vs. 43.

Behold. Luke has already used *idou* nine times in the infancy narrative; and the formulas *kai idou* (NOTE on 1:20) and *idou gar* (NOTE on 1:44) have a certain significance. The use here is more trivial.

worried. The verb *odynasthai* occurs four times in Luke/Acts and nowhere else in the NT. It implies mental and spiritual pain or sadness, and in Luke 16:24–25 and Acts 20:38 the anguish concerns life itself.

49. *Why were.* Literally, "How is it that?"

for me. The "me" in this question and the "I" in the next question are in the emphatic position in Greek, coming at the very end of both questions.

he said to them . . . you. The "you" is plural, and so Jesus is answering not only his mother's question but also *both* parents' amazement and worry.

in my Father's house. The Greek *en tois tou patros mou* is literally "in the . . . of my father," with the plural of the definite article used instead of a specific substantive. I shall discuss below in descending order of likelihood various interpretations that have been proposed. For fuller discussion and references, see Laurentin, *Jésus,* 38–72; Temple, "What."

A) "In the dwelling-place (house) of my (heavenly) Father." The Lucan context where the parents are searching for Jesus makes appropriate supplying *a noun of locale.* The neuter plural of the definite article with the preposition *en* is well attested in the meaning "in the dwelling-place of," e.g., the LXX of Job 18:19, "Strangers will dwell in his place [*en tois autou*]," and of Esther 7:9, "A gallows has been set up in the premises of Aman [*en tois Aman*]." An important parallel is found in Josephus *Contra Apion* I 18;⚹118: "in the place (temple) of Zeus [*en tois tou Dios*]." Following these parallels, Luke's Greek phrase would then have the sense of the French *chez*. The more specific identification of "place" as "house" is encouraged by the fact that Jesus is in the Temple, which on several occasions is referred to as God's house (*oikos*); see Luke 19:46; John 2:16 ("my Father's house"); and also Luke 6:4 pertaining to the Tabernacle. This translation is supported by the Syriac, Armenian, and Persian versions, by the Greek Church fathers, and by many of the Latin fathers, following Augustine.

B) "In or about the things (business, affairs) of my (heavenly) Father." The Lucan context where Jesus is found in the Temple precincts "seated in the midst of the teachers, both listening to them and asking them questions," makes appropriate supplying *a noun of activity*. One may argue that the first part of Jesus' response is not, "Where were you looking for me?", but, "Why were you looking for me?" There is nothing in Jesus' divine sonship that should have led his parents to know where he would be (i.e., in the Temple precincts). But conceivably, knowing that he was God's Son, the parents could have known that he would be involved in God's affairs, e.g., by discussing the Law and asking religious questions; and so they should not have worried. This logic is a bit forced, and the grammatical basis is weaker than for the previous explanation. Laurentin, *Jésus*, 54, argues that *einai en* does not really mean "to be about, to be preoccupied by." Moreover, it is difficult to find an exact biblical parallel for the preposition *en* governing a neuter plural definite article in the meaning "in the affairs of." It is true that one can find in the Bible the neuter plural definite article with the meaning "things, affairs" (Mark 8:33; I Cor 7:32–34), but not used thus with the preposition *en*. For this reason, those who support this interpretation of Luke usually cite as examples the preposition *en* with the neuter plural of the demonstrative pronoun, e.g., "Cultivate these things; immerse yourself in them [*en toutois isthi*]" (I Tim 4:15). This translation is supported by the Latin, Coptic, Ethiopic, and Arabic versions; it was revived by medieval Latin writers, and made popular by the classical translations of the Reformation period (Wycliffe, Erasmus, Luther, Rheims, Authorized or King James). Occasionally writers combine it with the previous translation, e.g., "about the house (temple) and all the things of my Father" (Venerable Bede, Albert the Great); but they do so on the grounds that the "house" is part of the business or affairs.

C) "In or among the household (relatives) of my (heavenly) Father." The Lucan context where the parents had searched for Jesus among their relatives and acquaintances (*en tois syngeneusin*), and therefore among the household of Jesus' earthly father, makes appropriate supplying *a noun naming persons*. In reply to his parents' search Jesus could be conceived as telling them that they should have searched among the relatives or household of his heavenly Father (*en tois tou patros mou*). As we have seen, there are other scenes in Luke (8:19–21; 11:27–28) where Jesus contrasts an earthly family with an eschatological family composed of disciples related to God. The use of the (masculine) plural definite article is attested in Rom 16:10–11: "Greet those who belong to the household (family) of Aristobulus . . . Greet those who belong to the household of Narcissus" (*tous ek tōn Aristoboulou . . . tous ek tōn Narkissou*). Patristic support for this has been found in Theodoret (PG 75:1461CD) who actually supplied the Greek noun for household members (*en tois oikeiois tou patros mou*); but this text has been questioned by Laurentin, *Jésus,* 43–44, so that main support is modern, namely, J. Döderlein. The insurmountable obstacle to this interpretation is the impossibility that Jesus would have spoken of the teachers of the Law in the Temple as "the household (family) of my Father."

50. *they did not understand.* This is a verbal form (*synienai*) related to the noun *synesis* used in vs. 47 of Jesus, so that Luke is drawing a sharp contrast between the parents' lack of understanding and Jesus' astounding understanding. To avoid the implication of a lack of understanding on Mary's part, especially after she had received a revelatory annunciation from an angel, some scholars have resorted to complicated hypotheses: (a) The "they" is a synecdoche with the whole used for the part, so that only Joseph is meant. This view was mentioned already by Cardinal Cajetan, *In Quattuor Evangelia* (Paris: Guillard, 1540), fol. 218v. (b) The "they" refers to the bystanders of vs. 47, not to the parents of vss. 48–49. This view too was mentioned by Cajetan and is defended by Power, "Who." (c) The object of the lack of understanding, namely, "the event (word) of which Jesus spoke to them," was not Jesus' response in vs. 49 but some other saying of Jesus to his parents not narrated by Luke. Power, "Who," combines this with the preceding hypothesis: after his questions to them in vs. 49, Jesus consolingly explained matters to his parents, but "they [the bystanders] did not understand this word he spoke to them [the parents]." J. B. Cortés and F. M. Gatti, *Marianum* 32 (1970), 404–18, and J. M. Bover, EB 10 (1951), 205–15, propose that three days before, as Jesus' parents were leaving Jerusalem, Jesus told them that he was going to stay behind in Jerusalem, but "they *had* not understood the word he *had* spoken to them." (Notice the need of translating the aorist tenses as pluperfects.) In my judgment these hypotheses are wishful eisegesis, not worthy of serious discussion. Laurentin (*Jésus,* 77) is correct when he says that surely the "they" means the parents, that theirs is a real (not simulated) lack of understanding, and that this understanding concerns Jesus' remarks in vs. 49.

the event of which Jesus spoke to them. Here, once again, Luke uses *rēma* with the double meaning "word, event," as in 2:15 (see NOTE), 2:17,19. This time, more directly than in the preceding occurrences, the meaning is "word"; and yet to translate it thus would disguise from the reader the connection with previous uses. Moreover, the parents' lack of comprehension centers not only on the words of Jesus' question but on the whole course of action that leads to it.

51. *he went back down . . . to Nazareth.* Literally, "he went down . . . and came to Nazareth." The going down is the opposite of going up in 2:42; the "came to Nazareth" is the opposite of the "used to go to Jerusalem" in vs. 41. For Luke's use of departure verbs to end scenes in the infancy narrative, see NOTE on 1:23.

was obedient to them. This construction of the verb "to be" plus a participle of *hypotassein* emphasizes the continuity of the situation. The latter verb is standard in the Pauline corpus for describing family subordination. Pax, "Jüdische," 255, sees this as a historical reminiscence: at age twelve Jesus was beginning to be self-responsible but was not completely emancipated from parental control. However, Luke is more interested, first, in the contrast that although he was God's Son, Jesus allowed himself to obey human parents; and, second, in explaining how, although Jesus had already revealed his divine sonship, he did not publicly begin his mission till after his baptism.

kept with concern all these events. See NOTES on 2:19.

in her heart. This is omitted by OS^sin.

52. *made progress.* This is the only Gospel usage of the verb *prokoptein*. Winter, "On the Margin," 107, contends that "to make progress in wisdom" is a Hebraism, but see the Greek inscription quoted under "maturity" below.

in wisdom . . . and favor. These two nouns appear in the summary statement about Jesus' growth in 2:40; the noun "maturity," which is placed between them here, is new to the description. The three nouns are coordinate; and so it is difficult to agree with Glombitza, "Der zwölfjährige," that the basic emphasis is on wisdom, with maturity and grace as specifications.

maturity. The noun *hēlikia* covers a span both of years (age) and size (stature). The former usage is more common in the LXX and Philo, and is supported by the Latin Vulgate. There are two other Lucan usages of the word: in 12:25 the span is probably one of age; in 19:3 it is clearly a question of stature. J. Schneider, TDNT, II, 942, calls attention to a pagan inscription about a youth of Istropolis who is said to be "making progress [*prokoptein*] in *hēlikia* and advancing in the reverence of the gods"; and in this inscription too the meaning of *hēlikia* is not clear. Many modern commentators prefer the meaning "stature" because an increase of age is too obvious to need Lucan emphasis. However, Luke may mean a general maturing in manhood which would involve both age and stature.

before God and men. The preposition *para* with the genitive can mean "with, alongside of" and "before." There is LXX support for both ideas: the preposition *meta* ("with," "in the company of") governs "the Lord and men" in a description of the growth of Samuel in I Sam 2:26, while *enōpion* ("before," "in the sight of") governs the same phrase in Prov 3:4.

COMMENT

Since we move here from Jesus as an infant to Jesus at the age of twelve, the question of the relationship of this story to what has preceded is of major importance. Matthew's birth story came to an end when the parents brought the little child to Nazareth; why does Luke have an interlude in which Jesus is portrayed as a boy? We saw that the Lucan birth story was dominated by a christology centered on Jesus' conception and birth. Does this story also have a christological theme? Let us begin with a general discussion of these points before we interpret the subsections in detail.

A. *Structure, Christology, and Outline*

Even though the scene in 2:22–40 forms almost a perfect inclusion with the opening of the infancy narrative, and even though 2:39–40 prepares for the emergence of Jesus in the ministry as one coming from Nazareth and Galilee to proclaim a message of wisdom and God's favor, Luke does not terminate his pre-ministry account with the presentation in the Temple; and he does not move from 2:40 directly to the opening of the ministry in 3:1. He rather provides as a transition another scene involving Jesus and the Temple. How does this scene fit into Luke's overall plan for chs. 1–2? In Table IX we saw a number of analyses of Lucan structure, and in them two ways of treating 2:41–52 are clear. One suggestion (e.g., Laurentin) gives this scene a role similar to that of the visitation: just as the two annunciation narratives were followed by the visitation, the two birth narratives are followed by the story of the boy Jesus in the Temple. Yet that structural analysis has difficulties. The point of the visitation was to show the fulfillment of the sign given to Mary during the annunciation; it is as intimately related to the annunciation of Jesus' birth as 1:24–25 is related to the annunciation of JBap's birth. The story in 2:41–52 is not the fulfillment of anything that precedes.[1] Another and more plausible suggestion appears in the analyses of Burrows and Lyonnet, i.e., that there are two Temple scenes (2:22–40 and 2:41–52) which are parallel to each other.[2] As we shall see, these two scenes do have very similar introductions and very similar conclusions; they involve a journey to Jerusalem and a journey back to Nazareth. Yet, making allowance for this on the grounds that Luke partially patterned 2:41–52 upon 2:22–40, one may still maintain that the best solution is to recognize that Luke 2:41–52 was not part of the original diptych structure of the infancy narrative which came to an end with 2:40 (see § 9, B2 and Tables XI and XIV). Thus it would have no real parallel in what precedes but would be an independent story of Jesus' youth added by Luke in a second stage of composition. So that the joining would not be too artificial, Luke presumably made the beginning and ending of 2:41–52 match the beginning and ending of 2:22–40.

---

[1] The real parallel to the visitation in the diptych pattern is the presentation in 2:22–40, which continues the story of Jesus' birth even as the visitation continues the story of the annunciation of Jesus' birth.

[2] But making these scenes parallel destroys the relationship between Jesus' birth and the presentation (see Table XIV) mentioned in the previous footnote.

There are many factors that point in this direction. The scene of finding the boy Jesus in the Temple precincts occurs after an interval of twelve years, in the time span between the events surrounding the birth and the events surrounding the baptism. Chronologically, then, it can scarcely be called a section of the *infancy* narrative. Indeed, as we shall see, in its content and tone it is a canonical example of those stories of the "hidden life" of Jesus (i.e., his life with his family at Nazareth before the ministry) which appear in the apocryphal gospels of subsequent centuries.[3] But besides exhibiting a difference of chronology and content, this story does not depend for its intelligibility on what precedes in Luke.[4] Indeed, if one were to read it as a unit, one would have no suspicion that Jesus had been virginally conceived and that Joseph was not his natural father. Rather, Joseph is included among the "parents" of Jesus (vss. 41,43) and is specifically called Jesus' father (48).[5] When Jesus speaks of his heavenly Father, his parents do not understand (49–50). This is more than the astonishment of 2:33 which is the ordinary reaction in Luke to the miraculous; it is a real failure to grasp revelation, as we see from other instances of not understanding (8:10; 18:34; 24:45). Such a failure is surprising after the annunciation to Mary in 1:26–38, after the message of the angels in 2:1–20, and after the predictions of Simeon in 2:21–40. For these reasons many scholars have posited a pre-Lucan narrative behind 2:41–52—a narrative that Luke adapted and added. While in general I have rejected the thesis of pre-Lucan sources for 1:5 – 2:40, except for the canticles,[6] the thesis has serious possibilities here. Van Iersel has argued well that there are traces of an original composition and addenda;[7] and even some of those who think that the main body of the Lucan infancy narrative has been translated from Hebrew find the Greek style of 2:41–52 less marked by Semitisms.[8] However, as the NOTES show, there

[3] The best example is the second-century *Infancy Gospel of Thomas*, translated in Hennecke, NTApoc, I, 392–401. (This is to be kept distinct from *The Gospel of Thomas* which is part of the Gnostic collection of Chenoboskion.) Despite the title, it treats not of Jesus' infancy but of his youth: "I, Thomas the Israelite, tell and make known to you, my Gentile brethren, all the works of the childhood of our Lord Jesus Christ, and his mighty deeds which he did when he was born in the land." Stories are told therein of what Jesus did at age five (2:1), age six (11:1), age eight (12:2), and at age twelve (19:1)—the last mentioned being a retelling of Luke 2:41–52.

[4] Of course, as the story is now narrated, Luke has made some connections; see NOTE on "Jesus' parents" in vs. 41.

[5] This nomenclature must be used with caution; see footnote 25, § 15.

[6] I remind the reader of what I mean by source (footnote 19, § 9); I am not denying that Luke inherited items of information from tradition.

[7] Van Iersel, "Finding," 172, points to a basic story in 41–43,45–46,48–50, with a created framework and additions in 44,47. He regards the additions as of a legendary or storytelling nature (p. 165); and it is precisely the additions that fascinated later storytellers, as we can see from *Infancy Gospel of Thomas* 19:2, and from the various theories mentioned in the NOTES on "remained" in 43, and on "they did not understand" in 50.

[8] Laurentin, *Structure*, 142. Schlatter, *Lukas*, 205, stresses the Greek grammatical features, e.g., the genitive participle in 42–43, and the word order in "a day's journey" in 44. However, there remains more parataxis than subordination, so that Semitic features are not totally absent.

are marks of Lucan style throughout; and if there was a pre-Lucan story, one must recognize that Luke has thoroughly rewritten it.[9]

While we may not be able to reach certainty about the pre-Lucan origin of the story, our understanding of its relation to the birth material can be deepened by reflecting on its function. Besides supplying a chronological transition between infancy and ministry, it supplies a transition between revelation *about* Jesus by others (angels, Simeon) and revelation that Jesus himself will proclaim; for in 2:41–52 Jesus speaks for the first time. I have insisted that the key to understanding the conception/birth narratives lies in christology (§ 1, A2). In both Matthew and Luke the moment of the revelation of Jesus as God's Son has been moved back from the baptism (where it is in Mark's Gospel) to the conception/birth. I pointed out that the Fourth Gospel did not treat the "backwards" movement of christology in the same way: John has jumped over the conception/birth by proceeding directly back to the pre-existence of the Word. The movement may be exemplified in still another way in the "hidden life" stories where the revelation of who Jesus is occurs before the baptism but not so far back as the conception. The christological moment here occurs in Jesus' youth when he is old enough to express in word and in work his self-consciousness. The operative insight in all this "backwards" movement is that the heavenly voice at the baptism did not adopt Jesus and make him the divine Son, but revealed publicly what he already was. "Hidden life" stories show that he was God's Son even as a boy by having him work miracles just as he does in the ministry, and by having him speak in the high christological language of the ministry. These stories as found in the apocryphal gospels often portray the boy Jesus in the role of a magician; but such fantastic elaboration should not disguise the instinct that the unknown period of the boyhood could best be filled in through a creative use of what was known from the ministry.[10] I contend that this same instinct has been at work in Luke 2:41–52; and it is no accident that, at the end of his sequence of apocryphal "hidden life" stories about Jesus, the author of the *Infancy Gospel of Thomas* presented an adaptation of Luke 2:41–52. He had recognized kindred material.

It is a common instinct in many cultures and literatures to make the boy the father of the man by creating boyhood stories for great figures, stories

---

[9] Van Iersel, "Finding," 1634, 167. Of Morgenthaler's list of sixty-seven Lucanisms, no fewer than thirteen occur here. It is not inconceivable that between the birth story with its heavy OT background and Semitized style and the ministry story which is much less Semitized, Luke has chosen to present a transition story in a Greek that is also transitional.

[10] In the *Infancy Gospel of Thomas* the five-year-old Jesus makes birds out of clay, but in so doing he is accused of violating the Sabbath (2:3), even as in the ministry. He causes the son of Annas the scribe to wither up like a tree and bear no fruit (3:2) and thus anticipates his later hostility to the scribes and his action in causing the fig tree to wither. The villagers react by asking, "From where does this child come, since his every word is an accomplished deed" (4:1), a reaction that anticipates the amazement of the citizens of Nazareth about Jesus' teaching and his mighty works.

that anticipate the greatness of the subject. Often these stories feature surprising knowledge shown at an age between ten and fourteen, e.g., stories of the Buddha in India, of Osiris in Egypt, of Cyrus the Great in Persia, of Alexander the Great in Greece, and of Augustus in Rome.[11] Within the Jewish background, Josephus (*Life* 2;※9) reports this of himself: "While still a boy about fourteen years old, I won universal applause for my love of letters, with the result that chief priests and the leading men of the city used to come to me constantly for precise information on some particulars in our ordinances." At a later age Eliezer ben Hyrcanus ran away from home; and when he was found by his father, he was studying the Law.[12] The Jewish legends of Moses contemporary with the NT attribute to him extraordinary knowledge as a boy, and comment how God gave him understanding and stature and beauty of appearance.[13] In treating Samuel, Josephus[14] tells us that the boy began to act as a prophet at the completion of his twelfth year, thus dating the call of Samuel by God in the Temple (I Sam 3:1–18). In the LXX story of Susanna (vs. 45), Daniel as a youth ("of twelve" according to the Syro-Hexaplar) receives a spirit of "understanding" that makes him wiser than the elders (see also vs. 63). I am not suggesting that the story of Jesus was borrowed directly from any of these examples, but the clear pattern that emerges explains how a boyhood story about Jesus could have been fashioned. And the Moses and Samuel examples explain why a story of Jesus' boyhood would be attached to an infancy narrative, as a preparation for his ministry.[15]

In this pattern of boyhood stories of great figures, there is stress by anticipation on both the subject's wisdom and life work. Both aspects are present in the Lucan story, although the wisdom is less important. In vs. 46 Jesus is simply listening and asking questions, a sign of his interest in the Law and his piety. Only in vs. 47, which Van Iersel characterizes as a novelistic addition to a pre-Lucan story, is there stress on Jesus' brilliance.

---

[11] For details see Laurentin, *Jésus*, 147–58. The similarity of age is not surprising, granted the intent of the stories to show the greatness of the subject from the beginning of his maturity.

[12] Bultmann, *History*, 301.

[13] Josephus *Ant.* II ix 6;※※230–31, mentions specifically Moses' growth in *synesis* and *hēlikia*, two of the nouns that Luke (2:47,52) uses of Jesus. Philo, *Vita Moysis* I 5–6; ※※21ff., inserts between the stories of Moses' infancy and of his ministry a description of Moses' astounding learning. For the importance of the Moses legends as background for the Matthean infancy narrative, see § 4, B2a).

[14] *Ant.* V x 4;※348.

[15] Laurentin, *Jésus*, 88–91, argues that the order of Luke 2, including this section, is dictated by Mal 3:1–3: "I send my messenger to prepare the way before me, and the Lord whom you seek will suddenly come to His Temple. . . . He will sit." I pointed out in § 15A that the Malachi passage may well have influenced the placing of the presentation scene, for there the one hailed as Lord (Luke 2:11) comes to the Temple. But there is nothing in the Malachi passage to explain two Temple scenes in ch. 2 of Luke. Laurentin's stress on the sitting in Mal 3:3 as comparable to Jesus' sitting in Luke 2:46 neglects the fact that Mal 3:3 continues: "He will sit as a refiner and purifier of silver." The judgment motif in Malachi is found in the presentation (2:34–35), not in the present scene.

The center of the story is not the boy's intelligence but his reference to
God as his Father in vs. 49.[16] This is highly christological, for here we have
Jesus saying of himself what the heavenly voice will say at the baptism.
Accordingly, Van Iersel would correct Bultmann and Dibelius who
classified the present narrative as a legend. More properly it is to be
classified as an apophthegm or paradigm, i.e., a short story centered
around a saying.[17] However, one must not jump to the conclusion, as does
Laurentin, that if we are not dealing with legend, we are dealing with history. To be precise, we are dealing with a biographical apophthegm: the illustration of a saying (in this case, a christological saying) shaped out of a
life setting. The present setting and saying are no less and no more historical than are the divine voice and its setting at the baptism of Jesus. Jesus
was baptized; Jesus had a boyhood—those are historical facts. But in
Luke those historical reminiscences serve as the occasion for the articulation of a revelation apprehended by post-resurrectional faith, namely,
the divine sonship.

And so, whether one is liberal or conservative, one must desist from
using the present scene to establish a historical development (or lack of
development) in Jesus' self-awareness. It is not possible to argue from vs.
49 that Jesus as a boy knew he was the Son of God. It is equally impossible to argue from vs. 52 (which is a standard description of growth) that
Jesus grew in human knowledge. At most one can argue that Luke's appreciation of Jesus did not cause him to see any difficulty in stating that Jesus
grew in wisdom and God's favor,[18] and that Luke's christology did not
cause him to see any difficulty in affirming that, already as a boy, Jesus
was God's Son. Nor finally can we determine anything historical about
Mary's understanding of Jesus from the statement in vs. 50 that she and
Joseph did not understand when Jesus spoke of his Father. As already indicated, this story or a form of it may well have first circulated in circles
ignorant of the annunciation story and ignorant of the virginal conception.

16 Most authors who posit a pre-Lucan story think that it included this statement. In some
ways it might be simpler to suppose a story without it, centering on the child's prodigious
wisdom—a story to which Luke would have added the christological motif. Yet see footnote
7 above. Moreover, the genius of a boyhood story would seem to demand a statement by
Jesus, the present statement or some other.
17 Bultmann, *History*, 244–45, defines legends as religious, edifying traditions, non-historical in character. Sometimes they involve the marvelous or miraculous, but they differ
from miracle stories in the sense that they are not units in themselves and gain their point
only when set in context. Bultmann, 11, defines an apophthegm as a unit consisting of a saying of Jesus set in a brief context (the context often being of a secondary character).
"Paradigm" is the equivalent to apophthegm in the Dibelius terminology. See also Laurentin, *Jésus*, 158–61.
18 This saying caused great difficulty for later Christian theologians raised upon a Nicaean
christology of eternal pre-existence, for they could not admit that an incarnate Word (a
Johannine concept) could grow in wisdom or in grace (favor). Renié, "Et Jesus," lists their
theories on how such a growth could not mean a growth in the grace of union or sanctifying grace, but only the exterior manifestation of a grace already possessed. Today we would
see these as problems of systematic theology rather than of exegesis.

But the fact that Luke, who is aware of such traditions, sees no difficulty in reporting Mary's lack of understanding means that *for him* vs. 50 is only an instance of the standard misunderstanding that greets a parabolic revelation or a prophetic statement.[19] It is a stylized reaction in Gospel literature and tells us nothing historical of Mary's psychology.

As a transition from these general remarks to our discussion of the individual subsections of the scene, let me suggest the following outline:

> *General Statement* about Jesus' growth, his wisdom and favor (40)
> *Geographical Introduction:* Jesus and parents had gone up to Jerusalem (41–42)
> > *Setting:* The parents lost Jesus and searched for him (43–45)
> > *Core of the Story:* The parents found the child and were amazed; Jesus answered them by stressing his Father's claim (45–50)
> *Geographical Conclusion:* Jesus went down with his parents to Nazareth (51)
> *General Statement* about Jesus' progress in wisdom, maturity, and favor (52)

I have already discussed vs. 40 as belonging with vs. 39 in the conclusion to the preceding section (§ 15E), but in so doing I pointed out that vs. 40 is transitional to Jesus' life at a later age. If the first stage of Lucan composition ended with 2:40, that verse supplied a transition to the description of Jesus as a man about thirty years of age beginning his ministry (3:23). But once Luke inserted 2:41–52, vs. 40 came to supply a transition to the present story. Having told us that "the child grew up and became strong, *filled with wisdom and favored by God*," Luke now proceeds to give us an example of that wisdom and divine favor at age twelve. Indeed, as the outline above indicates, he sandwiches the scene in the Temple between vs. 40 and vs. 52, which almost repeats vs. 40. Verse 52 now constitutes the transition to the ministry of Jesus at age thirty. If one asks why in this hypothesis Luke did not shift vs. 40 to the place now occupied by 52, it is precisely because the retention of 40 helped him lead into the story of a Jesus who had grown in wisdom and favor since his appearance as an infant in the Temple.

---

[19] Laurentin, *Jésus,* 164, quite correctly makes this point, but his overall treatment is confused by crossing the line from Luke's presentation to Mary's psychological history—a confusion that stems from his unproved assumption that we have in the Lucan story a genuine reminiscence stemming from Mary. His whole book on Luke 2:41–52 is written in relation to the thesis that Mary knew Jesus' divinity from the annunciation on. He recalls (p. 180⁶) worries in Rome that if one were to deny this, one would not be "sufficiently generous to the Madonna"! At times it seems as if the discussion would attribute to Mary a Nicaean understanding of divinity; at least it would attribute to her a post-resurrectional understanding of divine sonship, an understanding which Luke may have had, but scarcely Mary during Jesus' lifetime. While I am a Roman Catholic and share with Laurentin an acceptance of Church dogma on Mary, I reject resolutely his using in an exegetical and historical study the principle: "One cannot suppose that Mary lacked knowledge that would befit the Mother of God" (p. 184). From the Christian acceptance of Mary as the Mother of God one may learn of her sanctity, but not of the history of her growth in knowledge.

B. *The Introduction and the Setting (2:41–45)*

Within the broader framework of vss. 40 and 52, Luke provides an inner framework of geographical introduction (41–42)[20] and conclusion (51a). These verses concern the "going up" to Jerusalem from Nazareth and the "going down" back to Nazareth. The action is necessary for the story, but Luke shows such a sense of geographical theology in the Gospel and Acts that we should not pass over the localizations too lightly. On the first level of Lucan composition of 1:5–2:40, there was a magnificent inclusion between the beginning and ending of the infancy narrative, with an elderly, upright man and woman and a Temple scene in both. When he added the present narrative, Luke preserved at least part of the inclusion, namely, the Temple scene in Jerusalem. This miniature inclusion packaging the pre-ministry career of Jesus in 1:5–2:52 anticipates the major inclusion which packages the whole Gospel, stretching from a beginning in the Jerusalem Temple to an ending in the Jerusalem Temple (24:53). This general emphasis on the Jerusalem Temple in the Lucan infancy narrative should not cause us to overlook what is new in 2:41–52, namely, the first Lucan mention of *going up from Nazareth or Galilee to Jerusalem*.[21] This will be the direction taken by Jesus in the great journey of the public ministry, stretching from 9:51 to 19:28, and it is fittingly anticipated here. The parallel is further underlined by the fact that this great journey (the only time during the ministry that Jesus goes to Jerusalem) will bring Jesus to the Temple at Passover time—the same place and time as in 2:41–52.

In addition to looking forward to the ministry, the cultic indications in vss. 41–42 point back to the Temple piety earlier underlined in 1:5–25 and 2:22–40 (§ 10, footnote 13). The Jesus of the public ministry will come to Jerusalem and the Temple to bear a threatening prophetic witness about the city and the holy place (19:41ff.), but in this scene Jesus and his parents come piously to fulfill the duties of the Law. Such a difference of atmosphere from the ministry is intelligible precisely because the parents of Jesus are involved. They are figures described in OT terms and typical of the sensibilities of Judaism; they are a bridge to the era of Jesus but do not yet articulate his prophetic insights and proclamation.

In particular, the introductory vss. 41–42 resemble the introductory vss. 22–24 of the preceding scene; in both the visit to the Temple is presented

20 While 41–42 now constitute a unit, Schmidt, *Rahmen*, 314, in his reconstruction of the pre-Lucan story, suggests that it began with vs. 42: "When Jesus was twelve years old." Verse 41 would then be a back-formation from 42 inserted to constitute a connective with the preceding scene. It supplies no information not phrased in another way in 42, except the identification of the feast.

21 In 2:22 it was from Bethlehem that the parents brought Jesus up to Jerusalem.

as the fulfillment of legal obligations. The similarity is furthered by the fact that, although both these introductions provide a rationale for what follows, they really do not affect the story line. As we saw, the purification/presentation motif is not central to 2:25–38 where the primary emphasis is on the prophetic testimony of Simeon and Anna. Here too the Passover motif does not appear in the central dialogue between Jesus and his parents. In discussing 22–24 we found that the passage shows only a general knowledge of Jewish ritual and contains inaccuracies of detail (§ 15B). The same may be true here depending on how literally we understand Luke. Does he think that "the feast of Passover" was the only occasion in the year when Jews were obliged to go up to Jerusalem (see NOTE on vs. 41),[22] or is he simply describing the general practice of Galilean Jews who went up only once a year?[23] Or is he dependent on the picture of the parents of Samuel who used to go up once a year to worship at the sanctuary of Shiloh (I Sam 1:3,21,24; 2:19)? In any case the setting reflects no more than a popular grasp of Jewish customs and cannot be invoked to defend a thesis of strict historical reminiscences.[24]

If vss. 41–42 supply the general introduction, vss. 43–45 offer a more specific setting. (A similar procedure can be seen in the preceding section where 2:22–24 are the general introduction and 2:25–27 are the specific setting.) Although Christian midrashic interest has fastened upon where the caravan stopped the first night, how large the traveling party was, and why the absence of the child was not noticed sooner (see NOTES), Luke shows no interest in such details. For instance, the fact that "they had gone a day's journey before they began to search for him among their relatives and acquaintances" needs no historical explanation: it is a literary device to heighten for the reader the anxiety of the parents.[25]

C. The Core of the Story (2:46–50)

As we saw in A above, boyhood stories tend to stress by anticipation the wisdom and the life work of the subject. It is no accident then that the

---

[22] In Acts 20:16 Paul is described as going up to Jerusalem for the day of Pentecost. Luke also shows a great number of foreign Jews in Jerusalem for Pentecost in Acts 2:9ff.; but while commentators often assume that Luke is presenting them as pilgrims present for the feast, Acts 2:5 describes them as Jews dwelling in Jerusalem.

[23] If Luke knows that an annual pilgrimage was not an exact fulfillment of the Law, he calls no attention to the defect. Rather he is interested in describing the parents of Jesus as models of observing the Law (2:22–24).

[24] In the first NOTE on vs. 42 I caution against too hastily invoking later Jewish customs to explain the Lucan scene.

[25] The verse that describes this (44) is highly Lucan in style, and is regarded by Van Iersel, "Finding," 165, as a secondary intrusion into a more primitive story—an intrusion introducing novelistic elements. I am uncertain of this since there are many Lucan elements in the surrounding verses; but certainly 44 could be omitted with no loss of logic. The loss would be one of drama.

Lucan story really begins when the parents find Jesus for whom they have been searching. The drama lies in the circumstances in which they find him (circumstances illustrative of his wisdom) and in what he says when he is found (a christological claim). The building of the narrative is such that the latter is more important than the former.[26]

1. Jesus Is Found in the Midst of the Teachers (46–48a)

The main narrative begins with a time indication: "after three days." Is this an anticipatory allusion to the resurrection? Laurentin strongly affirms this, calling attention to the expression "on the third day" which is employed six times by Luke in reference to the resurrection.[27] Yet Luke does *not* use that expression here, even though he may well have meant to date the finding of Jesus on the third day after the parents left Jerusalem (see NOTE). The expression he does use, "after three days," occurs twice more in Lucan writing (Acts 25:1; 28:17) simply as a time demarcation with no possible reference to the resurrection. It is quite true that in Mark 8:31; (9:31); 10:34 "after three days" serves as a reference to the resurrection, but Luke in his parallels to these passages does not use "after three days." Thus we have no evidence that Luke or his readers would have associated 2:46 with a resurrection motif. There I would leave the matter, were there not a possibility of a pre-Lucan form of the story in which stage "after three days" might have echoed a resurrection motif. Let me take the opportunity to mention a curious parallel.

It is possible that the story of Jesus' changing water to wine at Cana (John 2:1–12) may have had a pre-Johannine existence as a "hidden life" story, i.e., as a story about the young Jesus before he began his ministry and while he was still living in the bosom of his family.[28] This would explain many peculiar points: the setting of the miracle in the highlands of Galilee around Nazareth (where Jesus does not work miracles in the Synoptic tradition); the dating of the miracle to a period before Jesus went to Capernaum (which marks the beginning of his public ministry in Galilee in the Marcan tradition); the presence of his mother and brothers (2:12). I mentioned above (under A) instances of "hidden life" miracles and sayings from the apocryphal gospels; they often lack restraint both by way of the marvelous and by the fact that they are done for family convenience.

---

[26] Schmahl, "Lk 2,41–52," 254–55, argues convincingly that the primary accent of the scene is on vs. 49.

[27] Laurentin, *Jésus*, 101–2, 115; see Luke 9:22; 18:33; 24:7,21,46; Acts 10:40.

[28] See R. E. Brown, *Biblical Reflections on Crises Facing the Church* (New York: Paulist, 1975), 96–101. I owe the basic insight to B. Lindars, *The Gospel of John* (London: Oliphants, 1972), 127–28; also NTS 16 (1970), 318–24. Laurentin, *Jésus*, 125–26, draws fruitful attention to the similarities between Luke 2:41–52 and the Cana story; but since he treats both stories as history, he never sees the possibility that the source of relationship may lie in the fact that they are two examples of the same kind of literature, i.e., "hidden life" stories. He traces it rather to the interest of the two evangelists in Mary.

The Cana story supposes the miraculous production of an extraordinary amount of wine (the six stone jars mentioned in 2:6 would have had a capacity of over one hundred gallons) in order to save from embarrassment a friend of the family (2:1–2).[29] If one grants at least possibility to this theory of an underlying "hidden life" story, then it is noteworthy that it is dated "on the third day" (2:1). Once again this is not an expression that John ever uses to describe the resurrection (contrast 2:19–22); and so I doubt that for John, any more than for Luke, there is a covert reference to the resurrection. But if that notice belongs to a pre-Johannine level of the story,[30] then we may well wonder why there is a reference to "after three days" and "on the third day" in the two "hidden life" stories that have been preserved for us canonically in Luke and John respectively. Are these reminders, built into the stories themselves, that we have in such stories a post-resurrectional understanding of Jesus, indeed an understanding that gave rise to the story?[31]

Returning to the Lucan narrative of Jesus in the Temple, I would point to the fact that the boy Jesus is found listening to the teachers of the Law and asking them questions. This is meant to foreshadow the interests of the man Jesus, who will often be engaged in debates over the Law. However, here there appears none of the hostility to the teachers of the Law that will mark Jesus' attitude in the ministry toward the scribes and lawyers,[32] for once again "Temple piety" pervades. If vs. 46 portrays the boy Jesus as intellectually curious about things religious, vs. 47 calls attention to his insight. In the NOTE on "understanding," I have shown that for

---

[29] The thesis of a *pre-Johannine* Cana story is common whether or not those who hold it consider it to have been a "hidden life" story. Most reconstructions of that story exclude Jesus' response to his mother in 2:4, and so the reconstructed story gives a picture of Jesus obligingly performing a miracle at his mother's request. If there were a more extensive tradition of such "hidden life" miracles, we could better understand why Jesus' mother approaches him about the shortage of wine, evidently expecting him to do something (2:3). In the *Infancy Gospel of Thomas* the boy Jesus miraculously supplies his mother with water (11:1–2), and produces one hundred measures of wheat from one grain for his father (12:1–2).

[30] R. T. Fortna, *The Gospel of Signs* (NTSMS 11; Cambridge University, 1970), 29–30, in his careful reconstruction of pre-Johannine narrative, is cautious on this phrase ("on the third day"), saying that it is probably Johannine, but raising explicitly the possibility that it is not.

[31] One may object that post-resurrectional understandings of Jesus appear also in the stories of the public ministry and without any such references to time. But there we are generally dealing with post-resurrectional reinterpretation of an existing story rather than with the rise of a new story. Laurentin, *Jésus*, 108, points to a number of parallels (some rather fanciful) between Luke 2:41–52 and Luke 24; see also Elliott, "Does Luke." It is tempting to explain these on the grounds of the post-resurrectional origins of the two bodies of material, one (ch. 24) fashioned to narrate directly the significance of the risen Jesus, the other fashioned to show a continuity between the risen Jesus and the pre-ministry Jesus.

[32] Luke may underline this by using "teachers" here rather than "scribes" or "lawyers" (see NOTE). The form of the story in the *Infancy Gospel of Thomas* 12:2 introduces the notion of hostility: "All paid attention to him and were astounded how he, a child, put to silence the elders and teachers of the people."

Luke this is an illustration of the wisdom of Jesus mentioned in the two statements of growth which frame this incident (vss. 40 and 52). Thus, even if Van Iersel is right in claiming that vs. 47 was a secondary addition to a pre-Lucan story, its addition is in harmony with the Lucan conception of the incident. The astonishment that greets Jesus' understanding and his answers anticipates the amazement that will greet Jesus' teaching when he begins his ministry (Luke 4:32) and the amazement of the scribes at his answers (20:26). It is a motif that is expanded in apocryphal "hidden life" stories.[83]

The amazement is shared by Jesus' parents. In the present sequence where vs. 48a follows vs. 47, part of the source of their amazement is Jesus' understanding and his answers. But even if vs. 47 is a secondary Lucan addition, so that vs. 48a follows 46, this sequence would mean that in a pre-Lucan form of the story the parents were amazed at finding Jesus where they found him and doing what he was doing. This would make sense if, as many scholars have supposed, this was once an independent narrative of how the parents came to learn of the identity and vocation of Jesus as the Son of God. Of course, in the present position of the story, such a revelation has been given several times before, and so the amazement is at the way (and perhaps at the early age) in which an already known identity and vocation have begun to be expressed.

2. The Mother's Question Leads Jesus to Speak about His Father (48b–50)

In the dialogue that follows we move from amazement on the parents' part to a lack of understanding. The question asked by the mother which has a tone of reproach seems somewhat inconsistent with Luke's previous treatment of Mary.[84] If one posits a pre-Lucan story in which there was no antecedent narrative of a virginal conception, the tone of the question is quite understandable. But how does Luke reconcile having Mary dare to *reproach* the Son of the Most High whom she has virginally conceived in complete obedience to whatever God wanted? (This reproach is all the more startling since Luke tends to avoid reproaches to Jesus by the disciples during the ministry.[85]) Perhaps the answer is that in 51b Luke

---

83 The passage quoted in the previous footnote goes on to have Jesus "expounding sections of the Law and the sayings of the prophets." In the much later *Arabic Gospel of the Infancy* there are chapters (50–52) reporting how Jesus was questioned about the Law, about astronomy, and about philosophy; he answers all questions.

84 Laurentin, *Jésus*, 36, is misguided here by a sensitivity that springs from later mariology; for he finds Mary's question, "Why have you done this to us?", uttered in a tone of deference and affection. The Greek expression is a complaint or rebuke in Gen 3:14; 4:10; I Sam 13:11.

85 For instance, in 9:21–22 in reporting Jesus' reaction to Peter's confession, Luke drops the reproach by Peter found in Mark 8:32. The Lucan disciples are more reverential to Jesus.

protects Mary against any offense and preserves her image as the handmaid of the Lord by reporting that she kept with concern all these events in her heart.[86]

It is probably inexact to claim that Jesus returns the reproach in the first part of his answer to Mary (and to Joseph) in 49a: "Why were you looking for me?"[87] The tone of his question is more one of grief that his parents have known him so poorly.[88] It anticipates the affirmation in 50 that "they did not understand," and its utterance is meant to be harmonious with the stress on Jesus' obedience in 51. The climax of the story and the core of this biographical apophthegm comes at the end of Jesus' second question: "Did you not know that *I must be in my Father's house?*" In the NOTE I have defended this translation of an ambiguous Greek expression; here I would stress only that the word "house" does not occur in the Greek so that the reference to the Temple is at most indirect. This means that Laurentin and others are wrong when they draw a close parallel between this saying and that of John 2:16: "You shall not make *my Father's house* a house of business." There precisely Jesus does use the word "house" to stress the nature of the Temple, and the statement is part of the prophetic stance of Jesus in the ministry reinterpreting the cult. Here he is not reinterpreting the Temple as his Father's house. He is merely saying that his presence in the Temple and his listening to the teachers is indicative of where his vocation lies, namely, in the service of God who is his Father, not at the beck and call of his natural family. I would maintain that Laurentin[89] is also incorrect when he says that here Jesus is divine Wisdom found in the Temple along the lines indicated in Sirach 24:8–12: "The Creator of all things gave me [Lady Wisdom] a command. . . . In the holy Tabernacle I ministered before Him, and I was established in Zion." The imagery in Sirach stems from an identification of Wisdom with the Law, the commandments of which were thought to be kept in the Ark of the Covenant in the Holy of Holies of the Tabernacle (or Temple). In the Lucan story Jesus is not identified with Wisdom but grows in wisdom (2:40,52); he is found not in the Holy of Holies but in the Temple precincts; he is not engaged in cultic ministry for the feast is over; and his answer puts no emphasis on the Temple as his natural habitat.

If we take "in my Father's house" as primarily a christological statement identifying Jesus as God's Son (a significance that is present even if we

---

[86] The *Infancy Gospel of Thomas* 12:4 goes even further in redressing the picture of Mary; for after Jesus' answer to her, the scribes and Pharisees ask if she is the mother of this child and say, "Blessed are you among women because the Lord has blessed the fruit of your womb."

[87] In the first part of the second question, "Did you not know?", does Jesus really expect the parents to know?

[88] For a similar expression of sorrow at a failure to understand Jesus' relation to his Father, see John 14:8–10.

[89] *Jésus*, 135–39.

translate the phrase as "about my Father's business"),[40] the "I *must*" (Greek *dei*) is perfectly intelligible. A similar sense of obligation appears in subsequent Lucan passages precisely when Jesus is speaking of the role the Father has given him to play. "I must preach the good news of the kingdom of God to other cities also, for I was sent for this purpose" (4:43). "The Son of Man must suffer many things . . . be killed . . . and on the third day be raised" (9:22; see also 17:25; 22:37; 24:7,26). "Behold I cast out demons and perform cures today and tomorrow, and the third day I must finish my course; nevertheless, I must go on my way today, tomorrow, and the day following" (13:32–33). The fact that many of these "must" statements made in the ministry concern suffering causes Laurentin to connect the present statement with the passion and resurrection.[41] But this is to mistake the part for the whole: the passion and the resurrection are *part* of the "must" of Jesus' vocation, and it is to vocation in general and not to specifics that Jesus refers here.

A very close parallel to Jesus' response to Mary in Luke 2:49 may be found in the Cana story of John, already discussed in relation to Luke 2:46. We saw that a pre-Johannine form of the Cana story may have been a "hidden life" narrative wherein Jesus' miraculous power was employed for the convenience of his family circle. The saying of Jesus in John 2:4 (footnote 29 above) may not have been part of that narrative, so that in the original Jesus immediately acceded to his mother's request. But such a story could not be brought into the Fourth Gospel without undergoing the corrective of the authentic Gospel insight that Jesus was at the immediate disposal only of God whom he called "Father." Consequently John inserted into the narrative a rejection by Jesus of his mother's interference in favor of the timetable set up by his Father: "Woman, what has this concern of yours to do with me? My hour has not yet come."[42] For John the

---

40 I have presumed that even the pre-Lucan story was centered around this christological statement which gave rise to it (footnote 16 above), and that Van Iersel is correct in classifying it as a biographical apophthegm, rather than as a legend. P. Winter, "Lc. 2,49," has argued that the pre-Lucan story may not have been christological but a legend illustrative of the piety of Jesus. He points to the treatment of Exod 15:2 in the Fragmentary Targum (Yerushalmi) where Jewish children nursing at the breast signal to their parents the message: "For God is our father who gave us honey from the rock." In other words, against the background of nourishment supplied by earthly parents, the children assert the nourishing power of their heavenly Father. This implies an understanding of the *'elōhê 'ābî* of Exod 15:2 as "God my Father" rather than as "God of my father." Although Winter argues for an early date for this interpretation, it remains a highly speculative hypothesis.

41 Laurentin, *Jésus*, 102–3, also brings out the fact that some of the other "must" passages concern the fulfillment of the Scriptures; and so he posits that in Luke 2:49 too Jesus is referring to Scripture, namely, to Mal 3:1–3 (footnote 15 above). All of this is tied in with Laurentin's questionable emphasis on the resurrectional interpretation of "after three days." I regret that so many times I have had to disagree with Laurentin's suggestions; but since he has devoted a whole book to this pericope, his opinions must be debated. I find that here, as in his earlier *Structure* where he stressed Mary as the Daughter of Zion, his claims to discover symbolism defy control.

42 An intelligent case can be made for translating the last part of this statement as "Has not my hour come?" A. Vanhoye, *Biblica* 55 (1974), 157–67, defends this translation and

hour of Jesus is determined in relation to the Father (13:1). Thus, John may have taken a pre-ministry story and made it center around a statement by Jesus indicative of his vocation, a vocation in which his earthly family has no call upon him.[43] In this analysis the answer of Jesus to Mary both in John 2:4 and in Luke 2:49 anticipates the kind of statement found in the heart of the ministry in Mark 3:31–35 when his mother and brothers came seeking him: "Whoever does the will of God is my brother and sister and mother."

To a mother who came speaking of "your father and I" Jesus has proclaimed the priority of another Father's demands, and he is not understood by his earthly parents (vs. 50). If the hypothesis of a pre-Lucan story is accepted and this was originally a revelation of Jesus' divine sonship, the failure to understand is not only explicable but almost necessary. The appreciation of Jesus' divine sonship was post-resurrectional; in the attempts of the evangelists to show that Jesus was already God's Son during his ministry, even though he was not always recognized as such, misunderstanding by the audience becomes a standard narrative feature.[44] Be that as it may, in the present Lucan context where divine sonship has already been revealed to the parents, their misunderstanding[45] concerns the way in which that sonship is finding expression, i.e., the Father's "must" which calls Jesus away from family obligations. Some of Jesus' vocation statements in the ministry meet the same kind of misunderstanding (see Luke 4:22), and Luke seems to underline that factor. Accordingly, while Mark 9:32 reports that the disciples did not understand Jesus' second prediction of the passion, Luke 9:45 adds to the Marcan report these words: "It was concealed from them that they should not perceive it."

---

interprets it to mean that the relationship on a family level which had hitherto existed between Jesus and his mother is now giving place to the hour in which the Father's call must be given primacy. Notice how much closer this other translation brings John 2:4 to Luke 2:49: "What has this concern of yours to do with me?" matches "Why were you looking for me?"; and "Has not my hour come?" matches "Did you not know that I must be in my Father's house [or about my Father's business]?" Notice also the important parallel in John 7:3–6 where Jesus' brothers want him to go to Judea and work miracles there. In reply Jesus distinguishes between their time which is always here and "my time" which has not yet come. (It is the negation here that inclines me to retain a negative meaning in John 2:4: "My hour has not yet come.")

[43] Jesus ordered that his own disciples should not give priority to family (Mark 10:29–30; Matt 10:37; Luke 14:26).

[44] A good example is the transfiguration and its aftermath in Mark 9:2–13 and Matt 17:1–13. Sometimes Matthew and John have Jesus' divine sonship understood by the disciples during the ministry, but their denial of him during the passion is an implicit indication that they never understood fully.

[45] Wherever mariology has been strong, the thought that Mary was limited in her understanding of Jesus has been repugnant. While the Venerable Bede could allow the view that Mary received only a progressive revelation of the divinity of Jesus, by the thirteenth century it was generally agreed that Mary had full knowledge from the time of the annunciation. Peter Canisius (1521–1597) attacked theories of Mary's limited knowledge as product of the heresies of the Reformers, and only in modern times and gingerly could the question be raised again in Roman Catholicism. See E. F. Sutcliffe, "Our Lady and the Divinity of Christ," *The Month* 180 (1944), 347–51; also footnote 19 above.

And after the third prediction only Luke (18:34) reports misunderstanding: "But they understood none of these things; this saying/event [*rēma*] was hid from them, and they did not grasp what was said."[46]

D. *The Conclusion* (2:51–52)

As I pointed out in the outline in A above, there are two concluding verses: vs. 51 has a place reference matching the geographical introduction in 41–42; vs. 52 is a growth or progress statement matching the similar statement in 40. Yet vs. 51 goes beyond the geographical reference of going down to Nazareth by adding two items of information, namely, that Jesus was obedient to his parents and that his mother kept with concern all these events in her heart. As I have already suggested, each of these items modifies the picture presented in the core of the story.

First, let us consider the statement in 51b that Jesus was obedient. This is quite dramatic when it is set alongside Jesus' "understanding" which caused the hearers to be astounded and his parents to be amazed. It is even more dramatic when it is set alongside his claim to have a special obligation as God's Son, an obligation and vocation which his parents did not understand.[47] In part, such obedience was demanded by the logic of the subsequent Gospel narrative. It explains why, even though Jesus was already consciously God's Son, this did not become apparent in his behavior until many years later at the baptism. It also explains why the Galilean villagers never suspected that he was more than Joseph's son (Luke 4:22). But the stress on obedience also serves the motif of piety which runs through the whole story: the Jesus who goes to Jerusalem with his parents to keep the observance of the feast is also a Jesus who keeps the commandment of honoring his father and his mother. He did not normally answer his parents as he did in vs. 49.

Second, let us turn to the statement in 51c that Mary kept with concern

---

46 The logic in Luke 24:7,26,44 of having the risen Jesus comment upon the "must" statements of the ministry implies that they were not understood when uttered. I think that the parallelism between the "must" statement in 2:49 followed by a lack of understanding and the "must" statements of the ministry followed by a lack of understanding results from the fact that they all concern Jesus' divine vocation. I do not agree with McHugh, *Mother*, 124, that in 2:50 what Mary and Joseph did not understand was Jesus' dark allusion to his future passion and resurrection in Jerusalem. I suspect that McHugh means this allusion on a historical level which I would judge thoroughly implausible at age twelve; but I think it is almost as implausible on the level of Lucan intent. Not only the parents but also the readers could scarcely understand that in 2:49 Jesus was darkly alluding to his future passion and resurrection.

47 Although Jesus' understanding in 47 and the parents' lack of it in 50 have different objects, Luke intends a contrast between them. This contrast was too sharp for the more personal mariology of the *Infancy Gospel of Thomas* 12:4 which omits any equivalent to Luke 2:50; see footnote 36 above.

all these words/events (*rēma*) in her heart. If the reference to obedience softens the portrait of Jesus in the scene, the statement about Mary in this last part of vs. 51 softens the portrait of Mary. She may have been amazed at what Jesus did (48); she may not have understood what he said of himself (50); she may even have reproached him (48b); but she is not unresponsive to the mystery that surrounds him. Her lack of understanding is not permanent; for the fact that she keeps with concern such events in her heart is by way of preparation for a future understanding as a member of the believing community (Acts 1:14). Virtually the same thing was said of Mary in 2:19 after the shepherds reported what the angel had told them about this mysterious child.[48] There (§ 14D), when I discussed the implication of the terms Luke used to describe Mary's attitude, I pointed out that she was the only adult from the infancy narrative who would be carried over into the ministry of Jesus and the life of the Church. By stressing her lack of understanding in vs. 50, Luke is faithful to history; the christology of Jesus as God's Son was not understood until after the resurrection. By stressing Mary's retention of the things that happened, puzzling to understand their meaning, Luke is giving us a perceptive theological insight into history: there was a continuity from the infant Jesus to the boy Jesus to the Jesus of the ministry to the risen Jesus; and when Christian disciples like Mary believed in Jesus as God's Son after the resurrection, they were finding adequate expression for intuitions that had begun long before.

Verse 52 repeats in part what was said about Jesus in vs. 40, which in turn repeated in part what was said about JBap. For convenience let me line up the three statements of Luke 1:80; 2:40; and 2:52:

JBap: "And the child grew up and became strong in Spirit."
Jesus: "And the child grew up and became strong, filled with wisdom and favored by God."
Jesus: "And Jesus made progress in wisdom, maturity, and favor before God and men."

It is easy to see that 2:40 repeats 1:80 and expands it, while 2:52 takes the expansion in 2:40 and expands it further. In discussing the earlier passages (§ 13A and § 15E), I cited OT parallels from the stories of Isaac, Samson, and Samuel which threw light on the stereotyped character of such formulas. Such parallels are also instructive here, especially the double reference to the growth of Samuel, matching a double reference to the growth of Jesus: "And the child waxed mighty before the Lord" (I Sam 2:21) and "The child advanced and was good in the company of God and

---

[48] The statement in 2:19 followed an expression of amazement in 2:18, even as the statement in 2:51b follows expressions of astonishment in 2:47–48.

men" (I Sam 2:26). As I have explained (Table XIV), in the original diptych pattern Luke intended that the birth story of JBap and the birth story of Jesus should end with a conclusion transitional to the ministry, thus 1:80 and 2:39–40. When Luke added the story of the boy in the Temple, rather than moving the previous conclusion (2:39–40) to the end, he put in a second conclusion transitional to the ministry. He had the Samuel precedent for two growth statements, and these statements in 2:40 and 2:52 enabled him to have a framework featuring wisdom surrounding a story concerned with Jesus' understanding and christological insight.[49]

In analyzing what is reported in vs. 52, we see that it shares the terms "wisdom" and "favor" with vs. 40; and what was said about that verse applies here. The new term in 52 is "maturity" (*hēlikia*, "age, stature"; see NOTE) which is quite appropriate for describing a transition from boyhood to manhood. Josephus[50] tells us that Moses' "growth in understanding [*synesis*] was not in line with his growth in stature [*hēlikia*] but far outran the measure of his years. . . . When he was three years old, God gave wondrous increase to his stature [*hēlikia*]." Another new aspect in 52 is the shift from being "filled" with wisdom and favor (vs. 40) to making progress in these aspects.[51] Once again this is quite appropriate; for the story has shown that Jesus at age twelve already had wisdom, and so now it is a question of growth or progress in that wisdom before he begins his ministry as a man. The growth in favor may be related to the obedience that Jesus, the Son of God, shows his parents at Nazareth. The son who is obedient and keeps the commandments is assured in Prov 3:1–14: "You will find favor . . . in the sight of God and men." Here *charis*, "favor, grace," means a basic goodness manifested in a life that is harmonious with God's commandments. Jesus will be so abundantly endowed with it that even the villagers of Nazareth, who failed to recognize him as God's Son because of his perfect obedience to his parents, will have to acknowledge his "grace" once he begins to speak (4:22).

49 As indicated in the NOTE on vs. 47, the "wisdom" in vss. 40 and 52 is related to the "understanding" of vs. 47 but is wider; and so Jesus' perception of his vocation in 49 would be an instance of *sophia*, "wisdom."

50 Josephus *Ant.* II ix 6;#230.

51 For later theological difficulties about a growth in wisdom and favor (grace), see footnote 18 above.

Sectional Bibliography (§ 16)
(Luke 2:41–52)

Dupont, J., "Luc 2:41–52: Jésus à douze ans," *Assemblées du Seigneur* 14 (1961), 25–41.

——— "Jésus retrouvé au Temple," *Assemblées du Seigneur* NS 11 (1970), 40–51.

Elliott, J. K., "Does Luke 2:41–52 Anticipate the Resurrection?" ExpTim 83 (1971–72), 87–89.

Glombitza, O., "Der zwölfjährige Jesus. Luk.ii 40–52. Ein Beitrag zur Exegese der lukanischen Vorgeschichte," NovTest 5 (1962), 1–4.

Laurentin, R., *Jésus au Temple: Mystère de Pâques et foi de Marie en Luc 2,48–50* (Paris: Gabalda, 1966).

Pax, E., "Jüdische Familienliturgie in biblisch-christlicher Sicht," BibLeb 13 (1972), 248–61.

Power, M. A., "Who Were They Who 'Understood Not'?" ITQ 7 (1912), 261–81, 444–59.

Renié, J. E., " 'Et Jesus proficiebat sapientia et aetate et gratia apud Deum et homines' (Lc. 2,52)," in *Miscellanea Biblica et Orientalia A. Miller Oblata,* ed. A. Metzinger (Studia Anselmiana 27–28; Rome: Herder, 1951), 340–50.

Schmahl, G., "Lk 2,41–52 und die Kindheitserzählung des Thomas 19,1–5," BibLeb 15 (1974), 249–58.

Spadafora, F., " 'Et ipsi non intellexerunt' (Lc. 2,50)," *Divinitas* 11 (1967), 55–70.

Temple, P., "What Is To Be Understood by *en tois* (Lk. 2,49)?" ITQ 17 (1922), 248–63.

Van Iersel, B., "The Finding of Jesus in the Temple. Some Observations on the Original Form of Luke ii 41–51a," NovTest 4 (1960), 161–73.

Winter, P., "Lc. 2,49 and Targum Yerushalmi," ZNW 45 (1954), 145–79, with an appended note in ZNW 46 (1955), 140–41.

IX. EPILOGUE (§ 17)

As we look back on the Lucan infancy narrative, inevitably there is a tendency to compare it to the Matthean. Throughout I have insisted that the two stories are very different, that neither evangelist knew the other's work, and that efforts at harmonizing the narratives into one consecutive story are quite impossible. But beneath the differences and even irreconcilability, there is a common understanding of the birth of the Messiah. This is manifested in two ways: first, in the tendency to stress the intrinsic connection of that birth with what has preceded in Israel; second, in the tendency to develop the christological significance of the birth and thus its incipient continuity with what will follow in the Gospel. For both evangelists the infancy narrative is the place where the OT and the Gospel most directly meet.

Matthew has made the connection more obvious, as befits his methodical pedagogy. The Matthean genealogy runs through Israel's history from Abraham to Jesus, but its concluding reference to the begetting of Jesus already hints at the newness of the Christian concept of the Messiah—a Messiah who was God's Son conceived without male intervention. Matthew narrates a dramatic birth story patterned on memories of the patriarch Joseph and of the infant Moses, but much of that may have come to him from a source. Matthew's own work is most visible in the somewhat heavy-handed insertion of citations focusing the reader's attention on the great events and places of Israel's history—events and places in a certain sense "relived" in the career of the infant Jesus. The overall impact of Matthew's composition is triumphantly to assure his Christian readers (giving them proof that they may use against any synagogue adversaries) of God's prophetic plan that the Messiah be called Jesus, that he be conceived of a virgin and be born in Bethlehem, and yet be from Nazareth.

Luke is much less obvious. He has a genealogy, but he relates it to the baptism rather than to the conception. He refers to the OT but chiefly by way of atmosphere and subtle allusion. His pedagogy is one of carefully balanced scenes (diptychs) in which the dramatis personae carry the message. Seemingly, unlike Matthew, Luke does not draw upon already composed sources for the main section of the infancy narrative in 1:5 – 2:40.[1]

---

[1] For the meaning of "source," see footnote 19, § 9 above. I have posited that Luke drew upon sources in a second stage of composition when he added four canticles to the main infancy narrative, along with a story of the boy Jesus in the Temple (2:41–52).

It is more plausible that he composes the narrative from beginning to end himself, depending on some items of historical information and popular tradition,[2] weaving in motifs and characterizations brought forward from the OT and back from the Gospel. The OT motifs are not the same ones which dominate in Matthew (the patriarch Joseph, Moses, Balaam), but the patriarchal couples (especially Abraham and Sarah), the births of Samson and Samuel, and the post-exilic piety of the Anawim.[3] Just as Matthew and Luke approach the OT differently, so also they handle the Gospel themes differently. Matthew chooses to dramatize Joseph who never appears in the ministry, except as the named father of Jesus. Luke chooses Mary and JBap, using what is said of them in the Gospel accounts of the ministry as a guide to depicting them in the infancy narrative. The fact that the Lucan infancy narrative has a larger cast of characters means that the role of representing an obedient Israel responsive to God's revelation about His Son can be more widely distributed than in Matthew's infancy narrative where Joseph is the only major representative. In reading Luke, one gets the impression that most pious Jews were immediately attracted by Jesus.

It is true that Simeon predicts that the child will be "for the fall of many in Israel"; but this indication of future failure is much less dominant than in Matthew's depiction of Herod, the chief priests and the scribes who were alarmed over Jesus and hostile to him. Luke is content to leave the Jewish rejection of Jesus to be recounted in the Book of Acts; he reports no attempt on the life of the infant Jesus as does Matthew. For the latter, Bethlehem and Nazareth constitute a favorable framework for the career of the infant Jesus—sites selected as a fulfillment of God's prophecies. But Jerusalem is a place of hostility to Jesus, since "all Jerusalem" aligns itself with Herod in alarm over the Messiah's birth (2:3). But for Luke the cities of Jerusalem, Bethlehem, and Nazareth are all favorable places in the career of the infant. Indeed, Jerusalem is the site for both the beginning and end scenes of that career, and there cult and Law find meaning in the Messiah. Thus, the transition from the OT to the Gospel is much smoother in Luke than in Matthew and is exemplified in more ways. Matthew had encountered an ongoing struggle with Pharisaic Judaism in his own community's history and life, and he presents this struggle as beginning in the first days of the Messiah's life. For Luke that struggle was more remote (chronologically, or geographically, or both); and he shows

[2] By historical information I mean, for example, the names of JBap's parents and the fact that they were Levites. By popular tradition I mean, for .example, the tendency to cast in terms of an angelic annunciation the proclamation of the birth of the Davidic Messiah, a tendency shaped by OT accounts of birth annunciations (Table VIII).

[3] As we have seen, those figures in the Lucan infancy narrative who do not figure in the Gospel proper (Zechariah, Elizabeth, the shepherds, Simeon, and Anna) have their portraits painted in OT colors.

a consistently favorable picture of Jews who almost instinctively recognize the infant Jesus as the fulfillment of the Law, the prophets, and the cult. As the Spirit is poured out on their representatives (Mary, Zechariah, Simeon), they burst into poetic praise of what God has done for His people; and thus the days of the infancy anticipate the outpouring of the Spirit of prophecy at Pentecost. Luke is more interested in establishing the continuity of the Christian movement with Israel than in anti-synagogue apologetics. His heroine Mary will embody that continuity—she responds obediently to God's word from the first as a representative of the Anawim of Israel (1:38); she appears in the ministry as a representative of the ideals of true discipleship (8:19–21); and she endures till Pentecost to become a Christian and a member of the Church (Acts 1:14).

APPENDIXES

APPENDIX I: LEVIRATE MARRIAGE

Did Jesus Have Too Many Grandfathers?

In § 3, B1c, I mentioned briefly the levirate marriage solution to the differences between the Matthean and Lucan genealogies of Joseph and Jesus, but left a full discussion to this appendix because of the intricacies of the argument. If the reader will glance at Table IV, the most obvious difference between the two genealogies will be immediately apparent: according to Matthew, the father of Joseph and the grandfather of Jesus was *Jacob*, while according to Luke, the father of Joseph and the grandfather of Jesus was *Eli* (or Heli). Since the third century one solution proposed for this discrepancy has been that Jacob and Eli were brothers (full or half) who successively had the same wife by levirate marriage. According to the law of Deut 25:5–10, if the elder brother died without children, the younger brother would have married the elder's widow. The firstborn son (Joseph) would have been the legal son of the deceased elder brother, even though the natural son of the younger brother. Our oldest attested witness to this solution, Julius Africanus (*ca.* A.D. 225) proposed that Luke gave us the legal genealogy, while Matthew gave us the natural genealogy[1]—Joseph was the legal son of Eli and the natural son of Jacob. Most subsequent proponents of the levirate solution have switched the attributions, with Matthew giving us the legal genealogy, and Luke, the natural (Zahn, Westcott, Burkitt, Taylor, Moffatt).

Ingenious as it is, this solution faces serious difficulties:

a) Jacob and Eli would have been full or blood brothers if "Matthan" (Matthew's name for the grandfather of Joseph and father of Jacob) and "Matthat" (Luke's name for the same ancestor) are variants of a name borne by one man. But the father of Matthan/Matthat was *Eleazar* according to Matthew, while he was *Levi* according to Luke. Are we to assume a

---

[1] Africanus' views are reported in Eusebius *Eccl. Hist.* I vii. Evidently he had a Lucan list that omitted Matthat and Levi, for he describes Melchi as third from the end and Joseph's grandfather. He tells us that a woman named Estha married Matthan (Matthean list), a Davidid descended from Solomon, and bore him *Jacob.* When Matthan died, Estha married Melchi (Lucan list), a Davidid descended from Nathan, and bore him *Eli.* Thus Jacob and Eli were half brothers. Eli married but died childless; by levirate custom his half brother Jacob married Eli's widow who gave birth to Joseph. Africanus attributes this explanation to the Desposyni (the "Master's people"), i.e., the relatives of Jesus' family from the villages of Nazareth and Cochaba.

second levirate marriage to explain this? To avoid this difficulty, some have argued that Jacob and Eli were half brothers, with the same mother but different fathers (Matthan and Matthat respectively). Then, however, one has the dubious coincidence that their mother married two men who had almost the same names.

b) We are not certain how widely levirate marriage was practiced in Jesus' time,[2] although Mark 12:18–27 (and par.) would suggest that it was still a known custom.

c) The whole point of the levirate marriage was that a child be born to the deceased father. Therefore, it would be very strange, if Joseph were the son of a levirate marriage, to have a genealogical list tracing his ancestry through his natural father.

d) The levirate marriage hypothesis could explain, at most, only the discrepancies at the very end of the genealogies; it offers little help with the other divergencies between the lists. If we accept the levirate hypothesis that both genealogies of Jesus are family lists traced respectively through the legal and natural fathers of Joseph, how do we explain the fact that earlier in the lists Matthew traces the descent through Zerubbabel's son Abiud, while Luke traces it through Zerubbabel's son Rhesa?[3] Why does Matthew trace descent through David's son Solomon, while Luke traces it through David's son Nathan?

The theory of a levirate marriage solves so little and has so many difficulties that it should be abandoned as a solution in the problem of the two genealogies, and even in the more restricted problem of Jesus' overabundance of grandfathers.

---

[2] Among the law codes of the Pentateuch, levirate marriage is peculiar to the Deuteronomic Code (Deut 25:5–10). It was a practice of tribal origin, important not only for keeping property within the family, but also for spiritual reasons, since a man obtained a certain immortality through his offspring. The difficult demand imposed on the deceased's kin must not have been popular, for it underwent modification in the course of time. Indeed, the Deuteronomic law itself, which places the burden on the deceased's brother, may already represent the narrowing of a more ancient custom binding even distant kin (Ruth 4). Leviticus 18:16 and 20:21 may be interpreted in opposition to the levirate obligation.

[3] Or Prince Joanan; see p. 93 above.

APPENDIX II: DAVIDIC DESCENT

Historically, Was Jesus of the House of David?

Precisely because the genealogies of Matthew and Luke do not agree and because we cannot be certain of their historical value, we must face the question of the historical worth of the NT claim that Jesus was a Davidid. The majority of scholars, including Cullmann, Hahn, Jeremias, Michaelis, and Stauffer, still accept this claim as historical. Yet, increasingly the purported descent from David is explained as a theologoumenon, i.e., as the historicizing of what was originally a theological statement.[1] If I may give a simplified explanation, the process of historicizing Davidic sonship is thought to have gone somewhat in the following way: the Christian community believed that Jesus had fulfilled Israel's hopes; prominent among those hopes was the expectation of a Messiah, and so the traditional title "Messiah" was given to Jesus; but in Jewish thought the Messiah was pictured as having Davidic descent; consequently Jesus was described as "son of David"; and eventually a Davidic genealogy was fashioned for him.[2] That the latter stages of this theory are not incredible is clear when we see how the high priest Zadok got the levitical genealogy attributed to him in I Chr 6:1–8. Zadok's historical origins are unknown; he may even have been a Canaanite; but he had become high priest, and according to tradition, the high priesthood belonged to the levitical House of Aaron. Eventually Zadok had to be legitimized in his ancestry by being given an Aaronid genealogy.

Before we examine the NT evidence for the Davidic descent of Jesus, it may be wise to test some of the presuppositions of this theory of a historicized theologoumenon. How dominant in Jesus' time was the expectation that the Messiah had to be a Davidid?[3] The royal House of David had exercised no dominant power in Palestine since the end of the sixth century

---

[1] Scholars use "theologoumenon" in various ways, but I am using it in the sense indicated. Among the followers of this approach are Heitmüller, Goguel, and Conzelmann. Burger, *Jesus* (which is a major treatment of Jesus' Davidic descent), shows himself favorable to it.

[2] To what extent did "son of David" have genealogical implications? Bultmann has suggested that it was more theological than genealogical; but Michaelis, "Davidssohnschaft," 323, argues: "The Messiah could be called 'son of David' only when it was taken for granted that he was a Davidid." In other words, the title did not create the idea of Davidic descent but presupposed it.

[3] Fitzmyer, "Son of David," succinctly traces the history of the Davidic tradition.

B.C., the time of Zerubbabel, a Davidid who served as Persian governor (NOTE on Matt 1:12). However, the regaining of independence in the second century B.C. under the Maccabeans or Hasmoneans seems to have catalyzed monarchical hopes once more. The fact that the Hasmonean high priests aggrandized their position by assuming the title of king provoked among their enemies, especially among the Pharisees and the Essenes, a revived expectation of the restoration of the true royal line, the House of David. It is in a Pharisee writing of the late first century B.C., the *Psalms of Solomon* (17:23[21]), that we encounter for the first time in Jewish literature the title "son of David" for the expected king. This *Psalm* 17(4–8) laments that, while the Lord chose David to be king over Israel, sinners (i.e., the Hasmonean priest rulers) set up a monarchy in place of the throne of David. When the true king, the son of David, comes, he will shatter the unrighteous rulers and purge Jerusalem and gather together a holy people (17:23[21]ff.). The other enemies of the Hasmonean priests, the Qumran Essenes, also developed a strong expectation of a Davidic Messiah.[4] In *4Q Florilegium* (i 10–13), a commentary on biblical passages which is contemporary with Jesus' lifetime, the passage I Sam 7:11–14, which established the Davidic dynasty, is interpreted thus: "He is the branch [ṣemaḥ] of David who will arise with the Interpreter of the Law . . . at the end of time"; and this Davidic figure is associated with the fallen hut of David which is to be raised up to save Israel (Amos 9:11). In another biblical commentary (4QpIs^a 2:21–28), Isa 11:1–3 is interpreted to refer to the Davidic "branch" to whom God will give a throne of glory and a crown of holiness (see also *4Q Patriarchal Blessings*).

With the destruction of the Temple (A.D. 70), when the pluralistic Judaism of Jesus' lifetime was narrowed down to a Pharisee remnant, we find "son of David" becoming a regular messianic designation.[5] In the *Shemoneh Esreh* or *Eighteen Benedictions,* which became a standard Jewish prayer before the end of the first century A.D., we find a petition (14th Benediction) that the throne of David be re-established speedily in Jerusalem, and another petition (15th Benediction, Babylonian recension) that the offspring of David be exalted and caused to flourish. In an apocalypse written after the fall of Jerusalem (*IV Ezra* 12:32), the author looks forward to the Messiah, kept by the Most High till the end of days, who shall spring from the seed of David.

Thus, it is quite true that in the minds of Christians of Jewish descent, if Jesus was identified as the Messiah, there would be an accompanying expectation that he was a Davidid. Yet, if this were not true, there are

---

[4] The literature is enormous. See R. E. Brown, "The Teacher of Righteousness and the Messiah(s)," in *The Scrolls and Christianity,* ed. M. Black (SPCK Theological Collections, 11; London, 1969), 37–44, 109–12.

[5] For the Talmudic references, see Lohse, *"Huios,"* 485; and Lohse, "König," 341.

enough exceptions to cast doubt on the assumption that a fictional Davidic descendancy would have necessarily been created for him. In the early second century A.D. Rabbi Aquiba hailed Bar Kochba (Simon ben Kosibah) as a messianic figure even though he was not a Davidid. Moreover, other types of messianic expectation, divergent from Davidic messianism, flourished in first-century Palestine. For instance, some looked for a hidden Messiah whose origins would be unknown until he was suddenly revealed to Israel.[6] At Qumran, in addition to looking for the (Davidic) Messiah of Israel, the sectarians yearned for the coming of a Messiah of Aaron, i.e., an anointed high priest of levitical ancestry.[7] There is a serious possibility that if Jesus were not factually a Davidid, he could have been fitted into one or the other of these expectations. Indeed, the author of the Epistle to the Hebrews writes precisely to present Jesus as the great high priest. Yet he has to struggle with the well-established tradition that Jesus was a Davidid and not a Levite: "For it is evident that our Lord was descended from Judah, and in connection with that tribe Moses said nothing about priests" (Hebr 7:14). Thus, one can have real doubts about the assumptions behind the theologoumenon theory: some, at least, who believed that Jesus had fulfilled Israel's hopes would not have had to jump to the conclusion that he was of Davidic descent, even if the majority thought that way.

Besides a weakness in its assumptions, the theologoumenon theory must face two major objections. *First,* relatives of Jesus were known in the primitive church. If the family was not Davidic, would they have gone along with the theological assumption of Davidic ancestry? Can it be assumed that James, the "brother of the Lord" and the leader of the Jerusalem community as late as the 60s, would never have heard the claim that his close relative was a Davidid? And if he and the other Palestinian Christians who knew the facts about Jesus' family were so indifferent to history as to go along with the pretense of Davidic origins or to assume that merely a theological claim was being made, would Jesus' enemies not have raised some protest? One would expect to find traces of a polemic, especially on the part of the Pharisees, denying Jesus' Davidic status as falsified. But, while there are Jewish attacks on Jesus' legitimacy, there is no polemic against his Davidic descent as such. The unlikelihood of falsification is increased if there is any truth in the information gleaned from Hegesippus[8] that in the 80s or 90s the grandsons of Jude, another

---

6 Strains of this expectation appear in the Fourth Gospel and again, in the next century, in Justin *Dialogue*. See Brown, ABJ, I, 53.

7 Johnson, *Purpose*, 120–38. Another expectation concerned the Messiah from the House of Joseph, but it is not attested this early.

8 In Eusebius *Eccl. Hist.* III xx 1–6. A highly unlikely touch in the story is that Domitian himself interrogates the grandsons, but that may be an aggrandized memory of a local Roman interrogation under Domitian. It is, of course, possible that the story, far from supporting the Gospel information about Davidic descent, has been created by that information

"brother" of Jesus, were brought to trial before the Emperor Domitian on the grounds that they were descended from David and therefore politically dangerous. Had the theologoumenon about Jesus' origins become so traditional that members of the family were willing to die as Davidids? Early in the third century, Julius Africanus, who had been born in Palestine and lived part of his life there, reports that there were relatives of Jesus who lived in the Nazareth area after his lifetime and were familiar with the family genealogies.[9]

Second, the NT evidence attributing Davidic ancestry to Jesus is widespread, and some of it is early. The oldest datable NT reference is Rom 1:3 (the letter itself was written *ca.* 58, but Paul is quoting a creedal formula of earlier Christianity[10]): "The Gospel concerning His [God's] Son, who was born of the seed of David according to the flesh." Can such a formula of faith tell us anything about Jesus' historical origins? May it not represent a step in the process of historicizing a theologoumenon, as mentioned above? Yet it is cited by Paul who knew the Palestinian situation and was always sensitive to correction from Jerusalem. Would he have used it if he knew that Jesus was not really descended from David? Would not this have left him vulnerable to the Jerusalem followers of James (Gal 2:12) or to those who were questioning his apostolate precisely on the grounds that he knew little of the earthly Jesus? Scholars who tell us that Paul may never have inquired about Jesus' ancestry forget that to a man with Paul's training as a Pharisee, the Davidic ancestry of the Messiah would be a question of paramount importance, especially in the period before his conversion when he was seeking arguments to refute the followers of Jesus. Paul, who twice insists on his own Benjaminite descent (Rom 11:1; Philip 3:5), would scarcely have been disinterested in the Davidic descent of Jesus.

Another text that needs to be considered is Mark 12:35–37a, for it is often adduced as evidence that Jesus himself disclaimed Davidic origins.

(see Burger, *Jesus,* 123–27). Yet there is other evidence of Roman apprehension about the House of David. In Eusebius *Eccl. Hist.* III xii, Hegesippus is cited to the effect that, after the capture of Jerusalem in 70, Vespasian issued an order that the descendants of David should be ferreted out, so that no member of the royal house should be left among the Jews (see footnote 60, § 3). Later on in Eusebius (III xxxii 6) Hegesippus is cited again for the story that Symeon, bishop of Jerusalem and son of Clopas (the brother of Joseph, Jesus' father—a relationship that makes Symeon Jesus' cousin), was martyred as a descendant of David and a Christian at the age of 120 in the time of Trajan (98–117). The bishop's age makes us suspect the legendary character of the story.

9 In Eusebius *Eccl. Hist.* I vii 14. This passage states that these relatives or Desposyni (the "Master's people") expounded the Davidic genealogy of Jesus throughout Galilee. As Lohmeyer, *Matthäus,* 8, points out, this may mean that the genealogies were used in a type of missionary apologetics—a suggestion that makes us cautious about their objectivity.

10 See footnote 46, § 11. There is no agreement among scholars as to whether the formula originally circulated in a Semitic-speaking or a Greek-speaking community. Vielhauer, Hahn, and Burger argue for the latter, pointing out that the formula is not easily retroverted into Aramaic. The passage in II Tim 2:8, "Jesus Christ, raised from the dead, descended from David," may be an instance of another early formula, this time preserved in one of the deutero-Pauline Pastorals (Michaelis, "Davidssohnschaft," 322).

As Jesus taught in the Temple precincts, he asked, "How can the scribes say that the Messiah is the son of David?" After all, as Jesus pointed out, the psalmist (David) had declared, "The Lord [God] said to my lord [the Messiah] . . . ," thus calling the Messiah "lord."[11] So how could the Messiah be David's son? The *prima facie* import of this passage (an import defended by Wrede and others) is that Jesus is denying that the Messiah is descended from David.[12] One might hypothesize that Jesus, who claimed to be the Messiah, sought to prove that the Messiah did not need to be a Davidid precisely because he himself was not a Davidid.[13] But there are serious objections to this interpretation. Clearly none of the three evangelists who report this scene understood it in that way, for they affirm elsewhere that Jesus is a Davidid.[14] Moreover, if Jesus were really arguing in this manner, he would be basing himself on slim evidence; and his opponents could quote against him many other texts to the contrary.

An opposing interpretation is set forth by Bultmann who doubts that this is a genuine saying of Jesus, precisely because Jesus did *not* claim to be the Messiah. Therefore, "the proof that the Messiah could not be David's Son could hardly have had any meaning for Jesus." The passage, for Bultmann, may have reflected the theology of a small group in the early Church who denied that Jesus was the son of David, in favor of proclaiming him Son of Man or Son of God.[15] However, this theory also faces difficulties; for there is no clear NT evidence of an early Christian re-

---

[11] Jesus argues according to the exegetical presuppositions of his time; for, as we can see in the rabbinic tradition, the psalm was considered to be of Davidic authorship and to be messianic. (However, Danell, "St. Paul," 94, points out that in the later Jewish Targum on the Psalms, David applies the lordship to himself: "He [God] will make me lord of all Israel." Danell suggests that this change may reflect Jewish counterapologetics, to prevent the psalm from being used to prove Jesus' lordship.) Modern scholars would not agree that David was the author of the psalm or that it was he who was speaking; neither would they understand "my lord" to refer to the future Messiah (footnote 9, § 3). In the psalm the oracular prophet was speaking in praise of his lord, the reigning king, probably at the moment of coronation: "The Lord [God] said to my lord [the king]. . . ."

[12] In Matt 22:41–46 the same passage is made a challenge to the Pharisees; but this is reflective of a tendency in early Christian tradition to clothe dominical sayings with the context of a controversy dialogue (Bultmann, *History*, 51). Also, Matthew's form of the question ("What do you think of the Messiah—whose son is he?") seems to understand the issue in terms of the Messiah's being either the son of David or the Son of God. Matthew's answer is that he is both, but the discussion has moved beyond Mark. Luke's presentation (20:41–44) is much the same as Mark's.

[13] So J. Klausner, *Jesus of Nazareth* (New York: Macmillan, 1925), 320.

[14] See footnotes 2 and 3, § 5, for the comparative Synoptic use of "son of David." John never uses the title, and it has been suggested that John 7:42 shows ignorance of Jesus' Davidic origins. In that passage some people in Jerusalem object against Jesus, citing his Galilean origins: "Doesn't Scripture say that the Messiah, being of David's family, is to come from Bethlehem, the village where David lived?" However, the scene may well be an instance of Johannine irony wherein, unknown to them, Jesus actually meets the questioners' demands or criteria (see Brown, ABJ, I, 330). In the larger Johannine corpus of writings, there is clear retention of Jesus' Davidic origins in Rev 3:7; 5:5; 22:16—a later book of the NT, to be sure, but one that sometimes reflects old tradition (see Hahn, *Titles*, 244–45).

[15] *History*, 136–37. See the discussion below of *Barnabas* 12:10–11. The view of Burger, *Jesus*, 58, 71, resembles that of Bultmann, for he suggests that the pre-Marcan sense of the passage was a polemic against Davidic descent, a polemic he finds attested in Mark 6:1–3.

jection of Jesus' Davidic origins, and Rom 1:3–4 shows how in the pre-Pauline period the idea of his being both son of David and Son of God were reconciled. Even if one grants Bultmann's presupposition that Jesus did not claim to be the Messiah, one need not rule out the possibility that the saying came from Jesus. Jesus proclaimed God's rule (kingdom) over men, a kingdom that was now beginning to be realized. He related this proclamation to God's promises to Israel; and for many of his contemporaries those promises included a Davidic Messiah who would re-establish the independence, the glory, the prosperity, and the conquest of the kingdom ruled by David. Some of those who followed Jesus hailed him as this Messiah; but Jesus himself does not seem to have approved of the title, even though there is no persuasive evidence that he rejected it altogether.[16] (To have rejected it would have constituted for many a denial that he was the one through whom God would accomplish His promises.) Rather he seems to have objected to the way it was understood and to the implications that men drew from it. We know that Jesus rejected any insertion of family claims into his ministry (Mark 3:31–35; Luke 11:27–28), and so it was perfectly consistent that he question an understanding of the Messiah that would emphasize physical descent, instead of God's sovereignty in implementing His plans.

It is quite possible, then, to deal with Mark 12:35–37a as a saying which came, at least substantially, from Jesus himself and which did not deny the Davidic sonship of the Messiah.[17] The question that Jesus poses in that passage may be an example of the *haggada* type of question known from rabbinic writings—a question that concerns apparent contradictions between different verses of Scripture.[18] In this instance the apparent contradiction arises between the many passages accepted by the scribes as demonstrating that the Messiah is to be descended from David (David's son) and a passage wherein the Messiah is designated as David's lord. The normal solution of the *haggada* question is not that one passage is wrong and another is right, but that both are right in different contexts, or that they constitute different aspects of the truth. The passage in Mark is so short that we cannot be sure exactly how Jesus reconciled the two aspects of the Messiah (David's son and David's lord)[19]—the exegesis of Matt

16 For a brief survey of the evidence, see R. E. Brown, *Jesus God and Man* (New York: Macmillan, 1967), 79–86.

17 Cullmann, *Christology*, 131, argues that, while the Marcan passage denies that the Messiah *must be* of the physical lineage of David, it does not prove that he could not be of that lineage.

18 J. Jeremias, *Jesus' Promise to the Nations* (SBT 24; London: SCM, 1958), 52–53; D. Daube, *New Testament*, 158–69. This theory opposes the idea that Jesus' question, "How can the scribes say that the Messiah is the son of David?", is a rhetorical question demanding a negative answer, or a vexatious question confusing the opponents but not giving Jesus' own view.

19 G. Bornkamm, *Jesus of Nazareth* (New York: Harper, 1960), 228: "More likely is the interpretation which finds the point of the saying in the *relationship* between the Messiah's

1:18–25 in § 5 above shows how one of the evangelists reconciled them—
but our main interest here is in the fact that the passage does not really
support the thesis that Jesus denied his own Davidic descent and/or the
Messiah's.

The discussion of the Marcan passage would not be complete without
mention of a second-century writer who echoes it. Basing himself on an allusion to the son of God in a text of Exod 17:14 that he is using, the author of the *Epistle of Barnabas* 12:10 comments: "Now there is Jesus once
more, not as son of man but as Son of God. . . . Because they were going
to claim that Christ was son of David, David himself, foreseeing and fearing this error of sinners, prophesied: 'The Lord said to *my Lord.'*" Does
this author deny the Davidic descent of Jesus or simply that Davidic
sonship should not be so interpreted as to detract from Jesus' being the
Son of God?

In summary, while certainty is not possible, the NT evidence that Jesus
was really a Davidid outweighs, in my opinion, doubts to the contrary. In
§ 3, B1b, I rejected the thesis that Jesus was of direct royal lineage or
that his family was of the ancestral nobility, but there is no insuperable
difficulty in positing that Joseph belonged to one of the non-aristocratic,
lateral branches of the House of David.

However, we must recognize that there would be no irreparable theological damage to Christianity if Jesus were proved to have been of non-
Davidic descent. The Christian assertion that Jesus was the Messiah
required a radical reinterpretation of that concept, and a further reinterpretation which would leave aside a physical descent from David in the
Messiah's ancestry would be intelligible. Jesus' words in Mark 12:35–37a,
if they do nothing else, warn against putting a premium on lineal descent
from David. And while the Christian Church did accept as fact the
Davidic origin of Jesus,[20] its use of this descent was more in apologetics

---

being the son of David and also the Lord." Michaelis, "Davidssohnschaft," 235, thinks the
point lies in the question of whether it is *more important* that the Messiah is David's son or
that he is David's Lord. Hahn, *Titles*, 252–53, interprets the Marcan passage in terms of a
two-step christology, involving a distinction between "son of David," which emphasizes the
Messiah's earthly activity, and "Lord," a title that implies messianic enthronement in heaven
—an interpretation echoing Rom 1:3–4. J. Schniewind, *Das Evangelium nach Markus* (10th
ed.; Göttingen: Vandenhoeck, 1963), 164–65, thinks the Marcan passage implies that, while
Jesus is indeed the son of David, he is more, since he is the Son of Man in a unique sense.
Fitzmyer, "Son of David," 123–26, allows that Schniewind's interpretation may represent the
teaching of the evangelist, but thinks it unlikely that Jesus himself was making a reference
to the Son of Man.

20 See the emphasis in Ignatius *Smyrnaeans* 1:1: ". . . our Lord, that he is (in truth) of
the family [*genos*] of David according to the flesh" (also *Ephesians* 18:2; 20:2; *Trallians*
9:1). Indeed, Gentile Christians, not understanding legal sonship through Joseph, made the
virgin Mary a Davidid, so that Jesus' descent according to the flesh could be more assuredly
Davidic (see Fischer, "Abkunft"). On the other hand, some of the Ebionite branch of Jewish Christians were uneasy about attributing a Davidic descent to Jesus because they as-

than in theology.[21] The *Davidic* Messiah was too nationalistic a figure to have primacy in Christian thought.

---

sociated the royal line of David through Solomon with the building of the Temple. See H. J. Schoeps, *Jewish Christianity* (Philadelphia: Fortress, 1969), 86–87.

[21] The frequency of the "son of David" usage in Matthew (footnote 3, § 5), as Gibbs, "Purpose," points out, may reflect a polemic against the Synagogue which was denying that Jesus was the Messiah.

BIBLIOGRAPHY FOR APPENDIX II

Bultmann, R., *History*, 136–37.

Burger, C., *Jesus als Davidssohn* (FRLANT 98[80]; Göttingen: Vandenhoeck, 1970).

Cullmann, O., *The Christology of the New Testament* (London: SCM, 1959), esp. 127–33.

Daube, D., *New Testament*, 158–69.

Fischer, J., "Die davidische Abkunft der Mutter Jesu: biblische-patristische Untersuchung," *Weidenauerstudien* 4 (1911), 1–115.

Fisher, L. R., "Can This Be the Son of David?" in *Jesus and the Historian*, ed. F. T. Trotter (In Honor of E. C. Colwell; Philadelphia: Westminster, 1968), 82–97.

Fitzmyer, J. A., "The Son of David Tradition and Mt 22:41–46 and Parallels," in *Essays on the Semitic Background of the New Testament* (London: Chapman, 1971), 113–26. Originally published in *Concilium* 20 (1967—*The Dynamism of the Biblical Tradition*), 75–87.

Gibbs, J. M., "Purpose and Pattern in Matthew's Use of the Title 'Son of David,'" NTS 10 (1963–64), 446–64.

Hahn, F., *The Titles of Jesus in Christology* (London: Lutterworth, 1969), 240–78.

Hay, D. M., *Glory at the Right Hand: Psalm 110 in Early Christianity* (SBLMS 18; Nashville: Abingdon, 1973).

Kingsbury, J. D., *Matthew*, 99–103.

——— "The Title 'Son of David' in Matthew's Gospel," JBL 95 (1976), 591–602.

Lohse, E., *"Huios Dauid,"* TDNT, VIII, 482–88.

——— "Der König aus Davids Geschlecht," in *Abraham unser Vater*, ed. O. Betz *et al.* (Festschrift Otto Michel; Leiden: Brill, 1963), 337–45.

Michaelis, W., "Die Davidssohnschaft Jesu als historisches und kerygmatisches Problem," in *Der historische Jesus und der kerygmatische Christus* (Berlin: Evangelische Verlag, 1962), 317–30.

Neugebauer, F., "Die Davidssohn Frage," NTS 21 (1974–75), 81–108.

Suhl, A., "Der Davidssohn im Matthäus-Evangelium," ZNW 59 (1968), 57–81, esp. 62–69.

APPENDIX III: BIRTH AT BETHLEHEM

Historically, Was Jesus Born at Bethlehem?

The NT evidence for birth at Bethlehem is much less impressive than the wide attestation given to Davidic descent: only the second chapters of the infancy narratives of Matthew and Luke support Bethlehem as the birthplace of Jesus. "The overwhelming evidence to the contrary has made the thesis that Bethlehem was *not* the historical birthplace of Jesus the *communis opinio* of New Testament scholarship."[1] Let us examine the evidence for this brave assertion to see whether the complexities of the situation demand more nuance.

Once more the alternative of a theologoumenon has been offered. Indeed, if the reader will examine the theologoumenon explanation for Davidic descent offered at the beginning of the previous Appendix, most of it can be reused here—Jesus was thought to be the Messiah, "the son of David"; but in Jewish thought it was expected that the Davidic Messiah would be born in David's town of Bethlehem; and so the story was created that Jesus was born in Bethlehem. However, when one begins to examine the presuppositions of this theory of a historicized theologoumenon, a number of difficulties emerge:

a) It is probably true that many Jews of Jesus' time expected the Messiah to be born at Bethlehem, but we must be aware that our chief evidence for this is Christian, not Jewish. Expectation of the Messiah's birth at Bethlehem is attested in the NT independently in Matt 2:4–5 and John 7:41–42, but not until considerably later in Jewish writings.[2]

b) Even if there was such an expectation among first-century Jews, we

---

1 Burger, *Jesus*, 104. The majority of those who reject the historicity of birth at Bethlehem opt for Nazareth as the birthplace. A few (e.g., Stegemann) think that the connection of Jesus with Nazareth is itself a historicized theologoumenon, representing a misunderstanding of the title "the Nazorean" (see NOTE on Matt 2:23); and their candidate for the birthplace is Capernaum which was the center of Jesus' activity during the ministry (see Kennard, "Capernaum"). Occasionally one encounters a maverick suggestion of another site, like Chorazin.

2 Without reference to Micah 5:1, Bethlehem appears as the birthplace of the Messiah in passages like TalJer *Berakoth* 5a, and *Midrash Rabbah* 51 on Lam 1:16. As for Micah 5:1(RSV 5:2), L. Ginzberg, *Legends*, V, 130, traces the messianic interpretation of the passage back to relatively old rabbinic traditions. Origen, *Against Celsus*, I, 51, charges that Jewish scholars, lest they give comfort to Christians, suppressed the expectation that the Messiah would be born at Bethlehem.

cannot prove that it was strong enough to create the story of Jesus' birth at Bethlehem. I mentioned in the previous Appendix (footnote 6) the expectation of a hidden Messiah who would appear suddenly, without people knowing where he came from. (This expectation is described in John 7:27, in contrast to 7:42 which involves the expectation of the Messiah's birth at Bethlehem.) If Jesus had not been born at Bethlehem, why could Christians not have been content to present him as the hidden Messiah, who made his appearance at the Jordan to be baptized?

c) Luke 2:4,11 stresses that Jesus was born in Bethlehem inasmuch as it was the city of David, but that emphasis is not so prominent in Matthew. That the Messiah had to be born at Bethlehem appears in the formula citation of Matt 2:5; but if I am right in my reconstruction of the pre-Matthean magi story (§ 6, C2), birth at Bethlehem was part of that story without any explicit reasoning about its necessity. And so, it is not clear that the earlier level of the birth-at-Bethlehem stories really did involve the historicizing of a theologoumenon.

d) It is often claimed that the creation of the story of Jesus' birth at Bethlehem was by way of apologetics against the Jewish ridicule of a Messiah who came from Nazareth (John 7:41,52). But would the *invention* of the Bethlehem tradition really have met the objection? After all, the Bethlehem story made its appearance in a rather late stratum of NT writing, when Jesus *of Nazareth* had been proclaimed as the Messiah for some fifty years. So far as we know, he had been preached and accepted by many without the slightest awareness of his being born at Bethlehem. Birth at Bethlehem could never be more than a very secondary motif in the royalty of him who died as "Jesus *the Nazorean*, King of the Jews."

e) Later Jewish polemic did not feature a denial that Jesus was born at Bethlehem, even when his legitimacy was attacked. If there is any truth in Origen's charge of suppressed references to the Messiah's birth at Bethlehem (footnote 2), such suppression would represent a tacit acknowledgment of Christian tradition concerning the birthplace of Jesus.

These difficulties make us cautious about the claim that birth at Bethlehem was a historicized theologoumenon. On the other hand, there are at least equally grave objections against the claim that we are dealing with a historical fact. *First,* while the silence of the rest of the NT is serious, it would be less serious if the two witnesses to birth at Bethlehem (Matt 2:1,5,8,16; Luke 2:4,11,15) agreed in their presentation; but they do not.[3] Matthew tells us incidentally that the parents of Jesus lived in a

---

[3] On this score the evidence for birth at Bethlehem differs considerably from the evidence for the virginal conception which is also found clearly in only two places in the NT, the first chapters in Matthew and Luke. Although independent of each other, Matthew and Luke have the same setting (an angelic annunciation about Mary who is betrothed to Joseph, but still a virgin) and the same theological language (action of the Holy Spirit) in their reference to the virginal conception. It is important to realize that the passages in the first

house in Bethlehem (2:11) and that Judea was their homeland (2:22), and so the birth of their child in Bethlehem of Judea would be normal. Only the highly imaginative story of the magi and the star focuses the reader's attention on the symbolism of the place of birth.[4] And Matthew himself spells out the theological significance with his formula citation of Micah 5:1. For Luke, the parents live in Nazareth of Galilee, and so a specific reason is given why they were in Bethlehem where they had no home (2:7) when the child was born. As we shall see in Appendix VII, the device of the census employed by Luke for this purpose almost surely represents an inaccuracy. And so the historicity of the present Gospel *contexts* of birth at Bethlehem is scarcely reassuring. However, if I am right in my contention in the commentary (§ 14, C1) that exegetical reflection on Gen 35:19-21 and Micah 4-5 is present in both the pre-Matthean and pre-Lucan background, the tradition of birth at Bethlehem is considerably more ancient than its present context in the Gospels.

Second, there is not only a silence in the rest of the NT about Bethlehem as the birthplace of Jesus; there is positive evidence for Nazareth and Galilee as Jesus' hometown or native region: his *patris.*[5] When Matthew and Luke use this term, since they have already affirmed that Jesus was born at Bethlehem, *patris* designates the place where Jesus grew up, consistent with Matt 2:22-23 and Luke 2:51, the transitional geographical information at the end of the respective infancy stories. However, since Matthew and Luke seemingly got the term from Mark (6:1,4 and par.) who betrays no knowledge of birth at Bethlehem, it is possible that the original idea was that the *patris* of Nazareth and Galilee was where Jesus was born. Certainly, in the dialogue of Mark 6:2-3, none of Jesus' neighbors betrays any knowledge that Jesus had an auspicious beginning by being born in the Davidic city of Bethlehem. The neighbors are astonished that Jesus has become famous as a religious figure, precisely because such fame was not presaged by anything extraordinary in his previous family situation at Nazareth. In the Fourth Gospel (1:46;

---

chapters of Matthew and Luke which deal with virginal conception never mention birth at Bethlehem, and the passages in the second chapters of Matthew and Luke which deal with birth at Bethlehem do not imply or need a previous tradition of a virginal conception. Thus, the two traditions seem to be quite independent of each other.

4 In my reconstruction of the pre-Matthean level (§ 4, B2), birth at Bethlehem would have been part of two independent stories, the narrative of angelic dream appearances p. 109 and the magi-Balaam narrative p. 192; but both are popular reflections of OT tradition. Herod was buried on a cone-shaped hill (the Herodium) some five miles SE of Bethlehem and clearly visible from there. If Jesus was not actually born at Bethlehem, the associations of Herod with the Bethlehem area may have been a catalyst in attaching the Jesus-Herod story (part of the narrative of angelic dream appearances) to that town.

5 Mark 6:1,4; Matt 13:54,57; Luke 4:23,24. Although the immediate context of John 4:44 would indicate that *patris* there refers to Galilee, some scholars have argued that John thinks of Judea as Jesus' "own country." I doubt it (ABJ, I, 187); but even the scholars who maintain this view would regard such an identification of the *patris* as Johannine theology rather than historical fact.

7:41–42,52) there are slighting references to Jesus' Galilean origins, showing that there was no knowledge among the people that he had been born elsewhere.[6] Even if we leave aside the implausible publicity that Matt 2:3–5 attaches to Jesus' birth at Bethlehem, how can there have been such a general ignorance of Jesus' birthplace in Bethlehem when the parents would have had to come from there as strangers with their child to a small village in Galilee (Matthew's scenario), or to come back to the village with a child born to them during a short journey to Bethlehem (Luke's scenario)?

The evidence, then, for birth at Bethlehem is much weaker than the evidence for Davidic descent or even (see Appendix IV) the evidence for virginal conception; and these three Christian claims are not necessarily interdependent.

[6] A *different* question is whether the fourth evangelist himself had knowledge that Jesus was born elsewhere. Certainly there is irony in John's description (7:41–42) of those who think that Jesus cannot be the Messiah because the Messiah is supposed to come from Bethlehem. The primary level of that irony based on the folly of such an objection is that Jesus does not come from Nazareth as the speakers suppose—he comes from above, from God. There may be a secondary level of that irony which deems the objection folly even on the level of natural origins—unknown to the objectors, Jesus does come from Bethlehem. But we have no way of being certain of this secondary irony, since John betrays no knowledge of birth at Bethlehem. Thus, one cannot use 7:41–42 to argue either for or against the fourth evangelist's awareness of the tradition of birth at Bethlehem. See Brown, ABJ, I, cxxxvi and 330, for the intricacies of Johannine irony: John is perfectly capable of leaving unanswered a foolish objection by Jesus' opponents or interrogators because he knows that that Christian reader will see the fallacy (cf. 4:12)—a technique that creates problems for the modern reader who has to guess how much John's readers knew.

BIBLIOGRAPHY FOR APPENDIX III

(Some of the works on Davidic descent in the Bibliography for Appendix II treat birth at Bethlehem as well.)

Blinzler, J., "Die Heimat Jesu," *Bibel und Kirche* 25 (1970), 14–20—a reply to H. Stegemann's 1969 inaugural address at the University of Bonn, "Jesus aus Kapernaum."

Kennard, J. S., Jr., "Was Capernaum the Home of Jesus?" JBL 65 (1946), 131–41.

Ramsay, W. M., *Was Christ Born at Bethlehem?* (New York: Putnam, 1898).

APPENDIX IV: VIRGINAL CONCEPTION

Historically, Was Jesus Conceived without a Human Father?

This is the last of three consecutive historical questions to be treated in an appendix. Consignment to an appendix is appropriate, not only because, like the previous questions, it cuts across the two infancy narratives and is best treated after readers are familiar with both, but also because the question of historicity goes beyond the intentions of Matthew and Luke which were my primary concern in the body of the commentary. By saying this, I do not imply that Matthew and Luke presented the virginal conception only as a symbol and were indifferent to what really took place. I think that both of them regarded the virginal conception as historical, but the modern intensity about historicity was not theirs. For them, the primary import of the virginal conception was theological, and more specifically, christological. Therefore, I agree fully with Paul Minear[1] who has insisted that the answers given by the evangelists do not dovetail with our modern questions of historicity and dogmatic significance, and what are problems to us often were not problems to them. Yet, I disagree with Minear if he means that, therefore, we should not ask these questions of historicity and dogmatic significance. Certainly, they should not be the only or primary questions (whence this relegation to an appendix). But we are creatures of *our* times, and to ignore questions like historicity that come spontaneously out of our times would be irresponsible. We must ask these questions, even if we may have to settle for the answer that the biblical evidence does not resolve them, precisely because the Bible was not written for that purpose.

At the beginning of the discussion, let me explain my insistence on the term "virginal conception," rather than the more familiar "virgin birth." First, the precise question is not the manner of Jesus' birth or how he came forth from the womb, but the manner of his conception. Was he conceived without the intervention of a human father, i.e., without male seed impregnating his mother? In post-biblical Christianity there did develop a belief in virginal birth alongside virginal conception—a miraculous and

---

[1] Review of my book on the virginal conception in *Interpretation* 28 (1974), 465-67.

painless birth in which the hymen was not ruptured,[2] something already
hinted at in the second-century *Protevangelium of James* 19–20. But that
form of "virgin birth" is not our concern here. Second, I avoid the term
"virgin birth" because of its creedal implications. The ancient creeds tend
to speak of Jesus' being "born of the Virgin Mary";[3] and while the authors
of those creeds certainly thought that Jesus had been virginally conceived,
it is not clear that what they were proposing as a matter of Christian faith
was the biological manner of Jesus' conception. The expansion of the old
creeds through a combined reference to birth from the Virgin Mary and
death under Pontius Pilate was, at least in part, to counter a heresy that
questioned the reality of Jesus' humanity.[4] That humanity was affirmed by
historical references to his birth and death. "Born of the Virgin Mary"
echoes the Pauline formula "born of a woman, born under the Law" (Gal
4:4) and is designed to underline the historicity of *Jesus*—a much wider
question than the historicity of his conception without a human father.

Since I have written a small book on the virginal conception, I shall not
attempt to make this appendix exhaustive. My interest is to enable the
reader to see the problems and to become familiar with the evidence, as an
invitation to further study.

A. *The Silence of the Rest of the New Testament*

It is beyond dispute that there is no explicit reference to the virginal conception in the NT outside the infancy narratives. What is a matter of dispute is whether there are some implicit references.[5] Let us examine the
major texts that have been proposed.

The Pauline Letters. In Gal 4:4–5 Paul says, "When the time had fully

---

[2] This is the *virginitas in partu*, the middle term in the fourth-century triad about Mary's
virginity: *ante partum, in partu, et post partum* ("before, in, and after birth")—a triad that
shifts the focus of the virginal conception from christology to mariology. Roman Catholics
have traditionally considered all three stages of the virginity of Mary to be revealed doctrine, but a more nuanced position is now being taken by Catholic theologians on the *in
partu*. In the accompanying bibliography, see the articles by Clark, Plumpe, and Rahner on
virginitas in partu (virginal birth), and the book by Blinzler which treats of the *virginitas
post partum* (perpetual virginity of Mary).

[3] The Old Roman Baptismal Creed (Hippolytus): "born from [*de*] the Holy Spirit, of
[*ex*] the Virgin Mary"; the Apostles' Creed: "conceived by [*de*] the Holy Spirit, born of
[*ex*] the Virgin Mary"; Niceno-Constantinopolitan Creed (381): "was made flesh by
[*de*] the Holy Spirit from [*ex*] the Virgin Mary." See H. Denzinger and A. Schönmetzer,
Enchiridion Symbolorum (32nd ed.; Freiburg: Herder, 1963), ##10,30,150.

[4] J. N. D. Kelly, *Early Christian Creeds* (2nd ed.; London: Longmans, 1960), 144–45,
332–38.

[5] As an illustration of diversity on this question, compare Fitzmyer, "Virginal Conception,"
and Miguens, *Virgin*, two treatments written by Roman Catholics about a year apart, survey-
ing the NT evidence. Fitzmyer denies all implicit references and doubts that even Luke asserts the virginal conception clearly; Miguens speaks of "alleged silence" and finds support
for the virginal conception in much of the NT. See reviews of Miguens in CBQ 38 (1976),
576–77; and TS 38 (1977), 160–62.

come, God sent forth His Son, born of a woman, born under the Law, to redeem those who were under the Law." Influenced perhaps by the (mis)use of the term "virgin birth," some (Zahn, Miguens) have immediately thought of a virginal conception here, since only the mother is mentioned. To be precise, however, Paul is speaking about the reality of Jesus' *birth*, not about the manner of his conception. The phrase "born of a woman" is meant to stress what Jesus shared with those whom he redeemed, precisely because it is applicable to everyone who walks this earth.[5a] It no more supports the virginal conception of Jesus than the figurative phrase "born of the seed of David" in Rom 1:3 disproves it. A more serious argument for Paul's knowledge of the virginal conception has been advanced from Paul's custom of writing in terms of Jesus' being "born" (the verb *ginesthai* in Gal 4:4; Rom 1:3; Philip 2:7) rather than of his being "begotten" (the verb *gennan,* used of Ishmael and Isaac in Gal 4:23,24,29). However, both these verbs in the middle or passive can mean "be born" and "be begotten"; and neither one really tells us anything specific about the manner of conception. For example, Matthew, who believes in the virginal conception, does use the verb *gennan* of Jesus, once, at least, clearly with the meaning "begotten" (1:20; see NOTES on Matt 1:16 and on Luke 1:35). Without further indication of Paul's mind, it would be abusive to read a knowledge of virginal conception into Paul's use of *ginesthai.*[6]

Gospel of Mark. Mark never mentions Joseph by name; and in a passage where Matthew and Luke have the citizens of Nazareth speak of Jesus as "the son of the carpenter" and "the son of Joseph," Mark uses "the son of Mary" (Mark 6:3; Matt 13:55; Luke 4:22). Reconstruction of the pre-Gospel history of the passage is complicated,[7] but Miguens has argued at length that the silence about Joseph on Mark's part is deliberate because Mark knew that Jesus had no human father. A much simpler solution is preferable. Joseph makes no appearance during Jesus' ministry in any Gospel, and it is highly likely that he had died before Jesus' baptism. If Mark's villagers speak of Jesus as "the son of Mary," this may represent an identification of Jesus in terms of the one living and familiar parent, precisely since Mark 6:3 brings up the *presence* of the family in the village. (See Appendix V for the question of whether the designation of Jesus through his mother is also a slur on his legitimacy.) In any case, the

---

[5a] See Matt 11:11 and Luke 7:28: Among *those born* (begotten) *of women,* none is greater than JBap.

[6] In the accompanying bibliography, among the authors writing specifically on Paul's knowledge of the virginal conception, Cooke, Danell, and Robinson affirm it, Legault denies it.

[7] It is difficult to know whether two different traditions are involved; and, if not, to know which is the earlier form of the one tradition. See the fuller discussion in Appendix V, B1. There (footnote 24) I stress the unlikelihood of Miguens' contention, granted the Marcan context.

thesis that Mark's villagers are hinting at the virginal conception seems incredible in light of Mark 6:4 where Jesus compares himself to a prophet
without honor in his own country, among his own relatives, and in his own
house. A similar low estimate of the relations between Jesus and his family
is found in 3:21,31–35. There Mark first tells us that "his own" thought
that Jesus was beside himself (or frenzied) and went out to seize him;
then Mark tells us that Jesus' mother and brothers came and, standing
outside the place where he was, sent in to call him. Apparently, Mark includes Jesus' mother among the "his own" who thought he was frenzied.[8]
Mark goes on to have Jesus distinguish his natural family, who are standing outside, from those inside listening to him, a family constituted by
doing the will of God. Such an uncomplimentary view of Mary's relationship to Jesus is scarcely reconcilable with a knowledge of the virginal
conception. Matthew and Luke, who do have this knowledge, delete the
first and most offensive part of the Marcan scene, where "his own" think
that Jesus is beside himself (even as in their parallel to Mark 6:4 they
delete Jesus' uncomplimentary reference to relatives who do not honor the
prophet). Moreover, Luke drastically modifies the last part of the Marcan
scene so that Jesus no longer replaces his natural family but rather includes his mother and brothers among those who hear God's word and do
it (8:19–21; see § 11D).

Johannine Writings. Some scholars have found support for the virginal
conception in a variant reading of John 1:13: *"He who was* [instead of
'they who were'] begotten, not by blood, nor by carnal desire, nor by
man's desire, but by God."[9] This variant is not attested in even one Greek
ms. of the Gospel, and is plausibly a change made in the patristic period in
order to enhance the christological utility of the text. In addition, it has
been argued that John 7:41–42 shows the evangelist's knowledge of birth
at Bethlehem and, therefore, of the virginal conception. John's knowledge
of birth at Bethlehem is unsure, and that has nothing to do with a knowledge of the virginal conception (footnotes 3 and 6 in Appendix III). Finally, it is dubious that "the one begotten [*gennētheis*] of God" in I John
5:18 refers to Jesus rather than to the Christian;[10] but even if it does,
more dubious still is the attempt to see in it a reference to the virginal conception. The same phrase "begotten [or born] of God" is used in I John

---

[8] I suspect that Mark has joined two separate traditions, and that originally the "his own"
did not include his mother. The closest parallel to Mark 3:21 is John 7:5: "Even his
brothers did not believe in him."

[9] The only major scholarly support for this reading today is among French-speaking
Roman Catholics, e.g., M.-E. Boismard, F.-M. Braun, D. Mollat. See the exhaustive defense
by J. Galot, *Etre né de Dieu: Jean 1:13* (Analecta Biblica, 37; Rome: Pontifical Biblical Institute, 1969); and a succinct summary of the arguments against it in ABJ, I, 11–12.

[10] The best modern commentary on I John applies it to the Christian—R. Schnackenburg,
Die Johannesbriefe (3rd ed.; Freiburg: Herder, 1965), 280.

2:29; 3:9; 5:1,4 of Christians in general without any implication of virginal conception.[11]

In summary evaluation of the evidence, I would say that it is perfectly proper to speak of the silence of the rest of the NT about the virginal conception because not a single one of the "implicit references" has any compelling force. On the other hand, one would misinterpret this silence if one concluded from it that no other author of the NT (outside of Matthew and Luke) knew of the virginal conception, or that the historicity of the virginal conception is thus disproved. We have no way of knowing how widespread in NT times was a belief in the virginal conception. Even where the virginal conception was known and accepted, it would have become the subject of preaching (and therefore likely to be included in the kind of writing we have in the NT) only when its christological significance was seen. What the silence of the rest of the NT does call into question is the theory that the memory of the virginal conception was handed down by the family of Jesus to the apostolic preachers and was universally accepted as fundamental Christian belief.

B. *The Origin of the Idea of a Virginal Conception*

Before I take up the obvious question raised by the silence of the rest of the NT, let me comment on the distribution of references to the virginal conception in the two areas of the NT that mention it, the Matthean and Lucan infancy narratives. The virginal conception appears only in Matt 1:18–25 and Luke 1:26–39.[12] In the commentary (§ 4, B2, and § 9, B2) I presented my own form of the common scholarly hypothesis that the infancy narratives represent a combination of *different* pre-Gospel narratives and traditions. There is no clear evidence of the idea of a virginal conception in any of that pre-Gospel material other than the angelic annunciation of birth. (Thus, it is a problem not only of the silence of the rest of the NT, but also of large parts of the infancy tradition, e.g., the silence of such stories as the angelic dream appearance narrative, fashioned on the Joseph and Moses traditions; the magi and star narrative, fashioned on the Balaam tradition; the narrative of finding the boy Jesus in the Temple precincts.) Nevertheless, the agreement of Matthew and Luke on the angelic

11 If one objects that these other passages do not use the aorist passive tense of the verb as does I John 5:18, that tense is used of the Christian in John 1:13.

12 The reference to Mary as Joseph's "betrothed" in Luke 2:5 and to Jesus as "the supposed son" of Joseph in 3:23 are Lucan editorial touches designed to bring a conformity with 1:26–39 into material that otherwise shows no awareness of the virginal conception. In my article "Luke's Description," I expressed my disagreement with Fitzmyer's contention (footnote 5 above) that even Luke 1:26–39 need not be understood as a reference to a virginal conception (see § 11, B1).

annunciation of birth as the vehicle of the idea of the virginal conception
establishes rather firmly in my judgment that a complex of three items antedated the two Gospels: (1) the literary form of an angelic annunciation
of birth; (2) the theological message in the annunciation which placed
side by side the Davidic descent of the Messiah and the begetting of God's
Son through the power of the Holy Spirit; (3) the setting of the annunciation whereby it involved a young girl who was betrothed but still a virgin.

How do we explain the pre-Gospel origin of these three items? The first
was a well-known OT literary pattern (Table VIII) and a natural medium
for Christians of Jewish descent to have used for their reflections about the
birth of Jesus the Messiah. The second, as we have seen in the commentary (§ 5A; § 11C), is cast in the language of early Christian creedal
affirmation and involves a christological insight that was earlier associated
with the resurrection and the baptism. The real problem is to explain the
third item, the setting. When the creedal affirmation of the begetting of
God's Son through the power of the Holy Spirit became the message of an
angelic annunciation of the birth of the Messiah, why was the annunciation placed in a setting that involved the conception of that Messiah by a
virgin? Was the catalyst for this setting a historical or a non-historical factor?

1. Non-historical Catalysts

Many scholars have maintained that, when the early Christians sought
to give expression to their faith that Jesus did not become God's adopted
Son during his lifetime but already was God's Son from the first moment
of his existence on earth, they came rather easily to expressing that faith in
terms of his having been begotten without a human father—precisely because virginal conception was a well-known religious symbol for divine origins. Some scholars have supported this contention by pointing to stories
of virginal conceptions in pagan or world religions; others have found instances of virginal conception in the traditions of Judaism.

VIRGINAL CONCEPTION IN PAGAN OR WORLD RELIGIONS. Among the
parallels offered for the virginal conception of Jesus have been the conceptions of figures in *world religions* (the Buddha, Krishna, and the son of
Zoroaster), in *Greco-Roman mythology* (Perseus, Romulus), in *Egyptian
and Classical history* (the Pharaohs, Alexander, Augustus), and among
famous *philosophers or religious thinkers* (Plato, Apollonius of Tyana),
to name only a few.

The validity of these parallels hinges on three points. (a) Would such
legends or traditions have been known to Christians in NT times so that
they could have influenced the idea of the virginal conception of Jesus? As
for the figures of world religions, there are internal problems about the

dating of the traditions of their conceptions;[13] and there is no proof of a knowledge of those traditions by first-century Christians. Although converts to Christianity from paganism would know the various legends of Egypt, Greece, and Rome, one can scarcely attribute to pagan converts what we know of the setting of the virginal conception in an angelic annunciation of birth—the pattern of this annunciation is so closely modeled on OT exemplars that, at least, one must posit the intermediary of Greek-speaking Judaism.[14] Such an intermediary brings us to the second point. (b) How attractive or acceptable would these pagan legends have been to Greek-speaking Jewish Christians? Would they have wanted to fashion the conception of Jesus after them? Many of the legends involved gross or amoral sexual conduct on the part of the deity who was thought to have begotten the child; and Wisdom 14:24,26 and Rom 1:24 show how Greek-speaking Jews and Jewish Christians would react to such conduct. When, after the first century, Christians did compare the virginal conception of Jesus to the pagan birth legends, they could see no affinity but rather a sharp contrast between the two.[15] And that leads us to the third point. (c) Are any of these divinely engendered births really parallel to the non-sexual virginal conception of Jesus described in the NT, where Mary is not impregnated by a male deity or element, but the child is begotten through the creative power of the Holy Spirit?[16] These "parallels" consistently involve a type of *hieros gamos* where a divine male, in human or other form, impregnates a woman, either through normal sexual intercourse or through some substitute form of penetration.[17] In short, there is no clear example of *virginal* conception in world or pagan religions that plausibly could have given first-century Jewish Christians the idea of the virginal conception of Jesus.

VIRGINAL CONCEPTION IN JUDAISM. Here the proposed parallels are fewer. Many scholars, although they know that Isaiah did not speak of a virginal conception, think that his prophecy was thus interpreted by

---

13 Boslooper, *Virgin Birth*, had some one hundred pages of excellent analysis of all the parallels I have mentioned. On p. 138 he states that the most ancient Buddhism knew nothing of the virginity of the Buddha's mother, and that later came the tradition of her conception from the white elephant who entered her side. It is also difficult to date the tradition that, after Zoroaster's death, his seed which had been preserved in a body of cold water impregnated a virgin who bathed therein.

14 Indeed, some would insist on the intermediary of *Palestinian* Judaism since they think that Matthew's account betrays a knowledge of a difference in marriage customs between Galilee and Judea (but see NOTE on "betrothed" in Matt 1:18).

15 Tertullian *Apologeticum* xv, xxi; Origen *Against Celsus* I 37.

16 See NOTE on "through the Holy Spirit" in Matt 1:18.

17 In *Virginal Conception*, 62¹⁰⁴, I discuss four seeming exceptions: (a) Plutarch's description of how the Egyptians believe that the spirit of a god can bring about the beginnings of parturition in a woman; (b) Aeschylus' description of how Io was made a mother by Zeus' mystic breath; (c) Plutarch's description of how Apollo engendered Plato by power; (d) the Petra and Hebron mystery cult of Dusares, acclaiming the virgin-mother goddess. But I show that divine intercourse is really presupposed in all four.

Greek-speaking Jews (LXX of Isa 7:14)[18] and that this explains why
Hellenistic Jewish Christians phrased their ideas about the origins of God's
Son in terms of a virginal conception. But, as I stated in § 5, B2, there is
no reason to believe that the LXX of Isa 7:14 either referred to a virginal
conception or was so interpreted by Jews. It is Christian exegesis,
witnessed in Matt 1:22–23, that has reinterpreted Isa 7:14 in light of an
existing Christian tradition of the virginal conception of Jesus. At most,
Matthew has let his interpretation of Isa 7:14 color his account of the virginal conception, and there is no indisputable evidence that Luke was dependent upon Isa 7:14 (footnote 63, § 5).

A more serious possibility for a Jewish idea of virginal conception lies
in Philo's description of the generation of virtues in the human soul.[19]
Philo employs allegorically the stories of the births of the patriarchs who
were begotten through the instrumentality of God: "Rebekah, who is per-
severance, became pregnant from God." Wary of seeking reliable parallelism in such an obvious allegory, some have suggested that, underlying
the Philonic exegesis, was a Hellenistic Jewish theory that the real patriarchs were begotten directly by God without male intervention. Paul has
been thought to give witness to this in his distinction between Abraham's
two sons, one born according to the flesh, one born *according to the*
promise or *spirit* (Gal 4:23,29).[20] Yet Rom 9:8–10 makes it clear that,
for Paul, the patriarchal children of the promise were still conceived by intercourse between their parents. And so we remain without real proof of
the existence in Judaism of the idea of a virginal conception that might
have influenced Jewish Christians in their thinking about Jesus.[21]

---

[18] The LXX rendering of Ps 110:3, "From the womb, before the morning I have begotten
you," has suggested to some that the Alexandrian Jewish LXX translators were influenced
by Egyptian ideas of the conception of the Pharaohs by the god Amun-Ra. This is stressed
by Emma Brunner-Traut as an antecedent for the conception of Jesus. However, Amun-Ra
was thought to act through the father, so that the conception of the Pharaoh was not without intercourse.

[19] Philo *De Cherubim* 12–15; but see also the other texts amassed by Carman, "Philo's
Doctrine." For the complexities of Philonian symbolism in this question, see R. A. Baer,
Philo's Use of the Categories Male and Female (Leiden: Brill, 1970). Grelot, "La naissance," offers a meticulous discussion of the relevance of the Philonic material to the virginal conception of Jesus and comes to a negative conclusion.

[20] See Dibelius, "Jungfrauensohn," 27–42; R. H. Fuller, JR 43 (1963), 254.

[21] Let me mention some other dubious examples that have been proposed: (a) A late
midrashic tradition that the affliction of Israel during the Exodus (Deut 26:7) involved en-
forced sexual abstention and that the expression "God knew their condition" in Exod 2:25
involved direct generation by Yahweh in the birth of Moses. (See Daube, *New Testament*,
5–9; Davies, *Setting*, 63–64, 81–82.) The evidence is far too late to be applied with any assurance to NT times, and the interpretation that a virgin birth was intended is highly dubious. (See review of Daube in JJS 7 [1956], 234–35.) (b) A tradition of the virginal conception of Melchizedek in the Slavonic *Secrets of Enoch* (see D. Flusser in *The Crucible of
Christianity*, ed. A. Toynbee [London: Thames & Hudson, 1969], 299). The date of this
work is quite uncertain, with some scholars putting it as late as the seventh century A.D. The
virginal conception of Melchizedek occurs in a fragment of one ms. of Slavonic *Enoch*, a
fragment that has been attributed to an early Christian heretic (W. R. Morfill, *The Book of*

2. Historical Catalysts

Precisely because the idea of a virginal conception is not easily explicable through pagan and Jewish parallels, a reasonable number of critical scholars posit a historical substratum. They contend that early Christians phrased their theological insight about the begetting of God's Son through the Holy Spirit in terms of a virginal conception because that is what happened. Please note the order of ideas in this contention. We are not discussing here a simple view whereby it was revealed at the moment of the virginal conception that Jesus was the Son of God. Rather, accepting the common scholarly agreement that such a revelation was post-resurrectional, we are discussing whether the post-resurrectional insight was attached to (and thus came to interpret) a factual virginal conception. If we leave aside the objection that a miracle such as the virginal conception cannot be factual (a prejudice or, at least, an unprovable presupposition), we must still ask how the knowledge of the extraordinary way in which Jesus was conceived would have reached Christians, and why it would have surfaced relatively late and only in two NT writings. There are several proposed solutions to these questions.

FAMILY TRADITION. The most common proposal for a historical catalyst is a tradition coming down from one or both of the two people who were in a position to know what happened, Joseph and Mary. Let us immediately dismiss simplistic forms of this thesis. That the Matthean infancy narrative came from Joseph and the Lucan infancy narrative came from Mary has been deemed untenable from the start (§ 1B). So also is an offshoot of that thesis wherein there are posited two consecutive annunciations: to Mary at the beginning of the pregnancy (Luke) and to Joseph after several months of his wife's pregnancy (Matthew). As a wag has remarked, that theory presupposes that Mary and Joseph never spoke to each other. I have argued in the commentary that the Matthean and Lucan annunciation accounts are developed variants of a pre-Gospel annunciation tradition. I regard that tradition as a popular narrative shaped along the pattern of OT annunciations of birth (Table VIII), and thus there is

---

the Secrets of Enoch [Oxford: Clarendon, 1896], 85). (c) In the Coptic Gnostic material from Nag Hammadi, *The Apocalypse of Adam* (*CG* V, 78, 18–20), which *may* be of Jewish origin, refers, apparently in a hostile manner, to the third kingdom of him who came from a virgin womb. (d) A work originally composed in Hebrew, *Jubilees* 16:12–13 describes the conception of Isaac thus: "In the middle of the sixth month the Lord visited Sarah and did unto her as He had spoken, and she conceived." Some have tried to combine this with the evidence in Hellenistic Judaism for direct divine begetting of the patriarchs, mentioned above. However, *Jubilees* 16:1 suggests that what "the Lord did unto her" was to remove her barrenness so that Abraham could beget a child of her—in short, the biblical explanation.

no reason to think that a narrative about an annunciation came down from the parents.[22] However, since an annunciation by an angel of the Lord is simply a figurative way of describing divine revelation, the crucial question for discussion is *whether the experiential knowledge that the child had been conceived without a human father had come down to the Christian community from Mary,* with the accompanying insight that this was by God's action. (I say "Mary" because the complete absence of Joseph during the ministry of Jesus makes Mary a more plausible channel.)

Some have seen positive support for this in Luke's insistence that "Mary kept with concern all these events, interpreting them in her heart";[23] but the preservation of eyewitness tradition is scarcely what is meant by that statement which has close antecedents in Gen 37:11 and Dan 4:28 (LXX) in reference to *dreams* (§ 14D). The real difficulty about a preserved family (Marian) tradition of the virginal conception of Jesus is the failure of that memory to have had any effect before its appearance in two Gospels in the last third of the first century. There is a strong tradition that the brothers of Jesus did not believe in him during the ministry (John 7:5; Mark 3:21, followed by 3:31)—did Mary not communicate his divine origins to them? Did not the virginal conception carry for Mary some implication as to who Jesus was? In the few ministry scenes in which she appears, historical or not, there is no memory that she showed any such understanding (Mark 3:31–35; John 2:3–4). And certainly she communicated no profound christological understanding to his followers who came to understand only after the resurrection and, indeed, at first seem to have proclaimed that Jesus had *become* Messiah, Lord, or Son of God *through the resurrection,*[24] never mentioning the virginal conception. The family tradition thesis is not impossible, but it faces formidable difficulties.[25]

PUBLIC KNOWLEDGE OF THE EARLY BIRTH. In the situation posited by both Matthew and Luke, Mary became pregnant considerably before she came to live with her husband (pp. 142–43 above). In the logic of the nar-

22 Many Roman Catholic scholars, who recognize the non-historical features of Matthew's account, have argued that Luke 1:26–38 represents the personal remembrances of the Virgin Mary. In the commentary (§ 11 C and D), I have attempted to show that it is a Lucan rewriting of a pre-Gospel annunciation tradition, with the character of Mary filled in from what Luke knew of her through sayings of Jesus preserved in the Gospel account of the ministry.

23 Luke 2:19,51. These statements are sometimes combined with Luke 1:2 in a theory making Mary and her reminiscences one of Luke's eyewitness sources. The theory is challenged by the non-historical or inaccurate character of the events in Luke 2 in which Mary is supposed to have participated, e.g., the census.

24 See footnote 14, § 1, for the possibility of an earlier stage attaching these titles to the parousia. The NT texts cited in § 1, A2, and in § 5A speak of God making, declaring, constituting, and begetting Jesus under these titles.

25 The arguments against a family tradition have been strongly advanced by the Roman Catholic scholar A. Vögtle, "Offene."

rative, this means that at least one fact pertaining to Jesus' conception may have entered the public domain, namely, that Jesus was born noticeably early after his parents came to live together. Is this a historical fact? That it is found in both Gospels, with only Matthew having a discernible apologetic interest in it, suggests that it predated the two evangelists. As we have already seen (footnote 28, § 5), it is not easily explicable as a Christian creation, for a fictional setting far less open to scandal was possible. We know of a Jewish charge that Jesus was illegitimate (Appendix V); if that charge circulated in the first century, it may have arisen precisely from this situation. If, then, there is a reasonable likelihood of the historicity of this peculiar chronology of pregnancy, how may it have entered into the idea of a virginal conception? The opponents of Jesus would deem him illegitimate and Mary unfaithful; but Christians would have rejected such an explanation, for they had a widespread and firm belief that Jesus was totally free of sin (II Cor 5:21; I Pet 2:22; Hebr 4:15; I John 3:5) and both Matthew and Luke present his parents as holy and righteous (Matt 1:19; Luke 1:42). They would have sought a positive explanation of the irregularity of his conception (and perhaps it was here that family tradition was an auxiliary). Thus, the idea of the virginal conception of God's Son may have resulted from an interplay of many factors: a creedal affirmation (designated or begotten Son of God through the Holy Spirit), stemming from the early preaching, and a theology of sinlessness coming together to interpret the historical fact of conception by Jesus' mother before she came to live with her husband[26]—a mixture leavened perhaps by an ingredient of family tradition. This complicated solution, although it reflects items from the meager evidence we possess, leaves many questions unanswered (e.g., Mary's understanding of all this); and so it remains quite tenuous.

In my book on the virginal conception, written before I did this commentary, I came to the conclusion that the *scientifically controllable* biblical evidence[26a] leaves the question of the historicity of the virginal conception unresolved. The resurvey of the evidence necessitated by the commentary leaves me even more convinced of that. To believers who have never studied the problems critically before, this conclusion may seem radical. To many scholars who have long since dismissed the virginal conception as theological dramatization, this conclusion may seem retrogressively conservative. (And I would shock them more by affirming that I think that it is easier to explain the NT evidence by positing historical

26 This is not a theory of the narrative dramatization of a theologoumenon; it supposes historical fact interpreted by a theological stance.

26a I mean the type of evidence constituted by tradition from identifiable witnesses of the events involved, when that tradition is traceably preserved and not in conflict with other traditions.

basis than by positing pure theological creation.) I hope only that I have presented the evidence accurately enough to have induced the readers to further study and to their own conclusions about the evidence.

C. *Other Influential Factors*

With the NT evidence so inconclusive, it is not surprising that many other factors, historical and theological, have guided the discussion of the virginal conception and the conclusions reached. Let me simply list them here with some of the nuances brought by modern scholarship.

a) The post-biblical evidence of the second century is not particularly helpful in determining the historicity of the virginal conception. On the one hand, despite relatively few references to it in early second-century church writings, outside the apologists (only Ignatius among the "Apostolic Fathers"),[27] it is quite well attested in the apocryphal writings—an indicator of popular acceptance. On the other hand, there were groups that denied the virginal conception. Christian Gnostics who did so (Cerdo, Cerinthus, Satornilus, the Carpocratians, Marcion, and the Manicheans) were often influenced by doctrinal prejudices of a docetic or anti-worldly nature. Not the manner of conception but the fact of conception (taking flesh in a womb) was repugnant to them. More important for our purposes was the rejection of the virginal conception by some Jewish Christians who accepted Jesus as a Messiah of strictly human origin. The roots of these groups in Palestine raise the possibility, albeit *slight,* of a tradition of natural conception coming down in Palestine from the original Jews who believed in Jesus.

b) Theories of inspiration and inerrancy have been invoked to the effect that, if Matthew and Luke thought that Jesus had been virginally conceived, their affirmation must be historically true. Leaving aside oversimplifications in such theories which cut across ecclesiastical divisions, many Christians would give the religious affirmations of the evangelists a privileged rank.[28] In evaluating their testimony on the virginal conception, it is important to realize that in and through this concept the evangelists

27 More detail and references for the second-century writings may be found in my book, *Virginal Conception,* 47–52, where I enter into dialogue with the more negative picture presented by Von Campenhausen, *Virgin Birth.* P. Borgen, *Tidsskritt for Teologi og Kirke* 42 (1971), 37–44, argues that Ignatius' traditions about the virginal conception were independent of the NT and thus a separate witness.

28 In the Roman Catholic tradition, the acceptance of biblical criticism has caused a reinterpretation but not a rejection of the concepts of inspiration and inerrancy. Notice the qualified description of inerrancy in the Vatican II document *Dei Verbum* (iii 1): "The Books of Scripture must be acknowledged as teaching firmly, faithfully, and without error that truth which God wanted put into the Sacred Writings for the sake of our salvation." A faithful Catholic would have to ask: Should one rank the biological manner of Jesus' conception as a truth God wanted put into the Sacred Writings for the sake of our salvation?

are making a christological affirmation about Jesus as Son of God and son of David. They presuppose a biological virginity, but that is not the main point of their affirmation. Thus, a Christian who wishes to give proper respect to the evangelists' teaching is still faced with the delicate decision as to whether a questioning of the biological supposition brings into question the main christological affirmation.

c) Consistent church teaching has been invoked to support the historicity of the virginal conception,[29] and certainly one can cite a virtual unanimity from A.D. 200 to 1800. For many of us this is an extremely important, even deciding factor. But the point made in discussing the previous factor needs to be repeated here. The virginal conception under its creedal title of "virgin birth" is not primarily a biological statement, and therefore one must make a judgment about the extent to which the creedal affirmation is inextricably attached to the biological presupposition. Moreover, in the period of unanimity, opponents of the virginal conception were, for the most part, denying the divinity of Jesus. That is not necessarily true today. A leading Protestant theologian has denied the virginal conception because he thinks it conflicts with the pre-existent divinity of Jesus.[30] (See p. 141 above for the distinction between [virginal] conception christology and pre-existence christology.) Two points should be remembered. First, in orthodox Christian belief, Jesus would be God's Son no matter how he was conceived, since his is an eternal sonship not dependent upon the incarnation. Second, for ordinary Christians the virginal conception has proved an effective interpretative sign of that eternal divine sonship; and we should not underestimate the adverse pedagogical impact on the understanding of divine sonship if the virginal conception is denied.

d) The contrary argument that the virginal conception denies the real humanity of Jesus, since it makes him unlike us in origin, needs careful historical testing. In Matthew and Luke the virginal conception was connected with an articulation of the divine sonship of Jesus, but without even a trace of an implication against the full humanity of Jesus. Indeed, Matthew associates the virginal conception with a genealogy of Jesus' human ancestors. In church history, as we saw above, among the earliest *opponents* of the virginal conception were those who denied the humanity of Jesus. Thus, despite theoretical objections, the virginal conception and the virgin birth, as a real conception and a real birth, have been factors giving Jesus something basic in common with other men and women.

29 In *Virginal Conception,* 34-43, I have listed a series of typical statements reflecting the thought of the Western Church on the virginal conception. In Roman Catholic theology, according to the usual criteria, the virginal conception would be classified as a doctrine infallibly taught by the ordinary magisterium.
30 W. Pannenberg, *Jesus—God and Man* (Philadelphia: Westminster, 1968), 143: "In its content, the legend of Jesus' virgin birth stands in an irreconcilable contradiction to the Christology of the incarnation of the preexistent Son of God found in Paul and John."

e) In the history of Christian dogma, the virginal conception has been placed at the service of the concupiscence theory of the transmission of original sin—a theory relating the transmission of the sin to the sexual nature of human propagation and the sensual appetites aroused by procreation. It was explained that Jesus was free from original sin because he was conceived without intercourse. Despite the distinguished list of supporters of this theory, ranging from Augustine and Ambrose through Karl Barth,[81] it is not widely accepted today; and its application to the virginal conception is very foreign to the evangelists' presentation.

f) The virginal conception quickly became locked into a larger picture of Mary the (Perpetual) Virgin (footnote 2 above). The result is that those churches which have a strong Marian tradition tend to regard any questioning of the virginal conception as a threat to the theological position of her who has been designated the "Mother of God" since the Council of Ephesus (431). Be that as it may, all Christians should be wary of any implication that the conception of Jesus in wedlock would detract from his nobility or Mary's sanctity. In its origins, the virginal conception shows no traces whatsoever of an anti-sexual bias and should not be made to support one. For the evangelists it was a visible sign of God's gracious intervention in connection with the becoming of His Son; in no way did that intervention make ordinary conception in marriage less holy.

g) Unfortunately, however, the historical alternative to the virginal conception has not been a conception in wedlock: it has been illegitimacy through adultery by Mary (Appendix V). The only ones who denied the virginal conception and maintained that Jesus was Joseph's natural and legitimate son were the second-century Jewish Christians, but one searches in vain for that suggestion in Jewish and Samaritan literature. This situation should be kept in mind by modern scholars who reject the virginal conception and assume without proof that Jesus was the son of Joseph. Matthew's account clearly rules that out; and, as we have seen, a too early birth may be implied in the tradition as far back as we can trace it. Undoubtedly, some sophisticated Christians could live with the alternative of illegitimacy; they would see this as the ultimate stage in Jesus' emptying himself and taking on the form of a servant (Philip 2:7), and would insist, quite rightly, that an irregular begetting involves no sin by Jesus himself. But illegitimacy would destroy the images of sanctity and purity with which Matthew and Luke surround Jesus' origins and would negate the theology that Jesus came from the pious Anawim of Israel (§ 12, C2). For many less sophisticated believers, illegitimacy would be an offense that would challenge the plausibility of the Christian mystery.

h) The virginal conception was a miracle, even though the evangelists

---

[81] *Church Dogmatics*, I[2] (Edinburgh: Clark, 1956), 188–92; he makes a sophisticated distinction between the lack of original sin and the virginal conception.

do not spotlight its marvelous character. Since the time of Origen (*Against Celsus* I 37) there have been attempts in the opposite direction to make it more acceptable by comparing it to natural phenomena, e.g., instances of parthenogenesis in animals, or, in modern times, to the results of cloning and of experimental embryology. These attempts, though often well-intentioned, represent a misunderstanding of what Christian tradition intended by the virginal conception. It was an extraordinary action of God's creative power, as unique as the initial creation itself (and that is why all natural science objections to it are irrelevant, e.g., that not having a human father, Jesus' genetic structure would be abnormal). It was not a phenomenon of nature; and to reduce it to one, however unusual, would be as serious a challenge as to deny it altogether.

I would hope that these observations clarify to some extent the issues involved.

BIBLIOGRAPHY FOR APPENDIX IV

Alonso, J. M., and P. Schoonenberg, "La concepción virginal de Jésus, historia o leyenda? Un diálogo teológico," EphMar 21 (1971), 161–216.

———— "La concepción virginal entre católicos," EphMar 21 (1971), 257–302.

Blinzler, J., *Die Brüder und Schwestern Jesu* (SBS 21; Stuttgart: Katholisches Bibelwerk, 1967). *Post partum* virginity.

Boslooper, T., *The Virgin Birth* (Philadelphia: Westminster, 1962).

Broer, I., "Die Bedeutung der 'Jungfrauengeburt' im Matthäusevangelium," BibLeb 12 (1971), 248–60.

Brosch, H. J., and J. Hassenfuss (eds.), *Jungfrauengeburt gestern und heute* (Mariologische Studien 4; Essen, 1969).

Brown, R. E., *The Virginal Conception and Bodily Resurrection of Jesus* (New York: Paulist, 1973).

———— "Luke's Description of the Virginal Conception," TS 35 (1974), 360–62.

Brunner-Traut, Emma, "Die Geburtsgeschichte der Evangelien im Lichte ägyptologischer Forschungen," *Zeitschrift für Religions-und-Geistesgeschichte* 12 (1960), 97–111.

Carman, A. S., "Philo's Doctrine of the Divine Father and the Virgin Mother," AJT 9 (1905), 491–518.

Carpenter, H. J., "The Birth from the Holy Spirit and the Virgin Mary in the Old Roman Creed," JTS 40 (1939), 31–36.

Cheyne, T. K., *Bible Problems and the New Material for Their Solution* (New York: Putnam, 1904), esp. 74–75, on the virgin-mother goddess Dusares at Petra.

Clark, A. C., "Born of the Virgin Mary," *The Way*, Supplement 25 (1975), 34–45. *In partu* virginity.

Clarke, W. K. L., *New Testament Problems* (London: Macmillan, 1929), esp. 1–5, on the virgin-mother goddess.

Cooke, R. J., *Did Paul Know of the Virgin Birth?* (New York: Macmillan, 1926).

Craghan, J. F., "Mary's *Ante Partum* Virginity: The Biblical View," AER 162 (1970), 361–72.

Danell, G. A., "Did St. Paul Know the Tradition about the Virgin Birth?" *Studia Theologica* 4 (1951), 94–101.

Danieli, G., "A proposito delle origini della tradizione sinottica sulla concezione verginale," *Divus Thomas* (Piacenza) 72 (1969), 312–31.

Delius, W., *Texte zur Geschichte der Marienverehrung und Marienverkündigung in der Alten Kirche* (Kleine Texte 178; Berlin: De Gruyter, 1956).

Fitzmyer, J. A., "The Virginal Conception of Jesus in the New Testament," TS 34 (1973), 541–75.

Ford, Josephine M., "Mary's Virginitas Post-Partum and Jewish Law," *Biblica* 54 (1973), 269–72.

Frank, K. S., " 'Geboren aus der Jungfrau Maria,' " *Zum Thema Jungfrauengeburt* (Stuttgart: Katholisches Bibelwerk, 1970), 91–120.

Fuller, R. H., "The Virgin Birth: Historical Fact or Kerygmatic Truth?" *Biblical Research* 1 (1956), 1–8.

Galot, J., "La virginité de Marie et la naissance de Jésus," NRT 82 (1960), 449–69. *In partu* virginity.

Gese, H., "Natus ex Virgine," in *Probleme biblischer Theologie*, ed. H. W. Wolff (G. von Rad Festschrift; Munich: Kaiser, 1971), 73–89.

Grelot, P., "La naissance d'Isaac et celle de Jésus," NRT 94 (1972), 462–87, 561–85.

Hoben, A., *The Virgin Birth* (Historical and Linguistic Studies in Literature Related to the New Testament, Second Series, I[1]; University of Chicago Press, 1903).

Lattke, Gisela, "Lukas 1 und die Jungfrauengeburt," in *Zum Thema Jungfrauengeburt*, ed. K. S. Frank *et al.* (Stuttgart: Katholisches Bibelwerk, 1970), 61–89.

Legault, A., "Saint Paul a-t-il parlé de la Maternité Virginale?" ScEccl 16 (1964), 481–93.

Machen, J. G., *The Virgin Birth of Christ* (New York: Harper, 1930).

McHugh, J., *Mother*, 269–342.

Michel, O., and O. Betz, "Von Gott gezeugt," in *Judentum, Urchristentum, Kirche* (Festschrift J. Jeremias; BZNW 26; Berlin: Töplemann, 1960), 3–23. Qumran thought.

Michl, J., "Die Jungfrauengeburt im Neuen Testament," *Mariologische Studien* 4 (1969), 145–84.

Miguens, M., *The Virgin Birth: An Evaluation of Scriptural Evidence* (Westminster, Md.: Christian Classics, 1975).

Orr, J., *The Virgin Birth of Christ* (New York: Scribner's, 1907).

Piper, O. A., "The Virgin Birth: The Meaning of the Gospel Accounts," *Interpretation* 18 (1964), 131–48.

Plumpe, J. C., "Some Little-Known Early Witnesses to Mary's *Virginitas in Partu*," TS 9 (1948), 567–77.

Rahner, K., *"Virginitas in Partu,"* *Theological Investigations*, IV (Baltimore: Helicon, 1966), 134–62.

Robinson, W. C., "A Re-study of the Virgin Birth of Christ," *Evangelical Quarterly* 37 (1965), 198–211, published as a *Supplement to the Columbia Theological Seminary Bulletin* (1966), 1–14.

——— "The Virgin Birth—A Broader Base," *Christ Today* 17 (1972), 238–40.

Saliba, J. A., "Virgin Birth and Anthropology," TS 36 (1975), 428–54.

Schürmann, H., "Die Geistgewirkte Lebensentstehung Jesu," in *Einheit in Vielfalt*, ed. W. Ernst *et al.* (Festgabe Hugo Aufderbeck; Leipzig: St. Benno, 1974), 156–69.

Smith, M., " 'God's Begetting the Messiah' in 1QSa," NTS 5 (1958–59), 218–24.

Steinmetz, F. J., "Jungfrauengeburt—Wunderglaube und Glaube," *Orientierung* 37 (1973), 31–34.

Talbert, C., H., "The Concept of Immortals in Mediterranean Antiquity," JBL 94 (1975), 419–36.

Taylor, V., *The Historical Evidence for the Virgin Birth* (Oxford: Clarendon, 1920).

Vallauri, E., "L'Esegesi Moderna di Fronte alla Verginità di Maria," *Laurentianum* 14 (1973), 445–80.

von Campenhausen, H. F., *The Virgin Birth in the Theology of the Ancient Church* (London: SCM, 1964).

Wilkinson, J., "Apologetic Aspects of the Virgin Birth of Jesus Christ," SJT 17 (1964), 159–81.

APPENDIX V: THE CHARGE
OF ILLEGITIMACY

In the previous appendix we saw that one possible historical catalyst for the idea of the virginal conception of Jesus was a remembrance that he had been born unduly early after his parents had come to live together—a chronology explicit in Matthew and implicit in Luke, and seemingly antedating both. While to the opponents of Jesus such an early birth may have supplied evidence of illegitimacy, the first attested Christian explanation for it was in terms of a miraculous conception while his mother was a virgin, taking place in the period after marriage, but before she came to live at Joseph's house. Having considered in detail this Christian explanation, let us now look at the uncomplimentary explanation adopted by opponents. My procedure will be to start with facts and only secondarily to turn to hypotheses, even though this means treating later evidence before earlier evidence. Accordingly, let us begin with the Jewish charge of illegitimacy as it is clearly documented from the second century onwards in both Christian and Jewish witnesses. Then we shall discuss the possible origins of that charge in the New Testament.

A. *The Evidence from the Second Century and Later*

Our chief interest here will be to see if there are traces of a charge of illegitimacy that do not stem from a knowledge of the infancy narratives. The early apocryphal writings offer uncertain hints. The *Gospel of Thomas,* discovered at Nag Hammadi, has often been thought to contain some authentic material from the ministry of Jesus not otherwise preserved in the canonical Gospels.[1] The saying of Jesus, ✗105, "He who knows father and mother will be called 'the son of a prostitute,'"[2] is too obscure to be really helpful. But one explanation that has been offered involves John 8:39ff., the debate between Jesus and "the Jews" concerning illegitimacy.

---

[1] Although preserved in a fourth-century Coptic ms., *Thomas* was almost certainly composed in Greek in the second century.

[2] J. Doresse, *The Secret Books of the Egyptian Gnostics* (New York: Viking, 1960), 369, numbers it ✗109 and translates it as a question: "He who knows father and mother, shall he be called 'Son of a harlot!'?"

In 8:55 Jesus claims to know his Father, and yet "the Jews" hint at his being illegitimate (8:41—see the discussion below). If Grant and Freedman are right in seeing the "mother" in this saying in *Thomas* as a reference to the Holy Spirit, the slur on one who knows his mother may be a blasphemy against the Holy Spirit (Mark 3:29).[3] The *Acts of Pilate* (2:3)[4] is clearer: "The elders of the Jews answered and said to Jesus, 'What should we see? First, that you were born of fornication; second, that your birth meant the death of the children in Bethlehem; third, that your father Joseph and your mother Mary fled into Egypt because they counted for nothing among the people.'" Although it has been claimed that this represents a form of the story of Jesus' illegitimacy earlier than the one known to Celsus (which we are about to discuss),[5] it is more clearly dependent upon Matthew than is Celsus' story.

The anti-Christian work of Celsus, written *ca.* A.D. 177–180, drew upon Jewish sources; and in it we find a fully developed tale of Jesus' birth which we may reconstruct as follows:[6]

> It was Jesus himself who fabricated the story that he had been born of a virgin. In fact, however, his mother was a poor country woman who earned her living by spinning. She had been driven out by her carpenter-husband [*tektōn*] when she was convicted of adultery with a soldier named Panthera.[7] She then wandered about and secretly gave birth to Jesus. Later, because he was poor, Jesus hired himself out in Egypt where he became adept in magical powers. Puffed up by these, he claimed for himself the title of God.

This attack upon Jesus' origins was evidently widespread. In North Africa, Tertullian, writing *ca.* A.D. 197, mentions among the charges against Jesus (of Jewish origin) the defamation that he was the son of a prostitute (*quaestuiaria—De Spectaculis* xxx 6).

---

[8] R. M. Grant and D. N. Freedman, *The Secret Sayings of Jesus* (London: Collins, 1960), 180–81. Also H. Montefiore and H. E. W. Turner, *Thomas and the Evangelists* (SBT 35; London: SCM, 1962), 29. Since "spirit" is a feminine noun in Hebrew, some Gnostic writings play upon the theme that the Holy Spirit was the mother of Jesus. The Holy Spirit is mentioned in only one saying in *Thomas* (#44), but precisely in terms of blasphemy against the Holy Spirit.

[4] The origins of the *Acts of Pilate* are in the second century, although the form we have is clearly attested only in the fourth century.

[5] F. Scheidweiler, NTApoc, I, 445.

[6] Our knowledge of the work of Celsus comes from Origen's *Against Celsus*, written *ca.* A.D. 248. For this story of Jesus' birth, see *Against Celsus* I, 28,32,69.

[7] In other patristic writings, the name given by Origen in reporting Celsus' tale, namely, Panthera, is treated as a name of one of Jesus' family ancestors. Sometimes it is taken as a surname for Jacob, Jesus' grandfather (according to Matthew—Table IV); thus Epiphanius *Panarion* (*Adv. Haer.*) III lxxviii 7; PG 42:708D). Other times it is treated as the name of an ancestor of Mary, e.g., John Damascene, *ca.* 740, gives the sequence: Levi, Melchi, Panther, Barpanther, Joachim, Mary, which is a confused combination of material from the Lucan list and from the *Protevangelium of James* (Joachim as Mary's father); see *On the Orthodox Faith* iv 14; PG 94:1156–57; also Andrew of Crete [*ca.* 725] in Homily VI, *On the Circumcision;* PG 97:916.

The evidence cited in the previous paragraph represents a Christian report of Jewish polemics; such counterpolemic is not always trustworthy. But in this instance we have substantiation from Jewish writings which refer to Jesus as "the son of Panthera" (Jeshu ben Pantera) and place this designation in the mouths of rabbis of the Tannaitic period (in particular of the early second century A.D.).[8] While this designation does not necessarily mark Jesus as illegitimate (Pantera could be a family name), one is hard-pressed to dissociate the name from Origen's report of a Jewish story about adultery between Mary and Panthera. A rabbi of the early second century, Simeon ben Azzai is said (Mishnah *Jebamoth* 4:13) to have found in Jerusalem a genealogy, seemingly dating from the period before A.D. 70, in which it was stated: "So-and-so is illegitimate, born of a married woman." Since Jews in fear of Christian persecution became very circumspect about making derogatory references to Jesus, the "So-and-so" has been thought to stand for Jesus; and this has been called "the earliest authenticated passage ascribing illegitimate birth to Jesus."[9] However, there is no way to be certain that the passage did originally refer to Jesus.[10]

By the Amoraic period of rabbinic literature (A.D. 200–500), the belief in Jesus' illegitimacy was well established in Jewish circles, as Ben Pantera was identified with Ben Stada ("the son of Stada"), whose mother was Miriam (Mary), a hairdresser who had been unfaithful to her husband.[11] Ben Stada was supposed to have learned black-magic formulas in Egypt which he brought back inscribed or cut into his skin, and he is said to have been hanged (crucified) on Passover Eve. This story developed into the medieval legends of the *Toledoth Yeshu*[12] according to which, during the days of Alexander Jannaeus (early first century B.C.), a certain Joseph Pandera[13] forced himself on Miriam the wife of Johanan who gave birth

8 The references include Tosephta *Hullin* II 22–23, and the Jerusalem Talmud tractates *Aboda Zara* 40d and *Sabbath* 14d. They are given and evaluated in Goldstein, *Jesus*, 32–39. There are various spellings of the name (*Pnṭyr'*, vocalized *Panṭērā*), namely, Pantira, Pandera, Pantiri, and Panteri.

9 S. Kraus, "Jesus of Nazareth," *The Jewish Encyclopedia* (New York: Funk & Wagnalls, 1904), VII, 170.

10 Stauffer, "Jeschu," assumes this, but it is denied by Goldstein, *Jesus*, 67–68.

11 References to Ben Stada are attributed to rabbis of the Tannaitic period; but the comments in TalBab *Sabbath* 104b and *Sanhedrin* 67a, which identify him with Jesus or Ben Pantera, are of Amoraic date. The twofold name is explained by saying that Stada was the husband of Miriam, while Pantera was her lover (*Sabbath* 104b). See Goldstein, *Jesus*, 57–62; he joins the many Jewish scholars who deny the accuracy of this identification of Ben Stada and Ben Pantera.

12 The *Toledoth Yeshu*, although late, may contain some ancient material; see E. Bammel, NTS 13 (1966–67), 319. Thoroughly unlikely is the thesis of H. J. Schonfeld (*According to the Hebrews* [London: Duckworth, 1937]) that the *Toledoth Yeshu*, which dates in its earliest form to the fourth century, is a parody of the lost *Gospel According to the Hebrews* which contained truly ancient information about Jesus.

13 This name represents a combination of the Gospel information that Jesus was the "son of Joseph" with the Jewish story that he was the "son of Pantera."

to Yeshu (Jesus). When it became known that he was the illegitimate son of Joseph Pandera, Yeshu fled to Upper Galilee. Yeshu discovered the secret letters of the divine name which he sewed into a cut in his thigh and used for magical purposes. He claimed to be the Messiah and the Son of God and was ultimately put to death on Passover Eve.

The real question that we must ask about this Jewish charge of illegitimacy, attested from the second century in both Jewish and Christian sources, is whether it represents a tradition independent of the Gospels (and thus indirectly confirmatory of the Matthean narrative) or a polemic in response to and stimulated by the Gospels. The appearance of Egypt in the story favors an acquaintance (direct or indirect) with the Matthean infancy story; on the other hand, the mention of the Roman soldier Pandera is scarcely explicable from the Gospels,[14] although the addition of a name may have been a popular embellishment of a basic story that developed in its own way from Matthew's account. And so there is no way to know with certainty whether the post-NT Jewish charge of illegitimacy is an authentic recollection of Jewish charges that were circulating before Matthew composed his narrative.

B. *The Evidence from the New Testament*

Two passages in the New Testament, outside the infancy narratives, offer possible corroboration for the existence of a Jewish charge of illegitimacy, Mark 6:3 and John 8:41.

1. The Appellation "Son of Mary" in Mark 6:3

The first task is to determine the authentic reading of the Marcan verse, an issue that is affected both by a textual variant of Mark and by the readings of the parallel verse in the other Gospels:

> Mark 6:3 (major codices): "Is not this *the carpenter, the son of Mary,* and the brother of James, Joses, Judas, and Simon? Are not his sisters here among us?"
>
> Mark 6:3 (P[45]; family 13, OL, Bohairic, Armenian): "Is not this *the son of the carpenter and of Mary, etc.*"

---

[14] See A. Deissmann, "Der Name Panthera," in *Orientalische Studien T. Nöldecke gewidmet,* ed. C. Bezold (Giessen: Töpelmann, 1906), 871–75. The name Pantera was a common name among Roman soldiers. An inscription found in Germany mentions a Tiberius Julius Abdes Pantera, an archer from Sidon in Phoenicia who was transferred in A.D. 9 to Germany. This information makes quite implausible the theory that "Pantera" arose as a corruption of *parthenos,* "virgin," although it is not impossible that the similarity of the two words prompted the choice of the genuine name Pantera—thus, L. Patterson, "Origin of the Name Pantera," *JTS* 19 (1917–18), 79–80.

Matt 13:55: "Is not this *the son of the carpenter?* Is not *his mother called Mary,* and are not his brothers James and Joseph, Simon and Judas? Are not all his sisters here among us?"

Luke 4:22: "Is not this *the son of Joseph?*"

John 6:42: "Is not this Jesus, *the son of Joseph?* Do we not know *his father and mother?*"

The three Synoptic Gospels set this question on the lips of the townspeople of Nazareth on the occasion of Jesus' only visit to his hometown during his ministry, and the question is meant to stress the ordinary origins of Jesus as contrasted with his growing reputation for marvelous deeds and words. John sets the question on the lips of "the Jews" on the shores of the Sea of Tiberias, but it has the same meaning. There is a good chance that we are dealing with variant forms of the one basic tradition.

The manuscript evidence clearly favors the first reading of Mark 6:3, but we must reckon with the fact that P[45] is our oldest ms. of Mark.[15] As for the logic of which reading is more likely to have been produced by scribes, many scholars who favor the second reading argue that scribes, anxious to preserve the idea of the virginal conception of Jesus, found scandalous the (original) reading of Mark calling Jesus "the son of the carpenter and Mary"[16] and that they rearranged the wording so that Jesus was simply called "the son of Mary." But one must ask whether scribes would be likely to change Mark in a way that would bring that Gospel into disagreement with the parallel readings in Matthew and Luke, both of which designate Jesus in relation to his father ("the son of the carpenter"; "the son of Joseph"). It is more likely, in my opinion, that scribes, faced with the Marcan original of "the carpenter, the son of Mary," would change it to agree with Matthew and Luke by designating Jesus in relation to Joseph. By calling him "the son of the carpenter," the scribes would at the same time bring Mark into conformity with the Christian tradition that Joseph (rather than Jesus) was a carpenter.[17]

---

15 This papyrus is usually dated to the third century, and we have corroborating evidence for the second reading of Mark in that century from Origen. In refuting Celsus (VI 36) he objects to the claim that Jesus was a carpenter by trade on the grounds that "Jesus himself is not described as a carpenter anywhere in the Gospels accepted by the churches."

16 Yet Matthew, who believed in the virginal conception, did not think it scandalous to call Jesus "the son of the carpenter." True, there is a different situation in Matthew from what we find in Mark: Matthew's readers already know of the virginal conception through the infancy narrative, and Mark's readers do not have a similar help. But would a scribe think of this subtle difference, and would not the fact that Matthew had used the phrase make it innocuous?

17 Second- and third-century scribes might have been sensitive about the designation of Jesus as a carpenter because of a polemic against his lowly status, a polemic that we can see attested by Celsus' remarks (footnote 15 above). Blinzler, *Brüder,* 28–30, offers a series of arguments for preferring the first reading of Mark over the second. I find their collective force persuasive, even if no single argument is conclusive (as contended by McArthur, "Son," 48–51). Yet so careful a scholar as Vincent Taylor (*The Gospel According to Mark* [New York: Macmillan, 1952], 300) opts for "Is not this the son of the carpenter?" as the original reading.

As for the inner logic of Synoptic relationships, in determining which reading Matthew and Luke found in Mark, we must be careful. Those who favor the second reading of Mark argue that it better explains why Matthew and Luke agree in identifying Jesus in terms of Joseph—they both found Jesus identified as "the son of the carpenter" in Mark. But can we really speak here of Luke as modifying Mark?[18] Rather there seem to be two traditions of the basic saying, a longer one (Mark, Matthew) and a shorter one (Luke, John). In the longer form there are references to the carpenter, Mary, the brothers and the sisters; in the shorter form Jesus is simply called "the son of Joseph."[19] If we consider Mark with that theory in mind, the first reading of Mark may have been the original long form of the saying; and Matthew may have adapted it slightly to avoid having Jesus called a carpenter—an instance of the generally more reverential tone of Matthew.

It seems wise then to take the first and better attested reading of Mark as the original reading, but also to resign ourselves to being unable to get behind the longer and shorter forms of the saying to an earlier form. In other words, we have no way of knowing whether the most ancient tradition had Jesus called "the son of Mary" or "the son of Joseph," or perhaps even "the son of Joseph and Mary."[20] Admitting that, let us nevertheless discuss the possible implications of calling Jesus "the son of Mary," since that is at least *an* ancient Christian memory of the scene. If Christians could report that Jesus was known as "the carpenter, the son of Mary," does that tell us something about the attitude of Jesus' opponents, as Christians understood them? Is the reference to Jesus by his mother's name an expression of contempt for him (and her) or simply an expression that helps to underline the ordinary character of his background? To some extent the answer to that question depends on the accompanying appellation, "the carpenter." There is really no proof that this was a slur on him as an ignorant manual laborer.[21] Rather, in the context, it places him

18 Luke's narrative of the rejection of Jesus at Nazareth differs from Mark's in both order and content; and it is possible that Luke was using a source other than Mark for this scene.

19 The second line of John broadens this short form, so that John's tradition may be composite, combining a source similar to the Lucan tradition with a source similar to the Marcan/Matthean tradition.

20 The most ancient tradition would still not necessarily give us the *ipsissima verba* of the scene. There is a gap between oldest Christian memory and the actual historical scene, a gap over which we have little scientific control.

21 In the second and third centuries, after Christians had hailed Jesus as God, it was a slur on the part of Jewish apologists to dismiss him as a workman (footnote 15 above). But the situation envisaged in the Gospels is quite different. See P. H. Furfey, "Christ as *Tektōn*," CBQ 17 (1955), 324–35. *Tektōn* covers a broad range of artisans in stone, wood, and (in late Greek) metal. Many of the Latin Church Fathers, depending on the translation *faber*, held that Joseph and Jesus were blacksmiths or ironsmiths (e.g., Hilary *On Matthew* xiv)—H. Höpfl, "Nonne hic est fabri filius?" *Biblica* 4 (1923), 41–55. However, the dominant Greek usage and the evidence of the early translations favor the idea of a skilled worker in wood. Justin, *Dialogue* lxxxviii 8, specifies that Jesus made plows and yokes, and some have thought that Justin was preserving an oral tradition independent of the Gospels. Today,

in a work or occupation comparable to that of the other citizens of
Nazareth. The tone is one of ordinariness in contrast to his new reputation
as a miraculous healer and religious teacher. Therefore, the use of "the
carpenter" supplies no *a priori* basis for seeing in "the son of Mary" a
contemptuous designation.

Nevertheless, Mark 6:3 is the only instance in the New Testament
wherein Jesus is identified by his relationship to his mother; and one must
explain that peculiarity. In a painstaking study, McArthur has seriously
weakened the contention that referring to someone as the son of his
mother, rather than as the son of his father, is *a regular way* of indicating
that the mother is a widow or that the child is illegitimate and the father is
unknown. McArthur admits that in some cultures the tradition prevails
that an illegitimate son be designated by his mother's name, but he does
not find evidence for this in the OT or in rabbinical literature. He is
quite right in arguing that passages like Lev 24:10–11 and Judg 11:1
("Jephthah . . . the son of a harlot") throw little light on Jesus "the son
of Mary." Unfortunately, however, McArthur does not deal with all the
evidence brought forward by E. Stauffer, the most ardent defender of the
thesis that there is a reference here to illegitimacy.[22] Stauffer points out
that in Samaritan and Mandaean usage "Jesus, son of Mary" has a pejorative sense; and he calls attention to the later Jewish principle: A man is illegitimate when he is called by his mother's name, for a bastard has no father.[23] Yet, of course, we have no proof that such a principle was
operative in Jesus' time.

As I mentioned in discussing Mark in Appendix IV (A), the easiest
way of explaining the designation of Jesus as "the son of Mary" in the
context of the story in which it appears is that Joseph was dead and Mary,
the one living parent, was well known to all the villagers. As McArthur insists, this is not a revival of the thesis that the son of a widow was
identified by his mother's name; for an official record would still have
identified him as "Jesus, the son of Joseph." The identification here as

there is a tendency among scholars to recognize that Joseph and/or Jesus would not have
been carpenters in the sense of making or repairing items that any peasant could deal with.
Tektōn in its classical sense could cover shipbuilder and architect. In their Anchor Bible
Matthew (Garden City: Doubleday, 1971), 172–73, W. F. Albright and C. S. Mann connect
tektōn with the Aramaic word *naggāra*, and an ancient ossuary found in Jerusalem in 1968,
bearing the inscription "Simon—*builder* [*bānêh*] of the Temple." They think of Joseph and
Jesus as builders who traveled to other cities, and thus in the ranks of master craftsmen. On
the slimmer evidence of much later Talmudic sayings involving *naggār*, G. Vermes, *Jesus the
Jew* (London: Collins, 1973), 21–22, argues for the meaning "scholar, learned man"!

[22] There is a brief treatment in his *Jesus*, 23–25, and a full treatment in "Jeschu." I find
some of his supporting evidence far-fetched. For instance he argues that the reference to
Jesus as "a gluttonous man and a wine-bibber" (Matt 11:19; Luke 7:34) is a charge of
illegitimacy—see Deut 21:20 where it is a form of denunciation by genuine parents.

[23] In *Jerusalem und Rom* (Bern: Francke, 1957), 118, Stauffer lists this as the sixty-
second statement of Jewish law. Unfortunately, he is not overly careful in the dating of the
Jewish material he invokes as background for first-century discussions.

"the son of Mary" would be purely contextual, rather than normal, official, or genealogical.[24] (A good parallel is offered by Luke 7:12 where, in the context, it is perfectly understandable that the deceased is identified as "the only son of his mother who was a widow.") Does the Marcan context also suggest that, in the mind of the villagers, Jesus was the illegitimate son of Mary? Is it a feeling of uneasiness about such an implication that causes Matthew to modify the designation "the son of Mary" to the harmless "Is not his mother called Mary?" After all, there is a mention in Mark 6:3 of the scandal (*skandalizein*) of the villagers at the thought of Jesus as a religious figure. However, the mention of the brothers and sisters militates against this connotation. One can scarcely consider all of them to have been illegitimate; and Jesus is being put together with them in order to emphasize his ordinariness. Thus, Mark 6:3 offers no firm support for a Jewish charge of illegitimacy during the ministry or even at a period contemporary with the evangelists.

2. The Debate over Illegitimacy in John 8:41

The evidence here is indirect and depends on inferences from Johannine style and technique. In 8:31ff. there is a debate between Jesus and "the Jews" about their descent from Abraham, who is characterized as their father. In vs. 39 Jesus calls into question whether they really are Abraham's children since they are not doing works worthy of him; and in vs. 41 he begins to point sarcastically to their real father, namely, the devil (see vs. 44). This causes "the Jews" to protest: "We were not born illegitimate. We have but one father, God Himself" (8:41). Knowing the allusive character of the Johannine discourse, many have seen here an *ad hominem* argument against Jesus. He has been talking about his heavenly Father and about their real father, but were there not rumors about his own birth? The Jews may be saying, *"We* were not born illegitimate, but you were." The emphatic use of the Greek pronoun "We" allows that interpretation. Wead[25] would see the possibility of an ironic hint to the same effect earlier in the chapter (vs. 19), where, in response to a statement of Jesus about his (heavenly) Father, the Jews ask, "Where is this 'father' of yours?"

Since illegitimacy and true fatherhood are a concern in John 8, the hint of a Jewish charge of illegitimacy is more plausible here than in Mark 6:3. Yet, the charge is far from certain. Thus, as a result of studying both the

---

[24] *A fortiori*, it would not be theological. The contention that Mark would place his only reference to the virginal conception of Jesus (son of Mary but not of Joseph) on the lips of opponents in such a context is implausible and has been rejected in Appendix IV.

[25] D. W. Wead, *The Literary Devices in John's Gospel* (Basel: Reinhardt, 1970), 61-62. He classifies John 8:41 as irony.

later and the earlier evidence, I would have to judge that we simply do not know whether the Jewish charge of illegitimacy, which appears clearly in the second century, had a source independent of the infancy narrative tradition—a source that would help to confirm as historical the chronology of an early birth supposed by Matthew and (implicitly) by Luke.

BIBLIOGRAPHY FOR APPENDIX V

Blinzler, J., *Brüder,* 71–72, on "the son of Mary."

Goldstein, M., *Jesus in the Jewish Tradition* (New York: Macmillan, 1950).

McArthur, H. K., " 'Son of Mary,' " NovTest 15 (1973), 38–58.

Stauffer, E., "Jeschu ben Mirjam (Mk 6:3)," in *Neotestamentica et Semitica,* ed. E. E. Ellis and M. Wilcox (In Honour of M. Black; Edinburgh: Clark, 1969), 119–28.

APPENDIX VI: OTHER JEWISH
BACKGROUND FOR MATTHEW'S NARRATIVE

In § 4, B2, I discussed the pre-Matthean material used by the evangelist in the infancy chapters, stressing two *narratives:* (a) the main pre-Matthean narrative, fashioned on the themes of the patriarch Joseph and the infant Moses, and shaped on a structure of angelic dream appearances, as illustrated in Tables VI and VII; (b) a secondary narrative, fashioned on the story of Balaam, a magus who comes from the East and sees the Davidic star, as explained further in § 6, C2. However, scholars have detected still other Jewish narratives that may have served as pre-Matthean background. The most prominent concern Abraham, the Queen of Sheba, and Jacob/Israel; and we shall discuss them in that order.

Abraham is mentioned at the beginning of Matthew's genealogy (1:1,2,17); and the literary form of the annunciation of birth, which is so prominent in Matt 1:18–25, is clearly illustrated in the birth of Abraham's sons, Ishmael and Isaac (Table VIII).[1] However, the proposal here is to seek background in material concerning Abraham that is not found in the Bible but in later Jewish legend,[2] namely, material about the birth of Abraham. Astrologers of the wicked King Nimrod told their royal master that a son had been born to Terah (Abraham's father). They had seen a star rise and devour other stars, and this was a sign that the child would gain possession of this world and of the world to come; consequently they advised the king to slay male children. The writings that attest this story come quite late in the Christian era, and we have no evidence that the legend was known in the first century A.D. Moreover, the birth of Abraham in this legend seems to be patterned on the story of the birth of Moses which we have seen attested much earlier. The problem of dating detracts also from the utility of the references to Abraham found in the midrashic interpretations of Isa 41:2–3, a passage referring to the just one whom God brings forth from the East.[3]

The Queen of Sheba is mentioned by Jesus in Matt 12:42 ("Q" tradi-

---

[1] Abraham's literal obedience to divine commands (Gen 12:1,4; 22:2–3) has been invoked as a parallel to Joseph's obedience in Matt 1–2.

[2] See Ginzberg, *Legends*, I, 186–87, 207–9.

[3] The Isaian reference to Abraham has been expounded by Malina, "Matthew," drawing upon rabbinic material.

tion) as coming from the ends of the earth to hear the wisdom of Solomon. She has been thought to be a forerunner of the magi,[4] coming to a king in Jerusalem, testing his wisdom, and bringing gifts of gold, spices, and precious stones. The most impressive element in the parallelism is the gifts (I Kgs 10:2); but the description of gifts in Isa 60:6 ("all those from Sheba will come bringing gold and frankincense"—§ 6, B2) is closer to Matthew's wording than is the account in I Kings of the Queen of Sheba. Less convincing is the observation that the Queen visited Solomon, the son of David, as a parallel to Matt 1:1 which describes Jesus as "son of David";[5] for in a close parallelism between the two stories Solomon has to have some similarity to *Herod*. I would judge coincidental the fact that I Kgs 10:13 refers to the Queen's going back to her own land, while Matt 2:12 reports that the magi "went away to their own country by another route." Certainly there is no vocabulary similarity between the Greek of the two passages.

I have stressed that, in Matthew's theology of ch. 2, Jesus relives in miniature some of the main events of the history of Israel, such as the Exodus and the Exile. It is not surprising then that some scholars have sought the background of the Matthean story in the journey of Jacob/Israel to Egypt after his persecution by Laban.[6] This background has sometimes been proposed in opposition to the thesis that Matthew drew upon the birth of Moses legends,[7] for it is argued that nothing in the Moses story accounts for going down to Egypt. I do not find this argument persuasive because it fails to recognize that the pre-Matthean Moses story is tied in with the dreams of the patriarch Joseph who did go down to Egypt. While both Jacob/Israel and Joseph went down to Egypt, Joseph is more associated with Egypt than is Jacob, just as he is more associated with the Pharaoh and with dreams.[8] Nevertheless, I do not wish to exclude the possibility of a minor reference to Jacob/Israel in the pre-Matthean material, especially since the formula citation in Matt 2:17–18 mentions Rachel, Jacob's wife who was buried near Bethlehem. We remember that it was Joseph who arranged for Jacob/Israel to come to Egypt and it was Moses who led Israel out of Egypt, and Jacob may be said to have returned from Egypt in the person of his descendants. Attention may be called to Gen 46:4 where

---

4 The chief exponent of this is Bruns, "Magi."

5 Galbiati, "L'adorazione," 22.

6 The names of M. Bourke, C. H. Cave, and D. Daube are associated with this thesis. It was at first followed but subsequently modified to the point of abandonment by Vögtle, *Messias*, 43–45.

7 Bourke and Daube consider the Jacob/Israel parallels more important than the Moses parallels. I cannot accept that thesis since the main story involves the birth of a child and the slaughter of male children, an element totally lacking in the Jacob/Israel narrative. Moreover, Laban is not a king, as are Herod and the Pharaoh.

8 The birth-of-Moses story picks up directly from the Joseph story in Exod 1:8 when the Pharaoh who will deal with Moses is compared to the Pharaoh who knew Joseph. See p. 112 above.

God says to Jacob: "I shall go down with you to Egypt and I shall bring you back again."

Intrinsic to the thesis of a background in the Jacob/Israel story is an evaluation of the early midrashic developments of that story as witnessed in the ancient Passover Haggadah, i.e., the popular account of Israel's deliverance narrated in relation to the celebration of Passover.[9] In this account the old Israelite creedal statement of Deut 26:5–8, involving the affirmation, "A wandering Aramean was my father," is reinterpreted by a slight change of vowels to read: "An Aramean sought to destroy my father."[10] A comparison is then made between Laban the Aramean who sought to destroy Jacob and his family and the Pharaoh who sought to destroy the Hebrew male children.[11] The midrash also draws together two separate biblical events pertaining to Jacob/Israel: his difficulties with Laban (Gen 31) and his subsequent migration to Egypt during the famine (Gen 46). Thus, in sequence we have an attempt against Jacob and his family by Laban the Aramean, a flight to Egypt as directed by God in a dream, and a later return of Israel under Moses.[12] The similarity to the Matthean story is enhanced if we realize that a difference of only one consonant separated the ethnic description of Laban as an Aramean (*'rmy*) and the identification of Herod as an Idumean (*'dmy*).[13] We do not know how ancient was the curious identification of Balaam and Laban (Jerusalem Targum on Num 22:5),[14] an identification that takes on greater interest because of the later contention that Balaam was one of the advisors to the Pharaoh in Egypt. If the Jacob/Israel legend was scarcely the main background for the pre-Matthean tradition (footnote 7), there is no reason why elements of it may not have already been intermingled with the story involving the patriarch Joseph and the birth of Moses which gave shape to the main pre-Matthean narrative.

9 Finkelstein, "Oldest," 293, would date the origins of this midrash to *ca.* 200 B.C. Nevertheless, we do not have the same certitude about its existence when Matthew was writing as we have about the midrash on the birth of Moses attested in Josephus and Philo.

10 The same verbal root is involved, *'bd*, which in the Qal means "to be lost, wander," and in the Pi'el means "to make lost, destroy."

11 "An Aramean, namely Laban, wished to destroy my father, namely Jacob—and Laban was even worse than the Pharaoh; whereas the Pharaoh wanted to kill only the males, Laban wanted to kill all—and my father Jacob went down into Egypt" (Daube, *New Testament,* 189).

12 This sequence is already present in embryo in Deut 26:5–8.

13 Hebrew *resh* (r) and *daleth* (d) are notoriously easy to confuse in the script employed after the Babylonian Exile. Nevertheless, Herod is not identified as an Idumean in Matthew, and so the play on that designation is purely hypothetical.

14 Once this identification was made, Laban's attempt to destroy Jacob's whole family could be understood as a purge directed against the future Messiah whom Balaam saw as a star that would rise from Jacob.

Bibliography for Appendix VI

(See also part B of the Bibliography for § 4.)

Bourke, M., "Genus," 167–73.

Bruns, J. E., "Magi," 51–54.

Daube, D., *New Testament,* 189–92.

Finkelstein, L., "The Oldest Midrash: Pre-Rabbinic Ideals and Teachings in the Passover Haggadah," HTR 31 (1938), 291–317.

Malina, B., "Matthew 2 and Isa 41,2–3: a Possible Relationship?" SBFLA 19 (1967), 290–302.

APPENDIX VII: THE CENSUS
UNDER QUIRINIUS

> At that time an edict went out from Caesar Augustus that a census should be taken of the whole world. (This was the first census under Quirinius as governor of Syria.) And so all went to be inscribed in the census, each to his own city. Joseph also went up from Galilee, from the city of Nazareth, into Judea to the city of David which is called Bethlehem, because he was of the house and lineage of David, to have himself inscribed in the census. (Luke 2:1–5).

If this notice about the census stood by itself, there would be some problems about the extent and the manner of registration; but the chronology would cause no difficulty. Augustus reigned from 44/42 B.C. to A.D. 14; Publius Sulpicius Quirinius became governor or legate of Syria in A.D. 6 and conducted a census of Judea (not of Galilee) in A.D. 6–7. The last mentioned date would then be implicitly fixed for Luke as the year of the birth of Jesus. But the chronological information in ch. 2 of Luke does not stand by itself; and when we compare it with other chronological information that he has given us in 1:5 and 3:1,23, there seems to be an irreconcilable conflict.

In 1:5 Luke tells us that the annunciation of the birth of JBap took place "in the days of Herod, king of Judea." According to our best information Herod died in March/April 4 B.C. (NOTE on Matt 2:1). According to Luke 1:36 Mary's pregnancy began some six months after Elizabeth's; and so Jesus would have been born about fifteen or sixteen months after the annunciation of JBap's birth. This would fix the year of his birth at no later than 3 B.C. and would bring Luke into an approximate correspondence with the information in Matt 2 that Jesus was born in the last years of Herod's reign.[1] However, such a date is ten years before Quirinius became governor of Syria and conducted the census. There are three basic approaches in dealing with this conflict. First, one may seek to reinterpret the Herod chronology of Luke 1 to agree with the Quirinius census dating (A.D. 6–7) of Luke 2. Second, one may seek to reinterpret the Quirinius census chronology of Luke 2 to agree with the Herod dating (4–3 B.C.) of

---

[1] It would seem from Matt 2:16 (see NOTE there) that Matthew thought that Jesus was born at least two years before the death of Herod the Great and thus ca. 6 B.C.

Luke 1. Third, one may recognize that one or both of the Lucan datings are confused, and that there is neither a need nor a possibility of reconciling them. Basically this appendix will come to the conclusion that the third approach is the most plausible, but only after a thorough discussion of suggestions made in the first and second approaches.

The first approach may be dealt with briefly, for the chronology of Herod the Great's reign is too fixed to be changed in order to match a date of A.D. 6–7. One ingenious suggestion, however, is that Luke did not mean Herod the Great but Archelaus, who is occasionally called Herod[2] and who ruled as king of Judea from 4 B.C. to A.D. 6. One could theorize that the annunciation of JBap's birth took place toward the end of Archelaus' reign (A.D. 5–6) and that Jesus was born after Archelaus had been deposed and the newly installed Quirinius began the census (A.D. 6–7). Another suggestion recognizes the likelihood mentioned in § 10D that, in joining the births of JBap and Jesus, Luke reflects theology rather than history. It is then proposed that the Herod (the Great) dating of 4–3 B.C. is correct for the birth of JBap, while the Quirinius census dating of A.D. 6–7 is correct for the birth of Jesus.[3]

These and other suggestions which date the birth of Jesus in A.D. 6–7 bring Luke into conflict with Matthew. More importantly they contradict the remaining items of Lucan chronological information mentioned in the first paragraph, namely, 3:1,23. The combination of those two verses pertaining to the beginning of Jesus' ministry indicates that Jesus was about thirty years old in the fifteenth year of Tiberius (A.D. 27–28). This would agree with a birth in 4–3 B.C. at the time of Herod the Great, but hardly with a birth in A.D. 6–7.[4] This difficulty has caused most scholars who wish to preserve Lucan accuracy to prefer the second approach and to seek to redate the census that Luke mentions to an earlier period, harmonious with the reign of Herod the Great. Much of the rest of this appendix will be devoted to the difficulties encountered in the second approach.

Did Augustus ever issue an edict that the whole world, i.e., the Roman

[2] Derrett, "Further Light," 82–85, who proposes this thesis, points to the designation "Herod" for Archelaus on coins and in Dio Cassius. But neither Josephus nor the New Testament ever calls Archelaus "Herod" (see Matt 2:22). Derrett's thesis does not totally save the accuracy of the infancy narrative, for we shall see several difficulties in the Lucan description of the census.

[3] This is the thesis of Sherwin-White, *Roman Society*, 167, who thinks that Luke is correcting Matthew's tradition. Rather, the generally accepted independence of the two infancy narratives and the apparent lack of any Lucan knowledge of Matthew makes their mutual reference to Herod the Great persuasive in the dating of Jesus' birth.

[4] Various datings for the birth of Jesus which appear in early Church writers, whatever historical value they may have, would place that birth before A.D. 1. Tertullian, *Adversus Judaeos* viii, speaks of the twenty-eighth year after the death of Cleopatra, which means 2 B.C. Clement of Alexandria, *Stromata* I 21 (#145), speaks of 194 years before the death of Commodus, which means 2 B.C. Irenaeus, *Against the Heretics* II xxii 6, says that Jesus was past forty years of age when he died, which implies a birth *ca.* 10–7 B.C. Eusebius, *Eccl. Hist.* I v 2, speaks of Jesus' birth in the forty-second year of Augustus, which means 3–1 B.C.

Empire, be enrolled in a census? Certainly not in the sense in which a modern reader might interpret the Lucan statement! In the reign of Augustus there was no single census covering the Empire; and granted the different legal statuses of provinces and client kingdoms, a sweeping universal edict seems most unlikely. But Luke may not have meant a single census. The long peace under Augustus made empire-wide policies possible, and Augustus was interested in censuses for various purposes. During his reign there were three enumerations of Roman *citizens* for statistical purposes (28 and 8 B.C.; A.D. 13–14). Taxation and military service were the main goals for census of *non-citizens* in the provinces; and we know of censuses held at different times in Gaul and in Egypt. Thus, what Luke may be telling us in an oversimplified statement is that the census conducted (in Judea) by Quirinius as governor of Syria was in obedience to Augustus' policy of getting accurate population statistics for the whole Empire.

Would a Roman census have sent people back to their tribal or ancestral homes to be enrolled, as Luke describes in the case of Joseph? We have no clear parallel for such a practice. Since enrollment was primarily for taxation purposes, the general Roman pattern was to register people where they lived or in the nearby principal city of a district (the city from which the tax would be collected). A papyrus (Lond. 904, 20f.) describes a census in Egypt in A.D. 104 wherein a temporary dweller, in order to be enrolled, had to go back to the area of his regular domicile where he had a house. (Sometimes this is referred to as a *kata oikian* census.) Obviously this ruling was motivated by tax considerations about property and agriculture; and it offers little support for sending Joseph from Nazareth where he permanently resided (2:39) to Bethlehem where clearly he had no property or wealth, according to 2:7.[5] Nevertheless, one cannot rule out the possibility that, since the Romans often adapted their administration to local circumstances, a census conducted in Judea would respect the strong attachment of Jews to tribal and ancestral relationships. Even if Luke had little historical information about how the census of Quirinius had been conducted, he lived in the Roman Empire and may have undergone census enrollment himself. It is dangerous to assume that he described a process of registration that would have been patently opposed to everything that he and his readers knew.[6] Yet, if we cannot confirm or deny the pattern of enrollment in ancestral cities which Luke depicts, his

[5] Methodologically, we should resist all fanciful efforts to interpret Luke through the information in Matt 2:11 that the family lived in a house at Bethlehem, as if Joseph had to enroll in Bethlehem because he had property there. Rather Luke 2:7 and Matt 2:11 represent one of the conflicts between the two infancy narratives mentioned in § 1, B2. Nothing in Luke's description of the birthplace or of the family's almost immediate return to Nazareth encourages us to think that Joseph had any other reason to go to Bethlehem beyond that given, i.e., ancestral descent.

[6] While Luke does *not* describe a *kata oikian* census, a vague knowledge of such censuses in Egypt may have given seeming plausibility to what Luke describes.

narrative seems to presume that the census of Quirinius affected Galileans. This is not factual for the census of A.D. 6–7, since at that time Galilee was not under Quirinius' direct supervision but was a tetrarchy ruled by Herod Antipas. And so now we must raise directly the question as to whether there was an earlier census by Quirinius before Galilee and Judea were ruled separately.[7]

Was Quirinius governor (legate) of Syria during or shortly after the reign of Herod the Great, and thus around or before 4 B.C.? Drawing chiefly upon Josephus,[8] we can put together the following chronology for the legates of Syria:

23–13 B.C.:	M. Agrippa
ca. 10 B.C.:	M. Titius
9–6 B.C.:	S. Sentius Saturninus
6–4 B.C. or later:	Quintilius (or Quinctilius) Varus
1 B.C. to *ca.* A.D. 4:	Gaius Caesar
A.D. 4–5:	L. Volusius Saturninus
A.D. 6 to after 7:	P. Sulpicius Quirinius

If Quirinius served as governor of Syria twice, once in A.D. 6 and once earlier, the two possible time slots for the earlier governorship would be before M. Titius (and thus before 10 B.C.) or between Quintilius Varus and Gaius Caesar (and thus between 4 and 1 B.C.). Either possibility could be reconciled with the Lucan information. However, from what we know of the relatively well-documented career of Quirinius, it is unlikely that he had an earlier governorship at either of those periods. He served as consul in 12 B.C. (Tacitus *Annals* III 48). He was in Asia Minor sometime after 12 and before 6 B.C. leading the legions in the war against the Homonadenses. He was in the Near East, specifically in Syria, as an advisor of Gaius Caesar for several years before A.D. 4. But there is no mention of Quirinius having been legate in the nearly twenty years of his career from 12 B.C. to A.D. 6. Josephus, who describes several times the beginning of Quirinius' legateship in A.D. 6, gives no hint that Quirinius had served previously in that capacity.[9]

Two inscriptions have been brought into the discussion to lend support to an earlier governorship by Quirinius. The first is the Lapis Tiburtinus, an inscription on a marble slab found in 1764 in the neighborhood of Tivoli (Tibur) and now in the Vatican Museum.[10] This inscription or

---

[7] I shall concentrate on an earlier census under or by *Quirinius*, since Luke mentions him; but many of my remarks pertain to an earlier census under any Roman governor.

[8] There have been attempts to challenge Josephus' accuracy and rearrange this chronology to fit Luke's evidence, e.g., T. Corbishley, *Journal of Roman Studies* 24 (1934), 43–49, would date the legateship of M. Titius before 12 B.C. to make room for Quirinius between Titius and Saturninus.

[9] See *Ant.* XVII xiii 5;#355; XVIII i 1;##1–2.

[10] ILS, #918. The text is conveniently found in Ramsay, *Was Christ*, 273, but tendentiously identified there as "the Inscription of Quirinius."

titulus, composed after A.D. 14, describes an unnamed person who was a major official victorious in war, and who twice served as legate, the second time serving as legate in Syria. The thesis that this is a reference to Quirinius is a pure guess with as many dissenters as adherents.[11] The other inscription was found on a marble base in Antioch of Pisidia by W. M. Ramsay in 1912.[12] The inscription is dedicated to G. Caristianus Fronto, a colonist of Antioch who served "as prefect of P. Sulpicius Quirinius, the chief magistrate [*duumvir*], and as prefect of M. Servilius." Quirinius is identified as a chief magistrate, while Servilius is not; but Ramsay argues that Quirinius and Servilius were of equal status, and indeed Quirinius was legate of Syria at the same time that Servilius was legate of Galatia during the Homonadensian war (before 6 B.C.). Obviously Ramsay's theory goes considerably beyond what the inscription says. His thesis that Quirinius served as legate of Syria during the Homonadensian war is highly dubious: the war took place in the Taurus mountains, and for military operations there Galatia was a far more practical base than Syria. Thus neither inscription lessens the difficulty of proving that Quirinius had an earlier governorship in Syria during which he might have conducted a census.

Indeed, even if without evidence one does posit this earlier governorship of Quirinius, how does one explain a Roman census of Palestine during the reign of Herod the Great? A client king who paid tribute to Rome, Herod had his own taxes and tax collectors; and there is no evidence that the Romans collected taxes based on a census within his realm (see Josephus *Ant.* XVII ii 2;⸬27). The known census of Quirinius in A.D. 6–7 was conducted precisely because Herod's son Archelaus had been deposed, and Judea was now coming under direct Roman government and taxation. But let me bring to the reader's attention four contrary indications that have been offered as support for the thesis that a Roman census was possible in Herod the Great's realm. *First,* Augustus became very displeased with Herod in 8 B.C. and wrote, threatening to treat Herod no longer as a friend but as a subject (*Ant.* XVI ix 3;⸬290). It has been suggested that this might have led to the imposition of Roman taxes and a Roman census. But, in point of fact, the evidence is that Augustus did not make good on his threat and withdraw his friendship.[18] *Second,* Josephus (*Ant.* XVII ii 4;⸬42) mentions an oath of allegiance to the emperor taken by the Jewish people *ca.* 7 B.C., under Herod the Great's direction. But the claim that this involved an acceptance of direct Roman taxation and a Roman census is gratuitous. A variant of this suggestion has been pro-

---

11 Sanclemeate assigned the *titulus* to Quirinius in 1793, and Mommsen and Ramsay are among the more famous supporters of that identification. Schürer, *History,* I, 1, 353–54 (rev. ed., I, 258–59), and Sherwin-White, *Roman Society,* 164–66, are general supporters of Lucan historicity who think that the inscription has nothing to do with Quirinius. The exhaustive article by Syme on the *titulus* builds a plausible case for referring the inscription to L. Calpurnius Piso, and exposes devastatingly the weakness of the Quirinius attribution.

12 It is published by him in "Luke's Narrative," 401.

18 See E. Bammel, "Die Rechtsstellung des Herodes," ZDPV 84 (1968), 73–79.

posed by Barnett, *"Apographē,"* who contends that Luke is not referring to a census for the purpose of taxation, but to a registration or enrollment (NOTE on "census" in 2:1) that Herod required for the purpose of the oath-taking. Of course, there is no evidence of such a registration, and Barnett has to suppose that Luke 2:2 should be translated: "This was an enrollment conducted *before* Quirinius was governor of Syria"—a translation that makes us wonder why Luke would have mentioned Quirinius at all. *Third,* Josephus twice makes reference to the fact that Herod the Great remitted to the people part of their taxes, and from that it is deduced that there must have been census records.[14] In fact, however, it proves only the existence of records, not of a census, much less of a Roman census. *Fourth,* an instance of Roman taxation of a client kingdom has been pointed to in the narrative of Tacitus, *Annals* VI 41, where *ca.* A.D. 36 Prince Archelaus the Younger conducted a census according to the Roman custom among the Cietae who were his subjects in the Cilician section of Cappadocia. But the passage does not say that *the Romans* imposed this census on Archelaus or his subjects.[15] Moreover, the imposition of the taxes was bitterly resented by the Cietae and led to a revolt. The imposition of a Roman census and Roman tax in the realm of Herod the Great should have produced exactly the same result; so the silence of Josephus, not only about such a census and tax under Herod, but also about a revolt or protest against Rome over such a practice, is an eloquent argument that there was no Roman census of Palestine before the census under Quirinius in A.D. 6–7—an event, with its concomitant revolt, carefully described by Josephus.

Let us consider for a moment Josephus' description of the Quirinius census. Judea was reduced from the position of an Herodian tetrarchy and became a Roman province annexed to Syria in A.D. 6 (759 A.U.C.); and Josephus (*Ant.* XVIII i 1;※※1–10) reports that Quirinius, who had been dispatched by Augustus to become legate of Syria, visited Judea "in order to make an assessment of the property of the Jews and to liquidate the estate of Archelaus." At first the Jews were shocked to hear of the registration of property, but most of them yielded at the intercession of the high priest. However, Judas the Galilean led a rebellion, becoming the founder of the nationalistic Zealot movement (*Ant.* XVIII i 6;※23). Certainly the Josephus narrative would not lead us to suspect that the Jews were previously accustomed to Roman census and taxation! In speaking of

14 *Ant.* XV x 4;※365; XVI ii 5;※64. It is the thesis of A. Schalit, *König Herodes* (Berlin: De Gruyter, 1969), 256–98, that there were censuses in Palestine on a six-year cycle, so that 8 B.C. marked the third census. A cycle of censuses every fourteen years is attested in Egypt, but there is no clear evidence for such a practice in Palestine.

15 Tacitus, *Annals* II 42, tells how in A.D. 17 Tiberius humbled King Archelaus the Elder, turned his kingdom into a province, and rearranged the tax revenues. Thus, the Cappadocian kingdom was under a more direct Roman tax control than was the kingdom of Herod the Great.

"the first census under Quirinius," surely Luke is referring to this well-known (and even notorious) census of A.D. 6–7,[16] a census to which he again refers in Acts 5:37.

Before I pass a general judgment on the historicity of Luke 2:1–5, let me mention some final efforts to save Lucan accuracy. It has been proposed that the present reading of Luke 2:2 is a mistake or textual corruption and that we should read "under Saturninus as governor of Syria." (I did not mention this as a textual variant in the NOTE on 2:2, for there is no manuscript evidence that supports it.) Since Saturninus[17] was governor in the period 9–6 B.C., this would at least synchronize the census with the reign of Herod the Great, although it still labors under the lack of evidence for a Roman census during that reign. The support for identifying Saturninus as the census taker is a passage in Tertullian, *Adversus Marcion* IV xix 10: "At that time there were censuses that had been taken in Judea under Augustus by Sentius Saturninus, in which they might have enquired about Jesus' ancestry." The fact that Tertullian speaks of censuses (plural) is often overlooked,[18] and it is assumed that he was referring to the census in Luke 2:1–5. Some have thought that he had a superior text of 2:2 which read "Saturninus"; others have thought that he was correcting the "Quirinius" reading in Luke after consulting Roman census records. However, there is no real evidence that Tertullian had the Lucan census in mind.[19] The passage occurs as part of an argument against the Docetists; and Tertullian wants to show that Luke 8:19–21 ("My mother and my brother are those who hear the word of God and do it") does *not* mean Jesus denied having any human ancestry. Accordingly, Tertullian points to the census records as a possible way of proving such ancestry. Probably he is assuming that such records existed for Palestine, even as they existed in Tertullian's own time. This is not just a guess about Tertullian's reasoning, for we have evidence of his assumptions in relation to the death of Jesus. In the *Apologeticum*, v 2 and xxi 24, he tells us that

16 An inscription of Aemilius Secundus, also called the Lapis Venetus (ILS, #2683), mentioning the census of Quirinius has been known since the seventeenth century but was deemed spurious. In 1880 a missing fragment from it was discovered in Venice and showed the inscription to be genuine (dated to shortly after A.D. 14). Ramsay and others have invoked it to support an earlier census of Quirinius, but there is no real reason to believe that it refers to a census other than that of A.D. 6–7. The text may be found in Ramsay, *Was Christ*, 274.

17 S. Sentius Saturninus was a self-made man who backed Pompey but eventually won favor under Augustus. He served as a consul in 19 B.C. and then as legate in Germany in A.D. 4–9. Little is known of the intermediate twenty-three years. Tertullian tells us that he was a proconsul in Africa, and Josephus (*Ant.* XVII v 2; #89) attributes to him a legateship in Syria before that of Varus.

18 Censuses (plural) under Augustus are mentioned again by Tertullian, *Adversus Marcion* IV xxxvi 8–9. For a careful evaluation of the whole problem, see Evans, "Tertullian's."

19 A problem would be created if Tertullian did mean that Jesus was born during the governorship of Saturninus (9–6 B.C.), since he reports elsewhere (*Adversus Judaeos* viii 11) that Jesus was born in the forty-first year of Augustus (3–2 B.C.). See also footnote 4 above.

Pilate must have reported the facts about the crucifixion to Tiberius who communicated them to the Senate, where there were debates about the divinity of Christ, in which Tiberius favored Christ!

Another ingenious attempt to rescue Luke is to propose that the census he mentions was a two-step process—a census begun under Saturninus or Varus (thus close to Herod's reign), but completed under Quirinius. However, Luke does not say that the census was completed under Quirinius, but that it took place (*egeneto*) under Quirinius. Stauffer[20] has recently revived a form of the two-step thesis, by distinguishing two terms: (a) the *apographē* (literally, "registration") of taxable property and persons, entailing an appearance at the registry office; and (b) the *apotimēsis* (literally, "evaluation") or actual tax assessment on the basis of the registration. According to Stauffer, Luke is describing the *apographē* (using that word), which was the first step in the Palestinian census and took place under Saturninus *ca.* 7 B.C., when Herod was still alive. It was then that Jesus was born. Josephus describes the *apotimēsis* or second step in the census which took place under Quirinius in A.D. 6–7. A fourteen-year process in a census is not unusual, Stauffer argues, since the census in Gaul took forty years. But, besides the difficulty of proving even a Roman *apographē* in Herod's reign, Stauffer's thesis faces major terminological obstacles. Luke speaks of an *apographē* under Quirinius, not of an *apotimēsis* under Quirinius; and Josephus uses both terms to describe the census of Quirinius (*Ant.* XVIII i 1; ※ ※2–4), so that neither ancient author supports Stauffer's distinction. Another form of the two-step process is the proposal that there was a Jewish census conducted by the priests in Herod's time, and that Luke has confused this with the Roman census ten to fifteen years later. But this is tantamount to a recognition that Luke was inaccurate.

When all is evaluated, the weight of the evidence is strongly against the possibility of reconciling the information in Luke 1 and Luke 2. There is no serious reason to believe that there was a Roman census of Palestine under Quirinius during the reign of Herod the Great. (Indeed, as regards the non-biblical "evidence," it is doubtful that anyone would have even thought about an earlier census if he were not trying to defend Lucan accuracy.) The information in Luke 1 may be correct: Jesus may indeed have been born during or at the end of the reign of Herod the Great. But Luke seems to be inaccurate in associating that birth with the one and only census of Judea (not of Galilee) conducted in A.D. 6–7 under Quirinius. Luke also seems to be inaccurate about that census in Acts 5:36. There, Gamaliel, supposed to be giving a speech in the early or mid 30s (shortly after the death of Jesus), mentions the uprising of Theudas, which did not

---

20 His thesis is presented briefly in *Jesus,* and in detail in "Dauer."

occur till some ten years after Gamaliel's speech,[21] and compounds the error by implicitly dating the census and uprising of Judas the Galilean (A.D. 6–7) *after* Theudas. R. Syme[22] offers the following highly plausible explanation of Luke's confusion:

> Two striking events in Palestinian history would leave their marks in the minds of men. First, the end of Herod in 4 B.C., second the annexation of Judaea in A.D. 6. Either might serve for approximate dating in a society not given to exact documentation. Each event, so it happened, led to disturbances. More serious were those in 4 B.C., according to Josephus. Varus the legate of Syria had to intervene with the whole of his army. But the crisis of A.D. 6 was the more sharply remembered because Roman rule and taxation were imposed. Thus, in Acts 5:37, the speech of the Pharisee Gamaliel: "In the days of the census."

As I have shown in the commentary (§ 14, B1), even if Luke was inaccurate on this dating of the census of Quirinius and mistakenly thought that it could have been associated with the birth of Jesus, we must recognize that the association enabled Luke to explain why Joseph and Mary were in Bethlehem when the child was born. It also served admirably the interests of Lucan theology, giving the nativity a backdrop of world and Israelite history.

[21] According to Josephus (*Ant.* XX v 1; #97), the uprising of Theudas took place when Fadus was procurator of Judea (A.D. 44–46).
[22] "Titulus," 600.

BIBLIOGRAPHY FOR APPENDIX VII

(See also the Bibliography for § 14.)

Barnett, P. W., "*Apographē* and *apographesthai* in Luke 2:1–5," ExpTim 85 (1973–74), 377–80.

Braunert, H., "Der römische Provinzialzensus und der Schätzungsbericht des Lukas-Evangeliums," *Historia* 6 (1957), 192–214.

Derrett, J. D. M., "Further Light," 82–95.

Evans, C. F., "Tertullian's References to Sentius Saturninus and the Lukan Census," JTS 24 (1973), 24–39.

Higgins, A. J. B., "Sidelights on Christian Beginnings in the Greco-Roman World," *Evangelical Quarterly* 41 (1969), 197–206, esp. 198–201.

Lee, G. M., "The Census in Luke," CQR 167 (1966), 431–36.

Moehring, H. R., "The Census in Luke as an Apologetic Device," in *Studies in the New Testament and Early Christian Literature,* ed. D. E. Aune (In Honor of A. P. Wikgren; NovTestS 33; Leiden: Brill, 1972), 144–60.

Ogg, G., "The Quirinius Question Today," ExpTim 79 (1967–68), 231–36.

Ramsay, W. M., "Luke's Narrative of the Birth of Jesus," *The Expositor,* series 8, vol. 4 (Nov. 1912), 385–407, 481–507.

———— *Was Christ,* esp. 95–248.

Schürer, E., *History,* I, II, 105–43. In the rev. ed. by G. Vermes and F. Millar (Edinburgh: Clark, 1973), I, 399–427.

Sherwin-White, A. N., *Roman Society and Roman Law in the New Testament* (Oxford: Clarendon, 1963), 162–71.

Stauffer, E., "Die Dauer des Census Augusti—Neue Beiträge zum lukanischen Schatzungsbericht," in *Studien zum Neuen Testament und zur Patristik* (Festschrift E. Klostermann; TU 77; Berlin: Akademie, 1961), 9–34.

———— *Jesus,* 27–36.

Syme, R., "The Titulus Tiburtinus," in *Vestigia: Akten des VI Internationalen Kongresses für Griechische und Lateinische Epigraphik, 1972* (Beiträge zur Alten Geschichte, 17; Munich: Beck), 585–601.

APPENDIX VIII: MIDRASH AS A
LITERARY GENRE

The discussion and literature about Jewish midrash (plural: midrashim) is extensive, but this appendix is confined to the use of the term in relation to the infancy narratives of Matthew and Luke. Some authors use the term for one or both of these infancy narratives; others use it for the putative sources, e.g., a midrash on the birth of Moses as a source for Matthew. Especially in the former usage, it is not always clear whether the term is being applied as a title for a literary genre, or less formally as the designation of a technique or style—is the author saying that the infancy narrative itself is to be classified as a midrash, or only that there is midrashic style in the infancy narrative?[1] In Roman Catholic discussions, particularly on a popular level, "midrash" has been thought to be a scholarly word for fiction, so that the designation "midrash" would be tantamount to saying that the infancy narratives are fables and that the events related in them did not occur. I shall begin by explaining why there is such a variety in the usage and understanding of the term, and then seek to be precise about the way in which the term may or may not be applicable to the infancy narratives as discussed in this volume.

In Biblical Hebrew the verb *dāraš* means "to seek, inquire, investigate, study"; and according to the pattern of Hebrew noun formation, *midraš* should designate the product of such study or investigation. The noun first appears in the Bible in II Chr 13:22; 24:27 in references to a midrash of the Book of Kings and a midrash of the Prophet Iddo. However, since these works have not been preserved for us, scholars can only guess what the Chronicler meant by such a designation.[2] More helpful is Sirach 51:23 where the author invites those who need instruction to lodge in his "house of midrash," seemingly a place of learning—a usage anticipating the post-biblical *bêt-ham-midraš* or "school." The Dead Sea Scrolls help us to detect what the term might mean in Jesus' time. It appears in 1QS vi 23; viii

---

[1] The work of Wright, *Literary Genre*, is a most helpful attempt to clarify this situation in favor of a stricter use of "midrash" as a literary genre or classification. Those who criticize him, e.g., Le Déaut, "Apropos," favor a much broader use in reference to an interpretative technique. Since literary genre is for the most part an artificial classification, more precision makes it more useful for differentiation. Personally I find Le Déaut's application of the term so broad as to be of little help in classification.

[2] For these guesses see Wright, *Literary Genre*, 34–37.

15,26; and CD xx 6 in the sense of "investigation, study, interpretation," especially of the Law. Particularly interesting is the use of midrash in 4QFlor i 14 as a title for a passage interpreting Ps 1:1 through a number of biblical citations woven together in an interpretative way.[3]

With the latter instance "midrash" is on its way toward the usage best known to us, i.e., as a designation in post-Christian Judaism for works which gather the legal statements, stories, and homilies of the rabbis around the biblical text, especially the text of the Pentateuch (Torah). From the second century A.D. on there are preserved rabbinic midrashim wherein there is a line-by-line commentary on a book like Exodus or Numbers in the style: "Rabbi X said, '. . .'; and Rabbi Y said, '. . . .'" Halakic midrash (*hᵃlākâ*, "rule, law") was a term used to designate interpretation by way of legal statements, whereas non-legal interpretation was called haggadic (*haggādâ*, "story"). In discussing rabbinic midrashim, one should distinguish between midrash as a composition consisting of these collected interpretations of Scripture, and the midrashic process which produced the interpretations. (Many other rabbinic works not called midrashim exhibit instances of midrashic interpretation.) The connection between the Scripture being discussed and the collected interpretations which might throw light on the Scripture was often rather loose; and so eventually "midrash" came to designate a free, homiletic exposition, with "haggadic midrash" having the connotation of fables or folklore used to illustrate the Bible.

This varied history explains the diversity of the use of midrash in discussing the infancy narratives. However, by way of specification and limitation,[4] let us look at two definitions or descriptions of rabbinic midrash distilled from its chief characteristics. The first is that of Renée Bloch:[5]

> Rabbinic midrash is a homiletic reflection or meditation on the Bible which seeks to reinterpret or actualize a given text of the past for present circumstances.

[3] The term pesher (*pešer*) also appears in this passage; and it would seem that midrash is a wider term for interpretative comments upon the Scripture, with pesher as a more specific genre. Most of the examples of pesher at Qumran are line-by-line reinterpretations of biblical works as if they were prophecies referring to the life and times of the Qumran (Essene) community. See footnote 13, § 4.

[4] Methodologically Le Déaut, "Apropos," 281, objects to such limitation on the grounds that there must be a correspondence between our classification (literary genres) and the ways in which the writers intended to express themselves. However, B. Vawter, CBQ 22 (1960), 33, is surely correct when he insists that ancient writers were not aware of many of the precise modern classifications, even if the terms we have adopted are ancient. The lack of ancient writers' conscious advertence makes literary forms no less definable and applicable.

[5] Wright, *Literary Genre*, 19, has distilled this definition from the headings of Bloch's treatment in "Midrash," cols. 1265–66: It has its point of departure in the Scriptures; it is of a homiletic character; it is an attentive study of the text; there is an adaptation to the present.

More detailed is the formula offered by Wright:[6]

> Rabbinic midrash is a literature concerned with the Bible; it is a liter-
> ature about a literature. A midrash is a work that attempts to make a
> text of Scripture understandable, useful, and relevant for a later gen-
> eration. It is the text of Scripture which is the point of departure, and
> it is for the sake of the text that the midrash exists. The treatment of
> any given text may be creative or non-creative, but the literature as a
> whole is predominantly creative in its handling of biblical material.
> The interpretation is accomplished sometimes by rewriting the biblical
> material. . . .

Wright would be the first to admit that such a definition has a precision
that goes beyond the awareness of the ancient practitioners of midrash. He
is also aware that in applying this definition to the Bible, he is somewhat
anachronistic; for it is a definition derived from a later (rabbinic) body of
material. Nevertheless, there are examples in the Bible of what Bloch and
Wright have classified as midrash. One of the clearest is the homily in Wisdom 11–19 based on the account of the plagues in Exod 7–12.

Thus, it is not impossible that the term midrash might be applicable to
the infancy narratives. Let me make the following observations in light of
Wright's description of rabbinic midrash:

1) In subsequent Christianity midrashim in the strictest sense have been
composed upon the basis of the infancy narratives of Matthew and Luke.
Already in the second century the *Protevangelium of James* rewrote the
biblical material in a creative way. One of the midrashic tendencies was to
combine Luke and Matthew and add details not mentioned by either, e.g.,
magi and camels meet shepherds with oxen and a donkey before a cave.
Matthew does not mention camels; but that detail is an interpretation of
the gifts of the magi against the background of Isa 60:6, a text which, as
we saw (§ 6, B2), may have been in Matthew's mind. Luke does not mention oxen and a donkey; but that detail is an interpretation of the Lucan
stress on a manger against the background of Isa 1:3, a text, which, as we
saw (§ 14, B2), may have been in Luke's mind. In these details and in the
combining of the two narratives we have real attempts at imaginative interpretation in order to make the Scripture understandable for a later generation. Much more in the style of haggadic midrashim would be the stories identifying the magi and describing their subsequent careers (§ 6D),
and the stories of the holy family's flight into Egypt (NOTE on Matt
2:14).

2) In the pre-Gospel background of the infancy narratives there were
midrashim on OT Scripture. Matthew's story of the birth of Jesus seems to

have drawn its coloring from Jewish midrashim interpreting the birth of Moses in Exod 1–2. As I pointed out in § 4, B2, the existence of such a midrash is attested in the *Antiquities* of Josephus and in the *Life of Moses* by Philo, works contemporary with the NT. More speculative is the existence of a midrash about the birth of the Messiah at Bethlehem or Migdal Eder—a midrash on Micah 4–5 and Gen 35:19–21 which I suspect underlies both Matthew and Luke (§ 14, C1). Other possible midrashic background has been mentioned in Appendix VI. But let it be clear: this is not the same as saying that either infancy narrative is a midrash on Exodus or on Micah or on other biblical passages. I am suggesting that Matthew and Luke drew not only from the Bible but also from midrashim that had interpreted biblical books with added detail.

3) Thus far in relation to the infancy narratives, I have commented upon post-Gospel and pre-Gospel midrashim. Now we must ask more precisely about the Gospel infancy narrative themselves. May they be classified as midrashim? If one follows Wright's definition, the infancy narratives would be midrashim if they were a literature about a literature, i.e., if they took as their basis texts of Scripture which they wished to make understandable. Some approaches to the infancy narratives would argue that this is exactly what the authors have done in whole or in part. One theory is that Matthew's narrative was created to illustrate the five fulfillment texts. However, I have argued in the opposite direction, i.e., that Matthew added the fulfillment citations to an already existing narrative (§ 4, A2). If Matthew did draw upon a midrash based on the birth of Moses, he did not compose the resultant story of Jesus' birth in order to make the story of Moses' birth more intelligible. In the Lucan infancy narrative, the canticles are centos of OT references, and some would identify anthological style with midrash.[7] However, the joining of OT citations to express the sentiments of infancy narrative speakers does not give us the same genre as commenting on the meaning of the OT passages.[8] Similarly, I have suggested that Luke painted the portrait of his characters (Zechariah, Elizabeth, Simeon, Anna) from OT models (Abraham, Sarah, the parents of Samuel, Eli), but he is scarcely seeking to make the OT characters more intelligible. Thus, I would have to judge that neither Matthew's in-

---

[7] A. Robert, "Littéraires (Genres)," DBSup V, col. 411, describes anthological style as one which "reuses, either literally or equivalently, the words or formulas of earlier Scriptures"; he calls attention to its frequency in the later parts of the OT. Wright, *Literary Genre*, 121–32, argues against Bloch and Robert who would equate this process and genre with midrash.

[8] As we saw, the Lucan canticles represent a standard way of writing hymns in the period just before Christ; for they have close parallels in the hymns of the Books of Maccabees and in the Qumran *Hodayoth*. When I discussed the question of the literary genre of the Magnificat and Benedictus, I turned to the well-accepted literary types or classifications of psalms, in particular to the classification "hymn of praise" (§ 12, D1).

fancy narrative nor Luke's meets Wright's criteria for midrash. The birth stories were composed, not to make the OT Scriptures more intelligible, but to make Jesus more intelligible. Part of his intelligibility is that he stands in continuity with and in fulfillment of the OT Scriptures.

4) Having stated that "midrash," taken in its strict sense, is *not* a term that describes well the literary genre of either infancy narrative, I should now emphasize that the style of exegesis exemplified in midrash *does* have a place in the composition of the infancy narrative. (It is for this reason that Le Déaut and others argue for the applicability of the term midrash to the infancy narratives and indeed to much of the NT use of the OT.) The subject of the interpretation is a person, so that both narratives develop the christological insight that Jesus was the Son of God from the first moment of his conception. The same kind of mind that would compose a midrash in order to make Scripture understandable composed birth stories to make that christological insight understandable. Sometimes the composition of a midrash upon the Scriptures involved adding what the author thought were historical details; sometimes it was an exercise of creative imagination. Similarly for the infancy narratives: they are a mélange of items of history or verisimilitude (§ 6, C1),[9] of images drawn from the OT or Jewish tradition, of images anticipated from the Gospel account of the ministry—all woven together to dramatize the conception and birth of the Messiah who was God's Son. This process of composition constitutes a theology in itself: even if the christological insight is new, it is best interpreted against the background of the births of the patriarchs, of Moses, and of Samuel, and against the background of the hopes of Isaiah, Micah, and Daniel. The presence of characters shaped on OT models shows a continuity between the old and the new. When it comes to finding a classification for the resultant mélange, perhaps we should settle for the literary genre of "infancy narratives of famous men," recognizing a common tendency to shape stories about the infancy and boyhood of those who have become famous, in order to show a unity in the pattern of the whole career (footnote 17, § 9). Infancy narratives of the Messiah would inevitably be colored by the expectations of the Messiah and by reflection on the Scripture texts which had come to embody those expectations. Such a broad classification would allow for the fact that, while the Matthean and Lucan birth stories have the same general christology and the same tendency to fill in lacunae through use of OT models, they are very different in style and stress.

[9] Often it is still possible to detect likely items of history, e.g., the information about the parents of JBap; other times it is not. This limitation must make us cautious in either direction. One may plausibly suspect that the story of the magi is largely an imaginative adaptation of the Balaam story, but one cannot dismiss the possibility of an underlying historical incident that we can no longer detect.

5) Implicitly this whole discussion has indicated that one may not classify the infancy narratives as belonging to the literary genre of factual history. However, even as my rejection of the classification "midrash" does not mean that I fail to recognize the presence of midrashic technique, so also my rejection of the classification "factual history" does not mean that I fail to recognize the probable presence of items of historical value.[10] Nevertheless, I stated very clearly in the very first section (§ 1B) that I did not think it possible to maintain intelligently that the two infancy narratives as they now stand are totally historical. Furthermore, I pointed out there and throughout the commentary that available evidence inclines against the historicity of large parts of them. Be this as it may, I do not think that the approach to the infancy narratives delineated in the preceding paragraph imperils either the fundamental message of the infancy narratives (that Jesus was God's Son from his conception) or the insight that God guided the composition of Scripture for the instruction of His people (the inspiration of the Scriptures). The acceptability of this approach involves a recognition that there are ways other than history by which a people can be instructed. I have little hope that those for whom history is the only biblical genre will be open to such an approach.[11] But when they dismiss this approach with the careless charge that we who hold it have "reduced" the infancy narratives to midrash, there is a double error. First, many of us would maintain that midrash is not a satisfactory designation for the literary genre of these stories; and second, midrash is not to be equated with fiction—which is the simplification (not to say, vilification) intended.

[10] Besides the caution in the preceding footnote, see Appendixes II, III, and IV where I have discussed the historicity of such major issues as Davidic descent, birth at Bethlehem, and virginal conception.

[11] Granted the fact that biblical criticism is new on the Roman Catholic scene and still highly suspect among Catholics of a more conservative outlook, it is fortunate that the official teaching of the Roman Catholic Church contains an emphasis on the presence in Scripture of many different literary genres besides that of history (Pope Pius XII, "Divino Afflante Spiritu," ##35–39, in *Rome and the Study of Scripture* [7th ed.; St. Meinrad: Grail, 1962], 97–99). Those Catholics who maintain that the factual historicity of the infancy narratives is affirmed by the Second Vatican Council's statement about the four Gospels "whose historical character the Church unhesitatingly asserts" (*Dei Verbum* 19) are wrong on two scores. First, everything in that statement applies only to the accounts of the *ministry* of Jesus for which there were apostolic witnesses; second, the "historical character" of the Gospels, the statement goes on to make clear, must be understood in a modified sense —modified by the manner of transmission and the intent of the evangelists which was not to write literal history (See above, § 1, footnote 4).

BIBLIOGRAPHY FOR APPENDIX VIII

(See also the Bibliographies for § 4 [part B] and Appendix VI.)

Bacher, W., *Die exegetische Terminologie der jüdischen Traditionsliteratur* (2 vols.; Leipzig: Hinrichs, 1899–1905).

Bloch, Renée, "Midrash," DBSup (Paris: Letouzey, 1957), V, cols. 1263–81.

Doeve, J. W., *Jewish Hermeneutics in the Synoptic Gospels and Acts* (Assen: Van Gorcum, 1954).

Ellis, E. E., "Midrash, Targum, and New Testament Quotations," in *Neotestamentica et Semitica*, ed. E. E. Ellis and M. Wilcox (In Honour of M. Black; Edinburgh: Clark, 1969), 61–69.

Gertner, M., "Midrashim."

———— "Terms of Scriptural Interpretation: A Study in Hebrew Semantics," *Bulletin of the School of Oriental and African Studies* 25 (1962), 1–27.

Lauterbach, J. Z., "Mishnah and Midrash," JQR 5 (1914–15), 503–27; 6 (1915–16), 23–95, 303–23.

Le Déaut, R., "Apropos a Definition of Midrash," *Interpretation* 25 (1971), 259–82.

Lehrman, S. M., *The World of the Midrash* (London: Yoseloff, 1962).

Miller, M. P., "Targum, Midrash, and the Use of the Old Testament in the New Testament," *Journal for the Study of Judaism* 2 (1971), 19–82.

Seeligmann, I. L., "Voraussetzungen der Midraschexegese," VetTestS 1 (1953), 150–81.

Vermes, G., *Scripture and Tradition in Judaism* (Leiden: Brill, 1961).

Wright, A., *The Literary Genre Midrash* (Staten Island: Alba, 1967).

APPENDIX IX: THE FOURTH ECLOGUE
OF VIRGIL

Although Virgil (70–19 B.C.) lived a century before the evangelists, this poem, composed in 40 B.C., mentions a Virgin (line 6) and a divinely descended Child (49) before whom all the earth will tremble in homage (50) in a golden age of peace (9,17) when the remaining "traces of guilt" will disappear (13,14). Small wonder that Christians saw in the Fourth Eclogue a pagan prediction of the virgin birth of Jesus the Messiah who took away original sin.[1] It was an interpretation that brought Virgil into the ranks of the prophets and won for the Cumaean Sibyl,[2] whom he quotes (4), honorable mention alongside David in the *Dies Irae*. However, Virgil does not suggest that the Child was conceived by the Virgin,[3] and the divine parentage of the Child is purely figurative. And so Jerome, who often provided a voice of common sense amidst patristic exaggeration, was perfectly correct when he dismissed this prophetic messianic interpretation of the Fourth Eclogue as the product of ignorance.[4]

Nevertheless, the Eclogue is worth our consideration for the light it may cast on two other points. First, it gives us the background into which educated Gentile hearers of the Matthean and Lucan infancy narratives may have fitted what they heard about the birth of Jesus. Second, the Eclogue has often been thought to reflect indirectly a knowledge of some of the themes of Isa 7–11 in the pagan world.

As we begin the first point, let us examine the context in which Virgil wrote his poem. In 40 B.C., through the mediating role of Asinius Pollio, Octavian (Augustus) and Mark Anthony, heirs of the great Julius Caesar assassinated in 44, made the Peace of Brundisium, seemingly bringing to an end a hundred years of savage civil war that had wracked Italy. It is to this century of disaster that Virgil refers when he speaks of "the race of

[1] The earliest attestation of the Christian messianic interpretation of the Fourth Eclogue seems to be in Lactantius' *Divinae Institutiones* VII 24; PL 6:810, written *ca.* 313. The interpretation was popularized in Constantine's *Oratio ad sanctorum coetum* 19–21; PL 8:455ff.

[2] Latin writers knew at least ten Sibyls, but the Sibyl of Cumae was the most famous. In particular, it would have been well known to Virgil, since Cumae was in Campania near Naples where Virgil spent much of his career.

[3] The Virgin of line 6 is Lady Justice (Dikē), daughter of Jupiter and Themis, who was driven from earth by the wickedness of men during the long wars. Her return signals the end of war.

[4] Jerome *Epistola* LIII 7; PL 22:544–45.

iron" (8) and the traces of "guilt" and of "sin" (13,31). His relief at its end may have been more than patriotic; for ancestral estates had been confiscated to pay off the victorious soldiers of the battle of Philippi (42 B.C.) in which Octavian and Anthony defeated Brutus, and Virgil's estate had been restored to him only by the clemency of Octavian through the intercession of Asinius Pollio. For Virgil all this seemed to indicate that the long expected golden age was at hand.[5] In Etruscan calculation there was a cycle of ten periods of history, with the first and tenth to be ruled by Saturn; and the reign of Saturn was returning (6).[6]

Virgil chooses to express his enthusiastic hopes for the future in the symbolism of the birth of a Child whose life will be concomitant with the coming of peace into the world. To be precise, it is not the Child who brings peace into the world, but he rules in a pacified world. This peace will not only mark the end of war and of economic need which produces commercial competition (31–33, 37–39), but also will restore the harmony of nature (28–30, 39–45), a harmony symbolized by the fruitfulness of field and flock, as befits a "bucolic" poem. The idea of someone sent by the gods to do this is common to many cultures, but Virgil may have been moved to use the symbolism of the Child by a birth related to the period of composition,[7] i.e., 40 B.C. and the consulship of Pollio. Many have thought that the Child might be Asinius Gallus, the son of Pollio. The objection to this is that the Child is pictured as a world ruler (17). It is true that Asinius Gallus would become a candidate for the principate after the reign of Octavian Augustus, but Virgil can scarcely have foreseen an event of fifty years later. Rather he is talking about a Child who has a foreseeable chance of coming soon to "rule over a world made peaceful by the virtues of his father" (17). The most likely candidate is a child of Mark Anthony or a child of Octavian, and perhaps Virgil is imprecise because he does not want to take sides. Anthony was marrying Octavia, the sister of Octavian; and Octavian himself had married Scribonia who was pregnant in 40 B.C.[8] The child of either marriage might

---

[5] For speculation on the "golden age," see Benko, "Thoughts," 137–38. Williams, "Version," 33, relates the ideal presentation of this age to the prophecy of the Cumaean Sibyl. Horace wrote his Epode XVI in the spring of 40, also influenced, but in a more negative way, by Philippi and the victory of Octavian and Anthony. There is a literary relationship between Virgil's Fourth Eclogue and Horace's Epode, with Virgil perhaps influenced by Horace.

[6] The departure of the virginal Lady Justice because of war marked the end of the first period of Saturn, and her return introduces the new reign of Saturn (6). The next-to-the-last of the ten Etruscan periods of time was thought to be ruled by Apollo (10).

[7] Williams, "Version," 39–40, stresses the novelty of the connection that Virgil makes between the Child's birth and the beginning of the golden age, and suggests that Virgil got the inspiration for focusing on the Child from the writings of Theocritus, who was also the inspiration for the pastoral theme of the Eclogues or Bucolics.

[8] Their child turned out to be Julia born in 39. Other have thought of M. Marcellus, the child of Octavia whom Octavian would eventually adopt.

accomplish Virgil's hopes, and personify the new spirit of peace come into the world.[9]

This background should enable us to see how well those who shared Virgil's aspirations would receive the accounts of the birth of Jesus. We saw in the commentary (NOTES on Matt 2:1–2) that Matthew's account of magi from the East bringing gifts and paying homage to a new king had analogies in first-century Roman history, as Oriental potentates brought regal gifts to Jerusalem and Rome. We saw that Luke's dating Jesus' birth in the context of an empire-wide census conducted by Augustus, the great peacemaker, would evoke a comparison between the two figures (§ 14, B1). How much more would readers familiar with the Fourth Eclogue see in the child placed in the manger and honored by shepherds a parallel to the dreamed-of Child whose cradle would be a cornucopia of flowers (23) and whose advent would free the flocks from fear (22)! The Jesus whose birth was hailed as that of a Savior and Lord (Luke 2:11) would evoke for the Jew the dreams of Isa 11 (§ 14, C2), but would be no less meaningful for the educated Gentile.

This last observation brings us to the second point in our discussion of the Fourth Eclogue. Is there a chance that indirectly Virgil's imagery has been influenced by the imagery in Isa 7–11, or at least by Jewish thought? Resemblances have been found between Isaiah's and Virgil's descriptions of a child to be born. In line 27 Virgil dates prosperity from the time that the Child can know in what valor consists, while Isa 7:16 dates victory from the time just before the child knows to refuse evil and choose good. In line 60 Virgil speaks of the Baby recognizing its mother, while Isa 8:4 speaks of the child having the knowledge to cry "My father" or "My mother." Further resemblances have been detected in the images used to describe the peace that will reign in nature.[10] In line 22 Virgil says, "The herds will not be afraid of the mighty lions," while Isa 11:6 says, "The leopard will lie down with the young goat; and the calf and the young lion and the fatling together; and a little child will lead them." Virgil (24) imagines that the serpent will perish,[11] while Isa 11:8 has the suckling child play over the hole of the asp. Virgil (30) has oaks yielding honey,

---

[9] The reference to the Child as a descendant of the gods in 49 is no obstacle to this identification, for Virgil could apply such language to earthly rulers. In the *Aeneid*, VI 792–94, Virgil addresses Octavian, "Hail to you, Augustus Caesar, son of a god, who will once more establish the golden age amid the fields where Saturn once reigned." The fact that later Virgil could shift his poetic hopes from the Child to Octavian himself indicates the symbolic nature of the Child.

[10] That care must be shown in evaluating such resemblances is underlined by the fact that many of these same images appear in Horace's Epode XVI as well (footnote 5 above), e.g., references to flocks that will go unharmed (61), to the lessening in number of poisonous serpents (52), and to the abundance of honey (47).

[11] Williams, "Version," 37: "No writer before Virgil says that snakes did not exist in the Golden Age" at the beginning. Virgil thinks that only later did the gods put poison into serpents (*Georgics* I 129).

while Isa 7:22 has everyone who is left in the land eating butter and honey. Moreover, the general pattern of the Eclogue has a mixture of bad with good while the Child is growing up (31–36),[12] even as the aftermath of the child's birth in Isa 7:14 is a mixed one.

The resemblances are, at most, indirect; but the possibility that Near Eastern imagery has influenced Virgil is enhanced when we note that much of the flora mentioned belongs to that region: the *baccar* or rustic nard of 19, the *colocasia* or Egyptian bean-lily of 20, and the *Assyrium amomum* or aromatic Assyrian shrub of 25. The image of lions threatening sheep in 22 is more at home in the Near East than in Italy. It has been suggested that the sequence of the happy coming of the Child (18–30), the revival of war with other nations (31–36), and final triumph (37–45) is parallel to the sequence in Jewish apocalyptic: the coming of the Messiah, the eschatological war, and the reign of peace.[18]

If there is any truth in these suggestions, how could such Jewish ideas have reached Virgil? Many have found the key in Virgil's appeal to the Cumaean Sibyl (4).[14] The Sibylline Oracles which had been kept in the temple of Jupiter Capitolinus in Rome were destroyed by fire in 83–82 B.C. The ensuing search for Sibylline Oracles to replace the originals drew upon private collections from a wide area (Erythrae in Greece, Sicily, Africa, Troy, Samos, etc.) and brought in prophecies of a Semitic origin. So far as we know there was no collection at Cumae, and Virgil would scarcely have had access to the collection in Rome which were read by the Quindecemviri and promulgated with the consent of the Senate. But undoubtedly a knowledge of the type of oracles which had been gathered was widespread, and the Capitoline collection was only a selection. We know of no Sibylline oracle that would give us an exact antecedent for Virgil's Eclogue, but only a fraction of the oracles have been preserved. Many scholars have turned attention to the Jewish oracles in Book III dating from the second century B.C. Lines 367ff. speak of an era of peace that will come to Europe and Asia, and line 372 (a dubious text) speaks of the blessedness of him whose life is lived in pastoral or bucolic circumstances. Lines 652ff. speak of God's sending a king who will give every land relief from the bane of war; but then follows the same sequence mentioned above: renewed war before the final victory. It is in the final victory that luscious honey comes from heaven, that trees bear abundant fruit and flocks are rich, that fountains of milk burst forth and fields are abundant, as the earth is no longer convulsed by the din of battle (746–752). Lines

---

12 Williams, *ibid.*, 40, maintains that the presence of difficulties slowing down the full development of the golden age is novel with Virgil.

18 Erdmann, *Vorgeschichten*, 85.

14 See footnote 2 above. Another proposed (but unverifiable) channel of Jewish influence on Virgil was through his patron Pollio who seemingly had Jewish connections (Josephus *Ant.* XV i 1;※※1–4).

788–795 are clearly influenced by the passages of Isaiah discussed above: the lambs and goats are not bothered by wild animals; lions eat hay like oxen; serpents and asps sleep with babes and do not harm them. The resemblances to Virgil's Fourth Eclogue are just as indirect as are the proposed resembances of Isaiah to the Eclogue; but they keep open the possibility that the Sibylline Oracles were a route through which Israelite prophetic expectations reached the Gentile world[15]—ideas that would have made the message of the infancy narratives readily acceptable.

[15] Later the Sibylline Oracles became the vehicle of Christian theology, e.g., Mary's virginity *in partu* (Appendix IV, footnote 2) in Book I, line 323; and Mary's perpetual virginity in Book VIII, 240–65. See the discussion by J. B. Bauer, "Die Messiasmutter in den Oracula Sibyllina," *Marianum* 18 (1956), 118–24.

BIBLIOGRAPHY FOR APPENDIX IX

Alföldi, A., "Der neue Weltherrscher der vierten Ekloge Vergils," *Hermes* 65 (1930), 369–84.

Benko, S., "Some Thoughts on the Fourth Eclogue," *Perspectives in Religious Studies* 2 (1975), 125–45.

Boll, F., "Die Vierte Ekloge des Virgil," in *Kleine Schriften zur Sternkunde des Altertums,* ed. V. Stegemann (Leipzig: Koehler, 1950), 332–56.

Büchner, K., *P. Vergilius Maro: der Dichter der Römer* (Stuttgart: Druckenmüller, 1956), esp. 175–93.

Erdmann, G., *Vorgeschichten,* 70–140.

Heidel, W. A., "Virgil's Messianic Expectations," *American Journal of Philology* 45 (1924), 205–37.

Jachmann, G., "Das Vierte Ekloge Vergils," *Annali della Scuola Normale Superiore di Pisa* 21 (1952), 13–62.

Lagrange, M.-J., "Le prétendu messianisme de Virgile," RB 31 (1922), 552–72.

Mayor, J. B., *et al., Virgil's Messianic Eclogue* (London: Murray, 1907).

Norden, E., *Die Geburt des Kindes* (Leipzig: Teubner, 1931).

Williams, G., "A Version of Pastoral: Virgil, *Eclogue* 4," in *Quality and Pleasure in Latin Poetry,* ed. T. Woodman and D. West (Cambridge University, 1974), 31–46, 139–46.

TRANSLATION OF THE FOURTH ECLOGUE[a]

[1] O Muses of Sicily, let me sing on a somewhat loftier note. [2] The theme of orchards and lowly tamarisk shrubs does not please everyone. [3] If we sing of woodlands, let them be worthy of a consul.[b]

[4] Now there has come the last age of which the Cumaean Sibyl sang; [5] a great orderly line of centuries begins anew; [6] now too the Virgin returns; the reign of Saturn[c] returns; [7] a new human generation descends from the high heavens. [8] Upon *the Child* now to be born, under whom the race of iron [9] will cease and a golden race will spring up over the whole world, [10] do you, O chaste Lucina,[d] smile favorably, for your own Apollo is now king.

[11] This glorious age will begin in your consulship, [12] O Pollio, as the mighty months[e] commence their course. [13] Under your leadership whatever traces of our guilt remain[f] [14] will disappear, freeing the earth from its perpetual fear. [15] He [the Child] will receive divine life and will see [16] heroes mingling with gods, and will himself be seen by them. [17] And he will rule over a world made peaceful by the virtues of his father.

[The Future Springtime of the Child's Infancy] [18] But first for you, O Child, without cultivation the earth will give as her little gifts [19] vines of ivy everywhere climbing wild and intermingling with rustic nard, [20] and the Egyptian bean-lily mixed together with the smiling acanthus. [21] Without being called, the goats will come home, their udders swollen with milk; [22] and the herds will not be afraid of the mighty lions. [23] For your pleasure your cradle will produce a cornucopia of flowers. [24] The serpent will perish, as will the deceptive poison herb, [25] while the aromatic Assyrian shrub will spring up in every field.

[The Future Summer of the Child's Education] [26] As soon as you can read about the praises heaped on heroes and the accomplishments of your parent, [27] and can know what valor consists in, [28] the plain will slowly become golden with waving grain, [29] and the ripening grape will hang from the wild briers, [30] and the stern oaks will yield dewy drops of honey. [31] However, some traces of the sin of old will perdure, [32] causing men to attempt the sea in ships, to build walls around [33] cities, and to plow the earth with furrows. [34] There will then be a second Argo with a second Tiphys to pilot it, [35] carrying chosen heroes; there will be a second series of wars, [36] and once more a great Achilles will be sent to Troy.[g]

[The Future Manhood of the Child] [87] Next, when the years have made you a strong man, [88] even the merchant will leave the sea, and the ship built with pine [39] will cease its merchant journeys.[h] Every land will be fruitful; [40] yet the earth will not feel the rake, nor the vine feel the pruning hook. [41] Indeed, the sturdy plowman will set his oxen loose from the yoke. [42] No longer will one learn to dye wool various colors; [43] for by himself the ram in the meadows will change his fleece, [44] at times a sweetly blushing shade of purple, at times saffron yellow; [45] and spontaneously the grazing lambs will be clothed in vermillion.

[46] The Fates cried to the spinning wheels of destiny: "Let such times come soon," [47] voicing in unison the fixed divine will.

[The Triumph of the Child] [48] Enter into your high honors—the time is virtually at hand— [49] O dear Descendant of the gods, O mighty Ally of Jove! [50] Behold the world trembles in homage with its massive dome: [51] the expanse of earth and sea, and the reaches of the sky! [52] Behold how all things rejoice at this age to come! [53] Now I wish that in a long enough life the last part [54] and sufficient inspiration allow me to tell of your deeds. [55] Then will I not be outdone in song either by Thracian Orpheus, [56] even if his mother Calliope assists him, [57] nor by Linus, even if fair Apollo, his father, helps him. [58] Indeed were Pan himself to vie with me in the presence of a judge from his native Arcadia, [59] he would judge himself defeated.

[60] Come forth, O Baby Boy, and recognize your mother with a smile,[i] [61] whom ten long months have brought to the weariness of labor. [62] Come forth, O Baby Boy, on whom parents have not yet smiled, [63] whom no god has honored at his table, and no goddess in her bed.

a. The first three lines constitute a transition from the bucolic theme of the preceding Eclogues, which was inspired by the Greek pastoral poet of Sicily, Theocritus. Lines are numbered in the translation, the overall pattern being three lines at the beginning and four at the end (a total of seven), and fifty-six lines in between, sometimes in patterns of sevens.

b. The reference is to Asinius Pollio (see line 12) who was consul in 40 B.C.

c. The subsequent lines will refer to the theory of ages designated by four metals, in the sequence gold, silver, bronze, iron. The warlike iron age is nearly over, and the first age of gold is returning. Virgil associates this golden age with Saturn; for others it was the age of Kronos.

d. Lucina is the goddess of childbirth; she is often identified as Diana or Artemis, the sister of Apollo mentioned in the next line. Apollo will be king because the prophecy he uttered through the Sibyl will be fulfilled.

e. The months are the ten months of the pregnancy that will give birth to the Child (line 61).

f. The "traces of guilt" and the "traces of the sin of old" in 31 are the remaining effects of the Roman civil wars.

g. Lines 31–36 admit that there will be an intervening period in which war will still occur, but now this will be a foreign war, such as that of Achilles against Troy, and no longer a war of Roman against Roman.

h. Since the earth in every country will be fruitful, there will be no need to buy products from other countries.

i. It is not clear whether the Child is to smile on the mother, or vice versa.

SUPPLEMENT
TO
THE BIRTH
OF THE MESSIAH

Updating the Work from 1976 through 1992
by Dialogue with the Literature Written in That Period

I have explained the goal of this Supplement in the second Foreword (for the new updated edition) at the beginning of the volume. Readers of *The Birth of the Messiah* (henceforth BBM) should find it easy to use: When they have finished reading a section (§) in BBM, they need simply turn to the same section number in the Supplement for recent studies on the same topic and my comments on them. In order that those who choose to read the Supplement as a unit may see how the thought expressed here is related to what I said earlier, there will be references back to the pertinent pages of BBM (using a page number and "above" to designate that work, without "p." or "pp." unless there would be an ambiguity). Abbreviations used in the Supplement are contained in the list of abbreviations at the front of this book; Matt, Mark, Luke, and John are used for both the Gospels that bear those names and the (unknown) evangelists who produced them. A long bibliography will conclude the Supplement, consisting of the books and articles written on the infancy narratives between 1976 and 1992—the material with which I enter into dialogue in these pages.

GENERAL INTRODUCTION

§1 Recent Scholarship and the Infancy Narratives in General

The topic of this section of BBM was the general character and historicity of the two infancy narratives. Inevitably reviews of my book since 1976 have led to reflection on these issues; and so it seems appropriate to devote a few pages at the beginning of this Supplement to a discussion of the reviews.[1] I shall start with the issue of historicity and then turn to the character or nature of the infancy narratives.

---

[1] Gleanings from contributive reviews will be incorporated under specific topics below. (As examples of solid reviews, one more conservative, one more liberal, see in the bibliography Marshall and Dunn. The review by McHugh and my response may also be of interest.) In limited space it seems best to ignore positive reactions that have repeated or summarized my views.

A. The Issue of Historicity. The infancy narratives describe some events that are miraculous. Predictably very liberal evaluators of BBM reacted by being bemused or even annoyed that I refused to decide in principle that the supernatural cannot have occurred and chose to evaluate equally on exegetical grounds the probability of both the natural and the miraculous elements. I shall discuss this type of liberal reaction below under Appendix IV, which discusses the virginal conception. Negative responses came also from the other end of the spectrum, namely, from very conservative reviewers who were disturbed that I did not simply accept both narratives as factual. Let me comment on that here.

It would not be fruitful to discuss at length such reactions when they are based on reviewers' assumptions that I regard as false or as misunderstandings of BBM.[2] Yet to clear the air, since such assumptions and misunderstandings are perennial, let me at least list the following affirmations made by reactors to BBM with the firm indication that *I reject them as erroneous:* (a) Because the Bible is the inspired word of God and/or Christianity is a historical religion, the infancy narratives must be historical (see 34 above) and indeed they must be able to be harmonized. (b) A lack of certainty about their historicity reflects rationalism, a denial of the miraculous, and/or adherence to the skepticism of Strauss, Harnack, or Bultmann.[3] (c) BBM stated that in general the infancy events are not historical or are "purely symbolic" or are simply theologoumena (understood by the objector as the fictional dramatization of theological concepts).[4] (d) BBM proposed that Matt's account of the virginal conception was created to respond to Jewish calumny sparked by the birth of Jesus too soon after Joseph and Mary came to live together.[5] (e) From the Roman Catholic viewpoint, the church has officially taught that the infancy narratives are historical.[6] (f) BBM's

[2] I have not bothered to include in the bibliography many reviews that exemplify this, e.g., E. Black, HPR 81 (#3, 1980–81), 13–23; (#4), 24–32; R. T. France, *The Churchman* 1 (#2, 1978); L. Johnston, *Heythrop Journal* 19 (1978), 439–41; R. Laurentin, *Marianum* 41 (1979), 76–100; M. Miguens, *Communio* (Eng.) 7 (1980), 24–25; W. G. Most, HPR 79 (#7, 1978–79), 77–79; S. Muñoz Iglesias, EB 36 (1977), 132–34; F. Spadafora, *Lateranum* 48 (1982), 138–54.

[3] See 25–26, 188 above for my own disavowal of such rationalism. Generalizing, Young ("Unspoken") attributes all doubts of modern scholars about infancy-narrative historicity to their rejection of the supernatural.

[4] For cautious warnings against a carelessly negative attitude on historicity, see above: p. 25; p. 37, n. 26; p. 188; p. 189, n. 28; p. 308, n. 36; p. 347; p. 527, n. 26; p. 529, n. 29; p. 561, n. 9.

[5] Stramare ("Annunciazione" 209) gives this false impression by quoting part of my sentence that runs from the bottom of 28 to the top of 29 above (Italian translation, p. 23) but omitting the "if" clause that is an essential modifier. He also ignores the conclusion reached on 542 above (Italian 738) that we have no way of knowing that the Jewish charge was in circulation when Matt wrote and therefore that it did not derive from Matt rather than vice versa. Ironically, that conclusion allows for Stramare's own view of Jewish dependence on Matt.

[6] J. Redford (*Clergy Review* 64 [1979], 5–11) maintained that the Vatican II document *Dei Verbum* (1965) affirmed the historicity of the infancy narratives. (See also the views of

observations imply that for Roman Catholics the historicity of the virginal conception is an "open question."[7]

Sometimes, especially within Catholic circles, a tone of polemics has marked the debate opened up by BBM. Indeed, despite the fact that in BBM I appreciated the earlier work of R. Laurentin on Luke 1–2 (1957), I gave the title "More Polemical than Instructive" to my evaluation of his later work *Évangiles*, which manifested hostility toward historical criticism, at times misrepresenting Fitzmyer's views and mine and lapsing into journalistic excess.[8] His defensive advocacy of historicity has reached even minor details, for example: The shepherds actually heard the angels sing the Gloria on Christmas eve (p. 461). Grelot ("Cantique" 482–88) points out several logical fallacies in Laurentin's claim (451) that if the Nunc Dimittis has been conserved and transmitted, as Luke 1:1–4 invites us to think, and Mary was present at the scene, it is to her memory one owes the transmission of the canticle, unless one refuses historicity *a priori*. Laurentin admits that Mary's memories were probably transmitted through the Jerusalem Christian community (544). Well, then, how does one draw a line between redaction by the community and creative activity, especially when the source was oral? And how much of the final product was due to Luke? Did he simply translate this supposed source into Greek or rewrite it? (Grelot thinks Luke himself composed the canticle in Greek.) Claims of historicity have to take into account all such variables. Like Laurentin, but with less polemics and more serious scholarship, Muñoz Iglesias, who earlier did important work directing Catholic attention to OT midrashic elements in Matt's account, has now become highly protective of historicity.[9]

Calkins in n. 89 below.) That is erroneous on two grounds: First, the pertinent section of *Dei Verbum* specifically cites the 1964 Pontifical Biblical Commission (PBC) statement on "The Historical Truth of the Gospels," which affirms that even in recounting the public ministry of Jesus, because of the development of tradition, the Gospels are not necessarily literal accounts. A process of adaptation, expansion, selection, and reordering has gone on in the years that separate Jesus from the Gospel writers. Second, neither of those documents deals with Jesus' infancy. The PBC statement treats only the period "when Christ our Lord joined to himself disciples who followed him from the beginning, saw his deeds and heard his words." When I was appointed to the PBC (1972), a former consulter gave me documentation on the aborted attempt *after Vatican II* to have the Commission prepare a statement on the historicity of the birth narratives—an unintelligible effort if the matter was already settled. See the response to Redford by F. J. Moloney, *Clergy Review* 64 (1979), 161–66.

[7] I stated the exact opposite in VCBRJ 25, n. 28.

[8] E.g. (p. 439): "Ce sont les excréments de la recherche historique." Laurentin's book repeats and elaborates a spate of earlier articles that I have not listed in the bibliography. His polemics fed ultraconservative organs in the USA (e.g., *National Catholic Register*, March 22 and 29, 1981), where they were used to "disprove" my pernicious errors. The tone of the assault caused consternation abroad: D. O'Donovan (*The Wedding Feast* [Melbourne: Spectrum, 1985], 81–104) attempted to save me from Laurentin's "berating," "subjectivity," and "resentment." I should note that not all mariologists found BBM a threat; see the review by E. R. Carroll, *Sunday Visitor*, Dec. 25, 1977.

[9] E.g., MIE 4.345–47 gives a long table showing how the two infancy narratives can be harmonizingly interwoven as evidence for the theory that both evangelists made selections

By assigning issues of historicity largely to appendixes, BBM was able to focus on the evangelists' rich christology, abundant use of the OT, and grasp of the infancy story as true Gospel. In my judgment an obsession with "proving" historicity is regressive, forcing prolonged discussion of areas in which the evangelists show no primary interest. The problem boils down to one's basic presupposition. I presuppose only that the two evangelists, in presenting the story of Jesus' conception, wished to teach Christians about his identity and role. I make no prejudgment about the type of literature in which they have chosen to do this. If the Bible is a library containing many different types of literature,[10] one may not presuppose that the infancy narratives are histories as some do.[11] The person who asserts historicity has as much to prove as the person who opts for a nonhistorical classification, and both must be aware that there is a wide range of classification between history and fiction.

Because of disagreements between the two infancy narratives, because of the lack of confirmation of their material anywhere else in the NT, because of the failure of highly public events in the narratives to be confirmed extrabiblically,[12] because of seeming inaccuracies (census affecting Galileans under Quirinius in Herod's time), and because of total uncertainty about the evangelists' sources for what is narrated, I made a careful judgment (36 above), denying that both accounts can be "completely historical," and thinking it unlikely that either account is

---

from a much longer body of infancy material. MIE 4.374–75 lists what is plausibly historical in Matt 1–2, amounting to seventy-five percent of the storyline. For instance, the magi were possibly migrant merchants of aromatic perfumes who were knowledgeable about an astral horoscope that could be interpreted as announcing the birth of the king of Israel. My disappointment in such speculations (and in the tone of Muñoz Iglesias's argumentation that sometimes oversimplifies positions and treats them as ridiculous) does not lessen my appreciation for the immense coverage of literature in MIE, which may be the longest work ever done on the infancy narratives and from which one can learn much.

[10] Pope Paul VI stated this in his address at the Vatican Library International Book Year Exhibit (March 25, 1972); see J. J. Megivern, *Official Catholic Teachings: Bible Interpretation* (Wilmington, NC: Consortium, 1978), 1037.

[11] France, a Protestant, in a series of articles on the Matthean infancy narrative (which otherwise make some good points) argues that history is to be assumed unless the contrary can be proved. Segalla ("A Proposito"), a Catholic favorable to Laurentin, finds my method too destructive and marked by "pregiudizio critico" (p. 120). How can Segalla (123) simply affirm that the traditions underlying Matt came substantially from a historical record? Is there not prejudice ("non critico," however) in that assumption? Among the Italian reactions to BBM, De Rosa, "Storia," is refreshingly clear in stating that while the theological thrust (= christology centered on Jesus as the Son of God) is discernible, historicity depends on the literary genre of these artistic and quasi-midrashic accounts, which may not be the same for Matt and for Luke. Encouraging also in emphasizing a theological thrust are two reflective essays in German. Kremer ("Erfassen"), always a balanced exegete, rejects a purely mythological approach in favor of recognizing the image value (*Bildsprache*), so that the infancy accounts can be taken seriously without, however, transforming them into factual reports designed to answer our historical interest. Fiedler ("Geschichten") enters into discussion of recent writing, including BBM, because he thinks of the opening chapters of Matt and Luke as primarily theology and proclamation.

[12] E.g., star over Bethlehem, all Jerusalem disturbed, slaughter at Bethlehem.

"completely historical." That left open the possibility that either or both are partially historical, and elsewhere I pointed to the importance of issues where these two independent infancy accounts agreed. In particular, I warned above (189, n. 28) that sweeping statements of nonhistoricity ("There were no magi") are quite unprovable. The historicity of the infancy narratives should be tested on the same grounds that serve for establishing the historicity of secular events.[13] (That insistence does not exclude the supernatural; comparably on the modern scene churches that accept supernatural occurrences and miracles do not hesitate to subject claims about such happenings to the usual tests of credibility.) Nor will it do to show that the events described in the infancy narratives are possible and the stories have verisimilitude—most historical fiction meets those criteria. Claims to certitude about historicity gained from unspecified tradition, from the experiences of later mystics, or from general piety are employing those tools to solve issues for which they have no relevance. If some find me too "rigorous" (or less kindly, skeptical and rationalist) when I admit that I do not know whether or not some events are historical, they should be more rigorous in proving what they claim to know. But enough of what I regard as unpersuasive historicizing; let me now turn to more fruitful discussion raised by the book.

B. The Character of the Infancy Narratives. In a substantive review, pressing a theory of comparative midrash that he has applied to other biblical literature, Sanders suggests that I feared to class the infancy narratives as midrash lest I bias the reader against historicity. That was not my reason; and paradoxically Laurentin, as well as many Spanish commentators on the infancy narratives (Muñoz Iglesias, Olivera), who are most insistent on the midrashic or "derashic" approach, always insist that they are supposing historicity.[14] If anything, I find the issue of midrash more confused than it was when I wrote Appendix VIII in BBM. Perhaps one will never get an agreement on terminology, but the following points may help. (a) If as a guide for identifying midrash one uses the earliest extant Jewish works known as the midrashim from the 2nd century A.D., namely, detailed, even if free, commentaries on OT texts verse by verse, then neither Gospel infancy narrative is a midrash. (Indeed, it is striking that in the NT there are no commentaries on the

---

[13] In the interpretation of Scripture Roman Catholics posit a positive role for church teaching when matters clearly affecting faith are involved (see below under Appendix IV in reference to the virginal conception), but that category would scarcely include the historicity of the magi, star, census, etc.

[14] Laurentin (*Évangiles* 57) contends that any definition of midrash as fiction is degrading and comes from rationalist exegesis. Díez Macho gives to a book (*Historicidad*) that deals in part with his midrashic approach a Spanish title meaning "The Historicity of the Infancy Narratives."

books of the Jewish Scriptures comparable to the Qumran pesharim and the rabbinic midrashim.) However, Laurentin (*Évangiles* 57) is aggressively opposed to using rabbinic midrashim as a norm for midrash: "People have falsely and abusively defined midrash in terms of late decadent forms." He and others do not regard midrash as a particular literary genre but as a manner of investigation.[15] (b) On 561 above I affirmed that there is midrashic technique in the narratives, and there is no real difference between Sanders and me on the fact that the OT has influenced the infancy narratives. Therefore if one chooses to define midrash as the use of midrashic techniques, some of the differences about classification of the Gospel infancy narratives may be purely terminological. (c) Sanders describes midrashic purpose as calling on Scripture to interpret contemporary life. That would seem to make the Scriptures the key to interpreting the present. In my conception that is not what the evangelists were doing. The focal point of the evangelists' attempt at self-understanding was Jesus, not the Scriptures; they wrote "commentaries" on Jesus from whom they interpreted all else. Laurentin (*Évangiles* 58), citing Perrot, recognizes this and says the coming of Christ has revolutionized or inverted midrash. Then, however, I would ask a question: If the process of the infancy narratives is the inverse of what the midrashic process normally was, and if the narratives are not like the Jewish Scripture commentaries that are known as midrashim, what do we gain by calling the infancy narratives midrash? (d) One must make a clear distinction as to whether we are referring to a description of what happened in the production of the infancy narratives or to a modern imitation of a process that flourished in the 1st century. A. Díez Macho first proposed that "Midrash" be used for the writings and "midrash" for the method, but then began to use the name "derash" for the interpretive method (*Sefarad* 35 [1975], 37–89). The latter term is largely employed by those writing in Spanish, and frequently invokes rabbinic hermeneutical rules.[16] By historical criticism we can detect midrashic procedures used by NT authors, but many of those who claim to be giving modern derashic interpretations are doing so in distinction from or even in opposition to historical criticism.[17] (e) The proportion in

[15] See Nolan, *Royal* 55; and the literature cited on 120–21 above.

[16] In reading different references to derash, I am not sure that all its proponents understand the process in the same way. To illustrate, according to Testa's summary ("XXXI" 133–34), Ortensio da Spinetoli's 1990 paper on recent infancy-narrative research states that it is commonly admitted that Matt used midrashic techniques, and then goes on to define midrash thus: a rereading of the present history in the light of the past. (The interest is not on history but on interpretation; it is creative and prophetic exegesis.) Yet the very next paper in the summary, Sofia Cavalletti's on midrashic readings of the infancy narratives, suggests that "midrash" be kept for specific writings, while "derash" be used for the manner of interpreting Scripture—one that is difficult to define, of which there are different definitions, and which escapes rigorous systematization.

[17] Olivera ("Interpretación"), as his title indicates, offers a derashic interpretation of Matt 1:18–25; in n. 20 below I indicate my difficulties with his approach. Testa ("XXXI"

the infancy narratives between authentic tradition about Jesus and imaginative reflection on him in terms of OT symbolism is not easy to discern, and that is why there will remain a problem about historicity whether or not we accept the category "midrash" for the infancy narratives.

In the opposite direction C. H. Talbert presses for a greater role for the Greco-Roman milieu, not simply by way of background (e.g., 168, 174, 415, 564 above) but in terms of basic form. For him the Gospels are like Greco-Roman biographies dominated by the myth of the Immortals.[18] In reaction to this hypothesis let me make some distinctions that will also apply below when I discuss proposed Greco-Roman parallels to various details in the infancy narratives. Those in the 1st century familiar with Greco-Roman literature and/or stories about gods, demigods, and heroes probably interpreted what they heard or read about Jesus against that background; if they became believers and were properly catechized, they quickly found out that there were major differences. But that tells us nothing about what the evangelists thought they were writing. If one proposes that they were writing the equivalent of Greco-Roman biographies of gods or demigods or heroes, has one proof that they had read such literature? Luke evidences a knowledge of wider literature, but the other evangelists do not. The claim that everyone at the time would have been unconsciously influenced by such a genre is impossible to substantiate and hard to imagine. Leaving aside formal biographies, one can make a better case that even Jews would have known (sometimes derisively) popular stories about the gods, but would they have wanted to imitate them in describing the Son of the Lord God of Israel? Most lines in the infancy narratives have patent OT parallels; it is very difficult to show that the evangelists drew upon the proposed and far more distant Greco-Roman parallels. The two evangelists could have written their infancy narratives without ever having heard or read biographies and tales composed by pagan writers; the

---

142) regards the derashic method as absurd at least for scientific theology. He gets the impression that some of its advocates want to support a mariology that has no real biblical foundation.

18 Besides his review of BBM, see *What Is a Gospel?* (Philadelphia: Fortress, 1969); his article "Prophecies" applies his views to the Lucan infancy narrative. In Testa's summary ("XXXI" 134–35) L. Troiani's 1990 paper on Greco-Roman heroes and demigods points out certain features that might have caused pagans to receive and interpret Jesus by fitting him into the hero category. (By the end of the 2nd century Celsus shows that this comparison was in vogue, although personally he rejects it.) Those who reacted to Troiani's paper observed that while heroes might ascend into heaven, heroes did not rise from the dead. If one is attracted by the biography approach to the Gospels, the distinctions made by P. L. Shuler, *A Genre for the Gospels* (Philadelphia: Fortress, 1982), are helpful. There existed a type of Greco-Roman literature of which the primary concern was to show the greatness of figures, using certain patterns to achieve that purpose. Recognizing that laudatory biography is a loosely defined genre without uniformity he would apply it to Matt, which is nevertheless marked by its own kerygmatic dimension.

orientation of the Gospel narratives could have come from Hebrew or LXX forms of the biblical stories of the Patriarchs, Moses, and David (enlarged by subsequent oral lore), plus some Jesus tradition and theological reflection. It was precisely this Jewish background (whether Hebrew or Greek) that made me willing (561 above) to settle for describing Matt 1–2 and Luke 1–2 simply as belonging to the genre of "infancy narratives of famous men," i.e., stories of birth and youth shaped in retrospect after the subjects had become famous. Brenner ("Female") uses the designation "birth of the hero" and describes a paradigm that fits the births of Isaac, Jacob, Moses, and Samson. Divine guidance or help, overcoming the difficult circumstances of the birth, prepares readers for the future career of a figure who is remembered as a hero.[19] Viviano ("Genres" 34), citing R. L. Fox, points out that often such retrospective infancy narratives are quite fanciful; and so the problem of historicity remains no matter how one classifies the Gospel accounts of Jesus' beginnings.

Viviano argues that a very ancient classification may have been "myth" if the (Jewish Christian) opponents attacked by I Tim 1:4 as occupying themselves with myths, genealogies, and midrashic speculations were reading something like Matt 1–2. When Viviano himself applies "myth" to the Matthean infancy narrative, he does not use it negatively but in the sense of a foundation legend in which history and fiction could both function. He finds support for the idea of foundation or origins in the use of *genesis* by Matt 1:18; and he compares Matt 1–2 to Gen 1–11: These chapters are not ordinary history but prehistory, i.e., symbolic narratives representative of primal reality. Despite the positive thrust of Viviano's theological perceptions, I fear that in communicating the infancy narratives to a present-day audience, "myth" will automatically raise obstacles too difficult to overcome.

A feverish interest in hermeneutics has left its mark on general approaches to the infancy narratives in these past years. Overall the results are positive but two mistakes sometimes mar the advocacy of a particular type of criticism. First, it is not unusual to find a virtually exclusive claim for one (new) approach, especially over against historical criticism, whereas I would evaluate all the approaches as complementary. In an article on Matt that manifests excellent sense, Harrington ("New") shows what each of the various kinds of historical and literary criticism can contribute to the study of the infancy narratives.

---

[19] It also fits the infancies of Sargon and Oedipus and a host of others, but we know that the evangelists knew about the Israelite figures of the Bible. According to Testa's summary ("XXXI" 135), C. Grottanelli's 1990 paper pointed out in ancient Mediterranean culture *models* of the presentation of the infancy of great mythical or historical persons with a variety of motifs, some of which parallel the stories of Jesus' infancy.

Second, the technicalities of the interpretive method can become almost an end in themselves, so that those who are searching for the worthwhile exegetical gain from the application of a method run up against a barrier of jargon and hermeneutical philosophy. This is a critique particularly applicable to structuralist/semiotic hermeneutics.

Laurentin (*Évangiles*) would consider one of his major contributions a semiotic approach to the infancy narratives (one-third of *Évangiles*). F. Martin ("Naître") offers a semiotic approach to Matt 2; and the models of A. J. Greimas influence the structuralist study of chap. 2 of Matt by Couffignal ("Conte") and of the whole Lucan infancy narrative by Agnes Gueuret (article and book). There are also semiotic/structuralist analyses of Luke 1–2 by Panier (*Naissance*), of Luke 1 by Merritt ("Angel's"), and of Luke 2 by Lauverjat ("Luc"). Although this semiotic contribution to infancy narrative research is largely in French, not all Francophonic biblical scholars are enthusiastic. L. Monloubou asks point-blank whether Laurentin's semiotics adds anything new to the interpretation and gives an answer that I translate:

> Our author [Laurentin] thinks so. According to my perception, this surging ocean of semiotics whose foaming waves swept over the tranquil beaches of exegesis is now in the process of retreating. It has left certain places on the exegetical beach reshaped; it also leaves various debris. An improper amount of importance given to the formal elements of a text irresistibly recalls the excesses of formal logic so appreciated by a decadent scholasticism (EV 93 [Nov. 24, 1983], 648).

My own reactions vary: Some semiotic studies are so complex and filled with created jargon that I cannot understand them; others I can understand but do not see that they have added much to what had already been perceived by other methods;[20] still others have interesting observations that I have not seen before and will bring into the discussions below.

An interest in sociology echoing liberation theology is manifest in the

---

[20] I have almost the same reaction to some modern examples of derash (nn. 16–17 above). Olivera ("Interpretación") reads Matt 1:18–15 derashically, invoking rabbinic rules and using some of the language of literary criticism, but comes up with little that traditional exegetes have not long recognized. Moreover, I find exaggerations. For Olivera (295) the purpose of Matt's "derashic" reading of the OT (e.g., of the conceptions of Isaac, Jacob, Samson, Samuel) is to show the superiority of Christ over those previous figures. In my judgment, although Matt certainly thinks of Jesus as superior, the OT echoes show primarily the continuity and consistency of God's way of acting. Olivera's appeal (297) to the derashic "tartey mishma" (one word with a double meaning) to explain how *parthenos* means both "young girl" and "virgin" in 1:23 ("The *parthenos* will be with child") is unnecessary. The type of woman covered by *hē parthenos* is *usually* young and virginal. In 1:23 "the virgin" aspect of the range of meaning dominates because that is what Matt indicates in the context. Why do we need a double meaning? His paragraph on 289 giving reasons why v. 26 does not belong with 1:18–25 is truly puzzling; there is no v. 26 in chap. 1.

recent literature, especially in reference to the opposition to Jesus by Herod (§6) and the Lucan Magnificat (§12). For instance, see the studies by Gaitán Hurtado, Herrera Aceves, Horsley, Krüger, Mezzacasa, O'Day, and Verweyen, with a response by Ernst, in the bibliography below. Their views will be discussed in the respective sections.

Specific comments on the use of narrative criticism in the studies by Bauer and Heil will appear in §3 below; here let me call attention to a general example. Gros Louis ("Different") offers a popular but very perceptive overview of what literary criticism, paying attention to narrative, can contribute to understanding Matt 1–2 and Luke 1–2. Although the two evangelists work with the same basic event, each employs narrative with a different effect. The numerical pattern of the Matthean genealogy shows that the direction is not human but from above, as does the use of dream revelations to move the action in a direction that the human subjects would not have expected.[21] The five prophecies are placed after the events to which they pertain, thus giving the impression that the prophecies did not give rise to the events; rather the events recalled the prophecies. Luke's narrative gives greater attention to character development, and the greater prominence of women moves it away from male domination. Significant moments in the Lucan account are followed not by fulfillment citations of OT prophecies, but by canticles that serve as the responses of those involved commenting on God's role in what has happened. Without dreams, the Lucan flow of action is more logically and historically motivated, e.g., movement to Bethlehem directed by a census. The annunciation of the conception of JBap is in a public setting while that of the conception of Jesus is more private, a difference catching the "still, small voice" atmosphere of God's activity in the OT (I Kings 19:12). Simple as these observations of Gros Louis are, I found them more persuasive than some of the complex semiotic/structuralist studies.

If we move beyond different hermeneutical approaches, scholars agree overall that the two infancy narratives share an interest in christology and OT background. The narratives also introduce themes that will reappear later in the body of the Gospel and offer characters and reactors that can serve as a model for the life of the readers. In Roman Catholic circles there has been considerable attention to the figure of Mary in the infancy narratives, where she has a greater presence than anywhere else in the NT;[22] sometimes the borderline between biblical exegesis and mariology is blurred in such research.

---

[21] Tupper ("Bethlehem") notes that theologically the portrayal of special incidents of divine providence through dream interventions occurs in the wider context of God's general providential guidance. I would see the latter exercised in the genealogical history.

[22] E.g., Núñez, "Maria"; Ripoll "Infancy" (Mary is fitted into other infancy-narrative emphases); see also MNT 74–97, 107–62.

Although treatment of the noncanonical infancy stories is beyond the focus of a commentary devoted to Matt 1–2 and Luke 1–2, they have been the subject of continued scholarly interest. In covering Jesus' life before the public ministry the apocryphal material is, in common estimation, later than and often derivative from the canonical accounts or traditions. Bovon ("Geburt") points to three cycles of stories that were told and written about: (a) the life of Mary before the birth of Jesus;[23] (b) the flight to Egypt; and (c) the childhood miracles of Jesus. Vorster ("Annunciation" 34–37), pointing out that the *Protevangelium of James* retells the canonical story of Jesus' birth from a virgin, analyzes well the pattern of such retelling. In one way the same underlying semantic structure is preserved; in another way the retelling, which is never exact, has its own purpose and thus becomes in principle another story. Kretschmar ("Natus" 422–26) finds in the *Protevangelium* a strong contrast between Mary and Eve: In giving birth to her son without pain Mary has been delivered from the curse of God on Eve, and thus is the first one to be redeemed from the sin of Adam and Eve.[24] Thus we are not seeing here a mariology where Mary is treated for her own sake (pace Cullmann) but a working out of christology.

THE MATTHEAN INFANCY NARRATIVE[25]

§2 General Observations

This section will concentrate on the relation of Matt 1–2 to the rest of the Gospel. The heart of this issue is *biblos geneseōs* in Matt 1:1 (49–

---

[23] See also n. 96 below on the particular emphasis on Mary's virginity in this literature.

[24] Ignatius (*Eph.* 19:1) sees the virginity of Mary as a separate mystery from her giving birth, but in his treatment the virginity has an antidocetic motive absent from the *Protevangelium*.

[25] In comment on the proper designation, "infancy narrative" is a modern taxonomic designation according to form and content. It is better than "birth narrative" because Matt and Luke give relatively little attention to the birth itself, and more to the infancy; but no single title will cover a span that extends from Abraham's begetting Isaac to Jesus' visit to the Temple at age twelve. "Infancy gospels" should be seen as another post-NT designation, for neither Matt nor Luke reproduces Mark 1:1 in calling the written work *euaggelion* (Matt 26:13, "this gospel," is ambiguous in light of 24:14; 4:23; 9:35). Nolan (*Royal* 108) argues for "The Gospel of the origins of Jesus Christ" as faithful to Matt's intent expressed in 1:1, but that neglects the conception/birth connotation in *genesis* (1:18). Marín Heredia ("Más" 320) prefers the designation "Theological Prologue," leaving out all descriptive indication of the content.

Most often it is recognized that neither evangelist knew the other's infancy narrative. For the thesis that Luke knew Matt's, see §9A below. More implausibly Gundry (*Matthew*) contends that Matt's infancy narrative is a midrash on Luke's. Not only does Gundry have to indulge in flights of fancy to establish this (e.g., Matt changed the slaying of doves in Jerusalem to the slaying of children in Bethlehem), but he has to ignore the almost total lack of surface connection between the two narratives (a feature very strange if one is a prolonged midrash on the other or if one evangelist knew the other's account). Leaney ("Virgin") simply assumes that Matt's infancy narrative is later than Luke's and states that Matt undertook "the task of answering the question, 'In view of the Annunciation being only to Mary, how was Joseph reassured as to her purity?' "

50, 58–59 above). Does that phrase refer: (a) to just the genealogy; (b) to the genealogy plus the rest of chap. 1; (c) to the whole of chaps. 1–2; (d) to 1:1–4:16; (e) or, most widely, to the whole Gospel?

(a) Tatum ("Origin") in a sense spans both (a) and (d), arguing that 1:1 introduces only 1:1–17, while 1:18 governs the section up to 4:16. I find that unlikely because of the appearance of *genesis* in both 1:1 and 1:18, with the second resuming the first. Indeed, Scott ("Birth" 89) points to the clever reverse-order connection between them: "*genesis* of Jesus Christ" in 1:1, and "of Jesus Christ the *genesis*" in 1:18.

(b) On 59 above I argued for at least an extension of the title to the whole of chap. 1 if vv. 18–25 were interpreted to explain v. 16. Luz (*Matthew* 103–4) agrees, although he prefers the translation of the key word *genesis* in 1:1 as record of "origin" rather than "birth" because chap. 1 of Matt does not treat the birth but the origin of Jesus Christ. The suggestion has a point; yet "origin" for *genesis* does not do justice to the "begetting" motif in all the etymologically related uses of *egennēsen* and the single use of *egennēthē* in 1:2–17.

(c) There would be a certain logic in applying the title in 1:1 to the whole of Matt 1–2 since those chapters constitute the entire story of the infancy; but then one would have to go beyond the begetting/conception/birth aspect of *genesis*. Thériault ("Règle") thinks he can find a three-fold motif (ancestral or Davidic; royal; ordinary and difficult) in the three "fourteen" sections of the genealogy (1:1–18); in the narrative of 1:18–2:23 (1:18–25; 2:1–12; 2:13–23);[26] and then in Matt 3–28—an interesting suggestion, but overextended and oversystematized.

(d) Bauer ("Literary" 454–55) sees the beginnings of Jesus reaching to 4:16, as do others, not necessarily because they draw this meaning from 1:1 but in large part because they regard 1:1–4:16 as the first major division of the Gospel.[27] Above (49–54, 105) I expressed doubt about this way of dividing Matt. A reason for preferring a first division consisting of chaps. 1–2 is the parallelism between 1:18–2:23 and the end of Matt—a parallelism that has been developed by scholars in the intervening years, as I point out in BDM.[28]

[26] E.g., East/star-vision/gold // Jerusalem/scriptural-prophecy/myrrh // Bethlehem/star-guide/frankincense. A different pattern of threes is proposed by Swaeles ("Des êtres"), one that matches both infancy narratives: At Bethlehem Luke 2:1–20 has creche/shepherds/angels; at Bethlehem Matt 2:1–10 has house/magi/star; at Jerusalem Luke 2:22–38 has Temple/Law/Prophets. There is certainly a functional equivalence between the Lucan shepherds and Matthean magi, but this enlarged parallel patterning seems forced.

[27] Marín Heredia ("Más" 320–21) prefers the division 1:1–4:16 because those verses contain seven prophetic fulfillment citations, a significant number, and there are inclusions, e.g., between the star of 2:1–12 and the people sitting in the darkness seeing a great light (4:12–16). Radaelli ("Racconti") thinks that one can find twelve episodes in Matt 1:1–4:25, which constitutes a prologue to the Gospel comparable in role to Mark 1:1–28 in that Gospel.

[28] Of course, one can meet my objection by subdividing 1:1–4:16 into 1:1–2:23 and 3:1–4:16 and making the two subdivisions relatively autonomous.

(e) Application to the whole Gospel is favored by Van Elderen ("Significance" 7). Dormeyer ("Mt 1,1") speculates that Matt substituted his 1:1 ("The book of the *genesis* of Jesus Christ") for Mark 1:1 ("The beginning of the gospel of Jesus Christ, the Son of God") to function as the Gospel title—Mark's title would appeal only to insiders (Christian believers) since it has little OT resonance, and Matt wanted to reach out to believers and unbelievers showing Jesus as the eschatological fulfillment of salvific expectation. DAICC (1.150–55) argues strongly that as already exemplified in Philo, *"Genesis"* was the Greek title of the OT book. Accordingly Matt's *biblos geneseōs* would have been understood as a title for the whole Gospel: "Book of the *New* Genesis wrought by Jesus Christ, son of David, son of Abraham." The word I have italicized, however, is not in the Greek; without it I doubt that Matt would have been satisfied to give his work the title of a scriptural book—even the first book—since he would have regarded Jesus as surpassing what had already been written. Moreover, rendering the genitive form of Jesus as an agent is problematic since the genealogy that follows leads to Jesus, not from him. At the end of the discussion DAICC mentions with favor another possibility: a polyvalent sense of *genesis*.[29] In covering the genealogy it can have a sense of origin/ begetting; in covering what follows the genealogy it can have the sense of birth; then it can have the sense of history or life-story; and finally it can have all the overall sense of (new) creation. That is an attractive proposal, but would Matt's readers have caught the fluctuating nuances?[30]

No matter how one conceives the mechanics of the relationship of Matt 1–2 to the rest of the Gospel, one thing is certain: The theological motifs of those chapters anticipate the theology of the rest of the Gospel.[31] In writing BBM, I found that far more important than the precisions just discussed, and happily the emphasis on theology continues. Scott ("Birth"), who thinks of the first major Matthean unit as 1:1– 4:16, capitalizes on the fact that Matt reports what happened before and after the birth of Jesus, but not the birth itself. In a certain sense the birth in this unit is the reader's, for here he/she is given what is necessary to make sense of the whole story of Jesus which is to follow. Charlier ("Du berceau") perceptively recognizes that Matt does not give us family reminiscences but retrojects into the infancy aspects of

---

29 See J. C. Fenton, *The Gospel of Matthew* (rev. ed.; London: Penguin/Westminster, 1977), 36.

30 I do not deem such a question irrelevant since the most basic sense of a passage is what it conveys in the dialogue between the evangelist and the audience he envisages or reaches.

31 Van Elderen ("Significance" 12) lists the presence of God, universalism, Davidic and Son-of-God christologies, and continuity with the OT.

Jesus' adult career, with a special anticipation of the passion (see 183 above). Via ("Narrative") points out that Matt introduces the reader to the marvelous at the level of discourse ("It was found that she was with child—through the Holy Spirit") before he presents Joseph on the narrative level. This observation implicitly warns us against making history primary and also prepares us for the manifest divine activity in the Gospel to follow.

A twofold theological function of the Matthean infancy narrative is commonly accepted. First, Matt 1–2 anticipates the christology of the Gospel by portraying Jesus as the Messiah, the Savior, the Son of God, and God with us (Emmanuel). Second, Matt 1–2 constitutes a catechesis on OT themes preparatory to recounting the story of Jesus' public ministry, as newly stressed by Ahirika ("Theology"). The important contribution of Nolan (*Royal*) has Matt 1–2 legitimizing the Savior as Son of David and Son of the Kyrios in such a correlative way that the basic christology is centered on "the Royal Son of God." Nolan documents in Jesus' time images of David and of the Davidic kings which include sanctity, fidelity to the Lord, speaking in the Spirit, wisdom, and elements of healing and prophecy—a Davidic picture influencing the whole Gospel. In Matt 1–2, Davidic elements beyond the obvious include the hope of the Gentiles (magi) related to the world kingdom of David and the coming of the magi with their gifts related to the visit of the Babylonian envoys to Hezekiah's treasury in Isa 39:1–2. At times Nolan's Davidic quest becomes a bit obscure and perhaps farfetched, e.g., the Hosea citation in Matt 2:15 is really an echo of Numbers (p. 209); the slaughter of the Bethlehem children becomes a slaughter of Davidids, like the pogrom against the royal family of Jerusalem (II Chron 21). Although I appreciate the strength of this Davidic thrust,[32] I regret that Nolan takes a stand against a Moses typology in Matt 2, despite his wise warning (p. 205) not to posit a single literary model. The story of a man named Joseph who receives revelation in dreams and goes to Egypt, of the slaughter of male children up to age two by a wicked king, and of the escape of one child who will save his people is obviously closer to the story at the end of Genesis and the beginning of Exodus (Joseph and Moses in Egypt) than to that of David.[33] The goal of Matt's infancy narrative is to be inclusive of the whole story of Israel with overt references to the great salvific events of the Exodus (Moses) and the Exile. If the Matthean Jesus was the royal Son of God, he was also the lawgiver and interpreter of the new, eschatological covenant.

---

[32] In the Matthean section of his "Sauveur," Feuillet too is very insistent on the importance attributed by Matt to Jesus' Davidic descent.

[33] Although below I shall point out some defects in Crossan ("From"), he is undeniably right in stressing that Matt's background is the OT story of Moses with its haggadic developments.

§3 The Genealogy of Jesus (Matt 1:1–17)

This topic has been the subject of numerous studies since 1976: two books and over thirty articles. We may consider it under four headings: attempts to reconcile Matt's genealogy with Luke's, attempts to understand Matt's genealogy more perceptively, the issue of the women in the genealogy, and the enduring utility of Matt's genealogy.

A. *Attempts to Reconcile Matt's Genealogy with Luke's.* On 76–79 and 84–94 above I compared the two genealogies of Jesus: Matt's genealogy that traces names descending from Abraham to Jesus, and Luke's that traces names ascending from Jesus back to Adam and God.[34] I maintained that they are both genealogies of Joseph, that their very sharp differences cannot be reconciled plausibly by appealing to levirate marriage (503–4), that Matt's genealogy (in patterns of fourteen) may have been composed by adding the names of Joseph and Jesus to an unofficial genealogy of the royal lineage of the expected Messiah, that Luke's genealogy (in patterns of seven) bears signs of popular (rather than archival) provenance among Greek-speaking Jews,[35] that neither gives assurance of being exact family history, and that the primary purpose of each is christological.[36] Orsatti (*Saggio* 34–35), having surveyed ancient Near Eastern genealogies and the variety of their purposes, judges that the essential insights to be gleaned from the two Gospel genealogies read in their context are that Jesus was rooted in human and Israelite history, was of Davidic origin, and had no human father.[37]

In itself an attempt to reconcile the two genealogies is unobjectionable, but very often such an attempt stems from the religious assumption that they must be reconciled because they could not exist in Scripture

---

[34] Stramare ("Significato" 205) makes the interesting point that there is an ascending element in Matt as well, for the opening verse of the genealogy identifies Jesus in ascending order as "son of David, son of Abraham." Similarly D. R. Bauer ("Literary" 457) notes that "Jesus Christ, son of David, son of Abraham" (1:1) is the reverse order of the genealogy (1:2–16), which goes from Abraham through David to Jesus called the Christ. Despite the correctness of the observation, the term "chiasm" that he applies may be too pretentious for the relation between two such unequal segments. Why not settle for an artistic topical sentence?

[35] G. J. Steyn (ETL 65 [1989], 409–11; also NTA 35 [1991], #175) has argued strongly that the biblical names in the pre-Abrahamic section of Luke's genealogy (3:34–38) were not drawn from Hebrew text but from the LXX. He points particularly to the name Cainan (*Kainam*; #64 on 76 above), which is absent from the Hebrew (or Samaritan) of Gen 11:12–13 and 10:22,24. See also Kurz (n. 44 below), 181. This is another argument against the thesis that Luke reproduces a family genealogy (which would scarcely reflect the LXX).

[36] Matt's purpose is to show that Jesus is appropriately designated Son of Abraham and Son of David; Luke's is to show that he is the Son of God. See Plum, "Genealogy"; Hempelmann, "Dürre."

[37] For the rest he thinks (p. 39) that early Christians may have had two different genealogies, one of them with famous names depicting legal royal descent, the other *perhaps* somewhat closer to reality.

unless they were both historically accurate records of Jesus' ancestors.[38] I do not think that such an evaluation is theologically necessitated or even justified. Both genealogies can be truly scriptural and inspired by God if only one or neither was a historically accurate family record. (Indeed, pressing further, I would ask: If one appeals to God's intention to argue that the genealogies *must* be historically reconcilable, why did God not inspire each evangelist to give us the same record?) Genealogies serve different purposes,[39] and no assumption can be made that the format demands genuine lineal descent.

I must wonder whether, without the religious assumption just discussed, Masson would have devoted his immense Angelicum thesis (*Jésus*) to reconciling the genealogies.[40] He argues that Shealtiel (both genealogies) was the husband of Jechoniah's daughter and the adopted son of Jechoniah: Matt gives the legal male parents from Solomon to Jechoniah, while Luke gives the natural parents of Jechoniah from Neri back through Nathan to David. (Yet in this monarchical era Luke has names not attested elsewhere at all for this period, or attested only in the postexilic period, or only levitically!) As for the names from Shealtiel to Joseph (also differing in the two lists), Masson makes another appeal to legal and natural differences.[41] Nettelhorst ("Genealogy") contends that Luke traces the genealogy back through Joseph's father while Matt traces it through Joseph's maternal grandfather. One can never disprove such hypotheses; but there is absolutely nothing in the Gospel text to justify them. And what is gained if such diverse genealogies are reconciled when the other parts of the two infancy narratives are apparently quite irreconcilable?

Feuillet's attempt ("Observations") to reconcile the genealogies (Matt

[38] In his own (typed) Roman house organ J. F. McCarthy (*Living Tradition* 11 [May 1987], 9) presents four ways in which both genealogies can be harmonized and historical: (a) levirate marriage or adoption; (b) Matt gives Joseph's genealogy; Luke gives Mary's; (c) Matt gives Joseph's; Luke gives Joseph's and Mary's; (d) Matt and Luke both give Joseph's and Mary's.

[39] It is interesting that many of those who would reconcile the genealogies show little interest in the sociological evidence of how genealogies function (65 above). In that area Wilson's *Genealogy* is a development of his previous work. Working in the same direction, Karin Plum ("Genealogy") analyzes the function of the biblical genealogies (chiefly to substantiate collective identity) and adds observations about the simultaneous roles of biblical women in relation to kinship, national identity, historical setting, and theology. For instance, genealogies feature men because they constituted society in a patriarchal world, and women enter the genealogy only when something special happens. Yet at the same time women are important in the literary consciousness, as manifested in the patriarchal stories that give prominence to matriarchs.

[40] Overstreet ("Difficulties") also betrays passion for demonstrating scriptural accuracy by harmonizing the genealogies.

[41] He argues that Mary was a Davidid (despite Luke 1:36 that has Mary related to a Levite); Pixner ("Maria" 44–45) thinks she may have been descended both from Levi and David. Lerle ("Ahnenverzeichnisse" 113) mentions a Jewish tradition about Mary, daughter of Heli (see Luke 3:23, which refers to Joseph as son of Heli), who was hung by her breasts (see Luke 11:27).

gives a genealogy through Joseph, Luke through Mary) is based on his interpretation of Luke 3:23: "Jesus . . . being the son, *as it was supposed,* of Joseph, the son of Eli (Heli) . . . the son of David . . . the son of Adam, the son of God." The reader would know from Luke 1 that Jesus was not the son of Joseph but of Mary and so is meant to assume that all the subsequent names are Mary's ancestors. This is implausible. Feuillet cannot dismiss so easily as he does the fact that it took close to 1,500 years for an interpreter to have recognized *specifically* that Luke intended the suggested parentage.[42] It is true that Luke has indicated to the reader that Jesus was not biologically begotten by Joseph; but he has called Joseph the father (*patēr*) of Jesus (2:48) and has twice stressed that Joseph was of the house of David (1:27, 2:4)—indeed in the latter instance he has spoken of Joseph as being of the lineage of or fatherly descent (*patreia*) from David. In the Lucan story flow how could Luke's hearers/readers interpret a genealogy that does not mention Mary, but does mention Joseph and traces ancestors through David, as anything other than a genealogy of Joseph? The "as it was supposed" takes into account that Joseph was not the biological begetter of Jesus but does not change the whole direction of the genealogy. If Mary was of the house of David, why would it be necessary to tell readers about Joseph's lineage? Later church writers did attribute Davidic descent to Mary (not necessarily through the Lucan genealogy); but often that stemmed from an inability to understand that in a Jewish mindset, through Joseph's acknowledgment, Jesus could be legally, even if not biologically, Joseph's son and thus share Joseph's Davidic descent.[43]

B. Attempts to Understand Matt's Genealogy More Perceptively. For a discussion of the application of Matt 1:1, see §2 in this Supplement. Clearly the genealogy in Matt 1:1–17 with its OT names (even as the genealogy in Luke 3:23–38) was shaped in Jewish-Christian circles. How would it have been understood by Gentile Christians with a background in Greco-Roman literature? Mussies ("Parallels") fills in a lacuna in Wettstein by offering classical parallels to almost every aspect of the

---

[42] Jean Nonni (= Annius of Viterbo) in 1502. Before Feuillet it was defended in the 20th century by P. Vogt and J. Herr. Nettelhorst ("Genealogy" 170), himself very conservative, describes this view as "nothing but wishful thinking."

[43] The Lucan genealogy gives the name Eli (or Heli) to the father of Joseph. Arguing that Luke really means to tell us that this is the name of Mary's father, Feuillet notes that the *Protevangelium of James* gives the name of Mary's father as Joachim. Feuillet then points to II Kings 23:34, where the name of King Eliakim is changed to Jehoiakim, as a sign of the equivalence of the names Eli and Joachim. See also Bartina, "Padre." Even without this rather tenuous identification, the *Protevangelium* does attribute Davidic descent to Mary; but that may be another of the many instances in which it misunderstands Jewish customs. Mussies ("Parallels" 40–42) has helpful remarks pointing out that Tertullian, Julius Africanus, and other ancient harmonizers who went this route did not grasp that genealogies might represent relationships other than family ties.

Matthean genealogy (placing, omission of some names, counting the generations).[44] Indeed, on pp. 43–44 he points out that famous figures like King Agamemnon and King Theseus could be attributed different ancestors by different authors, even as happened with Jesus. In my judgment Mussies's observations reflect on the broad acceptability of the Gospel genealogies, not on their formation.

The numerology of the genealogy continues to fascinate. Although Matt 1:17 states that in each of the three divisions there are 14 generations (pl. of *genea*), there are only 13 begettings (*egennēsen*) in the first division and 13 in the third division.[45] Lerle ("Ahnenverzeichnisse") counts 14 names (not begettings) from Abraham to David, 14 names from David (recounted) to Josiah, 14 names from Josiah (recounted) to Joseph[46]—though Matt specifically makes the break at Jechoniah, not Josiah, and counts 14 generations, not names. The prize for the most imaginative suggestion (alas, not the most plausible) goes to Hammer ("Intention"), who believes that the body of Matt consists of two large parts (chaps. 1–12 and 13–25—comparable to Dan 1–6 and 7–12!), each of which is divided into three sections containing 14 pericopes. Hammer thinks he can show how the career of one of the names in the Matthean genealogy applies to each pericope. Chopineau ("Notarikon") suggests the key is ADAM (Abraham, David, Messiah—the three sections), who is not mentioned by Matt (only by Luke). Most still seem willing to derive the 14 from the numerical value of the Hebrew consonants for David's name (*dwd* = 4+6+4; p. 80, n. 38 above). Pesch ("Er wird" 2.1396) makes the point that in the first segment of the genealogy, there are 4 patriarchal names from Abraham to Judah, 6 names from the Egyptian period to the conquest (Perez to Salmon/Rahab), and 4 names from the entrance to the Promised Land till David the king.

C. The Women in the Genealogy. The five women (four from the OT [Tamar, Rahab, Ruth, the wife of Uriah] and Mary) have been the subject of much reflection. Schnider and Stenger ("Frauen") pay attention to where the women are placed in relation to the begettings or the males: Sequentially there are 3 begettings before Tamar, 7 males (but only 6 begettings) before Rahab, and 3 males (after Ruth) before the

---

[44] For a similar effort in relation to Luke's genealogy, see W. S. Kurz in *Luke-Acts,* ed. C. H. Talbert (New York: Crossroad, 1984), 169–87.

[45] Twelve instances of *egennēsen* by men and one (the last) of *egennēthē* from a woman. The fact that the last begetting (the thirteenth—from Mary) already involves Jesus makes me reject even on a numerical basis Schaberg's contention (*Illegitimacy* 38–39) that there has been omitted an element that would have made 14, namely, the physical begetting of the illegitimate Jesus by the biological father. Two notices pertaining to the one child violates the whole counting system. Let me note also that Schaberg's proposal does not solve why there are also only 13 begettings in the first section.

[46] Along the same lines Newman ("Matthew") has 14 names from Abraham to David, 14 names from David (recounted) to Josiah, 14 from Jechoniah (Josiah is not recounted) to Jesus.

wife of Uriah. They assure us that 3 + 7 (+ 1) + 3 is common in apocalyptic; however, one would like an example of the use in that context of 14, the only numeral to which Matt calls attention.[47] Lagrand ("How") observes this pattern for the first four women: Male *egennēsan* Male *ek* Female. But in Jesus' birth the passive of *gennan* is used, and the *ek* covers both Mary (1:16) and the Holy Spirit (1:20). I would judge that the combination phrased in this manner clearly makes the Spirit the co-principal in bringing about the birth of Jesus but avoids making the Spirit's role that of a male begetter.[48] Quinn ("Is") argues that "Rachab" of Matt 1:5 is not the harlot of Joshua 2 and 6, whose name is always "Raab" in the LXX and Church Fathers—she is an unknown. My article (*"Rachab"*) disagrees by pointing out that the Matthean genealogy has several unusual orthographies for biblical names, that Rachab in Quinn's hypothesis would be the only nonbiblical personage in the first two sections, and that Rachab's husband Salmon appears in the list after a name associated with the desert wanderings,[49] the appropriate time for the biblical woman of Jericho.

What the five women of the genealogy have in common seems to be the most discussed point. As I pointed out on 71–74 above, three of the OT women are non-Israelites and Bathsheba is named through her husband who was a Hittite[50]—possibly a preparation for a Matthean Jesus who tells his disciples to make disciples of all nations, but, of course, not a factor that unites them with Mary. All four OT women have irregular or even scandalous aspects to their lives; yet by their endeavor they carry on the line of the Messiah[51]—a plausible preparation for the irregular situation of Mary in Matt 1:18–20, although Mary is not

---

[47] A similar objection can be leveled against an attempt to see the Matthean genealogy as consisting of six "weeks," with Mary inaugurating the eschatological Sabbath in bearing Jesus (see Foresti, "Maria").

[48] Ancients tried in various ways to catch the complexity of the roles of Mary and the Spirit, which are not simply male and female. A common gnostic motif is to portray both Mary and the Spirit as female, or Mary may be portrayed as male. *Odes Sol.* 19:10 reads: "Like a man she brought forth by her will"; and *Gos. Thomas* 15 refers to "one who was not born of woman" (Jesus?), while 114 has Jesus lead Mary (but which Mary?) so that she may be made male, become a living spirit, and enter the kingdom of heaven.

[49] I.e., his father Nahshon; see Num. 2:3, 7:12.

[50] This designation is traditional, e.g., II Sam 11:26; 12:15 (without the name "Bathsheba"). More problematical is whether Matt and/or his readers would have known that she was the daughter of Eliam (II Sam 11:3), identifiable as the son of Ahithophel (23:34), and thus seemingly the granddaughter of David's trusted advisor who treacherously conspired with Absalom against him and whose suicide provided Matt a model for Judas' treachery and suicide (Matt 27:3–10).

[51] The endeavor of Tamar and Ruth was in seeking to have a child to continue the lineage of their deceased husbands when no relative offered himself as a replacement. The endeavor of Bathsheba (the wife of Uriah) was in making certain that her son, Solomon, succeeded to the throne of his father David when another son, Adonijah, seemed about to seize the inheritance. The endeavor of Rahab was not in relation to her child (since the OT tells us nothing of her marriage or the birth), but in relation to the entrance of the Israelites into the Promised Land where the Davidic dynasty would be established. The parallelism among the women is not perfect.

portrayed by Matt as an example of endeavor. (It is not impossible that Matt would have the readers/hearers think of the direct intervention of God through the Holy Spirit as taking the place of human endeavor in this last instance.)

Beyond these similarities among the women new suggestions have been offered, e.g., by Heil ("Narrative") through his brand of narrative criticism.[52] Yet his suggestions about the impact of the women in the Matthean genealogy are in my judgment unconvincing because he fastens on elements that are dubious or obscure.[53] Since Abraham and Isaac forbade their sons to marry Canaanites, Heil makes a major point that Tamar was not a Canaanite. Yet the Bible never says that Tamar was not a Canaanite; the affirmation that she was an Aramean appears in the pre-Gospel period only in *Jubilees*.[54] Would Matt's readers/hearers know of that identification? Clearly inflated is Heil's claim: "By explicitly naming her Matthew reminds the reader that Judah continued the Abrahamic line not by his Canaanite wife but by the non-Canaanite Aramean, Tamar." Heil then goes on to say that Rahab, who is a Canaanite, is included to fulfill the universalist promise that all the people of the earth would be blessed in Abraham (Gen 12:3). In other words, one can find support from Abraham for Matt's choice of the women whether they were Canaanite or not! Would those who knew the Bible contrast Tamar's sinful union with Judah and Ruth's sinless union with Boaz, as Heil does, when the Book of Ruth (4:12) prays that the offspring to be given by the Lord to Boaz from Ruth will be like Perez, the child Tamar bore to Judah? For Heil "the wife of Uriah" is mentioned to emphasize David's sinfulness in terms of adultery and murder; but his narrative criticism calls no attention to Matt's stress that through her Solomon was born.

Bauer's attempt at narrative criticism ("Literary") hews closer to the text, but again is disappointing when it reaches "the bottom line." Arguing that there is no perfect common factor among the five women, he wants to separate Mary from the others; but then (463) he decides that a common characteristic is "they were all relatively powerless, marginalized, and in need of help." In such a patriarchal list reflecting patriarchal society could not almost any woman Matt chose to mention

---

[52] Without using the formal terminology of narrative criticism, I would insist on the need to follow the structure and storyflow of the narrative, and on the primacy of the given text over hypothetical reconstructions.

[53] In the ANALYSIS of §48 of BDM I explain why I find unproductive Heil's structuring of Matt 26–28 that runs against the surface indications of the text, a view in which I am not alone as I indicate there.

[54] Heil cites also the *Testaments of the Patriarchs*, which he would date to the 2nd century B.C.—a disputable claim.

be seen as marginalized and powerless? The (unmentioned) barren wives of the first patriarchs were certainly in need of help. Thus the characteristic proposed by Bauer does not explain why these four OT women were named. He is ignoring the obvious: These five women do have in common that their union with their partners before or at conception was scandalous or irregular,[55] something not true of most OT women. Muñoz Iglesias (MIE 4.104–17; also "Las mujeres") argues that what the women have in common is that they were not of the tribe of Judah, and that Matt included them to offset the objections that Jesus could not be the Messiah because his mother was not a Davidid of the tribe of Judah. (This is almost the mirror opposite of Johnson's theory mentioned on 72 above.) Muñoz Iglesias thinks that Luke's implicit indication that Mary was of priestly descent had probably circulated, but he does not want his thesis to depend on that. But without it, there is nothing that would call the attention of the readers/hearers of Matt to Mary's descent from a tribe other than Judah. Would they even be interested in Mary's descent since Jesus' legal relationship to the messianic line had nothing to do with his mother?[56] It is far better to pay attention to what Matt's text does tell us about Mary and relate that to the situation of the OT women: She was found to be with child before she had come to live with Joseph, and the child was not his—in other words, externally an irregular and potentially scandalous situation that in God's providence gave unique significance to her child.

No one can rival the newness of Jane Schaberg's insight that the factor the five women had in common was that their giving birth was marked by illegitimacy.[57] Below in Appendix IV I shall discuss Schaberg's claim that Jesus was illegitimate (because Mary was raped); but in reference to the OT women I would query whether any of the births associated with them by Matt was really looked on as illegitimate.[58] Certainly the birth of Solomon was not: The child of David's adultery with Bathsheba had died, and she and David were married when Solomon was conceived.[59] The passage quoted above from Ruth (4:12)

---

[55] Unhappily, Mattison's objection to this position ("God/Father" 199) flows from a misapprehension. Thinking that I said there was something irregular about "the begettings [of children] out of these women," she objects that what is extraordinary in two cases is not the begetting. On the page in BBM (73) cited by her I spoke deliberately of the *unions* of these women with their partners.

[56] On the legal fatherhood of Joseph, see Salas, "José."

[57] She discusses the genealogy in *Illegitimacy,* 20–41. Her *Concilium* article gives a brief summary.

[58] Even were the OT women mothers of illegitimate children, that would prove little about Mary. In their case Matt is very consistent: X (male) begot Y (male) from Z (the respective OT woman), leaving no doubt of male agency. But when he comes to Mary (1:16), he says, "from her was begotten Jesus," with no reference to a male begetter.

[59] For a good survey of Jewish interpretations of Bathsheba, see Madeleine Petit, "Bethsabée," who distinguishes between the first part of Bathsheba's life and the second part, in which she was venerated as queen-mother.

gives a marriage blessing that mentions with esteem the children both of Ruth and Tamar.[60] Outside of genealogies the Bible never narrates Rahab's union with Salmon; and there is no reason to think they were not married or that their child was illegitimate. Her former career as a prostitute did not prevent the rabbis from positing that once Israel entered the Promised Land, she worshiped the true God, lived the exemplary life of a convert, married Joshua, and became the ancestress of eight prophets.[61] On 73–74 above I spoke of the irregular or scandalous unions of the OT women in Matt's genealogy; but the suggestion of illegitimacy is, in my judgment, imposed on the Matthean text by Schaberg as a backreading from her (wrong) thesis that Jesus was illegitimate. The fragility of her thesis is illustrated by Freed's careful analysis ("Women") of Jewish thought about the four women in order to argue in the opposite direction, namely, that Matt, in order to prove against Jewish polemic that Jesus' birth was *not* illegitimate, introduced the women as examples of virtue despite contrary appearance! I do not agree with Freed about Matt's purpose, but he is right about the effect of Matt's citing the women.

Above (74) I stated that in Matt's view of Mary God's "intervention through a woman was even more dramatic than the OT instances; there God had overcome the moral or biological irregularity of the human parents, while here He overcomes the total absence of the father's begetting." Schaberg several times makes the point that there are no interventions in the instances of the OT women: no divine voices or miracles. I may not have chosen the perfect word;[62] but it should have been clear that divine "intervention" was meant in the sense of the divine planning explained a few pages earlier (68), namely, that although Matt's genealogy seems to concentrate on the human role in the conception of the Messiah ("A begot B"), in the biblical mentality a genealog-

[60]Judah was sinful; but Tamar was righteous (Gen 38:26—Philo can even use her to model chastity: *On the Preliminary Studies* 124). Would their child(ren), conceived in loyalty to the levirate principle, be illegitimate? As for Ruth, Josephus (*Ant.* 5.9.3–4; #330,335), a contemporary of Matt, states that nothing scandalous occurred between her and Boaz, and that their son Obed was born one year after they were married. Ruth 4:12, which blesses the children of Tamar and Ruth, challenges Blomberg's insistence on social stigma and marginalization of the children of the women in the genealogy. In the biblical estimation, how was Solomon marginalized because of his birth when Sir 47:12 says: "Because of his [David's] merits, he had as his successor a wise son who lived in security"?

[61]TalBab *Megilla* 14b; Midrash Rabba 2.1 on Ruth 1:1; and 8.9 on Num 5:10. There is no way of knowing how much of this midrashic development was known in Matt's time (although already Josephus, *Ant.* 5.1.7; #30, stresses that Rahab received enduring honor); but it does illustrate that one cannot assume a pejorative view of Rahab's subsequent life.

[62]Seemingly independently, however, Freed ("Women" 15) uses the same word in speaking of the women: "But in each case, it came to be thought that God intervened, not only in the relationship with the men in their lives, but also to transform their lives from those of questionable, if not sinful, natures to states of innocence or virtue."

ical "begetting" not only involves the passing of physical life from parent to child but also "reflects the working out of *God's* plan of creation in a history of salvation."[63] Matt most certainly intends to call attention to the fact that in order to bring about the birth of the Messiah, God made use of these women who were more active than their male partners in very difficult situations where circumstances were stacked against them. The ecumenical MNT (81) phrases very exactly what I intended by "divine intervention" in the genealogy: "The four OT women, marked by irregular marital unions, were vehicles of God's messianic plan."[64] That, rather than by illegitimate births, is how Matt used them to prepare for Mary, the fifth woman, "of whom was begotten Jesus, called the Christ," without the male sexual participation of Joseph.

As an addendum to my proposal about irregular marital unions I find value in Robin Mattison's suggestion ("God/Father" 201–2) that one should pay attention to the failures of the men who begot the children from these women. If one concentrates on the other begettings, one might think that the Davidic line depends on the faithfulness and obedience of the fathers; but Judah and Boaz failed in their levirate duties and David sinned against Uriah in taking the latter's wife. The begetting of the final member in Matt's Davidic genealogy involves the Holy Spirit and is quite independent of right or wrong human fathering.[65] Janice Anderson ("Mary's" 200) contributes other helpful insights. Despite Matt's highlighting the OT women as models of faith, "for the most part their roles remain in the context of the female private sphere, rather than the male official public sphere."[66] (After all, it is only with the *Protevangelium of James*, which devotes six chapters to the conception and birth of Mary, that the begetting of a woman in the messianic line becomes as important as the begetting of the men.) Anderson maintains (197) that in comparison with Matt's OT women, Mary's virginity exalts what God has done, partially undermining the patriarchal control. "God's nonsexual creation of Jesus in her womb exacerbates

---

[63] Orsatti (*Saggio* 101) correctly sees as a major theme of the Matthean genealogy a theological reading of Israel's history controlled by God in the light of the Christ-event.

[64] Similarly Orsatti (*Saggio* 72–73): "Behind these persons God is seen as 'the Lord of history' who guides and determines the events."

[65] She points out (203) that although no woman speaks in Matt 1, male begetting is not of the same value for religious identity at the end of the chapter. "We can see that in Matthew's genealogy we have a full-blown attempt to persuade readers to change their understanding of patriarchy." I disagree, however, with her analysis of Joseph's righteousness in terms of his thinking of the traditional vocation to keep a pure genetic line; not the purity of the Davidic line but the purity of marriage is the concern of Joseph that I find in the text.

[66] Her earlier article ("Matthew" 10) points out that Matt's concentration on Joseph can be seen in part as an attempt to come to grips with "the female difference": Birth belongs to the female sphere, and Jesus' birth even more so because there was no male assistance. Featuring Joseph evens things out from a patriarchal viewpoint.

tensions already present in the earlier scriptural traditions where God [not the male participant] ultimately controls reproduction."[67]

D. The Enduring Utility of Matt's Genealogy. One may see theological insights appropriate to Matt's time in the genealogy: continuity with the heritage of Israel's patriarchs and kings, the Davidic descent of Jesus, the preparation for the conception of Jesus in Mary's womb, foreshadowing of the Gentiles, etc. (see 66ff. above). Nevertheless, as Matt is read by or to audiences today, what utility does the genealogy have? The title of Hempelmann's article wrestling with this issue quotes a German romantic poet of the early 1800s who called the genealogy an "arid page in the Holy Book." As Hempelmann points out, aesthetically the genealogy strikes people as monotonous and pointless; historically it bothers scholars by its mistakes and omissions; morally it troubles preachers by listing ancestors for Jesus who were dishonest, brutal, or immoral; and philosophically, as an opening page of the NT, it does not offer much by way of helpful or salvific message. He goes on to counterargue that the genealogy illustrates God's condescension by way of involvement in our history. Independently I offered thoughts for preaching the genealogy (Brown, *Coming* 16–26) as a challenge to the idea that God works only through the saintly. The unworthies named in the genealogy illustrate the graciousness and gratuity of God's choice, and the list of mostly incompetent or scandalous kings raises the issue of an institution (the kingdom) that could be sacred despite and not because of its leadership. In other words, from the portrayal of God's dealing with those who lived before the coming of the Messiah one can learn much about God's dealing with those who have lived after that coming. Ulrich Zwingli maintained that if one understood the genealogy correctly, it contained the essential theology of the Reformation. I would be bolder: It contains the essential theology of the Old and New Testaments.

§4 Composition of Matt 1:18–2:23: Formula Citations; Pre-Matthean Background

In this section I shall treat recent contributions to the formation of the body of the Matthean infancy narrative.

A. Formula (Fulfillment) Citations. Luz (*Matthew* 116, 130, 143–44) attributes four of the five fulfillment citations to the scribes in the community who reflected on the infancy story before the evangelist wrote the Gospel; the distinguishing characteristic is the use of a non-

---

[67] In "Matthew" 10, Anderson states: "Although Jesus is Son of David through Joseph, he is Son of God through Mary."

LXX textual form, which at most Matt redacted. By exception Isa 7:14, which follows the LXX, was added by Matt himself. Like many other commentators I suggested (100 above) that Matt added all five formula citations in chaps. 1–2 to an already existing narrative shaped by other factors. (I see no reason why the evangelist may not have known both Hebrew and Greek and worked with several traditions of the Scriptures.) Yet I insisted that despite his use of tradition, Matt was more a creative author than a redactor and wove both earlier narrative and citations into his overall theological view. In different ways recent contributions reinforce the picture of Matt's creative vision. Pesch ("Er wird") has a sarcastic paragraph about "the chorus of current [German] critics" on the Matthean formula citations in chaps. 1–2. These critics spend their time pointing out that every one of the citations presents a difficulty from the viewpoints of textual and historical criticism, for none represents the text/meaning that modern scholars would find in the masoretic text of the respective passage. Surely it is a duty of commentators to point out such anomalies; a fairer criticism would be centered on whether commentators stop there and fail to elucidate the Matthean theology of the citation.[68] Pesch's own contribution in insisting that the citations fit the general messianic thrust of chaps. 1–2 is important and helpful, but not unique.[69] Menken ("References") places the citation from Jeremiah in Matt 2:17–18 in the context of Matt's general interest in Jeremiah[70] as the prophet who, not only by his words but also by his personal life, shows that the rejection of the Messiah was foreseen by God in the divine plan.

France, "Formula," shows how the addition of formula citations shaped the earlier tradition, even though that tradition may have motivated the addition of the citation—a mutual interaction. The original OT context from which the passage was taken and the changes from the MT or LXX that Matt made in citing the passage helped him to make theological points, some of which would have been easily understood by all of Matt's audience, others of which would have been recognized by those better trained in the biblical background. Yet it is hard to know how far to press reader comprehension. Kronholm ("Kommande") argues that the figure whose birth was foretold in Isa 7:14 was King

---

[68] In his critique Pesch cites Luz, Gnilka, and Schnackenburg, all of whom actually do pay attention to Matthean theology. He does not discuss BBM.

[69] Over against textual/historical criticism Pesch illustrates in various ways Matt's messianic use of the citations: The "they" of Matt's form of Isa 7:14 ("They will call his name Emmanuel") represents the members of the Christian community at the time Matt was writing the Gospel; part of the emphasis in Jesus' being called "a Nazorean," a messianic designation, is that Christians in Syria were called Nazoreans. See 152 and 212 above for similar explanations.

[70] Matt is the only NT author to mention Jeremiah by name, and all three Matthean references to Jeremiah are to be attributed to the evangelist.

Hezekiah (147 above), and one can use rabbinic treatments of Hezekiah (sometimes in messianic contexts) to illumine Matt's intention. Whether Matt's readers would have understood a reference to Hezekiah is a problem, however, as well as the dating of the rabbinic material.

Oberweis ("Beobachtungen") points out small ways in which the formula citation of Isa 7:14 influenced aspects of the surrounding story in Matt 1–2.[71] After Herod (called a king in 2:3,9) died, Matt 2:22 says Archelaus was king over Judea. Historically, however, Josephus (*Ant.* 17.11.4; #318; *War* 2.6.3; #93) is specific that Augustus did not make Archelaus a king. The Matthean description is to be explained from Isa 7:16b, which says that before the child whose conception was described in 7:14 learns good and evil (= before he is two years old), the land of those *two kings* will be deserted. In Matt 2:16 Herod massacres all the boys of two years of age and under in Bethlehem *and the regions all around it*. Why the generalities of time and place, when in 2:5,7 Herod had received precise knowledge? Isa 7:16 fixed the age, while the place description was determined by I Sam 10:2 that influenced the Ramah citation in Matt 2:18 (205 above). These observations are important: They establish that Matt did not simply drop the citations into a fixed narrative. Yet they scarcely establish Oberweis's suggestion that the formula citations are more important in shaping the total Matthean infancy account than are OT narratives and their pre-Christian midrashic developments.

B. Pre-Matthean Material Influential in the Matthean Infancy Account. On 104–19 above I detected three factors that may have contributed to Matt's narrative: a pattern of angelic dream appearances; the biblical stories of Joseph, Moses, and Balaam, combined with midrashic developments of the Moses story; and a pattern of angelic annunciations of birth (see also 155–59). Leaving the last until §11A below, I shall now discuss recent contributions to the discussion of the dream pattern, and the biblical/midrashic background.[72] In this discussion attention should be paid to the warning of Broer ("Jesusflucht" 86–87) of a tendency to underestimate the freedom of the evangelist as a composer and to attribute too much of the end product to sources precisely because

---

[71] Normally Matt is understood to have followed the popular etymology whereby the name Jesus was taken to have meant "YHWH saves." Oberweis, however, makes a case for Matt's use of the more scientific etymology "YHWH helps" (see 131 above). He maintains that the explanatory clause "for he will save his people from their sins" refers to God, so that the name Jesus is explicated by "Emmanuel which means 'God with us.'" In turn this is parallel to "He will be called a Nazorean" in 2:23. Van Aarde ("Immanuel") thinks that for Matt Jesus can be described as Emmanuel, the Torah incarnate.

[72] Luz (*Matthew*) thinks that there was a pre-Matthean oral narrative with some formula citations already woven in. The degree to which Matt has reshaped it while writing it down for the first time varies.

intellectually it may be easier to construct such sources than to analyze the evangelist's creativity.

The Dreams Described by Matt. In explaining that the story of the OT Joseph was the background of Matt's portrayal of the NT Joseph, beyond the patriarch's going to Egypt and bringing Jacob there and thus saving Israel from famine, I pointed out that it was significant that the OT Joseph was an interpreter of dreams. Gnuse ("Dream") has made an important contribution through a careful study of dreams both in the Bible and the classical world. The Matthean dreams, which structurally are much less complex than the classical parallels, draw upon forms in Genesis[73]—not the visual dreams explained by Joseph but auditory message dreams such as received by Abimelech, Jacob, and Laban. Gnuse offers a detailed analysis of the structure of the five Matthean dream reports, pointing to the remarkable similarity of pattern and the special emphasis on fulfillment in the accompanying narrative. The transcendent deity who is the ultimate source of the dream revelation supplies an interesting contrast to the immediacy of the "God-with-us" presence in Jesus.

Bartina ("Sueños") studies various kinds of dreams as vehicles of divine revelation in the Bible: e.g., relatively simple divine communication in sleep, and ecstasy involving extrasensory perception (subdivided into visions easy to understand and figurative symbolic visions that need interpretation). From the terminology used by Matt Bartina judges that Joseph received his divine messages through ecstatic communication. This judgment has implications for evaluating Joseph, since mystics who receive such gifts are often in an elevated form of the spiritual life permanently conformable to special action by God. I doubt that from what Matt tells us one can make any decision about ecstasy.[74] We have no way of knowing whether the formulator of the description had any specific type of dream communication in mind; we may be simply dealing with a popular, imaginative way of describing divine revelation, without any reflection about Joseph's stage of development beyond that he was a just man. Nor do we know whether Matt's audience would have thought that the appearance of an angel who gives a message in a dream was different from other angelic communicative appearances outside dreams, except that dreams would add an exotic tone for both Jew and Gentile.

OT and Midrashic Narratives. Beyond the general background supplied for Matt's Joseph by the OT patriarch of the same name, the major

---

[73] He argues they have not been drawn from the dreams in the midrashic stories about Moses found in Josephus, as proposed by Crossan ("From").

[74] Matt's *kat' onar* ("in a dream") has no parallel in the Bible. Bartina's assumption (48) that the original of Matt was written in Semitic is very dubious.

influence on Matt's account of the birth of Jesus came from the story of Moses with its various components; namely, a birth at the time when the Pharaoh was killing the Hebrew male children; the flight to Sinai and return after the Pharaoh's death; and the journey through Moab to the Promised Land involving the wicked king Balak, and Balaam, the wise man or magus (and his companions) from the East who saw the star.[75] On 114 above I pointed out midrashic developments of the Mosaic birth-segment in Josephus and Philo (writers of the 1st century A.D.). In a popular article Crossan ("From Moses") concentrates on the Mosaic-birth background. The treatment is problematic in several ways, however, for he neglects the OT Joseph and Balaam contributions, and into the midrashic developments centered on the birth of Moses he brings the 12th-century-A.D. *Sepher ha-Zikronot*, assuming that minor narrative details there "record a structure already present in the first century" (p. 21). This type of assumption, in my judgment, is dangerous, often leading to an unscientific, anachronistic application of Jewish materials to the NT. Crossan is correct, however, in adding to the midrashic background pseudo-Philo's *Biblical Antiquities*, which I largely neglected when I wrote BBM.[76] Harrington ("Birth") analyzes pseudo-Philo's account of the birth of Moses and Samson, pointing out the differences from the OT narratives and the parallels to Matt's and Luke's birth narratives.[77]

§5 An Angel Explains to Joseph the Conception of Jesus, and so He Takes His Wife Home (Matt 1:18–25)

This section is centered on an angelic annunciation explaining to Joseph that Mary his wife has conceived from the Holy Spirit. The

---

[75] I contended that a story or stories about Jesus echoing this Moses background already had the dream motif incorporated into it/them on the pre-Matthean level. Such a story heavily shaped by Scripture probably came from the same milieu that Matt drew on for his special material in the passion narrative: Judas and the blood money; the dream of Pilate's wife; Pilate's washing his hands to signal his innocence of Jesus' blood; the guards at the tomb and the earthquake. Common factors are strongly generative OT background, dreams, extraordinary wonders of nature, an extremely hostile portrayal of the Jewish leaders, and a portrayal of the Gentiles as quick to believe. I do not attempt to decide whether such material when it reached Matt, who rephrased it in its present form, was still oral or had already been committed to writing.

[76] At that time the majority of scholars seemed to date it after A.D. 70, but contemporaneously with my book there appeared an important new edition of Pseudo-Philo (SC 229–230; Paris: Cerf, 1976) that went against the tide and made a strong case for a pre-70 dating (230.66–74).

[77] Pseudo-Philo (9:1–10) has Amram beget Moses despite a general Hebrew decision to abstain from sexual relations because of Pharaoh's killing the male children. (Crossan ["From" 23] reads that as Amram refusing divorce, but the notion of divorce he imports from later Jewish tradition.) Pseudo-Philo also recounts that the spirit of God came upon Miriam (= Mary, Moses' older sister) and that she received a dream revelation about the child that would be born to her parents. See also 627 below.

annunciation format will be discussed under §11A below. My treatment here will concern what Matt means by conception from the Holy Spirit, the Matthean portrayal of Joseph, and the issue of other children of Mary raised by Matt 1:25.

A. Conception from the Holy Spirit. Above (133) I stressed that 1:18ff. logically followed 1:1–17 as Matt explains why in 1:16 he did not follow the usual pattern and say that Joseph begot (*egennēthē*) Jesus.[78] The most extraordinary (and the weakest) part of Jane Schaberg's thesis that Jesus was begotten by a rapist involves her interpretation of the description in 1:18,20 of Mary's pregnant state: *echousa ek pneumatos hagiou* and *gennēthen ek pneumatos hagiou* ("having child/begotten from[79] the Holy Spirit").[80] For Schaberg (68), it means that God is involved symbolically or figuratively but not literally: God parents or wills (fits into the divine plan) the child who was physically begotten through the sexual union of Mary and the unnamed man to whom she was not married. However, if in 1:16 *ex hēs egennethē* is applied to Mary as one from whom the child is literally brought into life, why does the similar phrase applied to the Holy Spirit four verses later not designate the other agent literally productive in bringing the child to life? Nor does Schaberg really take into account the context in which Joseph is receiving assurance about Mary's surprising pregnancy, an assurance that one would expect to concern and identify the agency of the begetting. Extraordinarily forced is Schaberg's contention that Matt chose a form of Isa 7:14 which specifically mentions *hē parthenos*[81] and which he attributed to "the prophet," all the while thinking of Deut 22:23–27 that speaks of a virgin who was raped and made pregnant.

Schaberg's claim that a rapist was Jesus' true father, in my judgment, destroys the theological identity of Jesus intended by Matt in 1:18–25. Jesus is not the son of an unknown. He is truly *Son of God* through creative generation in the womb of Mary from the Holy Spirit of God; Jesus is truly *Son of David* through acceptance by the Davidid Joseph,

[78]On 61–63 above I discussed the different readings proposed for 1:16, and opted for "Joseph, the husband of Mary; of her was begotten Jesus, called the Christ." In the intervening years Globe ("Some"), Luz, and others have been of the same mind.

[79]Mussies ("Joseph's" 178) criticizes my translating *ek* as "through," with the implication that I was stacking the evidence in favor of a creative action of the Holy Spirit rather than male begetting. Such a bias never occurred to me, and actually in 1:16 I translated it as "of." In the context *ek* indicates parental agency—but how? "Begotten from" someone is not admirable English, but I shall use it to avoid misinterpretation.

[80]This weakness is recognized by Blomberg ("Liberation"), who on other points is quite sympathetic to Schaberg's arguments; he sides with a reviewer who said that here Schaberg "strains the readers' credulity to the breaking point."

[81]Cazelles ("Septante") gives a very careful discussion of Isa 7:14 (in light of the Matthean appeal to the text). One will find confirmed there many of the points made above (145–49); but, without detailed discussion of the point, he thinks that the LXX does refer to a virginal conception, not simply the future conception of one who is at the moment a virgin.

who named as his son the child thus conceived in Mary's womb. Milavec ("Matthew's") brings out very well this interplay of Joseph's role and the Spirit's role in Jesus' identity. Gordon ("Paternity") argues that in principle the twofold sonship would not have seemed odd in antiquity: In the royal line the Pharaoh inherited the throne of his Pharaonic father, but he was hailed as son of Ra.[82] I insisted in BBM that conception from/through/of the Spirit of Matt (and Luke) was a notion of Jesus' sonship very different from John's notion of a preexistent divine Son ever at the Father's side. Raatschen ("Empfangen" 274–75) stresses that point; but then goes on to dub preexistence as "Gentile theology" that unwarrantedly was joined with Matt's views of the conception! The Prologues to John and Hebrews are scarcely Gentile theology, and why is the joining of preexistence and conception christology not to be considered a perceptive theological development? (See NJBC art. 81.##12–24.)

Above (589) I judged useful Mussies's evidence that Matt's genealogy could have been understood by those with only a Greco-Roman background. However, I can find little favorable to report about his thesis ("Joseph's") that Matt's birth account may have been rooted in Egyptian soil and may have meant that a divine agent mated as a male with Mary to beget Jesus. It is not impossible that some with a pagan background who heard or read Matt might have understood his account in that way, but I contend that it is utterly implausible that such was Matt's intended meaning. Mussies begins (177) with a misstatement that my main argument against such an interpretation is that *pneuma* is neuter. I made that point in an eight-word clause "Not only is the Holy Spirit not male" (124 above),[83] but it was certainly not my main argument. More important is the fact that there is absolutely nothing in Matt (or Luke) to suggest a sexual union. The well-worn examples of gods uniting with humans are quite irrelevant unless one can show that Matt not only knew them but thought them plausible. Mussies does not establish that. Every line of Matt's infancy narrative echoes OT themes: Are we to think that he accepted all that background but then violated

[82] That comparison is useful on the level of how Gentiles might have comprehended Matt's message; but as I shall insist against Mussies below, that does not prove Matt would think Ra begot the Pharaoh in the same way as the Holy Spirit begot Jesus—a comparison that (wisely) Gordon explicitly refuses to make.

[83] Mussies's refutation contends that a *pneuma* can beget as a mate. He draws on Plutarch who, denying that male gods have sexual intercourse with and deposit semen in earthly women (*Quaestiones conviviales* 8.1.717–18), reports an Egyptian idea that a god can beget a child; for "it is not impossible for a divine spirit [*pneuma theou*] to approach a woman and engender the beginnings of birth" (*Numa* 4,4). Does Plutarch's use of *pneuma theou* against the background of the sexual proclivities of male gods really constitute an enlightening parallel for what Matt intended by *pneuma hagion* against a Hebraic background where the one God has no sexual identity—especially given the parallelism that Matt 28:19 establishes among the Father, the Son, and the Holy Spirit?

horrendously the stern OT conception that God was not a male who mated with women?

B. The Portrayal of Joseph. Before Mary and Joseph had come together (1:18: *synerchesthai*) and before he had sexual relations with her (1:25: *ginōskein*), it was found she was with child. On 124 above I pointed out that *synerchesthai* could mean to have sexual relations; but I maintained that here it meant to live together in the same house. In other words, the marriage (contract) had been effected (which is why Matt calls them husband and wife) but the second stage of moving in together had not. Stramare ("Annunciazione" 207–9) complains that this chronology is really in the eye of the commentator and that Matt prescinded from the various stages of marriage. He ignores the *paralambanein* in 1:20,24 that makes good sense only if Mary was not living with Joseph and he was being told "to take along" his wife to his home (129 above).

The scene is centered on Joseph's reaction to the news. In the light of Jane Schaberg's thesis explained above, Robin Mattison's observation ("God/Father" 201) is worth quoting: "Matthew is not concerned about Mary's role in an illegitimate begetting. The author is concerned with illegitimate decision-making on the part of Joseph. . . ."[84] Above (125–29) I laid out three interpretations of the difficult 1:19, which describes Joseph's attitude.[85] I opted for the interpretation that Joseph, having no knowledge that Mary had conceived through the Holy Spirit, naturally thought she had been with another man. Accordingly, being *dikaios* ("upright, just, or righteous" = Law-observant)[86] but not willing to expose Mary to public disgrace, he decided to divorce her quietly. Brawley ("Joseph" 69–72) makes a helpful contribution by pointing this out as literary irony. The evangelist and the readers know what Joseph does not know; yet he wants to do what is right according to the revelation he has, i.e., the Law. Only when he receives more direct revelation (from an angel) will he change the action he planned.[87] I

---

[84] See my disagreement in n. 65 above, however, on the precise focal point of the decision.

[85] Vicent Cernuda ("Domicilio") offers a variant. Joseph living at his home in Bethlehem hears that Mary living at Nazareth is pregnant. He is not informed as to the reason why and so he decides not to judge her and publicly repudiate her. Rather he will let her parents take care of the matter; and if she is not sent south to Bethlehem, the marriage contract will be automatically canceled. Despite its ingenuity this theory is simply another harmonization of Matt and Luke; there is nothing in Matt to suggest that either Joseph or Mary had ever been in Nazareth before the journey described in 2:23.

[86] It is true that Deut 22:23–27 (see below) does not speak of divorce and does not specify what the engaged husband of a woman violated against her will should do, but divorce could represent Joseph's more stringent respect for the Law's negative view of a woman who had relations with a man other than her husband. (The later Targum Pseudo-Jonathan 23 on the Deut passage specifies "her husband may put her away from him by a bill of divorce.") López Rosas ("San José") stresses that the just Joseph, by going beyond the limited specifications of the Law, contributed to the realization of God's saving plan.

[87] Brawley is correct in insisting that Joseph is called upright in relation to his decision to divorce Mary; his righteousness is not defective at that moment but his knowledge is. The second instance of righteousness (by implication, when he does what the angel told

deemed it no accident that other interpretations that had Joseph from the beginning know the true source of Mary's pregnancy were popular largely among Roman Catholics, for those interpretations reflect sensitivities attested at a later period about the sanctity that Joseph must have had, never thinking an unworthy thought of Mary—sensitivities that I respect but am unwilling without evidence to attribute to 1st-century authors. Luz (*Matthew* 119–20) dubs as the "Catholic" hypothesis the "reverential awe" interpretation whereby Joseph, knowing that Mary had conceived through the Holy Spirit, decided to separate from her out of awe/fear because she belonged to God. Indeed, largely Catholic support for the hypothesis has not been lacking since I wrote BBM: Romaniuk ("Joseph"), Stramare ("Son"), and Herranz Marco ("Substrato," appealing to Aramaic).[88] Calkins ("Justice" 13) resorts to this argument: "If God chose his most perfect creature to be the *Theotokos*, the God-bearer, would he have chosen as her husband someone who could not share or respect her 'secret'?"[89] The assumption that Matt knew 4th-century theology about the "Mother of God" is more than dubious; and invoking what God must surely have done is risky given the biblical principle that God's thoughts are not our thoughts. Cantwell ("Parentage") extends the knowledge of the virginal conception to the families of the two spouses[90] and heightens Joseph's fear of the numinous (Mary was guarded by the Spirit from profanation even as the demon guarded Tobiah's Sarah). Beyond the weakness of such argumentation, I hope that Luz's designation of this approach as "Catholic" does not take hold. I continue to judge the "reverential awe" approach as running against the clear sense of the text; the long Catholic commentaries by Gnilka and Muñoz Iglesias do not advocate

---

him to do) can be used by Matt to appeal to his audience: The new revelation in Christ leads them to a righteousness that may seem at times in conflict with the Law but is based on the same principle as the Law: God's will. This would be in harmony with Matt (13:52) which does not praise new rather than old but new (God's revelation in and about Jesus) and old (the Law).

[88] Outside Catholic circles, Van Elderen ("Significance" 10) thinks that "the divine role in Mary's pregnancy seems to be known to Joseph initially, possibly from Mary."

[89] Maintaining that Matt expected readers to know that Mary had told Joseph of her "secret" (the divine origins of her pregnancy), Calkins supposes that Matt and his readers knew something like the Lucan account of the annunciation to Mary. Challenging my objection that we have no evidence of that, he wrongly invokes the Vatican II document *Dei Verbum* (#19) as demanding the basic harmony of the two accounts. (See n. 6 above on this issue.) Within the Catholic context it is not contrary to reason to think that centuries-long church teaching might play a role in deciding a major christological issue stemming from the NT, e.g., whether Jesus was conceived virginally of Mary, or a significant issue in age-old mariological devotion, e.g., Mary-ever-virgin. But where does one find evidence that there is binding church teaching that can be used today to settle minor exegetical points, e.g., how did Matt intend to present Joseph's mindset? That expectation is a distortion of the proper relation between faith and reason.

[90] Ammassari ("Famiglia") contends that throughout Jesus' career all kept a reserved silence about his conception. To explain the relationship between Joseph and Mary he calls upon later Christian examples of celibate marriages.

it; and at least among American Catholic scholars trained in the last twenty years I suspect it has very little following.

The proposal that Joseph's righteousness consisted of his willingness to obey the Law (127 above) has been strengthened through modifications brought to my explanation by Bourke, Dubarle, and Tosato. If we consider Deut 22:23–27 rather than 22:13–21, Joseph need not have thought Mary was culpably pregnant through adultery, for she could have been the innocent victim of rape. Presumably his decision to divorce Mary quietly meant that he would not demand a trial to determine the cause of the pregnancy (a trial perhaps usually demanded if money was to be returned), and so he would implicitly offer the father of Mary's child the opportunity to marry her. I pointed on 128 above to an Aramaic act of marriage-repudiation from Murabba'at (between a Joseph and a Mary); but MIE 4.164 has made more extended use of it, stressing that it is a good example of a private repudiation where no cause is offered and seemingly no tribunal is involved. Thus the objection to Matt's portrayal of quiet divorce on the basis of later rabbinic evidence of how repudiations had to be delivered[91] may not be applicable this early.

C. *"He did not know her until" (Matt 1:25): Other Children of Mary?*
The text affirms that Joseph had no sexual relations with Mary before Jesus' birth.[92] The issue of whether, after that birth, Joseph and Mary had children lies outside the scope of a commentary on the Gospel infancy narratives. Nevertheless, the divided stance of Christians on the issue causes it to be frequently discussed. Above (132) I contended that Matt 1:25 does not settle the issue, and I explained the various positions about the "brothers and sisters" of Jesus held in antiquity and today. Gilles (*Frères*) contends that the NT offers no justification for thinking that Jesus was the only son of Mary. However, a book done by Protestants and Catholics together (MNT 72) recognized that the continued virginity of Mary after the birth of Jesus is not a question directly raised by the NT, but once subsequent church history focused attention on the exact family relationship of the "brothers" and "sisters" of Jesus, "it cannot be said that the NT identifies them *without doubt* as blood brothers and sisters and hence as children of Mary." A Roman Catholic, Meier ("Brothers" 27) thinks that "from a purely philological

---

[91] López Rosas ("San José" 190) raises the possibility that Mishna *Giṭṭin* 8.1 offers a somewhat less public form of divorce: If someone throws a letter of divorce to his wife in her house, or her courtyard, or her lap, or her work-basket, then she is divorced.

[92] K. Luke ("Luke 2:14") points to the development of v. 26 in the Syriac tradition. Drawing on the Koran he posits that Tatian wrote in the Diatessaron: "In chastity he dwelt with her." Ephraem, commenting on the Diatessaron, wrote that the sight of Mary never aroused concupiscence in Joseph; but Ephraem assumes that Joseph and Mary entered marriage, a step of which Tatian, an Encratite, would not have approved.

and historical point of view, the most probable opinion is that the brothers and sisters of Jesus were his siblings."[93] He never makes clear whether he thinks that the Roman Catholic theological position that Mary remained a virgin all her life is so dogmatically affirmed that it solves for Catholics this issue of further children, which historical criticism cannot resolve with certitude.[94] He does affirm, however, that the thrust of historical criticism should cause Catholics to reflect on "the hierarchy of truths" (terminology of Vatican II) and recognize the perpetual virginity of Mary to be an issue lower in that index—an issue on which churches united on more central issues might be able to tolerate diverse views.

Meier spends much of the article devastating the thesis (held in the Western Church from the 4th century on) that these "brothers and sisters" were cousins of Jesus, a thesis that in truth faces enormous difficulties. In *Marginal* (324) Meier dismisses virtually without discussion the earlier portrayal in the *Protevangelium of James* that identified these figures as children of Joseph by a previous marriage. He simply characterizes the *Protevangelium* as "a wildly imaginative folk narrative that is outrageously inaccurate about things Jewish." That is true, but Vorster ("Annunciation" 42) wisely warns that it "does not imply that the story is completely worthless for historical construction."[95] Nor does it exempt us from the duty of examining a tradition about the "brothers and sisters" circulating in the first half of the 2nd century[96] that is surprisingly independent of the surface indications of the NT on this issue and cannot be derived from them (as can much else in the *Protevangelium*). Meier is more thorough in "Brothers" (5–6, 27), recognizing that the *Protevangelium* solution (also accepted by Epiphanius) is held by most Eastern Christians, has occasional Protestant support, and is not irrational.[97] Incidentally, he is quite correct in

[93] This is a stronger affirmation than J. A. Fitzmyer makes in *A Christological Catechism* (2nd ed.; New York: Paulist, 1990), 38: On the basis of the NT evidence alone the possibility of kinsmen in the broad sense rather than siblings "is not to be ruled out." It is also stronger than my affirmation in *Responses to 101 Questions on the Bible* (New York: Paulist, 1990), 93: The NT evidence "might well lead to the conclusion that these were Mary's children, if there were no evidence to the contrary."

[94] Earlier in Germany there was church reaction to the contention of R. Pesch (*Das Markusevangelium* [2 vols.; HTKNT 2; 1976], 1.322–25) that the brothers and sisters of Jesus mentioned in Mark 6:3 were children of Mary, but it never came to a point of official condemnation.

[95] Vorster (51–52) would also demand nuance in the judgment that the *Protevangelium* was written to glorify Mary; for him the purpose of the story is rather "a retelling of the birth story of Jesus from the perspective of his mother."

[96] For the treatment of Mary and her virginity in 2nd-century apocrypha, see the bibliography entries under Bagatti, Kretschmar, and Vorster.

[97] J. Beutler ("*adelphos*" in *Exegetisches Wörterbuch zum NT* 1.68), reporting that E. Stauffer opts for the *Protevangelium* explanation of the brothers, comments that it is possible but not compelling.

pointing out that this would make the brothers "stepbrothers," rather than "half-brothers" as I and others have mistakenly called them.

§6 Date of Jesus' Birth (before Herod's Death), the Magi, the Star, Herod (Matt 2:1–12)

The whole of chap. 2 deals with the aftermath of Jesus' birth in a context in which a geographical progression from Bethlehem[98] through Egypt to Nazareth plays a major role (53–54 above). Using a structuralist approach, F. Martin ("Naître") offers a dramatic (but debatable) presentation of factors in the chapter. I list some of his observations and invite readers to judge for themselves, for I may be too pedestrian to appreciate them. It is significant, according to Martin, that Herod is immobile while the magi are mobile. The appearance of the magi looking for the King of the Jews shakes up both scriptural and paternity expectations. The gifts they present constitute a loss for the pagans before they point significantly to the Messiah. That God's Son is called out of Egypt means a loss for that country of what it could have possessed.

Above (178) I divided 2:1–12 into two scenes: vv. 1–6 and 7–12. Schmahl ("Magier") uses the "pay homage" of 2:2,8,11 to divide 2:1–12 into four parts. Even without that one can subdivide according to storyflow into 2:1–2, 3–6, 7–8, 9–12 (magi/Herod/Herod/magi). Schmahl's comments highlight that the major contrast in this section is between the pious Gentile magi and the wicked Jewish leaders (Herod, chief priests, scribes)—not between the Jesus of the genealogy and Herod, as we shall see proposed below under D.

A. Date of Jesus' Birth (before Herod's death in 4 B.C.). According to Matt, Jesus was born "in the days of Herod the king" (and Luke 1:5 places the annunciation of JBap's conception "in the days of Herod, king of Judea"). Above (166–67) there was only a brief note pertaining to the date of Herod the Great's death: "While other possibilities are 5 B.C. and 1 B.C., the best evidence favors March/April 4 B.C. [= 750 A.U.C.]." I do not have a major commitment to that date, but recent discussions offer no compelling reason to change despite some contrary voices. (Were there not a strong desire to establish the historicity of various NT indications about Jesus' age during the public ministry, one suspects that theses of a later date would not be proposed.) On 166 above I found convincing Barnes's refutation of the thesis of Filmer that Herod's death should be dated in 1 B.C., a dating now defended by Thorley ("When")[99] and E. L. Martin (*Birth*; "Nativity"), and rejected

---

[98] On the historicity of birth at Bethlehem, I shall report briefly on recent opinion in §14D below.

[99] Jesus was born in 2 B.C.—a claim he justifies by Luke's census and Matt's star. For Luke's census see pp. 666–68 below.

by Bernegger ("Affirmation");[100] Johnson ("Eight");[101] Hoehner ("Date"); and Maier ("Date"). In particular, E. L. Martin assumes Matthean historicity (not dealing with the issue of verisimilitude; see 190 above) and harmonizes Matt with Luke, which he assumes to be equally historical. Using Rev 12:1–5 as a reference to the physical birth (rather than to the birth of the Messiah through passion and resurrection), Martin has Jesus born Sept. 11, 3 B.C., just after sunset at the beginning of Rosh Hashanah.[102] Jupiter rose as a morning "star" in the East in conjunction with Venus on Aug. 12, 3 B.C., and there were continued astronomical phenomena for the next 18 months. The magi presented gifts on Dec. 25, 2 B.C. when Jupiter stopped over Bethlehem in a meridian position in the constellation of the Virgin. Thus as Jesus began his ministry in Oct./Nov. A.D. 28, he was two months past his thirtieth birthday, precisely as in Luke 3:1,23. It is regrettable that Martin mars his thesis with such extravagantly precise hypotheses, reflecting overhistoricizing. I shall return to the issue of dating below when I discuss the star.

B. The Magi. Part of the post-1976 literature on this subject, some of it acerbic, has concerned their historicity. Yamauchi ("Episode" 22) laments that Roman Catholic scholars (he mentions me as an example) are now accepting interpretations that were earlier proposed by antisupernatural critics of Christianity.[103] I would ask two questions: First, for modern Catholic scholarship to gain Yamauchi's approval, would he have us accept as logical a *post hoc, propter hoc* attitude? That could reduce us to silence since almost every critical biblical position was earlier advanced by skeptics. Most of my coreligionists who use biblical criticism are perfectly aware of its origins but accept as wise the attitude of the church catholic since the time it first encountered Greek philosophy: Christians should put at the service of the gospel every truth or valid insight available, no matter the viewpoints of those who first phrased it. Second, in reference to my own position, although Yamauchi cites BBM 117 where I state that the immediate inspiration for the magi story came from the account of Balaam in Num 22–24,[104] it would have

---

[100] Like Barnes before him, Bernegger leaves open the possibility that Herod died earlier than 4 B.C., specifically in Dec. 5 B.C.

[101] He directs his arguments against Martin. Fitzmyer (*Luke* 1.401) opts for the 4 B.C. death.

[102] Maier ("Date" 126–30), who fixes the birth of Jesus in 5 B.C., presents some interesting arguments for November as the month. Wojciechowski ("Mt 2,20") would have Jesus born in 8–7 B.C.

[103] In the other direction Luz (*Matthew* 132, n. 28) detects "a peculiar neorationalism in the endeavor to save the historicity of the narrative." At the root of the problem I would find the erroneous supposition that scriptural narrative must be historical—a supposition that restricts the divine freedom to use various types of literature to guide God's people.

[104] Marín Heredia ("Más" 323–25) emphasizes the Balaam background. While not rejecting it, Luz (*Matthew* 131) states: "Literal reminiscences of the story of Balaam in Numbers 22–24 are almost completely missing in 2:1–12." He admits that Moses traditions probably have fructified the story; yet are there literal reminiscences of the Moses story

helped his readers if he had also informed them that I never said that there is no historical substratum in the magi story,[105] and that on 188 I refused specifically to dismiss the history of the magi story "simply on the grounds that the events are supernatural; for a presupposition that miracles are impossible is unscientific." It would have helped *me* if, in his otherwise informative article, Yamauchi answered even one of the three obstacles to historicity that I mentioned on 188–89 above (similar to obstacles detected by Luz, *Matthew* 132–33). Instead he has chosen to stress that astrology was known in the ancient world and among Jews. This argument shows only verisimilitude, i.e., whether writing fact or fiction, Matt composed a story that had a plausible context. Yamauchi is not alone; with less subtlety Firpo (*Problema*) relegates virtually all doubts about historicity to imitation of Strauss's rationalism and elevates unprovable harmonizations to the level of the factual. Salvoni ("Visita") is conservative but admits that the account is not pure history. Couffignal ("Conte") recognizes that the magi/Herod story has the characteristics of the birth-of-the-hero and wicked-ruler stories (above 227, n. 39) marked by a folkloric atmosphere.

Aus ("Magi") develops an interesting proposal involving the Persian king Cyrus that might be added to my supposition of a Balaam background.[106] Isa 45:1 entitles Cyrus: "the Lord's Anointed" (*Māšîaḥ*, *Christos*). Through him all people from the rising of the sun to its setting are to know the one God (45:6); and (45:14) as a service to God the wealth of Egypt and of Ethiopia, and the Sabeans, "men of stature,"[107] are to be brought. The geographical names relate this passage to Isa 60:6, where from Midian, Ephah, and Sheba come gold and incense, and bearers proclaim the good news (LXX: *euaggelein*) of the salvation of the Lord. Herodotus (*History* 1.204) tells us that having consulted magi about the meaning of his dream visions, King Astyages of the Medes tried to kill the male child (Cyrus) whom his daughter bore to Cambyses the Persian because the magi had predicted that the child would be king. If this development were known to Matt and his readers, this might be another component in the shaping of Matt's magi story.[108]

---

in 2:1–12 either? With the exception of the quote (2:20) from Exod 4:19 Matt's echoes of Joseph (the patriarch), Moses, and Balaam are subtly blended into a substratum. I explicitly refused to use late Jewish traditions in regard to Balaam (194 above), and so I am surprised that Luz thinks that the lateness of the traditions is an argument against my position. What is certainly early but not mentioned by Luz is that Philo called Balaam a *magus* even as he applied that term to those who advised the Pharaoh against Moses.

[105] Léon-Dufour (Review) in an otherwise favorable evaluation of BBM, finds it too skeptical about the magi, for the story is not impossible. Actually that is what I affirmed in n. 28 on 189 above.

[106] See also DAICC 258–59; Jesus recapitulates not only the experience of Israel but also that of "the hero with a thousand faces."

[107] Aus would read *mdh* ("stature") as *mdy* (Media); thus Medes come.

[108] Above under §5A I rejected Mussies's suggestion that Matt's "begotten of the Holy Spirit" might have been influenced by stories wherein a male god or divine spirit (Plutarch) engendered a child of an earthly woman. For a pious Jewish writer stories about pagan

The magi in subsequent Christian piety (197–200 above) remain the subject of continued interest. Daum (*Königin*) surveys art, legend, and archaeology. Duchesne-Guillemin ("Wise") concentrates on explaining why the magi are illustrated in some Western art as a young man, an adult, and an old man, pointing to a tradition preserved by Persian magi that Zoroaster would come back to life in the person of three sons and to a tradition about the Greek god of eternity, Aion, who could be represented as a child, an adult, and an old man. Charbel ("Mt") posits Nabatean Petra as the home of the magi—a specification of the Arabia hypothesis (169–70 above). To the usual background of the fulfillment citation in Matt 2:6 (Mic 5:1[2]; 2 Sam 5:2), Salvoni ("Vaticinio") and Heater ("Matthew") would add Gen 49:10, where Micah's (LXX) *archōn* and Matt's *hēgoumenos* ("ruler") are in parallelism. Petrotta ("Even Closer") finds that Matt's changes from Micah were based on an oral rather than a graphic reading, with Matt's preference for "rulers" in line 2 (184–85 above) a deliberate change from MT "clans/thousands" to emphasize Jesus' superiority over his predecessors in the Davidic genealogy.

C. The Star. There continues to be abundant literature devoted to this subject. Charlesworth ("Jewish") has gathered the evidence for Jewish interest in astrology (also Yamauchi, "Episode" 28–39). Above (195) I maintained that with the star, Matt echoed biblical symbolism (Balaam's vision of the Davidic star rising from Jacob[109]). Yet I noted that Matt's hearers/readers with Greco-Roman background would not have found bizarre a story where the birth of the King of the Jews was heralded by a star; for there were classical instances where heavenly bodies presaged great men and events (170). Küchler ("Wir") has enlarged that picture. The star was associated with depictions of the Dioscuri (Castor and Pollux, who were looked on as saviors) and of Alexander the Great; it was imprinted on the coins of Julius Caesar, Augustus, and Herod the Great. Thus, Küchler contends, readers of various backgrounds could have understood the appearance of a star as a claim that Jesus was king, nay even emperor.

Pp. 171–73 above reported that the three leading contenders for identification as Matt's star were a supernova, a comet, and a planetary conjunction;[110] and that still remains true. As evidence for a **nova/**

---

gods that were anathema to monotheism would be very different from a story about Cyrus, who remained an exalted figure for Josephus, the pseudepigrapha, and rabbinical literature (as Aus documents).

[109] Deichmann ("Erscheinung") points to an article that I overlooked: E. Kirschbaum, "Der Prophet Balaam und die Anbetung der Weisen," *Römische Quartalschrift* 49 (1954), 129–71. It shows the frequency of the Balaaam interpretation among the Church Fathers. Deichmann examines another patristic interpretation wherein the star was interpreted as an angel who guided the magi.

[110] Boa and Proctor (*Return*) make a proposal for the star I overlooked—a UFO! Sachs and Walker ("Kepler's") have meticulously examined what Kepler proposed astronomi-

supernova in the approximate time before Jesus' birth (previously lacking), Clark ("Astronomical") cites a Han-dynasty Chinese astronomical notice describing in the eastern portion of the heavens a phenomenon that appeared during March/April of 5 B.C., and he judges this to have been a nova.[111] Since a nova would have brightened quickly, it could have made an impression on the magi.

Phipps ("Magi") claims that the appearance of Halley's **comet** in A.D. 66 made an impression on the mind of the evangelist, for that was also the year when King Tiridates and his companions (called magi) came to Rome from Armenia. The evangelist may also have spoken with aged people who remembered that the comet had come in 12 B.C. during the reign of Herod the Great, and so a story sparked by events of the evangelist's own time could easily have been adapted as a setting for the birth of Jesus. Humphreys ("Star"), rejecting all other interpretations,[112] also opts for a comet, but not Halley's. He thinks that the above-mentioned Chinese astronomers were referring to a comet in 5 B.C. The planetary conjunctions of 7 and 6 B.C. alerted the magi to the coming birth, but they did not set out until the comet of 5 B.C. appeared. Humphreys (404) gives a "new chronology": Jesus was born between March 9 and May 4 in 5 B.C. (more probably April); the magi arrived between April 20 and June 15 that year.

As for the **planets** E. L. Martin (*Star*) thinks of conjunctions of Venus and Jupiter on Aug. 12, 3 B.C. (appearing like a morning star) and on June 17, 2 B.C. (like an evening star), with Jupiter appearing over Bethlehem on Dec. 25, 2 B.C. Involved with Jupiter was Regulus, the king star, which appeared to gain a halo. Making a different use of planets, Ferrari-D'Occhieppo ("Star") suggests that the magi came from the last descendants of the Old Marduk priesthood at the shrine of the god in Babylon who had now become syncretistic, incorporating worship of Ahuramazda and Yahweh and influenced by the messianic hopes of the Hebrew prophets. They observed on Sept. 15, 7 B.C. the planetary conjunction of Jupiter and Saturn.[113] On Nov. 12 of that year, as they

---

cally about the possible star phenomena of 14–4 B.C.—a study that sent me to check with relief that 171 above was accurate on the subject.

111 The word used (*hui-hsing*) normally refers to a comet, although there is an example when it describes what we know to have been a supernova. Because no motion is traced in the notice, Clark argues that it was not a comet. There is also a Korean notice of a *po-hsing* (again a word that generally refers to a comet) in 4 B.C. If there is no inaccuracy in the date, Clark theorizes that it might be another, later sighting of the same phenomenon.

112 A nova/supernova would not have seemed to move through the sky; a conjunction of planets would not have looked like a star appearing at a specific time or standing over Bethlehem.

113 Not Mars; see 172 above. Hughes (*Star*) also opts for a conjunction of Saturn and Jupiter in Pisces that dates Jesus' birth to Tuesday, Sept. 15, 7 B.C. Yet Clark ("Astronomical" 447) challenges that date; the conjunctions of the two planets in 7 B.C. were May 22, Oct. 6, and Dec. 1. He also maintains that the conjunctions would not have been spectacular and attracted notice. Sachs and Walker ("Kepler's") stress that the conjunction was not close enough to give the appearance of a single star and that a reliable

went from Jerusalem to Bethlehem, Jupiter appeared 50° above the horizon in the direction they were going (and thus apparently going before them). Shortly after Saturn became visible, the axis of a cone of zodiacal light pointed to a northwestern hill of Bethlehem (and thus apparently the star stood still). A simplified form of the technically written report of these magi was preserved in Aramaic among the family records of Joseph's relatives and became the source of Matt. The form of the *Protevangelium of James* (21:1–22:1) preserved in the 4th-century Bodmer papyrus may have more direct access to the technical report, for it correctly mentions plural "stars" (= comets) in relation to Jesus' birth. Given such a plethora of imaginative suggestions, I must judge that there is no greater consensus now than there was when BBM was written as to what astronomy/astrology can tell us about the star.

At times the relation between biblical scholars and astronomers (or those who invoke astronomy) are strained and phrased in language that approaches patronizing from both sides. Strobel's short book (*Stern*) makes a great deal of the astronomical phenomena of 7 B.C.; but in "Astronomie, Astrologie, Theologie" in *Theologische Rundschau* 54 (1989), 422–26, H.-H. Voigt complains that Strobel too simplistically supposes that Matt 2:1–12 is recounting historical events. And many biblical scholars look on the suggestions in the preceding paragraph as fodder for "Sunday Supplement" features at Christmastime. On the other side, astronomers often present their new insight with the assurance that this will show the skeptical biblical scholar that the Matthean account is historical. Ferrari-D'Occhieppo ("Star" 41) mentions "the view of those theologians who assumed that the story of the Magi as a whole was nothing but a pious myth" and implicitly sets out to challenge it.

It might help the discussion if the range of historical possibilities were spelled out. *Really no one, including the astronomers, takes everything in the Matthean account as literal history.* Matt says that the magi saw the star (not planets, not a comet) of the King of the Jews at its rising (or in the East), and that it went before them from Jerusalem to Bethlehem and came to rest over where the child was. In recent literature I have not found an astronomical proposal that fits that literally. If we leave aside literal exactitude, and allow some type of likeness, symbolism, or poetic rephrasing in the Matthean account,[114] as even astronomers must, then there are possibilities ranging from substantially factual, to partially factual, to totally theologically creative.

---

collation of four MSS of the Babylonian "almanac" for the period does not pay unusual attention to it.

[114] MIE 4.211, very conservative about historicity, states that the impression of movement is a literary artifice.

Let me discuss three: (1) Very substantial Matthean facticity: An astronomical phenomenon (supernova, planets, comet) took place at the time of Jesus' birth which foreign astrologers interpreted as predicting the birth of a Jewish king, and they came to Jerusalem during Herod's reign to find the child. Herod was upset and killed some male children at Bethlehem. This is possible, but to maintain it one must face the obstacles I listed on 188–89 above. (2) Partial Matthean facticity: After the crucifixion and resurrection, as Christians came to recognize in faith what God had done in Jesus, they reflected on his birth against the background of the OT and Jewish expectations. An astronomical phenomenon had taken place sometime before his birth, and this was interpreted as the fulfillment of the star that Balaam said would rise. Perhaps some who acclaimed the birth of Mary's child were interpreted as magi in light of the stories of Balaam, and possibly of Tiridates and/ or of Cyrus. (3) Total theological creativity by Matt or his source: Stories of the sort just listed gave rise to the whole of the star/magi/ Herod story. Personally I do not find (1) plausible; I think that (2) is quite possible for parts of the story (e.g., the star) and that (3) is quite possible for other parts of the story (e.g., Herod killing the children; flight to Egypt). Those are my opinions; I do *not know* how factual or historical is Matt's story of the magi, the star, and Herod's slaughter of the children; and given the state of the evidence, *neither does anyone else, whether biblical scholar or astronomer*. Claims that astronomy has proved the historicity of the magi/star story are exaggerated, for any astronomical discovery can be fitted into explanation (2) as well as into explanation (1).

D. Herod. Matt's extremely hostile portrayal is obvious; clearly the evangelist regards Jesus, not Herod, as King of the Jews. Yet I have hesitation about the thesis of Gubler ("Wo") that the main point of the passage was a choice between Jesus and Herod. She argues that in rebuilding the Temple as if he were another Solomon, Herod was laying claim to David's heritage, while Jesus, born in Bethlehem, David's birthplace, was the true Davidic heir. Probably I did not do sufficient justice to Matt 2:2 on 170 above, where I simply pointed out that what I translated as "the newborn King of the Jews" could be translated "he who has been born [namely,] the King of the Jews."[115] I remain uncertain, however, whether one can use "born the King" as a strong contrast with Herod who was not born a king. Matt wrote about one hundred years after Herod became king; how many of Matt's readers would have

---

[115] C. Burchard (ZNW 69 [1978], 143–45) argues that since the journey of the magi took time after they had seen the star and since Herod massacres all the boys of two years of age or under (2:16), Jesus is scarcely newborn. The term could cover a wide range, however.

known the origins of the reign of Herod the Great? In reading Matt 2 would they have immediately thought of Herod's building the Temple? In the last decade while writing BDM, I came to recognize that Matt's depiction of Herod the Great's hostility toward Jesus was functionally parallel to Luke's depiction of Herod Antipas' hostility toward Jesus (Luke 13:31; Acts 4:25–28). One may well wonder whether early Christian hearers of the Gospel stories kept the various Herods distinct.

Horsley ("Liberating"; *Liberation*) would find in the Jesus/Herod contrast a nascent revolutionary confrontation. Jesus' birth exacerbated conflict, eliciting violence against innocent people. This thesis becomes exaggerated, in my judgment, when he compares it to the violence exercised by South American governments against campesinos, etc. Certainly people thus oppressed can find the Matthean story meaningful and identify with the victims; but in the Matthean mindset Herod has the children killed not because the people of Bethlehem belong to a social stratum that threatens him but because he fears Jesus. Modernizing the sociopolitical situation of Jesus' time is often a hindrance in discerning what the author wished to convey to his first hearers/listeners (even if that is not the only level of meaning with which we need to be concerned). I judge quite exaggerated the proposal of Blomberg ("Liberation") that the main thesis of Matt 1–2 is the legitimacy of Jesus vs. the illegitimacy of Herod as king. He creates this contrast by a (confusing) treatment of the genealogy, where he is intrigued by Schaberg's thesis that Jesus is illegitimate—a thesis that he finally rejects but from which he wants to save the suspicion of illegitimacy. As I have argued above, there is little or nothing to suggest illegitimacy in the genealogy.

E. Individual Items. The exact role that Matt envisions for the star in 2:2,9–10 continues to be discussed (see the top of 174 above). Segalla (*Storia* 15) proposes that there were two different pre-Matthean strains, one in which the star was a sign (2:1–2), the other in which it was a guide (2:9b–11); Broer ("Jesusflucht" 81) would see at least in the present account this twofold role for the star. MIE 4.211, however, rejects the twofold functioning: The star is never said to guide the magi; at most it accompanies them. On 184–87 above I discussed the citation of Micah 5:1 and II Sam 5:2 in Matt 2:5–6, observing that the Micah portion matched neither the standard Hebrew nor the LXX text. Petrotta ("Closer") argues that the divergences were not of a textual origin but represent Matthean theologizing. In a second article ("Even Closer") he argues that Matt has done his theologizing by playing on Hebrew alliterations (see bottom of 185 above).

The issue of "the house" in 2:11 is a good test of methodology. Matt has never mentioned Joseph and Mary being anywhere but Bethlehem; he has told us that Joseph took Mary (home) in 1:24; he tells in 2:11 that the magi came into the house where they found the child with Mary his mother; and in 2:22–23 he explains that the reason that the family did not return to Bethlehem and went instead to Nazareth was apprehension about Archelaus. Yet MIE 4.212 judges it very adventurous to affirm that the house was the habitual domicile of the Holy Family; it prefers the idea that since the magi took time to come, some relative or friend had offered hospitality to the family in his house. Obviously MIE is assuming something for which there is not an iota of evidence in Matt, namely, the Lucan story of Joseph and Mary dwelling in Nazareth and coming as strangers to Bethlehem and there being no place for them at the lodgings. I would contend that it is exegesis faithful to what Matt reports to interpret the house in Matt 2:11 as the habitual dwelling place, and not only adventurous but also bad methodology to interpret Matt by something that he never mentions. Besides the background for the gold and frankincense of the magi in Isa 60:6 (and Ps 72:10–11—see 187–88 above), MIE 4.214 would explain the myrrh with a reference to Ps 45:9, where the king (perhaps reinterpreted as the Messiah) has robes fragrant with myrrh.

§7. Slaughter at Bethlehem; Flight to Egypt (Matt 2:13–23)

In the pattern suggested for Matt 2 on 53–54 above, I pointed out that vv. 1–12 relate to the "where" (*Ubi:* Bethlehem) of Jesus' birth, while vv. 13–23 relate to the "whence" (*Unde:* eventually leading to Nazareth) of Jesus' destiny set in motion by Herod's hostile reaction. Graves ("Story") stresses the guiding import of the geographical locations (Egypt, Bethlehem, Nazareth) in each of the formula citations of 2:13–23. France ("Herod") and Maier ("Infant") argue for the historicity of the basic account.[116] On 225–28 (also 204) above, I have listed all the evidence they cite; most of it supports verisimilitude, not historicity; and so my opinion of *non liquet* has not changed. Luz (*Matthew* 147) points out correctly that theodicy (God saving Jesus but not the innocent children) is not an issue that seems to occur to Matt here; rather he is concerned with the victory of Jesus over Herod, who cannot be a true king if he kills Israel's children. The parallel between the killing of the Bethlehem children by Herod and the killing of the Hebrew children by the pharaoh (with the main character escaping in each case) is easily recognizable. Broer ("Jesusflucht") points to another parallel that shows how widely the story could have been understood: Suetonius (*Augustus* 94.3) reports that some months before the birth of Augustus

---

[116] Wojciechowski ("Mt 2,20") associates the slaughter of the children with the period just after 7 B.C. when Herod the Great slew his own sons Alexander and Aristobulus.

a wondrous sign seen in Rome predicted the coming birth of one who would become king. The Senate tried to prevent that by ordering that no child born in the coming year should be reared, but the order was sidetracked because too many senators whose wives were pregnant hoped that the promised child might be theirs.

Using the flight into Egypt but combining Matt harmonistically with Luke and modernizing the picture, Bruce ("Flight") points to Joseph as a model for fathers: Loyally he endures anxiety even though he cannot foresee where things will end; he is innovative and not immobilized by complexities; and he does his duty even though he does not fully understand the reasons. Taking into account both apocryphal (203 above) and patristic material, Brändle ("Huida") argues that Joseph is more than the obedient protector of the child, for the revelation to him reveals the mystery of Christ.

Luz (*Matthew* 145), who speaks of an "unhistorical Bethlehem tradition" underlying the narrative, speculates that Jesus' stay in Egypt might be a historical kernel because the oldest form of Jewish tradition on this score, involving the adult Jesus as a day laborer in Egypt, does not seem dependent on Matt. However, I find it hard to isolate that item from the polemical context in which it is set (Origen, *Celsus* 1.28,38), namely, that Jesus learned magic in Egypt. It could represent an echo of the Gospel picture of Jesus or his father as a carpenter. A new and implausible suggestion about the going of Jesus to Egypt is made by M. Smith:[117] Jesus was in fact a magician; but to counter the Jewish polemic that he went to Egypt to learn magic, Matt has created the story that he was taken there as a child, implicitly before he could learn. If Matt were primarily answering such polemics, why would he not simply have denied that Jesus was ever in Egypt?

Above (214–16, 219–22), joining many other interpreters, I expressed the view that in 2:13–23 Matt is presenting Jesus as symbolically reliving the OT experience of Joseph going to Egypt and Israel returning in the Exodus. Advocating the basic historicity of the narrative, MIE 4.266–67 would refute this suggestion by contending that Matt understood Hosea 11:1 as a reference to the place from which God called *to* His Son. Yet a glance at OT commentaries shows wide support for the interpretation that Hosea was referring to the Exodus from Egypt; and not without reason from ancient times has it been suggested that Matt was reading Hosea 11:1 through Num 24:8, "God led him out of Egypt," a passage in Balaam's oracle that clearly refers to the Exodus. It is significant that Matt's first reference to Jesus as God's Son, which comes in the Hosea reference, sets him in the history of God's people (DAICC 263): "Son" is a divine title, but we are far here from a metaphysical approach.

[117] *Jesus the Magician* (New York: Harper & Row, 1978).

As for the citation of Jer 31:15 in Matt 2:17–18, DAICC (267) may be right in suspecting that Jer 31:31–34, which speaks of "a new covenant," had riveted Christian attention on chap. 31. Besides being mentioned in a negative setting in the Jer 31:15 passage, Ramah is shown in terror in Isa 10:29 and is the site for a warning trumpet in Hosea 5:8, so that it may have been considered "a city of sadness *par excellence*" (DAICC 269).

The plural in Matt 2:20, "Those who were seeking the child's life are dead," is explicable as an echo of the plural in the Moses account of Exod 4:19; and in the storyline the plural is meant to remind readers that the chief priests and scribes of the people cooperated with Herod in 2:4. Wojciechowski ("Mt 2,20"), recalling that Herod's son Antipater was executed five days before his father's death, would identify the father and son as the "those"; but again I must ask whether Matt's readers would have understood such an arcane reference. See 598 above for Oberweis's suggestion of why Matt 2:22 states that Archelaus "was king" over Judea.

The claim that "the prophets [plural]" said "He will be called a *Nazōraios*" (2:23) continues to puzzle.[118] Tatum ("Matthew") warns of mistranslation: not "He will be called a Nazorean," but "that he should be called . . ."—a qualified quotation. He correctly sees a bifocal reference to both Nazareth and an OT passage. Rüger ("Nazareth") traces *Nazōraios* and *Nazarēnos* to the Hebrew place name *Nāṣĕrat*, which was related to the *nēṣer* of Isa 11:1.[119] Ahirika interprets "the prophets" as Isa 11:1 (*nēṣer*) and Judg 13:5 (*nāzîr*), while Pritz ("He") thinks of all the prophets (the [d] hypothesis on 208 above), explaining that the anticipation of the Messiah (designated here by *Nazōraios*) was a unifying factor. Pesch ("Er wird") would see this final fulfillment citation as the summary of all the messianic expectation in the genealogy and the preceding narrative.

THE LUCAN INFANCY NARRATIVE

§9 General Observations

In this section of BBM I discussed the Lucan Gospel in general before I turned to overall issues in the infancy narrative (the Lucan Preface, historicity, function, sources, and structure).

---

[118] See 207–13, 223–25 above. Allan ("He shall"), citing Judg 13:2–7, and Taylor ("Jesus"), citing Isa 49:6, resort to views mentioned on 210, 213 above.

[119] See 211 above. Drawing on the *nēṣer* in Isa 11:1 and contending that the primary meaning of *Nazōraios* is related to Davidic descent, Pixner ("Maria" 45–49) proposes that the place name Nazara/Nazareth stems from a clan of Davidids who came back from Babylon at the end of the 2nd century B.C. and settled there. Pritz ("He") finds an echo of *Nôṣĕrî*, a Talmudic designation of Jesus, used in the plural for Christians, and of *nēṣer*, especially as used in Isa 11:1—the same three consonants appear in each, and TabBab *Sanhedrin* 43a associates Isa 11:1 with a disciple of Jesus.

A. The Lucan Gospel. Studying the infancy narrative does not require a full consideration of the Synoptic problem since Mark is not involved. In their recent commentaries both Fitzmyer and Bovon accept the two-source hypothesis (Luke drawing on Mark and Q), a view that I also found the most workable in my work on the passion (BDM §2). Implicit in that approach is that Luke and Matt wrote independently of each other; see Fitzmyer, *Luke* 1.73–75 for the difficulties of assuming otherwise.

In recent literature only a few scholars have tried to maintain that Luke's infancy account drew on Matt's despite the enormous diversity between the two.[120] Their thesis is difficult to discuss since it is largely an exercise of extraordinary imagination. The most recent effort in that direction is Goulder's *Luke*. Previously[121] I pointed out the implausibility of Goulder's proposals in the idiosyncratic book that he wrote on the Matthean Gospel (*Midrash*), viz., that Matt had meditated on Paul's letters and wrote his Gospel as a lectionary based on the Jewish liturgical calendar. The implication of that book (which I deemed "a high-quality diversion") was that the Matthean infancy narrative was almost entirely the fruit of the evangelist's imagination, e.g., Matt created the list of Jesus' postexilic ancestors by perusing the OT and picking out names that might have interesting symbolic value because of roles played (in preexilic times) by those who bore those names, e.g., Eliakim and Zadok. The new book makes the Lucan infancy narrative the fruit of that evangelist's imagination exercised in meditation on Matt's infancy narrative through expanded OT motifs. One might well surmise that two such remarkably imaginative Gospel writers are mirror reflections of the imaginative Goulder himself. The larger Goulder thesis that Luke composed his Gospel by juggling Mark, Matt, and a midrashic reading of OT passages has come under devastating refutation by Downing, "Paradigm," who has studied the use of sources by ancient writers and finds none remotely resembling Goulder's Luke in procedure. Indeed Downing maintains that Luke's interweaving of passages from a scroll copy of Matt as postulated by Goulder is almost a physical impossibility—there would be no way to have the whole of Matt's Sermon on the Mount visible at the same time as Goulder's thesis demands. For Downing (35), Goulder's thesis supposes "an apparently ordinary first-century writer's ability and willingness to ignore simple and rational contemporary compositional conventions and scribal techniques and to pioneer new, complex, and self-defeating ones all his own." In evaluat-

---

[120] See J. Drury, *Tradition and Design in Luke's Gospel* (London: DLT, 1976), 122–25, and Wilkens, "Theologische" (as well as his earlier writings). Drury was heavily influenced by Goulder's writing on Matt.

[121] *Union Seminary Quarterly Review* 31 (4; Summer 1976), 297–99.

ing the Matt book I judged that a very high percent of Goulder's *new and original* ideas, albeit ingenious, were wrong; and my view of the Luke book would not be much different. I express that judgment unhappily; he is gentlemanly in his debate with BBM, which he read most carefully and to which he pays a closing tribute (*Luke* 1.267). In treating individual infancy sections below I shall try to do him justice by pointing out what I found of worth in his *Luke*.

B. The Preface (Luke 1:1–4). On 238 above I discussed the Lucan Preface (1:1–4), arguing that it did not justify a claim that Luke drew the infancy narrative from eyewitness tradition and that therefore Luke's was a factual account. In the more recent conservative literature there is continued appeal to the Preface's references to "the original eyewitnesses and ministers of the word from the beginning" and to a systematic or "orderly account" as proving that Luke was writing carefully constructed history by using Mary memoirs. However, Fitzmyer (*Luke* 1.294, 298), Marshall (*Gospel* 42), and Bovon (*Evangelium* 1.37) are in agreement that "eyewitnesses and ministers of the word" refers to one group, viz., the disciples (apostles) from the beginning of their encounter with Jesus (Acts 1:21–22). Consequently, it is not a reference to Mary. Moreover, the Luke who moved around segments of the Marcan passion narrative and suppressed all memory of the Galilean postresurrectional appearances of Jesus (hinted at by Mark) has a different sense of orderliness from what conservative defenders of exact infancy history might imagine. According to Busse ("Evangelium" 176–77) the *asphaleia* ("assurance, reliability") that Luke 1:4 promises for the words reported has to do with the message's congruence with Scripture by way of realizing the hopes expressed therein. Finally, it should be noted that despite the frequent claim that Christians have always thought of the Lucan infancy narrative as Mary's memoirs, that position is not so frequent among the Church Fathers as one might imagine (see, for instance, Buby, "Research" 261).

C. Function of the Lucan Infancy Chapters. The literature on Luke 1–2 in the last decade was more abundant than that on Matt 1–2. Disproportionately Roman Catholic,[122] the quantity reflects the greater mariological potentialities of Luke, e.g., Laurentin's *Évangiles* is over eighty percent a Lucan treatment. Cardinal Ratzinger ("You") works reflectively with motifs from Luke's presentation of Mary and motifs in later theology to show that "the Church fails to carry out part of that which

[122] The fact that three of the four volumes of Muñoz Iglesias's huge MIE are devoted to Luke 1–2 would alone almost tilt the scale. (In the bibliography below I have been very select in listing his articles since many of those that preceded MIE would be reflected therein.) The important work of Legrand is all dedicated to the Lucan account.

she has been commanded to do if she does not extol Mary." As a challenge to the dearth of Protestant exegesis of Luke 1–2 in German,[123] Klaiber ("Lukanische") supports Luther's judgment that it contains examples of justification through faith. For instance, in regard to the conception, he argues that the emphasis is not on Mary's virginity as such but on God's creative power in the conception.

That Luke 1–2 belongs to the structure of the Gospel and is not an alien body of material (242 above) scarcely needs to be defended anymore; scholarship has turned to detecting a unified plan in all of Luke-Acts. Busse ("Evangelium") points out that the heavy OT echoes of Genesis and the Former and Latter Prophets (Abraham and Sarah; Hannah, Samuel, and Eli) in Luke 1–2 corresponds to the program laid out by Jesus for himself (and the Christian preachers) in Luke 24:27: "Beginning with Moses and all the Prophets, he interpreted to them what referred to him in all the Scriptures." The strong presence of JBap in Luke 1–2 corresponds to the emphasis in Acts 1:22; 10:37; 13:24 that has Jesus' proclamation of the good news begin with the baptizing by John.[124] An interesting contribution to the problem of precisely how Luke 1–2 is related to the rest of the Gospel is Tyson's "Birth." He points out, as have many others, that at one point in the course of its history the Lucan Gospel may have begun with 3:1. Yet considerations of various sorts show that Luke 1–2 has close connections with the body of the Gospel and forms a legitimate beginning. What is the correct way to designate the relationship? "Overture" is not really satisfactory; for although there are melodies in the overture that are picked up in the body of an opera, there is no action in the overture and most often it is played without presenting the characters of the opera. Tyson thinks rather of a prologue to the Greek drama where there is action and often an introduction of the characters who will be featured. Indeed, sometimes there is a disjunction between the prologue and the body of the play because the prologue deals with what happened before the time of the play and often on a different level—more mythical or heavenly compared to the earthly, human action of the first act. Such a comparison gives us a sense of how some in Luke's audience may have understood the opening of Luke's work.

Motifs in the infancy narrative that are practical for Christian life have received attention. I wrote BBM in part to show that the infancy narratives are not folklore devoid of real theology and fit only for naive romantics. H. Anderson ("Preaching") points out that unless people feel a connection between their own stories and the biblical stories, they

---

123 He wrote before Bovon's commentary on Luke.
124 Luke probably got the idea from Mark 1:1–4, where "the beginning of the gospel of Jesus Christ" is JBap's activity in the desert.

find no validation from preaching the Scriptures; and so he seeks by brief reflections on the Gospel infancy stories to relate them to family birth stories. Carolyn Thomas ("Nativity") observes that Matt and Luke both use the personages of their infancy narratives to reflect their distinctive understandings of discipleship as a model to the readers. But Luke's characters are more fully depicted and offer richer possibilities. Baudler ("Aspekte") finds a model for the upbringing of children in the Jesus who, though loved by his parents, is not their possession and is called to his own task by God.[125] The prominence of Mary in the Lucan infancy narrative has attracted many Roman Catholic studies (e.g., Núñez, "Maria"). Although Hernández Martínez ("Madre") recognizes that Luke's primary presentation of Mary is as mother of Jesus, her ongoing value that makes her a model for others is as the first one to believe.[126] Deborah Middleton ("Story" 563) argues that the Lucan Mary is not the crassly submissive figure rejected by feminists but a new model of discipleship for all humanity, male and female alike. The social justice that is characteristic of the Lucan Jesus is introduced in Mary's Magnificat; this is an aspect of Luke's allowing his theology to be dependent on a woman. Casalegno ("Maria") relates Mary to portrayals of other women in the whole Lucan Gospel and Acts, i.e., women especially blessed, women faithful to God's word, and women involved in the apostolic task. Sister T. Bernhard ("Women's") is also interested in the paradigmatic value of Mary among other women in Luke: She is placed at the beginning of the Gospel to match the women who went to proclaim the resurrection to the Eleven at the end of the Gospel (24:9). There are also the women who minister to Jesus in Galilee (8:1–3). Mary can be looked on as the first priest of the new dispensation, and the Lucan focus on women can support the ordination of women and their full role in evangelism. Those who react to Bernhard's suggestions by observing correctly that this goes considerably beyond Luke's conscious intention should recognize that so also (in differing degrees) do other paradigmatic uses of Mary sparked by Luke, e.g., as Our Lady, the Madonna, the Mother of the Church, etc. One attractive feature of Luke's portrayal of Mary as the first disciple, the first one to hear the will of God pertinent to Jesus and to do it, is its malleability at the hands of subsequent generations as they seek to find an ideal for the thrust of discipleship in their own times. Yet the hermeneutical controls to be exercised are not clear.

[125] Barbara Ort's *Kindheitsgeschichte* is an analysis of German catechetical use of the Lucan infancy narrative from 1777 to 1967.

[126] While Gabriel charges Zechariah with not having believed his words (1:20), Elizabeth, Zechariah's wife, praises Mary for having believed the things spoken to her by the Lord (1:45).

D. Sources behind the Lucan Infancy Narrative? On 244–47 above I discussed the issue of whether Luke used sources here, e.g., a Jewish-Christian source for the canticles (see §12 below), a Marian source for the stories about Jesus and Mary, and a JBap source.[127] At one extreme of recent discussions is Muñoz Iglesias, who posits that the whole infancy narrative came to Luke from an early Jewish-Christian source written in Hebrew, so that basically all that Luke did was translate it into Greek. At the other extreme is Goulder who posits that Luke used imagination on Mark, Matt, and the OT and had no special sources or traditions.[128] Schweizer ("Aufbau") posits a JBap source (plus two hymns from a Jerusalem priestly tradition) and a Jesus source, which were joined before Luke's editing.[129] The hand of Luke is seen in 1:48b,80(?); 2:1–2,19,34–35,40(?), and 51b. Bovon (*Evangelium* 1.21–22) recognizes that the canticles were not composed by Luke himself and speaks of legends or traditions pertinent to JBap and Jesus;[130] he does not find it easy to decide whether they were joined by Luke or by a predecessor. The position I held in BBM is substantially that adopted by Fitzmyer (*Luke* 1.309), who contends that most of the infancy narrative was freely composed by Luke on the basis of pre-Lucan information, but there was a Jewish-Christian source for the canticles. While he allows a JBap source for 1:5–25,57–66b, I still prefer to speak of JBap tradition or information shaped by Luke.[131]

The issue of the languages of these putative sources (as distinct from vaguer "traditions") has also been prominent. On 246 above the view that the Greek of the infancy narratives is more semitized than the rest of the Gospel was balanced by Cadbury's statement about the presence of Luke's personal style. That combination has been confirmed by Tam

127 According to Testa's summary ("XXXI" 135–36), E. Manicardi in his 1990 paper on tradition and redaction would propose separate sources for the stories of the shepherds, the presentation, Anna, and Jesus at age twelve. As explained in the text above, instead of multiplying sources, MIE posits one very early source in Hebrew. The thrust of that, as I mentioned in this Supplement under §1, causes MIE to assume a great deal of historicity. E.g., although other scholars have puzzled over why Luke has Zechariah struck mute after his question to Gabriel while Mary's question receives no reproof, and why Luke has Elizabeth in seclusion for five months, MIE 2.124, 130 would answer simply that these were historical facts.

128 He is almost odd-man-out among recent scholars in denying that Luke drew on some JBap tradition and holding that Luke made up all the material himself. Mark 6:14–29 is good evidence that stories about JBap circulated after his death.

129 Although he speaks of traditions, the detailed allotment of verses seems to imply sources: *JBap tradition*: 1:5–25,57–66 + Hymns; *Jesus tradition*: 2:8–20(except 19),22–39(except 34–35),41–46,48–51a; *joined tradition*: 1:26–38,39–45,56,76–79,80(?); 2:3–7,21,34–35(?),40(?).

130 He is quite confident in assessing what Luke has added to his sources, and even suggests that the source may have had a thrust different from that of Luke's account, e.g., JBap may have been presented therein as a priestly Messiah whereas Luke allows him to be only a prophet (*Evangelium* 1.56).

131 In the course of writing BDM I came to doubt that Luke had a source for the passion narrative. Rather, working with Mark, he had in addition traditions, some or all oral.

("Literary" 327), who claims that the concentration of Lucanisms in chaps. 1–2 is the highest in the Gospel and at least as high as in Acts. In whole or in part was Luke 1–2 once composed in Hebrew or Aramaic? Farris ("Discerning") thinks a refined application of R. A. Martin's statistical method[132] tilts the probability toward Hebrew sources. Nevertheless, an enduring problem is that ninety percent of Luke's vocabulary is found in the LXX; and where there are Hebraisms and Aramaisms, we do not know whether they represent a direct translation from Hebrew and Aramaic or the influence of a Septuagint where the Greek was translated from Hebrew and Aramaic. Fitzmyer (*Luke* 1.118–25), pointing out that there is no evidence that Luke knew Hebrew, comments on puzzling Hebraisms and argues that most of them are explicable as Septuagintisms. He also thinks that Aramaisms are best treated as Septuagintisms as long as one cannot show the direct influence of Aramaic—a judgment that has enormous importance since Fitzmyer is one of the foremost Aramaists in the world. Grelot ("Cantique"), a French scholar who has specialized in Semitics, argues in a similar way, and concludes that 2:29–32 was originally composed in Greek.

In a long, careful study of the phraseology of the Lucan infancy narrative Ó Fearghail ("Imitation") argues strongly for conscious imitation of LXX style rather than translation from a Semitic original. He diagnoses the theological function of that imitation (73): By re-creating the atmosphere of the (Greek) Bible Luke recalls God's interventions of the past to explicate God's intervention in the present.[133] Like many others I saw a setting for the Lucan canticles in early Christian prayer-life, but Dawsey ("Form") would associate the whole Lucan birth story with public worship praising God. He suggests that the semitized Greek may be a type of Christian "Synagogue Greek." Why has Luke preserved the liturgical tone? Maintaining that the Gospel was intended to be read from beginning to end at a worship session, Dawsey thinks the tone of Luke 1–2 helped the congregation to make the transition from the secular to the sacred at the emotional level.

E. *Structure.* Analysis and structure of Luke 1–2 were the subject of 239–45, 248–52 above and continue to be an issue. Mather ("Search") is right in seeing that Luke continues OT narrative techniques and style in describing Jesus' birth.[134] Laurentin (*Évangiles*), Panier (*Naissance*),

---

132 See Martin's *Syntactical Evidence of Aramaic Sources in Greek Documents* (Cambridge, MA: SBL, 1974).

133 Another possibility he points out is that after a Hellenistic preface (1:1–4), Luke 1:5ff. plunges readers into a Palestinian world with both parts of a mixed Gentile and Jewish audience in mind.

134 He overdoes, however, the JBap/Jesus parallelism by detecting it throughout Luke. Clearly JBap and Jesus are associated or contrasted in other passages but scarcely in a way comparable to the parallelism of Luke 1–2.

and Merritt ("Angel's") offer a semiotic analysis of Luke 1–2. The
results are not always productive (see Monloubou's comment on 581
above). Merritt, for instance, states (97) that while the parallelism
between the narratives concerning JBap and Jesus is generally recognized, its significance is not. Following a suggestion made in a structuralist study by Spivey, he would find a key in the binary opposition
between nature and culture that is central to the Lévi-Strauss analysis
of mythology. By his food, clothing, and wilderness locale JBap represents nature; as a city-dweller and the son of a carpenter Jesus represents culture. Is this comparison pertinent to the Lucan *infancy* narrative? In Luke Jesus is never identified as the son of a carpenter. His
parents live in rural Galilee. JBap's father is a priest who is introduced
to the readers in the Temple of Israel's capital city[135] and who lives in
the nearby Judean hillside. The wilderness is mentioned only at the end
of the JBap portion of the story as his future. Suggestions from a
semiotic approach made by Panier I consider more significant.[136] He
shows another way of looking at the picture (*Naissance* 140–44): JBap
dominates chap. 1; Jesus dominates chap. 2; JBap dominates 3:1–20;
Jesus dominates from 3:23ff. Chap. 1 begins and ends with JBap scenes;
the Jesus story is introduced within that framework; and the visitation
serves to bring back on track the JBap story after the lack of faith by
Zechariah.

In terms of overall structure Schweizer ("Aufbau"), Fitzmyer (*Luke*
1.134–36), and Bovon (*Evangelium* 1.vii) agree with BBM in treating
1:5–2:52 as a unit separate from 3:1–4:13; but many others[137] join these
chapters. The problem is somewhat relativized when those who opt for
1:5–4:13 admit that there are two partially autonomous subdivisions of
which the first is 1:5–2:52 (compare n. 28 above). Kirchschläger ("Beo-

---

[135] Luke tends to "citify" the Gospel picture; for Nazareth, Capernaum, and Nain are
all called cities even if they were only villages. This may be a retrojection from Luke's
own situation where Christians were mostly in cities (Bovon, *Evangelium* 1.226). Merritt
("Angel's") sees another binary opposition between the sacred (cultic, ascetic, prophetic)
themes associated with JBap and the more secular themes associated with Jesus. However, when Jesus first speaks he identifies the Temple as belonging to his Father; prophetic
themes surround his presentation in the Temple; and his mother's keeping these things in
her heart is a prophetic/apocalyptic theme. Thus I find both binary oppositions strained.
A contrast between priestly descent and Davidic descent is far more obvious (without
semiotic assistance).

[136] He writes clearly and with a knowledge of the views of scholars who have approached
the text from a different hermeneutical stance. At times, however, his wording suggests
that their work was not really paying attention to the literary flow of the passage. I would
argue that semiotics (and his in particular) pays attention to different aspects of the literary
flow, a flow already studied and valued by other approaches.

[137] E.g., Meynet ("Dieu") and Talbert ("Prophecies"). Brodie ("New") contends that
Luke 1–2 rewrites Chronicles, while Luke 3–4 rewrites Ezra-Nehemiah! Wilkens ("Theologische") posits triads throughout: first triad: 1:5–25/26–28/39–56; second: 1:57–80/2:1–
40/41–52; third: 3:1–20/3:21–4:13/4:14–44. In treating sonship in Luke, M. Wren, SJT 37
(1984), 301–11, sees the JBap-Jesus story continued in chaps. 3–4 (3:1–20 JBap; 3:21–4:13
Jesus; 4:14–30 recognition, epiphany).

bachtungen") proposes to structure 1:5–2:52 in two divisions along the line of those presented on 249 above (under B), but with three subsections on each side (annunciation, birth, and summary for JBap and for Jesus).[138] He stresses the theological pattern of promise and fulfillment between the annunciations and the birth narratives.

In a very careful technical article Higgins ("Tatian's") reconstructs the use of the Luke 1–2 in the *Diatessaron*. While much of the study is of textual import, the *Diatessaron* testifies to an ongoing Christian reflection on the infancy after the written Gospels.

§10   Annunciation of the Birth of John the Baptist (Luke 1:5–25)

Ford ("Zealotism") promotes the implausible hypothesis that the family of JBap was a Zealot circle.[139] Did the Zealot movement exist so early? In writing BDM (§31, A2g) I was convinced by those who argue that the Zealots arose during the Jewish revolt against Rome (specifically in A.D. 67–69, the period in which Josephus concentrates his references to them). Actually Luke portrays JBap's parents in a very nonrevolutionary manner; they are examples of priestly and Temple pietism. Luke will also portray Jesus' parents as obeying laws involving the Temple and sacrifices (2:22–24,39,41). In two instances, at his presentation and at age twelve, Jesus will be warmly received in the Temple. This fits in with Luke's picture of early Jewish Christians who went obediently to the Temple daily (Acts 2:46; 3:1; 5:12). That is why I affirmed on 268 above: "Luke wants to make it clear that if opposition rose between the Temple/priesthood and the following of Jesus, it was not because there was an inherent contradiction between Christianity and the cult of Israel. Rather there was continuity, as illustrated both in Jesus' origins and in the origins of the Church." Horsley (*Liberation* 91–100) is highly critical of my views, and observes (92): "To locate significance in John's priestly parents as representatives of the institutions of Judaism simply perpetuates an outmoded and historically ungrounded theological scheme." He goes on to comment on Jewish sociopolitical opposition to the high priesthood ranging from the Herodian period to the Jewish revolt, constructing this opposition from Josephus, rabbinic documents, etc. I would reply in two ways. First, I have no objection to sociopolitical analysis of this period. However, as I emphasize in BDM, I find that often it has been done without sufficient precision. In particular, I

---

138 The visitation and the finding of Jesus in the Temple are not assigned to either side.
139 Her evidence includes the parents as "righteous"; Zechariah as a visionary; militancy in the Benedictus; a political atmosphere in the anti-Augustan angelic proclamation to the shepherds.

disagree with Horsley's approach in many details. How much of the rabbinic material written from 150 to 400 years after the life of Jesus is an accurate description of this early situation? Beyond historical control in those documents there is the problem of rabbinic anti-Sadducee prejudice. In reconstructions one must also recognize that Josephus had his own prejudices. Even more important, as I explain below (650), the period from A.D. 6–30/33 was not the same politically as either the Herodian period or the post-44 period. The tendency to subsume both JBap and Jesus into a revolutionary movement against political rulers often badly intermingles evidence from the three periods. Second, in BBM and this Supplement I am diagnosing Luke's portrayal of the scene that has its own theological validity no matter what the historical sociopolitical situation was. Scholars can more easily come to agreement about the former than about the latter; and, in my judgment, Luke most certainly does *not* present JBap's parents, JBap, Jesus' parents, or Jesus as revolutionaries against the Roman order. Is the diagnosis of Gospel theology to be based on dubious reconstructions such as Horsley's or on Luke's own presentation, even if the latter goes beyond history?

In a different vein Beckwith ("St. Luke") thinks he can use Luke's indication about the priestly courses (1:5,8) to show that Jesus was born in the period from mid-January to early February, or late June to early August—with the former more likely because of the winter dates assigned by Hippolytus (Dec. 25) and Clement of Alexandria (Nov. 18). Most would judge that this puts more credence than warranted in patristic dating two centuries after the event.

As to specifics, to the parallelism between Abraham and Zechariah documented on 269 above, one may add that like Abraham in Gen 26:5, Zechariah observed God's "commandments and ordinances." Luke 1:5–7 gives some general information about JBap's parents that I theorized was most likely derivative from tradition (265–66 above). In particular, I rejected Goulder's overly imaginative attempts to derive names like Zechariah and Elizabeth from midrashic use of the OT. In repeating his theories Goulder (*Luke* 1.217) observes that I was inaccurate in saying he had not explained the assignment of Zechariah to the division of Abijah. Let me correct that oversight: Goulder says Luke created the assignment on the basis of I Chron 24:10–11, where the priestly division/course[140] of Abijah precedes that of Jeshua (LXX: Iēsous), and in Luke's Gospel Zechariah preceded Jesus. In my judg-

---

[140]G. Schwarz's brief study of *ephēmeria* in 1:5 gives results similar to my explanation of the term (258 above) as the "division" or "watch" (= course of service) of Abijah. Deriving it from Hebrew *mišmār*, he is rejecting H. Schürmann's German rendering of it as "class of service."

ment this type of proposal lacks control. If in I Chron Abijah's division/
course were separated from that of Jesus by one intervening course,
surely Goulder would tell us that Luke created the assignment of
Zechariah to Abijah's course because Zechariah preceded JBap who
preceded Jesus.

Harrington ("Birth" 322–23) points out that pseudo-Philo's *Biblical
Antiquities* 42 heightens the parallelism between the conception of JBap
and that of Samson (a parallelism noted in BBM). For instance, beyond
the biblical details in Judges 13, pseudo-Philo makes Samson's birth an
answer to his mother's prayers; she is told before birth what to call him;
the child is the one who is not to taste wine; and the mother keeps
silence.[141] Goulder (*Luke* 1.205–6) charts parallels between the angelic
vision of Zechariah and that of Cornelius in Acts 10. Luke does establish
parallels between figures in the two parts of his work, e.g., between the
legal trials of Jesus and of Paul, and between the deaths of Jesus and of
Stephen; and such a parallel here helps to show that this account is a
Lucan composition, not simply a borrowing from a putative JBap
source. Middleton ("Story" 556) points out the irony in having the
father of JBap, i.e., the father of the Elijah-like prophet of the messianic
age, bear the name of Zechariah, the prophet who marks the end of the
age of prophecy (Zech 13:2–6).

Luke's desire to concentrate on what would show JBap's activity as
preparatory for Jesus' work has shaped whatever JBap tradition may
underlie this annunciation scene. Thus nothing is said about the baptizing ministry, which was certainly central in JBap's life. How does the
appearance of an angel with his message signify that Zechariah's
"prayer is heard" (1:13)? As Busse ("Evangelium" 173) points out,
prayer and an answering heavenly appearance are frequently connected
in Luke (3:21–22; 9:28–29) and Acts (9:11–12; 10:9–11). Because of the
angel's prediction in the latter part of Luke 1:13 about the son to be
born, Bovon (*Evangelium* 1.54) thinks that Zechariah's personal prayer
was what was heard. I would contend (modifying what I wrote on 260
above) that Zechariah's general priestly service on behalf of Israel has
been heard; for while the child to be born answers Zechariah's unspoken
yearning for offspring, it is specified that the child "will turn many of
the sons of Israel to the Lord their God" (1:16) and "make ready for
the Lord a prepared people" (1:17e).[142] The sons and daughters of Israel

---

[141] I see no reason why two roughly contemporary works, Luke and pseudo-Philo, may
not be attesting independently to a developed Samson tradition. Far beyond the evidence
is Winter's thesis ("Proto-Source") that the JBap document on which Luke drew was
inspired by pseudo-Philo's account of Samson's birth. In the other direction MIE 2.45–
46, which dates pseudo-Philo after A.D. 70, suggests that the Latin form in which it has
been preserved was influenced by the Latin translation of Luke.

[142] A double goal: restore relations to God and repair relations among each other ("to
turn the hearts of the fathers toward the children"). However, as Panier (*Naissance* 172)
points out, JBap is "great *before* the Lord" and goes "*before* Him" (1:15a,17a), and this

will find their voice in Zechariah's Benedictus as the people of the God of Israel speaking as "we" (1:71ff.), and the last reference to the newborn JBap in the infancy narrative (1:80) anticipates the day of his public appearance to Israel.

On 278–79 above I explained the problem of interpreting Luke 1:17cd. MIE 2.116–18 states that the reason commentators like me have had difficulties is because we have tried to understand each line as referring to reciprocal reconciliation and have not taken into account derashic techniques whereby the verb in the first line means one thing (convert) whereas in the second line the same verb has a different sense (reconcile). So far as I can see MIE throws no specific light on those to whom Luke would assign the roles of "children," "fathers," "disobedient," and "just," which, of course, is a major part of the problem in interpreting the verse. More helpfully Bovon (*Evangelium* 1.57–58), who wrestles with this problem, points out that family opposition between fathers and children echoes an apocalyptic motif and is part of the eschatological atmosphere of the announcement. On 263 above I observed that the seeming illogic in Luke 1:22 (where Zechariah cannot speak but the people realized that he had seen a vision) may be solved by appealing to a tradition of appearances in the sanctuary. To the Josephus reference I gave, one may add the chronologically later references offered by Buth ("What Is") from Mishna *Yoma* 5.1 indicating a reluctance of the high priest to pray at length in the sanctuary lest the people outside be disturbed.[143] This tradition obviates the need to suppose that Zechariah communicated to the crowd what had happened, for Luke mentions signs-communication only after he tells us that the crowd realized that Zechariah had seen a vision.

Since this annunciation is to Zechariah, his wife Elizabeth, although mentioned, has not functioned as more than background. Yet in the storyline 1:25, where we are told that the Lord took away "my disgrace among men," begins to focus readers' attention on Elizabeth's positive role, especially when Zechariah has been reduced to silence because he did not believe the angel's words. In the next scene the angel's message to Mary in 1:36–37 ("Your relative Elizabeth, despite her old age, has also conceived a son. . . . Nothing said by God can be impossible") ignores Zechariah and moves Elizabeth to center stage. It is not surprising, then, that although the annunciations are to Zechariah and Mary, the visitation (1:39–56) is entirely a scene between Elizabeth and Mary.

---

spatial orientation shows God's role in accomplishing the goal. My temporal understanding of the "before" (261 above) may be too narrow.

[143] TalJer *Yoma* 5.2 (42c), portraying the people as anxious when the high priest stayed too long in the sanctuary, reports the appearance of the Holy One.

§11 Annunciation of the Birth of Jesus (Luke 1:26–38)

This section covers a number of topics, including the pattern of annunciations, the virginal conception of Jesus, Mary as Daughter of Zion, and some individual exegetical issues.

A. **The Annunciation Pattern** (292–98 above). Table X above drew attention to the parallels between the Lucan annunciations foreshadowing the conceptions of JBap and of Jesus by Elizabeth and Mary respectively.[144] Athalya Brenner has pointed to OT patterns involving two women and childbirth. Sometimes the women are rivals (Sarah and Hagar, Leah and Rachel, Hannah and Peninnah); sometimes they are cooperating relatives (Naomi and Ruth, Moses' mother and his sister). She suggests ("Female" 269–71) that Luke combines a variation of both patterns. Elizabeth and Mary are relatives and cooperative; yet there is a contrast between their respective offspring.

Table VIII above (156) suggests that Luke 1:26–38 follows the stereotyped pattern of biblical annunciations of birth, even if some features were not frequent or present in OT birth-annunciation exemplars (e.g., a qualifying phrase describing the visionary and the urging not to be afraid). Another table (157 above) shows that those missing features are found in OT divine commissions to heroes (Moses, Gideon), giving a change of life (and in a sense, a new birth). This combination of features was interpreted on 318 above, where I insisted that the annunciation of Jesus' birth in Luke also involved the beginning of Mary's confrontation with the mysterious plan of God—in other words, a type of a commissioning of Mary as the first Christian disciple.[145] Some writers (most often Roman Catholic) have diagnosed the main purpose and form of Luke 1:26–38 not as the annunciation of Jesus' birth but as the vocation/ commissioning of Mary, analogous with the call of Gideon in Judg 6:11– 24 (so Bellet, de la Potterie ["Annuncio"], Hubbard, Mullins, Ó Fearghail, Stock,[146] Verweyen). Unwarrantedly, in my judgment, this ap-

---

144 The earlier Table VIII compared the Matthean annunciation to Joseph and the Lucan annunciation to Mary. I posited a pre-Gospel tradition of the birth of Jesus, the Davidic Messiah, which each evangelist used in his own way (156–59 above). Goulder (*Luke* 1.221) holds that Luke, nobly trying to be fair to women, having read Matt's account of the angelic annunciation made to the distrustful Joseph, felt that courtesy required the invention of an annunciation to Mary who, on the pattern of women he knew in the early church, was undoubtedly faithful.

145 See also MNT 125–26. According to Testa's summary ("XXXI" 136–37), B. Prete's 1990 paper on the literary genre of the annunciation points out four different approaches to the issue: (a) annunciation of miraculous birth; (b) annunciation of vocation or calling; (c) apocalyptic structure (not genre) involving revelation by a heavenly being of the beginning of a new era; (d) a covenant whereby God proposes and Mary accepts. Some recognize a mixture of different elements. Prete himself opts for an annunciation genre that Luke makes the vehicle of a christological message which is at the heart of the scene, and I would agree with that.

146 In reporting Stock's views, I draw upon his technical article "Berufung." The more

proach refuses to regard as determinative the Lucan parallel annunciation of JBap's *birth* and the Matthean parallel annunciation of Jesus'
birth. That most of the verses in Luke 1:26–38 concern Jesus (what he
will do; who he is) and that the annunciation scene is prefaced to a
Gospel about Jesus[147] should make it evident that the primary purpose
of this scene is not mariological—indeed, this revisionist approach
makes me see why some might think we Catholics have our priorities
confused. Fortunately, in the recent literature there are Catholic scholars who do not agree with such an approach; e.g., Fitzmyer, Legrand
(*Annonce* 90–96), and Muñoz Iglesias ("Procedimiento" 33; MIE 2.10–
20) continue to hold that the scene is primarily an annunciation of Jesus'
birth wherein his significance is interpreted.[148] As for other scholars'
positions, Conrad ("Annunciation") stresses that the main elements of
the Lucan pericope are clearly those of birth annunciations, as can be
seen from a wider number of examples.[149] Zeller ("Ankündigung")
studies the Gospel annunciations of birth in the context of OT and other
annunciations (including varieties of subject, object, obstacles); he holds
that the real goal is to inform the readers of the divine message
(including the theological identity and fate of the child, continuity with
the OT and the divine plan), not to inform the recipient of the annunciation in the scenario. On 48 Zeller disagrees with Stock's interpretation
that would shift the focus from christology to mariology. Vorster ("Annunciation" 49–52) traces the development of the annunciation scene in
the *Protevangelium*; and even there, in a more mariological setting, it
remains primarily oriented toward birth. In discussions of the genre of
Luke 1:26–38, as Prete reminds us (n. 145 above), we cannot ignore
content as a determinative factor. In the three Lucan annunciations (to

recent, popular article "Von Gott" offers a useful portrait of Mary that can be applauded
even if one has qualifications about the scholarly positions taken in "Berufung."

[147] The Gideon scene is a very defective parallel for Luke 1:26–38. The element of
sending ("Go in your power and deliver Israel"), which makes the Gideon annunciation a
commissioning, is missing in Luke: There is no sending of Mary. The Gideon annunciation
is followed by more than two chapters (Judg 6:25–8:35) describing how Gideon carried out
his commission. The Gospel that follows the annunciation to Mary is the story of the
Jesus whom she conceives. The visitation to Elizabeth is scarcely a completion of a
mission given to Mary by the angel, and her role in the rest of the Gospel is brief. Legrand
(*Annonce* 95–96) is bluntly honest when he says that if one wishes to speak of a
commissioning/vocation scene in the Lucan narrative, the only possibility is a mission of
Jesus, Son of David and Son of God.

[148] Soares Prabhu ("Rejoice" 262) speaks of "a call narrative in which a birth oracle
replaces the commissioning"; it is rather a birth annunciation with secondary features of
a call narrative.

[149] Part of the discussion centers on the absence of "Do not be afraid" in OT birth
annunciations. Stock finds no parallel in the presence of the phrase in the JBap annunciation because, he says, Zechariah's fear is emotional while Mary's fear concerns the
message. This neglects the Matthean parallel, where Joseph is told not to be afraid to take
Mary his wife. The "Do not be afraid" is common to three birth annunciations with
different aspects of anxiety; see Conrad, "Annunciation" 661. He stresses that the motif
is found in Gen 15:1 preceding the annunciation of Ishmael's birth in Genesis 16, and the
expression is related to birth stories in Gen 35:17; I Sam 4:20.

Zechariah, to Mary, to the shepherds), the christological amplitude of
the second and third is notable and is what Luke is really interested
in.[150] The christological message concerning the infant Jesus is given by
angels, even as angels are the vehicle of the postresurrectional christological proclamation—that parallel is explicable because the birth message is a postresurrectional christological formulation. We need to keep
the centrality of christology in mind because much of the discussion to
be reported below is mariological.

   B. *Components of the Address to Mary.* In stressing that the *chaire,
kecharitōmenē*, and *ho kyrios meta sou* of Luke 1:28 are extraordinary,
Stock ("Berufung") uses arguments that may have the effect of confusing the issue. Of course, once the whole scene is read, one can look
back and find that "the Lord is with you" means more because the
Spirit of God is coming upon Mary. One must deal with the hermeneutical issue, however, that readers who knew this phrase and *chaire* as
ordinary greetings (biblical or otherwise) would not have seen such a
fuller meaning on their first encounter with 1:28, but rather only from
the context. Many (Delebecque, Muñoz Iglesias,[151] Stock, Zedda) continue to argue that *chaire* means "rejoice."[152] Stock's contention ("Berufung" 490) that otherwise this is the only one of the three Lucan
annunciations that does not mention joy (see *chara* in 1:14; 2:10) and
that the command to rejoice is fulfilled in the Magnificat (*agallan*, not
chairein, however) misses the point that the element of religious rejoicing here "comes from the context of the annunciation, and not because
chaire should be given an unusual translation which evokes an OT
passage" (see 34 above).

   The perfect passive participle verb form *kecharitōmenē* ("one who
has been graced"; "highly favored one"; "full of grace") has featured
strongly in discussions, especially in the articles of de la Potterie. In his
"*Kecharitōmenē*" (359–65) he analyzes two different approaches. First
there is the Protestant approach (to which now, alas, must be added a
few Catholics like Fitzmyer and me, and Ortensio da Spinetoli, who by
1982 had probably been influenced by us) where (a) the source of
gracing, God, is emphasized; (b) the gracing consists of election or
predestination of Mary; (c) the concentration is on her future role as

---

[150] In the third annunciation, Prete observes, the christological message is not tightly
related to the context, so that one could move from 2:1–7 to 2:21 easily without the
annunciation. In the second the christological message is more clearly directed to the
readers than to Mary.

[151] MIE 2.152–53, esp. n. 49: Without doubt *chaire* means joy in Luke's intention, for
how could Luke forget to imitate the LXX meaning? Did every word Luke wrote have to
imitate the LXX, especially when he and his readers heard *chaire* as an ordinary greeting
every day of their lives?

[152] Bovon (*Evangelium* 1.73) thinks it is just a greeting as the next verse indicates, but
Marshall (*Gospel* 65) holds that an echo of the LXX "rejoice" usage is possible.

mother of God's Son. Second there is the hitherto unanimous Catholic approach where (a) the recipient of the grace, Mary, is emphasized; (b) the gracing involves the sanctification of Mary; (c) the gracing is anterior to her maternity even if it has been done with a view toward the maternity. He argues with examples that *charitoun* is a factitive verb which in a religious context would express the transforming of the person acted upon.[153] Emphasizing the perfect tense, de la Potterie ("Annuncio" 62–65; "*Kecharitōmenē*" 492) denies that *kecharitōmenē* of 1:28 refers to the grace of the motherhood of God's Son which she is about to receive; rather it is a grace that she has already received to prepare for the motherhood. The aorist in 1:30 ("You found favor with God"; also "the Lord *is* with you" in 1:28) is the second step as she receives a precise role in the design of God, namely, the grace to become mother of God's Son (1:31), which is the third step. (By seeing 1:30 simply as explicating 1:28 Fitzmyer and I have gone in the minimalistic Protestant direction of discerning here that the *only* grace of Mary is to have been chosen as mother.) Thus in 1:28 the angel is asking Mary to rejoice because she has already been transformed by grace. "Annuncio" contends that this transformation involves the sanctity of Mary understood in such a way that Pope Pius IX was explicating its implicit sense when he defined the Immaculate Conception. But it also involved her orientation, indeed, secret desire, to remain a virgin ("*Kecharitō-menē*" 498ff.). Quotations from the patristic and medieval period justify this.

In general comment let me discuss first the Protestant-Catholic alignment, and then de la Potterie's interpretation. The technique of identifying a few Catholic scholars as moving in the Protestant direction (and implicitly for that reason suspect) is not particularly helpful. True, there are perennial Protestant-Catholic differences over Mary that may affect the way we have understood how she was graced; but de la Potterie gives a minimalist estimation of what he dubs the Protestant position and does not do justice to the complexity of the Catholic positions. In almost the opposite direction, Buzzetti ("Traducendo") shows how each of the classically different approaches to *kecharitōmenē* catches an aspect of truth. He suggests the translation "The Lord has filled you [*ti ha colmata*] with grace," which gives primary emphasis to God as the source, but the fullness of Mary's state is not neglected. Schützeichel's study of Calvin's commentary on the Magnificat (§12 below) recognizes

---

153 I have no objection to that observation, but I have problems when "*Kecharitōmenē*" (376–78) calls attention to a Byzantine hymn that refers to Mary as "immaculate virgin" from which it is inferred that the transformation rendered her without sin and led her to desire virginity (498–508). The hymn tells how Christians were understanding a Lucan phrase centuries later in the context of a developed mariology. Does it really tell us how Luke meant and his readers understood Mary's status of being graced?

exaggerated Marian statements by both sides that have to be evaluated
in the context in which they were uttered. Yet he stresses that what
Calvin opposed was a laudatory description of Mary that fails to acknowledge God as the source of all that she has received. For Calvin,
God's choice of Mary to be the Messiah's mother was responsible for
her faith, humility, and willingness to obey—virtues manifest in the
annunciation account that make her the teacher of those who read
Luke's account. Thus there is a transformation of Mary in the outlook
of this quintessentially Protestant commentator. Moreover, de la Potterie's description of the division does not alert the reader to the current
diversity among Catholics in infancy narrative research.[154] Catholics
today would have a wide range of views of the implications of *kecharitōmenē*. The resemblance to past Protestant exegesis results from the
employment of historical-critical methods since Pope Pius XII changed
the direction of Catholic scholarship with his encyclical *Divino Afflante
Spiritu*, but that does not automatically make all who use those methods
insensitive to the very positive picture Luke paints of Mary. Muñoz
Iglesias, who in reference to another verse specifically denies he has
been influenced by Protestant scholarship (MIE 2.188), contends that
the *charis* does not refer to sanctifying grace and is not a matter of
Mary's merits. It is a privilege freely given in the choice of her for the
maternal role with all that this choice involves but not formally with all
the graces that the divine maternity would involve (2.157–58).

I would detect two factors at the root of de la Potterie's obvious
discontent: (a) In other writings and statements he has taken a learned
but exaggerated stance against historical-critical exegesis not only as
wrong but even as harmful. Combined with that is the implication that
his own exegesis is objective. Yet the type of precision that he bases on
Greek tenses is highly questionable. *Kecharitōmenē* does involve an
already existing state of Mary in God's favor, but there is nothing in the
text that says how far back this goes in Mary's life. Nor does Luke
betray an interest in making the favor precise. The context implies
virtues similar to those just reported in Calvin's analysis of how God
prepared Mary. In my judgment, by finding in the Lucan *kecharitōmenē*

[154] Testa's and Leonardi's summaries of the 1990 Italian Biblical Association meeting
on the infancy narratives chronicle very diverse approaches. Among French scholars
Léon-Dufour, Grelot, Legrand, Carmignac, and Laurentin exemplify different positions.
Spanish-speaking scholarship covers a wide range of liberation, midrashic, and Semitic
interpretations. I believe I know personally those who by writing and reputation would be
considered the most prominent American Catholic NT scholars; and again there would be
no uniformity. Yet I doubt that many of them would hold that by *kecharitōmenē* the
evangelist had in mind a gracing of Mary that consisted of a life (nay, conception) that had
been totally free from sin, or that he was trying to convey her preferential desire to remain
a virgin. Most might hasten to assure me, however, that such an exegetical view does not
lessen their belief in Mary's immaculate conception or perpetual virginity, a belief based
on church reading of the Lucan scene, which is biblical interpretation in the larger sense.

a secret desire of Mary to remain a virgin, de la Potterie fails to read the account as a narrative about the conception of Jesus and overanalyzes it as a coded mariological presentation.[155] (b) For him the Scriptures must be interpreted through the patristic and medieval views with which he fortifies his discussions. In general, we should note that in the broad range of patristic interpretations there are views quite harmonious with modern critical positions on the infancy narratives, as illustrated by Buby who in passing ("Research" 258, 264–65, etc.) compares ideas in patristic nativity sermons to those in BBM. Even beyond those instances many Catholic historical-critical exegetes have respect for patristic and scholastic interpretations because they reflect the reading of Scripture in the church and have been formative for Roman Catholic beliefs (scarcely a Protestantizing tendency). However, we do not necessarily regard them as a guide to Luke's mind and therefore as a guide to what the text meant when it was first written. Confusion of the two stages in the hermeneutic process is not helpful.

As for my own interpretation, I do *not* think that in Luke's mind the only grace Mary received was to be mother of God's Son. I stated clearly in my CBQ (49 [1986], 664) review of research that I would insist on more nuance: In Luke's view God surely chose carefully the vessel of his Spirit and Mary was already looked on by God with favor. Since in the biblical view God's plans are long in existence, I have no problem with the idea that the favor was long-standing. Moreover, since God's favor is effective and does transform, in Luke's view Mary had thereby been prepared for accepting God's will that she would have had no way of foreseeing, namely, for conceiving Jesus as a virgin. In the flow of the narrative, however, where the whole point is that Mary is to bring forth God's Son, we must see a very tight connection between the *charitoun/charis* of 1:28,30 and Mary's conceiving Jesus. The favor of God presupposes and is directly oriented to the conception that is about to take place.[156] Speculation about what other elements might have been present in the favoring of Mary by God is beyond any detectable Lucan interest.

In recent discussion of the issue by scholars outside the Roman Catholic debate, Klaiber ("Lukanische") goes too far in his fear of a synergism based on Mary's cooperation. He argues that it is not because

155 Pixner ("Maria" 41–43) goes further and thinks it plausible that Mary had made a vow of virginity because the Temple Scroll (11QMiqd 53,15–54,3) mentions women's vows that imply some kind of self-denial. Besides the difficulty of transferring the Qumran mindset to an ordinary village girl, it is not clear that this is a vow of lifetime virginity.

156 Fitzmyer, *Luke* 1.345–46: The "favor is to be understood of the unique role that she is to perform in conceiving God's Messiah." Similarly Muñoz Iglesias, "Anuncio" 336. Fuller ("Note" 203) is very precise: "The 'favored' means that God has predestined, elected and called Mary for a specific role in salvation history . . . the giving also of the grace which is necessary to sustain the role."

Mary believes that the Messiah is born; rather, because God will send His Son in a wondrous way, Mary's faith is made possible—*sola fide/ sola gratia.* Fuller is more balanced: Mary's *genoito* (1:38: "Let it happen") stems from the *kecharitōmenē*; yet it remains an act of her own will—neither *sola fide/sola gratia* nor synergism ("Note" 204–5).

C. The Virginal Conception. This subject will be discussed in detail in Appendix IV below; here let me note only a few contributions specifically to the Lucan depiction. *Does Luke intend to narrate a conception of Jesus by Mary without male intervention?* Most recent scholars answer affirmatively whether or not they think that such a virginal conception was historical or was in a pre-Lucan narrative. Fitzmyer (*Luke* 1.338) graciously acknowledges a change of mind from an earlier article (see above 299) by affirming that Luke's account docs imply a virginal conception even if it is not so specific as Matt. Yet Scheifler ("Vieja") and G. Vermes before him argue that in Mishnaic usage (*Niddah* 1.4) a virgin is a girl who has not yet menstruated, and therefore the story that Luke tells about conception by Mary a virgin (1:27) merely has her conceive precociously early but by normal intercourse with Joseph.[157] The Mishna is giving a legal narrowing of the term, not to my knowledge attested in Judaism earlier. One has to ask whether "virgin" bore that connotation in a popular narrative a century and a quarter before. Moreover, if that is what Luke meant why did he not have Mary object, "How can this be since I am too young?" instead of "How can this be since I do not know (a) man?" Obviously the latter is what Luke meant by a virgin.[158]

Jane Schaberg (*Illegitimacy* 82–101) admits this but still contends that, like Matt but independently, Luke writes of and intends to convey an illegitimate conception of Jesus by Mary (permitting but not requiring this reading). For Schaberg at the time of the annunciation Mary was a virgin married to Joseph but who had not had sexual relations. Mary was seduced or most likely raped and impregnated between the annunciation and the visitation, and the terror provoked by that pregnancy (which did not come from Joseph her husband[159]) prompted her to go with haste to Elizabeth. Normally a woman who became pregnant in

---

[157] Tosepta *Niddah* 1.6: "Who is a virgin? Any girl who has never seen a drop of blood in her life; and even if she be married and have children, I call her a virgin until she shall have seen the first drop of menstrual blood."

[158] Instead of "I do not know man" in 1:34, K. Luke ("Koranic") points out that the Koran presupposes the reading, "Man does not know me." He traces it to the *Diatessaron* and Tatian's affection for encratism. Like most modern commentators Bovon (*Evangelium* 1.76) rejects the idea that Mary had a vow or promise of virginity, but he does leave open the possibility that the phrasing of her statement reflects the ascetic ideals of Hellenistic Judaism.

[159] At least Schaberg does not posit, as does Bostock ("Virgin"), that Zechariah took sexual advantage of Mary during her presence in his house!

Mary's situation had "no one to save her" (Deut 22:27), but Elizabeth's prophetic words that she is blessed among women show that God has turned her state to glory. She can sing a song of gratitude (the Magnificat, especially Luke 1:46–50) because God becomes her savior. God has regarded the humiliation of this handmaid (i.e., her illegitimate pregnancy) and extended mercy to her because of her fear of God.

Given that Luke does not indicate anything overtly about Mary's being violated, what are the keys in 1:26–38 to reading his mind on this subject? One is in the description of 1:27: "a virgin betrothed to a man" echoing a phrase in the LXX of Deut 22:23: "If there be *a virgin betrothed to a man*, and if another, having found her in the city, should have lain with her. . . ." Schaberg thinks Luke is preparing the readers for a story involving the rape of Mary. Yet notice that the italicized phrase is quite neutral in itself; without the second "if" clause it has no suggestion of irregularity. (Often Luke picks up phraseology from the LXX without necessarily reproducing the context in which it occurs; see Fitzmyer, *Luke* 1.114–16.) Certainly the pious religious context in which Luke presents his picture of the virgin named Mary would not prompt readers to think that he was introducing them to the story of a woman who lost her virginity through violation. Rather, since "a virgin betrothed to a man" could serve as the description of a woman who had entered the first stage of marriage, a stage passed through by almost every Jewish woman, that would most likely have been what the readers were meant to assume about Mary.

The other evidence for Schaberg lies in the strange question of Luke 1:34 implying that Mary has not had relations with a man at the time of the annunciation and yet avoiding the normal supposition that she would become pregnant through her husband. Does Luke intend the reader to understand that the pregnancy will be in the imminent future *before* her being taken home by Joseph and having sexual relations with him? Schaberg answers in the affirmative. (I think that more specifically for Luke the conception took place immediately upon Mary's affirmation, "Be it done to me"). The issue is how?[160] Is there any surface indication in the Lucan phrasing of Mary's question or of the angelic answer to suggest that she will be raped? The question is formulated so as to bring an answer, and that is given in terms of the overshadowing power of

---

[160] Schaberg (87–88) wrongly assumes that since scholars see Mary's question in relation to the answer (a literary solution), they ignore the psychological import of the question for Mary as she speaks in the scene. Mary's "How" question reflects a psychology of wanting to know what she must do in relation to what had been promised. According to Schaberg Mary is going to be raped. The angel, foreseeing that, assures her that God will protect her. How does this assurance help Mary to know how she is to conceive the messianic child since presumably the angel's answer does not tell her that she is going to be raped?

God and the agency of the Holy Spirit. In *Illegitimacy* 110–24 Schaberg seeks to explain that answer in a way that avoids a virginal conception. She rightly argues that overshadowing is not sexual; she argues that the passage echoes the Daughter of Zion motif (dubious: see D below), which often portrays a woman oppressed and violated. For Schaberg the coming of the Holy Spirit means protection—despite the fact that Mary is going to be ravaged, God will make the child holy and worthy to be called the Son of God. Mary responds by accepting what will be done to her. "Awkwardly, Luke makes Mary a victim of forces unknown to her" (138).

Schaberg's thesis has aroused anger as it has been sensationalized (in the press and to some extent by Bishop Spong); and so it should be emphasized that she has sought to argue as a scholar, is generally fair to other views, and shows no intentional tone of irreverence in her depiction of Mary as a rape victim. The reason her thesis will remain utterly implausible to most other scholars need have nothing to do with an establishment position or fear of church reaction. She is assuming that a rape happened and is interpreting Luke in that light; yet despite her attempt to read beneath the text there is not the slightest real hint in Luke of a rape. She admits (82,84) that Luke's execution of his intention was flawed since Luke's audiences in all likelihood would miss Luke's intent unless they had the advantage of knowing that Matt had preserved (more clearly) the original tradition of an illegitimate conception. Let me make two concluding comments on that particular contention. First, it is very weak exegetically to contend that an author expressed his central concern so incompetently that his contemporary audience would miss it. That should be resorted to only as a last possibility, for often it serves as a ploy for imposing on a text what it does not say. Second, since the mid-2nd century most readers of the Gospels have had Matt's infancy account, and it has not cast the light on Luke that Schaberg assumes. There have been other scholars who have thought that Jesus was illegitimately conceived (or legitimately conceived by Joseph) but have held that Luke did not know of that conception, or rejected it, or tried to disguise it. Schaberg may be the first to hold the thesis that Luke knew of *and intended to convey* an illegitimate conception (probably by rape). The fact that Bishop Spong has adopted her view in his popularization *Born* does not rectify the status to which she has implicitly reduced Luke: so incompetent that it took nineteen hundred years for someone to recognize the central meaning he intended in a major passage—a meaning that even after its discovery most others still cannot recognize. One should not decry solitary scholarship, but it does leave one open to the suspicion that the proposed insight is in the interpreter's eye rather than in the author's intent.

Acceptance of the most likely interpretation, namely, that Luke
intends to describe a virginal conception, still leaves items to be discussed. On 299–300 above I expressed doubt that Luke's account was
shaped by Isa 7:14. Fitzmyer (*Luke* 1.336) adds arguments to support
that view, but Bovon (*Evangelium* 1.66) posits Lucan dependence on
the Isaiah passage and thinks that early Christian reflection on this
passage helps to explain the genesis of the idea of the virginal conception. (Bovon considers the historicity of the virginal conception to be
unprovable and of no import [1.70].) His main thrust, however, is by
way of comparative religion (1.64–69), suggesting that scholars are too
hesitant about the pagan parallels. Yet Mussner ("Semantische") points
out that the semantic universe of Luke 1:26–38 (topography, names,
theology, OT allusions) exists within the horizon of Israel and has little
to do with the alleged pagan parallels.

In a word study of *parthenos,* Dodd ("New . . . I") maintains that it
preserved a neutral sense in Hellenistic Greek so that in 1:26–27 Luke
is simply saying that Mary is a *girl* betrothed to Joseph—virginity
becomes apparent only when she says in 1:34, "I do not know (a) man."
Carmignac's reply ("Meaning") insists on the sense "virgin" in 1:27
preparing for 1:34, and he is probably right if we remember analogously
how 1:7 prepared for 1:18 in the annunciation of JBap's birth.[161] Probably, however, one cannot appeal for support to the thesis of Vicent
Cernuda ("Paralelismo") that *gennan* is used of the generation of JBap
(1:13,57) because a father is involved and *tiktein* is used of that of Jesus
(1:30–31; 2:6–7,10–11) because no father is involved.[162] The latter verb
is too standard a feature of OT births for us to be sure that it would have
conveyed any special meaning to Luke's readers. LaVerdiere in a
popular article ("Virgin's") points to the dramatic force of the postpositive placing of "and the virgin's name was Mary" in 1:26. The naming
of the mother of Jesus there (a naming found only in four books of the
NT: Matt, Luke, Mark [once], Acts [once]) has somewhat the same
resonance as the naming of Jesus in 1:31, and the designation *parthenos*

---

[161] We may draw out the analogy: The old age of Zechariah and Elizabeth is recalled in
the reaction to the annunciation because that state in life normally offers an obstacle to
conception; so also is the virginity of Mary recalled because that state normally offers an
obstacle to conception. This means Mary's virginity is mentioned as her state, not as a
desire.

[162] I do not think that in this theory the apparent exception of *gennan* for Jesus in 1:35
is adequately explained as appropriate because it portrays an active intervention of the
Spirit in the begetting of Jesus. In "Dialéctica" Vicent Cernuda tries with great imagination to substantiate a similar distinction in Matt, pointing to *tiktein* for Jesus' birth in
1:21,25. As for exceptions, although in 2:2 *tiktein* is correctly used of Jesus by the
believing magi, *gennan* is used of him in 2:4 by the disbelieving Herod. The uses of
gennan in 1:16,20; 2:1, referring to the conception and historical birth of Jesus, are not
descriptions with full theological import. Thus there are many exceptions that require
forced explanations.

twice used of her there will never be given to another in the Gospel of Luke.[163] As for the agency of the virgin's conception, the Spirit/Power of 1:35, Panier (*Naissance* 185) observes that this is not a substitute masculine principle but manifests the other and divine character (*l'altérité divine*) of the intervention—a remark all the more perceptive in terms of what I rejected in notes 82, 83 above.

D. The Daughter of Zion. The idea that *kecharitōmenē* is a new name for Mary leads Stock ("Berufung" 474) to see in her both an individual and a collective figure (like "beloved" used both for Jesus and for Israel), an insight supporting the Daughter of Zion symbolism. That Mary speaks collectively in the Magnificat as the representative of the poor and oppressed of Israel (the *ănāwîm*) is clear from Luke without such oversubtleties. The thesis that in 1:26–38 Luke intends to describe Mary as the Daughter of Zion was queried on 320–27 above as insufficiently established—a query later strengthened by the ecumenical study MNT (128–32). I was one of the editors of the study, and Lemmo ("Maria") suggests that I unduly influenced this conclusion. In fact, several Protestant members (not only "Lutheran" as he incorrectly limits them) were most insistent on the lack of convincing evidence. Since then the Daughter of Zion identification has been challenged by scholars of diverse background.[164] Lemmo himself has argued for the identification; and Serra ("Esulta") takes up the challenge of MNT (130) to find evidence that Luke's readers would have perceived the subtle connections (based on *chaire*) that proponents posit between Luke 1:28 and some OT Daughter of Zion passages.[165] He examines early Jewish and Christian literature for evidence that such passages were widely known, finding it not for Joel 2:21–27 or Zeph 3:14–17, but for Zech 2:14–15 and 9:9. Not all the evidence he cites for the latter is sufficiently early to be helpful for Luke (e.g., *Pesiqta Rabbati*); yet *Sib. Or.* 3.785–87 and 1QM 12:13–14; 19:5–6 show that many Jews would have known "Rejoice, Daughter of Zion." Also Christians reflected on Zech 9:9 as an eschatological proclamation (see Matt 21:5 and John 12:15). If this somewhat strengthens the possibility that Luke thought of Mary as the Daughter of Zion, less convincing is Serra's thesis ("Annunciazione")

[163] Does that imply that already by the end of the 1st century she was being remembered by some Christians as "the Virgin Mary"?

[164] Fitzmyer (*Luke* 1.345); Muñoz Iglesias ("Anuncio" 332; MIE 2.153–54), Marshall (*Gospel* 65), and Bovon (*Evangelium* 1.73). On the other hand, support for the Daughter of Zion reference is offered by Ratzinger ("You") and Soares Prabhu ("Rejoice"). In "Madre" 246–51, having stressed more a primary image of Mary as believer, Hernández Martínez gives a refreshingly balanced presentation of the issues and concludes that a certain identification of Mary as the Daughter of Zion cannot be discounted.

[165] Zedda argues not only from the *chaire* Daughter of Zion passages but also from uses of synonyms, e.g., *euphrainein*. Would the hearers/readers of Luke catch "parallels" based on synonyms?

that this is a covenant scene where God is speaking to the chosen people and Mary is answering for Israel. LaVerdiere ("Be it") is closer to the truth in recognizing that Luke has Mary speak words demanded of every Christian.[166] The influence of the Gospel ministry reflecting back on Mary in Luke 1–2 is often wrongly overshadowed by discussions of Mary as Daugher of Zion.[167]

E. Individual Items. Above (288) I agreed with most scholars that the presence of "Blessed are you among women" in some of the textual witnesses to 1:28 was almost certainly due to borrowing from 1:42; and Fitzmyer and Bovon agree in their commentaries. Now, however, Cortés-Quirant ("Bendita") has argued for the authenticity of the blessing in 1:28 on the internal grounds that it explains better why Mary is startled at what was said (1:29), and on the external grounds that the strong textual evidence against it is almost exclusively Alexandrian (and thus, perhaps, a scholarly editing to prevent repetition).

Although Mary, like Zechariah, is startled (1:29), Panier (*Naissance* 160–61) points to a difference: Zechariah is startled at what he saw (1:12), but Mary at what Gabriel said. Panier would give the *potapos* ("*of what sort* the greeting might be") a somewhat spatial sense: She wondered about the source of the angel's words since he was only a porte-parole or intermediary spokesman. A helpful explanation of "You will call his name Jesus" in 1:31 (often interpreted through Matt 1:21: "for he will save his people") is supplied by Faber van der Meulen ("Zum jüdischen"), who argues that Luke does not stress the meaning of the name but its being given before birth. Such prenatal naming in Josephus and Egyptian and Greek literature is a sign of unique divine care and even identity.

I contended (310–16 above) that the two elements in the annunciation 1:32a–33b and 1:35bcd had a different but complementary christological import: Jesus would be Son of David (described in OT language in 1:32a–33b) and Son of God (described in the language of the Christian kerygma in 1:35bcd).[168] Marshall (*Gospel* 68) doubts that distinction. He would interpret "Son of the Most High" in 1:32a in terms of divine sonship because it precedes the reference to Davidic sonship in 1:32b. I would argue that such a thesis fails to make full use of the background in II Sam 7 spelled out on 310 above. "Son of the Most High" is

166 See also my "Mary" article (*America*).
167 On 327–28, 344–45 above I deemed also unproven the attempt to see Mary as the Ark of the Covenant; so also MNT 132–34; MIE 2.240–45; Hernández Martínez, "Madre" 251–58.
168 See also Fitzmyer (*Luke* 1.338–40; Bovon, *Evangelium* 1.65,77). In Appendix IV, B below I shall discuss the development of christology. Here I note only the suggestion of Escudero Freire ("Alcance") who would make Jesus' reference to "my Father" in 2:49 and the self-consciousness of his sonship that this language implies the key to the application of "Son of God" to him in 1:35.

mentioned first because it is the highest honor given to the Davidic claimant.[169] Working with the distinction between 1:32a–33b and 1:35bcd, Legrand ("Angel") contends that the messianic outlook of the first has not been completely spiritualized into christology. Those with an Anawim mentality who produced the Magnificat and the Benedictus and awaited the consolation of Israel (2:25) may have still expected the restoration of the messianic kingdom to Israel.[170] Luke wanted to make his Hellenistic Christian readers who had a spiritualized view of the role of Christ aware that their Jewish-Christian brothers and sisters kept alive a more material expectation (perhaps catalyzed by the Jewish revolt of A.D. 66–70). Obviously the validity of this thesis depends on whether Luke was abreast of the situation of the Christians in the Palestine area after A.D. 70.

In Lucan infancy monographs of the last fifteen years Legrand's *Annonce* ranks very high for solid exegesis free from mariological eisegesis. Amid many valuable individual insights his main theme is the annunciation as an apocalyptic proclamation by Daniel's angel of the last week of years, accomplishing God's promises and embodying the eschatological manifestation of divine power. Mary's question "How can this be since I do not know (a) man?" makes sense as seeking an explanation of the apocalyptic mystery, which is always unveiled to an individual when it comes to enactment (*Annonce* 125). Panier (*Naissance* 161–63) stresses the difference between Mary's reaction to the angelic message and that of Zechariah. The father of JBap poses a question (1:18) whereas Mary enters into a dialogue with the angel (1:34–37) and has the last word, a positive affirmation. Zechariah's question "How am I to know?" requests verification (and thus can be interpreted as doubt[171]). Mary's question "How can this be?" concerns the way in which she can properly respond to what has been told her (and thus can be interpreted as faith). Also, since the angel's role is by nature transient, this question that removes the intervention of a man places the woman or mother as the only human parent and thus (unconsciously on her part but strongly in the storyline) draws our attention to her as the sole human figure in center stage. In the last paragraph of §10

169 Although I would keep "Son of the Most High" within a Davidic and messianic framework, in the Lucan storyline it is not unrelated to the higher christology of Jesus' being Son of God in a sense that goes beyond Davidic descent—after all, it is "the power of the Most High" (1:35) that brings about the conception of the Son of God. JBap, who prepares for Jesus, is "prophet of the Most High" (1:76).

170 In his judgment Jesus' answer to the question in Acts 1:6 corrects only the timetable, not the idea, of restoration.

171 Panier (166) insists, however, that the muteness is more than a chastisement of doubt; it is a sign that attests paradoxically that the word has been received by Zechariah despite his misunderstanding. It is contrasted with Mary's continuing to speak after her question as she gives voice to the word she has received.

in this Supplement I pointed out that Elizabeth had been moved to center stage in the JBap storyline (and thus the visitation would involve Elizabeth and Mary); but Zechariah is still in the wings and will return to our attention in the birth story (§13) to deliver the Benedictus. Joseph will never be more than a shadow figure or speak in the Jesus story. Understood in that way, although highly christological, this annunciation scene has also offered justification for mariological developments.

On 291 above I mentioned (but did not spell out) that there are three possible translations of the clause *to gennōmenon hagion klēthēsetai huios theou* in 1:35: (a) The holy one to be born will be called Son of God; (b) The one to be born (will be) holy; he will be called Son of God; (c) The one to be born will be called holy—Son of God. I preferred (c) on grammatical grounds, and MIE 2.196–209 opts for it on the analogy of Isa 4:3. Legrand (*Annonce* 288–91) favors (a) because, as we see in Rom 1:3–4, the kerygmatic emphasis should be on the designation "Son of God" and (c) reduces that to a secondary apposition. Fitzmyer (*Luke* 1.351) favors (b) but not decisively; Zedda ("*Lc.* 1,35b") in a careful study prefers a form of (b): The one who will be born holy [= who will be holy by birth] will be called Son of God. This rendering means that because of Jesus' holy birth he will be recognized as Son of God, and therefore it was fitting that he be born of a virgin. I would grant that being born of a virgin rather than from normal parental union, although not constitutive of divine sonship (which is from eternity), has served in theology as a sign that Jesus was God's Son. Yet any suggestion that a virgin birth was more fitting can have the deleterious effect of suggesting that birth from married sexual union is less holy. By way of final observation, no matter how one translates the Greek, the phrasing *to gennōmenon hagion* indicates that the holiness of the child will be a rooted part of his being, not simply something to be acquired as with others.

§12 The Visitation; Canticles; The Magnificat (Luke 1:39–56)

I shall begin with a brief treatment of the visitation (which has not been the subject of much recent writing) and then devote longer subsections to the Lucan infancy canticles in general (on which there have been books by Farris and Muñoz Iglesias) and to the Magnificat in particular (the subject of some thirty-five individual items in the Supplement Bibliography below, including books by Gomá Civit and Valentini[172] and an issue of EphMar).

---

[172] His *Magnificat* is substantially the doctoral thesis that he presented at the Pontifical Biblical Institute in Rome in 1983. He offered his findings first in several articles that I have not included in the bibliography since they are repeated in the book.

A. *The Visitation*. As to why this scene consists of a dialogue between Elizabeth and Mary, see the last paragraph of §10 in the Supplement above. The journey of Mary to Elizabeth takes on particular significance in an overall Lucan context that places so much emphasis on journeys in order to show the development and progress of the gospel, e.g., the journey of Jesus to Jerusalem, and the journeys of Paul. To my brief note (331–32 above) on "hill country" (*oreinē*: 1:39), I should add that this word occurs eighteen times in Judith,[173] a statistic that increases the parallelism between the visitation scene and that biblical book (347 above). I have mentioned that in Schaberg's thesis the "haste" with which Mary goes to Elizabeth reflects her desperate situation, namely, her pregnancy stemming from having been seduced or (more likely) raped after the annunciation. In my judgment that is wrong. I explained (331 above) that the haste reflects part of Mary's reaction to the revelation of the angel that has told her of God's omnipotence in bringing about the conception, for Elizabeth's pregnancy is the sign of that omnipotence (see Fusco, "Messagio" 1.310). This interpretation is confirmed by the parallel haste with which the shepherds react in 2:16 to the angels' announcement of Jesus' birth at Bethlehem that also includes a sign. Clearly the latter has nothing to do with rape.

In the storyflow the first words spoken after Jesus has been conceived are Elizabeth's blessing on Mary and on the fruit of her womb in 1:42; these partially replace the benediction that the mute Zechariah was unable to give in 1:22 and constitute an artistic parallel to the blessing that is Jesus' last action on earth in this Gospel (24:50–51). Then Elizabeth again blesses Mary, this time as one who "believed that the Lord's words to her would find fulfillment" (1:45). On 334 above I pointed out that one could translate the verbal form by "will" instead of "would," and Bovon (*Evangelium* 1.86) emphasizes that final fulfillment is still far away. The whole of Jesus' life and death will fulfill the Lord's words to Mary.

B. *The Lucan Canticles*. When BBM was published, the thesis (which I rejected) that the canticles were originally *Jewish* compositions taken over by Christians (or Luke) had undergone a revival through Winter's hypothesis that they were Maccabean war songs. Since then the thesis of Jewish origin has had virtually no following except for Bovon, who has given it a new expression. In *Evangelium* 1.82–83 he lists some general parallels of words and ideas between the Magnificat and the *Psalms of Solomon*, a Pharisee composition, and suggests that Luke took the canticle over from Pharisee circles. The evidence is very slim, but even then it leaves open the possibility that among the early Christians who shaped the canticles were converted Pharisees.

---

173 Out of a total of forty Greek OT occurrences; Gomá Civit, *Song* 34.

On 350–55 above I contended that the four canticles (Magnificat, Benedictus, Gloria, Nunc Dimittis) were taken over in Greek by Luke and were adapted and inserted in the infancy narratives because they fit well the characters to whom he attributed them. Their ultimate origin was among early Jewish Christians of Anawim (*'anāwîm*) mentality, perhaps in Jerusalem. Laurentin (*Évangiles*) in his drive to relate the Lucan infancy narrative to Mary's memories has resisted this theory. *Sans doute*, he maintains, Mary took up and actualized in the community of Jerusalem the Magnificat she had spoken long ago; moreover Mary's memory preserved the Benedictus and Nunc Dimittis (449–51).[174] Alas, he remarks, even (the conservative) Cardinal Daniélou attributed the Gloria to Christian liturgy instead of to angels singing to shepherds, but knowledge of the supernatural experiences of the saints should make one more cautious (461).[175] Muñoz Iglesias, another conservative *ancien* in infancy-narrative research, disagrees ("Génesis" 22): "The obvious literary artifice of Luke 1–2 in expressing in poetic form the reaction of the principal characters of the narrative seems to be a sufficiently clear indication that the author does not pretend that such lyrical effusions should be considered rigorously historical." As MIE 1.315–18 indicates, he would trace the canticles to Palestinian Jewish Christians before A.D. 70. Fitzmyer (*Luke* 1.358–61), excluding the Gloria which was a Lucan composition, accepts that the other three were taken over by Luke in Greek and seemingly inserted. He is sympathetic to my thesis of their origin among early Jewish Christians; similarly Grigsby ("Compositional": all four canticles); Valentini (*Magnificat*: Magnificat); Monloubou (*Prière* 224–25: three, with emphasis on liturgical assemblies); and Farris (*Hymns*).[176]

The language in which the canticles was composed remains a major issue. Naturally those who think that the whole Lucan infancy narrative was translated from either Hebrew or Aramaic (§9D in this Supplement) think the same of the canticles. But because the canticles have a poetic style and are not tightly attached to their context, it is possible to theorize that Luke himself composed the rest of the infancy narrative in Greek and added to it canticles that he translated from Hebrew or Aramaic.[177] As I have stressed in Tables XII and XIII above (also 458),

[174] This hypothesis is necessary because those two canticles appear on the lips of old men, respectively Zechariah and Simeon, who would have been dead by the time of the early Christian community.

[175] At the opposite extreme I simply mention the idiosyncratic thesis of Trèves ("Magnificat"), who identifies them as 2nd-century-A.D. compositions stemming from the second Jewish revolt against Rome, reflecting *IV Ezra* and the *Syriac Apocalypse of Baruch*!

[176] As we shall see, both Grelot and Valentini think that the Nunc Dimittis was composed by Luke himself and inserted in his own narrative at a later stage. Farris thinks that the canticles were inserted in an already existing (pre-Lucan) infancy narrative.

[177] The appeal to style remains a much-disputed criterion for determining authorship. From features in the Magnificat similar to features found elsewhere in Luke, Goulder (*Luke* 1.229–30) argues that it was composed in Greek by the author (Luke) responsible

almost every phrase in the canticles echoes OT expressions.[178] They were composed in the manner of contemporary Hebrew hymns such as those found in the Dead Sea Scrolls.[179] However, similar Jewish hymns existed also in Greek (e.g., those in I Macc, even if originally composed in Hebrew), so that the pattern does not decide the language question. Muñoz Iglesias has devoted the first of his four-volume MIE to the canticles, showing phrase by phrase the original Hebrew that he thinks underlay them; and in an appendix he gives the Hebrew reconstructions offered by others (Delitzsch, Zorrell, Sahlin, etc.).[180] Valentini and Farris also opt for composition in Hebrew.[181] Yet specialists in Semitic disagree. Fitzmyer (*Luke* 1.359) states bluntly: "There is no evidence that the Magnificat ever existed in a Semitic (Hebrew or Aramaic) form."[182] Grelot ("Cantique") has argued phrase by phrase that the Nunc Dimittis was composed in Greek. Faced with such disagreement, it seems prudent to be conservative: The canticles exist in a semitized Greek, and the major exegetical emphasis should be spent on understanding them in that language, not on reconstructing a hypothetical Semitic original that is highly disputable.

The function of the canticles in the storyline remains difficult to analyze since they are so easily detachable. For instance, one of the arguments that the Magnificat has been added to an existing infancy story is the fact that it mentions clearly neither Jesus or JBap. Of course, there are some themes that the canticles share with the accompanying narrative (composed by Luke), but those may stem from Luke's being influenced by the type of liturgical and theological thought the canticles represent. If there is truth in the thesis that they come from an early Jewish-Christian community, Acts shows familiarity with Jewish-Christian communities. At the bottom of 335 and top of 336 above, I observed that the Magnificat and the Benedictus may be looked on as

---

for the rest of the infancy narrative and of the Gospel. From similarities in the Magnificat to the rest of the infancy narrative, Muñoz Iglesias ("Génesis" 14–17) argues that it was composed in Hebrew by the author (not Luke) responsible for the rest of the infancy narrative and translated by the author (Luke) responsible for the rest of the Gospel.

178 In reference to the Magnificat, Reiterer ("Funktion") has studied the OT background in detail. He sees the Mary of the canticle standing in continuity with the revelatory and prayer traditions of God's people (142), so that her victory hymn is a hinge between OT prophecy and NT eschatology (135).

179 I pointed out some parallels of wording and expression in various Qumran passages, and Rinaldi ("Chiarificazioni") has directed attention to more Qumran background for the Magnificat.

180 He theorizes that Luke translated the whole of chaps. 1–2 from Hebrew into Greek with few adaptations.

181 Farris is following R. A. Martin's statistical method (n. 132 above).

182 In "Génesis," published in 1986, Muñoz Iglesias repeats the argumentation he used in MIE 1 (published in 1983) but, so far as I can see, still ignores Fitzmyer's *Luke* that was published in 1981. Since Fitzmyer agrees with my positions on many key points about the Magnificat, Muñoz Iglesias could have added his name to those whom he considers "arbitrary" and guilty of "flagrant circular reasoning." See n. 9 above.

responses by Mary and Zechariah to the annunciations they had received earlier in the chapter, even though much of the wording is not directly related to what was announced. The canticles have been compared to opera arias that catch the sentiment of the character without playing much of a role in the plot or context. Remembering that Miriam has the same name as Mary, Bovon (*Evangelium* 1.83) makes the suggestion that Moses' song in Exod 15:1–19 and Miriam's song in 15:20–21 offered a pattern for the two speakers.

C. Magnificat.[183] I shall discuss the abundant new contributions on the first of the Lucan canticles under a number of subheadings.

Treatments by Luther and Calvin. Much of the Magnificat literature is by Roman Catholics interested in mariology; by contrast it is worth noting essays devoted to treatment of the canticles by the reformers. Lippold ("Revision") compares three modern editions (1956, 1975, 1984) of the *Lutherbibel*, concentrating on differences in the rendering of the Magnificat as it is adapted to contemporary German.[184] Schöpfer ("Christ") makes an interesting comparison between the treatments of the Magnificat by Albert the Great and Luther; surprisingly Albert emerges as more christological, and Luther as more mariological. In dealing with "He who is mighty has done great things with me" (1:49a), for instance, Albert concentrates on the might of God manifested in various ways, especially through the incarnation; Luther begins with Mary's relationship to God and the necessity for belief in God's might. Burger ("Luthers") analyzes the development of Luther's thought on the Magnificat, using fourteen sermons delivered between 1516 and 1544. Luther began by stressing the inner attitude or humility of Mary; then after 1520 under the influence of Erasmus he shifted attention to the low social state of Mary. The latter approach enabled the reformer to emphasize that Mary had nothing of herself and that all came from God. Yet by the 1530s, recognizing that social state alone was not the key to value, Luther returned to the concept of humility; in 1539 he stated: "This too is a miracle that the virgin was not proud."

Studies of Calvin's attitude have always been less frequent, and so Schützeichel ("Berühmte") meets a felt need. In interpreting the canticle the Geneva reformer placed all emphasis on the gracious and merciful power of God active in and on Mary, as she acknowledges in her opening lines when she confesses her own lowliness that God has regarded and lifted up. (See also 632–33 above.)

---

[183] Valentini's book, *Magnificat*, gives a useful and competent review of modern scholarship on issues of literary genre and structure, as well as detailed exegesis and a study of how the canticle fits into Luke's overall theology.

[184] I have not included in the Supplement Bibliography an article by E. Thaidigsmann in *Neue Zeitschrift für Systematische Theologie* 29 (1987), 19–38, which studies Luther's treatment of the Magnificat for his theology of perception and faith.

The Picture of Mary Who Speaks the Canticle. This is an obvious concern for the very few who think that these are Mary's original words. Yet it is also an issue for those who think it is a hymn composed by early Jewish Christians or even by the evangelist himself: What is the picture given of Mary when in the Lucan narrative it is placed on her lips?[185] In the theory advanced on 353–54 above, namely, that Luke added a few lines[186] to adapt the community hymn to the individual spokesperson, there was still the contention that the piety vocalized by the whole hymn was thought to suit the spokesperson (347). For instance, in the Magnificat Mary can be looked on as the spokeswoman of those with an Anawim mentality and as the first Christian disciple (357). Gomá Civit (*Song* 136–37) gives three titles to the Magnificat: the song of Israel, the voice of the humble (Anawim), and the soul and spirit of Mary. Reiterer ("Funktion") uses the OT background of the Magnificat to show the import of Mary's prayer for Christian life today. In their writings, each in his own way, Bailey ("Song"), Fitzmyer (*Luke* 1.361), Karris ("Mary's"), Farris (*Hymns* 118), Monloubou,[187] and Robinson ("Musings") seem also to hold this "representative" or paradigmatic interpretation of Mary. I have found particularly helpful the view that Mary's Magnificat anticipates the preaching of the Lucan Jesus in the body of the Gospel (see Brown, "Mary"). Mary, who received a christological message from the angel that her child would be Son of David and Son of God, translated that into a reversal of values whereby those of low degree would be exalted and the rich and powerful of this world would be cast down.[188] The Jesus of the ministry who was

185 The thesis that Elizabeth was the spokesperson (rejected on 334–36 above) has had little support in the literature since 1976. Agnes Gueret offered semiotic arguments for it in "Sur," but did not retain it in her subsequent *Engendrement*. Valentini ("Controversia") gives a useful review of the whole debate over the attribution of the Magnificat beginning with Loisy. Bogaert ("Épisode") tells of an article by De Bruyne which was too dangerous to publish amid the anti-Modernist furor—an article offering more Latin ms. evidence for attributing the Magnificat to Elizabeth.

186 I regarded v. 48 as the Lucan addition; Valentini (*Magnificat* 252) sees Luke's hand in vv. 48b and 54a. Marshall (*Gospel* 83) prefers the view of Schürmann that the personal sentiments suitable to Mary in v. 48 formed the basis of the hymn to which the general elements in vv. 51–55 have been added. I think it more likely that the general elements were formed on the model of Hannah's canticle to create a hymn celebrating the advent or appearance of the Messiah which needed the addition of v. 48 to be brought into the infancy narrative.

187 He makes an interesting point (*Prière* 227): The church knew of Mary; and while contemplating the great things God had done in her, the church deepened the perception of the great things God had done in its own life. This was done by reflecting on what God had done in Israel, without which aspect neither Mary nor the church could understand God—thus a complicated interdependence. McGovern ("Maria"), while calling Mary the ideal disciple, interprets the *doulē* reference of 1:38,48 as constituting Mary "the servant of the Lord."

188 To the OT background for this offered on 359 above may be added Wis 10:14, a reference that shows the idea is not foreign to the wisdom literature. Several scholars point to a sympathy for the reversal of values in Greco-Roman literature as evidence that Luke's message would have been widely understood.

introduced at his baptism by the heavenly voice as God's Son would also not simply repeat that christological message but reinterpret it into beatitudes on the poor and the hungry. Yet some mariologists with their stress on Mary as Daughter of Zion would go further. Vogels ("Magnificat" 282) sees the salvific history of the people of Israel being realized by her; Serra ("Fecit" 306, 343) thinks that Mary is the instrument of grace for the entire people of God, both the OT and NT people. Such insights, harmonious as they may be with Catholic theology, seem to reflect mariological development of a post-Lucan period.[189] The "I" of the Lucan Mary is closer to the representative "I" of Hab 3:18 which she quotes, even if she is a unique representative.

Closely related is the issue of verbal tenses in the Magnificat, especially the six aorists of vv. 51–53. (a) Are those aorists gnomic, translating Hebrew perfects and describing the way God had habitually acted toward the mighty/lowly, the rich/hungry (and is now acting and implicitly will continue to act)?[190] Thus Dupont, Herrera Aceves, Karris (who opts for both gnomic and inceptive), and Muñoz Iglesias. (b) Or are the aorists equivalent to prophetic perfect tenses[191] describing what God will do? This could favor an eschatological interpretation or could be used by those who think Mary may have historically uttered these words. Laurentin (*Évangiles* 201–2) refers to the Magnificat as Mary's prophecy[192] and opts for the future import of the aorists. (c) Or should the aorists be taken literally as describing a particular event in the past?[193] Contending that the hymn was composed by Jewish Christians after Jesus' life, I saw (363 above) the aorists as a reference to the

---

[189] The attempt of George Bernard (a pseudonym), to render the Magnificat into more vital language ("Pondering"), catching the élan of a song of joyous praise, is an interesting idea. Unfortunately, it is spoiled by a theology lacking in chronological perspective. Because of the Immaculate Conception Mary's spirit is said to "rejoice in God my Pre-Redeemer." The canticle has to be attributed to Mary herself because she is the mother of Christ's disciples, and they would not dare gratuitously to put the Magnificat on the lips of their mother. Apparently "Bernard" thinks that all mariology, including 2nd-millennium formulations, was known to Mary and/or to Luke.

[190] But if so, why has the Magnificat not retained the present tenses used for the actions of the Lord by Hannah's canticle (specifically in the LXX of I Sam 2:6–8) on which it was modeled? Another form of this approach is to see the aorists as liturgical presents, where the divine deliverance is experienced in the "now" of the liturgy (see Monloubou, *Prière* 228).

[191] Buth ("Hebrew") contends that the present and aorist tenses in the Magnificat represent a translation of the Hebrew *waw*-consecutive construction; he reconstructs the Magnificat in Hebrew.

[192] One of the aspects of the Lucan portrait of Mary elucidated by Cardinal Ratzinger ("You") is that of prophetess as she keeps in her heart the meaningful events of which she has been a witness for the future unfolding of their full meaning.

[193] Gomá Civit (*Song* 94–95) points out that there is truth in all three interpretations of the aorists: an exultant "today" that would embrace in undivided continuity the whole past and future of the people of God. Goulder (*Luke* 1.227–28) dismisses the whole issue by arguing that Luke employs different tenses in the canticle and "we ought to allow them their true force." In particular the aorists in 1:51–53 refer to OT actions of God—a view that Marshall (*Gospel* 83) deems "not very likely in the context."

salvation brought through the death and resurrection of Jesus; so also Hamel ("Magnificat"). Of course, as Farris (*Hymns* 115–16) rightly insists, all eschatological tension should not be eliminated, for the salvation wrought by Jesus also anticipates what God has yet to accomplish. Thus the Magnificat describes a decisive past event with decisive future consequences.

The decision about tense value has implications for the sociopolitical issues raised by many authors. Schottroff rejects strongly the gnomic and prophetic renderings: Rather, the Magnificat portrays a once-for-all apocalyptic act of God—noticeably different from the philanthropic poverty-theology of the rest of Luke (the rich are to give away wealth as alms to the poor). The Magnificat is closest to the social radicalism of the pre-Lucan Beatitudes in positing a revolutionary reversal of the inequities of wealth and power in this world with the destruction of the rich and mighty. Schottroff sympathizes with Marx's challenge that the church (and the evangelists) have betrayed the poor by spiritualizing the most ancient strands of Christian radicalism, which she locates among early members of the "Jesus movement." Most other interpreters would not draw this radical distinction between Luke's overall view on poverty and that of the Magnificat, arguing that Luke adopted a canticle that was harmonious with his own outlook and pointing to Luke's obvious admiration for the early community he describes in Acts as sharing their goods.

Reflecting on the Mary presented in the canticle, Verweyen ("Mariologie") points to the implications for the liberation of women from social constraints. Without the heavy overlay of political philosophy obvious in Schottroff, Gail O'Day ("Singing") makes an interesting comparison of three canticles placed on women's lips in the Bible, all with the theme of an all-powerful God who liberates by transforming impossibility into possibility. Miriam's song (Exod 15:1–18)[194] sees God triumphing over the Pharaonic oppressor and thus a God who will not allow the powerful to oppress the powerless. Hannah's song (I Sam 2:1–10) comes from one who was barren, an effective metaphor for being without hope of human solution; God, who can give life even to the dead, causes the impossible to happen. Mary's song has expressed obedience to a God for whom nothing is impossible, an obedience with a generative impact. Her Magnificat is not a privatistic reflection about herself but part of the larger experience of Israel's knowledge of God. Describing herself as one of low estate (see "slave" on 361 above), Mary establishes solidarity with the poor and oppressed and proclaims that God is "from generation

194 For the attribution to Miriam rather than to Moses, see Exod 15:20–21; and P. Trible, "Bringing Miriam out of the Shadows," BR 5 (#1, 1989), 14–25, 34.

to generation" (1:50) on the side of the lowly against the mighty, of the poor against the rich. This type of reflection leads us into another aspect of recent Magnificat investigations.

Liberation Theology Studies. The interesting history of Magnificat studies in the 20th century by Scholer ("Magnificat") estimates the detection of the social (and political) situation behind the Magnificat to be one of the major new developments in the post-1975 period. There are two general issues that are difficult, however. First, within the 1st Christian century studies sometimes fail to distinguish between the situation of Luke and his readers (*ca.* A.D. 80, after the Roman misrule of Palestine in A.D. 44–66 and the Jewish revolt of 66–70) and the situation of Jesus during his public ministry and of the first Palestinian Christians who may have composed the Lucan canticles (in particular, in A.D. 6–30/33). In the earlier period there was not the same Roman misrule as the later period and little by way of attested revolutionary movement, once the new Roman province of Judea had been success-fully established. Reading the political atmosphere of the later period into the earlier period creates confusion, a problem that I had to treat in analyzing the causes of Jesus' crucifixion (BDM §31A). In reading the political reconstruction behind some treatments of the infancy narra-tives, e.g., Horsley's *Liberation*, I would plead for a recognition that phrases that may have had little sociopolitical dynamism when first recited may have acquired much more when echoed by Jewish Chris-tians after 70. Second, beyond the pre-70 issue, it is often not clear whether the author is interpreting what Luke meant and his readers would have understood in the social context of the 1st century, or the meaning (not unrelated) that the canticle can have in our own times, especially in the third world (viz., Latin America and India). Gallo ("Dios") is helpful by referring specifically to rereading, a justifiable process as the Scriptures are made meaningful to new communities in each century. He supplies examples from the Puebla document (1979) of the Latin American bishops meeting in Mexico and the words spoken there by Pope John Paul II appealing to Mary's canticle. Similarly Herrera Aceves ("Magnificat" 368–73) refers to the treatment of the Magnificat by the same pope in his encyclical on Mary, *Redemptoris Mater*, and looks at the canticle from the hermeneutical viewpoint of the famous liberation-theology motif: God's preferential option for the poor. He asks whether this is exegetically founded or only accommo-dated. Herrera Aceves (367, 375) himself would distinguish (a) the sociopolitical and cultural situation in which the readers find themselves; (b) the meaning of the text uncovered by scientific exegesis; and (c) the context in which the other two are integrated. He finds it helpful to distinguish various semantic fields in the Magnificat: the aspect of

Mary's personal experiences; an extended temporal aspect wherein she speaks for all generations; the theological aspect of God's action; and the anthropological aspect of the contrasted groups (especially in 1:51–53) who are opposed religiously as well as sociopolitically. Such distinctions are helpful against a tendency to read the Magnificat from one exclusive stance.

Two studies concentrate *ex professo* on the picture of God in the canticle (Dupont, "Magnificat"; Gallo, "Dios"): the portrayal of a God who favors the poor and the hungry over the rich and the powerful. Most treatments concentrate on Mary as the spokesperson of the Anawim or the oppressed and of the canticle as their ("radical," "subversive") song. Several writers (e.g., Horsley, *Liberation* 84–85) remind us that as a woman canticle singer Mary is in the line of Deborah and Judith, both of whom were concerned with physical liberation of Israel from its enemies. Drawing on the four Gospels Raja ("Mary") discusses Mary's relationship to various types of marginalized people. Beyond the Magnificat which associates her with the downtrodden, Mark 3:20–21 places her with those who are slower in understanding, and John 19:25–27 has her standing with the desolate.[195] Morry ("Magnificat") sees the canticle as expressing God's intervention in authentic human existence. After detailed exegesis Gomá Civit (*Song* 106) states, "The cry of all the humble and oppressed, of all time and of the present, is recognized in the Mary of the Gospel."[196] God is "the God of the humble" (60), and she is the "Virgin of Liberation" (107). With diversities Herrera Aceves ("Magnificat"), Krüger ("Magnificat"), and Mezzacasa ("Cantico") are also among those who see the canticle speaking to the liberation expectations of the oppressed—an interpretation that puts more emphasis on the mighty/powerless contrast than on the rich/poor, content/hungry. Rinaldi ("Chiarificazioni") draws on Lucan parallels in the Qumran pesher on Psalm 37 to show the wider ambitions of those who designated themselves as poor, e.g., 4QpPs 37, 1.9–10: The congregation of the poor shall possess the land.[197]

Hamel ("Magnificat" 73–76), however, maintains that what the Magnificat foresees will be in part spiritual, not merely material, and thus not necessarily a spectacular revolution. It is an invitation to social justice without hate.[198] Dupont ("Magnificat" 336–37) finds three levels

---

[195] I find aspects of Raja's presentation quite forced, e.g., a desolate mother at the foot of the cross is not what John describes; rather the Johannine mother of Jesus is assigned a triumphal role as part of the completion of Jesus' work. Raja's claim (216–17) that Mary's personal name was ambivalent because Miriam was jealous of Moses supposes that such a frequent name at this time (seven Marys in the NT) carried with it for readers/hearers the whole history of the OT antecedent.

[196] On 109 he utters an important caution: If tomorrow Lazarus should take the place of the rich man at the head of the table and begin to act as he acted, the world will be as much in need of liberation as it is today.

[197] Also 2.10ff. On 359 above I offered another Qumran parallel to the Magnificat.

[198] Covering the whole of Luke, W. L. Swartley ("Politics or Peace [*Eirēnē*] in Luke's

of change in the Magnificat: a religious level (those who fear God will receive mercy: 1:50); a sociopolitical level (1:52–53); and an ethnic level (Israel: 1:53). Writing on the other side of the issue, Ernst ("Evangelium"), responding to critiques of his Luke commentary, insists that the Magnificat is not a sociopolitical manifesto, for (416) "Jesus is neither a social reformer nor a social revolutionary" and the rich/poor issue is not the central problem of Luke's Gospel (419). The poor are a religious category, and their needs are met by the proclamation of the kingdom rather than by a visible change whereby the rich will become financially poor and vice versa. As I reflect on this dispute in regard to the poor, greater clarity is needed as to whether Jesus' attitude, the attitude of early Christians, or Luke's attitude is meant.[199] I doubt that any of these would correspond to Schottroff's reconstruction of the social radicalism of early Christianity mentioned above. (As I pointed out on 416–17, a setting in which Joseph and Mary register in the census of Quirinius—a census that historically caused a famous uprising, as Luke knows [Acts 5:37]—portrays them as nonrevolutionary and obedient to civil authority.) Yet I recognize that as the proclamation of Jesus was accepted and acculturated among different strata in the Greco-Roman world, more radical sociopolitical ramifications were realized.[200]

The Form and Structure of the Magnificat. On 355–56 above I gave brief attention to the form: The Magnificat resembles the psalm type known as the hymn of praise (although in this period the classical types had broken down), rather than the eschatological hymn proposed by H. Gunkel. Farris (*Hymns* 68–85) accepts Westermann's description of the three main canticles as "declarative psalms of praise" (the Gloria, however, is a victory "shout of praise").[201] Valentini (*Magnificat* 21–51) gives a detailed study of this issue, showing that part of the shift from Gunkel[202] was an insistence that the classification by form should be

Gospel," in *Political Issues in Luke-Acts*, eds. R. J. Cassidy and P. J. Scharper [Maryknoll: Orbis, 1983], 18–37, especially 32–35) points out that "peace" in Luke covers peace between God and humanity but also embraces social, economic, and political realities, "showing clearly the inadequacy of existing political and religious alternatives."

199 I think Scholer ("Magnificat" 218–19) is correct in his personal judgment that the social impact of the Magnificat, especially as regards material possessions, was real both in Jesus' ministry and the early church, but "the Magnificat is not promoting a specific social agenda and/or socio-political 'this worldly' program."

200 On 363–64 above, I insisted that while the poverty and hunger of the oppressed in the Magnificat are primarily spiritual, "we should not forget the physical realities faced by early Christians"—realities that I then developed. Farris, Hamel, and Scholer saw this social interest in BBM; but curiously Dupont missed it, thinking that I would relativize social issues. See also my remarks on the Magnificat in the "Mary" article in *America* (pp. 98–99 in the *Biblical Exegesis* reprinting).

201 Gunkel drew a sharp distinction between hymns and thanksgivings. C. Westermann, arguing for more biblical terminology, joined those two categories as "psalms of praise," subdivided into descriptive (*beschreibend*) and declarative (*berichtend*). See R. E. Murphy, CBQ 21 (1959), 83–87; C. Westermann, *Praise and Lament in the Psalms* (Atlanta: Knox, 1981).

202 In which a major role belongs to G. Castellino, "Osservazioni sulla struttura letteraria del 'Magnificat,'" in *Studi dedicati alla memoria de Paolo Ubaldi* (Milan: Vita

based on more than literary criteria and take into account the life situation in which psalms or hymns were composed. In comparison to Qumran hymns, the Lucan canticles as a group are less stereotyped in their format; the Magnificat is closer to the canonical psalms in the regularity of its parallelisms.

As for structure,[203] a two-strophe pattern (vv. 46b–49, 50–55) is favored by Panier (*Naissance*) and Valentini (*Magnificat* 125). In analyzing the two strophes Bailey ("Song") has each climaxing with lowliness/exaltation; Bovon (*Evangelium* 1:83) finds three components in each; and Karris ("Mary's") sees the first strophe centered on Mary and the second as universalized.

Using many criteria, Monloubou (*Prière* 221ff.) distinguishes between vv. 46b–50, where there are more contrasted pictures, and vv. 51–55, where parallelism is stronger.[204] Yet he recognizes the different character of the ending of the Magnificat; and indeed many scholars in one way or another have expanded beyond the two-strophe approach. Vogels ("Magnificat") detects three strophes: vv. 46b–49 (what God has done for Mary), vv. 50–53 (for the people/Anawim), vv. 54–55 (for Israel).[205] Farris (*Hymns* 114–16) thinks a structuring into strophes is too formal—there are two "motive" clauses (vv. 48 and 49a) that are expanded.

Delorme ("Monde"), Krüger ("Magnificat"), and Mínguez ("Poética") offer semiotic analyses. Delorme speaks of a paradoxical logic. Similar to Vogels in the preceding paragraph, Krüger divides the Magnificat into three proclamations of God's action: on behalf of Mary (vv. 46–50); on behalf of the poor (vv. 51–53); and on behalf of Israel, God's servant (vv. 54–55). Mínguez works with connections between words to divide the canticle (the whole theme of which is praise) into vv. 46–49 and 50–55. In the first part, for instance, Mary's proclaiming "the greatness of the Lord" (v. 46b) is related to God's having "done great things" for Mary (49a); moreover "Savior" (47) and "has regarded" (48a) are chiastically arranged to match "has done" and "He who is mighty" (49a). Beyond that and consciously avoiding the designation

---

e pensiero, 1937), 413–29. I should mention that some scholars (H. Schürmann, G. Schneider) have opted for a mixed form: eschatological hymn and personal hymn of praise.

[203] Above (358–60) I proposed this structure: Introduction (vv. 48–49), First Strophe (vv. 48–50), Second Strophe (vv. 51–53), Conclusion (vv. 54–55). Both Fitzmyer (*Luke* 1.360) and Dupont ("Magnificat") favor such a division. Valentini (*Magnificat* 53–69) summarizes differing recent theories of structure.

[204] He mentions a study I overlooked in BBM: J. Irigoin, "La composition rhythmique du Magnificat," *Zetesis* (E. de Strycker Festschrift; Antwerp/Utrecht: Nederlandsche Boekhandel, 1973), 618–28.

[205] Also Reiterer ("Funktion" 133). Gomá Civit (*Song*) has a somewhat similar division: God and Mary (vv. 46–50); God and the humble (vv. 51–53); God and Israel (vv. 54–55). The division proposed by Gunkel in 1921 was vv. 46b–47, 48–53, 54–55.

"structural analysis," Meynet ("Dieu") uses complicated rhetorical analysis to argue that the parallel to the annunciation of JBap's birth to Zechariah is not simply the annunciation to Mary but also the visitation and the Magnificat—the whole of 1:26–56.[206] As for the Magnificat itself, vv. 46–49a involve Mary's "I"; vv. 49b–55 concentrate on a divine "He." There are concentric chiasms in each part,[207] and the middle verse is 49b: "And holy is His name." Contri ("Magnificat") finds a similarity to the Philippians hymn in the theme of humiliation/exaltation and in the focus on the incarnation.[208]

Many of these interpretations are interesting ways of reading and appreciating the Magnificat; yet we may well suspect that the interpreters are often seeing more subtlety than Luke consciously intended.[209]

Specific Issues. After so much reflection on the canticle from the viewpoints of mariology and liberation theology, it is important to concentrate on the meaning of the canticle in its setting and in itself. Panier (*Naissance*) helpfully reminds us that it is not simply a general response by Mary after Elizabeth has blessed her. It is a response specifically to Elizabeth's affirmation: "Fortunate is she who believed that the Lord's words to her would find fulfillment" (1:45). The Magnificat, then, praises the mighty things accomplished and manifested in the words God addressed to Mary (through an angel)—corresponding to the angel's assurance, "Nothing said by God can be impossible" (1:37). When Mary spoke as "I" in 1:34, she spoke as a female who had no relations with a male. Now by phrasing her praise in indirect language with her "soul" and "spirit" as the agents in 1:46b,47, Mary signals implicitly that she does not think of God's overshadowing on a sexual level. The Holy Spirit came upon her (1:35b), and Mary's spirit has found gladness (1:47). She can affirm with confidence the holiness of the name of the One who is mighty (1:49), because the child she has conceived through God's power will be called holy (1:35).

The distant otherness of God has been somewhat overcome through the child conceived in Mary's womb as God's Son; thus in an almost

---

[206] Meynet stresses the *structural* relationships between the Magnificat and Hannah's canticle. Goulder judges the relationship to be so strong that Luke composed the Magnificat on the model of Hannah's canticle.

[207] The fluidity of the Magnificat in the analyses of Mínguez ("Poética") and Meynet ("Dieu") in a sense defies traditional divisions into strophes. Occasionally the proposed relationships require imagination, e.g., Meynet proposes an overall chiastic inclusion between "she who believed . . . said" (45a, 46a) and "He spoke to Abraham [who, as we know from Paul, believed]" (55a, 55b). Thus the chiasm (which structures the Magnificat) begins before the Magnificat itself. Mezzacasa ("Cantico") also detects a chiastic structure.

[208] One can debate whether incarnation in a precise sense is present in the Philippians hymn; it is absent from the Magnificat. Moreover, the Philippians hymn is explicitly christological while the Magnificat is soteriological.

[209] Penna ("Canto") and others stress the unitary character of the canticle, and that is more important than how to divide it.

spatial sense she can say, "My spirit rejoices *in* God my Savior" (1:47). This has been studied by Mello ("In Deo") in the light of the LXX of Hab 3:18, "I shall rejoice in God my Savior" (358 above), a text rendered by Jerome as "I shall rejoice in God my Jesus [*in Deo Jesu meo*]," reflecting a tradition that read *yiš'î* as *Yĕšû'î*. Mello deals with the Lucan image of Jesus as Savior (see 2:11) and rereads the Magnificat from the viewpoint of "my Savior" being Jesus. Reiterer ("Funktion" 138) thinks "Savior" is a play on the Hebrew underlying Jesus' name (131, 640 above).[210]

"He [God] has scattered the proud in the imagination [*dianoia*] of their heart [*kardia*]" (1:51b) has caught the attention of several commentators. Gomá Civit (*Song* 89) points out that in the LXX both *dianoia* and *kardia* render the Hebrew word for heart (*lēb, lēbāb*) and they are set in parallelism in Luke 10.27; thus in the Magnificat Luke has God scattering the "proud of mind and heart." Valentini (*Magnificat* 181–85) believes that *dianoia* reflects the active force of the Hebrew root *ḥšb*, thus, "plan, project, scheme"; Fitzmyer (*Luke* 1.368) points to the LXX of Baruch 1:22 for *dianoia* in the sense of "plotting."

§13 Birth and Naming of John the Baptist; the Benedictus (Luke 1:57–80)

As with the preceding section I shall begin with a brief treatment of the narrative part of the scene (describing JBap's birth and naming, which has received little attention in recent writing) and then present a longer subsection on the Benedictus (which, although not nearly as popular as the Magnificat, has had more attention than the birth/naming).

A. Birth and Naming of the Baptist (1:57–66,80). The discussions continue as to whether there was once a separate JBap source in which this scene was the continuation of 1:5–25. Fitzmyer is sympathetic to that thesis, and Marshall thinks it possible. I favor the position that Luke shaped a continuous narrative out of fragmentary traditions about JBap and his parents. Goulder (*Luke* 1.237) shows how the story of

---

[210] Laurentin (*Évangiles* 201): " 'In God my *Savior*' is an allusion to the name of Jesus, transparent in the Hebrew substratum." The assumption that there was a Hebrew form of the Magnificat is dubious; nevertheless there could have been a play on the Hebrew underlying "Jesus" independently of that. There is evidence that such a play was associated with the Magnificat early, e.g., Origen, *Homilies on Luke* 7.8 (SC 87.162): "Maria *magnificat* Dominum Jesum." Below I shall object to the thesis that Luke played on the meaning of JBap's personal name, for Luke avoids Aramaic and Hebrew expressions and there is no evidence that his audience would have understood such a play requiring a knowledge of Hebrew etymology. I am willing to make an exception for "Jesus," since the meaning of that name may have been a part of common Christian teaching.

Sarah giving birth to Isaac and of Abraham naming him and circumcising him on the eighth day could have supplied Luke guidance. On 369 above I mentioned that there is not much early evidence for the custom of naming a child at the time of circumcision (rather than at birth).[211] Marshall (*Gospel* 88) points to the Hellenistic custom of naming a child soon after birth (Macrobius, *Saturnalia* 1.16.36) and thinks that this may have influenced Jewish practice in Palestine; so also Bovon. Luke puts stress on the fulfillment of the name-giving by the angel, and so some have thought that he was playing on the meaning of the name John (= "Yahweh has given grace"). However, Luke systematically avoids Semitic names and terms found in Mark, and so we may suspect that he addressed an audience that would not understand them. Since he offers no etymology of "John" (and indeed shows little interest in etymologies), his sole interest in confirming the prenatal naming was probably in showing that both JBap and his role were foreordained by God.

In n. 2 on 376 above I dismissed as pure fiction the thesis that 1:80, which refers to JBap's growing up and being in the desert, is related to JBap's having been brought to Qumran as the child of a priest and reared at the desert monastery (as an Essene). Neither Marshall nor Bovon is attracted by that thesis, but surprisingly Fitzmyer (*Luke* 1.389,454) is. The fact that there are resemblances between Qumran thought and the proclamation attributed to JBap as an adult need not mean that he was an Essene but merely that he had contacts with that ambiance. I find it unlikely that if JBap were an Essene, an echo of that would not have appeared in the traditions about him preserved in the NT or Josephus.

B. The Benedictus (1:67–79). I shall first discuss new studies of the structure of the Benedictus, then its setting and meaning.

The Structure. I opted for a simple structure for the Benedictus,[212] even as I did for the Magnificat (n. 203 above). I was consciously

---

[211] Since Goulder thinks that Luke had no tradition to guide him, he regards the suggested naming of the child after his father and the naming on the eighth day as Lucan slips in his totally fictional account. Bovon (*Evangelium* 1.101) is much more perceptive in recognizing how limited is our knowledge of Jewish customs at this period.

[212] See 380 above: Introduction (v. 68a), First Strophe (vv. 68b–71b), Second Strophe (vv. 72–75), Third Strophe (vv. 76–77), Conclusion (vv. 78–79). Fitzmyer (*Luke* 1.378) agrees with my view that vv. 76–77, referring specifically to JBap, are a Lucan insertion into an otherwise adopted hymn taken over from a Jewish-Christian source. However, he would argue that v. 70 is also Lucan in its composition. Vanhoye ("Intérêt") objects to this approach to vv. 76–77 because those verses have connections with the rest of the canticle. That is not surprising, however, since Luke composed the verses to fit into the canticle. Similarly only a short section of the Magnificat refers specifically to Mary, and so the thesis that a reference to JBap has been added to the Benedictus is not arbitrary. As for my contention that v. 77 is unlike the rest of the hymn in having few OT parallels (381 above; also 373), it is still true that "knowledge of salvation" and "forgiveness of sins" do not occur in the OT; but Vanhoye points to approximations: Ps 98:2: "The Lord has made His salvation known"; Lev 4:20: "The priest shall make atonement for them and the sin shall be forgiven them."

rejecting the complicated chiastic structure proposed by A. Vanhoye (383 above).[213] Using Vanhoye's basic outline but simplifying it, Croatto ("Benedictus" 210) proposes two symmetrical blocks of material in 1:68–72 and 1:73–79 with the theme of prophet at the center of each (1:70 and 1:76a) and with three matching items leading up to and away from each center. The first block deals with salvific works of the past, the second with christological deeds.[214] Then (215) Croatto culminates his analysis with a total scheme where the center of the concentric arrangement (twelve items ascending and descending on either side) is 1:72b, "remembering His holy covenant." Thus the Benedictus becomes a memorial of the covenant. Auffret ("Note") has drawn on and developed Vanhoye's structure with even more complicated connections between words. Rousseau ("Structures") has taken up the work of both and enlarged it, detecting four principal structures of awesome complexity.[215] The structures illuminate theological themes; they communicate a spiritual experience that can only be transmitted by symbols; and some of them were designed to help the memory. One has to admire the enormous work that has gone into such diagnoses of meticulous structure, but I am left with an enduring suspicion that the biblical author would be surprised at the ingenuity attributed to him. And, alas, I must repeat my basic complaint: I have not really learned much about the author's thought that I did not already know from a much simpler analysis. Without help from those studies it is perfectly obvious that the theme of prophetism is strong, mentioned in the introduction and 1:70,76a, and that there is a certain parallel between God raising up a horn of salvation at the beginning of the canticle and God's mercy in the visit of the rising light from on high at the end of the canticle. Marshall (*Gospel* 86) complains that the proposed chiastic structure does nothing to explain the progression of thought in the canticle. Farris (*Hymns* 129) finds Auffret (and Vanhoye) farfetched.

[213] In response Vanhoye ("Intérêt" 1532) contends that it is not "complicated" to find ABCDEF in one half and FEDCBA in the second half. I suspect that I am not alone in finding the concentric charts of Vanhoye and of the scholars (to be mentioned above) who follow his basic approach extremely complicated; but Vanhoye has previously worked out a large chiastic pattern for the Epistle to the Hebrews, and so this way of thinking is not foreign to him.

[214] On 218–19 Croatto adds reflections on the Magnificat because he thinks that the salvation-history motifs in the two canticles are the same.

[215] (a) Between the blessing/peace motif that marks the beginning and the end (vv. 68a and 79b), and the covenant/oath that marks a midpoint (vv. 72–73), the first part has seven words that appear also, but in chiastic arrangement, in the second part—an adaptation of Vanhoye. (b) "Prophets" (v. 70) and "prophet" (v. 76a) are the middle of the seven words, and there are concentric chiastic schemas based on them: *poiein* and *sōtēria* before "prophets" and *sōtēria* and *poiein* after it; *didonai* and *enōpion* before "prophet" and *enōpion* and *didonai* after it—an enlargement of Auffret's insights. (c) Verbs in the aorist plus four infinitives in the first part of the Benedictus deal with God's blessing (vv. 68–75); verbs in the future plus four infinitives in the latter part deal with the prophecy (vv. 76–79). (d) A complex series of parallel stichs have quasi-mathematical correspondences. Notice that (a) is centered on vv. 72–73, and (c) is centered on 75–76.

Many (some of them rejecting the Vanhoye thesis) opt for a simple bipartite analysis of the Benedictus (usually 68–75, 76–79). This is preferred by Panier, a semiotist. Marshall thinks the first part is a *berakah* or blessing, and the last part a *genethliakon* or birthday hymn. MIE (1.194) proposes that the first part is a hymn of thanksgiving (praise) to God; the second part is a canticle about the future mission of JBap. María del Carmen Oro finds in the first part the archaic christology of the Jewish Palestinians centered on Jesus as the servant from the house of David (which Luke borrowed), while the second part is centered on Jesus as the *anatolē ex hypsous* (which Luke added).[216] In harmony with its general approach to the canticles, MIE 1.188–92 contends that the Benedictus was written in Hebrew by a Jewish Christian, probably from levitical circles related to the family of Zechariah.[217]

The Setting. Whatever the origin of the canticle,[218] its basic meaning for exegesis must be related to and flow from its present context. Although it follows immediately after the birth, circumcision, and naming of JBap, Panier (*Naissance* 211) points out that in the longer sequence Zechariah is responding also to what was proclaimed to Mary (and made known to Elizabeth) about the conception and forthcoming birth of God's Son. Thus the Messiah will also enter into the reason why God is being blessed.[219]

The main point of Vanhoye's most recent contribution ("Intérêt") is to place the canticle within the overall Lucan stress on prophecy. In

[216] In part her division depends on tenses, aorists in the first part and futures in the second; but a good case can be made for reading an aorist in v. 78 (see 373 above and 660 below). Vanhoye ("Intérêt" 1531) criticizes her siding with those who deny the unity of the canticle. (I accept unity except for the Lucan addition in vv. 76–77.) According to Vanhoye, although many of his points are accepted in the rhetorical exegesis practiced by R. Meynet, the latter ultimately rejects Vanhoye's structure in favor of a two-part arrangement (benediction and oracle). Vanhoye admits that one cannot show that Luke wrote the canticle; he may have taken it over because he was attracted by its emphasis on prophetism.

[217] MIE leaves aside the discussion of Vanhoye and his followers as pertaining to literary structure (although those who think the canticle was composed in Hebrew will have a different outlook from those who think it was composed in Greek).

[218] Let me give another example of Goulder's fertile imagination: "The Benedictus is based on the Song of David, in just the same way as the Magnificat is on the Song of Hannah" (*Luke* 1.243)—Goulder's Luke made up most of the infancy narrative from the OT, and the two "songs" occur in the same general context (I Sam 2:1–10 and II Sam 22:2–51). There are a few phrases in the Song of David parallel to the Benedictus, e.g., "horn of salvation" (II Sam 22:3); "from my strong enemies, from those that hate me" (22:18); but these are psalm expressions as well (386–87 above). "From above" in 22:17 is more persuasive. Yet that does not make less exaggerated Goulder's claim that would make the Song of David the principal source, comparable to the much more persuasive influence of the Song of Hannah on the Magnificat.

[219] Because I think that 1:78–79 refers to the Messiah and not to JBap, I would not accept the thesis that the first half of the Benedictus (1:68–73), corresponding to the annunciation to Mary, refers to the conception of the Messiah, and that the second half (1:76–79) refers to the birth of JBap (even though I recognize that JBap is mentioned specifically in 1:76–77).

particular he insists that v. 76 with its *kai sy de* should be translated: "Now you too, child, will be called prophet of the Most High," thus adding JBap to the "holy prophets from of old" through whose mouths God spoke (v. 70). The Benedictus is called a prophecy from one filled with the Spirit, and in it Zechariah honors what God has done.[220] Carter ("Zechariah") asks an interesting question: Given the fact that only a small section of the Benedictus refers to JBap, why has this hymn been placed on the lips of Zechariah, instead of, for instance, on the lips of Simeon or some other infancy-narrative figure? Vanhoye's observation may be a partial answer: Zechariah utters prophecy (1:67) and JBap is also a prophet. But Carter goes further. Zechariah is introduced in 1:5–9 as a priest who worships God in the Temple and as one who is upright (*dikaios*), and Carter sees the Benedictus spoken by Zechariah as continuing both those facets of his character. (This would fit in with the way in which 1:59–64 resumes themes from 1:8–25.) Worship begins in 1:64 as Zechariah speaks in praise of God; his first words are "Blessed be the Lord, the God of Israel" (1:68). In 1:74–75 this theme of worship flows into the second theme of uprightness, for one of the results of God's action is that "we might serve/worship God in holiness and uprightness [*dikaiosynē*] before Him all the days of our lives."

Beyond the general context, a closer preparation for the Benedictus is what has happened to Zechariah at the naming of JBap. Zechariah was mute since the moment in the Temple when Gabriel rendered him thus and he was unable to speak to the people outside (1:20–22). In part he says now what he would have said then (but made all the more eloquent by all that has happened in the visitation and the birth narratives), and so it is not surprising that the early lines of the Benedictus speak of God's accomplishing the redemption of the people who are called God's own.[221] Zechariah identifies himself in solidarity with that people, and that is why there is such a strong tone of "us" throughout the canticle—stronger than the single passage where Mary speaks of "our" fathers in the Magnificat (1:55a). Panier (*Naissance* 211) reminds us that the most immediate context is the question raised by all the neighbors and dwellers in the hill country of Judea who wonder "What then is this child going to be?" (1:66). That is answered specifically in 1:76–77,[222] but also in the other verses inasmuch as part of JBap's identity in God's plan is his relation to Jesus. Thus he has a role in the

---

[220] Carter ("Zechariah" 244) points out that there are vocabulary similarities between the Benedictus and the speeches in Acts (where Luke gives great attention to the activity of the Spirit).

[221] That is why I argued above (627) that the affirmation by Gabriel to Zechariah that his prayer had been heard (1:13) had to refer to the public prayer for Israel.

[222] It constitutes one of the reasons why I argue that those verses were added by Luke to fit the canticle directly to the context.

redemption, salvation, and fulfillment of prophetic promises that constitute the substance of the canticle.

Specific Issues. On 386 above I offered the (Babylonian form of the)
Fifteenth Benediction of the *Shemoneh Esreh* ("Eighteen Benedictions") as a parallel for Luke 1:68–69, i.e., as an example of the
sentiments and vocabulary of the Benedictus verses in Jewish prayers.
Maintaining that this Benediction is a major source for the Lucan
canticle, Manns ("Prière") contends that its Babylonian form is the
oldest; it has been truncated in the Palestinian form because Jews knew
that Christians used it. Parallels in the Hebrew of Sirach 51:12 show
Manns that the Benediction is of Palestinian origin. He also claims that
this parallelism helps to date the Benediction, but does not explain his
logic. I would judge dating a much larger problem than Manns acknowledges in making the Lucan canticle depend on the Shemoneh Esreh; but
then he assumes that the evangelists knew the rereadings of Scripture in
the targumim and the midrashim of the synagogue—despite the fact that
all the extant Jewish works called targumim (except that on Job from
Qumran) or midrashim were composed after the Gospels were written.

Should an aorist tense ("visited") or a future ("will visit") be read
for the verb *episkeptesthai* ("to visit") in 1:78? My choice for the aorist
(373 above) remains a minority view, now rejected by Bovon, Fitzmyer,
Marshall, and Muñoz Iglesias. Most often the basis of the rejection is
that the "rising light" of v. 78 refers not to JBap who has been born but
to Jesus who will be born, and so logically Zechariah should be speaking
of the rising light that will visit. I agree that it refers to Jesus and that v.
78 belongs to the original Benedictus; but the Benedictus was composed
after the resurrection and is looking back on the coming of Jesus. It is
Luke who has put it in its present context and created the problem of
its being spoken before Jesus' birth. One can argue that when Luke did
this, he changed the verb to the future to fit the oncoming birth of Jesus;
but since it is incredible that copyists of the NT had a pre-Lucan form
of the Benedictus, those copyists who changed Luke's form back to the
aorist must have misunderstood the rising light as a reference to JBap.
All that seems an unnecessary complication: If Luke left the verb in its
original aorist, the change to the future would have been by the hand of
copyists who found it illogical to say that the light had come when Jesus
had not yet been born.

Another part of my reasoning is the parallelism between the beginning
and the end of the Benedictus. In the beginning (1:69) the canticle uses
figurative language: God "has raised up for us a horn of salvation in the
House of David His servant." That reference to the Messiah is in the
aorist tense. This is matched at the end (1:78) by more figurative
language: "Through the heartfelt mercy of our God by which there has

visited us a rising light [*anatolē*] from on high." As I have just mentioned, almost all agree that this is a messianic reference; and on 373–
74 above I point out the Davidic background. An aorist here would be
part of the parallelism. The "horn of salvation" symbol is used in
fulfilling the promises to "us," with many references to the Israelite
past (prophets of old, our fathers, the holy covenant, Abraham). The
"rising light from on high" symbol is used with "appearing to those
who sat in darkness and the shadow of death, guiding our feet into the
way of peace." This could also refer to Israelites/Jews, as the background given on 388–89 above shows. However, it is not impossible that
the Benedictus had the same twofold focus as the Nunc Dimittis: "This
salvation that you made ready in the sight of all the peoples: a light to
be a revelation to the Gentiles and to be a glory for your people Israel"
(2:30–32). The work of the Davidic heir (who was raised up by God or
came down from God) on behalf of both Israel and the Gentiles would
then be celebrated by the Benedictus. When the Benedictus was composed in the postresurrectional era, the spread of the Gospel was already
a reality. In the present infancy-narrative context Zechariah in his
canticle rejoices that the newborn JBap will go before the Lord and thus
have a share in granting to an enlarged people of God a knowledge of
salvation (1:76–77).

§14 Birth and Naming of Jesus (Luke 2:1–21)

This is the core Christmas scene, and so always receives much
attention. In the last decade and a half short exegetical or theological
studies of the whole passage include Kaufmann ("Geburt"), Kirchschläger ("Geburt"), Legrand ("Christmas"),[223] Steffen (*Weihnachtsgeschichte*), and Vögtle (*Weihnachten*). In addition, the individual parts of
the scene have been the subject of many treatments, of which a surprising number are concerned with historicity, e.g., of the census that
brought Jesus' parents to Bethlehem, and of Mary as an eyewitness to
all that happened. After two general subsections on the scene as a
whole, I shall discuss the individual parts, moving sequentially through
them.

A. **Structure, Composition, Overall Approaches.** The *structure* proposed
for 2:1–20 on 410 above recognizes three main divisions of about the
same length (vv. 1–7, 8–14, 15–20), each with two subdivisions. Pesch
("Weihnachtsevangelium" 103–5) also opts for these three main divisions (including v. 21 in the last) but finds nine subdivisions in each,

---

[223] BBM (434) drew on "L'évangile," his 1968 study of Luke 2:8–20; I would be in close
agreement with the theology of the new article as well.

giving the total of twenty-seven. (That elaborate a structuring is more often in the eye of the beholder than in the eye of the composer.) In particular he calls attention to the names/titles "Caesar Augustus" at the beginning, "Savior" and "Lord Messiah" in the middle (v. 11), and "Jesus" at the end. Fitzmyer (*Luke* 1.392) organizes into three uneven divisions (vv. 1–5, 6–7, 8–20), with three subdivisions in the last. Fusco ("Messaggio" 294), recognizing that the tripartite pattern of division (of the type I proposed) is held by almost all authors, works with it in detail (294–302) to discuss the issue I raised on 410–11: Attention is drawn to the middle scene where heaven and earth touch in the angelic annunciation to the shepherds, and yet the climax comes in the third division where the protagonists of the first and second divisions meet and respond to God's message embodied in the child. He wants to put the most emphasis on the last part that is not only the conclusion of the narrative but also the theological apex in the seeing of the sign, i.e., the newborn in the manger.

Eulenstein ("Und den" 95–102) uses the same type of tripartite division to trace an interesting sequence. Vv. 1–7 offer a stark contrast: beginning with an imperial edict of Caesar Augustus and ending with two parents who cannot even find a lodging place and have to place their baby in an animal manger. That whole scene is on the human level. Vv. 8–14 shift to a higher level in terms of a surprising divine intervention by an angel of the Lord and a multitude of the heavenly host. Their message reinterprets the elements of the first part, giving them meaning that one could not suspect from the human level. The third part (vv. 15–20) returns to the human level and the reaction that people of different types have to what was reinterpreted by God's intervention.

As for *composition,* unfortunately Bovon (*Evangelium* 1.115–16) repeats unconvincing arguments[224] for treating the birth story in chap. 2 (which he judges a Lucan composition, except for vv. 6–7,21) as originally separate from the story of Jesus' conception in chap. 1 (a pre-Lucan legend). Even those who posit a pre-Lucan source[225] need not go

---

[224] I dealt with many of them on 411 above. In particular, it is not true that Mary is introduced in 2:5 as if she had not been mentioned before; rather, the state of her pregnancy is repeated because it is now public and close to term and leads into the story that follows. Indeed, "his betrothed," which might otherwise be awkward, makes sense only after the situation established by 1:27. Nor is Joseph being introduced for the first time; the storyline here needs greater emphasis on Davidic origin than was supplied by the passing Davidic reference in 1:27. Remarkably weak is the claim that two different christologies are involved, dividing off 1:26–28 that stresses Davidic kingship from 2:11 that stresses "Savior." Davidic kingship continues to be stressed in 2:1–20 in the several references to David and in the title "Messiah Lord" of 2:11. The reason "Savior" (scarcely a totally different christology) appears in 2:11 is because of the Roman ambiance introduced in 2:1–2. Employing a Jewish title for God but one also used for Hellenistic rulers, Luke develops his picture to show that Jesus is meaningful to Gentiles as well.

[225] Most who do, offer variants of what I described on 411 above. For example, M. Riebl ("Weihnachten") detects the hand of Luke in 2:1–7,19, whereas 2:8–18,20 probably came to him from a source (thus the highly christological section). Pesch ("Weihnachts-

in that direction, e.g., Marshall (*Gospel* 97) thinks that on the pre-Lucan level the underlying narrative in chap. 2 was already joined to the narrative in chap. 1. I doubted the existence of a pre-Lucan source; and Fitzmyer (*Luke* 1.392–93) agrees, preferring to speak of Lucan composition employing varying amounts of tradition—an analysis I judge applicable to the annunciation in 1:26–38 as well.

As an example of *overall approaches* to the narrative, inclusions between the Lucan birth and death stories[226] are fully developed by Heck ("Krippenkind"), who finds the man of sorrows foreshadowed by the child in the manger. Neither the situation in which he was born (no room in the lodgings) nor the one in which he died (on the cross) was normal. He was born at night, and darkness covered the whole earth before he died. After birth he was swaddled in cloth strips and laid in an animal's manger; after death he was wrapped in a linen cloth and laid in a tomb that was not his own. To physical eyes the child in the manger and the condemned on the cross were powerless; but with his birth were associated the titles "Savior," "Messiah," and "Lord," and with his death "Messiah," "Son of God," and "King." The first to hear the news of the birth of the Messiah were shepherds; the first to profit from the death of the King of the Jews was a wrongdoer crucified with him. Those who saw the child in the manger went off praising and glorifying God; those who saw the condemned die on the cross glorified God saying, "This man was just," and returned home striking their breasts.

Panier's treatment (*Naissance* 249–59), giving attention to the narrative flow, supplies perceptive insights that unify both chaps. 1–2 and chap. 2 within itself. The beginning of chap. 2, which is focused on the census of the whole world, makes a good sequence to the end of the Benedictus where the rising light from on high appears to those who sat in darkness. At the end of chap. 1 JBap has gone off the scene to return at the beginning of chap. 3, and in his absence Jesus has the stage to himself. If the time in 2:1 seems to be that of Caesar Augustus, it is also the time of JBap's departure to the desert (1:80); and later in 2:22 it will be the time of the Law and of the customs it legislates. Beyond time indications a space sequence dominates Jesus' birth story. From the universal space of the whole world targeted by Caesar Augustus' census the scene shifts to the specific space of the city of David[227]—the symbolic site of Jewish kingship now lies within the ambiance of the Roman empire. The announcement of the angels is centered in another

---

evangelium" 99), however, treats the whole of 2:1–21 as pre-Lucan with only very minor Lucan touches.

[226] There is no reason to think that the parallel events in the death narrative caused the creation of the events in the birth narrative (pace Goulder and Sanderson); the vocabulary is entirely different.

[227] Goulder (*Luke* 1.246) contrasts this with the anonymous place of JBap's birth.

space where the shepherds are. Yet the central character has literally "no place" and is laid in a manger, so that the angelic message about the Lord Messiah comes to focus on that. (A symbol, I would add, that is a challenge to both the Roman concept of imperial power and the Jewish concept of kingship.) In terms of active personages in 2:1–40, the angels, the shepherds, Simeon, and Anna do not appear in more than one segment; Mary is the unifying figure throughout the segments. The child here has a semiotic function: Reactions to him are constitutive of the narrative. He is a sign; but unlike the signs given to Zechariah and Mary in the annunciations his role is more than confirmatory and punctiliar. He is an enduring sign that invokes interpretation and vocalization.

Beyond the general hermeneutical approaches to the infancy narratives discussed in BBM and in §§1 and 9 of this Supplement, recent discussion causes me to mention the approach of E. Drewermann to the Lucan birth story. He would turn the interpretation of Scripture into an exercise of depth psychology as a way of making its message meaningful to people.[228] As with dreams in Jung's psychology, the biblical narrative becomes a tissue of symbols telling us about our own existence, e.g., the virgin birth of God's Son is a symbolic way of expressing an acceptance of the status of each of us as God's child. Frankemölle ("Geburt") rejects not only the method but the results: The birth of Jesus does not signify our common hidden potentialities but God's intervening activity embodied in the unique figure of Jesus Christ. Drewermann's aberrations are not a pressing problem on the English-speaking scene, but his attempt to reject historical-critical exegesis and to substitute a totally different approach is an enduring issue. Historical-critical exegesis can get bogged down in factual details, sources, and theories of composition and become barren. In both BBM and this Supplement I have reacted to that. Nevertheless, a painstaking attempt to determine what was said and what it meant and the constant self-correction involved in scholarly dialogue about that meaning remain our greatest protection against uncontrolled, ingenious readings that make the text mean what we want it to mean (sometimes on behalf of a cause that is respectable but needs to be supported in other ways). To show how what was said and meant remains meaningful is part of the larger task of interpretation building on historical-critical exegesis, but not substituting for it.

B. Background of the Scene. The source of Luke's account is hard to discern, except for those who assume that it is all strict history derived

---

[228] His *Tiefenpsychologie und Exegese* (2 vols.; Olten: Walter, 1984–85) has been answered by G. Lohfink and R. Pesch, *Tiefenpsychologie und keine Exegese* (Stuttgarter Bibelstudien 129; Stuttgart: KBW, 1987).

from Mary—they have their own, almost insurmountable problems, as I argued in §14 of BBM above and will continue to argue below.[229] Most other scholars posit a combination of diverse factors: confused historical memories (e.g., a later census of Judea under Quirinius; Augustus' practice of commanding censuses as he solidified recently instituted imperial control; a tradition of Jesus' birth at Bethlehem); a christology phrased in a language that echoes Roman imperial propaganda ("To you this day there is born in the city of David a Savior who is Christ the Lord"); an idealism about Mary who survives into the story of the public ministry; and some possible echoes of the Jewish Scriptures (about Bethlehem, shepherds).

Goulder (*Luke* 1.247) maintains that the birth of Jesus is patterned on the birth of JBap and receives its substance from Matt's account. There are strong parallels between Matt and Luke, as I point out on 412 above; but most often the phrasing of the parallels is so different that it requires far less imagination to see two independent developments from some common traditional elements than to posit that Luke read the Matthean story and deliberately changed the material so much that one can scarcely recognize it.[230]

With unhesitating confidence that the rest of scholarship is wrong, Aus ("Weihnachtsgeschichte" 55–57) finds the source of the whole Lucan birth story in haggadic (= a form of midrashic) reflection on the story of Moses' birth! Many have suggested that point of origin for Matt 2 but confined themselves to elements of the developed Moses story attested by the time of the NT. Aus, reaching to works the written form of which date from 400 to 700 years after the birth of Jesus, combines material from them with great verve, all the while extending unwarranted assurance that this reflects early tradition. For the shepherd and census motifs, for instance, he goes to TalBab *Soṭa* 11a–13a where just before Moses' birth Hebrew women had sex with their husbands in the sheepfolds, to Midrash Rabbah on Canticle 2:15, §2 where Egyptian children keep a list (= census) of pregnant Hebrew women, and to

---

[229] Similar problems exist for Muñoz Iglesias, who argues that the source was written in Hebrew by an early Palestinian Christian of priestly background. This hypothetical author could not have been mistaken on such fundamental issues as the census, origin in Nazareth, etc. Consequently MIE has to spend much effort (3.38–68) on the census only to come up with what I regretfully regard as a desperate solution: We have before us an overly literal (and therefore confusing) Greek rendering of the Hebrew original that actually concerned a census before Quirinius and under Saturninus in 7 B.C. Instead of resorting to a Hebrew source that one cannot prove to have existed, the plausibility of which some of the best Semitists in the world deny, I prefer to settle for what we have, namely, reasonably clear Greek that reports something erroneous.

[230] The reasons offered for Luke's changes (*Luke* 1.248–50) are once more a tribute to Goulder's remarkable imagination: In Acts Luke evinces a dislike of maguses like Simon (Acts 8:9,11) and Bar-Jesus (13:6,8) and so he gets rid of Matt's magi; he does not like political overtones, so he gets rid of the murderous Herod, etc.

Targum Jonathan which gives a messianic interpretation of Jer 33:13 (a verse that mentions one who counts the flock). Without historically datable evidence that would show these ideas to have been known and combined in the 1st century, all this must be considered unsubstantiated speculation.

C. The Census of Quirinius (2:1–5). This was discussed both under §14 above (412–18) and in Appendix VII.[231] I pointed out that there were two difficulties about historicity: (a) There is no evidence that an edict went out from Caesar Augustus for a census to be taken of the whole world. (b) The first census undertaken by Quirinius as governor of Syria did not concern Galilee but Judea (which was being made a Roman province) and took place in A.D. 6 (thus some ten years after Herod's death).[232] My own judgment was that Luke confused the troubled times accompanying the formation of the province of Judea and the troubled times accompanying the death of Herod ten years previously.[233]

As for difficulty (a), Wiseman ("There") argues that in A.D. 6 there was a worldwide edict of Augustus instructing provincial governors to provide up-to-date lists of Roman citizens because he was about to impose on them an inheritance tax. Quirinius would have combined this with a provincial census; and so Luke 2:1–2 was correctly referring to two actions that took place in A.D. 6 even if he unified them and mistakenly associated Jesus' birth with them. In defense of Lucan dating, some would argue that there was a census by Augustus in 2 B.C. Yet to my knowledge, only in 5th-century Christian writing do we begin to see "census" used for what happened in 2 B.C., which Augustus himself described simply as his having been made "Father of my Country" by the Roman people.

A much more helpful direction is indicated by Benoit's thesis ("Quirinius" col. 697) that the "census of the whole world" under Augustus was a Lucan generalization based on Augustus' drive to classify the empire, as illustrated by many local censuses conducted at different times. This generalization set the birth of Jesus in the context of the unification and pacification of the whole world, associated in Luke's time with the memory of this now-worshiped imperial savior.[234] Several

---

[231] I shall not concern myself with recent literature that simply repeats proposed solutions already discussed and rejected there. Lawrence ("Publius") is a prime example of that.

[232] Luke mentions Herod in relation only to the conception of JBap (1:5ff.), not to the birth of Jesus; however, his story places Jesus' birth about fifteen months after the conception of JBap (1:36). Haacker ("Erst") thinks Luke's confusion stems from combining a JBap story that correctly placed his birth under Herod and a Jesus story that correctly placed his birth in the time of Quirinius (= ten years later). However, a birth of Jesus in A.D. 6 would mean that he was only about twenty-two when he began his public ministry—younger than all the Gospel indications for that ministry.

[233] I see no evidence that Luke had direct, firsthand knowledge of details about the birth of Jesus. In 3:1–3 he is quite precise about the beginning of the public activity of JBap, whereas in 3:23 he reports about Jesus only that he was "about thirty years of age."

[234] Fitzmyer (*Luke* 1.394) is favorable to this approach: "The birth in the city of David

other contributions add to the notion that Luke was deliberately counterposing Augustus to Jesus. Although I gave some information about
"Caesar Augustus" on 394 above, I did not discuss the thesis that in 2:1
Luke used *Augoustos,* a Greek transliteration from the Latin, as a
personal name for Caesar (i.e., for the emperor), even though in Acts
25:21,25 he uses *Sebastos,* the Greek equivalent of the Latin, as a
title.[235] Morris ("Why") proposes an explanation for such a personal-
name use in 2:1: In the birth-story contrast between Jesus and the
emperor, Luke would not have wanted to employ the laudatory imperial
title. It was better in that comparison to use two individual names,
Augustus who was Caesar and Jesus who was the Messiah (2:11). The
suggestion that Luke's "This day is born a Savior" (2:11) is a Christian
counterclaim to the imperial propaganda associated with the celebration
of Augustus' birth is enhanced by discoveries in Rome showing the care
expended on observance of the emperor's day: Calculations about the
direction of the sun's rays on that day had a role in aligning monuments
related to Augustus in the city, namely, his obelisk on Montecitorio, his
Ara Pacis, and his mausoleum. Smith ("Caesar's") has enlarged the
picture of the counterposing of Christ and Caesar by considering not
only Luke's allusions to the empire in the Gospel but also those in Acts,
where the issue of obedience to Roman decrees comes up in reference
to Paul.[236]

As for (b), the dating of the census of Quirinius, there have been
many attempts to save Lucan historicity. Most often that has taken the
form of positing two censuses, one (undocumented) in all Palestine *ca.*
4 B.C. when Herod was still alive and the recorded one in Judea in A.D.
6.[237] Benoit ("Quirinius") is willing to posit an otherwise not clearly

gives the story a Jewish atmosphere, but that is transformed by the larger reference to
Roman history." MIE 3.133–35 rejects it, perhaps because such echoing of imperial
propaganda would not fit the theory that the whole narrative was composed in Hebrew by
a very early Palestinian Christian. Yet Pesch ("Weihnachtsevangelium" 106–16), who also
thinks the whole birth story was pre-Lucan, makes the contrast between Augustus and
Jesus a major motif.

235 A title is what Latin *Augustus* ("August, Venerable") was when in 27 B.C. it was first
given to Octavian. Morris ("Why") cites F. F. Bruce, I. H. Marshall, and J. A. Fitzmyer
as recognizing this distinction.

236 It has long been recognized that the Lucan account of the trial and death of Jesus
was colored by anticipation of similar scenes in Acts (Stephen, Paul), but this is a healthy
reminder to extend the interrelationship of Luke and Acts to the infancy narrative. Beyond
the NT evidence discussed in the text above, Buchheit ("Hippolyt") shows how the
earliest Church Fathers to discuss the census of Augustus reacted theologically. Hippolytus, followed by Ambrose, denigrated the census as an exercise of this-worldly power over
against the peaceful kingdom brought by Jesus. (Strangely this view is still advocated by
Pesch ["Weihnachtsevangelium" 109–10], who contends that in the birth story Augustus
is not a peaceful figure but an oppressor of Jewish freedom, offending against the law of
God. I find nothing of that in Luke's narrative.) But Origen saw it as an example of the
power of the empire being put to the service of God. The birth that took place in
Bethlehem because of the census of the world would lead to the sanctification of the
world.

237 Thus with variations Brindle, "Census"; E. L. Martin (various publications); and
Thorley, "Nativity." Those who think that Herod died two or three years later than 4 B.C.

attested census in 4 B.C. and to see this as the beginning of a policy toward Palestine by Augustus that culminated in the later census of Quirinius. Some would insist on two governorships for Quirinius and thus totally preserve Lucan factuality; others would admit that Luke made a mistake by attributing the first census to Quirinius, who in fact was governor at the time of the second census. Benoit points out that Josephus tended to confuse the death of Herod the Great (4 B.C.) and the deposition of Herod's son Archelaus (A.D. 6), of whose rule he knew little—a confusion shared by Luke. On behalf of two governorships, E. L. Martin ("Nativity" 90) invokes the Lapis Tiburtinus (550–51 above), which describes an unnamed person who served twice as legate, the second time in Syria. He contends (perhaps correctly) that it refers to Q. Varus who was legate in Syria twice (7/6–4 B.C. and 2 B.C.–A.D. 1); but then he speculates that both S. Saturninus[238] and Quirinius governed in between the two legateships. In this theory Quirinius would have had his first governorship before 2 B.C. (when according to Martin's dating Herod was still alive) during which he conducted the census described by Luke. However, Benoit's comprehensive (and conservative) review of the evidence ("Quirinius" cols. 704–15) challenges the proposed double governorship of Quirinius (4–2 B.C. and A.D. 6–7) as "exceedingly doubtful" and better given up.

So also, in my judgment, should the proposal of two censuses. Acts 5:37 shows knowledge of only one census ("the census"). The so-called textual justification for two censuses, "This was the *first* census under Quirinius as governor" (Luke 2:2), has been correctly challenged by Haacker ("Erst"). It does not mean the first of two; it means that this was the first census[239] carried out under Roman auspices in the province of Judea—a census conducted when Augustus was emperor and Quirinius was governor.

D. The Journey to Bethlehem, the Birth, and No Room at the Katalyma (2:3–7). Caesar Augustus' census of the whole world, conducted when Quirinius was governor of Syria, is stated to have brought Joseph and Mary from Nazareth to Bethlehem where Jesus was born. Once more there are two historical problems: (a) The explanation that each was to be inscribed in his own city is unsupported by Roman practice (396 above). (b) That Mary and Joseph lived in Nazareth before Jesus' birth conflicts with Matt's evidence.

As for (a), Fitzmyer (*Luke* 1.405) confirms the absence of proof that

---

(§6A in this Supplement) are free to place the census later (especially since it is not attested).

238 Martin is trying to save the accuracy of Tertullian's report (553 above) that there were censuses taken by Saturninus.

239 He points to a similar use of *prōtos* by Josephus (*Ant.* 7.3.2; #67): "David was the first to drive the Jebusites out of Jerusalem," not "First, David drove the Jebusites out."

in a Roman census people were expected to return to their native lands or their ancestral towns. Later Roman examples pertinent to people who had to go to be registered in a district different from the one in which they resided because they had property there continue to be cited (e.g., Marshall, *Gospel* 101) despite the very clear facts that Luke does not attribute the necessity to property but to lineage, does not use *apotimēsis,* which is the proper term for registering goods or income, and refers to "no place for them in the lodgings," discouraging the supposition that Joseph had property in Bethlehem. G. D. Kilpatrick ("Luke") suggests that Luke may have got the idea from the instruction in Lev 25:10 that in the Jubilee year[240] all were to return to their own property or family estate.

As for (b), above in Appendix III, lest the issue get disproportionate emphasis by being treated in the body of the commentary, I studied the arguments for and against the historicity of locating Jesus' birth at Bethlehem, pointing out that the supporting evidence was weaker than for Davidic descent. (Meier, *Marginal* 216, would admit only that it cannot be ruled out; DAICC 226 concludes that it may owe more to apologetics than to history.) Some conservative reviewers have reacted indignantly as if Christian faith were under discussion; but Vallauri ("Natus") is willing to recognize less than absolute moral certainty. At least Matt and Luke agree on Bethlehem as the birthplace, but they do not agree on where Mary and Joseph lived before the birth. Despite constantly renewed attempts at harmonization (n. 85 above), absolutely nothing in the Matthean narrative would lead readers to think other than that Bethlehem was the original domicile of Joseph and Mary. Not only does Matt 2:11 mention their house, but also the tone of Matt 2:22–23 shows that they were moving from Bethlehem to Nazareth for the first time. Luke's picture that Joseph and Mary had to go from Nazareth to Bethlehem for census purposes is often preferred on the grounds that Luke is more likely to be giving us a substantially factual account—a preference especially on the part of those who think Luke is translating Mary's memoirs. Yet there are those who hold that if birth at Bethlehem is historical, Matt is more likely factual: Mary and Joseph were inhabitants of Bethlehem before Jesus' birth.[241] That position would imply that the census was a Lucan construction, based on confused memories of Roman censuses, in order to explain the two fixed traditions that came to the evangelist: birth at Bethlehem, and Nazareth as Jesus' hometown.

The birth is described laconically in 2:7. Greater attention is given to a result of the journey from Nazareth to Bethlehem, namely, the

---

[240] In many ways Jesus' opening explanation of his ministry in Luke 4:18–19 echoes the theme of the Jubilee year.

[241] J. Murphy-O'Connor, *The Holy Land* (Oxford Univ. Press, 1980), 147.

unanticipated locale in which the newborn had to be placed. I translated 2:7: "There was no place [*topos*] for them in the lodgings [*katalyma*]." Reflections on how to understand Luke's enigmatic statement are ancient. Must ("Diatessaric") points to a translation in the Western tradition stemming from Tatian's *Diatessaron* to the effect: "There was no other place for them (to put him) in the house[242] [or shed]." Trudinger ("No Room"), accepting the traditional translation "inn" for *katalyma,* rejects the image of the hard-hearted innkeeper turning Joseph and Mary away from the door.[243] Rather, all that Luke was saying is that because travelers were sheltered in one crowded room, "it was not the [fitting] place for them in the inn" to have a birth take place. Though I preferred the more general meaning "lodgings"[244] since Luke 10:34 uses *pandocheion* for "inn," I would agree that there is no justification in the text to imagine more than is implied by Trudinger to explain why the baby was laid in a manger[245] (presumably in a place where animals normally were). Working with the face value of "no place," LaVerdiere ("No Room") points out that while the expression is neutral without any clear connotation of rejection, it is open to that interpretation. In the ministry Jesus will have nowhere to lay his head (Luke 9:58); he will encounter a rejection of hospitality by a Pharisee (7:44–46) and by Samaritans (9:52–53). Thus in the larger Lucan picture the fact that there was no place at his birth may anticipate the career of the Son of Man who will be rejected (9:22).

Kerr ("No room") rejects the translation "inn" and imagines that Joseph, knowing that it took a long time to register for the census, went with Mary to Bethlehem ahead of time (see 2:6a: "while they were there") and was residing with relatives or friends. (I find nothing in the context to support such a residence.) On the analogy of I Sam 9:22, Mark 14:14, and Luke 22:11, Kerr argues that *katalyma* was a room in the house of these relatives or friends, specifically a room for guests. If it was a small room, Luke is telling us that Mary needed a larger place; if a large room with many guests there, she needed more privacy. And so she went to a room with a manger where normally the animals were

242 In passing (136) she suggests that the "house" that shows up in the Estonian witness to the reading may reflect *oikia,* a suggestion meaning that the *katalyma* of Luke 2:7 had been harmonized with the *oikia* of Matt 2:11.

243 As typical of that view he cites Luther's sermon condemning people of that time who would prefer thieves and cutthroats lounging around the inn. Safrai ("No Room") proposes an innkeeper who is correct rather than hard-hearted: He refused accommodations to (the obviously pregnant) Mary because if she went into labor and gave birth in the place where people were lodged, the other guests would have been inconvenienced by having to go out from it.

244 So too LaVerdiere ("No Room" 555): "The term *katalyma* refers to any place where a traveler can find hospitality while on a journey." See 399–401 above.

245 MIE 3.98 rejects the idea of "no fitting place" and opts for "not enough place"; I have no objection to that as a possibility.

temporarily sheltered, though they would have been moved out for this occasion. A similar view is proposed by Byrne ("No Room"), Kipgen ("Translating"), and especially by Bailey ("Manger") who has received attention in the press by his stress on modern Palestinian peasant customs. The guest room (often on the roof) had insufficient space, and so Mary was moved to the main family dwelling room where animals lived with people (the latter presumably sleeping on an elevated ledge) and where there was a manger on the floor. However, Ottey ("In a stable") persuasively rejects the thesis that Luke's *katalyma* means a guest room.[246] In six LXX instances the word renders Hebrew *mālôn*, which is a place where one stays overnight. In I Sam 1:18 (no Hebrew original) it is the place where Elkanah and Hannah stayed on the way to Shiloh, and that story is certainly part of Luke's background in the infancy narrative. Moreover, the unverifiable assumption of historicity in the guest-room interpretation (sometimes accompanied by a triumphalism about what other scholars have missed because they do not know Palestinian ethnography) is distracting; for if Luke describes something ordinary, that does not make it historical. Indeed, one may intelligently wonder whether an explanation that renders the scene quite ordinary really does justice to the sense of awe and "sign" with which Luke surrounds the swaddled baby lying in a manger—a topic to be discussed in relation to v. 12 below.[247]

I translated 2:7 as "She gave birth to a son, her firstborn." LaVerdiere ("Jesus") thinks it should be rendered: "She gave birth to her son, the firstborn," with *prōtotokos* having the force of a christological title relating Jesus to the Father (Col 1:15,18; Heb 1:6; Rev 1:5) and fulfilling Luke 1:35, "The one to be born will be called . . . Son of God." In "Wrapped," LaVerdiere goes to the OT usage of "swaddling" in Wis 7:1–6 (see 419 above) to show that the birth of the Father's firstborn involved a truly human child whose entry into life was the same as that of all.[248] Serra ("E lo avvolse") gives examples of some dozen different patristic interpretations of the swaddling;[249] and he himself (133) sees a

---

[246] Bovon (*Evangelium* 1.122) does opt for a guest room in a private house, but in a type of bed-and-board situation, not the house of an acquaintance or relative.

[247] Let me mention here the misleading character of the speculation that this is the manger where the shepherds of v. 8 normally kept food for their animals and that is why they knew where to find the baby. The shepherds are told in v. 12 about a baby in *a* manger, not in *the* manger, as if it were one known to them. In v. 16 they found Mary and Joseph and that is how they found the baby.

[248] Some bring into the discussion of "swaddling" a reference in Midrash Rabbah on Lam 1:16 §51 (also TalJer *Berakot* 2:4[5a]) where felt garments for the King Messiah as a child are supplied to the mother. The similarity is only partial, and the date of the tradition may be as late as the 5th century A.D.

[249] E.g., contrast of the child wrapped in swaddling with the glory that shone around the shepherds; contrast of the one who belonged in the immensity of the heavens or who is ruler of all now restricted by wrappings; the irony that the star led the magi to adore a child wrapped in swaddling; the wrappings showing the reality of the humanity; the swaddling of the child contrasted to the nudity of the risen Lord; etc.

common element in the symbolism of limited, precarious, earthly situation. I would see possibilities of that symbolism in the manger, but I think the evidence insufficient for the swaddling. I would also caution that Luke shows no awareness of incarnation theology wherein a preexistent divine being is now reduced to a humble human state.

E. The Angel of the Lord Tells Shepherds of the Birth of the Messiah (2:8–12).[250] Reflections on recent literature can be divided under two subheadings: the symbolism of the shepherds, and the angelic announcement that gives a sign.

Symbolism of the Shepherds. Recognizing that functionally the revelation to the shepherds and their coming to Bethlehem to see the Messiah is the Lucan parallel to Matt's account of the magi receiving revelation about the birth of the King of the Jews and coming to Bethlehem to see, Haudebert ("Bergers") asks why Luke has chosen shepherds as the recipients of such revelation.[251] (Luke 1:58 has only Elizabeth's neighbors and relatives hear of the birth of JBap and rejoice with her.) At least six different symbolisms have been appealed to.

(a) Comparative-religion symbolism, e.g., the Oedipus myth of the royal child found by a shepherd (420–21 above, n. 40). Popular earlier, this background had lost much of its appeal when BBM was written; and it is rejected by Fitzmyer, Marshall, and others. Yet it has been revived by Bovon (*Evangelium* 1.123). Once more it is not impossible that hearers of the Gospel educated in Greco-Roman mythology thought of this when they heard Luke's story, but it is not plausible in my judgment that such a Semitic story has its primary symbolism derived from pagan mythology. Luke's desire to show Jesus as greater than Caesar Augustus is understandable; a desire to compare him to pagan gods is much less plausible.

(b) Symbols of rustic virtues (nobility, gentleness, etc.). This is probably the way the image of the shepherd strikes many today, especially those who have no personal experience of pasturing and must depend on literature or art. In antiquity Virgil painted some idyllic pictures of the shepherd that could have influenced those with a Greco-Roman education. However, little emphasis is placed on this aspect of

---

250 The shepherds are taking turns watching "at night." Combined with 2:9b where "the glory of the Lord shone round them," and 2:32a where Jesus is referred to as "a light . . . to the Gentiles," this indication has contributed greatly to the depiction of Christmas where, against a dark background, Mary is shown with the baby surrounded by light and shining brightly. Sudbrack ("Geburt") discusses the light motif for Christmas in art (and patristic and mystic writing), and thinks of it as an essential theological component of God's revelation in Jesus. Eastern and Western writers cite Ps 36:10: "In your light we see light."

251 For MIE a question like that would be relativized: The shepherds are historical, and the pre-Lucan account was reporting history. With Fitzmyer (*Luke* 1.395) I judge that no matter where he got the idea, Luke introduced the shepherds into this scene; and I want to know what connotation he intended by them.

shepherds in the OT, and it would seem banal in the midst of the theologically charged Lucan infancy narrative.

(c) Symbols for sinners or those outside the Law (thus Temme, "Shepherds," and Goulder, *Luke* 1.251–52). It could be theologically fruitful to have the first revelation of the newborn Lord and Savior to those who otherwise would have been considered religious outcasts. Goulder states that Jesus knew bad company right from the start. Although on 420 above I warned that one should not too easily assume that shepherds represented sinners, I cited a later talmudic text and too easily made the affirmation that often in Jesus' time they were considered as dishonest, outside the Law.[252] With more consideration I would insist that we do not know what kind of attitude would be evoked in the 1st century by a reference to shepherds without anything in the context to specify it; and contemporary, not later, Jewish evidence is needed to show that shepherds would be looked on as outside the Law. The fact that Jesus is compared to a shepherd (John 10:11; Mark 14:27; Matt 25:32; Heb 13:20), that he is portrayed as regretting that the people are like sheep without a shepherd (Mark 6:34), and that he exalts the image of a shepherd who searches for the lost sheep (Luke 15:3–7) does not suggest a priori that a Christian audience would react unfavorably to the shepherd figures Luke presents here.

(d) Symbols for the poor, either financially or in spirit, such as the Anawim (supported in times past by Lagrange and George; recently by Marshall). Luke's general Gospel predilection for the poor has already been underlined in the Magnificat, and Ezekiel's parable of the shepherds (which was used by the early Christians as background for Jesus the shepherd) has God pasturing those who are despoiled. Nevertheless, the sheep rather than the shepherds are more likely to represent the downtrodden; and since the shepherds have flocks, they would not easily be representative of those without possessions. We should recognize that after the portentous references to Augustus and Quirinius in 2:1–2, shepherds present a contrasting atmosphere of ordinariness; but that is not the same as representing the poor or downtrodden. Fitzmyer (*Luke* 1.396), who rejects identification of the shepherds with the poor,

---

252 Temme ("Shepherds") appeals to Ezekiel's condemnatory comparison of the priests to shepherds whose action would harm their flock. The argument does not work, for the presupposition behind the condemnation is a favorable picture of what shepherds should be. It offers no reason to think that a simple mention of shepherds would produce a bad image. While not looking on the shepherds as sinners, Horsley (*Liberation* 103–6) would fit them into a peasantry despised by the aristocrats and looking for revolutionary deliverance. He points to Anthrongaeus, a shepherd who had himself designated king and led an armed band at the time of Herod the Great's death (Josephus, *Ant.* 17.10.7; #278–81). There is insufficient evidence, in my judgment, that politically shepherds would be particularly restive; and there is no evidence whatsoever that Luke had any interest in portraying them as such. See my remarks at the beginning of §10 in this Supplement.

thinks of them as representing the lowly of human society (see Luke 1:38,52).

(e) Symbols for the apostles or church pastors. Luke's shepherds not only hear the angelic message; they set forth with haste to Bethlehem and make known the event as it was told them (2:16–17); and then they return glorifying and praising God (2:20). Therefore, even though the shepherds are not specifically said to have believed the angelic announcement which they heard and reiterated, they could be forerunners of "future believers who will glorify God for what they have heard and will praise God for what they have seen."[253] In an early article ("L'évangile" 169, 177) Legrand went much further by seeing them as symbols or types of the apostles going forth to proclaim the Gospel. I rejected that because the shepherds did not go forth from Bethlehem to proclaim the Gospel[254] but to glorify God, a rejection reiterated by Haudebert ("Bergers" 183–84). Moving beyond the apostolic symbolism, several other writers would make them symbols of the church overseers or presbyters who are called shepherds in the NT. From the fact that the manger is a feeding trough LaVerdiere[255] maintains that Luke is foreshadowing the shepherds of the Christian community who are to feed the flock which is the church of God (Acts 20:28–29). I find that overimaginative: There is no hint of a "Table of the Manger" in Luke 2, and Luke never calls the pastors of the church shepherds (the Acts passage speaks only of a flock).

(f) Symbols of Davidic background. Twice Bethlehem is called the city of David (normally a designation for Jerusalem; 396 above), and David was a shepherd in the Bethlehem area when he was called by Samuel to be anointed king (I Sam 16). Many are willing to settle for that general an echo (e.g., Fitzmyer, *Luke* 1.396); but on the basis of the fact that Lucan shepherds are pasturing their flock, a more specific reference has been proposed involving Bethlehem as Migdal Eder, "the Tower of the Flock." Having criticized Aus at the beginning of this section, let me chastise myself for having invoked the Targum Pseudo-Jonathan of Gen 35:21 in support of this connection, even though I warned of its later dating. Fitzmyer (*Luke* 1.396) is quite right in rejecting it methodologically as 7th-century-A.D. evidence. Nevertheless the Migdal Eder possibilities explained on 421–23 above still remain,

---

[253] Thus 429 above. More simply, if one understands the Gloria to refer to "people of good will," one may agree with Haudebert ("Bergers" 185) that the shepherds personify that group.

[254] Without going to that extreme of making them apostolic forerunners, MIE 3.112–14 stresses their proclaiming role. I insist that the angels are the main proclaimers in the birth scene.

[255] "At the Table of the Manger"; so also A. Serra's 1990 paper on the shepherds of 2:8–20, according to Testa's summary ("XXXI" 138–39).

and have found support both from Haudebert ("Bergers" 182) and MIE 3.118–21.[256] With or without the Migdal Eder element, a Davidic-background symbolism remains the most plausible answer to why Luke portrays shepherds in the Bethlehem area as the first to hear the news that a Savior has been born in the city of David.

The Angelic Announcement and the Sign It Gives. This can be further broken down into two subtopics: the announcement itself and the sign.

(a) The announcement. Many scholars have spoken of the angelic appearance here as a third Lucan annunciation. On 424 above I pointed out that it has many of the features of the standard annunciation pattern (with the exception that the birth has already taken place), but on 411–12 I warned that its real parallel is not the two prebirth annunciations of Luke 1:5–38 but the postbirth story in Matt 2:1–12. Parker ("Birth") would sharpen the analysis: One should keep distinct annunciations made before birth and announcements of a birth that has taken place.[257] He offers examples for the latter from Ugaritic literature and from the OT, e.g., Jer 20:15 ("A male child [son] has been born to you") and Isa 9:5 ("A boy has been born to us; a son has been given to us").[258] The announcement in 2:11 manifests features of this pattern, including the passive verb, the joy that accompanies the birth of a son, and, I would add, the tone of solemnity. If, as observed above, the announcement echoes Roman imperial proclamations, it also echoes the language of the OT.

The announcement concerns the present: "This day there is born. . . ." Yet there is also a future component: "A great joy that will be for the whole people." Fusco ("Messaggio" 1.311) makes this tension the explanation of v. 19 as to why Mary kept with concern all these events, interpreting them in her heart. Only the future would show her how this child will bring joy to all the people. The basic information

[256] The latter points out (correctly) that shepherds are not mentioned in the references to that site, but the parallelism with Luke is based on the flock(s). That Migdal Eder in Micah 4:8 represents Jerusalem is not a major difficulty; for the Luke who has shifted the designation "the city of David" from Jerusalem to Bethlehem may also have shifted this other symbolic title from one to the other.

[257] I have no objection to that distinction, and indeed it may have the advantage of keeping Luke 2:8–12 closely integrated to what precedes (and thus it may implicitly reject Bovon's claim [*Evangelium* 1.115] that form-critically v. 8 begins a section that is distinct from the rest of the chapter). Yet there is hypercriticism in Parker's contention on 146–47 that the elements of the birth annunciation pattern (appearance of the angel of the Lord, fear, an objection or request for a sign, and the giving of a sign) should not be counted for they are general features of individual theophanies and have no essential relationship to announcements before or after birth. The pattern is set up by features that usually occur; the only essential feature is the forthcoming birth and that does not constitute a pattern. Also why should the fact that features are also associated with a theophany make them any less characteristic features of birth annunciations? Frankly, however, I have no interest in such a classification debate beyond what the classification contributes to exegesis.

[258] See also Ruth 4:17a; Job 3:3. On 424–25 I called attention to Isa 9:5(6) as the primary background for the Lucan birth announcement.

about the unusual combination *christos kyrios* ("Messiah Lord") in 2:11 was given on 402–3 above. Hann ("Christos") has made an important new contribution. He points out that all the texts of *Psalms of Solomon* that preserve 17:32(36) read *christos kyrios*, so that it should be preferred despite the many scholars who emend that text to *christos kyriou* ("the Messiah/anointed of the Lord"). It is quite true that the Hebrew of Lam 4:20 reads "the anointed of the Lord"; but how do we know that the LXX *christos kyrios* (most often emended to *christos kyriou*) is a mistranslation rather than a use of an alternate form of the title? Hann maintains that in the Hellenistic era not only did the absolute title "Messiah" begin to substitute for the preexilic royal designation "the Lord's Messiah/anointed," but also compound titles appeared, e.g., Dan 9:25: "Messiah/anointed prince." Later the Targum Neofiti of Gen 49:10 exemplifies "King Messiah," which will become a common title in Judaism. This type of usage was influenced by a Hellenistic royal pattern, e.g., "King Lord" for the Herodian rulers. Therefore Luke 2:11 is simply an early instance of the compound title "Messiah Lord" or "Lord Messiah."[259]

(b) The sign. The issue of why "a baby wrapped in strips of cloth and lying in a manger" is a sign (2:12)[260] is still not fully clear (418–20, 425 above). MIE 3.88–89 counterposes it to the Jewish expectation of the appearance of an adult: They are to see a newly born Messiah.[261] Trémel ("Signe"), who sees a parallel between the going to Bethlehem at the beginning of Luke and the going to Jerusalem at the end, would compare the child in a manger/stable to the paradox of Jesus on the cross, and compare "this will be a sign" to OT formulas of promise (see also the thesis of Heck about inclusions on 663 above). Most frequently the sign is interpreted to involve the lowliness of the situation of the child who is Savior and Lord Messiah.[262]

[259] As for the meaning of "Lord," Fitzmyer (*Luke* 1.202) and MIE 3.141–42 contend that although the title sets Jesus on a level alongside God, it does not identify him with God (vs. Laurentin, de la Potterie, and others).

[260] On 403 above I accepted the Vaticanus reading of "a sign" rather than the broadly attested reading of "the sign," which I regarded as a copyist's assimilation to the definite article in OT parallels. Fitzmyer agrees, but Marshall and Fusco prefer "the sign." In particular, the latter asks ("Messaggio" 1.306) why I would attribute the OT assimilation to the copyists rather than to Luke himself. Answer: because if Luke wrote "the sign," then the copyist of Vaticanus by changing it to "a sign" would be undoing a clear OT parallel—an unlikely procedure.

[261] For MIE the issue of why such apparently minor details as the wrapping and placing of the child are the precise elements of the sign is to a certain extent relativized by the contention (3.92) that these are historical memories—something that, of course, we do not know. Fusco ("Messaggio" 1.333) holds that although it is difficult to imagine the invention of a detail like the manger, its origins remain obscure.

[262] Fusco ("Messaggio" 1.314–15) objects that although this idea of a paradoxical sign (wherein insignificance and poverty are the countersigns of the exalted one) is a valid development for preaching, it is not really an intrinsic meaning of the text. It is almost as if the message has to interpret the sign rather than vice versa.

The most extended treatment of the sign is offered by Fusco ("Messaggio" 1.302–33), who makes many excellent observations. This is not a sign like those implicit in the annunciation to Zechariah (muteness) or to Mary (Elizabeth's conceiving). Those visible divine interventions really are extraneous to the heart of the message, even if they give assurance of divine omnipotence. The sign here is part of the message. In somewhat the same direction Bovon (*Evangelium* 1.126) speaks of the offense in the close identity of this sign and the referent: Jesus is the sign of christology. But Fusco (1.322–27) would insist that Jesus *in the manger* is the sign of christology,[263] not through lowliness but because that localization seen and accepted by the shepherds reverses Isa 1:3, the text to which I called attention on 419 above. There the salvation offered by God to Israel was being refused; now it is being accepted.

F. *The Gloria* (2:13–14). Several problems continue to be actively debated in relation to the canticle of the "heavenly host."[264]

Place among the Canticles and Structure. On 425–27 above I explained some of the unique features of the Gloria. Nevertheless I thought it shared enough features with the other three infancy narrative canticles to be grouped in the (Greek) collection that Luke drew upon to vocalize reaction to and reflection on what God was revealing about JBap and Jesus.[265] Most other scholars adopt toward the Gloria the same position they take toward the other canticles, e.g., MIE 1.242–92 argues for composition in Hebrew. Fitzmyer (*Luke* 1.397), however, although agreeing that the other three canticles are pre-Lucan Greek compositions, contends that Luke himself composed this one. In truth the Gloria is so short that decision is rendered very difficult.

Another issue is whether 2:14 should be treated as a tricolon or bicolon (couplet); I opted for a bicolon (404–5, 427 above). That is the dominant view among recent writers (Bovon, Fitzmyer, Luke, Marshall, and MIE).[266]

"Good will." More than a half-dozen articles betray a continued fascination with the wording and translation of the second line of 2:14, which begins with "and on earth peace" and then continues with a

263 Panier (*Naissance* 258–59) makes a similar point in a semiotic way: They went not to see the child but to see the word/event that had taken place as it had been told to them (2:15,17).

264 This LXX expression is not always positive in its connotation; in Jer 7:18 it refers to strange gods. That the heavenly host gave praise at the birth of Jesus may have a stronger connotation than reporting that angels gave praise.

265 K. Luke ("Luke 2:14") does not hesitate to affirm that the Gloria was a hymn of the Anawim. Marshall (*Gospel* 111) estimates that the Gloria is in effect a proclamation of the results of the birth of Jesus rather then a hymn of praise directly addressed to God. Bovon (*Evangelium* 1.128) says that it follows the christological revelation of 2:10–12 as liturgical commentary and choral conclusion.

266 R. S. Kilpatrick ("Greek") observes that now the preference for the bicolon or distich is usual.

phrase that is difficult to translate: *en anthrōpois eudokia(s)*. At the outset let me mention the continued discussion of one solution mentioned on 405 above: that *eudokias* was a Lucan addition to a pre-Lucan canticle. Schwarz ("*Anthrōpoi*"), continuing in a direction already indicated by his earlier work ("Lobgesang"), argues from three Syriac versions that the original Lucan text lacked *eudokias*, which was a Greek liturgical expansion of the text. However, the Syriac evidence is scarcely conclusive, for some Syriac translators tried to "improve" the NT text by shrewd guesses (see Matt 1:16; John 18:13). P.-R. Berger ("Menschen") contends that the Syriac evidence is clearly secondary and rejects Schwarz's attempt to retrovert Luke 2:14 into Aramaic.

Accepting a form of *eudokia* as original, I was inclined to render the disputed Greek as "and on earth peace *among people favored [by God]*" (403–4 above). Basically there are two problems: one textual, whether to read the genitive *eudokias* or the nominative *eudokia*, and the other interpretative, assigning a meaning to the choice made. Eulenstein ("Und den" 94) reminds us how intimately those two problems were connected at the Reformation. The Vulgate, favoring the genitive, read "hominibus bonae voluntatis"; and in the eyes of Luther this rendering, "Peace on earth to people [men] of good will," implied that God would give peace only to those who deserve it—a theology of merit! The nominative, making it possible to read "Peace and good will to people [men]," favored a theology of divine graciousness reaching out to all, no matter how they were disposed. On an interpretative level Luther's outlook would be supported by the only other use of *eudokia* in Luke (10:21), where God's attitude is involved, and by the overall tendency of the LXX and the rest of the NT to ascribe *eudokia* to God more often than to people.[267] Dodd ("New . . . II") agrees that the passage refers to divine election in which God favors some people. On purely textual grounds, however, Luther's preference for the nominative has little support.[268]

By the time BBM was written there was an added factor that seemed to support the best in both approaches, namely, the better Greek reading (the genitive), and yet allotting to God (rather than to human behavior) the initiative as to who would be favored. Phrases had been found in Qumran Hebrew and Aramaic describing "a man/children of His good will" (403–4 above; also Fitzmyer, *Luke* 1.411–12).

Yet there have been objections to that solution. In a careful study of

---

[267] Hebrew (or Aramaic) nouns in the Qumran literature that might underlie *eudokia* are also divine attributes.

[268] According to R. S. Kilpatrick ("Greek"), almost all editors prefer *eudokias* to *eudokia*, even though syntactically the latter is a much easier reading. Goulder (*Luke* 1.254) states, "The genitive is no longer in dispute."

Greek usage, R. S. Kilpatrick ("Greek") argues that there are three possible translations of the genitive *eudokias* that can be arranged in this order of increasing Greek syntactical difficulty: "among people who bless [God]"; "among people of [i.e., with an inner disposition toward] good will"; "among people of [God's] good pleasure [= favored by God]." The last translation is the most difficult because it would normally require an *autou* ("His"). Smyth ("Peace") argues that for the genitive to refer to "God's good will," the possessive must be expressed. The proposed Qumran parallels have a "his" (or "your") to make clear that God's attitude is meant, and the same is true of LXX usage where God's *eudokia* is meant. Guerra Gómez ("Hominibus") in a painstakingly careful study insists that the entire Latin evidence supports "bonae voluntatis" as a human attitude.[269]

Perhaps, consciously or unconsciously, we have let the discussion be too influenced by the Reformation problematic: divine election of some to receive peace, or some meriting peace by their behavior. Berger ("Lk 2:14") does not see this as a delimiting selection of people, for *eudokia* means God's saving power. Hansack ("Lukas 2,14") argues that even the Latin (with *bonae voluntatis* or *benevolentiae* as renditions) allowed for divine kindness. Mueller ("Application") draws together the entire phrase: "peace coming from his [God's] good pleasure with mankind." If we accept the better Greek reading, namely, the genitive, and if we follow the easier Greek syntax supported by the Latin, namely, "people of good will," we can still recognize that the reason they are people of good will is not because of their own merit but because God's grace/favor/good will has moved them in that direction (so also Bovon, *Evangelium* 1.129). If we accept Eulenstein's progression of the three parts of the narrative (§14A in this Supplement), we could posit that the *eudokias* that ends the second part in 2:14b should come from God since that part deals with heavenly intervention, whereas those favored (*anthrōpoi*) are exemplified by the people who react in the third part.

G. Reactions to the Happenings (2:15–20). C. Burchard (ZNW 69 [1978], 145–46) has devoted a brief note to the use of *dierchesthai heōs* in 2:15: "Let us *go over* to Bethlehem." From the other two Lucan examples (Acts 9:38: travel from Lydda to Joppa; Acts 11:19: travel to Phoenicia), he concludes that the shepherds are pictured at a distance from Bethlehem. Accordingly 2:8, placing the shepherds "in that same region," probably means no more than that they were somewhere in Judea (2:4).[270] I am not certain that we can derive such a precise picture from Luke's Greek.

---

269 Yet K. Luke ("Luke 2:14" 191–99) calls upon versional evidence, especially the Ethiopic, to support interpreting the text as God's good will to people. Many variants in the Syriac tradition read "hope" rather than "good will."

270 Bovon (*Evangelium* 1.123) prefers as a translation "the above-mentioned region" to "the same region."

In the passage, "They made known the event *as it was told them* concerning this child" (2:17), Ellingworth ("Luke"), maintaining that the shepherds understood the angel in 2:10–12 to be bringing a message from God, would translate the italicized words (= divine passive) as "what God said to them" (see also 2:20). Page 405 above noted that the Greek *rēma* ("word") is used in 2:15,17,19 to cover the double connotation of the Hebrew *dābār*, "word, deed/thing" and thus is a semitism. Burchard ("Note") observes that although *rēma* was virtually unused in Koine Greek (and Philo and Josephus) except in the sense of "verb," it is frequent in the Greek Bible and related literature with the same sense as *logos*[271] ("word," which also renders *dābār*). In general the NT uses *logos* more frequently than *rēma*, but half the NT uses of *rēma* are in Luke-Acts. *Rēma* dominates in *Joseph and Asenath*, a work written originally in Greek and surely not translated from Hebrew, manifesting the same double meaning "word" and "deed/thing." Therefore, Burchard (294) challenges the thesis that Lucan *rēma* points to a Hebrew or Aramaic original. Drawing also on Acts 10:37, he suggests that Luke may have chosen the semitized Greek *rēma* to represent the Christian message in Jewish context.

A crucial verse in Roman Catholic discussions is 2:19, which I translated (430–31): "Mary kept with concern all these events, interpreting them in her heart," arguing that the emphasis was not on Mary as the eyewitness source of historical knowledge, but on an apocalyptic and sapiential interpretation, and a gradual penetration of christological import. (Fitzmyer [*Luke* 1.398] is much of the same mind.) In BBM I had already drawn on Serra's article "Motivi," but now his *Sapienza* represents a major study of the issue in a more conservative direction. He presupposes basic historicity, i.e., that the shepherds who were directed by the angels to the child left an enduring impression in Mary's maternal memories. Luke would have interpreted this in terms of divine revelation, seeing a parallel to the apostles (shepherds of the church) who received revelation about Christ from angels at the tomb. In Serra's view Mary is the unique witness of the infancy narrative, animated by the Spirit to give the right explanation; she is the daughter of wisdom in the grand sapiential tradition of the OT, reflecting on the crucial covenant events. Bellia ("Confrontando") moves in an even more conservative direction, accepting the sapiential approach but criticizing the postresurrectional aspect of Serra's thesis and his overdependence on extrabiblical parallels. Nor does he totally appreciate Legrand's apocalyptic emphasis with its postresurrectional insights. Luke is telling us that Mary made a *realistic* comparison of factual events, not merely

---

[271] In fact, in some parts of the LXX *rēma* is more frequent than *logos*.

symbolic scenes. I see no way to substantiate all this. Luke is presenting Mary as a model, but what information he had about her personal outlook during Jesus' lifetime or after the resurrection no one knows.

H. Circumcision (2:21). On 432 I contended that the circumcision/naming in v. 21 "is so intermediary that it can be treated with either the birth scene [vv. 1–20] or with the purification/presentation [vv. 22–40]." Nevertheless, using parallelism with the JBap scene as a guide, I put it with vv. 1–20. Legrand ("On l'appela" 491) supports the relationship to 2:1–20, arguing that what follows v. 21 concerns obedience to the Law, whereas this verse concerns obedience to the angel's command. So also do Bovon (*Evangelium* 1.115,121) and Pesch (*Weihnachtsevangelium* 99); the latter points to all the OT birth stories that include the naming of the child. Fitzmyer, however, uses the parallelism differently and places v. 21 with vv. 22–40, as do Laurentin (*Évangiles* 238), Gueret, Marshall, and Stramare. Much of this discussion presupposes a precision in Lucan structure that might surprise the evangelist.

In a short, meditative article, pointing out that a name becomes an inalienable part of one's identity, and stressing that "Jesus" means "God saves," Kleiner ("Sie") shows how the whole Gospel is a message of salvation. Whether that was Luke's intent or not, Luke 2:21 should be read in the light of the many references to "the name" in Acts, e.g., 2:38, "Be baptized every one of you in the name of Jesus Christ for the forgiveness of sins"; 3:6, "Silver and gold I have none, but what I have I give you: In the name of Jesus Christ, the Nazorean, walk"; 4:12, "Nor is there any other name under heaven given to the human race by which we are to be saved." In most early Christian thought the "name" is "Lord," but that is predicated inseparably of Jesus.

§15 Presentation, Simeon, Nunc Dimittis, Anna (Luke 2:22–40)

As in the previous section, I shall devote a subdivision to general issues and then treat the individual topics in the sequential order of the story.

A. General Approaches. If 2:1 began with the atmosphere of imperial Rome, and 2:4 shifted the scene to Bethlehem, the city of the Davidic king, we now move to Jerusalem, site of the Temple and its liturgy. The principal reference of the angelic pronouncements in 2:1–21 was dominantly what already existed: The Savior is born; the baby is swaddled and lying in a manger. The principal reference of Simeon's pronouncements is dominantly future: The salvation has been made ready, but it is to be a revelation and a glory; and the child is set for the fall and rise, etc. Thus even logically 2:22–40 is a sequence to 2:1–21. If heavenly voices testified to the identity of the child in 2:1–21, the Law and the Prophets complete the picture here. Three references to the Law in 2:22–24 set an atmosphere; yet that is followed by three references to the Spirit in 2:25–27 (Bovon, *Evangelium* 1.136). The Law frames the passage, mentioned at both the beginning and the end (2:22,39), but in the midst of that Simeon prophesies and Anna the prophetess makes her appearance.

B. The Purification and the Presentation in the Temple (2:22–24). In addition to an objective summary of the modern exegetical dispute that I shall describe in the next paragraph, Köhler ("Pour") gives a brief but interesting history of the importance of the Feast of the Presentation in the liturgy and the Church Fathers.[272] He concludes his survey with Pope Paul VI's apostolic exhortation *Marialis Cultus* issued on that feast in 1974.

Exegetically, Luke 2:22 offers a famous difficulty: "When the time came for *their* purification according to the Law of Moses, they brought him [Jesus] up to Jerusalem to present him to the Lord." The context would suggest that it means the purification of the two parents (Luke 2:27: "the parents brought in Jesus to perform for him what was customary according to the Law"); and that the Law required the child to be brought to the Temple. Yet only the mother needed to be purified, and there was no need to bring the child to the Temple for dedication (see 448 above). On 436 I dismissed the alternative readings "her purification" and "his [Jesus'] purification" as scribal improvements to avoid the difficulty; so also Marshall (*Gospel* 116). Robert ("Comment") points out that Jerome supported the "his" reading on the grounds that Jesus would have had to be considered by people ritually impure as were all other firstborn sons. Also in favor of "his" Lagrange argued that Luke used not *katharsis* ("purification") but *katharismos*, which in Exod 30:10 has the sense of an expiatory sacrifice, and that it was in the context of that sacrifice that Jesus had to be brought to the Temple. Nevertheless, Robert judges the thesis too fragile.[273]

Some scholars have tried to avoid the implication of a mistake by Luke in writing "their" (especially those who think he got this account from Mary, who scarcely would have been confused on this point). For instance, they have argued that "their" refers to Jesus and Mary as a

---

[272] Bovon too (*Evangelium* 1.139) stresses how important the Feast of the Presentation became. Epiphanius shows that by the end of the 4th century it was celebrated in Jerusalem forty days after Epiphany. Origen devoted four homilies to the presentation, and Hesychius of Jerusalem (early 5th century), two.

[273] The vocabulary argument is weak; *katharsis* is never used in the NT, while *katharismos* is used some seven times. The use of the latter, nineteen times in the LXX, need not have a special significance.

compressed way of covering the presentation of Jesus and the purification of Mary.[274] Laurentin in his semiotic exegesis (*Évangiles* 240) is at pains to reinterpret "their purification" as meaning "of the people" of Jerusalem. There is no buying back of Jesus but a redemption of Jerusalem (2:38). Marshall too (*Gospel* 117) thinks that Jesus was offered (like Samuel) and not redeemed. Stramare ("Presentazione" 45–51) combines expiatory sacrifice by Jesus with "their" purification; and he holds that Jesus is not bought back because he remains in the Temple consecrated to God's service, e.g., even at age twelve in 2:43. I rejected all this on 449 above; and Robert "Comment" 451–54), having patiently examined the proposed arguments, contends that contextually and grammatically these are really not justifiable. (In passing he observes perceptively that semiotic/structuralist exegesis really does not solve a problem like this: It simply formalizes an insight with which the analysis started; and if the insight is wrong, the formalizing confirms the error.) The "their" does refer to the parents, although Robert would argue that such usage does not mean that Joseph had to be involved in the same way as Mary. He would understand 2:22 to mean: "When the time came for the purification prescribed for them in the Law of Moses."[275] That is certainly better than the hypotheses of Lagrange, Laurentin, and Stramare; but it still is not what Luke wrote. Why not simply admit that Luke was confused on this point (as on the census)? I saw the inaccuracies as proof that Luke did not grow up in Judaism or in Palestine. Fitzmyer (*Luke* 1.424) states: "Luke, not being a Palestinian Christian, is not accurately informed about this custom of the purification of the woman after childbirth." Goulder (*Luke* 1.255) comments, "Luke knows the LXX rather than real Jewish liturgical practice."

Accepting "their" and acknowledging Luke's inaccuracies, BBM concentrated on Luke's theology of the presentation, modeled after the presentation of Samuel. Fitzmyer has gone in much the same direction. I mentioned also possible influences of Malachi 3:1 and Dan 9:21–24 on the scene. Laurentin (*Évangiles* passim) and Stramare ("Presentazione," 40–41) enlarge the parallels to Malachi, but MIE 3.167–69 rejects most of the added Malachi proposals as well as the Daniel reference, accepting basically only the model from the story of Samuel. (See also Miyoshi, "Jesu," whose theory I explain below under the Nunc Dimittis.) Stramare, however, claims that the scene is not primarily related to the Samuel story but to the anointing of the Davidic king

---

274 That is also the view of Bovon (*Evangelium* 1.136,140), and of Miyoshi ("Jesu" 100–1) who calls on the model of the Nazirite Samuel and his mother.

275 Along similar lines MIE 3.176–77 cites as a parallel usage Jer 25:34 (LXX: 32:34). That passage, however, really does not mean "The days of the slaughter have come for you" but "The days have come for you to be slaughtered," even as Luke means that the days of the parents to be purified had come.

(I Samuel 16) and of the Holy of Holies (Dan 9:24). The objection that
there is no anointing in the Lucan scene can be answered, he thinks, by
an appeal to the meaning of Christ/Messiah as "anointed" (see Luke
2:11,26). There is a great divergence of method here, for Laurentin and
Stramare in my judgment are closer to writing NT theology[276] than to
giving an exegesis of Luke. Appeals to John and Hebrews are not a key
to Luke's mind, and vague assurances that there were some contacts
between Lucan and Johannine traditions tell us absolutely nothing about
Luke's knowledge of a theology of incarnation or of Jesus as the
sacrificial Lamb of God.

   C. Simeon and the Nunc Dimittis (2:25–32). In reference to Simeon I
would have little to add from recent literature to the discussion on 451–
54 above. As Bovon (*Evangelium* 1.141–42) notes, his appearance and
interpretative function are not unlike that of Ananias in the Paul story
(Acts 22:12–15), and his foreboding oracle in Luke 2:34–35 resembles
that of Agabus in Acts 21:10–11. The microcosmic relationship between
Simeon and Jesus duplicates the macrocosmic relationship between
Israel's expectations and their fulfillment. Bovon (1.146) expresses
surprise that Simeon never blesses the child; but given the indirect
relationship of the previous canticles to the events they follow, that is
not too surprising. As for the contents of the Nunc Dimittis, we learn
from it that Simeon is near the departure time of his life (2:29). On the
brink of death his eyes can see a salvation (2:30) in a way that is not
given to others until after death (Panier, *Naissance* 260)—almost an
anticipated beatific vision.

   The Nunc Dimittis has been the focus of frequent studies. In a very
abstract treatment, Marconi ("Bambino") approaches it from the viewpoint (mysterious for me, alas) of "esthetics" (*esthēs*, "clothing"),
which is "a hermeneutical category of seeing and a semantics of the
divine in the Lucan writings." He calls attention to the issue of seeing,
which is not a surprising motif since the revelation of God is centered in
the child that has been born.[277] In particular, Marconi (643) contrasts
the picture that Simeon would "not see death before he had seen the
Lord" with the OT theme where to see God would mean death. The
heart of the Nunc Dimittis is to "have *seen* this salvation that you made
ready in the *sight* of all the peoples," an attitude echoed in Jesus'
enthusiastic proclamation to his disciples: "Blessed are the eyes that
see what you see"—a sight that prophets and kings desired but did not
see. I do not pretend to understand all the nuances of Marconi's

---

[276] By that I mean a theology derived from looking at the whole NT and interpreting one
work in light of the other—a theology scarcely possible before there was a canonical
collection and therefore a theology reflecting the thought of later centuries.
[277] E.g., that the shepherds see is central in Luke 2:15,17,20.

approach, but he has called my attention to a different tone in the Nunc Dimittis from that of the Benedictus and the Magnificat: a more *christological* focus on what God has done. It also has a quite different poetic pattern.

This raises the issue of whether the Nunc Dimittis came to Luke from the same source as the Magnificat and Benedictus, as held likely by BBM, Fitzmyer, Marconi, Farris, and others. Bovon (*Evangelium* 1.145–46) thinks that like the Benedictus and Magnificat this canticle was pre-Lucan; but they were of Jewish origin (§12B in this Supplement), while this one might be either Jewish or Christian. Valentini (*Magnificat* 100–5) may be right in claiming that this is a later canticle than the other two. According to Testa's summary ("XXXI" 137–38), Valentini in his 1990 paper on the canticles has adopted the position ably defended by Grelot ("Cantique") that the Nunc Dimittis is an original Lucan composition, added to the already existing infancy narrative at a later period. I admit that I am more open to this view than I was when I wrote BBM because it explains better not only the differences from the Magnificat and Benedictus, which are community productions, but also the likelihood (to be explained below) that it lays out the program for the spread of the Christian message described in Acts. Nevertheless, if Luke composed the Simeon story first and then composed this hymn to add to it, why did he not make the hymn fit the context better? Having told us that Simeon was waiting for the consolation of Israel and wanted to see the Lord's Messiah, why does the hymn not use that vocabulary to tell us what he experienced when he held the child in his arms and blessed God?

I stressed strongly on 458 above that Deutero-Isaiah supplied the language and imagery of the hymn. Kellermann ("Jesus" 11, 16), who thinks the canticle was a pre-Lucan composition (with the possible exception of 2:29b, "since you have kept your word"),[278] agrees about Deutero-Isaiah but cites as the principal passage the LXX of Isa 51:1,3–6, which I did not cite.[279] Miyoshi ("Jesu"), in his quest for how this canticle is related to the presentation in the Temple, argues that 2:22–38 is throughout a Lucan composition, drawing not on a written source but on Jewish-Christian oral tradition. Isa 51–52 has supplied Luke with the

[278] On 21–22,25 he recognizes the possibility that the Magnificat came from Jewish Christians with an Anawim mentality, but for the Nunc Dimittis he would stress a group from Hellenistic diaspora Judaism with a missionary thrust toward the Gentiles inspired by Deutero-Isaiah. His footnotes do not reveal whether he is cognizant of the large body of English and Spanish literature on the origin of the canticles.

[279] I am very dubious of Kellermann's contention (17) that the Lord's anointed of 2:26 is not the Davidic Messiah but the spirit-filled, anointed servant prophet (Isa 59:21; 61:1; 52:7). Certainly for Luke *christos* is the Davidic Messiah, given the various references to David earlier in the infancy narrative. However, Kellermann (18) speculates that Luke had available a Jewish-Christian pesher on (a LXX style text of) Isa 61:1–2.

Septuagintal language for the canticle. The presentation of Samuel in
the sanctuary is the dominant parallel for the whole scene, with the
added element that Samuel was a Nazirite (as seen in the Qumran
Samuel material). The sacrifice for the purification of a Nazirite (Num
6) was the same as that for the purification of a mother after birth (Lev
12)—two young pigeons or doves. The "light" imagery of the priestly
blessing which ends Num 6 (also "peace, face") has influenced the
Nunc Dimittis. The fact that tannaitic literature (2nd century A.D.)
relates the priestly blessing of Num 6 to the revelation motif of Isa 52
(52:10: the Gentiles see salvation after Jerusalem has been redeemed)
completes the circle of relationship for Miyoshi. In evaluation, I recognize that a Christian application of Nazirite imagery to Jesus is not an
impossibility, despite the fact that he was not ascetic in clothes, food,
or drink; it is one of the possible additional meanings of *Nazōraios* in
Matt 2:23. Nevertheless, finding it in Luke 2:29–32 as a main motif
would suppose considerable subtlety on the part of Luke's audience/
readers. Bovon (*Evangelium* 1.138–39) judges it unlikely.

K. Berger ("Canticum") discusses the genre of the Nunc Dimittis as
a thanksgiving uttered before death, citing some excellent examples
from the Greco-Roman world and from Hellenistic Judaism as well
(testamentary literature, but especially *Jubilees* 22:7–9). He comments
impressively on the background of individual expressions and in this
connection also stresses the relation of the canticle to the eschatological
universalism of Isa 40–52.

Koet ("Simeons") raises the interesting question of the relationship
of the Nunc Dimittis to the theology of Luke–Acts about the salvation
of the Gentiles[280] and Israel. At the end of his double work does Luke
think Israel has been rejected? Koet calls this into question. The
background of the canticle in the second part of Isaiah brings to mind
the servant role where Israel is to be the instrument of bringing light to
the Gentiles. The words of Simeon to Mary in 2:34–35 (who praised
God for what had been done for Israel) predict that the path will not be
easy: There will be the fall and rise of many of Israel. This theme is
worked out in Acts, e.g., 13:46–47 where, having been rejected by the
Jews, Paul and Barnabas turn to the Gentiles and describe themselves
as having been made "a light to the Gentiles." One may wonder further
whether the order of phrases in 22:32ab is significant: a light first to be
a revelation to the Gentiles and then to be a glory for God's people

---

[280] See 440 above justifying the translation: "a light to be a revelation to the Gentiles
and to be a glory for your people Israel." Simón Muñoz ("Cristo") thinks it reflects a
Hebrew passive infinitive meaning "a light to be revealed/illumined." He comments that
Luke's use of the plural of *ethnos* ("nations") when he means "Gentiles" reflects Hebrew
gôyim. In my judgment both instances are perfectly intelligible in this type of semitized
Greek without resorting to a Hebrew original for the canticle.

Israel? That might mean that Acts 28:25–28 is not definitive in saying that this people (the Jews) will not be converted.

In 2:33 Luke reports that the father and mother were astonished at these things said about the child. Some scholars continue to argue from this that the original form of the story knew nothing of the virginal conception or of the annunciation. I and others who judge this to be Lucan composition would see "father and mother" to be ordinary parlance that Luke expects readers to understand in light of what they have already been told, and the astonishment here (as in 2:18) to be a standard reaction to divine revelation. In any case this is certainly how the verse must be read in the existing storyline.

D. Simeon's Oracle of Warning (2:34–35). On 460 above I called this the second oracle of Simeon. It is not a poetic canticle of the same quality as the Nunc Dimittis and has received much less attention in recent literature. If the Nunc Dimittis is the product of Simeon's blessing God (2:28), this oracle is the product of Simeon's blessing the parents.[281] The fact that "blessed" (*eulogēsen*) introduces both the canticle filled with hope and the dire oracle has led Buth ("What Kind" 7) to reflect that there are five kinds of blessings in the Bible, so that the appearance of two different species here is not unusual. In particular the blessing that involves the oracle of 2:34–35 is the "type of blessing where the contents are a prophetic prayer," as in Gen 27:27–29 (see Gen 49). If the Nunc Dimittis describes what the readied salvation will accomplish for both the Gentiles and Israel, the words of this second oracle describe how the accomplishment will be affected by human response. It is not a matter of understanding but of contradiction; not a matter of acceptance by the mind, but of piercing effects on the soul and the unveiling of inmost thoughts.

For Marshall (*Gospel* 122) the first line involving the fall and rise of many in Israel means that those who fall will then rise. Rather, in my judgment it means some will fall and others will rise (so also Fitzmyer, Bovon). The context is one of discerning judgment, and both OT and Lucan passages point in that direction (460–61 above). The reference to a sword[282] piercing "through *your own* soul" in v. 35a is not directed to

---

[281] Does "Simeon blessed them and said to Mary" (2:34) refer to two actions: a blessing on both and an oracle to Mary? Buth ("What Kind" 10) prefers one action: Simeon spoke a prophetic blessing over the parents that had a special meaning for Mary. The MT of Gen 48:15 offers an example of such an epexegetical understanding of a blessing clarifying its direction: Jacob/Israel blesses Joseph but says words calling God's benediction on Joseph's sons.

[282] On 463–64 above I opted for Ezek 14:17 as the principal background for the Lucan sword (*romphaia*) imagery, although I mentioned the attractiveness of Isa 49:1–2, where the mouth of the servant is like a sword (*machaira*). Koet ("Simeons" 2.1565) adds to the picture Isa 51:19, where a sword (*machaira*) brings destruction on Israel, and argues that *romphaia* and *machaira* are synonymous in the LXX. On the same principle he can point to Luke 21:24, where Jesus predicts that many in Israel will fall by the edge of the *machaira*. Goulder (*Luke* 1.258), arguing that Luke drew the virginal conception from Isa

Israel personified by Mary as the Daughter of Zion but to Mary as a person. She will be tested severely; but, given the little that Luke reports of Mary during and after the public ministry of Jesus, we can be no more precise than that. It is disheartening to see that the tendency to interpret Luke by John continues in terms of understanding this as her sufferings at the cross.[283] Luke never mentions her as present during the passion, either in Jerusalem or at the foot of the cross; and it is most unlikely that he means to refer to something he never describes.

E. Anna the Prophetess (2:36–38). This figure, bearing the name of Samuel's mother and thus continuing the parallels between the infancy of Jesus and that of Samuel, continues to attract attention. There is an enduring suspicion that the biographical information about her in 2:36–37, lavish for a minor character, has special significance, although Bovon (*Evangelium* 1.148) thinks the abundance may reflect a need to reinforce her identity because of the lower status given to women at the time. According to Wilcox ("Luke") a parallel for this "daughter of Phanuel" (a Hebrew/Aramaic name pattern) of the tribe of Asher is found in Serah who is listed as the sister of Asher's sons in Gen 46:17. She went down to Egypt with Jacob and was still listed in a census taken by Moses (Num 26:46). Rabbinic sources deduced from that her great age and made her the one who told Moses where the bones of Joseph were buried that he might take them to the Promised Land. Comparable to Anna's awaiting the liberation/redemption of Israel, Serah's knowledge made her the last custodian of "the mystery of liberation/redemption." She was looked on as a prophetess and even said to have entered Paradise still alive. However, these references are in the *Pirqe Rabbi Eliezer* and the Targum Pseudo-Jonathan, much later works; and that makes a parallel between Luke's Anna and Serah of uncertain value.

The problem of why there are two figures, Simeon and Anna, who greet Jesus in Jerusalem is solved by Figueras ("Syméon") in terms of Luke's reference to the Law and the Prophets. Later in order to symbolize the Law and the Prophets Luke will use Moses and Elijah, who in 9:30–31 will speak to Jesus about what he is to accomplish in Jerusalem. Here Simeon, who is "upright and devout," symbolizes the Law while Anna is called a "prophetess."[284]

7:14, stresses Isa 8:15 as the passage from which he drew the theme of falling. Koet (2.1560) objects that the latter Isaian passage concerns a stone over which one will fall and there is no reference to a stone in Luke 2:34. On 1.263 Goulder traces the sword to Ps 22:21 (*romphaia*; see 462 above).

[283] E.g., Marshall (*Gospel* 123). MIE 3.198 comments that evidently the keenest sorrow of Mary was in relation to the opposition to Christ that culminated on the cross. This is not "evident" exegetically, for there is not the slightest word about that in any Gospel.

[284] Figueras's explanation of Anna, however, goes beyond plausibility when "daughter of Phanuel" and "tribe of Asher" and "till she was 84" are all explained in light of prophecy: Phanuel is where Jacob saw God face to face; Asher is where Elijah prophesied: 84 = Daniel's 70 weeks of years + 7 + 7.

On 442, 467 above I asked whether the indication that Anna "had married as a young girl" (presumably 12/14 years old) and had "lived with her husband seven years" and as "a widow until [= for?] eighty-four years" meant that her total age was 84 (thus previously E. J. Goodspeed, G. Schneider, and now Bovon, Fitzmyer, Goulder) or about 103–105 (12/14 + 7 + 84; my preference; so also Wilcox, Marshall). Elliott ("Anna's Age") adds grammatical arguments in support of the latter. Varela ("Luke"; also Elliott) points out that Anna was with her husband 7 years and a widow 84 years, which is 12 × 7: numerically a perfect married span and an even more perfect widowhood. MIE 3.203–4 brusquely discounts this as "fantastic" and uses the same adjective for any relationship between Anna's age and that of the widow Judith who lived to be 105, proposed by many scholars. Although Wilcox ("Luke") points out that a late midrash described Judith as "one of the daughters of the prophets," he does not see much to be gained from the comparison of Anna and Judith. Marshall (*Gospel* 123–24) sees resemblances between Anna and Judith but does not think that the former was modeled on the latter. With or without these added symbolisms, if Anna lived to 105 years, a centenarian prophetess of stature bears the final witness to Jesus in the first days of his life.

§16 Jesus in the Temple at Age Twelve (Luke 2:22–40)

Since BBM was written there have been comparatively few articles devoted to this scene. Beyond issues of general approach, I shall discuss how to evaluate what Jesus is described as doing in the Temple, the phrase he uses in reference to his Father, and the ending of the scene.

A. General Approach. On 479–84 above I contended that although 2:41–52 has been adapted by Luke to its present context following the narrative of Jesus' infancy, it probably was once an independent story[285] and was rewritten and added here by Luke at a second stage of composition (at the same time that he added the canticles?). Fitzmyer (*Luke* 1.436) largely agrees; Bovon (*Evangelium* 1.152,154) thinks that it was an isolated anecdote[286] that Luke took from a Jewish-Christian

[285] On 480 I point out that the failure of the parents to understand when he speaks about his Father (2:49–50), as if they had received no revelation about Jesus' being God's Son, is much more of a problem than their astonishment in 2:33, which is the ordinary reaction to the miraculous. To support that observation (against Goulder, *Luke* 1.267, who sees no difference) I would add the importance of context. The presenting of the newborn infant in the Temple by his parents and the immediate recognition of his exalted dignity as the Lord's Messiah can scarcely have circulated by itself without some kind of background story about the birth of that child from these parents. However, the story of Jesus as a boy of twelve whose home is in Nazareth could stand by itself without any reflection on where or how he was born. With that possibility I find highly significant for the origin of this story an apparent unconsciousness on the parents' part of any previous extraordinary data that would account for Jesus' behavior and manner of speaking in the Temple.

[286] I.e., a story about an individual centered on a bon mot. Fitzmyer (*Luke* 1.436)

milieu, worked over, and used to conclude his prehistory (but not in any second stage of composition).

On 481 above I noted a progressive christological pattern: At the conception an angel revealed that Jesus is God's Son; now in the Temple Jesus reveals that he is God's Son; at the baptism God (the Father) will reveal that Jesus is the beloved Son.[287] Panier (*Naissance* 263–68) traces the continuity in another way. There has been much spatial movement in chap. 2: Nazareth-Bethlehem-Jerusalem-Nazareth and now back to Jerusalem. Jesus was conceived in one place, born in another, greeted in a third, and reared in the first. The initial words spoken by Jesus focus on the search for which place is his own: "Why were you looking for me?" Jesus' answer that defines the place in terms of his Father takes on more significance in the light of what has preceded. An angel spoke to Mary, and she was blessed for believing that the Lord's words to her would be fulfilled (1:45). Angels' words interpreted the birth of Jesus, and the shepherds went to Bethlehem to see the word/event that had taken place (2:15). They made known the word spoken to them, and all were astonished at these words (2:17–18). Simeon spoke concerning him. Now at last Jesus speaks, confirming the words previously spoken of him by referring to his Father. As Panier (264) phrases it, "Jesus is in truth at the place where the word of his Father is spoken and received."

Legrand ("Deux"), following a suggestion by Dupont ("Jésus re-trouvé"), would establish a parallelism between 2:41–50 (a journey to Jerusalem) and 24:13–33 (a journey to Emmaus). There are, of course, some vague general similarities: one ends the infancy narrative, the other ends the Gospel; in each there is a misunderstanding (by the parents, by the disciples); in each there is reference to Jerusalem. Beyond those, although Legrand evenhandedly points out differences between the two narratives, I find farfetched the resemblances he is interested in (417): The two anticipate two great articulations of the Lucan work to follow. Luke 2:41–50 suggests the great journey to Jerusalem that will culminate in the taking up of Jesus; Luke 24:13–33 evokes the departure of the disciples on the roads of the world and their experience of the absence of the master. The latter is clear in the sense that Jesus orders a preaching mission to all nations in 24:47. But how is the former clear? Does the fact that Jesus went to Jerusalem as a boy constitute real preparation for Luke's making a major theological focus of Jesus' journey to Jerusalem before he died? The proposed prepara-tions for the taking up of Jesus (e.g., the Temple where Jesus is found

---

speaks of a pronouncement story; I referred to it as a biographical apophthegm (483 above).

[287] Yet I insist that this arrangement tells us nothing about the origins of the Temple story, for the unity might result from Lucan structuring.

will not contain him) are overly subtle. As much as I appreciate Legrand's study of the annunciation, regretfully I judge his effort on the present passage more a reading into the text than a reading out of it.

B. Jesus at Age Twelve and His Activities in the Temple (2:41–47). Sparked by the reference to Jesus at age twelve joining his parents in going up to Jerusalem for Passover, popularizations continue to speak of Jesus' Bar Mitzvah, an identification that I rejected on 472–73 above.[288] As I mentioned (so also most commentators), there are talmudic indications of various legal capabilities or responsibilities assumed or assumable at age thirteen or twelve. Others point to a reference in Mishna *'Abot* 5.21(24) to being ready for the commandments at age thirteen. Van der Horst ("Notes") finds the rabbinic parallels for the obligations of a thirteen-year-old so persuasive that he posits an original Aramaic story in which *at age thirteen* Jesus determined the will of God by discussing Scripture as the rabbis did. Yet we do not know how much of this later evidence applies to Jewish practice in Jesus' or Luke's time. Indeed, Luke's narrative does not indicate that at age twelve Jesus went with his parents because he was obligated to do so—more simply he may now have been old enough for the parents to want him to come or for him to want to go.

The indication that after three days Jesus was found in the midst of the teachers leads to maximalist reflections by Manns ("Luc" 345–48). He supposes that in the 1st century at feasts the Jewish teachers had the custom of receiving youngsters in the Temple area to prepare them for their religious inauguration. He appeals also to the Targum Neofiti of Exod 19:10,15ff. where Moses tells the people to prepare themselves for three days, with the result that on the third day the glory of the Shekinah is made manifest and the Law is given. Thus we are being told in Luke that in this Temple scene Jesus received the Law given through Moses. This type of explanation, probably anachronistic in drawing on later documents, supposes a technical Jewish background that neither Luke nor his readers may have possessed. More simply Luke's picture of teachers in the Temple may have been affected by his portraits in Acts 3:11; 5:12,21,25 of the apostles teaching in Solomon's portico of the Temple. "After three days" need have no special significance given the frequency of patterns of three in storytelling. (I also rejected on 487 above the connection that Laurentin would make with resurrection on the third day, a rejection reiterated by Bovon, de Jonge,[289] Fitzmyer, and Marshall.)

---

[288] I have seen the statement that the first specific reference to Bar Mitzvah is supplied by the 15th-century *Sepher Ṣiyyoni* but have not been able to verify it.

[289] In "Sonship" 337, de Jonge judges that Laurentin's exposition, which follows in the allegorical tradition of Clement and Origen, by its soaring flight leaves behind the text and factual details, and thus the original meaning intended by the author. In particular (336)

In 2:46–47 Luke portrays Jesus "seated in the midst of the teachers, both listening to them and asking them questions." We are told that all who heard him were astounded at "his understanding [*synesis*] and his answers." Given the present sequence in the total infancy narrative, this is more than an indication that Jesus was precociously bright.[290] Whatever parallels may have been operative in the composition of the present story, the preceding narrative that Jesus was conceived without a human father and that he is the Son of God has prepared readers for God-given understanding and answers. In the flow of the present narrative Jesus listens and asks questions, and so apparently he does not know everything;[291] yet, as he will do later in life, he gives insights and answers for which he needs no formal human instruction. (For instance, he will pronounce with utter assurance on the eschatological will of God, often as foreshadowed in the Scriptures.) The amazement of those at the Temple scene anticipates the beginning of the public ministry and the wonderment of the people in the Nazareth synagogue at the gracious words that come from the mouth of Joseph's son (4:22; see 492 above).[292] Of course, one need not exaggerate, as does Laurentin in finding in the Jesus of this scene the personification of divine Wisdom described in Sirach 24 (rejected on 490 above and by Fitzmyer, *Luke* 1.437). Nor should one make Jesus here a teacher.[293] Significantly that is not stated

---

the *dei* of 2:49 does not necessarily evoke the resurrection of the Son of Man, for in Luke that verb governs wider necessities. (Consider 4:43, the next instance of its occurrence: "I must preach the gospel of the kingdom.") Although he acknowledges that W. Browning, D. Macpherson, and J. Drury also see a reference to the resurrection, Sylva ("Cryptic" 139–40) rejects their arguments.

[290] De Jonge ("Sonship") insists on the importance of the precociously-intelligent-child motif in Hellenistic biography (including Jewish stories—see 481–82 above).

[291] In more detail than I gave on 483 above, Fitzmyer (*Luke* 1.438–39) warns against psychologizing the narrative as if we were being given insights into what the historical Jesus knew at age twelve or what the historical Mary understood about her son as he was growing up. Yet that fallacy is virtually inevitable if one assumes that we have here Mary's biographical account of the pre-public-ministry life of Jesus.

[292] Goulder (*Luke* 1.264–66), maintaining that Luke's imagination is trying to reach into the inner being of Jesus ("the Little Know-All, or to put it less offensively, the Son of the Omniscient God"), thinks that Luke got the idea of Jesus' having divine insight from the implication of Matt 3:15, where Jesus is aware of righteousness before his baptism. In my judgment the completely different wording by which prebaptismal knowledge is expressed in Matt, Luke, and John suggests independent formulations of a common Christian evaluation.

[293] Marshall (*Gospel* 128): "There is no thought of his precociously teaching the experts"; also Fitzmyer (*Luke* 1.442). Legrand ("Deux" 412–13) argues that there is support in the text for Jesus as a teacher because he is seated in the midst of teachers even as Daniel was seated in the midst of judges (Dan 13:50), and Daniel was exercising a judging function. This is inexact. I pointed to similarities between the young Jesus and the young Daniel on 482 above in terms of remarkable wisdom given by God to youths. But that does not mean that Daniel and Jesus are alike in all details. Daniel is invited in 13:50 by the elders (*presbyteroi*; note: not judges): "Come sit with us and inform us since God has given you 'elderliness' [*presbeion*]." If Jesus were invited by the teachers, "Come sit with us because God has given you the status of a teacher," then Luke would be saying that Jesus was a teacher. Daniel does not ask the elders questions; Jesus asks the teachers questions.

in a narrative where others are given the title "teachers"; only in the future will Jesus' teaching earn him that title (7:40 and passim). Here the *sophia* ("wisdom") attributed to him (2:40) is manifested in understanding and answers.

C. **The Phrase** en tois tou patros mou (2:49).[294] On 475–77 above I discussed this imprecise phrase, "in the . . . of my Father," which is subject to three possible translations.[295] The third possibility, "in/among the relatives/household of my Father," has relatively little following. Of the two more popular possibilities, in preference to "in/about the things/business/affairs of my Father" I chose "in the house of my Father" (= Temple; so also Fitzmyer, Marshall). Recently, however, there seems to be a movement away from attributing one exclusive connotation to the phrase. Bovon (*Evangelium* 1.160) contends that the enigmatic statement fits the literary form of the anecdote, which concentrates on a bon mot.[296]

Weinert ("Multiple") contends that Luke intended all three possibilities in the phrase: locale [Temple], function, and persons. The preposition *en* in 2:43–46 is used to cover the Temple, the caravan, the company of the relatives, and the midst of the teachers, reminding the reader of the pilgrimage motif that is so important for the story. The committed people were on a pilgrimage, going to a distant sacred place to be altered for the better; and Jesus remained in the place to which they were going, namely, he remained in the "Father's company."

A dual reference is agreed upon, apparently independently, by Kilgallen ("Luke") and Sylva ("Cryptic"). The parents should have known not only that Jesus would be found in his Father's house but also that he would be engaged in his Father's affairs, namely, teaching.[297] This scene of Jesus' first activity is meant to anticipate Jesus' future action in the Lucan account of the ministry where he is emphatically a teacher (see 4:15). In particular it anticipates Jesus' future action in the Temple where he will teach every day (19:47; 21:37) when he is in Jerusalem. I am sympathetic to having this episode which concerns Jesus at age

---

[294] Luke 2:48 has prepared for Jesus' answer by having Mary complain, "Your father and I have been so worried." Bovon (*Evangelium* 1.159–60) observes that the normal Greek order would be "I and your father," but Luke has reversed the order because Jesus will speak of "my Father." This might answer Fitzmyer's surprise (*Luke* 1.443) that by speaking of Joseph as Jesus' father, Luke has not brought this story, which he has taken over, into conformity with the virginal conception in chap. 1.

[295] Van der Horst ("Notes") would trace the ambiguity to Aramaic, as seen in talmudic examples.

[296] Bovon would also see a double-meaning answer (house and affairs) responding chiastically to a double issue raised in Mary's questioning of Jesus: "Why have you done this to us? Behold your father and I have been . . . looking for you."

[297] Sylva would translate: "concerned with my Father's words in the Temple." He points out (138) that during the ministry the Lucan Jesus does not work miracles in Jerusalem, so that words are characteristic of his activity there.

twelve both culminate what has gone before in relation to the infant
Jesus and his parents and prepare for what is to come when the adult
Jesus will have left home and begun a public ministry. I doubt, however,
that we can understand the Greek phrase so precisely as teaching.
Reading the present episode before one has read the account of the
ministry would not give the impression that what Jesus has been doing
during his time in the Temple involved teaching (especially since, as
indicated immediately above, it is never said that Jesus teaches). At
most the account might make one think that what pertained to his Father
involved the probable subject of the exchange in the Temple precincts
between the teachers and Jesus, i.e., sacred matters and the Law. That
subject matter would also be the subject matter of Jesus' ministry,
including the ministry in Jerusalem, and thus still allow the scene to
prepare for what would come.

If the Greek phrase is given a dual meaning, perhaps the best phrasing
alongside "in my Father's house" would be the more comprehensive
"about my Father's affairs." Feuillet ("Sauveur" 141–43) argues
strongly for this, extending the coverage as far as the resurrection. (One
might compare Jesus' answer to his mother in John 2:4; see 491–92
above.) De Jonge ("Sonship") would see the phrase covering not only
the Father's house but also the divine plan—that is why the parents
could not understand Jesus' words.

In an extract from his 1974 Gregorian University dissertation, Escudero Freire ("Alcance") relates Jesus' consciousness of his Father in
2:49 (contrasted with Joseph as father in 2:48) to the conception of Jesus
as Son of God without a human father in 1:35. That is true in the present
sequence, but not necessarily if 2:49 were once part of a story that stood
by itself.

D. The Ending (2:51). Sylva ("Cryptic" 132–33) embraces the view of
de Jonge ("Sonship") that the pericope of Jesus in the Temple ends with
the first part of 2:51, so that the second part of 2:51, "His mother kept
with concern all the words/events [pl. of *rēma*] in her heart," is the
conclusion of the whole infancy narrative. He argues that v. 50, which
says that the parents of Jesus did not understand the word/event of
which Jesus spoke to them, uses *rēma* in the singular, and thus the
plural at the end of v. 51 has a wider reference. Also the better mss.
lack a "these" before "words/events," and that would be expected
were the reference to what immediately preceded (see 2:19)—in fact, I
unconsciously supplied a "these" in my translation of 2:51 (478 above).
There is some truth in these observations; yet the suggestion in v. 51
that Mary was seeking to interpret correctly puzzling words/events
cannot be divorced from the stated lack of understanding in v. 50.

Perhaps we can see a double function in the ending of v. 51, concluding
the Temple episode but also all the events that had preceded.

In 2:52 Couroyer ("À propos") concentrates on the third noun:
"Jesus made progress in wisdom, maturity, and *charis*." Appealing to
an article of Renié ("Et Jesus") that I cited in BBM (and followed in my
translation), Couroyer supports the thesis that *charis* does not mean
"grace," but the more secular "beauty, charm, favor," by appealing to
a Phoenician inscription from Memphis in Egypt. The basic idea is that
God's Son also won *human* recognition for his excellence.

APPENDIXES

In the light of literature written between 1976 and 1992 the Appendixes in BBM are being supplemented in this update in three different ways. (a) The material in only one, namely IV, has required a lengthy separate discussion that appears below. (b) The material pertinent to four other Appendixes (I, V, VII, VIII) was best treated under appropriate sections in the Supplement above. Appendix I on levirate marriage was largely informative; that marriage continues to be invoked to harmonize the Matthean and Lucan genealogies without any really new insights (see §3A).[298] Jane Schaberg's book *Illegitimacy* has added a new theory indirectly pertinent to V; her views are treated in reference to the Matthean genealogy (§3C) and to the Matthean and Lucan annunciations of Jesus' conception (§5A, §11C), as well as under Appendix IV below. The discussion of the Quirinius census (VII) has continued, but most of it was directly related to Luke 2:1–2 where the census is mentioned (§14C). Midrash (VIII) is very actively discussed; see 577–79, 598–600 above. (c) In reference to the four other Appendixes (II, III, VI, IX) there has been practically nothing new on Davidic descent (II) or birth at Bethlehem (III)[299] and nothing that I would choose to add pertinent to BBM's treatment of the items of other Jewish background (VI)[300] and of the Fourth Eclogue of Virgil (IX).

APPENDIX IV.
THE VIRGINAL CONCEPTION OF JESUS

I shall discuss this under two headings: debate over historicity, and observations about the relation of the virginal conception to christology.[301] Except in headings, to save space I shall use the abbreviation v.c. for the very frequent appearances of "virginal conception."

---

[298] In this paragraph all § references are to the Supplement.

[299] Yet see comments on 614–15, 669 above.

[300] On 544–45 above I rejected the parallels drawn between Matt's Herod story and the tradition about Laban, but kept open the possibility of a minor echo of the Jacob story. MIE 4.268–72 rejects both, partially out of lack of enthusiasm for the major relationship between Matt's description of Joseph and the OT Joseph story (which would involve Jacob).

[301] There are frequent surveys of this topic in mariological magazines: *Ephemerides*

A. Debate over the Historicity of the Virginal Conception. At the very beginning of this Supplement I mentioned some liberal reaction criticizing BBM because I was not willing simply to dismiss either or both of the two infancy narratives simply as fiction or myth (in the ordinary sense of the latter term). A particular point in the reaction concerned my attitude toward the v.c. of Jesus recounted in both narratives. That topic, it seems, introduces issues disturbing to conservatives and liberals alike.

On purely exegetical grounds "I came to the conclusion that the *scientifically controllable* biblical evidence leaves the question of the historicity of the virginal conception unresolved";[302] yet there was better evidence for historicity than against. But as I noted, since this issue has repercussions for faith in Christ, many go beyond the limited results of exegesis and affirm the historicity of the v.c. on theological grounds. For Roman Catholics, I stated: "I think that according to the usual criteria applied in Roman Catholic theology the virginal conception would be classified as a doctrine infallibly taught by the ordinary magisterium."[303] I have found in the recent literature (sometimes specifically in reaction to my position) four other views about the historicity of the v.c. that I shall now proceed to discuss.

(1) *Exegetical Evidence Establishes the Historicity of the Virginal Conception.* I contended that on exegetical grounds alone one could not resolve the issue in favor of the historicity of the v.c. Some have

Mariologicae, Marian Studies, Marianum. A very brief, competent, and dispassionate survey of the issues is offered by Longenecker ("Whose"). Roman Catholics have had a disproportionately large role in the discussion of the last quarter-century since this was really the first time that the modern form of the historicity issue forcefully emerged on their scene; the contributions range from intelligent through the almost incoherently indignant. I shall avoid aspects of the recent discussions that simply repeat points already made in BBM.

302 Stated in VCBRJ 66–67, and repeated on 527–28 above (although Laurentin, *Évangiles* 429, thinks I "made progress" between the two books!), this observation may not be relativized by claiming that there is no "scientifically controllable evidence" for anything in Scripture. Obviously the type of evidence invoked in the physical sciences is not at issue, but, as BBM indicated, "the type of evidence constituted by tradition from identifiable witnesses of the events involved, when that tradition is traceably preserved and not in conflict with other traditions." Jesus died on a cross—that is an item that meets the criterion of scientifically controllable evidence.

303 VCBRJ 35; BBM 529, n. 29. J. R. Sheets, "Virginal Conception: Fact and Faith," *Chicago Studies* 14 (1975), 279–96, regards me as "conceding" this in an attempt to test infallibility and complains that I never explain the usual criteria. I had not thought that necessary since they are well known to theologians. The extraordinary magisterium involves a *de fide* statement in creeds, or definitions by universal councils or popes speaking *ex cathedra.* If that explicit and specific teaching is lacking, one turns to see if the ordinary magisterium offers guidance, i.e., what has been generally taught and believed as revealed truth. As witnesses to that, one consults Scripture, the writings of Church Fathers and of theologians, the liturgy, catechisms, belief of the faithful, etc. Scholars who have studied these witnesses give us their judgment whether a particular doctrine has been infallibly taught by the ordinary magisterium as revealed. Occasionally they have changed their view because new factors have clarified what is the heart of church teaching (as distinct from a passing expression of that teaching). In the traditional understanding scholars are not the ultimate authority but only a guide.

attempted to find additional convincing exegetical evidence. My early survey evaluation of the pertinent evidence (TS 33 [1972], 3–34) was reprinted and refined in VCBRJ and was followed by J. A. Fitzmyer's similar overview (TS 34 [1973], 541–75). Independently, we reached the conclusion that the only NT evidence supporting the v.c. was in Matt 1 and Luke 1; and that conclusion has been confirmed in the 1978 ecumenical MNT (in which a dozen NT scholars participated).[304] The agreement of Matt and Luke on the v.c. is very important but not totally conclusive, given the silence of the rest of the NT and even the rest of Matt and Luke on the topic. Predictably, more conservative scholars have reacted to BBM by invoking on behalf of the v.c. passages like Gal 4:4; John 1:13 (minor Latin reading[305]); John 6:41–42 (irony); or Mark 6:3—evidence that I (and Fitzmyer) had already discussed and rejected. Sometimes the claims for greater evidence reach an extravagant level, e.g., Laurentin's contention (*Évangiles* 7, 385) that there was at Nazareth "the very firm local tradition assuring that Jesus was not the son of Joseph"; indeed "the Gospels constantly avoid calling Jesus 'son of Joseph,' except in the mouth of his adversaries (Matt 13:55; John 1:45 [an adversary?]; 6:42) or in contexts where this language of ordinary life is clearly rectified (Luke 2:33,48–49)." That is certainly a curious way of disguising that Jesus is called son of Joseph (or of the carpenter) five times and son of Mary only once! In relation to that "son of Mary" in Mark 6:3, Winandy had argued that it is unique in the Bible to have a man called by his mother's name. Then I Chron 2:16, "the sons of Zeruiah" (specifically identified as David's sister; also II Sam 17:25), was pointed out; but Winandy ("Note") has now argued that Zeruiah was a man!

Impressive simply by its length (536 pp.) is the study of the v.c. by de Freitas Ferreira (*Conceição*), who looks at the evidence cautiously but conservatively.[306] Overall he is correct in contending (485) that the exegetical arguments do not disprove the v.c., but too optimistic when he claims (482) that the silence of most of the NT is fully comprehensible from the very nature of the subject and that the idea of the v.c. circulated in restricted Palestinian circles without significant repercussions or global significance for the kerygma. I would comment that there is simply no way to establish the latter claim. De Freitas (493) maintains that the only plausible explanation for Jewish-Christian faith in the v.c.

304 So also Wilckens ("Empfangen" 62–63); he would locate Matt and Luke and Ignatius of Antioch (who also knew of the v.c.) all in the Syria area.

305 Cranfield ("Some" 179) does not accept the Latin reading where the singular refers to Jesus' birth, but thinks with C. K. Barrett that the plural description of the birth of the Christians presupposes the v.c. of Jesus.

306 He betrays his sympathies in the deprecatory terms he uses for arguments against the v.c. (e.g., "delusions").

is a family tradition; in BBM (527) I allowed family tradition as possibly a leavening factor but scarcely the only explanation.

More often conservative disagreement with my position about the limited NT evidence simply skipped further exegetical discussion and made a theological assertion: Both the evangelists affirm the v.c., and Scripture is inerrant. That is an insufficient argument. Theologically my understanding of inspiration and inerrancy (and that of my church[307]) does not require me to accept everything a biblical author affirms as factually historical.

(2) *Church Teaching Does Not Require Belief in the Virginal Conception.* Some Roman Catholic theologians suggested that I was wrong in thinking that a literal v.c. is infallibly taught by the ordinary magisterium of the church; they would argue that it may be purely symbolic. For instance, Monika Hellwig, in her article "The Dogmatic Implications of the Birth of the Messiah," interprets the v.c. symbolically (Mary/the church, rather than Joseph/Israel, brought forth the Messiah) and sees no obstacle to Jesus' having been conceived illegitimately through the rape of Mary.[308] Although I discussed Roman Catholic Church teaching in VCBRJ, I did not consider that an exegetical commentary such as BBM, intended for readers of many backgrounds, was the appropriate place for an internal Catholic debate about theology; and that judgment continues into the Supplement. Let me make only two remarks that may be of interest beyond the restricted area of inner Roman Catholic debates. First, I wrote that "I think" that a literal v.c. is infallibly taught.[309] I was and am aware of the limited value of that judgment since I am not a systematic theologian who has devoted a life study to the criteria for determining such an issue (as are some who disagree). Nevertheless, I would maintain that the majority of Catholic systematic theologians would evaluate the literal v.c. as infallibly taught.[310]

[307] I find a good working tool in the affirmation of Vatican Council II (*Dei Verbum* 11) that the Scriptures convey "without error the truth that God wanted put into the sacred writings for the sake of our salvation"—an affirmation that leaves the task of determining by exegesis, theology, and church tradition what God so wanted.

[308] In his little book written in a popular style for general audiences (*First*), Richards is at times properly cautious about historicity, e.g., "We can no longer put our finger on the present reality underlying his [Matt's] story" (27). Yet he clearly feels sympathy for those theologians who affirm that "there was no virginal birth in the literal sense outside the story" (89–91).

[309] That caution "I think" (VCBRJ 35) infuriated some ultraconservative Catholic commentators on the book. For them the infallible character of teaching on the v.c. was so apparent that I was being less than a true Catholic by only thinking that it was infallibly taught. Teaching by the extraordinary magisterium (n. 303 above) is specific; and it would be slyly challenging for a Roman Catholic to say that he or she *thinks* that something thus defined (e.g., the Immaculate Conception of Mary) is infallibly taught. The ordinary magisterium by its very nature is not so specific, and only the official teaching authorities of the church can state with absolute assurance that something is infallibly taught by the ordinary magisterium. Therefore neither I nor my reviewers have that right.

[310] See J. P. Kenny, "Was Mary in Fact a Virgin?" *Australasian Catholic Record* 56

Second, if in Roman Catholic thought church authority constitutes the final voice on what is infallibly taught by the ordinary magisterium, that authority has shown itself very unfriendly to those who have questioned the v.c. I cite the following simply as a barometer of official church attitude (and not with any evaluative judgment on the justice of the individual cases). In Spain, the Jesuit José Scheifler of Deusto University near Bilbao suggested ("Vieja"; see 635 above) that the v.c. could be treated as a legend. The article brought indignant petitions by over 10,000 Spaniards, a restatement of belief by the Spanish bishops' commission on faith (early 1978), and a warning from the Jesuit General.[311] In the United States, R. McBrien's views on the v.c. were part of what caused Roman authorities to request a review of his *Catholicism* (2 vols.; Minneapolis: Winston, 1980). The omission of the sentence "For good reasons, therefore, one might reject the historicity of the v.c. of Jesus without necessarily incurring the burden of heresy" (1.516) was one of the changes worked out when a "Study Edition" appeared in 1981.[312] The authorization of Ute Ranke-Heinemann to teach Catholic theology at the University of Essen was removed by the German bishops in 1987 for understanding "the Virgin Birth not biologically, but theologically."[313]

(3) *Theological Arguments Cannot Guide Exegesis in the Issue of the Virginal Conception.* Some liberal critics contended that I was unscientific and unconsciously (or even consciously) dishonest in introducing a theological factor such as church teaching. Critical exegesis should be all determinative, and scholars like me who show deference to church teaching (or any religious guidance) have most likely distorted their exegesis to reach conclusions in harmony with that bias. After some *pro forma* praise of my work as "magisterial and enormous," Kermode's review of BBM quickly got to my weakness: I had submitted the book for a *nihil obstat* and *imprimatur*,[314] and consequently I rejected the

---

(1979) 282–300; also F. Salvoni, "Verginità di Maria oggi," *Ricerche Bibliche e Religiose* 11 (1976), 21–35, chastising H. Küng for rejecting the v.c., for which there is more serious authority than for the perpetual virginity.

311 Part of the Spanish opposition was directed against a work by Xavier Pikaza of Salamanca, *Los origenes de Jesus* (1976), which I have not seen. Pikaza defends his book as theological exegesis in *Salmanticenses* 24 (1977), 351–61. As for Scheifler, although *Sal Terrae* printed a more conservative rebuttal of his views and had closed the debate, the editors stated that they were forced by a mandate from their Jesuit superiors to include still another rebuttal by I. de la Potterie, S.J., finding the v.c. in John (66 [1978], 569–78).

312 Even then, a bishop's plan to grant an *imprimatur* was blocked.

313 This is her phrasing of the situation in *Eunuchs for the Kingdom of Heaven* (New York: Doubleday, 1990), 348. I am puzzled by the account she gives on the preceding page of the opinions favorable to her position from prominent German Catholic theologians. While she would deny the historicity of the v.c., of the virgin birth (giving birth and remaining physically intact), and of the perpetual virginity of Mary, I am not certain that any of those cited would agree with her in *denying* the v.c., even if they might not affirm that it was infallibly taught.

314 The Latin names of Catholic church evaluations enable him to appeal to Milton, who observed that English would not "provide servile letters enow to spell such a dictatory

view that Matt might have midrashically made up the v.c. because that would be inconsistent with the teaching of the church. "Giving up the virgin birth might be bad for people." (It does not seem to occur to Kermode that if it is the truth, to give it up would indeed be bad for people.[315]) With similar acidity but less elegance, J. L. McKenzie found me "evasive" and "protecting my rear" in not denying the v.c. (etc.)— in his view, an exegete is not obliged to discuss further the legitimacy of articles of faith seemingly based on ancient misunderstandings of biblical texts.[316] The Episcopalian Bishop Spong (*Born* 124) has the same critique of me: "As a Roman Catholic he must constantly discipline his scholarship in the service of the official teaching and dogma of his tradition. That makes it difficult for him to follow his scholarship if it leads to ecclesiastically unacceptable conclusions. . . . But the ground on which the doctrines of his church depend has been, nonetheless, eroded by the demands of his scholarship." Of the almost six hundred pages of BBM above, very few are even remotely affected by issues of church doctrine,[317] so that the portrayal of my constant internal conflict is overdone, to say the least.

What is ironic is that those who deny the v.c. sometimes do not recognize that they too are passing judgment from a theological vantage point. Let us consider two recent books: Parrinder, *Son of Joseph*, and Spong, *Born*. They are highly quixotic in their treatment of the biblical evidence for and against the v.c.; for in quoting the scholarship of others, whether they are aware of it or not, they leave out much of what gets in the way (Spong even more than Parrinder). Each has an agendum shaped by a view of modern Christian life. Parrinder writes in order to

---

presumption." Actually, since I think that church teaching can be an enlightening context for scriptural interpretation, I have never felt it a limitation of my freedom to have my books published with a public assurance that the biblical views that I have stated are free of doctrinal error from a Roman Catholic viewpoint. At the opposite end of the spectrum from Kermode, ultraconservative Catholics also resent the *imprimatur* when it is given to a book such as mine that embodies modern biblical criticism because that affirmation interferes with their desire to impose their narrow views as church doctrine and to condemn as heretical what, in fact, is perfectly tolerable within the range of Catholic thought.

[315] Gary Wills (Universal Press syndicated column, week of June 12, 1978) cited Kermode's review as an example of sophisticated religious narrowness, for it constitutes a failure to recognize that objective scholarly study of the Scriptures should take into account the religious transmission of the text.

[316] McKenzie expressed himself explicitly in an interview with K. Briggs, *New York Times* (Dec. 25, 1977): "Referring to his disbelief in the virgin birth, he conceded that '. . . I think it is important to belief that Jesus was fully a man with two sets of chromosomes, two parents.'" As part of protecting an almost universal church heritage from the past (the only "rear" worth protecting), I see nothing contradictory in believing that Jesus was fully a man even when there was only one human parent—the issue of chromosomes can be left to the creator Spirit who brought him into human existence.

[317] The only doctrinal issues in the infancy narratives are the christological identity of Jesus and the v.c. Since the former is supported by many other sections of the NT, the only doctrinal issue peculiar to Matt 1–2 and Luke 1–2 is the v.c. which is mentioned not at all in chap. 2 of either Gospel and only in a few verses of chap. 1.

affirm the paternity of Joseph and the full family life at Nazareth. Joseph was young and ardent and in love with Mary; they had normal sex, and Jesus was the first of their many children.[318] The idea of the v.c. has been propagated by celibate priests whose views are incompatible with a truly Christian appreciation of sex and marriage. Spong (*Born*) thinks that Jesus was illegitimate, perhaps the child of rape. The v.c. is propagated to further repressive tendencies, particularly within Roman Catholicism, e.g., subjecting women by giving them a sense of guilt about their own sexuality.[319] Virginity for both authors seems to be an idealization of sexual repression, manipulated for the political purposes of keeping a celibate clergy in power. Ranke-Heinemann's rejection of the v.c. is linked to her book-length attack on the Catholic fear of pleasure in sex. Whether or not one agrees with such political and sexual theology,[320] it certainly influences the outlook of the respective critics on the v.c., sometimes at the very moment they are decrying the influence of traditional theology on other exegetes. Leaving that and the question of Catholic-bashing to other commentators (see the evaluation by Daley, "Born"), I would prefer to query whether this approach really helps in discerning the theology of the v.c. as presented by Matt and Luke. Those evangelists may be considered unconsciously patriarchal; but neither of them presents the conception of Jesus in a context of the superiority of celibacy, or of the impurity of women's sexuality, or of keeping women out of priestly or hierarchical power. They present the conception as the unexpected manifestation of the creative power of God and as an aspect of the mystery of the divine and the human in

318 Although that situation may seem to Parrinder the logical alternative to a v.c., in fact, if one denies the v.c., the evidence for Joseph as the father is slim. Cranfield ("Some" 177, 185–86), having stated that a positive proof of the v.c. by exegesis is out of the question, deems "it virtually certain that Joseph was not biologically the father of Jesus." Two mutually hostile traditions about Jesus' birth, Christian and Jewish, came to agree on that point. The Christian claim that Joseph was not the father (Matt, Luke) can scarcely have arisen by reaction to Jewish calumny—that would have been answered by saying Joseph *was* the father—so that, unless one wants to say that Jewish polemic about Jesus' illegitimacy was based entirely on misunderstanding, it helps to show that Christians were claiming an unusual conception.

319 Schaberg (*Illegitimacy* 10) is not too far from the suspicions/accusations of Parrinder and Spong: "One wonders if it [the v.c.] is a projection of male fantasy and wishes: for a tame and pure woman who is asexual or does not exercise her sexuality; for a woman especially untroubling to the celibate male psyche. . . ." Schaberg admits that by the time of Justin and some early creedal expressions (thus by mid-2nd century) Christians had come to the idea of a v.c. Therefore, I presume her statement about the origin of the idea of a v.c. refers to the 1st and early 2nd century. Knowing our evidence for that period, I can only wonder who and where were the celibate male Christians who were fantasizing in this manner. (Since Paul does not mention a v.c., he can scarcely be listed as the culprit.) Or are the fantasies attributed generically to 20th-century clerical celibates being retrojected on 1st-century Christian males?

320 One does not find in such writing an equal voice for the view that there might be a genuine spirituality of celibacy, and/or that it might serve as a valuable testimony challenging the omnipresent glorification of sex in our times. One may compare to their narrowness of view the very sensitive "Mary, Virgin and Wife: A Dialogue," by W. M. Thompson and P. F. Chirico (*Chicago Studies* 28 [1989], 137–59).

Jesus—an issue that does not seem to be of major import to some who would reject the v.c.[321]

However, lest it seem that I am avoiding the underlying issue by calling attention to the exaggerations and bias of some who denounce the theology of the v.c., let me concentrate on the more basic issue of whether church tradition may legitimately play a role in exegesis. I have argued elsewhere[322] that because of the very nature and origin of the NT, in the passages pertinent directly to Christian doctrine, exegesis can legitimately incorporate into a *full* biblical interpretation the faith of the community that both produced and preserved the NT—indeed an exegete should profit from this connatural faith enrichment.[323] The notion shared by the Roman Catholic McKenzie and the Episcopalian Spong that church doctrines are irrelevant because their grounds have been eroded by modern scholarship represents an inversion of the ancient Christian attitude toward the relationship between doctrine and Scripture. Doctrine was not simply derived from the Scriptures;[324] for when the Scriptures were written, they gave expression to what was already believed and taught. And surely that is true in the case of the infancy narratives: Belief that Mary conceived as a virgin did not first come from reading what Matt and Luke wrote; rather Matt and Luke wrote their accounts to express a faith that they already had in the v.c. In the instance of genuine church doctrine, the Holy Spirit would be seen as playing a role in leading the church, including its spokespersons,

321 Spong (especially 36–40) presents a Jesus who was not of divine origin, but a gifted, humble, generous, and self-giving human being whose friends certainly did not understand him as a messiah. Yet they underwent an Easter experience or internal realization that enabled them to see patterns of total dependence on God in Jesus so that his life reflected God's life. Spong is complimentary in what he writes about me as a NT scholar (e.g., *Born* 124); I hope I am not ungracious if in return I remark that I do not think a single NT author would recognize Spong's Jesus as the figure being proclaimed or written about.

322 *The Critical Meaning of the Bible* (New York: Paulist, 1981), 23–44; *Biblical Exegesis and Church Doctrine* (New York: Paulist, 1985), 26–53.

323 McKenzie, who sarcastically complains about a Catholic scholar's difficulty "to wean himself from his training, which has drilled him to salute the papal flag," cited me wrongly: Brown "sees no reason why a Catholic's understanding of the infancy narratives should differ from a Protestant's understanding." On 9 above I spoke of Catholic and Protestant agreement about "what Matthew and Luke meant [past tense] in their infancy narratives"; but disagreement about what the infancy narratives mean (present tense) may well arise because of a Catholic's adherence to the church's dogmatic teaching, sometimes papally "ensigned."

324 Nor was it an alien interpretation imposed on Scripture, as sometimes assumed in modern discussions, particularly by those who resent the doctrines of their own church which they regard as alien to themselves. Undoubtedly I am influenced by my status as a Catholic priest. Is it inconceivable that the positions of some liberal critics are influenced by their reaction to the tradition in which they were brought up? Spong (*Born* xiv) is clear that he prefers Schaberg's exegesis because she has an independent freedom of inquiry while I am bound by the dogmatism of the Roman tradition. It does not seem to occur to him that Schaberg, in her dealing with Catholic doctrine and feminism, might be reacting to her history as a former nun. He is more perceptive in his own case that he is influenced by the fact that he grew up as a biblical fundamentalist (*Born* 3), even if he seems to regard any recognition that the NT supports the divinity of Jesus as a fundamentalist position.

to the penetration of the mystery of Christ. Consulting such a church insight does not make modern biblical exegesis a subservient slave, for exegesis has often had an important corrective function, helping to specify more exactly the thrust of the doctrine and to understand the limitations of past phrasing. Why, then, should exegetes be allergic to learning from church doctrine as if their own exegesis were the only guide to biblical truth?[325] Given the many changes that approaches to the Bible have undergone in the 20th century, doctrine and consequently faith cannot be thought to depend solely on the infallibility of modern biblical criticism.

(4) *Exegetical Evidence Disproves the Virginal Conception*. This view is the opposite of (1) above. On 528–31 above I argued that although the limited NT evidence is not conclusively probative, to posit historical fact as an explanation of Matt's and Luke's agreement on the v.c. is more conformable to the evidence than to posit fictional creation. For some, however, conception without a human father is simply incredible and cannot be historical. One may wonder whether the attitude that a miraculous conception cannot have happened is more intellectually profound than the opposite contention that because it is described in the Bible it must have happened.[326] Insisting that no a priori attitude can settle the issue, we may divide those who would disprove the v.c. on the basis of evidence into two groups: those (a larger number) who think Matt and Luke intended readers to believe that Jesus was conceived without a human father, and those who do not think the evangelists had this intention (so that a literal v.c. was a misreading). In evaluating their thoughts we should remember that most critics think Matt and Luke wrote independently of each other, and thus the solution must explain how whatever is proposed could have happened in two separate instances.

(a) Matt and Luke intended readers to believe that Jesus was conceived without a human father. If there was in fact no v.c., then both either lied or were themselves deceived. Some scholars have thought that the idea of a v.c. arose out of Christian *apologetics*: Jesus was illegitimate, and the v.c. was created to cover that up. This contention is not even slightly plausible unless suspicions of illegitimacy were very old and it was well known that Joseph was not Jesus' physical father.

[325] Spong has made the exegesis of Schaberg and Goulder mainstays in his theory that Mary was a sexually violated teenage girl; but he does not deal at length with the implausibilities in their exegesis. His readers would need to be aware that those two exegetes in their respective approaches represent an extreme minority. Evaluators may well ask whether Spong found in them convenient support for a thesis about the impossibility of a miraculous birth toward which he was already inclined.

[326] Hattrup ("Neues") correctly points out the limitations of the mechanistic worldview behind the automatic rejection of the v.c. He thinks that such a worldview is now passé philosophically and even scientifically.

Otherwise Christian apologetics would have answered a charge of illegitimacy much more simply: by an affirmation of Joseph's fatherhood.
There is no pre-Gospel evidence of Jesus being attacked as illegitimate,
and it is very difficult to find in the NT writings clear evidence that such
a charge was being made by anti-Christian opponents (Appendix V on
534–42 above). Most who hold for the illegitimacy of Jesus do not seek
to be specific about details, but occasionally in the recent literature the
proposal is spelled out and is thus open to more precise evaluation. For
instance, drawing on the scene in Thomas Hardy where Tess of the
D'Urbervilles tells her husband-to-be that she was seduced and meets
rejection, Bostock ("Virgin") imaginatively describes how Joseph had
to forgive Mary for being pregnant, and how she had to forgive him for
his first reaction in wanting to divorce her. He combines that with the
Lucan scene which came earlier and posits that Zechariah had relations
with Mary in the three months she was at his house! Bostock calls
attention to sacred marriages in the pagan world where a virgin cohab-
ited with a king or priest so that the child would be regarded as the son
of a deity. The idea was known in Judaism and therefore understood
("Divine" 330).[327] This somewhat bizarre explanation seems to suppose
that his begetting JBap was a permanent cure to Zechariah's being
hampered sexually by being on in years.

More widely proposed is the *theologoumenon* approach: The v.c. was
originally an imaginative or poetic way of phrasing the theological truth
that Jesus was God's Son, but very quickly it was misunderstood to be
literal. Those who hold this should be able to explain what would have
led two Christian writers with Jewish background, independently of
each other, to phrase their theological insight in such a strange way. Or
if a phraseology involving the v.c. was already in existence before Matt
and Luke wrote, one must explain what caused Christians to move
toward such phraseology so quickly. Can it be shown that the idea of a
v.c. of religious figures was so familiar that people would have moved
toward it spontaneously? Is there an explanation beyond those discussed in detail and rejected by the studies just mentioned in (1) above
(VCBRJ, Fitzmyer)?[328] In a popular article Barrett ("Can" 29) maintains

[327] Bostock claims that to believe in a v.c. places "our religion in a remote supernatural
realm" ("Virgin" 261). All people have human fathers, and we may assume Jesus had
one; a virginal conception denies the reality of the incarnation. However, this argument
that if Jesus had no human father, he would not be truly human leaves me with a problem
about human beginnings. Whether by direct creation or by evolution, logically the first
human(s) had no human parent(s)—were the first humans not human? If one believes in a
transcendent God, at some point one has to allow that God's power to act beyond human
potentialities. A religion that takes seriously God's supernatural intervention is not so
horrendous as Bostock seems to assume. For Christians, after all, the conception of God's
Son is a unique moment.

[328] These explanations include borrowing from pagan myths about God's mating with
women and concretizing the reference to a virgin in the Greek of Isa 7:14. See VCBRJ 61–
65; also Cranfield, "Some." It is difficult to classify Leaney's contribution, which ranges

that perhaps Matt and Luke did not mean the v.c. literally but intended only to highlight the role of God. To show that God's action is not separate from that of *two* human parents, Barrett points to the statement in Ruth 4:13 that Boaz went into Ruth, and the Lord gave her conception. Yet Matt is specific that Joseph had not gone into Mary when her pregnancy was made known to him.[329] In a rather evenhanded survey of the problems posed by the infancy narratives, Crouch ("How" 36) resorts to the Philonic patriarchal allegories and the Pauline (Gal 4:29) terminology of Isaac's birth according to the Spirit discussed on 524 above, but without mention of Grelot's detailed refutation and of Rom 9:8–10, which indicate that no factual conception without a human father was meant either by Philo or Paul. DAICC (1.216) correctly points out that although one cannot say that the historical evidence clearly confirms the miraculous conception of Jesus, no satisfactory mundane explanation has procured a critical consensus: "None of the proposed parallels [to the v.c.], either pagan or Jewish, seemingly accounts for the story we find in the NT." Cranfield ("Some" 177) states of the v.c.: It is "right to acknowledge that up to the present no proof of its non-historicity has been produced."

(b) Matt and Luke did not intend readers to believe that Jesus was conceived without a human father. Most often this thesis posits that the two evangelists understood themselves to be writing in figurative language of a theologoumenon, so that the literalist misunderstanding was not shared by them but originated with their subsequent readers/hearers. The same objections to the theologoumenon approach mentioned above apply here and perhaps even more forcefully. Under the previous rubric the misunderstanding would have occurred at a pre-Gospel stage on which the two evangelists drew. Now one must posit that suddenly late in the century independently two evangelists phrased this strange theologoumenon in such a misleading way.

Jane Schaberg (*Illegitimacy*) has a unique approach. Both evangelists knew that Jesus was conceived illegitimately (by an unknown man

---

very widely and offers observations (e.g., as to what constitutes folklore) rather than arguments. Although for him Mary is almost a symbolic figure standing for Israel who has no husband (but God), he seems to think that Luke intended a virginal conception. Yet apparently Luke was aware of other possibilities (as exhibited elsewhere in the NT), and those alternatives "make it unnecessary to believe the account in Luke" ("Virgin" 100).

[329] The oldest extant commentary on the canonical Gospel narratives, the *Protevangelium of James* 11:2–3, specifically blocks Barrett's interpretation: It has Mary ask whether she would conceive of the Lord God as every woman bears, and the angel tells her no. Barrett argues fallaciously when he says that Paul's statement that Jesus "was descended from David *according to the flesh*" (Rom 1.3) would be meaningless if Joseph were not Jesus' father. That statement, meant to describe Jesus' human heritage, was most likely shaped without any advertence to the issue of how Jesus was conceived and cannot be used to solve that issue. At most one may ask whether the evangelists who wrote of the v.c. would have chosen such phrasing, even though they might have "lived" with it.

seducing or, more probably, raping Mary) and were trying to convey
that to the readers in such a way as to indicate that God had reversed
human values and made this conception by a victimized woman the
source of salvation—the child could be looked on therefore as God's
child through the work of the Holy Spirit. The family had known the
truth about the child and felt that God had saved Mary from her despised
condition (whence the name "Jesus"). Hitherto women had been involved in assuring that the illegitimacy tradition was not forgotten or
totally distorted. "Because of its traumatic nature and its potential
damage to the Jesus movement, and because of its faith demand, the
tradition was a difficult one to communicate" (155). Despite the evangelists' intention to communicate the truth, being men, they wrote so
indirectly that they tamed or blunted the illegitimacy of Jesus, making it
hard for the readers to experience the grief and danger of the historical
circumstances. Consequently Christian readers soon became unaware
of the illegitimacy of Jesus and interpreted the event as a v.c. without a
human parent, something that the evangelists never intended. In the
Supplement above I have examined in detail the indications of illegitimacy proposed by Schaberg and found them extremely tenuous. Often
she has to impose on texts connotations that run against their face value.
She cannot offer from the first two centuries a single clear Christian
affirmation that Jesus was illegitimate. One can debate whether Paul
knew the v.c. when he wrote that Jesus was "born of a woman"; but he
scarcely knew that Jesus was the child of seduction or rape when he
wrote that "he was born under the Law" (Gal 4:4).[330] Clearly unlikely is
the proposal that Matt and Luke independently happened to create very
different stories that apparently stressed Mary's virginity (even though
they knew and wanted to convey that she had been seduced or raped)
so that all subsequent commentators until Schaberg misread them to
refer to a v.c.

B. The Relation of the Virginal Conception to New Testament Christology.
The v.c. as presented in Matt 1 and Luke 1 is primarily an issue of
christology. How does this manner of conception fit into the rest of the
NT picture(s) of Jesus as the Messiah and the Son of God? In various
ways that has been a continuing concern in recent study.[331] Prete
("Significato") is seemingly favorable to the thesis that the v.c. is not

[330]Given the OT tendency to visit the sins of the parents on the children, if Mary had
been seduced, would there have been such insistence on the sinlessness of Jesus (John
8:46; 14:30; I Pet 1:19; 3:18; I John 3:5,7; Heb 4:15)? If Christians knew of a rape of Mary,
the portrayed presumptions of family claims (Mark 3:31–35) and of family normality (6:3)
are indeed strange.

[331]It is well known that Jesus' (virginal) conception or birth was later used as an
argument against docetism; but, combining the evidence in Ignatius (*Eph.* 19:1 in the light
of *Trall.* 9:1), Wickings ("Nativity") thinks that the usage of the v.c. to affirm Jesus'
humanity went back to the 80s.

derived simply from family tradition but involves Jesus' statements about his Father, interpreted in the light of postresurrectional faith.

Some of the discussion has been focused on the proposal I made in BBM (e.g., 29–32, 134–38) about the place of the v.c. in NT christology, namely, that a postresurrectional evaluation of Jesus was gradually read back and allowed to interpret the Jesus of the ministry and even the beginnings of Jesus' life as a child. Some critics immediately jumped to the wrong conclusion that this approach was the same as that of the rationalist approach of A. von Harnack.[332] However, the rationalist form of a developmental NT christology would posit that postresurrectional Christian thought made Jesus what in fact he had not been, namely, made a simple human being divine. On 134 above I specifically alerted readers against that interpretation of the evidence I offered: "Orthodox Christians need have no conflict with such a thesis of a growing retrospective evaluation of Jesus, provided it is understood that the evaluation involves an appreciation of a reality that was already there—Jesus was who he was during his lifetime, even if it took his followers centuries to develop a partially adequate theological vocabulary in which to articulate his greatness."[333]

Other reactions to my proposal are more complicated and worth discussing by way of ongoing clarification. I pointed out that from the preserved literature of the NT what we can detect about early preaching shows that the second coming and the resurrection were moments fastened upon for expressing the christological identity of Jesus (as Messiah, Lord, Son of God, etc.). Then in the written-Gospel accounts of the public ministry the baptism was the moment fixed on for overtly identifying Jesus christologically; that is where Mark begins. Matt and Luke, written after Mark, identify Jesus christologically àt his conception, while John, who does not describe the conception or birth, identifies him christologically (as the Word) in a preexistence with God before the creation. Thus the second coming, resurrection, baptism, conception were "christological moments," i.e., scenes in the life of Jesus that became the vehicle for giving expression to postresurrectional christology. (These are not necessarily moments when revelation of developed christology actually took place.[334])

332 E.g., de Freitas Ferreira (*Conceição* 291); Muñoz Iglesias, review in n. 2 above. MIE 2.65–66 oversimplifies by linking with Harnack less conservative Catholics and then advancing refutations that would be quite irrelevant to a more subtle form of the thesis.

333 Since some of the conservative objectors are Roman Catholics, it is not inappropriate to call to their attention the 1964 Instruction of the Roman Pontifical Biblical Commission "On the Historical Truth of the Gospels," which is official Catholic teaching. It speaks of the divinity of Jesus being clearly perceived *after* he rose from the dead, and of the apostles drawing on that fuller understanding when they passed on to their listeners what the Lord had done and said. That is harmonious with the backward development of christology that I have detected in the Gospels.

334 Fitzmyer (*Luke* 1.208, 446–47) seems confused on that point, even though he accepts my general approach. I cannot exclude the possibility that revelation did take place

Let me invoke the example of the baptism as a christological moment, for three Gospels use this scene as the occasion to describe a revelation from heaven that Jesus is God's beloved Son through and with the activity of the Holy Spirit. By *the ordinary rules of biblical evidence* one can judge that Jesus was actually baptized by JBap, but not how much was revealed about what to whom on that occasion,[335] nor whether factually the heavens were opened, a voice sounded from above, and a dove descended.[336] Similarly, two Gospels use the "moment" of Jesus' conception to describe a revelation from an angel that Jesus is God's Son through the activity of the Holy Spirit. Of course, Jesus was conceived; but, as I have reiterated above, one cannot decide by the ordinary rules of biblical evidence that he was conceived without a human father, even if the earliness of the tradition (before our written Gospels) and the lack of other plausible explanations of that tradition make historicity the stronger likelihood. Nor can one know how much was revealed to whom on that occasion,[337] nor whether an angel appeared and spoke, anticipating the language of the early Christian kerygma (Rom 1:3–4) about Son of David and Son of God.[338] None of the above invalidates the postresurrectional understanding of revelation that Jesus was God's Son through the Holy Spirit or the evangelists' teaching that he was this from the first moment of his conception and, a fortiori, from the time when he first began a public ministry.

Some have accused me of accepting an outmoded theory of a chronologically linear development of NT christology[339]—one that can be

---

historically at a particular moment (see the next note), but that is quite secondary to the pedagogical use of the moment.

[335] The chief intention of the three Gospel accounts is to tell *readers* who Jesus is, not whether they are to think that JBap or the bystanders saw or heard anything. John 1:32 describes a vision (internal or external?) of JBap, without implying that anyone else was present. One may *suspect* that Jesus' decision to accept baptism from JBap was for him a moment of unique perception about the direction his life should then take. We need not suppose, however, that the perception was phrased by him in the christological language used to describe the baptism in the Gospels.

[336] One may *suspect* that these constitute an insightful biblical dramatization of a revelation that the evangelists were trying to communicate.

[337] Matt has a revelation to Joseph; Luke has a revelation to Mary. Mary's conception of a child without a human father would have had to mean something to her (and to anyone else who knew of it; see 526–27 above) in terms of God's power being manifested in this child. That does not mean that Mary had to be able to express the identity of Jesus with postresurrectional clarity. Subsequent behavior ascribed to her in the public ministry in Mark, Matt, and John, where she does not seem to understand the direction Jesus' life is taking, would militate against that.

[338] Even more clearly than for the baptism, the Gospel description (angelic annunciation) is a standard dramatization of the insight that God set aside someone even before birth for a task; see 155–59 above, and Muñoz Iglesias, "Procedimiento."

[339] DAICC (1.200–1) deems "simplistic" my contention that "the moment of Jesus' divine sonship, first tied to the resurrection, was moved back to the ministry and baptism and then to the conception." I gather that this is the phrasing of the authors rather than an exact quotation from me. The closest I can find that I come to that phrasing is on 481 above, but what I said there is more happily phrased, as my (added) italics indicate: "The moment *of the revelation* of Jesus as God's Son has been moved back from the baptism (where it is in Mark's Gospel) to the conception/birth." What is simplistic about thinking

refuted easily since some early elements in the NT suggest preexistence. Neither I nor anyone else knows how Christian thought progressed chronologically. Surely all Christians did not think the same about Jesus at any given period in the 1st century (or in any century since). Evidence for preexistence thought is early; but more than likely some Christians, using the analogy of divine Wisdom, moved to the idea of a preexistence with God without ever reflecting on the conception/birth of Jesus as a significant factor in his divine identity. Also more than likely, while others were reflecting on preexistence or on conception from the Holy Spirit, some were still content with formulas such as those in Acts that God raised up Jesus and made him Lord and Messiah or begot him as Son.[340] Thus no one should attempt to fit into a smooth chronological development the actual christological outlook of 1st-century Christians in various parts of the world (about which we can only guess). What I was proposing was a logical (not a chronological) way of understanding the pattern of christological thought we find in the NT. It is a *fact* that christological statements about what Jesus became (or was declared to be or was made) through the resurrection appear in passages reflecting pre-Pauline tradition in the epistles and in sermons in Acts that have a possibility of preserving language from a period before the Gospels were written. Mark, the earliest Gospel, however, does not present a christology whereby Jesus becomes or is made the Son of God through the resurrection. It teaches readers that Jesus was God's Son at the baptism. What he was before is clarified in the Gospels written after Mark. Thus in terms of the sequence of Jesus' life, Christians may well have moved backwards in the sense that they saw more quickly the christological implications of the event that came at the end of Jesus' earthly career (the resurrection) but was closest in time to their own lives and conversion—an event to which some of those who preached to them could bear witness because of the appearances of the risen Lord. It is not simplistic to think that only gradually and in retrospect did they work out the christological implications for earlier parts of Jesus' life, especially for the birth that none of the apostles witnessed or is not recorded as having been preached. Obviously that working out would have taken place at different times in different places.

R. H. Fuller in his own long endeavor to understand NT christology

---

that some Christians in their reflection may have moved back from the resurrection to the baptism to the conception in terms of which event was understood to be the first to reveal who Jesus was? For a fuller statement of how I understand the development of NT chronology, see NJBC, article 81, ##12–24. A view very much like mine is held by Wilckens, "Empfangen" 62–64.

[340] One could utter those formulas without being very precise to what extent they added an identity that Jesus did not already possess. They probably meant different things to different people. They are recorded by the author of Acts and by Paul, neither of whom believe that Jesus first became the Son of God through the resurrection.

has rendered me the service of exploring and developing my suggestions.[341] I used Rom 1:3–4 as an indication of a pre-Pauline, common
theology of the double identity of Jesus as Son of David and Son of
God, applied to the resurrection; and I contended that the infancy
Gospels applied this christology to the v.c. (but with the two identities
now simultaneous, not a "two step" process).[342] Fuller thinks the Son-
of-God aspect of Jesus in the infancy narrative is more closely related
to God's sending his Son as a savior in the pre-Pauline Gal 4:4–5 (which,
he recognizes, in itself has nothing to do with the v.c.)—a type of
prophetic sending not related to Davidic origins.[343] I am perfectly
content to accept this as an added element in the retrojected christological evaluation used to interpret the conception of Jesus, but I am not
sure that I would keep it as distinct from the Son of David/Son of God
pattern as Fuller does (although in "Conception" 43, he admits they are
easily combined). After all, a primary example that he gives of this
prophetic sending-of-the-son christology (Mark 12:1–12) is soon followed (Mark 12:35–37) by a discussion of Son of David/Son of God
according to Psalm 110! His type of investigation, however, is far more
programmatic for where infancy narrative research should go[344] than
fanciful conjectures about how much of the annunciation scenes was
historical and whether the parents of Jesus had to know all this christology before Jesus was born.

[341] Besides articles in the bibliography below, see his "Pre-Existence Christology: Can
We Dispense with It?" *Word & World* 2 (1982), 29–33.
[342] Fuller maintains that for Paul the formula had come to include preexistence (which
may well be true). Why then is preexistence of the incarnational type lacking in the
infancy narratives? It is from *pre*-Pauline usage, I would answer, that the infancy
narratives derived the Son of David/Son of God christology. Thus, the antiquity of
preexistence christology tells us nothing about its influence on Luke or his sources.
[343] Fuller argues (against Bultmann) that this sending has nothing to do with preexistence or (against E. Schweizer) with divine wisdom.
[344] See Miyoshi ("Entstehung" 46, 56) who brings into the picture another postresurrectional formula (Acts 1:8) and relates the Son of David/Son of God motif to the self-
understanding of Jewish and Gentile Christianity in terms of the importance of the descent
of the Spirit.

SUPPLEMENT BIBLIOGRAPHY

A few works written before 1977 but not included in BBM are included. Of the numerous commentaries on the whole Gospels of Matt and Luke written in the period 1976–1992, I have included only those I regard as the most substantial, namely, Davies/Allison, Gnilka, and Luz on Matt; and Bovon, Fitzmyer, and Marshall on Luke. (Two others, Gundry on Matt and Goulder on Luke, are incorporated because they propose theories on which I shall have to comment.) The arrangement of entries is alphabetical by author and then usually chronological for plural entries under the same author. (Family names beginning in *de, di, du* and in *van, von* are listed under *d* and *v* respectively.) Before each entry one of three letters appears: **B** (= Both) when the entry pertains to both the Matthean and Lucan infancy narratives; M (= Matthew) when the entry pertains to the Matthean infancy narrative; and *L* (= Luke) when the entry pertains to the Lucan infancy narrative. Immediately following the author's name is the indication (§) as to which section(s) in BBM the entry most closely pertains. If an entry pertains to an Appendix, that is indicated by the Roman numeral by which that Appendix is numbered in BBM.

M   Ahirika, E. A. (§2), "The Theology of Matthew in the Light of the Nativity Story," *Biblebhashyam* 16 (1990), 5–19.

M   Allan, G. (§7), "He shall be called a Nazirite?" ExpTim 95 (1983), 81–82.

B   Ammassari, A. (§5), "La famiglia del Messia," BibOr 19 (1977), 195–203.

B   Anderson, H. (§1), "Preaching as Validation: The Christmas Story and Family Birth Stories," NTR 4 (4; 1991), 78–83.

M   Anderson, J. C. (§3), "Matthew: Gender and Reading," *Semeia* 28 (1983), 3–27, esp. 7–10.

B   ——— (§3), "Mary's Difference: Gender and Patriarchy in the Birth Narratives," JR 67 (1987), 183–202.

L   Auffret, P. (§13), "Note sur la structure littéraire de Lc i.68–79," NTS 24 (1977–78), 248–58.

M   Aus, R. D. (§6), "The Magi at the Birth of Cyrus, and the Magi at Jesus' Birth in Matt 2:1–12," in *New Perspectives on Ancient Judaism*, eds. J. Neusner *et al.* (2 vols.; Honor H. C. Kee; Lanham, MD: University Press of America, 1987), 2.99–114.

L   ——— (§14), "Die Weihnachtsgeschichte im Lichte jüdischer Traditionen vom Mose-Kind und Hirten-Messias (Lukas 2,1–20)," *Weihnachtsgeschichte, Barmherziger Samariter, Verlorener Sohn* (Berlin: Institut Kirche und Judentum, 1988), 11–58.

B Bagatti, B. (IV), "La verginità di Maria negli apocrifi del II-III secolo," *Marianum* 33 (1971), 281–92.

L Bailey, K. E. (§12), "The Song of Mary: A Vision of a New Exodus (Luke 1:46–55)," *Near East School of Theology Theological Review* 2 (#1, 1979), 29–35.

L —— (§14), "The Manger and the Inn," *Ibid.* 2 (#2, 1979), 33–44.

B Barrett, J. E. (IV), "Can Scholars Take the Virgin Birth Seriously?" BR 4 (#5, 1988), 10–15, 29.

L Bartina, S. (§3), "¿El padre de la Virgen María se llamó Joaquín o Eliaquín? (Lc 3,23)," EphMar 39 (1989), 95–99.

M —— (§4), "Los sueños o éxtasis de San José (Mt 1, 20–24; 2, 13–14,19–22)," CJ 39 (1991), 43–53.

L Baudler, G. (§9), "Aspekte für eine christliche Erziehung nach den lukanischen Kindheitserzählungen," TPQ 134 (1986), 28–38.

M Bauer, D. R. (§3), "The Literary Function of the Genealogy in Matthew's Gospel," SBLSP 1990, 451–68.

L Beckwith, R. T. (§10), "St. Luke, the Date of Christmas and the Priestly Courses at Qumran," *Revue de Qumran* 9 (1977), 73–94.

L Bellet, P. (§11), "Estructura i forma: anunciació de naixement i forma d'elecció profética (Lc 1, 26–38)," *Revista Catalana de Teologia* 7 (1982), 91–130.

L Bellia, G. (§14), "'Confrontando nel suo cuore'. Custodia sapienziale di Maria in Lc 2,19b," BibOr 25 (1983), 215–28.

L Benoit, P. (§14, VII), "Quirinius," DBSup 9 (1978), cols. 693–720.

B Benson, G. P. (IV), "Virgin Birth, Virgin Conception," ExpTim 98 (1986–87), 139–40. Reply to Bostock's first article.

L Berger, K. (§15), "Das Canticum Simeonis (Lk 2:29–32)," NovTest 27 (1985), 27–39.

L Berger, P.-R. (§14), "Lk 2:14: *anthropoi eudokias*. Die auf Gottes Weisung mit Wohlgefallen beschenkten Menschen," ZNW 74 (1983), 129–44.

L —— (§14), "Menschen ohne 'Gottes Wohlgefallen' Lk 2:14?" ZNW 76 (1985), 119–22.

L Bernard, G. (§12), "Pondering over the Magnificat," HPR 91 (#2, 1990–91), 21–25. Author's name is a pseudonym.

M Bernegger, P. M. (§6), "Affirmation of Herod's Death in 4 B.C.," JTS NS 34 (1983), 526–31.

L Bernhard, T. (§9), "Women's Ministry in the Church: A Lukan Perspective," SLJT 29 (1986), 261–63.

M Blomberg, C. L. (§3), "The Liberation of Illegitimacy: Women and Rulers in Matthew 1–2," BTB 21 (1991) 145–50.

M Boa, K., and W. Proctor (§6), *The Return of the Star of Bethlehem* (Garden City, NY: Doubleday, 1980).

M Boers, H. (§4), "Language Usage and the Production of Matthew 1:18–2:23," in *Orientation by Disorientation* (Honor of W. A. Beardslee; Pittsburgh: Pickwick, 1980), 217–34.

L Bogaert, P.-M. (§12), "Épisode de la controverse sur le *Magnificat*. À propos d'un article inédit de Donatien De Bruyne (1906)," *Revue Bénédictine* 94 (1984), 38–49.

B Bostock, G. (IV), "Virgin Birth or Human Conception?" ExpTim 97 (1985–86), 260–63.

B —— (IV), "Divine Birth, Human Conception," ExpTim 98 (1986–87), 331–33. Response to Benson.

B Bourke, M. M. (§1), Review of BBM, CBQ 40 (1978), 120–24.

L Bovon, F. (§9), "Die Geburt und die Kindheit Jesu," BibKir 42 (1987), 162–70. Earlier French original in *Bulletin des Facultés Catholiques de Lyon* 104 (1980), 19–29.

L —— (§9), *Das Evangelium nach Lukas* (2 vols.; EKKNT 3; Zurich: Benziger, 1989), 1.43–162. See review by J. Dupont, *Biblica* 72 (1991), 397–403.

M Brändle, F. (§7), " 'La huida a Egipto': Reflexiones bíblico-teológicas," CJ 29 (1981), 25–36.

M Brawley, R. L. (§5), "Joseph in Matthew's Birth Narrative and the Irony of Good Intention," *Cumberland Seminarian* 28 (1990), 69–76.

L Brenner, A. (§11), "Female Social Behaviour: Two Descriptive Patterns within the 'Birth of the Hero' Paradigm," VetTest 36 (1986), 257–73.

L Brindle, W. (§14, VII), "The Census and Quirinius: Luke 2:2," JETS 27 (1984), 43–52.

L Brodie, L. T. (§9), "A New Temple and a New Law. The Unity and Chronicles-based Nature of Luke 1:1–4:22a," JSNT 5 (1979), 21–45.

M Broer, I. (§§6,7), "Jesusflucht und Kindermord," TKP 74–96.

B Brown, R. E. (§§3–5, 10–13), *A Coming Christ in Advent: Matt 1 and Luke 1* (Collegeville: Liturgical Press, 1988). Reprints articles from *Catholic Update* (1986) and *Worship* (1986–88).

B —— (§§6,7,14–16), *An Adult Christ at Christmas: Matt 2 and Luke 2* (Collegeville: Liturgical Press, 1978). Reprints articles from *Worship* (1975–77).

B —— (§11), "Mary in the New Testament and in Catholic Life," *America* 146 (#19, May 15, 1982), 374–79; reprinted in his *Biblical Exegesis and Church Doctrine* (NY: Paulist, 1985), 86–100.

B —— (§1), "More Polemical than Instructive: R. Laurentin on the Infancy Narratives," *Marianum* 47 (1985), 188–207, reprinted in his *Biblical Exegesis* 74–85, 156–61.

M —— (§3), "*Rachab* in Mt 1,5 Probably Is Rahab of Jericho," *Biblica* 63 (1982), 79–80 (see Quinn).

M Bruce, J. A. (§7), "The Flight into Egypt: The Dreams of Fathers," SLJT 27 (1984), 287–96.

L Buby, B. (§9), "Research on the Biblical Approach and the Method of Exegesis Appearing in the Greek Homiletic Texts of the Late Fourth and Early Fifth Centuries, Emphasizing the Incarnation Especially the Nativity and Mary's Place within It," *Marian Library Studies* 13–14 (1981–82), 223–394.

L Buchheit, V. (§14), "Hippolyt, Origenes und Ambrosius über den Census Augusti," VK 50–56.

L Burchard, C. (§14), "A Note on *Rēma* in JosAs 17:1f.; Luke 2:15,17; Acts 10:37," NovTest 27 (1985), 281–95.

L Burger, C. (§12), "Luthers Predigten über das Magnifikat (Lc. 1,46–55)," in *Théorie et pratique de l'exégèse,* eds. I. Backus and F. M. Higman (Geneva: Droz, 1990), 273–86.

L Busse, U. (§9), "Das 'Evangelium' des Lukas. Die Funktion der Vorgeschichte im lukanischen Doppelwerk," in *Der Treue Gottes Trauen,* eds. C. Bussmann and W. Radl (G. Schneider Festschrift; Freiburg: Herder, 1991), 161–77.

L Buth, R. (§12), "Hebrew Poetic Tenses and the Magnificat," JSNT 21 (1984), 67–83.

L —— (§15), "What Kind of Blessing Is That?" *Jerusalem Perspective* 3 (3; 1990), 7–10.

L —— (§10), "What Is the Priest Doing? Common Sense and Culture," *Jerusalem Perspective* 4 (1; 1991), 12–13.

L Buzzetti, C. (§11), "Traducendo *kecharitōmenē* (Lc. 1,28)," in *Testimonium Christi* (Onore di J. Dupont; Brescia: Paideia, 1985), 111–16.

L Byrne, M. (§14), "No Room for the Inn," *Search* 5 (2; 1982), 37–40.

M Calkins, A. B. (§5), "The Justice of Joseph Revisited," HPR 88 (#9, 1987–88), 8–19.

M Cantwell, L. (§5), "The Parentage of Jesus: Mt 1:18–21," NovTest 24 (1982), 304–15.

L Carmignac, J. (§11), "The Meaning of *Parthenos* in Luke 1.27—A Reply to C. H. Dodd," BibTrans 28 (1977), 327–30.

L Carter, W. (§13), "Zechariah and the Benedictus (Luke 1,68–79)," *Biblica* 69 (1988), 239–47.

L Casalegno, A. (§9), "Maria e algumas figuras femininas nos escritos lucanos," *Perspectiva Teológica* 23 (1991), 191–206.

M Cazelles, H. (§5), "La Septante d'Is 7,14," in *La Mère de Jésus-Christ et la Communion des Saints dans la Liturgie,* eds. A. M. Triacca and A. Pistoia (Rome: Edizioni Liturgiche, 1986), 45–54.

M Charbel, A. (§6), "Mt 2,1–12: Os Magos no ambiente do Reino Nabateu," *Revista de Cultura Bíblica* 7 (1983), 90–100.

M Charlesworth, J. H. (§6), "Jewish Astrology in the Talmud, Pseudepigrapha, the Dead Sea Scrolls, and the Early Palestinian Synagogues," *Harvard Theological Review* 70 (1977), 183–200.

M Charlier, J.-P. (§2), "Du berceau au tombeau. Préface et postface de l'évangile de Matthieu," *Vie Spirituelle* 133 (1979), 8–25, 172–91.

M Chopineau, J. (§3), "Un notarikon en Matthieu 1/1. Note sur la généalogie de l'Évangile de Matthieu," ETR 53 (1978), 269–70.

M Clark, D. H. *et al.* (§6), "An Astronomical Re-Appraisal of the Star of Bethlehem—A Nova in 5 BC," QJRAS 18 (1977), 443–49.

L Conrad, E. W. (§11), "The Annunciation of Birth and Birth of the Messiah," CBQ 47 (1985), 656–63.

L Contri, A. (§12), "Il 'Magnificat' alla luce dell' inno cristologico di Filippesi 2,6–11," *Marianum* 40 (1978), 164–68.

L Cortés-Quirant, J. B. (§11), "'Bendita tú sobre todas las mujeres'. ¿Gabriel o Isabel? Breve estudio de crítica textual," EB 49 (1991), 271–76.

M   Couffignal, R. (§§6,7), "Le conte merveilleux des mages et du cruel Hérode," *Revue Thomiste* 89 (1989), 97–117.

L   Couroyer, B. (§16), "À propos de Luc II, 52," RB 86 (1979), 92–101.

B   Cranfield, C. E. B. (IV), "Some Reflections on the Subject of the Virgin Birth," SJT 41 (1988), 177–89.

L   Croatto, J. S. (§13), "El 'Benedictus' como memoria de la alianza (Estructura y teología de Lucas 1,68–79)," *Revista Bíblica* 47 (1985), 207–19.

M   Crossan, J. D. (§4), "From Moses to Jesus: Parallel Themes," BR 2 (#2, 1986), 18–27.

B   Crouch, J. E. (§1, IV), "How Early Christians Viewed the Birth of Jesus," BR 7 (#5, 1991), 34–38.

B   Daley, B. (IV), "Born of a Virgin," *The Tablet* 246 (Dec. 19/26, 1992), 1598–1603. Review of Parrinder and Spong.

M   Daum, W. (ed.) (§6), *Die Königin von Saba: Kunst, Legende und Archäologie* (Stuttgart. Belser, 1988).

M   Davies, W. D., and D. C. Allison (§2), *A Critical and Exegetical Commentary on the Gospel According to Saint Matthew* (3 vols.; ICC; Edinburgh: Clark, 1988–   ), esp. 1.149–284. Abbreviated as DAICC.

L   Dawsey, J. M. (§9), "The Form and Function of the Nativity Stories in Luke," *Melita Theologica* 36 (1985), 41–48.

B   de Freitas Ferreira, J. (IV), *Conceição Virginal de Jesus* (Analecta Gregoriana 217; Rome: Gregorian Univ., 1980).

M   Deichmann, F. W. (§6), "Zur Erscheinung des Sternes von Bethlehem," VK 98–106.

L   de Jonge, H. J. (§16), "Sonship, Wisdom, Infancy: Luke ii. 41–51a," NTS 24 (1977–78), 317–56.

L   de la Potterie, I. (§11), "L'annuncio a Maria," in *La Madre del Signore*, ed. C. Vagaggini (Bologna: EDB, 1982), 55–73.

L   ——— (§11), "*Kecharitōmenē* en Luc 1,28. Étude philologique exégétique et théologique," *Biblica* 68 (1987), 357–82, 480–508.

L   del Carmen Oro, M. (§13), "Benedictus de Zacarías (Luc 1,68–79)," *Revista Bíblica* 45 (1983), 145–77.

L   Delebecque, E. (§11), "Sur la salutation de Gabriel à Marie (Lc 1,28)," *Biblica* 65 (1984), 352–55.

L   Delorme, J. (§12), "Le monde, la logique et le sens du Magnificat," SeB 53 (1989), 1–17.

B   De Rosa, G. (§1), "Storia e teologia nei racconti dell' infanzia di Gesù," *Civiltà Cattolica* 129 (#4, 1978), 521–37.

B   Díez Macho, A. (§1), *La historicidad de los Evangelios de la Infancia* (Madrid: Fe Católica, 1977).

L   Dodd, C. H. (§11), "New Testament Translation Problems I," BibTrans 27 (1976), 301–11, esp. 301–3 on *parthenos*.

L   ——— (§14), "New Testament Translation Problems II," BibTrans 28 (1977), 101–16, esp. 104–10 on *eudokein, eudokia*.

M   Dormeyer, D. (§2), "Mt 1,1 als Überschrift zur Gattung und Christologie des Matthäus-Evangeliums," FGN 2.1361–83.

L Downing, F. G. (§9), "A Paradigm Perplex: Luke, Matthew and Mark,"
   NTS 38 (1992), 15–36. Response to Goulder, *Luke*.

M Dubarle, A. M. (§5, IV), "La conception virginale et la citation d' Is., VII,
   14 dans l'Évangile de Matthieu," RB 85 (1978), 362–80.

M Duchesne-Guillemin, J. (§6), "The Wise Men from the East in the Western
   Tradition," in *Papers in Honour of Professor Mary Boyce*, ed. J. Duchesne-Guillemin (2 vols.; Leiden: Brill, 1985), 1.149–57.

B Dunn, J. D. G. (§1), Review of BBM, SJT 33 (1980), 85–87.

L Dupont, J. (§12), "Le Magnificat comme discours sur Dieu," NRT 102
   (1980), 321–43.

M Edwards, O. (§6), "Herodian Chronology," *Palestine Exploration Quarterly*
   114 (1982), 29–42.

L Ellingworth, P. (§14), "Luke 2.17: Just who spoke to the shepherds?"
   BibTrans 31 (1980), 447.

L Elliott, J. K. (§15), "Anna's Age (Luke 2:36–37)," NovTest 30 (1988),
   100–2.

L EphMar (§12), whole issue 36 (1–2; 1986), 5–147 is devoted to the Magnificat.

L Ernst, J. (§12), "Das Evangelium nach Lukas—kein soziales Evangelium,"
   Theologie und Glaube 67 (1977), 415–21.

L Escudero Freire, C. (§16), "Alcance Cristológico de Lc. 1,35 y 2,49,"
   Communio 8 (1975), 5–77. Also as *Alcance cristológico y traducción de
   Lc 1,35* (Seville: Centro de Estudios Teológicos, 1975).

L Eulenstein, R. (§14), " '. . . und den Menschen ein Wohlgefallen' (Lk
   2,14)," *Wort und Dienst* 18 NS (1985), 93–103.

L Faber van der Meulen, H. E. (§11), "Zum jüdischen und hellenistischen
   Hintergrund von Lukas 1,31," in *Wort in der Zeit*, eds. W. Haubeck and
   M. Bachmann (K. H. Rengstorf Festschrift; Leiden: Brill, 1980), 108–22.

L Farris, S. C. (§9), "On Discerning Semitic Sources in Luke 1–2," in GP2
   201–37.

L ——— (§12), *The Hymns of Luke's Infancy Narratives* (JSNTSup 9; Sheffield: JSOT, 1985).

M Ferrari-D'Occhieppo, K. (§6), "The Star of the Magi and Babylonian
   Astronomy," CKC 41–53.

B Feuillet, A. (§3), "Observations sur les deux généalogies de Jésus Christ de
   saint Matthieu (1,1–17) et de saint Luc (3,23–38)," EV 98, Ser. 10, #44
   (1988), 605–8 + 294.

B ——— (§1), "Le Sauveur messianique et sa Mère dans les récits de l'enfance
   de Saint Matthieu et de Saint Luc," *Divinitas* 34 (1990), 17–52, 103–50.

B Fiedler, P. (§1), "Geschichten als Theologie und Verkündigung—die Prologe
   des Mattäus- und Lukas-Evangeliums," TKP 11–26.

L Figueras, P. (§15), "Syméon et Anne, ou le témoignage de la loi et des
   prophètes," NovTest 20 (1978), 84–99.

M Firpo, G. (§6, VII), *Il problema cronologico della nascita di Gesù* (Brescia:
   Paideia, 1983).

L Fitzmyer, J. A. (§9), *The Gospel According to Luke (I–IX)* (2 vols.; AB 28;
   Garden City, NY: Doubleday, 1981), esp. 303–448.

L Ford, J. M. (§10), "Zealotism and the Lukan Infancy Narratives," NovTest 18 (1976), 280–92.

M Foresti, F. (§3), "Maria, genitrice del sabato escatologico. Considerazioni sul significato di Mt. 1,1–17," BibOr 26 (1984), 31–43.

M France, R. T. (§2), "Scripture, Tradition and History in the Infancy Narratives of Matthew," GP2 239–66.

M —— (§7), "Herod and the Children of Bethlehem," NovTest 21 (1979), 98–120.

M —— (§4), "The Formula-Quotations of Matthew 2 and the Problem of Communication," NTS 27 (1980–81), 233–51.

M Frankemölle, H. (§14), "Die Geburt im Stall," *Diakonia* 19 (1988), 402–10.

M Freed, E. D. (§3), "The Women in Matthew's Genealogy," JSNT 29 (1987), 3–19.

B Fuller, R. H. (§1), Review of BBM, CBQ 40 (1978), 116–20.

B —— (IV), "The Conception/Birth of Jesus as a Christological Moment," JSNT 1 (1978), 37–52.

B —— (IV), "New Testament Roots to the Theotokos," MS 29 (1978), 46–64.

L —— (§11), "A Note on Luke 1:28 and 38," in *The New Testament Age*, ed. W. C. Weinrich (Honor of Bo Reicke; 2 vols.; Macon, GA: Mercer, 1984), 1.15–27.

L Fusco, V. (§14), "Il messaggio e il segno. Riflessioni esegetiche sul racconto lucano della natività (Lc 2.1–20)," PS 1.293–333.

L Gaitán Hurtado, A. (§12), "El Magnificat, canto de liberación y esperanza," *Revista Vida Espiritual* 108 (April–June 1992), 19–52.

L Gallo, L. A. (§12), "El Dios del Magnificat: una relectura desde la situación latinoamericana," VF 465–85.

B Gilles, J. (§5), *Les "frères et soeurs" de Jésus* (Questions religieuses; Paris: Aubier, 1979).

B Globe, A. (§1), "Some Doctrinal Variants in Matthew 1 and Luke 2 and the Authority of the Neutral Text," CBQ 42 (1980), 52–72.

M Gnilka, J. (§2), *Das Matthäusevangelium* (2 vols.; HTKNT 1.1–2; Freiburg: Herder, 1986, 1988), esp. 1.1–62.

M Gnuse, R. (§4), "Dream Genre in the Matthean Infancy Narrative," NovTest 32 (1990), 97–120.

L Gomá Civit, I. (§12), *The Song of Salvation. The Magnificat* (Middlegreen [UK]: St. Paul, 1986). Spanish orig. 1982.

M Gordon, C. H. (§4), "Paternity at Two Levels," JBL 96 (1977), 101.

L Goulder, M. D. (§9), *Luke: A New Paradigm* (2 vols.; JSNTSup 20; Sheffield: JSOT, 1989), esp. 1.205–69.

M Graves, T. H. (§7), "A Story Ignored: An Exegesis of Matthew 2:13–23," *Faith and Mission* 5 (1987), 66–76.

L Grelot, P. (§15), "Le Cantique de Siméon (*Luc*, II, 29–32)," RB 93 (1986), 481–509.

L Grigsby, B. (§12), "Compositional Hypotheses for the Lucan 'Magnificat,'" EvQ 56 (1984), 159–72.

B   Gros Louis, K. R. R. (§1), "Different Ways of Looking at the Birth of Jesus," BR 1 (#1, 1985), 33–40.

M   Gubler, M.-L. (§6), "Wo nehmen wir den Stern her?" *Diakonia* 19 (1988), 410–15.

L   Gueret, A. (§12), "Sur Luc 1,48–55," *Centre Protestant d'Études et de documentation* Supplement (April 1977), 1–12.

L   ——— (§9), "Luc I-II. Analyse sémiotique," SeB 25 (1982), 35–42.

L   ——— (§9), *L'engendrement d'un récit, l'évangile de l'enfance selon Saint Luc* (LD 113; Paris: Cerf, 1983).

L   Guerra Gómez, M. (§14), " 'Hominibus bonae voluntatis.' Análisis fililógico-teológico y traducción (Lc 2,14 y 'Gloria' de la Misa)," *Scripta Theologica* 21 (1989), 755–75. Longer form in *Burgense* 30 (1989), 31–86.

M   Gundry, R. H. (§2), *Matthew* (Grand Rapids: Eerdmans, 1982), esp. 13–41.

L   Haacker, K. (§14), "Erst unter Quirinius? Ein Übersetzungsvorschlag zu Lk 2,2," *Biblische Notizen* 38–39 (1987), 39–43.

L   Hamel, E. (§12), "Le Magnificat et le renversement des situations," *Gregorianum* 60 (1979), 55–84.

M   Hammer, W. (§3), "L'intention de la généalogie de Matthieu," ETR 55 (1980), 305–6.

L   Hann, R. R. (§14), "Christos Kyrios in PsSol 17.32: 'The Lord's Anointed' Reconsidered," NTS 31 (1985), 620–27 (related to Luke 2:11).

L   Hansack, E. (§14), "Lukas 2,14: 'Friede den Menschen auf Erden, die guten Willens sind'?" BZ NS 21 (1977), 117–18.

B   Harrington, D. J. (§§4,10,11), "Birth Narratives in Pseudo-Philo's *Biblical Antiquities* and the Gospels," in *To Touch the Text*, eds. M. Horgan and P. Kobelski (Honor of J. A. Fitzmyer; New York: Crossroad, 1989), 316–24.

M   ——— (§5), "New and Old in New Testament Interpretation: The Many Faces of Matthew 1:18–25," NTR 2 (1; 1989), 39–49.

B   Hattrup, D. (IV), "Neues von der Jungfrauengeburt," *Theologie und Glaube* 82 (1992), 249–55.

L   Haudebert, P. (§14), "Les bergers en Luc 2,8–20," KMRL 179–85.

M   Heater, H. (§6), "Matthew 2:6 and Its Old Testament Sources," JETS 26 (1983), 395–97.

L   Heck, E. (§14), "Krippenkind—Schmerzensmann. Eine bibeltheologische Betrachtung zu Lukas 2,1–20," GL 61 (1988), 451–59.

M   Heil, J. P. (§3), "The Narrative Roles of the Women In Matthew's Genealogy," *Biblica* 72 (1991), 538–45.

B   Hellwig, M. K. (IV), "The Dogmatic Implications of the Birth of the Messiah," *Emmanuel* 84 (1978), 21–24.

M   Hempelmann, H. (§3), " 'Das dürre Blatt im Heiligen Buch.' Mt 1,1–17 und der Kampf wider die Erniedrigung Gottes," *Theologische Beiträge* 21 (1990), 6–23.

B   Hendrickx, H. (§1), *Infancy Narratives* (2d ed.; London: Chapman, 1984). A uniquely useful, small handbook.

L   Hernández Martínez, J. M. (§11), "La madre de Jesús, la primera creyente (Perspectivas mariológicas de Lc. 1–2)," EphMar 34 (1984), 239–58.

M   Herranz Marco, M. (§5), "Substrato arameo en el relato de la Anunciación a José," EB 38 (1979–80), 35–55, 237–68.

L   Herrera Aceves, J. J. (§12), "El Magnificat, canto de liberación," *Efemerides Mexicana* 6 (1988), 367–90.

L   Higgins, A. J. B. (§9), "Luke 1-2 in Tatian's Diatessaron," JBL 103 (1984), 193–222.

M   Hoehner, H. W. (§6), "The Date of the Death of Herod the Great," CKC 101–11.

M   Horsley, R. (§6), "Liberating Christmas," *Christianity and Crisis* 48 (1988–89), 436–38.

B   ⸻ (§6), *The Liberation of Christmas. The Infancy Narratives in Social Context* (New York: Crossroad, 1989).

L   Hubbard, B. J. (§11), "Commissioning Stories in Luke-Acts," *Semeia* 8 (1977), 103–26, esp. 115–16.

M   Hughes, D. (§6), *The Star of Bethlehem Mystery* (London: Dent; New York: Walker, 1979).

M   Humphreys, C. J. (§6), "The Star of Bethlehem—a Comet in 5 BC—and the Date of the Birth of Christ," QJRAS 32 (1991), 389–407; also *Tyndale Bulletin* 43 (1992), 31–56.

M   Johnson, D. (§6), " 'And they went eight stades toward Herodeion,' " CKC 93–99 (date of the death of Herod the Great).

L   Karris, R. J. (§12), "Mary's Magnificat and Recent Study," *Review for Religious* 42 (1983), 903–8.

L   Kaufmann, L. (§14), "Geburt des Messias: Text und Kontext einer guten Nachricht [Lk 2:1–21]," *Orientierung* 44 (1980), 250–53.

L   Kellermann, U. (§15), "Jesus—das Licht der Völker. Lk 2,25–33 und die Christologie im Gespräch mit Israel," *Kirche und Israel* 7 (1992), 10–27.

B   Kermode, F. (§1), Review of BBM, *NY Review of Books* (June 29, 1978), 39–42.

L   Kerr, A. J. (§14), " 'No room in the kataluma,' " ExpTim 103 (1991–92), 15–16.

L   Kilgallen, J. J. (§16), "Luke 2.41–50: Foreshadowing of Jesus, Teacher," *Biblica* 66 (1985), 553–59.

L   Kilpatrick, G. D. (§14), "Luke 2,4–5 and Leviticus 25,10," ZNW 80 (1989), 264–65.

L   Kilpatrick, R. S. (§14), "The Greek Syntax of Luke 2.14," NTS 34 (1988), 472–75.

L   Kipgen, K. (§14), "Translating *Kataluma* in Luke 2.7," BibTrans 34 (1983), 442–43.

L   Kirchschläger, W. (§14), "Die Geburt Jesu von Nazaret (Lk 2,1–20)," TPQ 131 (1983), 329–42.

L   ⸻ (§9), "Beobachtungen zur Struktur der lukanischen Vorgeschichten Lk 1–2," *Bibel und Liturgie* 57 (1984), 244–51.

L   Klaiber, W. (§9), "Eine lukanische Fassung des *sola gratia*. Beobachtungen zu Lk 1,5–56," in *Rechtfertigung*, eds. J. Friedrich *et al.* (E. Käsemann Festschrift; Tübingen: Mohr, 1976), 211–28.

L   Kleiner, J. R. (§14), " 'Sie gaben ihm den Namen Jesus' (Lk 2,21)," GL 57 (1984), 456–58.

L   Köhler, T. (§15), " 'Pour le présenter au Temple' (Lc 2,22)," VF 513–21.

L   Koet, B. (§15), "Simeons Worte (Lk 2,29–32.34c–35) und Israels Geschick," FGN 2.1549–69.

B   Kremer, J. (§1), "Das Erfassen der bildsprachlichen Dimension als Hilfe für das rechte Verstehen der biblischen 'Kindheitsevangelien' und ihre Vermittlung als lebendiges Wort Gottes," in *Metaphorik und Mythos im Neuen Testament*, ed. K. Kertelge (Quaestiones Disputatae 126; Freiburg: Herder, 1990), 78–109.

L   Kretschmar, G. (§1), " 'Natus ex Maria virgine'—Zur Konzeption und Theologie des Protevangeliums Jacobi," in *Anfänge der Christologie*, eds. C. Breytenbach *et al.* (F. Hahn Festschrift; Göttingen: Vandenhoeck & Ruprecht, 1991), 417–28.

M   Kronholm, T. (§5), "Den kommande Hiskia," *Svensk Exegetisk Årsbok* 54 (1989), 109–17.

L   Krüger, R. (§12), "El Magnificat de Lucas 1,46–55," *Cuadernos de Teología* 9 (1988), 77–83.

M   Küchler, M. (§6), " 'Wir haben seinen Stern gesehen . . .' (Mt 2,2)," BibKir 44 (1989), 179–86.

M   Lagrand, J. (§§3,5), "How Was the Virgin Mary 'Like a Man' (*'yk gbr'*)? A Note on Mt. i 18b," NovTest 22 (1980), 97–107.

B   Laurentin, R. (§1), *Les Évangiles de l'Enfance du Christ* (2d ed.; Paris: Desclée, 1982). Eng. ed.: *The Truth of Christmas. Beyond the Myths.* (Petersham, MA: St. Bede's, 1986).

L   Lauverjat, M. (§9), "Luc 2: une simple approche," SeB 27 (1982), 31–47.

L   LaVerdiere, E. (§14), "Jesus the First-Born," *Emmanuel* 89 (1983), 545–48.

L   ——— (§11), "Be it done to me," *Emmanuel* 90 (1984), 184–90, 196.

L   ——— (§14), "Wrapped in Swaddling Clothes," *Emmanuel* 90 (1984), 542–46.

L   ——— (§14), "No Room for Them in the Inn," *Emmanuel* 91 (1985), 552–57.

L   ——— (§14), "At the Table of the Manger," *Emmanuel* 92 (1986), 22–27.

L   ——— (§11), "The Virgin's Name Was Mary," *Emmanuel* 92 (1986), 185–89.

L   Lawrence, J. (§14, VII), "Publius Sulpicius Quirinius and the Syrian Census," *Restoration Quarterly* 34 (1992), 193–205.

L   Leaney, A. R. C. (IV), "The Virgin Birth in Lucan Theology and in the Classical Creeds," in *Scripture, Tradition and Reason*, eds. R. Bauckham and B. Drewery (Honor of R. P. C. Hanson; Edinburgh: Clark, 1988), 65–100.

B   Legrand, L. L. (§1), Review of BBM, ITS 5 (1978), 291–94.

L   ——— (§11), *L'Annonce à Marie (Lc 1, 26–38)* (LD 106; Paris: Cerf, 1981).

L   ——— (§14), "The Christmas Story in Lk 2:1–7," ITS 9 (1982), 289–317.

L   ——— (§14), "On l'appela du nom de Jésus (Luc, II, 21)," RB 89 (1982), 481–91.

L ───── (§16), "Deux voyages: Lc 2:41–50; 24:13–33," in *À cause de l'Évangile*, ed. F. Refoulé (Mélanges J. Dupont; LD 123; Paris: Cerf, 1985), 409–29.

L ───── (§§10,11), "The Angel Gabriel and Politics. Messianism and Christology," ITS 26 (1989), 1–21.

L Lemmo, N. (§11), "Maria, 'Figlia di Sion', a partire da Lc 1,26–38. Bilancio esegetico dal 1939 al 1982," *Marianum* 45 (1983), 175–258.

B Leonardi, G. (§1), "I vangeli dell'infanzia di Matteo e di Luca. XXXI Settimana Biblica Nazionale dell' Associazione Biblica Italiana (10–14 settembre 1990)," *Studia Patavina* 37 (1990), 299–311 or 737–49. See Testa below.

B Léon-Dufour, X. (§1), Review of BBM, RechScRel 66 (1978), 128–31.

M Lerle, E. (§3), "Die Ahnenverzeichnisse Jesu," ZNW 72 (1981), 112–17.

L Lippold, E. (§12), "Die Revision der Lutherbibel von 1984, dargestellt am Beispiel des Magnifikat Lk 1,46–55," *Jahrbuch für Liturgik und Hymnologie* 29 (1985), 127–34.

B Longenecker, R. N. (IV), "Whose Child Is This?" *Christianity Today* 34 (1990), 25–28.

M López Rosas, R. (§5), "San José en la Sagrada Escritura. La justicia de San José según Mateo 1,18ss.," *Efemerides Mexicana* 7 (1989), 179–93.

L Luke, K. (§11), "The Koranic Recension of Luke 1:34," ITS 22 (1985), 380–99.

L ───── (§14), "Luke 2:14 in Some Ancient Versions," ITS 24 (1987), 185–219.

M Luz, U. (§2), *Matthew 1–7* (Minneapolis: Augsburg, 1985), esp. 100–64. This is vol. 1 of *Das Evangelium nach Matthäus* (3 vols.; EKKNT 1; Zurich: Benziger, 1985–).

L McGovern, J. J. (§12), "Maria, 'Sierva de Yahweh' en Lc 1, 38–49," *Estudios Teológicos* 7 (1980), 3–15.

B McHugh, J. (§1), Review of BBM, *Ampleforth Review* (1980), 43–57, with my response in 57–60 (also my *Biblical Exegesis and Church Doctrine* [New York: Paulist, 1985], 69–74).

B McKenzie, J. L. (§1), Review of BBM, *National Catholic Reporter* (Dec. 2, 1977), 10.

M Maier, P. L. (§7), "The Infant Massacre—History or Myth?" *Christianity Today* 20 (1975), 299–302.

M ───── (§6), "The Date of the Nativity and the Chronology of Jesus' Life," CKC 113–30.

L Manns, F. (§16), "Luc 2,41–50 témoin de la bar Mitswa de Jésus," *Marianum* 40 (1978), 344–49.

L ───── (§13), "Une prière juive reprise en Luc 1,68–69," *Ephemerides Liturgicae* 106 (1992), 162–66.

L Marconi, G. (§15), "Il bambino da vedere. L'estetica lucana nel cantico di Simeone e dintorni," *Gregorianum* 72 (1991), 629–54.

M Marín Heredia, F. (§§6,7), "Más allá de las apariencias: Mt 2,1–23," *Carthaginensia* 7 (1991), 319–30.

B Marshall, I. H. (§1), Review of BBM, EvQ 51 (1979), 105–10.

L ——— (§9), *The Gospel of Luke* (Grand Rapids: Eerdmans, 1978), esp. 45–130.

M Martin, E. L. (§6, VII), *The Birth of Christ Recalculated* (2d ed.; Pasadena: Foundation for Biblical Research, 1980).

M ——— (§6), "The Nativity and Herod's Death," CKC 85–92.

M ——— (§6), *The Star that Astonished the World* (Portland, OR: ASK, 1991).

M Martin, F. (§§6,7), "Naître entre juifs et paiens," SeB 51 (1988), 8–21. Also *Filologia Neotestamentaria* 1 (1; 1988), 77–93.

M Masson, J. (§3), *Jésus, Fils de David dans les généalogies de St Mt et de St Lc* (Paris: Téqui, 1982).

L Mather, P. B. (§9), "The Search for the Living Text of the Lucan Infancy Narrative," in *The Living Text*, eds. D. E. Groh and R. Jewett (Honor of E. W. Saunders; Lanham, MD: University Press of America, 1985), 123–40.

M Mattison, R. D. (§3), "God/Father: Tradition and Interpretation," *Reformed Review* 42 (1989), 189–206 (on Matt 1:1–17).

B Medisch, R. (§1), Review of BBM, *Theologie der Gegenwart* 22 (1979), 242–47.

B Meier, J. P. (§1), *A Marginal Jew* (3 vols.; New York: Doubleday, 1991–   ), 1.205–52.

B ——— (§5), "The Brothers and Sisters of Jesus in Ecumenical Perspective," CBQ 54 (1992), 1–28.

B Mejia, J. (§1), Review of BBM, *Documentation Celam* 3 (1978), 235–46.

L Mello, A. (§12), "*In Deo Jesu meo*: Abacuc 3,18 e il Magnificat," SBFLA 38 (1988), 17–38.

M Menken, M. J. J. (§7), "The References to Jeremiah in the Gospel according to Matthew (Mt 2,17; 16,14; 27,9)," ETL 60 (1984), 5–24.

L Merritt, H. W. (§11), "The Angel's Announcement: A Structuralist Study," in *Text and Logos: The Humanistic Interpretation of the New Testament*, ed. T. W. Jennings, Jr. (Atlanta: Scholars, 1990), 97–108, on Luke 1.

L Meynet, R. (§12), "Dieu donne son Nom à Jésus. Analyse rhétorique de Lc 1,26–56 et de I Sam 2,1–10," *Biblica* 66 (1985), 39–72.

L Mezzacasa, F. (§12), "El cantico de liberación de María. Una reflexión catequética de Lc. 1,46–56," *Cuadernos de Teología* 9 (1988), 133–50.

L Middleton, D. F. (§§9–11), "The Story of Mary: Luke's Version," *New Blackfriars* 70 (1989), 555–64.

M Milavec, A. (§5), "Matthew's Integration of Sexual and Divine Begetting," BTB 8 (1978), 108–16.

L Mínguez, D. (§12), "Poética generativa del Magnificat," *Biblica* 61 (1980), 55–77.

L Miyoshi, M. (§15), "Jesu Darstellung oder Reinigung im Tempel unter Berücksichtigung von 'Nunc Dimittis' Lk II 22–38," *Annual of the Japanese Biblical Institute* 4 (1978), 85–115.

B ——— (IV), "Zur Entstehung des Glaubens an die jungfräuliche Geburt Jesu in Mt 1 and Lk 1," *Ibid.* 10 (1984), 33–62.

L   Monloubou, L. (§12), *La Prière selon saint Luc* (LD 89; Paris: Cerf, 1976), esp. 219–39 on the Magnificat.

L   Morris, R. L. B. (§14), "Why *Augoustos*? A Note to Luke 2:1," NTS 38 (1992), 142–44.

L   Morry, M. F. (§12), "The Magnificat: Reflections," MS 38 (1987), 63–77.

L   Mueller, T. (§14), "An Application of Case Grammar to Two New Testament Passages," *Concordia Theological Quarterly* 43 (1979), 320–25, on Luke 2:14.

B   Mulholland, M. R. (§1), Review of BBM, *Biblical Archaeology Review* 7 (1981), 46–59.

L   Mullins, T. Y. (§11), "New Testament Commission Forms, Especially in Luke-Acts," JBL 95 (1976), 603–14.

B   Muñoz Iglesias, S. (§1), *Los Evangelios de la Infancia* (5 vols.; Madrid: Biblioteca de Autores Cristianos [= BAC], 1983–ᅠ; abbreviated as MIE):

L   Vol. I: *Los Cánticos del Evangelio de la Infancia segun Sun Lucas* (BAC 508; 1983; 2d ed. 1990).

L   Vol. II: *Los anuncios angélicos previos en el Evangelio lucano de la Infancia* (BAC 479; 1986).

L   Vol. III: *Nacimiento e infancia de Juan y de Jesús en Lucas 1–2* (BAC 488; 1987).

M   Vol. IV: *Nacimiento e infancia de Jesús en San Mateo* (BAC 509, 1990).

B   ——— (IV), "La concepción virginal de Cristo en los Evangelios de la Infancia," EB 37 (1978), 5–28, 213–41.

B   ——— (§11), "El procedimiento literario del anuncio previo en la Biblia," EB 42 (1984), 21–70.

L   ——— (§11), "El anuncio del Angel y la objeción de María," EB 42 (1984), 315–62.

L   ——— (§9), "María y la Trinidad en Lucas 1–2," *Estudios Trinitarios* 19 (1985), 143–61.

L   ——— (§12), "Génesis histórico-literaria del Magnificat," EphMar 36 (1986), 9–27.

M   ——— (§2), "Tradición y redacción en la infancia de Jesús según Mateo 1–2 (A propósito de un libro reciente del prof. G. Segalla)," *Marianum* 52 (1990), 228–34.

M   ——— (§3), "Las mujeres en la genealogía de Jesús segun San Mateo," *III Symposio Bíblico Español*, eds. J. Carreira des Neves *et al.* (Estella, Navarra: Verbo Divino, 1991), 347–60.

M   Mussies, G. (§3), "Parallels to Matthew's Version of the Pedigree of Jesus," NovTest 28 (1986), 32–47.

M   ——— (§5), "Joseph's Dream (Matt 1:18–23) and Comparable Stories," in *Text and Testimony*, eds. T. Baarda *et al.* (Honor of A. F. J. Klijn; Kampen: Kok, 1988), 177–86.

L   ——— (§13), "Vernoemen in de antieke wereld. De historische achtergrond van Luk. 1,59–63," *Nederlands Theologisch Tijdschrift* 42 (1988), 114–25.

L   Mussner, F. (§11), " 'Das semantische Universum' der Verkündigungsperikope (Lk 1,26–38)," *Catholica* 43 (1992), 228–39.

L   Must, H. (§14), "A Diatessaric Rendering in Luke 2.7," NTS 32 (1986), 136–43.

M   Nettelhorst, R. P. (§3), "The Genealogy of Jesus," JETS 31 (1988), 169–72.

M   Newman, B. M., Jr. (§3), "Matthew 1.1–18: Some Comments and a Suggested Restructuring," BibTrans 27 (1976), 209–12.

M   Nolan, B. M. (§2), *The Royal Son of God. The Christology of Matthew 1–2 in the Setting of the Gospel* (Göttingen: Vandenhoeck & Ruprecht, 1979).

B   Núñez, E. A. (§1), "Maria de Nazaré," *Vox Scripturae* 1 (1991), 43–52.

M   Oberweis, M. (§4), "Beobachtungen zum AT-Gebrauch in der matthäischen Kindheitsgeschichte," NTS 35 (1989), 131–49.

L   O'Day, G. (§12), "Singing Woman's Song: A Hermeneutic of Liberation," *Currents in Theology and Mission* 12 (1985), 203–10 (on Luke 1:46–55).

L   Ó Fearghail, F. (§11), "The Literary Forms of Lk 1,5–25 and 1,26–38," *Marianum* 43 (1981), 321–44.

L   ——— (§9), "The Imitation of the Septuagint in Luke's Infancy Narrative," *Proceedings of the Irish Biblical Association* 12 (1989), 58–78.

M   Olivera, F. (§5), "Interpretación derásica de *Mt* 1,18–26," *Mayéutica* 17 (1991), 281–304.

L   Olley, J. W. (§14), "God on the Move—A Further Look at *Kataluma* in Luke," ExpTim 103 (1991–92), 300–1.

M   Orsatti, M. (§3), *Un saggio di teologia della storia. Esegesi di Mt. 1,1–17* (Studi Biblici 55; Brescia: Paideia, 1980).

L   Ort, B. (§9), *Die Kindheitsgeschichte Jesu nach Lukas in der Geschichte der Katechese* (Frankfurt: Lang, 1977).

L   Ottey, J. L. (§14), " 'In a stable born our brother,' " ExpTim 98 (1986–87), 71–73.

M   Overstreet, R. L. (§3), "Difficulties of New Testament Genealogies," *Grace Theological Journal* 2 (1981), 303–26.

L   Panier, L. (§9), "La nomination du Fils de Dieu," SeB 59 (1990), 35–51 (on Luke 1–2).

L   ——— (§9), *La naissance du fils de Dieu. Sémiotique et théologie discursive. Lecture de Luc 1–2* (Paris: Cerf, 1991), esp. 121–270.

L   Parker, S. P. (§14), "The Birth Announcement," in *Ascribe to the Lord*, eds. L. Eslinger and G. Taylor (Memory of P. C. Craigie; JSOTSup 67; Sheffield: JSOT, 1988), 133–49.

B   Parrinder, G. (IV), *Son of Joseph: the Parentage of Jesus* (Edinburgh: Clark, 1992).

L   Penna, R. (§12), "Il Canto di Maria in Luca 1,46–55," *Mater Ecclesiae* 13 (1977), 73–85.

M   Pesch, R. (§7), " 'Er wird Nazoräer heissen,' Messianische Exegese in Mt. 1–2," FGN 2.1385–1401.

B   ———, ed. (§1), *Zur Theologie der Kindheitsgeschichten; der heutige Stand der Exegese* (Munich: Schnell & Steiner, 1981). Abbrev. TKP.

L   ——— (§14), "Das Weihnachtsevangelium (Lk 2,1–21): Literarische Kunst—Politische Implikationen," TKP 97–118.

M   Petit, M. (§3), "Bethsabée dans la tradition juive jusqu'aux Talmudim," *Judaica* 47 (1991), 209–23.

M Petrotta, A. J. (§6), "A Closer Look at Matt 2:6 and Its Old Testament Sources," JETS 28 (1985), 47–52.

M ——— (§6), "An Even Closer Look at Matt 2:6 and Its Old Testament Sources," JETS 33 (1990), 311–15.

M Phipps, W. E. (§6), "The Magi and Halley's Comet," *Theology Today* 43 (1986–87), 88–92.

L Pikaza, X. (§12), "María liberadora (Transfondo evangélico y novedad mariana del Magníficat)," EphMar 38 (1988), 295–334.

B Pixner, B. (§11), "Maria im Hause Davids. Tempelrolle und Jungfrauengeburt," GL 64 (1991), 41–51.

B Plum, K. F. (§3), "Genealogy as Theology," *Scandinavian Journal of the Old Testament* 3 (1989), 66–92.

L Prete, B. (§11), "Il significato di Luca 1,34 nella struttura del racconto dell' annunciazione," *Marianum* 40 (1978), 248–76.

M Pritz, R. (§7), " 'He Shall Be Called a Nazarene,' " *Jerusalem Perspective* 4 (6; 1991), 3–4.

M Quin, J. C. (§2), "The Infancy Narratives with Special Reference to Matt. 1 and 2," IBS 9 (1987), 63–69.

M Quinn, J. D. (§3), "Is Rachab in Mt 1,5 Rahab of Jericho?" *Biblica* 62 (1981), 225–28 (see Brown, "*Rachab*").

M Raatschen, J. H. (§5), "Empfangen durch den Heiligen Geist. Überlegungen zu Mt 1,18–25," *Theologische Beiträge* 11 (1980), 262–77.

B Radaelli, A. *et al.* (§2), "I racconti dell' infanzia nel contesto del prologo dell' Evangelo," RBR 15 (1980), 7–26, 199–227.

B Raja, R. J. (§12), "Mary and the Marginalized," *Vidyajyoti* 51 (1987), 215–29.

L Ratzinger, J. (§11), " 'You are full of grace': Elements of biblical devotion to Mary," *Communio* 16 (1989), 54–68.

L Reiterer, F. V. (§12), "Die Funktion des alttestamentlichen Hintergrundes für das Verständnis der Theologie des Magnifikat," *Heiliger Dienst* 41 (1987), 129–54.

B Richards, H. J. (§1), *The First Christmas: What Really Happened?* (Mystic, CT: Twenty-Third, 1986). Earlier British editions: London: Collins, 1973; Oxford: Mowbray, 1983.

L Riebl, M. (§14), "Weihnachten mit Lukas. Auslegung und Anwendung von Lk 2,1–20," *Bibel und Liturgie* 59 (1986), 226–32.

L Rinaldi, B. (§12), "Chiarificazioni sul Magnificat," EphMar 37 (1987), 201–5.

B Ripoll, F. (§1), "The Infancy Narratives and Mary," *Biblebhashyam* 3 (1977), 287–302.

L Robert, R. (§14), "Comment comprendre 'leur purification' en Luc II, 22?" *Revue Thomiste* 90 (1990), 449–55.

L Robinson, B. (§12), "Musings on the Magnificat," *Priests & People* 1 (1987–88), 332–35.

M Romaniuk, K. (§5), " 'Joseph, son époux, qui était un homme juste et ne voulait pas la dénoncer . . .' (Mt 1,19)," *Collectanea Theologica* 50 (1980), 123–31.

L   Rousseau, F. (§13), "Les Structures du Benedictus (Luc 1.68–69)," NTS 32 (1986), 262–82.

M   Rüger, H. P. (§7), "Nazareth/Nazara/Nazarēnos/Nazoraios," ZNW 72 (1981), 257–63.

M   Sachs, A. J., and C. B. F. Walker (§6), "Kepler's View of the Star of Bethlehem and the Babylonian Almanac for 7/6 B.C.," *Iraq* 46 (#1, 1984), 43–55.

L   Safrai, S. (§14), "No Room in the Inn?" *Jerusalem Perspective* 4 (6; 1991), 8.

M   Salas, A. (§3), "José, el Padre," *Biblia y Fe* 6 (1980), 304–32.

M   Salvoni, F. (§6), "Il vaticinio di Michea," RBR 10 (1975), 31–42.

M   ——— (§6), "La visita dei Magi e la fuga in Egitto," RBR 14 (1979), 171–201.

B   Sanders, J. A. (§1), Review of BBM, *Union Seminary Quarterly Review* 33 (1978), 193–96.

B   Schaberg, J. (IV), *The Illegitimacy of Jesus* (San Francisco: Harper & Row, 1987).

M   ——— (§3), "The Foremothers and the Mother of Jesus," *Concilium* 206 (1989), 112–19.

L   Scheifler, J. R. (§11, IV), "La vieja Natividad perdida," *Sal Terrae* 65 (1977), 835–51.

M   Schmahl, G. (§6), "Magier aus dem Osten und die Heiligen Drei Könige," *Trierer Theologische Zeitschrift* 87 (1978), 295–303.

M   Schmidt, A. (§5), "Der mögliche Text von P. Oxy. III 405, Z. 39–45," NTS 37 (1991), 160 (a textual variant of Matt 1:22–25).

L   Schmidt, P. (§12), "Maria und das Magnificat," *Catholica* 29 (1975), 230–46.

M   Schnider, F., and W. Stenger (§3), "Die Frauen im Stammbaum Jesu nach Mattäus," BZ NS 23 (1979), 187–96.

M   ——— (§5), " 'Mit der Abstammung Jesu Christi verhielt es sich so . . .' Matt 1:18–25," BZ NS 25 (1981), 255–64.

L   Schöpfer, J. (§12), "Der Christ steht vor Gott. Albertus Magnus und Martin Luther kommentieren das Magnificat," GL 58 (1985), 460–66.

L   Scholer, D. M. (§12), "The Magnificat (Luke 1:46–55): Reflections on Its Hermeneutical History," in *Conflict and Context*, eds. M. L. Branson and C. R. Padilla (Grand Rapids: Eerdmans, 1986), 210–19.

L   Schottroff, L. (§12), "Das Magnificat und die älteste Tradition über Jesus von Nazareth," *Evangelische Theologie* 38 (1978), 298–313.

L   Schützeichel, H. (§12), " 'Das berühmte und denkwürdige Lied der heiligen Jungfrau': Calvins Auslegung des Magnificat," in *Creatio ex amore*, eds. T. Franke *et al.* (A. Ganoczy Festschrift; Würzburg: Echter, 1989), 300–11.

L   Schwarz, G. (§14), " '. . . anthrōpoi eudokias' (Lk 2:14)," ZNW 75 (1984), 136–37.

L   ——— (§10), "Ex ephēmerias Abia? (Lukas 1,5)," *Biblische Notizen* 53 (1990), 30–31.

L Schweizer, E. (§9), "Zum Aufbau von Lukas 1 und 2," in *Intergerini Parietis Septum*, ed. D. Y. Hadidian (Honor of Markus Barth; Pittsburgh: Pickwick, 1981), 309–35.

M Scott, B. B. (§2), "The Birth of the Reader," *Semeia* 52 (1990), 83–102.

B Segalla, G. (§1), "A proposito di due libri recenti sui vangeli dell' infanzia," *Studia Patavina* 30 (1983), 117–30.

M ———— (§4), "Tradizione e redazione in Matteo 1–2," *Teologia* 8 (1983), 109–36.

M ———— (§§5–7), "Matteo 1,18–2,23: dalla tradizione alla storia," *Teologia* 10 (1985), 170–202.

M ———— (§2), "Matteo 1–2: dalla narrazione teologica della tradizione alla teologia kerygmatica della redazione," *Teologia* 11 (1986), 197–225.

M ———— (§2), *Una storia annunciata. I racconti dell'infanzia in Matteo* (Brescia: Morcelliana, 1987). Contains revised versions of the three *Teologia* articles above.

L Serra, A. (§12), " 'Fecit mihi magna' (Lc 1,49a). Una formula comunitaria?" *Marianum* 40 (1978), 305–43.

L ———— (§11), "L'Annunciazione a Maria (Lc 1,26–38). Un formulario di Alleanza?" *Parole di Vita* 25 (#3, 1980), 164–71.

L ———— (§14), *Sapienza e Contemplazione di Maria secondo Luca 2.19,51a* (Scripta Pont. Facultatis Theologicae 'Marianum' 36; Rome, 1982).

L ———— (§11), " 'Esulta, Figlia di Sion!' Principali letture di Zc 2,14–15 e 9,9a–c nel Giudaismo antico e nel cristianesimo del I–II secolo," *Marianum* 45 (1983), 9–54.

L ———— (§14), " 'E lo avvolse in fasce' (Lc 2,7b)," VF 81–133.

L Simón Muñoz, A. (§15), "Cristo, luz de los gentiles. Puntualizaciones sobre Lc 2,32," EB 46 (1988), 27–44.

B Sloyan, G. S. (§1), "Conceived by the Holy Ghost, Born of the Virgin Mary," *Interpretation* 33 (1979), 81–84. Review of BBM.

L Smith, R. (§14), "Caesar's Decree (Luke 2:1–2): Puzzle or Key?" *Currents in Theology and Mission* 7 (1980), 343–51.

L Smyth, K. (§14), " 'Peace on Earth to Men . . .' (Luke 2.14)," IBS 9 (1987), 27–34.

L Soares Prabhu, G. M. (§11), " 'Rejoice, Favored One!' Mary in the Annunciation-Story of Luke," *Biblebhashyam* 3 (1977), 259–77.

B Spong, J. S. (IV), *Born of a Woman* (San Francisco: Harper, 1992).

L Steffen, U. (§9), *Die Weihnachtsgeschichte des Lukas* (Hamburg: ARH, 1978).

L Stock, K. (§11), "Die Berufung Marias (Lk 1,26–38)," *Biblica* 61 (1980), 457–91.

L ———— (§§11, 12), "Von Gott berufen und von den Menschen seliggepriesen. Die Gestalt Marias in Lucas 1,26–56," GL 64 (1991), 52–63.

M Stramare, T. (§5), "Son of Joseph from Nazareth. Problems Concerning Jesus' Infancy," CJ 26 (1978) 31–71.

L ———— (§15), "La presentazione di Gesù al Tempio (Lc. 2,22–40)," CJ 29 (1981), 37–61.

L ——— (§14), "La circoncisione di Gesù," BibOr 26 (1984), 193–203.

M ——— (§3), "Significato della genealogia di Gesù in Matteo," BibOr 27 (1985), 205–13.

M ——— (§3), "Per un riesame della genealogia di Matteo," BibOr 28 (1986), 3–13.

M ——— (§5), "L'annunciazione a Giuseppe in Mt. 1,18–25: Analisi letteraria e significato teologico," BibOr 31 (1989), 3–14, 199–217.

M Strobel, A. (§6), *Der Stern von Bethlehem* (Fürth: Flacius, 1985).

B Sudbrack, J. (§1), "Die Geburt des Lichts. Zur Ikonographie von Weihnachten," GL 57 (1984), 451–55.

B Swaeles, R. (§2), "Des êtres, des choses et des lieux au temps de Noël-Epiphanie," *Communautés et Liturgies* 68 (1986), 323–42.

L Sylva, D. D. (§16), "The Cryptic Clause *en tois tou patros mou dei einai me* in Lk 2:49b," ZNW 78 (1987), 132–40.

B Talbert, C. H. (§1), Review of BBM, *Perspectives in Religious Studies* 5 (1978), 212–16.

L ——— (§9), "Prophecies of Future Greatness: The Contributions of Greco-Roman Biographies to an Understanding of Luke 1:5–4:15," in *The Divine Helmsman*, eds. J. L. Crenshaw and S. Sandmel (Honor of L. H. Silberman; New York: Ktav, 1980), 129–41.

L Tam, D. S. (§9), "The Literary and Theological Unity Between Lk. 1–2 and Lk. 3–Acts 28" (Ph.D. dissertation; Duke Univ., 1978).

M Tatum, W. B. (§4), " 'The Origin of Jesus Messiah' (Matt 1:1,18a): Matthew's Use of the Infancy Traditions," JBL 96 (1977), 523–35.

M ——— (§7), "Matthew 2.23—Wordplay and Misleading Translations," BibTrans 27 (1976), 135–38.

M Taylor, D. B. (§7), "Jesus—of Nazareth?" ExpTim 92 (1980–81), 336–37.

L Temme, J. M. (§14), "The Shepherds' Role," TBT 29 (1991), 376–78.

B Testa, G. (§1), "XXXI Settimana Biblica Nazionale dell' ABI (10–14 settembre 1990) (I vangeli dell' Infanzia)," *Divus Thomas* 93 (1990), 132–44. Summary of nine papers given at the meeting, also summarized by Leonardi (above); I have used Testa's summary and checked it against Leonardi's.

M Thériault, J.-Y. (§2), "La Règle de Trois. Une lecture sémiotique de Mt 1–2," *Science et Esprit* 34 (1982), 57–78.

B Thomas, C. (§§1, 9), "The Nativity Scene," TBT 28 (1990), 26–33.

L Thorley, J. (§14, VII), "The Nativity Census: What Does Luke Actually Say?" *Greece and Rome* 26 NS (1979), 81–84.

B ——— (§6, VII), "When Was Jesus Born?" *Greece and Rome* 28 NS (1981), 81–89.

M Tosato, A. (§5), "Joseph Being a Just Man (Matt 1:19)," CBQ 41 (1979), 547–51.

L Trémel, B. (§14), "Le signe de nouveau-né dans la mangeoire. A propos de Lc 2,1–10," in *Mélanges Dominique Barthélemy,* eds. P. Casetti *et al.;* (Fribourg: Editions Universitaries, 1981), 593–612.

L Trèves, M. (§12), "Le Magnificat et le Benedictus," *Cahiers du Cercle Ernest-Renan* 27 (1979), 105–10.

L Trudinger, L. P. (§14), " 'No Room in the Inn': A Note on Luke 2:7," ExpTim 102 (1990–91), 172–73.

M Tupper, E. F. (§7), "The Bethlehem Massacre—Christology Against Providence?" RevExp 88 (1991), 399–418.

L Tyson, J. B. (§9), "The Birth Narratives and the Beginning of Luke's Gospel," *Semeia* 52 (1990), 103–20.

L Valentini, A. (§12), "La controversia circa l'attribuzione del Magnificat," *Marianum* 45 (1983), 55–93.

L ——— (§12), *Il Magnificat. Genere letterario. Struttura. Esegesi* (Bologna: Dehoniane, 1987).

L Vallauri, E. (§14), "Natus in Bethlehem," *Laurentianum* 19 (1978), 413–41.

M van Aarde, A. G. (§5), "Immanuel as die geïnkarneerde tora," *Hervormde Teologiese Studies* 43 (1987), 242–77 (see NTA 34 [1990], #112).

L van der Horst, P. W. (§16), "Notes on the Aramaic Background of Luke ii 41–52," JSNT 7 (1980), 61–66.

M Van Elderen, B. (§2), "The Significance of the Structure of Matthew 1," CKC 3–14.

L Vanhoye, A. (§13), "L'intérêt de Luc pour la prophétie en Lc 1,76; 4,16–30 et 22,60–65," FGN 1529–48, esp. 1529–35 on the Benedictus.

L Varela, A. T. (§15), "Luke 2.36–37: Is Anna's Age What is Really in Focus?" BibTrans 27 (1976), 446.

L Verweyen, H. (§11), "Mariologie als Befreiung. Lk 1,26–45,56 im Kontext," *Zeitschrift für katholische Theologie* 105 (1983), 168–83.

M Via, D. O., Jr. (§2), "Narrative World and Ethical Response: The Marvelous and Righteousness in Matthew 1–2," *Semeia* 12 (1978), 123–49.

M Vicent Cernuda, A. (§2), "La dialéctica *gennō-tiktō* en Mt 1–2," *Biblica* 55 (1974), 408–17.

L ——— (§§9,11), "El paralelismo de *gennō* y *tiktō* en Lc 1–2," *Biblica* 55 (1974), 260–64.

B ——— (§5), "El domicilio de José y la fama de María," EB 46 (1988), 5–25.

M Viviano, B. T. (§2), "The Genres of Matthew 1–2: Light from 1 Timothy 1:4," RB 97 (1990), 31–53.

L Vögtle, A. (§14), *Was Weihnachten bedeutet. Meditation zu Lukas 2,1–20* (Freiburg: Herder, 1977).

B Vorster, W. S. (§§1,11), "The Annunciation of the Birth of Jesus in the Protevangelium of James," in *A South African Perspective on the New Testament*, eds. J. H. Petzer and P. J. Hartin (Presented to B. M. Metzger; Leiden: Brill, 1986), 33–53.

L Weinert, F. D. (§16), "The Multiple Meanings of Luke 2:49 and Their Significance," BTB 13 (1983), 19–22.

B Wickings, H. F. (IV), "The Nativity Stories and Docetism," NTS 23 (1976–77), 457–60.

L Wilckens, U. (§11), " 'Empfangen vom Heiligen Geist, geboren aus der Jungfrau Maria'—Lk 1,26–38," TKP 49–73.

L Wilcox, M. (§15), "Luke 2,36–38. 'Anna bat Phanuel, of the tribe of Asher, a prophetess . . . ,' " FGN 2.1571–79.

L   Wilkens, W. (§9), "Die theologische Struktur der Komposition des Lukas-evangeliums," TZ 34 (1978), 1–13.

M   Wilson, R. R. (§3), *Genealogy and History in the Biblical World* (New Haven: Yale University, 1977).

B   Winandy, J. (IV), "Note complémentaire sur la conception virginale dans le Nouveau Testament," NRT 104 (1982), 425–31.

L   Wiseman, T. P. (§14, VII), " 'There went out a Decree from Caesar Augustus . . . ,' " NTS 33 (1987), 479–80.

M   Wojciechowski, M. (§§6,7), "Mt 2,20: Herod and Antipater? A supplementary clue to dating the birth of Jesus," *Biblische Notizen* 44 (1988), 61–62.

M   Yamauchi, E. M. (§6), "The Episode of the Magi," CKC 15–39.

B   Young, J. (§1), "The Unspoken Premise," HPR 93 (#3, 1992–93), 55–58.

L   Zedda, S. (§11), "Il *Chaire* di Lc 1,28 alla luce di un triplice contesto anticotestamentario," PS 1.273–92.

L   ——— (§11), "*Lc* 1,35b, 'Colui che nascerà santo serà chiamato Figlio di Dio,' " RivBib 33 (1985), 29–43, 165–89.

M   Zeller, D. (§1), "Die Ankündigung der Geburt—Wandlungen einer Gattung," TKP 27–48.

BIBLIOGRAPHICAL INDEX OF AUTHORS

This is not an index of the discussions of an author's views; rather it lists the page on which a reader may find bibliographical information about an author's book or article. Throughout the book (including the Supplement) references to an author's work are made by giving the author's last name and one or two significant words from the title (most often the opening word[s]), and this abbreviated title is included in the index. Where no title is given in the index, the title and bibliographical information about the author's work (often a work peripherally associated with the topic of the infancy narratives and mentioned only once) will be found in the text or a footnote on the page indicated.

INDEX OF SUBJECTS

A few authors are listed here, not for bibliographical purposes (see preceding index), but because there is a discussion of their views.